Using Platinum Edition

Using

HTML 4.0, Java 1.1, and JavaScript 1.2

Second Edition

Using

HTML 4.0, Java 1.1, and JavaScript 1.2

Using Platinum Edition

Second Edition

Eric Ladd and Jim O'Donnell, et al.

Platinum Edition Using HTML 4.0, Java 1.1, and JavaScript 1.2

Library of Congress Catalog No.: 97-69812

ISBN: 0-7897-1477-9

00 99 98 6 5 4 3 2 1

Interpretation of the printing code: the rightmost double-digit number is the year of the book's printing; the rightmost single-digit number, the number of the book's printing. For example, a printing code of 98-1 shows that the first printing of the book occurred in 1998.

Screen reproductions in this book were created using Collage Plus from Inner Media, Inc., Hollis, NH and Capture from Mainstay, Camarillo, CA.

Contents at a Glance

I Design

II HTML, Graphics, XML and VRML

III Scripting Languages

IV Dynamic HTML

Table of Contents

V Webcasting

VI CGI and Server-Side Scripting

31 Programming CGI Scripts 855

32 Custom Database Query Scripts 887

33 CGI and Database Security 915

Credits

SENIOR VICE PRESIDENT OF PUBLISHING
Richard K. Swadley

PUBLISHER
Jordan Gold

GENERAL MANAGER
Joe Muldoon

MANAGER OF PUBLISHING OPERATIONS
Linda H. Buehler

EXECUTIVE EDITOR
Tim Ryan

DIRECTOR OF EDITORIAL SERVICES
Lisa Wilson

MANAGING EDITOR
Patrick Kanouse

DIRECTOR OF SOFTWARE AND USER SERVICES
Cheryl D. Willoughby

SENIOR ACQUISITIONS EDITOR
Jeff Taylor

DEVELOPMENT EDITORS
Jon Steever
John Gosney
Tim Ryan

SENIOR EDITOR
Elizabeth A. Bruns

COPY EDITORS
Nancy Albright
Kelli M. Brooks
Michael Brummitt
Keith Cline
San Dee Philips

PRODUCT MARKETING MANAGER
Kourtnaye Sturgeon

TECHNICAL EDITORS
Bill Bruns
Jodi Cornelius
Ryan Miller

BOOK DESIGNER
Ruth Harvey

COVER DESIGNER
Sandra Schroeder

PRODUCTION TEAM
Mike Henry
Linda Knose
Tim Osborn
Staci Somers
Mark Walchle

INDEXERS
Bruce Clingaman
Ben Slen

Composed in *Century Old Style* and *ITC Franklin Gothic* by Que Corporation.

Eric and Jim gratefully dedicate this book to Father Edward S. Kacerguis, Resident Catholic Chaplain at Rensselaer Polytechnic Institute, in recognition of his many years of steadfast friendship and support. Thanks, FrEd!

About the Authors

Eric Ladd (erl1@access.digex.net) is an Internet/World Wide Web consultant living in Washington, DC. He currently works (by day) as a Project Manager for Advanced Technology Systems in Arlington, Virginia, where he leads a team of Internet developers that support the Federal Deposit Insurance Corporation (FDIC). By night, he toils endlessly for Macmillan Computer Publishing, co-authoring *Platinum Edition Using HTML 3.2, Java 1.1, and CGI*, *Special Edition Using Microsoft Internet Explorer 4*, and contributing to over half a dozen other titles.

Eric earned two degrees in mathematics from Rensselaer Polytechnic Institute in Troy, New York, where he also taught calculus, linear algebra, differential equations, and complex variables for six years.

Outside of work and writing, Eric enjoys hitting the gym, biking, country dancing, and being dragged around the city of Washington by his Boxer Zack.

Jim O'Donnell was born on October 17, 1963, in Pittsburgh, Pennsylvania (you may forward birthday greetings to **odonnj@rpi.edu**). After a number of unproductive years, he went to Rensselaer Polytechnic Institute, where he spent 11 years earning three degrees, graduating for the third (and final) time in 1992. He is now employed as an Aerospace Engineer in metropolitan Washington, DC.

Jim has been working as an author and technical editor for Macmillan Computer Publishing for over three years, contributing to over 30 books. This is the fourth book for him and his co-author Eric, whose credits also include *Special Edition Using Microsoft Internet Explorer 4*. When Jim isn't writing or researching for Macmillan Computer Publishing, he can often be found on IRC (IRC Nick: JOD); you can also visit The House of JOD at **http://www.rpi.edu/~odonnj/**. When he isn't on the computer, Jim likes to run, play ice hockey, read, collect comic books and PEZ dispensers, and play the best board game ever, Cosmic Encounter.

Jerry Ablan (munster@mcs.net) is best described as a computer nut. He has been involved with computers since 1982, and has programmed in many languages. He is Director of Technology for MindBuilder **(http://www.mindbuilder.com),** an interactive multimedia firm near Chicago.

He currently lives in a Chicago suburb with his wife Kathryn, daughter Cassandra, their dog Flatus the Great, three cats, and a tank full of fish.

He is the author of *Developing Intranet Applications with Java*; co-author of *Teach Yourself More Java 1.1 in 21 Days*, and *Web Site Administrator's Survival Guide*; and a contributing author to *Special Edition Using Java*; *Platinum Edition Using HTML 3.2, Java 1.1, and CGI*; and *Intranets Unleashed*.

Steve Banick has settled into a peaceful coexistence with his wife Christina, and his two barky dogs (Spooky and Density). Steve can be haggled with at his creative services and graphic design firm, Steven Banick and Associates. Believing you should practice what you preach, he is available on the Web at **http://www.Banick.com**, and via email at **Steve@Banick.com**.

His published works as a contributing and lead author include: *Special Edition Using Microsoft Commercial Internet System*, *Special Edition Using Microsoft Visual InterDev*, *Web Management with Microsoft Visual SourceSafe 5.0*, *Special Edition Using Microsoft Internet Information Server 4.0*, *Frontpage Unleashed*, and *Using Microsoft Frontpage 98*.

Luke Cassady-Dorion is a software engineer at Metis LLC (**http://www.metisllc.com**), a leading health-care software development firm. With the aid of various distributed-object technologies, including CORBA, Luke has deployed a series of enterprise-wide solutions written entirely in Java. Luke is the author of numerous articles on distributed computing and Java, including the recently published book *Industrial Strength Java*. Luke can be reached for comment at **luke@luke.org**.

Ramesh Chandak graduated with a Fellowship in Advanced Engineering Study from MIT (Cambridge, MA), and has a total of 8 years of work experience in the IT industry. Ramesh has worked extensively with Internet, Microsoft, Sybase, Powersoft, and Java technologies. In addition, Ramesh has authored 7 books, tech edited 12 books, and published 20+ technical articles for several leading publishers on client/server, databases, multimedia, and Internet technologies.

Dr. Donald Doherty is a neuroscientist and a computer expert. He received his Ph.D. from the Department of Psychobiology at University of California, Irvine. Don's computer experience includes programming large-scale computer models of brain systems. He's written on a wide range of computer topics. His books include *Teach Yourself JavaBeans in 21 Days*. Don is a Research Associate in the Department of Neurobiology at the University of Pittsburgh School of Medicine. Visit his Web site at **http://ourworld.compuserve.com/homepages/brainstage/**.

Mike Ellsworth is Development Manager, Advanced Technology and the Webmaster for A.C. Nielson Company. He established the corporate web site and has developed two information delivery services for Nielson: BrokerNet and SalesNet. While developing these Web services, he did extensive CGI programming, including interfacing with legacy systems. He holds a degree in psychology from Duke University and received writing training at the University of Denver. Mike and his family live in Minnesota.

Paul Santa Maria has been programming for over 15 years. He earned his M.S. in Software Engineering in 1994 and now is a Principal Systems Engineer with FileNet Corporation in Southern California.

Mike Morgan is founder and president of DSE, Inc., a full-service Web presence provider and software development shop. The DSE team has developed software for such companies as Intelect, Magnavox, DuPont, the American Biorobotics Corporation, and Satellite Systems Corporation, as well as for the Government of Iceland and the Royal Saudi Air Force. DSE's Web sites include the prestigious Nikka Galleria, an online art gallery. DSE's sites are noted for their effectiveness—one of the company's sites generated sales of over $100,000 within 30 days of being announced.

Mike is a frequent speaker at conferences on Internet technology, and has taught computer science and software engineering at Chaminade University (the University of Honolulu) and in the graduate program of Hawaii Pacific University. He has given seminars for the IEEE, National Seminars Group, the University of Hawaii, Purdue University, and Notre Dame.

Mike holds a master of science in systems management from the Florida Institute of Technology and a Bachelor of Science in Mathematics from Wheaton College, where he concentrated his studies on computer science. He is currently a student in the Organizational Leadership Ph.D. program at Regent University.

Mike can usually be found in his office at DSE, drinking Diet Pepsi and writing HTML and C++. He lives in Virginia Beach with his wife, Jean, and their six children. You reach him at **Mike.Morgan@mail.dse.com**.

Michael Morrison (mmorrison@thetribe.com, www.thetribe.com) is a writer and skateboarder living in Nashville, Tennessee. Michael is the author of *Presenting JavaBeans* and *Teach Yourself Internet Game Programming with Java in 21 Days*; he is also a contributing author to *Teach Yourself Java in 21 Days, Professional Reference Edition*, and *Late Night Visual J++*. When not working late into the night by the sounds of Miles Davis and Phish, Michael enjoys skateboarding on ramps of all shapes and sizes.

Melissa Niles is a systems administrator and web programmer for InCommand Inc., a company located in Yakima, Washington that specializes in Internet and Intranet applications.

Bliss Sloan, perhaps better known on AOL as One Tahiti, is a programmer, consultant, and writer who works from her cabin in the back woods of southern Appalachia. She currently hosts AOL's "Beyond HTML: Advanced Web Topics" message board. She can be reached at **OneTahiti@aol.com**.

Ryan Sutter is a freelance writer, programmer analyst, Webmaster and founder of a small record company called Nuclear Gopher Productions. By day, he works for Performark Incorporated. By night he writes techie books, plays with his 3 year old son Sydney, plots world-domination for Nuclear Gopher Productions and eats too much pizza. Ryan has been a computer nut since he purchased his first Commodore VIC20 for $40.00 at K-Mart in 1982. In the 15 years since, he has coded in BASIC, C, Clipper, Visual Basic, dBase, Powerbuilder, Java, HTML, JavaScript, C++, Objective-C, Perl and then some. He is a fanatic about cross-platform computing via Internet standards and Java. He is also a guitarist, a Minnesota Vikings fan and a terrible chess player. He can be reached at **rockboy@nucleargopher.com**.

Acknowledgments

A tome like this doesn't write itself. It is the result of the orchestrated efforts of many; all of whom deserve recognition. We would like to thank the entire staff at Que that helped with this book—especially Jeff Taylor, Jon Steever, Elizabeth Bruns and Todd Pfeffer—for their support and assistance over the course of this project. Also we would like to thank the cadre of contributing authors and technical editors, without whom this book would have been woefully incomplete. Finally, we want to express a special note of thanks to Doshia Stewart, who got the whole thing started, and to Jane Brownlow and Jill Byus, for helping to make our time spent working with Que so pleasant.

Eric is grateful for the support and understanding of many people while he disappeared yet again to write another book. Thanks to Dad in Ilion, Brenda in San Diego, and to many good friends and co-workers: Bob Leidich, Tara Bridgman, Mark Ribeiro, Anthony Smith, Rick Thibault, Kevin Levy, Randy Bowers, Michael Hodges, Erik Jones, and the crew at Remington's. You can all try calling me again—you won't get the voice mail… really!

Once again, Jim would like to thank his family for understanding and his absence while he worked on this book. Jim would also like to extend a special thank you to his roommates—Richard and Darby—for putting up with him during the long writing process. Finally, Jim would like to say hello and thanks to the rest of his friends, the Tuesday Night Poker Crew, and to his teammates on the DC Nationals. I'm going to Disney World!!! (Well, Richard is, anyway…)

We'd Like to Hear from You!

Que Corporation has a long-standing reputation for high-quality books and products. To ensure your continued satisfaction, we also understand the importance of customer service and support.

Tech Support

If you need assistance with the information in this book, please access Macmillan Computer Publishing's online Knowledge Base at **http://www.superlibrary.com/general/support**. If you do not find the answer to your questions on our Web site, you may contact Macmillan Technical Support by phone at 317/581-3833 or via e-mail at support@mcp.com.

Also be sure to visit Macmillan Computer publishing's Web resource centers for all the latest information, enhancements, errata, downloads, and more. It's located at **http://www.mcp.com/**.

Orders, Catalogs, and Customer Service

To order other Que or Macmillan Computer Publishing books, catalogs, or products, please contact our Customer Service Department at **800/428-5331** or fax us at **800/835-3202** (International Fax: 317/228-4400). Or visit our online bookstore at **http://www.mcp.com/**.

Comments and Suggestions

We want you to let us know what you like or dislike most about this book or other products. Your comments will help us to continue publishing the best books available on computer topics in today's market.

Tim Ryan, Executive Editor
Macmillan Computer Publishing
201 West 103rd Street
Indianapolis, Indiana 46290 USA
Email: tryan@mcp.com
Fax: 317/581-4663

Please be sure to include the book's title and author as well as your name and phone or fax number. We will carefully review your comments and share them with the author. Please note that due to the high volume of mail we receive, we may not be able to reply to every message.

Thank you for choosing QUE!

Introduction

In this chapter

The Hypertext Markup Language (HTML) and the World Wide Web altered the face of the Internet and of personal computing forever. At one time regarded as the province of universities and government organizations, the Internet has grown to touch more and more lives everyday. Even further, the multimedia content that can be provided via HTML and other web technologies such as JavaScript, Java, CGI, and others makes the web an exciting place to be.

Through the efforts of standards organizations such as the World Wide Web Consortium and the VRML Architecture Group, and those of companies such as Netscape, Microsoft, Macromedia, and Sun Microsystems, the HTML and the other languages and technologies used to present information over the web have continued to develop and evolve. The number of possibilities for providing information content over the web is astounding, and growing every day.

That is where *Platinum Edition Using HTML 4, Java 1.1, and JavaScript 1.2*, Second Edition steps in to help. This book is the single source you need to quickly get up to speed and greatly enhance your skill and productivity in providing information on the World Wide Web.

How to Use This Book

This book was designed and written from the ground up with two important purposes:

- First, *Platinum Edition Using HTML 4, Java 1.1, and JavaScript 1.2*, Second Edition makes it easy for you to find the most effective means to accomplish any task that needs to be done or present most any kind of information that can be served on the web.
- Second, this book covers the major web technologies—not only HTML, Java, and JavaScript, but also VRML, Microsoft's VBScript web browser scripting language, XML, CGI, and both Microsoft's and Netscape's implementations of Dynamic HTML—in a depth and breadth that you won't find anywhere else. It has been expanded well beyond the best-selling *Special Edition Using HTML 4*, Fourth Edition, including almost 500 additional pages of in-depth technical detail, tips, techniques, and troubleshooting solutions. It also includes a CD-ROM filled with web software, helpful documentation, and code from the examples in this book.

With these goals in mind, how do you use this book?

If you are familiar with HTML and with setting up web pages and web sites, you may be able to just skim through the first couple of chapters to see what some of the issues in page and site design are, and you can glance through the basic HTML elements discussed in the first two or three parts. Even if you are familiar with HTML, there may be some information in those parts that will be new to you, especially some of the new HTML 4.0 information. You can then read the advanced sections on HTML, as well as the sections on other web technologies such as JavaScript and Java, XML, CGI, VRML, and Dynamic HTML to determine which of those elements you want to include in your web pages.

Platinum Edition Using HTML 4, Java 1.1, and JavaScript 1.2, Second Edition was written with the experienced HTML programmer in mind. Your experience may be limited to a simple web home page you threw together, or you may be designing and programming professional web sites. Either way, you will find comprehensive coverage of HTML and other web technologies. Throughout the book there are techniques for creating quality, effective web pages and web sites.

How This Book Is Organized

Part I: Design

Chapter 1, "Web Site Design," discusses the issues concerned with how to establish a consistent look-and-feel and organization to your web pages so that they come together to form a coherent whole.

Chapter 2, "Web Page Design," gives you an overview of some of the issues that need to be considered when designing and laying out your web pages.

Part II: HTML, Graphics, XML, and VRML

Chapter 3, "HTML 4.0 Tag Reference," gives you a quick reference to all the HTML 4.0 tags, in a format that is easy to understand and use.

Chapter 4, "Imagemaps," shows how graphics can be used as imagemaps—graphic navigation aids formatted to enable the user to link to other URLs by clicking on sections of the graphic. The chapter discusses both server-side and client-side imagemaps.

Chapter 5, "Advanced Graphics," talks about the basic HTML tag used to include graphics in an HTML document and discusses the different graphics formats and display options supported. The chapter also discusses some of the many uses to which graphics can be put.

Chapter 6, "Tables," discusses the use of HTML tables, both to present data and information in a tabular format and also to achieve great control of the relative placement and alignment of HTML text, images, and other objects.

Chapter 7, "Frames," shows you how to split the web browser window into different frames and how to use each to display a different HTML document. Some of the potential uses to which frames can be put are also shown and discussed.

Chapter 8, "Forms," discusses HTML forms—the primary way that user input and interactivity is currently supported in web pages.

Chapter 9, "Style Sheets," takes a look at a recommended and increasingly popular formatting option available in HTML: cascading style sheets. Style sheets are a way of setting up a custom document template that gives the web page author a great deal more control over how web pages will look to those viewing the pages.

Chapter 10, "FrontPage Components," discusses the additional capabilities you can add to your web pages by using Microsoft's FrontPage Components (formerly known as web bots) and a web server with the FrontPage Extensions installed.

Chapter 11, "Key Access and Security Concerns for Web Administrators," discusses some of the security issues that designers of web pages and web sites, particularly ones that involve the transmission of financial and other sensitive information, need to be aware of when designing their sites.

Chapter 12, "NetHelp," introduces you to the NetHelp system for producing specially formatted help files geared toward web applications and delivery.

Chapter 13, "Introduction to XML," introduces you to XML—a new markup language that has the potential to provide increased capabilities for formatting information for the web, the Internet, and beyond.

Chapter 14, "Creating VRML Objects and Worlds," explains the basics of the Virtual Reality Modeling Language (VRML) and shows how you can use it to create simple three-dimensional objects. The chapter also shows you how to change their color, shape, and appearance. The chapter then reviews the next step in the VRML authoring process, taking simple VRML objects and building them up into more complicated objects and into whole VRML worlds. An example of the creation of a simple VRML world is used to explain the process.

Part III: Scripting Languages

Chapter 15, "Introduction to JavaScripting," discusses Netscape's JavaScript web browser scripting language and shows some of the uses to which you can put it in a web page.

Chapter 16, "The Web Browser Object Model," discusses the object model included with Netscape Navigator and Microsoft Internet Explorer. That object model enables you to use scripting languages to interact with HTML documents.

Chapter 17, "Using Inline JavaScripting," shows you how to use the `javascript:` protocol to add JavaScript capabilities inline to your HTML documents without resorting to the `<SCRIPT>` tag.

Chapter 18, "Manipulating Windows and Frames with JavaScript," shows you how to use JavaScript to create and use web browser windows, dynamically generate HTML documents, and manipulate and cross-communicate between multiple windows and frames.

Chapter 19, "Using JavaScript to Create Smart Forms," shows you how you can use JavaScript to pre-process information entered into HTML forms and thus ensure that only valid data is submitted to the web server.

Chapter 20, "Cookies and State Maintenance," shows you how to interface with and manipulate web browser cookies with JavaScript. This enables you to remember information from one page to another in a web site and across multiple visits to a web site from a single user.

Chapter 21, "Using JavaScript to Control Web Browser Objects," shows you how you can use Netscape's LiveConnect and Microsoft's ActiveX technologies to access and manipulate Java applets, plug-in content, ActiveX Controls, and other objects through JavaScript.

Chapter 22, "Scripting with Microsoft VBScript and JScript," discusses one component of Microsoft's ActiveX Technologies: ActiveX Scripting. ActiveX Scripting enables programmers and users to create custom-scripted applications in Internet Explorer and other compatible applications in Visual Basic, Scripting Edition (VBScript), and JScript—Microsoft's open implementation of Netscape's JavaScript language.

Part IV: Dynamic HTML

Chapter 23, "Introduction to Dynamic HTML," introduces you to the Dynamic HTML implementations of Netscape and Microsoft—two very different ways of adding increased animation and interactivity to web pages.

Chapter 24, "Advanced Netscape Dynamic HTML," goes into greater depth to show you more of Netscape's version of Dynamic HTML, centered around Netscape's use of manipulating style sheet attributes, the nonstandard <LAYER> tag, and Netscape's downloadable font technology.

Chapter 25, "Advanced Microsoft Dynamic HTML," explores the set of web technologies that Microsoft has dubbed Dynamic HTML, including extensions to Microsoft's Web Browser Object Model and the use of ActiveX Controls and other web browser objects to implement new capabilities to Microsoft's web browser.

Part V: Webcasting

Chapter 26, "Introduction to Webcasting," gives you an overview of the new *push* technologies becoming available. Push technologies enable you to automatically send content to users of compatible web clients.

Chapter 27, "Adding Live or Streamed Media to Your Web Site," addresses some of the special issues related to providing live or on-demand streamed media—audio, video, or both that plays continuously over an open Internet connection between server and client.

Chapter 28, "Microsoft Netshow and Other Technologies," shows how you can use Microsoft's Netshow application, and applications from other vendors, to add live content to your web pages.

Chapter 29, "CDF and Active Desktop Components," describes Microsoft's Channel Definition Format standard. This standard enables you to configure an HTML document or other web browser object to become a live, dynamic component right on a user's desktop.

Chapter 30, "Netscape Netcaster," discusses Netscape's push technology, known as the Netcaster and how it can be used to deliver automatically updated information over the web.

Part VI: CGI and Server-Side Scripting

Chapter 31, "Programming CGI Scripts," describes the basics of the Common Gateway Interface (CGI) and how you can use programs, scripts, and processes that can be run on the web server with web browsers.

Chapter 32, "Custom Database Query Scripts," discusses database processing that can be done at the server to provide an interactive user interface over the Internet between someone using a web browser and a central store of information.

Chapter 33, "CGI and Database Security," discusses the security issues involved with running and using CGI processing in much greater depth. The discussion also examines what to do with bad data and how to help ensure the safety of your server against malevolent attacks.

Chapter 34, "Web Database Tools," discusses some of the tools and utilities that you can use to set up databases for access over the web.

Chapter 35, "Indexing and Adding an Online Search Engine," goes through the steps and software necessary to add an online search engine to you web site and thus give your users quick and ready access to anything on your site.

Chapter 36, "Server-Side Includes," explains Server-Side Includes (SSI)—what they are, how they are used, and some example applications that show them in action.

Chapter 37, "Active Server Pages," discusses the Active Server Pages component of Microsoft's Internet Information Server web server, and how you can use them to dynamically configure and tailor the output of your web site according to the capabilities of your clients.

Part VII: Java

Chapter 38, "Developing Java Applets," discusses the basics of designing, writing, and debugging Java applets by using a variety of software development tools.

Chapter 39, "User Input and Interactivity with Java," examines how you can use Java applets to add another way of soliciting user input and adding interaction and interactivity between web pages and users.

Chapter 40, "Graphics and Animation," shows some of the different graphics capabilities of Java and how you can use Java to create both static and dynamic images within a web page.

Chapter 41, "Creating and Implementing Live Chats," explains how live, real-time chat capabilities can be added to web pages through Java.

Chapter 42, "Network Programming," explains how you can use Java sockets to interface Java applets with other sources of data and information anywhere on the Internet.

Chapter 43, "Security," explains some of the special security issues related to writing, providing, and running Java applets provided over the web.

Appendixes

Appendix A, "JavaScript 1.2 Language Reference," provides a reference to the properties, functions, and statements included in the JavaScript language.

Appendix B, "What's on the CD?" describes the software, utilities, code, and documentation that you will find on the CD-ROM that accompanies this book.

Special Features in the Book

Que has over a decade of experience writing and developing the most successful computer books available. With that experience, we've learned what special features help readers most. Look for these special features throughout the book to enhance your learning experience.

Notes

Notes present interesting or useful information that isn't necessarily essential to the discussion. This secondary track of information enhances your understanding of Windows, but you can safely skip notes and not be in danger of missing crucial information. Notes look like the following:

NOTE Microsoft Internet Explorer 4 supports the inline display of Windows Bitmap (.BMP) graphics in addition to GIFs and JPEGs.

Tips

Tips present advice on quick or often overlooked procedures. These include shortcuts that save you time. A tip looks like the following:

Using an asterisk (*) as the value of your ALT attribute gives users with nongraphical browsers a bullet-like character in front of each list item.

Cautions

Cautions serve to warn you about potential problems that a procedure may cause, unexpected results, and mistakes to avoid. Cautions look like the following:

CAUTION

Don't let an animation run indefinitely. An animation that's going constantly can be a distraction from the rest of the content on your page.

Troubleshooting

No matter how carefully you follow the steps in the book, you eventually come across something that just doesn't work the way you think it should. Troubleshooting sections anticipate these common errors or hidden pitfalls and present solutions. A troubleshooting section looks like this:

TROUBLESHOOTING

There's a small, hyperlinked line at the bottom right of my linked images. How do I get rid of it?

Your problem most likely stems from HTML code like the following:

```
<A HREF="author.html">
<IMG SRC="ericzack.jpg" WIDTH=300 HEIGHT=400 ALT="Eric and Zack">
</A>
```

By having a carriage return after the <IMG> tag but before the </A> tag, you often get an extraneous line at the bottom right corner of the linked image. By placing the </A> tag immediately after the <IMG> tag

```
<A HREF="author.html">
<IMG SRC="ericzack.jpg" WIDTH=300 HEIGHT=400 ALT="Eric and Zack"></A>
```

it should take care of that annoying little line.

On the Web References

Throughout this book, you will find On the Web references that point you to World Wide Web addresses where you can find additional information about topics. On the Web references look like the following:

ON THE WEB

http://hoohoo.ncsa.uiuc.edu/ This site is the home of the NCSA web server, providing complete documentation that will help you configure the NCSA server.

Cross References

Throughout the book, you will see references to other sections, chapters, and pages in the book. These cross references point you to related topics and discussion in other parts of the book. Cross references look like the following:

▶ **See** "Web Browser Object Model," **p. 636**.

Other Features

In addition to the previous special features, there are several conventions used in this book to make it easier to read and understand.

Underlined Hot Keys or Mnemonics Hot keys in this book appear underlined, like they appear onscreen. In Windows, many menus, commands, buttons, and other options have these hot keys. To use a hot-key shortcut, press Alt and the key for the underlined character. For example, to choose the Properties button, press Alt and then R.

Shortcut Key Combinations In this book, shortcut key combinations are joined with plus signs. For example, Ctrl+V means hold down the Ctrl key while you press the V key.

Typefaces This book also has the following typeface enhancements to indicate special text, as show in the following table.

Typeface	Description
Italic	Italics are used to indicate new terms.
Boldface	Boldface is used to indicate text you type, Internet addresses, and other locators in the online world.
`Computer Type`	This typeface is used for onscreen message, commands, and code.
`Computer Italic Type`	This typeface is used to indicate placeholders in code and commands.

PART I

Design

CHAPTER 1

Web Site Design

by Eric Ladd

In this chapter

The Many Facets of Web Design

Designing web sites is both a complex and rewarding activity. Hours of careful thought are needed at the planning stage. You need to take the time to think about who will be reading your pages—how they see and understand information, what types of computers they use, what browser software they have, and how fast their connections are. After you have profiled your audience, you must then consider the message that you want to communicate via the web site and how best to convey that message to your target audience. Finally, you need to consider the possibilities and limitations of web publishing to determine how you will actually create the site. Web site design is a struggle among these competing forces. As a designer, you must decide how you will meet the requirements of each one.

This chapter, and the following chapter, give you some things to think about during the planning stages for both entire sites and for individual pages. After you have a good handle on site and page planning, you will be ready to move on to later chapters. These later chapters introduce you to Hypertext Markup Language (HTML), the document description language used to author web pages. With knowledge of HTML and intelligent design, you can create sites that are accessible to the broadest audience possible and that effectively communicate what you have to say.

Know Your Audience

Web site design should be driven by audience considerations. It doesn't matter how powerful a server you have, how skilled a Java programmer you are, or how flashy your graphics are if your message is lost on the end user. If there is just one concept you take away from this chapter, let it be that you keep your audience uppermost in your mind during the design process.

Audience characteristics can fall into many categories. Because most sites have to be designed to provide maximum audience appeal, this chapter looks at two broad, yet important, categories:

- **How will users move through the information?** A web site is different from a single web page in that there are many major sections within a site that a user can visit. By developing an awareness of how people think about the information you're presenting, you can design a structure that is intuitive and that harnesses the natural associations your audience members are likely to make.
- **What technologies do your users have?** The primary reason that many sites avoid the high-end stuff such as Java applets or Macromedia Director movies presented through Shockwave is because end users don't have a machine, a browser, or a connection to support them. With all the diversity in web-surfing technology, it is helpful to take some time to learn about the tools your audience is using. This enables you to create a more accessible design.

How Will Users Move Through the Information?

You can't know how all your users think, but you can usually make some valid generalizations that can guide you during the design process. As you assess different cognitive characteristics of your audience, think about how you can use those characteristics to achieve the following design objectives:

- *Make use of association.* Association is a mental process in which one concept is paired with another. In general, people are prone to making certain associations, whereas other associations may be particular to a specific user group. Identify whatever associations between informational items you think your audience will make. After you identify the associations, you can express them on your site through the use of hypertext links. A hypertext link is highlighted text on a page that, when clicked by the user, instructs the browser to load a new document. Presumably the new document is related to the hypertext link that the user clicked on to load it.
- *Make use of consistency.* A consistent approach to the many aspects to your site—look and feel, navigation, presentation of information, and so on—reduces the amount of mental effort the user needs to make to get around. Introduce your approaches to these things as early as you can and carry it through the entire site. Microsoft's consistent approach, onscreen appearance, and structuring of information about its software products make it easy to research any Microsoft product after you understand the layout for one of them (see Figure 1.1).

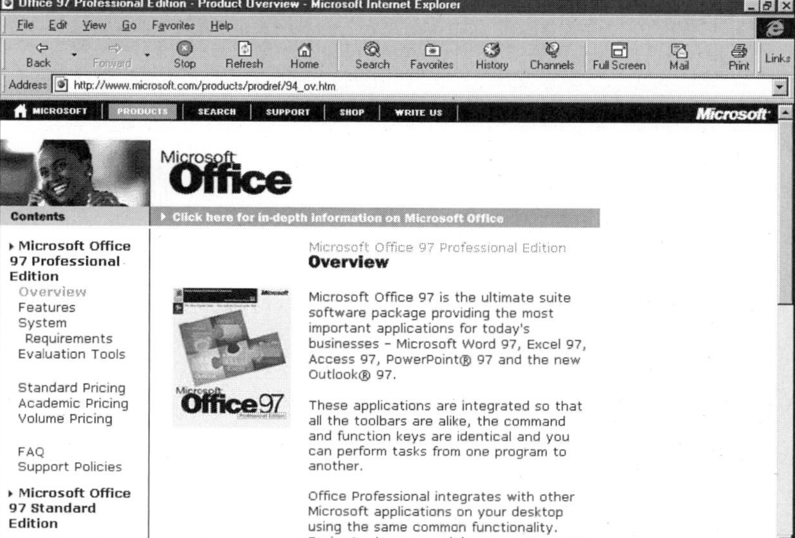

FIG. 1.1
Consistent use of graphics, navigation options, and content structure help visitors get around your site.

- *Make use of context.* Provide users with a context to which they can relate. Make sure they can get to all the important sections of your site from any other section (see Figure 1.2). This is critical because you can never predict on which page a user will enter your site. If you provide context on the home page only, users entering the site at a subordinate page will be unaware of the available options.

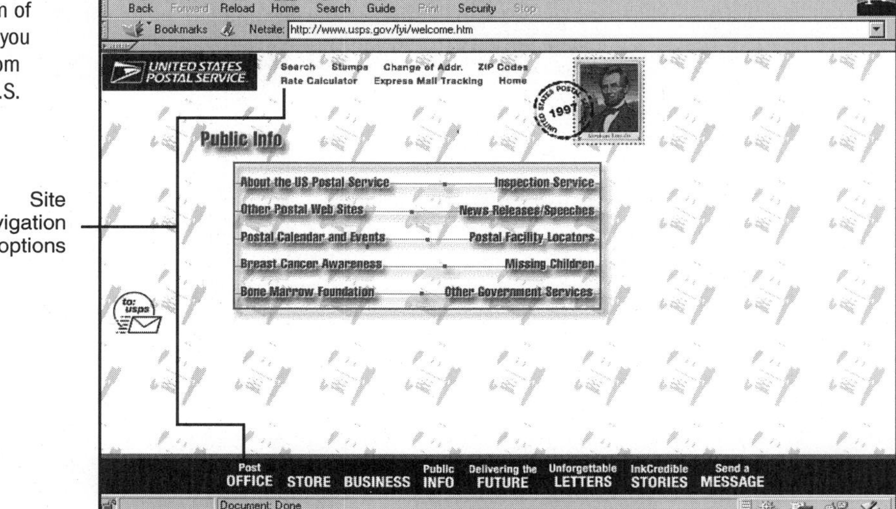

FIG. 1.2 Navigation options at the top and bottom of each page enable you to get anywhere from anywhere on the U.S. Post Office's site.

What Technologies Do Your Users Have?

The equipment your audience has access to is another key characteristic you must assess. Thankfully, HTML is platform independent, and so the type of machines your audience is using should be largely irrelevant. As long as your audience can run some type of browser program, they should be able to view your pages.

Other technology concerns do influence design decisions. These include

- *Monitor.* Because the web is an almost totally visual medium, it helps to know what monitors you are designing for. If you are not certain, it is best to design to a lower-end standard: a 14-inch monitor, set at 640×480, with the standard 256-color Windows palette. Remember that not everyone has the sophisticated monitors that many designers have.
- *Browser software.* Netscape Navigator and Microsoft Internet Explorer support all the latest extensions to HTML, but not every browser does. Some browsers such as Lynx are text-only, meaning users won't be able to see your graphics. Additionally, a good number of your users will be visiting your site from America Online (AOL), CompuServe, Prodigy, or some other online service. Each service's browser has its own

quirks that you must consider when designing; AOL's browser could not process the HTML table tags for the longest time, for example, so AOL users missed out on some attractive layouts that used tables.

▶ To learn more about the new HTML form provisions for visually impaired users, **see** "Forms," **p. 211**.

Visually impaired users may be using Braille or speech-based browsers, meaning that all your visible content will be lost on them unless you provide text alternatives for graphics, Java applets, and other embedded content. The World Wide Web Consortium is expanding the accessibility of many HTML constructs for users with speech-based browsers. Many HTML 4 additions for the form tags, for example, were driven by the need for forms to be more usable by the blind or visually impaired.

Remember that if you design to a higher-end graphical browser, you need to make alternative content available to people using less capable browsers as well.

- *Helper applications and plug-ins.* Even though many of today's browsers are incredibly powerful, they can't do it all alone. Audio clips, video clips, multimedia content, and some image formats require the use of a separate viewer program (a helper application) or a program that works with the browser to display content inline (a plug-in). Before you load up your site with these elements, make sure your audience has (or at least has access to) the additional software needed to view them.

The home page of many sites provides a notice that informs users of combinations of browser software and plug-ins the site is best viewed with (see Figure 1.3). Many of these notices also include links to pages where you can download the software. This is a helpful service that can maximize a user's experience when visiting your site.

- *Connection speed.* Some designers put together pages on a local drive and browse the pages right on the same machine. Other designers may port finished pages to a server and view them over a high-speed connection. Neither type of designer will appreciate the exasperation of having to wait for a page to download over a 14.4Kbps modem. Consider the types of connections your users will have and design appropriately. This may compel you to scale back on multimedia content and perhaps even some graphics content as well. Another way you can show respect for those with slower connections is to make available versions of your pages that are largely text, with minimal or no graphics.

NOTE More and more web page authoring programs come with tools that estimate how long it will take a given page to download. The FrontPage 98 Editor, for example, displays an estimated download time over a 28.8Kbps connection for whatever page you are editing. This time displays near the bottom right of the Editor window along the status bar.

Allaire's HomeSite includes a Document Weight function that computes estimated download times for 14.4, 28.8, and 57.6Kbps connections.

FIG. 1.3
Pepsi's site tells users which browsers and plug-ins will enhance their visit.

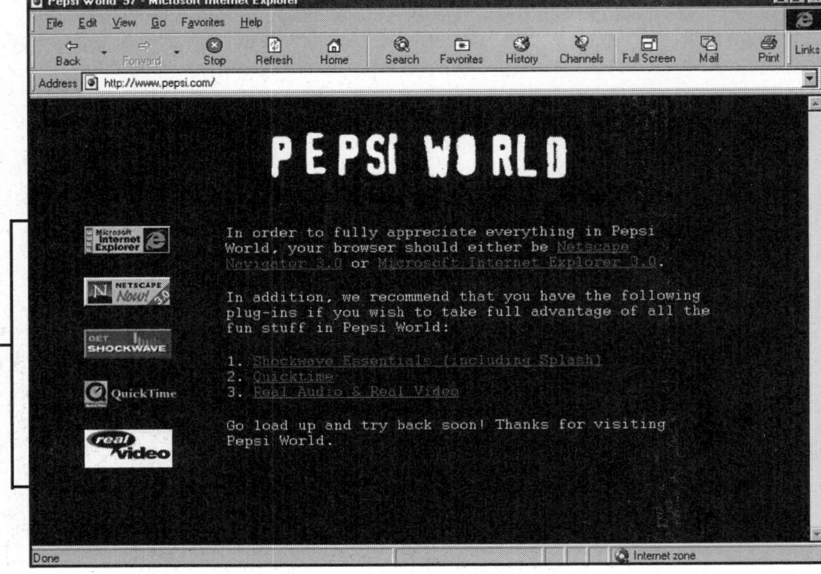

List of browsers and plug-ins

TIP Set up separate links to large multimedia items and indicate the file size parenthetically next to the link (see Figure 1.4). This enables users to decide whether they want to download the file.

FIG. 1.4
Adobe supports its software products with several downloadable files, some of which are quite large.

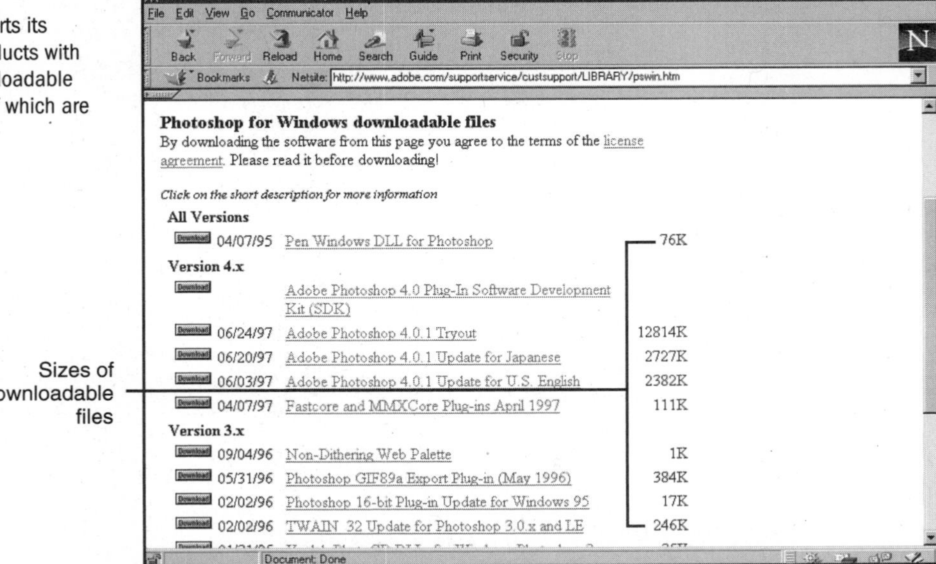

Sizes of downloadable files

Considering Your Own Objectives

It is possible to spend so much time assessing audience factors that you can forget your reasons for wanting to create a web site. User considerations are of paramount importance, but during the design process, you should not lose sight of your own motivations.

While planning your site, you should compose a mission statement or list of objectives that articulates why you want to create a web site. This statement or list is another factor that should contribute to the site's design.

Use your mission statement or objective list to ground yourself during the design process. Keep checking your design against your reasons for designing the site in the first place. By balancing end-user considerations with your own objectives, you will produce a site that has broad appeal and that helps you attain your communications goals.

Post your mission statement or objective list in a public place on a whiteboard or on newsprint so that you and your design team (if you have one) can always be reminded of why you're doing what you're doing.

Structuring Information

Audience characteristics and your own objectives for creating a site are the "human factors" that go into web site design. As you begin to focus on the site itself, you will discover that two other factors are vying for a visitor's attention: the information you're presenting and the graphics look of the site. Just as you had to strike a balance between audience characteristics and your objectives, you need to do the same for these site-related factors as well.

Two approaches for structuring content have emerged during the web's short history: the drill-down structure (also known as the layered structure) and the flat structure.

The Drill-Down Structure

Most early web sites made use of the drill-down structure. A *drill-down structure* means that the information in the site is layered several levels beneath the home page of the site and that users must drill down through those layers to see it. The idea is much like having to navigate down through several folders and subfolders to find a desired file in Windows 95 or Macintosh (or down through several directories and subdirectories to find a desired file in DOS or a UNIX system). Yahoo! uses this structure on its site (see Figure 1.5). The drilling down occurs as you move from general to specific topics.

NOTE One advantage of the drill-down approach for site administrators is that they can interpret the number of levels a visitor drills down through as a measure of the visitor's interest in the site's content. ■

FIG. 1.5
You drill down through several more general topics as you key in on a specific topic on Yahoo!'s site.

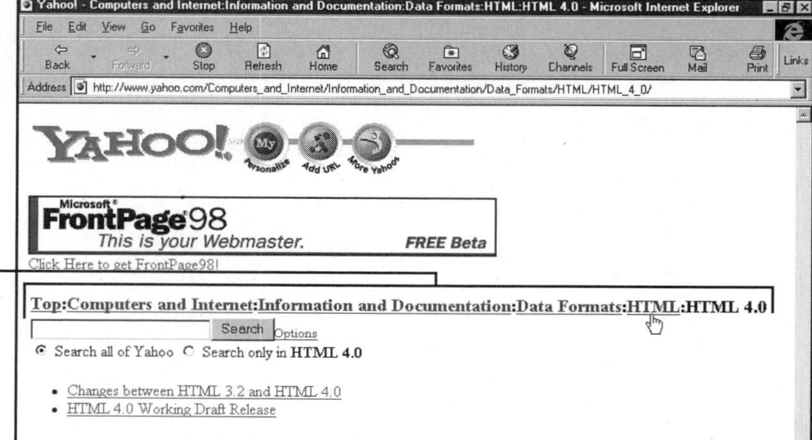

Drill-down structure (Each segment represents a deeper layer.)

The drill-down approach provided a systematic way to structure content on early sites, but users quickly grew tired of having to plow through so many levels to get the information they wanted and then having to navigate back up through the levels to move on to another part of the site. User feedback about so much layering led designers to consider different techniques. The flat structure emerged from these deliberations.

The Flat Structure

The flat structure isn't so much of its own structure as it is a lessening of the drill-down approach. Every site will probably have one or two levels of drill down (from the home page to any subordinate page, for example), but you can seek to minimize the number of layers so that there are fewer barriers between users and the information they want. There are two ways to do this:

- *Limit the number of subdirectories you use.* You are more likely to end up with a drill-down structure if you use a lot of subdirectories (or subfolders) on your server to store and organize your HTML documents. Try to keep your documents up as close to the root level as you can.

Draw a map of your site hierarchy in outline form and try to identify places where you can reduce the number of information layers.

- *Increase navigation options.* Give users access to as much as possible on every page. Figure 1.6 shows the AT&T Universal Card home page, which makes available a list of links to all major areas of the site and links to other AT&T services.

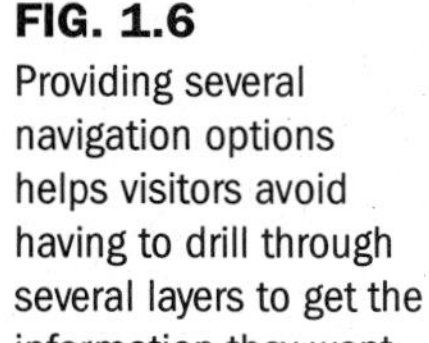

FIG. 1.6
Providing several navigation options helps visitors avoid having to drill through several layers to get the information they want.

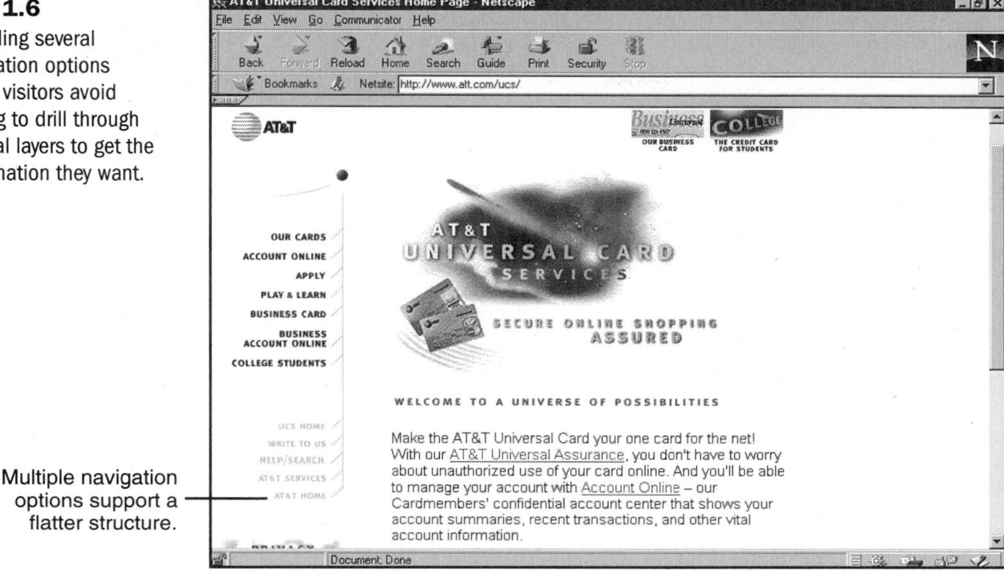

Developing a Look

A sharp graphics look is important to your site as well. Often it is the graphics that hook a visitor and influences him to stop and read your content. Additionally, a consistent look provides a unique identity for the site.

The rule of thumb you should remember when developing a look and feel is that it should enhance the delivery of your message without overpowering it. A well-done look and feel initially draws in users and then fades into the background as the users move around within the site. If you throw in too much glitz, you run the risk of detracting from what you really want to get across.

The next four sections share some other design ideologies to keep in mind while developing a look and feel for your site.

Less Is Often More

The fact that browsers can display images does not justify heaping a whole bunch of them on to all your pages to create a high-impact look. Don't forget that some users have text-only browsers and others have slow connections. These people will not have the ability or the patience to view a site that relies heavily on a lot of graphics for its look.

Try to keep the number of graphics you use to a minimum. Graphics for logos and navigation are almost essential, but beyond that give careful consideration to the images you put in your pages. Make sure that they add value to the site by enhancing the presentation of your content.

After you decide on a set of images to use, continue to use the same images throughout the site. This helps promote a consistent look. Additionally, after the images are stored in users' caches, users spend less time waiting for pages to download.

Backgrounds

A good background should stay exactly there, in the background. If a background is so obtrusive that it interferes with presentation of content in the foreground, you are less likely to get your point across.

Many sites these days have gone to a plain white background. Although this may seem rather ordinary, it supports a clean and professional look that many users appreciate and it keeps download times to a minimum (see Figure 1.7).

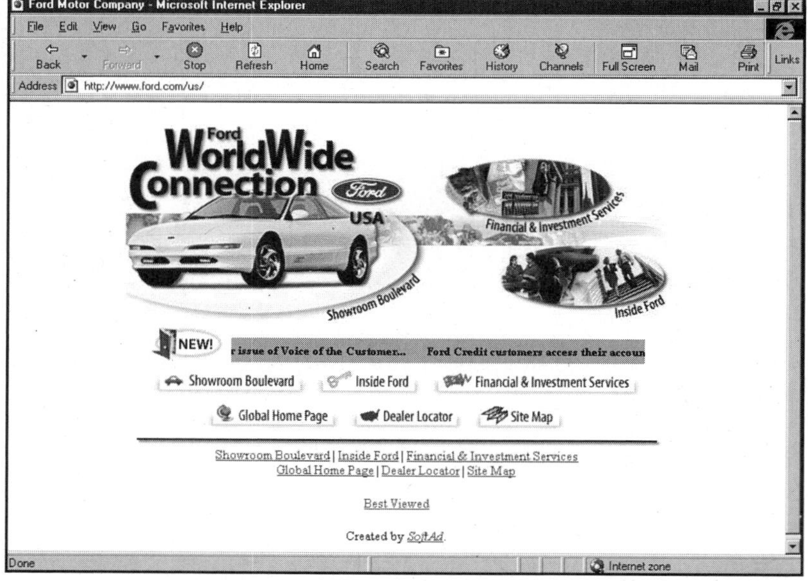

FIG. 1.7
Ford Motor Company's white background looks crisp and professional and provides good contrast for items in the foreground.

HTML supports the use of other colors as backgrounds. If you choose a color other than white, you need to make sure that there is sufficient contrast between the background color and all elements in the foreground. If you change the background color to black, for example, you need to also change the color of your body text. If you don't, you will have black text on a black background and your content will be invisible!

You can also use images in the background (see Figure 1.8). Background images are read in and tiled to fill the entire browser window. Again, the critical thing is that the background image does not intrude on the content in the foreground. Additionally, you want to design your image so that it tiles seamlessly. Being able to see the boundaries where the tiling occurs can distract users from the information you want them to see.

You can use a background color and background image simultaneously on your pages; the color you use, however, should be the same as the dominant color in the image. The background color will be rendered immediately by the browser and then the background image will be placed and tiled after the image is read in. This way, if there is a delay in downloading the image, you still have a colored background that approximates the color scheme of the image. After the image has transferred, its appearance onscreen should not be too distracting because of the close match between it and the background color.

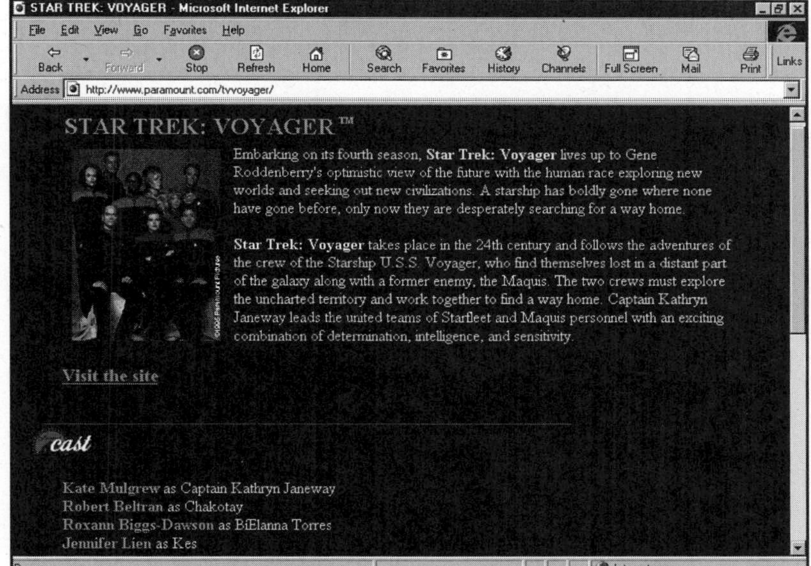

FIG. 1.8
Paramount's logo looms large behind information about its television programs, but not so large that it's overpowering.

Color Choices

HTML provides control over other page colors too. Controlling background and body text color was mentioned in the preceding section. You can control the color of three different types of hypertext links as well: unvisited, visited, and active (a link is active only for the instant that the user clicks on it). Colors for all three types should be chosen so that they provide good contrast with the background color or image. Beyond that, it is a good visitor service to color visited links a different color from unvisited links because this provides a visual cue to users as to where they have been in the site.

Hypertext link colors are a nice way to work in your company's color scheme if you're designing for a corporate site. Painting link colors in this way subtly promotes corporate identity throughout the site.

Iconography: Is It Intuitive?

Many designers choose to represent major sections of a site with *icons*, small images that are meant to convey what type of content is found in each section. The site in Figure 1.9 makes good use of icons, including books for the Publications and Documents section and a podium for the Speeches section.

The critical test that icons must pass is the intuitiveness test. Because you are using a small image to communicate a possibly complicated idea, you need to make sure that users can make a fairly quick association between the image and the idea. The best way to do this is to test the icons with potential users. Get some people together who know nothing about the site you're designing and show them your icons. As they see each icon, ask them to write down what web site information or functionality might be associated with it. After you have gathered their responses, share the icons with them again, this time giving the significance of each icon. Ask for their feedback on whether they think the icon truly represents what you want it to. By combining user responses from the first viewing with feedback from the second viewing, you should be able to make a good assessment of how intuitive your icons are.

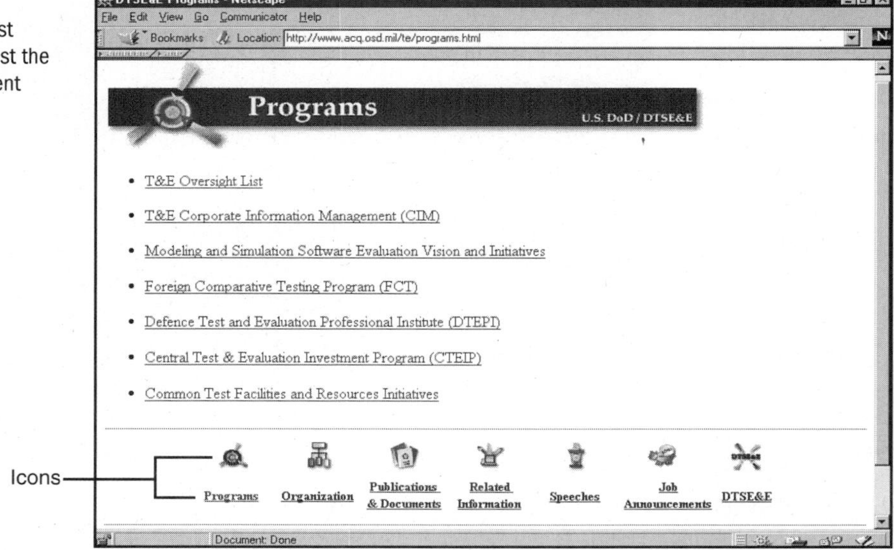

FIG. 1.9
Icons should almost immediately suggest the nature of the content they link to.

Using Pre-Packaged Graphics Themes

Just because you may not have a dedicated graphic artist to help you come up with a visual identity, you are not necessarily resigned to having a bland site. Many ready-to-use sets of images that you can download and use freely in your design are available.

Perhaps the easiest set of pre-packaged themes to use comes as part of the FrontPage 98 Editor. You can choose from one of seven different themes, previewing them all in the Themes dialog box (see Figure 1.10). Each theme includes banner, background, button, bullet, horizontal rule, and navigation images, as well as specs to set up heading and body text styles.

If you do have a little graphics expertise yourself, it would be a simple matter to import any of the graphics in the theme into a capable graphics program such as Photoshop or PaintShop Pro and customize them for your site. You might, for example, add your company's name to the banner image so that it is always visible to the reader.

If you are having trouble coming up with a look and feel for your site, feel free to look at and experiment with a pre-packaged theme from FrontPage or any other source. They are an easy way to put a very attractive face on your site with a minimal amount of effort.

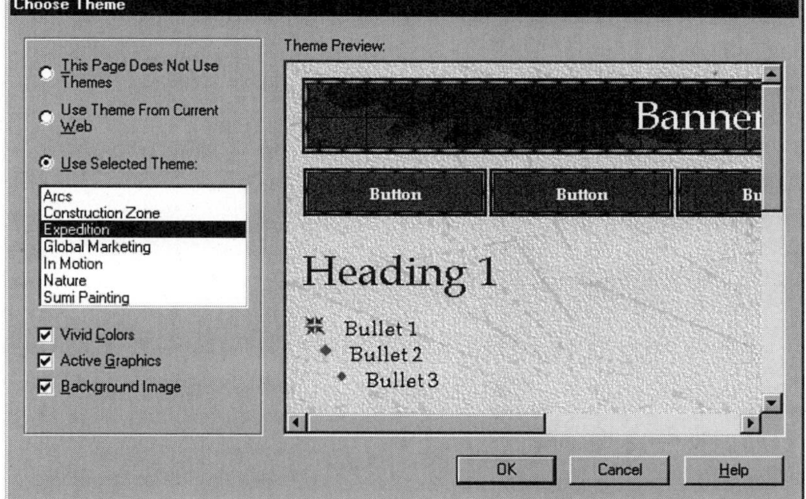

FIG. 1.10
The FrontPage Editor comes with seven different built-in graphics themes that you can preview and use.

Desirable Site Elements

Expectation is another powerful mental process that you can harness. Anticipating and meeting users' expectations will impress them and make it more likely that they will come back to your site.

Over time, web users have come to rely on certain functionality being present on most web sites. The next several sections catalog these features so that you can consider building them into the design for your site.

Tables of Contents

A site-wide table of contents lays out everything available on the site—usually as hypertext links so that users can click and go where they want (see Figure 1.11). Depending on the size of your site, it may take some time to compile and code a comprehensive table of contents. Remember, however, that users will appreciate the quick access to all parts of your site.

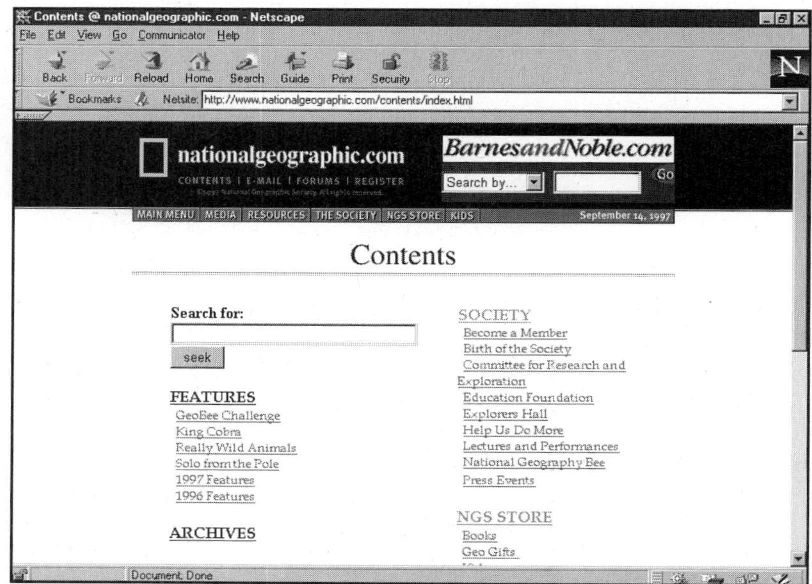

FIG. 1.11
National Geographic's table of contents is a list of links to all major areas of the site.

Microsoft's FrontPage 98 comes with a Table of Contents Component that you can use to automatically generate and update a table of contents for your site.

Search Engines

Indexing your site to make it searchable is a great way to make any part of your site available without a lot of drill down. Figure 1.12 shows the US Airways search page. Many such pages are as simple as the one input field you see in the figure.

Outfitting your site with a search engine may be easier than you think. Some search-engine programs such as ICE are publicly available and fairly painless to install. Major server programs such as Netscape Enterprise Server and Microsoft's Internet Information Server are coming bundled with search-engine software.

▶ For more information on search engines, **see** "Indexing and Adding an Online Search Engine," **p. 953**.

FIG. 1.12
Making your site searchable spares users hours of effort trying to find the information they need.

Navigation Tools

▶ To learn more about setting up site navigation, **see** "Desirable Page Elements," **p. 41**.

Comprehensive navigation options should be available to users on every page. At the very least, you need to provide links to every major content section of your site (see Figure 1.13). Additionally, you should think about providing links to important functional areas of the site such as the Table of Contents and the search engine discussed in the previous sections.

What's New

People who visit your site frequently will appreciate a What's New section so that they can quickly find out what has changed since their last visit (see Figure 1.14). This spares them having to go through the whole site to discover new content.

You can maintain your What's New section manually or you can have it generated on-the-fly by your web server by using publicly available common gateway interface (CGI) scripts. These scripts check the files on your site for their last changed dates and display a list of files that have been altered within a specified period of time. The pages generated by these scripts don't tend to be very descriptive, so it is best to maintain your What's New section manually if you have the resources.

You can also use software such as NetMind's URL Minder to dispatch an email to visitors when something on your site changes.

FIG. 1.13
Netscape places links to major sections of its site at the top of its home page.

Navigation options

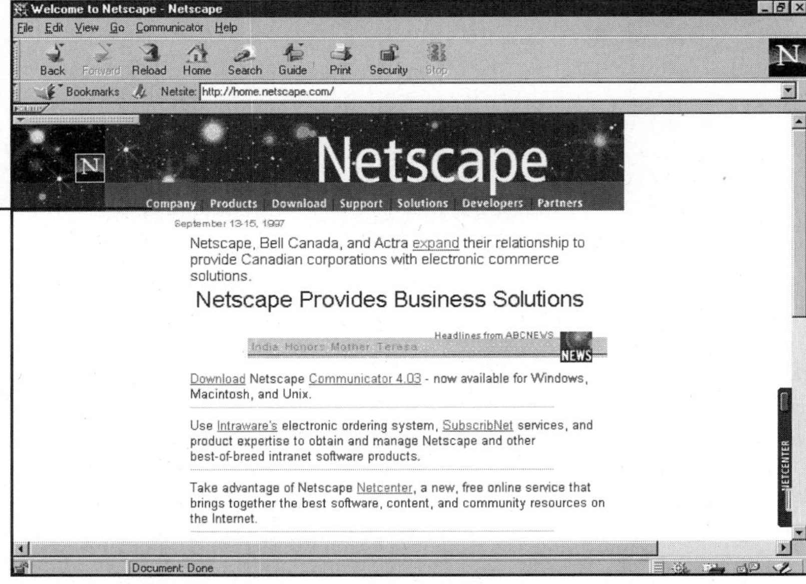

FIG. 1.14
Visitors to the Lurker's Guide to Babylon 5 can find out about new content at a glance.

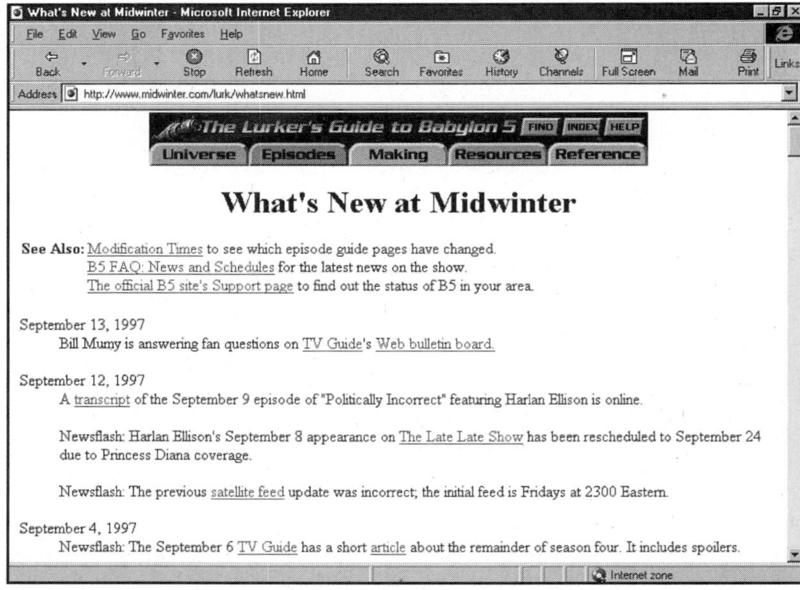

Guest Books

Sign in, please! Guest books provide a record of visitors to the site. Signing the guest book is almost always voluntary, but there are usually links to the guest book page from the home page that encourage visitors to sign.

▶ To learn how to create an HTML form, **see** "Forms," **p. 211**.

A guest book uses HTML forms to gather information about the visitor and then archives the information on the server (see Figure 1.15). Try to keep your guest book form short. Users who are willing to sign may change their minds if they see that they have to fill out an extensive form.

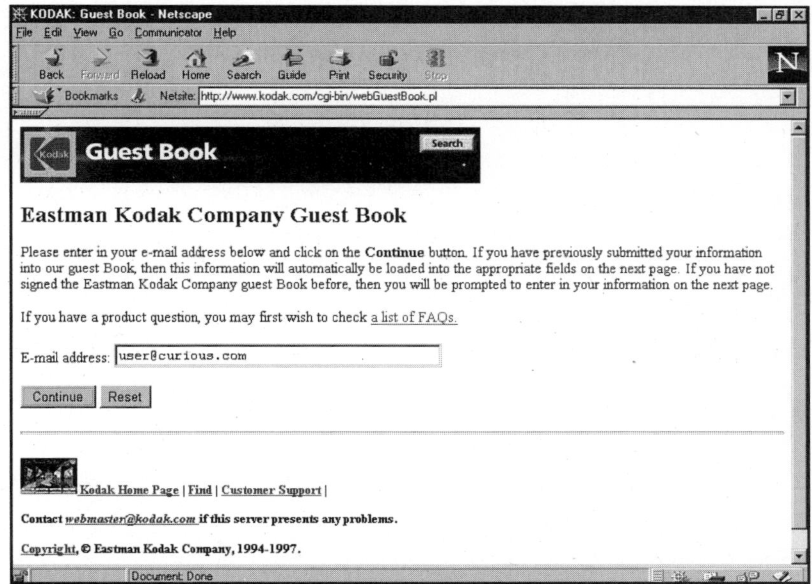

FIG. 1.15
Kodak's online guest book begins by asking for your e-mail address and then enables you to add more comments if you wish.

Feedback Mechanism

▶ **See** "Desirable Page Elements," **p. 41**, for more information on ways to collect visitor feedback.

You should always be gathering feedback on your site so that you can build on and improve it. Putting a feedback mechanism on your site is a great way to collect opinions from people as they visit.

Feedback mechanisms can take two different forms. A simple way to support user feedback is to place an email hypertext link on your pages. By clicking on the link, users open a mail window in their browsers where they can compose and send a feedback message to you.

The second approach is to create an HTML form that asks specific questions (see Figure 1.16). This requires a bit more effort than setting up an email link, but it does provide the advantage of gathering responses to a standard set of questions.

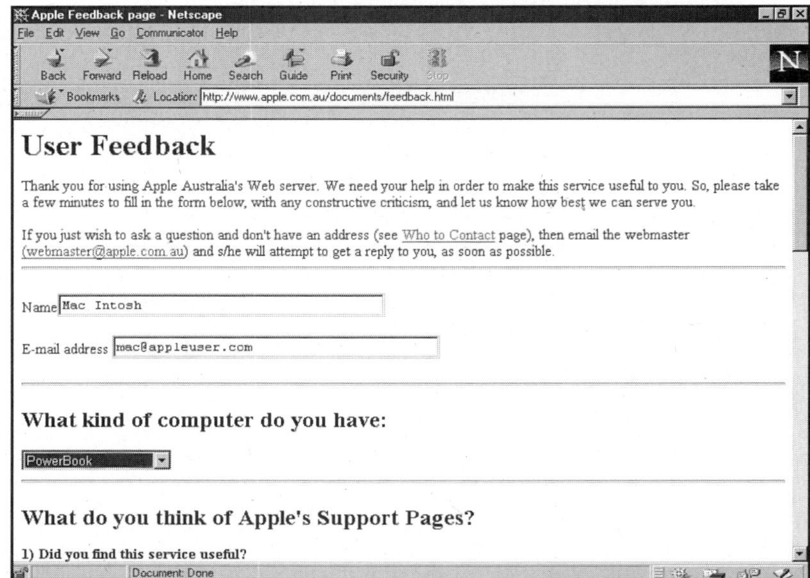

FIG. 1.16
Visitors to Apple's Australian site can provide more than just an email for feedback.

Mailing Lists

A mailing list gateway enables users to subscribe to mailing lists that will keep them up to date on changes to the site or on some other topic of interest. Figure 1.17 shows the mailing list subscription page from the Macmillan Computer Publishing site.

Threaded Discussion Groups

Threaded discussion groups are very much like having Usenet newsgroups right on your site. Users can participate in discussions about the site or topics relevant to content on the site by posting their ideas and opinions or by responding to posts by others.

If you are unsure as to how you can set threaded discussion on your site, you can check out some solutions available from various software vendors. Allaire produces a product called Allaire Forums to support browser-based threaded discussions (see Figure 1.18). By using Forums's Cold Fusion engine, users can read and post to any of a number of related groups.

Chat Channels

Chat channels enable users to interact in real time. Some sites support a general chat channel where users can discuss the site or topics that relate to site content. Another application of chat channels is to provide a question-and-answer session with a subject-matter expert or celebrity.

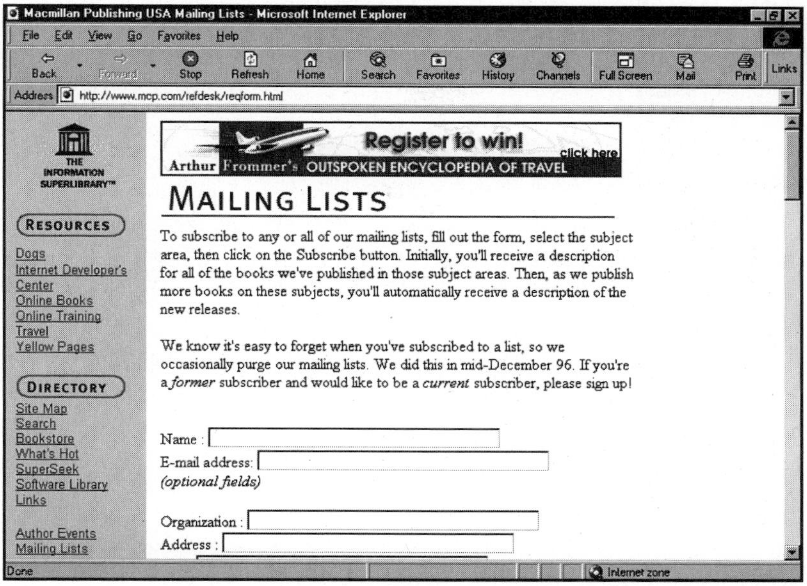

FIG. 1.17
Macmillan Computer Publishing supports several mailing lists on a myriad of subjects.

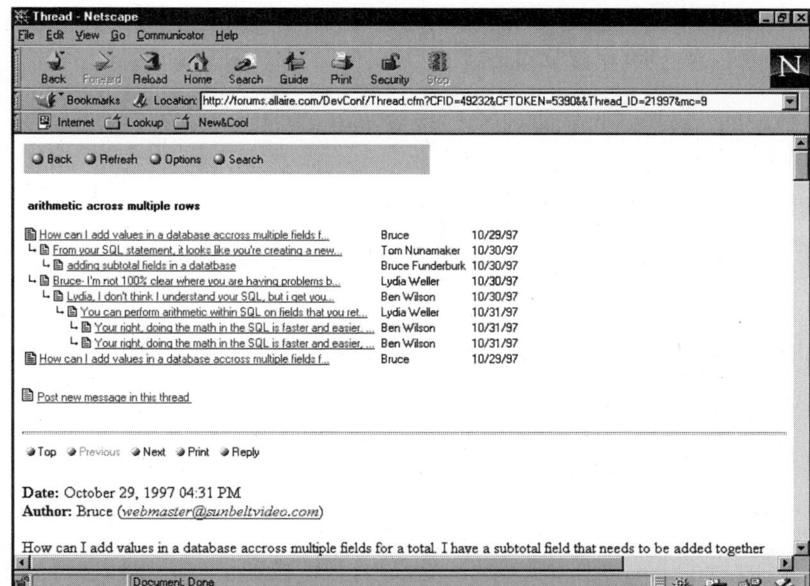

FIG. 1.18
Allaire provides threaded discussion groups for developers who use Allaire products.

Most chat servers have a feature that enables you to record a chat session. Reviewing the transcripts of a chat is a terrific way to gather feedback and other ideas for improving your site.

▶ For more information on chat channels, **see** "Creating and Implementing Live Chats," **p. 1239**.

Multimedia Content

As browsers become better able to display multimedia content inline, you will see more and more of it on web sites. The biggest impediment continues to be bandwidth. Most multimedia files are quite large and may take several minutes to download.

You have many options when it comes to providing multimedia content, including

- Audio
- Video
- Macromedia Director movies
- Virtual Reality Modeling Language (VRML)

Most multimedia files require a helper application or plug-in to view them, so be sure to notify users about what viewer programs they need to download before they get to pages with multimedia content.

Audio clips are especially popular on music sites where they enable a visitor to preview parts of an album before buying. Audio files come in several formats including .wav, .au, and .aiff for sound bytes and .mid for music.

Streamed audio is different from other audio formats in that the sound is played as information is received by the browser rather than after the entire file is downloaded. Progressive Network's RealAudio (.ra or .ram) is the leading streamed audio format. You can learn more about RealAudio by directing your browser to **http://www.realaudio.com/**.

Computer video files also come in several formats. The most popular are MPEG (.mpg), QuickTime from Apple (.qt or .mov), and Video for Windows from Microsoft (.avi, short for Audio Video Interleave). Computer video files are also huge, usually on the order of 1MB of information or more for a video clip that lasts only a few seconds. Combine this with limited bandwidth and you can see why web video hasn't attained the prominence of other multimedia forms.

Nonetheless, progress is being made on the web video front. Streaming can enable video to be displayed as it is received, although this technique is still in a formative stage. Microsoft made a bold move by making ActiveMovie technology available for Internet Explorer 4. ActiveMovie eliminates the need for video helper applications by enabling Internet Explorer to display MPEG, QuickTime, and Video for Windows files inline. Additionally, Real Video by Progressive Networks provides support for streaming video content.

▶ For more information on streaming multimedia, **see** "Adding Live or Streamed Media to Your Site," **p. 735**.

Macromedia Director is an authoring tool for composing multimedia presentations or movies. A movie draws on text, graphics, audio, and video information to create interactive applications that can be run on Macintosh and Windows platforms or that can be delivered over the Internet (see Figure 1.19).

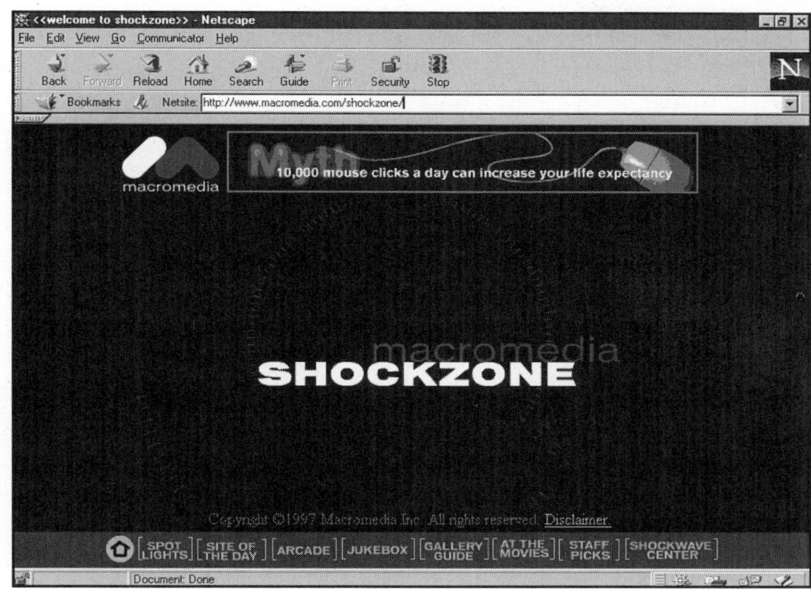

FIG. 1.19
Macromedia's Shockwave Gallery showcases a number of web sites that include Shockwave animations.

Director movies are viewed in a browser using Shockwave, a plug-in freely available from Macromedia. Because Director movie files are typically quite large, Macromedia also provides a utility called AfterBurner, which compresses the movie file and optimizes it for transfer over the Internet.

VRML (rhymes with "thermal") originally stood for Virtual Reality Markup Language. It was later changed to Virtual Reality Modeling Language because VRML code isn't really markup. It is a description language that enables you to render interactive 3D environments in real time over the web. VRML worlds are viewed with a VRML browser or with a web browser with a VRML plug-in.

▶ For more information, **see** "Creating VRML Objects and Worlds," **p. 361**.

Testing Your Design

After you have completed your design work and have a first cut of your site developed, you should consider testing the design and looking for ways to improve it before final roll-out. These last three sections give you some different tests to try.

Pilot the Site

Taking the site for a test drive with some potential users is a great way to gather ideas for making it better. To do this, round up some people who have some degree of web-surfing experience but who have not seen the site. Turn them loose on the site and encourage them to look for things that they would change. You can even give them a feedback form to fill out with a standard set of questions and an open-ended question for other thoughts they may have.

If you do pilot your site with a group of users, watch them as they do it! You'll be amazed at what you can learn from facial expressions and body language.

Try It with Different Browsers

As you developed the site, you probably used just one browser. After you are finished, you owe it to your audience to view the site in other browsers, including at least one non-graphical browser. Record any corrections needed and go back to your HTML files and look for ways to address the problems you find.

As an extension to trying out your site with different browsers, you can also change your monitor's resolution so that you can see what your site looks like at 640×480, 800×600, and 1024×768 pixels.

Try It at Different Connection Speeds

To accomplish this one, you may have to send people home to sign on from there. It is, however, well worth the effort. Have them check the pages on the site and time how long it takes for each to download. One popular rule of thumb suggests that it should not take more than 15 seconds for each page to download. Identify pages that take longer than this and look for ways to scale back the amount of information. ●

CHAPTER 2

Web Page Design

by Eric Ladd

In this chapter

Page Design Follows Site Design

Many of the issues that go into designing a web site also go into the design of a single web page, but some page design considerations are unique. Ideally, page design should follow site design; and when you get ready to start a page, you should already have a good sense of what the page needs to accomplish, given its place in your site design.

A book this size could be written on all the issues that go into the design of quality web pages. This chapter summarizes only the major concepts and elements of a good design. By looking at the work of others and doing design yourself, you will build up your own good design sense and the skills you need to implement a first-rate web site.

Check out the Usenet www.authoring newsgroups to learn about design concepts, approaches, and philosophies used by other web designers around the world.

Know Your Audience

The cardinal rule for web site design is also the cardinal rule for page design. Knowing your audience and designing to that audience requires you to gather as much information about them as possible, including

- Equipment configuration (hardware, software, and Internet connection)
- Learning characteristics (how to best present information so that they understand it)
- Motivations for surfing the web (business, professional, personal, entertainment, or educational reasons)
- Demographic factors (age, amount of education, geographic location, language)
- Cultural characteristics (any other factors that could influence how they read a page)

You need to gather all this informhation before you start designing pages. As with all things, finding out as much as you can beforehand will save you a whole lot of headaches later.

In addition to gathering as many user characteristics as you can, you should keep in mind the following two things that are common to all users:

- They are visiting your pages because they are interested in the information you have put there.
- They are using some type of web browser to visit your site.

Knowledge of these two factors provides a good basis for beginning your web page design. The next two sections investigate some of the specifics of each.

NOTE Unless you have the luxury of developing for a very homogeneous group of people, you will probably have to design your pages to be accessible to the broadest audience possible. In the absence of proper information about your audience, designing for maximum readability is the best rule of thumb.

Corporate Intranets: Designing for a Homogenous Group

If you are working on an intranet page for your company, one thing you can typically take advantage of is a common platform. Many companies that put up intranets get a site license for their browser of choice. After you know that everyone is using the same browser, you can design to that browser's level of performance. If your intranet users are using Netscape Navigator 4, for example, you can design pages with frames, client-side imagemaps, Java applets, and the <LAYER> tag (a Netscape extension to standard HTML). If everyone is using Internet Explorer 4, however, you could use one of the Microsoft proprietary tags such as <MARQUEE>. Additionally, everyone is most likely running the software on the same platform with the same connection speed, so you can design to those parameters as well.

Another advantage that you can harness in a corporate intranet design situation is a common culture. Most firms have a "way of doing things" that can be captured on the intranet pages. This gives the pages a context to which all your users can relate.

Designing for an audience whose members are more or less the same is a luxury that few people get to experience. If you find yourself in this situation, be sure to make full use of the characteristics common to your users.

Choosing Information

When you choose information for a page and choose how you are going to format that information, you should think about how you can minimize the effort the reader has to make to understand your message. If a page has relevant content that is presented in a well-organized layout, readers are much more likely to get something out of it than if the page is crammed with a lot of extraneous information and is displayed in a cluttered way.

When choosing what information to put on a page, keep the following two, often competing, parameters in mind:

- What information does the page need to get across to accomplish your communication objectives?
- What information is your audience genuinely interested in reading?

The first point in the preceding list presupposes that you have good and proper reasons for wanting to post content on the web in the first place. Assuming that you have key communication objectives you want to reach, distill the messages that support those objectives down to their bare essence. Dressing up your messages with frivolous content, or burying them in irrelevant information, means the reader has to make a greater effort to extract them. This reduces the likelihood that your readers will come away with what you want them to.

NOTE If you haven't formulated what goals you hope to achieve by creating web pages, go back to the drawing board and write some down. Your set of goals should be one of the driving forces behind your decisions about what qualifies as appropriate content. ■

On the other side of the coin is what the audience is interested in. A visitor to your web page also has specific objectives in mind. In a perfect world, your audience visits your pages because they want to read the messages you want to convey. When visitors leave your web page and understand your message, both of you have satisfied your objectives.

Of course, the objectives of a web page author and a web page reader are not always convergent. In these cases, you may need to include content on your pages that attracts the audience you want. There is a fine balance that you have to achieve, however. You must include enough content to get people to your page without including so much that it obscures the message you want to get across.

Presenting the Information

After you have selected the information to go on a page, you then need to think about how you want to display it. Between standard HTML and extended HTML (browser-specific HTML instructions that are not part of the standard), there are many ways to place content on a page that permit both creativity and good organization. These include

- *Paragraphs.* You probably learned back in grade school that every paragraph should speak to a unique idea. The same holds true for web page paragraphs; you can use them to convey an important concept. Figure 2.1 shows a page from the White House for Kids site that breaks up simple facts about the history of Washington, DC into paragraphs.

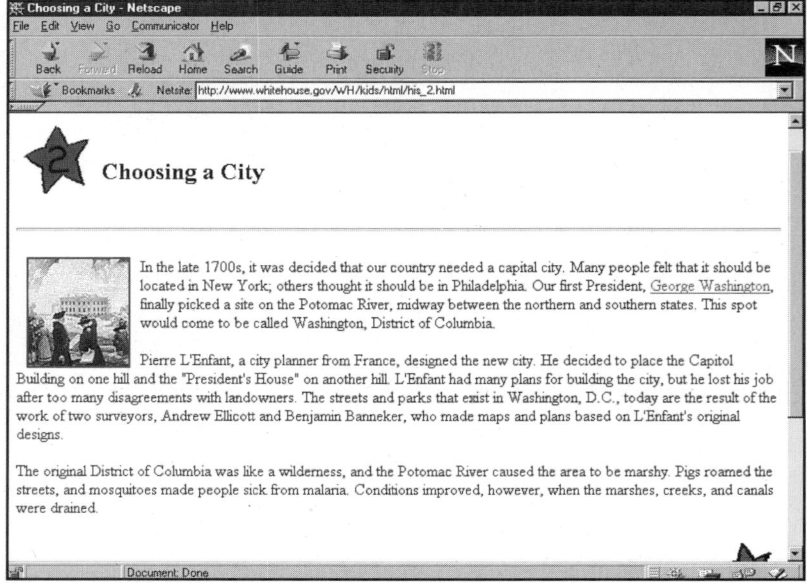

FIG. 2.1
Each paragraph should put forward one major point that supports your communications goals.

- *Lists.* HTML includes extensive support for lists. Placing items in a bulleted or ordered list makes for a readable and easy-to-understand presentation of information. Ordered lists are also useful for conveying a sequential relationship among the list items. A definition list provides a means of presenting a term, followed by its definition. Figures 2.2 and 2.3 illustrate some of the layouts possible with HTML lists.

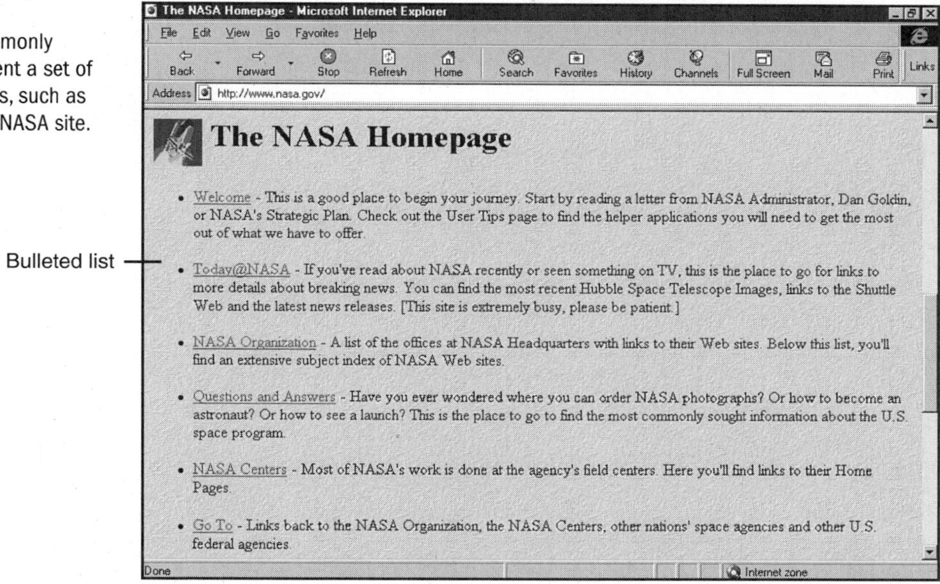

FIG. 2.2
Lists are commonly used to present a set of hypertext links, such as those on the NASA site.

- *Images.* Graphics content is one of the forces that has made the web so popular, and users almost always expect graphics on a web page. Clever use of images can communicate your message to those who visit your pages (see Figure 2.4). Images can also be used as page backgrounds, hyperlink anchors, and as site navigation aids.
- *Font styles.* You can make key words and phrases stand out from regular text by using one of HTML's many font formats. Text can be rendered in bold, in italic, or in a fixed-width font such as Courier (see Figure 2.5). Additionally, you can use other HTML instructions to change the size, color, and typeface of text. Now that they are standard, HTML style sheets provide even greater flexibility for page authors applying style information to their pages.

  ▶ For more information, **see** "Style Sheets," **p. 235**.

- *Multimedia content.* As computers become more powerful and connection speeds become faster, multimedia content such as audio, video, and Macromedia Director movies will become standard fare on web pages. These page elements are highly engaging and a great way to draw users to your site.

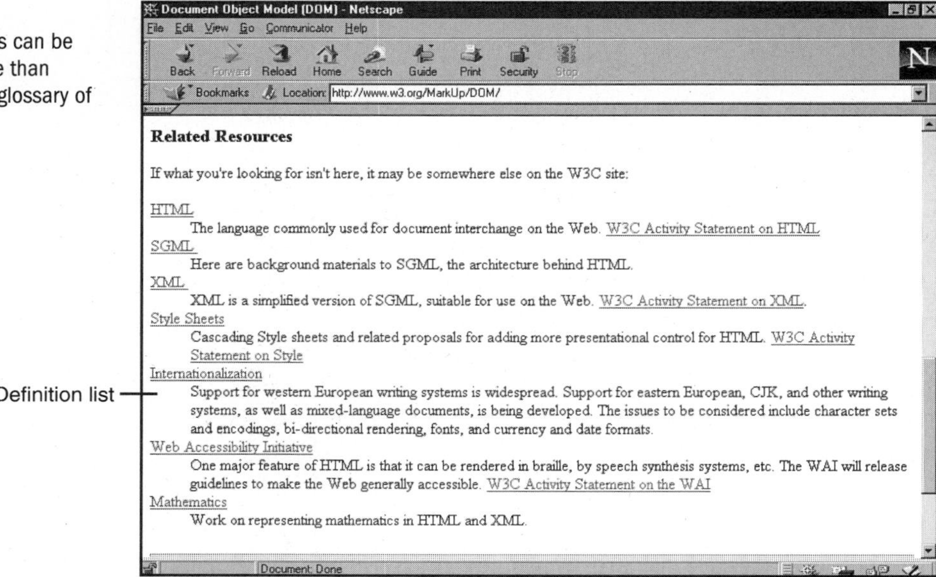

FIG. 2.3
Definition lists can be used for more than presenting a glossary of terms.

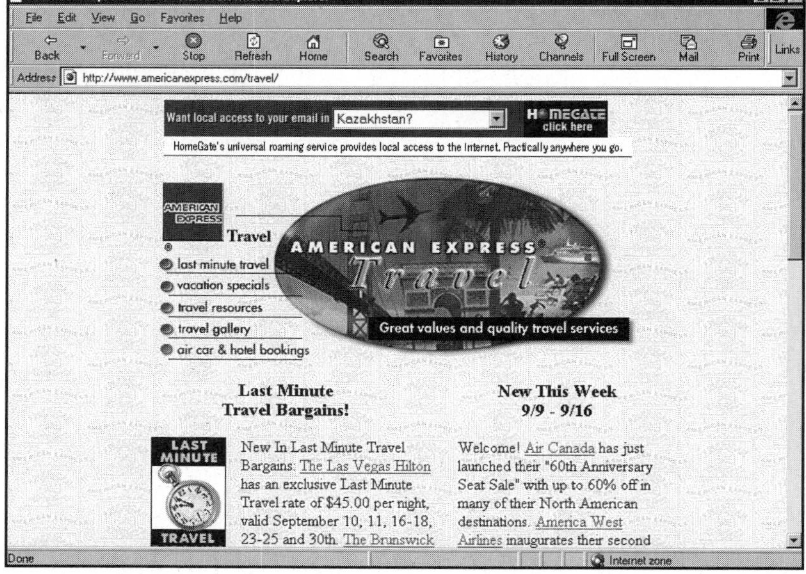

FIG. 2.4
American Express's travel site uses images for its background, for the banner graphic, and for special offers.

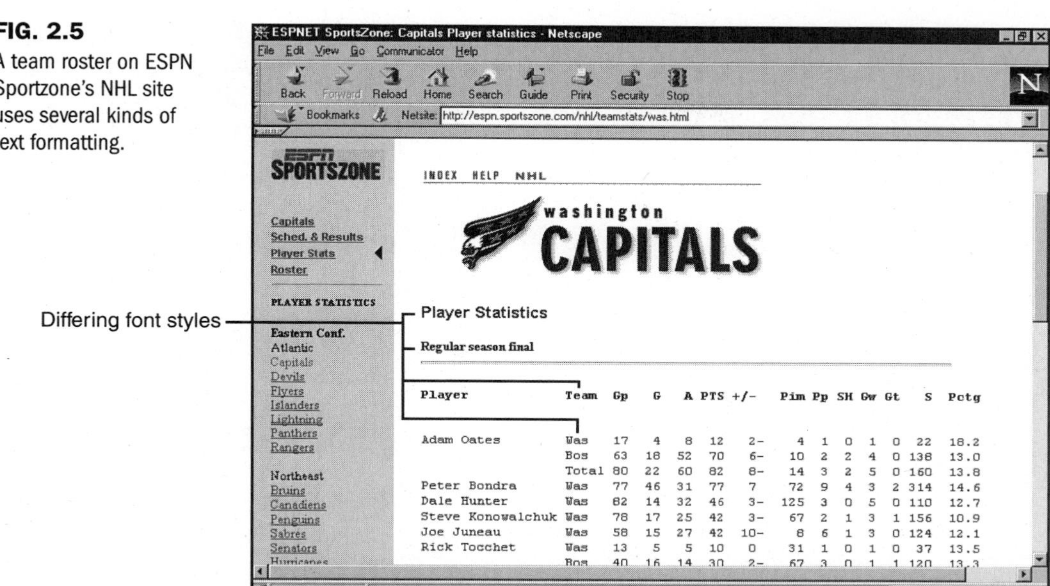

Player	Team	Gp	G	A	PTS	+/-	Pim	Pp	SH	Gw	Gt	S	Pctg
Adam Oates	Was	17	4	8	12	2-	4	1	0	1	0	22	18.2
	Bos	63	18	52	70	6-	10	2	2	4	0	138	13.0
	Total	80	22	60	82	8-	14	3	2	5	0	160	13.8
Peter Bondra	Was	77	46	31	77	7	72	9	4	3	2	314	14.6
Dale Hunter	Was	82	14	32	46	3-	125	3	0	5	0	110	12.7
Steve Konowalchuk	Was	78	17	25	42	3-	67	2	1	3	1	156	10.9
Joe Juneau	Was	58	15	27	42	10-	8	6	1	3	0	124	12.1
Rick Tocchet	Was	13	5	5	10	0	31	1	0	1	0	37	13.5
	Bos	40	16	14	30	2-	67	3	0	1	1	120	13.3

FIG. 2.5
A team roster on ESPN Sportzone's NHL site uses several kinds of text formatting.

- *Tables*. HTML tables enable you to put information into an easy-to-read, tabular form (see Figure 2.6). Tables also permit very precise alignment control inside their component cells; many resourceful HTML authors have made creative use of this feature to produce onscreen layouts that could not be achieved any other way (see Figure 2.7).

▶ **See** "Tables," **p. 165**

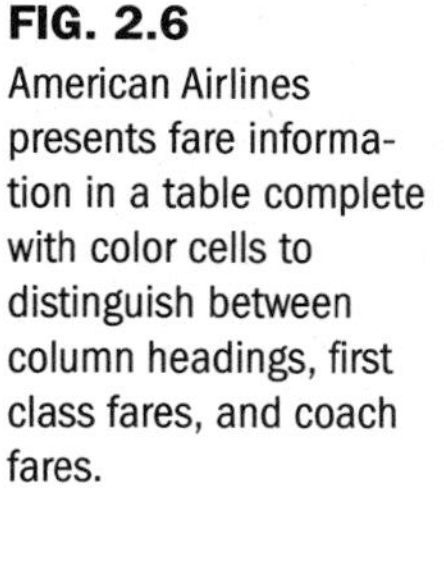

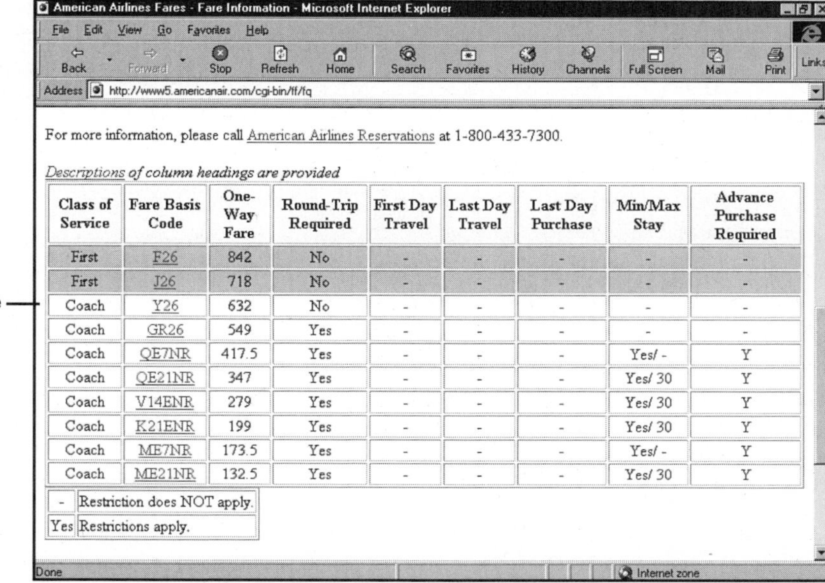

For more information, please call American Airlines Reservations at 1-800-433-7300.

Descriptions of column headings are provided

Class of Service	Fare Basis Code	One-Way Fare	Round-Trip Required	First Day Travel	Last Day Travel	Last Day Purchase	Min/Max Stay	Advance Purchase Required
First	F26	842	No	-	-	-	-	-
First	J26	718	No	-	-	-	-	-
Coach	Y26	632	No	-	-	-	-	-
Coach	GR26	549	Yes	-	-	-	-	-
Coach	QE7NR	417.5	Yes	-	-	-	Yes/ -	Y
Coach	QE21NR	347	Yes	-	-	-	Yes/ 30	Y
Coach	V14ENR	279	Yes	-	-	-	Yes/ 30	Y
Coach	K21ENR	199	Yes	-	-	-	Yes/ 30	Y
Coach	ME7NR	173.5	Yes	-	-	-	Yes/ -	Y
Coach	ME21NR	132.5	Yes	-	-	-	Yes/ 30	Y

-	Restriction does NOT apply.
Yes	Restrictions apply.

FIG. 2.6
American Airlines presents fare information in a table complete with color cells to distinguish between column headings, first class fares, and coach fares.

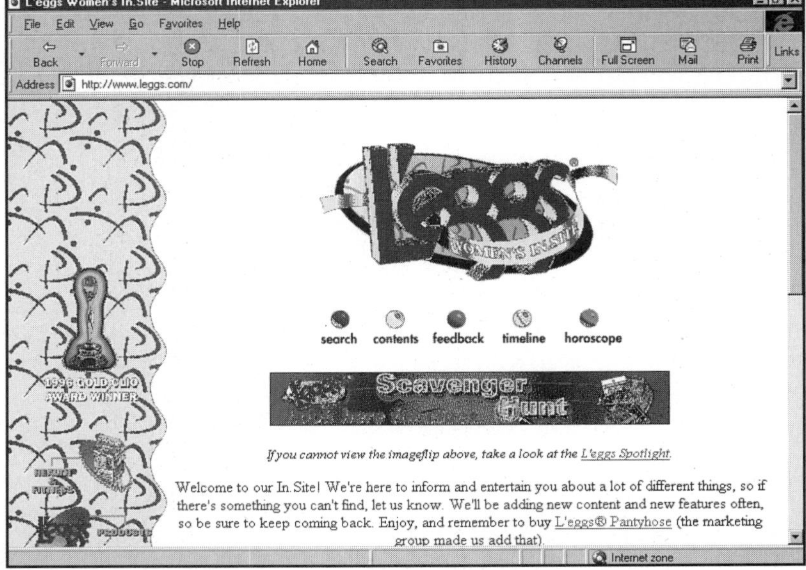

FIG. 2.7
The award-winning L'eggs site uses a table to produce the navigation area on the left side of the screen and the content area on the right.

- *Frames*. When you split a browser window into two or more regions, the individual regions are called frames. Each frame is capable of displaying its own document, and so you can have multiple pages onscreen simultaneously. Figure 2.8 shows a web page that makes effective use of frames.

▶ **See** "Frames," **p. 191**.

FIG. 2.8
Gateway 2000 keeps navigation choices in a borderless frame along the top of the browser screen.

The page elements noted in the preceding list give you a design palette to work with. It is up to you to decide which elements best communicate your message in a way that is clear to your audience.

HTML Standards and Browser Compatibility

The current draft HTML standard is HTML 4, which incorporates most of the page elements discussion in the previous list. Even the frame tags are part of HTML 4 spec, including the concept of "floating frames" as proposed by Microsoft.

NOTE *Floating frames* are frames that you can place on a page just as you would an image.

Most mainstream browsers are already in compliance with the HTML 4 tags that create paragraphs, lists, and font effects as well as those that place images, multimedia content, tables, and frames on a page. If you discover that some of your audience will be using a browser that is not HTML 4-compliant, you should research which tags the browser does not support and make sure you don't use those tags in your page design unless you can provide some kind of alternative way to view the content. Fortunately, there are a couple of approaches to providing alternatives. The next two sections discuss these approaches.

Alternative HTML

One of the great features of HTML is that it enables you to provide alternative content if your primary content is not viewable. The HTML instruction that places an image on a page, for example, also supports the display of a text-based alternative to the image for users with text-only browsers or for users who have turned image loading off on their graphical browsers. As you read the chapters on HTML in this book, make note of the ways that you can provide alternative content on your pages. Using these techniques will also help to maximize your audience.

Alternative HTML Pages

Sometimes users cannot view an entire page. One case of this is a framed page. Although most users will probably be using a browser that can process frames, you still need to be sensitive to "frames-challenged" browsers. You can do this by creating non-frames versions of your framed pages. Many sites that use frames provide links to pages that contain the same information but don't use frames (see Figure 2.9).

Desirable Page Elements

As users traverse the web, they become accustomed to seeing certain items on pages. They come to rely on these items being present to enhance their web browsing experience. This section looks at a few common page elements that are also good end-user services.

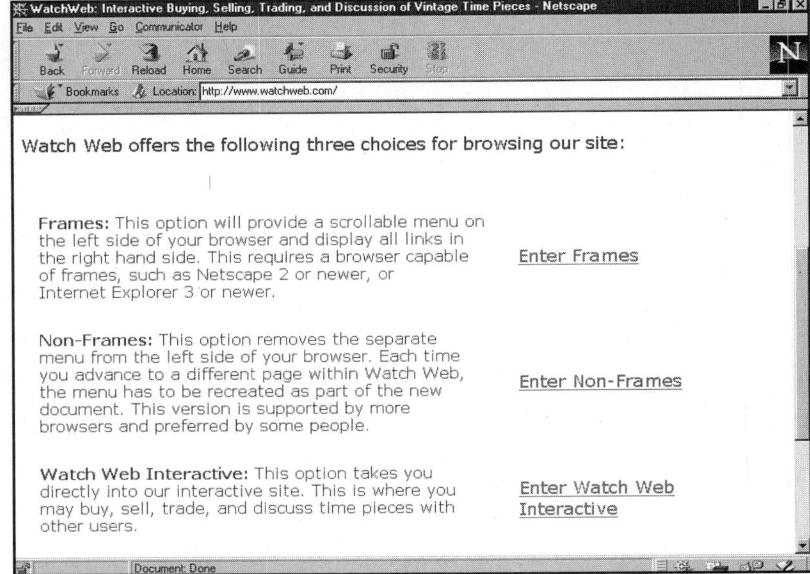

FIG. 2.9
WatchWeb offers both framed and non-framed versions of its pages.

Last Updated Date

Everyone craves fresh content, so it makes sense to have some kind of "freshness dating" on your pages. A last updated date tells visitors how recently the information on a page has changed (see Figure 2.10). Assuming they remember the last time they visited your page, they can use the last updated date to decide whether there is any new content that they need to check out if they are a regular visitor.

▶ To learn how to automate your last updated dates, **see** "FrontPage Components," **p. 257**.

Server-side includes are a good way to have the server automatically stamp your pages with last updated dates. See Chapter 37, "Active Server Pages," for more information.

CAUTION

Having a last updated date can create image problems for you if you don't keep refreshing your pages. Users will be unimpressed if they see a last updated date of six months ago!

FIG. 2.10
The Washington Post notes last update dates and times so that readers know that the content is continuously refreshed throughout the day.

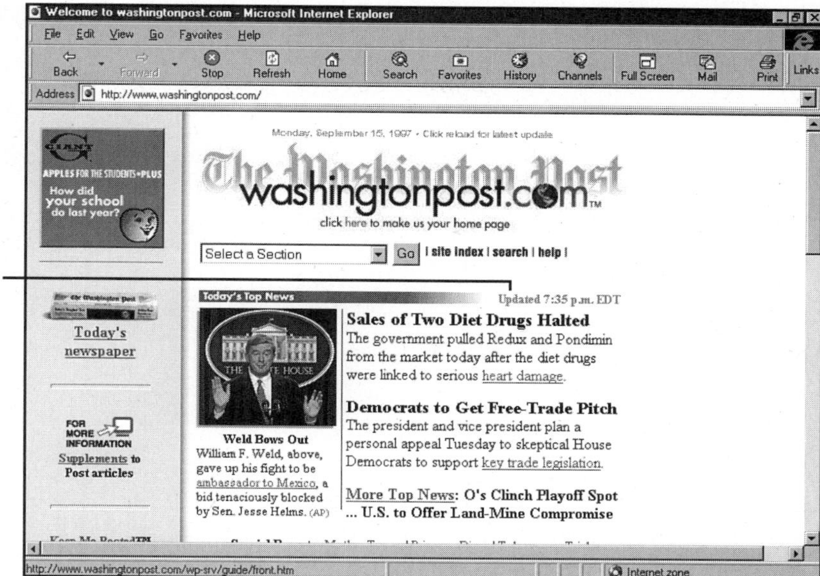

Contact Information

User feedback is important to your efforts to maintain and improve your pages. Many web pages have contact information at the bottom, typically the email address of the webmaster or the page author. Others take you to a separate HTML page to collect feedback (see Figure 2.11). These email addresses are often hyperlinked so that users can click on them and compose a feedback message.

NOTE It is better to include your email address right in the hyperlink so that visitors can just click to send mail. That way, if someone is seeing a printout of the page only, she still knows where to send the feedback.

Navigation Tools

It frustrates users when they get that "You can't get there from here" feeling. To avoid the web equivalent of this, it is imperative that you place navigation tools on your pages. Depending on where users are, they will have different expectations about which navigation tools should be available.

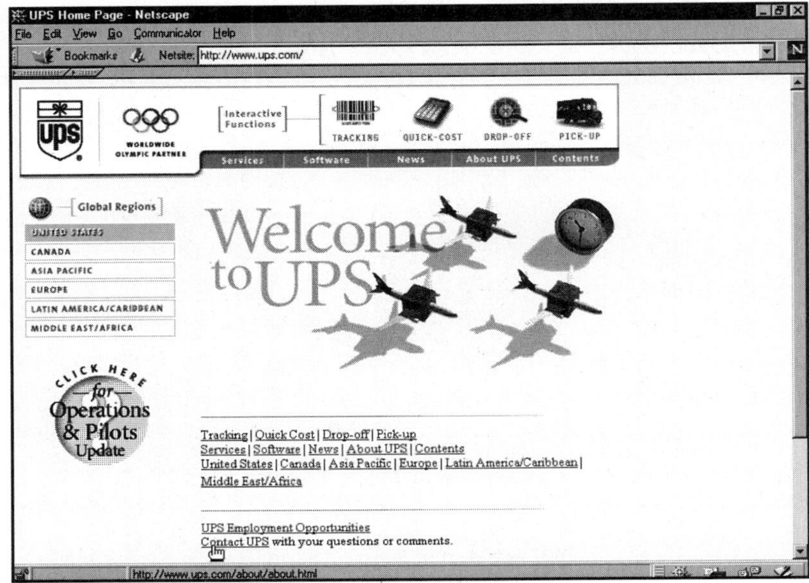

FIG. 2.11
You can contact the United Parcel Service through a link at the bottom of its web page.

A visitor hitting the home page of a site will most likely be looking for some type of clickable image or imagemap that can take her to the major subsections of the site (see Figure 2.12). A home page that is well-designed will also include a set of hypertext links that duplicate the links on the imagemap. This enables people with text-only browsers, or people with image loading turned off, to navigate from the home page as well.

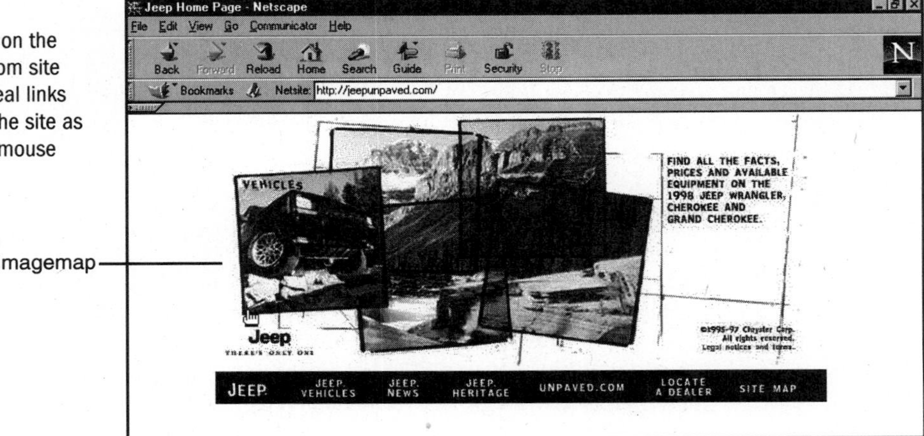

FIG. 2.12
The imagemap on the jeepunpaved.com site changes to reveal links to sections of the site as you move your mouse over the map.

When on an "inside" page of a site, users typically look for navigation bars either at the top or bottom of the page (see Figures 2.13). Some pages have navigation bars at both the top and bottom so that the user has the option of using the closest one. In other cases, a page will have a set of links across the top of the page that points to the major areas of the site and another set along the bottom of the page pointing to functional areas.

FIG. 2.13
Microsoft puts major site links right at the top of each of its products pages.

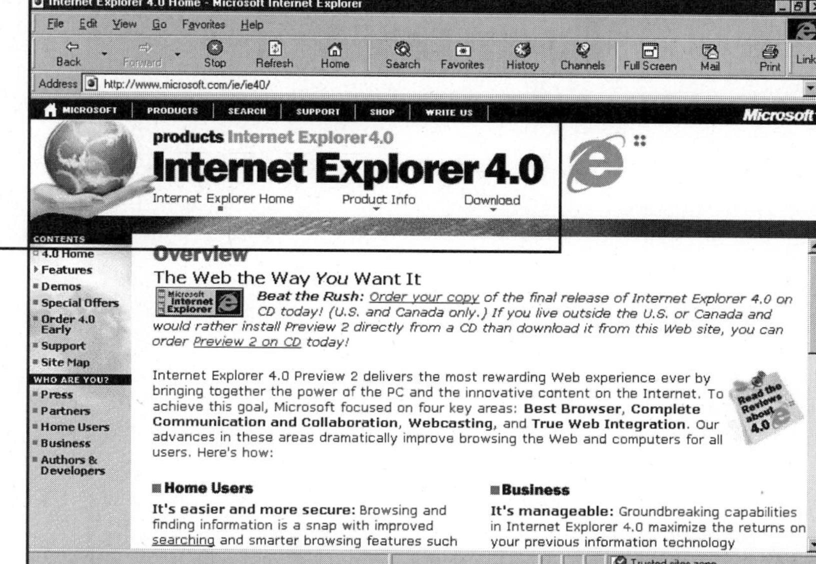

Navigation bar

Counters

Some people think counters, which are graphics displays of the number of people who have visited a page (see Figure 2.14), are annoying. Counters can be annoying if they are used in a grandstanding or self-indulgent way. They can be a useful service, however, if they are built into pages in an unobtrusive way. Counters are helpful to

- Users, who can get a sense of how many other people are interested in the content on the page.
- Page authors, who can better track the traffic on their pages.

▶ To learn how to add a counter to one of your pages, **see** "FrontPage Components," **p.257** or "Custom Database Query Scripts," **p. 887**.

There are two ways you can go about placing a counter on a page. One approach involves programming the counter yourself. This is a fairly straightforward thing to do, but it does require that your web page server supports Common Gateway Interface (CGI) programs. If you want to avoid programming altogether, you drop the FrontPage Hit Counter Component on your page and let it do all the work for you.

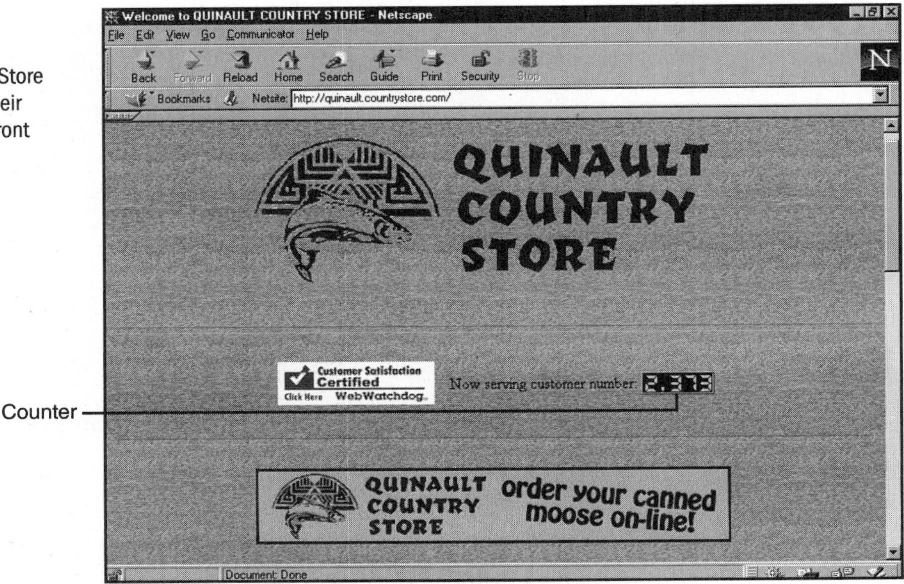

FIG. 2.14
Shoppers at the Quinault Country Store are counted on their way through the front door.

If you don't have CGI support on your server, you can use one of the online counter services. Figure 2.15 shows you the counter service at **http://www.digits.com/**. This popular service walks you through the setup process and tells you exactly what HTML code to place in your files to increment the counter.

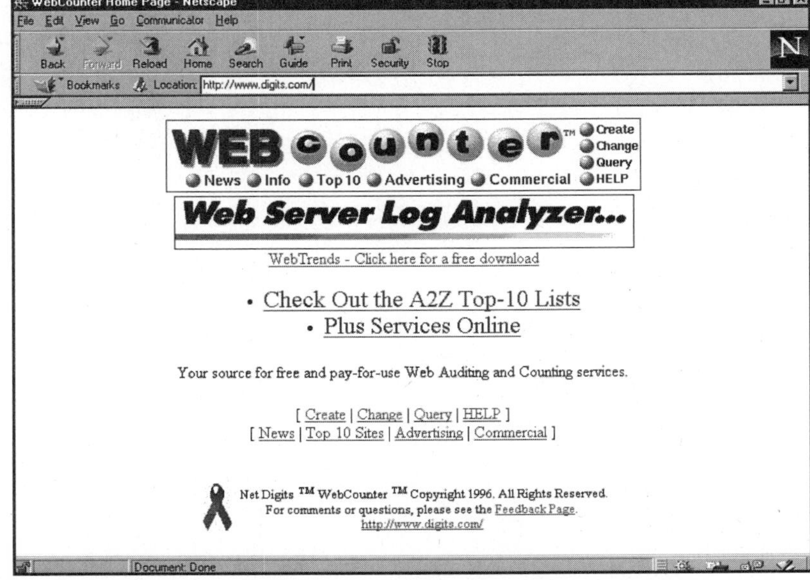

FIG. 2.15
WebCounter is an online service that provides page counters to sites otherwise unable to implement them.

> **CAUTION**
>
> When you use an online counter service, the images that make up the counter display have to be transferred from your host service. This can delay page loading and make visitors to your web pages impatient.
>
> Don't put a counter on every page you create. Usually a counter on the home page of a site is sufficient.

Breaking Up Long Pages

You should avoid placing too much content on a single page. Forcing users to scroll through large amounts of text serves only to annoy them. If you have a lot of content, try to think of ways to divide it over several pages so that users can read it in smaller, more digestible chunks.

Sometimes long pages are unavoidable. For those instances, you can make use of some of the graphics elements techniques, discussed in the following section, to make reading long pages less of an effort for your audience.

Graphics Elements

Graphics elements are a terrific way to break up a sea of text. Graphics give users' eyes a break from line after line of content. Intelligent placement of the graphics can also create interesting and attractive layouts.

With the HTML you will learn in this book, you will be able to use the following three effective graphics elements:

- Horizontal rules
- Images
- Pull quotes

Horizontal Rules A *horizontal rule* is just a simple horizontal line across the width of a page (see Figure 2.16). Simple proves very effective in this case because a horizontal rule can break up a long page into smaller sections and give the readers' eyes a reprieve from an abundance of text.

Images *Images* can break up a lot of text and they are particularly effective when text wraps around them (see Figure 2.17). HTML 4 includes instructions for placing "floating images" that permit text wrapping.

Pull Quotes A *pull quote* is a key phrase or sentence from a manuscript that is repeated in larger, bold text. Pull quotes provide you with a doubly powerful page element: They break up big blocks of text and they reiterate important points (see Figure 2.18).

It is easy to make a pull quote by using HTML tables. You can do this by floating a table in the middle of your document's text and placing a large, formatted excerpt from the text in the table. It is also a good idea to have the table borders turned off and to use horizontal lines above and below the excerpted text.

FIG. 2.16
Netscape separates descriptions of various features on its site with horizontal rules.

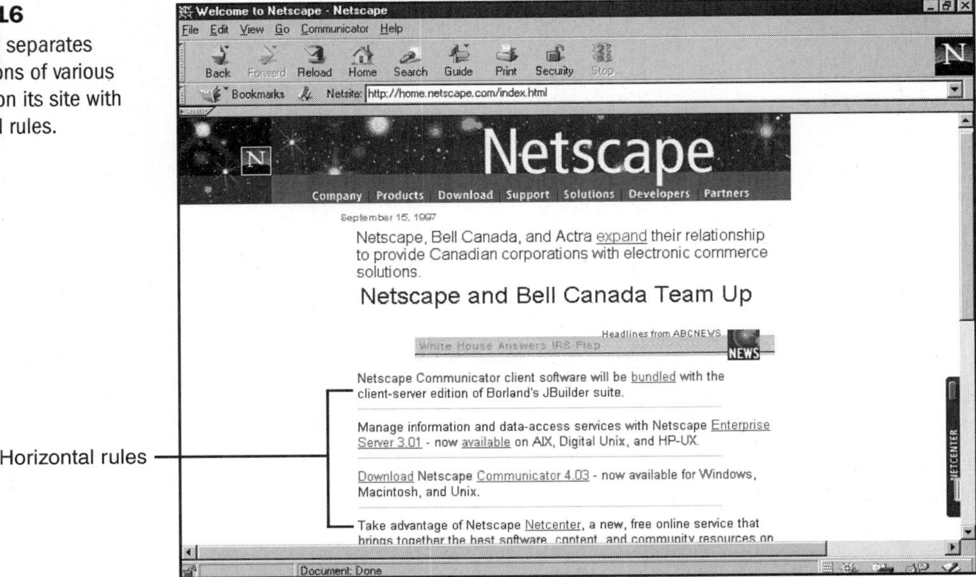

FIG. 2.17
A CNN story about the troubled space station Mir wraps around a picture of the station.

FIG. 2.18
Pull quotes give readers' eyes a break from long passages while repeating a key idea.

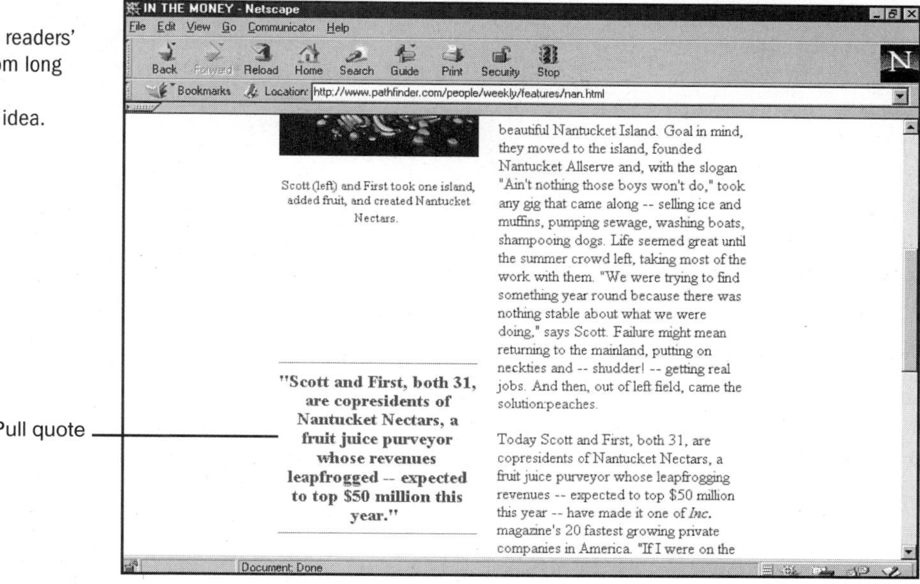

Table of Contents

If a page is really long, you should make the extra effort to set up a small table of contents at the top of the page (see Figure 2.19). By clicking on different entries in the table of contents, users can jump right to the section of the document they are interested in and not have to scroll through the document to find it.

FIG. 2.19
Long documents placed on a single page should have a table of contents at the top to assist the reader in navigating the document.

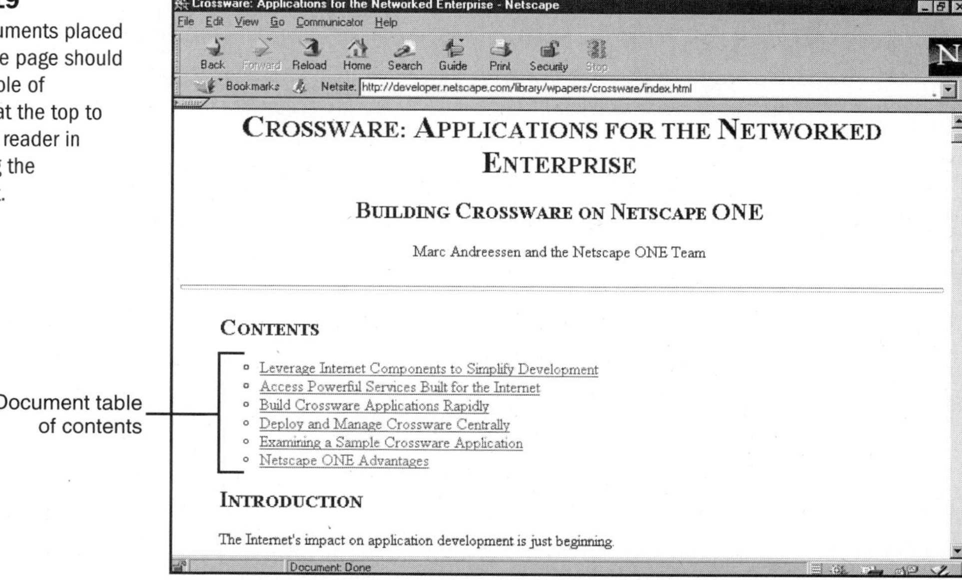

PART II

HTML, Graphics, XML and VRML

CHAPTER 3

HTML 4.0 Tag Reference

by Eric Ladd

In this chapter

Reference Scope

This chapter is unique in the book because it is written to serve as a reference for all the tags included in the recommended HTML 4.0 standard. It is a one-stop catalog of each tag, including the tag's attributes, syntax, and sample uses. By necessity, the chapter covers a large amount of information, but you'll soon come to appreciate the value of having all the relevant facts about all HTML tags, together with tips on how to use them, right at your fingertips.

NOTE This chapter covers only the tags included in the HTML 4.0 Document Type Definition (DTD) as published by the World Wide Web Consortium (W3C). Browser-specific extensions to HTML 4.0 are beyond the scope of this chapter, but may be covered elsewhere in the book. For example, the `<LAYER>` tag introduced by Netscape Communications Corporation is discussed in detail in Chapter 23, "Introduction to Dynamic HTML," and Chapter 24, "Advanced Netscape Dynamic HTML."

For the most up-to-date status of HTML 4.0, consult **http://www.w3.org/TR/PR-html40/**, where you will find links to the most current version of the standard and the version just prior to that.

How This Chapter Is Organized

Because of the vast coverage of the chapter, the information presented has been carefully structured to make it as easy as possible for you to look up the tags you need. At the highest level, the chapter is organized into major sections that cover a group of related tags. The major sections include

- Document structure tags
- Text-level formatting tags
- Block-level formatting tags
- List tags
- Hyperlink tags
- Image and imagemap tags
- Table tags
- Form tags
- Frame tags
- Executable content tags

In some cases, tags covered in this chapter get a more thorough treatment in a later chapter of the book. Look for cross-references to point you to this expanded coverage.

Within a given section, several tags are discussed in detail. Specifically, you'll find the following information about each tag:

- The tag's keyword—For example, the `<INPUT>` tag's keyword is `INPUT`.

- What kind of tag it is—Every HTML tag is either a *container tag* or a *standalone tag*. A container tag activates an effect and has a companion tag that discontinues the effect. For example, `<I>` is a container tag that, together with its companion closing tag `</I>`, causes all text found between them to be rendered in italics. The `<I>` tag turns on the italics effect and the `</I>` tag turns it off.

  A standalone tag does not have a companion tag. For example, the `<IMG>` tag simply places an image on a page. `<IMG>` has no effect that was turned on and needs to be turned off, so there is no need for a closing tag.

NOTE Standalone tags are sometimes called *empty tags*.

- The tag's function—A description of the effect or page element that the tag controls.
- The tag's syntax—HTML is derived from the Standard Generalized Markup Language (SGML) by applying SGML constructs according to a certain set of rules. These rules define a tag's syntax.
- The tag's attributes—An attribute modifies how a tag's effect is applied. Some tags take no attributes, and others may be able to take several. Additionally, attributes can sometimes take on only one of a set number of values. In these cases, the possible values of the attribute are listed along with the attribute. Use of some attributes may be required (such as the `SRC` attribute for the `<IMG>` tag), and use of others may be optional. A tag's required attributes, if any, are noted in each attribute discussion.
- Sample usage—You can learn more about how a tag is used by looking over the sample code given in the tag description.
- Related tags—Some tags work in conjunction with others to produce an effect. In these cases, you'll find a listing of the other HTML tags related to the one being described. Very often, you'll find that the related tags are discussed in the same section.

Within a section, tags are listed alphabetically by keyword, unless they need to be used in a certain order, in which case, they are presented in the order in which they are typically used.

Document Structure Tags

Every HTML document has three major components: the HTML declaration, the head, and the body. The document structure tags are those that define each component.

<HTML>

Type:

Container

Function:

Declares the document to be an HTML document. All document content and supporting HTML code goes between the `<HTML>` and `</HTML>` tags.

Syntax:

```
<HTML> ... </HTML>
```

Attributes:

None.

Example:

```
<HTML>
... all content and HTML code goes here ...
</HTML>
```

Related Tags:

Although the <HTML> tag is typically the first tag in a document, it is sometimes preceded by a <!DOCTYPE> tag that specifies what level of HTML conformance the document displays. A document conforming to the HTML 4.0 standard might have a <!DOCTYPE> tag that reads

```
<!DOCTYPE HTML PUBLIC "-//W3C//DTD HTML 4.0//EN">
```

Technically, <!DOCTYPE> is an SGML tag, not an HTML tag, so it is acceptable for it to be outside the <HTML> and </HTML> tags.

<HEAD>

Type:

Container

Function:

Contains the tags that comprise the document head.

Syntax:

```
<HEAD> ... </HEAD>
```

Attributes:

None.

Example:

```
<HTML>
<HEAD>
... tags making up the document head go here ...
</HEAD>
... all other content and HTML code goes here ...
</HTML>
```

Related Tags:

A number of tags can be placed between the <HEAD> and </HEAD> tags, including <BASE>, <ISINDEX>, <LINK>, <META>, <SCRIPT>, <STYLE>, and <TITLE>. Each of these is described next.

<BASE>

Type:

Standalone

Function:

Declares global reference values for the HREF and TARGET attributes. The reference or base HREF value is used as a basis for computing all relative URL references. The base TARGET name is used to identify the frame into which all linked documents should be loaded.

Syntax:

```
<BASE HREF="base_url">
```

or

```
<BASE TARGET="frame_name">
```


Attributes:

The <BASE> tag takes either the HREF or the TARGET attribute. A given <BASE> tag can contain only one of these, so if you need to specify a base URL and a base target frame, you need to have two <BASE> tags in the head of your document. These two attributes work as follows:

- HREF—Specifies the reference URL that is used to help compute relative URLs. For example, if the BASE HREF URL is **http://www.myserver.com/sports/hockey/skates.html** and you use the relative URL **pucks.html** elsewhere in the document, the relative URL will really point to **http://www.myserver.com/sports/hockey/pucks.html**.
- TARGET—Specifies the default frame name to which all links are targeted.

NOTE When used in a <BASE> tag, HREF is typically set to the URL of the document.

Example:

```
<HEAD>
<BASE HREF="http://www.myserver.com/index.html">
<BASE TARGET="bigframe">
...
</HEAD>
```

This code sets the document's base URL to **http://www.myserver.com/index.html** and the base frame for targeting hyperlinks to the frame named "bigframe".

<ISINDEX>

Type:

Standalone

Type:

Standalone

Function:

Denotes the linking relationship between two files.

Syntax:

```
<LINK HREF="url_of_linked_file" TITLE="title" REL="forward_relationship"
REV="reverse_relationship">
```

Attributes:

The <LINK> tag takes the following attributes:

- HREF—Set equal to the URL of the file to which you're making the linking reference.
- TITLE—Gives the link a descriptive title.
- REL—Specifies the relationship of the linked file to the current file.
- REV—Specifies how the current file relates to the linked file.

Function:

Produces a single-line input field used to collect query information.

Syntax:

```
<ISINDEX PROMPT="Please enter the value to search for.">
```

Attributes:

The PROMPT attribute specifies what text should appear before the input field. In the absence of a PROMPT attribute, the text will read "This is a searchable index. Enter search criteria:".

Example:

```
<HEAD>
<ISINDEX PROMPT="Enter the last name of the employee you want to search for:">
...
</HEAD>
```

NOTE <ISINDEX> was used in the early days when the <FORM> tags had yet to come onto the

Table 3.1 shows some possible values for REL and REV and what these values mean.

Table 3.1 Possible values for the *REL* and *REV* attributes.

Value	Meaning
Copyright	Web site's copyright page
Glossary	Glossary of terms for a site
Help	Site help page
Home	Site home page
Index	Site index page
Made	mailto URL pointing to the email address of the page author
Next	Page that logically follows the current page
Previous	Page that precedes the current page
Stylesheet	File containing style information for the page
TOC	Site table of contents
Up	Page that is above the current page in a site's hierarchy

NOTE Because there are so many different types of linked files, it is permissible to have more than one <LINK> tag in a document.

Example:

```
<HEAD>
<LINK HREF="/style/styles.css" REL="Stylesheet">
<LINK HREF="/index.html" REL="Home">
<LINK HREF="/help.html" REL="Help">
<LINK HREF="back_one.html" REV="Next"
...
</HEAD>
```

<SCRIPT>

Type:

Container

Function:

Contains script code referenced in the body of the document.

Syntax:

```
<SCRIPT LANGUAGE="scripting_language">
... script code goes here ...
</SCRIPT>
```

Attributes:

The <SCRIPT> tag can take the following attributes:

- DEFER—Specifying the DEFER attribute tells the browser that the script does not generate any document content. This enables the browser to continue parsing and rendering the document without having to execute the script.
- LANGUAGE—Set equal to the scripting language used to write the script. LANGUAGE is being deprecated in favor of using the TYPE attribute.
- SRC—Specifies the URL of a file containing the script code, if not contained between the <SCRIPT> and </SCRIPT> tags.
- TYPE—Set equal to the MIME type of the script code, usually text/javascript or text/vbscript. TYPE is a required attribute under HTML 4.0.

Example:

```
<SCRIPT LANGUAGE="VBScript">
<!--
Sub ScriptEx
document.write("<HR>")
document.write("<H1 ALIGN=CENTER>Thank you for your submission!</H1>")
document.write("<HR>")
-->
</SCRIPT>
```

NOTE Script code is often placed between <!-- and --> tags so that browsers that can't process scripts will treat the code as a comment.

<STYLE>

Type:

Container

Function:

Specifies style information for the document.

Syntax:

```
<STYLE TYPE="mime_type" MEDIA="media_type" TITLE="title">
... style information goes here ...
</HTML>
```

Attributes:

THE <STYLE> tag takes the following three attributes:

- MEDIA—Specifies what media types the styles are to be used for (visual browser, speech-based browser, Braille browser, and so on).
- TITLE—Gives the style information a descriptive title.

- TYPE—Set equal to the Internet content type for the style language. This means that you will most likely say TYPE="text/css1" to denote the use of the style language put forward in the Cascading Style Sheets, Level 1 specification. TYPE is a required attribute of the <STYLE> tag.

Example:

```
<STYLE TYPE="text/css1">
<!--
   BODY {font: 10 pt Palatino; color: silver margin-left: 0.25 in}
   H1 {font: 18 pt Palatino; font-weight: bold}
   H2 {font: 16 pt Palatino; font-weight: bold}
   P {font: 12 pt Arial; line-height: 14 pt; text-indent: 0.25 in}
-->
</STYLE>
```

NOTE Style information is usually contained between <!-- and --> tags so that browsers that cannot process it will treat the style information as a comment.

<TITLE>

Type:

Container

Function:

Gives a descriptive title to a document. Use of the <TITLE> tag is required by the HTML 4.0 DTD for many good reasons. Titles show up in browser window title bars and in bookmark and history listings. In each of these cases, you provide an important reader service when you specify a title, because the browser will display just the document's URL otherwise. Additionally, web search engines such as Yahoo! and AltaVista frequently look for title information when they index a document.

Syntax:

```
<TITLE> ... document title goes here ... </TITLE>
```

Attributes:

None.

Example:

```
<TITLE>
The Advantages of a Corporate Web Site
</TITLE>
```

TIP Try to keep titles to 40 characters or less so that browsers can display them completely.

<BODY>

Type:

Container

Function:

Contains all content and tags that comprise the document body.

Syntax:

```
<BODY BGCOLOR="background_color" BACKGROUND="background_image"
   LINK="unvisited_link_color" ALINK="active_link_color"
   VLINK="visited_link_color" TEXT="text_color">
 ... document body goes here ...
</BODY>
```

Attributes:

The <BODY> tag takes the following attributes, which focus on global background and coloring properties. Each color-related attribute can be set equal to one of the 16 reserved color names (BLACK, WHITE, AQUA, SILVER, GRAY, MAROON, RED, PURPLE, FUSCHIA, GREEN, LIME, OLIVE, YELLOW, NAVY, BLUE, and TEAL) or to an RGB hexadecimal triplet.

- ALINK—Set equal to the color you want to paint active links (a link is active the instant the user clicks it).
- BACKGROUND—Set equal to the URL of an image to use in the document background. The image will be horizontally and vertically tiled if it is not large enough to fill the entire browser screen.
- BGCOLOR—Set equal to the color you want to paint the document's background.
- LINK—Set equal to the color you want to paint unvisited links (a link is unvisited if a user has yet to click it).
- TEXT—Set equal to the color you want to paint the body text of the document.
- VLINK—Set equal to the color you want to paint visited links (a link is visited if a user has already clicked it).

NOTE All the attributes listed have been deprecated in favor of using style sheet characteristics to specify the same information.

Example:

```
<BODY BGCOLOR="white" TEXT="#FF0088" LINK="#DD0F00" VLINK="#00FF9A">
... all document body content and HTML code goes here ...
</BODY>
```

Related Tags:

Dozens of tags are allowed between the <BODY> and </BODY> tags. In fact, with the exception of some of the frame-related tags, any tag in the rest of the chapter can be placed between <BODY> and </BODY>.

Putting together what you've learned in this section, you can come up with a generic HTML document template such as the following:

```
<HTML>
<HEAD>
<TITLE>Document Template</TITLE>
... <META>, <BASE>, <LINK>, <SCRIPT>, <STYLE>, <ISINDEX> tags ...
</HEAD>
<BODY>
... document body content and tags ...
</BODY>
</HTML>
```

When creating a new document, you can use this code to get started and then fill in tags and other information according to your needs.

Text-Level Formatting Tags

HTML provides a host of tags that you can use to change how text is displayed on a browser screen. After all, 12-point Times Roman gets a little tired after a while, and it's nice to give a reader an occasional break from a sea of ordinary text.

Text-level formatting can occur in one of two ways. An HTML tag that formats text can make changes to the font properties of the text (*font formatting* or *physical styles*), or it can describe how the text is being used in the context of the document (*phrase formatting* or *logical styles*). The next two sections introduce you to the tags used for each type of formatting.

Font Formatting

<B>

Type:

Container

Function:

Contains text to be rendered in boldface.

Syntax:

```
<B> ... bold text goes here ... </B>
```

Attributes:

None.

Example:

```
<B>Stop!</B> Make sure you activate SSL on your browser before proceeding.
```

<BASEFONT>

Type:

Standalone

Function:

Sets base size, color, and typeface properties for the body text font.

Syntax:

```
<BASEFONT SIZE="size" COLOR="color" FACE="list_of_typefaces">
```

Attributes:

<FONT> can take any combination of the following attributes:

- COLOR—Set to any of the 16 reserved, English-language color names or an RGB hexadecimal triplet. The default font color is black.
- FACE—Set to a list of typefaces that the browser should use to render the text. The browser will use the first face in the list if that face is available. If not, it will work through the rest of the list and use the first face it finds available.
- SIZE—Set equal to an integer value between 1 and 7. This number is mapped to a font size in points by the browser, according to the user's preferences. The default SIZE value is 3.

Example:

```
<BASEFONT SIZE=5 COLOR="navy" FACE="Arial,Helvetica,Times">
```

Related Tags:

The <FONT> tag is typically used if you need to modify any of the base font properties specified in the <BASEFONT> tag.

NOTE The W3C has deprecated the use of the <BASEFONT> tag. Specifying font properties, such as size, color, and typeface, can now be done with style sheets.

<BIG>

Type:

Container

Function:

Contains text to be rendered in a font size bigger than the default font size.

Syntax:

```
<BIG> ... big text goes here ... </BIG>
```

Attributes:

None.

Example:

```
It's <BIG>really</BIG> important that you check this out!
```

Related Tags:

The <SMALL> tag has the opposite effect (see later in this chapter).

<FONT>

Type:

Container

Function:

Contains text whose font properties are to be modified.

Syntax:

```
<FONT SIZE="size" COLOR="color" FACE="list of typefaces">
... text with modified font properties ...
</FONT>
```

Attributes:

Note that the <FONT> tag has the same attributes as the <BASEFONT> tag. <FONT> is used to change font properties from the base values provided in the <BASEFONT> tag or from their default values. SIZE can be set to a value between 1 and 7, or it can be set equal to how much larger or smaller you want the font size to go (-1 for one size smaller, +3 for three sizes larger, and so on). COLOR and FACE work exactly as they did for the <BASEFONT> tag.

Example:

```
<FONT SIZE=+1 COLOR="red">Caution:</FONT> You should scan all downloaded
files with a virus checker before executing them.
```

Related Tags:

<FONT> changes properties specified in the <BASEFONT> tag.

NOTE For changing font properties, the <FONT> tag has been deprecated in favor of style sheets.

<I>

Type:

Container

Function:

Contains text to be rendered in italics.

Syntax:

```
<I> ... italicized text goes here ... </I>
```

Attributes:

None.

Example:

```
My favorite paper is <I>The Wall Street Journal</I>.
```

<S>, <STRIKE>

Type:

Container

Function:

Contains text to be marked with a strikethrough character.

Syntax:

```
<S> ... strikethrough text goes here ... </S>
```

or

```
<STRIKE> ... strikethrough text goes here ... </STRIKE>
```

Attributes:

None.

Example:

```
Content that has been struck from the record will be denoted as
follows: <S>removed content</S>.
```

NOTE Both the <S> and <STRIKE> tags have been deprecated by the W3C. You should use style sheets to render strikethrough text instead.

<SMALL>

Type:

Container

Function:

Contains text to be rendered in a font size smaller than the default font size.

Syntax:

```
<SMALL> ... smaller text goes here ... </SMALL>
```

Attributes:

None.

Example:

```
It's a <SMALL>small world</SMALL> after all!
```

Related Tags:

The `<BIG>` tag has the opposite effect (see the `<BIG>` tag section earlier in the chapter).

<SUB>

Type:

Container

Function:

Contains text to be a subscript to the text that precedes it.

Syntax:

```
<SUB> ... subscript text goes here ... </SUB>
```

Attributes:

None.

Example:

```
In the above equation, x<SUB>1</SUB> and x<SUB>2</SUB> are the unknowns.
```

<SUP>

Type:

Container

Function:

Contains text to be rendered as a superscript to the text that precedes it.

Syntax:

```
<SUP> ... superscript text goes here ... </SUP>
```

Attributes:

None.

Example:

```
The area of a square equals s<SUP>2</SUP>, where s is the length of one side.
```

<TT>

Type:

Container

Function:

Contains text to be rendered in a fixed-width font. Typically, this font is Courier or some kind of typewriter font.

Syntax:

```
<TT> ... text to be in fixed-width font goes here ... <TT>
```

Attributes:

None.

Example:

```
The computer will then display the <TT>Login:</TT> prompt.
```

<U>

Type:

Container

Function:

Contains text to be rendered with an underline.

Syntax:

```
<U> ... text to be underlined ... </U>
```

Attributes:

None.

Example:

```
Longest book I've read: <U>War and Peace</U>.
```

The <U> tag has been deprecated by the W3C. If you need to underline text, you can do so using style sheets. However, keep in mind that a user might confuse your underlined text with hypertext and try to click it. Also, in keeping with general typesetting rules, if you italicize for form or style, you should not underline.

Phrase Formatting

Recall that phrase formatting indicates the *meaning* of the text it marks up and not necessarily how the text will be rendered on the browser screen. Nevertheless, text marked with a phrase formatting tag will typically have some kind of special rendering to set it apart from unmarked text.

<ACRONYM>

Type:

Container

Function:

Contains text that specifies an acronym.

Syntax:

```
<ACRONYM> ... acronym goes here ... </ACRONYM>
```

Attributes:

None.

Example:

```
Hypertext Markup Language <ACRONYM>(HTML)</ACRONYM> is derived from the
Standard Generalized Markup Language <ACRONYM>SGML</ACRONYM>.
```

<ADDRESS>

Type:

Container

Function:

Contains either a postal or electronic mail address. Text marked with this tag is typically rendered in italics.

Syntax:

```
<ADDRESS> ... address goes here ... </ADDRESS>
```

Attributes:

None.

Example:

```
If you have any comments, please send them to
<ADDRESS>feedback@myserver.com</ADDRESS>.
```

<CITE>

Type:

Container

Function:

Contains the name of a source from which a passage is cited. The source's name is typically rendered in italics.

Syntax:

```
<CITE> ... citation source goes here ... </CITE>
```

Attributes:

None.

Example:

```
According to the <CITE>New York Times</CITE>, crime in the
city is on the decline.
```

<CODE>

Type:

Container

Function:

Contains chunks of computer language code. Browsers commonly display text marked with the `<CODE>` tag in a fixed-width font.

Syntax:

```
<CODE> ... code fragment goes here ... </CODE>
```

Attributes:

None.

Example:

```
<CODE>
for n = 1 to 10
   value(n) = (n++)^2;
</CODE>
```

<DEL>

Type:

Container

Function:

Contains text that has been deleted from the document. The tag is intended mainly for documents with multiple authors and/or editors who would want to see all the content in an original draft, even though it may have been deleted by a reviewer.

NOTE The idea of logically marking up deleted text is similar to the idea of using revision marks in Microsoft Word. When revision marks are turned on, you can see the deleted text even though it is technically no longer part of the document.

Syntax:

```
<DEL> ... deleted text goes here ... </DEL>
```

Attributes:

None.

Example:

```
She just got a big<DEL>, huge</DEL> raise.
```

In this example, the use of the word huge is redundant, so an astute copy editor would delete it.

Related Tags:

The <INS> tag has a similar function for inserted text.

<DFN>

Type:

Container

Function:

Denotes the defining instance of a term. Internet Explorer will display text tagged with <DFN> in italics, whereas Netscape Navigator will use no special formatting.

Syntax:

```
<DFN> ... term being introduced goes here ... </DFN>
```

Attributes:

None.

Example:

```
Freud proposed the idea of a <DFN>catharsis</DFN> - a release
of psychic tension.
```

<EM>

Type:

Container

Function:

Contains text to be emphasized. Most browsers render emphasized text in italics.

Syntax:

```
<EM> ... emphasized text goes here ... </EM>
```

Attributes:

None.

Example:

```
All employees <EM>must</EM> sign their timesheets before submitting them.
```

<INS>

Type:

Container

Function:

Contains text that has been inserted into the document after its original draft.

Syntax:

```
<INS> ... inserted text goes here ... </INS>
```

Attributes:

None.

Example:

```
The New World was discovered by <DEL>Magellan</DEL>
<INS>Columbus</INS> in 1492.
```

NOTE Note how <DEL> and <INS> are used together to strike some text and then insert a correction in its place.

Related Tags:

The <DEL> tag logically represents deleted text.

<KBD>

Type:

Container

Function:

Contains text that represents keyboard input. Browsers typically render such text in a fixed-width font.

Syntax:

```
<KBD> ... keyboard input goes here ... </KBD>
```

Attributes:

None.

Example:

```
When prompted for the item code, enter <KBD>179-990A</KBD>.
```

<Q>

Type:

Container

Function:

Contains a direct quotation to be displayed inline.

Syntax:

```
<Q CITE="URL_of_cited_document"> ... quotation goes here ... </Q>
```

Attributes:

If you're quoting from an online source, you can set the `CITE` attribute equal to the source's URL.

Example:

```
<Q>To be or not to be.  That is the question.</Q>, he said dramatically.
```

Related Tags:

The `<BLOCKQUOTE>` tag can also be used to denote quoted text, but block quotes are displayed with increased right and left indents and not in line with the rest of the body text.

<SAMP>

Type:

Container

Function:

Contains text that represents the literal output from a program. Such output is sometimes referred to as *sample text*. Most browsers will render sample text in a fixed-width font.

Syntax:

```
<SAMP> ... program output goes here ... </SAMP>
```

Attributes:

None.

Example:

```
A common first exercise in a programming course is to write a program
to produce the message <SAMP>Hello World</SAMP>.
```

<STRONG>

Type:

Container

Function:

Contains text to be strongly emphasized. Browsers typically render strongly emphasized text in boldface.

Syntax:

```
<STRONG> ... strongly emphasized text goes here ... </STRONG>
```

Attributes:

None.

Example:

```
Do <STRONG>not</STRONG> install the software until you've closed
all other running applications.
```

<VAR>

Type:

Container

Function:

Denotes a variable from a computer program. Variables are typically rendered in a fixed-width font.

Syntax:

```
<VAR> ... program variable goes here ... </VAR>
```

Attributes:

None.

Example:

```
The <VAR>RecordCount</VAR> variable is set to the number of records
that the query retrieved.
```


Block-Level Formatting Tags

Block-level formatting tags are usually applied to larger content than the text-level formatting tags. As such, the block-level tags define major sections of a document, such as paragraphs, headings, abstracts, chapters, and so on. The tags profiled in this section are the ones to turn to when you when you want to define the block-level elements in a document you're authoring.

<BLOCKQUOTE>

Type:

Container

Function:

Contains quoted text that is to be displayed indented from regular body text.

Syntax:

```
<BLOCKQUOTE CITE="URL_of_cited_document"> ... quoted text goes here ...
</BLOCKQUOTE>
```

Attributes:

If you're quoting from an online source, you can set the CITE attribute equal to the source's URL.

Example:

```
Fans of Schoolhouse Rock will always be able to recite the preamble
of the United States Constitution:
<BLOCKQUOTE>
We, the people, in order to form a more perfect Union ...
</BLOCKQUOTE>
```

Related Tags:

The <Q> tag is used to denote quoted text that is to be displayed in line with the body text.

Type:

Standalone

Function:

Inserts a line break in the document. Carriage returns in the HTML code do not translate to line breaks on the browser screen, so authors often need to insert the breaks themselves. The <BR> tag is indispensable when rendering text with frequent line breaks, such as addresses or poetry. Unlike the <P> tag or the heading tags, <BR> adds no additional vertical space after the break.

Syntax:

```
<BR CLEAR="LEFT¦RIGHT¦ALL">
```

Attributes:

The CLEAR attribute tells which margin to break to when breaking beyond a floating page element such as an image. Setting CLEAR="LEFT" breaks to the first line in the left margin free of the floating object. CLEAR="RIGHT" breaks to the first clear right margin, and CLEAR="ALL" breaks to the first line in which both the left and right margins are clear.

Example:

```
President William Jefferson Clinton<BR>
The White House<BR>
1600 Pennsylvania Avenue NW<BR>
Washington, DC 20500
```

<CENTER>

Type:

Container

Function:

Centers all text and other page components it contains.

Syntax:

```
<CENTER> ... centered page components goes here ... </CENTER>
```

Attributes:

None.

Example:

```
<CENTER>
<H2>Annual Report to Stockholders</H2>
by Caroline A. Krauss, CEO
</CENTER>
```

NOTE The W3C has deprecated the `<CENTER>` tag in favor of using the `<DIV>` tag (see the following tag) or style sheets for centering.

Part I Ch 3

<DIV>

Type:

Container

Function:

Defines a section or division of a document that requires a special alignment.

Syntax:

```
<DIV ALIGN="LEFT|RIGHT|CENTER|JUSTIFY">
...
</DIV>
```

Attributes:

The `ALIGN` attribute controls how text contained between the `<DIV>` and `</DIV>` tags is aligned. You can set `ALIGN` equal to `LEFT`, `RIGHT`, `CENTER`, or `JUSTIFY`, depending on the kind of alignment you need.

Example:

```
<DIV ALIGN="JUSTIFY">
This is a fairly long paragraph that should be rendered with non-ragged
left and right margins.  HTML authors can accomplish this effect by
setting the ALIGN attribute equal to JUSTIFY.  ALIGN=LEFT will make the
text flush left, but the right margin will be ragged.
</DIV>
```

<HR>

Type:

Standalone

Function:

Places a horizontal line on the page.

Syntax:

```
<HR ALIGN="alignment" NOSHADE SIZE="thickness"
WIDTH="pixels_or_percentage_of_screen">
```

Attributes:

The unmodified `<HR>` tag places a line, 1 pixel thick, across the page. The line will have a shading effect to give the illusion of being three-dimensional. You can change how the default line is displayed by using combinations of the following attributes:

- `ALIGN`—You can set `ALIGN` equal to `LEFT`, `RIGHT`, or `CENTER` to change how the horizontal line is aligned on the page. Note that this matters only when you've changed the width of the line to be something less than the browser screen width. The default value of `ALIGN` is `CENTER`.
- `NOSHADE`—Placing the `NOSHADE` attribute in an `<HR>` tag suppresses the shading effect and yields a solid line.
- `SIZE`—`SIZE` controls the thickness of the line. You set `SIZE` equal to the number of pixels in thickness you'd like the line to be.
- `WIDTH`—A line's `WIDTH` can be specified in one of two ways. You can set it equal to a number of pixels, or you can set it equal to a percentage of the user's browser screen width (or table cell, if you're placing a line inside a cell). Because you can't know the screen resolution settings of every user, you should use the percentage approach whenever possible.

Example:

```
<HR NOSHADE WIDTH=80% SIZE=4>
<DIV ALIGN="CENTER"><B>Welcome!</B></DIV>
<HR NOSHADE WIDTH=80% SIZE=4>
```

<H1>-<H6>

Type:

Container

Function:

Establishes a hierarchy of document heading levels. Level 1 has the largest font size. Increasing through the levels causes the font size to decrease. All headings are rendered in boldface and have a little extra line spacing built in above and below them.

NOTE Although the headings tags are meant to be used in a strictly hierarchical fashion, many authors use them out of sequence to achieve the formatting effects they want.

Syntax:

```
<Hn ALIGN="LEFT|RIGHT|CENTER|JUSTIFY"> ... Level n heading ... </Hn>
```

where n = 1, 2, 3, 4, 5, or 6.

Attributes:

The ALIGN attribute controls how the heading is aligned on the page. You can set a heading's alignment to values of LEFT, RIGHT, CENTER, or JUSTIFY. The default alignment is LEFT.

Example:

```
<H1 ALIGN="CENTER">Table of Contents</H1>
<H2>Chapter 1 - Introduction</H2>
...
<H2>Chapter 2- Prior Research</H2>
...
```


<P>

Type:

Container

Function:

Denotes a paragraph. Most browsers ignore the use of multiple <P> tags to increase the amount of vertical space in a document.

Syntax:

```
<P ALIGN="LEFT|RIGHT|CENTER|JUSTIFY">
paragraph text
</P>
```

Attributes:

The ALIGN attribute controls how text in the paragraph is aligned. You can set ALIGN to LEFT (the default), RIGHT, CENTER, or JUSTIFY.

Example:

```
<P ALIGN="CENTER">
Every line of text in this paragraph is centered,
which probably makes it look somewhat strange
since most people are accustomed to a JUSTIFY alignment
for lots of text.
</P>
```

<PRE>

Type:

Container

Function:

Denotes text to be treated as preformatted. Browsers render preformatted text in a fixed-width font. Whitespace characters, such as spaces, tabs and carriage returns, found between the <PRE> and </PRE> tags are not ignored. This makes preformatted text a viable option for presenting tables of information.

Syntax:

```
<PRE WIDTH="width_of_widest_line">
... preformatted text goes here ...
</PRE>
```

Attributes:

The <PRE> tag's WIDTH attribute is set to the number of characters in the widest line of the preformatted text block. This information helps some browsers choose the font size for displaying the text.

Example:

```
<PRE WIDTH=34>
Catalog No.  Item          Price
AZ-1390      Polo Shirt    $29.99
FT-0081      Sweater       $52.99
CL-9334      Belt          $16.99
</PRE>
```

<SPAN>

Type:

Container

Function:

Generic container tag for applying style information.

Syntax:

```
<SPAN STYLE="style information">
range of text over which style is to be applied
</SPAN>
```

Attributes:

You can set the STYLE attribute to a sequence of as many *characteristic: value pairs* as you need to specify the style information you're applying. Valid style characteristics are those put forward in the Cascading Style Sheets Level 1 specification.

Example:

```
<SPAN STYLE="font-weight: bold; color: red; text-indent: 0.25 in">
Here is some bold, red, text that's indented by one quarter of an inch.
</SPAN>
```

List Tags

Technically, HTML lists are a form of block-level formatting, but because lists are such a useful way of presenting content, the list tags merit their own section in the chapter.

HTML 4.0 continues to support five types of lists, although tags for two of the five have been deprecated. Using the tags in this section, you can create the following types of lists:

- Definition lists
- Directory lists
- Menu lists
- Ordered (numbered) lists
- Unordered (bulleted) lists

Most HTML lists use the list item tag, `<LI>`, so this tag is covered first, followed by the tags you use to create each type of list.

<LI>

Type:

Container

Function:

Denotes an item in a list.

Syntax:

```
<LI TYPE="list_type" START="start_value"> ... list item goes here ... </LI>
```

Attributes:

The `<LI>` tag can take two different attributes:

- `START`—(Ordered lists only.) You can change the starting value of the numbering sequence from the default of `1` to any other value you choose.
- `TYPE`—(Ordered and unordered lists.) You can modify the numbering scheme in an ordered list or the bullet character in an unordered list by setting `TYPE` to one of the different list types available. Ordered list types include `1` (Arabic numerals), `A` (uppercase alphabet), `a` (lowercase alphabet), `I` (uppercase Roman numerals), and `i` (lowercase Roman numerals). The unordered list types include `DISC` (solid circular bullet), `SQUARE` (solid square bullet), and `CIRCLE` (open circular bullet).

NOTE Even if you are not using an Arabic numeral numbering scheme, you should still set START equal to a numeric value. Browsers know to map the START value to any numbering scheme you've specified in a TYPE attribute. For example, the code

```
<LI TYPE="a" START="4">
```

will produce an ordered list beginning with the lowercase letter d.

Example:

```
<LI>Larry</LI>
<LI>Curly</LI>
<LI>Moe</LI>
```

Related Tags:

The <LI> tag is always used in conjunction with one of the other HTML list tags: <DIR>, <MENU>, <OL>, and <UL>.

<DIR>

Type:

Container

Function:

Creates a directory listing. Items in a directory list are bulleted and generally short—usually not more than 20 characters in length. Directory lists were originally intended for rendering narrow columns of information, such as indexes or telephone directory listings.

NOTE The <DIR> tag has been deprecated by the W3C. You should use an unordered list (<UL>) instead.

Syntax:

```
<DIR COMPACT>
<LI>List item 1</LI>
<LI>List item 2</LI>
...
</DIR>
```

Attributes:

The optional COMPACT attribute instructs a browser to reduce the spacing between list items so that the list is rendered in the smallest amount of vertical space possible.

Example:

```
<DIR>
<LI>Mary Garrison, x521</LI>
<LI>Tom Hinkle, x629</LI>
<LI>Pat Joseph, x772</LI>
</DIR>
```

Related Tags:

List items in a directory list are specified with the `<LI>` tag.

<DL>

Type:

Container

Function:

Denotes a definition list.

Syntax:

```
<DL COMPACT>
 ... terms and definitions go here ...
</DL>
```

Attributes:

The `COMPACT` attribute is optional and allows you to compress the list into the smallest vertical space possible on the browser screen.

Example:

```
<DL>
<DT>Browser</DT>
<DD>A program that allow a user to view World Wide Web pages</DD>
<DT>Server</DT>
<DD>A program that fields requests for web pages</DD>
</DL>
```

Related Tags:

Terms in a definition list are specified with the `<DT>` tag, and their definitions are specified with the `<DD>` tag.

<DT>

Type:

Container

Function:

Contains a term to be defined in a definition list.

NOTE Some browsers will automatically render a definition list term in boldface.

Syntax:

```
<DT> ... term being defined goes here ... </DT>
```

Attributes:

None.

Example:

```
<DL>
<DT>Creatine</DT>
<DD>A nutritional supplement that promotes muscle development</DD>
...
</DL>
```

Related Tags:

Use of the <DT> tag makes sense only in the context of a definition list (between the <DL> and </DL> tags). The <DD> tag is used to give the term's definition.

<DD>

Type:

Container

Function:

Contains a term's definition. The definition is typically indented from the term, making it easier for the reader to see the term-definition structure of the list.

Syntax:

```
<DD> ... term definition goes here ... </DD>
```

Attributes:

None.

Example:

```
<DL>
<DT>HTML</DT>
<DD>A document description language used to author web pages</DD>
...
</DL>
```

Related Tags:

The <DD> tag should be used only when contained by <DL> and </DL> tags. A term, specified by a <DT> tag, should precede each definition.

<MENU>

Type:

Container

Function:

Creates a menu listing. Menu list items are typically short—usually not more than 20 characters in length. Most browsers render a menu list in the same way they render a bulleted list.

NOTE The use of menu lists has been deprecated by the W3C. You should use the unordered list tag (<UL>) instead.

Syntax:

```
<MENU COMPACT>
<LI>Menu list item 1</LI>
<LI>Menu list item 2</LI>
...
</MENU>
```

Attributes:

The optional COMPACT attribute is used to reduce vertical spacing between list items.

Example:

```
<MENU COMPACT>
<LI>Hamburgers</LI>
<LI>Hot dogs</LI>
<LI>BBQ chicken</LI>
</MENU>
```

Related Tags:

List items in a menu listing are specified with the <LI> tag.

<OL>

Type:

Container

Function:

Creates an ordered or numbered list.

Syntax:

```
<OL TYPE="1¦A¦a¦I¦i" START="start_value" COMPACT>
<LI>List item 1</LI>
<LI>List item 2</LI>
...
</OL>
```

Attributes:

The <OL> tag can take the following attributes:

- COMPACT—Instructs the browser to reduce vertical spacing between list items.
- START—You can change to a position other than the first position in the ordering scheme by using the START attribute. For example, setting START to 3 with TYPE set equal to I produces a list that begins numbering with III (3 in uppercase Roman numerals).

- TYPE—Controls the numbering scheme used when rendering the list. The default value of 1 indicates the use of Arabic numerals, but you can also choose from uppercase letters (A), lowercase letters (a), uppercase Roman numerals (I), or lowercase Roman numerals (i).

Example:

```
Book Outline
<OL TYPE="A">
<LI>HTML</LI>
<LI>Dynamic HTML</LI>
<LI>Java</LI>
<LI>JavaScript</LI>
</OL>
```

Related Tags:

List items in an ordered list are specified with the <LI> tag.

<UL>

Type:

Container

Function:

Creates an unordered or bulleted list.

Syntax:

```
<UL TYPE="DISC¦SQUARE¦CIRCLE" COMPACT>
<LI>List item 1</LI>
<LI>List item 2</LI>
...
</UL>
```

Attributes:

The <UL> tag can take the following attributes:

- COMPACT—Reduces the vertical spacing between list items.
- TYPE—Allows you to specify which bullet character to use when rendering the list. This can be helpful when nesting bulleted lists because browsers have a default progression of bulleted characters that they use. You can override the browser's choice of bullet characters in the nested lists by using TYPE.

Example:

```
Web Browsers
<UL TYPE="SQUARE">
<LI>Netscape Navigator</LI>
<LI>Microsoft Internet Explorer</LI>
<LI>NCSA Mosaic</LI>
</UL>
```

Related Tags:

List items in an unordered list are specified with the <LI> tag.

Hyperlink Tags

The capability of linking web resources makes the web so fascinating. By following links, you can be looking up job opportunities one moment and then be reading up on the latest mixed drink recipes the next! Linking between documents is accomplished with the one simple tag described in this section.

<A>

Type:

Container

Function:

The <A> tag can do one of two things, depending on which attributes you use. Used with the HREF attribute, the <A> tag sets up a hyperlink from whatever content is found between the <A> and </A> tags and the document at the URL specified by HREF. When you use the <A> tag with the NAME attribute, you set up a named anchor within a document that can be targeted by other hyperlinks. This helps make navigating a large document easier because you can set up anchors at the beginning of major sections and then place a set of links at the top of the document that point to the anchors at the beginning of each section.

NOTE Hypertext links are typically colored and underlined. A linked graphic will be rendered with a colored border. If you don't want a border around your linked image, be sure to specify BORDER=0 in the <IMG> tag you use to place the image.

Syntax:

```
<!-- Setting up a hyperlink -->
<A HREF="URL_of_linked_document" TARGET="frame_name"
   REL="forward_link_type" REV="reverse_link_type"
   ACCESSKEY="key_letter" TABINDEX="tab_order_position">
... hyperlinked element goes here ...
</A>
```

or

```
<!-- Setting up a named anchor -->
<A NAME="anchor_name">
... text to act as named anchor ...
</A>
```

Attributes:

The <A> tag can take a host of attributes, including

- ACCESSKEY—An access key is a shortcut key a reader can use to activate the hyperlink. For example, if you set the access key to the letter "C," Windows users can press Alt+C on their keyboards to activate the link.
- HREF—Gives the URL of the web resource to which the hyperlink should point.
- NAME—Specifies the name of the anchor being set up.
- REL—Describes the nature of the forward link (see Table 3.1 for possible values).
- REV—Describes the nature of the reverse link (see Table 3.1 for possible values).
- TABINDEX—Specifies the link's position in the document's tabbing order.
- TARGET—Tells the browser which frame the linked document should be loaded into.

Examples:

The following code sets up a simple hyperlink:

```
You can learn more about our
<A HREF="prodserv.html TARGET="main" ACCESSKEY="P">
products and services</A> as well.
```

To follow the link, a user can click the hypertext `products and services` or press Alt+P (on a Windows machine) or Cmd+P (on a Macintosh).

This code establishes a named anchor within a document:

```
...
<A NAME="toc">
<H1>Table of Contents</H1>
</A>
...
```

With the anchor set up, you can point a hyperlink to it by using code such as this:

```
<A HREF="index.html#toc">Back to the Table of Contents</A>
```

Image and Imagemap Tags

Without images, the web would just be another version of Gopher. Web graphics gives pages powerful visual appeal and often adds significantly to the messages that authors are trying to convey.

Placing an image on a page is as simple as using the HTML <IMG> tag. In its most basic form, the <IMG> tag needs only one attribute to do its job. However, <IMG> supports as many as 10 different attributes that you can use to modify how the image is presented.

▶ **See** "Advanced Graphics," **p. 135**

<IMG>

Type:

Standalone

Function:

Places an inline image into a document.

Syntax:

```
<IMG SRC="URL_of_image_file"
  WIDTH="width_in_pixels" HEIGHT="height_in_pixels"
  ALT="text_description" BORDER="thickness_in_pixels"
  ALIGN="TOP¦MIDDLE¦BOTTOM¦LEFT¦RIGHT"
  HSPACE="horizontal_spacing_in_pixels"
  VSAPCE="vertical_spacing_in_pixels"
  ISMAP USEMAP="map_name">
```


Attributes:

As you can see from the tag's syntax, `<IMG>` can take several attributes (each attribute is described in detail in this section):

- `SRC`—Specifies the URL of the file containing the image.
- `WIDTH` and `HEIGHT`—Gives the width and height of the image in pixels. Specifying this information in the tag means that the browser can allot space for the image and then continue laying out the page while the image file loads.
- `ALT`—A text-based description of the image content. Using `ALT` is an important courtesy to users with nonvisual browsers or with image loading turned off.
- `BORDER`—Controls the thickness of the border around an image. An image has no border by default. However, a hyperlinked image will be rendered with a colored border. If you don't want the border to appear around your image, you need to set `BORDER=0`.
- `ALIGN`—Controls how text flows around the image. `TOP`, `MIDDLE`, and `BOTTOM` alignment aligns text following the image with the top, middle, or bottom of the image, respectively. However, when the text reaches the end of the current line, it will break to a position *below* the image. If you want text to wrap around the entire image, you need to use the `LEFT` or `RIGHT` values of the `ALIGN` attribute to float the image in the left or right margin. Text will wrap smoothly around a floated image.
- `HSPACE` and `VSPACE`—Controls the amount of whitespace left around the image. `HSPACE` is set to the number of whitespace pixels to use on the left and right sides of the image. `VSPACE` controls the number of whitespace pixels left above and below the image.
- `ISMAP`—Identifies the image as being used as part of a server-side imagemap.
- `USEMAP`—Set equal to the name of the client-side imagemap to be used with the image.

Example:

```
<IMG SRC="/images/logo.gif" WIDTH=600 HEIGHT=120
  ALT="Welcome to XYZ Corporation" USEMAP="#main"
  VSPACE=10>
```

One popular use of images is to set up *imagemaps*—clickable images that take users to different URLs, depending on where they click. Imagemaps are popular page elements on many sites because they provide users with an easy-to-use graphical interface for navigating the site.

Imagemaps come in two flavors: server-side and client-side. When a user clicks on a server-side imagemap, the coordinates of the click are sent to the server, where a program processes them to determine which URL the browser should load. To accomplish this, the server must have access to a file containing information about which regions on the image are clickable and with which URLs those regions should be paired.

With client-side imagemaps, the client (browser) processes the coordinates of the user's click, rather than passing them to the server for processing. This is a much more efficient approach because it reduces the computational load on the server and eliminates the opening and closing of additional HTTP connections. In order for the browser to be able to process a user's click, it must have access to the same information about the clickable regions and their associated URLs as the server does when processing a server-side imagemap. The method of choice for getting this information to the client is to pass it in an HTML file—usually the file that contains the document with the imagemap, although it does not necessarily have to be this way. HTML 4.0 supports two tags that enable you to store imagemap data in your HTML files: `<MAP>` and `<AREA>`. A discussion of these tags rounds out the coverage in this section.

▶ **See** "Imagemaps," **p. 117**

<MAP>

Type:

Container

Function:

Contains HTML tags that define the clickable regions (hot regions) of an imagemap.

Syntax:

```
<MAP NAME="map_name">
... hot region definitions go here ...
</MAP>
```

Attributes:

The `NAME` attribute gives the map information a unique name so it can be referenced by the `USEMAP` attribute in the `<IMG>` tag that places the imagemap graphic.

Example:

```
<MAP NAME="navigation">
<AREA SHAPE="RECT" COORDS="23,47,58,68" HREF="search.html">
<AREA SHAPE="CIRCLE" COORDS="120,246,150,246" HREF="about.html">
...
</MAP>
```

With the imagemap data defined by the map named navigation, you would reference the map in an <IMG> tag as follows:

```
<IMG SRC="navigation.gif" USEMAP="#navigation">
```

If the map were stored in a file different from the document's HTML file, you would reference it this way:

```
<IMG SRC="navigation.gif" USEMAP="maps.html#navigation">
```

Related Tags:

The <AREA> tag is used to define the individual hot regions in the imagemap. The named map is referenced by the USEMAP attribute of the <IMG> tag.

<AREA>

Type:

Standalone

Function:

Defines a hot region in a client-side imagemap.

Syntax:

```
<AREA SHAPE="RECT¦CIRCLE¦POLY¦DEFAULT" COORDS="coordinate_list"
  HREF="URL_of_linked_document" TARGET="frame_name"
  ALT="text_alternative" TABINDEX="tab_order_position" NOHREF>
```

Attributes:

The <AREA> tag takes a number of attributes, including

- ALT—Provides a text alternative for the hot region in the event that the image does not load or the user has image-loading turned off. ALT text is also used by spoken-word browsers for the visually impaired.
- COORDS—Specifies the coordinates that define the hot region. Coordinates are given as a list of numbers, separated by commas. No coordinates are needed when specifying a DEFAULT region.
- HREF—Set equal to the URL of the document to associate with the hot region.
- NOHREF—Using the NOHREF attribute in an <AREA> tag essentially deactivates the hot region by having it point to nothing.
- SHAPE—Specifies the shape of the hot region being defined. Possible values of SHAPE include RECT for rectangles, CIRCLE for circles, POLY for polygons, and DEFAULT for any point on the image not part of another hot region.
- TABINDEX—Defines the hot region's position in the tabbing order of the page.
- TARGET—Specifies into which frame to load the linked document.

NOTE Each type of hot region has a specific number of coordinate points that you need to specify to completely define the hot region. A rectangular region is defined by the coordinates of the upper-left and lower-right corners, a circular region by the coordinates of the center point and a point along the edge of the region, and a polygonal region by the coordinates of the polygon's vertices.

Example:

```
<MAP NAME="main">
<AREA SHAPE="POLY" COORDS="35,80,168,99,92,145" HREF="profile.html">
<AREA SHAPE="CIRCLE" COORDS="288,306,288,334" HREF="feedback.html">
<AREA SHAPE="DEFAULT" HREF="index.html">
</MAP>
```

Related Tags:

<AREA> tags are allowed only between <MAP> and </MAP> tags.

Table Tags

HTML tables are not only a great way to present information, but a useful layout tool as well. HTML 4.0 expands the table tags in several important ways:

- Support for rendering parts of the frame around a table, rather than "all or nothing."
- Control over which boundaries to draw between cells.
- Table header, body, and footer sections can be defined as separate entities.

This section looks at all the table-related tags and their many attributes.

▶ **See** "Tables," **p. 165**

<TABLE>

Type:

Container

Function:

Contains all HTML tags that comprise a table.

Syntax:

```
<TABLE ALIGN="LEFT¦CENTER¦RIGHT" BORDER="thickness_in_pixels"
  BGCOLOR="color" WIDTH="pixels_or_percentage_of_browser_width"
  COLS="number_of_columns" CELLPADDING="pixels" CELLSPACING="pixels"
  FRAME="outer_border_rendering" RULES="inner_border_rendering">
...
</TABLE>
```

Attributes:

The <TABLE> tag can take the following attributes to modify how the table is presented:

- ALIGN—Controls how the table is aligned on the page. Possible values are LEFT, CENTER, and RIGHT. Tables that are left- or right-aligned will float in the margin and text can wrap around them.
- BORDER—Specifies the thickness of the table border in pixels.
- BGCOLOR—Set equal to the background color to use in the cells of the table.
- CELLPADDING—Controls the amount of whitespace between the contents of a cell and the edge of the cell.
- CELLSPACING—Specifies how many pixels of space to leave between individual cells.
- COLS—Set equal to the number of columns in the table. Knowing this value enables the browser to compose the table faster.
- FRAME—Controls which parts of the table's outer border are rendered. FRAME can take on the values shown in Table 3.2.

Table 3.2 Values of the *FRAME* attribute of the *<TABLE>* tag.

Value	Purpose
ABOVE	Displays a border on the top of a table frame
BELOW	Displays a border at the bottom of a table frame
BORDER	Displays a border on all four sides of a table frame
BOX	Same as BORDER
HSIDES	Displays a border on the left and right sides of a table frame
LHS	Displays a border on the left side of a table frame
RHS	Displays a border on the right side of a table frame
VSIDES	Displays a border at the top and bottom of a table frame
VOID	Suppresses the display of all table frame borders

- RULES—Controls which parts of the table's inner borders are displayed. RULES can be set equal to one of the values shown in Table 3.3.

Table 3.3 Values of the *RULES* attribute of the *<TABLE>* tag.

Value	Purpose
ALL	Displays a border between all rows and columns
COLS	Displays a border between all columns

continues

Attributes:

<TFOOT> can take the same ALIGN and VALIGN attributes as the <THEAD> tag:

- ALIGN—Controls the horizontal alignment within the cells of the table footer. ALIGN can take on values of LEFT, RIGHT, CENTER, or JUSTIFY.
- VALIGN—Controls the vertical alignment in the footer cells. VALIGN can take on values of TOP, MIDDLE, BOTTOM, or BASELINE.

Example:

```
<TFOOT ALIGN="JUSTIFY" VALIGN="TOP">
<TR>
<TD><I>Source:</I> The Washington Post, 9/22/97</TD>
...
</TR>
</TFOOT>
```

Related Tags:

You specify the rows and cells in the table footer by using the <TR>, <TH>, and <TD> tags.

<TBODY>

Type:

Container

Function:

Defines the body section of the table.

Syntax:

```
<TBODY ALIGN="LEFT¦CENTER¦RIGHT¦JUSTIFY" VALIGN="TOP¦MIDDLE¦BOTTOM¦BASELINE">
...
</TBODY>
```

Attributes:

<TBODY> can take the following attributes:

- ALIGN—Controls the horizontal alignment within the cells of the table body. ALIGN can take on values of LEFT, RIGHT, CENTER, or JUSTIFY.
- VALIGN—Controls the vertical alignment in the body cells. VALIGN can take on values of TOP, MIDDLE, BOTTOM, or BASELINE.

Example:

```
<TBODY ALIGN="LEFT" VALIGN="BASELINE">
<TR>
<TD>Brenda Lynn</TD>
<TD>SD-4949</TD>
<TD>x619</TD>
...
</TR>
</TBODY>
```

Related Tags:

You specify the rows and cells in the table body by using the <TR>, <TH>, and <TD> tags.

<COLGROUP>

Type:

Container

Function:

Groups a set of columns so that properties may be assigned to all columns in the group rather than to each one individually.

Syntax:

```
<COLGROUP SPAN="number_of_columns" WIDTH="width_of_column_group"
  ALIGN="LEFT¦RIGHT¦CENTER¦JUSTIFY" VALIGN="TOP¦MIDDLE¦BOTTOM¦BASELINE">
...
</COLGROUP>
```

The <COLGROUP> and </COLGROUP> tags have no content or code between them if the properties put forward in the <COLGROUP> tag are to apply to each column in the group. You can also use the <COL> tag between <COLGROUP> and </COLGROUP> to specify column properties for a sub-group of the larger group.

Attributes:

<COLGROUP> can take the following attributes:

- ALIGN—Controls the horizontal alignment within the column group. ALIGN can take on values of LEFT, RIGHT, CENTER, or JUSTIFY.
- SPAN—Tells the browser how many columns are in the group.
- VALIGN—Controls the vertical alignment in the column group. VALIGN can take on values of TOP, MIDDLE, BOTTOM, or BASELINE.
- WIDTH—Specifies how wide (in pixels or in terms of relative width) the enclosed columns should be.

Example:

```
<COLGROUP SPAN=3 ALIGN="CENTER" VALIGN="TOP">
</COLGROUP>
<TR>
<TD>Column 1 - center/top alignment</TD>
<TD>Column 2 - center/top alignment</TD>
<TD>Column 3 - center/top alignment</TD>
<TD>Column 4 - default alignment</TD>
</TR>
</TFOOT>
```

Related Tags:

The <COL> tag can be used between the <COLGROUP> and </COLGROUP> tags to refine column properties for a subset of the column group.

<COL>

Type:

Standalone

Function:

Specifies properties for a column or columns within a group.

Syntax:

```
<COL SPAN="number_of_columns" WIDTH="width_of_column_subgroup"
  ALIGN="LEFT¦RIGHT¦CENTER¦JUSTIFY" VALIGN="TOP¦MIDDLE¦BOTTOM¦BASELINE">
```

Attributes:

<COL> can take the following attributes:

- ALIGN—Controls the horizontal alignment within the column cells. ALIGN can take on values of LEFT, RIGHT, CENTER, or JUSTIFY.
- SPAN—Tells the browser how many columns to which to apply the property.
- VALIGN—Controls the vertical alignment in the column cells. VALIGN can take on values of TOP, MIDDLE, BOTTOM, or BASELINE.
- WIDTH—Specifies the width (in pixels or in terms of relative width) of the column or column group.

Example:

```
<TABLE BORDER=1>
<COLGROUP>
   <COL ALIGN=CENTER>
   <COL ALIGN=RIGHT>
</COLGROUP>
<COLGROUP>
   <COL ALIGN=CENTER SPAN=2>
</COLGROUP>
<TBODY>
   <TR>
      <TD>First column in first group, center aligned</TD>
      <TD>Second column in first group, right aligned</TD>
      <TD>First column in second group, center aligned</TD>
      <TD>Second column in second group, center aligned</TD>
   </TR>
</TBODY>
</TABLE>
```

<TR>

Type:

Container

Function:

Defines a row of a table, table header, table footer, or table body.

Syntax:

```
<TR BGCOLOR="color" ALIGN="LEFT|RIGHT|CENTER|JUSTIFY"
  VALIGN="TOP|MIDDLE|BOTTOM|BASELINE">
...
</TR>
```

Attributes specified in a <TR> tag apply only to the row that the tag is defining and will override any default values.

Attributes:

The <TR> tag can take the following attributes:

- ALIGN—Controls the horizontal alignment within the cells in the row. ALIGN can take on values of LEFT, RIGHT, CENTER, or JUSTIFY.
- BGCOLOR—Controls the background color of cells in the row. You may set BGCOLOR equal to one of the 16 reserved color names or to a hexadecimal triplet describing the desired color.
- VALIGN—Controls the vertical alignment of the cells in the row. VALIGN can take on values of TOP, MIDDLE, BOTTOM, or BASELINE.

Example:

```
<TR BGCOLOR="white" VALIGN="TOP">
<TD>Cell #1</TD>
<TD>Cell #2</TD>
...
</TR>
```

Related Tags:

Cells in a row are defined using the <TD> or <TH> tags.

<TD>, <TH>

Type:

Container

Function:

Defines a cell in a table. <TH> creates a header cell whose contents will be rendered in boldface and with a centered horizontal alignment. <TD> creates a regular data cell whose contents are aligned flush left and in a normal font weight. Vertical alignment for both types of cells is MIDDLE by default.

Syntax:

```
<TD ALIGN="LEFT¦RIGHT¦CENTER¦JUSTIFY" VALIGN="TOP¦MIDDLE¦BOTTOM¦BASELINE"
  BGCOLOR="color" NOWRAP ROWSPAN="number_of_rows"
  COLSPAN="number_of_columns">
```

or

```
<TH ALIGN="LEFT¦RIGHT¦CENTER¦JUSTIFY" VALIGN="TOP¦MIDDLE¦BOTTOM¦BASELINE"
  BGCOLOR="color" NOWRAP ROWSPAN="number_of_rows"
  COLSPAN="number_of_columns">
```

Attributes:

Both the <TH> and <TD> tags can take the following attributes:

- ALIGN—Controls the horizontal alignment within the cell. ALIGN can take on values of LEFT, RIGHT, CENTER, or JUSTIFY.
- BGCOLOR—Controls the background color of the cell. You may set BGCOLOR equal to one of the 16 reserved color names or to a hexadecimal triplet describing the desired color.
- COLSPAN—Specifies the number of columns the cell should occupy.
- NOWRAP—Suppresses text wrapping within the cell.
- ROWSPAN—Specifies the number of rows the cell should occupy.
- VALIGN—Controls the vertical alignment of the cell. VALIGN can take on values of TOP, MIDDLE, BOTTOM, or BASELINE.

Example:

```
<TR VALIGN="BOTTOM">
<TH>Column 1 - center/bottom alignment</TH>
<TD VALIGN="MIDDLE">Column 2 - left/middle alignment</TD>
<TD ALIGN="JUSTIFY">Column 3 - justify/bottom alignment</TD>
<TD COLSPAN=2>Columns 4 and 5 - left/bottom alignment</TD>
</TR>
```

Form Tags

HTML forms are a web surfer's gateway to interactive content. Forms collect information from a user, and then a script or program on a web server uses the information to compose a custom response to the form submission.

For all the form controls that are available to you as a document author, there are surprisingly few tags you need to know to produce them. These tags, together with some new tags introduced in the HTML 4.0 spec that improve form accessibility for the disabled, are covered in this section.

▶ **See** "Forms," **p. 211**

<FORM>

Type:

Container

Function:

Contains the text and tags that comprise an HTML form.

Syntax:

```
<FORM ACTION="URL_of_processing_script" METHOD="GET¦POST"
  TARGET="frame_name" ENCTYPE="MIME_type_of_file_to_upload"
  ACCEPT-CHARSET="acceptable_character_sets">
...
</FORM>
```

The <FORM> tag and its attributes are sometimes referred to as the *form header*.

Attributes:

The <FORM> tag takes the following attributes:

- ACCEPT-CHARSET—Set equal to a list of character sets that the form's processing script can handle.
- ACTION—Set equal to the URL of the script or program that will process the form data. ACTION is a required attribute of the <FORM> tag.
- ENCTYPE—Used when you're expecting a file upload as part of the form data submission and is set equal to the expected MIME type of the file.
- METHOD—Refers to the HTTP method used to send the form data to the server. The default METHOD is GET, which appends the data to the end of the processing script URL. If you set METHOD="POST", the form data will be sent to the server in a separate HTTP transaction.
- TARGET—Allows you to target the response from the processing script or program to a specific frame.

Example:

```
<FORM ACTION="/cgi-bin/addentry.pl" METHOD="POST" TARGET="response">
...
</FORM>
```

Related Tags:

The following tags are valid only when used between the <FORM> and </FORM> tags: <INPUT>, <SELECT>, <OPTION>, <TEXTAREA>, <BUTTON>, <LABEL>, <FIELDSET>, and <LEGEND>. Each of these tags is described in this section.

<INPUT>

Type:

Standalone

Function:

Places one of the following form controls:

- Text, password, or hidden fields
- Check boxes
- Radio buttons
- File upload fields
- Image-based buttons
- Scripted buttons
- Submit and reset buttons

Syntax:

```
<!-- Text and password fields -->
<INPUT TYPE="TEXT¦PASSWORD" NAME="field_name" VALUE="default_value"
  SIZE="field_size" MAXLENGTH="maximum_input_length"
  DISABLED READONLY>
```

or

```
<!-- Hidden field -->
<INPUT TYPE="HIDDEN" NAME="field_name" VALUE="field_value">
```

or

```
<!-- Checkbox -->
<INPUT TYPE="CHECKBOX" NAME="field_name" VALUE="field_value"
  CHECKED DISABLED>
```

or

```
<!-- Radio button -->
<INPUT TYPE="RADIO" NAME="field_name" VALUE="field_value"
  CHECKED DISABLED>
```

or

```
<!-- File upload -->
<INPUT TYPE="FILE" NAME="field_name" VALUE="default_value"
  ACCEPT="acceptable_MIME_types" DISABLED>
```

or

```
<!-- Image-based button -->
<INPUT TYPE="IMAGE" SRC="URL_of_image_file" ALT="text_description"
  ALIGN="TOP¦MIDDLE¦BOTTOM¦LEFT¦RIGHT" USEMAP="map_name" DISABLED>
```

or

```
<!-- Scripted button -->
<INPUT TYPE="BUTTON" VALUE="button_label" onclick="script_name"
  DISABLED>
```

or

```
<!-- Submit/reset button -->
<INPUT TYPE="SUBMIT¦RESET" VALUE="button_label" DISABLED>
```

Attributes:

The `<INPUT>` tag is easily the most versatile of all the HTML tags. It has a large number of attributes, although not all are applicable in every situation. The following list examines each variant of the `<INPUT>` tag (which corresponds to changing values of the `TYPE` attribute) and notes what each applicable attribute does in that situation.

- Text and password fields (`TYPE="TEXT¦PASSWORD"`)—The `NAME` attribute gives the input field a unique name so it can be identified by the processing script. The `VALUE` attribute is appropriate for a text field when you want to prepopulate the field with a default value. `LENGTH` is set equal to the number of characters wide the input field should be on screen. `MAXLENGTH` sets an upper limit on how many characters long the input from the field can be. The `DISABLED` attribute deactivates the field, and `READONLY` leaves the field active while disallowing the user from typing any new input into it.
- Hidden fields (`TYPE="HIDDEN"`)—`NAME` and `VALUE` specify the name of the field and the value to pass to the server.
- Check box (`TYPE="CHECKBOX"`)—`NAME` gives the check box field a unique name, and `VALUE` is set equal to the value you want passed to the server if the box is checked. Including `CHECKED` makes the box preselected, and `DISABLED` disables the check box altogether.
- Radio buttons (`TYPE="RADIO"`)—`NAME` gives a name to the entire set of radio buttons. All buttons can have the same `NAME` because their corresponding `VALUE`s have to be mutually exclusive options. The `CHECKED` attribute preselects a radio button and `DISABLED` shuts down the radio button.
- File upload (`TYPE="FILE"`)—`NAME` gives the field a unique name, and `VALUE` is set to the default value of the field (presumably a filename). The `ACCEPT` attribute provides a set of acceptable MIME types for upload. Specifying the `DISABLED` attribute deactivates the field.
- Image-based button (`TYPE="IMAGE"`)—The `SRC` attribute tells the browser where it can find the image file for the button. `ALT` provides a text-based alternative to the image should the image file not be available. You can use `ALIGN` to control how the image is aligned on the page. `USEMAP` is set equal to a client-side imagemap name, allowing you to take different actions, depending on where the user clicks. Using the `DISABLED` attribute shuts off the button.
- Scripted button (`TYPE="BUTTON"`)—Whatever you specify for the `VALUE` attribute will be the text that appears on the face of the button. The `onclick` attribute is set equal to the name of the script that is to execute when the button is clicked. If you specify the `DISABLED` attribute, the scripted button will be deactivated.

- Submit and reset buttons (TYPE="SUBMIT¦RESET")—The VALUE attribute specifies what text to place on the button. If DISABLED, the submit or reset button will be turned off.

Example:

```
<FORM ACTION="/cgi-bin/bigform.cgi">
Login Name: <INPUT TYPE="TEXT" NAME="login" SIZE=12>
Password: <INPUT TYPE="PASSWORD" NAME="passwd" SIZE=12>
<INPUT TYPE="HIDDEN" NAME="browser" VALUE="IE4">
Sex: <INPUT TYPE="RADIO" NAME="sex" VALUE="F">Female
     <INPUT TYPE="RADIO" NAME="sex" VALUE="M">Male
<INPUT TYPE="BUTTON" VALUE="Check data" onclick="validate()">
<INPUT TYPE="SUBMIT" VALUE="Login">
<INPUT TYPE="RESET" VALUE="Clear">
</FORM>
```

<SELECT>

Type:

Container

Function:

Sets up a list of choices from which a user can select one or many.

Syntax:

```
<SELECT NAME="field_name" SIZE="visible_rows" MULTIPLE DISABLED>
...
</SELECT>
```

Attributes:

You can use the following attributes with the <SELECT> tag:

- DISABLED—Deactivates the field.
- MULTIPLE—Allows the user to choose more than one of the options by holding down the Ctrl key and clicking.
- NAME—Gives the field a unique name so it can be identified by the processing script.
- SIZE—Set equal to the number of options that should be visible on the screen.

NOTE If you set SIZE=1 and don't specify MULTIPLE, the field will be displayed as a drop-down list. Otherwise, the field appears as a scrollable list of options.

Example:

```
<SELECT NAME="toppings" SIZE=5 MULTIPLE>
<OPTION>Mushrooms</OPTION>
<OPTION>Onions</OPTION>
<OPTION>Sausage</OPTION>
...
</SELECT>
```

Related Tags:

Individual options in the list are specified using the <OPTION> tag.

<OPTION>

Type:

Container

Function:

Defines an option in a <SELECT> field listing.

Syntax:

```
<OPTION VALUE="option_value" SELECTED DISABLED>
... option text ...
</OPTION>
```

Attributes:

The <OPTION> tag takes the following attributes:

- DISABLED—Makes the option unavailable.
- SELECTED—Preselects an option.
- VALUE—Specifies a value to pass to the browser if the option is select. If no VALUE is given, the browser will pass the option text to the server for processing.

Example:

```
<SELECT NAME="state" SIZE=5>
<OPTION VALUE="AL">Alabama</OPTION>
<OPTION VALUE="NM" SELECTED>New Mexico</OPTION>
<OPTION VALUE="OK">Oklahoma</OPTION>
...
</SELECT>
```

Related Tags:

The <OPTION> tag is valid only between the <SELECT> and </SELECT> tags.

<TEXTAREA>

Type:

Container

Function:

Sets up a multiple-line text input window.

Syntax:

```
<TEXTAREA NAME="field_name" ROWS="number_of_rows"
  COLS="number_of_columns" DISABLED READONLY>
... default text to appear in window ...
</TR>
```

Attributes:

The <TEXTAREA> tag can take the following attributes:

- COLS—Set equal to the number of columns wide the text window should be.
- DISABLED—Deactivates the text window.
- NAME—Assigns a unique name to the input window so that the processing program can identify it.
- READONLY—Leaves the window active, but the user will not be able to change the default text that is displayed.
- ROWS—Set equal to the number of rows high the text window should be.

Example:

```
<TEXTAREA NAME="feedback" ROWS=10 COLS=40>
We appreciate your comments!  Please delete this
text and type in your feedback.
</TEXTAREA>
```

<BUTTON>

Type:

Container

Function:

Places a button on the form. This type of button is different from the one rendered by <INPUT> because it has improved presentation features, such as three-dimensional rendering and up/down movement when clicked.

Syntax:

```
<BUTTON TYPE="SUBMIT¦RESET" NAME="button_name" VALUE="button_value"
  DISABLED>
... text for button face or <IMG> tag ...
</BUTTON>
```

If there is text between the <BUTTON> and </BUTTON> tags, that text will appear on the face of the button. If there is an <IMG> tag between <BUTTON> and </BUTTON>, the image will be used as the button.

Attributes:

You can use the following attributes with the <BUTTON> tag:

- DISABLED—Disables the button.
- NAME—Gives the button a unique name.
- TYPE—Set to SUBMIT or RESET, depending on the type of button you're defining.
- VALUE—Specifies what is passed to the server when the button is clicked.

Example:

```
<BUTTON NAME="secure_connect" VALUE="secure">
<IMG SRC="images/clickme.gif">
</BUTTON>
```

<LABEL>

Type:

Container

Function:

Denotes a form field label. Labels are typically text next to the field that prompts the user for the type of input expected. This works fine for text-based browsers, but it makes forms inaccessible for users who are visually impaired and who use speech-based or Braille browsers. Marking field labels with the <LABEL> tag makes it possible to prompt these users for the necessary input.

Syntax:

```
<LABEL FOR="field_ID" ACCESSKEY="shortcut_key" DISABLED>
... label text goes here ...
</LABEL>
```

Attributes:

The <LABEL> tag takes the following attributes:

- ACCESSKEY—You can set up a shortcut key for placing the cursor in the field corresponding to the label by using the ACCESSKEY attribute. For example, if you set ACCESSKEY="K", the users can access the field by pressing Alt+K (Windows) or Ctrl+K (Macintosh).
- DISABLED—Deactivates the label.
- FOR—Set equal to the value of the ID attribute for the field that goes with the label.

Example:

```
<LABEL FOR="PW" ACCESSKEY="P">Enter your password:</LABEL>
<INPUT TYPE="PASSWORD" ID="PW" NAME="passwd">
```

Related Tags:

<LABEL> is typically used with the <INPUT>, <SELECT>, or <TEXTAREA> tags.

<FIELDSET>

Type:

Container

Function:

Groups related form input fields.

Syntax:

```
<FIELDSET>
... related input fields ...
</FIELDSET>
```

Attributes:

None.

Example:

```
<FIELDSET>
Login: <INPUT TYPE="TEXT" NAME="login">
Password: <INPUT TYPE="PASSWORD" NAME="passwd">
</FIELDSET>
```

Related Tags:

The `<LEGEND>` tag can be used to give a field grouping a specific name.

<LEGEND>

Type:

Container

Function:

Names a group of related form fields.

Syntax:

```
<LEGEND ALIGN="LEFT¦RIGHT¦TOP¦BOTTOM" ACCESSKEY="shortcut_key">
... legend text goes here ...
</LEGEND>
```

Attributes:

The `<LEGEND>` tag has two attributes:

- `ACCESSKEY`—Set equal to a keyboard key to be used as a shortcut key.
- `ALIGN`—Controls how the legend text is horizontally aligned with respect to the group of fields and can be set equal to `LEFT`, `RIGHT`, `TOP`, or `BOTTOM`.

Example:

```
<FIELDSET>
<LEGEND ALIGN="TOP">User Login Information</LEGEND>
Login: <INPUT TYPE="TEXT" NAME="login">
Password: <INPUT TYPE="PASSWORD" NAME="passwd">
</FIELDSET>
```

Related Tags:

`<LEGEND>` gives a name to a set of fields grouped together by the `<FIELDSET>` tag.

Frame Tags

In framed layouts, the browser window is broken up into multiple regions called *frames*. Each frame can contain a distinct HTML document, allowing you to display several documents at once rather than just one.

There are only a few tags you need to know to set up a framed page. These tags are covered in this section.

▶ **See** "Frames," **p. 191**

<FRAMESET>

Type:

Container

Function:

Divides the browser window into frames.

Syntax:

```
<FRAMESET ROWS="list_of_row_sizes" COLS="list_of_column_sizes">
...
</FRAMESET>
```

Attributes:

<FRAMESET> can take the ROWS or COLS attribute, but not both at the same time. ROWS specifies how the browser screen should be broken up into multiple rows. ROWS is set equal to a list of values that describe the size of each row. The number of items in the list determines how many rows there will be. The values in the list determine the size of each row. Sizes can be in pixels, percentages of screen depth, or relative to the amount of available space. COLS works the same way, except it will divide the screen into columns.

Example:

```
<!-- Divide the screen into three columns: 100 pixels, 50% of screen,
  and whatever is left over. -->
<FRAMESET COLS="100,50%,*">
...
</FRAMESET>
```

Related Tags:

<FRAMESET> only breaks up the screen into multiple regions. You must use the <FRAME> tag to populate each frame with content. Also, you can use the <NOFRAMES> tag to specify alternative content for browsers that cannot process frames.

NOTE <FRAMESET> tags may be nested to create even more complex layouts.

Part I Ch 3

<FRAME>

Type:

Standalone

Function:

Places content into a frame.

Syntax:

```
<FRAME SRC="URL_of_document" NAME="frame_name" FRAMEBORDER="0¦1"
  MARGINWIDTH="width_in_pixels" MARGINHEIGHT="height_in_pixels"
  NORESIZE SCROLLING="YES¦NO¦AUTO">
```

Attributes:

The `<FRAME>` tag can take several different attributes:

- `FRAMEBORDER`—Setting `FRAMEBORDER` to `1` turns on the frame's borders; setting it to `0` turns them off.
- `MARGINHEIGHT`—Specifies the size (in pixels) of the top margin of the frame.
- `MARGINWIDTH`—Specifies the size (in pixels) of the left margin of the frame.
- `NAME`—Gives the frame a unique name so it can be targeted by other tags (such as `<A>`, `<FORM>`, and `<AREA>`).
- `NORESIZE`—Suppresses the user's ability to drag and drop a frame border in a new location.
- `SCROLLING`—Controls the presence of scrollbars on the frame. Setting `SCROLLING` to `YES` makes the browser always put scrollbars on the frame, setting it to `NO` suppresses the scrollbars, and setting it to the default of `AUTO` lets the browser decide whether the scrollbars are needed or not.
- `SRC`—Tells the browser the URL of the HTML file to load into the frame. `SRC` is a required attribute of the `<FRAME>` tag.

Example:

```
<FRAMESET COLS="25%,75%"> <!-- Make 2 columnar frames -->
   <!-- Populate frame #1 -->
   <FRAME SRC="leftframe.html" NORESIZE NAME="left" FRAMEBORDER=0>
   <!-- Populate frame #2 -->
   <FRAME SRC="rightframe.html" NORESIZE NAME="right" FRAMEBORDER=0>
...
</FRAMESET>
```

Related Tags:

The `<FRAME>` tag is valid only between the `<FRAMESET>` and `</FRAMESET>` tags.

<NOFRAMES>

Type:

Container

Function:

Provides an alternative layout for browsers that cannot process frames.

Syntax:

```
<NOFRAMES>
... non-frames content goes here ...
</NOFRAMES>
```

Attributes:

None.

Example:

```
<FRAMESET COLS="25%,75%"> <!-- Make 2 columnar frames -->
   <!-- Populate frame #1 -->
   <FRAME SRC="leftframe.html" NORESIZE NAME="left" FRAMEBORDER=0>
   <!-- Populate frame #2 -->
   <FRAME SRC="rightframe.html" NORESIZE NAME="right" FRAMEBORDER=0>
<NOFRAMES>
Your browser cannot process frames.  Please visit the
<A HREF="/noframes/index.html">non-frames version</A>
of our site.
</NOFRAMES>
</FRAMESET>
```

Related Tags:

`<NOFRAMES>` is valid only between the `<FRAMESET>` and `</FRAMESET>` tags. Your `<NOFRAMES>` content should be specified before any nested `<FRAMESET>` tags.

<IFRAME>

Type:

Container

Function:

Places a floating frame on a page. *Floating frames* are best described as "frames that you can place like images."

Syntax:

```
<IFRAME SRC="URL_of_document" NAME="frame_name" FRAMEBORDER="0¦1"
  WIDTH="frame_width_in_pixels_or_percentage"
  HEIGHT="frame_height_in_pixels_or_percentage"
  MARGINWIDTH="margin_width_in_pixels"
  MARGINHEIGHT="margin_height_in_pixels"
  SCROLLING="YES¦NO¦AUTO" ALIGN="TOP¦MIDDLE¦BOTTOM¦LEFT¦RIGHT">
... text or image alternative to the floating frame ...
</IFRAME>
```

Attributes:

The <IFRAME> tag can take the following attributes:

- ALIGN—Controls how the floating frame is aligned, and can be set to TOP, MIDDLE, BOTTOM, LEFT, or RIGHT. TOP, MIDDLE, and BOTTOM alignments make text appear next to the frame, starting at the top, middle, or bottom of the frame. Setting ALIGN to LEFT or RIGHT floats the frame in the left or right margin and allows text to wrap around it.
- FRAMEBORDER—Setting FRAMEBORDER to 1 turns on the floating frame's borders; setting it to 0 turns them off.
- HEIGHT—Specifies the height of the floating frame in pixels.
- MARGINHEIGHT—Specifies the size (in pixels) of the top margin of the floating frame.
- MARGINWIDTH—Specifies the size (in pixels) of the left margin of the floating frame.
- NAME—Gives the floating frame a unique name so it can be targeted by other tags (such as <A>, <FORM>, and <AREA>).
- SCROLLING—Controls the presence of scrollbars on the floating frame. Setting SCROLLING to YES makes the browser always put scrollbars on the floating frame, setting it to NO suppresses the scrollbars, and setting it to the default of AUTO lets the browser decide whether the scrollbars are needed or not.
- SRC—Tells the browser the URL of the HTML file to load into the floating frame. SRC is a required attribute of the <IFRAME> tag.
- WIDTH—Specifies the width of the floating frame in pixels.

Example:

```
<IFRAME SRC="floating.html" WIDTH="50%" HEIGHT="50%" ALIGN=LEFT
  SCROLLING="NO" NAME="floater" FRAMEBORDER=1>
Your browser does not support floating frames. :(
</IFRAME>
```

Executable Content Tags

One of the ways in which web pages have become more dynamic is through their support of executable content such as Java applets and ActiveX controls. These page elements are downloaded to the browser and run in its memory space to produce dynamic content on the browser screen.

HTML 4.0 supports two ways to place executable content: the <APPLET> tag for Java applets and the <OBJECT> tag for other executable objects. These tags, along with the supporting <PARAM> tag, are profiled in this section.

<APPLET>

Type:

Container

Function:

Places a Java applet on a page.

Syntax:

```
<APPLET WIDTH="width_in_pixels" HEIGHT="height_in_pixels"
  CODEBASE="base_URL_for_applet" CODE="applet_class file"
  OBJECT="serialized_applet_file" NAME="applet_name"
  ARCHIVE="archive_list" ALT="text_alternative"
  ALIGN="TOP¦MIDDLE¦BOTTOM¦LEFT¦RIGHT"
  HSPACE="pixels" VSPACE="pixels">
...
</APPLET>
```

Attributes:

As the following list demonstrates, many of the `<APPLET>` tag's attributes are just like those for the `<IMG>` tag:

- `ALIGN`—Positions adjacent text at the `TOP`, `MIDDLE`, or `BOTTOM` of the applet window, or you can float the window in the `LEFT` or `RIGHT` margins.
- `ALT`—Provides a text-based alternative to the applet.
- `ARCHIVE`—Set equal to a comma-delimited list of archive locations.
- `CODE`—Specifies the class file.
- `CODEBASE`—Set equal to the URL of the code.
- `HEIGHT`—Specifies the height of the applet window in pixels. `HEIGHT` is a required attribute of the `<APPLET>` tag.
- `HSPACE`—Controls the amount of whitespace (in pixels) to the left and right of the applet window.
- `NAME`—Gives the applet a unique name so that it can be referenced by other Java applets.
- `OBJECT`—Provides the name of a serialized applet file.
- `VSPACE`—Controls the amount of whitespace (in pixels) above and below the applet window.
- `WIDTH`—Specifies the width of the applet window in pixels. `WIDTH` is a required attribute of the `<APPLET>` tag.

Example:

```
<APPLET WIDTH=250 HEIGHT=200 CODE="marquee.class" NAME="marquee"
  ALT="Scrolling text marquee applet" ALIGN="RIGHT"
  HSPACE=5 VSPACE=12>
  <PARAM NAME="message" VALUE="Hello World!">
...
</APPLET>
```

Related Tags:

Parameters are passed to a Java applet using the `<PARAM>` tag.

<PARAM>

Type:

Standalone

Function:

Passes a parameter to a Java applet (<APPLET>) or other executable object (<OBJECT>).

Syntax:

```
<PARAM NAME="parameter_name" VALUE="parameter_value"
  VALUETYPE="DATA¦REF¦OBJECT" TYPE="internet_media_type">
```

Attributes:

The <PARAM> tag can take the following attributes:

- NAME—Provides the name of the parameter.
- TYPE—Tells the browser what the parameter's Internet media (MIME) type is.
- VALUE—Specifies the value of the parameter.
- VALUETYPE—Provides more detail about the nature of the VALUE being passed and can be set to DATA, REF, or OBJECT.

Example:

```
<APPLET WIDTH=300 HEIGHT=224 CODE="test.class ALT="Test applet"
   ALIGN="TOP" NAME="test" >
   <PARAM NAME="tolerance" VALUE="0.001" VALUETYPE="DATA">
   <PARAM NAME="pi" VALUE="3.14159" VALUETYPE="DATA">
...
</APPLET>
```

Related Tags:

<PARAM> tags can be used only between the <APPLET> and </APPLET> tags or between the <OBJECT> and </OBJECT> tags.

<OBJECT>

Type:

Container

Function:

Places an executable object on a page.

Syntax:

```
<OBJECT CLASSID="implementation_info" CODEBASE="URL_of_object"
  CODETYPE="MIME_type" TYPE="data_MIME_type"
  STANDBY="message_while_loading" USEMAP="map_name"
  ALIGN="TEXTTOP¦MIDDLE¦TEXTMIDDLE¦BASELINE¦TEXTBOTTOM¦LEFT¦CENTER¦RIGHT"
```

```
  WIDTH="width_in_pixels_or_percentage" NAME="object_name"
  HEIGHT="height_in_pixels_or_percentage"
  HSPACE="pixels" VSPACE="pixels" BORDER="pixels">
...
</OBJECT>
```

Attributes:

The `<OBJECT>` tag has an exhausting list of attributes, but many of them are like those for the `<IMG>` tag so they are fairly easy to understand:

- `ALIGN`—Controls how content adjacent to the object area is aligned. Note that this `ALIGN` attribute has many more possible values than `ALIGN` attributes for other tags.
- `WIDTH` and `HEIGHT`—Specifies the dimensions of the object area as a number of pixels or as a percentage of available space.
- `BORDER`—Set equal to the number of pixels that the border thickness should be.
- `HSPACE` and `VSPACE`—Controls the amount of whitespace around the object area.

Additionally, `<OBJECT>` can take these attributes:

- `CLASSID`—Identifies which implementation or release of the object you're using.
- `CODEBASE`—Set equal to the URL of the object.
- `CODETYPE`—Describes the code's MIME type.
- `STANDBY`—Allows you to display a message to the user while the object is loading.
- `TYPE`—Specifies the MIME type of the data passed to the object.
- `USEMAP`—Points to client-side map data, if imagemaps are used.

Example:

```
<OBJECT WIDTH=100% HEIGHT=100 CODETYPE="application/x-oleobject"
  CLASSID="CLSID: 1A4DA620-6217-11CF-BE62-0080C72EDD2D"
  CODEBASE="http://activex.microsoft.com/controls/iexplorer/marquee.ocx"
  HSPACE=5 VSPACE=10 ALIGN=MIDDLE BORDER=0>
  <PARAM NAME="image" VALUE="greeting.gif">
  <PARAM NAME="speed" VALUE="7">
  <PARAM NAME="repeat" VALUE="1">
...
</OBJECT>
```

Related Tags:

Parameters passed to the object are given by the `<PARAM>` tag.

CHAPTER 4

Imagemaps

by Eric Ladd

In this chapter

What Are Imagemaps?

If you use a graphical browser, you have probably noticed that many major web sites have a large clickable image on their main page. These images are different from your run-of-the-mill hyperlinked graphic in that your browser loads a different document, depending on where you click. The image is somehow "multilinked" and can take you to a number of different places. Such a multilinked image is called an *imagemap*.

The challenge in preparing an imagemap is defining which parts of the image are linked to which URLs. Linked regions in an imagemap are called *hot regions* and each hot region is associated with the URL of the document that is to be loaded when the hot region is clicked. After you decide the hot regions and their associated URLs, you need to determine whether the web server or the web client will make the "decision" about which document to load, based on the user's click. This choice is the difference between server-side imagemaps and client-side imagemaps. Either approach is easy to implement after you know the information needed to define the hot regions.

This chapter walks you through the necessary steps for creating both server-side and client-side imagemaps and introduces you to some software programs that make the task of defining hot regions much less tedious.

Server-Side Imagemaps

A server-side imagemap is one in which the server determines which document should be loaded, based on the user's click on the imagemap. To make this determination, the server needs the following:

- *The coordinates of the user's click.* This information is passed to the server by the client program.
- *A program that takes the click coordinates as input and provides an URL as output.* Most servers have a routine built in that handles this task.
- *Access to the information that defines the hot regions and their associated URLs.* This information is critical to the processing program that checks the hot regions to see whether the user's click corresponds to an URL. When the program finds a match, it returns the URL paired with the clicked hot region. The file on the server that contains this information is called a *map file.*

Additionally, you need two other "ingredients" to complete a server-side imagemap:

- *An image.* An imagemap is like any other graphic in that you need to have a GIF or a JPEG file that contains the image.
- *Proper setup in your HTML file.* When you place the imagemap graphic, you use the `<IMG>` tag with a special attribute to alert the client program that the image is to be used as a server-side imagemap.

As an HTML author, you need to be most concerned about two of the items just listed: the map file and the setup in the HTML file. The next two sections discuss these aspects of creating an imagemap.

Preparing the Map File

The map file is a text file that contains information about the hot regions of a specific imagemap graphic. For this reason, a separate map file is necessary for each imagemap graphic you want to use. The definition specifies the type of hot region as a rectangle, circle, polygon, or point.

These regions, as their names suggest, refer to the geometric shape of the hot region. Their defining coordinates are determined as pixel points relative to the upper-left corner of the imagemap graphic, which is taken to have coordinates (0,0). The following list identifies basic imagemap shape keywords and their required coordinates:

- `rect`. Indicates that the hot region is a rectangle. The coordinates required for this type of shape are the upper-left and lower-right pixels in the rectangle. The active region is the area within the rectangle.
- `circle`. Indicates that the hot region is circular. Coordinates required for using a circle are the center-point pixel and one edge-point pixel (a pixel on the circle itself). The active region is the area within the circle.
- `poly`. Indicates that the hot region is a polygon. To specify the polygon, you need to provide a list of coordinates for all the polygon's vertices. A polygonal region can have as many as 100 vertices. The active region is the area within the polygon.
- `point`. Indicates that the region is a point on the image. A point coordinate is one specific pixel measured from the upper-left corner of the imagemap graphic. A point is considered active if the click occurs closest to that point on the graphic, yet not within another active region.
- `default`. A catch-all that defines all areas of an imagemap graphic that are not specified by any other active region.

Part II Ch 4

An imagemap definition file should, whenever possible, be configured with a default HTML link. The default link takes the user to an area that isn't designated as being an active link. This URL should provide the user with feedback or helpful information about using that particular imagemap.

CAUTION

An imagemap definition file should never contain both a point and a default region. If point regions are defined and a user does not click a hot region, the server sends the user to the URL associated with the closest point region and the default URL will never be used.

Following each type of region in the imagemap definition file is the URL that is returned to the user when a click within that area is recorded. Active regions in the definition file are read from the first line down. If two regions overlap in their coordinates, the imagemap program uses the first region it encounters in the file.

CAUTION

URLs in map files should always be absolute or fully qualified URLs—that is, the URL should specify a protocol, server name, and filename (including the directory path to the file).

NOTE You can use the pound sign (#) to comment on a line in the imagemap definition file. Any line with a pound sign at the beginning is ignored by the imagemap program. Comments are useful for adding information such as the date of creation, the physical path to the imagemap graphic, or specific comments about the server configuration.

Two primary types of map file configurations exist: one for the original CERN-style imagemaps and one for the NCSA server's implementation of imagemaps. Both use the same types of hot regions and the same coordinates to define each type. However, the formatting of this information in each map file is different. For this reason, you should check with the system administrator about the particular imagemap setup of the server you are using.

CERN Map File Format Lines in a CERN-style map file have the following form:

```
region_type coordinates URL
```

The coordinates must be in parentheses, and the x and y coordinates must be separated by a comma. The CERN format also doesn't allow for comments about hot regions. A sample CERN-style hot region definition might look like the following:

```
poly (133,256) (42,378) (298,172) http://www.your_firm.com/triangle.html
```

NSCA Map File Format NCSA developed a slightly different format from CERN's for map file information. Their format is as follows:

```
region_type URL coordinates
```

The coordinates don't have to be in parentheses, but they do have to be separated by commas. The equivalent of the map data line presented previously in NCSA format is as follows:

```
rect http://www.yourserver/triangle.html 133,256 42,378 298,172
```

Setting Up the Imagemap

Because of the differences in imagemap processing programs on different servers, you can use two techniques for setting up imagemaps.

Pointing Directly at the Processing Scripting The first approach, most commonly used with NCSA and CERN servers, involves a direct call to the imagemap processing program on the server. The HREF attribute is set equal to the URL to the imagemap processing script followed by a slash (/) and the name of the map defined in the server's imagemap.conf file. In the preceding example, the name of the map is mainpage. The actual graphic is then included with the <IMG> tag. The <IMG> tag also includes the ISMAP attribute, indicating that the image placed by the tag is to be a server-side imagemap. Using this approach, your imagemap link might look like this:

```
<A HREF="/cgi-bin/imagemap/mainpage">
<IMG SRC="images/mainpage.gif" ISMAP></A>
```

For this example to work, the imagemap.conf file must also include a line pointing to a map file for the imagemap mainpage. That line might look like the following:

```
mainpage : /maps/mainpage.map
```

Entries in the imagemap.conf file enable the imagemap program to find the map files you create. You need a similar entry in the imagemap.conf file for each imagemap you want the server to process.

NOTE The CERN server includes a slightly different version of the imagemap script, called htimage, that eliminates the need for the imagemap.conf file. Instead, htimage enables you to specify an URL to the map file directly. Using htimage rather than imagemap in the preceding example, you write the following:

```
<A HREF="/cgi-bin/htimage/maps/mainpage.map">
<IMG SRC="images/mainpage.gif" ISMAP></A>
```

You can use CERN's htimage script even if you run the NCSA server.

Pointing Directly at the Map File Linking to the imagemap script on the server is somewhat easier under Netscape and Windows HTTP servers. For this program, you just use the following line with an NCSA-style map file:

```
<A HREF="/maps/mainpage.map">
<IMG SRC="images/mainpage.gif" ISMAP></A>
```

These servers don't require the imagemap.conf file, so you can "eliminate the middle-man" and point directly to the map file. When the server detects a call for a map file, it automatically invokes the imagemap processing program.

Example: A Main Page Imagemap

Figure 4.1 shows an image to be used as an imagemap on the main page of a typical corporate site. The coordinates to define the hot regions in the image are given in Table 4.1.

Table 4.1 Coordinates and URLs for main page imagemap example.

Shape	Coordinates	URL
Rectangle	(24,21),(191,128)	**http://www.yourserver.com/sitemap.html**
Circle	(139,249),(186,323)	**http://www.yourserver.com/search.html**
Polygon	(281,55),(442,106),(483,215),(421,283),(393,187),(261,267),(242,139),(384,124)	**http://www.yourserver.com/whatsnew.html**

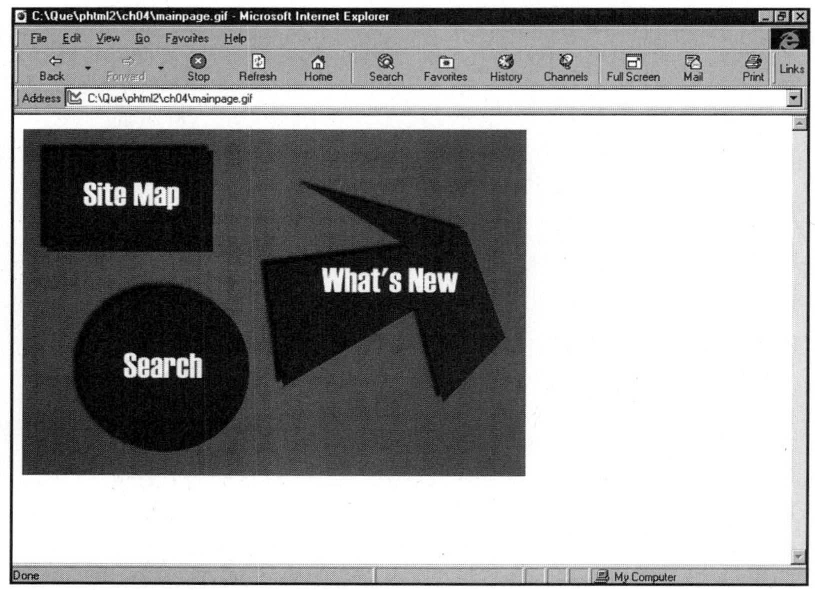

FIG. 4.1
An imagemap on a home page typically provides navigation links to all major areas of a site.

To set this up in a CERN-style map file, you use the following:

```
rect (24,21) (191,128) http://www.yourserver.com/sitemap.html
circle (139,249) (186,323) http://www.yourserver.com/search.html
poly (281,55) (442,106) (483,215) (421,283) (393,187) (261,267) (242,139)
(384,124) http://www.yourserver.com/whatsnew.html
```

For a server that works with the NCSA map file format, you use this:

```
rect http://www.yourserver.com/sitemap.html 24,21 191,128
circle http://www.yourserver.com/search.html 139,249 186,323
poly http://www.yourserver.com/whatsnew.html 281,55 442,106 483,215
421,283 393,187 261,267 242,139 384,124
```

With a map file set up in one style or another, you then set up the imagemap with:

```
<A HREF="http://www.yourserver.com/cgi-bin/imagemap/mainpage">
<IMG SRC="images/mainpage.gif" ISMAP ...></A>
```

for servers that use an imagemap.conf file or with:

```
<A HREF="http://www.yourserver.com/maps/mainpage.map">
<IMG SRC="images/mainpage.gif" ISMAP ...></A>
```

for servers that automatically go to the map file.

NOTE If you are using a server with an imagemap.conf file, you also need a line in that file matching the name "mainpage" with the map file mainpage.map:

```
mainpage : /maps/mainpage.map
```

Example: A Navigation Imagemap

Another very common use of imagemaps is for navigation bars at the top or bottom of a web page. Figure 4.2 shows a typical navigation graphic with the hot regions defined by the information in Table 4.2.

Table 4.2 Coordinates and URLs for navigation imagemap example.

Shape	Coordinates	URL
Rectangle	(11,19),(101,80)	**http://www.yourserver.com/index.html**
Rectangle	(130,20),(230,79)	**http://www.yourserver.com/search.html**
Rectangle	(264,20),(368,79)	**http://www.yourserver.com/whatsnew.html**
Rectangle	(396,20),(463,78)	**http://www.yourserver.com/sitemap.html**
Rectangle	(493,20),(587,79)	**http://www.yourserver.com/feedback.html**

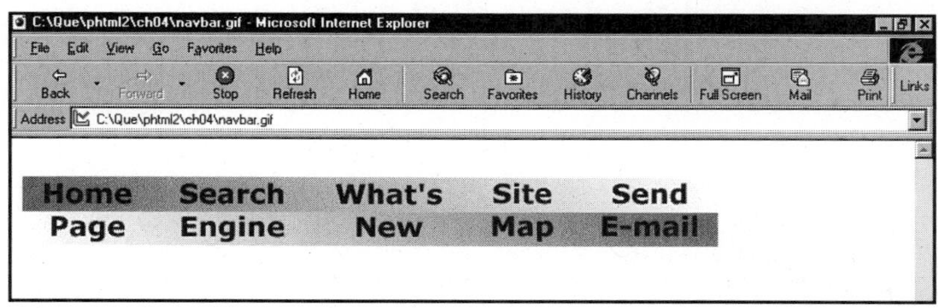

FIG. 4.2
A footer graphic frequently supports navigation options from each page in a site.

The CERN format map file for this imagemap looks like the following:

```
rect (11,19) (101,80) http://www.yourserver.com/index.html
rect (130,20) (230,79) http://www.yourserver.com/search.html
rect (264,20) (368,79) http://www.yourserver.com/whatnew.html
rect (396,20) (463,78) http://www.yourserver.com/sitemap.html
rect (493,20) (587,79) http://www.yourserver.com/feedback.html
```

If you are preparing a map file in NCSA format, use the following:

```
rect http://www.yourserver.com/index.html 11,19 101,80
rect http://www.yourserver.com/search.html 130,20 230,79
rect http://www.yourserver.com/whatsnew.html 264,20 368,79
rect http://www.yourserver.com/sitemap.html 396,20 463,78
rect http://www.yourserver.com/feedback.html 493,20 587,79
```

After your map file is done in the appropriate format, you set up the imagemap with:

```
<A HREF="http://www.yourserver.com/cgi-bin/imagemap/navigate">
<IMG SRC="images/navbar.gif" ISMAP ...></A>
```

or with:

```
<A HREF="http://www.yourserver.com/maps/navigate.map">
<IMG SRC="images/navbar.gif" ISMAP ...></A>
```

depending on whether the server uses an imagemap.conf file.

Client-Side Imagemaps

Having the server do the work of finding out where the user clicked and where to send the user based on the click places a lot of additional burdens on server resources. The client has to open another HTTP connection to the server to pass the coordinates and get the response back regarding what URL to load next. The computations the server has to do to find out what hot region the user clicked are straightforward, and there is no reason they can't be done by the client. Slow transmission times between client and server mean that users may have to wait quite a while from the time they click the mouse to the time the new URL loads.

Until recently, the compelling reason for having the server do the imagemap computations was that the map file data resided on the server. If there were a way to get this information to the client, the client could do the computations and the imagemap process would become much more efficient. This is the spirit behind client-side imagemaps.

Client-side imagemaps involve sending the map data to the client as part of an HTML file rather than having the client contact the server each time the map data is needed. This process may add to the transfer time of the HTML file, but the increased efficiency is well worth it.

Advantages

The movement toward client-side imagemaps has been fueled by the promise of a number of advantages, including the following:

- *Immediate processing.* After the browser has the map file information, it can process a user's click immediately instead of connecting to the server and waiting for a response.
- *Offline viewing of web pages.* If you're looking at a site off a hard drive or a CD-ROM drive, there's no server at all to do any imagemap computations. Client-side imagemaps allow imagemaps to be used when you're looking at pages offline.

- *No special configurations based on server program.* Client-side imagemaps are always implemented the same way. You don't need to format the map data differently, depending on whether a server expects CERN or NCSA imagemaps, because no server is involved.

Previously, the only disadvantage of using client-side imagemaps was the fact that it wasn't standard HTML and, therefore, not implemented by all browsers. Now that client-side imagemaps have been adopted as part of HTML for a few years, you would be hard pressed to find a graphical browser that does not yet support them.

Defining a Map

A client-side imagemap is defined using HTML tags and attributes, usually right in the HTML file that contains the document with the imagemap. The map data is stored between the `<MAP>` and `</MAP>` container tags. The `<MAP>` tag has the mandatory attribute NAME, which is used to give the imagemap data a unique identifier that can be used when referencing the data.

Inside the `<MAP>` and `</MAP>` tags, hot regions are defined by standalone `<AREA>` tags—one `<AREA>` tag for each hot region. The `<AREA>` tag takes the attributes shown in Table 4.3.

Table 4.3 Attributes of the *<AREA>* tag.

Attribute	Purpose
ALT	Provides a text-based alternative to the hot region
COORDS	Lists the coordinates of points needed to define the hot region
HREF	Supplies the URL to be associated with the hot region
NOHREF	Specifies that there is no URL associated with the hot region
SHAPE	Set equal to the keyword (`rect`, `circle`, `poly`, and `default`) that specifies the shape of the hot region
TARGET	Identifies the frame where the linked document should be rendered

NOTE The `point` keyword is not supported in HTML 4.0.

The triangle link set up during the discussion of server-side imagemaps, for example, would take the following form as a client-side imagemap:

```
<MAP NAME="triangle">
<AREA SHAPE="poly" COORDS="133,256,42,378,298,172"
HREF="http://www.yourserver.com/triangle.html" ALT="Triangle Link">
</MAP>
```

The preceding HTML sets up a map named "triangle" that has one hot region. Note that the numbers in the list of coordinates for the `COORDS` attribute are all separated by commas and that the URL in the `HREF` attribute is fully qualified.

The <AREA> tag can also take a NOHREF attribute, which tells the browser to do nothing if the user clicks on the hot region. Any part of the image that is not defined as a hot region is taken to be a NOHREF region—if users click outside a hot region, they don't go anywhere by default. This approach saves you from setting up an <AREA SHAPE="DEFAULT" NOHREF> tag for all your maps.

NOTE You can have as many <AREA> tags as you like. If the hot regions defined by two <AREA> tags overlap, the <AREA> tag listed first gets precedence.

Setting Up the Imagemap

With the imagemap data set up in HTML form, you next need to set up the imagemap itself. To do this, you just use the <IMG> tag along with the USEMAP attribute. USEMAP tells the browser that the image to be used is a client-side imagemap. It is set equal to the name of the map that contains the appropriate map data. For the client-side imagemap defined previously, the setup would look like this:

```
<IMG SRC="images/mainpage.gif" USEMAP="#triangle">
```

The pound sign (#) before the map name indicates that the map data is found in the same HTML file. If the map data is in another file called maps.html (which is perfectly okay), your <IMG> tag would look like the following:

```
<IMG SRC="images/mainpage.gif" USEMAP="http://www.your_firm.com/
➥maps.html#triangle">
```

TIP If you have standard navigation imagemaps on your site, you should consider storing the map data for them in a single HTML file for easier maintenance.

Example: A Main Page Imagemap

To set up the map information to make the image shown earlier in Figure 4.1 a client-side imagemap, you could use the following HTML:

```
<MAP NAME="mainpage">
<AREA SHAPE="rect" COORDS="24,21,191,128"
HREF="http://www.yourserver.com/sitemap.html" ALT="Site Map">
<AREA SHAPE="circle" COORDS="139,249,186,323"
HREF="http://www.yourserver.com/search.html" ALT="Search">
<AREA SHAPE="polygon"
COORDS="281,55,442,106,483,215,421,283,393,187,261,267,242,139,384,124"
HREF="http://www.yourserver.com/whatsnew.html" ALT="What's New">
</MAP>
```

Then, to set up the imagemap, you would use

```
<IMG SRC="images/mainpage.gif" USEMAP="#mainpage">
```

if the map information were in the same file. If the map information were stored in the file maps.html, you would modify the preceding <IMG> tag to read as follows:

```
<IMG SRC="images/mainpage.gif" USEMAP="http://www.yourserver.com/maps.html#main">
```

Example: A Navigation Imagemap

To use the image in Figure 4.2 as a client-side imagemap, you first need to set up the map information in an HTML file:

```
<MAP NAME="navigate">
<AREA SHAPE="rect" COORDS="11,19,101,80"
HREF="http://www.yourserver.com/index.html" ALT="Home Page">
<AREA SHAPE="rect" COORDS="130,20,230,79"
HREF="http://www.yourserver.com/search.html" ALT="Search">
<AREA SHAPE="rect" COORDS="264,20,368,79"
HREF="http://www.yourserver.com/whatsnew.html" ALT="What's New">
<AREA SHAPE="rect" COORDS="396,20,463,78"
HREF="http://www.yourserver.com/sitemap.html" ALT="Site Map">
<AREA SHAPE="rect" COORDS="493,20,587,79"
HREF="http://www.yourserver.com/feedback.html" ALT="Feedback">
</MAP>
```

With the map data in place, you can reference it with the <IMG> tag:

```
<IMG SRC="images/navbar.gif" USEMAP="#navigate">
```

if the map data is in the same HTML file. Because the same navigation maps are often used on several pages on a site, you might want to put the map data in a single map file and reference the file each time you need the map:

```
<IMG SRC="images/navbar.gif" USEMAP="maps.html#navigate">
```

As noted earlier, this is an efficient way to manage imagemaps common to many pages.

Using Server-Side and Client-Side Imagemaps Together

Client-side imagemaps are a great idea because they permit faster imagemap processing and enhance the portability of your HTML documents. Unfortunately, you can't be certain all graphical browsers support the client-side imagemap approach just described. If you know that there are some members of your audience who don't have a browser capable of processing client-side imagemaps, you should consider combining server-side and client-side imagemaps, until all browsers support client-side maps.

To combine a server-side imagemap with a client-side imagemap for the main page example discussed earlier, you can modify the earlier HTML as follows:

```
<A HREF="http://www.yourserver/maps/mainpage.map">
<IMG SRC="images/mainpage.gif" USEMAP="#mainpage" ISMAP></A>
```

Flanking the `<IMG>` tag with `<A>` and `</A>` tags makes it point to the mainpage.map file on the server. You need to include the `ISMAP` attribute in the `<IMG>` tag to let the browser know that the image is linked as a server-side imagemap as well.

NOTE You can link NCSA- and CERN-style server-side imagemaps to client-side imagemaps by having the HREF in the <A> tag point to the imagemap script, instead of pointing directly to the map file.

Providing a Text Alternative to an Imagemap

When using an imagemap—in particular, a server-side imagemap—it is important to provide a text-based alternative to users who have a text-only browser or who have image loading turned off. These users won't even be able to view your image, so the entire imagemap will be lost on them if a text-based alternative is not supplied.

Additionally, not all web robots can follow the links set up in a server-side imagemap. By providing a text-based set of links that replicate the links in the imagemap, you give the robots a way to better index your pages.

NOTE Text-based alternatives are less critical for client-side imagemaps because of the ALT attribute of the <AREA> tag. You are still free to include such alternatives, however, if you are willing to make the effort.

Most sites place their text-based alternatives to an imagemap just below the imagemap graphic. Usually the links are in a smaller font size and are separated by vertical bars or some such separator character (see Figure 4.3).

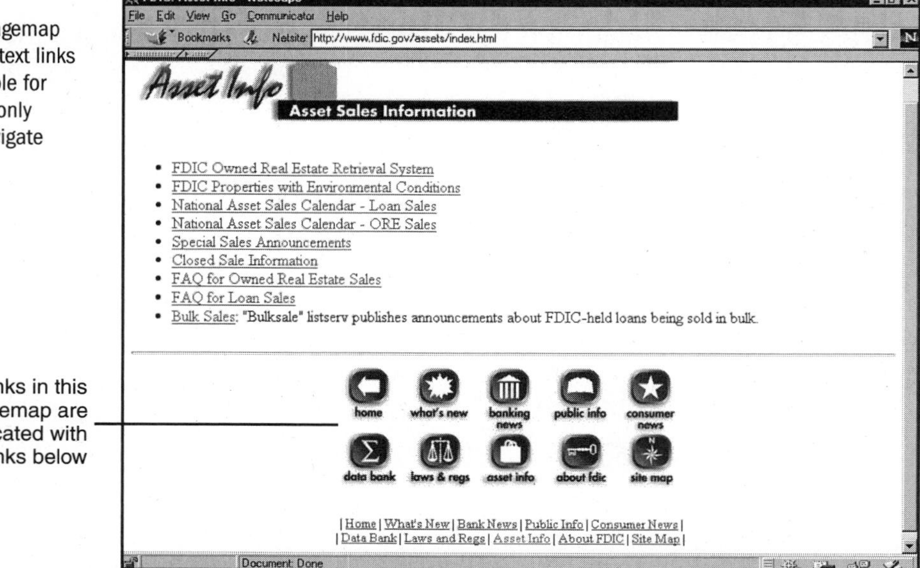

FIG. 4.3 Duplicating imagemap links with hypertext links makes it possible for users with text-only browsers to navigate your site.

Imagemap Tools

Whether you are creating a server-side or client-side imagemap, it can be cumbersome determining and typing in all the coordinates of all the points needed to define hot regions. Luckily, programs are available to help you through this process. They enable you to load your imagemap image, trace out the hot regions right onscreen, and then write the appropriate map file or HTML file to implement the imagemap. The following sections describe two of these programs: Mapedit and Microsoft's FrontPage.

Mapedit

Mapedit 2.31 is a shareware imagemap tool produced by Boutell.Com, Inc. This version of Mapedit supports client-side images and targeting of individual frames when using an imagemap within a framed document.

Using Mapedit is easy. From the File menu, choose Open/Create to begin. In the dialog box that appears, you won't see a choice between doing a server-side or a client-side imagemap. Rather, you first tell Mapedit which map file or HTML file you want the map data to go to. Based on the type of file you specify, Mapedit can figure out if you want a server-side or a client-side map. Finally, tell Mapedit the file containing the image for the imagemap. When you click OK, the image file is loaded into the Mapedit window, and you're ready to start defining hot regions.

You can choose Rectangle, Circle, or Polygon tools from the Mapedit Tools menu or from the toolbar just below the menus. Each tool enables you to trace out a hot region shaped like the name of the tool. To use the Rectangle tool, point your mouse to the upper-left corner of the rectangular hot region and click the left mouse button. Then move your mouse pointer to the lower-right corner of the region. As you do so, a black rectangular outline is dragged along with the pointer, eventually opening up to enclose your hot region (see Figure 4.4).

FIG. 4.4
Mapedit's hot region tracing tools are very easy to use.

With the mouse pointer pointing at the lower-right corner, left-click the mouse again. When you do, you see a dialog box like the one shown in Figure 4.5. Type the URL associated with the hot region you are defining into the dialog box, along with any comments you want to include, and click OK. Mapedit puts this information into the file it is building and is then ready to define another hot region or to save the file and exit.

FIG. 4.5
After your hot region is defined, Mapedit prompts you for the URL to associate with it.

Mapedit's Circle and Polygon tools work similarly. With the Circle tool, you place your mouse pointer at the center of the circular region (which is sometimes difficult to estimate!) and left-click. Then move the pointer to a point on the circle and left-click again to define the region and call up the dialog box. To use the Polygon tool, just left-click the vertices of the polygon in sequence. When you hit the last unique vertex (that is, the next vertex in the sequence is the first one you clicked), right-click instead to define the region and reveal the dialog box.

If you are unhappy with how your trace is coming out, just press the Esc key to erase your trace and start over.

Other Mapedit Tool menu options enable you to move an entire hot region (Move), add points (Add Points), or remove points (Remove Points) from a polygon and test the imagemap file as it currently stands. The Edit Default URL option, under the File menu, enables you to specify a default URL to go to if a user clicks somewhere other than a hot region. Mapedit's test mode (choose Tools, Test+Edit) presents the imagemap graphic to you and enables you to click it. If you click a hot region, the URL dialog box opens and displays the URL associated with the region you clicked.

NOTE Mapedit is available for all Windows platforms, Macintosh, and many kinds of UNIX. You can find Mapedit on the CD-ROM that comes with this book. After a 30-day evaluation period, you must license Mapedit at a cost of $25. Site licenses are also available. Educational and nonprofit users do not have to pay for a license, but should register their copies of Mapedit.

Microsoft FrontPage

The FrontPage Editor comes with an Image toolbar that activates whenever you select an image. In addition to basic image operations such as cropping, rotating, and changing contrast, buttons on the Image toolbar can also help you set up hot regions in an imagemap. The imagemap-related buttons are the first five you see on the left end of the toolbar (see Figure 4.6).

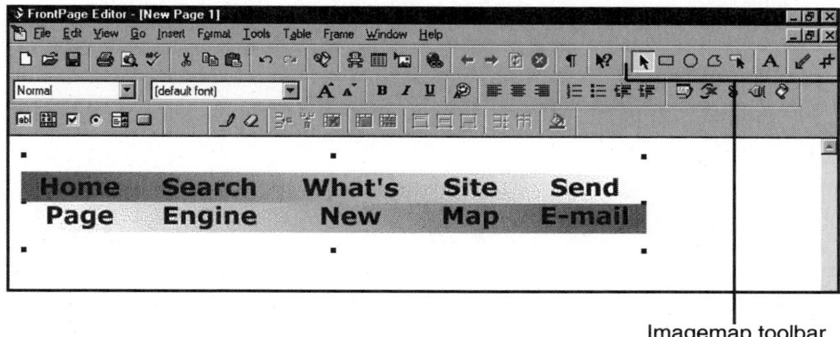

FIG. 4.6
FrontPage's Image toolbar includes buttons for setting up imagemaps.

▶ **See** "How FrontPage Handles Imagemaps," **p. 275.**

An important thing to note about FrontPage's imagemap handling is that, by default, it is done using a preprogrammed page object called a *bot*. When you look at the code FrontPage generates to support an imagemap, you will see something like this:

```
<!--webbot bot="ImageMap"
polygon=" (201,163) (237,139) (303,148) (329,180) (310,208) pageone.htm"
rectangle=" (228,309) (278, 397)  pagetwo.htm"
circle=" (281,83) 60  pagethree.htm" src="map.gif"
alt="map.gif (18273 bytes)" align="right" width="600" height="380" -->
```

This is a call to the FrontPage Imagemap bot—a piece of executable code that resides on a FrontPage-compliant web server. If you're not using a FrontPage-compliant server, this code won't do you or your visitors any good. Fortunately, you can instruct FrontPage to write client-side imagemap code instead by performing these steps:

1. In the FrontPage Explorer, choose Tools, Web Settings, and then click the Advanced tab.
2. Make sure the Generate Client-Side Imagemaps option near the top of the dialog box is checked.
3. Select the Netscape option from the Style drop-down list.
4. Click OK.

This tells FrontPage that it should not use the Imagemap bot and the code you find in your HTML files should be consistent with the HTML standard for client-side imagemaps.

After you have loaded an imagemap graphic, you can select the Rectangle, Circle, or Polygon tool by clicking its button on the toolbar. When using the Rectangle tool, click the upper-left corner of the rectangular hot region and then click the lower-right corner. As you move from upper left to lower right, a rectangular trace will be dragged across the hot region. After you click on the lower right, you will see the dialog box shown in Figure 4.7. Here you can enter the URL to be associated with the hot region.

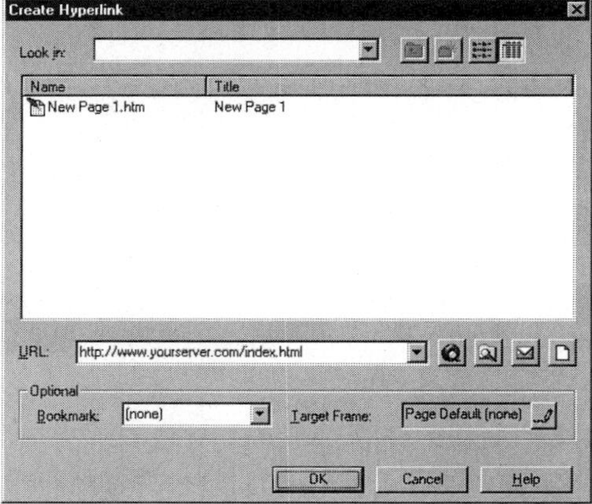

FIG. 4.7
You can enter an URL for a hot region or link to a page available in the open FrontPage web.

The FrontPage Circle tool works much the same as Mapedit's—click at the center of the circle, move the mouse pointer to a point on the edge of the circle, and then release the mouse button to open the dialog box you saw in Figure 4.7. To use the FrontPage Polygon tool, click the first vertex of the polygon, followed by each of the other vertices, until you hit the last one. Then click again on the first vertex and the URL box will appear.

If you are dissatisfied with how a trace is coming out, switch to the Select tool (first button on the Image toolbar), select the trace, and then press the Delete key.

Live Image

Live Image is an easy-to-use imagemapping tool for Windows 95 and Windows NT. If you have used a program called Map This! in the past, Live Image may seem very familiar. Indeed, Live Image is an enhanced version of Map This!, but the enhancements come (literally) with a price. A single-user license for Live Image will set you back $29.95.

Figure 4.8 shows the Live Image interface. The large area on the right side of the window is where the imagemap graphic loads. On the left is a listing of the hot regions you have defined. You can drag the separator bar between the two sides to a new position, if you want to change the size of either.

Live Image's interface is very intuitive, particularly those buttons you use to create hot regions. Just click the button corresponding to the shape of the hot region you want to define and then trace the hot region with your mouse. When you finish, you will see a dialog box like the one in Figure 4.8 prompting you for a URL, target frame, and any comments you want to associate with the region. Note also that hot regions are shaded on the graphic.

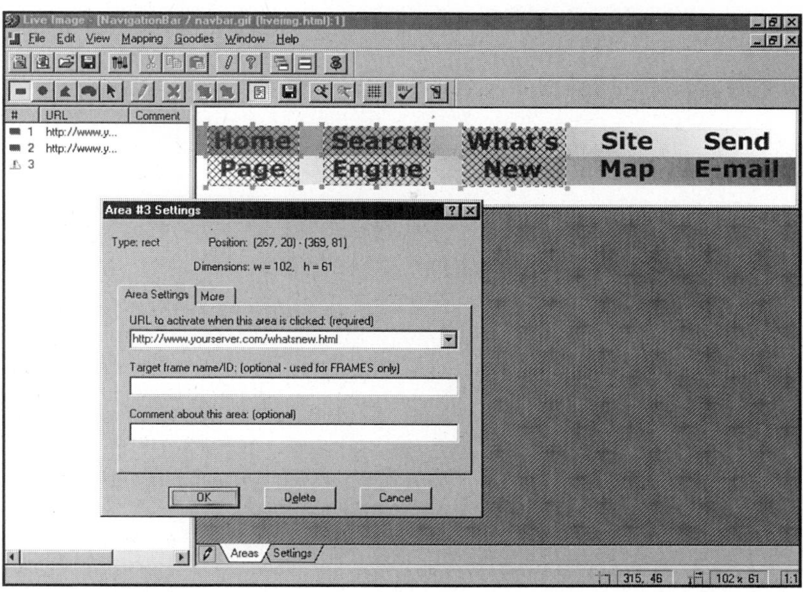

FIG. 4.8
Live Image enables you to see both the imagemap graphic and your hot regions simultaneously.

You also get a lot of extras in Live Image that you don't in other imagemap programs. In addition to being able to zoom in and out on the graphic, for example, you can also set up a grid over the image to assist you with very precise hot region traces. You can control the fineness of the grid and can even have points in your hot region trace snap to the grid.

Live Image enables you to test an imagemap in two ways. The first is through a "simulated browser" built into Live Image. When you test this way, you move your mouse pointer over the imagemap graphic and you will see URLs show up at the bottom of the screen as you pass over a hot region. The second way is to load the HTML file that Live Image produces into an actual browser and test it there.

Some of the other distinguishing features of Live Image include the following:

- An URL Checker that tests the URLs you associate with your hot regions to make sure they are valid
- Support for morphing one type of hot region into another
- The ability to work with more advanced types of files such as Cold Fusion templates or Active Server Page files
- JavaScript support for mouse-related events (`onMouseOver` and `onMouseOut`)
- Several example imagemaps and extensive help files
- A Settings tab where you can specify a map's name, author, default URL, and other information

Although you do have to pay a little bit of money for Live Image, you get quite a lot in return. You can learn more about Live Image by visiting **http://www.mediatec.com/**. ●

CHAPTER 5

Advanced Graphics

by Eric Ladd

In this chapter

Sorting Through the Graphic Possibilities

It is unlikely that the web would be so popular if it didn't support graphical content. Graphics give web pages visual appeal that keeps users surfing for hours. Graphics are also essential for people designing and posting web pages, as graphics often convey a message more powerfully than text alone.

Placing an image on a web page is a relatively easy matter—there's only one HTML tag you need. This tag also has many attributes that give you a good bit of control over how your graphics are presented.

Intelligent use of images requires planning, so you need to think about what idea you want to put forward, how to best represent the idea graphically, and what format is most appropriate for the graphic. The thought you put into your graphic content should be at least as much as you put into textual content—perhaps even more so because a reader gets a sense of an image just by quickly looking at it, whereas reading and comprehending text-based information requires more time. And there's more to making a web graphic than just creating the illustration. You need to consider the appropriateness of one of the many special effects that are possible with the GIF and JPEG formats. For GIFs, this means asking yourself questions such as the following:

- Should the GIF be transparent?
- Should it be interlaced?
- Should it be animated?

When considering JPEGs, you can ask:

- How much should the JPEG be compressed?
- Should it be a progressive JPEG (analogous to an interlaced GIF)?

Additionally, you need to think about color, depth, textures, filters, drop shadows, embossing, and all the other possible graphic effects. Through everything, you also need to keep the size of your graphics files as small as you can so that they don't take too long to download. How can you possibly balance all these constraints?

This chapter helps you to answer these questions so that your graphics content is as effective as it can be. This chapter starts with an in-depth discussion of the <IMG> tag and how this simple tag brings great variety to how images are presented. Then the discussion examines the two major web graphics storage formats and the merits and drawbacks of each. Finally, the chapter focuses on many of the web graphics effects previously noted, why you might want to use each one, and how to create them with readily available software (including some software on the CD-ROM that comes with this book). Mastering the content of this chapter will not necessarily make you a first-rate digital media design guru, but it will give you an awareness of what is possible in the realm of web graphics.

Layout Considerations When Using the <*IMG*> Tag

After you have an image stored and ready to be posted on the web, you need to use the HTML <IMG> tag to place the image on a page. <IMG> is a standalone tag that takes the attributes shown in Table 5.1. According to the HTML 4.0 DTD, only SRC is mandatory. You will quickly find, however, that you want to use many of them.

Table 5.1 Attributes of the <*IMG*> tag.

Attribute	Purpose
ALT	Supplies a text-based alternative for the image
ALIGN	Controls alignment of text following the image
BORDER	Specifies the size of the border to place around the image
HEIGHT	Specifies the height of the image in pixels
HSPACE	Controls the amount of white space to the left and right of the image
ISMAP	Denotes an image to be used as part of a server-side image map
SRC	Specifies the URL of the file where the image is stored
USEMAP	Specifies a client-side imagemap to use with the image
VSPACE	Controls the amount of white space above and below the image
WIDTH	Specifies the width of the image in pixels

The Basics

Even though the SRC attribute is the only attribute technically required in an <IMG> tag, you should get into the habit of considering three others as mandatory:

- HEIGHT *and* WIDTH. By providing image HEIGHT and WIDTH information, you speed up the page layout process and enable users to see pages faster. A browser uses the HEIGHT and WIDTH values in the <IMG> tag to reserve a space for the image and actually places the image after it has finished downloading. Without these two attributes, the browser has to download the entire image, compute its size, place it on the page, and then continue laying out the rest of the page. If a page has a lot of graphical content, leaving off HEIGHT and WIDTH can seriously delay presentation of the page and annoy visitors.
- ALT. Don't forget that some users don't have graphical browsers and can't see your images at all. You should provide a text alternative to your image for these users with the ALT attribute (see the text-only version of Yahoo!'s main page in Figure 5.1). Also, because web robots can't parse images, they often use the ALT description in an <IMG> tag to index the image.

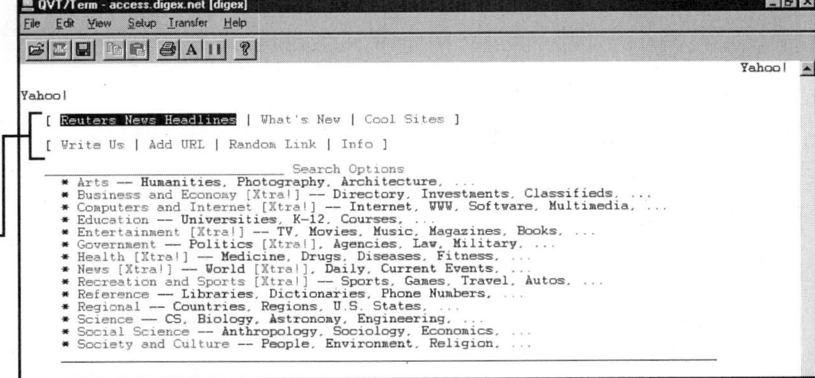

Text alternatives to images

FIG. 5.1 Providing a text-based alternative for each image is an important courtesy to users with text-only browsers.

Your basic `<IMG>` tag then should look like the following:

```
<IMG SRC="URL_of_image_file" WIDTH=width_in_pixels
HEIGHT=height_in_pixels ALT="alternative_text_description">
```

Most sites make conscientious use of these attributes in each `<IMG>` tag. Figure 5.2, for example, shows images on AltaVista's main page along with the corresponding HTML source code in Listing 5.1.

FIG. 5.2 All the images on AltaVista's page are set up with `WIDTH`, `HEIGHT`, and `ALT` attributes.

Listing 5.1 <*IMG*> tags from the AltaVista site.

```
<IMG src="/av/gifs/av_logo.gif" alt="[AltaVista] "  BORDER=0 ALIGN=middle
  HEIGHT=72 WIDTH=161>
<a href="/av/content/av_network.htm">
<IMG src="/av/gifs/av_map.gif" ismap alt="[AltaVista Network] "  BORDER=0
 ALIGN=middle  HEIGHT=72 WIDTH=127 usemap=#header></a>
<a href="http://ad.doubleclick.net/jump/altavista.digital.com/
sponsor-button/left_badge">
<img src="http://ad.doubleclick.net/ad/altavista.digital.com/
sponsor-button/left_badge" ismap width=90 height=72 border=0
align=middle alt=AD></a>
<a href="http://ad.doubleclick.net/jump/altavista.digital.com/
sponsor-button/right_badge">
<img src="http://ad.doubleclick.net/ad/altavista.digital.com/
sponsor-button/right_badge" ismap width=90 height=72 border=0
align=middle alt=AD></a>
```

NOTE You can also use the `HEIGHT` and `WIDTH` attributes to scale the size of your images on some browsers. If you have an image that is 232 pixels wide by 160 pixels high, for example, its dimensions can be halved with the use of the following tag:

```
<IMG SRC="graphic.gif" WIDTH=116 HEIGHT=80 ALT="Reduced image">
```

Similarly, you could scale the image size up by using a `WIDTH` greater than 232 and a `HEIGHT` greater than 160.

Although this is one way to modify the size of images, it is probably not the best way because browsers don't always do the best job at resizing. Additionally, this does not change the download time because the file size is still the same.

Your best bet is to use a program such as Photoshop or LView Pro to resize the graphic before placing it on your web page. Not only are these programs better suited to resize an image, they also enable you to preserve the aspect ratio (ratio of width to height) during the resize.

Adding a Border

The `BORDER` attribute gives you a simple way to instruct the browser to place a border around an image. `BORDER` is set equal to the number of pixels wide you want the border to be. Figure 5.3 shows an image with several different border sizes. The default border is no border.

FIG. 5.3
Borders look good when placed on photos; they give the picture the appearance of being framed.

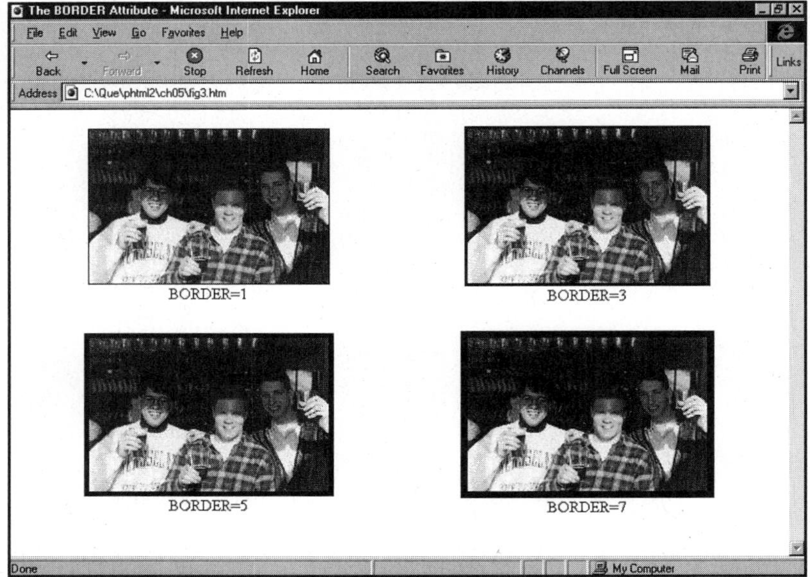

Adding Space Around Your Image

White space around an image is called *gutter space* or *runaround*. Putting a little extra space around an image is a good way to give it some more breathing room on the page and make it stand out better.

Runaround is controlled by the `HSPACE` and `VSPACE` attributes. Each is set to the number of pixels of extra space to leave to the right and left of an image (`HSPACE`) or above and below an image (`VSPACE`). Figures 5.4 and 5.5 show some images with varying amounts of `HSPACE` and `VSPACE`.

NOTE `HSPACE` and `VSPACE` don't have to be used independently of each other. In fact, they are very often used together. The following code would leave 10 pixels of space all the way around the image, for example:

```
<IMG SRC="picture.jpg" HSPACE=10 VSPACE=10 ...>
```

CAUTION

You cannot increase space on just one side of an image. Remember that `HSPACE` adds space to both the left and the right of an image and that `VSPACE` adds space both above and below the image.

FIG. 5.4
HSPACE controls the distance between an image and things to the right and left of the image.

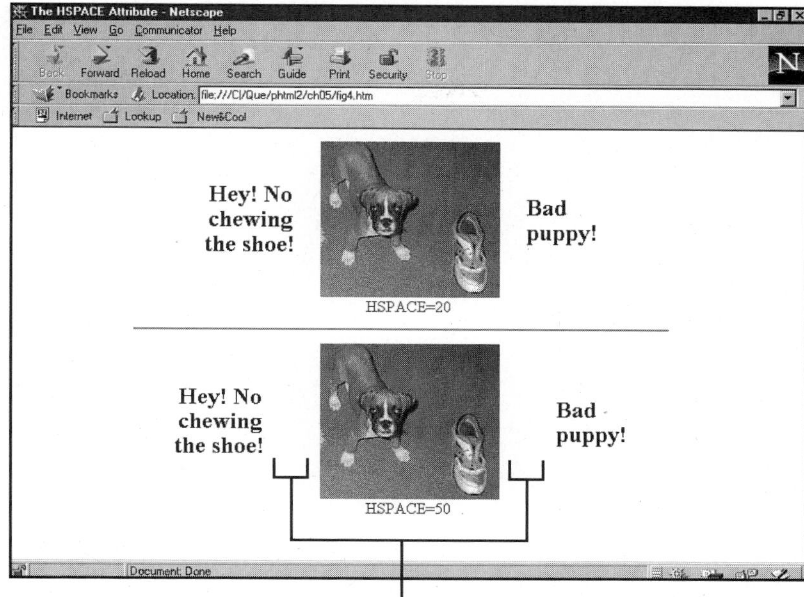

FIG. 5.5
VSPACE can open up room above and below an image.

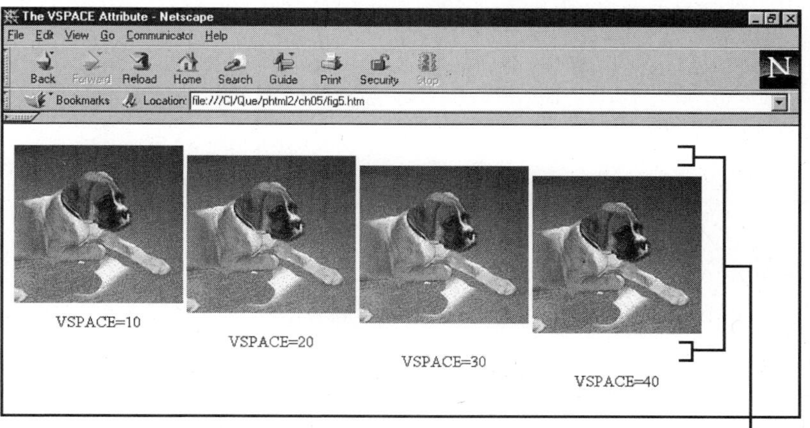

The *ALIGN* Attribute and Floating Images

The `ALIGN` attribute of the `<IMG>` tag can take on one of the five different values summarized in Table 5.2. `TOP`, `MIDDLE`, and `BOTTOM` refer to how text should be aligned following the image. `LEFT` and `RIGHT` create floating images in either the left or right margin.

Table 5.2 Values of the *ALIGN* attribute in the *<IMG>* tag.

Value	Purpose
`TOP`	Aligns the top of subsequent text with the top of the image
`MIDDLE`	Aligns the baseline (the line on which the text appears to sit) of subsequent text with the middle of the image
`BOTTOM`	Aligns the baseline of subsequent text with the bottom of the image
`LEFT`	Floats the image in the left margin and allows text to wrap around the right side of the image
`RIGHT`	Floats the image in the right margin and allows text to wrap around the left side of the image

Figure 5.6 shows text aligned with `TOP`, `MIDDLE`, and `BOTTOM` (the default alignment). One important thing to note with `TOP` and `MIDDLE` alignments is that when the text reaches a point where it needs to break, it breaks at a point below the image and leaves some white space between the lines of text.

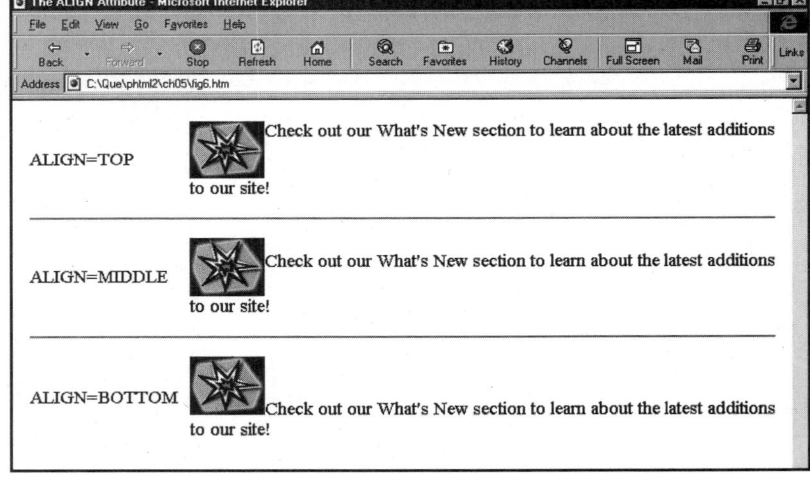

FIG. 5.6
Of `TOP`, `MIDDLE`, and `BOTTOM` alignment, only `BOTTOM` allows text to properly wrap around an image.

Values of `LEFT` and `RIGHT` for the `ALIGN` attribute were adopted as part of the HTML 3.2 standard to allow for floating images that permit text to wrap around them. Figure 5.7 shows some floated images (pictures of Jack Kent Cooke and the Redskins logo in the "A New Beginning" box) on the Washington Post's web page. Listing 5.2 shows the corresponding HTML source code.

FIG. 5.7
Floating images sit in one margin and allow text to wrap around them.

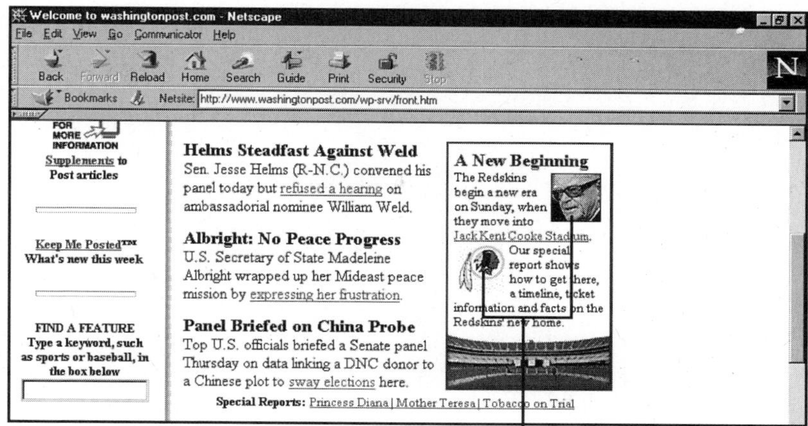

Listing 5.2 HTML code to produce floating images.

```
<font size="+1"><b><font color="#8C0018">A New Beginning
</font color></b></font><br>
<IMG src="/wp-srv/sports/images/redskins/redesign/jkc_small2.jpg"
border="0" width="50" height="50" vspace="3" align="right" alt="spacer">
<font size="-1">The Redskins begin a new era on Sunday, when they move
into <A href="/wp-srv/sports/redskins/longterm/1997/stadium/special/
front.htm">Jack Kent Cooke Stadium</a>.
<IMG src="/wp-srv/sports/images/redskins/redesign/skinlogo_small.jpg"
border="0" width="50" height="50" vspace="2" align="left" alt="spacer">
Our special report shows how to get there, a timeline, ticket information
 and facts on the Redskins' new home.<br clear="all"></font>
```


Floating images opened the door to many creative and interesting layouts. In fact, it is even possible to overlap images by floating one in the left margin and one in the right margin.

The advent of floating images created a need for a way to break to the first left or right margin that is clear of a floating image. To satisfy this need, the `CLEAR` attribute was added to the `<BR>` tag. Setting `CLEAR` to `LEFT` breaks to the first instance of a left margin that is clear of floating images (see Figure 5.8). `CLEAR=RIGHT` does the same thing, except it breaks to the first right margin. You can clear both margins by setting `CLEAR=ALL`. The code to produce Figure 5.8 is as follows:

```
<IMG SRC="cheers.jpg" ALIGN=LEFT>
<FONT SIZE=6><B>CHEERS!</B> Raise your glass to a good time at the
Clubhouse Pub!</FONT>
<BR CLEAR=LEFT>
The Clubhouse Pub offers a complete line of domestic and imported
draft and bottled beer, wine, soda, and juices. Be sure to also
check out our food menu for those times when you get the munchies.
```

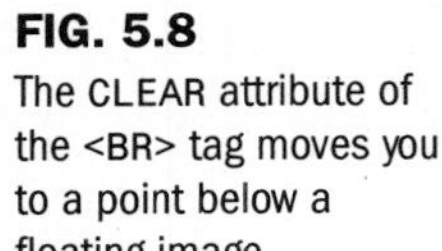

FIG. 5.8
The CLEAR attribute of the <BR> tag moves you to a point below a floating image.

ISMAP and USEMAP

Imagemaps are clickable images that load different pages depending on where you click the image. They are frequently found on the main page of a site where they typically serve as a navigational tool to the major sections of the site.

▶ **See** "Imagemaps," **p. 117**.

The ISMAP attribute of the <IMG> tag is a standalone attribute that tells the browser that the image is to be used as part of a server-side imagemap.

The USEMAP attribute of the <IMG> tag is set equal to the name of a client-side imagemap. With client-side imagemaps, map information is named and sent directly to the browser. Setting USEMAP equal to a map name instructs the browser to use the map information associated with that name.

Images as Hyperlink Anchors

As explained in Chapter 3, "HTML 4.0 Tag Reference," the <A> container tag is used to create hypertext anchors. By clicking the hypertext, you instruct your browser to load the resource at the URL specified in the HREF attribute of the <A> tag.

There's no law that says hyperlink anchors can only be text. Very often you will find images serving as anchors as well. By linking images to other web pages, you create a button-like effect—the user clicks the button and the browser loads a new page.

To use a graphic as a hyperlink anchor, put the <IMG> tag that places the graphic between <A> and </A> tags:

```
<A HREF="welcome.html">
<IMG SRC="images/hello.gif" ALT="Hello there!"></A>
```

This results in the linked image shown in Figure 5.9. Notice that the image has a border even though there was no BORDER attribute specified. Hyperlinked images automatically get a border colored with the same colors that you set up for hypertext links using the LINK, VLINK, and ALINK attributes of the <BODY> tag.

Borders around hyperlinked images are typically distracting, especially if the image is a transparent GIF. Notice in Figure 5.9 how the border shows the extent of the otherwise transparent bounding box around the image. To eliminate the border, include BORDER=0 inside the <IMG> tag.

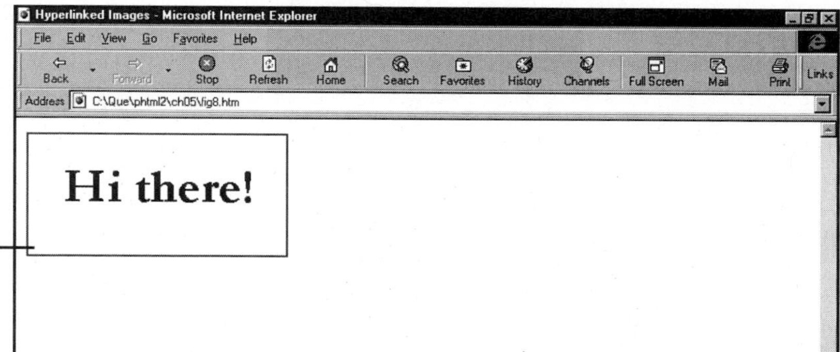

FIG. 5.9 A hyperlinked image will automatically get a border unless you specify BORDER=0.

TROUBLESHOOTING

There's a small, hyperlinked line at the bottom right of your linked images. How do you get rid of it?

Your problem most likely stems from HTML code such as the following:

```
<A HREF="author.html">
<IMG SRC="ericzack.jpg" WIDTH=300 HEIGHT=400 ALT="Eric and Zack">
</A>
```

By having a carriage return after the <IMG> tag but before the </A> tag, you often get an extraneous line at the bottom-right corner of the linked image (see Figure 5.10). By placing the </A> tag immediately after the <IMG> tag

```
<A HREF="author.html">
<IMG SRC="ericzack.jpg" WIDTH=300 HEIGHT=400 ALT="Eric and Zack"></A>
```

it should take care of that annoying little line.

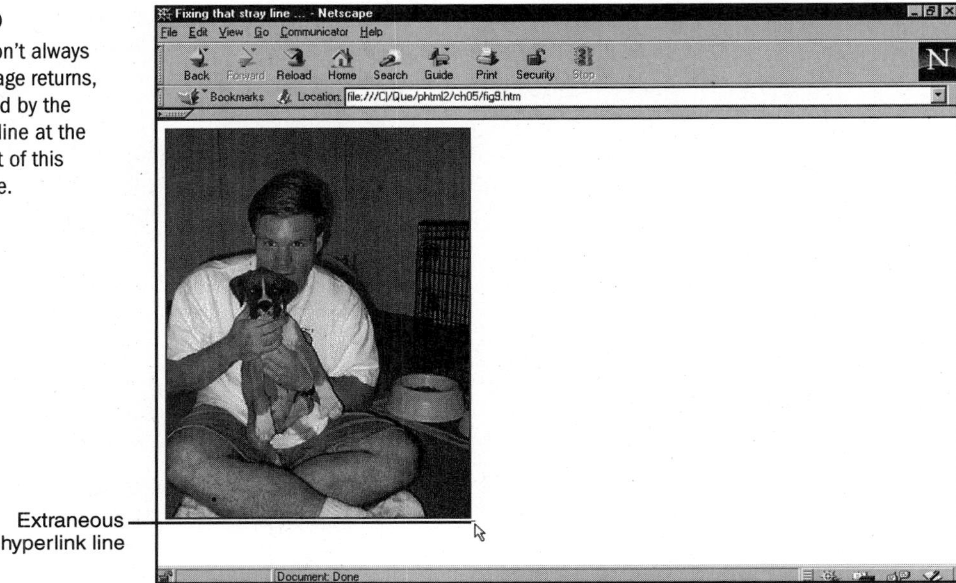

FIG. 5.10
Browsers don't always ignore carriage returns, as evidenced by the extraneous line at the bottom right of this linked image.

Images as Bullet Characters

Some people opt to create their own bullet characters for bulleted lists instead of using the characters that browsers provide. To do this, you need to place the bullet graphic with an <IMG> tag and follow it with a list item:

```
<IMG SRC="bullet.gif" WIDTH=12 HEIGHT=12 ALT="*">HTML 4.0<BR>
<IMG SRC="bullet.gif" WIDTH=12 HEIGHT=12 ALT="*">Java<BR>
<IMG SRC="bullet.gif" WIDTH=12 HEIGHT=12 ALT="*">JavaScript 1.2<BR>
```

TIP Using an asterisk (*) as the value of your ALT attribute gives users with non-graphical browsers a bullet-like character in front of each list item.

There are several things to note about this HTML:

- You must have a separate <IMG> tag for each bullet.
- You may need to experiment with the ALIGN attribute to find the best alignment between bullets and list items.
- You have to place line breaks manually with a <BR> tag at the end of each list item.

Usually, this is enough to deter many page authors from using their own bullet characters. If you are still determined to use custom bullets, however, there's one more alignment issue you need to be aware of: If a list item is long enough to break to a new line, the next line starts below the bullet graphic, not indented from it (see Figure 5.11). This detracts from the nice indented presentation that users expect from a bulleted list.

One way to avoid this problem is to make list items short enough to fit on one line. If that isn't possible, you should consider setting up your list with custom bullets in an HTML table.

▶ **See** "Tables," **p. 165**.

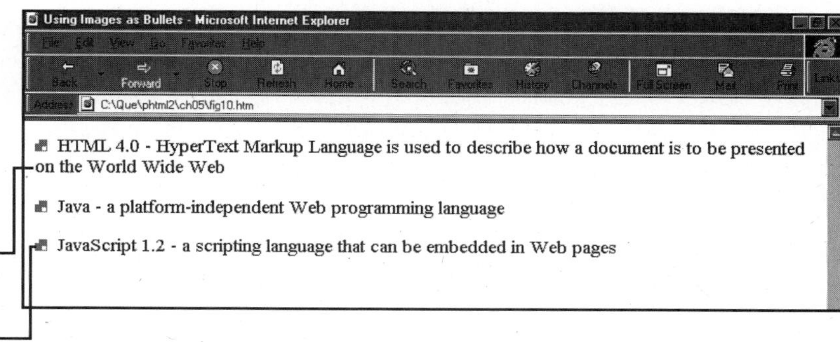

FIG. 5.11
If you are using a custom bullet graphic, you will also be responsible for things such as text wrapping and alignment.

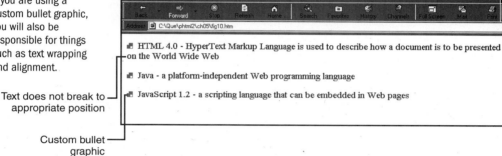

Images as Horizontal Rule

Some sites also use a custom graphic in place of a horizontal rule (see Figure 5.12). This is a nice way to subtly reinforce a site's graphic theme.

Alignment problems are less of an issue with a custom rule, but there are a couple of rules to keep in mind:

- Assume a screen width of 640 pixels and keep your rule sized accordingly. Don't let the rule's width exceed 640 pixels.
- The default alignment for rule placed with the `<HR>` tag is centered. You can replicate this effect for your custom rule by placing the `<IMG>` tag for the rule graphic between `<P ALIGN=CENTER>` and `</P>` tags.
- Use a row of dashes for your `ALT` text in the `<IMG>` tag so that text-only users can get a rule effect as well.

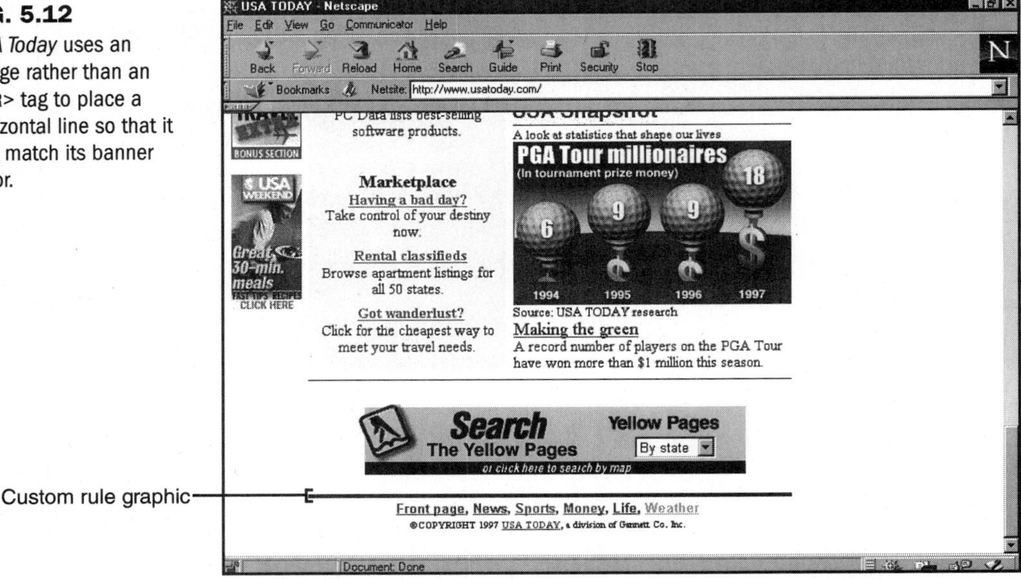

FIG. 5.12
USA Today uses an image rather than an <HR> tag to place a horizontal line so that it can match its banner color.

Graphic Storage Formats

Technically, web graphics can be stored in any format, but only two formats display inline on all of today's popular graphical browsers: GIF and JPEG. Other graphics formats have to be displayed by a helper application that is launched by the browser when it detects a format it can't display.

NOTE Microsoft Internet Explorer 4 supports the inline display of Windows Bitmap (.BMP) graphics in addition to GIFs and JPEGs.

GIF

Graphics Interchange Format (GIF) was originally developed for users of CompuServe as a standard for storing image files. The GIF standards have undergone a couple of revisions since their inception. The current standard is GIF89a.

Graphics stored in GIF are limited to 256 colors. Because full-color photos require many more colors to look sharp, you shouldn't store full-color photos as GIFs. GIF is best used with line art, logos, and icons. If you do store a full-color photo as a GIF, its palette is reduced to just 256 colors and the photo will not look as good on your web page.

In spite of a limited number of colors, the GIF89a standard supports the following three web page effects:

- *Interlacing*. In an interlaced GIF image, non-adjacent parts of the image are stored together. As a browser reads in an interlaced GIF, the image appears to fade in over several passes. This is useful because the user can get a sense of what the entire image looks like without having to wait for the whole thing to load.
- *Transparency*. In a transparent GIF, one of the colors is designated as transparent, allowing the background of the document to show through. Figure 5.12 illustrates a transparent and non-transparent GIF. Notice in the non-transparent GIF that the bounding box around the text is visible. By specifying the color of the bounding box to be transparent, the background color shows through and the text appears to just be sitting on the background.

  Transparent GIFs are very popular and many of the graphics programs available today support the creation of transparent GIFs. On the PC, LView Pro is one program that creates transparent GIFs. PhotoGIF is a plug-in to Photoshop that enables you to create both transparent and interlaced GIFs. JASC's PaintShop Pro is a very reasonably priced graphics program that supports transparent GIFs. You can even use Microsoft FrontPage to create transparent GIFs from existing images (see Figure 5.13).

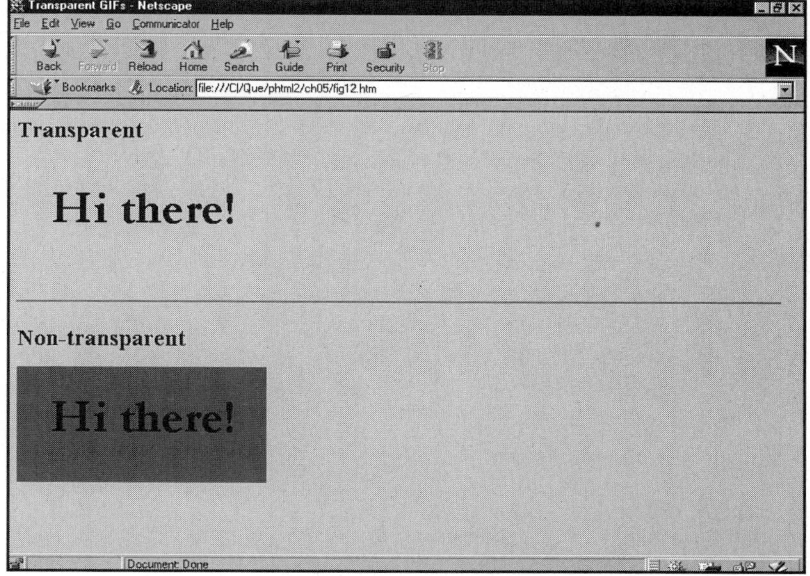

FIG. 5.13
The background color in a transparent GIF takes on the page's background color to make objects in the image appear to sit right on the page.

- *Animation*. Animated GIFs are created by storing the sequence of images used to produce the animation in one file. A browser that fully supports the GIF89a standard is designed to present the images in the file one after the other to produce the animation. The programs that enable you to store the multiple images in the GIF file also enable you to specify how much delay should occur before beginning the animation and how many times the animation should repeat. Web designers are making widespread use of animated GIFs because they are much easier to implement than server push or even Java animations (see Figure 5.14). A server push animation requires a CGI program to send the individual images down an open HTTP connection.

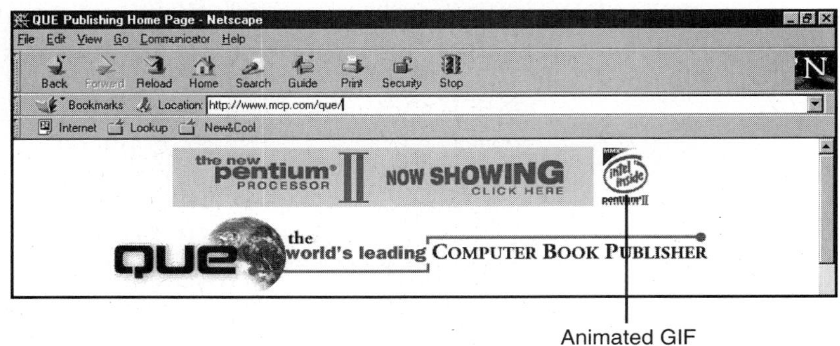

FIG. 5.14 Many advertising banners seen on web sites are animated GIFs.

JPEG

Joint Picture Experts Group (JPEG) refers to a set of formats that support full-color images and stores them in a compressed form (see Figure 5.15). JPEG is a 24-bit storage format that enables for 2^{24} or 16,777,216 colors! With that much color data, it is easy to see why some form of compression is necessary.

Although JPEG is great for full-color images, it does not permit some of the nice effects that GIF does. Transparency is not possible with JPEG images because the compression tends to make small changes to the image data. With the exception of a server push approach, animation is not yet possible with JPEGs. There is an analogy to interlaced GIFs, however. The progressive JPEG (p-JPEG) format has recently emerged, which gives the effect of an image fading in just as an interlaced GIF would.

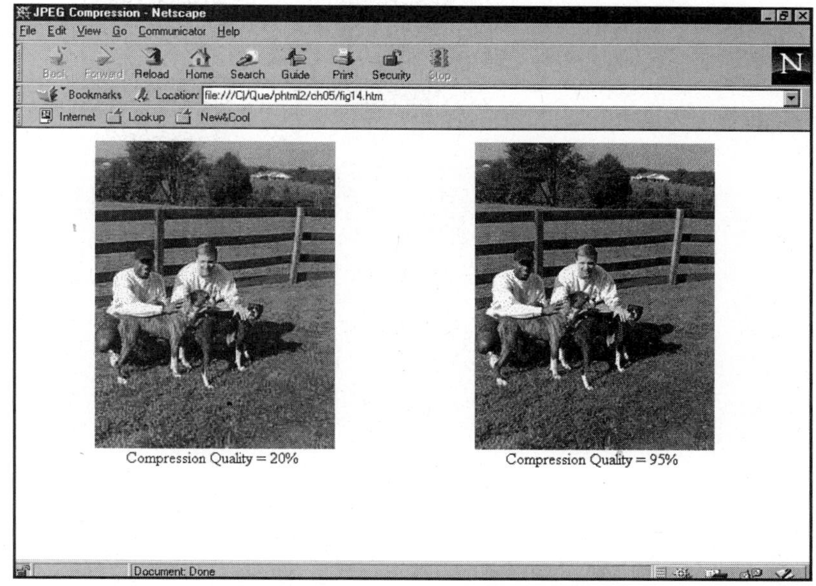

FIG. 5.15
The image on the left is more highly compressed and, therefore, more grainy than the image on the right.

Choosing a Format

The question of which format to use is often a daunting one for beginning designers. Fortunately there are some ways to focus your thinking as you make this choice:

- Do you need to create a transparency effect? If the answer is yes, you will have to use a GIF because it is the only widely accepted format that supports transparency.
- Do you need to produce an animation? Unless you want to code a server push animation, it is easier to place animations on your pages by using animated GIFs.
- Is your graphic a full-color image? Full-color images, particularly photographs of things in nature, are best stored as JPEGs so that you can harness its support for more than 16 million colors.
- Does your graphic have any sharp color changes or boundaries? Some graphics change quickly from one color to another rather than fading gradually over a continuum of colors. Because of the mathematics behind the compression algorithm, JPEGs don't cope well with sudden color changes. Use GIF to handle images such as these.
- Do you need a fade-in effect? This isn't too much of a discriminator because both GIF and JPEG support some type of fade-in effect—interlacing for GIF and p-JPEG for JPEG.

A good rule of thumb is to use JPEG for color photos and to use GIFs for all other graphics and illustrations. Because transparency and animation are not usually needed for full-color images, this rule is not seriously limiting.

The Portable Network Graphics Format

A proposal currently before the World Wide Web Consortium (W3C) describes a new image format that is intended to take the place of the very popular GIF format. This new format is called the Portable Network Graphics (PNG) format and it has already been made a recommendation by the W3C.

PNG has many powerful features that exceed those of the GIF format, including

- Better compression ratios with no loss
- File integrity and corruption checking
- Two-dimensional interlacing
- 8-bit color palette and 16-bit grayscale support
- Alpha channel for transparency

PNG is fully supported by Internet Explorer and many other browsers. Netscape Navigator, however, requires a plug-in to view PNG graphics. Netscape plans to implement inline PNG support in a later version of Navigator 4.0 or Navigator 5.0 A host of image editors and converters support PNG as well. For a very thorough listing of PNG-capable software, check out **http://www.wco.com/~png/pngapps.html**.

To learn more about the PNG specification, direct your browser to **http://www.boutell.com/boutell/png/**.

Using the Browser Safe Color Palette

Lynda Weinman, a popular author on the topics of web graphics and color, has advanced the idea of a "browser safe palette"—a set of colors rendered the same way by *any* browser on *any* platform. Netscape Navigator and Microsoft Internet Explorer both use the same default 256-color palette when rendering web pages, but because of slight differences between the PC and the Macintosh, 40 of these colors can appear differently, depending on the platform. If you remove these 40 colors from the default palette, the remaining 216 colors comprise a palette that should appear exactly the same regardless of a user's hardware or software.

The browser safe color palette is freely available from **http://www.lynda.com/hex.html**, ordered both by hue and by RGB color values. You are welcome to download the palette and use it to make your GIF images and other colored page elements as browser friendly as possible. Macintosh users can check out Pantone's ColorWeb color selection application at **http://38.219.133.4/pantone/catalog/colorwebss.html**.

Creating Transparent GIFs

When you make a transparent image, you designate one color in the image's palette to be the transparent color. Pixels colored with the transparent color allow the background color to show through. Figure 5.12 showed you transparent and non-transparent versions of the same image.

This technique is useful in getting rid of the "bounding box" that typically surrounds a graphic. When you compose an image in a graphics program, the workspace is almost always rectangular. Your image goes inside this rectangular region (the bounding box), and invariably there is some amount of space between the image and the edges of the box. By choosing the color of the excess space pixels to be transparent, you make them disappear on the browser screen. This is what happened in Figure 5.12. The bounding box pixels in the image using the transparency option were the ones designated as transparent, so they let the white background show through and give the effect of the oval sitting right on top of the web page.

TIP Think twice before putting a border around a transparent GIF because it will outline the bounding box and ruin the transparency effect.

NOTE Microsoft's Image Composer is an image editing program that makes use of "sprites" or images whose shape is that of the object they portray and not necessarily a rectangle. The inspiration for sprites came from extending the idea of transparency.

Many popular graphic programs support transparent GIFs. One such program that you will find on the CD-ROM with this book is LView Pro. LView Pro is a terrific shareware program that is well worth the $40.00 you will pay for the license.

Creating a transparent GIF in LView Pro involves the following two simple steps:

1. Designating a color as the background color.
2. Instructing LView Pro to note the background color as the transparent color when saving the file.

Figure 5.16 shows the LView Pro interface. On the right side of the screen, you will find the Color Selection Dialog Bar. Along the top of the bar, three rectangles display, from left to right, the foreground color, the background color, and the transparent color. To change the transparent color, move your mouse pointer to the color in the color palette (at the bottom of the Dialog Bar) that you want to be the new transparent color, press the Alt key, and click either mouse button. You should see the color in the third rectangle at the top change to the color you selected.

With the background color set, all you need to do is tell LView Pro to make that color transparent in the GIF file. You do this by choosing File, Preferences, Graphics File Formats, and clicking the GIF tab. Checking Save Transparent color information (GIF89a only) ensures that LView Pro will designate your chosen background color as transparent (see Figure 5.17).

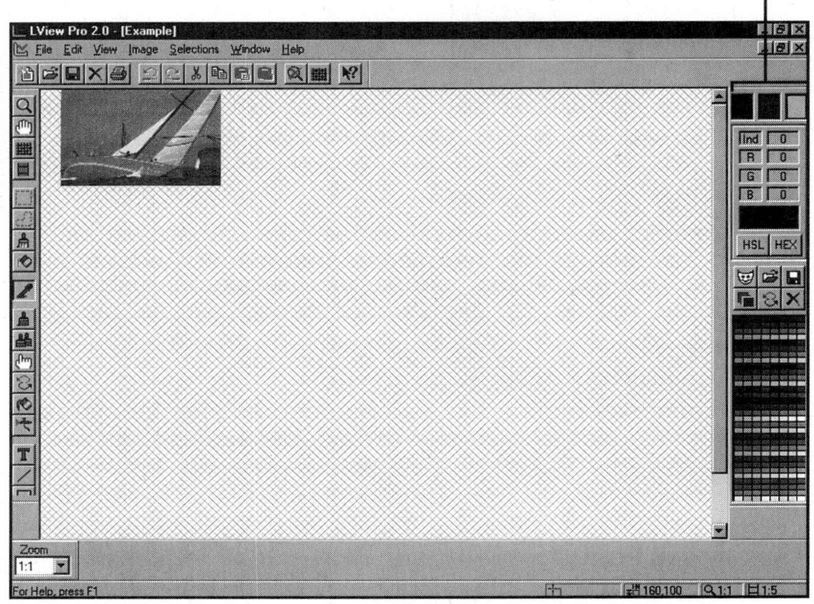

FIG. 5.16
LView Pro gives you access to an image's entire color palette, enabling you to choose one color as the background color.

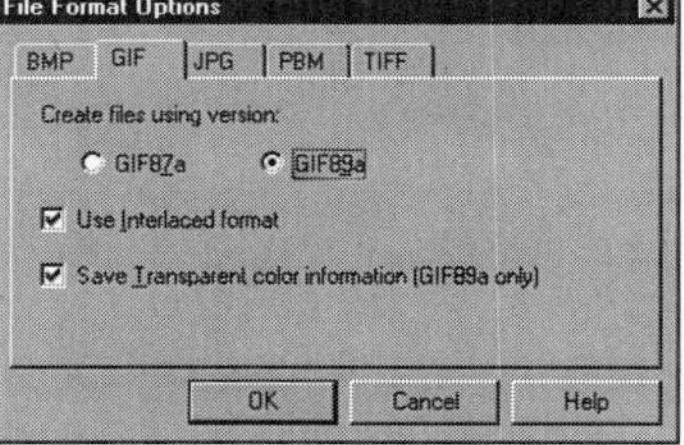

FIG. 5.17
Instructing LView Pro to save transparent color information means that pixels painted with the background color will be designated as transparent.

Why Aren't There Transparent JPEGs?

Transparency is only supported in the GIF format. A JPEG image cannot use a transparency effect because the algorithm used to compress a JPEG file is lossy. This means that during decompression, some pixels are not painted with the exact same color they had before the compression. These color changes are so small that they are typically imperceptible to the human eye, although you may be able to detect color differences after several cycles of compression and decompression. However, a computer can detect the difference and therein lies the demise of the transparent JPEG. To understand further, consider the following example:

You scan in a photograph of a field of flowers and you want to save it as a JPEG. The JPEG format supports over 16.7 million colors. Suppose that you choose color number 3,826,742 as the transparent color and save the file. During the compression and subsequent decompression, some data loss occurs in the file. As a result of the loss, a pixel originally painted with color number 3,826,742 is now colored with color number 3,826,740. The pixel was supposed to be transparent, but because its color number was changed by the compression, it will not be. The pixel will be painted with color number 3,826,740 and not let the background show through.

The reverse situation can happen as well. Suppose a pixel originally colored with color number 3,826,745 ends up being painted with color number 3,826,742. This is the transparent color, so the pixel will adopt the background color rather than color number 3,826,745 as originally intended.

As long as JPEG continues to be a lossy format, it will be impossible to use transparency with them. If you have to use a transparent graphic, you must use a GIF.

Making an Image "Fade In"

Even when image files are made as small as possible, it can still take a while for them to download. Initially browsers had to load and process the entire file before it began to present the image onscreen. This meant users had to sit there staring at a blank screen for minutes at a time. Web user attention spans being what they are, people would often give up in frustration and move on to another page instead of wait for an image to finish downloading.

Since those early days, two approaches to reducing user frustration have emerged. Both involve having an image "fade in" as the image data is read by the browser. The user sees a blurry, incomplete image at first, but then the image quality improves as more data is read in. The key thing for users is that they immediately see an approximation to the finished image on their screens. This keeps them engaged and makes it less likely that they will move on to another page.

The "two" approaches to fading an image on to a page are actually variations on the same idea, modified for different storage formats. In each case, the image data is not stored in "top-to-bottom" order. Instead the image data is reordered so that adjacent rows of pixel information are no longer stored contiguously in the file. As the browser reads down the file, it places the rows of noncontiguous data up on the screen. The result is an incomplete image that fills itself in as the rest of the image data is read (see Figures 5.18 and 5.19). A GIF stored in this way is called an interlaced GIF. The same idea applied to a JPEG file yields a progressive JPEG or p-JPEG.

A different kind of fade-in effect is to have a black-and-white version of an image load first, followed by the full-color version. You can accomplish this by using the LOWSRC attribute of the <IMG> tag. LOWSRC is set equal to the URL of the black-and-white image file. This file loads and is rendered more quickly because it is generally much smaller than its full-color equivalent (less color information to store means a smaller file size). The full-color version is then rendered in place of the LOWSRC image after it is read in. This gives the appearance of the black-and-white image being "painted" with color.

FIG. 5.18
An image that "fades in" appears blocky at first, but you can still make out enough detail to have an idea of what it is.

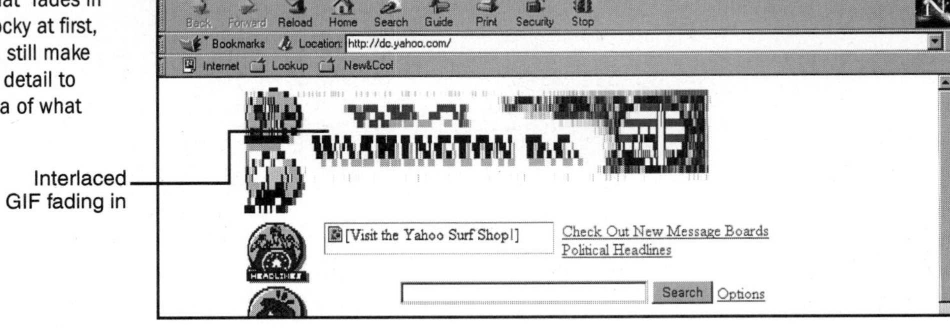

FIG. 5.19
As more data is read in, the image comes into sharper focus and eventually reaches its final form.

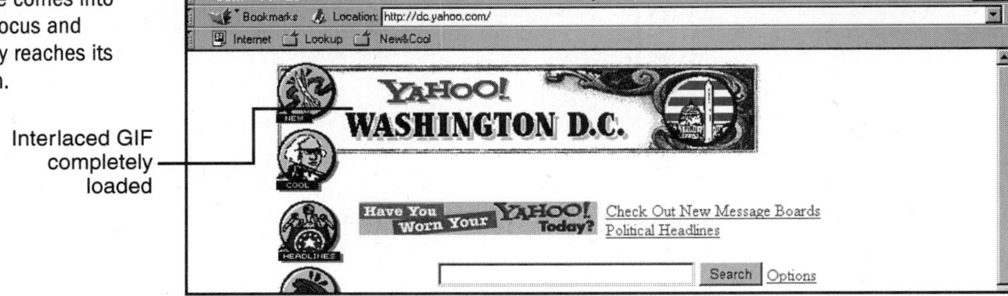

Making Interlaced GIFs

Creating an interlaced GIF is a simple matter with LView Pro. To instruct LView Pro to save a GIF in interlaced form, just select File, Preferences, Graphics File Formats, and then click the GIF tab. Checking the Use Interlaced format will do the trick. To deactivate saving in the interlaced format, just uncheck the box.

Progressive JPEGs

p-JPEGs are relatively new, but LView Pro is current enough to have the capability to help you make them. To activate saving in a progressive JPEG format, choose File, Preferences, Graphics File Formats, and then click the JPG tab. Check the Use Progressive JPEG Compression Format box, and you're good to go (see Figure 5.20).

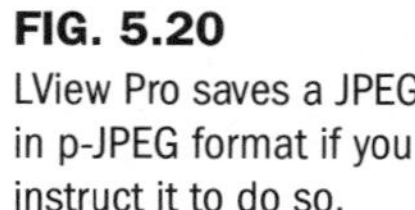

FIG. 5.20
LView Pro saves a JPEG in p-JPEG format if you instruct it to do so.

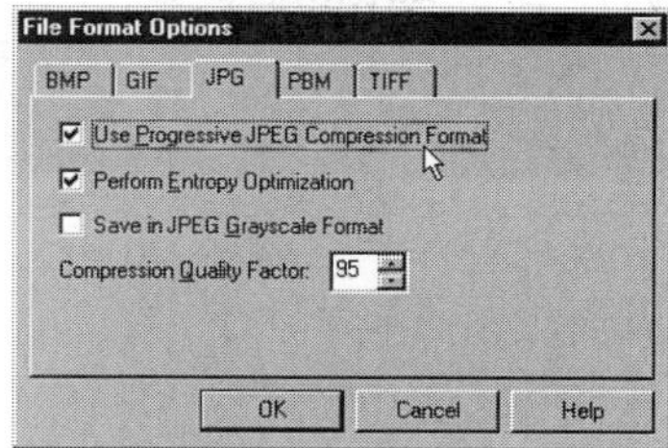

Creating Animated GIFs

One of the biggest crazes to hit the web in the past year has been doing animations with animated GIFs instead of relying on a dynamic document technique such as server push or client pull. The irony is that animated GIFs have been around since 1989—at least in theory. The GIF89a standard has always supported multiple images stored in the same GIF file, but no one caught on until recently that you can do web animations this way.

It is surprising that this development didn't happen sooner, given the fact that GIF animations are so much easier to implement than server push animations. A server push animation requires a server that is CGI-capable, a program to pipe the individual frames of the animation down an open HTTP connection, and a browser that can handle the experimental MIME type used. All you need for a GIF animation is a program to help you set up the GIF file and a browser that is completely compliant with the GIF89a standard. That you don't need any CGI programming is a relief to those publishing on a server that either does not have CGI or that restricts CGI access to certain users.

One program that will help you build animated GIFs is the GIF Construction Set from Alchemy Mindworks (see Figure 5.21). The text you see in the window denotes the different blocks that comprise the animated GIF. The animated GIF always begins with a header block and can be followed with images, text, comments, controls, and looping instructions. Each of these can be placed by clicking the Insert button.

You don't even need to be familiar with the GIF Construction Set's GIF building "language" to use the program. By choosing File, Animation Wizard, you are taken through a series of dialog boxes that ask whether the animation is for the web, whether it should loop once or indefinitely, whether the frames are line drawings or photorealistic, how much delay there should be between frames, and what files contain the images for the individual frames (see Figure 5.22). The GIF Construction Set uses this information to author the animated GIF file for you automatically.

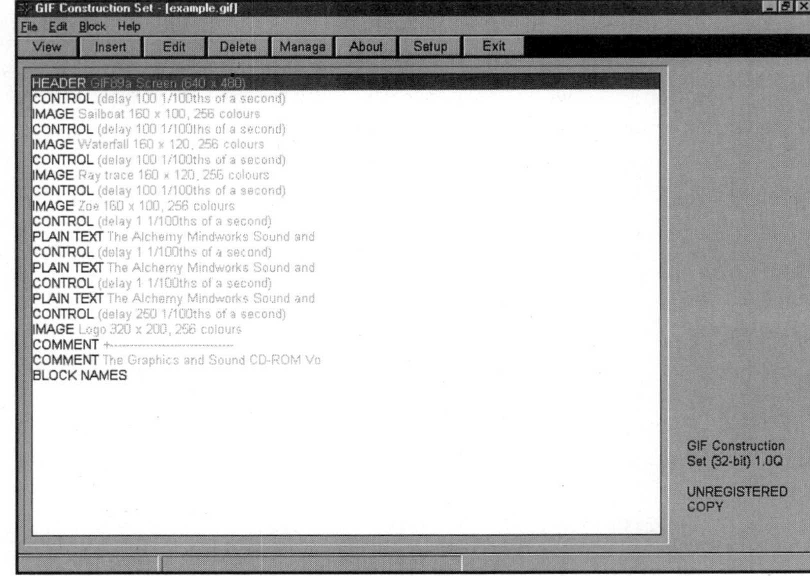

FIG. 5.21
An animated GIF file also contains animation properties such as how many times to loop the animation and how long to wait between loops.

CAUTION

Don't let an animation run indefinitely. An animation that is going constantly can be a distraction from the rest of the content on your page.

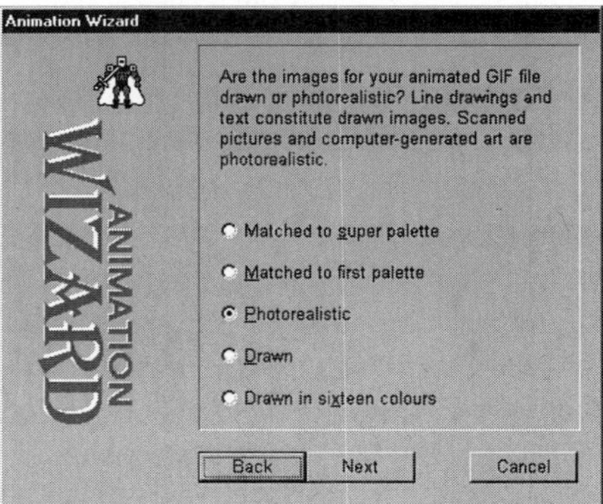

FIG. 5.22
The Animation Wizard automates the entire process of creating an animated GIF.

The GIF Construction Set is robust enough to support you in other web graphics endeavors. It can do the following:

- Create transparent GIFs
- Convert AVI videos to animated GIFs

- Add transition effects to still graphics
- Create animated text banners
- Add words to images as blocks of plain text

You can download the GIF Construction Set from Alchemy Mindwork web site at **http://www.mindworkshop.com/alchemy/gifcon.html**. Registering your copy of the GIF Construction Set will set you back $20 plus $5 for shipping.

NOTE FrontPage 98 also provides support for animation of page elements. You can make images or text fly onto the page from any part of the browser screen thanks to the Java applets resident in the FrontPage Editor.

Using Image Effects that Create Depth

Although a computer screen is inherently two-dimensional, web graphic artists try not to let that get them down. They draw on a variety of techniques that give web pages the illusion of depth. Creating these effects usually involves the use of a higher-end graphics program such as PaintShop Pro or Photoshop. These are well worth the time and expense, however, because they give web pages a richness that is hard to beat.

Light Sources

Photoshop enables you to apply three different types of light sources in 1 of 10 different styles to an image from the Lighting Effects dialog box shown in Figure 5.23. You call up the dialog box by choosing Filter, Render, and then selecting Lighting Effects from the Render pop-up menu.

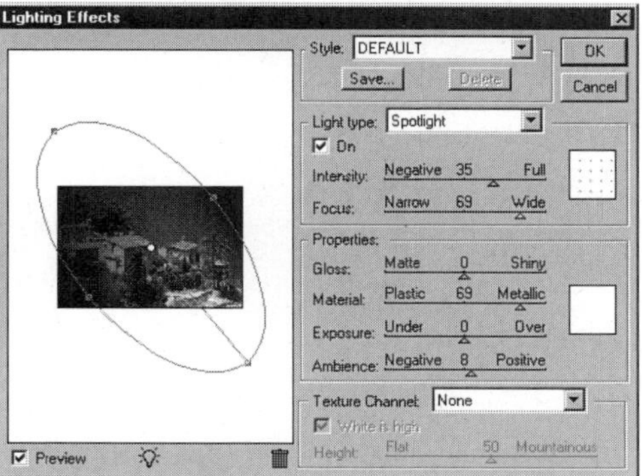

FIG. 5.23 Let there be light—on your web pages, that is.

The cardinal rule to remember when lighting the images on your pages is to illuminate each object with the same light source at the same position. Think of it as the sun shining on your page. There is only one sun in the sky and all the objects on the page are getting light from it simultaneously. If you light different objects with different light sources at different positions, the lighting will seem counter-intuitive to those who view the page. You should try to make the lighting seem as natural as possible so that the page is more inviting.

Drop Shadows

Placing drop shadows behind page elements is a great way to make them appear elevated just off the page (see Figure 5.24). An easy way to make a drop shadow is to make a copy of the page element, paint it black, and drop it in behind and to one side of the element being shadowed. If you are using Photoshop, you can achieve increased realism by copying the page element to a subordinate layer, painting it black, expanding it by several pixels, blurring it a few times, and positioning it as desired.

CAUTION

Make sure that the location of your drop shadows is consistent with your light sources.

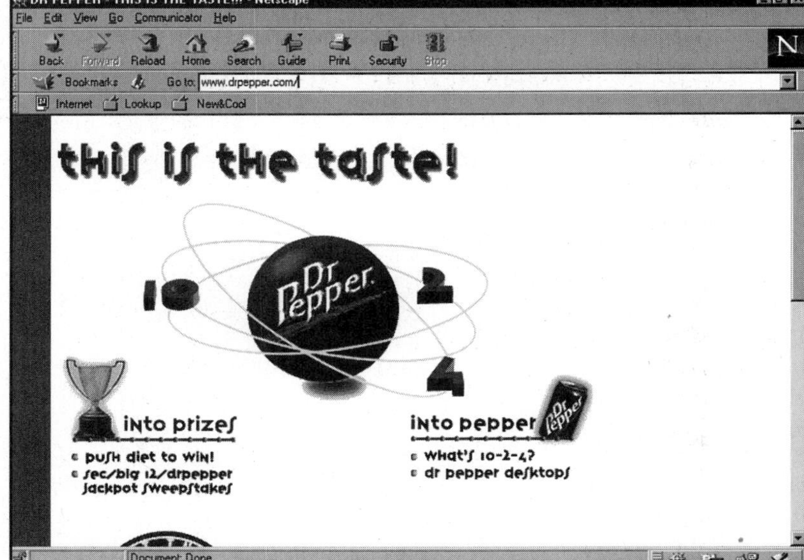

FIG. 5.24 Combinations of light and shadow make an image appear to be floating over the page.

Embossing

Embossing a graphic element makes it appear to be "raised up" and gives it a much more textured appearance (see Figure 5.25). Photoshop has a built-in embossing filter that you can use by selecting Filters, Stylize, and then selecting Emboss from the Stylize pop-up menu.

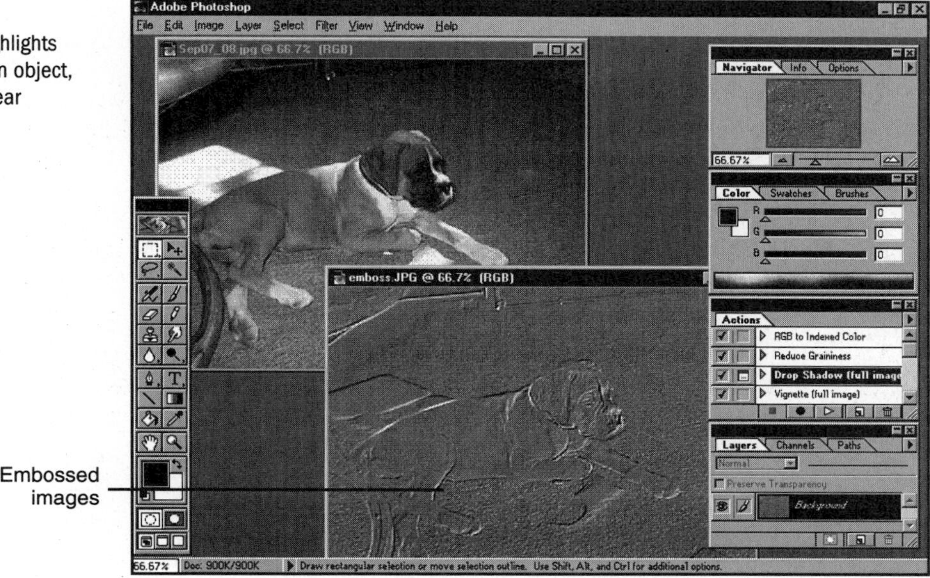

FIG. 5.25
Embossing highlights the edges of an object, making it appear raised.

Ray Tracing

Ray tracing is a technique for making two-dimensional images look very three-dimensional. You can usually tell a ray-traced image by its very distinct use of perspective (objects get smaller as they move away from you).

To create your own ray-traced images, you need a special program. Windows users can check out Caligari Truespace; Strata Vision is a good program for the Macintosh. For more information on other ray-tracing software, consult **http://www.yahoo.com/Computers_and_Internet/Graphics/Ray_Tracing/**.

Keeping File Sizes Small

One of the greatest courtesies you can extend to your users is to keep your graphics files small. Invariably, it is the graphics that take the longest time to download. By keeping the file sizes small, you minimize the time that users spend waiting to see your pages. Your typical 30K to 50K graphics file may load in a few seconds over a T1 connection, but it may take several minutes for users dialing up with a 28.8Kbps or 14.4Kbps connection.

You can enlist a number of techniques to help keep your file sizes down. These include:

- Making the image dimensions as small as possible
- Using thumbnail versions of images
- Saving GIFs with natural color gradients as JPEGs

- Increasing the amount of JPEG compression
- Using fewer bits per pixel to store the image
- Adjusting image contrast
- Suppressing dithering

Each technique is discussed briefly over the next several sections.

Resizing the Image

Larger images take up more disk space—it is as simple as that. The reason for this is straightforward: There are more pixels in a larger image, so more color information must be stored.

The height and width of your graphics should be no larger than they have to be. By keeping the onscreen dimensions of your images small, you contribute to a smaller overall file size.

If you resize an image in a graphics program to make it smaller, be sure to keep the aspect ratio (ratio of width to height) the same. This prevents the image from looking stretched or squashed.

Using Thumbnails

Thumbnails are very small versions of an image—usually a photograph. By placing a thumbnail of an image on a page, you reduce file size by using an image that has a smaller width and height than the original.

Thumbnails are usually set up so that users can click them to see the full image. If you do this, you should include the size (in kilobytes) of the file that contains the full image so that users can make an informed decision about downloading it.

CAUTION

Recall that you can resize an image by reducing the WIDTH and HEIGHT attributes in the <IMG> tag. However, this does not save on download time and browsers generally don't do the best job of resizing the image.

Storing GIFs as JPEGs

JPEGs are created with a very efficient (albeit lossy) compression scheme. The compression works best on images with a lot of natural color gradation. This is why JPEG is the format of choice for color photos placed on the web.

If you have a GIF with a lot of color gradation, you can experiment with saving as a JPEG to see whether you can compress the file size further. It may not always work, but it is worth a try. You don't have to worry about color loss either because JPEG can accommodate millions of colors to GIF's 256 colors.

Conversely, if you have an image with large blocks of contiguous color, you are better off storing it as a GIF because GIF's compression scheme is geared toward exploiting adjacent pixels painted the same color.

Increasing the JPEG Compression Ratio

JPEG compression often achieves very impressive compression ratios (on the order of 50:1) with very little loss in image quality. You can crank the ratio higher (refer to Figure 5.19) to make your file size smaller, but the image will not look as good when it is decompressed and decoded. A highly compressed JPEG will take slightly longer to decompress as well.

Reducing Color Depth

GIFs can use a palette of up to 256 colors. This corresponds to eight bits per pixel (2^8 equals 256). But what if you don't need that many colors? Sometimes GIFs use just two or three colors. That little color information can be stored in much less than eight bits per pixel. It would seem like some of that storage space could be recovered, resulting in a smaller file size.

It turns out that you can reduce the number of bits per pixel used to store color information. This is called reducing the image's color depth. Lowering the color depth is a great way to reduce file size because you can often cut the amount of space you are using in half or better.

Suppose, for example, that you have a GIF that uses six distinct colors. The number six is between four (2^2) and eight (2^3), so you would need three bits per pixel to describe the color information. (Two bits per pixel only supports the first four colors, so you have to go to the next highest exponent.) By reducing the color depth from eight bits per pixel to three bits, you realize a savings of over 60 percent!

LView Pro gives you an easy way to reduce your color depth. By choosing Image, Color Depth, you get the dialog box you see in Figure 5.26. A true color image is one that uses 24-bit color (for example, a JPEG); the color depth for these images cannot be changed. Palette-based images are ones that draw their colors from a palette of no more than 256 colors. For palette images, LView Pro enables you to choose 256 colors (eight bits per pixel), a palette with a custom number of colors, or a predefined palette read in from a file.

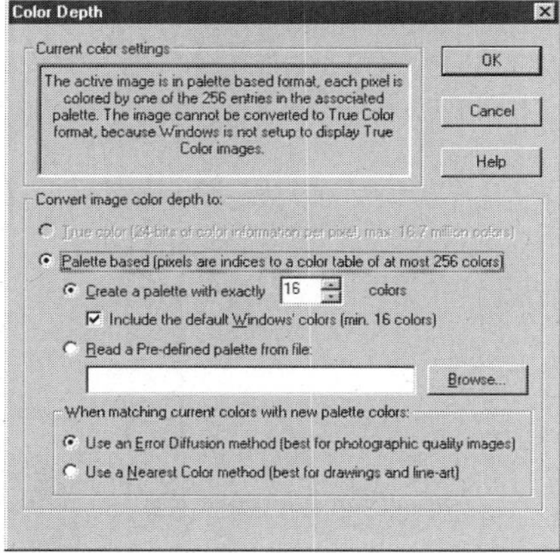

FIG. 5.26
Reducing a GIF's color depth can greatly reduce the amount of space needed to store the image.

Adjusting Contrast

Contrast in an image refers to the brightness of objects relative to one another. Making changes to the contrast in your image generally effects the size of the resulting image file. If your file is still too big, therefore, tweaking the contrast may be a way to bring it down more.

One way to change contrast in your images is to adjust the gamma correction. Increasing the gamma correction into positive values tends to brighten the entire image and reduce overall file size because there are fewer colors to store. Conversely, negative gamma correction values darken an image and increase its file size. You can change the gamma correction in LView Pro by selecting Image, Color Adjustment, Pre-defined, and then selecting gamma correction from the list of available image parameters.

No Dithering

Dithering makes an image appear to have more colors in its palette than it actually does. This is accomplished by combining colors in the existing palette to produce colors that are not in the palette. Dithering can be helpful with GIF images with a lot of subtle color gradations. Otherwise, for images with just a few solid colors, you probably won't want to use dithering.

One thing to be aware of when using dithering is that it tends to increase file size. This occurs because fewer pixels in a row have the same color. The compression scheme used with GIF files exploits adjacent pixels that have the same color. When there are fewer same-colored pixels, the compression can't make the file as small.

> **CAUTION**
>
> Dithering can also create an unattractive graininess in your images. If you enable dithering, be sure to look at your image before you put it on the web to make sure that the dithering does not detract from it.

CHAPTER 6

Tables

by Eric Ladd

In this chapter

Introduction to HTML Tables and Their Structure

Tables have been around for a while, but the table tags weren't officially made part of HTML until the HTML 3.2 draft was released. Browsers such as Netscape Navigator and Microsoft Internet Explorer were supporting the table tags almost as soon as they were proposed and, now that tables are standard HTML, these companies are extending the tags to produce tables that are even more full-featured.

This chapter introduces you to tables as they have been written into the HTML 4.0 specification. Although tables are intended for the display of columnar data, you'll find, as you progress through this chapter, that tables are much more than that—they are a bona fide page design tool as well.

To understand the table tags better, it helps to take a moment to consider how HTML tables are structured. The fundamental building blocks of an HTML table are cells, which can contain a data element of the table or a heading for a column of data. Related cells are logically grouped together in a row of the table. The rows, in turn, combine to make up the entire table.

If you can keep this breakdown in mind as you read the next few sections, the syntax of the table tags will make much more sense to you. Remember:

- Cells are the basic units of a table; they can contain data elements or column headers.
- Cells are grouped together into rows.
- Rows are grouped together to produce an entire table.

The Table Tags

Before delving into the more advanced uses of tables, it's instructive to look at a table used for the purpose tables are intended: to display columns of data. The next three sections present the tags you need to create a simple table for this purpose.

All table-related tags occur between the `<TABLE>` and `</TABLE>` container tags. Any table-related tags occurring outside of these tags will be ignored.

A good habit you should get into immediately is to put the `</TABLE>` tag into your HTML file when you put the `<TABLE>` tag in. If you don't have a `</TABLE>` tag and you go to browser to preview your work, the browser won't render the table. This is because the browser reads through all of the code to produce a table before rendering it. It has to do this to compute how much space it needs for the table and, after the amount of space is known and allocated, the browser goes back and fills in the cells. Without a `</TABLE>` tag, a browser can't know that it has hit the end of a table and, therefore, won't render any of it.

NOTE If you're using an HTML-editing program that lets you compose a table onscreen, you won't have to worry about the `<TABLE>` and `</TABLE>` tags or any other table-related tag. The program will write the code to produce the table for you.

Creating a Table Row

Tables are made up of rows, so you need to know how to define a row. The <TR> and </TR> tags are used to contain the HTML tags that define the individual cells. You can place as many <TR> and </TR> tag pairs as you need inside a table, each pair accounting for one row.

So far, then, the code for a basic HTML table with m rows looks like:

```
<TABLE>
   <TR> ... </TR>   <!-- Row 1 -->
   <TR> ... </TR>   <!-- Row 2 -->
   ...
   <TR> ... </TR>   <!-- Row m -->
</TABLE>
```

Indenting your table code helps you keep better track of individual cells and rows.

Creating a Table Cell

Table cells come in two varieties: header cells for headers that appear over a column of data and data cells for the individual entries in the table.

A table header cell is defined with the <TH> and <TH> tag pair. The contents of a table header cell are automatically centered and appear in boldface, so you typically don't need to format them further.

In a standard table, headers usually comprise the first row so that each column in the table has some type of heading over it. If the basic table you're developing has n columns of data, the HTML for the table would look like:

```
<TABLE>
   <TR>    <!--Row 1 -->
      <TH>Header 1</TH>
      <TH>Header 2</TH>
      ...
      <TH>Header n</TH>
   </TR>
   <TR> ... </TR>   <!-- Row 2 -->
   ...
   <TR> ... </TR>   <!-- Row m -->
</TABLE>
```


Data cells usually make up the bulk of the table and are defined by <TD> and </TD> tags. Text in data cells is left justified by default. Any special formatting, such as boldface or italics, has to be done by including the appropriate formatting tags inside the <TD> and </TD> pairs.

If we let data cells constitute the rest of the basic table we're constructing, we have the basic template shown in Listing 6.1:

Listing 6.1 A basic table template.

```
<TABLE>
   <TR>    <!-- Row 1 -->
      <TH>Header 1</TH>
      <TH>Header 2</TH>
      ...
      <TH>Header n</TH>
   </TR>
   <TR>    <!-- Row 2 -->
      <TD>Data element 1</TD>
      <TD>Data element 2</TD>
      ...
      <TD>Data element n</TD>
   </TR>
   ...
   <TR>    <!-- Row m -->
      <TD>Data element 1</TD>
      <TD>Data element 2</TD>
      ...
      <TD>Data element n</TD>
   </TR>
</TABLE>
```

The HTML above makes for a nice template that you can use whenever starting a table. By filling in the headers and data elements with some genuine information, we can produce a table like the one you see in Figure 6.1.

```
<TABLE>
   <TR>    <!-- Row 1 -->
      <TH>Quarter</TH>
      <TH>Sales ($M)</TH>
      <TH>Expenses ($M)</TH>
      <TH>Profit ($M)</TH>
   </TR>
   <TR>    <!-- Row 2 -->
      <TD>1st</TD>
      <TD>11.4</TD>
      <TD>10.1</TD>
      <TD>1.3</TD>
   </TR>
   <TR>    <!-- Row 3 -->
      <TD>2nd</TD>
      <TD>12.0</TD>
      <TD>11.5</TD>
      <TD>0.5</TD>
   </TR>
   <TR>    <!-- Row 4 -->
      <TD>3rd</TD>
      <TD>10.2</TD>
      <TD>8.1</TD>
      <TD>1.1</TD>
   </TR>
</TABLE>
```

FIG. 6.1
Tabular data is much easier to read on a web page when placed in an HTML table.

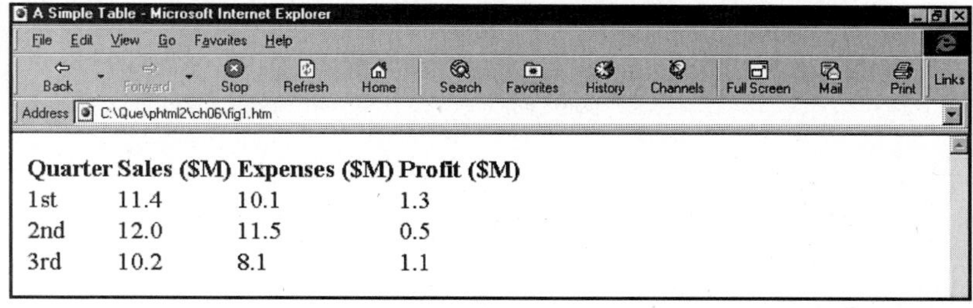

NOTE If the contents of a table cell are too wide to fit across the cell, a browser will break the contents onto multiple lines. If you want the content of a cell to be placed on one line with no breaking, include the `NOWRAP` attribute in the `<TD>` or `<TH>` that defines the cell.

Alignment

The beauty of HTML tables is the precise control you have over the alignment of content in individual cells and over the table itself. There are two types of alignment that you can specify:

- Horizontal alignment refers to the alignment of an element across the width of something; for example, the alignment of a header across the width of a cell, or the alignment of a table across the width of the page. Horizontal alignment is controlled by the `ALIGN` attribute. You can set `ALIGN` equal to `LEFT`, `CENTER`, or `RIGHT`.
- Vertical alignment refers to the alignment of an element between the top and bottom of a cell. You control the vertical alignment of cell contents by setting the `VALIGN` attribute to `TOP`, `MIDDLE`, or `BOTTOM`.

NOTE You cannot specify vertical alignment for an entire table because a page's length isn't fixed like its width is.

Aligning the Entire Table

You can use the `ALIGN` attribute in the `<TABLE>` tag to specify how the table should be aligned relative to the browser window. Setting `ALIGN` to `LEFT` or `RIGHT` floats the table in the left or right margin, respectively. Floating tables behave much like floating images in that you can wrap text around them. This is how you produce a page element such as a pull quote (see Figure 6.2).

Using the `CENTER` value of `ALIGN` centers the table in the browser window, though not all browsers support this. If you can't center a table this way, you can enclose the HTML that produces the table between the `<CENTER>` and `</CENTER>` tags. This should become unnecessary, though, as browsers come into compliance with the HTML 4.0 standard.

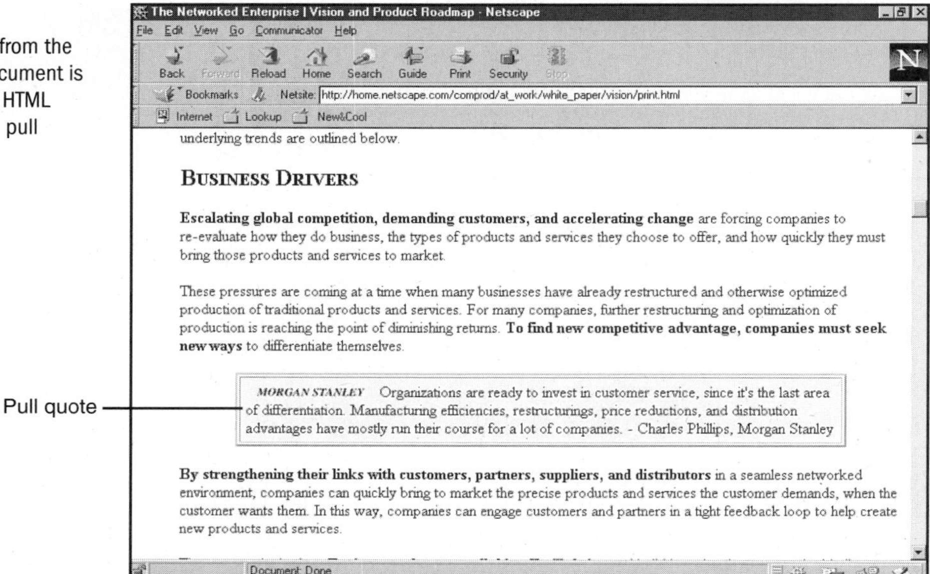

FIG. 6.2
Text excerpted from the body of the document is placed into an HTML table to form a pull quote.

Alignment Within a Row

If you want the vertical or the horizontal alignment to be the same for every cell in a given row, you can use the `VALIGN` and `ALIGN` attributes in the row's `<TR>` tag. Any alignment specified in a <TR> tag will override all default alignments.

NOTE The default vertical alignment for both header and data cells is `MIDDLE`. The default horizontal alignment depends on the type of cell: Header cells have a `CENTER` alignment and data cells have a `LEFT` alignment.

Alignment Within a Cell

HTML 4.0 permits alignment control all the way down to the cell level. You can prescribe vertical or horizontal alignments in both header and data cells by using the `VALIGN` or `ALIGN` attributes in `<TD>` tags. Any alignment specified at the cell level overrides any default alignments and any alignments specified in a `<TR>` tag.

Setting alignments in individual cells represents the finest level of control of table alignment. In theory, you can manually specify vertical and horizontal alignments in every single cell of your tables if you need to. Unfortunately, it's easy to get lost among all of those `VALIGN` and `ALIGN` attributes, especially when it comes to deciding which will take precedence. If you have trouble mastering table alignment, remember the following hierarchy:

- Alignments specified in <TD> or <TH> tags override all other alignments but apply only to the cell being defined.
- Alignments specified in a <TR> tag override default alignments and apply to all cells in a row, unless overridden by an alignment specification in a <TD> or </TH> tag.
- In the absence of alignment specifications in <TR>, <TD>, or <TH> tags, default alignments are used.

Controlling Other Table Attributes

In addition to tweaking alignments, you have a say in other aspects of the tables you create as well. These include:

- Background color
- Captions
- Width of the table
- Borders
- Spacing within and between cells
- How many rows or columns a cell should occupy

The next six sections walk you through each of these table features and discuss the HTML tags and attributes you need to know to produce them.

Background Color

An easy way to add some contrast to your table to make it stand out from the rest of the content on a page is to give the table a background color different from the document's background color. By adding the BGCOLOR attribute to the <TABLE> tag, you can color the table background with an English-language color name or any RGB hexadecimal triplet just as you would specify the document's background color in the <BODY> tag.

Determining a desired color's RGB hexadecimal code is one of the more tedious tasks in web page authoring. Fortunately, many people have made color resources available on the web that allow you to choose a color and have the RGB Hex code returned to you. For a wide selection of such sites, point your browser to **http://www.yahoo.com/Computers_and_Internet/Internet/World_Wide_Web/Page_Design_and_Layout/Color_Information/**.

Many browsers also support the use of BGCOLOR in the <TR>, <TD>, and <TH> tags, enabling you to present rows and cells in different colors. One effective use of this technique is to paint the top row of the table (presumably the row containing the column headers) with one background color and the remaining rows with a different color. This further distinguishes the items in the top row as column heads. You can make rows of data stand out by alternating a white and gray background color as well.

Adding a Caption

To put a caption on your table, enclose the caption text between the <CAPTION> and </CAPTION> tags. Captions appear centered over the table and the text may be broken to match the table's width (see Figure 6.3). You can also use physical style tags to mark up your caption text. The HTML to produce Figure 6.3 follows:

```
<TABLE>
   <CAPTION><B>Profit/Loss - 1Q-3Q 1997</B></CAPTION>
<TR>    <!-- Row 1 -->
      <TH>Quarter</TH>
      <TH>Sales ($M)</TH>
      <TH>Expenses ($M)</TH>
      <TH>Profit ($M)</TH>
   </TR>
   <TR>    <!-- Row 2 -->
      <TD>1st</TD>
      <TD>11.4</TD>
      <TD>10.1</TD>
      <TD>1.3</TD>
   </TR>
   <TR>    <!-- Row 3 -->
      <TD>2nd</TD>
      <TD>12.0</TD>
      <TD>11.5</TD>
      <TD>0.5</TD>
   </TR>
   <TR>    <!-- Row 4 -->
      <TD>3rd</TD>
      <TD>10.2</TD>
      <TD>8.1</TD>
      <TD>1.1</TD>
</TR>
</TABLE>
```

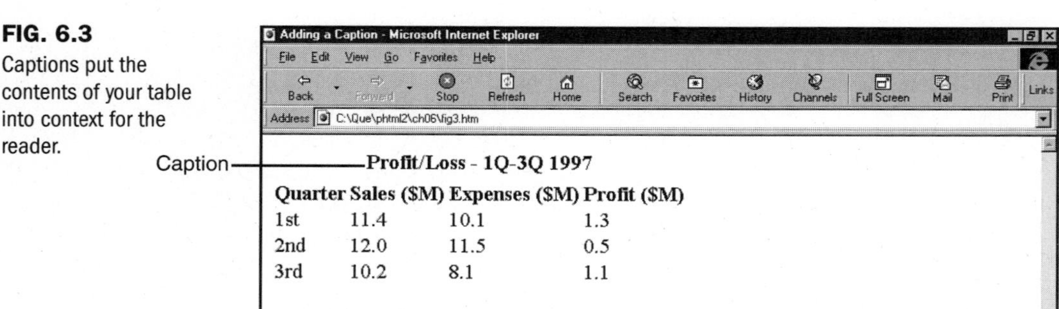

FIG. 6.3 Captions put the contents of your table into context for the reader.

If you prefer your caption below the table, you can include the ALIGN=BOTTOM attribute in the <CAPTION> tag. You can also left-justify or right-justify your caption by setting ALIGN to LEFT or RIGHT, respectively.

TIP Put your caption immediately after the <TABLE> tag or immediately before the </TABLE> tag to prevent it from unintentionally becoming part of a table row or cell.

Setting the Width

The WIDTH attribute of the <TABLE> tag enables you to specify how wide the table should be in the browser window. You can set WIDTH to a specific number of pixels or to a percentage of the available screen width.

WIDTH is often used to force a table to occupy the entire width of the browser window. If we change the <TABLE> tag in the HTML code in the previous section to:

```
<TABLE WIDTH=100%>
```

the table is rendered as shown in Figure 6.4. The statistics are centered in their columns for easier readability.

TIP Because you can't know how every user has set his screen width, you should set WIDTH equal to a percentage whenever possible. The only exception to this is if the table has to be a certain number of pixels wide to accommodate an image in one of the cells or to achieve a certain layout effect.

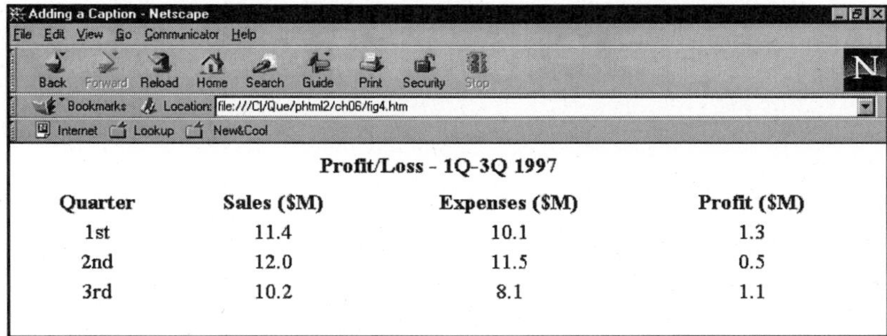

Profit/Loss - 1Q-3Q 1997

Quarter	Sales ($M)	Expenses ($M)	Profit ($M)
1st	11.4	10.1	1.3
2nd	12.0	11.5	0.5
3rd	10.2	8.1	1.1

FIG. 6.4 You have control over how much of the browser screen width a table occupies, thanks to the WIDTH attribute.

Some browsers such as Netscape Navigator 4 and Internet Explorer 4 support the use of the WIDTH attribute in a <TD> or tag to control the width of individual columns. This is not proper HTML, according to the HTML 4.0 DTD, and support for using WIDTH in this way is tenuous, at best.

Adding a Border

You can place a border around your table by using the BORDER attribute of the <TABLE> tag. BORDER is set to the number of pixels wide you want the border to be. A version of our hockey statistics table with a two-pixel border is shown in Figure 6.5. The modified <TABLE> tag that accomplishes this effect is:

```
<TABLE WIDTH=100% BORDER=2>
```

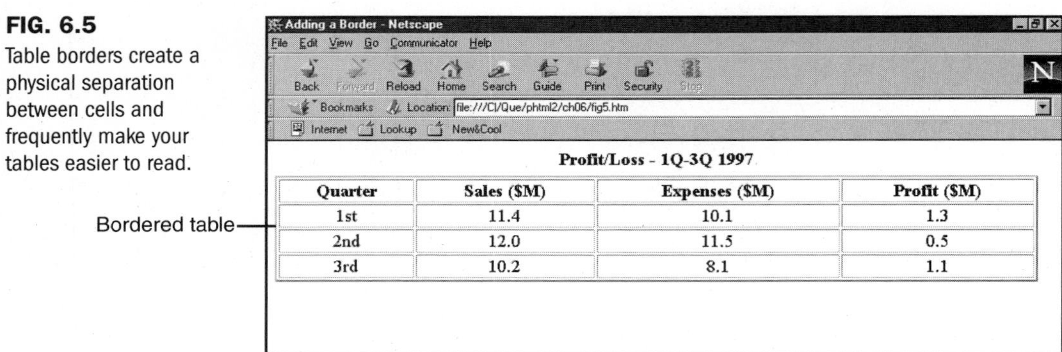

Profit/Loss - 1Q-3Q 1997

Quarter	Sales ($M)	Expenses ($M)	Profit ($M)
1st	11.4	10.1	1.3
2nd	12.0	11.5	0.5
3rd	10.2	8.1	1.1

FIG. 6.5 Table borders create a physical separation between cells and frequently make your tables easier to read.

You can also set BORDER equal to zero. This means that no border will be used and that the browser should give back any space it has reserved to put in a border. This is an especially good approach to use when using a table to position page elements because you want the table that creates the structure to be transparent to the reader.

Spacing Within a Cell

The distance between an element in a cell and the boundaries of the cell is called cell padding. The CELLPADDING attribute of the <TABLE> tag enables you modify the amount of cell padding used in your tables. Typically, web page authors increase the cell padding from its default value of 1 to put a little extra white space between the contents and the edges of a cell (see Figure 6.6). This gives the whole table a bit more "room to breathe." The <TABLE> tag used to produce Figure 6.6 is

```
<TABLE WIDTH=100% BORDER=2 CELLPADDING=6>
```

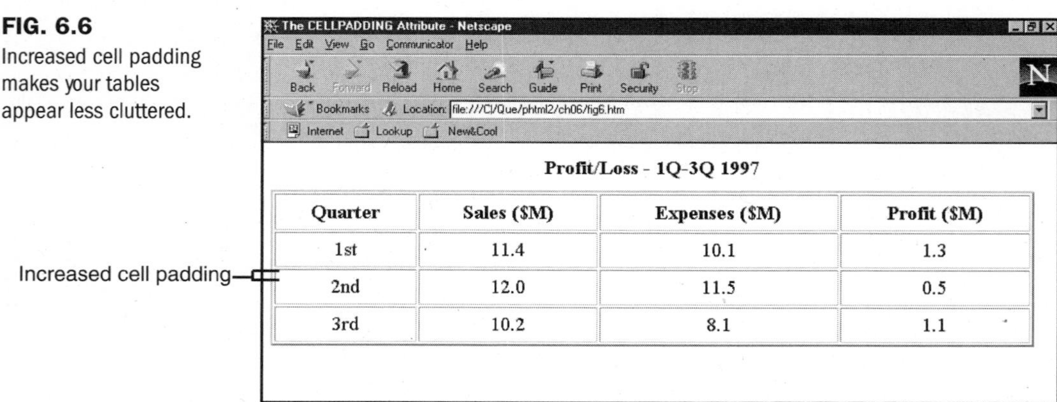

Profit/Loss - 1Q-3Q 1997

Quarter	Sales ($M)	Expenses ($M)	Profit ($M)
1st	11.4	10.1	1.3
2nd	12.0	11.5	0.5
3rd	10.2	8.1	1.1

FIG. 6.6 Increased cell padding makes your tables appear less cluttered.

Spacing Between Cells

You also have control over the space between cells. By increasing the value of the CELLSPACING attribute of the <TABLE> tag, you can open a table up even further (see

Figure 6.7). Notice that the border used between the cells also increases. The <TABLE> tag used in Figure 6.7 is

```
<TABLE WIDTH=100% BORDER=2 CELLSPACING=6>
```

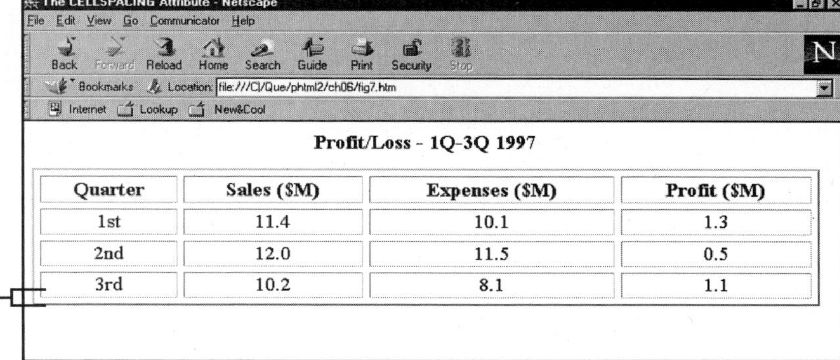

Quarter	Sales ($M)	Expenses ($M)	Profit ($M)
1st	11.4	10.1	1.3
2nd	12.0	11.5	0.5
3rd	10.2	8.1	1.1

FIG. 6.7 Increasing the amount of space between cells can give the illusion of your border being thicker than it really is.

Spanning Multiple Rows or Columns

By default, a cell occupies or spans one row and one column. For most tables, this is usually sufficient. When you start to use tables for layout purposes, though, you'll encounter instances where you want a cell to span more than one row or column. HTML 4.0 supports attributes of the <TH> and <TD> tags that permit this effect.

Using the *COLSPAN* Attribute

The COLSPAN attribute inside of a <TH> or <TD> tag instructs the browser to make the cell, defined by the tag, take up more than one column. You set COLSPAN equal to the number of columns the cell is to occupy.

COLSPAN is useful when one row of the table is forcing the table to be a certain number of columns wide while the content in other rows can be accommodated in a smaller number of columns. Figure 6.8 shows a table that makes good use of the COLSPAN attribute. In the figure, the page author used the COLSPAN attribute to get the table header UPCOMING SCHEDULE to occupy three columns of the table. The HTML that accomplishes this would look like:

```
<TABLE>
<TR>
<TD COLSPAN=3>UPCOMING SCHEDULE</TD>
</TR>
...
</TABLE>
```

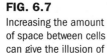

FIG. 6.8
Forcing a cell to occupy more than one column is helpful in creating compelling page layouts.

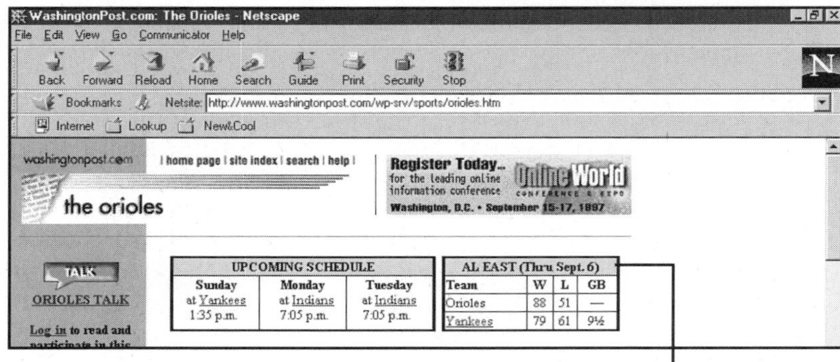

Table header spans four columns.

Using the *ROWSPAN* Attribute

`ROWSPAN` works in much the same way as `COLSPAN`, except that it enables a cell to take up more than one row. Figure 6.9 shows a home page for which the layout was done with a table. The large image in the center is in a single cell that spans three rows (`ROWSPAN=3`). The HTML code to place the image might look like:

```
<TABLE>
<TR>
<TD> ... contents of first cell ... </TD>
<TD ROWSPAN=3><IMG SRC="largeimage.gif" ...></TD>
<TD> ... contents of third cell ... </TD>
</TR>
...
</TABLE>
```

FIG. 6.9
A large central image surrounded by various site links is possible, thanks to the ROWSPAN attribute.

Image spans three rows.

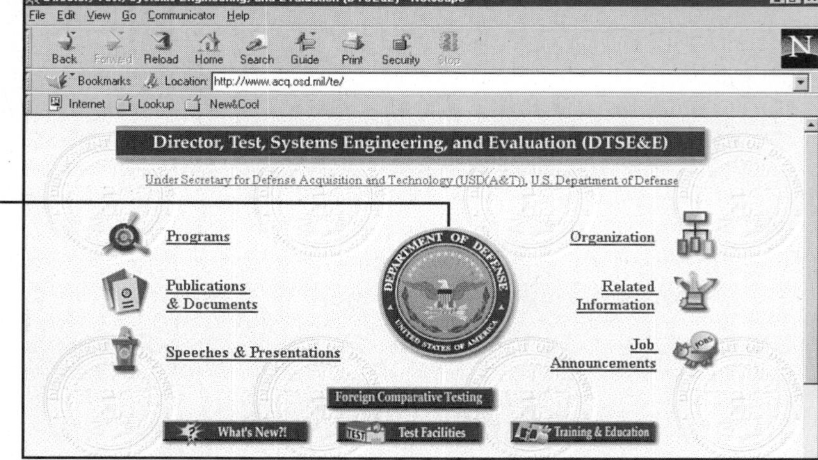

What Elements Can Be Placed in a Table Cell

HTML tables were developed with the intent of presenting columns of information, but that information does not necessarily have to be text-based. There are many types of page elements that you can place in a given table cell:

- **Text**—Text is the most obvious thing to put in a table cell, but don't forget that you can format the text with physical and logical styles, heading styles, list formatting, line and paragraph breaks, and hypertext anchor formatting.
- **Images**—You can place an image in a table cell by enclosing an `<IMG>` tag between the `<TD>` and `</TD>` tags that define the cell. This is useful for designing page layout with tables because you aren't constrained to only text.
- **Blank Space**—Sometimes, it's useful to put a blank cell in a table. You can accomplish this by putting nothing between the cell's defining tags (`<TD></TD>`) or by placing a non-breaking space between the tags (`<TD> </TD>`). Use of the nonbreaking space is preferable because, if you have borders turned on, a cell with a nonbreaking space picks up a 3-D effect that makes it appear to rise up out of the table.
- **Form Fields**—The ability to place form fields inside of a table cell is very important, especially when you consider that the prompting text in front of form fields is of varying lengths. By putting prompting text and form fields in a table, you can align them all and make the form much more attractive.
- **Other Tables**—You can embed one table inside of another, though this can induce quite a headache for most people! Previously, only Netscape Navigator and Microsoft Internet Explorer supported tables within tables, but now that it is part of the HTML 4.0 standard, other browsers should support it as they come into compliance with the new standard.

If you plan to embed a table within a table, it's helpful to do a pencil-and-paper sketch first. The sketch should help you code the tables more efficiently.

Table Sections and Column Properties

The W3C has added several table-related tags to the HTML 4.0 spec that enable you to split tables into logical sections and to control alignment properties of rows or columns of data.

Table Sections

The `<THEAD>`, `<TBODY>`, and `<TFOOT>` container tags denote the start of a table header, body, and footer, respectively. By explicitly distinguishing the different parts of your table, you can control your column attributes. The separation of the table header and footer also makes it easier for the browser to render and print tables that are broken across several pages. Additionally, it makes it simple to set up a static header or footer in frames at the top and bottom of a browser screen and to place the body of the table in a scrollable frame between the header and footer frame.

<THEAD> contains the rows that comprise the table header and <TFOOT> contains the rows that comprise the footer. In the absence of <THEAD> and <TFOOT> tags, the <TBODY> tag becomes optional. You can use multiple <TBODY> tags in long tables to make smaller, more manageable chunks. All three tags can take both the ALIGN and VALIGN attributes to control horizontal and vertical alignment within the sections they define.

NOTE All three tags are only valid between the <TABLE> and </TABLE> tags.

A typical table created with these tags might look like:

```
<TABLE>
    <THEAD>
        <TR>
            ...
        </TR>
    </THEAD>
    <TBODY>
        <TR>
            ...
        </TR>
        <TR>
            ...
        </TR>
        ...
        <TR>
            ...
        </TR>
    </TBODY>
    <TFOOT>
        <TR>
            ...
        </TR>
    </TFOOT>
</TABLE>
```

NOTE When these tags were first introduced by Microsoft, the use of the </THEAD>, </TBODY>, and </TFOOT> tags was optional. However, in the interest of good coding style, you should include the section closing tags when dividing your tables into sections.

Used in conjunction with the column grouping tags discussed in the next section, the table section tags are an ideal way to control how different properties are applied to different parts of a table.

Setting Column Properties

The <TR> tag supports attributes that enable you to specify all sorts of properties for an entire row of a table. In particular, you get very good control over both horizontal and vertical alignment with the ALIGN and VALIGN attributes. Microsoft has taken this a step further by making it possible to apply horizontal alignment properties to columns of data as well as rows.

You have two options when applying alignment properties to columns. The <COLGROUP> tag is appropriate when applying properties over several columns. It takes the attributes ALIGN, which can be set to LEFT, CENTER, or RIGHT; VALIGN, which can be set to TOP, MIDDLE, BOTTOM, or BASELINE; WIDTH, which is set equal to the desired width of the group; and SPAN, which is set to the number of consecutive columns that the properties apply to. In the following example:

```
<TABLE BORDER=1>
   <COLGROUP ALIGN=RIGHT SPAN=2>
   <COLGROUP ALIGN=CENTER>
   <COLGROUP ALIGN=LEFT SPAN=3>
   <TBODY>
      <TR>
         <TD>First column group, right aligned</TD>
         <TD>First column group, right aligned</TD>
         <TD>Second column group, center aligned</TD>
         <TD>Third column group, left aligned</TD>
         <TD>Third column group, left aligned</TD>
         <TD>Third column group, left aligned</TD>
      </TR>
   </TBODY>
</TABLE>
```

the six columns are split into three groups. The first two columns have right-aligned table entries, the third column has centered entries, and the last three columns have left-aligned entries (see Figure 6.10).

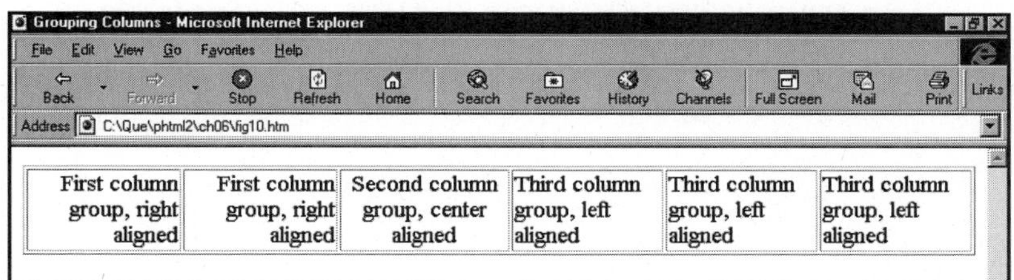

FIG. 6.10 Grouping columns allows you to simultaneously assign common alignment properties to a number of columns.

If columns in a group are to have differing properties, you can use <COLGROUP> to set up the group and then specify the individual properties with the <COL> tag. <COL> takes the same attributes as <COLGROUP>, but these attributes only apply to a subset of the columns in a group. For example, the HTML:

```
<TABLE BORDER=1>
   <COLGROUP>
      <COL ALIGN=CENTER>
      <COL ALIGN=RIGHT>
   </COLGROUP>
   <COLGROUP>
      <COL ALIGN=CENTER SPAN=2>
   </COLGROUP>
   <TBODY>
      <TR>
```

```
            <TD>First column in first group, center aligned</TD>
            <TD>Second column in first group, right aligned</TD>
            <TD>First column in second group, center aligned</TD>
            <TD>Second column in second group, center aligned</TD>
        </TR>
    </TBODY>
</TABLE>
```

splits the four columns of the table into two groups of two columns each. The first group's columns use center and right alignments, whereas both columns in the second group use center alignment (see Figure 6.11).

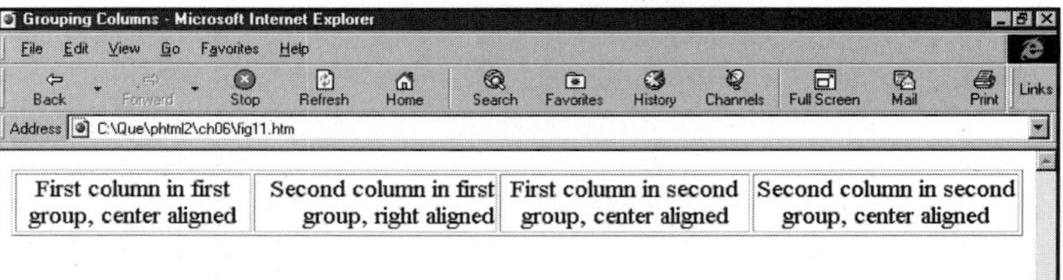

FIG. 6.11 You can also group columns and still assign alignment parameters on an individual basis.

Other Attributes of the *<TABLE>* Tag

Because of the new support for dividing tables into logical sections and the grouping of columns, the W3C has introduced some new attributes for the `<TABLE>` tag that let you control inner and outer borders of a table. Inner borders are controlled by the `RULES` attribute. You can think of inner borders as the dividing lines between certain components of the table. `RULES` can take on the values shown in Table 6.1.

Table 6.1 Values of the *RULES* attribute of the *<TABLE>* tag.

Value	Purpose
ALL	Display a border between all rows and columns
COLS	Display a border between all columns
GROUPS	Display a border between all logical groups (as defined by the `<THEAD>`, `<TBODY>`, `<TFOOT>`, and `<COLGROUP>` tags)
NONE	Suppress all inner orders
ROWS	Display a border between all table rows

The `FRAME` attribute controls which sides of the outer borders are displayed. In the context of tables, `FRAME` refers to the outer perimeter of the entire table and not frames like those discussed in Chapter 7, "Frames." `FRAME` can take on the values summarized in Table 6.2.

Table 6.2 Values of the *FRAME* attribute of the <*TABLE*> tag.

Value	Purpose
ABOVE	Displays a border on the top of a table frame
BELOW	Displays a border at the bottom of a table frame
BORDER	Displays a border on all four sides of a table frame
BOX	Same as BORDER
HSIDES	Displays a border on the left and right sides ofa table frame
LHS	Displays a border on the left-hand side of a table frame
RHS	Displays a border on the right-hand side of a table frame
VSIDES	Displays a border at the top and bottom of a table frame
VOID	Suppresses the display of all table frame borders

Tables as a Design Tool

Although tables were developed for presenting columnar data, they have evolved to the point where they can do much more. There are three primary driving forces behind the rise of tables as a design tool:

- You aren't restricted to only putting text in table cells.
- You can make a cell occupy more than one row or column.
- You get incredibly fine control over the alignment of content in individual cells.

Creating a Complex Layout

CNN's Fitness and Health page is a complex combination of embedded tables (see Figure 6.12). The navigation images you see down the left-hand side are contained in the first cell of the overall table that creates the structure for the page. Within that cell, another table creates the set of CNNPlus links.

The second cell in the main table contains the lead story (on dental health) and the Medical Library—a set of links created by a second embedded table.

Aligning Images of Different Sizes

Figure 6.13 shows you AT&T's WorldNet service home page. Note that each of the major links has an image to its left. Because each image is of a slightly different size, it was necessary to place each in its own table cell and then use the ALIGN attribute to give them all a centered look.

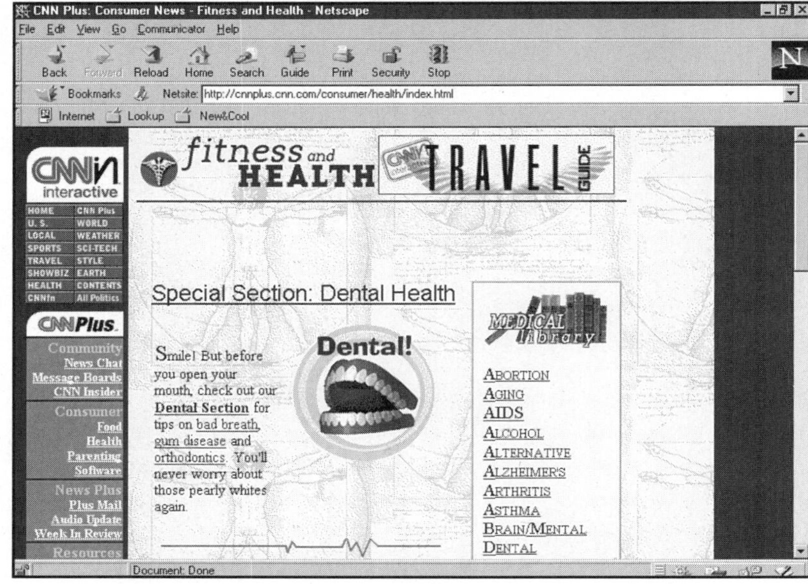

FIG. 6.12
CNN's pages typically use tables to create a columnar look to the information.

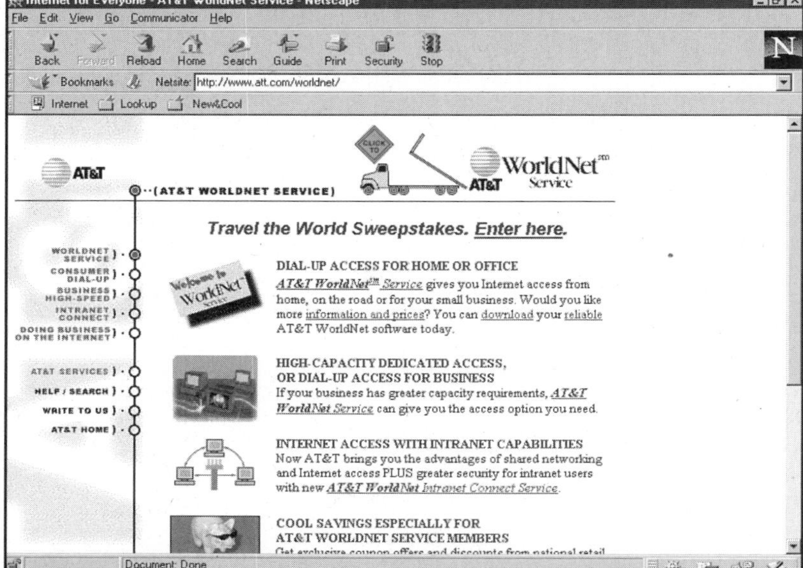

FIG. 6.13
Different image sizes can offset adjacent text and make it look unaligned. By placing images in a table, everything lines up cleanly.

Aligning Form Fields

The search page on amazon.com's web site would be a mess if it weren't for the different form fields placed in table cells (see Figure 6.14). This is because the prompting text in front of the fields (Author, Subject, Title, and so on) are of varying lengths. If the fields started right after each word, none of them would line up. By placing both the prompting text and the form fields in common table rows, the alignment is perfect.

FIG. 6.14
Using a table to align form fields is an essential part of making a form readable and usable.

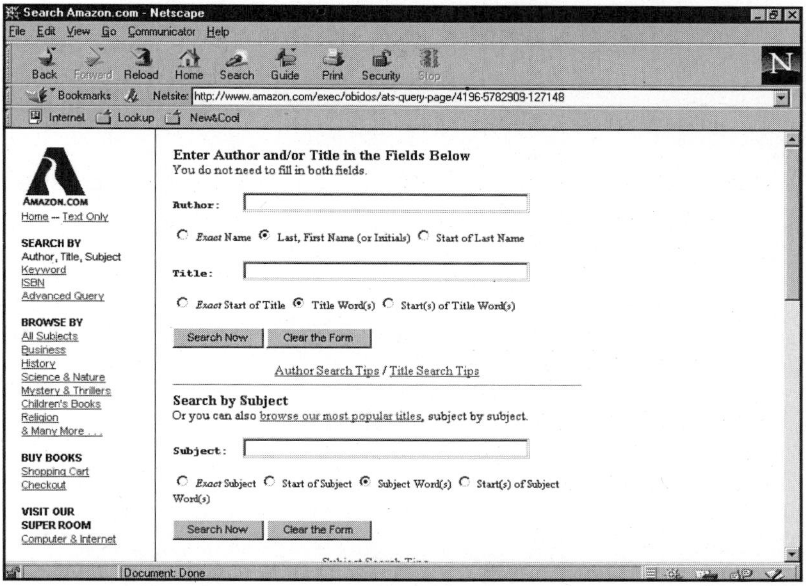

Creating Tables with Web Page Authoring Tools

The table tags have vexed some content developers from the beginning as it is hard for some folks to keep track of all of their <TR>, <TH>, and <TD> tags. It didn't take long for many popular document authoring tools to provide support for the creation and modification of HTML tables—particularly WYSIWYG support that spares a developer from seeing any table tags at all. This chapter closes with a look at how four different authoring tools can help you create tables.

Microsoft FrontPage 98

The FrontPage Editor gives you extensive table support from the moment you start a table. In particular, there are three ways for you to create a new table:

- Choose Table, Draw Table to activate the Table Drawing tool.This lets you draw the boundaries of your table and then draw the lines to form the rows and columns (see Figure 6.15).
- Choose Table, Insert Table to launch a dialog box that prompts you for basic table information such as how many rows and columns, width, border size, alignment, cell padding, and cell spacing. Once these parameters are collected, FrontPage creates the shell of the table for you.

- Click the Insert Table button on the toolbar. This reveals a 4-row by 5-column grid that you can drag your mouse pointer over to specify the dimensions of your table. After you have the proper size selected, simply release your mouse button and FrontPage will place the empty table on the page.

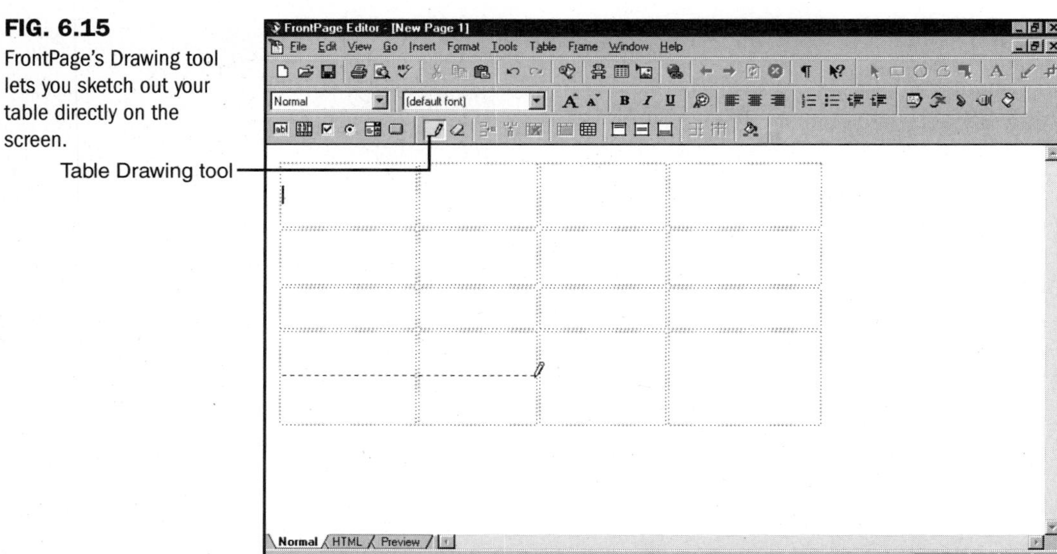

FIG. 6.15 FrontPage's Drawing tool lets you sketch out your table directly on the screen.

The end product of any of the previous actions is a blank table waiting to have content placed in the cells. If you place text into the cells, you can simply type it in. You can also place images, horizontal rule, blank space, and other tables in individual cells in much the same way you would on the full-sized page.

FrontPage's extensive Table menu also helps you out with many table-related tasks that are cumbersome to create otherwise. For example, you can choose to insert a caption, cell, row, or column into an existing table—something that can be tedious to do if you were working with the raw HTML code. The Table menu can also assist with:

- **Cell Operations**—You can choose to delete or merge a set of cells or to split one cell into multiple cells.
- **Selection Operations**—It's often a tricky thing to select a particular cell, row, or column within a table. The Select options on the Table menu make it a simple matter. For example, to select a column, you can place the cursor in a cell that occupies the column that you want to select; then choose Table, Select Column. You can select the contents of the entire table this way as well.
- **Even Distribution**—When you draw a table by hand, you might not get your rows or columns to be exactly the same size. To even things out, you can select the rows or columns and choose one of the distribute evenly Table menu options to make each row or column the same size.

- **Text/Table Conversion**—Switching between plain text and table format is a breeze with FrontPage's options that let you convert between the two.
- **Properties**—You can call up Properties dialog boxes for your table's caption, a selected cell, or for the entire table (see Figure 6.16).

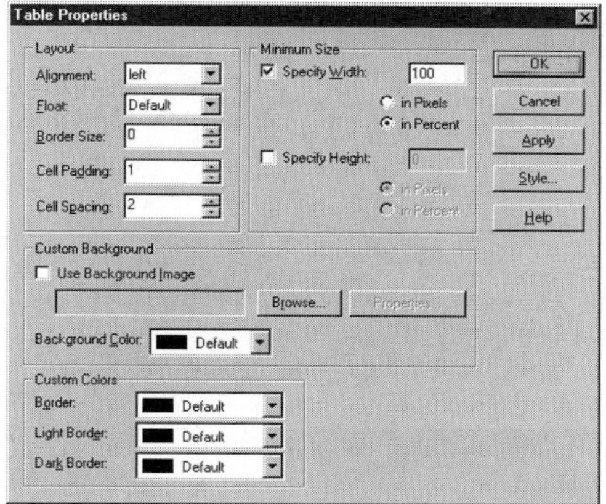

FIG. 6.16
Global table properties are easy to change, as are those for individual cells.

Many of the options on the Table menu are also replicated on the FrontPage Table toolbar. If you don't see the toolbar, choose View, Table Toolbar to activate it.

Netscape Composer

Netscape's integrated web document authoring tool Composer checks in with a fair amount of table support as well. By clicking the Table button on the Composer toolbar or by choosing Insert, Table, Table, you get the table kickoff dialog box shown in Figure 6.17. Here you can specify all of the parameters that Composer needs to set up a new table. After you click OK, Composer will place a blank table on the page according to your specs. When the blank table is in place, you're free to fill in the individual cells with whatever content you choose.

Should you need to insert or delete any cells, rows, or columns, Composer can help you. You can find the insert options under the Insert menu. Choosing Insert, Table, reveals a set of items that you can insert. Similarly, you can choose Edit, Delete Table to see a list of table components that you can remove.

As with the FrontPage Editor, Composer gives you access to cell, row, or table properties, but all of the property settings are lumped together into one dialog box. To call up the properties, right-click on a cell in the table and choose Table Properties from the pop-up menu that appears. Figure 6.18 shows you the result of this action. Note that there are tabs in the dialog box for table, row, and cell level properties.

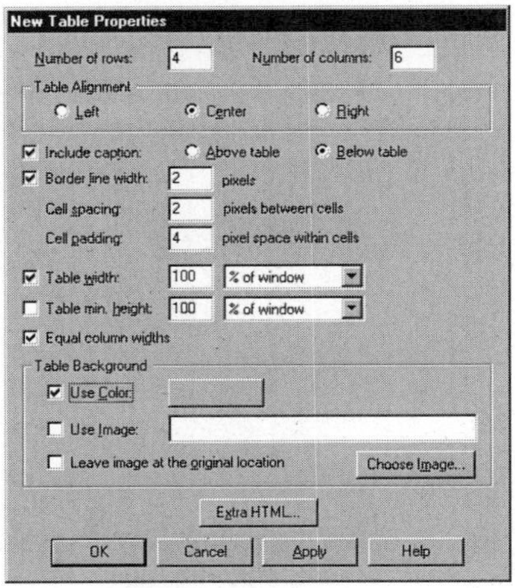

FIG. 6.17
Netscape Composer prompts you for any global table attributes you want to specify when first setting up a table.

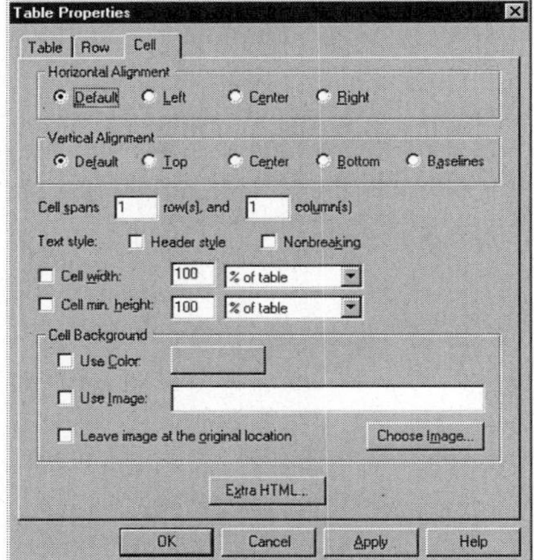

FIG. 6.18
Need to tweak your table? Netscape Composer lets you do it all from one place.

Allaire HomeSite

Allaire's HomeSite HTML editor gives you a number of ways to work with tables. Probably the fastest way to start is to use the Quick Table button at the end of the Tables toolbar. Clicking this button reveals a 12-row by 6-column grid that you can drag your mouse pointer over to choose the size of your table. After you select the appropriate size, HomeSite writes in the necessary HTML tags to support the table.

NOTE The Quick Table option only produces the HTML tags to create the structure of the table. It's up to you to go back through the code and place content in the table.

Your other option for starting is to use the Table Wizard that you can activate by clicking the Table Wizard button on the Tables toolbar or by pressing Ctrl+Shift+T. The wizard is simply a single dialog box, as shown in Figure 6.19. On the top tab, you can choose the size of your table, the caption text, border properties, the table's width, cell spacing, cell padding, and alignment settings. As you assign values to these properties, HomeSite will adjust the table it displays in the lower part of the dialog box. You can place your cursor in any of the cells in the display and put whatever content you want in them.

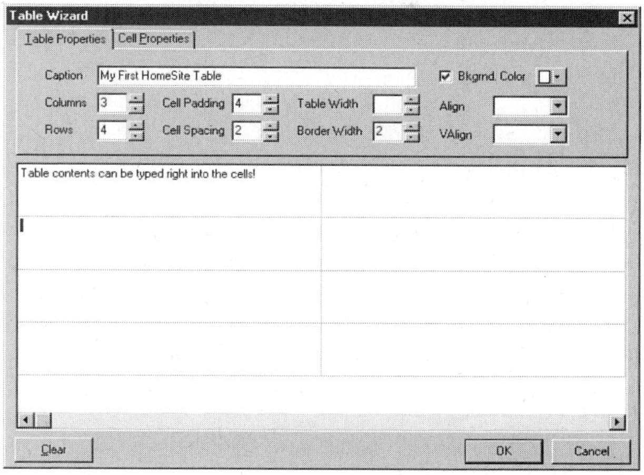

FIG. 6.19
The HomeSite Table Wizard is a near WYSIWYG tool for creating a table.

To change properties for an individual cell, place your cursor in the cell you want to change and switch to the Cell Properties tab in the Wizard dialog box. There you can adjust the cell's width, height, alignment values, text wrapping properties, and spanning values.

If you're the kind who likes to get down into the guts of things and work with HTML tags, you'll want to make use of the buttons on the HomeSite Tables toolbar. The buttons with a blue bar across the top of them place table-related tags (`<TABLE>`, `<TR>`, `<TH>`, and `<TD>`) by means of a dialog box that prompts you for an attributes that should go into the opening tag. The buttons to the right of those that don't have a blue bar simply place the tag pair in the document and leave it to you to fill in any needed attributes. You can use these buttons to place `<TABLE>`, `<TR>`, `<TD>`, `<TH>`, and `<CAPTION>` tag pairs.

Adobe PageMill

You can easily create tables with PageMill's intuitive table support. To begin, click on the Insert Table tool on the toolbar shown in Figure 6.20. After you click the tool, you can specify the number of desired rows and columns in the ensuing dialog box. Alternatively, you can click the Insert Table tool and drag the mouse—either vertically or horizontally—the proper distance to denote the number of desired rows and columns. The default width of the table is the width of the PageMill document window. However, it's simple to modify the table to change the width of a table, as discussed later in this section.

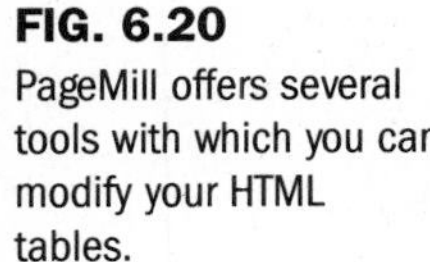

FIG. 6.20
PageMill offers several tools with which you can modify your HTML tables.

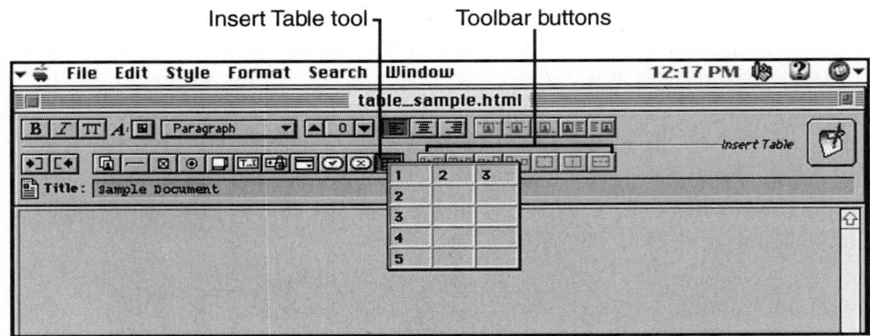

You can resize tables in PageMill simply by selecting a table and dragging the tab on the right-hand side to resize it. The number of rows and columns will remain the same, but their lengths will remain proportional to the size of the table.

Using the toolbar buttons illustrated in Figure 6.20, you can perform several operations on your table cells. When you properly select the space or contents of your tables, you can use the toolbar buttons to do the following:

- Join or divide cells
- Delete or insert columns
- Delete or insert rows

You can manipulate the look of your table through the PageMill Attributes Inspector. The Inspector is a utility that enables you to specify the attributes for objects (tables, graphics, and so on), forms, frames, and pages, with each attribute set arranged on a different tab. To access the Inspector, select Show Attributes Inspector from the Window menu.

TIP Leaving the width field blank in the Inspector instructs PageMill to size the table just wide enough to accommodate the contents of the table cells.

The Inspector allows you to place a caption at the bottom or on top of the tables, as seen in Figure 6.21. You can also specify the table border, cell spacing, and cell padding.

The inspector will also allow you to modify the contents of a table cell. Simply select the cell to be modified and the Inspector displays the cell attributes. Once again, you can specify the table width using the width parameter on the Object tab. With the Inspector, you can set certain cells as header cells and suppress word-wrapping as well. Finally, using the Inspector, you can specify the vertical and horizontal alignment of the cell contents.

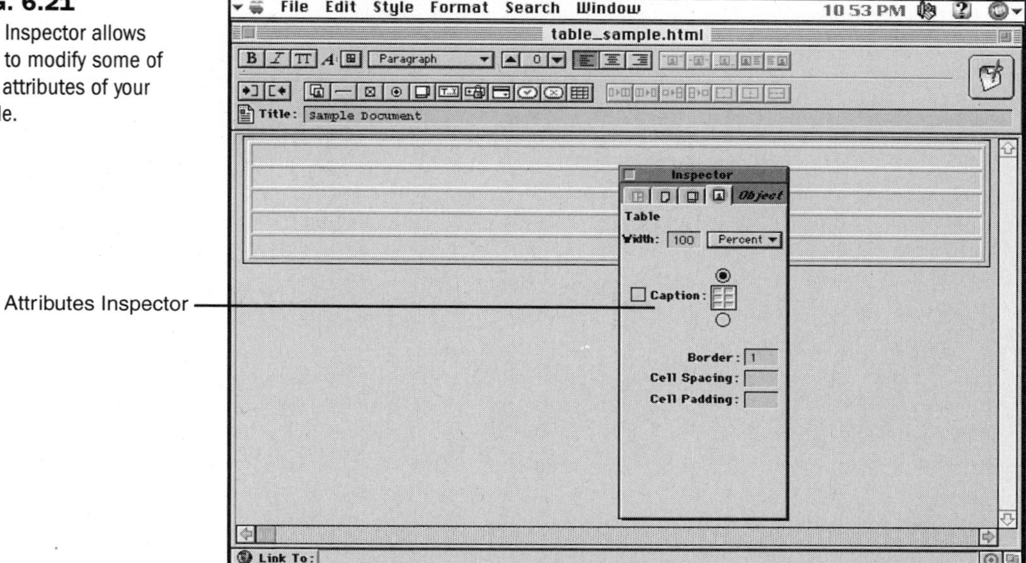

FIG. 6.21
The Inspector allows you to modify some of the attributes of your table.

CHAPTER 7

Frames

by Eric Ladd

In this chapter

Frames tend to lend themselves well to applications in which you want one set of content to remain on the browser screen all the time, while another set of content changes. This is easily accomplished by splitting the browser window into two frames: one for static content and one for changing content. Items typically found in static content frames include

- Navigation tools
- Tables of contents
- Banners and logos
- Search interface forms

Users interact with the static content (click a hypertext link, enter search criteria into a form, and so on), and the result of their action appears in the changing content frame.

Setting Up a Frames Document

After you've made the decision to use frames on your site, you need to know the HTML tags that make it possible. The next several sections walk you through how to create framed pages and how to provide alternatives for those who can't view frames.

A good first step, especially for intricately framed layouts, is to draw a pencil-and-paper sketch of how you want the framed page to look. In addition to helping you think about how to create the most efficient layout, your sketch also helps you determine how to order your <FRAMESET> tags, if you have more than one.

The *<FRAMESET>* Tag

The first step in creating a framed document is to split up the browser screen into the frames you want to use. You accomplish this with an HTML file that uses the <FRAMESET> and </FRAMESET> container tags instead of the <BODY> and </BODY> tags. <FRAMESET> and </FRAMESET> are not just container tags. Attributes of the <FRAMESET> tag are instrumental in defining the frame regions.

Each <FRAMESET> tag needs one of two attributes: ROWS, to divide the screen into multiple rows, or COLS, to divide the screen into multiple columns. ROWS and COLS are set equal to a list of values that instructs a browser how big to make each row or column. The values can be a number of pixels, a percentage of a browser window's dimensions, or an asterisk (*), which acts as a wildcard character and tells the browser to use whatever space it has left. For example, the following HTML:

```
<FRAMESET ROWS="35%,25%,10%,30%">
...
</FRAMESET>
```

breaks the browser window into four rows (see Figure 7.3). The first row has a height equal to 35 percent of the browser screen height; the second row has a height equal to 25 percent of the browser screen; the third row has a height equal to 10 percent of the screen; and the fourth row has a height equal to 30 percent of the screen. Similarly, the following HTML:

```
<FRAMESET COLS="150,100,3*,*">
...
</FRAMESET>
```

splits the window into four columns (see Figure 7.4). The first column is 150 pixels wide; the second is 100 pixels wide; and the remaining space is divided between the third and fourth columns, with the third column three times as wide (3*) as the fourth (*).

CAUTION

Don't put a ROWS and a COLS attribute in the same <FRAMESET> tag. Frames-capable browsers can only do one or the other at a time.

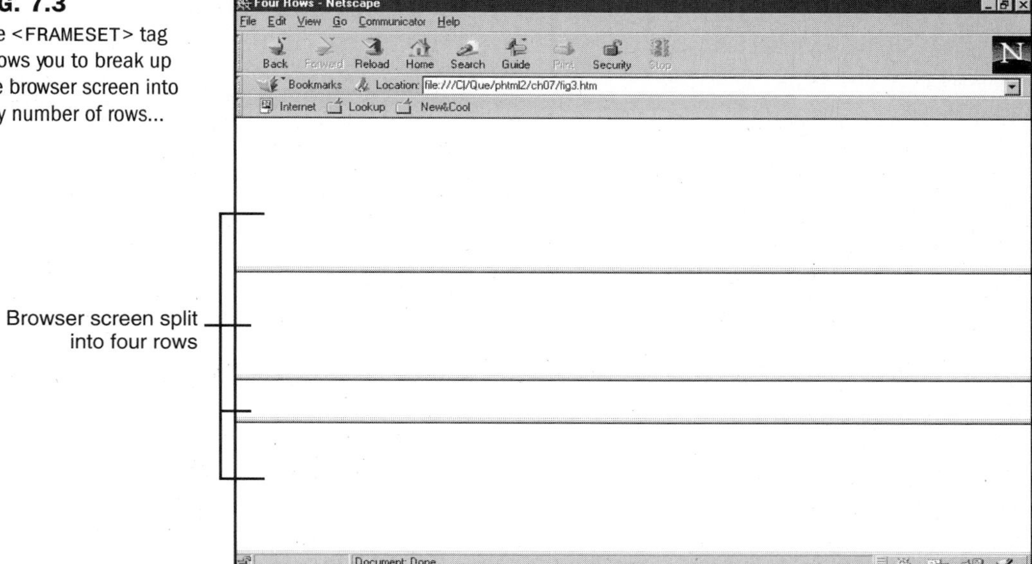

FIG. 7.3
The <FRAMESET> tag allows you to break up the browser screen into any number of rows...

The <FRAMESET> tag can also take two script-related attributes: onload and onunload. These event handlers execute the script code you assign to them when the framed layout is loaded and unloaded, respectively.

TIP Some browsers still recognize the FRAMEBORDER attribute of the <FRAMESET> tag, which you can use to set the thickness of the border between frames. You can even set FRAMEBORDER to zero so that frames appear seamless (no visible boundaries between frames so that the layout looks continuous). The HTML 4.0 spec calls for FRAMEBORDER to be an attribute of the <FRAME> tag discussed later in the chapter.

FIG. 7.4
...or into any number of columns. You have control over how big each row or column will be.

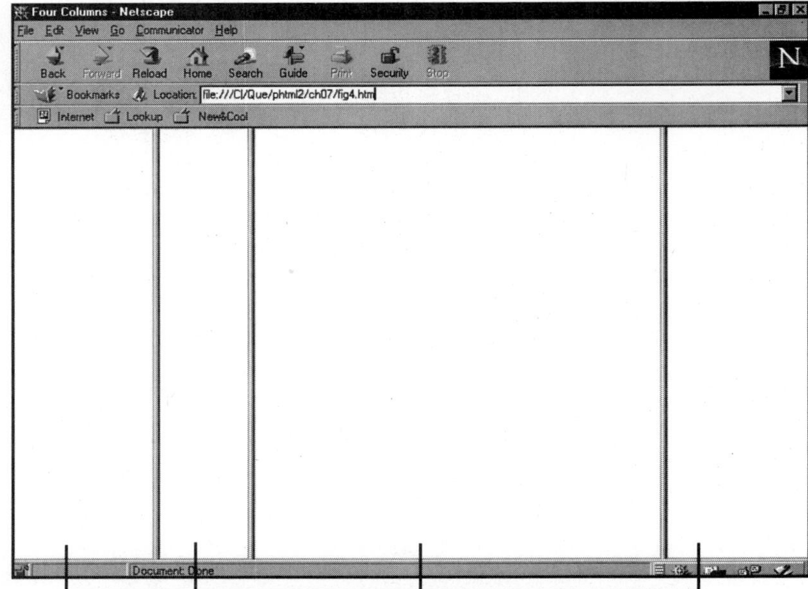

Browser screen split into four columns

Nesting <FRAMESET> Tags to Achieve Complex Layouts

To produce really interesting layouts, you can nest `<FRAMESET>` and `</FRAMESET>` tags. Suppose you want to split the browser window into six equal regions. You can first split the screen into three equal rows with the following HTML:

```
<FRAMESET ROWS="33%,33%,33%">
...
</FRAMESET>
```

This produces the screen shown in Figure 7.5.

Next you need to divide each row in half. To do this, you need a `<FRAMESET>...</FRAMESET>` pair for each row that splits the row into two equal columns. The HTML `<FRAMESET COLS="50%,50%">…</FRAMESET>` does the trick. Nesting these tags in the HTML at the beginning of this section produces the following:

```
<FRAMESET ROWS="33%,33%,33%">
     <FRAMESET COLS="50%,50%"> <!-- Split Row 1 into two columns -->
          …
     </FRAMESET>
     <FRAMESET COLS="50%,50%"> <!-- Split Row 2 into two columns -->
          …
     </FRAMESET>
     <FRAMESET COLS="50%,50%"> <!-- Split Row 2 into two columns -->
          …
     </FRAMESET>
</FRAMESET>
```

FIG. 7.5
The first step in producing a complex framed layout is to split the browser screen up into rows or columns.

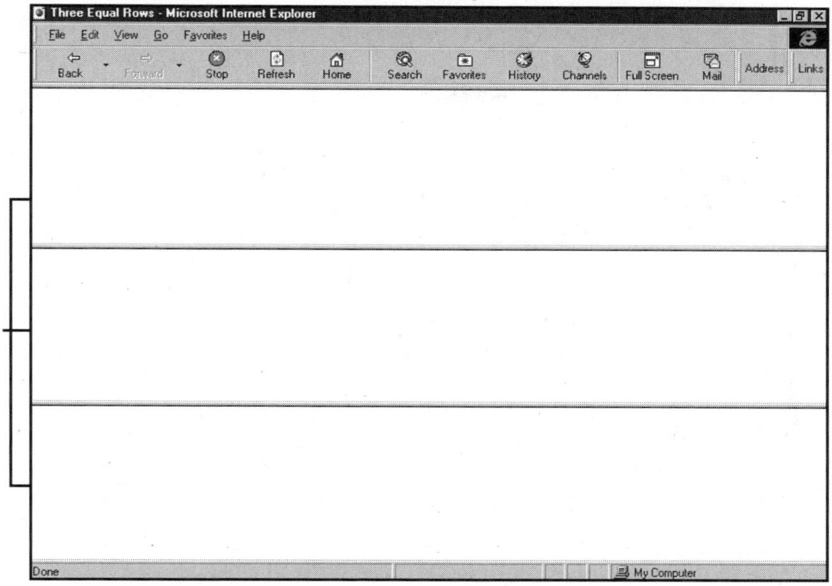

Three equal rows

The previous HTML completes the task of splitting the window into six equal regions. The resulting screen is shown in Figure 7.6.

FIG. 7.6
You further subdivide the initial rows or columns to produce the final layout.

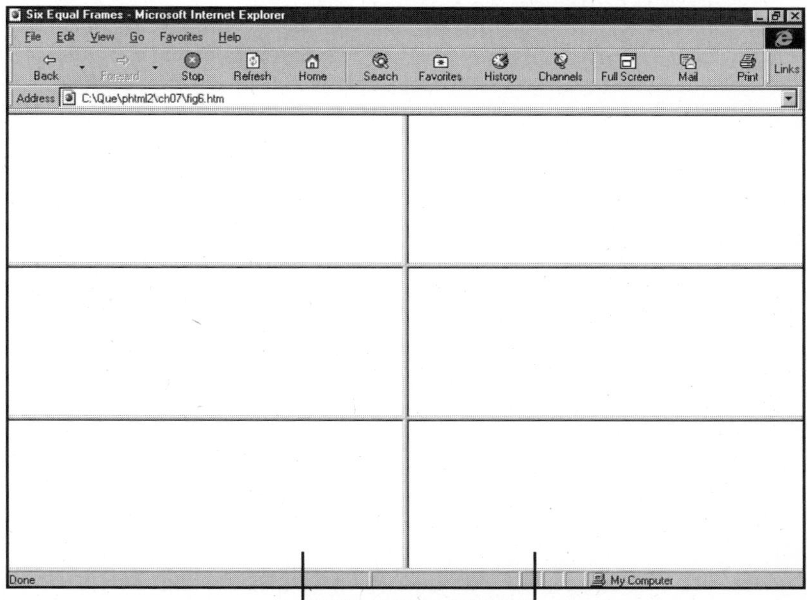

Splitting each row in half yields six equal frames.

Not sure whether to do a <FRAMESET> with ROWS or COLS first? Take a look at the sketch of what you want the browser window to look like. If you have unbroken horizontal lines that go from one edge of the window to the other, do your ROWS first. If you have unbroken vertical lines that go from the top of the window to the bottom, do your COLS first.

Of course, you're not limited to making regions that are all the same size. Suppose you want an 80 pixel high banner graphic to appear all the way across the browser screen and, below the banner, you need a 175 pixel wide column for a table of contents; the balance of the width is for changing content. In this case, you could use the following HTML:

```
<FRAMESET ROWS="80,*">  <!-- Split screen into two rows. -->
     …                <!-- Placeholder for banner graphic row. -->
     <FRAMESET COLS="175,*">  <!-- Split row 2 into two columns. -->
          …    <!-- Placeholder for table of contents. -->
          …    <!-- Placeholder for changing content frame. -->
     </FRAMESET>
</FRAMESET>
```

The ellipses you see in the previous code are placeholders for the tags that place the content into the frames that the <FRAMESET> tags create. You put a document in each using the <FRAME> tag discussed in the next section.

Placing Content in Frames with the *<FRAME>* Tag

Using <FRAMESET> tags is only the beginning of creating a framed page. After the browser window is split into regions, you need to fill each region with content. The keys to doing this are the <FRAME> tag and its many attributes.

With your frames all set up, you're ready to place content in each frame with the <FRAME> tag. The most important attribute of the <FRAME> tag is SRC, which tells the browser the URL of the document you want to load into the frame. The <FRAME> tag can also take the attributes summarized in Table 7.1. If you use the NAME attribute, the name you give the frame must begin with an alphanumeric character.

Table 7.1 Attributes of the *<FRAME>* tag.

Attribute	Purpose
FRAMEBORDER=1¦0	Turns frame borders on or off
MARGINHEIGHT=n	Specifies the amount of white space to be left at the top and bottom of the frame
MARGINWIDTH=n	Specifies the amount of white space to be left along the sides of the frame
NAME="name"	Gives the frame a unique name so it can be targeted by other documents

`NORESIZE`	Disables the user's ability to resize the frame
`SCROLLING=YES¦NO¦AUTO`	Controls the appearance of horizontal and vertical scrollbars in the frame
`SRC="url"`	Specifies the URL of the document to load into the frame

To place content in each of the regions you created at the end of the previous section, you can use the following HTML:

```
<FRAMESET ROWS="80,*">  <!-- Split screen into two rows. -->
     <FRAME SRC="banner.html">
     <FRAMESET COLS="175,*">  <!-- Split row 2 into two columns. -->
          <FRAME SRC="table_of_contents.html">
          <FRAME SRC="changing_content.html">
     </FRAMESET>
</FRAMESET>
```

The resulting screen appears in Figure 7.7.

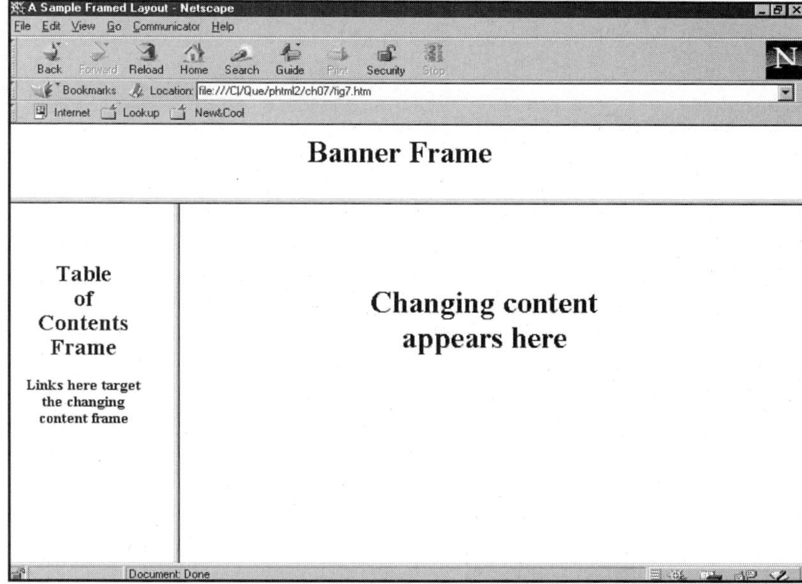

FIG. 7.7 Each frame in your layout should have a corresponding <FRAME> tag that populates it with content.

Certainly, the `SRC` attribute in a `<FRAME>` tag is essential. Otherwise, the browser would not know where to look for the content that is to go into the frame.

You'll probably find yourself using the other attributes frequently as well. In particular, `MARGINWIDTH` and `MARGINHEIGHT` let you set up left and right (`MARGINWIDTH`) and top and bottom (`MARGINHEIGHT`) margins within each frame. Putting a little white space around the content in each frame enhances readability, especially when you have `FRAMEBORDER` set to zero.

The NORESIZE and SCROLLING attributes are handy when you want to modify the user-controlled aspects of a frame. Recall that a user can change the size of a frame by clicking a border of a frame and dragging it to a new position. NORESIZE is a Boolean attribute that, when present in a <FRAME> tag, suppresses the user's ability to change the size of the frame. You might want to do this if it is imperative that the size of a frame not change so that it can always accommodate a key piece of content. SCROLLING can be set to YES if you always want horizontal and vertical scrollbars on the frame, and to NO if you never want scrollbars. The default value of SCROLLING is AUTO, in which the browser places scrollbars on the frame if they're needed and leaves them off if they're not needed.

CAUTION

Be careful about setting SCROLLING to NO. You should do this only if you are absolutely sure that all the content in a frame will always be visible. Otherwise, users might find themselves in a situation where content runs off the side or bottom of a frame and they have no way to scroll around to see it.

Targeting Named Frames

Probably the trickiest thing about frames is getting content to appear where you want it to appear. This is where naming the frames you create becomes critical. By naming the changing content frame main, you can then use the TARGET attribute in all of your <A> tags to direct all hyperlinked documents to be loaded into that frame:

```
<FRAMESET ROWS="80,*">  <!-- Split screen into two rows. -->

     <FRAME SRC="banner.html">
     <FRAMESET COLS="175,*">  <!-- Split row 2 into two columns. -->
          <FRAME SRC="table_of_contents.html">
          <FRAME SRC="changing_content.html" NAME="main">
     </FRAMESET>
</FRAMESET>
```

With frames set up by the preceding code, an example link in the file table_of_contents.html might look like this:

```
<A HREF="software/index.html" TARGET="main">
Software Products
</A>
```

The TARGET attribute tells the browser that the file software/index.html should be loaded into the frame named main (the changing content frame) whenever a user clicks the hypertext Software Products in the table of contents frame.

If all the links in table_of_contents.html target the frame named main, you can use the <BASE> tag in the head of the document to set a value for TARGET that applies to all links:

```
<HEAD>
<TITLE>Table of Contents</TITLE>
<BASE TARGET="main">
</HEAD>
```

With this <BASE> tag in place, every hyperlink targets the changing content window named main.

Netscape set aside some reserved frame names when it introduced the frame-related tags. These magic target names include:

- _blank targets a new blank window that is not named.
- _self targets the frame where the hyperlink is found.
- _parent targets the parent <FRAMESET> of the frame where the hyperlink is found. This defaults to behaving like _self if there is no parent document.
- _top targets the full window before any frames are introduced. This creates a good way to jump out of a nested sequence of framed documents.

While the TARGET attribute is useful for targeting the effects of hyperlinks, you can use it in other HTML tags as well. Placing the TARGET attribute in a <FORM> tag instructs the browser to target the response from the form submission to the specified frame. This enables you to set up a search form in one frame and have the search results appear in a separate frame.

The other tag you can use TARGET in is the <AREA> tag, which is used to define a hot region in a client-side imagemap. This permits the document associated with a hot region to be loaded into the frame of your choice.

Respecting the Frames-Challenged Browsers

If you create a document with frames, people who are using a browser other than Netscape Navigator 4.0 or Microsoft Internet Explorer 4.0 might not be able to see the content you want them to see because their browsers don't understand the <FRAMESET>, </FRAMESET>, and <FRAME> tags. As a courtesy to users with frames-challenged browsers, you can place alternative HTML code between the <NOFRAMES> and </NOFRAMES> container tags. Any HTML between these two tags is understood and rendered by other browsers. A frames-capable browser, on the other hand, ignores anything between these tags and works just with the frame-related HTML.

Some users have a browser that can render frames, but the users dislike framed documents. For this portion of your audience, you should consider having a non-frames version of all your pages available (see Figure 7.8). This way, users who like frames can stick with them and those who don't like frames have a way to view the same content without being burdened with an uncomfortable interface.

When making framed versions of existing pages, don't discard your non-frames content. Very often, you can use the non-frames HTML documents as the alternative content found between the <NOFRAMES> and </NOFRAMES> tags.

CAUTION

The <NOFRAMES> and </NOFRAMES> tags must occur after the initial <FRAMESET> tag, but before any nested <FRAMESET> tags.

FIG. 7.8
Providing a non-frames version of your framed content is an important user courtesy.

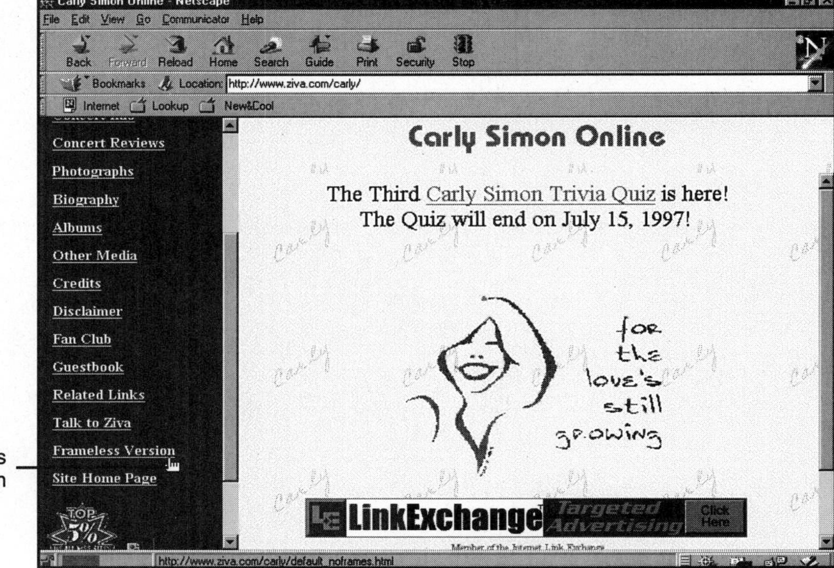

Creating Floating Frames

Microsoft introduced the concept of a floating frame with Internet Explorer 3. You can think of a floating frame as a smaller browser window that you can open in your main browser window—much like the picture-in-a-picture feature that comes with many television sets. Just as with regular frames, you can load any HTML document you want into a floating frame. The primary difference is that floating frames can be placed anywhere on a page that you can place an image. In fact, you'll find the HTML syntax for placing floating frames to be very similar to that for placing an image.

You place a floating frame on a page by using the `<IFRAME>` and `</IFRAME>` tags. A browser that can do floating frames ignores anything between these two tags, allowing you to place an alternative to the floating frame (most likely text or an image) on the page as well. This way, browsers that don't know how to render floating frames can ignore the `<IFRAME>` and `</IFRAME>` tags and act on what is found between them. The `<IFRAME>` tag can take the attributes summarized in Table 7.2.

Table 7.2 Attributes of the *<IFRAME>* tag.

Attribute	Purpose
`ALIGN=LEFT¦RIGHT`	Floats the floating frame in the left or right margin
`FRAMEBORDER=0¦1`	Controls the presence of the beveled border around the floating frame

HEIGHT=pixels¦percent	Specifies the height of the floating frame
HSPACE=n	Specifies how many pixels of white space to leave to the left and right of the floating frame
NAME="frame_name"	Gives the floating frame a unique name so it can be targeted by hyperlinks
SCROLLING=YES¦NO¦AUTO	Controls the presence of scrollbars on the floating frame
SRC="url"	Specifies the URL of the document to load into the floating frame
VSPACE=n	Specifies how many pixels of white space to leave above and below the floating frame
WIDTH=pixels¦percent	Specifies the width of the floating frame

The `<IFRAME>` tag has three required attributes: `WIDTH`, `HEIGHT`, and `SRC`. `WIDTH` and `HEIGHT` specify the width and height of the floating frame in pixels or as a percentage of the browser screen's width and height. `SRC` tells the browser the URL of the document to load into the floating frame. Thus, your basic floating frame HTML looks like this:

```
<C2><IFRAME WIDTH=250 HEIGHT=112 SRC="http://www.your_firm.com/floating.html">
<C2>Text or image based alternative to the floating frame
</IFRAME>
```

Figure 7.9 shows an example of a floating frame.

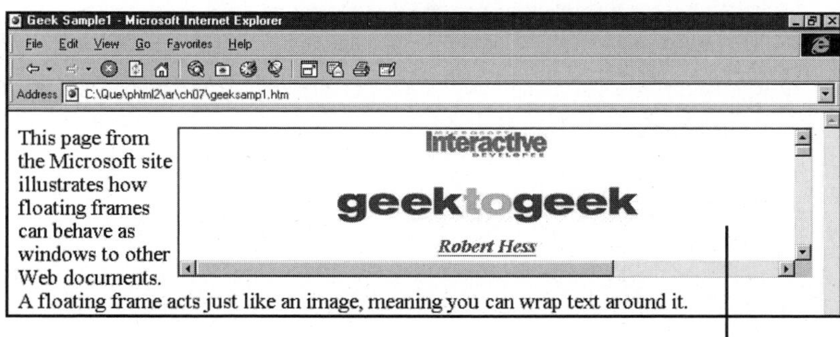

FIG. 7.9
Floating frames let you place a new document right in the middle of the main document.

In addition to the three required attributes, the `<IFRAME>` tag takes several other attributes that give you good control over the floating frame's appearance. These include:

- `FRAMEBORDER`—You might notice in Figure 7.9 that the floating frame has a beveled border that gives it the appearance of being recessed in the main browser window. If you prefer a more seamless look, you can use the `FRAMEBORDER` attribute in the `<IFRAME>` tag. Setting `FRAMEBORDER=0` eliminates the beveled border.

- SCROLLING—A browser that can render floating frames puts a scrollbar on the floating frame if the document it contains exceeds the dimensions of the frame. You can suppress the scrollbars by specifying SCROLLING=NO in the <IFRAME> tag. If you always want scrollbars present, you can set SCROLLING equal to YES.
- HSPACE and VSPACE—If your floating frame needs some clear space around it, the HSPACE and VSPACE attributes of the <IFRAME> tag work the same way they do for the <IMG> tag: HSPACE adds clear space to the left and right of the floating frame, and VSPACE adds clear space above and below. HSPACE and VSPACE values are in pixels.
- ALIGN—You can float the floating frame in the left or right margins by specifying ALIGN=LEFT or ALIGN=RIGHT. Any text following the floated frame wraps around it to the right or left, respectively. You can use the <BR> tag with the appropriate CLEAR attribute to break to the first line clear of floated frames.
- NAME—Naming a floating frame allows you to target it with the TARGET attribute in an <A> tag. Thus, you can set up links to documents and have them appear in the floating frame.

Support for Developing Framed Layouts

When the frame tags first came on the scene, many content developers were challenged by their complexity. Things were made worse by having to do all of the code by hand and without the luxury of any kind of WYSIWYG preview capability. Fortunately, most top-notch content development programs now include some support for authoring framed documents. This chapter closes with a look at three such programs.

Microsoft FrontPage 98

The FrontPage 98 Editor has its own Frames menu from which you can initiate just about any frames-related task. To get started with a framed layout, choose Frames, New Frames Page to call up the dialog box you see in Figure 7.10. Here you find a list of ten preconfigured framed layouts that FrontPage can set up for you automatically.

NOTE You can access this same list of available framed layouts by choosing File, New and then clicking the Frames tab.

As you highlight the different selections, you see a preview of how each one breaks up the browser screen. After you find the one you want, click OK and the framed layout is loaded into the Editor. Figure 7.11 shows the Header, Footer, and Contents layout.

Note in Figure 7.11 that each frame initially has three buttons in it. The Set Initial Page button lets you assign an existing document to that frame. Clicking the button allows you browse to find the file. The New Page button clears out the frame and lets you work just as you would in the full FrontPage Editor window. You click this button if you have not yet prepared any content for the frame.

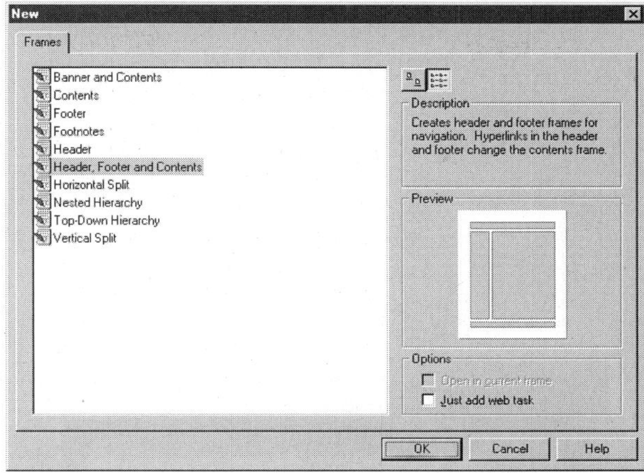

FIG. 7.10
The FrontPage Editor can set up <FRAMESET> tags for ten different framed layouts.

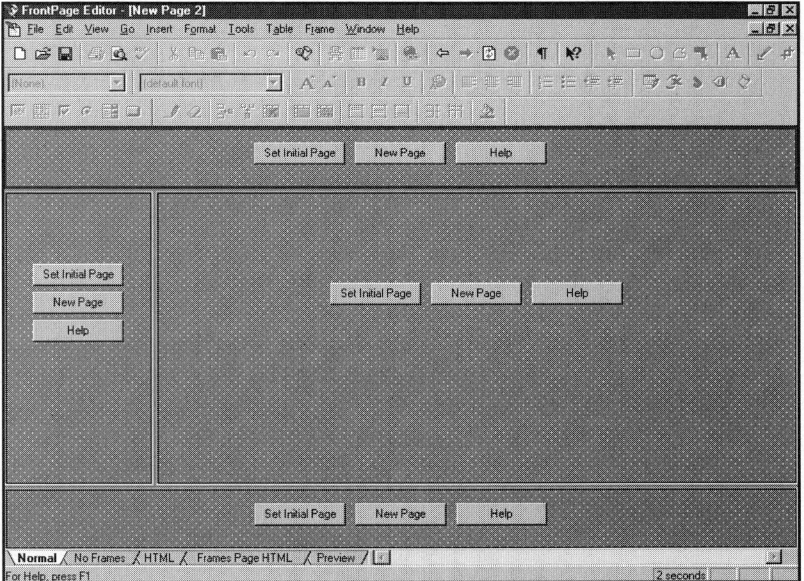

FIG. 7.11
A selected frame layout is loaded into the FrontPage Editor where you can work on each frame individually.

Another thing to notice is how the tabs near the bottom of the Editor window change. When you are working with a framed layout, you get two extra tabs: No Frames, to show you what your framed document will look like on a browser that doesn't support frames, and Frames Page HTML, which contains all of the <FRAMESET> tags that make the layout possible.

After you have a framed layout in place, you can start using the other options found under the Frames menu. The Split Frame option lets you subdivide your select frame (denoted by a blue outline) into two equal rows or columns. Choosing Delete Frame eliminates the selected frame and reduces the framed layout to whatever frames are left after the deletion. The Set Initial

Page option repeats the functionality of the button bearing the same label. If you prefer to create the content for a frame in a full-sized window, you can choose the Open Page in a New Window option. The Save Page and Save Page As options let you save the content you've developed for a frame.

The last two options in the Frames menu let you alter properties of either the entire framed layout or one of the frames within the layout. Choosing the Frames Page Properties option opens the dialog box shown in Figure 7.12 where you can specify attributes of the whole layout such as whether to display borders, how much spacing to use between frames, what kinds of margins to use, what to use as a background, and how to title the layout.

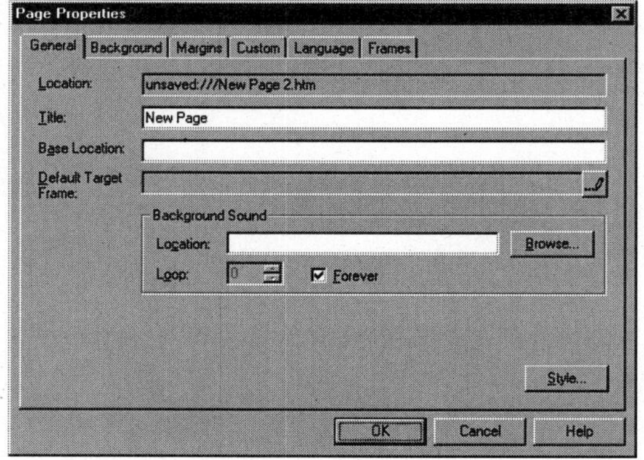

FIG. 7.12
Because the framed layout is created by an HTML document, you can alter many of the same properties for the layout as you can for any document.

The Frame Properties option launches the dialog box shown in Figure 7.13. Here you can modify the attributes of the select frame, including whether the frame can be resized, whether it should have scrollbars, what its height and width should be, what margins should be used inside the frame, and what the frame's initial page should be. There is also a Frames Page button that opens the Frames Page Properties dialog box you saw in Figure 7.12.

Allaire HomeSite

Allaire's HomeSite tends to be focused on creating an HTML document at the source code level, allowing you to work directly with the HTML tags. HomeSite provides good support for creating a framed layout, including a wizard that walks you through the set up of the layout and then writes out the appropriate HTML tags that reproduce the layout on a browser screen.

Most of HomeSite's frames support resides on the Frames toolbar, which is found on the Frames tab of the HomeSite SpeedBar (see Figure 7.14). The various buttons on the bar provide very different levels of support, and you are free to choose whichever ones are best suited to your authoring preferences.

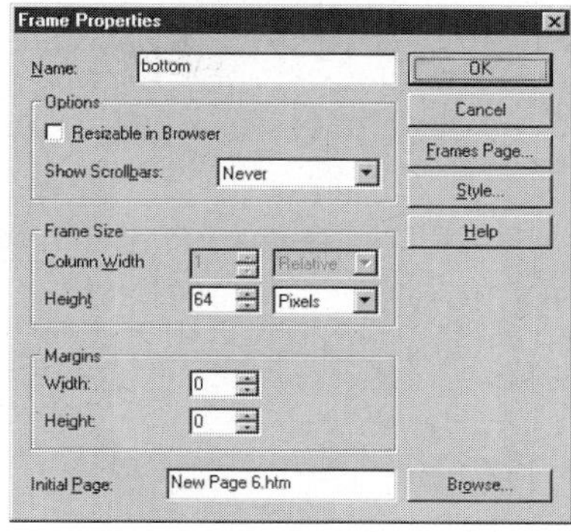

FIG. 7.13
Each frame in the layout has its own set of properties that you can tweak as needed.

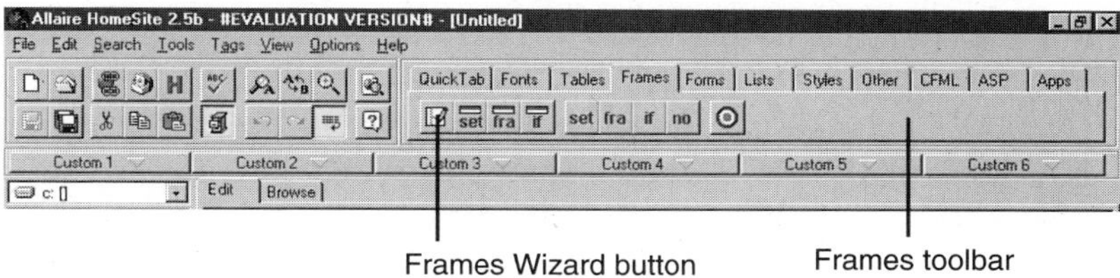

FIG. 7.14
The HomeSite Frames toolbar gives you access to a frames wizard, dialog boxes that collect frame tag attributes, or just the frame tags themselves.

The left-most button on the toolbar launches the HomeSite Frames Wizard. Like most wizards, the Frames Wizard takes you through a sequence of dialog boxes wherein you specify how you want your framed layout to be set up. After the wizard has all the information it needs, it writes the `<FRAMESET>` tags that create your desired layout. When you fire up the wizard you're first asked if you want to split the screen into rows or columns. You can choose to have between one and nine of each. Next, you have the option of subdividing each of your initial rows or columns into smaller frames. You can have from one to nine of these subdivisions as well. With this information collected, the wizard gives you a preview of what your layout will look like (see Figure 7.15). In the same dialog box where you see the preview, you can also establish the properties of each of the individual frames including its name, source document URL, margin width and height, whether there should be scrollbars, and whether the user should be able to resize the frame.

TIP You can also invoke the Frames Wizard by pressing Ctrl+Shift+W.

After you set the parameters for each of the frames in your layout, click the Finish button to instruct HomeSite to create the `<FRAMESET>` and `<FRAME>` tags that will support the layout. HomeSite writes this code right into the main editing window.

NOTE After you set up the `<FRAMESET>` and `<FRAME>` tags, you still need to create the files that will populate each frame.

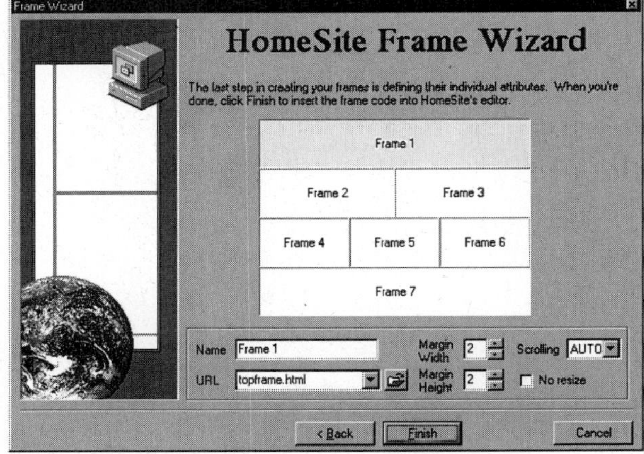

FIG. 7.15
HomeSite's Frames Wizard is more flexible than the preset frames configurations you get with FrontPage.

The Frames Wizard is HomeSite's most automated form of frames support. Just to the right of the Frames Wizard button are three other buttons that open dialog boxes for setting up `<FRAMESET>`, `<FRAME>`, and `<IFRAME>` tags, respectively. If you're the type of author who likes placing your own tags, but don't mind a little help setting up the attributes, then you'll make use of these buttons. As Figure 7.16 shows, you can specify every attribute of the `<IFRAME>` tag from the dialog box and then click OK to write the entire tag into your document.

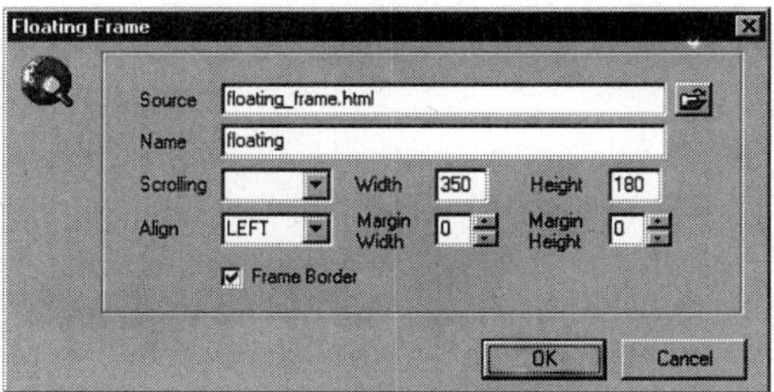

FIG. 7.16
Other buttons on the Frames toolbar are more tag focused, allowing you to set up an entire tag in one step.

The remaining five buttons on the toolbar simply place a tag in the document, after which it falls to you to go back and add in any attributes you need. The first four buttons place the `<FRAMESET>`, `<FRAME>`, `<IFRAME>`, and `<NOFRAMES>` tags, respectively, including closing tags where appropriate. The right-most button on the toolbar adds a `<BASE>` tag to your document with the `TARGET` attribute so you can set up global targeting within the document.

Adobe PageMill

Frames are simple to construct using PageMill; the requisite frameset and HTML source code are transparently generated while you construct the frames using drag-and-drop techniques.

To build a framed document in PageMill, start out with a blank page. Hold down the Alt key while dragging from one of the window margins. You'll notice that, in effect, you drag a border across the page. You can create horizontal or vertical frame elements in this manner.

Holding the Alt key while moving borders allows you to create new frames. Dragging the borders without holding the Alt key simply moves the borders.

When creating frames in PageMill, several files are actually constructed. The base document, which starts out as a blank page, contains the frameset. This file describes the names of the different frames as well as their sizes and other attributes. The HTML code used to populate the different frames named in your frameset is stored in various other files. Opening the frameset file in PageMill launches the entire suite of frames. In contrast, opening the HTML source code for one of the frames merely brings up the frame contents in an isolated PageMill window.

You can select frames in your PageMill document simply by clicking their contents. When selected, the frame borders are highlighted. You save the frames individually by selecting them and saving them individually. If you resize any of the frames, you are prompted to save the frameset. PageMill arbitrarily assigns names to the individual frames; when saving the frame HTML, PageMill creates file names with the frame name appended with an .html suffix.

PageMill allows you to individually save frames, save the frameset, or, most usefully, save the entire set of frames. Located under the File menu, you will see the Save Everything command, which saves the individual frame HTML as well as the frameset in the proper files.

To modify your frames, you might want to use the utility called the PageMill Attributes Inspector. As described in the last chapter, the Inspector is a utility that allows you to specify the attributes for objects (tables, graphics, and so on), forms, frames, and pages, with each attribute set arranged on a different tab. To access the Inspector, select Show Attributes Inspector from the Window menu. The Frame tab is one of the four major tabs available in the Attributes Inspector.

As depicted in Figure 7.17, the Frame tab allows you to modify attributes of the individual frames. Simply select one of the frames in the frameset and activate the Inspector.

You might notice that you can change the names of the different frames to something that is perhaps more relevant. Furthermore, the width of the frame can be changed or expressed using different bases; you can express the frame width as:

- A percentage of the browser window width
- A set number of pixels
- Relative to other frames in the frameset

Notice in Figure 7.17 that you can also set the height and width of the frame margins. Furthermore, you can specify whether the frames will contain margins and if the user will have the ability to manually resize the frame.

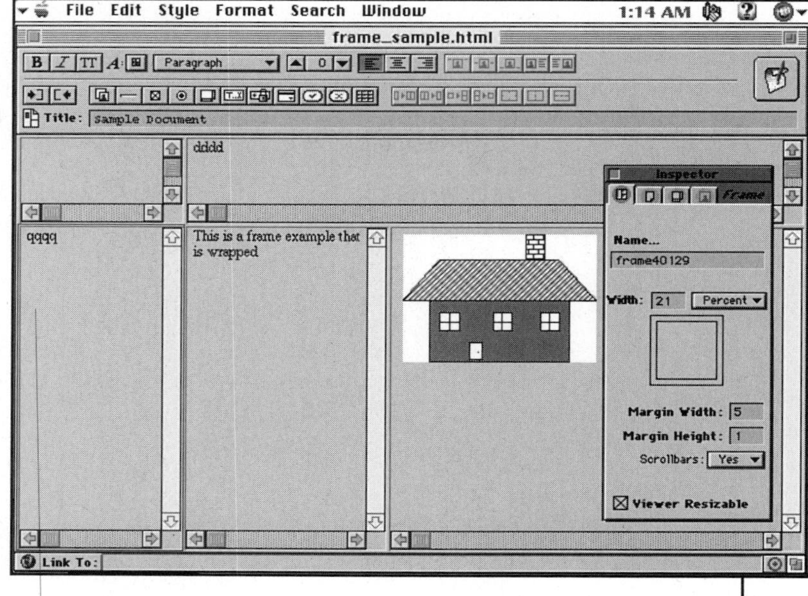

FIG. 7.17
It's easy to modify a series of frames using the PageMill Inspector.

Naturally, you want to set up hypertext links between your different frame documents. This is accomplished by assigning targets to the links described in different frames. PageMill has a special function that aids in assigning targets to your individual URLs.

Triple-click a link to select it; then click and hold on the link after it's selected. A box appears that gives you a variety of choices from which you can send pages corresponding to the link. You can do the following:

- Open the link in the existing frame
- Open the link in a new window
- Open the link in the same frame of a new window
- Open the link in the same window

You might notice that there is a map at the bottom of the pop-up box that mimics the structure of the open frameset document. You can also drag the mouse over to one of the representative frames in the pop-up image to denote a target frame for a given link.

CHAPTER 8

Forms

by Eric Ladd

In this chapter

Overview: Forms and CGI

One of the big sensations on the web today is a customized page, set up according to your own specifications—but how do you let the server know what your specs are? Is there a way that users can provide information to servers and get a personalized response in return? The answer, of course, is yes, and the way to do it is with HTML forms.

Forms are the visible or front-end portion of interactive pages. Users enter information into form fields or controls—user interface elements that are similar to those found on Windows and Macintosh operating systems—and click a button to submit the data. The browser then packages the data, opens an HTTP connection, and sends the data to a server. Things then move to the transparent or back-end part of the process.

Web servers are programs that know how to distribute web pages. They are not programmed to process data from every possible form, so the best they can do is hand off the form data to a program that does know what to do with it. This hand-off occurs with the help of the Common Gateway Interface or CGI—a set of standards by which servers communicate with external programs.

The program that processes the form data is typically called a CGI script or a CGI program. The script or program performs some manipulations of the data and composes a response—typically an HTML page. The response page is handed back to the server (via CGI) which, in turn, passes it along to the browser that initiated the request.

▶ To learn more about CGI programming, **see** "Programming CGI Scripts," **p. 855**.

Forms and CGI are opposite sides of the same coin. Both are essential to create interactive pages, but it is the forms side of the coin that the user sees. This chapter examines how to create Web forms and gives an overview of some of the behind-the-scenes activity that has to occur to produce the custom pages and other dynamic functionality that Web users have come to love.

NOTE When a CGI script or program composes an HTML page, it is said to be generating HTML on-the-fly. The capability to generate pages on-the-fly is what makes custom responses to database and forms submission possible.

Creating Forms

HTML's form support is simple and complete. A handful of HTML tags create the most popular elements of modern graphical interfaces, including text windows, check boxes and radio buttons, pull-down menus, and push buttons.

Composing HTML forms might sound like a complex task, but you need to master surprisingly few tags to do it. All form-related tags occur between the <FORM> and </FORM> container tags. If you have more than one form in an HTML document, the closing </FORM> tag is essential for distinguishing between the multiple forms.

Adding a </FORM> tag immediately after creating a <FORM> tag is a good practice; then you can go back to fill in the contents. Following this procedure helps you avoid omitting the closing tag after you finish. Many of today's popular HTML editing programs take care of placing the </FORM> tag for you, so be sure to check to see if the editor you're using does this.

Each HTML form has three main components: the form header, one or more named input fields, and one or more action buttons.

The *<FORM>* Tag

The form header and the <FORM> tag are actually one and the same. The <FORM> tag takes the three attributes shown in Table 8.1. The ACTION attribute is required in every <FORM> tag.

Table 8.1 Attributes of the *<FORM>* tag.

Attribute	Purpose
ACCEPT	Specifies a list of MIME types that the server will process correctly
ACCEPT-CHARSET	Provides a list of character sets that are acceptable to the server
ACTION	Specifies the URL of the processing script
ENCTYPE	Supplies the MIME type of a file used as form input
METHOD=GET¦POST	Tells the browser how it should send the form data to the server
TARGET	Gives the name of the frame where the response from the form submission is to appear

ACTION is set equal to the URL of the processing script so that the browser knows where to send the form data after it is entered. Without it, the browser has no idea where the form data should go. An ACTION URL has the following form:

protocol://server/path/script_file

METHOD specifies the HTTP method to use when passing the data to the script and can be set to values of GET or POST. When you're using the GET method, the browser appends the form data to the end of the URL of the processing script. The POST method sends the form data to the server in a separate HTTP transaction.

METHOD is not a mandatory attribute of the <FORM> tag. In the absence of a specified method, the browser uses the GET method.

CAUTION

Some servers might have operating environment limitations that prevent them from processing an URL that exceeds a certain number of characters—typically one kilobyte of data. This limitation can be a problem when you're using the GET method to pass a large amount of form data. Because the GET method appends the data to the end of the processing script URL, you run a greater risk of passing an URL that's too big for the server to handle. If URL size limitations are a concern on your server, you should use the POST method to pass form data.

The ENCTYPE attribute was introduced by Netscape for the purpose of providing a file name to be uploaded as form input. You set ENCTYPE equal to the MIME type expected for the file being uploaded. ENCTYPE does not create the input field for the file name; rather, it just gives the browser a heads-up as to what kind of file it is sending. When prompting for a file to upload, you need to use an <INPUT> tag with TYPE set equal to FILE.

As an example of these three <FORM> tag attributes, examine the following HTML:

```
<FORM ACTION="process_it.cgi" METHOD=POST ENCTYPE="text/html">
Enter the name of the HTML file to validate:
<INPUT TYPE="FILE" NAME="html_file">
<INPUT TYPE="SUBMIT" VALUE="Validate it!">
</FORM>
```

The form header of this short form instructs the server to process the form data using the program named process_it.cgi. Form data is passed using the POST method, and the expected type of file being submitted is an HTML file.

New <FORM> tag attributes in HTML 4.0 include TARGET, which is used to direct the response from the processing script to a particular frame; ACCEPT, which denotes the MIME types of files that the server processing the form can handle correctly (this is useful when a user is submitting a set of files to the server because you can then check to make sure that all of the submitted files are of an acceptable MIME type); and ACCEPT-CHARSET, which specifies the character sets the server understands.

The <FORM> tag can also take two event handlers—onSubmit and onReset. This gives you the ability to execute some script code when the form is submitted or reset, respectively. For example, if you write a JavaScript function that validates the data a user enters into a form, you could invoke the script using an event handler as follows:

```
<FORM ACTION="processit.cgi" onSubmit="validateform()">
```

Named Input Fields

The named input fields typically comprise the bulk of a form. The fields appear as standard GUI controls such as text boxes, check boxes, radio buttons, and menus. You assign each field a unique name that eventually becomes the variable name used in the processing script.

If you are not coding your own processing scripts, be sure to sit down with your programmer to agree on variable names. The names used in the form should exactly match those used in coding the script.

You can use several different GUI controls to enter information into forms. The controls for named input fields appear in Table 8.2.

Table 8.2 Types of named input fields.

Field Type	HTML Tag(s)
Text Box	`<INPUT TYPE="TEXT">`
Password Box	`<INPUT TYPE="PASSWORD">`
Check Box	`<INPUT TYPE="CHECKBOX">`
Radio Button	`<INPUT TYPE="RADIO">`
Hidden Field	`<INPUT TYPE="HIDDEN">`
File	`<INPUT TYPE="FILE">`
Text Window	`<TEXTAREA>...</TEXTAREA>`
Menu	`<SELECT>...<OPTION>...</SELECT>`

The <INPUT> Tag

You might notice in Table 8.2 that the `<INPUT>` tag handles the majority of named input fields. `<INPUT>` is a stand-alone tag that, thanks to the many values of its `TYPE` attribute, can place most of the fields you need on your forms. `<INPUT>` also takes other attributes, depending on which `TYPE` is in use. These additional attributes are covered for each type, as appropriate, over the next several sections.

NOTE The `<INPUT>` tag and other tags that produce named input fields just create the fields themselves. You, as the form designer, must include some descriptive text next to each field so that users know what information to enter. You might also need to use line breaks (`<BR>`), paragraph breaks (`<P>`), and non-breaking space (` `) to create the spacing you want between form fields.

Because browsers ignore white space, lining up the left edges of text input boxes on multiple lines is difficult because the text to the left of the boxes is of different lengths. In this instance, HTML tables are invaluable. By setting up the text labels and input fields as cells in the same row of an HTML table, you can produce a nicely formatted form. To learn more about forms using table conventions, consult Chapter 6, "Tables."

Text and Password Fields Text and password fields are simple data entry fields. The only difference between them is that text typed into a password field appears on-screen as asterisks (*).

▶ **See** "Security," **p. 1281** to find out more about how to make your web pages secure.

CAUTION

Using a password field protects users' passwords from the people looking over their shoulders, but it does not protect the password as it travels over the Internet. To protect password data as it moves from browser to server, you need to use some type of encryption or similar security measure. Authentication of both the server and client by using signed digital certificates are two other steps you can take to keep Internet transactions secure.

A text or password field is produced by the HTML (attributes in square brackets are optional):

```
<INPUT TYPE="{TEXT¦PASSWORD}" NAME="Name" [VALUE="default_text"]
[SIZE="width"] [MAXLENGTH="max_width"]>
```

The `NAME` attribute is mandatory because it provides a unique identifier for the data entered into the field.

The optional `VALUE` attribute allows you to place some default text in the field, rather than have it initially appear blank. This capability is useful if a majority of users will enter a certain text string into the field. In such cases, you can use `VALUE` to put the text into the field, thereby saving most users the effort of typing it.

The optional `SIZE` attribute gives you control over how many characters wide the field should be. The default `SIZE` is typically around 20 characters, although this number can vary from browser to browser. `MAXLENGTH` is also optional and allows you to specify the maximum number of characters that can be entered into the field.

Figure 8.1 shows a form on Amtrak's reservations site used to prompt a logon ID and password. Notice how password text appears as asterisks. The corresponding HTML is shown in Listing 8.1.

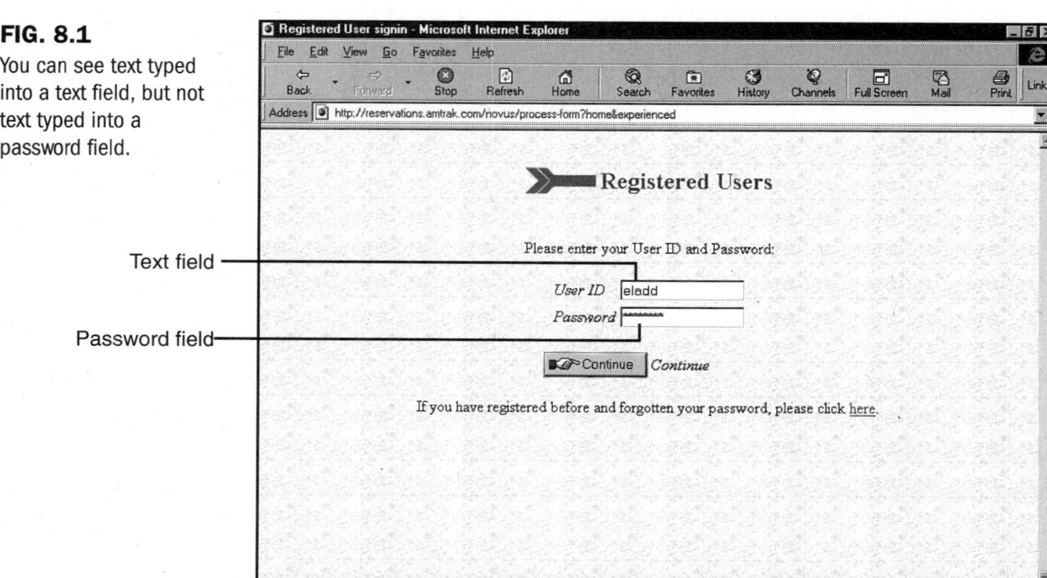

FIG. 8.1
You can see text typed into a text field, but not text typed into a password field.

Listing 8.1 HTML code to produce text and password fields.

```
<FORM ...>
<table>
<tr>
<TD ALIGN='LEFT'><EM>User ID</EM></TD>
<TD ALIGN='LEFT'><INPUT TYPE='TEXT' SIZE='16' MAXLENGTH='16' NAME='USERNAME'>
</TD>
</TR>
<TR>
<TD ALIGN='LEFT'><EM>Password</EM></TD>
<TD ALIGN='LEFT'><INPUT TYPE='PASSWORD' SIZE='16' MAXLENGTH='16'
NAME='PASSWORD'></TD>
</TR>
</TABLE>
...
</FORM>
```

Check Boxes Check boxes provide users with several choices, from which they can select as many of the choices as they want. An `<INPUT>` tag that is used to produce a check box option has the following syntax:

```
<INPUT TYPE="CHECKBOX" NAME="Name" VALUE="Value" [CHECKED]>
```

Each check box option is created by its own `<INPUT>` tag and must have its own unique `NAME`. If you give multiple check box options the same `NAME`, the script has no way to determine which choices the user actually made.

The `VALUE` attribute specifies which data is sent to the server if the corresponding check box is chosen. This information is transparent to the user. The optional `CHECKED` attribute preselects a commonly selected check box when the form is rendered on the browser screen.

Figure 8.2 shows a survey on the Ben & Jerry's Ice Cream site with several check box options. The HTML that produces the check boxes is shown in Listing 8.2.

NOTE If they are selected, check box options show up in the form data sent to the server. Options that are not selected do not appear.

Listing 8.2 HTML code to produce check boxes.

```
<FORM ...>
<B>What Ben & Jerry's products have you tried?</B> -- Choose all that apply.
<INPUT TYPE ="CHECKBOX" NAME="field18" VALUE="ice cream, ">Ice Cream
<INPUT TYPE ="CHECKBOX" NAME="field18" VALUE="low fat, ">Low Fat Ice Cream
<INPUT TYPE ="CHECKBOX" NAME="field18" VALUE="yogurt, ">Frozen Yogurt
<INPUT TYPE ="CHECKBOX" NAME="field18" VALUE="sorbet, ">Sorbet
<INPUT TYPE ="CHECKBOX" NAME="field18" VALUE="novelties">Frozen Novelties
...
</FORM>
```

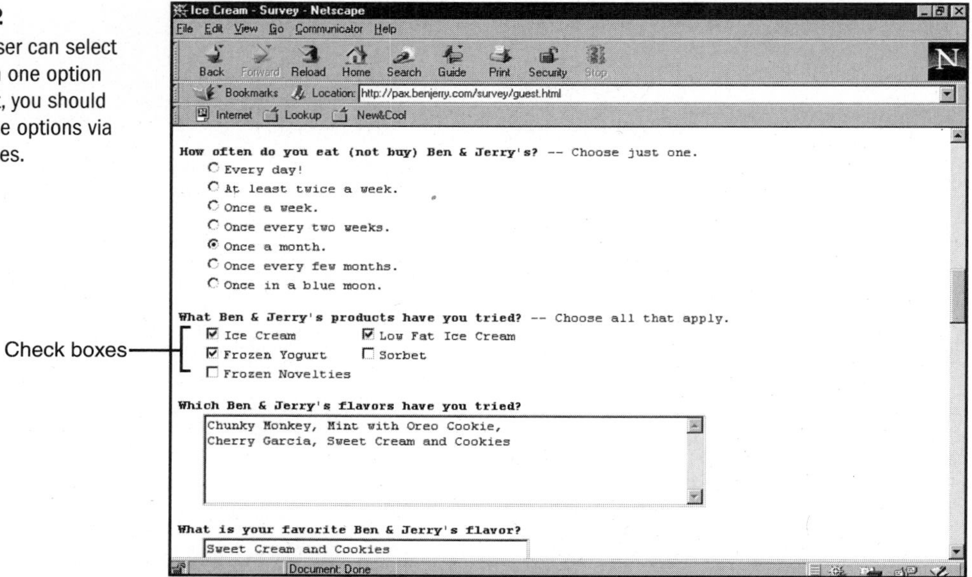

FIG. 8.2 When a user can select more than one option from a set, you should present the options via check boxes.

Radio Buttons Radio buttons are used to present users with a set of choices, from which they can choose *one* and *only one*. When you set up options with a radio button format, you should make sure that the options are mutually exclusive so that a user doesn't try to select more than one.

The HTML code to produce a set of three radio button options is as follows:

```
<FORM ...>
<INPUT TYPE="RADIO" NAME="Name" VALUE="VALUE1" [CHECKED]>Option 1<P>
<INPUT TYPE="RADIO" NAME="Name" VALUE="VALUE2">Option 2<P>
<INPUT TYPE="RADIO" NAME="Name" VALUE="VALUE3">Option 3<P>
...
</FORM>
```

The `VALUE` and `CHECKED` attributes work exactly the same as they do for check boxes, although you should have only one preselected radio button option. A fundamental difference with a set of radio button options is that they all have the same `NAME`. This is permissible because the user can select only one of the options.

Microsoft's site and Internet search page makes use of radio buttons as shown in Figure 8.3; the corresponding HTML is in Listing 8.3.

FIG. 8.3
Mutually exclusive options are best presented to users by means of radio buttons.

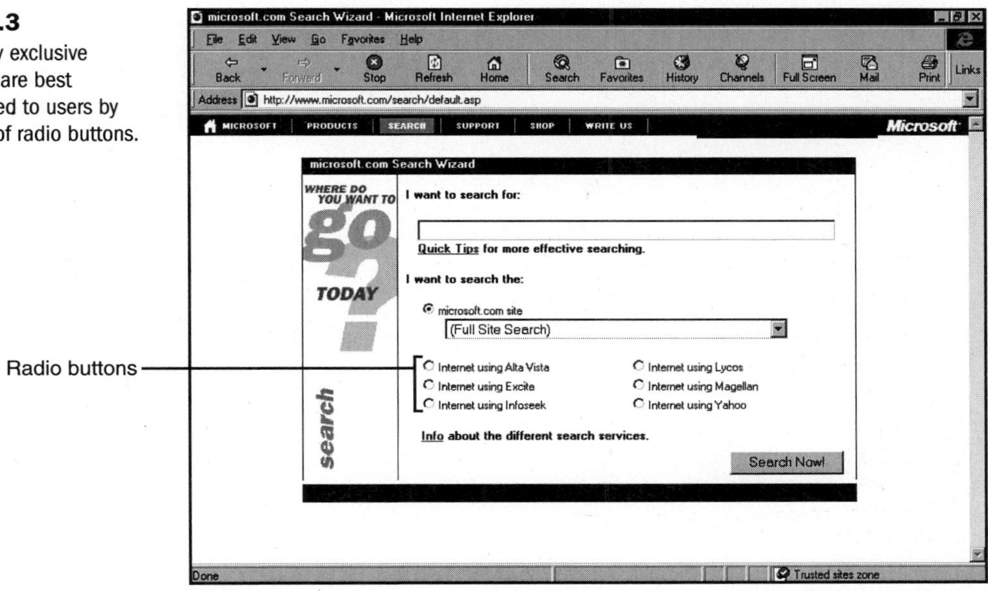

Listing 8.3 HTML code to produce radio buttons.

```
<FORM>
<TR>
<TD WIDTH="225" COLSPAN="1">
<FONT FACE="MS Sans Serif, Arial, Helv" SIZE="1">
<BR>
     
<INPUT NAME="SearchType" TYPE="RADIO" VALUE="altavista">Internet using Alta
Vista<BR>
     
<INPUT NAME="SearchType" TYPE="RADIO" VALUE="excite">Internet using Excite<BR>
     
<INPUT NAME="SearchType" TYPE="RADIO" VALUE="infoseek">Internet using
Infoseek<BR>
</FONT>
</TD>
<TD WIDTH="225" COLSPAN="1">
<FONT FACE="MS Sans Serif, Arial, Helv" SIZE="1">
<BR>
<INPUT NAME="SearchType" TYPE="RADIO" VALUE="lycos">Internet using Lycos<BR>
<INPUT NAME="SearchType" TYPE="RADIO" VALUE="magellan">Internet using
Magellan<BR>
<INPUT NAME="SearchType" TYPE="RADIO" VALUE="yahoo">Internet using Yahoo<BR>
</FONT>
</TD>
</TR>
...
</FORM>
```

Hidden Fields Technically, hidden fields are not meant for data input. You can send information to the server about a form without displaying that information anywhere on the form itself. The general format for including hidden fields is as follows:

```
<INPUT TYPE="HIDDEN" NAME="name" VALUE="value">
```

One possible use of hidden fields is to allow a single general script to process data from several different forms. The script needs to know which form is sending the data and a hidden field can provide this information without requiring anything on the part of the user.

Because HTTP is a stateless protocol (information from the user's session is not tracked), it is not possible for the input from one form to be carried forward to another. Thus, another application of hidden fields is doing just that. This lets you split up a long form into several smaller forms and still keep all of the user's input in one place by passing it from one form to the next in the sequence. For example, suppose that in the first of a sequence of several forms, you collect a visitor's name and mailing address. That information is passed to the script that processes the form. Because part of what this script has to do is build the next form in the sequence, it would be an easy matter to have the script to include hidden fields in the next form that carry the name and address information forward.

NOTE Because hidden fields are transparent to users, it doesn't matter where you put them in your HTML code. Just make sure they occur between the <FORM> and </FORM> tags that define the form that contains the hidden fields.

Files You can upload an entire file to a server by using a form. The first step is to include the ENCTYPE attribute in the <FORM> tag. To enter a file name in a field, the user needs the <INPUT> tag with TYPE set equal to FILE:

```
<FORM ACTION="whatever.cgi" ENCTYPE="application/x-www-form-urlencoded">
What file would you like to submit: <INPUT TYPE="FILE" NAME="your_file">
...
</FORM>
```

Being able to send an entire file is useful when submitting a document produced by another program—for example, an Excel spreadsheet, a résumé in Word format, or just a plain Notepad text file.

NOTE You can also use the ACCEPT attribute when you have an <INPUT> field of type FILE to specify the MIME types of files that are acceptable for upload.

Multiple Line Text Input

Text and password boxes are used for simple, one-line input fields. You can create multiline text windows that function in much the same way by using the <TEXTAREA> and </TEXTAREA> container tags. The HTML syntax for a text window is as follows:

```
<TEXTAREA NAME="Name" [ROWS="rows"] [COLS="columns"]>
Default_window_text
</TEXTAREA>
```

The NAME attribute gives the text window a unique identifier just as it does with the variations on the <INPUT> tag. The optional ROWS and COLS attributes allow you to specify the dimensions of the text window as it appears on the browser screen. The default number of rows and columns varies by browser.

The text that appears between the <TEXTAREA> and </TEXTAREA> tags shows up in the input window by default. To type in something else, users need to delete the default text and enter their text.

Multiline text windows are ideal for entry of long pieces of text such as feedback comments or e-mail messages (see the Federal Express feedback page in Figure 8.4 and corresponding code in Listing 8.4). Some corporate sites on the Web that collect information on potential employees might ask you to copy and paste your entire résumé into multiline text windows!

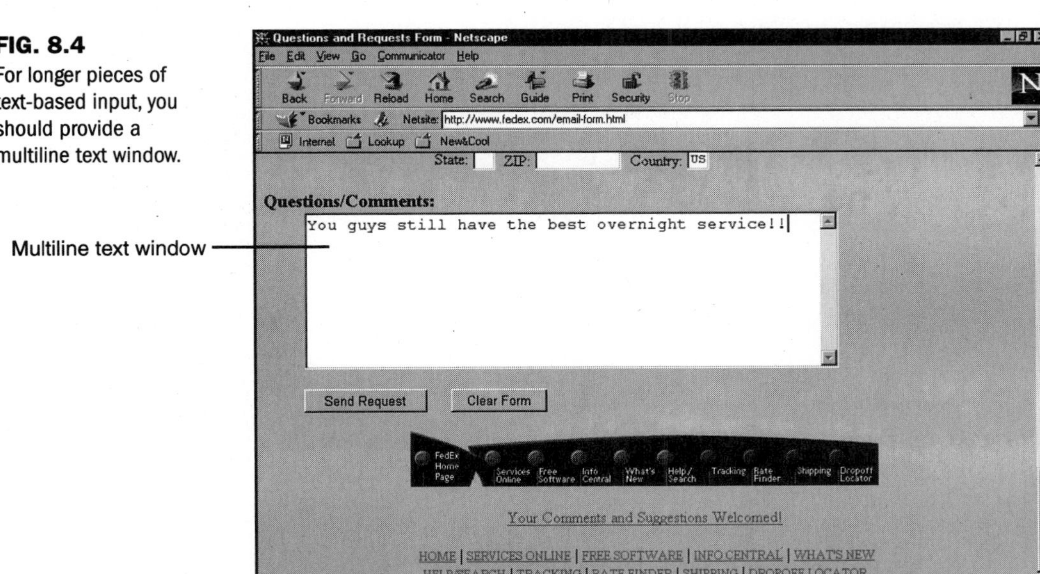

FIG. 8.4
For longer pieces of text-based input, you should provide a multiline text window.

Listing 8.4 HTML code to produce a multiline text window.

```
<FORM ...>
<H3>Questions/Comments:
<TEXTAREA NAME="comments" ROWS="8" COLS="51">
</TEXTAREA>
</H3>
...
</FORM>
```

A useful attribute of the <TEXTAREA> tag that is supported by Netscape Navigator 4 and Internet Explorer 4 is WRAP—a Boolean attribute that, when present, instructs the browser to wrap text within the input window, rather than let it scroll. Users will appreciate your use of this attribute, as it spares them from having to remember to press the Enter key each time they want to move to a new line in the text window.

Menus

The final technique for creating a named input field is to use the <SELECT> and </SELECT> container tags to produce pull-down or scrollable option menus (see Figure 8.5 and Listing 8.5). The HTML code used to create a general menu is as follows:

```
<FORM ...>
<SELECT NAME="Name" [SIZE="size"] [MULTIPLE]>
<OPTION [SELECTED]>Option 1</OPTION>
<OPTION [SELECTED]>Option 2</OPTION>
<OPTION [SELECTED]>Option 3</OPTION>
...
<OPTION [SELECTED]>Option n</OPTION>
</SELECT>
...
</FORM>
```

In the <SELECT> tag, the NAME attribute again gives the input field a unique identifier. The optional SIZE attribute lets you specify how many options should be displayed when the menu renders on the browser screen. If you have more options than you have space to display them, you can access them either by using a pull-down window or by scrolling through the window with scroll bars. The default SIZE is 1. If you want to let users choose more than one menu option, include the MULTIPLE attribute. When MULTIPLE is specified, users can choose multiple options by holding down the Ctrl key and clicking the options they want.

NOTE If you specify the MULTIPLE attribute and SIZE=1, a one-line scrollable list box displays instead of a drop-down list box. This box appears because you can select only one item (not multiple items) in a drop-down list box.

Listing 8.5 HTML code to produce a drop-down list.

```
<FORM ...>
<SELECT NAME="WebResourceURL">
<OPTION VALUE="/products/ColdFusion/30/Overview/">What is Cold Fusion 3.0?
<OPTION VALUE="/products/download/download.cfm?section=products
&Product_ID=75">How do I download Cold Fusion 3.0?
<OPTION VALUE="/products/download/download.cfm?section=products
&Product_ID=41">Where do I download HomeSite?
<OPTION VALUE="/products/coldfusion/30/Feature/index.cfm">
What features are in Cold Fusion 3.0?
<OPTION VALUE="/products/coldfusion/30/Example/">
Can I see some examples of CF 3.0?
<OPTION VALUE="/products/coldfusion/30/overview/tescustomers.cfm">
What do customers say about CF 3.0?
```

```
<OPTION VALUE="https://www.allaire.com/store">
How do I purchase Allaire Software?
<OPTION VALUE="/company/background/background.cfm">Who is Allaire?
<OPTION VALUE="/services/services.cfm">How do I get technical support?
<OPTION VALUE="http://www.allaire.com/products/forums/20/index.cfm">
What is Allaire Forums?
<OPTION VALUE="http://www.allaire.com/partners/partners.cfm">
Does Allaire have a partner program?
</SELECT>
...
</FORM>
```

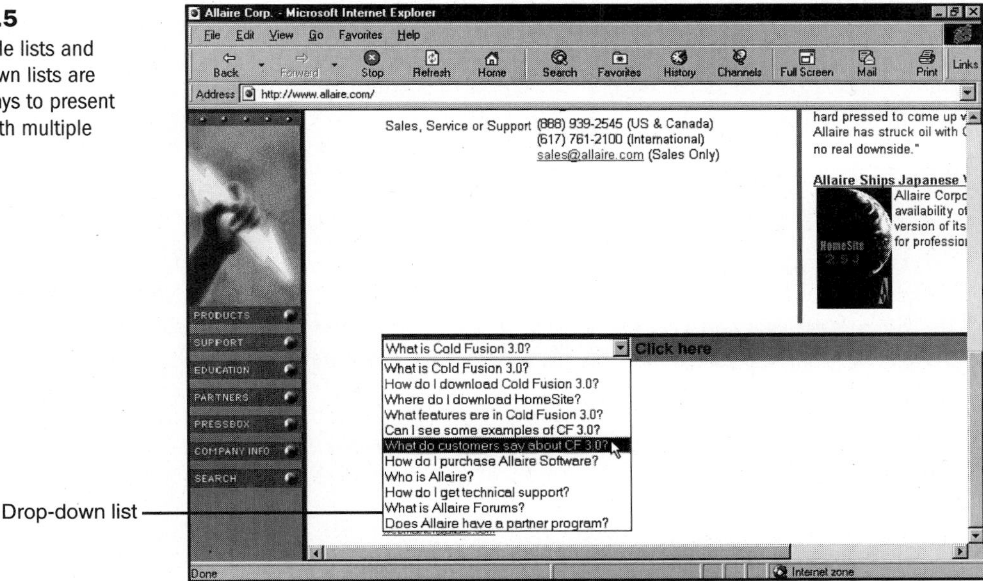

FIG. 8.5
Scrollable lists and drop-down lists are other ways to present users with multiple options.

Each option in the menu is specified inside of its own `<OPTION>` container tag. If you want an option to be preselected, include the `SELECTED` attribute in the appropriate `<OPTION>` tag. The value passed to the server is the menu item that follows the `<OPTION>` tag unless you supply an alternative using the `VALUE` attribute. For example:

```
<FORM ...>
<SELECT NAME="STATE">
<OPTION VALUE="NY">New York</OPTION>
<OPTION VALUE="DC">Washington, DC</OPTION>
<OPTION VALUE="FL">Florida</OPTION>
...
</SELECT>
...
</FORM>
```

In the preceding menu, the user clicks a state name, but it is the state's two-letter abbreviation that passes to the server.

Action Buttons

The handy <INPUT> tag returns to provide an easy way of creating the form action buttons you see in many of the preceding figures. Buttons can be of two types: Submit and Reset. Clicking a Submit button instructs the browser to package the form data and send it to the server. Clicking a Reset button clears out any data entered into the form and sets all the named input fields back to their default values.

Regular Submit and Reset Buttons Any form you compose should have a Submit button so that users can submit the data they enter. The one exception to this rule is a form containing only one input field. For such a form, pressing Enter automatically submits the data. Reset buttons are technically not necessary but are usually provided as a user courtesy.

To create Submit or Reset buttons, use the <INPUT> tags as follows:

```
<INPUT TYPE="SUBMIT" VALUE="Submit Data">
<INPUT TYPE="RESET" VALUE="Clear Data">
```

Use the VALUE attribute to specify the text that appears on the button. You should set VALUE to a text string that concisely describes the function of the button. If VALUE is not specified, the button text is Submit Query for Submit buttons and Reset for Reset buttons.

Using Images as Submit Buttons You can create a custom image to be a Submit button for your forms and you can set up the image so that clicking it instructs the browser to submit the form data (see Figure 8.6 and Listing 8.6). To do this, you set TYPE equal to IMAGE in your <INPUT> tag and you provide the URL of the image you want to use with the SRC attribute:

```
<INPUT TYPE="IMAGE" SRC="images/submit_button.gif">
```

You can also use the ALIGN attribute in this variation of the <INPUT> tag to control how text appears next to the image (TOP, MIDDLE, or BOTTOM), or to float the image in the left or right margins (LEFT or RIGHT).

Imagemapped Submit Buttons

A future possibility for image-based submit buttons is to also include the USEMAP attribute so that clicking different parts of the image would cause different instructions to be sent to the server. The various instructions would be set up using the <AREA> tag, just as you set up different URLs in a client-side imagemap. Some details about how the browser would gather and pass the coordinates of the click still need to be ironed out before this becomes standard though.

Listing 8.6 HTML code to produce an image-based Submit button.

```
<FORM ...>
<TABLE>
<TR>
<TD ALIGN=center VALIGN=top COLSPAN=3><BR>
```

```
<INPUT TYPE="image" BORDER=0
SRC="http://www.ual.com/images/retrieve_flts_button.gif">
</TD>
</TR>
</TABLE>
...
</FORM>
```

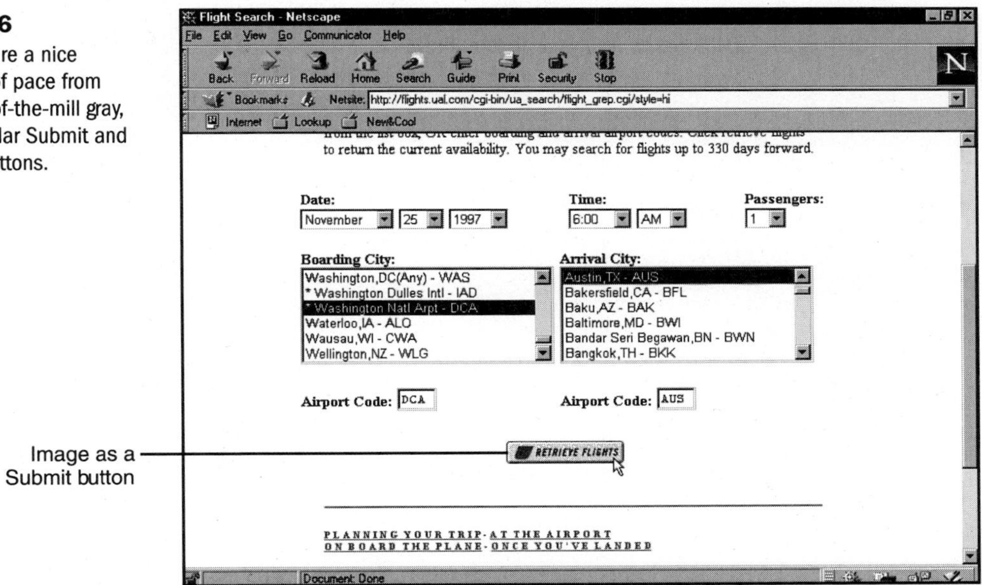

FIG. 8.6
Images are a nice change of pace from the run-of-the-mill gray, rectangular Submit and Reset buttons.

Scripted Buttons A new variant on action buttons is the *scripted button*—one that executes a client-side script when clicked. To create a scripted button, you still use the `<INPUT>` tag, but with `TYPE` set equal to `BUTTON`. The `VALUE` attribute still specifies what text should appear on the face of the button.

By default, a button created in this way has no behavior associated with it. To make the button do something when clicked, you need to also include the `onclick` event handler. You set `onclick` equal to a name of a script that has presumably been set up using the `<SCRIPT>` tag earlier in the document. Thus, the code to produce a fully defined scripted button might look like this:

```
<INPUT TYPE="BUTTON" VALUE="Check data" onclick="check_data()">
```

Set up in this way, the button sends an instruction to the browser to execute the script `check_data` whenever it is clicked.

▶ To learn more about JavaScript-enabled forms, see "Using JavaScript to Create Smart Forms," **p. 515**.

The *<BUTTON>* Tag The <BUTTON> tag was introduced with HTML 4.0 to allow action buttons with better presentation features. The first thing to note about the <BUTTON> tag is that it is a container tag, meaning a companion </BUTTON> tag must also be used. What goes between the <BUTTON> and </BUTTON> tags has everything to do with how the button looks on-screen. If there is just text between the tags, that text appears on the face of the button. If there is an <IMG> tag between them, the image is used as the button.

<BUTTON> takes the TYPE attribute, which can be set to SUBMIT, RESET, or BUTTON. Each of these options produces a button very similar to the ones you get by using the <INPUT> tag with the same TYPE values, but there are subtle differences in how the buttons appear on-screen. This is particularly so in the case of image-based buttons, which are rendered three-dimensionally (with a drop shadow) and which move down and then up when clicked.

<BUTTON> can take the NAME and VALUE attributes as well. You need to assign a name to a button when it is a submit button in a set of more than one. The VALUE attribute is what gets passed to the server when the button is clicked.

Labeling Input Fields

It was noted earlier in the chapter that it is up to you as a form author to include prompting text in front of your form fields to suggest to a user how he or she should fill in the field. The HTML 4.0 <LABEL> tag formalizes the relationship between the prompting text (the label) and the form field it is paired with. <LABEL> takes the FOR attribute, where FOR is set equal to the ID attribute value of the associated form field. In the following example:

```
<LABEL FOR="PW">Enter your password: </LABEL>
<INPUT TYPE="PASSWORD" NAME="PASSWD" ID="PW">
```

the prompting text Enter your password: comprises the label. Note how the label is associated with the subsequent field with the matching FOR and ID attributes.

How a label is rendered varies from browser to browser, so you should continue to place labels and their associated form fields in tables for proper alignment. Thus, the preceding example is better done as:

```
<FORM ...>
<TABLE>
<TR>
<TD><LABEL FOR="PW">Enter your password: </LABEL></TD>
<TD><INPUT TYPE="PASSWORD" NAME="PASSWD" ID="PW"></TD>
</TR>
</TABLE>
...
</FORM>
```

NOTE You can also implicitly associate a label with a form field by placing the tag that created the field between the <LABEL> and </LABEL> tags. Done this way, the previous password example looks like this:

```
<LABEL>Enter your password: <INPUT TYPE="PASSWORD" NAME="PASSWD"></LABEL>
```

While this might reduce how much you have to type, it's worth noting that this approach precludes you from putting your labels and form fields in their own table cells. ■

Although labels might not seem to do much for you, they're an important thing to include for visually impaired users who use a speech-based browser. In this case, the browser knows to treat the label as prompting text for a form field and instructs the user accordingly.

Additionally, you can associate an *access key* with your form field label by using the ACCESSKEY attribute. ACCESSKEY is set equal to a single letter from the user's keyboard. After it is set up, users can use the ACCESSKEY keystroke to go directly to the associated form field (an action called *giving focus* to the field) and fill it in. Expanding the previous password example to include an access key yields the following:

```
<FORM ...>
<TABLE>
<TR>
<TD><LABEL FOR="PW" ACCESSKEY="P">Enter your <U>p</U>assword: </LABEL></TD>
<TD><INPUT TYPE="PASSWORD" NAME="PASSWD" ID="PW"></TD>
</TR>
</TABLE>
...
</FORM>
```

The ACCESSKEY attribute in the <LABEL> tag associates the letter P with the form field label. Thus, whenever Windows users type Alt+P or Macintosh users type Cmd+P, they give focus to the password field, meaning that the cursor moves there and allows them to type in a password.

If you assign an ACCESSKEY to a form field label, make sure you make the key known to your users. In the preceding example, the letter p in password was put between <U> and </U> tags so that it would appear underlined. This is consistent with the way Windows programs label their access keys (for example, the underlined F in the File menu means you can press Alt+F to activate the menu).

You can use the ACCESSKEY attribute with the <A> tag as well. This way, users can jump to a linked document by pressing the access key rather than clicking the link.

Grouping Related Fields

Two other tags that were added to the HTML 4.0 form tags in recognition of non-visual browsers are the <FIELDSET> and <LEGEND> tags. <FIELDSET> allows you to group related form fields together in a logical group, and <LEGEND> lets you assign descriptive text to the group of fields. Neither of these might seem necessary on a standard visual browser, but for a visually impaired user with a speech-based browser, these extra features make a form much more accessible.

NOTE One advantage of using <FIELDSET> grouping on a visual browser is that it facilitates tabbing through the form field. After the browser knows about a group of fields, it can tab you through the fields in sequence.

<FIELDSET> does not have any attributes, but it does have a companion closing </FIELDSET> tag. To create a logical grouping of fields, you simply place the tags that create the fields between <FIELDSET> and </FIELDSET>.

Each logical <FIELDSET> grouping can have a <LEGEND> tag associated with it. The text between <LEGEND> and </LEGEND> is what captions the grouping, and you can use the ALIGN attribute in the <LEGEND> tag to align the legend text with respect to the grouped fields. Possible values for ALIGN in this case are TOP, BOTTOM, LEFT, and RIGHT.

NOTE Aligning the legend text only produces an effect on visual browsers.

<LEGEND> can also take the ACCESSKEY attribute so that you can set up an access key for the form field grouping.

As an example of how <FIELDSET> and <LEGEND> work together, consider the following example:

```
<FORM ...>
<FIELDSET>
<LEGEND ALIGN="LEFT">Shipping Address</LEGEND>
<TABLE>
<TR>
<TD COLSPAN=2>Address:</TD>
<TD COLSPAN=4><INPUT TYPE="TEXT" NAME="SH_ADDR"></TD>
</TR>
<TR>
<TD>City:</TD>
<TD><INPUT TYPE="TEXT" NAME="SH_CITY"></TD>
<TD>State:</TD>
<TD><INPUT TYPE="TEXT" NAME="SH_STATE"></TD>
<TD>Zip:</TD>
<TD><INPUT TYPE="TEXT" NAME="SH_ZIP"></TD>
</TR>
</TABLE>
</FIELDSET>
<FIELDSET>
<LEGEND ALIGN="LEFT">Billing Address</LEGEND>
<TABLE>
<TR>
<TD COLSPAN=2>Address:</TD>
<TD COLSPAN=4><INPUT TYPE="TEXT" NAME="BL_ADDR"></TD>
</TR>
<TR>
```

```
<TD>City:</TD>
<TD><INPUT TYPE="TEXT" NAME="BL_CITY"></TD>
<TD>State:</TD>
<TD><INPUT TYPE="TEXT" NAME="BL_STATE"></TD>
<TD>Zip:</TD>
<TD><INPUT TYPE="TEXT" NAME="BL_ZIP"></TD>
</TR>
</TABLE>
</FIELDSET>
...
</FORM>
```

In the preceding code, the form fields are grouped into two logical groups: shipping address fields and billing address fields. On a visual browser, the legend text Shipping Address and Billing Address appear above each logical grouping.

Disabled and Read Only Fields

Many of the HTML 4.0 form tags accept attributes that render the fields they produce as disabled, meaning the field is grayed out, or as read only, meaning the text appearing in the field by default cannot be changed. The `DISABLED` attribute takes care of disabling a field and can be used with the following tags:

- `<INPUT>`
- `<LABEL>`
- `<SELECT>`
- `<OPTION>`
- `<TEXTAREA>`
- `<BUTTON>`

For example, you might want to disable an option in a drop-down list if you know from other information gathered from the user that the option was inappropriate to present.

NOTE Disabled form fields are skipped over as a user tabs through the form. Also, any values assigned to a disabled field are not passed to the server when the form is submitted.

The `READONLY` attribute only works for the `<INPUT>` tag with `TYPE` set to `TEXT` or `PASSWORD` and the `<TEXTAREA>` tag, because these are the only tags that can be prepopulated with text. In these cases, the text is just presented for the user's information, not so that it can be changed.

NOTE Read only forms fields are included when tabbing through a form and values assigned to these fields are passed to the server upon form submission.

Form Field Event Handlers

The W3C has also added a number of scripting event handlers to work with many of the form tags to facilitate the execution of script code while a user fills out a form. Two of the most widely usable event handlers are `onfocus` and `onblur`. Recall that a field receives focus when you've tabbed to it or clicked it to make it active. At the moment a field receives focus, you can choose to execute a script by setting the `onfocus` attribute of the corresponding form field tag equal to the name of a script defined in the document.

▶ **See** "Using JavaScript to Create Smart HTML Forms," **p. 515**.

When you tab out of a form field that has focus, the field is said to blur. You can execute a script when a blur event occurs by setting `onblur` equal to the name of the script you want to run.

`onfocus` and `onblur` can be used with the following HTML form tags:

- <BUTTON>
- <INPUT>
- <LABEL>
- <SELECT>
- <TEXTAREA>

Additionally, the <INPUT>, <SELECT>, and <TEXTAREA> tags can take the `onselect` and `onchange` event handlers which launch scripts when the field is selected or changed, respectively.

Passing Form Data

After a user enters some form data and clicks a submit button, the browser does two things. First, it packages the form data into a single string, a process called encoding. Then it sends the encoded string to the server by either the `GET` or `POST` HTTP method. The next two sections close out the chapter by providing some details on each of these steps.

URL Encoding

When a user clicks the Submit button on a form, his browser gathers all the data and strings it together in `NAME=VALUE` pairs, each separated by an ampersand (`&`) character. This process is called encoding. It is done to package the data into one string that is sent to the server.

Consider the following HTML code:

```
<FORM ACTION="http://www.your_firm.com/cgi-bin/form.cgi" METHOD="POST">
     <INPUT TYPE="TEXT" NAME="first">
     <INPUT TYPE="TEXT" NAME="last">
     <INPUT TYPE="SUBMIT">
</FORM>
```

If a user named Joe Schmoe enters his name into the form produced by the preceding HTML code, his browser creates the following data string and sends it to the CGI script:

```
first=Joe&last=Schmoe
```

If the GET method is used instead of POST, the same string is appended to the URL of the processing script, producing the following encoded URL:

```
http://www.server.com/cgi-bin/form.cgi?first=Joe&last=Schmoe
```

A question mark (?) separates the script URL from the encoded data string.

Storing Encoded URLs

As you learned in the previous discussion of URL encoding, packaging form data into a single text string follows a few simple formatting rules. Consequently, you can fake a script into believing that it is receiving form data without using a form. To do so, you simply send the URL that would be constructed if a form were used. This approach can be useful if you frequently run a script with the same data set.

For example, suppose you frequently search the Web index Yahoo for new documents related to the scripting language JavaScript. If you are interested in checking for new documents several times a day, you could fill out the Yahoo search query each time. A more efficient way, however, is to store the query URL as a bookmark. Each time you select that item from your bookmarks, a new query generates as if you had filled out the form. The stored URL looks like the following:

http://search.yahoo.com/bin/search?p=JavaScript

Further encoding occurs with data that is more complex than a single word. Such encoding simply replaces spaces with the plus character and translates any other possibly troublesome character (control characters, the ampersand and equal sign, some punctuation, and so on) to a percent sign, followed by its hexadecimal equivalent. Thus, the following string:

```
I love HTML!
```

becomes:

```
I+love+HTML%21
```

HTTP Methods

You have two ways to read the form data submitted to a CGI script, depending on the METHOD the form used. The type of METHOD the form used—either GET or POST—is stored in an environment variable called REQUEST_METHOD and, based on that, the data should be read in one of the following ways:

- If the data is sent by the GET method, the input stream is stored in an environment variable called QUERY_STRING. As noted previously, this input stream usually is limited to only about one kilobyte of data. This is why GET is losing popularity to the more flexible POST.
- If the data is submitted by the POST method, the input string waits on the server's input device, with the available number of bytes stored in the environment variable CONTENT_LENGTH. POST accepts data of any length, up into the megabytes, although it is not very common yet for form submissions to be that large.

Creating Forms with Authoring Tools

Composing HTML forms is another one of those daunting tasks that faced early content developers. Trying to keep all of your <INPUT> tags and their NAMEs straight in your head can often get frustrating. And now that the form tags are expanding and becoming increasingly complex, it's more important than ever to have access to an authoring tool that can assist you with the task of creating a form. This section looks at the forms support you receive from Microsoft FrontPage 98, Allaire HomeSite, and Adobe PageMill.

FrontPage 98

The FrontPage Editor helps you compose forms in a couple of ways. The most obvious is the Form Toolbar which contains buttons for placing single line text fields, multiline text boxes, check boxes, radio buttons, drop-down menus, and action buttons. When you click any of these, the desired control appears on the page, along with submit and reset buttons (if you haven't started a form yet). The form is contained by a box with dashed rule, and any other controls you place in the box are part of that form (see Figure 8.7).

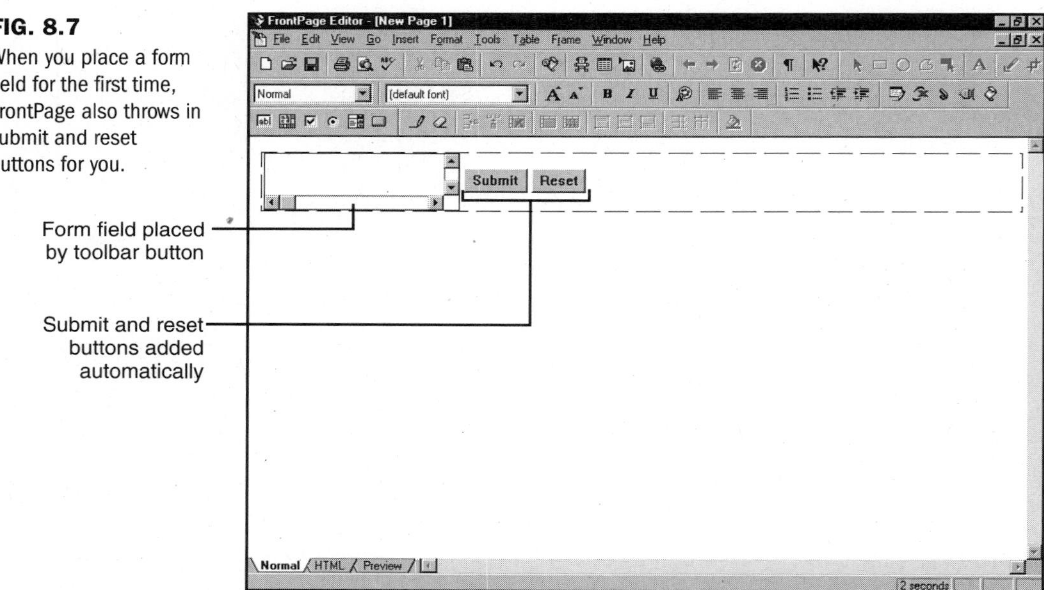

FIG. 8.7
When you place a form field for the first time, FrontPage also throws in submit and reset buttons for you.

After you have at least one form field on a page, you can access some different properties menus to specify the field's details. In particular, right-clicking a form control and then selecting Form Field Properties opens a properties dialog box for that control where you can type in the values for the attributes in the tag that creates the control. Additionally, you can choose Form Properties to specify attributes of the <FORM> tag, or you can choose Form Field Validation to set up some script code behind the form to do basic error checking on the user's input (see Figure 8.8).

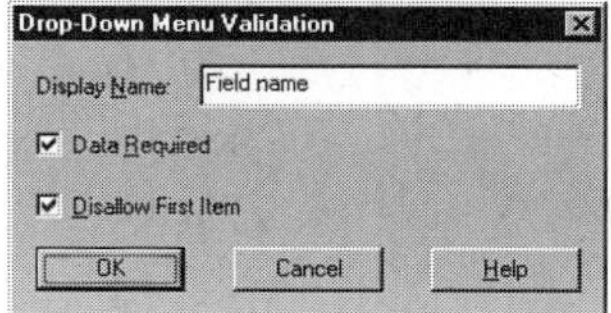

FIG. 8.8
The Drop-Down Menu Validation dialog box lets you require that data be selected and that the first item in the list be disallowed.

The other way FrontPage can assist you with form composition is through the Insert, Form Field option. Choosing this option reveals a pop-up list of available form fields, including a few that aren't on the Forms Toolbar like Image and Label. After you select a field, FrontPage places the field on the page and you can modify its properties in the same way you would for a field placed by using the toolbar.

Allaire HomeSite

Like FrontPage, Allaire's HomeSite also has a Forms toolbar with buttons that place most popular form controls. The Form button lives at the left end of the toolbar and is used to set up the `<FORM>` and `</FORM>` tags for the form. As the dialog box in Figure 8.9 shows, you can set up the form's `ACTION`, `METHOD`, `ENCTYPE`, and `TARGET` attributes all in one shot.

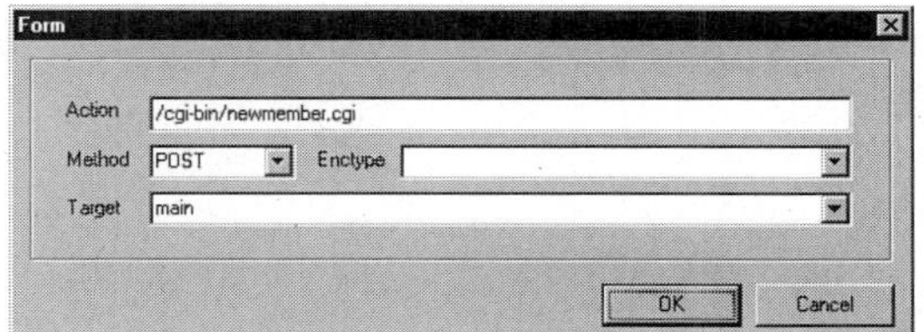

FIG. 8.9
The Form button should be the first one you click when setting up a form with HomeSite.

The other buttons in the toolbar call up a dialog box with appropriate fields that allow you to specify the attributes of the tag you're setting up. Figure 8.10 shows the dialog box you get when placing a multiline text window. Note how the dialog box has fields corresponding to the `NAME`, `ROWS`, and `COLS` attributes of the `<TEXTAREA>` tag.

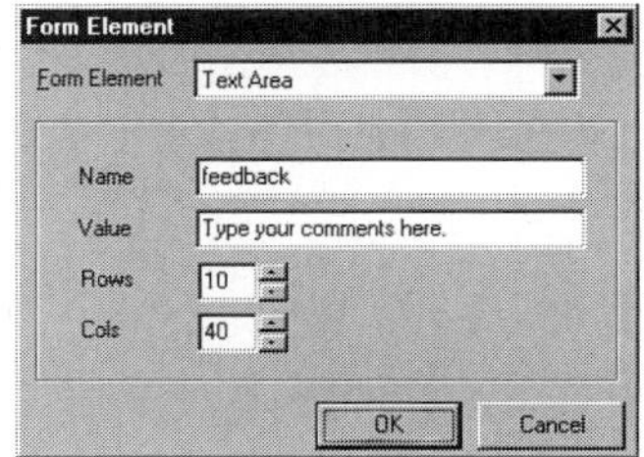

FIG. 8.10
Buttons on the Forms toolbar are context sensitive and present you with dialog boxes appropriate to the tag you're setting up.

NOTE HomeSite's Forms toolbar does not include a button for password fields.

Adobe PageMill

Like the preceding products, forms are easily created in PageMill with the toolbar buttons shown in Figure 8.11.

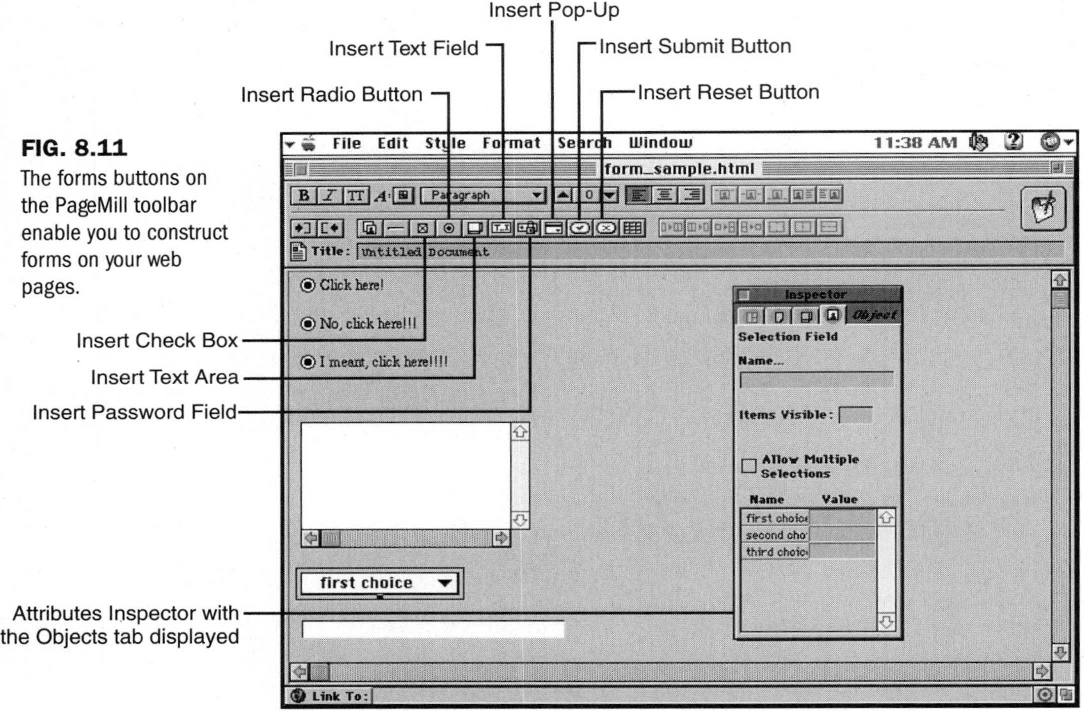

FIG. 8.11
The forms buttons on the PageMill toolbar enable you to construct forms on your web pages.

Creating forms is simple. Click any of the toolbar buttons in Figure 8.11 to create a form element. For check boxes and radio buttons, enter the accompanying text by clicking to the right of the elements. Elements like text areas, buttons, and pop-up menus can be selected and resized.

You can edit your form elements using the PageMill Attributes Inspector. As described in previous chapters, the Attributes Inspector is a utility that allows you to specify the attributes for objects (like tables, graphics, and forms), as well as frames, pages, and so on. Each attribute set is arranged on a different tab. To access the Inspector, select Show Attributes Inspector from the Window menu. The Object tab is one of the four major tabs available in the Attributes Inspector. The versatility of the Inspector becomes apparent when using forms. Select a form while the Inspector is active and you'll see the form's attributes displayed in the Object tab, as shown in Figure 8.11. Notice that the attributes change as you click different form elements. As these different elements have different attributes, you can modify them individually with the Inspector. ●

CHAPTER 9

Style Sheets

by Eric Ladd

In this chapter

What Are Style Sheets?

There are two competing forces in web page authoring: content and presentation. When HTML was first released, the tags were largely focused on content and descriptively defined the various parts of a document: a heading, a paragraph, a list, and so on. Over time, instructions were added to help with presentation issues at the font level. These instructions included tags for boldface, italics, and typewriter styles.

Then, as graphical browsers became standard equipment, there was a greatly increased focus on presentation. In particular, Netscape began introducing proprietary extensions to HTML that only its browser could render properly. These extensions generally produced attractive effects on pages and users began using Netscape en masse. Not to be left out, Microsoft began producing its own browser—Internet Explorer—and with it, its own proprietary HTML extensions. Content authors, who could only watch the new tags emerge, were frequently left confused and frustrated because it was hard to tell which browser to write for and how long it would be before the next new set of bells and whistles became available.

As designers push for more control over page attributes, such as indentation and line spacing, the evolution of HTML stands at a fork in the road. One path leads to the continued introduction of proprietary tags by the people making the browsers—a path that will lead HTML into even muddier waters. The other path leads to an explicit separation of content and presentation by introducing HTML style sheets—documents that provide specifications for how content should look on screen. By separating these two otherwise competing forces, HTML is free to evolve as a language that describes document content, and will be less susceptible to seemingly endless extensions by browser software companies.

The W3C's first stab at separating content and presentation was the Cascading Style Sheets, level 1 (CSS1) specification—a formal statement on how to specify style information. A W3C working group has just released the Cascading Style Sheets, level 2 (CSS2) specification. After a period of public review, it is likely that HTML 4.0 and CSS2 will provide the separation of content and design that the web community has come to need. This chapter reviews the HTML elements and the CSS1 and CSS2 rules you'll need to know to implement style sheets on your pages.

NOTE CCS2 builds on the CCS1 recommendation by adding features that enable authors to implement style sheets across different browsers (for example, speech-based browsers for the visually impaired) and to more easily maintain their style sheets. Additionally, CSS2 includes enhancements that will allow style information to be transmitted more rapidly over a network. For more information on the CSS2 proposal, point your browser to **http://www.w3.org/TR/WD-CSS2/cover.html**.

Before looking at the different ways to build style information into your pages, it is helpful to review some of the basics behind the concept of a style sheet.

Style sheets are collections of style information that are applied to plain text. Style information includes font attributes such as type size, special effects (bold, italics, underline), color, and alignment. Style sheets also provide broader formatting instructions by specifying values for quantities such as line spacing and left and right margins.

Style sheets are not really a new concept; word processing programs such as Microsoft Word have been making use of user-defined style for a number of years. Figure 9.1 shows a Word style definition in the Style dialog box. Notice how the style accounts for many of the presentation attributes mentioned previously.

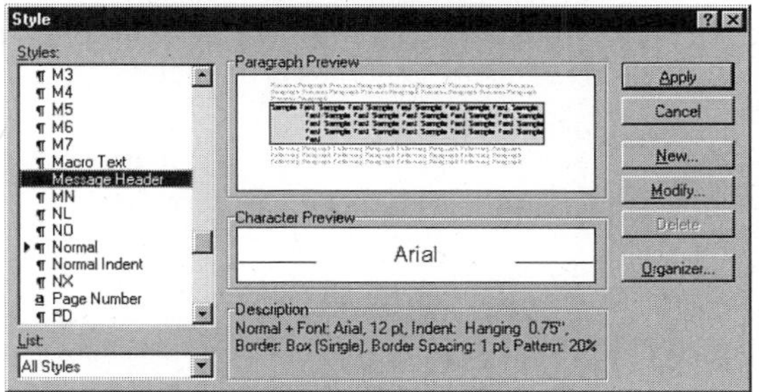

FIG. 9.1
Word processors enable users to store content presentation attributes together as a style.

Why Style Sheets Are Valuable

Simply put, style sheets separate content and presentation. Apart from freeing up HTML to develop as a content description language, it gives Web page designers precise control over how their content appears onscreen. Other benefits of style sheets include:

- **Central repositories of style information**—If you use a standard set of styles on all of your pages, you can store the corresponding style information in one file. This way, if you have to edit the style information, you just have to make the change in one place instead of in every file.
- **Little-to-no new HTML to learn**—With style information being stored in style sheets, there should be virtually no need for the introduction of new HTML tags for the purposes of formatting. This promises to reduce the confusion that often arises out of browser-specific extensions to HTML.
- **Consistent rendering of content**—Browsers vary slightly in how they render content, especially the logical text styles (emphasized text (`<EM>`), keyboard input (`<KBD>`), and so on). By assigning specific style information to logical style tags, web page authors can be assured that their content will look exactly the same on every browser.

Different Approaches to Style Sheets

The W3C is advocating the "Cascading Style Sheet" proposal for implementing style sheets. Cascading refers to the fact that there is a certain set of rules that browsers use, in cascading order, to determine how to use the style information. Such a set of rules is useful in the event of conflicting style information because the rules would give the browser a way to determine which style is given precedence.

Even though the style sheet specification is still under public review, many browsers (including Netscape Navigator 4.0 and Microsoft Internet Explorer 4.0) already support different ways of including style information in a document. The different approaches include:

- **Linked styles**—Style information is read from a separate file that is specified in the `<LINK>` tag.
- **Embedded styles**—Style information is defined in the document head using the `<STYLE>` and `</STYLE>` tags.
- **Inline styles**—Style information is placed inside an HTML tag and applies to all content between that tag and its companion closing tag. For example, you can left-indent an entire paragraph one half-inch by using the `<P STYLE="margin-left: .5 in">` tag to start the paragraph. If the content to which you want to apply style information isn't conveniently grouped by a set of container tags, you can also use the `<SPAN>` and `</SPAN>` tags to do the same job.

Linking to Style Information in a Separate File

One important thing to realize is that you don't have to store your style sheet information inside each of your HTML documents. In fact, if you anticipate applying the same styles across several HTML pages, it is much more efficient for you to store the style information in one place and have each HTML document linked to it. This makes it much easier to change the formatting of all your pages by changing the style sheet instead of changing every page.

Setting Up the Style Information

To set up a linked style sheet, you first need to create the file with the style information. This takes the form of a plain-text file with style information entries. Each entry starts with an HTML tag, followed by a list of presentation attributes to associate with the rendering of the effect of that tag. Some sample lines in a style sheet file might look like:

```
BODY {font: 12 pt Helvetica; color: blue; margin-left: 0.5in}
H1 {font 18 pt Palatino; color: red}
H2 {font 16 pt Palatino; color: AA4D60}
```

The first line sets the body text to 12 points Helvetica type rendered in blue with a one-half inch left margin. The second line redefines the level 1 heading to 18 point Palatino type rendered in red, and the third line sets the level 2 heading to 16 point Palatino type, rendered in the mauve color represented by the hexadecimal triplet `AA4D60`.

NOTE When setting colors in your style sheet file, you can use one of the sixteen English-language color names, or an RGB hexadecimal triplet, to describe the color.

Remember that the syntax for specifying a characteristic has the form

```
{characteristic: value}
```

Multiple characteristic/value pairs should be separated by semicolons. For example:

```
P {font: 10 pt Arial; line-height: 12 pt; color: silver; text-indent: .50 in}
```

CAUTION

There is a great temptation, when you first start to work with style sheets to use the syntax `characteristic=value`. Make sure you use the `{characteristic: value}` syntax previously noted.

The cascading style sheet specification lets you specify more than fonts, typefaces, and colors. Table 9.1 lists the different font and block level style attributes you can assign to a file containing style information.

Table 9.1 Font and block level characteristics permitted in style sheets.

Characteristic	Possible Values
font-family	Any typeface available to the browser through Windows (the default font is used if one of the specified fonts is not available).
font-size	Any size in points (pt), inches (in), centimeters (cm), or pixels (px); larger or smaller (relative-size values); xx-small, x-small, small, medium, large, x-large, xx-large (absolute-size values); or a percentage relative to the parent font's size.
font-weight	Normal, bold; bolder, lighter (relative weights).
font-style	Normal, italic, oblique.
font-variant	Normal, small-caps.
color	Any RGB hexadecimal triplet or HTML 4.0 English-language color name.
background-attachment	(Whether the background image stays fixed or scrolls with the content) scroll, fixed.
background-color	Transparent; any RGB hexadecimal triplet or HTML 4.0 English-language color name.
background-image	None; URL of image file.
background-repeat	Repeat-x (tile background image only in the horizontal direction), repeat-y (tile only in the vertical direction), repeat (tile in both directions), no-repeat (no tiling).
border-color	Any RGB hexadecimal triplet or HTML 4.0 English-language color name.
border-style	None, dashed, dotted, solid, double, groove, ridge, inset, outset.
border-bottom-width	Thin, medium, thick; any number of points (pt), inches (in), centimeters (cm), or pixels (px).

continues

Table 9.1 Continued

Characteristic	Possible Values
border-left-width	Thin, medium, thick; any number of points (pt), inches (in), centimeters (cm), or pixels (px).
border-right-width	Thin, medium, thick; any number of points (pt), inches (in), centimeters (cm), or pixels (px).
border-top-width	Thin, medium, thick; any number of points (pt), inches (in), centimeters (cm), or pixels (px).
float	Left, right, none; floats positioned content in left or right margin.
padding-bottom	Any number of points (pt), inches (in), centimeters (cm), or pixels (px); or a percentage of the parent element's width.
padding-left	Any number of points (pt), inches (in), centimeters (cm), or pixels (px); or a percentage of the parent element's width.
padding-right	Any number of points (pt), inches (in), centimeters (cm), or pixels (px); or a percentage of the parent element's width.
padding-top	Any number of points (pt), inches (in), centimeters (cm), or pixels (px); or a percentage of the parent element's width.
text-align	left, center, right, justify.
text-decoration	None, underline, overline, line-through, blink.
text-indent	Any number of points (pt), inches (in), centimeters (cm), or pixels (px); or a percentage relative to the indentation of the parent element.
text-transform	Capitalize, uppercase, lowercase, none.
line-height	Normal; any number of points (pt), inches (in), centimeters (cm), or pixels (px); or a percentage of the font size.
letter-spacing	Normal; any number of points (pt), inches (in), centimeters (cm), or pixels (px).
word-spacing	Normal; any number of points (pt), inches (in), centimeters (cm), or pixels (px).
margin-left	Auto; any number of points (pt), inches (in), centimeters (cm), or pixels (px); or a percentage of the parent element's width.
margin-right	Auto; any number of points (pt), inches (in), centimeters (cm), or pixels (px); or a percentage of the parent element's width.

Characteristic	Possible Values
margin-top	Auto; any number of points (pt), inches (in), centimeters (cm), or pixels (px); or a percentage of the parent element's width.
margin-bottom	Auto; any number of points (pt), inches (in), centimeters (cm), or pixels (px); or a percentage of the parent element's width.
vertical-align	Baseline, sub, super, top, text-top, middle, bottom, text-bottom; or a percentage of the current line-height.

NOTE Line-height in Table 9.1 refers to the leading or space between lines that the browser uses. Padding refers to the amount of space left around an element.

You can see from the table that you get control over a large number of presentation characteristics—certainly more than you get with HTML tags alone. In addition to the font and block level properties noted in Table 9.1, CSS2 includes characteristics that give you control over how your content is positioned on the browser screen. The content positioning characteristics, summarized in Table 9.2, enable you to precisely place any portion of your content exactly where you want it, even overlapping other content in some cases.

Table 9.2 Content positioning characteristics permitted in style sheets.

Characteristic	Purpose and Possible Values
position	Specifies how content is to be positioned; possible values are static (content cannot be positioned or repositioned), absolute (content is positioned with respect to the upper-left corner of the browser window), and relative (content is positioned with respect to its natural position in the document).
top	Specifies the vertical displacement of the positioned content; values can be in points (pt), pixels (px), centimeters (cm), or inches (in) and can have negative values (negative value moves content above its reference point on the screen).
left	Specifies the horizontal displacement of positioned content; values can be in points (pt), pixels (px), centimeters (cm), or inches (in) and can have negative values (negative value moves content to the left of its reference point on the screen).
clip:rect(x1,y1,x2,y2)	Defines the size of the clipping region (rectangular area in which the positioned content appears); (x1,y1) are the coordinates of the upper left corner of the rectangle and (x2,y2) are the coordinates of the lower right corner.

continues

Table 9.2 Continued

Characteristic	Purpose and Possible Values
overflow	Tells the browser how to handle positioned content that overflows the space allocated for it; possible values are visible, hidden, auto, and scroll.
visibility	Enables the document author to selectively display or conceal positioned content; possible values are show or hide.
z-index	Permits stacking of positioned content in the browser screen so that content overlaps; z-index is set to an integer value of 0 or higher (content with a smaller z-index will be positioned below content with higher z-index values).

Both Netscape and Microsoft have bundled their support for content positioning as part of the "dynamic HTML" capabilities of the fourth releases of each of their browsers. Although both browsers support content positioning by means of cascading style sheets, Netscape initially tried to implement positioned content through the proprietary `<LAYER>` tag. Currently, Navigator 4.0 supports both the CSS and the `<LAYER>` tag approaches.

NOTE Content positioning is discussed in detail in Chapter 23, "Introduction to Dynamic HTML," Chapter 24, "Advanced Netscape Dynamic HTML and Examples," and Chapter 25, "Advanced Microsoft Dynamic HTML and Examples."

Using the *<LINK>* Tag

Once you create your style sheet file, save it with a .css extension and place it on your server. Then you can reference it by using the `<LINK>` tag in the head of each of your HTML documents, as follows:

```
<HEAD>
<TITLE>A Document that Uses Style Sheets</TITLE>
<LINK REL=STYLESHEET HREF="styles/sitestyles.css">
</HEAD>
```

The `REL` attribute describes the relationship of the linked file to the current file, namely that the linked file is a style sheet. `HREF` specifies the URL of the style sheet file.

CAUTION

Style sheet files are of MIME type text/css, though not all servers and browsers register this automatically. If you set up a site that uses style sheets, be sure to configure your server to handle the MIME type text/css.

Embedded Style Information

Figure 9.2 shows the W3C's style sheet page, which makes use of an embedded style sheet. The style information is stored in the document head, as shown in the excerpt of HTML source code in Listing 9.1. The structure of the style information takes the same form that you saw for setting up style information in a separate file: an HTML tag name, followed by curly braces containing the style characteristics. For example, regular text in the document body is rendered in Verdana and colored according to the RGB triplet `#000` (shorthand for `#000000`), whereas text marked up with the <H1> tag is rendered with a negative 6% margin and painted with the RGB color `#900` (a dark red color).

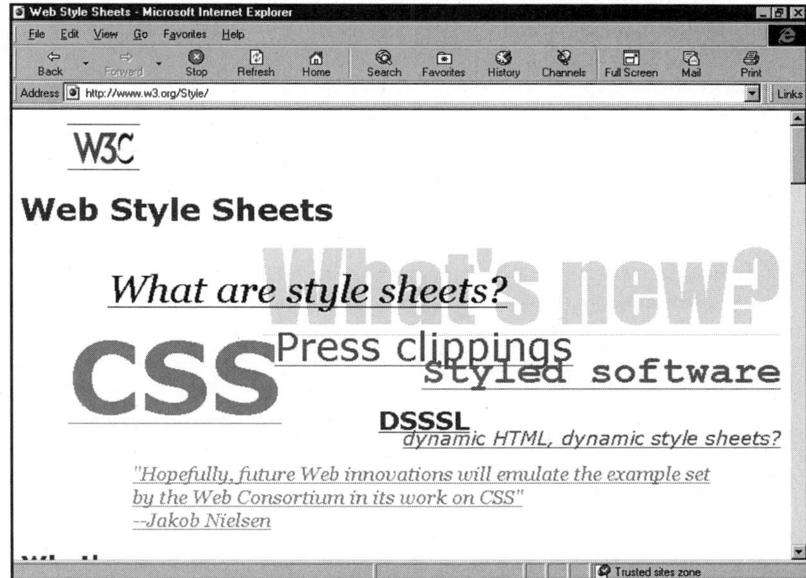

FIG. 9.2
The W3C's style sheet page makes use of a style sheet to show how to overlap text.

Listing 9.1 Embedded style information in the W3C's style sheet page.

```
<STYLE TYPE="text/css">
<!--
BODY {
  color: #000;
  background: #FFF;
  margin-left: 7%;
  font-family: verdana, helvetica, sans-serif;
}
H1, H2 {
  margin-left: -6%;
  color: #900;
```

continues

Listing 9.1 Continued

```
}
H3 {
  color: #900;
}
A:link { color: #900 }
A:visited, A:active { color: #009 }
.hide {
  display: none;
  color: white;
}
SPAN.date { font-size: 0.8em }
SPAN.attribution {
  font-weight: bold
}
BLOCKQUOTE {
  margin-left: 4em;
  margin-right: 4em;
  margin-top: 10pt;
  margin-bottom: 10pt;
  font-style: italic;
}

ADDRESS {
  text-align: right;
  font-weight: bold;
  font-style: italic
}
...
-->
</STYLE>
```

Using the *<STYLE>* Tag

As you can see in Listing 9.1, embedded style information is placed between the `<STYLE>` and `</STYLE>` tags. When the W3C released HTML 3.2, it reserved the use of these tags specifically for the purpose of embedded style information. The HTML 4.0 spec now formalized the use of the `<STYLE>` tag.

The `TYPE` attribute tells a browser what type of style information setup is used and is most often set equal to `text/css`. Specifying other types allows for some flexibility in the implementation of other style information specification schemes in the future. This also makes it easier for browsers that do not support style sheets to ignore the style information between the two tags.

Style information of the MIME type text/css is set up the same way that style information is set up in a linked style sheet file. The first entry on each line is the keyword from an HTML tag, followed by a list of characteristic/value pairs enclosed in curly braces. You can use any of the characteristics shown in Tables 9.1 or 9.2 when specifying your embedded style information.

Note that the style information you see in Listing 9.1 is enclosed in comment tags (<!-- and -->) so that browsers that do not understand style sheets will ignore the style information, rather than presenting it onscreen.

TIP Style information that is specified in the head of a document by using the <STYLE> tag will only apply for that document. If you want to use the same styles in another document, you need to embed the style information in the head of that document as well.

Only use embedded style information for page-specific styles. If you have more global style elements you want to implement, place them in a file and link the file as a style sheet in all of your documents. Centralizing as much style information as possible is the best way to ensure a consistent implementation.

Inline Style Information

You can specify inline styles inside an HTML tag. The style information given applies to the document content up until the defining tag's companion closing tag is encountered. Thus, with the following HTML

```
<P STYLE="text-align: center; color: yellow">
Yellow, centered text
</P>
<P>
Back to normal
</P>
```

the text `Yellow, centered text` will appear centered on the page and colored yellow. This style applies up until the </P> tag, at which point the browser reverts back to whatever style it was using before the inline style (see Figure 9.3).

NOTE Depending on which browser you use to render a piece of code containing style information, you may or may not see the desired effect because not all browsers support the CSS instructions. Internet Explorer 3.01 or higher and Netscape Navigator 4.0 both support CSS style instructions.

CAUTION

Don't forget the closing tag when embedding style information in an HTML tag. Otherwise, the effects of the style may extend beyond the point in the document where you wanted them to stop.

4. Squats (legs)
5. Curls (biceps)

TIP Using inline styles is fine for changes to small sections of your document. However, you should consider using a linked style sheet or the <STYLE> tag if your styles are to be more global.

Using Multiple Approaches

You aren't limited to using just one of the described style sheet approaches. You can use all three simultaneously if needed. One case in which you may want to do this is on a corporate site where you have the following:

- **Global styles**—Certain styles used on every page are best stored in a single style sheet file and linked to each page with the <LINK> tag. This might apply to styles mandated as a corporate standards such as the use of a plain white background and a single typeface.
- **Sub-section styles**—Large corporate sites typically have many subdivisions, each with its own look and feel. You can store styles to support a subdivision's look between the <STYLE> and </STYLE> tags in the head of each document in the subdivision. The

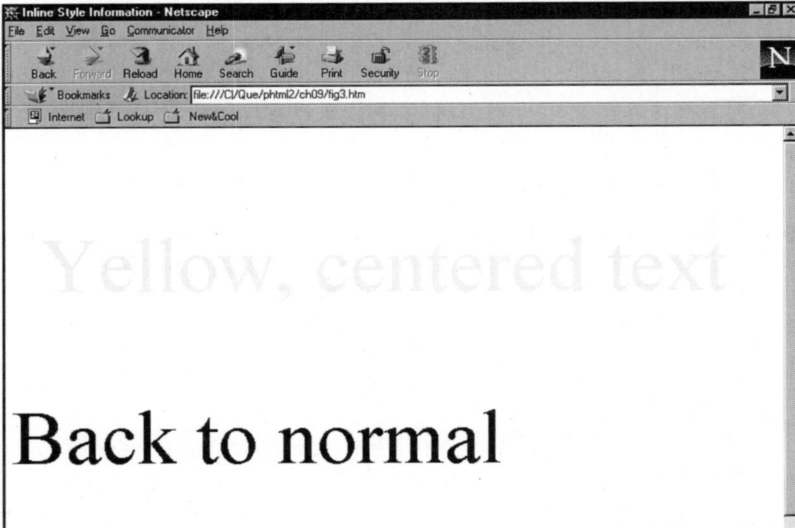

FIG. 9.3
Many HTML tags now accept a STYLE attribute that specifies style information to apply along with the effect of the tag.

subdivisions might represent different business units within the corporation, or it can just be a set of related documents such as product specs or white papers.

- **Page-specific styles**—If you need to make a small deviation from your chosen global or subsection styles, you can use an inline style to make the change where you want it. You might use a page-specific style if a page in one of your subdivisions has particular presentation requirements. For example, a key passage in a white paper might be highlighted by rendering it in bold and in color.

However, you shouldn't use all three approaches in the same document just for the sake of doing it. You should seek to optimize your use of style sheets by choosing the approach, or combination of approaches, that enables you to apply the styles you want, where you want them, without a lot of unnecessary code.

Remember style precedence when using multiple approaches . Recall that the idea behind a cascading style sheet is that there is a set of rules that browsers apply, in cascading order, to determine which style information takes precedence. You need to be aware of these rules so that you do not produce unintended style effects on your pages. In general, you'll be fine if you remember the following:

- Inline styles override both linked style sheets and style information stored in the document head with the `<STYLE>` tag.
- Styles defined in the document head override linked style sheets.
- Linked style sheets override browser defaults.

Keeping these rules in mind will make troubleshooting your style sheet setup much easier.

Tips for Style Sheet Users

Even though style sheets are relatively new, web authors are already coming up with some good rules of thumb for implementing them. The next few sections share some of these helpful hints.

Harnessing Inheritance

Inheritance refers to the fact that HTML documents are essentially set up as hierarchies, and that styles applied at one level of the hierarchy necessarily apply to all subordinate levels as well. This means that if you assign style information inside of a `<UL>` tag, the information also applies to all of the items in the unordered list because the `<LI>` tags are subordinate to the `<UL>` tag.

If you're not using embedded style information, you can make broader use of inheritance by setting up as much common style information in the `<BODY>` tag as you can. Because every tag between `<BODY>` and `</BODY>` is subordinate to the `<BODY>` tag, these tags will inherit the style information you specify in the `<BODY>` tag, and you should be spared from having to repeat it throughout the rest of the document.

Grouping Style Information

If you want to assign the same style characteristics to a number of tags, you can do so in just one line, rather than using a separate line for each tag. For example, if you want all three kinds of links—unvisited, visited, and active—to be rendered in the same style, you can list them all individually

```
A:link {font-size: 12 pt; font-weight: bold; font-decoration: underline}
A:visited {font-size: 12 pt; font-weight: bold; font-decoration: underline}
A:active {font-size: 12 pt; font-weight: bold; font-decoration: underline}
```

or you can define them all at once

```
A:link A:visited A:active {font-size: 12 pt; font-weight: bold;
font-decoration: underline}
```

Either set of code will make all hypertext links appear in 12-point type that is bold and underlined.

You can also group style information applied to just one tag. For example, if you redefined your level 2 headings as

```
H2 {font-size: 16 pt; line-height: 18 pt; font-family: "Helvetica";
font-weight: bold}
```

you can express the same thing as

```
H2 {font: 16pt/18pt bold "Helvetica"}
```

and save yourself a bit of typing.

Creating Tag Classes

The proposed style sheet specifications allow you to subdivide a tag into named classes and to specify different style information for each class. For example, if you want three different colors of unvisited links, you can set them up as

```
A:link.red {color: red}
A:link.yellow {color: yellow}
A:link.fuschia {color: fuschia}
```

The period and color name that follow each `A:link` sets up a class of the `A:link` tag. The class name is whatever follows the period. You use the class names in the `<A>` tag to specify which type of unvisited link you want to create, as follows:

```
Here's a <A CLASS="red" HREF="red.html">red</A> link!
And a <A CLASS="yellow" HREF="yellow.html">yellow</A> one ...
And a <A CLASS="fuschia" HREF="fuschia.html">fuschia</A> one!
```

If you use multiple style sheet approaches, make sure you define the same set of classes in all of them so that the same set of class names is available to the browser in each case.

Using the *ID* Attribute

You can also set up your own style names, if setting up a named class of an HTML tag doesn't suit your needs. For example, you can say:

```
<STYLE TYPE="text/css">
<!--
...
#style1 { font-size: 16 pt; text-decoration: underline }
#style2 { font-size: 20 pt; text-decoration: blink}
...
-->
</STYLK>
```

and then reference these styles using an `ID` attribute in a tag that can take the `STYLE` attribute, for example,

```
<BODY ID="style1" ...>
...
<P ID="style2">
Here is a paragraph done in style2 ...
</P>
...
</BODY>
```

In this code excerpt, all of the body text will be rendered in underlined, 16-point type as defined by the style1 identifier, and text in the paragraph that starts `Here is a paragraph done in style2 ...` will be 20-points high and blinking as specified by the style2 identifier .

NOTE Named identifiers have to start with the pound sign (#) when you define them in the style information section of your document. When you reference an identifier with the `ID` attribute, the pound sign isn't necessary.

Style Sheet Software Tools

Even though web style sheets are still fairly new, a number of document authoring software packages are rising to the occasion and providing support for including style information in your documents. Microsoft showed leadership in implementing the Cascading Style Sheet specification in Internet Explorer 3, so it should be no surprise that its web development tool, FrontPage, is leading the way in providing style sheet support for document authors.

Microsoft FrontPage

To use FrontPage's style sheet functions, you need to work in the FrontPage Editor—the FrontPage component used to create web documents.

In the FrontPage Editor, choosing Format, Stylesheet will reveal the Format Stylesheet dialog box you see in Figure 9.5. As you see in the figure, FrontPage assumes you're embedding your style information in the document head when you choose this option, as evidenced by the `<STYLE>` and `</STYLE>` tags you see in the dialog box.

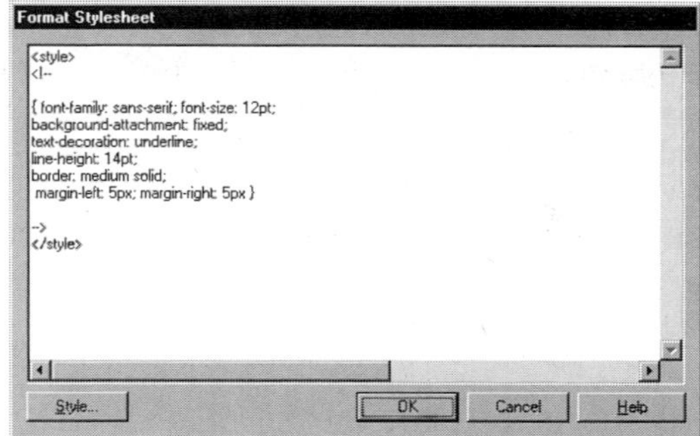

FIG. 9.5
The FrontPage Editor enables you to create embedded style specifications.

You can type the style information you want to apply directly into the dialog box, or you can click the Style button near the bottom left to open up the Style dialog box into which you can enter the information. Figure 9.6 shows you the Alignment tab of this dialog box, which enables you to specify values for margins, padding, and floating properties. Other tabs include:

- **Borders**—For specifying type, color and width of borders.
- **Font**—For choosing a type family and size.
- **Color**—For choosing a background color, a foreground color, or a background image (including how to tile the image).
- **Text**—For choosing text style, weight, and decoration, line height, letter spacing, and alignment properties.

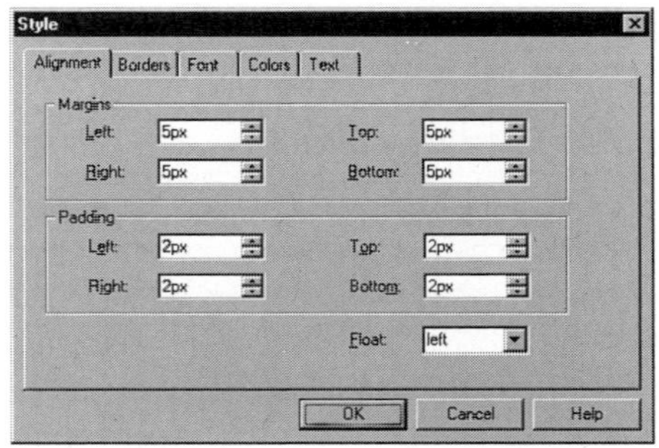

FIG. 9.6
If you can't remember all of those style characteristics, don't worry! FrontPage has them all stored in the Style dialog box.

After you finish setting up the style information, click the OK button to apply the styles. Depending on what characteristics you've specified, you may not see any effect on the FrontPage Editor's Normal tab. To make sure that your style information was properly built into the source code of the document, click the HTML tab to look at the raw code. You should see your style information contained in the document head.

FrontPage can also help you if you want to place style information in a separate file or if you want to use inline styles. If you need to create a separate style sheet file, you can still use the dialog boxes you see in Figures 9.5 and 9.6 to set up the style information. Then, after the style specifications are written into the document, you can copy and paste them to a blank document and then save the document as a text file with a .css extension.

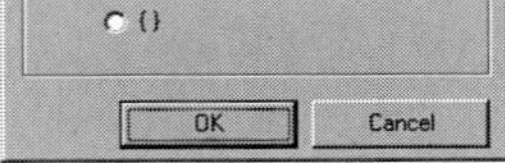

can place defined style information.

While you compose the page on the Normal tab, the code to produce the page is being generated on the HTML tab (see Figure 10.3). Authors who prefer to work with raw code can jump to this tab at any time to make quick edits as needed.

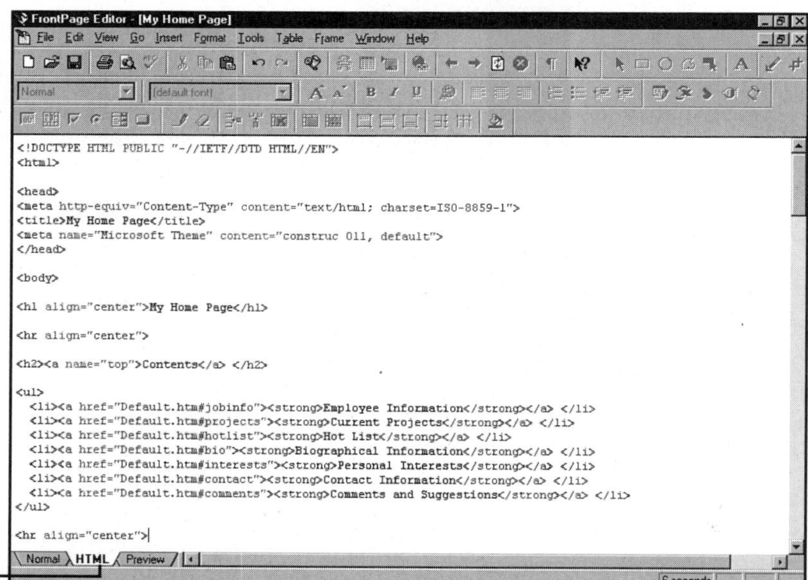

FIG. 10.3
FrontPage also lets you work with raw HTML code, though there is not much support for placing tags into the code other than typing them by hand.

Because it's important to test your work by looking at it in a browser, the FrontPage Editor also comes with a Preview tab that gives you an idea of how a page will look to an end user. Figure 10.4 shows you a preview of the WYSIWYG page you saw in Figure 10.2.

TIP Even if you look at your pages from the Preview tab, it's still a good idea to look at them in a full-fledged browser program, too.

On the server side of FrontPage, there needs to be support in place for FrontPage's many interactions with the web server. The FrontPage Explorer can read a web site (or *web*, in FrontPage lingo) right off a server and can publish a web you're working on back to a server. Additionally, automated functions such as FrontPage Components, page transitions, and hover buttons need to be processed by the server. It's easy to understand how you get the client side components of FrontPage in place—you just install them on your hard drive—but it's probably less clear as to how you get FrontPage's server-side component's installed.

If you use Microsoft's Internet Information Server (IIS) 3.0 or above, you're in luck because FrontPage's server-side components are already built into IIS. When you direct your client-side components to work with an IIS server, the integration between the two is seamless.

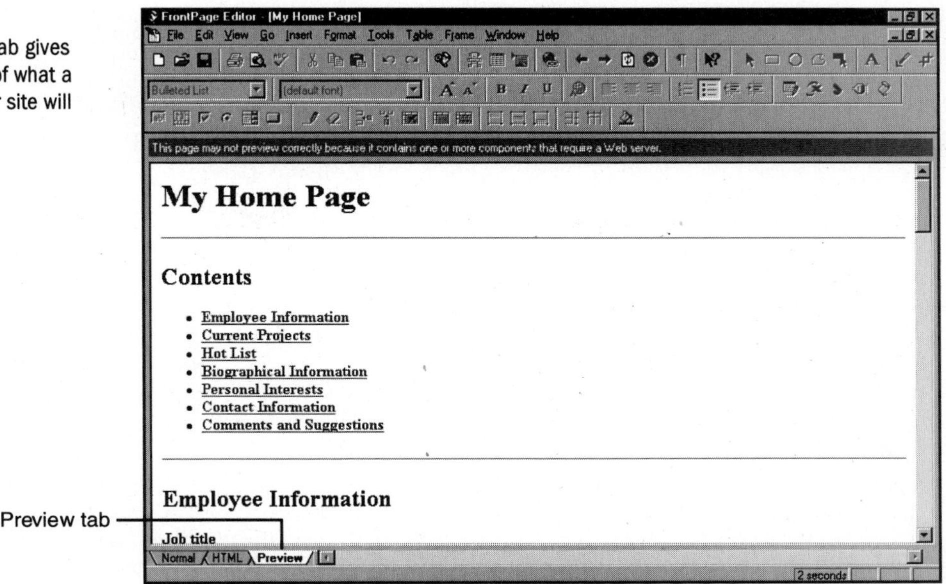

FIG. 10.4 The Preview tab gives you an idea of what a visitor to your site will see.

If you use any other server software, you have to compensate by installing the FrontPage Server Extensions on your server. The Extensions enable a non-IIS server to:

- Understand the code that the FrontPage Editor places into an HTML file when placing an automated function on a page.
- Act on that code by substituting an HTML tag, launching a program, downloading an applet, or whatever action is appropriate.

Microsoft has made FrontPage Server Extensions available for a wide variety of server platforms. Table 10.1 gives you the details on which servers have FrontPage Server Extensions available. After the Extensions are installed, FrontPage's client-side components will work seamlessly with your server.

Table 10.1 FrontPage server extensions.

Operating System	Web Servers
Solaris 2.4, 2.5	NCSA 1.5.2; CERN 3.0; Apache 1.0.5, 1.1.1, and 1.1.3; Netscape Commerce Server 1.12; Netscape Communications Server 1.12; Netscape Enterprise 2.0; Netscape FastTrack 2.0
SunOS 4.1.3, 4.1.4	NCSA 1.5.2; CERN 3.0; Apache 1.0.5, 1.1.1, and 1.1.3; Netscape Commerce Server 1.12; Netscape Communications Server 1.12; Netscape Enterprise 2.0; Netscape FastTrack 2.0

continues

Table 10.1 Continued

Operating System	Web Servers
IRIX 5.3, 6.2	NCSA 1.5.2; CERN 3.0; Apache 1.0.5, 1.1.1, and 1.1.3; Netscape Commerce Server 1.12; Netscape Communications Server 1.12; Netscape Enterprise 2.0; Netscape FastTrack 2.0
HP/UX 9.03, 10.01	NCSA 1.5.2; CERN 3.0; Apache 1.0.5, 1.1.1, and 1.1.3; Netscape Commerce Server 1.12; Netscape Communications Server 1.12; Netscape Enterprise 2.0; Netscape FastTrack 2.0
BSD/OS 2.1	NCSA 1.5.2; CERN 3.0; Apache 1.0.5, 1.1.1, and 1.1.3; Netscape Commerce Server 1.12; Netscape Communications Server 1.12; Netscape Enterprise 2.0; Netscape FastTrack 2.0
Digital UNIX 3.2c, 4.0	NCSA 1.5.2; CERN 3.0; Apache 1.0.5, 1.1.1, and 1.1.3; Netscape Commerce Server 1.12; Netscape Communications Server 1.12; Netscape Enterprise 2.0; Netscape FastTrack 2.0
Linux 3.0.3	NCSA 1.5.2; CERN 3.0; Apache 1.0.5, 1.1.1, and 1.1.3; Netscape Commerce Server 1.12; Netscape Communications Server 1.12; Netscape Enterprise 2.0; Netscape FastTrack 2.0
AIX 3.2.5, 4.x	NCSA 1.5.2; CERN 3.0; Apache 1.0.5, 1.1.1, and 1.1.3; Netscape Commerce Server 1.12; Netscape Communications Server 1.12; Netscape Enterprise 2.0; Netscape FastTrack 2.0
Windows 95	Microsoft Personal Web Server, FrontPage Personal Web Server, O'Reilly and Associates WebSite, Netscape FastTrack 2.0
Windows NT, Intel x86	Internet Information Server 2.0, 3.0; O'Reilly and Associates WebSite; Netscape Commerce Server 1.12; Netscape Communications Server 1.12; Netscape Enterprise 2.0; Netscape FastTrack 2.0; FrontPage Personal Web Server
Alpha NT Server 4.0	Internet Information Server 2.0, 3.0; Microsoft Peer Web Services

When you install the FrontPage Server Extensions, you are placing several different executable files on your server so that the FrontPage Editor can build calls to these executables into the HTML code it writes. This is the mechanism by which FrontPage supports the FrontPage components you'll read about next.

CAUTION

Because the FrontPage Server Extension files are installed below the root directory of your HTTP server, you leave your server vulnerable to attack by hackers who can try to run one of the executables in an attempt to overwrite content on your server.

What Are FrontPage Components?

FrontPage Components are objects you place on a Web page that represent a piece of programming. You can drop a FrontPage Component anywhere you want on a page using the FrontPage Editor. It is up to the server to identify and interpret the Component as it serves an HTML file containing a Component. How the server handles the Component varies with what the Component is supposed to do. For example, a server may invoke the programming represented by the Component when

- The file is published to the server
- The file is served to a browser
- The user performs a certain action

The main thing is that the user never detects that you didn't have to do any programming to put program-like functionality on your web pages. All you have to do is drop the Component on the page and let the server handle the rest.

FrontPage Components come in many flavors. Some are specific to certain types of HTML constructs such as forms or imagemaps. Others handle routine tasks such as counting how many visitors have accessed a page or maintaining a table of contents. The following list outlines the Components discussed in this chapter. By reading subsequent sections of the chapter, you'll learn how to place each Component on the page, what the Component looks like in the raw HTML listing, and how a server processes the Component.

- Comment Component
- Insert HTML Component
- Timestamp Component
- Include Page Component
- Scheduled Image Component
- Scheduled Include Page Component
- Table of Contents Component
- Hit Counter Component
- Substitution Component
- Confirmation Field Component
- Page Banner Component

In addition to covering the above Components, you'll also see how FrontPage uses a Component to handle imagemap processing and how FrontPage supports many other compelling effects such as banner ads, page transitions, and hover buttons.

Using the Comment Component

The Comment Component lets you add comments to your WYSIWYG page on the FrontPage Editor's Normal tab. The comment will appear in purple text and will be preceded by the word "Comment:". Comments are remarks intended for authors and editors working on the document. They are not meant for consumption by the end user, so you'll never see a comment show up on the Preview tab.

To insert a Comment Component on a page, follow these instructions:

1. Choose Insert, FrontPage Component or click the Insert FrontPage Component button on the toolbar (the button has a picture of a robot on it). When you do, you'll see the Insert FrontPage Component dialog box shown in Figure 10.5. The box presents a listing of the FrontPage Components so that all you need to do to place one is to select it and click OK.

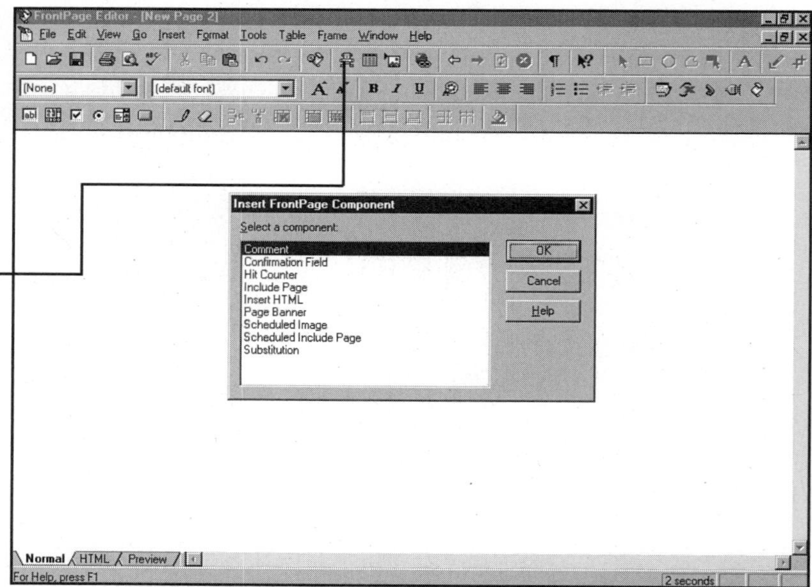

FIG. 10.5 The Insert FrontPage Component dialog box is your one stop for accessing most of FrontPage's Components.

Insert FrontPage Component button

2. Select the Comment Component and click OK. The Comment dialog box shown in Figure 10.6 will appear.
3. Type the text of your comment into this dialog box and click OK when you finish.

After you click OK, you'll see your comment appear on the Normal tab of the FrontPage Editor. As previously noted, the comment should be painted purple and be preceded with the word "Comment:". If you switch over to the HTML tab, you'll see something like the following:

```
<p><!--webbot bot="PurpleText"
preview="This is the first time I've placed a FP Component!" --></p>
```

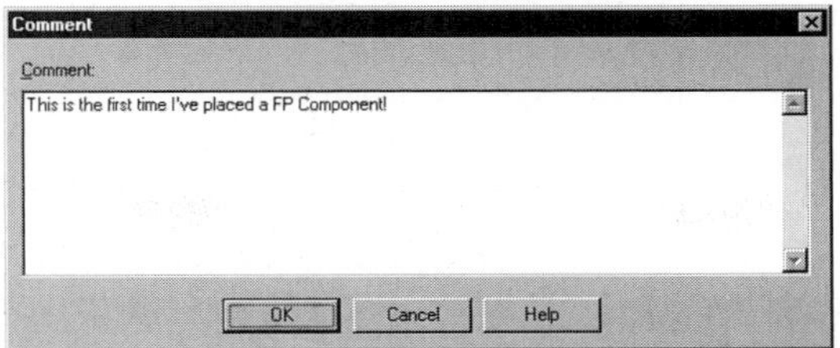

FIG. 10.6
The Comment dialog box collects the comments you want to place in your documents.

When interpreted by the server, this code will invoke the PurpleText bot on the server and render the content stored under the preview parameter as a comment.

NOTE There are a few things worth noting about the previous code. First, FrontPage still refers to Components as WebBots in the code. This isn't too big a deal because the FrontPage Server Extensions can handle the two different names and neither you nor a user should detect any difficulties.

The second thing to note is that the Component code is stored between HTML comment tags: <!-- and -->. This keeps the Component code hidden in the event that the raw code is served to a browser. You'll find that most of the FrontPage Components show up in the HTML code this way.

If you ever want to edit a comment, simply move your mouse pointer to it. When you do, you'll see the pointer cursor change to include a robot character. This means you're pointing at a FrontPage Component. Double-click on the comment to open up the Comment dialog box you saw in Figure 10.6 and make the changes to your comment there.

Using the Insert HTML Component

HTML is changing all the time. New tags are proposed, and often implemented, at an alarming rate. No web authoring program can keep releasing new versions to keep up with all the new tags, so most of them come with some means of inserting an unsupported HTML tag into a document's HTML code. In the case of the FrontPage Editor, this task is handled by the Insert HTML Component.

To insert an unsupported HTML tag, simply follow these steps:

1. Choose Insert, FrontPage Component, or click the Insert FrontPage Component toolbar button to call up a listing of available Components.
2. Select the Insert HTML Component to reveal the HTML Markup dialog box (see Figure 10.7).
3. Type in the tag you want to insert and then click OK. You won't see anything happen on the Normal tab, but you'll see something like the following on the HTML tab:

```
<!--webbot bot="HTMLMarkup" startspan -->
<FIELDSET>
<LEGEND ALIGN="CENTER">Age Information</LEGEND>
Birthdate: <INPUT TYPE="TEXT" NAME="DOB">
```

Using the Scheduled Image Component

Another web site task that's often hard to keep track of is posting and removing time-sensitive content. You may remember to post the content at a certain time, but it is easy to forget about removing it after it has expired unless you marked it on your calendar. FrontPage can help you with these situations with its Scheduled Event Components. The first of these is the Scheduled Image Component that you can use to place an image on a page at a specific time and to remove or replace it at a later time.

To place a Scheduled Image Component, follow these instructions:

1. Choose Insert, FrontPage Components, or click the Insert FrontPage Component toolbar button to display the list of available Components.
2. Highlight the Schedule Image option and then click OK. This calls up the Scheduled Image Properties dialog box you see in Figure 10.10. Here you can specify the image file to display, when to start displaying it, and when to stop displaying it. You also have the option of specifying an image to display before and after the scheduled times.

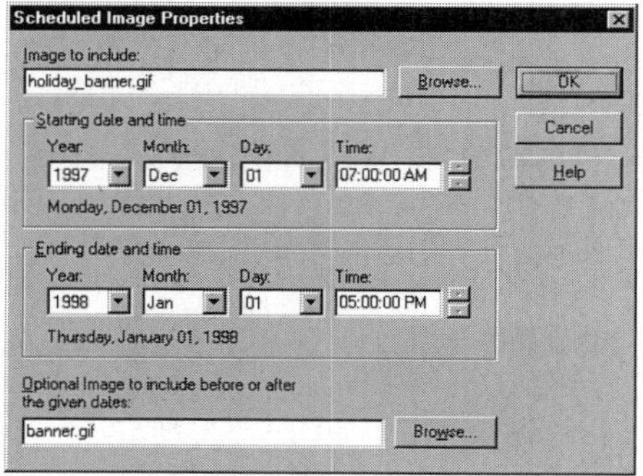

FIG. 10.10 Scheduled images are useful for sites that sell advertising. Ad graphics can be automatically placed and taken down with the Scheduled Image Component.

NOTE The image you choose to display doesn't have to be on your own server. You can specify a URL that points to an image file on another server as well. Keep in mind though that if the image file is removed from the remote server, your server won't be able to insert it when the page is served. For this reason, you may want to make a copy of the image on your server. That way, you'll always have access to it.

After you configure the Scheduled Image Component and click OK, the image or its alternate will show up on the Normal tab if FrontPage can access it. On the HTML tab, you see code similar to the following:

```
<!--webbot bot="ScheduledImage" u-src="holiday_banner.gif"
u-else-src="banner.gif" d-start-date="01 Dec 1997 07:00:00"
d-end-date="01 Jan 1998 17:00:00" -->
```

Using the Scheduled Include Page Component

The Scheduled Include Page Component works in a way that is similar to the Schedule Image Component. The primary difference is that the Scheduled Include Page Component builds in the contents of an entire page for a specified period of time, rather than just an image.

When you choose Insert, FrontPage Component, or click the Insert FrontPage Component toolbar button and then select the Scheduled Include Page Component, you'll see a dialog box that's virtually identical to the one you saw in Figure 10.10. The only difference is that you are prompted to provide the URL of an HTML file and not the URL of an image. Note that you can display one file during the scheduled time and specify an alternative file to use before and after the scheduled display times.

Assuming FrontPage can access it, your Scheduled Include Page (or its alternative, depending on the timing) will appear on the Normal tab of the FrontPage Editor. The code for the Scheduled Include Page Component on the HTML tab will look something like the following:


```
<!--webbot bot="ScheduledInclude" u-include="pageone-aprfool.htm"
u-else-include="pageone.htm" d-start-date="01 Apr 1998 00:01:00"
d-end-date="02 Apr 1998 00:01:00" -->
```

Using the Table of Contents Component

A table of contents can be another one of those site elements that is a "pain to maintain." Because tables of contents are also a valuable service to your visitors, it's important to make an effort to try to keep yours current. FrontPage can help you with this task by providing you with the Table of Contents Component.

To place a Table of Contents Component on your site, choose Insert, Table of Contents to reveal the Table of Contents Properties dialog box you see in Figure 10.11. Here you specify the file that is the starting point for your table of contents. FrontPage will follow all the links on the page and catalog the files it finds along the way. Then FrontPage traverses the links it finds on these files, and so on, until it has generated a table of contents for the entire site.

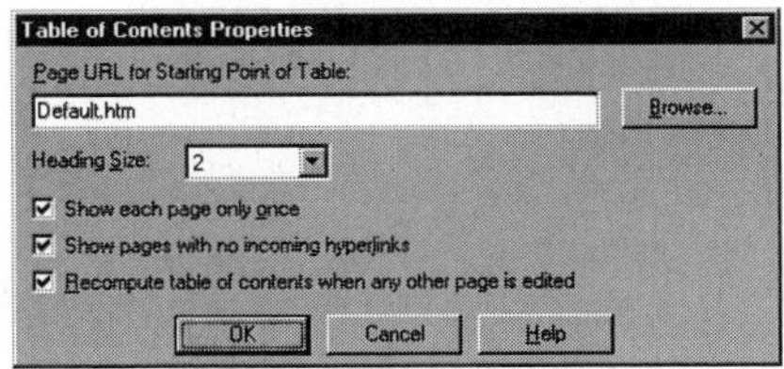

FIG. 10.11 FrontPage will automatically generate and maintain a site table of contents, sparing you from having to track all the changes.

NOTE The Table of Contents Component is not available from the dialog box you saw in Figure 10.5. You can select it only from the Insert menu.

Note also in the dialog box that you have control over the heading style used to render the table of contents. You can also specify that each file appear only once (a good idea if you have a lot of multiple linked files on your site) and that pages with no incoming hyperlinks appear (a good idea if you have many standalone pages). The Recompute feature is perhaps the nicest part of the Table of Contents Component because it will automatically redo the table if you make changes to any of the files.

When the Table of Contents Component is placed on your page, it will appear as a bulleted list of links on the Normal tab. You can follow the links by holding down the Control key while you click them. On the HTML tab, you'll see a call to the Outline bot as follows:

```
<!--webbot bot="Outline" u-url="Default.htm" b-aggressive-trimming="TRUE"
b-show-orphans="TRUE" b-manual-recalc="FALSE" i-heading="2" tag="BODY" -->
```

Using the Hit Counter Component

One popular element on the home page of many sites is a counter that indicates how many people have visited the page. When counters first started to appear on pages, they were simply text, but later web content providers got fancy and sent images to the browser to represent the digits in the visitor count. This allowed counters to take on various looks—some looked like a speedometer whereas other looked like an LED readout. Either way, counters add a little pizzazz to a page and give the page's owner a sense of how popular the page is with web surfers.

At one time you had to code a CGI script to retrieve the previous count, add one to it, and then display the result. Further coding was needed if you were going to parse the visitor count and send each digit as an image. But now, FrontPage relieves you of all that by providing a Hit Counter Component that you simply drop into place on a page.

To put a Hit Counter Component on one of your pages, simply do the following:

1. Choose Insert, FrontPage Component, or click the Insert FrontPage Component toolbar button to call up the list of available Components.
2. Select Hit Counter and click OK to call up the Hit Counter Properties dialog box shown in Figure 10.12. FrontPage lets you choose from five different counter digit styles, or you can specify your own custom style. Additionally, you can reset the counter to a desired value, and you can restrict the counter to be set a number of digits in length.

> **CAUTION**
>
> If you restrict the number of digits in your counter, make sure you leave at least enough digits to accommodate the traffic on your site.

When the Hit Counter appears on the Normal tab of the FrontPage Editor, you'll just see the text "[Hit Counter]" rendered in boldface. If you switch to the HTML tab, you'll see code such as the following:

```
<!--webbot bot="HitCounter" i-image="3" i-digits="5" b-reset="TRUE"
preview="&lt;strong&gt;[Hit Counter]&lt;/strong&gt;" u-custom
i-resetvalue="0" -->
```

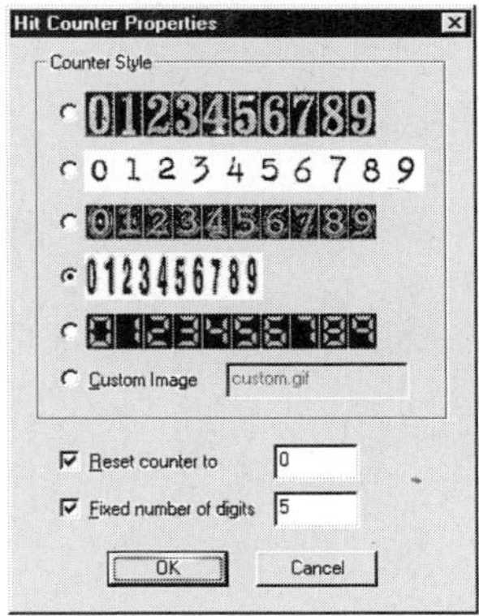

FIG. 10.12
Before FrontPage, hit counters required extensive server-side programming.

Using the Substitution Component

The Substitution Component inserts the value of a web or page configuration variable into a document. The default configuration variables available to the Substitution Component are

- Author
- Modified By
- Description
- Page URL

Any web setting parameters you specify in the FrontPage Explorer will be available to the Substitution Component as well (choose Tools, Web Settings; see Figure 10.13).

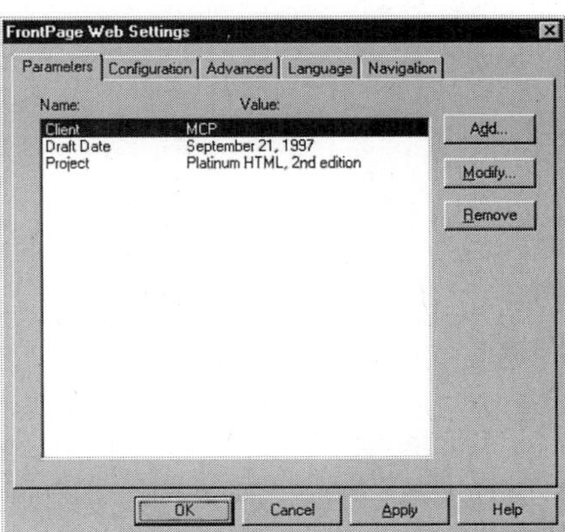

FIG. 10.13
You can establish global web parameters that are available for placement on a page using the Substitution Component.

To use the Substitution Component, follow these steps:

1. Choose Insert, FrontPage Component, or click the Insert FrontPage Component toolbar button to reveal the dialog box that lists the Components.

2. Select the Substitution option, and click OK to open the Substitution Component Properties dialog box you see in Figure 10.14.
3. Choose the configuration variable you want from the drop-down list, and click OK to place the Component.

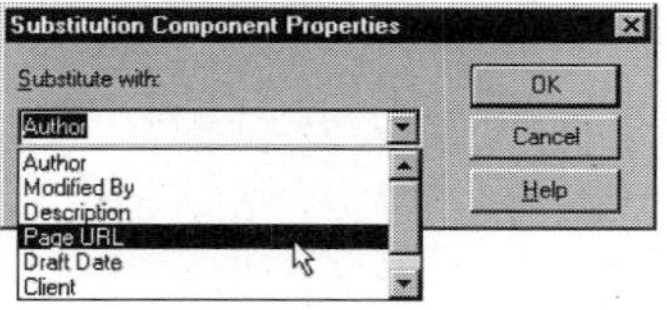

FIG. 10.14
The Page URL variable is a useful substitution for authors who like to display a document's URL in the document itself.

When the Substitution Component appears on the FrontPage Editor's Normal tab, you'll see the name of the variable you selected enclosed in square brackets. On the HTML tab, the Substitution Component is represented by code that resembles the following:

```
<!--webbot bot="Substitution" s-variable="vti_author" -->
```

Using the Confirmation Field Component

Forms are a web content provider's means of collecting information from end users. Data entered into a form is typically sent back to the server for some kind of processing, but before this happens, there are a few things you can do with the form data to ensure that it is as polished as it can be. One of these things is to confirm the data in the form's key fields, and the FrontPage Confirmation Field Component can help you do it.

The first thing you need to make a form field confirmation is, not surprisingly, a form. Assuming you've already used the FrontPage Editor to compose a form, go back through the form and write down the names (as assigned in the NAME attributes) of the form fields you want to confirm. You'll need the field names when inserting the Field Confirmation Component.

Next, you need to create a confirmation page where the Field Confirmation Component will reside. To do this, follow these steps:

1. In the FrontPage Editor, choose File, New and then select the Normal Page option.
2. Put whatever banner, background, and text you want on the page, leaving spaces where you want the form field confirmations to go.
3. Place your cursor at a position where you want a confirmation and then choose Insert, FrontPage Component, or click the Insert FrontPage Component toolbar button. From the Components list, select the Confirmation Field option.
4. Enter the name of the form field you want confirmed in the Confirmation Field Properties dialog box (see Figure 10.15) and click OK.

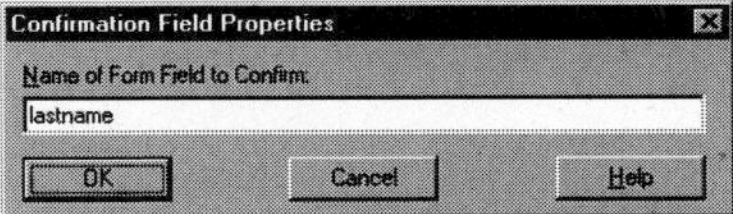

FIG. 10.15
Confirming the data submitted in a form field is as simple as typing the field's name into a dialog box.

5. Repeat steps 3 and 4 for each field you want to confirm.
6. Save the confirmation page to your open web.

With the confirmation page created, the last thing you need to do is to link the form with the confirmation page. You can accomplish this by performing these steps:

1. Open the form page in the FrontPage Editor, right-click on the form, and select the Form Properties option.
2. Click the Options button in the Form Properties dialog box.
3. In the Options for Saving Results of Form dialog box, click the Confirmation Page tab. You should see the dialog box shown in Figure 10.16.

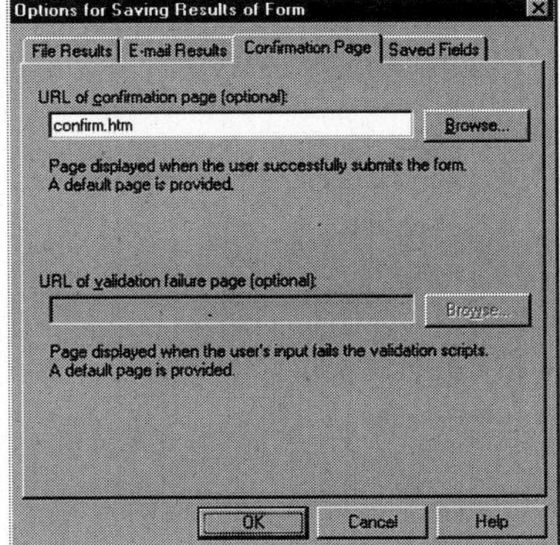

FIG. 10.16
You need to tell FrontPage if a form has an associated confirmation page.

4. Enter the URL of the confirmation page or browse to the page itself if it's in your open web.
5. Click OK in the Options for Saving Results of Form and Form Properties dialog boxes.

Now the chosen fields in the form will be confirmed before the data is sent along for processing. If you look at the Confirmation Field Components on the confirmation page, they will appear as the field name enclosed in square brackets. If you look at the HTML source code for the Confirmation Field Components, you'll see something such as the following:

```
<!--webbot bot="ConfirmationField" s-field="lastname" -->
```

When users submit a form with fields set up for confirmation, they will be presented with your confirmation page that will repeat back to them what they entered. If the data entered is incorrect, users can make changes to it from the confirmation page.

Using the Page Banner Component

The Page Banner Component places a banner across the top of the page in either an image-based or text-based format. If you choose an image and one of the FrontPage graphic themes has been applied, the banner graphic will have the same look and feel as the theme (see Figure 10.17). A text-based banner will also have the same look and feel as the text within the theme. By default, the banner will display the page's title, regardless of whether you use the image or text format.

FIG. 10.17
Banners display a page's title in either image- or text-based form.

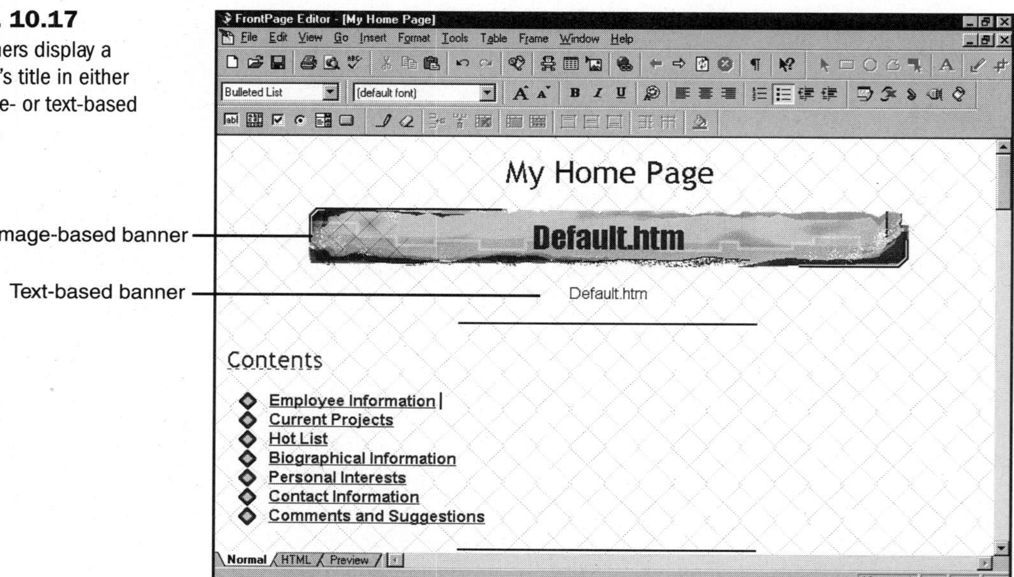

To place a banner on a page, place your cursor where you want the banner to appear and choose Insert, FrontPage Component, or click the Insert FrontPage Component toolbar button. In the dialog box that appears, select the Page Banner option and click OK. You'll then see the Page Banner Properties dialog box shown in Figure 10.18. All you need to do is to tell FrontPage whether you want the banner to be an Image or Text and it will do the rest.

As you saw in Figure 10.17, a banner shows up on the Normal tab just as it will look on a browser screen. When you look at the code for the banner, you'll see something resembling the following:

```
<!--webbot bot="Navigation" s-type="banner" s-rendering="graphics"
s-orientation b-include-home b-include-up -->
```

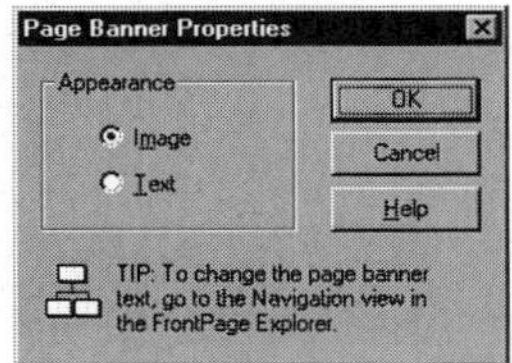

FIG. 10.18 When FrontPage knows whether you want an image or text in your banner, it can proceed with the banner creation.

How FrontPage Handles Imagemaps

The FrontPage Editor has toolbar buttons you can use to trace out hot regions on an image when creating an imagemap. After you've completed a trace, FrontPage prompts you for the URL to associate with the hot region. But what FrontPage does with the imagemap information after this may surprise you. This section looks at FrontPage's default approach to handling imagemaps and how you can adjust it to your needs.

After you complete the definition of your hot regions, you should switch to the HTML tab to examine the code FrontPage placed there to represent your imagemap. You probably expect to see the `<MAP>` tag and some `<AREA>` tags forming the imagemap code, but what you see instead is something like the following:

```
<!--webbot bot="ImageMap"
polygon=" (201,163) (237,139) (303,148) (329,180) (310,208) (259,204)
(213,202) (202,169) feedback.htm" rectangle=" (228,309) (278, 397)
services.htm" circle=" (281,83) 60  techsupport.htm" src="main.gif"
alt="main.gif (9219 bytes)" align="right" width="532" height="400" -->
```

As this code shows, FrontPage's default approach to processing imagemaps is to use a bot on the server, not to embed client-side imagemap code into the HTML file.

Although the Imagemap bot works fine, you may prefer to have FrontPage write out `<MAP>` and `<AREA>` tags so that you can have a truly client-side imagemap (using a bot means that the server is still involved). To set up FrontPage to use client-side imagemaps, go to the FrontPage Explorer, choose Tools, Web Settings, and then click the Advanced tab. This opens the dialog FrontPage Web Settings box you see in Figure 10.19. Near the top of the dialog box, you will see options for creating imagemaps. Make sure the Generate Client-Side Image maps box is checked, select the Netscape option from the Style drop-down list, and then click OK. You should then find that imagemaps you create in the future don't use the Imagemap bot.

Other Automated FrontPage Features

FrontPage comes with a number of other automated features and functions beyond the FrontPage Components. To close the chapter, this last section takes you on a brief tour of some of FrontPage's other high-end features. In each case, FrontPage is taking a task that was previously labor-intensive and reducing its setup to a few simple actions.

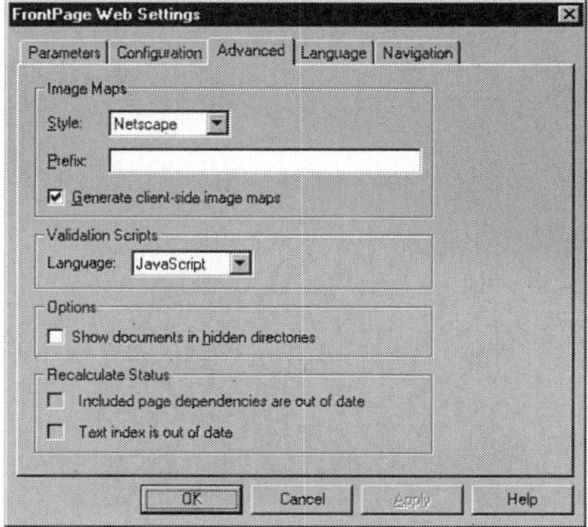

FIG. 10.19 You can alter FrontPage's approach to imagemap processing from the Advanced Web Settings dialog box.

- **Search, Discussion, Save Results, and Registration Bots**—If you've used previous versions of FrontPage, you might be wondering where some of the old FrontPage bots are among the FrontPage Components. Among the more popular of these are the Search, Discussion, Save Results, and Registration bots.

  The answer is that they are available in FrontPage 98, but they are not listed with the FrontPage Components. Instead, you have to look elsewhere to create instructions that use these bots. To use the Search bot, which sets up a minisearch engine in your FrontPage web, choose Insert, Active Elements, Search Form to launch the dialog box that will allow you to configure your search.

  You can use the Discussion bot to create a fully searchable threaded discussion group by choosing File, New FrontPage Web in the FrontPage Explorer. When you see the list of possible webs, choose the Discussion Web Wizard to walk through the steps of creating the threaded discussion.

  The Save Results bot is called the Save Results form handler in FrontPage 98. To use the form handler, right-click your form and select Form Properties from the pop-up menu you see. Then click the Options button to configure the saving location and format.

  Finally, the Registration bot is now tucked away in a User Registration page template in the FrontPage Editor. To load the template, choose File, New in the Editor, and choose the User Registration document from the list you see. A registration page lets web users self-register, rather than burdening you with all the data entry.

- **Hover Buttons**—Buttons that change their properties when a user's mouse pointer is over the button or when the user clicks the button. You can set up the button to be text- or image-based, and FrontPage can even bevel the image for you so that it looks more like a button.

  To create a hover button, choose Insert, Active Elements, Hover Button to reveal the Hover Button dialog box. If you want a text-based button, you can set it up here, including how the button should be colored and what onscreen effect it should possess (glow, beveling, and so on). If you want to use an image, click the Custom button to open the

Custom dialog box. In the lower half of the dialog box, you'll find fields for specifying the default button image and the image to display when a user's mouse is hovering over the image.

After your button is configured, click OK to place it on your page. If you peek at the HTML tag, you'll see that FrontPage renders the button by using a Java applet.

- **Page Transitions**—One of the neat features found in Microsoft's PowerPoint presentation creation software is a set of transitions you can use between slides in the presentation. Now Microsoft brings those transitions to the web through the FrontPage Editor. To add a transition to a page, choose Format, Page Transition to open the Page Transitions dialog box. Here you can choose from over 20 different transition effects. You can also set the duration of the transition and specify the event that triggers the transition (entering the page, leaving the site, and so on).

  After the transition is in place, you can look at the HTML code to see that FrontPage accomplished the transition by using a `<META>` tag in the document head. The tag contains an `HTTP-EQUIV` value that corresponds to the triggering event that you selected. Once the server detects the event, it uses dynamic HTML to produce the transition effect.

NOTE Because they use Microsoft's notion of dynamic HTML, FrontPage page transitions are best previewed with Internet Explorer 4.0.

- **Text Animations**—Text doesn't have to sit still with FrontPage. It can come flying onto the page from anywhere off the screen or it can spiral into place gracefully. To animate some text, highlight it with your mouse, choose Format, Animation, and then select one of the 14 available animations. When you preview the page in a Microsoft dynamic HTML-capable browser, you'll see the text move on to the screen according to the animation technique you chose.
- **Banner Ad Manager**—Sites that sell advertising can use the FrontPage Banner Ad Manager, which takes a list of ad graphics files and displays them in sequence. You can control how long each graphic appears, what the graphics link to, and the transition effect between graphics. To activate the Banner Ad Manager, choose Insert, Active Elements, Banner Ad Manager. The Banner Ad Manager enables you to specify the size of the banner, which images to display in the banner space, how banner transitions should occur, and how long each image should appear.

CHAPTER 11

Key Access and Security Concerns for Web Administrators

by Mike Morgan

In this chapter

Web Security on the Internet and Intranet

As soon as your computer is connected with one or more other computers you have a security problem. Anyone using the other computers can access your computer's memory and data. This chapter addresses the ways that the security of your computer can be threatened and provides some guidelines for its defense.

The first part of the chapter defines some terms and gives an overview of the major security threats. Next, the chapter describes what a local web administrator can do to keep his or her site secure. Finally, this chapter takes up the topic of security administration, discussing the larger issues of site security, security policy, and security administration tools, to show what a site administrator can do to keep a site safe.

The Internet and its cousin, corporate intranets, are built on a family of protocols known as the Transmission Control Protocol/Internet Protocol (TCP/IP). The heart of TCP/IP is its cability to connect any machine on the Internet to any other by routing packets from one machine to another. You can use the UNIX utility `traceroute` to see how your machine connects to other machines on the Internet. Suppose you work on a machine named `mickey`. If you enter

```
traceroute donald
```

you might get output like

```
traceroute to donald.com (—some IP address—), 30 hops max, 40 byte packets
1 minnie (—some IP address—) 20 ms  10 ms  10 ms
2 pluto  (—some IP address—) 120 ms  120 ms  120 ms
3 donald (—some IP address—) 150 ms  140 ms  150 ms
```

For that particular set of packets, your connection to `donald` passed through the machines `minnie` and `pluto`.

The `traceroute` output shows that when you pass information around the net(whether the Internet or a corporate intranet), others attached to the Internet may be able to intercept and read, or even change, the information. How likely is it that you or your organization will be the target of an attack? That's part of what you must determine in establishing your *security stance*.

ISO Standard X.509 details nine threats that a computer network might face:

- Identity Interception The threat that the identity of one or more users participating in an exchange may be disclosed.
- Masquerade A situation in which one user pretends to be another.
- Replay A special form of masquerade (and the most common form) in which an unauthorized user records the commands or passwords of an authorized user, then replays them to the system to gain access or privilege.
- Data Interception A situation in which a perpetrator gains access to confidential information.
- Manipulation A situation in which data is altered without authorization.
- Repudiation The threat that one user might deny that they participated in a particular exchange.

- Denial of Service   Prevention or interruption of access to a service, or delay of time-critical operations.
- Misrouting   A situation, in which a communication intended for one person is rerouted to another.
- Traffic Analysis   The ability to gain information by measuring factors such as frequency, rate, and direction of information transferred.

Most of these attacks can be mounted against either a site on the Internet or an intranet server. Many intranet sites have a firewall —a system to restrict access from machines not on the company's intranet. Just because your site is behind a firewall, don't assume "the natives are friendly." Even if your site is behind a firewall, you should still use the techniques described in this chapter to further protect your site against attack. If someone does manage to penetrate your network security, they will have to deal with still more security, at the server level.

This chapter addresses defenses against masquerade and replay attacks, with less emphasis on denial of service and data interception.

Identity interception is a fact of life with most network services. A user can participate in an exchange anonymously using special anonymity servers on the Internet or by spoofing the email system to appear as someone else. Hypertext Transfer Protocol (HTTP), typically used on the web for communications between browsers and servers, does not usually capture a user's name, therefore making personal identity safer with the web than with most other services.

Manipulation and repudiation are most easily prevented by using a digital signature system based on public keys. The public key system called Pretty Good Privacy (PGP) is described in this chapter. A different system, called Privacy Enhanced Mail (PEM) is described later in the chapter, in the context of Electronic Data Interchange (EDI). If you are using a commercial server such as Netscape or Microsoft server products, you can also exchange secure mail and news.

Many attacks may be thwarted by encrypting data before it is sent and using digital signatures to prove that data was not altered after it was sent. In general, the public domain servers such as NCSA and Apache do not support these features. (The secure version of Apache, formerly called Apache-SSL, Secure Apache, and Sioux, is now available commercially under the name Stronghold from C2Net Software, Inc. (**http://www.c2.net**).

Commercial servers, such as Netscape's FastTrack and Enterprise servers, Microsoft's Internet Information Server (IIS), O'Reilly's WebSite, and C2Net's Stronghold (formerly Secure Apache), do support a range of encryption and digital signature options. Encryption, digital signatures, and the infrastructure to support them are the most important reasons to consider a commercial server over a public domain (free) server.

Netscape's recent servers include a "Certificate Server," and all of their servers (not just the web servers) can be set up to look at the electronic signatures on a user's certificate before deciding whether or not to grant access.

No good defenses against misrouting and traffic analysis exist. If an attacker can gain access to the bitstream (either on the LAN or by grabbing it from the Internet), he or she can change mail headers (most of which are not encrypted) or perform traffic analysis. By using secure email, however, the user can ensure that misrouted messages cannot be read by someone other than the intended recipient.

NOTE This chapter uses the terms "hacker" and "cracker" in their technical sense. Perhaps surprisingly, the term "hacker" was coined to refer to the most productive people in a technical project—people who often worked extremely long hours to add clever technical features. The term "cracker" refers to a person who commits unauthorized penetrations of computer systems.

Balancing Between Security and Usability

Security is not without cost. Figure 11.1 illustrates the fact that one can achieve security only at the expense of ease-of-use and performance. A Web administrator can choose any operating point within this triangle but cannot be at all three corners simultaneously.

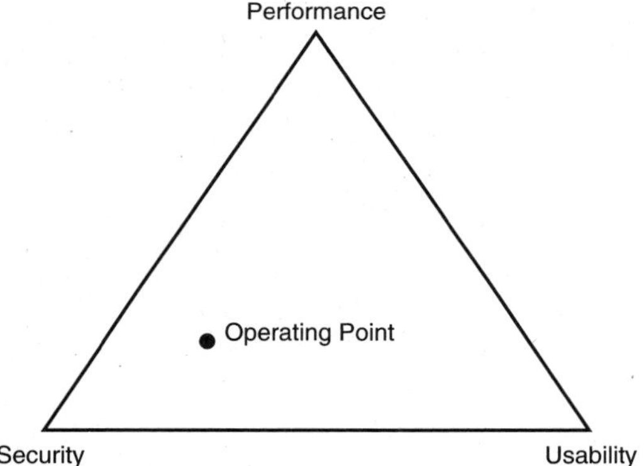

FIG. 11.1
A web administrator can operate a site anywhere within the triangle—but you can't be at all three corners at once!

With few exceptions, every step toward enhanced security is a step away from high performance and usability. Each system administrator, in concert with the Web administrators of the sites on the system, must determine where the acceptable operating points lie. One way to think about the trade-off between security and user issues is to compare the value of the information and service provided by the server to the likely threat. Security analysts often identify six levels of security threat:

1. Casual users These people might inadvertently compromise security.
2. Curious users These people are willing to explore the system but unwilling to break the law.
3. Greedy users These people are willing to divulge information for financial gain but are unwilling to break the law.

4. Criminals These people are willing to break the law.
5. Well-financed criminals These people have access to sophisticated tools.
6. Foreign governments These people have essentially unlimited resources.

For most systems, the value of the information and service justifies securing the system against at least the first two or three levels of threat. No system openly available on the Internet can withstand a concerted attack from the highest levels of threat. In the late 80s, computer security experts agreed that most attacks came from curious or greedy users. These days, however, experts widely agree that the threat has grown more sophisticated. Attacks now are often committed by a technically skilled, well-funded person who has strong motives for attacking a system. Indeed, the U.S. government has studied the topic of *information warfare*, a term that refers to the exploitation of computer infrastructure resources, such as those operated by banks, telephone companies, and transportation companies.

This chapter presents a series of security solutions, ranging from simple user authentication systems sufficient to keep out the casual user who might inadvertently compromise security, to fairly expensive systems that raise the cost of penetration high enough that potential infiltrators need good funding in order to succeed.

See the section on Security Administration Tools later in this chapter to learn some techniques that might deter, or at least detect, even the *most persistent criminal*.

Built-in Server Access Control

The easiest way to protect files is to use the access control mechanisms built into NCSA, Apache, and similar UNIX servers. These techniques are not powerful—they can be foiled with very little effort. Nevertheless, they're relatively easy to implement and they keep confidential files away from most casual browsers.

The Netscape web servers (FastTrack and Enterprise), as well as the new Netscape SuiteSpot technology, provide security capabilities well in excess of what is available in NCSA and its kin. If your site needs pinpoint control over access, check out the Netscape products. Also, if you need to run on a Windows NT platform instead of UNIX, you will want to look at the Netscape, Microsoft, and O'Reilly products.

For more information on the Netscape servers, see Part V of *Running a Perfect Netscape Site* (Que, 1996). Microsoft's entry, Microsoft Internet Information Server, is described in *Running a Perfect Web Site with Windows* (Que, 1996).

To understand how built-in server access control works, we need a little background information on the kind of response a server sends back after a client has requested a file. The response a client wants usually looks something like the following:

```
HTTP/1.0 200 OK
Date: Mon, 1 Sep 1997 17:24:19 GMT
Server: Apache/1.0.2
Content-type: text/html
```

```
Content-length: 5244
Last-modified: Tue, 26 Aug 1997 19:11:01 GMT
<!DOCTYPE HTML PUBLIC "-//IETF/DTD HTML 3.0//EN">
<HTML>
<HEAD>
.
.
.
</BODY>
</HTML>
```

As you can see, a variety of items precede the HTML. The information normally consists of a status line and header fields. The status line contains the status code (200, 401, ans so on) and classifies the response to the browser as informational, success, redirection, or client error. The header fields can cover a wide range of information. Possible header fields are general, request, response, and entity. One response header field in particular makes built-in server access control possible:

```
WWW-Authenticate
```

The WWW-Authenticate header field is included in responses with status code 401. Status code `401` (Unauthorized) is seen when the user accesses a protected directory. A `WWW-Authenticate` header field contains a challenge. Typically, a browser interprets a code 401 by giving the user an opportunity to enter a username and password.

The syntax is:

```
_WWW-Authenticate: 1#challenge_
```

The browser reads the challenge(s)—there must be at least one—and asks the user to respond. Most popular browsers handle this process with a dialog box prompting the user for a username and password. The next several sections describe how to configure your server to restrict specific files, allowing only those who return the correct username and password to access those files.

access.conf The NCSA server looks for a file named `access.conf` in the configuration directory. Here are two typical entries for `access.conf`:

```
<Directory /usr/local/etc/httpd/htdocs/morganm>
_<Limit GET>
_order allow, deny
_allow from all
_</Limit>
</Directory>
<Directory /usr/local/etc/httpd/htdocs/ckepilino>
_<Limit GET>
_order deny, allow
_deny from all
_allow from dse.com
_</Limit>
</Directory>
```

These entries tell the server who has access to the morganm and ckepilino directories, respectively. The first line of each entry names the directory. The next line shows that GET requests are restricted. The order directive specifies the order in which allow and deny directives should be applied. In the first example, GET requests are allowed to the morganm directory from any domain and denied from none. In the second example, the deny directive is applied first, so access is not allowed from anywhere. Then the allow directive is invoked, allowing access to the ckepilino directory only from dse.com, as an exception to the general denial rule.

htaccess You can place the same entries shown earlier in access.conf in a file named .htaccess in the directory you want protected. This approach decentralizes access control. Instead of requiring the site web administrator to manage access.conf, this approach enables each directory owner to set up localized security. To restrict access to the ckepilino directory, for example, make a file named .htaccess. Notice the period before the name—this makes the file invisible to casual browsers. Then put the following lines in the file:

```
<Limit GET>
_order deny, allow
_deny from all
_allow from dse.com
</Limit>
```

The same mechanism can be used to limit POST as well as GET.

User Authentication The next step in site protection is user authentication. For example, to restrict access to the morganm directory to the specific users jean, chris, and mike, put the following lines in the access.conf file:

```
<Directory /usr/local/etc/httpd/htdocs/morganm>]
_Options Indexes FollowSymlinks
_AllowOverride None
_AuthUserFile /usr/local/etc/httpd/conf/.htpasswd
_AuthGroupFile /dev/null
_AuthName By Secret Password Only!
_AuthType Basic
_<Limit GET>
__require user jean
__require user chris
__require user mike
_</Limit>
</Directory>
```

To do the same thing using an .htaccess file, use the following lines:

```
AuthUserFile /home/morganm/.htpasswd
AuthGroupFile /dev/null
AuthName By Secret Password Only!
AuthType Basic
<Limit GET>
_require user jean
_require user chris
_require user mike
</Limit>
```

In both cases, `AuthUserFile` specifies the absolute pathname to the password file. The location of this file is unimportant, as long as it's outside the web site's document tree. The `AuthGroupFile` directive is set to `/dev/null`—a way of saying that this directory does not use group authentication. The `AuthName` and `AuthType` directives are required and are set to the only options currently available in the NCSA server.

phtpasswd To create the password file that's specified by `AuthUserFile`, run the program `htpasswd`. This program does not always come with the server installation kit but is available from the same source. It must be compiled locally.

To run `htpasswd` the first time, type something like this:

```
htpasswd -c /home/morganm/.htpasswd jean
```

The `-c` option creates a new password file with the specified pathname. The username (in this case, `jean`) specifies the first user to be put into the file. `htpasswd` responds by prompting for the password.

Your subsequent calls to `htpasswd` should omit the `-c` option:

```
htpasswd /home/morganm/.htpasswd chris
htpasswd /home/morganm/.htpasswd mike
```

Once the password file is in place, it's easy to tell the server to read (or reread) the file. On UNIX, run the following command:

```
ps -ef ¦ grep httpd
```

NOTE On some versions of UNIX, `ps -aux` is the first command.

This command lists all the current copies of the web server, something like the following:

```
root 9514_1_0 16:55:45 - 0:00 /usr/local/etc/apache/src/httpd
nobody 9772_9514_0 16:55:45 - 0:00 /usr/local/etc/apache/src/httpd
nobody 11568_9514_0 16:55:45 - 0:00 /usr/local/etc/apache/src/httpd
nobody 11822_9514_0 16:55:45 - 0:00 /usr/local/etc/apache/src/httpd
nobody 12084_9514_0 16:55:45 - 0:00 /usr/local/etc/apache/src/httpd
nobody 11138_9514_0 16:55:45 - 0:00 /usr/local/etc/apache/src/httpd
```

Look for the one that begins with `root`. Its process ID is used as the parent process ID of all the other copies. Note the process ID of that parent copy. For this example, it's `9514`. Once you've obtained this number, enter the following line:

```
kill -HUP 9514
```

This command sends a hangup signal (`SIGHUP`) to the server daemon. For most processes, the hangup signal tells the server that an interactive user, dialed in by modem, has hung up. Daemons, of course, have no interactive users (at least not the sort who can get to them by modem), but by convention, sending `SIGHUP` to a daemon tells it to reread its configuration files. When the parent copy of `httpd` rereads `access.conf`, it learns about the new restrictions and starts enforcing them.

You can use similar techniques to set up authenticating groups, but requirements for group authentication are less common. See your server documentation if you want details.

Password-protection Scripts

The built-in access control mechanisms are easy to set up, and offer security against casual threats, but they will not resist a determined attack. Anyone with certain types of network monitoring equipment can read the username and password out of the packets. If there's an Ethernet LAN close to the server, for example, an Ethernet card can be put into "promiscuous mode" and told to read all traffic off the network. For even lower cost, a determined cracker can often guess enough passwords to penetrate most sites. Some servers honor a `GET` request for `.htaccess`, giving the cracker knowledge of where the password file is kept.

Even though the passwords are encrypted, methods exist to guess many passwords. Software is available to try every word in the dictionary in just a few minutes. A brute force search involving every word of six or fewer characters takes under an hour. Compromise of a site does not require compromise of every account—just one. Studies have found that, before users are taught how to choose and change passwords, as many as 50 percent of the passwords on a site fall victim to a simple cracking program. After training, about 25 percent of the passwords are still vulnerable.

Rules for choosing good passwords can be built into software. A password should be long (eight characters or more) and should not be any word appearing in a dictionary or related at all to the user's personal information. A password should not be the same as the username, or the same as any of the computer vendor's default passwords. The password should be entered in mixed case—or, better yet, with punctuation or numbers mixed in. Every user should change passwords regularly, and when a new password is chosen, it should not be too similar to the old password.

`passwd+` is designed to replace the UNIX system's standard password maintenance program (`/bin/passwd`). It catches and rejects passwords following certain patterns—it rejects many for being too short or matching a dictionary word. Many newer versions of UNIX have incorporated logic similar to `passwd+` into their own version of `passwd`. For web site password protection, logic similar to `passwd+` certainly could be incorporated.

It's important to make sure that passwords are written to the disk in encrypted form, and that the file holding the passwords is read-protected. The following three listings provide the basis for a simple password protection system. Like `.htaccess`, this system is vulnerable to network sniffing and replay. Unlike `.htaccess`, however, this system can be extended to include `passwd+`-style logic, so that the passwords hold up better against crackers.

NOTE If you're not familiar with CGI scripting, you might want to skip this section until you've read Chapter 31. If you're new to Perl, be sure to read *Teach Yourself Perl 5 in 21 Days*, Second Edition (Sams, 1996), or *Perl 5 Interactive Course* (Waite Group, 1997).

The CD-ROM that accompanies this book contains `login.cgi`. Connect an HTML form to `login.cgi` and use it to collect users' names and passwords. If they present a valid name and password, the script redirects them to a file in the protected subdirectory. If they are the site owner (as evidenced by their `$LEVEL` being equal to two), they are redirected to the `addUser.html` page.

User passwords are maintained with the script named `addUser.cgi`, also available on the CD-ROM. When `login.cgi` recognizes the site owner and sends them to `addUser.html`, they supply the data for the new user.

To get started, write a one-line Perl program to encrypt a password. If you want your password to be `OverTheRiver`, for example, run the script in Listing 11.1.

Listing 11.1 starter.pl Use this little script to generate the first password.

```
#!/usr/local/bin/perl
# By Michael Morgan, 1995
$encryptedPassword = crypt("OverTheRiver", 'ZZ');
print $encryptedPassword;
exit;
```

You get a reply like this one (the actual characters may vary):

```
ZZe/eiKRvN/k.
```

Copy the encrypted password into the owner's line in the password file (shown below). After that, delete the program from the disk.

Each line of the password file should look similar. If the owner of the files is named Jones, for example, the owner's line might read as follows:

```
jones:ZZe/eiKRvN/k.:1:2:
➥I. M. Jones, (804) 555-1212, (804) 555-1145, jones@xyz.com
```

Once the first line of the file has been built by hand, the owner can add subsequent users by using the script.

If a cracker can get a copy of the password file, then he can run CRACK or more sophisticated password crackers against it. Make sure that the password file is outside the document tree, forcing the cracker to test password guesses online. Next, add a counter to the preceding script, so that repeated attempts to access a user ID disable that account and notify the system administrator.

Realize that these mechanisms do nothing to keep *local* users out of the site. Remember that on any system with more than a few users, a computer-assisted cracker can probably guess at least one password. Make sure that key files like source code and password files are readable only by those who absolutely must have access.

Vulnerability Due to CGI Scripts and Server-side Includes

CGI scripts and server-side includes (SSIs) can make the server vulnerable. Many web administrators believe that because the server runs as the unprivileged user `nobody`, no harm can be done. But `nobody` can copy the `/etc/passwd` file, mail a copy of the file system map, dump files from `/etc`, and even start a login server (on a high port) for an attacker to telnet to. User `nobody` can also run massive programs, bringing the server to its knees in a "denial of service" attack.

If you allow SSIs or CGI scripts on your site, be sure to read Chapters 36, "Server-Side Includes," and 33, "CGI and Database Security."

Communications Security

Web site security works like a home burglar alarm. You don't expect to make your site impregnable, but making it difficult to crack encourages crackers to move on to less fortified sites. Once the private areas of the site are password-protected and the common CGI holes are closed, the remaining vulnerability at the web-site level resides in the communications links between the user and the site. An aggressive cracker can sniff passwords, credit card numbers, and other confidential information directly from the Internet.

Credit card companies have led the effort to encrypt communications links. Credit card theft on the Internet is expected to follow a different pattern than theft in conventional transactions. When a physical card is stolen, thieves know that they have just a few days—maybe just hours—before the card number is deactivated. They try to run up as large a balance as possible while the card is still good. In so doing, they often trigger security software. If, on the other hand, a thief could get access to thousands of credit card numbers, then he could use each number just once. Such illegal use is unlikely to trip any credit card company alarms, and therefore could lead to massive loss in the industry. With the rapid growth of the web and the number of online commercial transactions, it is wise to provide protection for confidential information like credit card numbers.

Credit card transactions are only one example of net information which needs protection. A number of software encryption protocols or systems can help make your information more secure as you communicate with others on the net. These systems can provide:

- Authentication
- Confidentiality
- Integrity
- Nonrepudiation

See the sidebar for a quick reference to these systems.

Some Encryption Protocols or Systems for Net Communications

CyberCash	A protocol. Provides security for payments sent on the net. Does not provide confidentiality for the message except for the credit card numbers. Similar to SET.
DNSSEC	Domain Name System Security, a standard. Secures DNS updates. Does not provide confidentiality or nonrepudiation services, just authentication and integrity.
F-SSH	Data Fellows Secure Shell. Provides strong security for remote terminal applications such as telnet. Available since mid-1996 in freeware and commercial versions for Unix and Windows 3.11, Windows 95, and Windows NT systems.
Kerberos	A security service. Secures higher-level applications. Does not provide integrity and nonrepudiation services; provides authentication and confidentiality only. Proposed for use in TLS.
PCT	A Microsoft protocol with various names, including Private Communications Technology. This improved on SSL 2.0 and is a parallel technology to SSL 3.0. Encrypts TCP/IP communications. Still supported by Microsoft.
PGP	Pretty Good Privacy. This application program secures email and files.
SET	A protocol. Provides security for payments sent on the net. Does not provide confidentiality for the message except for the credit card numbers. Similar to CyberCash.
S-HTTP	Secure Hypertext Transfer Protocol. Encrypts HTTP communications, at the TCP/IP application level. Not currently supported by Microsoft's or Netscape's browsers, although Netscape has pledged future support.
S/MIME	Secure MIME, a format for email encryption. Type of security used can be specified by the user. S/MIME is supported by Microsoft Outlook and Outlook Express email clients.
SSH	Secure Shell. Secures remote terminal applications such as telnet. Does not provide integrity and nonrepudiation services; provides authentication and confidentiality only. Older version of F-SSH.
SSL	Secure Sockets Layer, a protocol that works at the data-transport level. Encrypts TCP/IP communications. Widely used.
TLS	Transport Layer Security. Proposed to succeed SSL. Still in draft.

Secure Socket Layer

Most web administrators are aware that Netscape, Microsoft, C2Net, and O'Reilly, among others, offer secure web servers. The security in these products is based on a low-level encryption scheme, *Secure Sockets Layer* (*SSL*). The web is based on TCP/IP (Transmission Control Protocol/Internet Protocol), which consists of several software "layers"—you can replace the software implementing a layer with a new software component without changing the rest of the protocols. SSL is a Network layer encryption scheme. When a client makes a request for secure communications to a secure server, the server opens an encrypted port. The port is managed by software called the SSL Record Layer, which sits on top of TCP. Higher-level software, the SSL Handshake Protocol, uses the SSL Record Layer and its port to contact the client.

The SSL Handshake Protocol on the server arranges authentication and encryption details with the client using ***public-key encryption***. Public-key encryption schemes are based on mathematical "one-way" functions. In a few seconds, anyone can determine that 7×19 equals 133. On the other hand, determining that 133 can be factored by 7 and 19 takes quite a bit more work. A user who already has these factors (the "secret key") can decrypt the message easily.

Some commercial public-key encryption schemes are based on keys of 1024 bits or more, which should require years of computation to crack at current computing speeds. Using public-key encryption, the client and server exchange information about which cipher methods each understands. They agree on a one-time key to be used for the current transmission. The server might also send a certificate (called an *X.509.v3 certificate*) to prove its own identity.

NOTE Mathematically strong encryption schemes are classified by the U.S. Government as "munitions." In general, encryption software and algorithms developed in the U.S. cannot be exported. The U.S. government takes this issue very seriously. Some other nations have policies prohibiting the transmission of encrypted data through their telephone lines. These policies have been the topic of much debate on the Internet and elsewhere.

In many cases, software that is compatible with the strong encryption schemes available in the U.S. has been developed outside the United States, and is available as an "International" version. Be sure to read the license agreement that comes with your software. Users in the U.S. should use the U.S. version, and are restricted from taking (or sending) the product overseas. Users outside the U.S. may be able to use the international version, subject to the laws in their country.

In other cases, vendors have weakened the algorithm by reducing the key size from 1024 bits to 128 or even 40 bits, in order to avoid certain government restrictions.

In all cases, check the documentation that came with your browser or server, or get legal advice, to see what you can and cannot do with your software.

Some browsers indicate whether or not a session is secure. The Microsoft Internet Explorer, for example, displays a locked padlock icon in its status bar at the lower-right corner when a session is secure. The Netscape Navigator 4.0x shows an unlocked padlock icon if the session is not secure, and a locked padlock if the session is encrypted; in the Netscape 3.0x browser, a "key" icon in the lower-left corner of the window shows whether a session is encrypted or not. A broken key indicates a non-secure session. A key with one tooth shows that the session is running on a 40-bit key. A key with two teeth shows that a 128-bit key is in use.

End users should not assume that seeing an unbroken key or locked lock guarantees that their transmission is secure. They also should check the certificate. In Microsoft Internet Explorer, you can click the padlock icon in the status bar to access security information about your current session. In Netscape Navigator 4.0x, you can click the security icon on the iconbar; in 3.0x, you can access this information by choosing View, Document Info. If the certificate is not owned by the organization that the users think they're doing business with, they should verify the certificate by calling the vendor.

SSL is a powerful encryption method. Because it has a publicly available reference implementation, you can easily add it to existing software such as web and FTP servers. It's not perfect—for example, it doesn't flow through proxy servers correctly—but it's a first step in providing communications security.

Most browsers and web servers support SSL. A free implementation of SSL, named SSLeay, serves as the basis for security in Apache and NCSA httpd, as well as in Secure Mosaic.

The SSL 3.0 protocol may soon by replaced by an improved version, the ***Transport Layer Security (TLS)*** protocol, which itself is based on SSL 3.0. Drafts relating to the TLS protocol are available at the IETF web site (see below).

ON THE WEB

http://www.w3.org/Security/Faq/ The W3 Security FAQ, an excellent place to start reading about web security issues.

http://www.w3.org/Security/ An excellent page of security links at the W3 standards organization site.

ftp://ietf.org/internet-drafts/draft-ietf-tls-protocol-03.txt The IETF Internet draft for Transport Layer Security (TLS), which is based on SSL 3.0 and will supercede it.

ftp://ietf.org/internet-drafts/draft-ietf-tls-kerb-cipher-suites-01.txt An IETF draft memo on the "Addition of Kerberos Cypher Suites to...(TLS)"

http://home.netscape.com/newsref/std/SSL.html Deals with SSL 3.0 standards and licensing.

http://ietf.org/draft-ietf-tls-ssl-version3-00.txt The SSL 3.0 draft at the IETF standards organization.

ftp://ietf.org/internet-drafts/draft-luotonen-ssl-tunneling-03.txt The SSL tunneling draft at IETF.

http://home.netscape.com/eng/ssl3/ The top of a hierarchy containing the technical specifications of SSL 3.0.

ftp://ftp.psy.uq.oz.au/pub/Crypto/SSL/ The site to visit to download the SSL library SSLeay.

http://www.psy.uq.oz.au/~ftp/Crypto/ Contains the Frequently Asked Questions list for SSLeay.

Secure HTTP

A competing standard to SSL is *Secure HTTP* (*S-HTTP*) from Enterprise Integration Technologies. Like SSL, S-HTTP allows for both encryption and digital authentication. Unlike SSL, though, S-HTTP is an application-level protocol—it makes extensions to HTTP.

The S-HTTP proposal suggests a new document suffix, `.shttp`, and the following new protocol:

```
Secure * Secure-HTTP/1.1.
```

Using `GET`, a client requests a secure document, tells the server what kind of encryption it can handle, and tells the server where to find its public key. If the user who matches that key is authorized to `GET` the document, the server responds by encrypting the document and sending it back. The client then uses its secret key to decrypt the message and display it to the user. One of the encryption methods available with S-HTTP is PGP, described in the next section.

Neither Microsoft Internet Explorer 4.0x nor Netscape Navigator 4.0x currently supports S-HTTP, but Netscape has announced its commitment to future support for this protocol. (See **http://search.netscape.com/newsref/std/standards_qa.html** for more details.)

Pretty Good Privacy

The Pretty Good Privacy application, written by Phil Zimmerman, has achieved fame and notoriety by spreading "encryption for everyone." For several years, PGP hung under a cloud because it did not have clear license to use the public-key encryption algorithms. There was also an investigation into whether Zimmerman had distributed PGP outside the United States. (U.S. law prohibits the distribution of strong encryption systems.)

Those clouds have finally lifted. With the release of PGP 2.6, the licensing issues have been entirely resolved, and the U.S. government has announced that it has no interest in seeking indictments against Zimmerman.

If you live in the U.S. and are a U.S. citizen or lawfully admitted alien, you can get PGP from the server at MIT. If you live outside the U.S., you should use PGP 2.6ui. This version was built in Europe and does not violate U.S. export control laws.

ON THE WEB

http://web.mit.edu/network/pgp-form.html You can get PGP by visiting this URL and following the instructions given.

http://www.pgp.com Check out this site for more information on the commercial version of PGP.

Part of the agreement with the patent-holder, RSA Data Security, Inc., was that PGP could not be used for commercial purposes. A commercial version of the program, with proper licensing, is available from ViaCrypt.

Although PGP is available on all common platforms, its user interface is essentially derived from the UNIX command line. In other words, it's not particularly user-friendly. The ViaCrypt version has addressed this concern to some extent, but it's still fair to say that only a very small percentage of users use PGP on a regular basis. If S-HTTP were ever to move into the mainstream, more users might use PGP "behind the scenes" as the basis for session encryption.

One good use of PGP, apart from S-HTTP, is in dealing with information after a user has sent it to the server. Suppose that a hotel accepts reservations (with a credit card number for collateral) over the web. The hotel might use the Netscape Enterprise Server to ensure that credit card data is not sent in the clear between the user and the web site. Then, once the CGI script gets the credit card information, what can it do with it? If it stores it unencrypted on a hard disk, the numbers are vulnerable to a cracker who penetrates overall site security. If the card numbers are sent in the clear via e-mail to a reservation desk, they risk being sniffed en route over the Internet.

One solution is to use PGP to transfer the reservation message (including credit card data) by secure email. Start with a form mailer like Matt Wright's `formmail.pl` (available at Matt's Script Archive, **http://www.worldwidemart.com/scripts/**). Find the place in that script where it opens a file handle to `sendmail` and change it to the following:

```
open (MAIL, "¦ /usr/local/bin/pgp -eatf reservations ¦
➥mail reservations@localInn.com") ¦¦ &die("Could not open mail");
```

No user-supplied data has been passed to the shell. Now, put the reservations desk on the PGP public keyring. When the script runs, PGP encrypts (the `-e` option) the text (`-t`) from `STDIN` for user `reservations` into ASCII characters and adding *armor lines* (`-a`) to prevent tampering. The result is written to standard output because the filter option (`-f`) is turned on.

The reservations' clerk must have his own copy of PGP (it's available for PCs, Macs, and other common platforms). When the reservations' clerk receives the encrypted message, he decrypts it using his secret key, making sure to store the credit card data and other private information offline. He can also save the encrypted message on his local disk, using PGP and a secret passphrase.

PGP enables the user to input a *passphrase* instead of a password. Passphrases can be arbitrarily long and may have embedded white space and other special characters. Take advantage of this flexibility to make the passphrase difficult to guess.

Site Security

The first section of this chapter entitled, "Web Security on the Internet and Intranet," tells you what individual web administrators can do to enhance the security of their web site. Closing the door to HTTP infiltrators is of little use, if infiltrators can penetrate the site through FTP, `sendmail`, or Telnet. This chapter covers the steps the system administrator can take to make the site more resistant to attack.

General Security Measures, with Specifics for Windows NT

First, some general security tips apply no matter what operating system you are using. Whether your server is running Windows NT or a variety of Unix, you can enhance your overall site security. These tips apply to almost any system, from an operating system to a database. Specific examples are drawn from Windows NT.

Making Your "Admin" Account Less Accessible Rename the "admin" account(s) to make it more difficult for intruders to guess the name(s). Make another account—which you monitor closely—with a name that implies it is the administrator's account, but which has little power.

If possible, block the renamed administrator's account from being used at all unless a utility is run first. For example, on Windows NT, use the PASSPROP utility from the Resource Kit to keep the administrator's account from doing anything but logging on to domain controllers.

To minimize accidental damage to your system, and to make tracking admin usage easier, keep your use of the renamed administrator's account to a minimum. Don't do non-administrative work on an empowered account. Up to a point, the more barriers to climb to gain admin access, the better.

Rendering Your "Guest" Account Harmless If possible, make all your users log in with assigned usernames and passwords. For example, on Windows NT, C2CONFIG.EXE lets you "kill" the original guest account.

Sometimes you must have a guest account. If this is the case, rename the "guest" to something difficult to guess. Don't let it delete or write registry keys and files. If you must let the guest write files, let it be in a special "incoming" directory just for that purpose. Give the guest only as much power as necessary.

Make Your Workstations and Domain Controllers Secure Make sure you and your users log off as soon as you are done. When logging back on, use a secure logon program if one is available, such as the Ctrl + Alt + Del screen on Windows NT. To further guard against forgetful users, use a good password-protected screen saver.

Check and Recheck Security Settings and Admin Usage Remove unused user accounts. Review the list of users who have admin powers and monitor admin and guest usage. Check password and privilege settings in detail. Educate and re-educate users about the value of secure logins, prompt logouts, and difficult-to-guess passwords. Good security is an ongoing activity.

Exposing the Threat

Much of the material in this chapter provides explicit tips about how to attack a UNIX system. Some of this material is obsolete (but may still apply to systems that have had recent upgrades). All of this material is already widely disseminated among those people who are inclined to attack systems. The material is provided here so that system administrators can be aware of what kinds of attacks are likely to be made.

This section focuses on UNIX because most web sites are hosted on UNIX servers. UNIX is one of the most powerful operating systems in common use, and with that power, comes vulnerability.

Other operating systems, such as the various members of the Windows family, have somewhat less functionality and are consequently a bit less vulnerable. The Macintosh is unique in that it has no command-line interface, therefore, it is more resistant to certain kinds of attack.

Many checks for vulnerability are left undone, even though they are simple and they hardly detract from performance and usability. In many cases, the system administrator is unaware of the threat or believes that "it will never happen at my site."

A site need not be operated by a bank or a Fortune 500 company to have assets worth protecting. A site need not be used by the military for war planning to be considered worthy of attack. As the case studies in this section show, sometimes merely being connected to the Internet is enough to cause a site to be infiltrated.

Case Studies

Security needs to be a budgeted item, just like maintenance or development. Depending upon the security stance, the budget may be quite small or run to considerable sums. In some organizations, management may need to be convinced that the threat is real. The following case studies illustrate how other sites have been attacked and compromised, as well as government analyses of threats and vulnerabilities.

Making Sure You Have a Legitimate Version of SATAN

For some functions, SATAN must run with `root` privilege. One way an infiltrator might break into a system is to distribute a program that masquerades as SATAN or to add `.sat` tests that actually widen security holes.

To be sure you have a legitimate version of SATAN, check the MD5 message digest fingerprint. The latest fingerprints for each component are available at **http://www.cs.ruu.nl/cert-uu/satan.html**.

Electronic Data Interchange via the Internet

As businesses become more sophisticated, they have begun moving toward *Electronic Commerce*. Electronic Commerce includes the specialized area of *Electronic Data Interchange (EDI)*. True EDI adheres to rigorous standards and often is delivered over special networks.

A site owner can send email to a wholesaler ordering merchandise at any time, but that doesn't make the exchange EDI. EDI is characterized by four factors:

- Accepted standard messages, such as EDIFACT or X12, are used.
- There's direct processing of most messages by the receiving computer system.
- A prior relationship between the trading partners is theoretically unnecessary.
- Security is a factor in the communications.

The third factor might seem a bit odd. For many purchases, there's little need for a sales representative to contact a buyer personally. For commodity items, such personal contact prior to the sale represents an added expense for the seller that must be passed on to the buyer. The value added by such salespeople has traditionally been to make the buyer aware of their company as a supplier.

EDI is sometimes conducted over specialized value-added networks (VANs). These VANs serve to "introduce" trading partners who have no prior business relationship. Although each VAN is different, here's how EDI generally works:

1. Sellers register their businesses on one of the VANs, using standardized codes to identify what goods or services they sell.
2. Buyers post Requests for Quotations (RFQs) to the VANs in a standardized format.
3. The VAN delivers RFQs to the appropriate sellers by email.
4. A seller analyzes each RFQ and prepares a bid, which is posted on the VAN.
5. The VAN delivers the RFQ back to the buyer.

If the seller wins the bid, the buyer sends a PO message back through the VAN. A *contract award message* is posted, and in many cases (for example, if the buyer is the U.S. Government), the winning price is announced.

Two major sets of standards are used in EDI. The international standard, promulgated by the United Nations, is called EDIFACT. The U.S. standard is called X12. The ISO adopted EDIFACT in 1987 as its standard. The U.N. and ANSI have announced that EDIFACT and X12 will be merged.

N O T E The alignment plan was adopted by a mail ballot of X12 in December 1994/January 1995. That plan is available online at **http://polaris.disa.org/edi/ALIGNMEN/**. The text of the floor motion adopted at the February 1995 X12 meeting is available at the same site.

Find information on the Data Interchange Standards Association (DISA) at **http://www.disa.org/**.

Much of the impetus behind EDI has come from the U.S. Government. On October 26, 1993, President Clinton signed an Executive Memorandum requiring federal agencies to implement the use of electronic commerce in federal purchases as quickly as possible. The order specified that by the end of FY 1997, most U.S. Federal purchases under $100,000 must be made by EDI.

The President's order formed the Federal Electronic Commerce Acquisition Team (ECAT) that generated the guidelines for the Federal EDI initiative. ECAT has since been reorganized into the Federal Electronic Commerce Acquisition Program Office (ECA-PMO); its documents (and those of ECAT) are available on the Internet at **ftp://ds.internic.net/pub/ecat.library/**. The ECA-PMO also operates a web site at **http://snad.ncsl.nist.gov:80/dartg/edi/fededi.html** courtesy of the National Institute of Standards and Technology (NIST).

On the CD

The Federal implementation guidelines for purchase orders (in **ftp://ds.internic.net/pub/ecat.library/fed.ic/ascii/part-22.txt**) provide over 100 pages of details on how the U.S. government interprets X12 transaction set 850 (described later in more detail in the "ANS X12" section).

RFC 1865, dated January 1996 and titled "EDI Meets the Internet," was written by a small team led by Walter Houser of the U.S. Department of Veterans Affairs and reflects part of the federal focus and enthusiasm for EDI. Although much of EDI is conducted through VANs, Houser *et al.* points out that the EDI standards allow almost any means of transfer, and that the Internet is well-suited for most EDI functions. The RFC quotes the ECAT as saying, "The Internet network may be used for EDI transactions when it is capable of providing the essential reliability, security, and privacy needed for business transactions." You can read this RFC from the files on the CD-ROM that accompanies this book.

Although the largest portion of Federal EDI is conducted over the VANs, Houser et al. makes a strong case that tools are available on the Internet today to provide this essential reliability, security, and privacy.

N O T E For more information on the Federal EDI initiative, join the **FED-REG** mailing list. To subscribe, send a message to **fed-reg-request@snad.ncsl.nist.gov**. The message body should contain only the following line:

```
subscribe fed-reg
```

continues

continued

ECAT also operates a mailing list, appropriately named `ecat`. To subscribe, send a message to **listserv@forums.fed.gov**, containing only the following line:

```
subscribe ecat firstname lastname
```

For more general information on EDI, subscribe to the EDI-L mailing list. Send a message to **listserv@uccvma.ucop.edu** containing only the following line:

```
subscribe edi-l yourname
```

This mailing list also is transferred via gateway to the USENET newsgroup **bit.listserv.edu-l**.

New methods of EDI, including EDI over the Internet, are discussed on the EDI-NEW mailing list. Send a message to **edi-new-request@tegsun.harvard.edu** containing only the following line:

```
subscribe edi-new yourname
```

ON THE WEB

ftp://ftp.sterling.com/edi/lists/ To come up to speed quickly on EDI, review archives of the many EDI-related mailing lists stored at this site.

EDI Standards

The key to making EDI work on a large scale is the rigorous use of standards. In recent years, two groups of standards have emerged—an international standard promulgated by the United Nations, and a U.S. standard designed by the American National Standards Institute (ANSI). More recently, both organizations have agreed to build a unified standard, which will enable EDI to become truly worldwide. This section describes the two major standards sets and their proposed unification.

UN/EDIFACT The United Nations promulgates a set of rules "for Electronic Data Interchange For Administration, Commerce and Transport" (UN/EDIFACT). The full standards are available online at **http://www.premenos.com/**. Each document type (known in EDI circles as a *transaction set*) is quite robust. A purchase order can specify multiple items or services, for example, from more than one delivery schedule, with full details for transport and destination as well as delivery patterns.

The full UN/EDIFACT standard is available online at **http://www.itu.ch**.

ASC X12 The U.S. standards accrediting body is the American National Standards Institute (ANSI). ANSI defines EDI through its Accredited Standards Committee X12 and the EDI standard has taken on the name of that committee.

CAUTION

The ANSI EDI standards are voluminous. Before investing in EDI software, get the help of a good consultant. Before writing any EDI software of your own, read the standards. The X12 standard is available from:

Data Interchange Standards Association, Inc.
1800 Diagonal Road, Suite 200
Alexandria, Virginia 22314-2852
Voice: 1-703-548-7005
FAX: 1-703-548-5738

For more information on X12, subscribe to the **x12g** and **x12c-impdef** mailing lists. For the former, send email to **x12g-request@snad.ncsl.nist.gov** with the following message:

```
subscribe x12g
```

For the latter, send email to **x12c-impdef-request@snad.ncsl.nist.gov** with the following message:

```
subscribe x12c-impdef
```

The Grand Unification UN/EDIFACT and X12 are due to be merged, and many firms already are using one of these two standards as the basis for their in-house standard. Subscribe to the EDI mailing lists mentioned earlier or work with a EDI mapping software developer (some points of contact are coming up in the next section) to find out which standards may apply to your firm and your trading partners.

Secure Email

EDI is associated with real money and is a natural target of thieves. Here are a few ways that a thief can take advantage of unsecured EDI:

- Placing false purchase orders and stealing the merchandise.
- Changing the ship-to address of a legitimate purchase order to divert merchandise.
- Intercepting a seller's bid and undercutting the price.
- Monitoring how often a seller reports that they're out of stock in response to an order, to gauge production capacity.

To combat these problems, EDI needs two kinds of security:

- Digital signatures, including non-repudiation
- Encryption

Both needs can be met using the public key encryption systems that were introduced earlier in the chapter.

NOTE Netscape Navigator 4.0 has built-in secure email. Given Netscape's dominant position in the marketplace, secure email will become increasingly common. A respectable list of products are already S-MIME compatible. See "S-MIME Central" at RSA for details: **http://www.rsa.com/smime/html/products.html**.

PGP Recall that PGP (Pretty Good Privacy) is a private implementation of public key cryptography by Phil Zimmerman. His software is widely available in the U.S. and overseas, and a commercial version also is available.

PGP can provide encryption and digital signatures, as well as encryption of local files using a secret key algorithm. The PGP code is open for inspection and has been thoroughly checked by experts. It's not based on open standards (Internet RFCs), but it's not often named as part of an EDI or near-EDI communications standard.

PEM Privacy-Enhanced Mail (PEM) is defined in RFCs 1421 through 1424. PEM provides three major sets of features:

- Digital Signatures, including non-repudiation
- Encryption
- Certification

Certification deals with the issue of trust. Suppose that Bob sends a signed, encrypted message to Alice, for example. He has to have Alice's public key—if someone can slip in the wrong key and convince Bob that it's Alice's key, then that person subsequently can read Bob's message (see Figure 11.4).

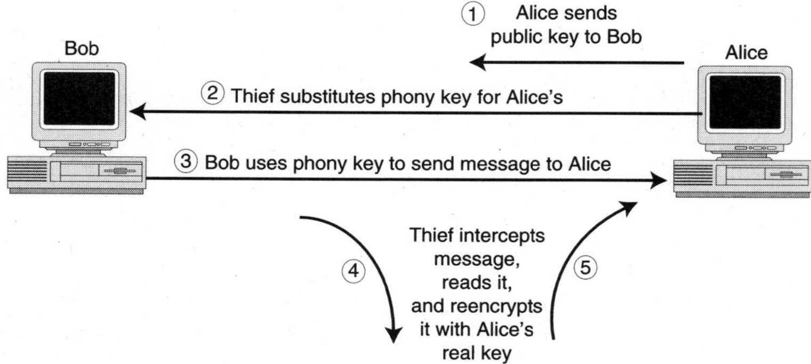

FIG. 11.4
Anyone who can trick Bob into using the wrong key can read the message that Bob intended for Alice.

Alice needs to know Bob's public key so that she can verify the signature. If someone can convince her to accept a forged key, then that person can send messages to her that appear to be from Bob (see Figure 11.5). The potential for abuse in EDI is obvious.

FIG. 11.5
Anyone who can trick Alice into accepting the wrong key can forge a message from Bob to Alice.

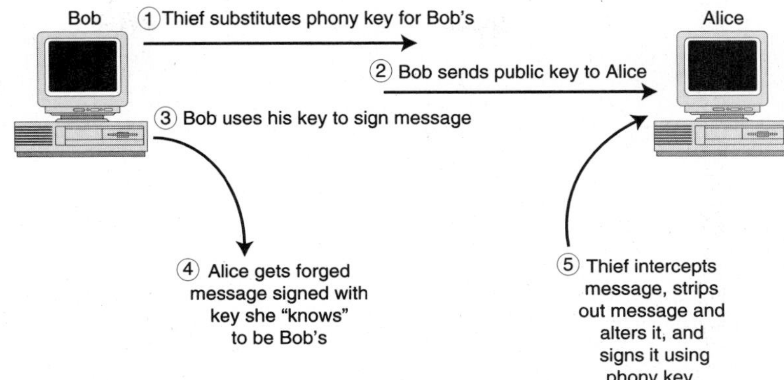
Bob
Alice
1 Thief substitutes phony key for Bob's
2 Bob sends public key to Alice
3 Bob uses his key to sign message
4 Alice gets forged message signed with key she "knows" to be Bob's
5 Thief intercepts message, strips out message and alters it, and signs it using phony key.

To reduce the likelihood of such forgeries, various certification hierarchies have been devised. If Bob and Alice know each other, they can exchange public keys through a private channel (for example, they can hand floppy disks to each other). If Bob and Alice are prospective trading partners, however, they probably have had no prior contact.

When Bob sends his first message to Alice using PEM, he can include a certificate from someone else saying that this public component really belongs to Bob. If Alice trusts the third party who has digitally signed the certificate, then Alice presumably can trust that the key presented as Bob's really belongs to Bob. We say "presumably" because the real strength of the certification lies in the certification policy of the third party. If they issue certificates to anyone who asks, then their certificates aren't worth much. If, on the other hand, they require three forms of personal ID, then their certificates have a higher value.

There are legitimate needs for certification authorities at different levels of assurance. A commercial authority preparing certificates that will be used to sign contracts requires a higher level of assurance than a low-assurance authority whose certificates are used for noncommercial purposes. This discussion ultimately leads to the question of who certifies the certifiers.

The *Internet PCA Registration Authority (IPRA)* described in RFC 1422 has been designated to certify *certification authorities (CAs)*. The "PCA" refers to *Policy Certification Authority.* A PCA is responsible for defining a certification policy and enforcing it among the CAs that it certifies.

Initially, IPRA is being operated by MIT on behalf of the Internet Society (ISOC). The plan is to transition IPRA to the Internet Society as soon as the Society is ready.

A hierarchy of PCAs and CAs is set up through IPRA, which intends to certify PCAs offering a range of levels of assurance. CAs then apply to PCAs for certification. Many CAs at the company or university level will certify users in much the same way as they now issue ID cards. Some CAs will require much higher (that is, commercial-grade) certification. Many CAs will also want to certify under more than one PCA. For example, a company might issue a low- or medium-assurance certificate to all employees who are on the Internet, but a high-assurance certificate to buyers who are authorized to legally commit the company to a transaction (such as a purchase). A portion of a certification path is shown in Figure 11.6.

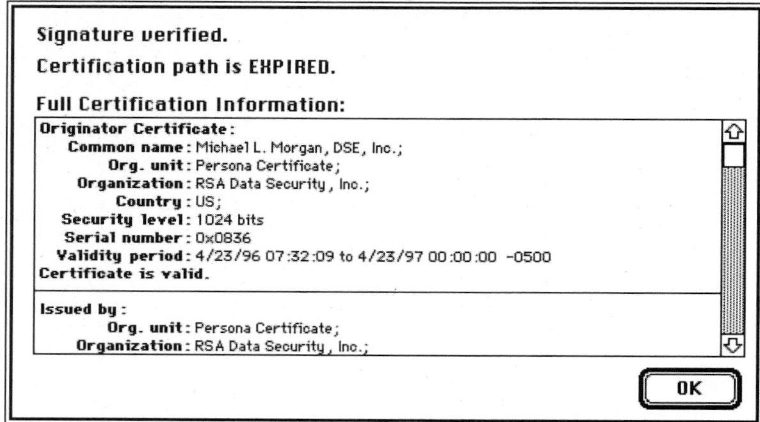

FIG. 11.6
Each certificate is dependent upon the one above it in the hierarchy—when one certificate expires, the path expires.

ON THE WEB

For more information on the IPRA, read RFC 1422, visit **http://bs.mit.edu:8001/ipra.html**, or send email to IPRA at **ipra-info@isoc.org**.

Mark Riordan has released a non-commercial program that implements much of PEM. It's called *Riordan's Implementation of PEM (RIPEM)* and is available to U.S. and Canadian citizens (or permanent immigrants to either country); information on getting access to the software is available at **ftp://ripem.msu.edu/pub/crypt/GETTING_ACCESS**.

Trusted Information Systems has released a non-commercial reference implementation of PEM named TIS/PEM. TIS/PEM has since been superseded by TIS/MOSS, the TIS MIME Object Security Services. TIS/MOSS extends TIS/PEM in that TIS/MOSS provides digital signature and encryption for Multi-purpose Internet Mail Extensions (MIME) objects. Thus, many types of files—documents in many formats, graphics, video, and even sound—can be signed and encrypted. TIS/MOSS supports the certification structures described earlier.

X.400

X.400 is the Open System Interconnect (OSI) mail standard that competes with various Internet standards. The Internet standards are developed using a fairly streamlined process based on circulation of Requests for Comments (RFCs) and voting by the Internet Engineering Task Force (IETF). X.400 is promulgated by the CCITT (now part of the International Telecommunications Union), so it has the force of international standardization behind it.

The way international standards are set, various telephone companies play a significant role in the process, which some observers believe leads to unnecessarily complex standards. It's certainly true that few readers would describe the international standards as well-organized or clearly written. Incompatible or non-conforming software often can be traced to differing interpretations of the standards documents.

The formal standards are spelled out in two sets of recommendations:

- Recommendations X.400, CCITT SG 5/VII, *Message Handling Systems: System Model—Service Elements*, dated October 1984.
- Recommendations X.400/ISO 10021, CCITT SG 5/VII ISO/IEC JTC1, *Message Handling: System and Service Overview*, dated April 1988.

Internet purists argue that X.400 has all the elegance of a standard designed by committee. X.400 fans argue back that the Internet was developed piecemeal and that new features must be grafted in—these features can't be a natural part of the design. For a detailed analysis of these arguments, see *The Internet Message: Closing the Book with Electronic Mail* by Marshall T. Rose (Prentice-Hall: 1993).

The U.S. Government has been a strong supporter of OSI, so X.400 is likely to play an important part in the continuing Federal EDI initiative. On the other hand, the Internet is growing far more quickly than X.400 and is likely to overtake anything that might be done in X.400.

File Transfer Protocol

Once two trading partners have "found" each other (possibly through email or a VAN), they might decide to exchange documents using the Internet *File Transfer Protocol* (*FTP*). They agree on whether to use X12 or EDIFACT, and then they establish FTP directories and give each other the password to their EDI directory.

Security For sensitive documents, two trading partners might agree also to use a public key encryption system, such as PGP or PEM. They then set up a blind "drop-box" for incoming documents, and an anonymous FTP "pickup center." Documents intended to be world-readable, such as RFQs, are placed in the FTP directory unencrypted, but with a digital signature from the originator. Sensitive documents, such as quotes, are signed by the seller, then encrypted using the buyer's public key, and are finally placed in the drop-box. If anyone breaks the receiving system's security (or steals the message from the Internet), that person is unable to read the message or change its contents.

FTP Macros The FTP macro capability can be used in FTP directories to cause certain programs to run on the FTP host. These scripts can be used to extract data from the firm's business software on demand, rather than storing all documents in an FTP directory.

FTP Programming If an application requires tighter integration than that provided by the FTP macros, a developer can write a program that obeys the FTP protocol but provides custom back-end processing. In his 1990 Prentice-Hall book *UNIX Network Programming,* W. Richard Stevens shows how to implement *Trivial File Transfer Protocol (TFTP)*, a simpler relative of FTP. Stevens' example requires over 2,000 lines of C code to provide a client and a server. Although some of this code consists of comments, the real FTP is more complex than TFTP. By the time your firm is ready to modify FTP, you're ready to start considering commercial EDI solutions.

Mapping Software

A number of firms, including Premenos (at **http://www.premenos.com/**) and TSI International (at **http://www.tsisoft.com/**), provide software that integrates with the client's business system on one side and the EDI standards on the other. Figure 11.7 illustrates this software.

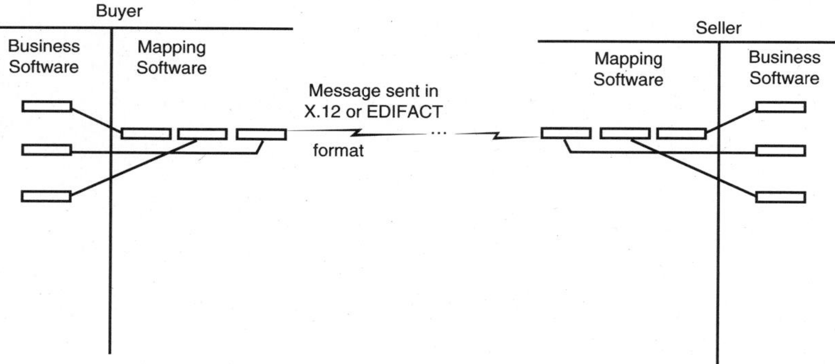

FIG. 11.7 Commercial EDI software maps from the client's business system to the EDI standards.

Some of this software, such as Templar from Premenos (**http://www.templar.com/**), offers confidentiality, integrity, authentication, and non-repudiation of origin as well as receipt. These companies also offer "shrink-wrapped" EDI that is set up for dealing with a specific major trading partner or industry.

Versions of EDI software are available for all machines from desktop models to mid-range UNIX boxes to MVS mainframes.

VANs

VANs once offered the only secure, reliable interface between trading partners. Surveys conducted during that time showed that most users were unhappy with their VAN, citing poor performance and high costs as reasons for dissatisfaction.

With the booming popularity of the Internet, more companies are looking for ways to leave their VANs. Many VANs, in response, are connecting to the Internet, hoping to deal with user's complaints as well as increase the size of their market. To see an example of a VAN that's aggressively promoting its services over the Internet, visit **http://www.compnet.com/**. The FAQ at **http://www.compnet.com/faq.html** is particularly useful. It contains price details, specific setup instructions for Macintosh and Windows machines, and information about how to begin to receive and respond to Federal RFQs immediately.

Internet EDI

The Internet is destined to play a larger role in EDI. A number of companies have banded together in a nonprofit consortium named CommerceNet to explore the general area of electronic commerce via the Internet. This consortium's home page is at **http://www.commerce.net/**. You can get an overview of the organization at **http://www.commerce.net/about/**. Also at that site is the charter of the CommerceNet EDI Working Group, which says, in part, that it will do the following:

> "Define an architecture that links buyers, sellers, and service providers through the Internet as well as proprietary networks…"

One of the group's objectives is to:

> "Support alternative business models where communications flow within a VAN, across VANs bridged by the Internet, or entirely on the Internet."

More detailed information on the progress of bringing EDI to the Internet is available by subscribing to the **IETF-EDI** mailing list. Send a message to **listserv@byu.edu** with the following message body:

```
sub ietf-edi yourname
```


Going Further: Additional Online Resources

There are several places you can turn for additional helpful information on the topics covered in this chapter.

You can get general information on public-key cryptography at

http://world.std.com/~franl/crypto/

RSA, the company that holds the patents on public-key encryption technology, provides online information at this site:

http://www.rsa.com/

You can get answers to your questions about PGP at:

http://www.cis.ohio-state.edu/hypertext/faq/usenet/pgp-faq/top.html

If you're looking for a book on PGP, you'll find the application thoroughly described in *PGP: Pretty Good Privacy* by Simson Garfinkel (O'Reilly: 1995).

General security tips, and tips about CGI security, await you at this site:

http://www.cerf.net/~paulp/cgi-security

This is a Frequently Asked Questions list addressing general security concerns:

http://www-genome.wi.mit.edu/WWW/faqs/www-security-faq.html

CHAPTER 12

NetHelp

by Eric Ladd

In this chapter

What Is NetHelp?

Psychologists have known for a while that knowledge retention is best when a person learns something when he needs to know it as opposed to learning something in a classroom setting. This is a primary reason for the success of context-sensitive help and other forms of electronic performance support that can come to the rescue with the answers you need at the moment you need them.

For most Windows-based applications, context-sensitive help is delivered using hooks that are built into the Windows operating system. This is fine up until you port your application to other platforms like UNIX or Macintosh—then you need to use other approaches. This is exactly what happened to the Netscape Communications Corporation. Netscape had versions of its Netscape Communicator suite that ran on Windows, Mac, and UNIX platforms and needed to provide help for each version. Rather than use the built-in Windows features for the Windows version of the software and different techniques for the other platforms, Netscape devised an approach to provide help that is HTML-based and, therefore, platform independent. This meant that the same help facility could be deployed on all three platforms without having to be re-tooled. Netscape's name for the new help system was *NetHelp*. NetHelp presents help context through Navigator, which uses JavaScript, Java, and other built-in components to deliver the content in an interactive way.

This chapter introduces you to some of the specifics behind NetHelp. In particular, you'll learn about how NetHelp systems are structured, how to prepare and deliver content through a NetHelp system, and how to use some of the tools that are available to NetHelp developers.

Figure 12.1 shows you the NetHelp system that launches when you press F1 in Netscape Navigator 4.0. The structure that you see in the figure is typical of all NetHelp systems. Navigation options down the left side of the window let you move through the system's table of contents as well as examine the index and search for a keyword. On the right side of the screen, you find a header graphic, detailed help information on a particular topic, and a navigation bar at the bottom that allows user to move forward or backwards, print out the help information being displayed, or exit the system. As a NetHelp system author, it is up to you to develop content for each one of these sections of the window.

Fortunately, developing NetHelp content is fairly easy. Because NetHelp is so tightly integrated with the Netscape Navigator browser, you can use any of the following in your help content:

- Text, formatted by any valid HTML tag, and hypertext
- Images, including animated GIFs
- Multimedia content like video clips or Macromedia Shockwave files
- JavaScript
- Java
- Dynamic HTML
- Style sheets

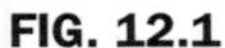

FIG. 12.1
NetHelp system windows have a standard structure and require content to be placed into each area.

Having access to so many different types of content allows you to create a help facility that is much more robust than just text, hypertext, and graphics alone. It also affords you several other benefits:

- **Your choice of authoring tool**—Because you are just writing HTML documents, you can use your favorite HTML authoring tool to develop NetHelp content. Other help systems require you to purchase a proprietary program to do content development.
- **Easy, centralized maintenance**—You can keep all of your NetHelp system files together in a single location and maintain those files as the "master" set of content for the system.
- **Single scripting language**—JavaScript is understood throughout the NetHelp interface so you can embed functions into your pages just like you would do with macros in WinHelp (a Windows-based application for authoring help content).
- **Customizable interface**—The structure of a NetHelp window is always the same, but it's up to you as to what you put into each part of the window. This means you can customize the look and feel of each one of your NetHelp systems.
- **Automatic table of contents and index**—The NetHelp Builder is a Java applet that scans your NetHelp system and builds a table of contents and a searchable index for the system.

Part II Ch 12

NOTE The NetHelp Builder applet is available as part of the NetHelp Software Development Kit (SDK) or as a standalone file. You can download the NetHelp Builder applet or the entire SDK from **http://home.netscape.com/eng/help/devkit/devkit-contents.htm**.

Now that you have a better understanding of what NetHelp is all about, you may be generating ideas for NetHelp systems for your own Web sites. While it is easy to set up links from a Web site or a Web-based application, you should also know that it's possible to invoke a NetHelp

what's in the Topic pane and to exit the system. When NetHelp is busy loading a page, you also see a progress bar in the Bottom pane.

As a NetHelp author, you are primarily responsible for producing content for the Header, Topic, and Bottom panes. Each of these is made up of HTML and graphics files that you create. Because you have full control over these parts of the window, it becomes an easy matter to customize the NetHelp interface with colors, custom graphics, buttons, and scripted events.

system from *any* binary application on any platform. Thus, you can use NetHelp to create context-sensitive help for any application that needs a help facility, not just for Web sites.

Before you charge into developing your first NetHelp system, it's helpful to take a few minutes to develop an understanding of how NetHelp windows are structured and of the different type

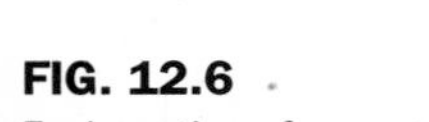

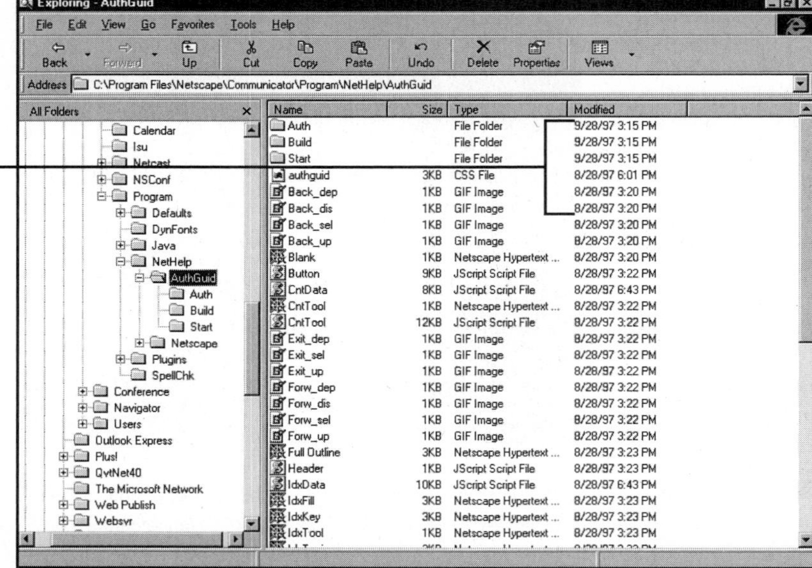

FIG. 12.6
Each section of your NetHelp system has its own directory.

- **Header File**—The Header File is an HTML file that populates the Header Pane with content. Usually the Header File contains a banner graphic and some type of navigation links to let you change among the available topics. Header Files are named according to the convention xxxxxHdr.htm.
- **Topic File**—The Topic File is an HTML file that contains the subsection and topic information. Subsections and topics are noted by being contained in `<H1>` and `<H2>` tags, respectively. They are also set up as named anchors with the `<A>` tag. `<A>` takes the `TOCSTRING` attribute which allows you to specify the text to use in the table of contents. Listing 12.1 shows the first few lines of such an HTML file for the NetHelp Author's Guide. The Section is Authoring, the subsection is Introduction, and the first topic is Authoring for NetHelp.

Listing 12.1 HTML code to define subsections and topics in a topic file.

```
<!-- =============== Section: Authoring =============== -->

<!-- =============== Subsection: Introduction =============== -->

<H1><A NAME="Introduction" TOCSTRING="Introduction"></A></H1>

<!-- =========== Topic: Authoring for NetHelp =========== -->

<H2><A NAME="Authoring_for_NetHelp" TOCSTRING="Authoring for NetHelp"></A>
Authoring for NetHelp</H2>
Now that you have read the
<A HREF="nethelp:AuthGuid/start:Welcome_to_NetHelp">Getting
```

```
Started</A> section and are familiar with the basics of NetHelp, you are
ready to begin creating your own NetHelp system.
<P>In this authoring phase you will:
...
```

- **Help Project File**—The Help Project File is named help.hpf and is generated automatically by the NetHelp Builder. Parameters in the Help Project File specify the name of the NetHelp window, its size, how the panes should be created, and how each subsection is divided into topics.

Even though the Project Help File is automatically generated, you can open it up in Notepad and make your own modifications to it. For example, you can change the default window size or specify a different way to frame the panes.

There can be other files in the section's directory, but there have to be at least the three files listed previously. Any other files are there to support the content in the Topic File. These might include graphic or other multimedia files.

Backing up a directory level, you'll find a number of implementation files in the folder that contains the system's sections. These are general files that support the creation of a NetHelp window. They have nothing to do with the content of your NetHelp system—they simply set up the framework into which you place your system content. A complete listing of these files would fill several pages, but some of the critical files follow:

- **Back_*.gif**—Four files that are used to render the Back button in the Bottom Pane. The four files each correspond to a different state of the button (not in use/grayed-out, mouse over the button, button pressed, button released).
- **Forw_*.gif**—Four files that render the Forward button in the Bottom Pane.
- **Exit_*.gif**—Four files that render the Exit button in the Bottom Pane.
- **Prnt_*.gif**—Four files that render the Print button in the Bottom Pane.
- **Tool_*.gif**—Three files that render the buttons that appear next to the Contents, Index, and Find buttons in the Locator Pane.
- **Wait.gif**—An animated GIF that is used to render the progress bar in the Bottom Pane.
- **NavUI.htm**—Places the buttons and accompanying JavaScript into the Bottom Pane.
- **ToolUI.htm**—Places the buttons and accompanying JavaScript for the Contents, Index, and Find buttons in the Locator Pane.
- **CntTool.htm**—Renders the Locator Pane when the table of contents is selected.
- **IdxTool.htm**—Renders the Locator Pane when the index is selected.
- **System.htm**—File that loads the core JavaScript files.
- **NSHIfrm.htm**—Divides the NetHelp window into panes and invisible frames for holding JavaScript code.
- **System.js**—A JavaScript file that defines a System object with handlers to process events like clicking buttons and links.

As you develop confidence in working with NetHelp, you can edit these files to further customize your NetHelp systems. For example, you can modify the NHSIfrm.htm file to break the NetHelp window up into panes that are sized differently from the default sizing. Another instance of needing to edit some of the implementation files is if you're using your own button and tool graphics. In this case, you need to update the HTML files with the names of your custom GIF files so that NetHelp doesn't use the default buttons.

Authoring a NetHelp System

Now that you have an understanding of the inner workings of a NetHelp system, you're ready to think about creating a system of your own. From the last section, you know that you have to:

1. Organize your help content into sections, subsections, and topics.
2. Create HTML and graphics files for Header and Topic Files.
3. Use the NetHelp Builder to create your table of contents and index.

The specifics of these steps are considered in the next three sections.

Planning Your Structure

The first step is really a planning step. It's best to approach the organization problem from the bottom level up. Take index cards and write a help topic on each one. Help topics should be chosen according to your anticipation of a user's need for assistance with a certain task or with part of an application's interface. After you have all of the topics written down, start sorting related topics into piles. When you're finished, each pile represents a subsection. For each of these piles, you need to create a Topic File containing the help content for each of the items on the index card.

NOTE NetHelp can best handle a long Topic File that contains several internal named anchors (created with the `<A NAME="name">` tag). Each anchor represents the start of the help content for a specific topic. With this kind of setup, the Topic File is really representing the subsection, not just a single topic. You can split the coverage of each topic into its own Topic File, but you have to go in and make edits to the implementation files so that the NetHelp system comes together properly.

Finally, you can gather related piles together to form your sections. Each one of these sections needs a Header File that displays a banner graphic and provides between-section navigation options in the Header Pane.

Creating the HTML Files

For each section you identify through your index card exercise, you need to create a Header File (section information and navigation) and a Topic File (subsection and topic information and navigation). Both of these files are just HTML files, but the Topic File requires the use of some special attributes so that the NetHelp Builder applet can do its job of creating the table of contents and index.

Listing 12.2 shows the Header File code for the Composer section of the NetHelp system that supports Netscape Communicator. Note that the file is relatively straightforward—the bulk of the code goes toward creating the table of linked graphics that allow users to change between sections.

Listing 12.2 Header file for composer section of Communicator NetHelp system.

```
<!DOCTYPE HTML PUBLIC "-//W3C//DTD HTML 3.2//EN">
<HTML>
<HEAD>
   <META NAME="GENERATOR" CONTENT="Mozilla/4.0b1 (Win95; I) [Netscape]">
   <META HTTP-EQUIV="Content-Type" CONTENT="text/html;
    charset=iso-8859-1">
<SCRIPT SRC = "../../Header.js" LANGUAGE = "JavaScript1.2"></SCRIPT>
</HEAD>
<BODY BGCOLOR="#FFFFFF">
<!-- Table to place banner graphic -->
<TABLE CELLSPACING=0 CELLPADDING=0 WIDTH="100%" >
<TR>
<TD ALIGN = "left" VALIGN = "top">
<IMG SRC ="composer.gif">
</TD>
</TR>
</TABLE>
<!-- Table to place between-section navigation links -->
<TABLE>
<TABLE BORDER = 0 CELLSPACING=0 CELLPADDING=0 WIDTH = 100%>
<TR>
<TD ALIGN = "center" VALIGN = "bottom"> 
<A HREF="nethelp:netscape/home:start_here">
<IMG SRC = "../shared/commIcon.gif" BORDER = 0 ALT = "Communicator Help">
</A>  
<A HREF = "nethelp:netscape/navigatr:A1">
<IMG SRC = "../shared/navIcon.gif" BORDER = 0 ALT = "Navigator Help">
</A>  
<A HREF = "nethelp:netscape/messengr:GETTING_STARTED">
<IMG SRC = "../shared/messIcon.gif" BORDER = 0 ALT = "Messenger Help">
</A>  
<A HREF = "nethelp:netscape/collabra:getting_started">
<IMG SRC = "../shared/collIcon.gif" BORDER = 0 ALT = "Collabra Help">
</A>  
<A HREF = "nethelp:netscape/composer:about_composer">
<IMG SRC = "../shared/compIcon.gif" BORDER = 0 ALT = "Composer Help">
</A>  
<A HREF = "nethelp:netscape/confernc:CONF_MAIN_ABOUT">
<IMG SRC = "../shared/confIcon.gif" BORDER = 0 ALT = "Conference Help">
</A> 
<A HREF = "nethelp:netscape/netcastr:net_main_about">
<IMG SRC = "../shared/netIcon.gif" BORDER = 0 ALT = "Netcaster Help">
</A>
</TD>
</TR>
</TABLE>
<BR>
</BODY>
</HTML>
```

One thing in Listing 12.2 that might seem perplexing to you is:

```
<SCRIPT SRC = "../../Header.js" LANGUAGE = "JavaScript1.2"></SCRIPT>
```

This is a modified `<SCRIPT>` tag that uses the `SRC` attribute to import the JavaScript code found in the file Header.js two directory levels above the directory the Header File lives in. With many common JavaScript files in use in a given NetHelp system, referencing them from a single file makes maintenance much easier.

Another item in the Header File listing that might seem new is the use of the nethelp URL form like you see in the line:

```
<A HREF = "nethelp:netscape/netcastr:net_main_about">
```

Netscape Navigator 4.0 is programmed to understand the nethelp URL to mean that it should launch a NetHelp window based on the contents of the netcastr section directory and that, after it's open, the NetHelp window should display the contents for the net_main_about topic. By using the nethelp URL, you can create context-sensitive links to content in your NetHelp system.

NOTE The full syntax of a nethelp URL is:

```
nethelp:system/section:topic
```

TIP You can also link to resources outside of your NetHelp system. When you do this, you should include the `TARGET="_blank"` attribute in your `<A>` tag so Netscape launches a clean browser window in which the external content can be displayed.

The Topic File is a little more involved. You've already had a preview of some Topic File code back in Listing 12.1. There you saw that subsections and topics were designated by level 1 and 2 heading tags, respectively. Also, each subsection and topic was marked as a named anchor using the `<A>` tag. Used in this context, the `<A>` tag can take three different attributes:

- `INDEXSTRING`—`INDEXSTRING` is set equal to a list of keywords to go into the index for the subsection. Words in the list are separated by the carat (^) character.
- `NAME`—`NAME` gives the anchor a unique name for targeting by other hyperlinks.
- `TOCSTRING`—`TOCSTRING` provides the text to be used in the subsection's or topic's listing in the table of contents.

CAUTION

Use of the `<H1>`, `<H2>`, and `<A>` tags supports the NetHelp Builder by giving it a predictable structure from which to build the table of contents and the index. It's important for you to follow these conventions so that your tables of contents and indexes are accurate.

Beyond these special uses of the heading tags and the `<A>` tag, it's business as usual in the rest of the Topic File. You might find that your Topic Files are rather long, especially if you are grouping help for all of your topics into a single Topic File.

Now that you've seen some of the nuances of the Header and Topic files, you're ready to create your own. If you need a jump start in creating these files, you can take a look at Listings 12.3 and 12.4 which present templates for generic Header and Topic files, respectively. The remainder of this section walks you through the listings and tells you how to insert your own content to create the necessary files for your NetHelp system.

To create a Header file, remember that you need a banner graphic and icons for each section. Listing 12.3 contains the generic Header file code. Note the comments in the listing that help you to understand the Header file structure and to know where to place your content.

Listing 12.3 HTML code for a generic NetHelp header file.

```
<HTML>
<HEAD>
   <!-- Import necessary JavaScript code -->
   <SCRIPT SRC="../../Header.js" LANGUAGE="JavaScript1.2">
   </SCRIPT>
</HEAD>
<!-- Start Header body, setting background color to white -->
<BODY BGCOLOR="#FFFFFF">
<!-- Place the banner graphic first. -->
<TABLE WIDTH="100%" CELLPADDING=0 CELLSPACING=0 BORDER=0>
   <TR>
      <TD VALIGN="TOP" ALIGN="CENTER">
         <IMG SRC="URL_of_banner_graphic">
      </TD>
   </TR>
</TABLE>
<!-- Now place the section icons and link them to their -->
<!-- respective Topic files using a nethelp URL. -->
<TABLE WIDTH="100%" CELLPADDING=0 CELLSPACING=0 BORDER=0>
  <TR>
     <TD VALIGN="BOTTOM" ALIGN="CENTER">
         
        <!-- Icon and link for section 1 -->
        <A HREF="nethelp:system_name/section1:starting_topic">
        <IMG SRC="URL_for_section1_icon" BORDER=0 ALT="Section 1 Name">
        </A>  
        <!-- Icon and link for section 2 -->
        <A HREF="nethelp:system_name/section2:starting_topic">
        <IMG SRC="URL_for_section2_icon" BORDER=0 ALT="Section 2 Name">
        </A>  
        <!-- Icon and link for section 3 -->
        <A HREF="nethelp:system_name/section3:starting_topic">
        <IMG SRC="URL_for_section3_icon" BORDER=0 ALT="Section 3 Name">
        </A>  
        ...
        <!-- Repeat for as many sections as you have. -->
        ...
        <!-- Icon and link for section x -->
        <A HREF="nethelp:system_name/sectionx:starting_topic">
        <IMG SRC="URL_for_sectionx_icon" BORDER=0 ALT="Section x Name">
```

continues

Listing 12.3 Continued

```
            </A>
         </TD>
      </TR>
</TABLE>
<!-- A line break puts a little white space below the row of icons. -->
<BR>
</BODY>
</HTML>
```

The <SCRIPT> tag in the Header file <HEAD> section takes care of reading in all of the necessary JavaScript code. In the document <BODY>, you need to first provide the URL of the banner graphic. The code is set up to use a vertical alignment of `TOP` and a horizontal alignment of `CENTER`, but you are free to change these according to your design preferences.

Next, for each section in your NetHelp system, you need to provide the URL of the icon that represents the section and the nethelp URL that points to the appropriate Topic file. This information goes into the second table you see in Listing 12.3. The table is made up of a single row whose only cell contains the linked section icons. Alignment in the cell is set to `CENTER` for the horizontal and `BOTTOM` for the vertical, but, as with the banner graphic alignment, you are welcome to change these values to whatever you like. The code as is presents all of the section icons in a row just below the banner graphic. Non-breaking spaces are used after each icon to provide a little white space.

NOTE It is important to leave the `BORDER=0` attribute in each <IMG> tag that places a section icon. Otherwise, because the icon is linked, users will see a colored border all the way around the image.

Also, make sure you use the `ALT` attribute to provide a text-based alternative for each icon. This ensures that something useful appears in place of the icon if the image file does not load properly.

When your Header file is done, you need to save it with the following naming convention: the name must end with the characters Hdr.htm, and the first five characters of the file name should be the first five characters of the Topic file name. So, for example, if your Topic file is named overview.htm, then your corresponding Header file must be named overvHdr.htm.

With the Header file finished, you can move on to create the Topic file. A Topic file template appears in Listing 12.4.

Listing 12.4 HTML code for a generic NetHelp topic file.

```
<HTML>
<HEAD>
   <!-- Import necessary JavaScript code -->
   <SCRIPT SRC="../../Topic.js"  LANGUAGE="JavaScript1.2">
   </SCRIPT>
   ...
```

```
    <!-- Document head can also contain title, style sheet link, etc. -->
    ...
</HEAD>
<BODY BGCOLOR="#FFFFFF">

<!-- Section name appears as a level 1 heading -->
<!-- The NAME attribute serves as the section name in a nethelp URL. -->
<!-- The TOCSTRING attribute is used by the Builder to construct -->
<!-- the table of contents. -->

<H1><A NAME="section_name" TOCSTRING="section_name"></A></H1>

<!-- Topics within the section appear as level 2 headings. -->
<!-- The NAME attribute serves as the topic name in a nethelp URL. -->
<!-- The TOCSTRING attribute is used by the Builder to construct -->
<!-- the table of contents. -->

<H2>
<A NAME="topic1_name"
TOCSTRING="topic1_name" INDEXSTRING="topic1^index^keywords"></A>
Topic 1
</H2>
Topic 1 Content

<!-- Repeat the above structure for each topic. -->

<H2>
<A NAME="topic2_name"
TOCSTRING="topic2_name" INDEXSTRING="topic2^index^keywords"></A>
Topic 2
</H2>
Topic 2 Content
...
<H2>
<A NAME="topicx_name"
TOCSTRING="topicx_name" INDEXSTRING="topicx^index^keywords"></A>
Topic x
</H2>
Topic x Content
...
</BODY>
</HTML>
```


The Topic file begins much like the Header file did, in that you need to read in the standard JavaScript code that supports the functionality of the Topic Pane. You do this with the <SCRIPT> tag shown in the document <HEAD>. Note that you can give the Topic file an HTML title or set up a link to a style sheet in the document <HEAD> as well.

The name of the section is set up next as a level 1 heading with the <H1> and <A> tags. The NAME attribute of the <A> tag is set equal to the section's name and is what you use for the section portion of a nethelp URL. The TOCSTRING attribute is set equal to whatever text you want to appear at the section's position in the table of contents.

For the business letter example in the preceding section, you might compose a DTD that looks like this:

```
<!ELEMENT letter (date, insideaddress, salutation, body, closing,
signature?)>
<!ELEMENT date (#PCDATA)>
<!ATTLIST date align (left¦right) "left">
<!ELEMENT insideaddress (#PCDATA ¦ br*)>
<!ELEMENT br EMPTY>
<!ELEMENT salutation (#PCDATA)>
<!ELEMENT body (p+)>
<!ELEMENT p (#PCDATA)>
<!ATTLIST p align (left¦justify¦right) "left">
<!ELEMENT closing (#PCDATA)>
<!ELEMENT signature (#PCDATA)>
```

This code may not be as clear as the markup it specifies, so here is a line-by-line description of what the DTD says:

- A `LETTER` has exactly one `DATE`, one `INSIDEADDRESS`, one `SALUTATION`, one `BODY`, one `CLOSING`, and an optional `SIGNATURE`.
- A `DATE` just contains text.
- The `DATE` element has an attribute called `ALIGN` that can take on values of `LEFT` and `RIGHT`. In the absence of a specification for `ALIGN`, its value should be taken to be equal to `LEFT`.
- An `<INSIDEADDRESS>` contains text and zero or more `<BR/>` elements.
- The `<BR/>` element is empty (that is, it has no end tag).
- A `<SALUTATION>` just contains text.
- The `<BODY>` is comprised of one or more `<P>` elements.
- The `<P>` element just contains text.
- The `<P>` element also has an `ALIGN` attribute that can equal `LEFT`, `JUSTIFY`, or `RIGHT`. Its default value is taken to be `LEFT`.
- The `<CLOSING>` element just contains text.
- The `<SIGNATURE>` element just contains text.

Just by knowing these rules, any XML parser could properly process your document. In addition to being useful for XML parsers and browsers, a DTD is useful in a few other situations:

- XML authoring tools use DTDs to validate the code you write. If the syntax in your XML document is incorrect, the program can detect and flag it for you. As the next section explains, the program should not even enable you to save the document unless it conforms to a DTD.
- An XML browser can't know the default values of any attributes without a DTD.
- Just as with HTML, XML ignores extra white space characters (spaces, carriage returns, tabs) beyond a single space. Specifically, if an element's content model is *mixed* (meaning it can be both text and other elements), white space within the element is taken to be significant. Elements that contain only other elements are said to have *element content*; white space in these elements is ignored.

Most importantly, DTDs enable you to publish your documents for consumption by others. To accomplish this, however, you must include instructions in your documents that tell an XML processing program how to find your DTD. Adding a simple <!DOCTYPE> element at the start of your XML file takes care of this. For the letter example, you might reference its DTD as follows:

```
<!DOCTYPE LETTER SYSTEM "http:/www.yourserver.com/DTDs/letter.dtd">
<LETTER>
<DATE ALIGN="RIGHT">
December 1, 1997
</DATE>
<INSIDEADDRESS>
...
</LETTER>
```

The first line in the code directs the XML processor to the DTD at **http://www.yourserver.com/DTDs/letter.dtd**. The processor can then download the DTD and use it to check the document for appropriate syntax and to determine default attribute values.

Valid and Well-Formed XML Documents

For all the value a DTD provides, you may be surprised to learn that DTDs are not absolutely necessary. If an XML document conforms to a few key rules, a parser should still be capable of handling it. Specifically, a document is said to be *well-formed* if:

- It contains one or more elements.
- The document conforms to the grammar put forth in the XML specification.
- There is one element called the *root or document element* whose start and end tags are not contained by any other element. The `<LETTER>` element would be the root element for the letter example.
- All other non-empty elements are properly nested.
- All attribute values are contained by quotation marks.
- All entities have either been declared in the DTD or are one of the following reserved entities: `&`, `<`, `>`, `'`, and `"`.

Even in the absence of a DTD, an XML parser should correctly parse a well-formed document. This means that the parser can build the document tree (the logical structure that the parser creates as it processes the document), but it cannot assess the proper use of the elements.

The key rule to remember about well-formed documents is this: If it is not well-formed, it is not XML. A document that is not well-formed will be summarily rejected by any XML parser. This seemingly rigid approach has the following two important advantages:

- It ensures that XML never "breaks" a browser the way extended HTML tags can. If a document is well-formed, an XML browser is guaranteed to be capable of rendering it. If a document isn't well-formed, the browser just ignores it.

- It forces XML authors to get into good coding habits, as opposed to the sloppy habits that have come to plague HTML documents. Because the rules of being well-formed are well established, any XML editing program should be capable of checking an author's work to determine whether it is well-formed before saving.

If there is a DTD specified for a well-formed document and the document conforms to the DTD, the document is said to be *valid.* Validity is a stronger requirement than being well-formed. However, because validity implies the presence of a DTD, it is certainly the preferred state of the two. The primary benefit of having a valid document is that it is widely publishable. A valid document must have a DTD, and if you make that DTD available with the document, any XML processing program can use the DTD to facilitate the parsing and rendering of the document. Because the DTD formally defines the document, it also becomes easier to bring other functionality to bear on the document, such as search engines, style sheets, non-visual browsers, and printing applications.

Linking with XML

The first phase of the W3C's rollout of XML was issuing the draft standard for basic XML grammar. That draft is really just a set of rules for how elements, entities, processing instructions, and so on must be structured for a document to be considered an XML document. The draft does not specify any particular elements because XML authors are free to create their own. The same is true for entities, except for the five reserved entity characters (`<`, `>`, `&`, `"`, `'`). Although the draft sounds vague, remember that, in a sense, it is supposed to be. The "extensibility" part of XML comes from the ability to form your own sets of elements and entities according to your needs.

One important idea that the draft of the grammar standard does not address is linking documents. If you are familiar with HTML, you know that you use an `<A>` element to link text or a graphics to another document. But because there are no specific elements in XML, you may be wondering how XML documents get linked together. The answer lies in the second phase of the XML rollout—the draft standard for XML linking (the XML Linking Specification [XLL]). In keeping with the "extensible and flexible" philosophy inherent in XML, the standard calls for more than just the traditional unidirectional linking you get with HTML. Instead, with XML, you can do extended linking that allows for multidirectional links or links to special kinds of information. The next three sections look at what is possible when linking XML documents.

Simple Links

The simple XML link is very much like the link you get with the `<A>` element in HTML. Because it is up to the XML author as to what to name an element, there is no specific element name reserved for use when linking. For the purposes of this section, the simple linking element is `<SIMPLINK>`. You are welcome to call the simple link element whatever you would like in your own documents.

What sets simple linking apart from basic linking in HTML is the much larger number of attributes that a simple link element can take. Table 13.1 summarizes these attributes.

Table 13.1 Attributes for a simple link element.

Attribute	Purpose
`ACTUATE="AUTO¦USER"`	Specifies what event should trigger the traversal of the link
`BEHAVIOR`	Provides more detail about how the traversal should occur
`CONTENT-ROLE`	Describes the meaning of the content in the document you're linking to
`CONTENT-TITLE`	Provides a title for the linked content that can be displayed to the user
`HREF`	Specifies the URL of the document you're linking to
`INLINE="TRUE¦FALSE"`	Says whether the link is inline
`ROLE`	Describes the meaning of the link
`SHOW="EMBED¦REPLACE¦NEW"`	Tells the processing application how to display the information in the linked document
`TITLE`	Provides a title for the link that can be displayed to the user
`XML-LINK`	Specifies what kind of XML link the element supports

Many of these attributes would strike even a veteran HTML author as strange; thus a few additional words of explanation are probably in order. The `ACTUATE` attribute tells the processing application when the link should be traversed. If it is set to `AUTO`, the link is traversed when it is encountered. `ACTUATE="USER"` means that the link should not be traversed until the user explicitly requests it. After the link traversal begins, the processing application can get more details about how to carry out the traversal from the `BEHAVIOR` attribute.

The `SHOW` attribute tells the processing application how to display the linked content with respect to the content it is currently displaying. Setting `SHOW` to `REPLACE` tells the application to overwrite the current content with the linked content. A `SHOW` value of `EMBED` means to embed the linked content inside the current content. Finally, setting `SHOW` to `NEW` directs the application to display the linked content in a new context that does not change the nature of the display of the current content (much like a web browser launching a new instance to display a page instead of replacing the loaded page).

A link is said to be *inline* if information in the specification of the link can be used to determine the resource to which the link points. In this context, it is appropriate to use the `CONTENT-ROLE` and `CONTENT-TITLE` attribute to provide meaning and title information for the content. The

HTML <A> tag is an example of an inline link because its HREF attribute describes where the link points. If the link is not inline, it is considered to be *out-of-line*. You can specify CONTENT-ROLE and CONTENT-TITLE attributes for an out-of-line link, but they have no meaning in that context. Out-of-line links are useful for creating multidirectional links, but they have meaning only in the context of a link group, which tells a processing application where to look for linking information.

The XML-LINK attribute tells the processing application what kind of XML link it is handling. In the case of a simple link, you would set XML-LINK="SIMPLE".

NOTE Attribute names that start with XML are reserved for the further standardization of the linking specification. This means that you should not introduce an attribute name that starts "XML-" in any of your XML markup.

When setting up your link element, you can specify some default attribute values in your DTD that eliminate the need for a lot of extra typing. You know that <SIMPLINK> is intended to be a SIMPLE link, for example, that it will most likely be inline, that users will probably want control over traversal of the link, and that the linked content should replace existing content. You can express all this in a DTD as follows:

```
<!ELEMENT simplink ANY>
<!ATTLIST simplink
     ACTUATE          (AUTO|USER)            "USER"
     BEHAVIOR          CDATA                 #IMPLIED
     CONTENT-ROLE      CDATA                 #IMPLIED
     CONTENT-TITLE     CDATA                 #IMPLIED
     HREF              CDATA                 #REQUIRED
     INLINE           (TRUE|FALSE)           "TRUE"
     ROLE              CDATA                 #IMPLIED
     SHOW             (REPLACE|EMBED|NEW)    "REPLACE"
     TITLE             CDATA                 #IMPLIED
     XML-LINK          CDATA                 #FIXED "SIMPLE"
>
```

With this DTD, you could specify a link as simple as:

```
<SIMPLINK HREF="linked_doc.xml">element_content</SIMPLINK>
```

Values of XML-LINK="SIMPLE", ACTUATE="USER", INLINE="TRUE", and SHOW="REPLACE" are understood from the DTD.

Extended Links

Extended links differ from simple links in that they can point to any number of resources which may or may not be co-located with the document in which the link is found. The result is a multilinked link that can take a user to one of many places.

Two types of elements are needed to specify an extended link. The first is one to contain link text for each individual linked resource and the second is one to contain the elements that define the linked resources. As stated earlier, you can name XML elements in whatever way you choose. For this discussion, however, the <EXTLINK> is the container element for the elements that specify individual resources and <LOCATOR> is the element that contains link text for each resource. What that yields for a general extended link syntax is

```
<EXTLINK ...>
   <LOCATOR ...>Link text</LOCATOR>
   <LOCATOR ...>Link text</LOCATOR>
   ...
   <LOCATOR ...>Link text</LOCATOR>
</EXTLINK>
```

Each of these elements has a number of attributes, but they are the same as those used with the <SIMPLINK> element to define simple links. <EXTLINK> takes the following attributes:

- ACTUATE
- BEHAVIOR
- CONTENT-ROLE
- CONTENT-TITLE
- INLINE
- ROLE
- SHOW
- TITLE
- XML-LINK

For the <EXTLINK> element, you should set XML-LINK equal to EXTENDED. Otherwise, values and functions of the attributes are the same as specified in Table 13.1. Note that <EXTLINK> does not take the HREF attribute. This is because it just contains the pointers to individual resources instead of pointing to something itself.

The <LOCATOR> element takes these attributes:

- ACTUATE
- BEHAVIOR
- HREF
- ROLE
- SHOW
- TITLE
- XML-LINK

<LOCATOR> elements do point to linked resources. Because of this, the HREF attribute is necessary. You should set the XML-LINK attribute in a <LOCATOR> element to LOCATOR. Beyond that, the attributes are the same as in Table 13.1.

By putting it all together and including a DTD that specifies default attribute values, you might see a sample extended link that looks like this:

```
You can find a lot of good online references about
<EXTLINK>
<LOCATOR HREF="http://www.w3.org/XML/">W3C XML Page</LOCATOR>
<LOCATOR HREF="http://www.ucc.ie/xml/">XML FAQ</LOCATOR>
<LOCATOR HREF="http://developer.netscape.com/news/viewsource/
bray_xml.html">Beyond HTML: XML and Automated Web Processing
by Tim Bray</LOCATOR>
XML
</EXTLINK>
```

In a browser, the text "XML" would be hyperlinked. However, when a user clicks the text, the browser needs to do something to present the multiple linking options. This might take the form of a pop-up menu that lists W3C XML Page, XML FAQ, and Beyond HTML: XML and Automated Web Processing by Tim Bray. Users could then choose from among these three options.

NOTE The XLL does not say how an XML browser has to render an extended link. The method of rendering is up to whomever is programming the browser.

Extended Pointers

Borrowing from the Text Encoding Initiative (TEI)—a project whose objective is to identify standards and guidelines for the electronic publication of scholarly work— XML also includes the notion of *extended pointers*, or *XPointers*. XPointers basically enable you to link to a position in a document's parsing tree (the logical structure the parser uses to represent the document). This saves you from having to set up named anchors like you do in an HTML document. In the business letter example, you could link to the following:

```
child(1,body) (3)
```

This would refer to the third child of the first (and only) BODY element in the letter.

Links can also point to a span of the document. For example, the code

```
child(3,p)..child(5,p)
```

selects the third, fourth, and fifth <P> elements of the letter.

CAUTION

It is possible to select something to link to that is not a valid XML document when you target the parsing tree. The XLL spec is not specific about how to handle these situations.

In addition to selection by element, the XLL draft spec also calls for selection by instance number and attribute name and value.

Extended Link Groups

With the possibility of extended, out-of-line links, a processing application may need to process a number of separate files to determine all the links and their resources. To facilitate this processing, XML supports the notion of an *extended link group*—a logical grouping of linked documents. The group is defined by and contained in a grouping element and each document in the group is specified by an empty document element. Calling the grouping and document elements <XLINKGROUP> and <DOCUMENT>, respectively, you could set up the following extended link group:

```
<XLINKGROUP XML-LINK="GROUP" STEPS=3>
   <DOCUMENT XML-LINK="DOCUMENT HREF="doc1.xml"/>
   <DOCUMENT XML-LINK="DOCUMENT HREF="doc2.xml"/>
   <DOCUMENT XML-LINK="DOCUMENT HREF="doc3.xml"/>
   ...
   <DOCUMENT XML-LINK="DOCUMENT HREF="docn.xml"/>
</XLINKGROUP>
```

The STEPS attribute of the <XLINKGROUP> elements recognizes that the linked documents may include extended link groups themselves and places a limit on how many document levels deep the processing application should go when processing the extended group. The HREF attribute of the <DOCUMENT/> element gives the URL of each linked document.

NOTE Values of the XML-LINK attribute in both the <XLINKGROUP> and <DOCUMENT/> elements could have been set up as defaults in the DTD.

Using Style Sheets with XML

One of the important points made at the start of this chapter was that XML elements do not specify how content is presented. Instead, an XML browser should use a style sheet to determine how content in each element should be displayed. The delivery of a draft specification for XML style sheet language (XSL) is expected to be complete at around the time this book is published; thus at the time of this writing, the exact details of how to mesh XML with style sheets are not known. However, the W3C has hinted at what XSL will be based on, so it is possible to speculate as to how the XML document style sheets will work.

The XSL spec will be based on the Document Style Semantics and Specification Language (DSSSL), an ISO standard for specifying how a document is to be formatted. It consists of two parts: a transformation language, which is used to apply structural transformations to SGML files; and a style language, which is used to provide formatting instructions. Together these languages take raw SGML code and prepare it for display through a browser. The XSL

Working Group is adapting DSSSL to work with XML. After their work is complete, XML authors will have a way to specify presentation for their documents just as they use a DTD to specify syntax.

▶ **See** "Style Sheets," **p. 235**

In addition to DSSSL, the XSL spec is expected to eventually support other style sheet formats as well. Chief among these is the Cascading Style Sheet (CSS) specification, which is already in use on the web.

Applications

At this point, you may be wondering how you might use XML in your work as a web content developer. XML's best and highest use is for the creation of specialized markup languages. Therefore, if you want to determine how you can use XML, think about the content that you are publishing and what special needs you have based on the nature of the content. Perhaps your content is related to a specific scientific discipline or maybe your documents have an unusual structure to them. You can capture these characteristics by using XML to define a customized markup language that supports them. If you take it a step further and develop a DTD for your XML application, you open yourself to the possibilities of making your documents more easily formatted and searched. This is because the applications that perform these tasks can use the DTD to teach themselves the rules you created for marking up the content.

Despite XML's newness, it is already being used by some companies as the foundation for specialized markup languages. Some of these applications include:

- *Open Financial eXchange (OFX)*. A markup format to be used with programs, such as Quicken and Microsoft Money, to exchange information with banks. XML supports this effort by providing the capability to give meaning to marked up content. This enables financial applications to understand the nature of the information they are processing.

  ▶ **See** "CDF and Active Desktop Components", **p. 809**

- *Channel Definition Format (CDF)*. Microsoft's vision for push technology on the web is supported by CDF. Web site administrators can turn all or part of their sites into "webcasting channels" by building a CDF file that drives the channel. XML is useful in creating CDF because it was necessary to create elements to define the channel and the schedule for updating the channel content.
- *Resource Description Framework (RDF)*. RDF is another effort by the W3C aimed at producing a language for specifying web document metadata. *Metadata* refers to information about the documents themselves rather than their content.
- *Mathematical Markup Language (MML)*. Mathematics is a discipline with many unique publishing requirements, especially when it comes to special characters such as operator symbols or Greek letters. MML allows documents with heavy mathematical content to be rendered on the web.

- *Chemical Markup Language (CML)*. Publications in chemistry need to be capable of expressing descriptions of chemical formulas, equations, and molecule structures. CML supports chemists who want to publish their research to the Internet.

The preceding list of applications covers a diverse range of content. No one of these areas could have been handled by HTML, yet XML has the flexibility to define an electronic publication markup language for each one.

References

XML is in the very early stages of development and is sure to evolve beyond the draft specifications that have already been put forward. What's more, these changes will probably occur very rapidly because there is such a push to stop extending HTML and to start using a more flexible alternative.

The following list identifies some online resources that you can use to keep apprised of all the developments surrounding XML. Be sure to check them frequently so that you know the status of the "next wave" for web document markup:

- The World Wide Web Consortium is the arbiter of the XML specification. You can find the W3C XML page at **http://www.w3.org/XML/**. Here you will find links to the most recent XML, XLL, and XSL drafts and listings of XML-related software such as parsers and browsers.
- The XML Frequently Asked Questions (FAQ) list at **http://www.ucc.ie/xml/** is an excellent reference with separate sections for general, user-, author-, and developer-related questions.
- Tim Bray, an editor of both the XML and XLL draft specs, has published an article entitled "Beyond HTML: XML and Automated Web Processing" at **http://developer.netscape.com/news/viewsource/bray_xml.html**.
- Norman Walsh maintains a good introduction to XML found at **http://www.berkshire.net/~norm/articles/xml/**.
- Jon Bosak of Sun Microsystems authored the highly regarded article "XML, Java, and the Future of the Web," which looks into the type of automated processing that will be possible with XML-based documents. You can find the article online at **http://sunsite.unc.edu/pub/sun-info/standards/xml/why/xmlapps.htm**.
- You can learn all about DSSSL, the basis for the XML style specification, at **http://www.jclark.com/dsssl/**.

CHAPTER 14

Creating VRML Objects and Worlds

by Jim O'Donnell

In this chapter

The Virtual Reality Modeling Language

The Virtual Reality Modeling Language (VRML) is a language intended for the design and use of three-dimensional, multi-person, distributed interactive simulations. To put it in simpler language, VRML's designers intend it to become the building blocks of cyberspace.

The World Wide Web is based on the Hypertext Markup Language (HTML), which was developed from the Standard General Markup Language (SGML) standard. SGML and HTML are fundamentally designed as two-dimensional text formatting toolsets. Mark D. Pesce, Peter Kennard, and Anthony S. Parisi presented a paper called *Cyberspace* at the First International Conference on the Web in May 1994, in which they argued that, because humans are superb visualizers and live and work in three dimensions, extending the Web with a third dimension would allow for better organization of the masses of data already on the Web. They called this idea the Virtual Reality Markup Language. The concept was welcomed and the participants immediately began searching for a format to use as a data standard. Subsequently, the M in VRML was changed from *Markup* to *Modeling* to accentuate the difference between the text-based nature of the Web and the three-dimensional nature of VRML.

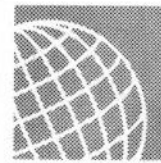

ON THE WEB

http://www.hyperreal.com/~mpesce/www.html You can go to this Web site to read the paper *Cyberspace.*

Silicon Graphics' Open Inventor was settled on as the basis for creating the VRML standard. Open Inventor is an object-oriented (C++) developer's toolkit used for rapid development of three-dimensional graphic environments. Open Inventor has provided the basis for a number of standards, including the Keystone Interchange Format used in the entertainment industry and the ANSI/ISO's X3H3 3D Metafile specification.

VRML's design specifications were guided by the following three goals:

- Platform independence
- Extendibility
- The capability to work over low-bandwidth connections

VRML Objects

The building blocks of VRML creations, usually called VRML worlds, are objects created in VRML. The VRML language specification contains a collection of commands, called nodes, for the creation of a variety of simple objects such as spheres, cubes, and cylinders, as well as objects consisting of an arbitrary collection of vertices and faces.

NOTE For a three-dimensional object, *faces* are the flat surfaces that make up the object and *vertices* are where the faces meet. A cube, for instance, has six faces and eight vertices.

VRML allows for the creation of more complex objects through the combination of simple objects. It is a hierarchical language, with *child* objects inheriting the properties of their *parents*. For instance, if a complex object was being defined to create a model of a human body, then by default, any properties defined for the body as a whole (such as color) would also apply to the simple objects that make up the body, such as the head, arms, legs, and so on. The rest of this chapter focuses on the creation of VRML objects.

VRML Worlds

The assemblage of VRML objects into a (hopefully) coherent whole defines a VRML world. There are many example VRML worlds on the Web that use the three-dimensional paradigm for different purposes. To define the placement and relationship of different objects to one another, you need to be able to specify their relative sizes and positions, using VRML's different coordinate systems. Additionally, VRML allows you to define what lighting sources are present in your world and what preset views are included.

Adding Motion and More with VRML 2.0

VRML 1.0 worlds are static. The only motion within them is the movement of the viewpoint representing the user as he uses a VRML browser to traverse through the VRML world. With the definition of VRML 2.0, VRML's capabilities were extended to allow the creation of dynamic worlds.

VRML 2.0 objects can now be given movement of their own, and three-dimensional sound (audio that sounds different depending on position of the listener with respect to the source) can be added. Another new capability introduced with VRML 2.0 is the ability to add behaviors to VRML objects. Behaviors—which can be scripted or specified in Java applets, for instance—are characteristics of objects that depend on their relationship to other objects on the VRML world, to the viewer, or to other parameters, such as time. For instance, a VRML 2.0 fish in an aquarium might swim away if you get too close to it.

Why (and How) Should You Use VRML?

As a Web author interested in VRML, you need to ask yourself what you would like to achieve with it. Unfortunately, there are two important characteristics of VRML that restrict its usefulness at the current time. The first is that VRML worlds tend to be *big*. Specifying three-dimensional objects as a collection of flat surfaces can lead to very large object descriptions, particularly when trying to model a curved surface. The other important characteristic is that the connection speed of the majority of people on the Internet is still limited to no higher than that achieved with a 28.8 or 33.6 modem.

Full-blown VRML worlds can take a long time to be transmitted over the Internet, which very often limits the audience to only those people looking for cool VRML worlds to look at. These worlds can also be extremely complicated to define and set up, requiring a lot more discussion than the space we have here. (Something along the lines of Sams' *Teach Yourself VRML 2 in 21 Days* is needed to adequately cover the subject.)

However, a very good use for VRML (one that doesn't have the problems of requiring huge files to be downloaded) is to add special effects to HTML Web pages. This is particularly true now that Netscape's Live3D plug-in, which adds Moving Worlds-based VRML capabilities to Netscape Navigator, is being distributed along with Netscape Navigator 3. This fact, and the ability to embed small VRML scenes into HTML Web pages, makes VRML an ideal addition to the Web author's bag of tricks.

Because of this, the primary focus of the VRML section of this book is to familiarize you with enough VRML that you can create small VRML scenes to achieve specific special effects within your Web pages. In the course of doing so, you will also learn enough of the VRML language and syntax to give you a good grasp on the language fundamentals, so that you can move on to the creation of larger VRML worlds, if you desire.

Basic VRML Syntax

VRML files are usually plain ASCII (though they are often gzipped to make them easier to transmit over the Internet), which means that you can create them using ordinary text editors. It is likely that you will use a VRML authoring program if you want to create a very large, complex VRML world—and even smaller worlds, if you have an authoring program available—where the details of VRML syntax will be hidden from you. It is a good idea to get a basic grasp of the important VRML language elements, though. Later, this will help you get the results you want.

Listing 14.1 shows a simple VRML file that displays a red sphere on a white background (see Figure 14.1):

Listing 14.1 redball.wrl A red VRML sphere.

```
#VRML V2.0 utf8

Background {
   skyColor 1 1 1
}
Transform {
   children [
      Shape {
         appearance Appearance {
            material Material {
               diffuseColor 1 0 0
            }
         }
```

```
            geometry Sphere {}
        }
    ]
}
```

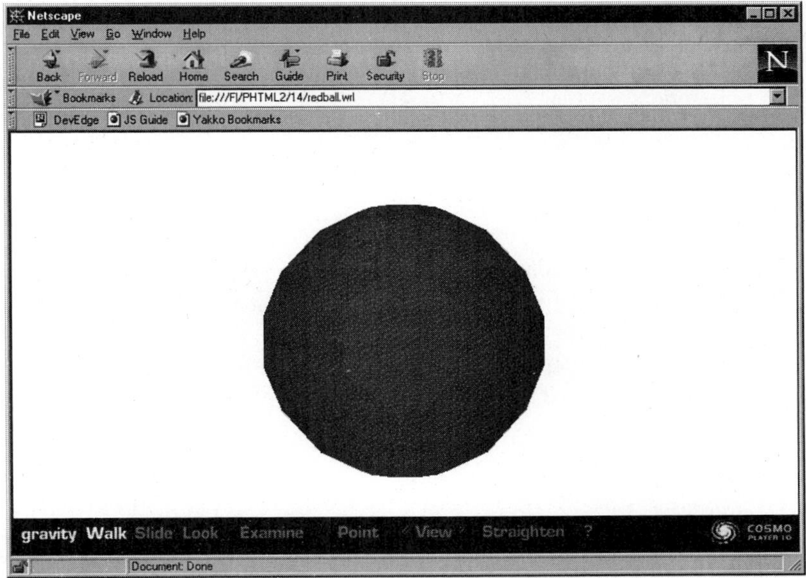

FIG. 14.1 Specifying simple objects can be done with just a few lines of VRML code.

The VRML comment character is the #; everything after a # on any line is a comment (such as "the color red"). The first line of the file begins with a #, so it is a comment. Unlike other comments in the file, this one is necessary. It identifies the file as being VRML and gives the version number of VRML used. VRML browsers require this information to be located at the start of any VRML file.

The first line of the file shown in Listing 14.1 reads `#VRML V2.0 utf8`. VRML 2.0 files generally have this comment in their first line, indicating conformance to the VRML 2.0 specification and that an international character set based on ASCII is being used.

Other than ignoring comments, the file format is entirely free-form. Anywhere there is white space—TABs, spaces, or carriage returns—you can have as much or as little space as you'd like. For instance, an equivalent listing to the one shown in Listing 14.1 is

```
#VRML V2.0 utf8
Background {skyColor 1 1 1} Transform {children [Shape {appearance
Appearance {material Material {diffuseColor 1 0 0}} geometry Sphere {}}]}
```

As with any programming language, you should structure and comment your VRML files well enough that they can be easily read and understood.

Nodes and Fields

If you are familiar with the C, C++, or Java programming languages, you probably recognize the curly braces ({ and }) to define blocks of related information. VRML files are made up of *nodes*, which look like this:

```
NodeType { configuration information }
```

VRML nodes are the language elements used to include the basic geometric shapes, transformations, lighting sources, and other objects. Each node has a number of *fields* defined for it that are used to configure how it looks or behaves.

The *NodeType* refers to one of the types of nodes that is supported by the VRML specification. The full VRML 2.0 specifications can be found on the CD that accompanies this book. Some of the nodes shown in Listing 14.1 are `Background`, `Transform`, `Shape`, `Material`, and `Appearance`.

Configuring Nodes with Fields The configuration information inside the braces consists mainly of *fields*. Some of the fields in the example are the `Material` node's `diffuseColor` field and the `Background` node's `skyColor` field. In general, each field has a name and a value. For the `diffuseColor` field, the value is 1 0 0, a set of three numbers that indicate the color to use for the `Sphere`, which follows (the three numbers list the color's components in the order red, green, blue).

Field values can be simple numbers, groups of numbers, strings, keywords, images, boolean values, and more. Some fields can have multiple values, in which case the values are separated by commas and surrounded by square brackets. For example, you could specify three colors for the `diffuseColor` field of the `Material` node as:

```
Material { diffuseColor [1 0 0,0.5 0.5 0,0 1 0] }
```

All of the fields for a given node have a default value or values associated with them—if you want to use the default, you can simply omit the field entirely.

Objects, Hierarchies, Separators

A VRML world can be thought of as a hierarchy of simple VRML objects. In VRML, the `Transform` node is used as the container for an object—that object is included inside the `Transform` node's `children` field. Not all `Transform` nodes contain any geometry (vertices and faces of VRML objects); some are used for grouping other objects together into a more complex object. This is how object hierarchies are specified in VRML. The attachment information is specified by placing objects within other objects, using the `Transform` node. In other words, the `Transform` node can contain *children* nodes to describe objects that are attached to it.

Grouping VRML objects into hierarchies and building them into full VRML worlds is discussed in greater depth later in this chapter.

Simple VRML Objects

The VRML 2.0 specification includes a number of nodes that let you specify geometric shapes. All VRML 2.0 objects are made up of one or more of these nodes, which are used within the

Shape node. The Shape node has two fields, an appearance field and a geometry field. It is in the place of the geometry field value that the VRML 2.0 geometric nodes are used. The nodes and syntax for each, along with an example VRML file, are shown in Listing 14.2.

Sphere

The `Sphere` node is very simple; it has only one field, called `radius`, that gives the radius of the sphere (the default radius is 1). Listing 14.2 shows an example of the default sphere, which is shown, as rendered by Cosmo Player within Netscape Navigator, in Figure 14.2.

Listing 14.2 sphere.wrl A simple VRML sphere.

```
#VRML V2.0 utf8

Background {
   skyColor 1 1 1
}
Transform {
   children [
      Shape {
         appearance Appearance {
            material Material {
               diffuseColor 0.5 0.5 0.5
            }
         }
         geometry Sphere {}
      }
   ]
}
```

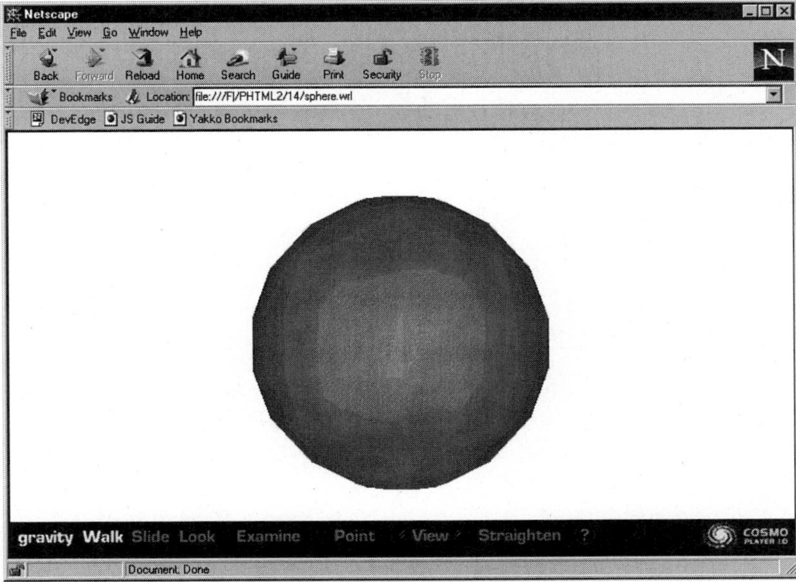

FIG. 14.2 A standard VRML sphere of radius 1.

NOTE The Appearance node is included in all of these examples to make the VRML objects a color that gives good contrast with the background so that you can see it easier. The syntax of this node is described later in the chapter.

Cone

A VRML Cone node is made up of two parts: the sides and the bottom. Both of these parts are optional. By default, a cone has both, but the sides and bottom field can be set to FALSE to turn them off. A cone has two other fields, height, specifying the height of the cone sides, and bottomRadius, specifying the radius of the bottom. The default values for these are a bottomRadius of 1 and a height of 2.

Listing 14.3 shows an example of a VRML cone, with sides but no bottom. As shown in Figure 14.3, when this cone is rotated to where you could normally see its bottom, nothing is shown.

Listing 14.3 cone.wrl A simple VRML cone.

```
#VRML V2.0 utf8

Background {
   skyColor 1 1 1
}
Transform {
   children [
      Shape {
         appearance Appearance {
            material Material {
               diffuseColor 0.5 0.5 0.5
            }
         }
         geometry Cone {
            bottomRadius 2
            height       6
            bottom       FALSE
         }
      }
   ]
}
```

Cylinder

A cylinder created by the VRML Cylinder node has three parts: the sides, the bottom, and the top. It has the same fields as the Cone field, with the addition of the top field to enable or disable the top of the cylinder, in addition to the bottom and sides. A longer, fatter cylinder is created through Listing 14.4, as shown in Figure 14.4.

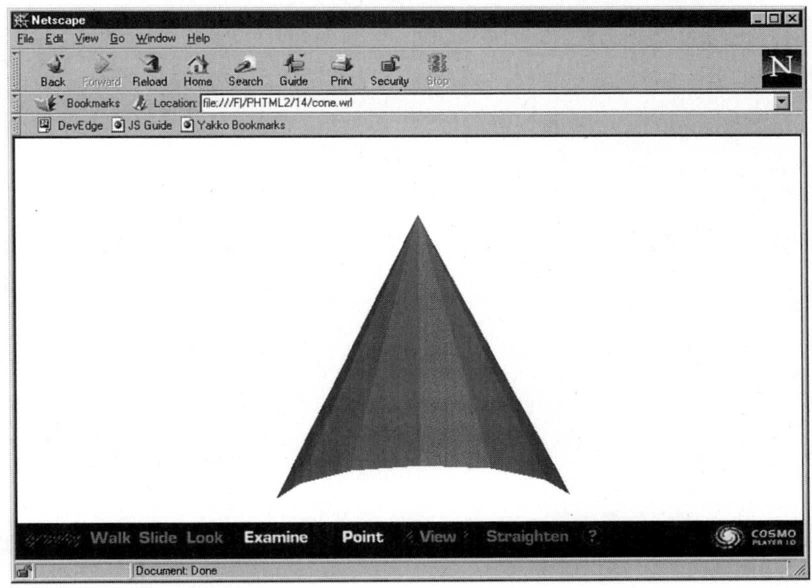

FIG. 14.3
A standard VRML cone; by specifying `bottom FALSE`, the bottom of the cone is not visible.

Listing 14.4 cylinder.wrl A simple VRML cylinder.

```
#VRML V2.0 utf8

Background {
   skyColor 1 1 1
}
Transform {
   children [
      Shape {
         appearance Appearance {
            material Material {
               diffuseColor 0.5 0.5 0.5
            }
         }
         geometry Cylinder {
            radius 2
            height 6
         }
      }
   ]
}
```

Part II Ch 14

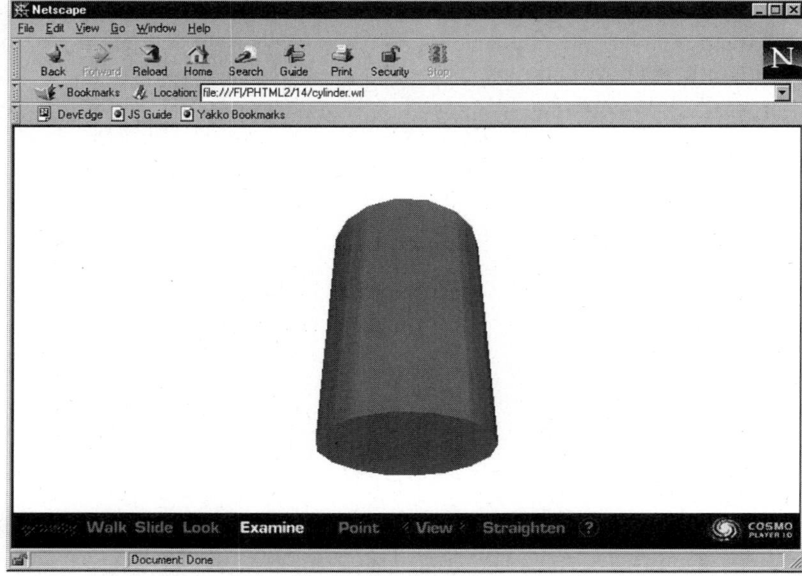

FIG. 14.4
A standard VRML cylinder.

NOTE While the Sphere, Cone, and Cylinder nodes would seem to specify curved surfaces in VRML, when the VRML file is parsed by a VRML browser, the objects are converted into vertices and faces through a process called *tessellation*. You should see this for yourself when you load a VRML example showing one of these curved surfaces into a VRML browser; rather than a single curved surface, you should be able to see a many individual faces.

Cube

A VRML `Cube` node creates a simple three-dimensional rectangular solid. Its single field is the `size` field, which is given three values to determine the cube's width, height, and depth (all of which have a default value of 2). Listing 14.5 shows an example of a more coffin-shaped VRML cube (see Figure 14.5).

Listing 14.5 cube.wrl A simple VRML cube.

```
#VRML V2.0 utf8

Background {
   skyColor 1 1 1
}
Transform {
   children [
      Shape {
         appearance Appearance {
            material Material {
```

```
                diffuseColor 0.5 0.5 0.5
            }
        }
        geometry Box {
            size 2 6 2
        }
    }
  ]
}
```

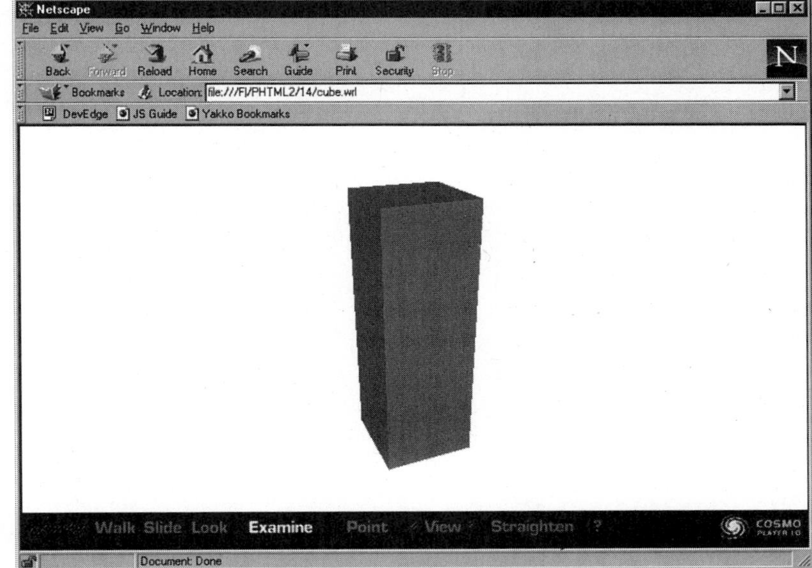

FIG. 14.5
A standard VRML cube; the length, width, and depth can be set to make any rectangular solid.

Text

The `Text` node allows you to create flat text objects in VRML. Because the resulting text is flat, it is possible that it is not visible when viewed, if looked at edge on. The `AsciiText` node has three fields: `string`, `fontStyle`, and `length`.

The `string` field specifies the string or strings to be displayed. Strings are specified in double quotes—if multiple strings are desired, each string is specified in double quotes, separated by commas, and enclosed in square brackets. The `length` field allows you to specify the length of each string; if the length selected is too large or small, the string is compressed or stretched to fill the space. A length of 0 allows that line to be any length.

The `fontStyle` field contains one `FontStyle` node; this is used to format the text. The syntax of the `FontStyle` node, along with sample field values is shown in the following:

```
FontStyle {
   family        ["SERIF"]
   style         "PLAIN"
   size          1.0          # (0,)
   horizontal    TRUE
   justify       "BEGIN"
   spacing       1.0          # [0,)
   language      ""
   leftToRight   TRUE
   topToBottom   TRUE
}
```

The `family`, `style`, and `size` fields determine the typeface and style of the text strings. The `horizontal`, `justify`, and `spacing` fields allow you to determine the format of the text and how the strings appear as a group. Finally, `language`, `leftToRight`, and `topToBottom` add support for non-English languages.

Listing 14.6 shows an example of the use of the `Text` node, with the results shown in Figure 14.6.

Listing 14.6 ascii.wrl Two-dimensional VRML ASCII text.

```
#VRML V2.0 utf8

Background {
   skyColor 1 1 1
}
Transform {
   children [
      Shape {
         appearance Appearance {
            material Material {
               diffuseColor 0.5 0.5 0.5
            }
         }
         geometry Text {
            string [
               "This Is",
               "A Test Of",
               "The Text Node"
            ]
            fontStyle FontStyle {
               justify "MIDDLE"
               spacing 2
            }
```

```
                    length [
                        0,
                        0,
                        0
                    ]
                }
            }
        ]
}
```

FIG. 14.6
VRML ASCII is two dimensional; if you rotate it so that you view it edge on, it isn't visible.

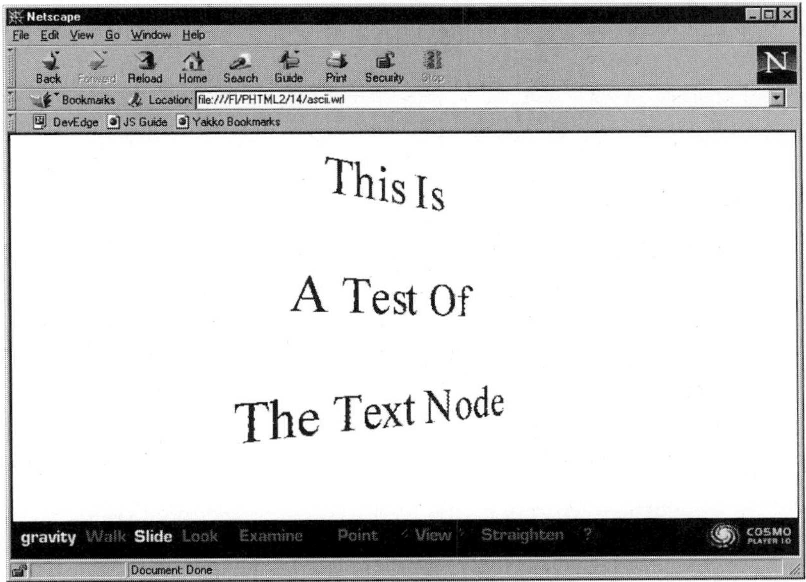

IndexedFaceSet

The nodes discussed so far are useful to start, especially if you're building simple worlds by hand. Most VRML files, however, make extensive use of another node, `IndexedFaceSet`. An `IndexedFaceSet` node is a way of describing an object using a set of vertices that are joined together by faces. Listing 14.7 shows an example of this, which creates a pyramid using five vertices and five faces to create the four sides and the base (see Figure 14.7).

Listing 14.7 pyramid1.wrl Arbitrary objects with VRML's *IndexedFaceSet.*

```
#VRML V2.0 utf8

Background {
   skyColor 1 1 1
}
DEF Pyramid Transform {
   children [
      Shape {
         appearance Appearance {
            material Material {
               diffuseColor 0.5 0.5 0.5
            }
         }
         geometry IndexedFaceSet {
            coord Coordinate {
               point [
                  -1 0 -1,
                   0 2  0,
                   1 0 -1,
                   1 0  1,
                  -1 0  1
               ]
            }
            coordIndex [
               0, 1, 2, -1,
               2, 1, 3, -1,
               3, 1, 4, -1,
               4, 1, 0, -1,
               0, 2, 3,  4, -1
            ]
            normalPerVertex FALSE
            solid           FALSE
            creaseAngle     0.5
         }
      }
   ]
}
```

The array of vertex coordinates is specified using the `coord` field of the `IndexFaceSet` node, which takes a `Coordinate` node as its value. The `Coordinate` node has a single field, `point`. The `point` field takes multiple values, each of which is a triplet of numbers giving the X, Y, and Z coordinates of one vertex. (Later in this chapter, you learn about VRML coordinate systems in greater detail.) There can be as many vertices as you need. Keep in mind, though, that each vertex only needs to be specified once, no matter how many faces it is used in.

The actual `IndexedFaceSet` node contains a field called `coordIndex` that stores a list of faces, as specified by the indices of vertices in the order they are used for each face. For instance, the sequence `0, 4, 1, -1` is used to create one face from the 0th, 4th, and 1st vertices (vertices are numbered from 0). The `-1` signifies the end of the current face, and the next face can begin with the next number.

FIG. 14.7
VRML indexed face sets can be used to construct arbitrary three-dimensional solids.

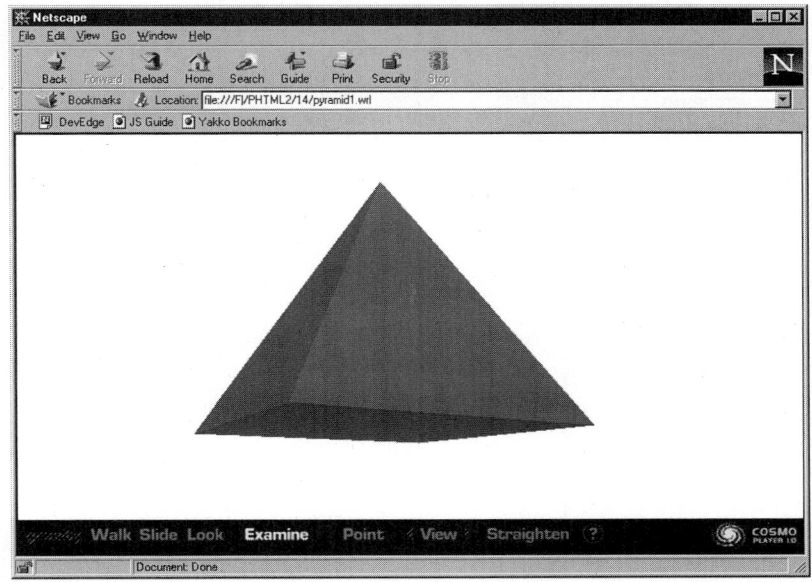

Some Hints on Using *IndexedFaceSet*

Although `IndexedFaceSet` is a very powerful tool, there are some things to watch out for when you are using it.

Make sure all the vertices in a given face are *coplanar*, meaning that the face is flat (this is true if either the X, Y, or Z component of each vertex in the face is equal). If one or more of the vertices are not in the same plane, then the object looks very strange when viewed from certain angles.

Avoid T-intersections. Two faces should always meet at a shared edge. If you have a face that touches another face without sharing common vertices, the round-off errors in the VRML browser causes viewing problems.

Avoid using too many faces, when possible, because that slows down rendering more than any other factor.

IndexedLineSet

Sometimes you do not want to create polygon-based figures but, instead, are satisfied to use lines. For example, the spokes of a bicycle wheel might best be represented by simple lines rather than `Cylinder` nodes. Not only is it easier, it also renders much faster.

To create sets of lines, use `IndexedLineSet`. The syntax is exactly the same as the `IndexedFaceSet` node. Figure 14.8 shows the same pyramid figure created in Listing 14.7, using `IndexedLineSet` instead. The listing, pyramid2.wrl, is on the CD-ROM but is not reproduced here because it is virtually identical to Listing 14.7.

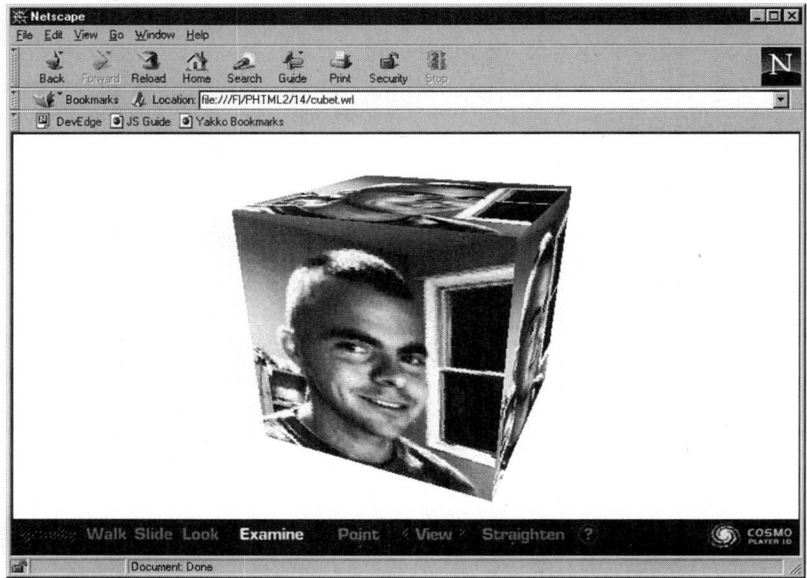

FIG. 14.10
Images can be mapped to the faces of VRML objects.

Because the faces were all flat in the preceding example, the image used wasn't noticeably distorted. That isn't the case when images are mapped to curved surfaces, such as those created by `Sphere`, `Cone`, or `Cylinder` nodes. Listing 14.10 shows another example, this time with an image mapped to a cylinder. As shown in Figure 14.11, the image appears undistorted on the top and bottom of the cylinder, but on the sides it is wrapped around the surface. Note that different graphics formats can be used as textures. The VRML 2.0 specification requires that VRML browsers support PNG and JPEG graphics, and recommends support for other graphics formats such as CGM and GIF.

Listing 14.10 cylindet.wrl Mapping images to curved surfaces gives a distorted result.

```
#VRML V2.0 utf8

Background {
   skyColor 1 1 1
}
Transform {
   children [
      Shape {
         appearance Appearance {
            texture ImageTexture {
               url "billy.jpg"
            }
         }
```

```
            geometry Cylinder {
               radius 2
               height 6
            }
         }
      ]
   }
```

FIG. 14.11 Images mapped to curved surfaces will usually be distorted.

VRML Modeling Software

As shown in the previous sections, creating simple VRML objects by hand is relatively easy. In the next section of this chapter, the discussion focuses on taking these simple objects, combining them into more complex ones, and assembling them into VRML worlds.

When creating a complicated VRML world, it is usually easiest to use a VRML authoring program. Even for the creation of simple VRML objects, the task is made very easy using a modeling program. As with any program of this type, what you lose in precise control of your VRML world, you usually more than make up for in increased productivity and ability.

There is an increasingly large number of VRML and other three-dimensional modelers and authoring programs available. Each program has its strengths and weaknesses. Information about many of them can be obtained through the VRML Repository, located at **http://www.sdsc.edu/vrml/**. Space does not permit discussing any of them here, but Figure 14.12 shows an example of three-dimensional text created using a VRML authoring program. It would be very difficult, if not impossible, to create something like that by hand. With a program designed for that purpose, however, it is extremely easy. The VRML file used to create Figure 14.12, is named `cpjod.wrl` and is included on the CD.

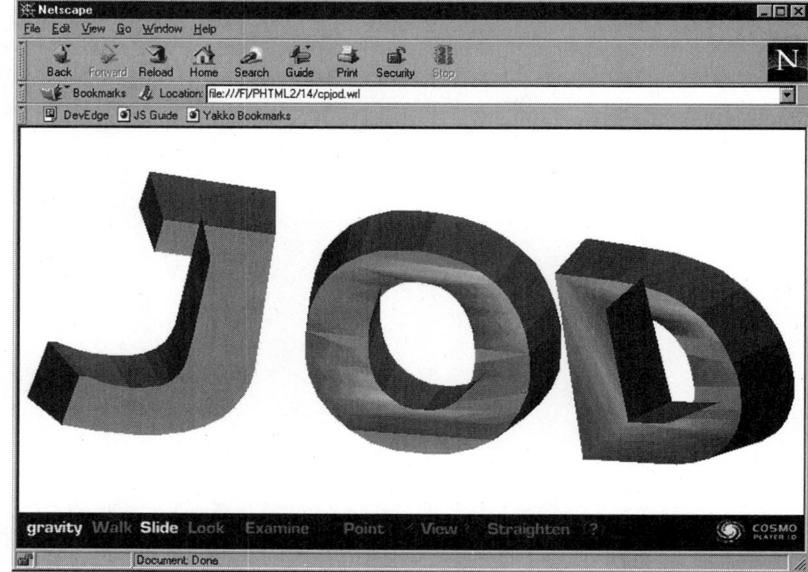

FIG. 14.12
Complex three-dimensional objects such as this can be created easily using a VRML authoring program.

TROUBLESHOOTING

Why are my VRML files created with a VRML authoring program so big?

As shown in the first half of this chapter, the VRML language makes use of a number of simple geometric shapes. You can create complex objects by assembling objects with more than one of these simple shapes. The most complex—and versatile—VRML node used to create shapes is the `IndexedFaceSet` node, which allows you to create arbitrarily complex, three-dimensional objects.

While this node is very versatile, it can also create fairly large VRML files. Most VRML authoring programs use the `IndexedFaceSet` node to create all objects, even ones, such as spheres and cylinders, that have other VRML nodes that can be used to define them. This means that, for a given shape, a hand-coded VRML file is usually smaller than one created via an authoring program—sometimes much smaller. Now, the ease of use of the authoring programs usually outweighs such considerations, but for VRML objects that consist of a small number of simple shapes, it might be worthwhile to create them by hand.

VRML Object Libraries

If you are interested in creating VRML objects for use in a VRML world, or with an embedded VRML special effect in a Web page, you should probably take a look around on the Web before starting from scratch. There are many places to get three-dimensional objects that you can use for your purposes, both in VRML files and in other formats that can be converted to VRML.

Probably the central clearinghouse of all things VRML, appropriately called the VRML Repository, is located at **http://www.sdsc.edu/vrml/**. This Web site contains a vast array of information about VRML, links to sites containing VRML browser and authoring software, and just about anything else you can think of that has to do with VRML.

Among the many other sites featuring VRML examples, applications, and objects is the VRML Models site located at **http://www.ocnus.com/models/models.html**. This site, like the VRML Repository library, features an indexed list of VRML objects and worlds. A unique feature of the VRML Models site is its VRML Mall, which is an actual three-dimensional gallery through which you can view all of its VRML objects.

Finally, the Mesh Mart, located at **http://www.meshmart.org/** was set up as a source of three-dimensional objects. While most of its objects are not in VRML format, they are available in formats that can be easily converted to VRML. Through the Mesh Mart, a program called **wcvt2pov.exe** is available that can convert between many different three-dimensional formats. It can read in files with the following formats:

- AOFF (*.geo) files
- AutoCAD (*.dxf) files
- 3D Studio (*.3ds) files
- Neutral File Format (*.nff)
- RAW (*.raw) files
- TPOLY (*.tpoly) files
- TrueType fonts (*.ttf) files
- Wavefront (*.obj) files

And write out files in these formats:

- AutoCAD (*.dxf)
- 3D Studio (*.asc)
- Neutral File Format (*.nff)
- OpenGL (*.c)
- POVRay V2.2 (*.pov, *.inc)
- PovSB (*.psb)

- RAW (*.raw)
- TPOLY (*.tpoly)
- VRML V2.0 (*.wrl)
- Wavefront (*.obj)

VRML Worlds

In the context of this discussion, a VRML world refers to a VRML file that is designed to be standalone and is loaded into a VRML-compatible Web browser on its own, without being embedded in an HTML-based Web page. Though there is no lower or upper limit on the size and complexity of a VRML world, these worlds tend to be fairly large. The three-dimensional VRML paradigm is often used to allow the user to "move through" the VRML world, visiting the parts of interest.

One example of good use of VRML worlds is demonstrated through sites that model an actual three-dimensional object, building, or geographic location, allowing remote users from all over the world to actually "see" what that object looks like, perhaps even to travel through it. For instance, a college or corporation could create a VRML world consisting of a three-dimensional model of their campus. Users could then move around the campus and see it from any conceivable angle. In addition, each building in the model could contain a hypertext link to an HTML Web page with information about that building. (For a discussion of adding hypertext links to VRML objects, see the "Linking to the Web" section later in this chapter.)

Another example of an appropriate use of a VRML world is any application that makes good use of VRML's three-dimensional capabilities. A commercial Web site might use VRML to set up a retail storefront that Web customers can move and browse through, much like a real store. The three-dimensional objects possible with VRML make it ideal for showing representations of mechanical parts or chemical models.

Inline VRML Scenes

Inline VRML scenes are best used to achieve a given special effect within an HTML Web page. By creating a very small, very specialized VRML scene and displaying it inline, you can achieve a variety of special effects. This is particularly true if you add some of the animation and movement extensions possible with VRML 2.0. An inline VRML scene can be used to achieve a similar effect to an animated GIF; depending on the desired effect, this can be done with a VRML file smaller than the GIF.

Design Considerations

After you come up with an idea for your VRML environment, you need to consider a number of other factors that influence the final design. As well as deciding what objects you want to put in the VRML environment and where they are with respect to each other, there are other factors that might limit what you can achieve. How big of a VRML environment should you create? How detailed should it be? How should it be shaped? How should everything be laid out? How should you create it?

Size and Detail

The first thing you should consider before drafting your environment is size—not in terms of the space it takes up in the virtual world, but the final size of your .WRL file. In a perfect world, everyone would have a high-powered graphics workstation and a T3 line connecting them to the Internet, and you wouldn't have to worry about how big your VRML file is, how long it takes to transmit over the Internet, or how long it takes to render after it arrives at the client machine.

In reality, however, things are quite different. Most people are running Pentium PCs over 28.8 and 33.6 Kbps modems. If you come up with a VRML world that is 10MB, you severely limit your audience because of the hour and a half download time and the time it takes for the client computer to render it. No matter why you are interested in providing VRML environments on the Web, no one will look at it if it takes that long.

Therefore, you need to consider how big you are going to make your VRML environment and how detailed it should be. It is a question of compromise. You can have a very large environment, but then you cannot add a great amount of small details. Or, if you only have a few objects in your environment, they can probably be displayed with a great deal of detail. It becomes a trade-off between size and detail.

That is why it is important to start the process with a purpose for your VRML environment. If you are trying to sell something and you want your customers to understand what they are getting, you should probably opt for multiple VRML environments, each of which displays a few objects—or even just one—in great detail. However, if you want to give your users a sense of what it's like to stand next to the Pyramids in Egypt, texturing each pyramid brick by brick isn't necessary. If you want to let your users tour a model of your entire electronics workshop, you might not need to include every oscilliscope and soldering iron. But, if you want them to see the tools used, you can limit your environment to a single workbench.

NOTE While separately modeling each brick in a pyramid, to use the example in the previous paragraph, is probably not necessary and a waste of memory and bandwidth, VRML does allow you to define and reuse objects within a VRML world. In this case, you could define one brick or a small set of bricks, and reuse these bricks to create your pyramid. Naming and reusing objects is described in greater detail later in this chapter.

Design and Layout

After you have decided how big your environment will be and what to include in it, the next step becomes deciding how it will look. A VRML environment is like any other space, virtual or not. If it looks cluttered and unkempt, people won't want to look at it. You need to decide how you want things to be laid out and how you want people to navigate through your environment. Is it a scene that they will be looking at from a distance? Or do you want them to jump in and poke around?

Again, the important factor in answering these questions is your environment's purpose. For example, if you are creating a VRML world that requires users to follow a particular sequence, then you need to find ways to direct their travels through your world. On the other hand, if you want people to freely explore your VRML world, you might want to have a more open environment. Even if you are recreating a space that exists in the real world, you need to consider what is necessary and not necessary.

VRML World Design Example

Throughout much of the rest of this chapter, the discussion focuses on the design of a very simple VRML world. We go through the process of initial layout, building VRML objects together into compound objects, and placing them in our world. Then, we find out about some of the ways to add realism to our VRML world through the use of textures, lighting, and the addition of multiple viewpoints. Finally, we find out how to link our VRML world up to other VRML worlds, HTML pages, or anything with an URL.

While the process of building this VRML world might be easier with a VRML authoring or three-dimensional modeling software package, this chapter instead shows how it is done by hand. By performing the steps of VRML world-building manually, you get a much better grasp of the fundamentals of the VRML language—and if you subsequently want to use a VRML authoring tool, this foundation makes it much easier.

Mapping Your VRML Environment

Rather than charging off and throwing together VRML objects that you might need in your world, the first step in the design process should be to sketch out what you want your world to look like. An important tool at this point of the design process is shown in Figure 14.13—a simple sheet of graph paper.

By using graph paper, including both a top view and a side view of what you would like to put in your world, you get a good idea of the following important points:

- What simple VRML objects do you need?
- What compound objects do you need and how should they be created from the simple ones?
- How much space do you need in your environment?
- Where should the VRML objects be placed in that environment?
- Where can you add lighting and camera views for the best effects?

FIG. 14.13
Initial VRML world design and layout, on paper or with a two-dimensional drawing package, is a crucial first step.

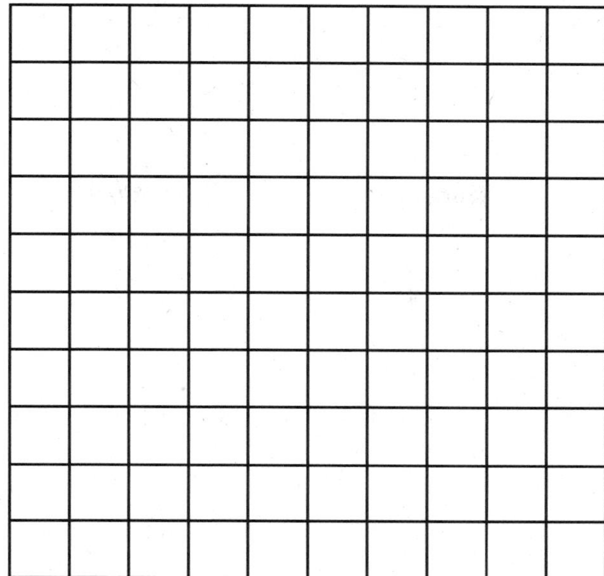

VRML Coordinate Systems

Although it is important to visualize the design of your VRML environment, it is stored as a set of coordinates and mathematical transformations. You need to convert your visual design into these coordinates and transformations—this is one of the reasons that sketching out your world on graph paper is a good idea. To fully understand how to accomplish this, you need to know a bit about the coordinate systems that VRML uses, as well as the vectors and matrices it employs.

Cartesian Coordinates

Cartesian coordinates, those used in VRML, are named after the geometry developed by Renè Descartes. They are basically the standard way of describing the two- or three-dimensional geometry of something. Figure 14.14 shows the default coordinate system used by VRML.

By default, when you begin looking at a VRML scene, the positive direction of the x-axis goes from left to right, the positive direction of the y-axis goes from down to up, and the positive direction of the z-axis goes from the back of the environment towards the front. This is called a right-handed coordinate system because if you curl the fingers of your right hand from the x- towards the y-axis, your thumb points along the z-axis.

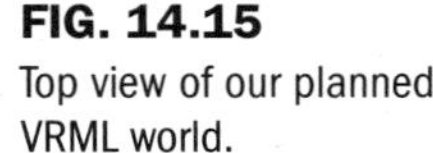

FIG. 14.15
Top view of our planned VRML world.

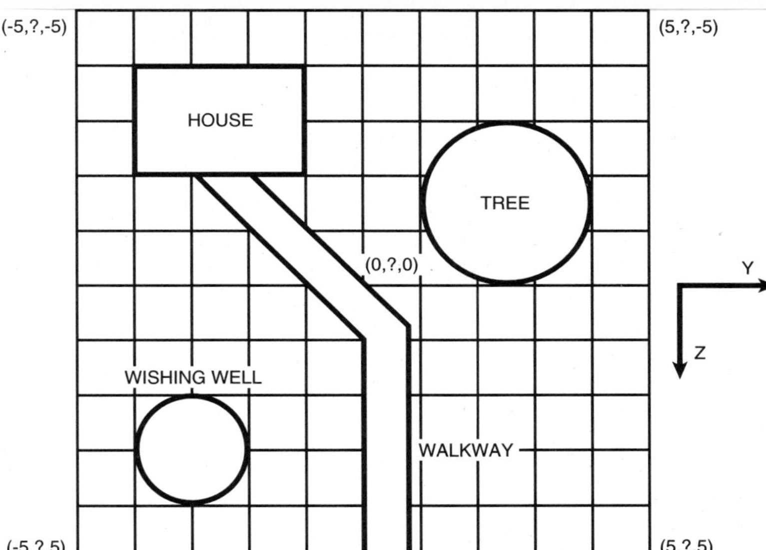

FIG. 14.16
Side view of our planned VRML world.

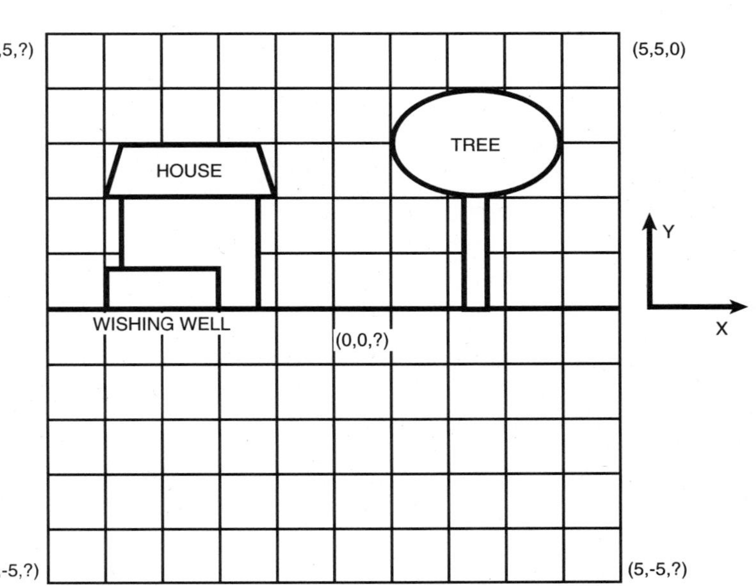

Part II Ch 14

FIG. 14.14
VRML's default Cartesian coordinate system.

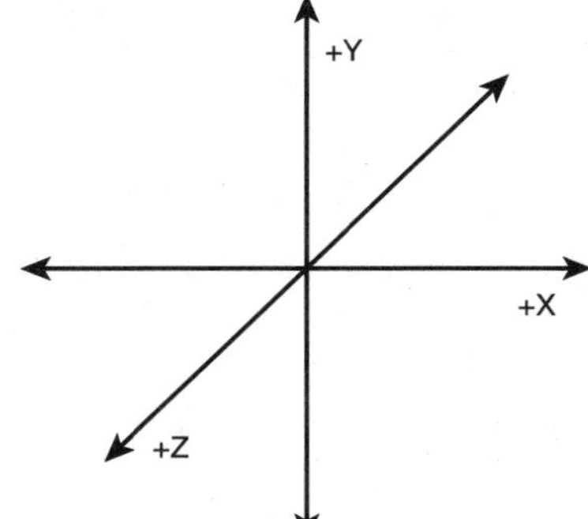

The right-handedness of the coordinate system also comes into play when you discuss rotations. The direction of a positive rotation about an axis is determined by the ***right-hand rule***. For instance, to determine the direction of a positive rotation about the z-axis, point your right thumb along the z-axis in its positive direction. The way your fingers curl define a positive rotation.

Vectors

A point in the Cartesian coordinate system is called a ***vertex***. A vertex is simply a location in space represented by three numbers, x, y, and z. A ***vector*** is related to a vertex in that it is also represented by x, y, and z coordinates. Whereas a vertex represents a point in space, a vector represents a direction. So, the vertex (1,0,1) represents the point x=1, y=0, and z=1. The vector (1,0,1) represents the direction you would be traveling in going from the origin, the point (0,0,0), to the vertex (1,0,1).

VRML Units

When specifying coordinates and rotation angles in VRML, you need to remember that the default measure of distance is a ***meter***, and the default measure of rotation angle is a ***radian***.

NOTE A *radian* is a unit used to measure angles and rotations. There are 2π radians in 360°, so you can determine the number of radians from a given number of degrees by multiplying by $180/\pi$, about 57.3.

NOTE Any node can be assigned a name by which it can be referred to later. This is done with the DEF prefix, as shown in Listing 14.11:

```
DEF Example Transform { ... }
```

You can see how to use node naming to your advantage to reuse VRML objects in the "Reusing VRML Objects with Instancing" section, later in this chapter.

CAUTION

If you load xample01.wrl, or some of the subsequent examples into your Web browser, you might think there is a problem. When xample01.wrl is first loaded, all that you probably see is a flat square. This is because the default entry view into VRML worlds of most VRML browsers results in you looking directly at the cube and viewing the flat plane edge on. Move around in the VRML world and you can see the objects. You learn how to redefine the entry view later in this chapter in the "Specifying Different Views to Your VRML World" section.

Transform: Using the *translation* Field

The `translation` field of the `Transform` node is one of the ways of moving VRML objects. Its value gives the x, y, and z distances to move the VRML object.

Building a VRML World: Part II

Listing 14.12 shows the beginnings of our VRML world, this time with the bottom part of the house moved to its correct position (as seen in the overhead view of Figure 14.18). This is accomplished by moving it with the `translation` field—the x, y, and z distances used for the move were found from our sketch.

When used, it moves the object from the origin of the VRML coordinate system so that it is centered at the point (*x*, *y*, *z*).

Listing 14.12 xample02.wrl Building a VRML world, part II.

```
#VRML V2.0 utf8

Background {
   skyColor 1 1 1
}
DEF Example Transform {
   children [
      Shape {
         appearance Appearance {
            material Material {
               diffuseColor 0 0.75 0
            }
         }
         geometry IndexedFaceSet {
            coord Coordinate {
```

```
               point [
                  -5 0 -5,
                   5 0 -5,
                   5 0  5,
                  -5 0  5
               ]
            }
            coordIndex [
               0, 1, 2, 3, -1
            ]
            normalPerVertex FALSE
            solid           FALSE
            creaseAngle     0.5
         }
      }
      Transform {
         translation -2.5 1 -3
         children [
            Shape {
               appearance Appearance {
                  material Material {
                     diffuseColor 0 0 0
                  }
               }
               geometry Box {
                  size 2.3333 2 1.3333
               }
            }
         ]
      }
   ]
}
```

FIG. 14.18
The `translation` field allows simple and compound VRML objects to be moved around the VRML environment.

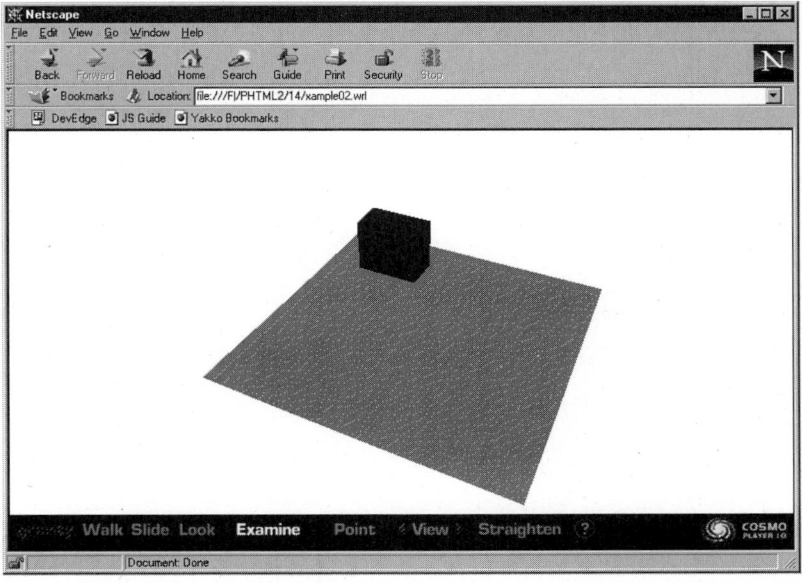

Creating Object Hierarchies

Unless your VRML world is very simple—even simpler than our example—you might find yourself very often building up more complex VRML objects from simpler ones. While it is possible to treat each of the objects separately—and move and scale each individually—it's a lot easier to create the compound object from the individual ones and then manipulate that object with one operation.

Transform: Using the *children* field

The `children` field of the `Transform` node was mentioned earlier in the chapter. It can be used as a container of other nodes, called *child* nodes. By using multiple `Shape` nodes or nesting multiple `Transform` nodes within one another, those nodes are grouped together into a compound VRML object.

Building a VRML World: Part III

Listing 14.13 shows the next addition to our VRML world, the addition of the roof to our house. Note that the roof is created with an `IndexedFaceSet` and positioned on top of the bottom part of the house within a `Transform` node. Then, the compound object representing the complete house is moved into the correct position within the VRML environment (see Figure 14.19).

Listing 14.13 xample03.wrl Building a VRML world, part III.

```
#VRML V2.0 utf8

Background {
   skyColor 1 1 1
}
DEF Example Transform {
   children [
#
# The Ground
#
      Shape {
         appearance Appearance {
            material Material {
               diffuseColor 0 0.75 0
            }
         }
         geometry IndexedFaceSet {
            coord Coordinate {
               point [
                  -5 0 -5,
                   5 0 -5,
                   5 0  5,
                  -5 0  5
               ]
            }
            coordIndex [
               0, 1, 2, 3, -1
```

```
            ]
            normalPerVertex FALSE
            solid           FALSE
            creaseAngle     0.5
         }
      }
      Transform {
         translation -2.5 1 -3
         children [
#
# The House
#
            DEF House Transform {
               children [
                  Shape {
                     appearance Appearance {
                        material Material {
                           diffuseColor 0 0 0
                        }
                     }
                     geometry Box {
                        size 2.3333 2 1.3333
                     }
                  }
                  Transform {
                     translation 0 1 0
                     children [
                        Shape {
                           appearance Appearance {
                              material Material {
                                 diffuseColor 0 0 1
                              }
                           }
                           geometry IndexedFaceSet {
                              coord Coordinate {
                                 point [
                                   -1.5    0 -1,       # Vertex Indices:
                                    1.5    0 -1,       #
                                    1.5    0  1,       #    0----1
                                   -1.5    0  1,       #    ¦4--5¦
                                   -1.1667 1 -0.6667,  #    ¦¦  ¦¦
                                    1.1667 1 -0.6667,  #    ¦7--6¦
                                    1.1667 1  0.6667,  #    3----2
                                   -1.1667 1  0.6667   #
                                 ]
                              }
                              coordIndex [
                                 0, 1, 2, 3, -1,
                                 4, 5, 6, 7, -1,
                                 0, 1, 5, 4, -1,
                                 1, 2, 6, 5, -1,
                                 2, 3, 7, 6, -1,
                                 3, 0, 4, 7, -1
                              ]
```

Part II Ch 14

continues

Listing 14.13 Continued

```
                                normalPerVertex FALSE
                                solid           FALSE
                                creaseAngle     0.5
                              }
                            }
                          ]
                        }
                      ]
                    }
                  ]
                }
              ]
            }
```

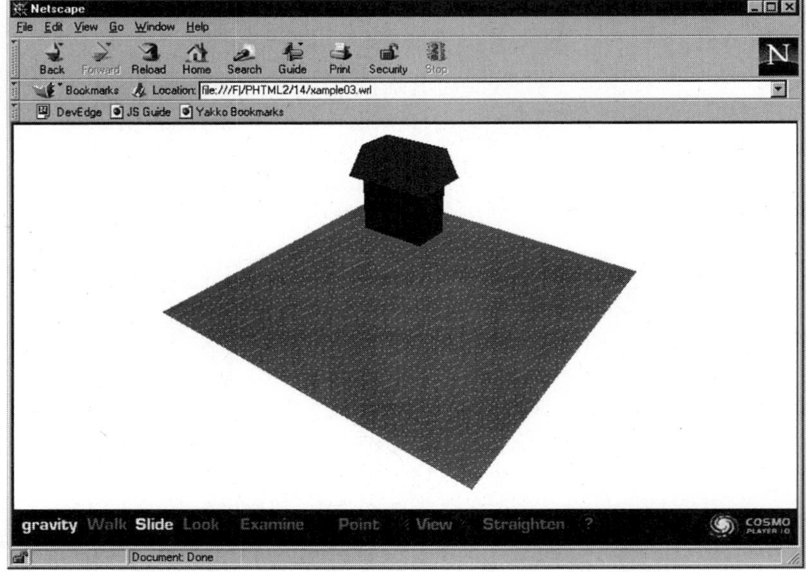

FIG. 14.19 Creating compound objects in VRML makes it much easier to create and manipulate complex scenes.

Convex and Concave Objects

VRML and VRML rendering engines used in VRML browsers are usually pretty good about figuring out what you want your shapes to look like. The simple shapes, of course, can hardly look like anything other than what they are. However, when putting together shapes with `IndexedFaceSet`, the VRML browser sometimes needs a few hints on what you want your shape to look like. This is particularly true when the shape you are creating is not convex.

Although there is a more precise mathematical definition, a convex shape is basically one in which there aren't any indentations. In general, you can travel a straight line from any given point inside the shape to any other point inside the shape, and every point you travel through also is inside the shape. The two-dimensional full moon shape is convex.

A concave shape is one that does have indentations, or concavities, within it. For instance, the two-dimensional crescent moon is concave; if you were to travel from one of the tips of the crescent to the other, you would travel across the area that is not part of the shape.

VRML assumes by default that the vertices you define and the face sets that you create are convex and can create them without too much trouble. When you need to define a concave shape, however, you might need to give it a hand.

IndexedFaceSet: Using the *ccw* and *convex* Fields

The `ccw` and `convex` fields of the `IndexedFaceSet` node is used to give VRML hints about face sets, vertex sets, and solids that might otherwise confuse it. Each of these fields takes a boolean value of `TRUE` or `FALSE`. To specify that a shape is not convex (and/or not defined in a counterclockwise manner), set the value of the field to `FALSE`.

Building a VRML World: Part IV

Listing 14.14 shows the definition of the walkway in our VRML world. The `ccw` and `convex` fields of the walkway's `IndexedFaceSet` node are set to `FALSE`, because it is a concave shape, and its vertices are defined in a clockwise manner. Note that the y components of each vertex used in the face is set to 0.01; this is so our walkway appears just above the ground. Figure 14.20 shows a sky view of the resulting walkway.

NOTE For the remaining parts of the VRML world building example, only excerpts of the VRML listing is printed in the text, as the rest of the VRML file remains unchanged from the previous part. The full listing for each part is on the CD that accompanies this book.

Listing 14.14 xample04.wrl (excerpt) Building a VRML world, part IV.

```
#
#  The Walkway
#
Shape {
   appearance Appearance {
      material Material {
         diffuseColor 1 1 1
      }
   }
   geometry IndexedFaceSet {
      coord Coordinate {
         point [
            -2      0.01 -2.3333, # Vertex Indices:
            -2      0.01 -2,      #     7-0
             0.6667 0.01  0.6667, #     6 1
```

Part II Ch 14

continues

Listing 14.14 Continued

```
                0.6667 0.01  5,      #      \ \
                0      0.01  5,      #       \ 2
                0      0.01  1,      #      5 |
               -3      0.01 -2,      #      | |
               -3      0.01 -2.3333  #      4-3
            ]
         }
         coordIndex [
            0, 1, 2, 3, 4, 5, 6, 7, -1
         ]
         normalPerVertex FALSE
         ccw             FALSE
         solid           FALSE
         convex          FALSE
         creaseAngle     0.5
      }
   }
```

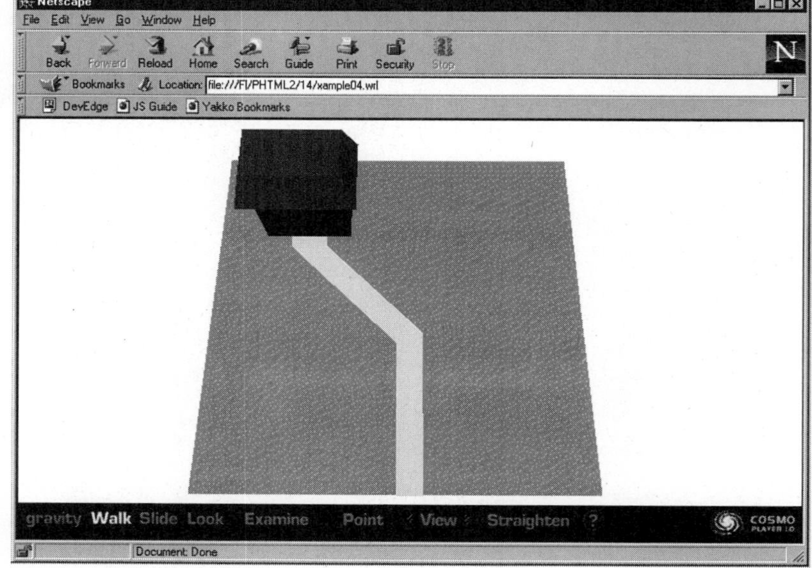

FIG. 14.20
The `ccw` and `convex` fields give the VRML browser the information it needs to correctly render concave shapes and solids.

Scaling VRML Objects

Other than translating VRML objects about the VRML environment, another transformation that can be done is scaling. Scaling allows you to scale VRML objects in the x, y, and z directions. The following are several instances in particular where scaling comes in handy:

- Non-uniform scaling can be used with simple VRML objects to easily generate new shapes—scaling a sphere to look like a football or a flying saucer, for instance.

- Scaling can be used to allow a VRML world builder to create a set of primitive objects using a given set of coordinates. The objects can then be used as is within any VRML environment by including them and scaling them to fit the other objects in the world.

Transform: Using the *scale* field

The `scale` field of the `Transform` node takes three numbers as its value, which specify the scale factor to be used for the x, y, and z directions. Scale factors greater than one make the object larger; less than one make it smaller.

Building a VRML World: Part V

We will design the tree in our VRML world using two simple VRML objects, a sphere for the top part of the tree and a cylinder for the tree trunk. As shown in Listing 14.15, the `scale` field is used to flatten out the sphere to make it look a bit more tree-like. As with the house, the compound object of the tree—scaled sphere and cylinder—is assembled within a `Transform` node, and then the whole thing is moved into position (see Figure 14.21).

Listing 14.15 xample05.wrl (excerpt) Building a VRML world, part V.

```
#
# The Tree
#
DEF Tree Transform {
   children [
      Shape {
         appearance Appearance {
            material Material {
               diffuseColor 0.5 0.25 0
            }
         }
         geometry Cylinder {
            radius 0.1667
            height 3
         }
      }
      Transform {
         translation 0 1.5 0
         scale       1.5 1 1.5
         children [
            Shape {
               appearance Appearance {
                  material Material {
                     diffuseColor 0 1 0
                  }
               }
               geometry Sphere {}
            }
         ]
      }
   ]
}
```

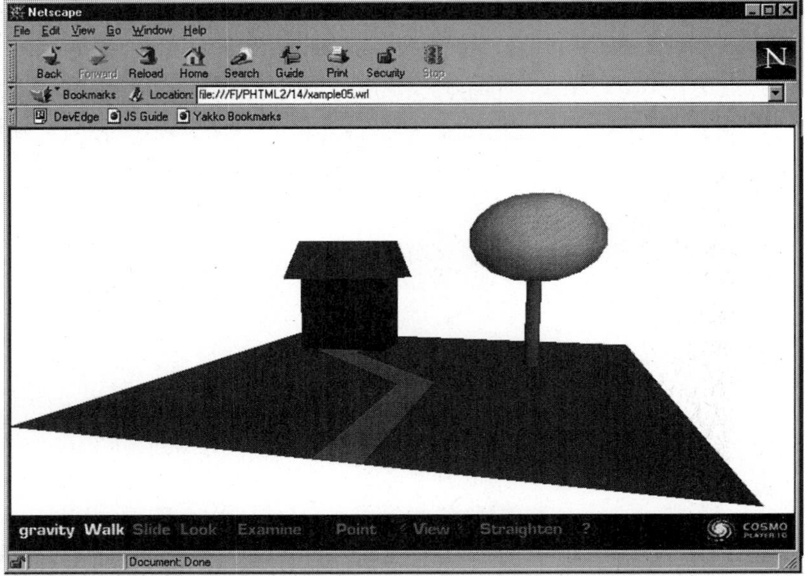

FIG. 14.21
There are many more possibilities offered by the simple VRML objects when the `scale` field is used to reshape them.

Reusing VRML Objects with Instancing

If you are creating a VRML environment that includes many copies of a given object—cars in a parking lot, pins in a bowling alley, or bubbles underwater, for instance—you don't want to have to define each one individually. Ideally, you could define one such object and then copy and paste the others. In fact, it would be even better if you could do this, but also make small changes, such as a different color or size, in each of the copies.

VRML supports *instancing*, which allows you to do exactly that. By defining an object and giving it a name, you can use that object again—redefining any of its characteristics, as well—by referring to it by its name.

Using the *DEF* and *USE* Keywords

The way to make use of instancing to generate multiple copies of defined VRML objects is through the `DEF` and `USE` keywords. `DEF` is used along with a VRML node to define a name for that node, as in:

```
DEF MyName NodeType {
   fieldName1 value
   fieldName2 value
}
```

This gives the node the name `MyName`. To use that node again, you just need to use the `USE` keyword. For instance, to define a red sphere and then reuse it as a blue sphere, you could do the following:

```
Transform { children [ Shape {
   appearance Appearance { material Material { diffuseColor 1 0 0 } }
   geometry DEF MySphere Sphere {} } ] }
Transform { children [ Shape {
   appearance Appearance { material Material { diffuseColor 0 0 1 } }
   geometry USE MySphere     } ] }
```

For a simple sphere, this doesn't really save you much, but if you need to create multiple copies of a more complicated object, it can be very helpful.

Building a VRML World: Part VI

Listing 14.16 shows the last piece in our VRML world, the wishing well. This is done by creating a white cylinder and placing a black cylinder inside it to make it look like a well. In this example, the first cylinder is named `Wall` by the `DEF` keyword, and the second cylinder reuses it through `USE Wall` (see Figure 14.22).

Listing 14.16 xample06.wrl (excerpt) Building a VRML world, part VI.

```
#
# The Wishing Well
#
DEF WishingWell Transform {
   children [
      Shape {
         appearance Appearance {
            material Material {
               diffuseColor 1 1 1
            }
         }
         geometry DEF Wall Cylinder {
            height 0.6667
         }
      }
      Transform {
         scale 0.8 1 0.8
         children [
            Shape {
               appearance Appearance {
                  material Material {
                     diffuseColor 0 0 0
                  }
               }
               geometry USE Wall
            }
         ]
      }
   ]
}
```

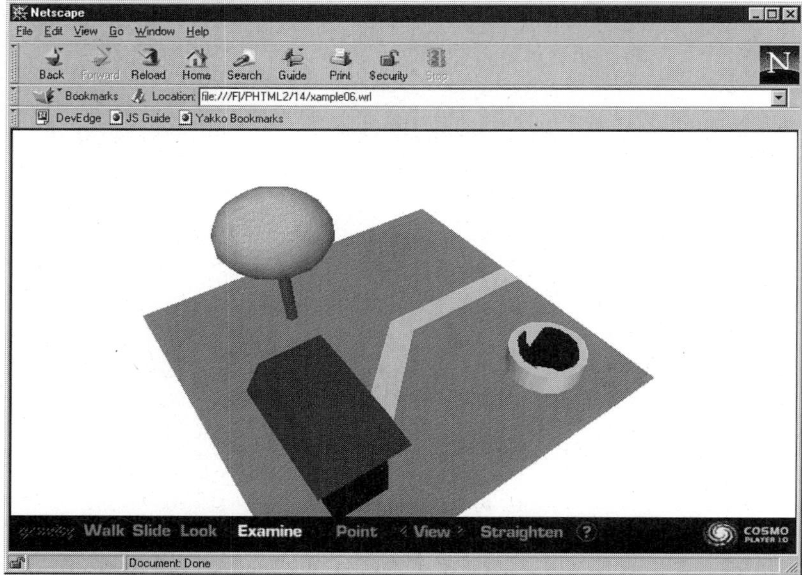

FIG. 14.22
Object reuse through the DEF and USE keywords can significantly reduce the size of your VRML world if you need to use many copies of similar objects.

Adding Realism with Textures

All of the objects in the VRML world are now defined. You'll now see some of the other effects that can be added to your world to add more realism or additional options for your users.

Earlier in this chapter, you learned a little about how to use the textures nodes to add realism to an object through the addition of image file textures. By default, VRML maps the image file specified by `ImageTexture` to each entire face of the solid in question—the six faces of a cube or the top, bottom, and curved surface of a cylinder, for instance. When mapping a texture to a surface to make it more realistic, it is best to tile small images repeatedly over the different faces.

Using the *TextureTransform* Node

Other than the `texture` and `material` fields, along with the corresponding nodes used to specify their values, the `Appearance` node also has a `textureTransform` field. The value of this field is specified by the `TextureTransform` node. Its `scale` field refers to how the coordinates of the object to which the texture is being mapped will be scaled, so scale factors greater than one result in the image appearing smaller on the object and tiled more times.

Building a VRML World: Part VII

Listing 14.17 shows an example of the texturing applied to our VRML world (the full listing on the CD shows the textures applied to all of the objects). In this case, a rocky appearance is given to the wishing well and other, more realistic, appearances are given to the other objects in the VRML world (see Figure 14.23).

Listing 14.17 xample07.wrl (excerpt) Building a VRML world, part VII.

```
#
# The Wishing Well
#
DEF WishingWell Transform {
   children [
      Shape {
         appearance Appearance {
            texture ImageTexture {
               url "rock.jpg"
            }
            textureTransform TextureTransform {
               scale 8 1
            }
         }
```

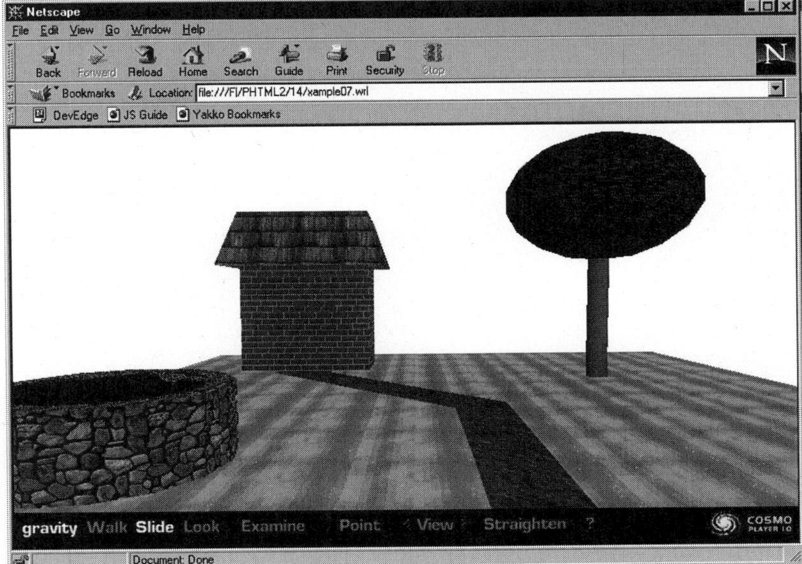

FIG. 14.23
While textures certainly lend a more realistic appearance to a VRML world, they do slow down the file transmission and rendering, so use them only when needed.

VRML Lighting

Lighting in VRML worlds comes from many different sources. It is possible to create lighting sources of several different types and include them in your world. Additionally, VRML browsers often have headlights attached to your current viewpoint, which emit light in the direction you are looking.

When designing your VRML world, you might have specific areas that you want to have light sources or camera views. If designing a VRML storefront, for instance, you might want to have lighting near each of your store's items. You'd definitely want the entry view of the VRML world near the entrance, but you might also want to create views that correspond to the different sections of your store. For our example, we will add some lighting and camera views to show the different effects possible.

Browser Headlights

We have not specified any lighting in the example VRML world we have been developing, so where is the light coming from? Different VRML browsers handle this differently. The Cosmo Player VRML plug-in for Netscape Navigator has a small amount of ambient light that is supplied in the absence of specified light sources. Additionally, it supplies a headlight that provides light originating from your current viewpoint. By setting the `headlight` field of the VRML `NavigationInfo` node to `FALSE`, your VRML worlds can automatically disable the headlight (although, depending on the VRML browser, the user can re-enable it—in Cosmo Player this is done by right-clicking anywhere in the VRML world and selecting Headlight). The syntax for this is:

```
NavigationInfo {
   headlight FALSE
}
```

Using the *DirectionalLight* Node

The `DirectionalLight` node is used to create a light source that emanates from a given direction. Its color and direction fields are used to specify what color light it is supplying and from where. For example, a yellow light coming straight down a VRML scene would be specified as:

```
DirectionalLight {
   color     1  1 0
   direction 0 -1 0
}
```

Directional lighting nodes, as well as other lighting nodes, can be placed anywhere in a VRML file. Be aware, however, that if lighting nodes are placed within a compound object that is translated or rotated, this can end up affecting the position or direction of the light.

Using the *PointLight* Node

A point light source is similar to a directional light source, except that it has a location instead of a direction—it emanates from that location in all directions. For example, a white light emanating from coordinates {1,1,1} would appear as:

```
PointLight {
   location 1 1 1
}
```

NOTE The default color for either type of light source is white, so white lights do not need to actually have the color field specified.

Using the *SpotLight* Node

The `SpotLight` node combines aspects of both the directional light and the point light. Like a spotlight, it has a location within the VRML world and has a direction indicating its primary focus. As you move away from its main direction, the light decreases in intensity until it cuts off completely at the value specified in the `cutOffAngle` field. For example, a white spotlight emanating from coordinates {1,1,1}, shining straight down, and with a cutoff angle of 30 degrees (about 0.52 radians) would appear as:

```
SpotLight {
   location 1 1 1
   direction 0 -1 0
   cutOffAngle 0.52
}
```

Building a VRML World: Part VIII

Listing 14.18 shows our VRML world with two light sources added, plus with the browser headlight turned off. The first light source added is a directional yellow light shining straight down. The second is a point source of white light shining from near the front of the VRML world. As shown in Figure 14.24 (and shown much more clearly if you view this example in your VRML browser), the lighting produces the following effects on the objects in the VRML world:

- **The House** The point source of white light brightens up the front of the house roof. The other three sides of the roof are much darker. This is because the white light is only hitting the front, and the yellow light from above does not brighten up the roof—because it is blue, it does not have any yellow component.
- **The Tree** Both the white and yellow lights brighten up the tree because there are yellow components in its green color. The backs of the tree and tree trunk are unlit by either source and are darker.
- **The Wishing Well** Both the white and yellow lights brighten up the wishing well. However, the white outer wall of the wishing well picks up the color of whatever light source is shining on it. So, the front of the well appears white, the top appears yellow, and the unlit back is darker.
- **The Walkway** The walkway is lit by both sources, and its white color also picks up the colors of the light source. Towards the front of the walkway, the white light source dominates and it appears white. Close to the house, it looks more yellow.

Listing 14.18 xample08.wrl (excerpt) Building a VRML world, part VIII.

```
NavigationInfo {
   headlight FALSE
}
DirectionalLight {
   color      1  1 0
   direction 0 -1 0
}
PointLight {
   location 0 1 5
}
```

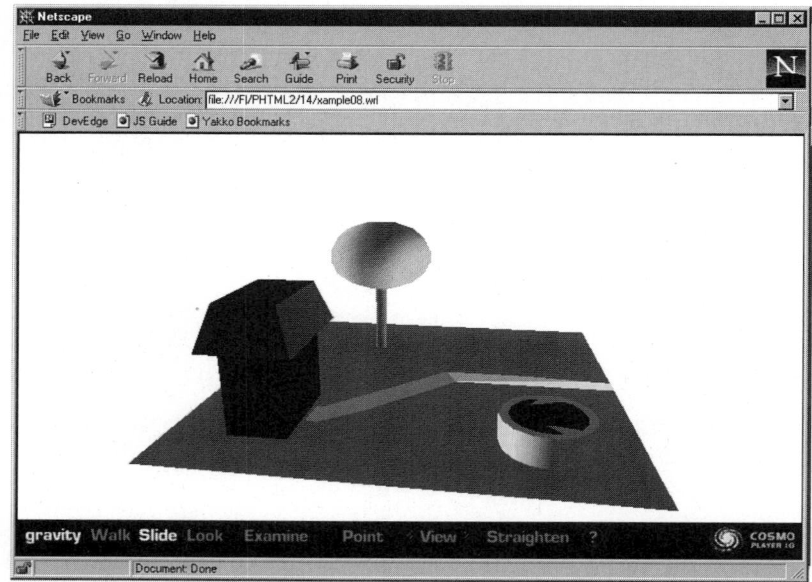

FIG. 14.24 Placement of VRML light sources can greatly affect the appearance and apparent color of objects in the VRML world.

NOTE To better illustrate the effects of colored light sources, this example does not apply the image textures discussed in the previous section. Instead, it goes back to the previous iteration, which gave a simple color to each VRML object.

Specifying Different Views to Your VRML World

It is possible to define the entry point that visitors to your VRML world will take. Additionally, you can also define multiple viewpoints. Most VRML browsers allow users to select between these viewpoints.

Using the *Viewpoint* Node

The `Viewpoint` node defines a viewpoint into a VRML world. The most important fields in this node are the `position`, `orientation`, and `description`, which determine where the viewpoint is located and pointed, and what each is called.

By default, the position of the camera is (0,0,1) and is pointed in the -z direction. The `position` field specifies an x, y, and z position. The `orientation` field has four values: the first three define an x, y, z vector direction, and the fourth is the angle to rotate the camera about the vector. Remember the right-hand rule to determine the correct rotation directions.

By default, VRML browsers use the first `Viewpoint` node encountered as its entry view. The others appear in the VRML browser as alternate viewpoints (for example, in Cosmo Player, they can be accessed by right-clicking and selecting the Viewpoints submenu).

Building a VRML World: Part IX

Listing 14.19 shows how multiple viewpoints can be defined in our VRML world. Figure 14.25 shows the initial viewpoint and how Cosmo Player allows the others to be selected.

Listing 14.19 xample09.wrl (excerpt) Building a VRML world, part IX.

```
Viewpoint {
   position    0 2 12
   description "Entry"
}
Viewpoint {
   position    5 2 -12
   orientation 0 1 0 2.7
   description "Behind"
}
Viewpoint {
   position    0 16 0
   orientation 1 0 0 -1.5708
   description "Above"
}
Viewpoint {
   position    0 48 0
   orientation 1 0 0 -1.5708
   description "Way Above"
}
```

Figures 14.26 through 14.28 show the different viewpoints that have been defined and can be selected for viewing our VRML world. The positions and orientations are the initial positions only. They can each be changed via the normal navigation through the VRML world.

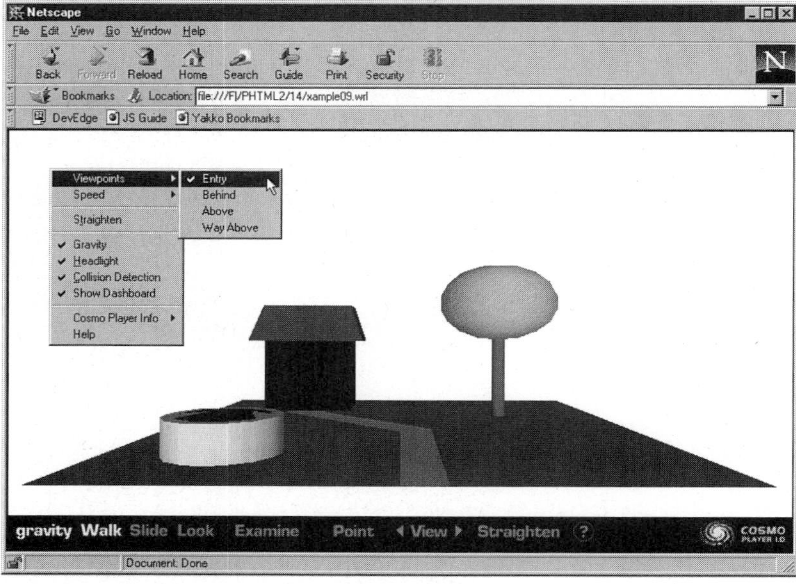

FIG. 14.25
The predefined VRML viewpoints can be selected by the user of the VRML browser.

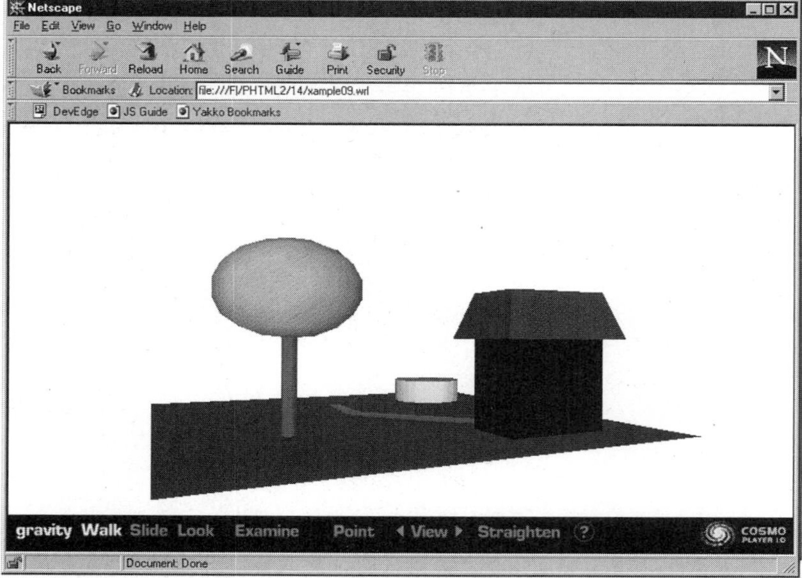

FIG. 14.26
By defining views for your users, you can allow them to easily travel where you would like them to go.

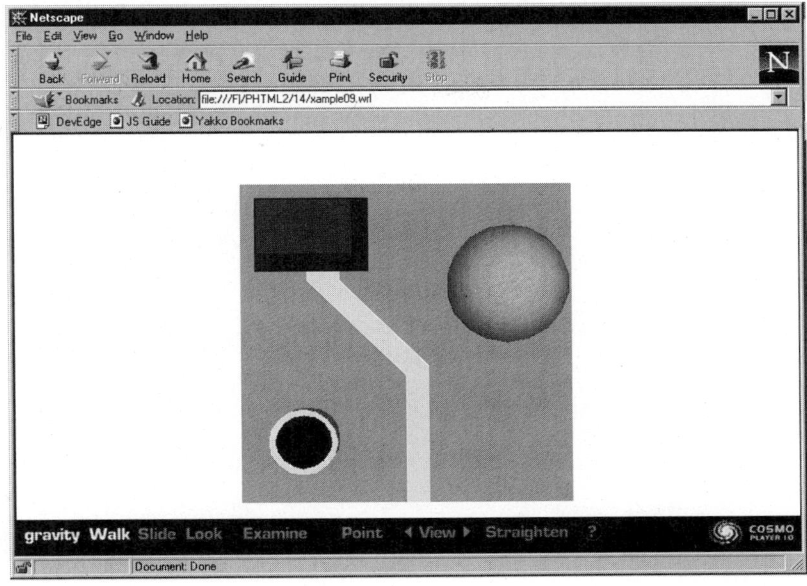

FIG. 14.27
The overhead view shows how close we came to our original top view drawing (see Figure 14.15) of our VRML world.

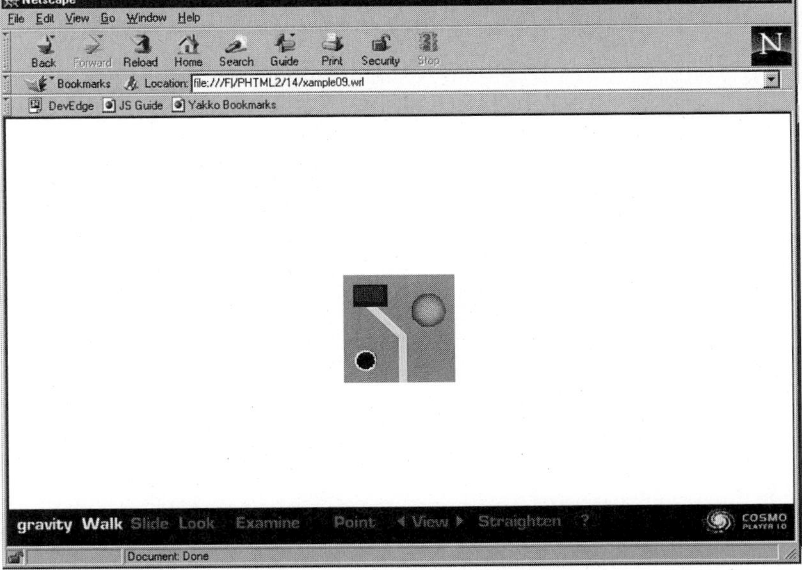

FIG. 14.28
It's possible to define bird's eye views of our VRML world.

Linking to the Web

VRML, like HTML, is a language meant to be used on the Internet and the Web. An essential element for this is the hypertext link. This allows VRML worlds to be linked to other VRML worlds. And, if the VRML browser supports it, URLs can also be followed to HTML Web pages and other Internet resources.

Using the *Anchor* Node

Hypertext links are implemented in VRML using the `Anchor` node. The important fields for this node are the `url` field, which is used to specify the URL hypertext link, `description` field, which gives a text description of the link, and `children` field, which is used to contain the VRML object that will serve as the anchor of the link.

Building a VRML World: Part X

Listing 14.20 shows how the hypertext link is implemented in our VRML world. In this case, it enables viewers of the VRML world to travel to my home page. When the cursor is placed over the appropriate object in the VRML browser, the pointer becomes the hand pointer, and the URL or description appears in the status bar (see Figure 14.29).

Listing 14.20 xample10.wrl (excerpt) Building a VRML world, part X.

```
#
# The House
#
Anchor {
   url         "http://www.rpi.edu/~odonnj"
   description "JOD's Home Page"
   children [
      VRML code for House object...
   ]
}
```

Other Features of VRML 2.0

The concepts discussed in this chapter should give you a solid, basic understanding of what you need to do to design and build three-dimensional worlds in VRML 2.0. However, what has been demonstrated here is only the tip of the iceberg for what you can do with VRML 2.0. The goal of the VRML 2.0 standard is to provide the tools to create three-dimensional worlds that include movement and sound and allow the objects within the world to be programmed with behaviors that allow them to react to your presence and the presence of other objects. For example, VRML fish can be programmed to swim away from you if you get too close.

FIG. 14.29
Embedding hypertext links in VRML objects allows VRML browsers to load and travel to other VRML worlds, and HTML-aware browsers to go to HTML Web pages.

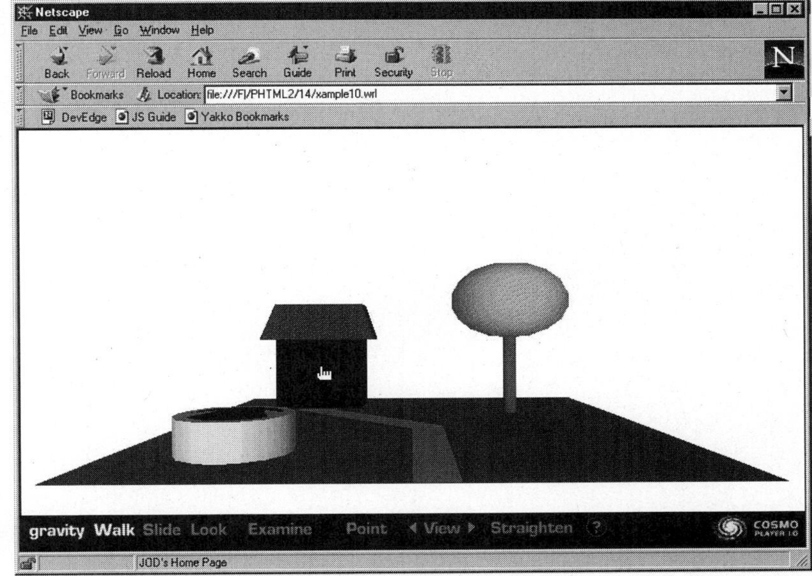

Some of the other capabilities of VRML 2.0 fall into the general categories of enhanced static worlds, interaction, animation, scripting, and prototyping. These are discussed in the VRML 2.0 specification. They are summarized in the following sections.

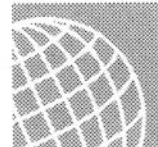

ON THE WEB

http://www.vrml.org/VRML97/DIS/ This Web site gives you access to the full, final specification for the VRML 2.0 language.

Enhanced Static Worlds

VRML 2.0 supports several new nodes and fields that allow the static geometry of VRML worlds to be made more realistic. You can create separate backdrops for the ground and the sky, using colors or images. Objects such as clouds and mountains can be put in the distance, and fog can be used to blur distant objects. Irregular terrain can be created, rather than using flat planes for your surface. VRML 2.0 also provides three-dimensional sound to further enhance realism.

Interaction

VRML 2.0 includes a new class of nodes, called sensor nodes, that can set off events in response to different inputs. Touch and proximity sensors react to the presence of the viewer either touching or coming close to an object. A time sensor is capable of keeping track of the passage of time, allowing time-correlated events to be added to your VRML world. And VRML 2.0 supports realistic collision detection and terrain following to ensure that your viewers bounce off of (or at least stop at) your walls and solid objects and can travel through your world while easily following things like steps and inclines.

Animation

VRML 2.0 interpolator nodes allow you to create predefined animations for any of the objects in your VRML world. These animations can be programmed to occur automatically or in response to some other factor, either an action of your viewer or at a given time. With these interpolators, you can create moving objects, objects such as the sun or the moon that change color as they move, or objects that change shape. The viewpoint can also be animated to create an automatic guided tour of your VRML world.

Scripting

The key to many of VRML 2.0's other features—particularly the movement of VRML 2.0 objects—is its support of scripting. Scripting is used to program objects' behaviors, not only allowing them to move but also giving them the capability to react realistically to objects around them. A script is the link that is used to take an event—generated by a sensor node, for instance—and generate the appropriate action.

Prototyping

The final category of enhancement to VRML 2.0 is the capability for prototyping. What this allows you to do is to create your own nodes. By grouping a set of nodes together to achieve a specific purpose, within a new prototype node, that node becomes available for reuse.

NOTE If you want to find out more about what you can do with VRML 2.0, *Teach Yourself VRML 2 in 21 Days* by Sams Publishing.

PART III

Scripting Languages

CHAPTER 15

Introduction to JavaScripting

by Jim O'Donnell

In this chapter

Introduction to JavaScript

JavaScript enables you to embed commands in an HTML page. When a compatible web browser, such as Netscape Navigator 2 or higher or Internet Explorer 3 or higher, downloads the page, your JavaScript commands are loaded by the web browser as a part of the HTML document. These commands can be triggered when the user clicks on page items, manipulates gadgets and fields in an HTML form, or moves through the page history list.

NOTE Microsoft's Internet Explorer web browser supports JScript, their own implementation of Netscape's JavaScript language. JScript is compatible with JavaScript, but there are some differences. When programming in JavaScript, it is always a good idea to test your scripts by using both browsers.

Some computer languages are *compiled*—you run your program through a compiler, which performs a one-time translation of the human-readable program into a binary that the computer can execute. JavaScript is an *interpreted* language—the computer must evaluate the program every time it is run. You embed your JavaScript commands within an HTML page, and any browser that supports JavaScript can interpret the commands and act on them.

JavaScript is powerful and simple. If you've ever programmed in C++ or Java, you will find that JavaScript is easy to pick up. If not, don't worry. This chapter will have you working with JavaScript in no time. This chapter examines the basic syntax of the language, and the other chapters in this section show you how to apply it. In the next two chapters, "The Web Browser Object Model" and "Using Inline JavaScripting," you will find out how to use JavaScript to interact with your web pages and how to build it in to your HTML. Chapters 18 through 21 then show you in greater detail how to use JavaScript with windows and frames, HTML forms, web browser cookies, and how to control other web browser objects—such as Java applets and ActiveX Controls—with JavaScript. Finally, the last chapter in this section, "Scripting with Microsoft VBScript and JScript" show you how to use the two scripting languages offered by Microsoft.

Why Use a Scripting Language?

HTML provides a good deal of flexibility to page authors, but HTML by itself is static; after being written, HTML documents can't interact with the user other than by presenting hyperlinks. Creative use of CGI scripts (which run on web servers) and the newer web technologies such as Java, ActiveX Controls, and Dynamic HTML, has made it possible to create more interesting and effective interactive sites. Even so, a scripting language is very often what ties all the elements of a web page together.

JavaScript enables web authors to write small scripts that execute on the users' browsers rather than on the server. An application that collects data from a form and then posts it to the server can validate the data for completeness and correctness before sending it to the server, for example. This can greatly improve the performance of the browsing session because users don't have to send data to the server until it has been verified as correct.

Another important use of web browser scripting languages such as JavaScript comes as a result of the increased functionality being introduced for web browsers in the form of Java applets, plug-ins, ActiveX Controls, and VRML objects and worlds. Web authors can use each of these things to add extra functions and interactivity to a web page. Scripting languages act as the glue that binds everything together. A web page might use an HTML form to get some user input and then set a parameter for an ActiveX Control based on that input. It is usually a script that carries this out.

What Can JavaScript Do?

JavaScript provides a fairly complete set of built-in functions and commands, enabling you to perform math calculations, manipulate strings, play sounds, open new windows and new URLs, and access and verify user input to your web forms.

Code to perform these actions can be embedded in a page and executed when the page is loaded. You can also write functions containing code that is triggered by events you specify. You can write a JavaScript method that is called when the user clicks the Submit button of a form, for example, or one that is activated when the user clicks a hyperlink on the active page.

JavaScript can also set the attributes, or *properties*, of ActiveX Controls, Java applets, and other objects present in the browser. This way, you can change the behavior of plug-ins or other objects without having to rewrite them. For example, your JavaScript code could automatically set the text of an ActiveX Label Control based on what time the page is viewed.

What Does JavaScript Look Like?

JavaScript commands are embedded in your HTML documents. Embedding JavaScript in your pages requires only one new HTML element: `<SCRIPT>` and `</SCRIPT>`. The `<SCRIPT>` element takes the attributes `LANGUAGE`, which specifies the scripting language to use when evaluating the script, and `SRC`, which can be used to load a script from an external source.

JavaScript itself resembles many other computer languages. If you are familiar with C, C++, Pascal, HyperTalk, Visual Basic, or dBASE, you will recognize the similarities. If not, don't worry—the following are some simple rules to help you understand how the language is structured:

- JavaScript is case-sensitive.
- JavaScript is pretty flexible about statements. A single statement can cover multiple lines and you can put multiple short statements on a single line—just make sure to add a semicolon (;) at the end of each statement.
- Braces (the { and } characters) group statements into blocks; a *block* may be the body of a function or a section of code that gets executed in a loop or as part of a conditional test.

NOTE If you program in Java, C, or C++, you might be puzzled when looking at JavaScript programs–sometimes each line ends with a semicolon, sometimes not. In JavaScript, unlike those other languages, the semicolon is not required at the end of each line.

JavaScript Programming Conventions

Even though JavaScript is a simple language, it is quite expressive. This section reviews a small number of simple rules and conventions that will ease your learning process and speed your use of JavaScript.

Hiding Your Scripts You will probably be designing pages that may be seen by browsers that don't support JavaScript. To keep those browsers from interpreting your JavaScript commands as HTML—and displaying them—wrap your scripts as follows:

```
<SCRIPT LANGUAGE="JavaScript">
<!-- This line opens an HTML comment
document.write("You can see this script's output, but not its source.")
//   This is a JavaScript comment that also closes the comment -->
</SCRIPT>
```

The opening `<!--` comment causes web browsers that do not support JavaScript to disregard all text they encounter until they find a matching `-->` so that they don't display your script. You do have to be careful with the `<SCRIPT>` tag, however; if you put your `<SCRIPT>` and `</SCRIPT>` block inside the comments, the web browser ignores them also.

Comments Including comments in your programs to explain what they do is usually good practice—JavaScript is no exception. The JavaScript interpreter ignores any text marked as comments; therefore, don't be shy about including them. You can use two types of comments: single-line and multiple-line.

Single-line comments start with two slashes (//), and are limited to one line. Multiple-line comments must start with /* on the first line and end with */ on the last line. Here are a few examples:

```
   // this is a legal comment
/ illegal -- comments start with two slashes
/* Multiple-line comments can
   be spread across more than one line, as long as they end. */
/* careful -- this comment doesn't have an end!
/// this comment's OK, because extra slashes are ignored //
```

CAUTION

Be careful when using multiple-line comments—remember that these comments don't nest. If you commented out a section of code in the following way, for example, you would get an error message.

```
/* Comment out the following code
 * document.writeln(DumpURL()) /* write out URL list */
 * document.writeln("End of list.")
 */
```

The preferred way to create single-line comments to avoid this is as follows:

```
/* Comment out the following code
```

```
* document.writeln(DumpURL()) // write out URL list
* document.writeln("End of list.")
*/
```

Using <NOSCRIPT> You can improve the compatibility of your JavaScript web pages through the use of the `<NOSCRIPT>...</NOSCRIPT>` HTML tags. Any HTML code placed between these container tags will not display on a JavaScript-compatible web browser, but will display on one that cannot understand JavaScript. This enables you to include alternative content for your users who are using web browsers that don't understand JavaScript. At the very least, you can let them know that they are missing something, as in this example:

```
<NOSCRIPT>
<HR>If you are seeing this text, then your web browser
   doesn't speak JavaScript!<HR>
</NOSCRIPT>
```

The JavaScript Language

JavaScript was designed to resemble Java, which in turn looks a lot like C and C++. The difference is that Java was built as a general-purpose object language; JavaScript, on the other hand, is intended to provide a quicker and simpler language for enhancing web pages and servers. This section describes the building blocks of JavaScript and teaches you how to combine them into legal JavaScript programs.

NOTE You can find a complete language reference for JavaScript in Appendix A, "JavaScript 1.2 Language Reference," and on the CD that accompanies this book. You can also find this information and more at Netscape's DevEdge Online web site at **http://developer.netscape.com**.

Using Identifiers

An *identifier* is just a unique name that JavaScript uses to identify a variable, method, or object in your program. As with other programming languages, JavaScript imposes some rules on what names you can use. All JavaScript names must start with a letter or the underscore character, and they can contain both upper- and lowercase letters and the digits 0 through 9. JavaScript supports two different ways for you to represent values in your scripts: literals and variables. As their names imply, *literals* are fixed values that don't change while the script is executing, and *variables* hold data that can change at any time.

Literals and variables have several different types; the type is determined by the kind of data that the literal or variable contains. The following are some of the types supported in JavaScript:

- *Integers*. Integer literals are made up of a sequence of digits only; integer variables can contain any whole-number value. You can specify octal (base 8) and hexadecimal (base 16) integers by prefixing them with a leading "0" or "0x", respectively.

- *Floating-point numbers*. The number 10 is an integer, but 10.5 is a floating-point number. Floating-point literals can be positive or negative and can contain either positive or negative exponents (which are indicated by an "e" in the number). For example, 3.14159265 is a floating-point literal, as is 6.023e23 (6.023×10^{23}, or Avogadro's number).
- *Strings*. Strings can represent words, phrases, or data, and are set off by either double (") or single (') quotation marks. If you start a string with one type of quotation mark, you must close it with the same type. Special characters, such as \n for newline, and \t can also be utilized in strings.
- *Booleans*. Boolean literals can have values of either `TRUE` or `FALSE`; other statements in the JavaScript language can return Boolean values.

Using Functions, Objects, and Properties

JavaScript is modeled after Java, an object-oriented language. An *object* is a collection of data and functions that have been grouped together. A *function* is a piece of code that plays a sound, calculates an equation, or sends a piece of email, and so on. The object's functions are called *methods* and its data are called its *properties*. The JavaScript programs you write will have properties and methods and will interact with objects provided by the web browser, its plug-ins, Java applets, ActiveX Controls, and other things.

NOTE Although the words "function" and "method" are often used interchangeably, they are not the same. A method is a function that is part of an object. For instance, `writeln` is one of the methods of the object `document`.

TIP Here's a simple guideline: An object's properties are the information it knows; its methods are how it can act on that information.

Using Built-In Objects and Functions Individual JavaScript elements are *objects*. String literals are string objects, for example, and they have methods that you can use to change their case, and so on. JavaScript can also use the objects that represent the web browser in which it is executing, the currently displayed page, and other elements of the browsing session.

To access an object, you specify its name. Consider, for example, an active document object named `document`. To use `document`'s properties or methods, you add a period (.) and the name of the method or property you want. For example, `document.title` is the title property of the `document` object, and `explorer.length` calls the length member of the string object named `explorer`. Remember, literals are objects too.

You can find out more about the objects built in to JavaScript and the web browser in the next chapter.

▶ **See** "Web Browser Object Hierarchy and Scoping," **p. 438**

Using Properties Every object has properties, even literals. To access a property, just use the object name followed by a period and the property name. To get the length of a string object named `address`, you can write the following:

```
address.length
```

You get back an integer that equals the number of characters in the string. If the object you use has properties that can be modified, you can change them in the same way. To set the color property of a house object, for example, just use the following line:

```
house.color = "blue"
```

You can also create new properties for an object just by naming them. If you define a class called `customer` for one of your pages, for example, you can add new properties to the `customer` object as follows:

```
customer.name = "Joe Smith"
customer.address = "123 Elm Street"
customer.zip = "90210"
```

Finally, knowing that an object's methods are just properties is important. You can easily add new properties to an object by writing your own function and creating a new object property using your own function name. If you want to add a `Bill` method to your `customer` object, you can do so by writing a function named `BillCustomer` and setting the object's property as follows:

```
customer.Bill = BillCustomer;
```

To call the new method, you use the following:

```
customer.Bill()
```

Array and Object Properties JavaScript objects store their properties in an internal table that you can access in two ways. You have already seen the first way—just use the properties' names. The second way, *arrays*, enables you to access all of an object's properties in sequence. The following function prints out all the properties of the specified object:

```
function DumpProperties(obj, obj_name) {
   result = ""     // set the result string to blank
   for (i in obj)
      result += obj_name + "." + i + " = " + obj[i] + "\n"
   return result
}
```

You can access all the properties of the `document` object, for instance, both by property name—using the dot operator (for example, `document.href`)—and by the object's property array (`document[1]`, although this may not be the same property as `document.href`). JavaScript provides another method of array access that combines the two: associative arrays. An *associative array* associates a left and a right side element; the value of the right side can be used by specifying the value of the left side as the index. JavaScript sets up objects as associative arrays with the property names as the left side and their values as the right. You can, therefore, access the `href` property of the `document` object by using `document["href"]`.

Programming with JavaScript

JavaScript has a lot to offer page authors. It is not as flexible as C or C++, but it is quick and simple. Most importantly, it's easily embedded in your web pages; thus you can maximize their impact with a little JavaScript seasoning. This section covers the gritty details of JavaScript programming and includes a detailed explanation of the language's features.

Expressions

An *expression* is anything that can be evaluated to get a single value. Expressions can contain string or numeric literals, variables, operators, and other expressions, and they can range from simple to quite complex. The following are examples of expressions that use the assignment operator (more on operators in the next section) to assign numeric or string values to variables:

```
x = 7;
str = "Hello, World!";
```

By contrast, the following is a more complex expression whose final value depends on the values of the `quitFlag` and `formComplete` variables:

```
(quitFlag == TRUE) & (formComplete == FALSE)
```

Operators

Operators do just what their name suggests: They operate on variables or literals. The items that an operator acts on are called its *operands*. Operators come in the following two types:

- *Unary operators*. These operators require only one operand and the operator can come before or after the operand. The `--` operator, which subtracts one from the operand, is a good example. Both `--count` and `count--` subtract one from the variable count.
- *Binary operators*. These operators need two operands. The four math operators (+ for addition, - for subtraction, * for multiplication, and / for division) are all binary operators, as is the = assignment operator.

Assignment Operators *Assignment operators* take the result of an expression and assign it to a variable. JavaScript doesn't enable you to assign the result of an expression to a literal. One feature of JavaScript not found in most other programming languages is that you can change a variable's type on-the-fly. Consider the HTML document shown in Listing 15.1.

Listing 15.1 Var-fly.htm JavaScript enables you to change the data type of variables.

```
<HTML>
<HEAD>
<SCRIPT LANGUAGE="JavaScript">
<!-- Hide this script from incompatible web browsers!
function typedemo() {
   var x;
   document.writeln("<HR>");
   x = Math.PI;
   document.writeln("x is " + x + "<BR>");
   x = false;
   document.writeln("x is " + x + "<BR>");
   document.writeln("<HR>");
}
//  Hide this script from incompatible web browsers! -->
</SCRIPT>
<TITLE>Changing Data Types on the Fly!</TITLE>
```

```
</HEAD>
<BODY BGCOLOR=#FFFFFF>
If your web browser doesn't support JavaScript, this is all you will see!
<SCRIPT LANGUAGE="JavaScript">
<!-- Hide this script from incompatible web browsers!
typedemo();
//   Hide this script from incompatible web browsers! -->
</SCRIPT>
</BODY>
</HTML>
```

NOTE `Math` is a JavaScript object used to access many of its math functions. The next chapter introduces you to more of the `Math` object's properties.

▶ **See** "JavaScript Objects," **p. 454**

This short program first prints the (correct) value of `pi` in the variable `x`. In contrast, if you try to set a floating-point variable to a Boolean value in most other languages you will either generate a compiler error or a runtime error. JavaScript happily accepts the change and print `x`'s new value: `FALSE` (see Figure 15.1).

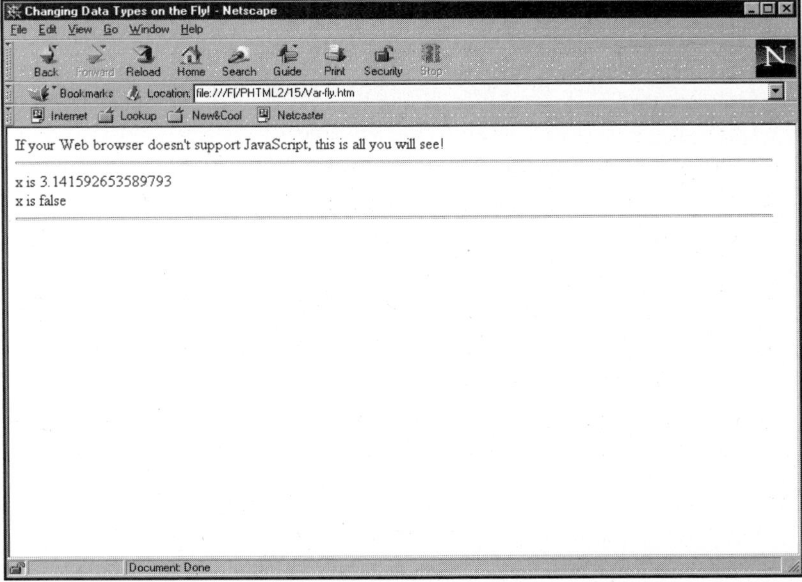

FIG. 15.1
Because JavaScript variables are loosely typed, not only their value can be changed, but also their data type.

The most common assignment operator, `=`, just assigns the value of an expression's right side to its left side. In the preceding example, the variable `x` got the integer value `7` after the expression was evaluated. For convenience, JavaScript also defines some other operators that combine common math operations with assignment. Table 15.1 shows these.

Table 15.1 Assignment operators that provide shortcuts to doing assignments and math operations at the same time.

Operator	What It Does	Two Equivalent Expressions
`+=`	Adds two values	`x+=y` and `x=x+y`
	Adds two strings	`string += "HTML"` and `string = string + "HTML"`
`-=`	Subtracts two values	`x-=y` and `x=x-y`
`*=`	Multiples two values	`a*=b` and `a=a*b`
`/=`	Divides two values	`e/=b` and `e=e/b`

Math Operators The previous sections gave you a sneak preview of the math operators that JavaScript furnishes. You can either combine math operations with assignments, as shown in Table 15.1, or use them individually. As you would expect, the standard four math functions (addition, subtraction, multiplication, and division) work just as they do on an ordinary calculator. The negation operator, `-`, is a unary operator that negates the sign of its operand. Another useful binary math operator is the modulus operator, `%`—this operator returns the remainder after the integer division of two integer numbers. For instance, in the expression

```
x = 13%5;
```

the variable `x` would be given the value of `3`.

JavaScript also adds two useful unary operators: `--` and `++`, called, respectively, the *decrement* and *increment* operators. These two operators modify the value of their operand, and they return the new value. They also share a unique property: You can use them either before or after their operand. If you put the operator after the operand, JavaScript returns the operand's value and then modifies it. If you take the opposite route and put the operator before the operand, JavaScript modifies it and returns the modified value. The following short example might help to clarify this seemingly odd behavior:

```
x = 7;   // set x to 7
a = --x; // set x to x-1, and return the new x; a = 6
b = a++; // set b to a, so b = 6, then add 1 to a; a = 7
x++;     // add one to x; ignore the returned value
```

Comparison Operators Comparing the value of two expressions to see whether one is larger, smaller, or equal to another is often necessary. JavaScript supplies several comparison operators that take two operands and return TRUE if the comparison is TRUE, and FALSE if it is not. (Remember, you can use literals, variables, or expressions with operators that require expressions.) Table 15.2 shows the JavaScript comparison operators.

Table 15.2 Comparison operators that allow two JavaScript operands to be compared in a variety of ways.

Operator	Read It As	Returns *TRUE* When
`==`	Equals	The two operands are equal.
`!=`	Does not equal	The two operands are unequal.
`<`	Less than	The left operand is less than the right operand.
`<=`	Less than or equal to	The left operand is less than or equal to the right operand.
`>`	Greater than	The left operand is greater than the right operand.
`>=`	Greater than or equal to	The left operand is greater than or equal to the right operand.

You might find it helpful to think of the comparison operators as questions. When you write the following,

```
(x >= 10)
```

you're really saying, "Is the value of variable `x` greater than or equal to `10`?" The return value answers the question, TRUE or FALSE.

TROUBLESHOOTING

You may be asking yourself, "Why do my tests for equality always succeed, even when I know that the two quantities are sometimes different?"

A common mistake in JavaScript, just as in C, C++, or Java, is mixing up the = operator—used to set one quantity equal to another—and the == operator—used to test two quantities for equality. The following code tests to see whether the variable a is equal to 10. If it is, this code writes out the following line:

if (a == 10)

document.writeln("a is equal to 10!")

On the other hand, the following code sets a equal to 10 and returns TRUE, and thus always writes out the following line:

if (a = 10)

document.writeln("a is equal to 10!")

Logical Operators Comparison operators compare quantity or content for numeric and string expressions. Sometimes, however, you need to test a logical value such as whether a comparison operator returns TRUE or FALSE. JavaScript's logical operators enable you to compare expressions that return logical values. The following are JavaScript's logical operators:

- &&, read as "and." The && operator returns TRUE if both its input expressions are TRUE. If the first operand evaluates to FALSE, && returns FALSE immediately, without evaluating the second operand. Here's an example:

```
x = TRUE && TRUE;       // x is TRUE
x = FALSE && FALSE;     // x is FALSE
x = FALSE && TRUE;      // x is FALSE
```

- ||, read as "or." This operator returns TRUE if either of its operands is TRUE. If the first operand is TRUE, || returns TRUE without evaluating the second operand. Here's an example:

```
x = TRUE || TRUE;       // x is TRUE
x = FALSE || TRUE;      // x is TRUE
x = FALSE || FALSE;     // x is FALSE
```

- !, read as "not." This operator takes only one expression and returns the opposite of that expression; !TRUE returns FALSE, for example, and !FALSE returns TRUE.

Note that the "and" and "or" operators don't evaluate the second operand if the first operand provides enough information for the operator to return a value. This process, called *short-circuit evaluation*, can be significant when the second operand is a function call. For example,

```
keepGoing = (userCancelled == FALSE) && (theForm.Submit())
```

If userCancelled is TRUE, the second operand, which submits the active form, is not called.

String Operators You can use a few of the operators previously listed for string manipulation as well. All the comparison operators can be used on strings too; the results depend on standard lexicographic ordering (ordering by the ASCII values of the string characters), but comparisons aren't case-sensitive. Additionally, you can use the + operator to concatenate strings, returning a string made up of the original strings joined together. The expression

```
str = "Hello, " + "World!";
```

would assign the resulting string "Hello, World!" to the variable str.

Controlling Your JavaScripts

Some scripts you write will be simple; they will execute the same way every time, one time per page. If you add a JavaScript to play a sound when users visit your home page, for example, it doesn't need to evaluate any conditions or do anything more than one time. More sophisticated scripts might require that you take different actions under different circumstances. You might also want to repeat the execution of a block of code—perhaps by a set number of times or as long as some condition is TRUE. JavaScript provides constructs for controlling the execution flow of your script based on conditions, as well as for repeating a sequence of operations.

Testing Conditions JavaScript provides a single type of control statement for making decisions: the `if...else` statement. To make a decision, you supply an expression that evaluates to `TRUE` or `FALSE`; which code is executed depends on what your expression evaluates to.

The simplest form of `if...else` uses only the `if` part. If the specified condition is `TRUE`, the code following the condition is executed; if not, it's skipped. In the following code fragment, for example, the message appears only if the condition (that the `lastModified.year` property of the `document` object says it was modified before 1995) is `TRUE`:

```
if (document.lastModified.year < 1995)
   document.write("Danger! This is a mighty old document.")
```

You can use any expression as the condition. Because you cannect expressions and combined them with the logical operators, your tests can be pretty sophisticated. For example,

```
if ((document.lastModified.year >= 1995) && (document.lastModified.month >= 10))
   document.write("This document is reasonably current.")
```

The `else` clause enables you to specify a set of statements to execute when the condition is `FALSE`. For instance,

```
if ((document.lastModified.year >= 1995) && (document.lastModified.month >= 10))
   document.write("This document is reasonably current.")
else
   document.write("This document is quite old.")
```

Repeating Actions JavaScript provides two different loop constructs that you can use to repeat a set of operations. The first, called a `for` loop, executes a set of statements some number of times. You specify three expressions: an *initial* expression that sets the values of any variables that you need to use, a *condition* that tells the loop how to see when it is done, and an *increment* expression that modifies any variables that need it. Here's a simple example:

```
for (count=0; count < 100; count++)
   document.write("Count is ", count);
```

This loop executes 100 times and prints out a number each time. The initial expression sets the counter, `count`, to zero. The condition tests to see whether `count` is less than 100 and the increment expression increments `count`.

You can use several statements for any of these expressions, as follows:

```
for (count=0, numFound = 0; (count < 100) && (numFound < 3); count++)
   if (someObject.found()) numFound++;
```

This loop either loops 100 times or as many times as it takes to "find" three items—the loop condition terminates when `count >= 100` or when `numFound >= 3`.

The second form of loop is the `while` loop. It executes statements as long as its condition is `TRUE`. You can rewrite the first `for` loop in the preceding example, for instance, as follows:

```
count = 0
while (count < 100) {
   if (someObject.found()) numFound++;
   document.write("Count is ", count)
}
```

Which form you use depends on what you are doing; `for` loops are useful when you want to perform an action a set number of times, and `while` loops are best when you want to keep doing something as long as a particular condition remains `TRUE`. Notice that by using curly braces, you can include more than one command to be executed by the `while` loop. (This is also `TRUE` of `for` loops and `if...else` constructs.)

JavaScript Reserved Words

JavaScript reserves some keywords for its own use. You cannot define your own methods or properties with the same name as any of these keywords; if you do, the JavaScript interpreter complains.

Some of these keywords are reserved for future use. JavaScript might enable you to use them, but your scripts may break in the future if you do.

Table 15.3 shows JavaScript's reserved keywords.

Table 15.3 JavaScript reserved keywords should not be used in your JavaScripts.

abstract	double	instanceof	super
boolean	else	int	switch
break	extends	interface	synchronized
byte	FALSE	long	this
case	final	native	throw
catch	finally	new	throws
char	float	null	transient
class	for	package	TRUE
const	function	private	try
continue	goto	protected	var
default	if	public	void
do	implements	return	while
import	short	with	in
static			

CAUTION

Because Netscape is still developing and refining JavaScript, the list of reserved keywords might change or grow over time. Whenever a new version of JavaScript is released, it might be a good idea to look over its new capabilities with an eye toward conflicts with your JavaScript programs.

Using JavaScript Statements

This section provides a quick reference to some of the more important JavaScript statements. Those listed here are in alphabetic order—many have examples. Here's what the formatting of these entries means:

- All JavaScript keywords are in `monospaced` font.
- Words in *monospace italics* represent user-defined names or statements.
- Any portions enclosed in square brackets (`[` and `]`) are optional.
- `{`*statements*`}` indicates a block of statements, which can consist of a single statement or multiple statements enclosed by curly braces.

The *break* Statement The `break` statement terminates the current `while` or `for` loop and transfers program control to the statement that follows the terminated loop.

Syntax

```
break
```

Example

The following function scans the list of URLs in the current document and stops when it has seen all URLs or when it finds a URL that matches the input parameter `searchName`:

```
function findURL(searchName) {
   var i = 0;
   for (i=0; i < document.links.length; i++) {
      if (document.links[i] == searchName) {
         document.writeln(document.links[i] + "<br>")
         break;
      }
   }
}
```

The *continue* Statement The `continue` statement stops executing the statements in a `while` or `for` loop, and skips to the next iteration of the loop. It doesn't stop the loop altogether like the `break` statement; instead, in a `while` loop, it jumps back to the condition. In a `for` loop, it jumps to the update expression.

Syntax

```
continue
```

Example

The following function prints the odd numbers between 1 and `x`; it has a `continue` statement that goes to the next iteration when `i` is even:

```
function printOddNumbers(x) {
   var i = 0
   while (i < x) {
      i++;
      if ((i % 2) == 0) // the % operator divides & returns the remainder
         continue
```

```
      else
         document.write(i, "\n")
   }
}
```

The *for* Loop A `for` loop consists of three optional expressions, enclosed in parentheses and separated by semicolons, followed by a block of statements executed in the loop. These parts do the following:

- The starting expression, `initial_expr`, is evaluated before the loop starts. It is most often used to initialize loop counter variables. You are free to use the `var` keyword here to declare new variables.
- A *condition* is evaluated on each pass through the loop. If the condition evaluates to `TRUE`, the statements in the loop body are executed. You can leave the condition out. If you do, it always evaluates to `TRUE`. If you leave the condition out, make sure to use `break` in your loop when it is time to exit.
- An update expression, `update_expr`, is usually used to update or increment the counter variable or other variables used in the condition. This expression is optional; you can update variables as needed within the body of the loop if you prefer.
- A block of statements are executed as long as the condition is `TRUE`. This block can have one or multiple statements in it.

Syntax

```
for ([initial_expr;] [condition;] [update_expr]) {
   statements
}
```

Example

This simple `for` statement prints out the numerals from 0 to 9. It starts by declaring a loop counter variable, `i`, and initializing it to 0. As long as `i` is less than 9, the update expression increments `i`, and the statements in the loop body are executed.

```
for (var i = 0; i <= 9; i++) {
   document.write(i);
}
```

The *for...in* Loop The `for...in` loop is a special form of the `for` loop that iterates the variable `variable-name` over all the properties of the object named `object-name`. For each distinct property, it executes the statements in the loop body.

Syntax

```
for (var in obj) {
   statements
}
```

Example

The following function takes as its arguments an object and the object's name. It then uses the `for...in` loop to iterate through all the object's properties and writes them into the current web page.

```
function dump_props(obj,obj_name) {
   for (i in obj)
      document.writeln(obj_name + "." + i + " = " + obj[i] + "<br>");
}
```

The *function* Statement The `function` statement declares a JavaScript function; the function may optionally accept one or more parameters. To return a value, the function must have a `return` statement that specifies the value to return. All parameters are passed to functions *by value*—the function gets the value of the parameter, but cannot change the original value in the caller.

Syntax

```
function name([param] [, param] [..., param]) {
   statements
}
```

Example

This example defines a function called `PageNameMatches`, which returns `TRUE` if the string argument passed to the function is the title of the current document.

```
function PageNameMatches(theString) {
   return (document.title == theString)
}
```

The *if...else* Statement The `if...else` statement is a conditional statement that executes the statements in `block1` if `condition` is `TRUE`. In the optional `else` clause, it executes the statements in `block2` if `condition` is `FALSE`. The blocks of statements can contain any JavaScript statements, including further nested `if` statements.

Syntax

```
if (condition) {
    statements
}
[else {
    statements}]
```

Example

This `if...else` statement calls the `Message.Decrypt()` method if the `Message.IsEncrypted()` method returns `TRUE`, and calls the `Message.Display()` method otherwise.

```
if (Message.IsEncrypted()) {
    Message.Decrypt(SecretKey);
}
else {
    Message.Display();
}
```

The *new* Statement The `new` statement is the way that new objects are created in JavaScript. If, for example, you defined the following function to create a `house` object

```
function house (rms,stl,yr,garp) { // define a house object
   this.room = rms;          // number of rooms (integer)
   this.style = stl;         // style (string)
   this.yearBuilt = yr;      // year built (integer)
   this.hasGarage = garp; // has garage? (boolean)
}
```

Example

You could then create an instance of a `house` object by using the `new` statement, as in the following:

```
var myhouse = new house(3,"Tenement",1962,false);
```

A few notes about this example. First, note that the function used to create the object doesn't actually return a value. The reason can work is that it makes use of the this object, which always refers to the current object. Second, although the function defines how to create the `house` object, none is actually created until the function is called using the `new` statement.

The *return* Statement The `return` statement specifies the value to be returned by a function.

Syntax

```
return expression;
```

Example

The following simple function returns the square of its argument, `x`, where `x` is any number.

```
function square( x ) {
   return x * x;
}
```

The *this* Statement You use `this` to access methods or properties of an object within the object's methods. The `this` statement always refers to the current object.

Syntax

```
this.property
```

Example

If `setSize` is a method of the `document` object, `this` refers to the specific object whose `setSize` method is called:

```
function setSize(x,y) {
   this.horizSize = x;
   this.vertSize = y;
}
```

This method sets the size for an object when called as follows:

```
document.setSize(640,480);
```

The *var* Statement The `var` statement declares a variable *varname*, optionally initializing it to have *value*. The variable name *varname* can be any JavaScript identifier, and *value* can be any legal expression (including literals).

Syntax

```
var varname [= value] [, var varname [= value] ] [..., var varname [= value] ]
```

Example

This statement declares the variables `num.hits` and `cust.no`, and initializes their values to zero.

```
var num_hits = 0, var cust_no = 0;
```

The *while* Statement The `while` statement contains a condition and a block of statements. The `while` statement evaluates the condition; if *`condition`* is `TRUE`, it executes the statements in the loop body. It then re-evaluates *`condition`* and continues to execute the statement block as long as *`condition`* is `TRUE`. When *`condition`* evaluates to `FALSE`, execution continues with the next statement following the block.

Syntax

```
while (condition) {
   statements
}
```

Example

The following simple `while` loop iterates until it finds a form in the current document object whose name is `"OrderForm"`, or until it runs out of forms in the document:

```
x = 0;
while ((x < document.forms[].length) && (document.forms[x].name != "OrderForm"))
{
   x++
}
```

The *with* Statement The `with` statement establishes *`object`* as the default object for the statements in `block`. Any property references without an object are then assumed to be for *`object`*.

Syntax

```
with object {
   statements
}
```

Example

This statement uses `with` to apply the `write()` method and set the value of the `bgColor` property of the `document` object.

```
with document {
   write "Inside a with block, you don't need to specify the object.";
   bgColor = gray;
}
```

JavaScript and Web Browsers

The most important thing you will be doing with your JavaScripts is interacting with the content and information on your web pages, and through it, with your user. JavaScript interacts with your web browser through the browser's object model. Different aspects of the web browser exist as different objects, with properties and methods that can be accessed by JavaScript. For instance, `document.write()` uses the `write` method of the `document` object. Understanding this web Browser Object Model is crucial to using JavaScript effectively. Also, understanding how the web browser processes and executes your scripts is also necessary.

When Scripts Execute

When you put JavaScript code in a page, the web browser evaluates the code as soon as it is encountered. Functions, however, don't get executed when they're evaluated; they just get stored for later use. You still have to call functions explicitly to make them work. Some functions are attached to objects—buttons or text fields on forms, for example, which are called when some event happens on the button or field. You might also have functions that you want to execute during page evaluation. You can do so by putting a call to the function at the appropriate place in the page.

Where to Put Your Scripts

You can put scripts anywhere within your HTML page, as long as they are surrounded with the `<SCRIPT>...</SCRIPT>` tags. One good system is to put functions that will be executed more than one time into the `<HEAD>` element of their pages; this element provides a convenient storage place. Because the `<HEAD>` element is at the beginning of the file, functions and VB Script code that you put there is evaluated before the rest of the document is loaded. Then you can execute the function at the appropriate point in your web page by calling it, as in the following:

```
<SCRIPT language="JavaScript">
<!-- Hide this script from incompatible web browsers!
myFunction();
//   Hide this script from incompatible web browsers! -->
</SCRIPT>
```

Another way to execute scripts is to attach them to HTML elements that support scripts. When scripts are matched with events attached to these elements, the script is executed when the event occurs. This can be done with HTML elements, such as forms, buttons, or links. Consider Listing 15.2, which shows a very simple example of attaching a JavaScript function to the `onClick` attribute of an HTML forms button (see Figure 15.2).

Listing 15.2 Button1.htm Calling a Javascript function with the click of a button.

```
<HTML>
<HEAD>
<SCRIPT LANGUAGE="JavaScript">
<!-- Hide this script from incompatible web browsers! -->
function pressed() {
    alert("I said Don't Press Me!");
}
//   Hide this script from incompatible web browsers! -->
</SCRIPT>
<TITLE>JavaScripts Attached to HTML Elements</TITLE>
</HEAD>
```

```
<BODY BGCOLOR=#FFFFFF>
<FORM NAME="Form1">
    <INPUT TYPE="button" NAME="Button1" VALUE="Don't Press Me!"
        onClick="pressed()">
</FORM>
</BODY>
</HTML>
```

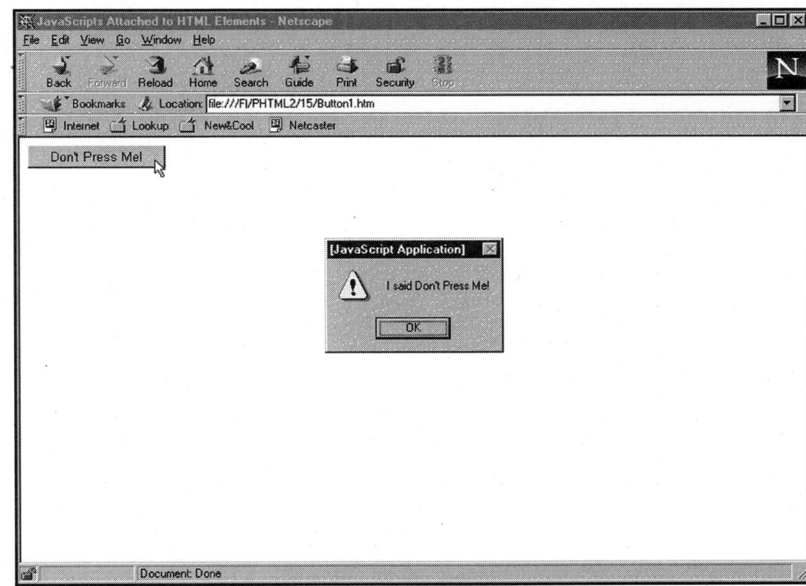

FIG. 15.2
JavaScript functions can be attached to form fields through several different methods.

JavaScript also provides you with an alternative way to attach functions to objects and their events. For simple actions, you can attach the JavaScript directly to the attribute of the HTML form element, as shown in Listing 15.3. Each of these listings produces the output shown in Figure 15.2.

Listing 15.3 Button2.htm Simple JavaScripts can be attached right to a form element.

```
<HTML>
<HEAD>
<TITLE>JavaScripts Attached to HTML Elements</TITLE>
</HEAD>
<BODY BGCOLOR=#FFFFFF>
<FORM NAME="Form1">
    <INPUT TYPE="button" NAME="Button1" VALUE="Don't Press Me!"
        onClick="alert('I said Don\'t Press Me!')">
</FORM>
</BODY>
</HTML>
```

Sometimes you have code that should not be evaluated or executed until after all the page's HTML has been parsed and displayed. An example would be a function to print out all the URLs referenced in the page. If this function is evaluated before all the HTML on the page has been loaded, it misses some URLs. Therefore, the call to the function should come at the page's end. You can define the function itself anywhere in the HTML document; it is the function call that you should put at the end of the page.

NOTE JavaScript code to modify the actual HTML contents of a document (as opposed to merely changing the text in a form text input field, for instance) must be executed during page evaluation.

CHAPTER 16

The Web Browser Object Model

by Jim O'Donnell

In this chapter

In Chapter 15, "Introduction to JavaScripting," you learned the basics of JavaScript—its syntax, control structures, and how to use it to access and manipulate objects. To be useful, however, there needs to be something to manipulate. How does JavaScript (or any other scripting language, for that matter) interact with your web browser?

The answer is the Web Browser Object Model. Each script-compatible web browser, mainly Netscape Navigator and Microsoft Internet Explorer, exposes a number of objects that can be used to control and interact with the browser. The sum total of these objects is the browser's object model.

As you would expect, the object models that Netscape and Microsoft have developed for their web browsers are not completely compatible. Not only are there differences between the models from the two vendors, but each revision of their web browsers also differs from the last—they are largely backward-compatible, but include a number of new capabilities. This chapter examines those elements of the Web Browser Object Model that are (for the most part) common to all Netscape and Microsoft web browsers, version 3 and higher. (Differences are noted in the discussion.) Later chapters discuss some of the major changes that have occurred with the advent of support for Cascading Style Sheets and Dynamic HTML.

See "Web Browser Object Model," **p. 636**

See "Internet Explorer 4 Document Object Model," **p. 680**

Web Browser Object Hierarchy and Scoping

Figure 16.1 shows the hierarchy of objects that the web browser provides and that are accessible to JavaScript. As shown, `window` is the topmost object in the hierarchy, and the other objects are organized underneath it. Using this hierarchy, the full reference for the value of a text field named `text1` in an HTML form named `form1` would be `window.document.form1.text1.value`.

Because of the object-scoping rules in JavaScript, however, it is not necessary to specify this full reference. *Scoping* refers to the range over which a variable, function, or object is defined. A variable defined within a JavaScript function, for instance, is only scoped within that function—it cannot be referenced outside the function. JavaScripts are scoped to the current window, but not to the objects below the window in the hierarchy. Thus for the preceding example, the text field value could also be referenced as `document.form1.text1.value`.

As in Figure 16.1, all web pages will have the `window`, `navigator`, `document`, `history`, and `location` objects. Depending on the contents of the web page, other objects may also be defined. The remainder of this chapter reviews the objects shown in Figure 16.1—what information is defined for them (properties), what functions they can perform (methods), and the actions to which they can respond (events).

The *Window* Object

The web browser creates at least one `window` object for every document. Think of the `window` object as an actual window, and the `document` object as the content that appears in the window. As briefly discussed in this chapter, and then in more detail in Chapter 18, "Manipulating Windows and Frames with JavaScript," one document can create more than one window, using the `window` object's `open()` method.

▶ **See** "Manipulating Windows and Frames with JavaScript," **p. 479**

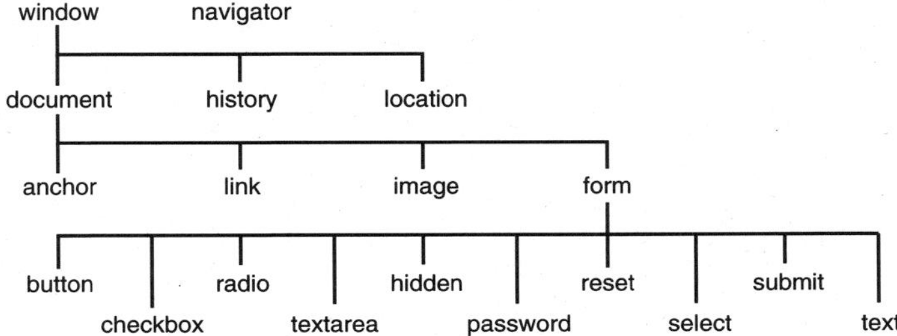

FIG. 16.1 Objects defined by the web browser are organized in an hierarchy and can be accessed and manipulated by JavaScript.

Window Object Properties

Your HTML documents can access and manipulate a number of attributes of the current web browser window through the `window` object. Some of the more useful `window` object properties are the following:

`closed`—specifies whether a window has been closed (Boolean).

`defaultStatus`—the default message that appears in the status line of the web browser window (string).

`length`—the number of frames in the current window (integer).

`name`—the name of a window (string).

`opener`—when a window is opened using the `open()` method, the name of the window from which it was created is in this property (string).

`parent`—refers to a window that contains a frameset (object).

`self` or **`top`**—refers to the current window (object).

`status`—can be used to read or set the contents of the web browser's status line (string).

In addition to the properties in the preceding list, remember that the `document`, `history`, and `location` objects are also properties of the `window` object.

Window Object Methods

You can use JavaScript to create or operate on existing windows by using the methods associated with the `window` object. The following are some of these methods:

`alert(`*`string`*`)`—puts up an alert dialog box and displays the message specified in *string*. Users must dismiss the dialog box by clicking the OK button before the web browser will allow them to continue.

`blur()`—removes the focus from the specified window.

`clearTimeOut(`*`timerID`*`)`—clears the timer function with ID *timerID* (see `setTimeOut()` method in this list).

`close()`—closes the specified window.

`confirm(`*`string`*`)`—puts up a confirmation dialog box with two buttons (OK and Cancel) and displays the message specified in *string*. Users can dismiss the dialog box by clicking Cancel or OK; the confirm function returns `true` if users click OK and `false` if they click Cancel.

`eval(`*`string`*`)`—evaluates *string* as JavaScript code and returns the result.

`focus()`—puts the focus on the specified window.

`open(`*`arguments`*`)`—opens a new window.

`prompt(`*`string`*`,[`*`inputDefault`*`])`—opens a prompt box, which displays *string* as a prompt and asks the user for input. If *inputDefault* is specified, it is shown as the default value of the prompt box.

`scroll(`*`x`*`,`*`y`*`)`—scrolls the window to the given *x* and *y* coordinates.

`setTimeOut(`*`expression`*`,`*`msec`*`)`—evaluates *expression* after the specified number of milliseconds have passed. This method returns a timer ID that can be used by `clearTimeOut`.

NOTE Each of the preceeding methods—as well as the events in the following section—are applied to the `window` object to which they belong. For instance, `blur()` or `self.blur()` would remove the focus from the window in which the document was. `MyWindow.blur()` would remove it from the window called MyWindow.

Window Object Events

Finally, the `window` object can respond to the following events:

`onBlur`—triggered when the focus is removed from the window

`onError`—triggered when an error occurs in the window

`onFocus`—triggered when the focus is applied to the window

`onLoad`—triggered when the web browser finishes loading a document into the window

`onUnload`—triggered when the user exits from the document within the window

Window methods can be placed in either the `<BODY>` or `<FRAMESET>` tag of the document. To attach a JavaScript function to the `onLoad` event, for example, you could use this `<BODY>` tag:

```
<BODY onLoad="alert('Document download complete!')">
```

Chapter 18 includes an extensive example of how to use JavaScript to create and manipulate windows.

▶ **See** "JavaScript Windows Example," **p. 495**

The *Location* Object

As mentioned earlier, one of the properties of every window is the `location` object. This object holds the current URL, including the hostname, path, CGI script arguments, and even the protocol. Table 16.1 shows the properties and methods of the `location` object.

Table 16.1 The *location* object contains information on the currently displayed URL

Name	What It Does
Properties	
`href`	Contains the entire URL, including all the subparts; for example, **http://www.rpi.edu:80/~odonnj/index.html**
`protocol`	Contains the protocol field of the URL, including the first colon; for example, **http:**
`host`	Contains the hostname and port number; for example, **www.rpi.edu:80**
`hostname`	Contains only the hostname; for example, **www.rpi.edu**
`port`	Contains the port; for example, **80**
`path`	Contains the path to the actual document; for example, **~odonnj/index.html**
`hash`	Contains any CGI arguments after the first `#` in the URL
`search`	Contains any CGI arguments after the first `?` in the URL
Method	
`assign(`*`string`*`)`	Sets `location.href` to the value you specify

Listing 16.1 shows an example of how you access and use the `location` object. First, the current values of the location properties are displayed on the web page (see Figure 16.2). As you can see, not all of them are defined. Additionally, when the button is clicked, the `location.href` property is set to the URL of my home page. This causes the web browser to load that page (see Figure 16.3).

Listing 16.1 Location.htm The *location* object enables you to access and set information about the current URL.

```
<HTML>
<HEAD>
<SCRIPT LANGUAGE="JavaScript">
<!-- Hide this script from incompatible Web browsers! -->
function gohome() {
   location.href = "http://www.rpi.edu/~odonnj/";
}
// Hide this script from incompatible Web browsers! -->
</SCRIPT>
<TITLE>The Location Object</TITLE>
</HEAD>
<BODY BGCOLOR=#FFFFFF>
<SCRIPT LANGUAGE="Javascript">
<!-- Hide this script from incompatible Web browsers! -->
document.writeln("Current location information: <BR> <HR>");
document.writeln("location.href = " + location.href + "<BR>");
document.writeln("location.protocol = " + location.protocol + "<BR>");
document.writeln("location.host = " + location.host + "<BR>");
document.writeln("location.hostname = " + location.hostname + "<BR>");
document.writeln("location.port = " + location.port + "<BR>");
document.writeln("location.pathname = " + location.pathname + "<BR>");
document.writeln("location.hash = " + location.hash + "<BR>");
document.writeln("location.search = " + location.search + "<BR> <HR>");
// Hide this script from incompatible Web browsers! -->
</SCRIPT>
<FORM NAME="Form1">
   <INPUT TYPE="button" NAME="Button1" VALUE="Goto JOD's Home Page!"
      onClick="gohome()">
</FORM>
</BODY>
</HTML>
```

NOTE The `document.write()` method is discussed later in this chapter in the "The `Document` Object" section.

The *History* Object

The web browser also maintains a list of pages that you have visited since running the program; this list is called the ***history list,*** and can be accessed through the `history` object. Your JavaScript programs can move through pages in the list by using the properties and functions shown in Table 16.2.

Table 16.2 The *history* object contains information on the browser's history list.

Property	Type	What It Does
`current`	Property	Contains the URL of the current history entry
`length`	Property	Contains the number of entries in the history list
`previous`	Property	Contains the URL of the previous history stack entry
`next`	Property	Contains the URL of the next history stack entry
`back()`	Method	Goes back one entry in the history list
`forward()`	Method	Goes forward one entry in the history list
`go(`*`num`*`)`	Method	Goes forward ***num*** entries in the history stack if ***num*** > 0, otherwise it goes backward -***num*** entries
`go(`*`string`*`)`	Method	Goes to the newest history entry whose title or URL contains *string* as a substring; the string case doesn't matter

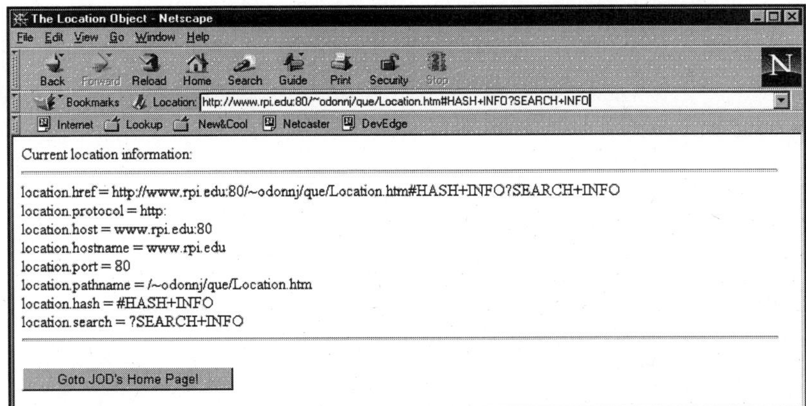

FIG. 16.2
Manipulating the `location` object gives you another means of moving from one web page to another.

The `history.length`, therefore, would return the number of entries in the history list. The methods `history.back()` and `history.forward()` would cause the web browser to load the previous and next entry in the history list, if any.

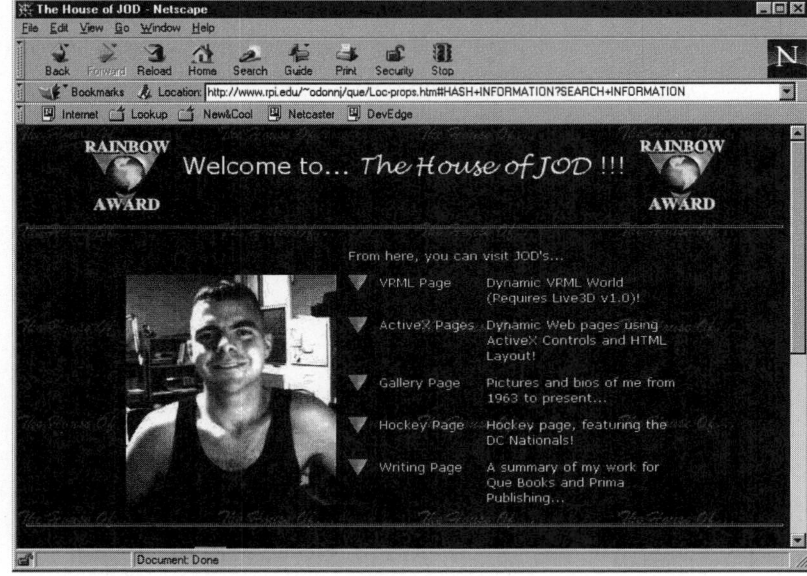

FIG. 16.3
By setting its `href` property, you can use the `location` object to change the URL your web browser is looking at.

The *Document* Object

Web browsers also expose an object called `document`. As you might expect, this object exposes useful properties and methods of the active document. The `location` object refers only to the URL of the active document, but `document` refers to the document itself. Chapter 18 discusses the `document` object in more detail, but its basic properties and methods are shown here.

▶ **See** "Filling Your Windows II: The `Document` Object," **p. 493**

Document Object Properties

You can access and manipulate a number of attributes of the current web browser document through the `document` object. Some of the more useful `document` object properties are the following:

`alinkColor`—the color of the document's active link

`bgColor`—the background color of the document

`cookie`—the document's cookie

`domain`—domain name of the server that served the document

`fgColor`—the foreground color of the document

`lastModified`—the date the document was last modified

`linkColor`—the color of the document's links

`referrer`—the URL of the document from which this document was called

title—the contents of the <TITLE> tag

URL—the complete URL of the document

vlinkColor—the color of the document's visited links

In addition to the properties in the preceding list, remember that the `anchor`, `link`, `form`, and `image` objects are also properties of the `document` object.

Document Object Methods

You can use JavaScript to operate on documents by using the methods associated with the `document` object. The following are some of these methods:

close()—closes the specified document.

eval(*string*)—evaluates *string* as JavaScript code and returns the result.

open()—opens a stream for a new document. This document is meant to be filled with the output of calls to the `document.write()` and/or `document.writeln()` methods.

write(*expression*, [*expression...*])—writes one or more HTML expressions.

writeln(*expression*, [*expression...*])—identical to `write()`, except this method appends a newline.

Listing 16.2 shows a JavaScript that accesses and displays some of the properties of the `document` object. Notice that the `Link` object is accessed through the `links` array, one for each URL link on the current web page (see the "JavaScript Object Arrays" section later in this chapter). Figure 16.4 shows the results of loading this web page.

Listing 16.2 Document.htm The *document* object enables you to access and set information about the current document.

```
<HTML>
<HEAD>
<TITLE>The Document Object</TITLE>
</HEAD>
<BODY BGCOLOR=#FFFFFF>
<A HREF="http://www.rpi.edu/~odonnj/">JOD's Home Page</A>
<A HREF="http://www.rpi.edu/~odonnj/que/Window.htm">The Window Object</A>
<A HREF="http://www.rpi.edu/~odonnj/que/Location.htm">The Location Object</A>
<A HREF="http://www.rpi.edu/~odonnj/que/Document.htm">The Document Object</A>
<HR>
<A HREF="mailto:odonnj@rpi.edu">Jim O'Donnell</A>
<HR>
<SCRIPT LANGUAGE="JavaScript">
<!-- Hide this script from incompatible Web browsers! -->
var n
document.writeln("<EM>Current document information:</EM><BR><PRE>")
document.writeln("document.title         = ,"document.title)
document.writeln("document.location      = ,"document.location)
document.writeln("document.lastModified  = ,"document.lastModified)
```

continues

Listing 16.2 Continued

```
for (n = 0;n < document.links.length;n++)
   document.writeln("document.links[,"n,"].href = ,"
      document.links[n].href)
document.writeln("document.linkColor     = ,"document.linkColor)
document.writeln("document.alinkColor    = ,"document.alinkColor)
document.writeln("document.vlinkColor    = ,"document.vlinkColor)
document.writeln("document.bgColor       = ,"document.bgColor)
document.writeln("document.fgColor       = ,"document.fgColor,"<PRE><BR>")
//  Hide this script from incompatible Web browsers! -->
</SCRIPT>
</BODY>
</HTML>
```

Some of the real power of the `document` object, however, is realized by making use of the objects underneath it in the hierarchy—particularly the different HTML forms elements available. This is because HTML forms are one of the primary ways of interacting with the user of a web page. The next few sections of this chapter discuss the objects used to interact with HTML forms.

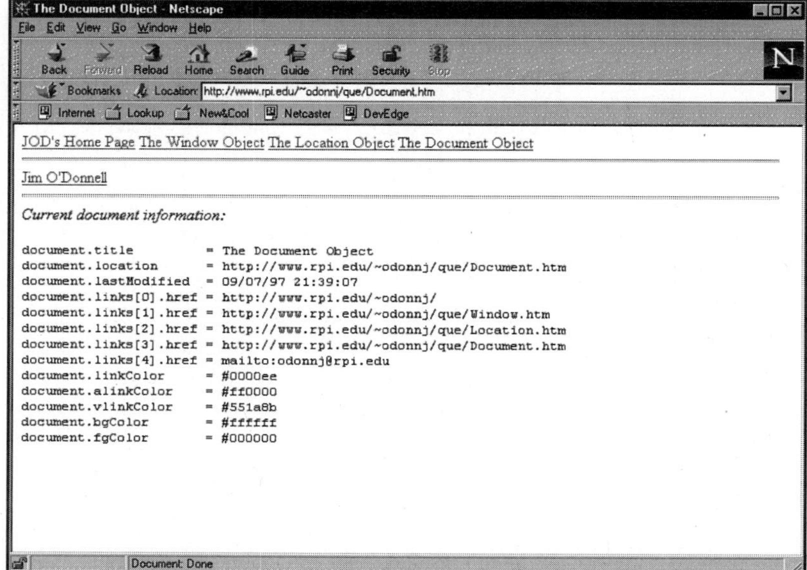

FIG. 16.4
`Document` object properties contain information about the current document displayed in the web browser.

JavaScript Object Arrays

Before you read about the other objects in the web browser object hierarchy, now is a good time to learn about JavaScript's object array. An *object array* is what JavaScript uses to reference objects when there is more than one of the object in the current window or document (known as multiple instances of the object). An HTML document is likely to contain more than one hypertext link, for example, so there will be more than one `link` and `anchor` object. Each form requires a separate `form` object, each image an `image` object, and so on.

JavaScript gives you multiple ways of referencing and accessing these objects. Consider the following excerpt of HTML code, for example:

```
<FORM NAME=MyForm1 ACTION=… METHOD=…>
   HTML Form elements…
</FORM>
<FORM NAME=MyForm2 ACTION=… METHOD=…>
   HTML Form elements…
</FORM>
```


The first way to use JavaScript to reference these forms is to use the conventional object hierarchy that you have seen thus far. To set the value of a text field named `MyText1` in the first form, for example, you would use something like this:

```
document.MyForm1.MyText1.value = "Some Value"
```

JavaScript, on the other hand, gives you several ways other ways to reference these objects, using JavaScript's object arrays. Objects are contained in an object array in the order in which they are defined in the document. Assuming that the two previously mentioned forms are the only two forms in the document, the first can be referenced using

```
document.forms[0]
```

and the second with

```
document.forms[1]
```

Thus the same text field could be set using

```
document.forms[0].MyText1.value = "Some Value"
```

The third way to reference objects in an object array is to use JavaScript's associative arrays. With associative arrays, the array element is referenced by including its name as the argument of the array. Using this method, the two forms would be referenced as

```
document.forms["MyForm1"]
```

and

```
document.forms["MyForm2"]
```

and the text field set using

```
document.forms["MyForm1"].MyText1.value = "Some Value"
```

These examples show the three different ways to reference JavaScript objects when multiple instances of them exist. Which way should you use? That depends on the application:

Object Hierarchy Referencing. For example,

```
document.MyForm1.MyText1.value
```

Use this method when you are dealing with one or two objects, each with a predefined name and separate actions associated with each.

Object Array with Numerical Index. For example,

```
document.forms[0].MyText1.value
```

Use this method when you want to repeat an action over multiple objects using a JavaScript `for` or `while` loop.

Object Associative Array. For example,

```
document.forms["MyForm1"].MyText1.value
```

Use this method when you want to operate on one or two objects only, but the specific object may vary.

CAUTION

If you are designing HTML documents and want to remain compatible with Netscape Navigator 2.0 (if you are programming for a corporate intranet that hasn't upgraded in a while, for instance), you can only use the numerical index method of referencing object arrays.

For a given HTML document, some of the predefined object arrays that JavaScript can access (depending on what is defined in the document) are the following:

`anchors`—one for each of the `<A>` tags containing a NAME attribute

`applets`—one for each `<APPLET>` tag

`arguments`—one for each argument of a JavaScript function.

`elements`—one for each element in an HTML form

`embeds`—one for each `<EMBED>` tag

`forms`—one for each HTML form

`frames`—one for each `<FRAME>` tag in a window containing a `<FRAMESET>`.

`history`—one for each entry in the history list for a window

`images`—one for each `<IMG>` tag

`links`—one for each `<AREA>` and/or `<A>` tag containing a `HREF` attribute

`mimeTypes`—one for each MIME type supported by the client web browser, its helper applications, plug-ins, and (primarily for Internet Explorer) ActiveX Controls

`options`—one for each `<OPTION>` tag

`plugins`—one for each plug-in installed on the client web browser

The *Link*, *Area*, and *Anchor* Objects

These objects are created within a document when there are hypertext links or targets created using the `<A>` or `<AREA>` tag. A `link` object is created when the `<A>` tag uses the `HREF` attribute and the `anchor` object is created when it uses the `NAME` attribute. `Area` objects are created for each `<AREA>` tag, used for creating client-side imagemaps.

▶ **See** "Client-Side Imagemaps," **p. 124**

Link and area objects are referenced through the link's object array. Each object in this array has the same properties as a location object (see Table 16.1 earlier in the chapter). In addition, these objects have the events listed in Table 16.3.

Table 16.3 Events of the HTML *form* object.

Event	When It Occurs
onClick	Triggered when a link object is clicked
onMouseOver	Triggered when the mouse passes over a link or area object
onMouseOut	Triggered when the mouse passes out of a link or area object

Anchor objects are also referenced using an object array, the anchors array. The only property of this object array, however, is the length property, which returns the number of elements in the array.

The *Form* Object

The HTML form object is the primary way for web pages to solicit different types of input from the user. JavaScript will often work along with HTML forms to perform its functions. The object model for HTML forms includes a wide variety of properties, methods, and events. If you use these with each form, JavaScript can manipulate and access those forms.

Form Object Properties

Tables 16.4, 16.5, and 16.6 show some of the properties, methods, and events attached to HTML form objects. These can be used in JavaScripts—the properties and methods can be used to access or manipulate information and to perform certain functions, and the events can be used to trigger JavaScript functions related to the form itself. If there is a form named Form1, for instance, the method document.Form1.submit() can be called in JavaScript to submit the form. On the other hand, if the <SUBMIT> button calls a function in response to an onSubmit event, the submission of the form can be disabled if the function returns a false value. This is a good way to perform form validation within the web browser and only allow submission of the form if all fields are validated.

Table 16.4 Properties of the HTML *form* object.

Property	What It Contains
name	The value of the form's NAME attribute
method	The value of the form's METHOD attribute
action	The value of the form's ACTION attribute

continues

Table 16.4 Continued

`elements`	The `elements` array of the form
`length`	The number of elements in the form
`encoding`	The value of the form's `ENCODING` attribute
`target`	Window targeted after submit for form response

Note that the HTML form elements that can be included within the form, `<INPUT>`, `<RADIO>`, `<CHECKBOX>`, and other forms tags, are also represented as objects and can be referenced by JavaScript. These form `element` objects are also properties of their parent form—they are discussed in the next section.

Table 16.5 Methods of the HTML *form* object.

Method	What It Does
`reset()`	Resets the form to its initial values
`submit()`	Submits the form

Table 16.6 Events of the HTML *form* object.

Event	When It Occurs
`onReset`	Triggered when the `<RESET>` button is clicked or the `reset()` method is called
`onSubmit`	Triggered when the `<SUBMIT>` button is clicked or the `submit()` method is called

Using Objects to Manipulate *Form* Elements

A good place to use JavaScript is in forms; this is because you can write scripts that process, check, and perform calculations with the data the user enters. JavaScript provides a useful set of properties and methods for text `<INPUT>` elements and buttons and the other form elements.

You use `<INPUT>` elements in a form to enable the user to enter text data; JavaScript provides properties to get the objects that hold the element's contents as well as methods for doing something when the user moves into or out of a field. Table 16.7 shows some of the properties, methods, and events defined for `<INPUT>` form `element` objects.

Table 16.7 HTML form *input* object properties, methods, and events.

Property	What It Contains
`name`	The value of the element's `NAME` attribute
`value`	The field's contents
`defaultValue`	The initial contents of the field
Method	**What It Does**
`focus()`	Moves the input focus to the specified object
`blur()`	Moves the input focus away from the specified object
`select()`	Selects the specified object
`submit()`	Submits the form according to its `ACTION` and `METHOD` attributes
Event	**When It Occurs**
`onFocus`	Triggered when the user moves the input focus to the field, either via the Tab key or a mouse click
`onBlur`	Triggered when the user moves the input focus out of this field
`onSelect`	Triggered when the user selects text in the field
`onSubmit`	Triggered when the form is submitted
`onChange`	Triggered only when the field loses focus and the user has modified its text; use this action to validate data in a field

Individual buttons and check boxes have properties too; JavaScript provides properties to get objects containing a button's data, as well as methods for doing something when the user selects or deselects a particular button. Table 16.8 shows some of the properties, methods, and events defined for button elements.

Table 16.8 HTML form *radio* and *checkbox* object properties, methods, and events.

Property	What It Contains
`name`	The value of the button's `NAME` attribute
`value`	The `VALUE` attribute
`checked`	The state of a check box
`defaultChecked`	The initial state of a check box

continues

Table 16.8 Continued

Method	What It Does
`focus()`	Moves the input focus to the specified object
`blur()`	Moves the input focus away from the specified object
`click()`	Clicks a button and triggers whatever actions are attached to it
`submit()`	Submits the form according to its `ACTION` and `METHOD` attributes
Event	**When It Occurs**
`onClick`	Triggered when the button is pressed
`onFocus`	Triggered when the user moves the input focus to the field, either via the Tab key or a mouse click
`onBlur`	Triggered when the user moves the input focus out of this field
`onSubmit`	Triggered when the form is submitted
`onChange`	Triggered only when the field loses focus and the user has modified its text; use this action to validate data in a field

For more details and examples of what you can do with JavaScript and the objects, properties, and methods associated with HTML forms, see Chapter 19, "Using JavaScript to Create Smart Forms."

▶ **See** "Client-Side Form Validation," **p. 516**

The *Image* Object

The last web browser object to be discussed in this chapter is the `image` object. One `image` object is created in a document by each `<IMG>` tag on the page. These objects are referenced through an image's `object` array; the object's array has a `length` property that you can use to find out how many images are present. Table 16.9 shows some of the other properties and events associated with the `image` object.

Table 16.9 HTML *image* object properties and events.

Property	What It Contains
`border`	The value of the `BORDER` attribute
`complete`	Indicates whether the image has been completely loaded
`height`	The value of the `HEIGHT` attribute
`hspace`	The value of the `HSPACE` attribute
`lowsrc`	The value of the `LOWSRC` attribute

Property	What It Contains
`name`	The value of the `NAME` attribute
`src`	The value of the `SRC` attribute
`vspace`	The value of the `VSPACE` attribute
`width`	The value of the `WIDTH` attribute
Event	**When It Occurs**
`onAbort`	Triggered when the user aborts the loading of an image, such as by clicking the Stop button
`onError`	Triggered when an error occurs when an image is being loaded
`onLoad`	Triggered when an image is completely loaded

Image Object Example

Listing 16.3 shows an example that uses the `onMouseOver` and `onMouseOut` events of the `link` object, along with the properties of the `image` object, to create a hypertext link whose anchor changes whenever the mouse is passed over it. This is often done to highlight hypertext link anchors as the mouse passes over them, to make them stand out more—for instance, the changed image can be a glowing version of the original image. Figure 16.5 demonstrates how this will appear in the web page.

Listing 16.3 Image.htm Use JavaScript to create changing HyperText link anchors.

```
<HTML>
<HEAD>
<SCRIPT LANGUAGE="JavaScript">
<!-- Hide this script from incompatible Web browsers! -->
function changeImage(i,j) {
   document.images[i].src = "clickme" + j + ".gif"
}
//  Hide this script from incompatible Web browsers! -->
</SCRIPT>
<TITLE>The Image Object</TITLE>
</HEAD>
<BODY BGCOLOR=#FFFFFF>
<A HREF="Document.htm" onMouseOver="changeImage(0,2)"
                       onMouseOut="changeImage(0,1)">
   <IMG SRC="clickme1.gif" WIDTH=200 HEIGHT=50 BORDER=0>
</A>
<HR>
<A HREF="Location.htm" onMouseOver="changeImage(1,2)"
                       onMouseOut="changeImage(1,1)">
   <IMG SRC="clickme1.gif" WIDTH=200 HEIGHT=50 BORDER=0>
</A>
</BODY>
</HTML>
```

Listing 17.2 Continued

```
<BODY BGCOLOR=#FFFFFF>
<H1>Tell Me About Pop-Up Messages</H1>
This is a pop-up message. Unlike a normal JavaScript alert box, pop-up messages
are composed of HTML and can therefore include <B>formatted</B> <I>text</I>.
To close the pop-up message window, just click the OK button below.
<FORM NAME="buttonForm">
<INPUT TYPE="button" VALUE="OK" onClick="window.close();">
</FORM>
</BODY>
</HTML>
```

For the most part, the Tell Me example Web page is a normal Web page with no frills. One important thing going on here is worth pointing out, however. When the OK button is clicked, the pop-up message has to go away. This means that the newly created browser window displaying the page must be killed. This is accomplished in the `onClick` event handler for the OK button. The `window.close()` method is called to destroy the window and thereby remove the pop-up message.

Displaying a Scrolling Message

While on the subject of displaying messages, it is important to review another useful type of message: a scrolling message. A *scrolling message* is a text message scrolled across the screen horizontally. Scrolling messages are interesting because they are animated and draw attention to themselves. Scrolling messages typically manifest themselves in one of two ways: either as a scrolling text form field or as a scrolling status bar. This example takes the latter approach and shows you how to display a scrolling message in the status bar of a Web browser.

CAUTION

The fact that scrolling messages are animated and draw attention to themselves can also be a negative. Web pages with too much animation can be extremely annoying to users. It is important to weigh the potential annoyance factor of animated Web elements before filling a page with them. In moderate usage, however, animation provides a powerful way to convey information on a Web page.

JavaScript makes displaying a scrolling message in the status bar of a Web browser surprisingly easy. Figure 17.3 shows the Scrolling Message example Web page with a message scrolling across the status bar of the browser. Unfortunately, it is difficult to get the scrolling animation across to you through the static pages of this book, but hopefully you will get the idea. If not, try opening the page for yourself. You can find the page (ScrollingMessage.htm) on the accompanying CD.

The source code for the Scrolling Message page is surprisingly simple considering the fact that the page is dynamically animating a string of text. Listing 17.3 contains the source code for the page.

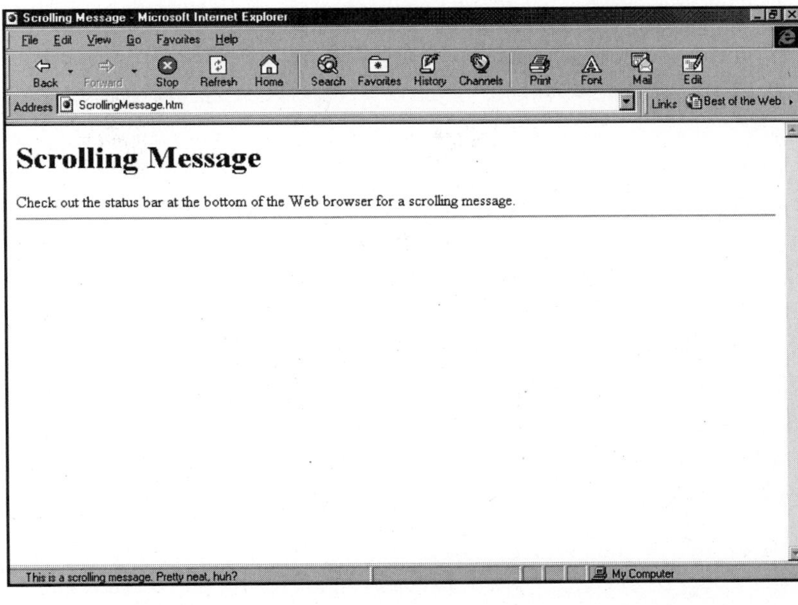

FIG. 17.3
The Scrolling Message example Web page with a message scrolling in the Web browser's status bar.

Listing 17.3 ScrollingMessage.htm Scrolling a message in the web browser's status bar with JavaScript.

```
<HTML>
<HEAD>
<SCRIPT LANGUAGE="JavaScript">
<!-- Hide this script from incompatible Web browsers!
var msg = "   This is a scrolling message. Pretty neat, huh?   ";
var pos = 0;

function scrollMsg() {
  window.status = msg.substring(pos, msg.length) + msg.substring(0, pos);
  if (++pos > msg.length)
    pos = 0;
  window.setTimeout("scrollMsg()", 200);
}
//   Hide this script from incompatible Web browsers! -->
</SCRIPT>
<TITLE>Scrolling Message</TITLE>
</HEAD>
<BODY BGCOLOR=#FFFFFF>
<H1>Scrolling Message</H1>
Check out the status bar at the bottom of the Web browser for a scrolling
message.
<HR>
<SCRIPT LANGUAGE="JavaScript">
<!-- Hide this script from incompatible Web browsers!
```

continues

Listing 17.3 Continued

```
scrollMsg();
//   Hide this script from incompatible Web browsers! -->
</SCRIPT>
</BODY>
</HTML>
```

The JavaScript code for the Scrolling Message example Web page involves a couple of global variables and a function, `scrollMsg()`. The `msg` variable is a string that stores the message being scrolled. The `pos` variable is an integer that keeps track of the position within the string being displayed. The scrolling of the message is accomplished by shifting the characters in the string being displayed. The `pos` variable basically keeps track of the scroll position within this string.

The `scrollMsg()` function sets the status bar of the browser window to a string containing a modified version of the message. The modified string consists of the latter part of the message string beginning at the scroll position, with the beginning of the string tacked on to the end. This is how the scrolling effect is achieved. The actual setting of the status bar is accomplished by setting the value of the `window.status` property.

After setting the message and updating the string position, the `scrollMsg()` function sets a timer to facilitate the animation part of the scrolling message. The `window.setTimeout()` method enables you to specify a piece of JavaScript code and a period of time (in milliseconds) after which you want the code executed. In this case, a call to the `scrollMsg()` function is provided as the code; the timeout period is set to 200 milliseconds, or 2/10 of a second. At this rate, the animation updates five times every second.

The only other JavaScript code in the example is the call to the `scrollMsg()` function near the bottom of the HTML code. This call is necessary to initially start the animation and get things going. Because the `scrollMsg()` function sets a timeout that results in another call to itself, there is no need to ever directly call it again.

Displaying Helper Messages

The last type of message covered in this chapter is helper messages, which are used to provide information about an HTML element such as a hyperlink or image. When the user moves the mouse over an HTML element, a helper message displays. It provides additional information about the element.

Like scrolling messages, helper messages typically display in one of two places: either in a text form field or in a browser's status bar. This example takes the latter approach and shows you how to display a helper message in the status bar of a Web browser. To make things more interesting, the helper message code builds on the scrolling message code and supports both helper messages and scrolling messages. Therefore if the mouse is not over an element that has a helper message associated with it, a scrolling message displays. When the mouse triggers a helper message, the helper message temporarily displays in place of the scrolling message. After a short period of elapsed time, the scrolling message appears again.

Figure 17.4 shows the Helper Message example Web page in action with a helper message being displayed. To get a better idea as to how the messages are displayed, you should open the page (HelperMessage.htm) yourself off of the accompanying CD.

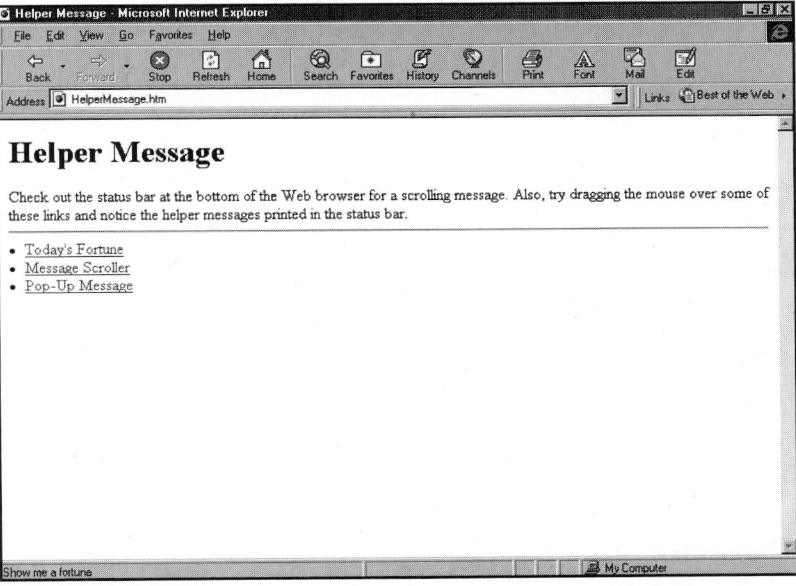

FIG. 17.4 The Helper Message example Web page with a helper message displayed in the Web browser's status bar.

The source code for the Helper Message page is based largely on the source code for the Scrolling Message example Web page. Even so, some changes are definitely in order to add support for helper messages. Listing 17.4 contains the source code for the page.

Listing 17.4 HelperMessage.htm Displaying helper messages with JavaScript.

```
<HTML>
<HEAD>
<SCRIPT LANGUAGE="JavaScript">
<!-- Hide this script from incompatible Web browsers!
var msg = "   This is a scrolling message. Pretty neat, huh?   ";
var pos = 0;
var showMsg = true;

function scrollMsg() {
  if (!showMsg) {
    window.setTimeout("scrollMsg()", 1500);
    showMsg = true;
    return;
  }
```

continues

Listing 17.4 Continued

```
  window.status = msg.substring(pos, msg.length) + msg.substring(0, pos);
  if (++pos > msg.length)
    pos = 0;
  window.setTimeout("scrollMsg()", 200);
}

function helperMsg(text) {
  showMsg = false;
  window.status = text;
}
//   Hide this script from incompatible Web browsers! -->
</SCRIPT>
<TITLE>Helper Message</TITLE>
</HEAD>
<BODY BGCOLOR=#FFFFFF>
<H1>Helper Message</H1>
Check out the status bar at the bottom of the Web browser for a scrolling
message.
Also, try moving the mouse over some of these links and notice the helper
messages
printed in the status bar.
<HR>
<LI><A HREF="Fortune.htm"
onMouseOver="helperMsg('Show me a fortune');return true;">
Today's Fortune</A>
<LI><A HREF="ScrollingMessage.htm"
onMouseOver="helperMsg('Scroll a message');return true;">
Message Scroller</A>
<LI><A HREF="PopUpMessage.htm"
onMouseOver="helperMsg('Pop up a message');return true;">
Pop-Up Message</A>
<SCRIPT LANGUAGE="JavaScript">
<!-- Hide this script from incompatible Web browsers!
scrollMsg();
//   Hide this script from incompatible Web browsers! -->
</SCRIPT>
</BODY>
</HTML>
```

First off, you may notice that the `msg` and `pos` global variables are still used to store the scroll message and scroll position, respectively. In addition, a `showMsg` Boolean variable keeps track of whether to show the scrolling message. If `showMsg` is set to `true`, the scrolling message displays; if it is `false`, a helper message displays instead. The `showMsg` variable is initialized to `true`, which means the page starts out showing the scroll message.

The latter half of the `scrollMsg()` function is essentially the same as it was in the Scrolling Message example Web page. However, there is new code added to the first part of the function to deal with which message is to be displayed. If the `showMsg` variable is set to `false`, it means a helper message is currently being displayed. Therefore, a 1 1/2 second timeout is set and the `showMsg` variable is set back to `true`. This results in the helper message hanging around for 1 1/2 seconds, after which the scroll message displays.

The `helperMsg()` function is responsible for displaying helper messages. It takes a string argument as the helper message and sets the status bar accordingly. Notice that it also sets the `showMsg` variable to `false`. This is necessary so that the `scrollMsg()` function yields for the helper message to be displayed. Otherwise, it would immediately replace the helper message with the scroll message.

The Web page gets started near the bottom of the HTML code when the `scrollMsg()` function is called. This gets the scroll message going, but it does not do anything to facilitate the helper messages. The helper messages display in response to events; three hyperlinks have event handlers that call the `helperMsg()` function. When the user moves the mouse over one of these hyperlinks, the `helperMsg()` function is called and an associated helper message displays.

You are not limited to displaying helper messages for text hyperlinks; you could just as easily associate them with image hyperlinks.

CAUTION

As with scrolling messages, you should use helper messages sparingly to get the best effect. Gratuitous or unnecessary use of helper messages can easily become annoying to users.

Displaying Random Fortunes

JavaScript-driven messages are powerful in their own right, but they don't do much in the way of making a Web site feel organic. In other words, it is hard to use messages alone to make a Web site have a constantly changing feel without actually changing the messages in the code. One way to breathe a little life into a site is to build a set of information and randomly select a portion of it to display at a given time. A good example of a practical application of this idea is a random fortune Web page, where a random fortune, or interesting quote, is displayed each time someone visits the page. Figure 17.5 shows a page that performs this exact task.

The idea behind the Fortune page is that users get to view different information each time they visit the page. This creates a more interesting experience for users and keeps them coming back. An easy way to simulate a future return to a Web page is to reload the page in a browser. This is also a good way to test the Fortune page and see more fortunes. Figure 17.6 shows the Fortune page after reloading it.

Notice that the fortune changed. If you happen to run the page (Fortune.htm) off of the accompanying CD, don't be surprised if you don't see the same fortunes as the ones shown in the figures. Remember, the idea is that the information is presented *randomly*, so it is unlikely that you would see the exact same fortunes as when capturing these figures were captured for placement on the CD.

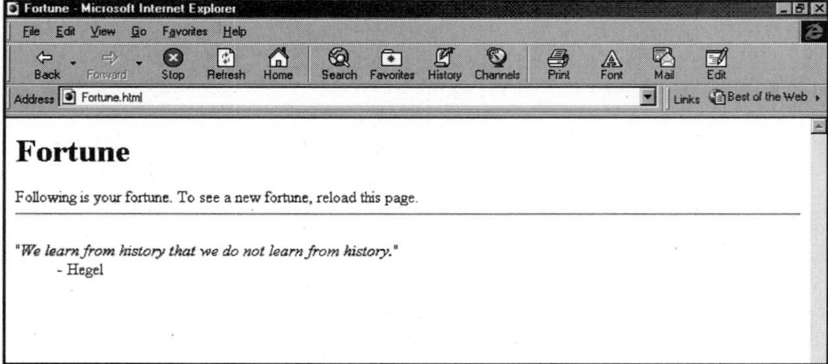

FIG. 17.5 The Fortune example Web page with a random fortune displayed.

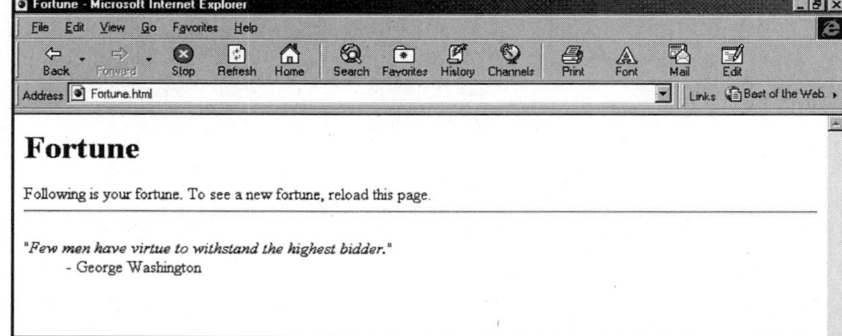

FIG. 17.6 The Fortune example Web page after being reloaded.

TROUBLESHOOTING

Sometimes the fortune does not appear to change when you reload the page. Why?

Although this may look like a bug in the program, the JavaScript code is functioning properly. The fortunes are selected based on a random number generated by the JavaScript code. The very nature of random numbers dictates that occasionally the same number comes up twice in a row. This is what is happening when you reload the page and see the same fortune. Because this example contains only eight fortunes, you have a one in eight chance of a fortune being chosen twice in a row.

The JavaScript code for the Fortune example Web page is considerably more involved than any you have seen thus far. Although it may look a little intimidating at first, rest assured that nothing very complicated is going on. The bulk of the code is the initialization of the array of fortunes. Listing 17.5 contains the complete source code for the Fortune page.

Listing 17.5 Fortune.htm Displaying random fortunes with JavaScript.

```
<HTML>
<HEAD>
<SCRIPT LANGUAGE="JavaScript">
<!-- Hide this script from incompatible Web browsers!
function getFortune() {
  // Create the arrays
  fortunes = new Array(8);
  sources = new Array(8);

  // Initialize the arrays with fortunes
  fortunes[0] = "We learn from history that we do not learn from history.";
  sources[0] = "Hegel";
  fortunes[1] = "Few men have virtue to withstand the highest bidder.";
  sources[1] = "George Washington";
  fortunes[2] = "Petty laws breed great crimes.";
  sources[2] = "Ouida";
  fortunes[3] = "The right to be let alone is the beginning of all freedom.";
  sources[3] = "Justice William O. Douglas";
  fortunes[4] = "America's one of the finest countries anyone ever stole.";
  sources[4] = "Bobcat Goldthwaite";
  fortunes[5] = "What's the Constitution between friends?";
  sources[5] = "Timothy J. Campbell";
  fortunes[6] = "The highest result of education is tolerance.";
  sources[6] = "Helen Keller";
  fortunes[7] = "Tyranny is always better organized than freedom.";
  sources[7] = "Charles Peguy";

  // Get a random index into the arrays
  i = Math.floor(Math.random() * fortunes.length);

  // Write out the fortune as HTML
  document.write("<DL>\n");
  document.write("<DT>" + "\"<I>" + fortunes[i] + "</I>\"\n");
  document.write("<DD>" + "- " + sources[i] + "\n");
  document.write("<DL>\n");
}
//   Hide this script from incompatible Web browsers! -->
</SCRIPT>
<TITLE>Fortune</TITLE>
</HEAD>
<BODY BGCOLOR=#FFFFFF>
<H1>Fortune</H1>
Following is your fortune. To see a new fortune, reload this page.
<HR>
<SCRIPT LANGUAGE="JavaScript">
<!-- Hide this script from incompatible Web browsers!
getFortune();
//   Hide this script from incompatible Web browsers! -->
</SCRIPT>
</BODY>
</HTML>
```

As you can see, the JavaScript code consists primarily of one big function, `getFortune()`. The `getFortune()` function is entirely responsible for getting a random fortune and writing it out to the Web page. The function starts by creating and initializing two arrays: `fortunes` and `sources`. These two arrays contain the fortune text and their respective authors. The initialization of the arrays just consists of assigning values to each array element.

With the fortune arrays created and initialized, the `getFortune()` function moves on to generating a random integer index into the arrays via a call to the `Math.random()` method. This index is then used as the basis for selecting a fortune from the arrays. The `document.write()` method is used to actually write the fortune to the Web page.

The `getFortune()` method is called near the end of the HTML code. Keep in mind that the location of the `getFortune()` method call in the HTML code is where the fortune will be placed on the Web page. This is because the fortune is generated and written to the page on-the-fly. This is a powerful, yet simple way to manipulate Web pages with JavaScript and give them a little more life.

Rotating Ad Banners

The commercialization of the Web has created an entirely new medium for marketing and promotion. Everything from software to cars is now being advertised on the Web through what are known as ad banners. An ad banner is just an image containing an advertisement that is placed on a Web page. Fortunately for graphic designers, a standard banner image size has finally been more or less agreed on. Most ad banner images are now 468 pixels wide-by-60 pixels tall.

Ad banners serve as an important part of the revenue for many Web sites. Consequently, it is important that they get their messages across effectively. Trying to coach you on the creation of ad banners is clearly beyond the scope of this book, but this discussion does examine how to automatically rotate between several banners to increase the amount of advertising exposure your site can generate and thus potentially increase your sponsorship revenue. These ad banners function much like billboards that alternate between different ads.

A JavaScript rotating ad banner enables you to specify multiple banner images and then alternate, or rotate, between them after a given period of time. In this way, you can have multiple advertisers supported in the same physical banner space. Additionally, with JavaScript you can provide a different hyperlink for each advertiser so that the user navigates to the correct Web site when he or she clicks on an ad banner.

Dynamically Changing Images with JavaScript

To implement a rotating ad banner in JavaScript, you have to be able to change an image dynamically from JavaScript code. This is accomplished by setting the `src` property for an HTML image object. All the images for a given Web page are stored in an array in the page's `document` object called `images`. To change an image on the page, you just access it in the `images` array and set its `src` property to a new value, like this:

```
document.images[0].src = "Scenic.gif"
```

JavaScript `image` objects also support a `lowsrc` property that contains a low-resolution image to be loaded and shown before the normal image defined in `src`. The idea is that the low-resolution image is significantly faster to load and gives the user something to look at while the complete image is loading. To assign a low-resolution image to an image object, just set the `lowsrc` property of the object, like this:

```
document.images[0].lowsrc = "Scenic_lr.gif"
```

This example code sets the first image in the `images` array, which corresponds to the first image listed in the HTML code. You can also access images in the array by name if you have set the `name` property for each image on the page in the HTML code. The following example shows how to set an image by name:

```
document.images["image1"].src = "Scenic.gif"
```

This example code uses the name of an image to find and access it within the `images` array. The associated HTML code for the image might look something like this:

```
<IMG NAME="image1" SRC="UnScenic.gif">
```


Implementing the Rotating Banner Example Web Page

Now that you understand how to use JavaScript code to change images, you are ready to implement a rotating ad banner. Figure 17.7 shows an example ad banner displayed in the Rotating Banner example Web page.

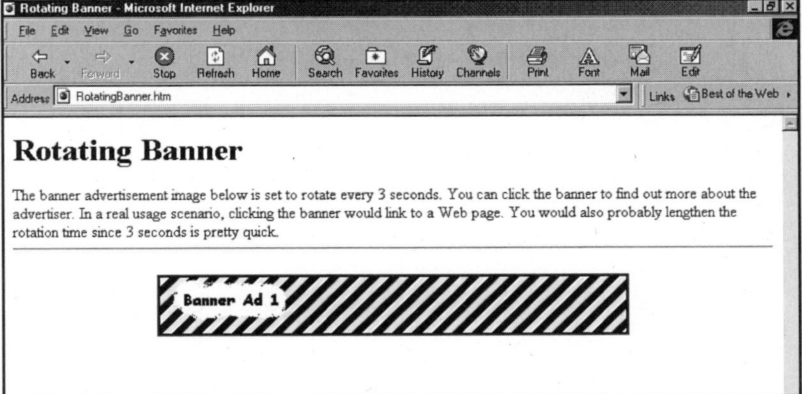

FIG. 17.7
The Rotating Banner example Web page with the first advertisement banner displayed.

The Rotating Banner page is set up so that the banner image changes every 3 seconds. Figure 17.8 shows a second banner displaying after 3 seconds have elapsed.

NOTE Practically speaking, 3 seconds is probably not enough time for a user to really take in an ad, but it makes the example a little more interesting to watch.

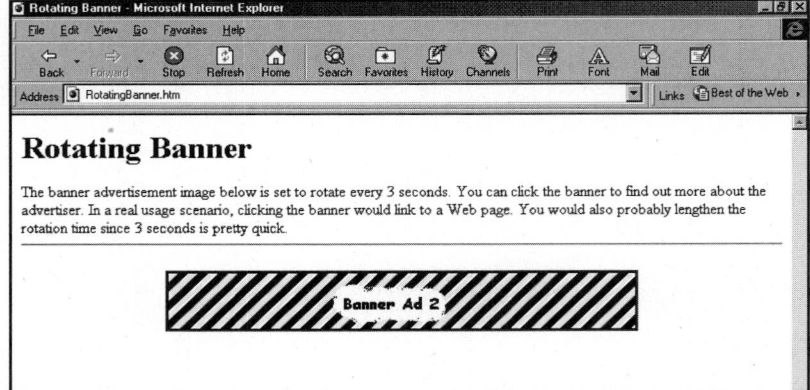

FIG. 17.8
The Rotating Banner example Web page after a few seconds with the second advertisement banner displayed.

The JavaScript code for the Rotating Banner page is pretty straightforward. The real key to the page's functionality is the dynamic setting of an image on the page. The capability to dynamically change an image could also be useful far beyond the scope of ad banners. By just changing an image based on user input, you could actually create games and other interactive programs in JavaScript.

Getting back to the Rotating Banner example, Listing 17.6 contains the complete source code for the Web page.

Listing 17.6 RotatingBanner.htm Displaying a rotating advertisement banner with JavaScript.

```
<HTML>
<HEAD>
<SCRIPT LANGUAGE="JavaScript">
<!-- Hide this script from incompatible Web browsers!
var bannerNum = 1;

function linkBanner() {
  window.alert("You just clicked Ad Banner " + bannerNum + ".");
}

function rotateBanner() {
  if (++bannerNum > 3)
    bannerNum = 1;
  document.images["banner"].src = "Banner" + bannerNum + ".gif";
  window.setTimeout('rotateBanner();', 3000);
}
//   Hide this script from incompatible Web browsers! -->
</SCRIPT>
<TITLE>Rotating Banner</TITLE>
</HEAD>
<BODY BGCOLOR=#FFFFFF onLoad="window.setTimeout('rotateBanner();', 3000);">
<H1>Rotating Banner</H1>
```

```
The banner advertisement image below is set to rotate every 3 seconds. You
can click the banner to find out more about the advertiser. In a real usage
scenario, clicking the banner would link to a Web page. You would also probably
lengthen the rotation time since 3 seconds is pretty quick.
<HR>
<P ALIGN=CENTER>
<A HREF="javascript:linkBanner();">
<IMG NAME="banner" SRC="Banner1.gif">
</A>
</P>
</BODY>
</HTML>
```


The Rotating Banner example Web page contains one global integer variable, `bannerNum`, that keeps track of which banner is currently being displayed. The different banners are named Banner1.gif, Banner2.gif, and Banner3.gif. Because these names follow a simple pattern, it is easy to use the `bannerNum` variable to determine the name of the banner to display. This is accomplished in the `rotateBanner()` function, which increments `bannerNum` and then uses it to set the name of the new banner image to display. Notice that a timeout is set so that the banner displays for 3 seconds before it rotates again.

You may be wondering how the banner rotation gets started to begin with. A timeout of 3 seconds is set in the browser window's `onLoad` event handler. When the timeout period elapses, the `rotateBanner()` function is called, thereby changing the banner and starting the rotation cycle.

As mentioned earlier, you can click on the ad banner and it will react differently based on the banner being displayed. Typically a banner takes you to an advertiser's Web page upon being clicked. In this example just an alert box displays, indicating the banner that was clicked. This is carried out in the `linkBanner()` function, which uses the `bannerNum` variable to build a string that is displayed to the user.

To actually link to a Web page from JavaScript code, you set the URL of the new page by using the `window.location.href` property, like this:

```
window.location.href="http://www.javasoft.com/"
```

Setting this property causes the browser to immediately open the given URL. This is a powerful capability and gives you a lot of flexibility in controlling the navigation of a Web site. To make the Rotating Banner example link to different sites, you would just modify the `rotateBanner()` function so that the `window.location.href` property is set to different sites based on the value of the `bannerNum` variable.

Playing Sounds

The last area this chapter touches on is using JavaScript to play sounds. Although the JavaScript language does not directly support sounds, it is very easy to use JavaScript as a means of tweaking HTML code into playing a sound programmatically. To understand how this works, first consider how a sound is played in a Web page purely through HTML code. Typically a sound file such as an AU or WAV file is associated with a hyperlink; when the hyperlink is clicked, the Web browser automatically launches a suitable player to play the sound. The key to the sound being played is the user clicking the hyperlink.

Playing a Sound with JavaScript

Because you want to be able to play a sound programmatically, you must figure out a way to simulate a hyperlink being clicked. A good way to do this is to set the `window.location.href` property directly. By setting this property in JavaScript, you effectively force the Web browser to play a sound file without requiring the user to interact with the page. Following is an example of how this is accomplished:

```
window.location.href="Rooster.au";
```

This simple line of JavaScript code causes the Web browser to load the sound file named Rooster.au and then use a suitable audio player to play it. This is a powerful and extremely easy way to liven up a Web page with sound.

Associating Sounds with Images

The Fun With Sound example Web page demonstrates how to associate a sound with an image. Figure 17.9 shows the Fun With Sound page with some images that trigger sounds when the mouse is moved over them.

CAUTION

Although sounds can often be informative and give Web pages a multimedia boost, they can just as easily turn users away if used too liberally. You don't have to bombard users with sounds to get their attention. Also keep in mind that sounds eat up bandwidth as they are being downloaded, so try to keep them short and sweet.

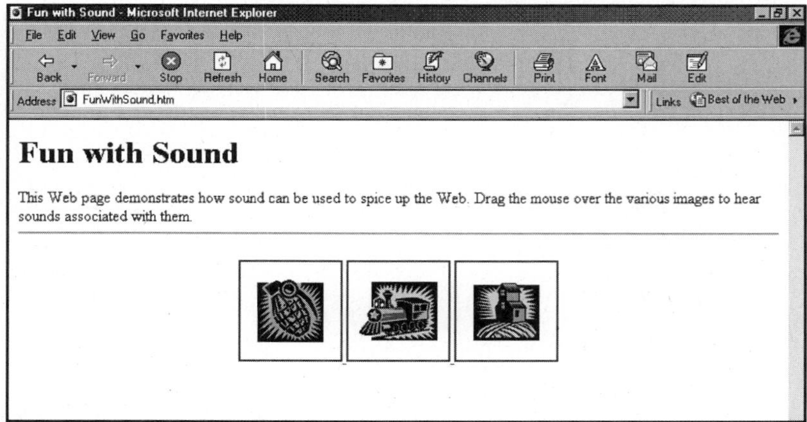

FIG. 17.9 The Fun With Sound example Web page with the sound-activating images displayed.

External sound players are typically involved in playing a sound in a Web page. This means that you usually see a window appear for the sound player whenever a sound plays. The sound player usually has options for pausing or restarting the sound as it plays. Figure 17.10 shows the sound player invoked by Microsoft Internet Explorer when an AU sound is played.

NOTE The AU sound format is popular on the Web primarily due to its use in Java applets. AU audio players are available for most major platforms. Windows WAV sounds can also be used in Web pages, but they are not always supported on platforms such as Solaris.

FIG. 17.10 Internet Explorer's default audio player.

The JavaScript code for the Fun With Sound example Web page is extremely simple. Listing 17.7 contains the complete source code for the page.

Listing 17.7 FunWithSound.htm Playing sounds with JavaScript.

```
<HTML>
<HEAD>
<SCRIPT LANGUAGE="JavaScript">
<!-- Hide this script from incompatible Web browsers!
function playSound(fileName) {
  // Load and play a sound
  window.location.href=fileName;
}
//   Hide this script from incompatible Web browsers! -->
</SCRIPT>
<TITLE>Fun with Sound</TITLE>
</HEAD>
<BODY BGCOLOR=#FFFFFF>
<H1>Fun with Sound</H1>
This Web page demonstrates how sound can be used to spice up the Web. Move
the mouse over the various images to hear sounds associated with them.
<HR>
<P ALIGN=CENTER>
<A HREF="#" onMouseOver="playSound('Grenade.au');">
<IMG SRC="Grenade.gif">
</A>
<A HREF="#" onMouseOver="playSound('Train.au');">
<IMG SRC="Train.gif">
</A>
<A HREF="#" onMouseOver="playSound('Rooster.au');">
<IMG SRC="Farmhouse.gif">
</A>
</P>
</BODY>
</HTML>
```

The JavaScript code for the Fun With Sound example Web page consists primarily of one function, `playSound()`, which is responsible for loading and playing a sound from a given file. This is accomplished by just setting the `window.location.href` property to the sound file name, like you saw earlier in this section.

The `playSound()` function is actually called in response to `onMouseOver` events triggered when the user moves the mouse over an image on the page. There are three such images, each of which triggers the `playSound()` method when the mouse is moved over it. The sound played for each image reflects the meaning of the image. A train whistle sound, for example, plays when the mouse is moved over the image of a train.

Notice that the images are actually defined as hyperlinks. This is necessary so that the `onMouseOver` event handler can be set. Because you don't actually want the images to be used as hyperlinks, the links are set to `"#"`. You saw this same technique earlier in the chapter with the Pop-Up Message example Web page.

CHAPTER 18

Manipulating Windows and Frames with JavaScript

In this chapter

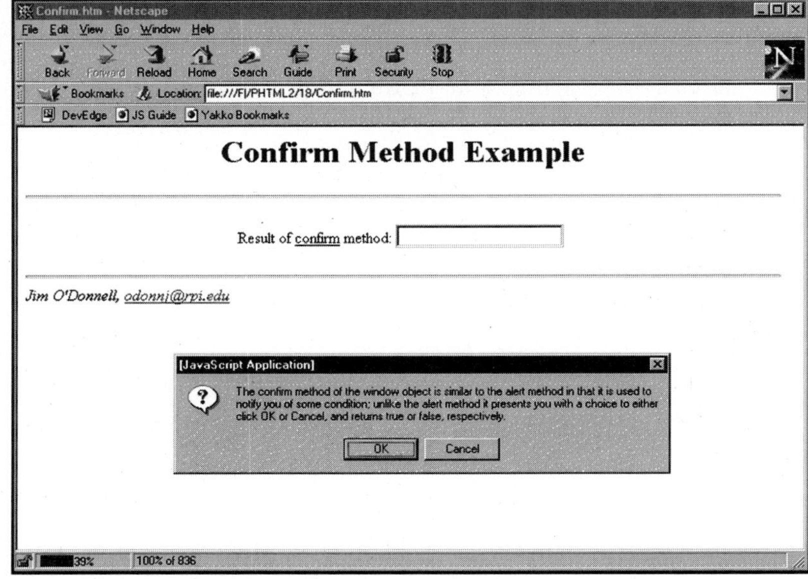

FIG. 18.7
You can use the `window.confirm()` method to create a "gateway" condition to your site. Users must agree to this condition before they can access your site.

Listing 18.8 Prompt.htm The user can enter any single line of input in the prompt.

```
<HTML>
<HEAD>
<TITLE>Prompt.htm</TITLE>
</HEAD>
<BODY BGCOLOR=#FFFFFF>
<CENTER>
<H1>Prompt Method Example</H1>
<HR>
<FORM NAME="MyForm">
Result of <U>prompt</U> method: <INPUT TYPE=TEXT NAME="MyText" SIZE=30>
</FORM>
<HR>
</CENTER>
<ADDRESS>
Jim O'Donnell, <A HREF="mailto:odonnj@rpi.edu">odonnj@rpi.edu</A>
</ADDRESS>
<SCRIPT LANGUAGE="JAVASCRIPT">
<!-- Hide script from incompatible browsers! -->
res = window.prompt("The prompt method of the window " +
   "object allows you to ask the user for input; you can " +
   "also specify a default input, such as URL of my home " +
   "shown below.","http://www.rpi.edu/~odonnj")
document.MyForm.MyText.value = res
//   Hide script from incompatible browsers! -->
</SCRIPT>
</BODY>
</HTML>
```

FIG. 18.8
Using the `window.prompt()` method's simple dialog box makes it easy to get simple input from your user.

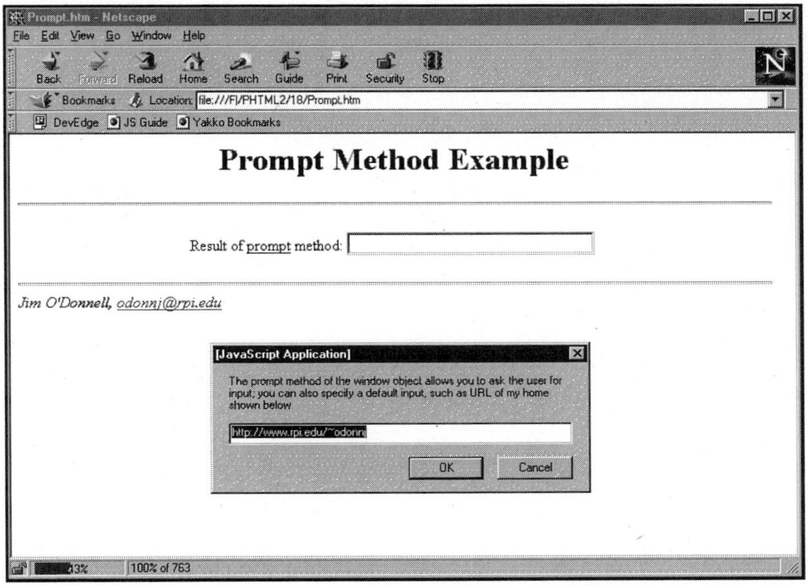

Filling Your Windows I: The *Location* Object

Instead of specifying a URL in the `window.open()` method, you have several other ways to specify the contents of a new `window` object. The first of these ways is the simplest of the two: by using the new window's `location` object. Referring back to the first example in this chapter, for instance, instead of specifying "Form1.htm" as the first argument of the `window.open()` method, you could do the same thing by using the following after the new window is created:

```
self.MyWindow.location.href = "Form1.htm"
```

Filling Your Windows II: The *Document* Object

A second way of specifying content for new windows—or for your original Web browser window, for that matter—is by using methods of the `document` object. The following document object methods are used to create content within an HTML document:

- **`document.open()`**—the `open()` method is used to open the document for writing. If the method is used within an existing web page, the content created will replace the current contents.
- **`document.write()`** or **`document.writeln()`**—each of these methods is used to write HTML code into the currently opened document. If these statements are encountered while the current document is being loaded—in the following example, the document is already open—the content they generate will be included along with the other contents of the page.

If these methods are used after the current document has been opened, but without a preceding `document.open()` method, they will generate an error. If the `document.open()` method is used, all the content generated will replace the current contents.

The only difference between the `write()` and `writeln()` method is that the `writeln()` method includes a new line after the content. This does not affect the HTML generated, but makes it easier to view.

- **`document.close()`**—this method closes and causes to be displayed a document opened using the `document.open()` method.

Listing 18.9 shows WindowJS.htm. This HTML document reproduces the first example shown in this chapter (shown in Listings 18.1 and 18.2) with only one file. Instead of loading a second HTML document into the new window, the `document.write()` method is used to dynamically generate the HTML to be displayed. The results of this file are identical to that shown in Figure 18.1, except for the fact that the title and heading are changed.

Listing 18.9 WindowJS.htm HTML documents can be generated on-the-fly.

```
<HTML>
<HEAD>
<TITLE>WindowJS.htm</TITLE>
</HEAD>
<BODY BGCOLOR=#FFFFFF>
<CENTER>
<H1>Window Example #5</H1>
<HR>
</CENTER>
<ADDRESS>
Jim O'Donnell, <A HREF="mailto:odonnj@rpi.edu">odonnj@rpi.edu</A>
</ADDRESS>
<SCRIPT LANGUAGE="JAVASCRIPT">
<!-- Hide script from incompatible browsers! -->
MyWindow = window.open("","MyWindow",
   "toolbar=no,location=no,directories=no,status=no," +
   "menubar=no,scrollbars=no,resizable=no," +
   "width=475,height=155")
str = "<HTML>" +
      "<HEAD>" +
      "<TITLE>Form1.htm</TITLE>" +
      "</HEAD>" +
      "<BODY BGCOLOR=#FFFFFF>" +
      "<CENTER>" +
      "<TABLE WIDTH=95% BORDER>" +
      "<FORM NAME='MyForm'>" +
      "<TR><TD><B>Form Element Type</B></TD>" +
      "     <TD><B>Name</B></TD>" +
      "     <TD> </TD></TR>" +
      "<TR><TD><B>TEXT</B> Element</TD>" +
      "     <TD><I>MyText</I></TD>" +
      "     <TD><INPUT TYPE='TEXT' NAME='MyText'></TD></TR>" +
      "<TR><TD><B>CHECKBOX</B> Element</TD>" +
      "     <TD><I>MyCheckBox1</I></TD>" +
      "     <TD><INPUT TYPE='CHECKBOX' NAME='MyCheckBox1'></TD></TR>" +
      "<TR><TD><B>CHECKBOX</B> Element</TD>" +
```

```
      "     <TD><I>MyCheckBox2</I></TD>" +
      "     <TD><INPUT TYPE='CHECKBOX' NAME='MyCheckBox2'></TD></TR>" +
      "<TR><TD><B>CHECKBOX</B> Element</TD>" +
      "     <TD><I>MyCheckBox3</I></TD>" +
      "     <TD><INPUT TYPE='CHECKBOX' NAME='MyCheckBox3'></TD></TR>" +
      "</FORM>" +
      "</TABLE>" +
      "</BODY>" +
      "</HTML>"
self.MyWindow.document.write(str)
self.MyWindow.document.close()
//   Hide script from incompatible browsers! -->
</SCRIPT>
</BODY>
</HTML>
```

JavaScript Windows Example

This example shows how it is possible to create an HTML forms-based control panel that uses JavaScript to load and execute other JavaScripts in their own windows. This is done through the use of the `window` web browser object, its properties and methods.

Listing 18.10 shows CpMain.htm, the top-level HTML document giving access to the control panel. The JavaScript in this example is very simple, and is included in the `onClick` attribute of the forms `<input>` tag. Clicking on the button executes the JavaScript window method `open`:

```
window.open('cp.htm','ControlPanel','width=300,height=250')
```

This creates a window named "ControlPanel" that is 300×250 pixels in size, and loads the HTML document Cp.htm.

Listing 18.10 CpMain.htm A JavaScript attached right to a forms button will create a new window when clicked.

```
<HTML>
<HEAD>
<TITLE>JavaScript Window Example</TITLE>
</HEAD>
<BODY BGCOLOR=#FFFFFF>
<CENTER><H3>Activate the control panel by clicking below</H3></CENTER>
<HR>
<FORM>
<CENTER>
<TABLE>
<TR><TD><INPUT TYPE="button" NAME="ControlButton" VALUE="Control Panel"
           onClick="window.open('Cp.htm','ControlPanel',
                                    'width=300,height=250')"></TD></TR>
</TABLE>
</CENTER>
</FORM>
</BODY>
</HTML>
```

When the button is clicked, Cp.htm is loaded into its own window, as shown in Figure 18.9. (Note that in this figure and the next, the windows have been manually rearranged so that they all can be seen.) This HTML document uses an interface of an HTML form organized in a table to give access through this control panel to other JavaScript applications, namely a timer and a real-time clock. Listing 18.11 shows Cp.htm. The JavaScript functions `openTimer()`, `openClock()`, `closeTimer()`, and `closeClock()` are used to open and close windows for a JavaScript timer and clock, respectively. These functions are attached to forms buttons that make up the control panel. Note that because the JavaScript variables `timerw` and `clockw` are defined outside of any of the functions they can be used anywhere in the JavaScript document. They are used to remember whether the timer and clock windows are open.

Listing 18.11 Cp.htm This HTML form calls JavaScripts to create and destroy windows for a timer and or a real-time clock.

```
<HTML>
<HEAD>
<SCRIPT LANGUAGE="JavaScript">
<!-- Hide this script from incompatible Web browsers! -->
var timerw = null;
var clockw = null;
function openTimer() {
   if(!timerw)
      timerw = open("CpTimer.htm","TimerWindow","width=300,height=100");
}
function openClock() {
   if(!clockw)
      clockw = open("CpClock.htm","ClockWindow","width=50,height=25");
}
function closeTimer() {
   if(timerw) {
      timerw.close();
      timerw = null;
   }
}
function closeClock() {
   if(clockw) {
      clockw.close();
      clockw = null;
   }
}
//   Hide this script from incompatible Web browsers! -->
</SCRIPT>
</HEAD>
<BODY BGCOLOR=#EEEEEE>
<FORM>
<CENTER>
<TABLE>
<TR><TD>To Open Timer...</TD>
    <TD ALIGN=CENTER>
       <INPUT TYPE="button" NAME="ControlButton" VALUE="Click Here!"
          onClick="openTimer()"></TD></TR>
<TR><TD>To Close Timer...</TD>
```

```
    <TD ALIGN=CENTER>
       <INPUT TYPE="button" NAME="ControlButton" VALUE="Click Here!"
          onClick="closeTimer()"></TD></TR>
<TR><TD>To Open Clock...</TD>
    <TD ALIGN=CENTER>
       <INPUT TYPE="button" NAME="ControlButton" VALUE="Click Here!"
          onClick="openClock()"></TD></TR>
<TR><TD>To Close Clock...</TD>
    <TD ALIGN=CENTER>
       <INPUT TYPE="button" NAME="ControlButton" VALUE="Click Here!"
          onClick="closeClock()"></TD></TR>
<TR><TD>To Open Both...</TD>
    <TD ALIGN=CENTER>
       <INPUT TYPE="button" NAME="ControlButton" VALUE="Click Here!"
          onClick="openTimer();openClock();"></TD></TR>
<TR><TD>To Close Both...</TD>
    <TD ALIGN=CENTER>
       <INPUT TYPE="button" NAME="ControlButton" VALUE="Click Here!"
          onClick="closeTimer();closeClock();"></TD></TR>
<TR><TD></TD></TR>
<TR><TD>To Close Everything...</TD>
    <TD ALIGN=CENTER>
       <INPUT TYPE="button" NAME="ControlButton" VALUE="Click Here!"
          onClick="closeTimer();closeClock();self.close();"></TD></TR>
</TABLE>
</CENTER>
</FORM>
</BODY>
</HTML>
```


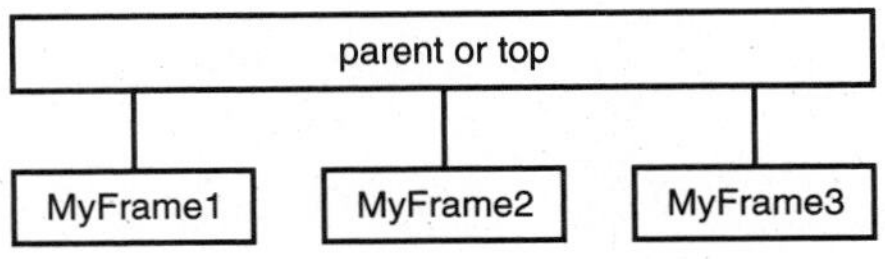

FIG. 18.9 The Control Panel button calls a JavaScript and creates a new browser window.

Listing 18.12 shows CpTimer.htm, the HTML document that implements the JavaScript timer. Note that both this listing and the next, which implements a JavaScript real-time clock, use the properties of the JavaScript `Date` object to access time information.

Listing 18.12 CpTimer.htm

```
<HTML>
<HEAD>
<SCRIPT LANGUAGE="JavaScript">
<!-- Hide this script from incompatible Web browsers! -->
var timerID = 0;
var tStart  = null;
function UpdateTimer() {
   if(timerID) {
      clearTimeout(timerID);
```

continues

Listing 18.12 Continued

```
      clockID  = 0;
   }
   if(!tStart)
      tStart   = new Date();

   var tDate = new Date();
   var tDiff = tDate.getTime() - tStart.getTime();
   var str;

   tDate.setTime(tDiff);

   str = ""
   if (tDate.getMinutes() < 10)
      str += "0" + tDate.getMinutes() + ":";
   else
      str += tDate.getMinutes() + ":";
   if (tDate.getSeconds() < 10)
      str += "0" + tDate.getSeconds();
   else
      str += tDate.getSeconds();

   document.theTimer.theTime.value = str;

   timerID = setTimeout("UpdateTimer()", 1000);
}
function Start() {
   tStart = new Date();
   document.theTimer.theTime.value = "00:00";
   timerID = setTimeout("UpdateTimer()", 1000);
}
function Stop() {
   if(timerID) {
      clearTimeout(timerID);
      timerID  = 0;
   }
   tStart = null;
}
function Reset() {
   tStart = null;
   document.theTimer.theTime.value = "00:00";
}
<!-- Hide this script from incompatible Web browsers! -->
</SCRIPT>
</HEAD>
<BODY BGCOLOR=#AAAAAA onload="Reset();Start()" onunload="Stop()">
<FORM NAME="theTimer">
<CENTER>
<TABLE>
<TR><TD COLSPAN=3 ALIGN=CENTER>
       <INPUT TYPE=TEXT NAME="theTime" SIZE=5></TD></TR>
<TR><TD></TD></TR>
<TR><TD><INPUT TYPE=BUTTON NAME="start" VALUE="Start"
            onclick="Start()"></TD>
```

```
    <TD><INPUT TYPE=BUTTON NAME="stop"  VALUE="Stop"
            onclick="Stop()"></TD>
    <TD><INPUT TYPE=BUTTON NAME="reset" VALUE="Reset"
            onclick="Reset()"></TD>    </TR>
</TABLE>
</CENTER>
</FORM>
</BODY>
</HTML>
```

Listing 18.13 shows CpClock.htm, the HTML document that implements the JavaScript real-time clock. Figure 18.10 shows the Web page with the control panel, timer, and real-time clock windows all open.

Listing 18.13 CpClock.htm

```
<HTML>
<HEAD>
<TITLE>Clock</TITLE>
<SCRIPT LANGUAGE="JavaScript">
<!-- Hide this script from incompatible Web browsers! -->
var clockID = 0;
function UpdateClock() {
   if(clockID) {
      clearTimeout(clockID);
      clockID  = 0;
   }
   var tDate = new Date();
   var str;

   str = "";
   if (tDate.getHours() < 10)
      str += "0" + tDate.getHours() + ":";
   else
      str += tDate.getHours() + ":";
   if (tDate.getMinutes() < 10)
      str += "0" + tDate.getMinutes() + ":";
   else
      str += tDate.getMinutes() + ":";
   if (tDate.getSeconds() < 10)
      str += "0" + tDate.getSeconds();
   else
      str += tDate.getSeconds();

   document.theClock.theTime.value = str;

   clockID = setTimeout("UpdateClock()", 1000);
}

function StartClock() {
   clockID = setTimeout("UpdateClock()", 500);
}
```


continues

Listing 18.13 Continued

```
function KillClock() {
   if(clockID) {
      clearTimeout(clockID);
      clockID  = 0;
   }
}
<!-- Hide this script from incompatible Web browsers! -->
</SCRIPT>
</HEAD>
<BODY BGCOLOR=#CCCCCC onload="StartClock()" onunload="KillClock()">
<CENTER>
<FORM NAME="theClock">
   <INPUT TYPE=TEXT NAME="theTime" SIZE=8>
</FORM>
</CENTER>
</BODY>
</HTML>
```

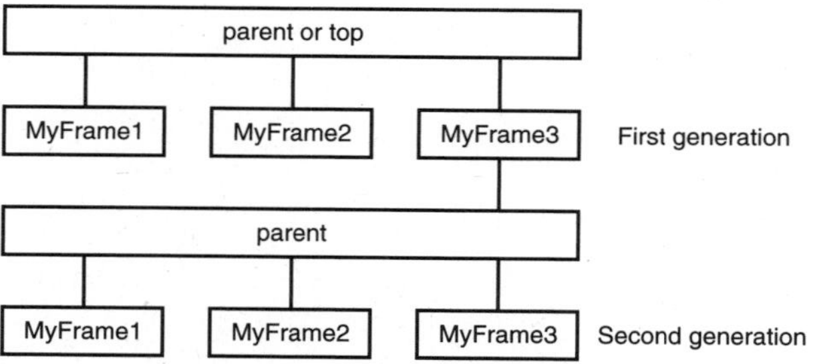

FIG. 18.10 Multiple browser windows can be created by JavaScript, each running its own JavaScripts and performing its functions independently.

Creating and Using Frames

Chapter 7, "Frames," showed you how to create and use frames in your web site. You can access and manipulate the contents of these frames by using the `frame` object. Each of the frames created in a document can be accessed through the `frames` object array, which is attached to the `document` object. The most important thing to remember about a `frame` object is that *it is a `window` object*. What this means is that each frame that is created is a separate `window` object, and all the properties, methods, and events associated with window objects can be applied.

▶ **See** "Frames," **p. 191**

Communicating Between Frames

After you have created a series of frames by using the `<FRAMESET>` and `<FRAME>` tags, how do you use JavaScript to access and manipulate each frame? As mentioned in the preceding section, each frame is a separate `window` object. Therefore, if you can figure out how to reference each frame, you can use the same techniques that were used with windows for each frame.

The Web Browser Object Model includes several properties that apply to frame and window objects that make referencing different frames much easier. These properties are the self, window, parent, and top properties. Their meanings are as follows:

- **`self`** or **`window`**—these properties are used to refer to the current window or frame.
- **`parent`**—this property is used to refer to the `window` or `frame` object that contains the current frame.
- **`top`**—this property is used to refer to the topmost window or frame object that contains the current frame.

Understanding the Frames Object Hierarchy

Consider a simple frame set created using the following HTML code:

```
<FRAMESET ROWS="50%,50%">
   <FRAMESET COLS="50%,50%">
      <FRAME SRC="Form.htm" NAME="MyFrame1">
      <FRAME SRC="Form.htm" NAME="MyFrame2">
   </FRAMESET>
   <FRAME SRC="Frameset2.htm" NAME="MyFrame3">
</FRAMESET>
```

This divides the window into three frames, two side-by-side on the top half of the window, and a third occupying the entire bottom half. The object model for this document will appear as shown in Figure 18.11.

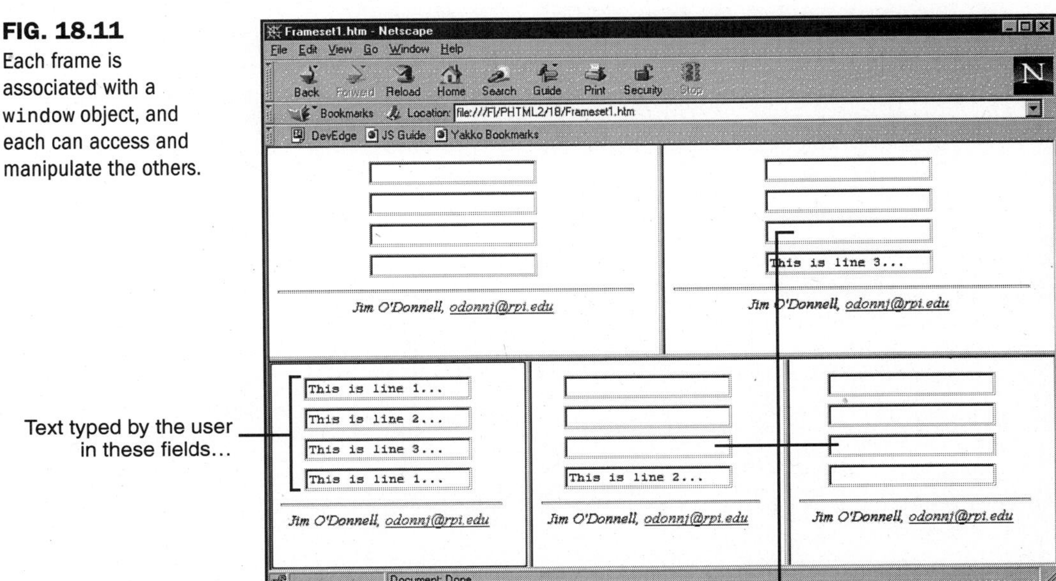

FIG. 18.11 Each frame is associated with a `window` object, and each can access and manipulate the others.

Given the object hierarchy shown in Figure 18.11, you would reference the frame objects as follows:

- To reference any of the child frames from the parent document, you could use `self.`**`frame_name`**. You could access the `document` object of the first frame, for example, through `self.MyFrame1.document`.
- To reference the parent document from any of the child frames, you could use `parent` or `top`. Any of the child frames could access the `document` object of the parent document, for example, through `parent.document`.

CAUTION

Whenever possible, you should use `parent` rather than `top`. The reason for this is that `parent` always refers to the immediate parent of the frame in question. You can use `top` to refer to the topmost parent containing your frame. If your document is included as a frame in someone else's HTML document, however, it is likely that your reference to `top` will result in an error.

- To reference a child frame from another child frame, you would just combine the two already discussed in this list. The `document` object of the second frame, for instance, could be accessed by either of the other child frames through `parent.MyFrame2.document`.

Now, what if you introduce another generation to your framed document. The third frame might load an HTML document that itself contains a `<FRAMESET>` tag to further divide up the window into more frames, as in the following:

```
<FRAMESET COLS="33%,33%,*">
   <FRAME SRC="Form.htm" NAME="MyFrame1">
   <FRAME SRC="Form.htm" NAME="MyFrame2">
   <FRAME SRC="Form.htm" NAME="MyFrame3">
</FRAMESET>
```

This would result in the object hierarchy shown in Figure 18.12.

This would result in a window showing a total of five frames. The top half of the window would show two frames, part of the first generation of `frame` objects. The bottom half of the window would show three frames, part of the second generation of `frame` objects. The following examples show you ways to reference the `document` object of the different generations of frames and parent frame sets:

- Reference first generation `MyFrame1 document` object from topmost parent:

  ```
  self.MyFrame1.document
  ```

- Reference second generation `MyFrame1 document` object from topmost parent:

  ```
  self.MyFrame3.MyFrame1.document
  ```

- Reference first generation `MyFrame1 document` object from the first generation frame (`MyFrame2`) or the second-level parent (`MyFrame3`):

  ```
  parent.MyFrame1.document
  ```

- Reference first generation `MyFrame1` `document` object from any of the second generation frames:

  `parent.parent.MyFrame1.document`, or

  `top.MyFrame1.document`

- Reference second generation `MyFrame1` `document` object from any of the other second generation frames:

  `parent.MyFrame1.document`

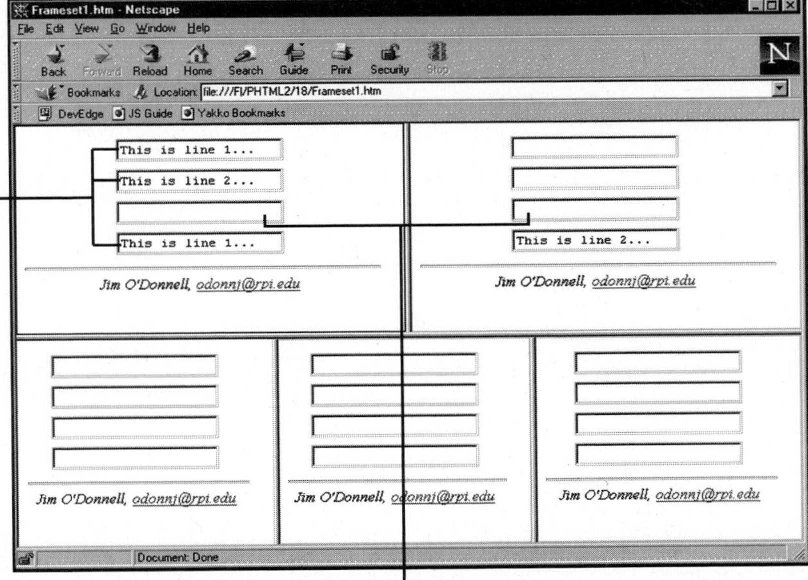

FIG. 18.12 Through multiple frame sets, it is possible to produce an intricate hierarchy of `frame` objects.

Multiple Frame Access Example

Listings 18.14 through 18.16 show an example of the kind of multiple frame, multiple generation frame setup discussed in the preceding section. Notice that a few things from this example demonstrate the object-oriented nature of JavaScript, which gives you the flexibility to accomplish multiple things.

- The same HTML document is loaded into each of the five frames that results from this example. Thus each form element has the same name. Because of the object hierarchy that results from the multiple frames, however, it is possible to uniquely specify each element.
- Likewise, both the first and second generation frames are given the same names. Again, the object hierarchy allows the frames to be uniquely addressed, accessed, and manipulated.

Listing 18.14 Frameset1.htm Top-level frame set.

```
<HTML>
<HEAD>
<TITLE>Frameset1.htm</TITLE>
</HEAD>
<FRAMESET ROWS="50%,50%">
   <FRAMESET COLS="50%,50%">
      <FRAME SRC="Form.htm" NAME="MyFrame1">
      <FRAME SRC="Form.htm" NAME="MyFrame2">
   </FRAMESET>
   <FRAME SRC="Frameset2.htm" NAME="MyFrame3">
</FRAMESET>
</HTML>
```

Listing 18.15 Frameset2.htm Second generation frame set.

```
<HTML>
<HEAD>
<TITLE>Frameset2.htm</TITLE>
</HEAD>
<FRAMESET COLS="33%,33%,*">
   <FRAME SRC="Form.htm" NAME="MyFrame1">
   <FRAME SRC="Form.htm" NAME="MyFrame2">
   <FRAME SRC="Form.htm" NAME="MyFrame3">
</FRAMESET>
</HTML>
```

Listing 18.16 Form.htm HTML document to be included in each frame.

```
<HTML>
<HEAD>
<TITLE>Form.htm</TITLE>
</HEAD>
<BODY BGCOLOR=#FFFFFF>
<CENTER>
<TABLE>
<FORM NAME="MyForm">
<TR><TD>
    <INPUT TYPE=TEXT NAME="MyText1"
       onChange="self.document.MyForm.MyText4.value =
            document.MyForm.MyText1.value">
    </TD></TR>
<TR><TD>
    <INPUT TYPE=TEXT NAME="MyText2"
          onChange="parent.MyFrame2.document.MyForm.MyText4.value =
            document.MyForm.MyText2.value">
    </TD></TR>
<TR><TD>
    <INPUT TYPE=TEXT NAME="MyText3"
       onChange="top.MyFrame2.document.MyForm.MyText4.value =
            document.MyForm.MyText3.value">
```

```
    </TD></TR>
<TR><TD>
<INPUT TYPE=TEXT NAME="MyText4">
    </TD></TR>
</FORM>
</TABLE>
<HR>
<CENTER>
<ADDRESS>
Jim O'Donnell, <A HREF="mailto:odonnj@rpi.edu">odonnj@rpi.edu</A>
</ADDRESS>
</BODY>
</SCRIPT>
</HTML>
```

The HTML form specified in the document shown in Listing 18.16 has small JavaScript functions attached to the `onChange` events of each of the first three text elements. The first copies any entered text into the fourth text element of the current frame. The second copies entered text into the fourth text element of the parent's `MyFrame2` frame. The third copies entered text into the fourth text element of the grandparent's `MyFrame2` frame.

Figure 18.13 shows how this works when text is entered into the first of the second generation frames. Line 1 is copied into line 4 in the same frame. Line 2 is copied into line 4 of the second of the second generation frames. Line 3 is copied into line 4 of the second of the first generation frames.

FIG. 18.13
Any frame can be accessed by scripts in any other frame in a multiple frame document.

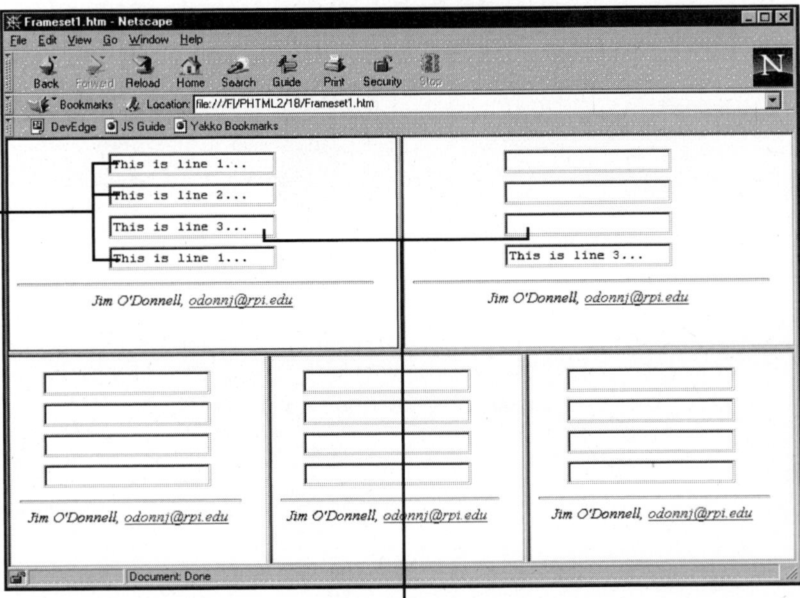

Figures 18.14 and 18.15 show the effects of typing the same lines into the first three lines in one of the first generation frames. Note that when the line 3 is entered, it overwrites line 4 of the second of the first generation frames. This is because parent refers to itself when you are already at the top level. Therefore, for first generation frames, `parent.parent` and `parent` are equivalent.

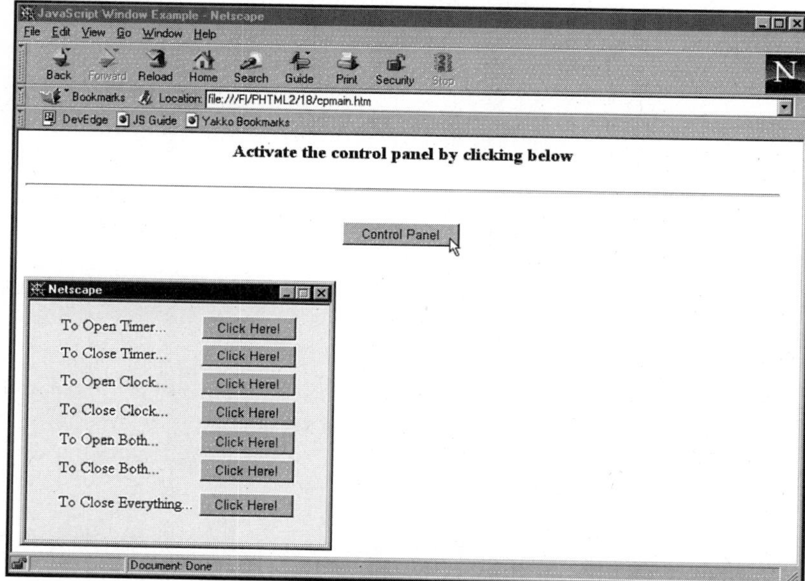

FIG. 18.14 You can use HTML frames to solicit input from the user and then use that input in other frames and windows.

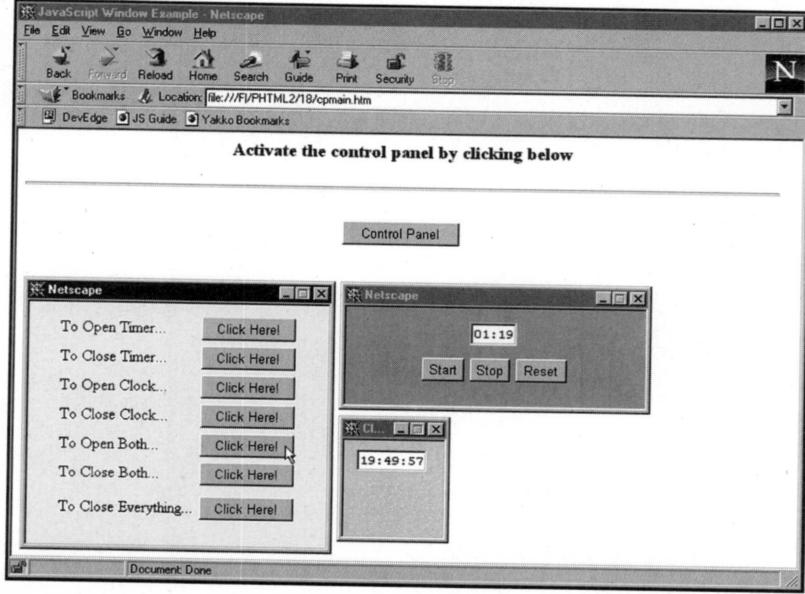

FIG. 18.15 The `parent` and `top` properties of the `frame` or `window` objects refer to themselves when you are already at the top level.

Using Hidden Frames

You can build frame-based pages another way too—this is by placing all the HTML and JavaScript code that you don't want changed into a hidden frame. Depending on the Web browser your users are using to look at your site, and how you specify the borders of your frames, this frame may not actually be completely invisible. It might appear as a tiny space with one or two borders shown on it. To specify a hidden frame, just add another frame to your frame set, but make sure the other frames take up all the available space. If you are using two frames, for example, as in the following:

```
<FRAMESET ROWS="50%,50%">
   <FRAME NAME="MyFrame1" SRC="Frame1.htm">
   <FRAME NAME="MyFrame2" SRC="Frame2.htm">
</FRAMESET>
```

You could add a hidden frame this way:

```
<FRAMESET ROWS="50%,50%,*">
   <FRAME NAME="MyFrame1" SRC="Frame1.htm">
   <FRAME NAME="MyFrame2" SRC="Frame2.htm">
   <FRAME NAME="MyHidden" SRC="Hidden.htm">
</FRAMESET>
```

With this, the first two frames take up 100% of the page, meaning that the last frame will be made as small as the browser can make it. You can then place the JavaScript code that you wish to persist in the hidden HTML document, and use the techniques shown in this chapter to manipulate the contents of the other frames in the document.

JavaScript Frames Example

In this example, you can see further examples of window manipulation using JavaScript—in addition, you will see how different frames can be accessed and manipulated. Listing 18.17 shows WfMain.htm. Like CpMain.htm in the previous example, this is the simple, top-level HTML document for this example. This one is even simpler in that it does not contain any JavaScript at all, simply setting up the frame set and frames for the example and indicating the HTML documents, WfTop.htm and WfText.htm, to be loaded into each frame.

Listing 18.17 WfMain.htm This main HTML document creates a frame set and loads two other documents into the resulting frames.

```
<HTML>
<TITLE>Windows and Frames</TITLE>
<FRAMESET ROWS="100,*">
   <FRAME SRC="WfTop.htm"  NAME="frame1" SCROLLING="no" NORESIZE>
   <FRAME SRC="WfText.htm" NAME="frame2">
</FRAMESET>
<NOFRAMES>
</NOFRAMES>
</HTML>
```

The document that makes up the uppermost frame, shown in Listing 18.18, creates a button bar of functions that you can use to manipulate the frames and windows of this example.

Listing 18.18 WfTop.htm The HTML and JavaScripts in this web page enable you to manipulate of the windows and frames in this example.

```
<HTML>
<HEAD>
<TITLE>Windows and Frames</TITLE>
<SCRIPT LANGUAGE="JavaScript">
<!-- Hide this script from incompatible Web browsers! -->
function bottomColor(newColor) {
   window.parent.frames['frame2'].document.bgColor=newColor;
}
function topColor(newColor) {
   window.parent.frames['frame1'].document.bgColor=newColor;
}
function navi() {
   window.open('WfVisit.htm','Visit',
       'toolbar=no,location=no,directories=no,' +
       'status=no,menubar=no,scrollbars=no,resizable=no,' +
       'copyhistory=yes,width=600,height=200');
}
function Customize() {
var PopWindow=window.open('wfcolor.htm','Main',
        'toolbar=no,location=no,directories=no,status=no,' +
        'menubar=no,scrollbars=no,resizable=no,copyhistory=yes,' +
        'width=400,height=200');

   PopWindow.creator = self;
}
function ConfirmClose() {
   if (confirm("Are you sure you wish to exit Netscape?"))
      window.close()
}
<!-- Hide this script from incompatible Web browsers! -->
</SCRIPT>
</HEAD>
<BODY>
<CENTER>
<FONT COLOR=RED>
<H2>Windows and Frames</H2>
<FORM>
<INPUT TYPE="BUTTON" VALUE="Back"
   onClick="parent.frame2.history.back()">
<INPUT TYPE="BUTTON" VALUE="Visit Other Sites"
   onClick="navi()">
<INPUT TYPE="BUTTON" VALUE="Background Colors"
   onClick="Customize()">
<INPUT TYPE="BUTTON" VALUE="Forward"
   onClick="parent.frame2.history.forward()">
```

```
<INPUT TYPE="BUTTON" VALUE="Exit"
   onClick="ConfirmClose()">
</CENTER>
</FORM>
</BODY>
</HTML>
```

The initial contents of the lower frame give some quick instructions on what each button does (see Listing 18.19). The resulting Web page, when this is loaded into a Web browser, is shown in Figure 18.16.

Listing 18.19 WfText.htm This informational web page also provides the jumping-off point to another site.

```
<HTML>
<HEAD>
<TITLE>Windows and Frames Text</TITLE>
</HEAD>
<BODY BGCOLOR=#FFFFFF>
<CENTER>
<H2>Welcome to Windows and Frames Using JavaScript</H2>
</CENTER>
<B>There are 5 control buttons on the control panel:<BR>
<OL><LI>Forward: Takes you to the front of the frame. (This only works
        after you actually choose to go somewhere and come back.)
    <LI>Visit Other Site: This window will let you type a site address and
        you will be able to visit that specific site.
    <LI>Background Color: Lets you choose the top and the bottom frame's
        background color.
    <LI>Back: Takes you back on a frame.
    <LI>Exit: Exits from Netscape.
</OL>
</B>
<CENTER>
Let's check the "back/forward" buttons. Let's<BR>
<FONT SIZE="+2"><A HREF="http://www.microsoft.com">Go Somewhere!!!</A>
</BODY>
</HTML>
```


One capability given by the upper frame toolbar is the ability to specify the background colors of either the upper or lower frame. Clicking the Background Colors button creates a window and loads the HTML document shown in Listing 18.20. This window uses HTML forms radio buttons to enable you to select from five choices of background color for each frame. Note that the `creator` object, and `topColor()` and `bottomColor()` methods used in Listing 18.20 to change the frame colors are set up in the `Customize()` function of the WfTop.htm HTML document (see Listing 18.18). Because this window is created by that function, it inherits those objects and methods, and can use them to change the frame background colors (see Figure 18.17).

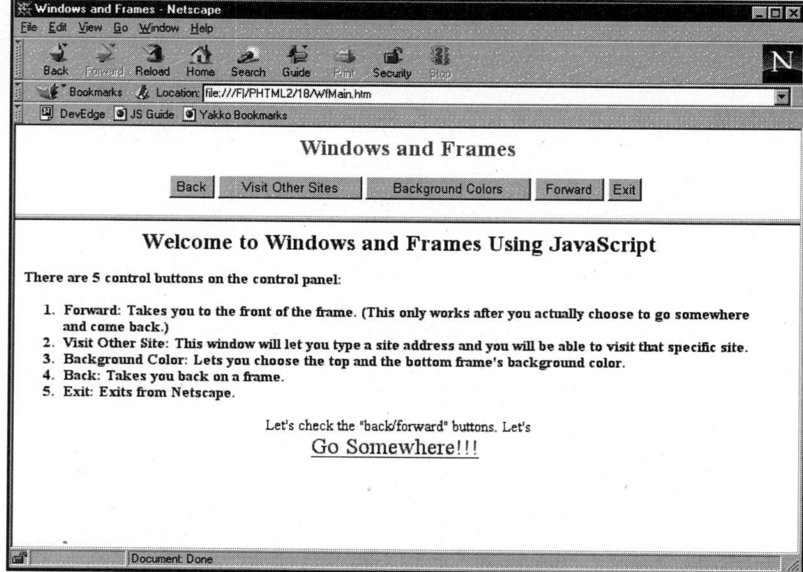

FIG. 18.16 JavaScript can use the browser `window` and `frame` objects to create and manipulate the browser and its frames.

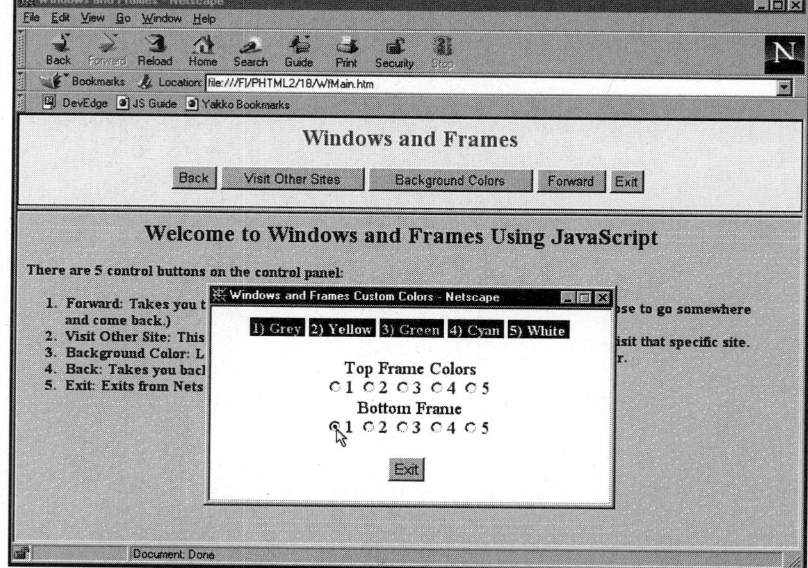

FIG. 18.17 The choices in this box enable you to dynamically change the background color of each frame.

Listing 18.20 WfColor.htm JavaScript enables you to manipulate the appearance of windows and frames being viewed.

```
<HTML>
<HEAD>
<TITLE>Windows and Frames Custom Colors</TITLE>
</HEAD>
<CENTER>
<TABLE>
<TR BGCOLOR="Black">
   <TH><FONT COLOR="#CFCFCF"> 1) Grey   </FONT></TH>
   <TH><FONT COLOR="#FFFF00"> 2) Yellow </FONT></TH>
   <TH><FONT COLOR="#00FF00"> 3) Green  </FONT></TH>
   <TH><FONT COLOR="#00FFFF"> 4) Cyan   </FONT></TH>
   <TH><FONT COLOR="#FFFFFF"> 5) White  </FONT></TH></TR>
</TABLE>
<FORM NAME="background">
<FONT SIZE=4>
   Top Frame Colors<br>
   <INPUT TYPE="RADIO" NAME="bgcolor"
       onClick="creator.topColor('#CFCFCF')">1
   <INPUT TYPE="RADIO" NAME="bgcolor"
       onClick="creator.topColor('#FFFF00')">2
   <INPUT TYPE="RADIO" NAME="bgcolor"
       onClick="creator.topColor('#00FF00')">3
   <INPUT TYPE="RADIO" NAME="bgcolor"
       onClick="creator.topColor('#00FFFF')">4
   <INPUT TYPE="RADIO" NAME="bgcolor"
       onClick="creator.topColor('#FFFFFF')">5
   <BR>
   Bottom Frame<BR>
   <INPUT TYPE="RADIO" NAME="bgcolor"
       onClick="creator.bottomColor('#CFCFCF')">1
   <INPUT TYPE="RADIO" NAME="bgcolor"
       onClick="creator.bottomColor('#FFFF00')">2
   <INPUT TYPE="RADIO" NAME="bgcolor"
       onClick="creator.bottomColor('#00FF00')">3
   <INPUT TYPE="RADIO" NAME="bgcolor"
       onClick="creator.bottomColor('#00FFFF')">4
   <INPUT TYPE="RADIO" NAME="bgcolor"
       onClick="creator.bottomColor('#FFFFFF')">5
   <P>
   <INPUT TYPE="BUTTON" VALUE="Exit" onClick="window.close()">
</FONT>
</FORM>
</CENTER>
</BODY>
</HTML>
```

Another way to use the button bar and attached JavaScript functions in the top frame is to manipulate the contents of the lower frame and the appearance of both. If you follow instructions and click the Go Somewhere!!! hypertext link in the lower frame, the URL included in the listing for that link (the Microsoft home page) is loaded into the lower frame.

By using a JavaScript function `navi()`, the Visit Other Sites button creates a window and loads in the HTML document WfVisit.htm, shown in Listing 18.21. This document uses an HTML form to query the user for an URL (see Figure 18.18) and then makes use of the web browser frame object to load the web page referenced by that URL into the lower frame (see Figure 18.19).

Listing 18.21 WfVisit.htm The HTML and JavaScript in this file allow others web pages to be loaded into the lower frame.

```
<HTML>
<HEAD>
<TITLE>Windows and Frames Navigator</TITLE>
<SCRIPT LANGUAGE="JavaScript">
<!-- Hide this script from incompatible Web browsers!
function visit(frame) {
   if (frame == "frame2")
      open(document.getsite.site.value,frame);
   return 0;
}
<!-- -->
</SCRIPT>
</HEAD>
<BODY BGCOLOR=#FFFFFF>
<CENTER>
<H2><B>Windows and Frames Navigator</B></H2>
<FORM NAME="getsite" METHOD="post">
<hR>
<INPUT TYPE="TEXT" NAME="site" SIZE=50>
<INPUT TYPE="BUTTON" NAME="gobut" VALUE="Go!"
   onclick="window.close();visit('frame2')">
<HR>
<INPUT TYPE="BUTTON" VALUE="Exit" onclick="window.close()">
</FORM>
</BODY>
</HTML>
```

The Back and Forward buttons also call JavaScript functions that use the `frame` object to move the lower frame backward and forward through its history list. The final button of the upper frame toolbar calls a JavaScript function that gives the user the ability to exit from the web browser, after first getting confirmation.

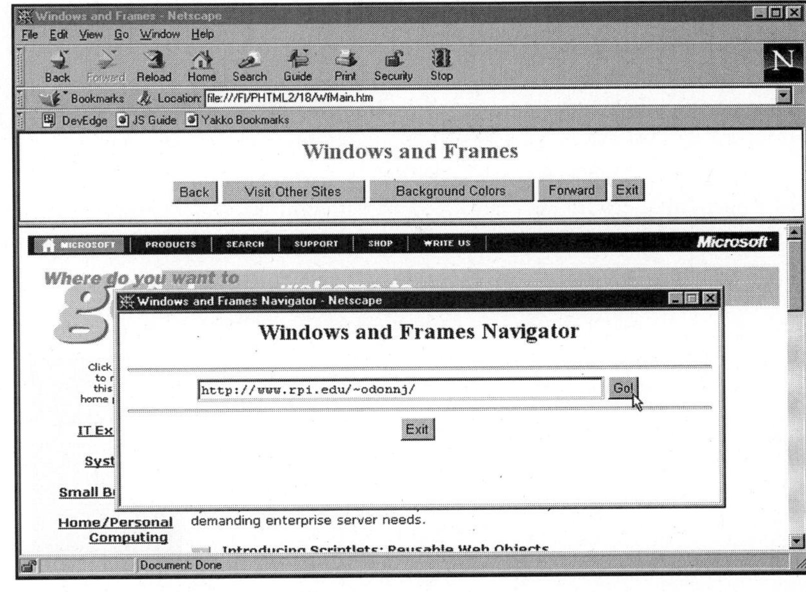

FIG. 18.18
Any valid URL can be typed into this HTML form to be loaded into the lower frame of the main browser window.

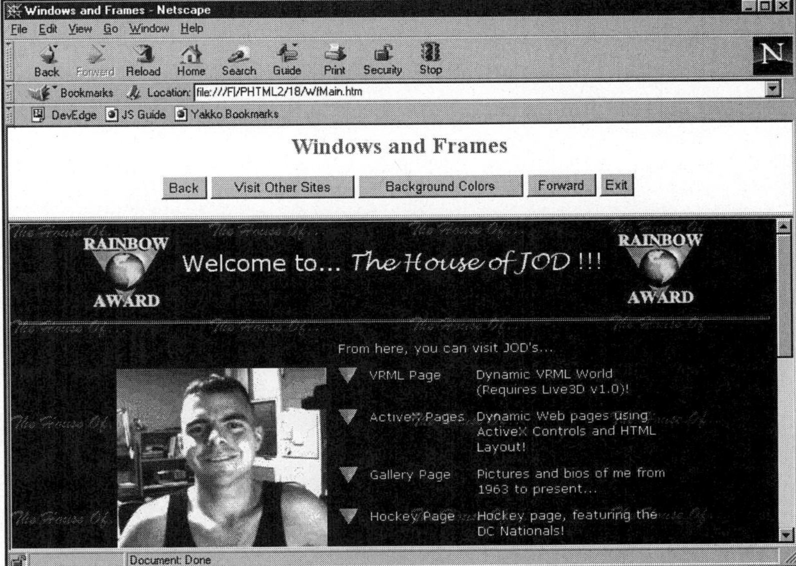

FIG. 18.19
After a few documents have been viewed in the lower frame, the Back and Forward buttons in the upper frames can be used.

CHAPTER 19

Using JavaScript to Create Smart Forms

by Jim O'Donnell

In this chapter

Client-Side Form Validation

One of the most common tasks for JavaScripting is to do form validation. Many web applications need to gather input from users. Traditionally this data is entered in the browser and then transmitted to the server. The server checks the validity of the data, and either stores the data on the server or sends back a message to the user requesting additional information or asking him to enter valid data. Not only does this slow down your web server, but it creates unnecessary web traffic as well. With just a few lines of code, you can validate much of this data on the client's machine and send it to the server only after it is complete.

This chapter discusses ways of using JavaScript to make your HTML forms smarter. First, a few examples give you some ideas on how to use JavaScript to prefill, validate, and format HTML form elements. After that, the discussion focuses on how you can make sure a credit card number is well formed—obviously, it is not possible to truly validate a credit card number at the client, but it is possible to determine whether the number is a valid format. Finally, this chapter reviews a couple of collections of JavaScript form validation scripts that are freely available on the web. These should get you well on your way to adding form validation to your web pages.

HTML Form Text Field Validation and Formatting with JavaScript

Listing 19.1 is an example of a traditional HTML page used to gather input from a user. Take a closer look at a few of the elements of this page.

Listing 19.1 Form.htm An HTML document using a standard HTML form.

```
<HTML>
<HEAD>
<TITLE>Forms Verification</TITLE>
</HEAD>
<BODY BGCOLOR="#FFFFFF">
<H1>Credit Card Payment Information</H1>
<HR>
<B>All information must be entered before the form can be submitted...</B>
<HR>
<FORM NAME="MyForm">
<TABLE>
<TR><TD>First Name:</TD>
    <TD> </TD>
    <TD><INPUT TYPE=TEXT NAME="FirstName" SIZE=20 VALUE=""></TD></TR>
<TR><TD>Last Name:</TD>
    <TD> </TD>
    <TD><INPUT TYPE=TEXT NAME="LastName"  SIZE=20 VALUE=""></TD></TR>
<TR><TD COLSPAN=3><HR></TD></TR>
<TR><TD>Payment Date:</TD>
    <TD> </TD>
    <TD><INPUT TYPE=TEXT NAME="PayDate"   SIZE=10 VALUE=""></TD>
    <TD>(enter as mm/dd/yy)</TD></TR>
```

```
<TR><TD>Payment Amount:</TD>
    <TD><B>$</B></TD>
    <TD><INPUT TYPE=TEXT NAME="Amount"    SIZE=10 VALUE=""></TD></TR>
<TR><TD>Credit Card Number:</TD>
    <TD> </TD>
    <TD><INPUT TYPE=TEXT NAME="CCNumber"  SIZE=20 VALUE=""></TD>
    <TD>(must be 13 or 16 digits long)</TD></TR>
<TR><TD>Expiration Date:</TD>
    <TD> </TD>
    <TD><INPUT TYPE=TEXT NAME="ExpDate"   SIZE=10 VALUE=""></TD>
    <TD>(enter as mm/dd/yy)</TD></TR>
</TABLE>
<HR>
<INPUT TYPE=SUBMIT NAME="MySubmit" SIZE=20 VALUE="SUBMIT INFORMATION">
</FORM>
</BODY>
</HTML>
```

This HTML document, when viewed in Internet Explorer, appears as shown in Figure 19.1.

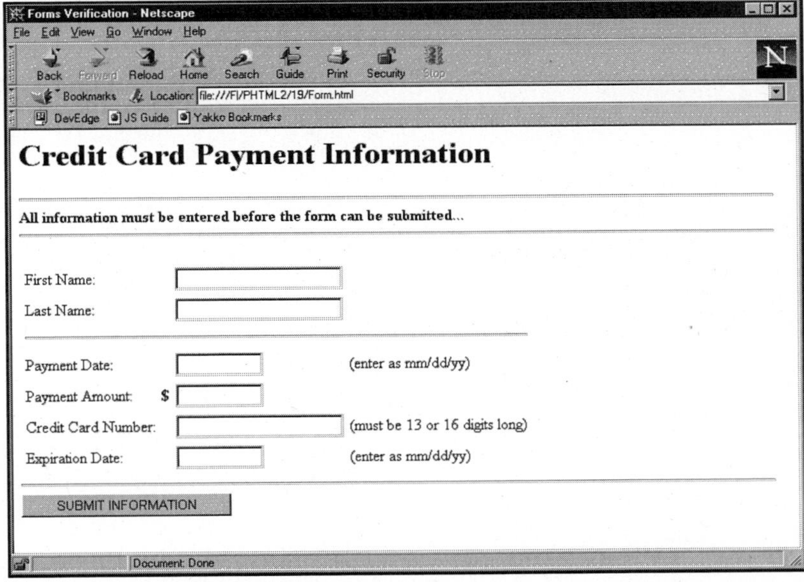

FIG. 19.1
You can use standard HTML Forms elements to set up a document for receiving user input.

The different elements of the HTML document, as shown in Listing 19.1, are as follows:

- `<FORM>...</FORM>` Tags

  These are the container tags that must surround the HTML Forms input elements. The `NAME="MyForm"` attribute is used to help identify the form from which that data came when the form is being processed. You might notice that neither the `METHOD` nor `ACTION` attribute for the `<FORM>` tag has been sent. This is because this form is being used as an example. Normally you would set `METHOD=POST`, and set the `ACTION` to the appropriate URL of where on your web server you want the data to be sent.

- `<INPUT TYPE=TEXT>` Tags

  Each of these tags is used to receive one piece of information from the user. Each is named, using the `NAME` attribute, to allow the resulting data to be identified.

- `<INPUT TYPE=SUBMIT>` Tag

  This tag puts the button on the form used to submit it. Like the other elements, it is named using the `NAME` attribute, and the `VALUE` attribute is used to customize the text appearing on the button.

▶ **See** "Creating Forms," **p. 212**

Scripting HTML Form Text Fields

HTML documents can include JavaScripts to perform a variety of client-side scripting functions to validate elements of the form before it is submitted to the web server. Note that not all the form validation can be done at the client—for instance, for this example you would definitely need to validate the payment information at the server—but some of the simpler things definitely can be done.

> **CAUTION**
>
> This is meant to be an illustrative example designed to show some of the types of user input that can be validated using JavaScript at the client. It is not meant to be a realistic example of how to implement a web-based payment system. If you want to do that, there are a lot of concerns with security and validation of payment information that are not addressed here. However, you can find some of this information elsewhere in this book.
>
> ▶ **See** "Verifying Input Is Legitimate," **p. 924**

A couple of different ways enable you to validate the information entered into a form. For text fields, the best way to do it is as you go. By calling a JavaScript from the `onChange` method of the HTML Form text field, you can validate the data entered into a field any time it has changed. Here is an example of the syntax used to do this:

```
<INPUT TYPE=TEXT NAME="PayDate" SIZE=10 VALUE=""
       onChange="checkDate(document.MyForm.PayDate)">
```

In this example, whenever the information in the text field named `PayDate` is changed, the JavaScript `checkDate()` function is called. The argument of the `checkDate()` function, in this case, is the text field object (assuming that the name of the form is `MyForm`).

Prefilling Entries

The only apparent change from the unscripted to scripted version of this example in Figure 19.2 is that the payment date has been prefilled. Because an obvious default entry exists for this field—the current date—it makes sense to let JavaScript do this and save the user a little bit of effort. This is done by executing the JavaScript statements shown in Listing 19.2 when the document is loaded:

Listing 19.2 FormScr.htm (excerpt).

```
//
////////////////////////////////////////////////////////////////////////
//
// This function formats a date as mm/dd/yy.
//
function formatDate(dateVar) {
   newDate = dateVar.toLocaleString()
   newDate = newDate.substring(0,newDate.indexOf(" "))
   return newDate
}
//
// Prefill payment date with current date
//
today = new Date()
document.MyForm.PayDate.value = formatDate(today)
```

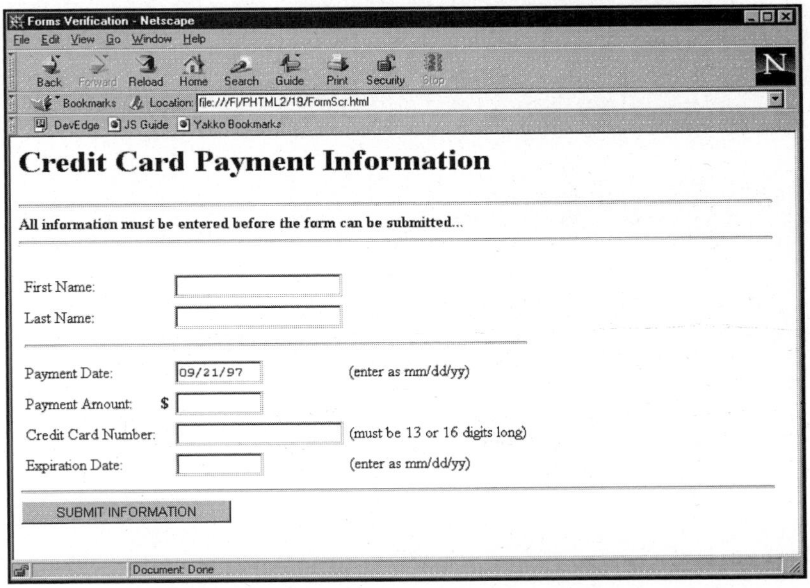

FIG. 19.2
Other than having the payment date entry prefilled, this JavaScripted form doesn't look very different from the unscripted version.

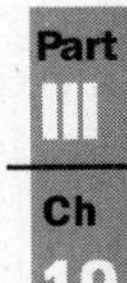

NOTE The complete listings of this HTML document and all the other documents used in this chapter are on the accompanying CD in the file named FormScr.htm.

The `today` variable is set equal to a JavaScript `Date` object containing the current date. The `formatDate()` function takes a `Date` object as an argument and returns a string with the date in the format "mm/dd/yy".

Note that the user can change this entry, picking a payment date that is after the current date. You might not want to allow the user to select a payment date prior to the current date, however—if his payment is late, for instance, you don't want him to be able to "predate his check." You can easily prevent this with JavaScript, as will be shown later in this chapter.

Formatting Proper Name Entries

Listing 19.3 shows the JavaScript function `capitalizeName()`. This function formats a proper name entry by capitalizing the first letter. This is not terribly important to do, as forms validation topics go, but it is a nicety. Another feature of this function (included here because of personal bias), is that it also capitalizes the letter immediately following an apostrophe.

Listing 19.3 FormScr.htm (excerpt) JavaScript subroutine to format proper name entries.

```
//
// This function capitalizes proper names; it also capitalizes the
// letter after the apostrophe, if one is present
//
function capitalizeName(Obj) {
//
// Set temp equal to form element string
//
   temp  = new String(Obj.value)
   first = temp.substring(0,1)
   temp  = first.toUpperCase() + temp.substring(1,temp.length)
   apnum = temp.indexOf("'")
   if (apnum > -1) {
      aplet = temp.substring(apnum+1,apnum+2)
      temp  = temp.substring(0,apnum) + "'" +
              aplet.toUpperCase() +
              temp.substring(apnum+2,temp.length)
   }
   Obj.value = temp
}
```

Validating and Formatting Currency Entries

Listing 19.4 shows the JavaScript function `checkAmount()`. This function validates and formats an entry meant to be an amount of money. Primarily, this entry needs to be a numeric value, but it is a little more forgiving than that; it will remove a leading dollar sign if the user has put one in. Then, after making sure that the value is numeric, the subroutine formats it as dollars and cents and writes it back out to the form field from which it came.

Listing 19.4 FormScr.htm (excerpt) JavaScript subroutine to validate and format currency.

```
//
////////////////////////////////////////////////////////////////////////
//
// This function checks to see if the value of the object that is
// passed to it is a valid currency, and then formats it.
//
function checkAmount(Obj) {
//
// Set temp equal to form element string
//
   temp = new String(Obj.value)
//
// Remove leading $, if present
//
   temp = temp.substring(temp.indexOf("$")+1,temp.length)
//
// Convert into a floating point number and format as dollars
// and cents
//
   temp = parseFloat(temp)
   temp = Math.floor(100*temp)/100
   temp = String(temp)
   if (temp.indexOf(".") == -1) {
      temp = temp + ".00"
   }
   if (temp.indexOf(".") == temp.length -2) {
      temp = temp + "0"
   }
//
// If zero value, make blank
//
   if (temp == "0.00") {
      temp = ""
   }
//
// Write back out to the form element
//
   Obj.value = temp
}
```


If you are not familiar with JavaScript, you might be confused a little by the `checkAmount()` function because it seems to treat the same variable alternatively as a number or as a string. Because JavaScript allows its variables to be dynamic types, you can use the same variable to store any kind of data that JavaScript recognizes. JavaScript generally treats data as the subtype—such as integer, floating point, or string—appropriate to the operation.

As a final note, you see that for an entry incorrectly formatted, `checkAmount()` will blank the entry. How your JavaScripts respond to incorrect entries is up to you. You can remove the

```
//
minLength = 13
maxLength = 16
//
function checkCCNumber(Obj) {
//
// Get object value
```

continues

incorrect entry—as is done in this example—leave it but set an error flag that prevents the form from being submitted until it is corrected, bring up an Alert box, or anything else you would like to do.

Validating and Formatting Date Entries

The JavaScripts implement a number of tests. In addition to making sure that the expiration date entered has not passed, the credit card number entered is checked to see whether it is well formed. The JavaScript checks employ both the prefix and length text, as well as the Luhn Algorithm check digit test. Figure 19.6 shows the results of a well-formed credit card number of the card type selected.

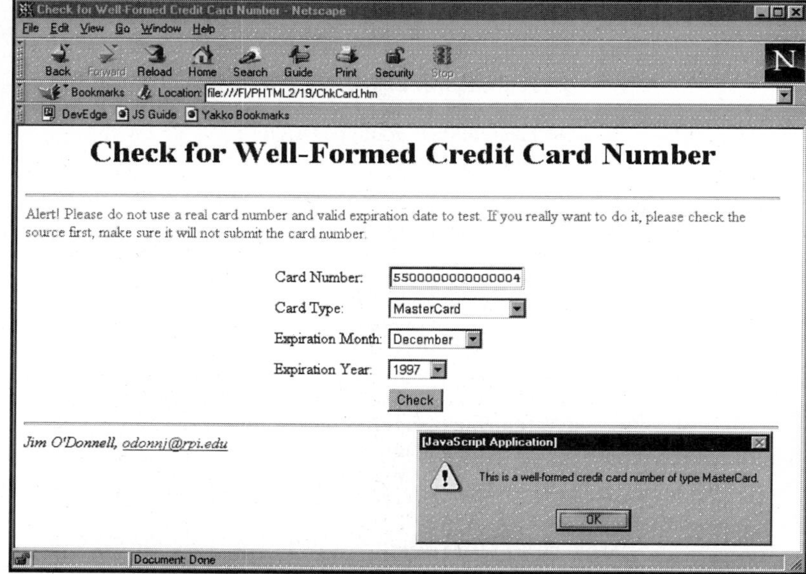

FIG. 19.6
Both the check digit and prefix and length test need to pass to correctly identify the card number as well formed for the given type.

As shown in Figure 19.7, the JavaScript tests are even smart enough to determine when a well-formed card number of a type other than the one selected has been entered. If the number is not a well-formed card number for any known type of card, an Alert box with that information appears (see Figure 19.8).

Netscape's Sample Form Validation Scripts

ON THE WEB

http://developer.netscape.com/library/examples/javascript/formval/overview.html A veritable treasure trove of freely available JavaScripts for form validation is available from the Netscape web site at the following URL:

The JavaScript source file that you can download from that site is called FormChek.js. In addition, a number of sample HTML files there show the functions in operation. The JavaScript functions defined there come under a number of general categories, as described in the header information in the FormChek.js file (summarized in the following sections).

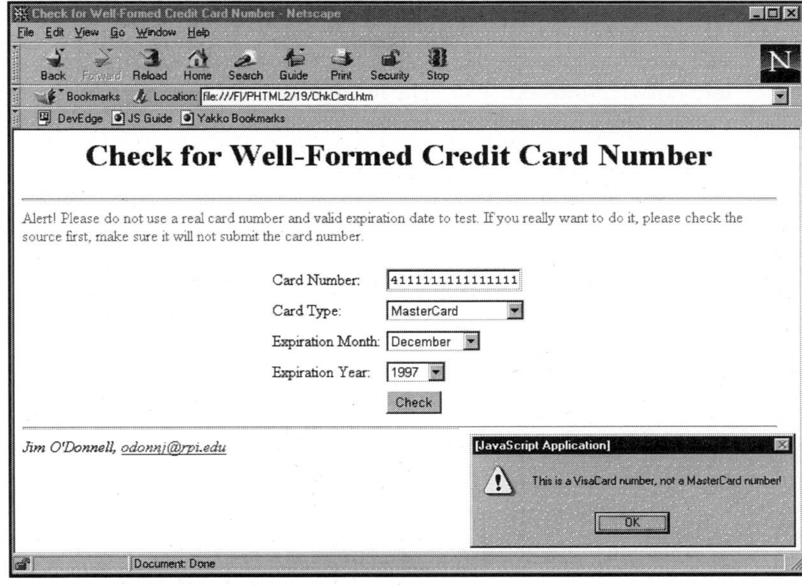

FIG. 19.7
Using the prefix and length information, it is possible to automatically determine the type of a mis-identified card.

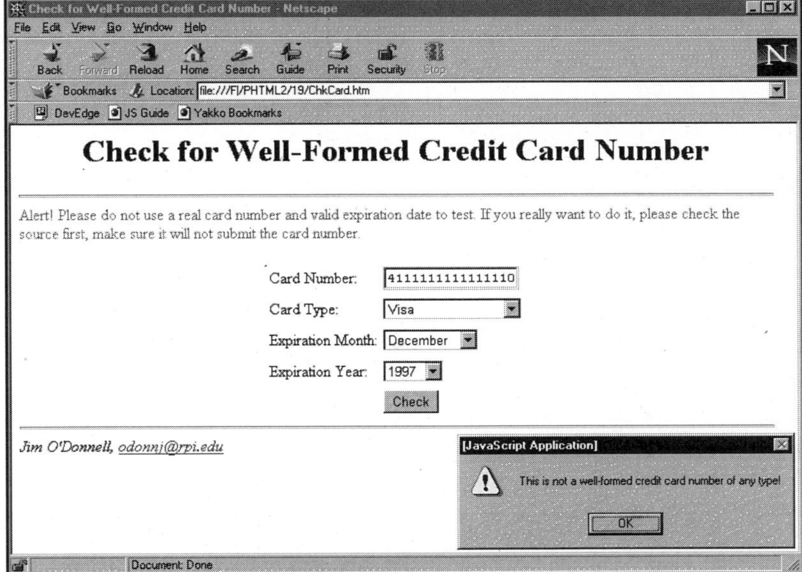

FIG. 19.8
If the check digit test is failed, the number cannot be a valid credit card number of any known type.

- isAmericanExpress(cc)

  True if string cc is a valid American Express number.
- isDinersClub(cc)

  True if string cc is a valid Diner's Club number.
- isCarteBlanche(cc)

  True if string cc is a valid Carte Blanche number.
- isDiscover(cc)

  True if string cc is a valid Discover card number.
- isEnRoute(cc)

  True if string cc is a valid enRoute card number.
- isJCB(cc)

  True if string cc is a valid JCB card number.
- isAnyCard(cc)

  True if string cc is a valid card number for any of the accepted types.
- isCardMatch(Type,Number)

  True if number is valid for credit card of type.

FormChek JavaScript Collection Example

Along with the FormChek.js JavaScript source file for forms validation, Netscape has a number of sample HTML documents that exercise the JavaScript functions. These functions, and the way they are implemented, provide a good example of ways to create smart HTML Forms with JavaScript.

Figure 19.9 shows one of the sample HTML documents, showing a partially filled-out form. Notice that the zip code and phone number have been formatted using a standard format. The data was not entered into those fields in that format—JavaScript functions were called to reformat and redisplay those fields in that standard format.

You should notice one other thing about Figure 19.9. Notice that the cursor is located in the Email field, and that the status line of the web browser window contains the text "Please enter a valid email address (like foo@bar.com)." This is a way of providing context-sensitive help to your user with a JavaScript that sets the `window.status` property—and thus the contents of the current status line—to an informative string for the current field being entered. This is done using the `onFocus` event of each `<INPUT>` tag, as shown here:

```
<INPUT TYPE="text" NAME="Email" onFocus="promptEntry(pEmail)"
                                onChange="checkEmail(this,true)">
```

The `onFocus` event is triggered when the cursor enters the form field in question. When this happens, the preceding code calls the `promptEntry()` function, which is as follows:

```
function promptEntry(s) {
   window.status = pEntryPrompt + s
}
```

FIG. 19.9
JavaScript can reformat your data to standardize the appearance of the information entered.

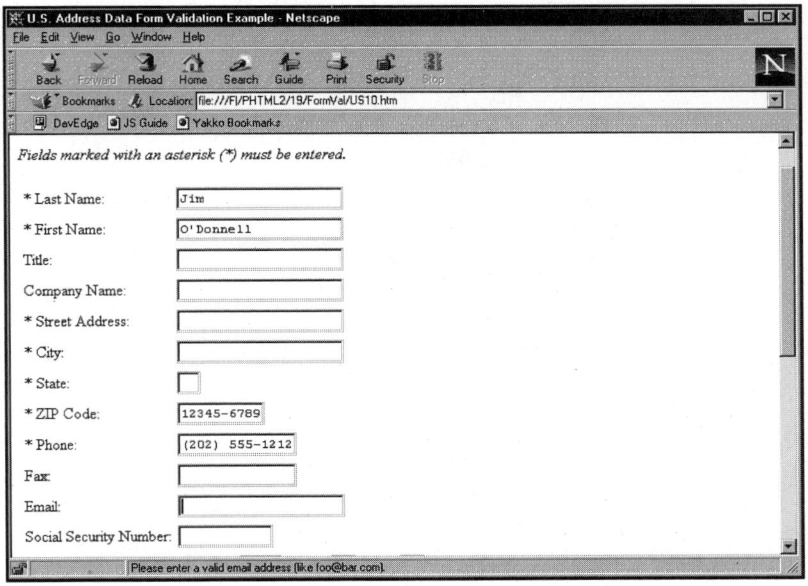

This function just sets the status line to the passed string. (`pEntryPrompt` and `pEmail` are predefined global strings that, in this case, result in the status line shown in Figure 19.9.)

What about the other side of the equation? How does the entered information get validated? The `onChange` event triggers a call to the `checkEmail()` function, which is as follows:

```
function checkEmail(theField,emptyOK) {
   if (checkEmail.arguments.length == 1) emptyOK = defaultEmptyOK;
   if ((emptyOK == true) && (isEmpty(theField.value))) return true;
   else if (!isEmail(theField.value,false))
      return warnInvalid(theField,iEmail);
   else return true;
}
```

The `checkEmail()` function calls the `isEmail()` function with the contents of the Email field, which returns `true` or `false`, depending on whether it was found to be valid. If it was not valid, the `warnInvalid()` function is called, shown in the following code, which displays the Alert box shown in Figure 19.10.

```
function warnInvalid(theField,s) {
   theField.focus()
   theField.select()
   alert(s)
   return false
}
```

In addition to displaying the Alert box, `warnInvalid()` also does two other things: It moves the cursor to the field in question, using the `theField.focus()` method, and then selects the current contents of the field with `theField.select()`. This makes it very easy for you to edit the contents of the field (see Figure 19.11).

FIG. 19.10
The FormChek JavaScript routines display and alert immediately when an invalid form field is found.

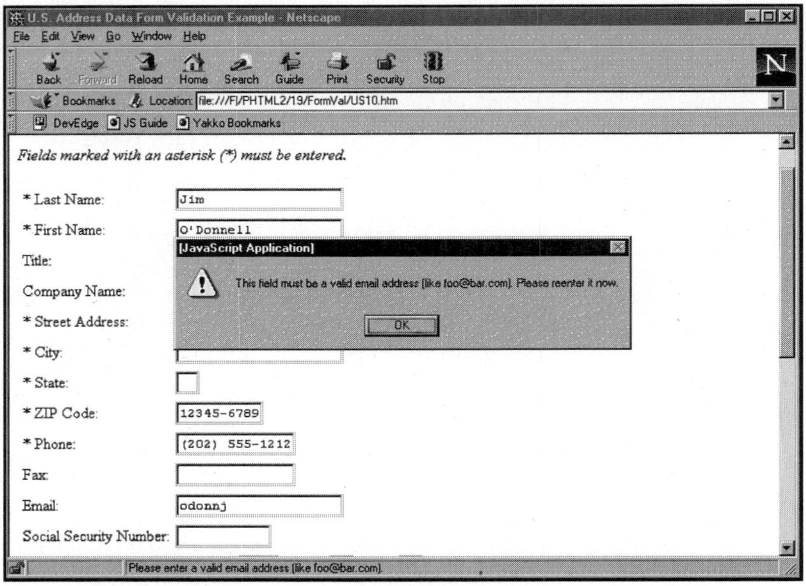

FIG. 19.11
You can make it easy for your users to correct invalid fields by selecting the current contents.

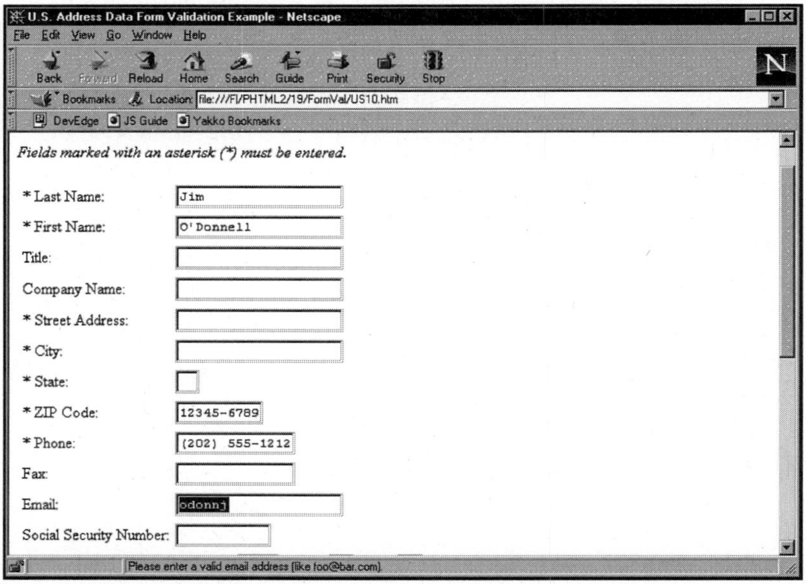

The FormChek routines also include credit card validation functions that perform the same prefix, length, and check digit tests as those discussed earlier in this chapter. As shown in Figure 19.12, these routines are not quite as forgiving if you enter a valid number with the wrong card type.

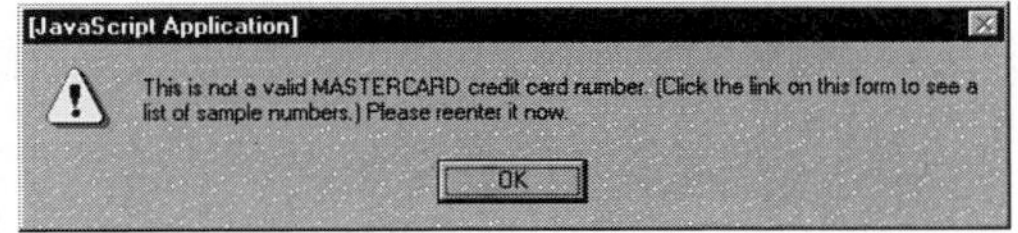

FIG. 19.12 If the credit card number you enter is not a valid number for the selected card type, you will receive this Alert box and be given the opportunity to re-enter the number.

When you attempt to submit the form, it calls a routine that forces checks to make sure that you have input valid data in all the required fields. If you have not, you get an alert box that tells you about the first such field, and the cursor is moved to that field (see Figure 19.13). When you have finally completed all required elements of the form correctly, you can successfully submit the form; in this example program, the dynamically generated HTML document shown in Figure 19.14 results.

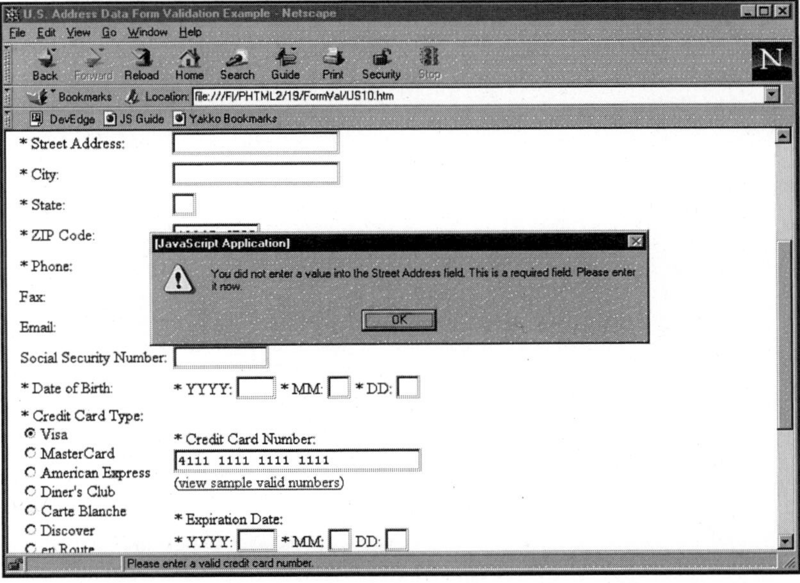

FIG. 19.13 You can easily make any field in your form a required field, and require your users to enter valid data there.

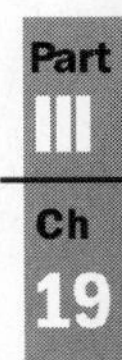

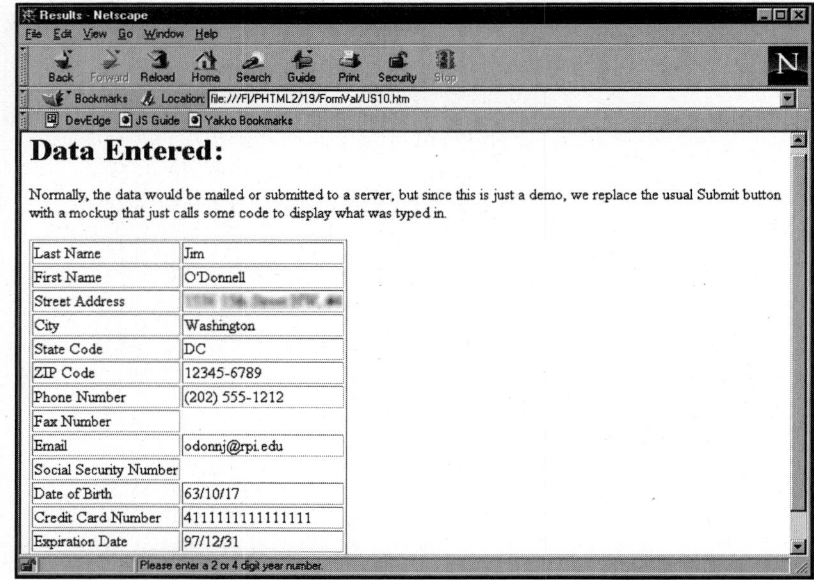

FIG. 19.14 Upon successful completion of the form, its data can be submitted for processing.

CHAPTER 20

Cookies and State Maintenance

by Bill Chosiad

In this chapter

The Trouble with Stateless HTTP

Web servers have very short memories. When you request a page, the server doesn't really know who you are, what you entered on a form three pages ago, or whether this is your first visit to the site or your 75th. One of the challenges of using the Hypertext Transfer Protocol (HTTP) is that it doesn't track the *state* of your interactions with the server. *State* refers to any information about you or your visit to a web site. It is maintained as you move from page to page within the site, and it may be used by the web server or a JavaScript program (or both) to customize your experience at the site. But if HTTP doesn't maintain the state, what does?

This chapter shows you how to get around HTTP's limitations by using cookies, URL query string parameters, and hidden form variables. Although the bulk of this chapter deals with cookies, time is spent investigating other techniques, as well as where and how they may best be used.

Maintaining State

Maintaining state means remembering information while the user moves from page to page within a web site. With this information in hand, you can set user preferences, fill in default form values, track visit counts, and do many other things that make browsing easier for users and give you more information about how your pages are used.

You can maintain state information number of ways:

- Store it in cookies
- Encode it in URL links
- Send it in hidden form variables
- Store it in variables in other frames
- Store it on the web server

Be aware, however, that some technical challenges regarding state maintenance can occur. While browsing a site, a user might suddenly zoom off to another web site and return minutes, hours, or days later, only to find that any saved state information is out of date or has been erased. He or she might return by clicking his browser's Back button, by using a bookmark, or by typing in the URL directly, causing state information encoded in the URL to be overwritten or lost.

The web developer must maintain state information regardless of whether the user navigates through the site using buttons on a form or a URL link on a page. This could mean adding information to both hidden form variables and every URL `<A HREF...>` tag that appears on the page.

With all these difficulties to overcome, these state maintenance mechanisms had better be useful. Luckily, they are. There are many advantages to maintaining state, both within a single site visit and from one visit to the next. Consider the following scenarios:

- *A shopping cart application*. Users could browse through the site while selecting items and adding them to a virtual shopping cart. At any time, they can view the items in the cart, change the contents of their cart, or take the cart to the checkout counter for purchase. Keeping track of which user owns which shopping cart is essential.
- *Custom home pages*. Both Netscape and the Microsoft Network have set up home pages where users can customize what they see when they arrive. After giving the user a choice of layouts, color schemes, and favorite destinations, it stores the preferences on the user's own computer through the use of cookies. The user can return to the site any time and get his previously configured page.
- *Frequent visitor bonuses*. By storing information on the client computer, this application keeps track of how many times a browser has hit a particular page. When the user reaches a certain level of hits, he gets access to more or better services.
- *Change banners*. You can make graphic banners and text change each time the user hits a page. This technique is often used to cycle through a list of advertisements.
- *Bookmarks*. Remember where a user was when he last visited the site. Was he reading a story, filling out a questionnaire, or playing a game? Let him pick up where he left off.
- *Games*. Remember current or high scores. Present new challenges based on past answers and performance.

Cookies: An Introduction

Cookies—sometimes called *magic cookies,* but more formally known as *persistent client state HTTP cookies* —enable you to store information on the client browser's computer for later retrieval. Although they have their drawbacks, cookies are the most powerful technique available for maintaining state within a web site.

Netscape came up with the original cookie specification. There doesn't seem to be any good reason why Netscape chose that particular name. In fact, on their cookie specification page, they even admit that "the state object is called a cookie for no compelling reason."

In their simplest form, cookies store data in the form of `name=value` pairs. You, the developer, can pick any name and value combination you want. More advanced cookie features include the capability to set an expiration date and to specify what web pages may see the cookie information.

Advantages of Cookies

One of the most powerful aspects of cookies is their persistence. When a cookie is set on the user's browser, it may persist for days, months, or, usually in a special cookie file. As with all files, this cookie file might be accidentally (or purposefully) deleted, taking all the browser's cookie information with it. The cookie file could be write-protected, thus preventing any cookies from being stored there. Browser software may impose limitations on the size and number of cookies that may be stored, and newer cookies may overwrite older ones.

Because cookies are associated with a particular browser, problems come up if users switch from one browser to another. If you usually use Netscape Navigator and have a collection of cookies, they will no longer be available for you to use if you decide to switch to Microsoft Internet Explorer.

Finally, if several people use the same computer and browser, they might find themselves using cookies that belong to someone else. The reason for this is that cookie information is stored in a file on the computer, and the browser has no way to distinguish between multiple users.

Disadvantages of Cookies

There are also some problems, both real and imagined, concerning the use of cookies. Because many browsers store their cookie information in an unencrypted text file, you should never store sensitive information, such as a password, in a cookie. Anyone with access to the user's computer could read it.

Newer web browsers, such as Netscape Navigator 4.0 and Microsoft Internet Explorer 4.0, might have a feature that alerts the user every time an attempt is made to set a cookie. These browsers could even be configured to prevent cookies from being set at all. This sometimes results in confusion on the user's part when a dialog box informs her that something strange involving a cookie is happening to her computer. If cookies are disabled, your carefully designed web application might not run at all.

Cookie Myths

The biggest problem facing cookies could be a psychological one. Some savvy web users believe that all cookies are a tool used by "Big Brother" to violate their privacy. Considering that cookies are capable of storing information about where users have visited on a web site, how many times they have been there, what advertising banners they have viewed, and what they have selected and placed on forms, some people think that their privacy is being invaded whenever a cookie gets set on their computer.

In reality, cookies are seldom used for these purposes. Although technically these things are possible, better and easier ways of getting the same type of information now exist without using cookies.

Other users complain about web sites being able to write information to their computers and taking up space on their hard drives. This is somewhat true. Web browser software limits the total size of the cookies stored to 1.2MB, with no more than 80KB going to any one web site. Consider, however, that this number probably is small when compared to the size of the pages and graphic images that web browsers routinely store in their page caches.

Other users are concerned that cookies set by one web site might be read by other sites. This is completely untrue. Your web browser software prevents this from happening by making cookies available only to the sites that created them.

If your users understand the usefulness of cookies, this "cookie backlash" shouldn't be a problem.

ON THE WEB

Netscape came up with the original cookie specification. You can find more information on the Netscape web site at **http://www.netscape.com/newsref/std/cookie_spec.html**.

Using Cookies

By now you have considered the pros and cons of cookies and have decided that they are just what you need to make your JavaScript application a success.

This section discusses a number of handy functions for reading and setting cookies, which will help you make your web sites smarter and more user friendly. Also included in this section are Internet references for finding additional information concerning cookies.

Retrieving Cookie Values

Cookie names and values are stored and set using the `cookie` property of the `document` object. To store the raw cookie string in a variable, you would use a JavaScript command such as the following:

```
var myCookie = document.cookie;
```

To display it on a web page, use the following command:

```
document.write ("Raw Cookies: " + document.cookie + "<BR>");
```

JavaScript stores cookies in the following format:

```
name1=value1; name2=value2; name3=value3
```

Individual `name=value` pairs are separated by a semicolon and a blank space. There is no semicolon after the final value.

To make it easier to retrieve a cookie, you probably want to use a JavaScript routine such as the one shown in Listing 20.1.

Listing 20.1 The *GetCookie* function.

```
function GetCookie (name) {
  var result = null;
  var myCookie = " " + document.cookie + ";";
  var searchName = " " + name + "=";
  var startOfCookie = myCookie.indexOf(searchName)
  var endOfCookie;
  if (startOfCookie != -1) {
    startOfCookie += searchName.length; // skip past cookie name
    endOfCookie = myCookie.indexOf(";", startOfCookie);
    result = unescape(myCookie.substring(startOfCookie, endOfCookie));
  }
  return result;
}
```

In Listing 20.1, the `myCookie` string helps avoid annoying boundary conditions by making sure all cookie string names start with a space and end with a semicolon.

From there, it is easy to find the start of the `name=` portion of the string, skip it, and retrieve everything from that point until the next semicolon.

Setting Cookie Values

The *`name=value`* combination is the minimum amount of information you need to set up a cookie. However, there is more to cookies than just this. Here is the complete list of parameters used to specify a cookie:

- *`name=value`*
- `expires=`*`date`*
- `path=`*`path`*
- `domain=`*`domainname`*
- `secure`

Cookie Names and Values The *`name`* and *`value`* can be anything you choose. In some cases, you might want it to be very explanatory, such as `FavoriteColor=Blue`. In other cases, it could just be code that the JavaScript program interprets, such as `CurStat=1:2:1:0:0:1:0:3:1:1`. In any case, the *`name`* and *`value`* are completely up to you.

In its simplest form, a routine to set a cookie looks like this:

```
function SetCookieEZ (name, value) {
  document.cookie = name + "=" + escape(value);
}
```

Notice that the value is encoded using the `escape` function. If there were a semicolon in the string, it might prevent you from achieving the expected results. Using the `escape` function eliminates this problem.

Also notice that the `document.cookie` property works rather differently from most other properties. In most other cases, using the assignment operator (=) causes the existing property value to be completely overwritten with the new value. This is not the case with the `cookie` property. With cookies, each new *`name`* you assign is added to the active list of cookies. If you assign the same *`name`* twice, the second assignment replaces the first.

There are some exceptions to this last statement, but these are explained in the section "Path" later in this chapter.

Expiration Date The `expires=`*`date`* tells the browser how long the cookie will last. The cookie specification page at Netscape states that dates are in the form of

```
Wdy, DD-Mon-YY HH:MM:SS GMT
```

Here's an example:

```
Mon, 08-Jul-96 03:18:20 GMT
```

This format is based on Internet RFC 822, which you can find at **http://www.w3.org/hypertext/WWW/Protocols/rfc822/#z28**.

The only difference between RFC 822 and the Netscape implementation is that, in Netscape Navigator, the expiration date must end with `GMT` (Greenwich Mean Time). Happily, the JavaScript language provides a function to do just that. By using the `toGMTString()` function, you can set cookies to expire in the near or distant future.

Even though the date produced by the `toGMTString()` function doesn't match the Netscape specification, it still works under JavaScript.

If the expiration date isn't specified, the cookie remains in effect until the browser is shut down.

Here is a code segment that sets a cookie to expire in one week:

```
var name="foo";
var value="bar";
var oneWeek = 7 * 24 * 60 * 60 * 1000;
var expDate = new Date();
expDate.setTime (expDate.getTime() + oneWeek);
document.cookie = name + "=" + escape(value) + ";
   expires=" + expDate.toGMTString();
```

Deleting a Cookie To delete a cookie, set the expiration date to some time in the past—how far in the past doesn't generally matter. To be on the safe side, a few days ago should work fine. Here is a routine to delete a cookie:

```
function ClearCookie (name) {
  var ThreeDays = 3 * 24 * 60 * 60 * 1000;
  var expDate = new Date();
  expDate.setTime (expDate.getTime() - ThreeDays);
  document.cookie = name + "=ImOutOfHere; expires=" + expDate.toGMTString();
}
```

When deleting cookies, it doesn't matter what you use for the cookie value—any value will do.

CAUTION

Some versions of Netscape do a poor job of converting times to GMT. Some common JavaScript functions for deleting a cookie consider the past to be one millisecond behind the current time. Although this is usually true, it doesn't work on all platforms. To be on the safe side, use a few days in the past to expire cookies.

Path By default, cookies are available to other web pages within the same directory as the page on which they were created. The `Path` parameter allows a cookie to be made available to pages in other directories. If the value of the `Path` parameter is a substring of a page's URL, cookies created with that path are available to that page. You could create a cookie with the following command, for example:

```
document.cookie = "foo=bar1; path=/javascript";
```

This would make the cookie `foo` available to every page in the `javascript` directory and all those directories beneath it. If, instead, the command looked like this

```
document.cookie = "foo=bar2; path=/javascript/sam";
```

the cookie would be available to `sample1.html`, `sample2.html`, `sammy.exe`, and so on.

Finally, to make the cookie available to everyone on your server, use the following command:

```
document.cookie = "foo=bar3; path=/";
```

What happens when a browser has multiple cookies on different paths but with the same name? Which one wins?

Actually, they all do. When this situation arises, it is possible to have two or more cookies with the same name but different values. If a page issued all the commands listed previously, for example, its cookie string would look like the following:

```
foo=bar3; foo=bar2; foo=bar1
```

To help be aware of this situation, you might want to write a routine to count the number of cookie values associated with a cookie name. It might look like this:

```
function GetCookieCount (name) {
  var result = 0;
  var myCookie = " " + document.cookie + ";";
  var searchName = " " + name + "=";
  var nameLength = searchName.length;
  var startOfCookie = myCookie.indexOf(searchName)
  while (startOfCookie != -1) {
    result += 1;
    startOfCookie = myCookie.indexOf(searchName, startOfCookie + nameLength);
  }
  return result;
}
```

Of course, if there is a `GetCookieCount` function, there would need to be a `GetCookieNum` function to retrieve a particular instance of a cookie. That function would look like this:

```
function GetCookieNum (name, cookieNum) {
  var result = null;
  if (cookieNum >= 1) {
    var myCookie = " " + document.cookie + ";";
    var searchName = " " + name + "=";
    var nameLength = searchName.length;
    var startOfCookie = myCookie.indexOf(searchName);
    var cntr = 0;
    for (cntr = 1; cntr < cookieNum; cntr++)
      startOfCookie = myCookie.indexOf(searchName, startOfCookie + nameLength);
    if (startOfCookie != -1) {
      startOfCookie += nameLength; // skip past cookie name
      var endOfCookie = myCookie.indexOf(";", startOfCookie);
      result = unescape(myCookie.substring(startOfCookie, endOfCookie));
    }
  }
  return result;
}
```

CAUTION

There is a bug in Netscape Navigator version 1.1 and earlier. Only cookies whose path attribute is set explicitly to / are properly saved between sessions if they have an `expires` attribute.

To delete a cookie, the name and the path must match the original name and path used when the cookie was set.

Domain Usually, after a page on a particular server creates a cookie, that cookie is accessible only to other pages on that server. Just as the `Path` parameter makes a cookie available outside its home path, the `Domain` parameter makes it available to other web servers at the same site.

You can't create a cookie that anyone on the Internet can see. You may only set a path that falls inside your own domain. This is because the use of the `Domain` parameter dictates that you must use at least two periods (for example, `.mydomain.com`) if your domain ends in `.com`, `.edu`, `.net`, `.org`, `.gov`, `.mil`, or `.int`. Otherwise, it must have at least three periods (`.mydomain.ma.us`). Your domain parameter string must match the tail of your server's domain name.

Secure The final cookie parameter tells your browser that this cookie should be sent only under a secure connection with the web server. This means that the server and the browser must support `HTTPS` security. (`HTTPS` is Netscape's Secure Socket Layer web page encryption protocol.)

If the `secure` parameter is not present, it means that cookies are sent unencrypted over the network.

NOTE You can't set an infinite number of cookies on every web browser that visits your site. Here are the number of cookies you can set and how large they can be:

- Cookies per each server or domain: 20
- Total cookies per browser: 300
- Largest cookie: 4KB (including both the `name` and `value` parameters)

If these limits are exceeded, the browser might attempt to discard older cookies by tossing out the least recently used cookies first.

Now that you have seen all the cookie parameters, it would be helpful to have a JavaScript routine set cookies with all the parameters. Such a routine might look like this:

```
function SetCookie (name, value, expires, path, domain, secure) {
  var expString =
            ((expires == null) ? "" : ("; expires=" + expires.toGMTString()))
  var pathString = ((path == null) ? "" : ("; path=" + path))
  var domainString = ((domain == null) ? "" : ("; domain=" + domain))
  var secureString = ((secure == true) ? "; secure" : "")
  document.cookie = name + "=" + escape (value) +
```

```
                      expString + pathString + domainString + secureString;
}
```

To use this routine, you call it with whatever parameters you care about and use `null` in place of parameters that don't matter.

A Cookie Example

The JavaScript program in Listing 20.2 provides an example of cookies in use. This program enables the user to create a personalized "News-of-the-Day" page containing links to sites of general interest in a number of different categories. The user's favorite links are stored in cookies. Figure 20.1 shows what the Favorites page looks like.

Listing 20.2 The *Favorites* script.

```
<HTML>
<HEAD>
<SCRIPT LANGUAGE="JavaScript">
<!-- Comment out script from browsers that don't know JavaScript
// This JavaScript code should run under Netscape Navigator 3.0
// and Microsoft Internet Explorer 3.0 and above. It will not run
// locally under Internet Explorer. If you use IE, you must load
// this page from a web server.
//===============================================================
// Here are our standard Cookie routines
//===============================================================
//---------------------------------------------------------------
// GetCookie - Returns the value of the specified cookie or null
//             if the cookie doesn't exist
//---------------------------------------------------------------
function GetCookie(name) {
  var result = null;
  var myCookie = " " + document.cookie + ";";
  var searchName = " " + name + "=";
  var startOfCookie = myCookie.indexOf(searchName)
  var endOfCookie;
  if (startOfCookie != -1) {
    startOfCookie += searchName.length; // skip past cookie name
    endOfCookie = myCookie.indexOf(";", startOfCookie);
    result = unescape(myCookie.substring(startOfCookie,
                                          endOfCookie));
  }
  return result;
}
//---------------------------------------------------------------
// SetCookieEZ - Quickly sets a cookie which will last until the
//               user shuts down his browser
//---------------------------------------------------------------
function SetCookieEZ(name, value) {
  document.cookie = name + "=" + escape(value);
}
//---------------------------------------------------------------
// SetCookie - Adds or replaces a cookie. Use null for parameters
```

```
//              that you don't care about
//---------------------------------------------------------------
function SetCookie(name, value, expires, path, domain, secure) {
  var expString = ((expires == null)
                  ? "" : ("; expires=" + expires.toGMTString()))
  var pathString = ((path == null) ? "" : ("; path=" + path))
  var domainString = ((domain == null)
                  ? "" : ("; domain=" + domain))
  var secureString = ((secure == true) ? "; secure" : "")
  document.cookie = name + "=" + escape(value)
                  + expString + pathString + domainString
                  + secureString;
}
//---------------------------------------------------------------
// ClearCookie  - Removes a cookie by setting an expiration date
//                three days in the past
//---------------------------------------------------------------
function ClearCookie(name) {
  var ThreeDays = 3 * 24 * 60 * 60 * 1000;
  var expDate = new Date();
  expDate.setTime (expDate.getTime() - ThreeDays);
  document.cookie = name + "=ImOutOfHere; expires="
                  + expDate.toGMTString();
}
//===============================================================
// Here are the object and the routines for our Favorites app
//===============================================================
//---------------------------------------------------------------
/* Here is our "favorite" object.
   Properties: fullName - The full descriptive name
               cook     - The code used for the cookie
               urlpath  - The full url (http://...) to the site
      Methods: Enabled - Returns true if the link's cookie is
                          turned on
               Checked  - Returns the word "CHECKED" if the
                          link's cookie is turned on
               WriteAsCheckBox - Sends text to the document in a
                                 checkbox control format
               WriteAsWebLink  - Sends text to the document in a
                                 <A HREF...> format
---------------------------------------------------------------*/
function favorite(fullName, cook, urlpath) {
  this.fullName = fullName;
  this.cook   = cook;
  this.urlpath  = urlpath;
  this.Enabled = Enabled;
  this.Checked = Checked;
  this.WriteAsCheckBox = WriteAsCheckBox;
  this.WriteAsWebLink = WriteAsWebLink;
}
//---------------------------------------------------------------
// Enabled - Checks to see if the cookie exists
// returns - true if the cookie exists
//           false if it doesn't
```

continues

Listing 20.2 Continued

```
//-----------------------------------------------------------------
function Enabled() {
  var result = false;
  var FaveCookie = GetCookie("Favorites");
  if (FaveCookie != null) {
    var searchFor = "<" + this.cook + ">";
    var startOfCookie = FaveCookie.indexOf(searchFor)
    if (startOfCookie != -1)
      result = true;
  }
  return result;
}
//-----------------------------------------------------------------
// Checked - Checks to see if the cookie exists (using Enabled)
// returns - 'CHECKED ' if the cookie exists
//           "" if it doesn't
//-----------------------------------------------------------------
function Checked () {
  if (this.Enabled())
    return "CHECKED ";
  return "";
}
//-----------------------------------------------------------------
// WriteAsCheckBox - The favorite may be either a regular URL or
//                   a section title.  If the urlpath is an empty
//                   string, then the favorite is a section title.
//                   The links will appear within a definition
//                   list, and are formatted appropriately.
//-----------------------------------------------------------------
function WriteAsCheckBox () {
  // Check to see if it's a title or regular link
  if (this.urlpath == "") {
    // It's a section title
    result = '<DT><STRONG>' + this.fullName + '</STRONG>';
  } else {
    // It's a regular link
    result = '<DD><INPUT TYPE="checkbox" NAME="'
      + this.cook + '" '
      + this.Checked()
      + 'onClick="SetFavoriteEnabled(this.name, this.checked);">'
      + this.fullName;
  }
  document.write(result);
}
//-----------------------------------------------------------------
// Global Variable:
// NextHeading - Sometimes we only want to print a heading if one
//               its favorites is turned on.  The NextHeading
//               variable helps us to do this. See WriteAsWebLink
//-----------------------------------------------------------------
var NextHeading = "";
//-----------------------------------------------------------------
// WriteAsWebLink - The favorite may be either a regular URL or
```

```
//                    a section title.  If the urlpath is an empty
//                    string, then the favorite is a section title.
//                    The links will appear within a definition
//                    list, and are formatted appropriately.
//---------------------------------------------------------------
function WriteAsWebLink() {
  var result = '';
  if (this.urlpath == "") {
    NextHeading = this.fullName;      // It's must be a Title
  } else {
    if (this.Enabled() || (GetCookie("ViewAll") == "T")) {
      if (NextHeading != "") {
        result = '<P><DT><STRONG>' + NextHeading+ '</STRONG>';
        NextHeading = "";
      }
      result = result + '<DD><A HREF="' + this.urlpath + '">'
             + this.fullName + '</A>';
    }
  }
  document.write(result);
}
//=================================================================
// Global Variables
//=================================================================
/*---------------------------------------------------------------
FaveList will be a list of all favorite objects, which are
then declared below.  favorites with an empty urlpath property
are section headings
---------------------------------------------------------------*/
var FaveList = new Array();
// Comics Section ------------------
FaveList[1] = new favorite("Comics", "", "");
FaveList[2] = new favorite("Dilbert", "cdilb",
  "http://www.unitedmedia.com/comics/dilbert/");
FaveList[3] = new favorite("Doonesbury", "cdoon",
  "http://www.uexpress.com/cgi-bin/ups/mainindex.cgi?code=db");
FaveList[4] = new favorite("Mr. Boffo", "cboff",
  "http://www.uexpress.com/cgi-bin/ups/new_mainindex.cgi?code=mb");
// General News Section ------------
FaveList[5] = new favorite("General News", "", "");
FaveList[6] = new favorite("CNN", "ncnn", "http://www.cnn.com/");
FaveList[7] = new favorite("NPR", "nnpr",
  "http://www.npr.org/news/");
FaveList[8] = new favorite("Boston Globe Quick Read", "nbos",
  "http://www.boston.com/globe/print/print.htm");
// Computer Industry Section --------
FaveList[9] = new favorite("Computer Industry", "", "");
FaveList[10] = new favorite("PC Week", "ipcw",
  "http://www.pcweek.com/");
FaveList[11] = new favorite("Infoworld", "iinfo",
  "http://www.infoworld.com/");
FaveList[12] = new favorite("CMP TechWire", "icmp",
  "http://www.techweb.com/wire/wire.html");
// Search Engines Section ----------
```

continues

Listing 20.2 Continued

```
FaveList[13] = new favorite("Search Engines", "", "");
FaveList[14] = new favorite("Yahoo!", "syah",
  "http://www.yahoo.com/");
FaveList[15] = new favorite("Alta Vista", "sav",
  "http://www.altavista.com/");
FaveList[16] = new favorite("excite", "sexc",
  "http://www.excite.com/");
// Misc. Section -------------------
FaveList[17] = new favorite("Misc.", "", "");
FaveList[18] = new favorite("Stock Quotes/Graphs", "mstock",
  "https://quotes.galt.com/cgi-bin/stockclnt");
FaveList[19] = new favorite("Today in History", "mtih",
  "http://www.thehistorynet.com/today/today.htm");
FaveList[20] = new favorite("Merriam-Webster's Word of the Day",
  "mwod", "http://www.m-w.com/cgi-bin/mwwod.pl");
FaveList[21] = new favorite("Quotes of the Day", "mquot",
  "http://www.starlingtech.com/quotes/qotd.html");
FaveList[22] = new favorite("Top 10 List", "mtop",
  "http://www.cbs.com/lateshow/lists/");
//=================================================================
// Page Writing Routines
//=================================================================
//---------------------------------------------------------------
// SendOptionsPage - Writes a page allowing the user to select
//                   her favorite preferences
//---------------------------------------------------------------
function SendOptionsPage() {
  document.write('<H1>Select Favorites</H1>');
  document.write('<FORM METHOD=POST>');
  // Here's the button for viewing the Favorites page
  document.write('<INPUT TYPE=button VALUE="Show Favorites" '
                 + 'onClick="'
                 +'ReloadPage()'
                 +';">');
  // The links will look nicer inside a definition list
  document.write('<DL>');
  for (var i = 1; i < FaveList.length; i++)
    FaveList[i].WriteAsCheckBox();  // Write each checkbox
  document.write('</DL><P>');
  ClearCookie("ViewAll");
  document.write('</FORM>');
}
//---------------------------------------------------------------
// LoadOptions - Sets the ShowOptions cookie, which makes the
//               option selection page appear when the page is
//               then reloaded.
//---------------------------------------------------------------
function LoadOptions() {
  SetCookieEZ("ShowOptions", "T");
  window.open(document.location.href, "_top", "");
}
//---------------------------------------------------------------
// ToggleView - Toggles ViewAll mode on and off.  When on, all
```

```
//              links will be displayed.  When off, only the
//              user's favorite selections will be displayed.
//---------------------------------------------------------------
function ToggleView() {
  if (GetCookie("ViewAll") == "T") {
    ClearCookie("ViewAll");
  } else {
    var fiveYears = 5 * 365 * 24 * 60 * 60 * 1000;
    var expDate = new Date();
    expDate.setTime (expDate.getTime() + fiveYears );
    SetCookie("ViewAll", "T", expDate, null, null, false);
  }
  window.open(document.location.href, "_top", "");
}
//---------------------------------------------------------------
// SendPersonalPage - Writes a page showing the categories and
//                    links which the user prefers. Only shows a
//                    heading if one of its favorites is enabled
//---------------------------------------------------------------
function SendPersonalPage() {
  if (GetCookie("ViewAll") != "T")
    document.write('<H1>Your Favorites:</H1>');
  else
    document.write('<H1>Links:</H1>');
  // Here are the buttons for viewing the options or
  // "View All" pages
  document.write('<FORM METHOD=POST>');
  if (GetCookie("ViewAll") == "T") {
    document.write('<INPUT TYPE=button VALUE="View Favorites" '
                   +'onClick="ToggleView();">')
  } else {
    document.write('<INPUT TYPE=button VALUE="View All" '
                   +'onClick="ToggleView();">');
  }
  document.write('<INPUT TYPE=button '
                 + 'VALUE="Select Personal Favorites" '
                 + 'onClick="LoadOptions();">');
  document.write('</FORM>');
  // The links will look nicer inside a definition list
  document.write('<DL>');
  for (var i = 1; i < FaveList.length; i++)
    FaveList[i].WriteAsWebLink();     // Write each link
  document.write('</DL><P>');
}
//================================================================
// Helper Functions
//================================================================
//---------------------------------------------------------------
// isEnabled - Returns True if the favorite identified by the
//             name parameter is enabled.
//---------------------------------------------------------------
function isEnabled(name) {
  var result = false;
  var FaveCookie = GetCookie("Favorites");
```


continues

Listing 20.2 Continued

```
    if (FaveCookie != null) {
      var searchFor = "<" + name + ">";
      var startOfCookie = FaveCookie.indexOf(searchFor)
      if (startOfCookie != -1)
        result = true;
    }
    return result;
  }
  //------------------------------------------------------------
  // AddFavorite- Enables the favorite identified by the name
  //              parameter.
  //------------------------------------------------------------
  function AddFavorite(name) {
    if (!isEnabled(name)) {
      var fiveYears = 5 * 365 * 24 * 60 * 60 * 1000;
      var expDate = new Date();
      expDate.setTime (expDate.getTime() + fiveYears );
      SetCookie("Favorites", GetCookie("Favorites")
                + "<" + name + ">", expDate, null, null, false);
    }
  }
  //------------------------------------------------------------
  // ClearFavorite- Disables the favorite identified by the name
  //                parameter.
  //------------------------------------------------------------
  function ClearFavorite(name) {
    if (isEnabled(name)) {
      var FaveCookie = GetCookie("Favorites");
      var searchFor = "<" + name + ">";
      var startOfCookie = FaveCookie.indexOf(searchFor);
      var NewFaves = FaveCookie.substring(0, startOfCookie)
        + FaveCookie.substring(startOfCookie+searchFor.length,
                                             FaveCookie.length);
      var fiveYears = 5 * 365 * 24 * 60 * 60 * 1000;
      var expDate = new Date();
      expDate.setTime (expDate.getTime() + fiveYears );
      SetCookie("Favorites", NewFaves, expDate, null, null, false);
    }
  }
  //------------------------------------------------------------
  // SetFavoriteEnabled - Turns the favorite identified by the name
  //                      parameter on (SetOn=true) or off
  //                      (SetOn=false).
  //------------------------------------------------------------
  function SetFavoriteEnabled(name, SetOn) {
    if (SetOn)
      AddFavorite(name);
    else
      ClearFavorite(name);
  }
  //------------------------------------------------------------
  // ReloadPage - Reloads the page
  //------------------------------------------------------------
  function ReloadPage() {
```

```
  window.open(document.location.href, "_top", "");
}

// End Commented Script -->
</SCRIPT>
</HEAD>
<BODY>
<SCRIPT LANGUAGE="JavaScript">
<!-- Comment out script from browsers that don't know JavaScript
/*-----------------------------------------------------------------
Here's where we select the page to send.  Normally we send the
personalized favorites page (by calling SendPersonalPage). However,
If the cookie ShowOptions is set, we'll send the options selection
page instead (by calling SendOptionsPage).
----------------------------------------------------------------*/
  if (GetCookie("ShowOptions") == "T") {
    ClearCookie("ShowOptions");
    SendOptionsPage();
  } else {
    SendPersonalPage();
  }
// End Commented Script -->
</SCRIPT>
<CENTER>
This is a very dull page unless you have a JavaScript
enabled browser.<BR>
</CENTER>
</BODY>
</HTML>
```

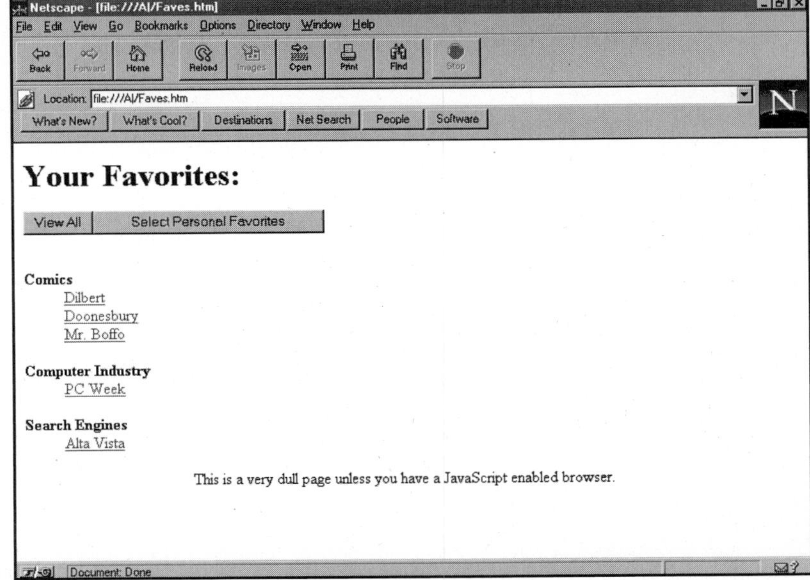

FIG. 20.1 The Favorites page.

Before JavaScript, a task like this would have been handled at the server. Each hit would have involved having the server run some type of script or program to read the user's cookies and generate his page on-the-fly. With JavaScript, all this processing takes place on the client's browser. The server just downloads the static page, and it might not even do that, because the page might come from the client's local cache. When the page is loaded, all the links, selected or not, are sent. The client, with the help of cookies and JavaScript, decides which ones to show the user.

This program makes use of three different cookies. The "Favorites" cookie contains a unique code for each favored link. The "ViewAll" cookie toggles between showing the user's favorites and all possible links. The program may also display either of two pages: one for displaying the selected links, and the other for changing the configuration and options. When the "ShowOptions" cookie is set, the Options selection page is displayed. Otherwise, the regular page is shown. Figure 20.2 shows what the configuration page looks like.

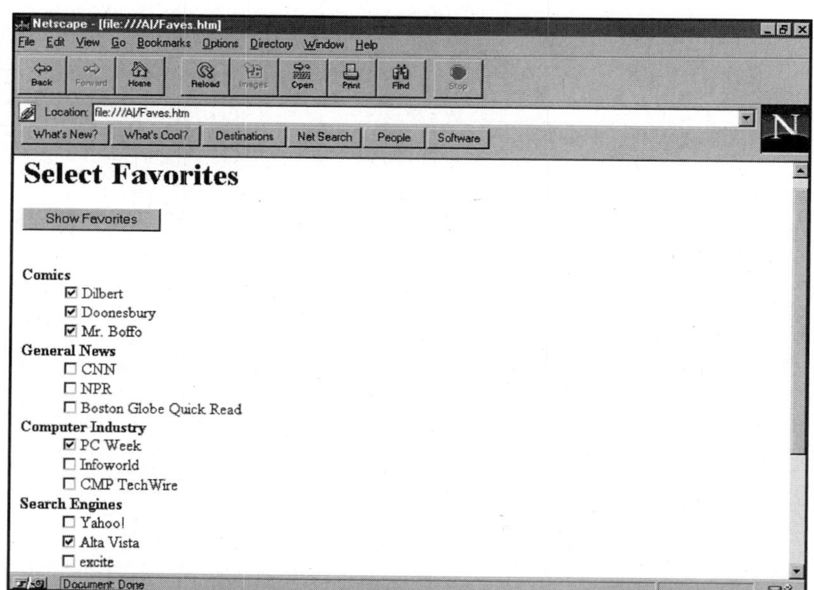

FIG. 20.2
The Favorites configuration page.

The program creates objects called "Favorites." Each favorite is, in essence, a web link to another page. The favorite contains information on the link's URL, a user-friendly page description, and the code that identifies it in the "Favorites" cookie string. The favorite also knows how to print itself on a web page as a regular link for the Favorites page or in a check box format for the Options page.

Where Are Cookies Going?

As mentioned earlier, cookies were designed and first implemented by Netscape. However, the Internet Engineering Task Force (IETF) has a committee—the Hypertext Transfer Protocol

(HTTP) Working Group—whose charter is to examine, document, and suggest ways to improve HTTP.

ON THE WEB

You can find a link to the HTTP Working Group's latest Internet Draft called "Proposed HTTP State Management Mechanism" at **http://www.ietf.cnri.reston.va.us/html.charters/http-charter.html**.

Although the draft specification resembles Netscape cookies in theory, if not in syntax, it does have a few notable differences. It doesn't encourage having cookies around much longer than the browser session. If the new specification is accepted, cookies are given a `Max-Age` lifetime rather than an `expires date`. All cookies expire when their time comes; but in all cases, they go away when the browser shuts down.

Reading the specification provides insight into the complexities that surround the inner workings of cookies; it is well worth the read, regardless of whether the specification is approved.

Which Servers and Browsers Support Cookies?

Although other ways of web programming, such as CGI and special server interfaces, require that the server as well as the browser understand cookies, only the browser matters to JavaScript. This means that you can generally use JavaScript with impunity as long as you know your clients are JavaScript-capable.

Many JavaScript web applications probably mix the language with other development tools, however, which would require the server to understand cookies. Because new servers and browsers are coming to the Net so quickly, it is impossible for a printed book to keep up with the latest software.

ON THE WEB

You can find cookie information at the following locations on the Web:

Netscape cookie spec page (referenced previously in this chapter): **http://www.netscape.com/newsref/std/cookie_spec.html**

Browsers supporting cookies: **http://www.research.digital.com/nsl/formtest/stats-by-test/NetscapeCookie.html**

Cookie Central: **http://www.cookiecentral.com/**

Andy's cookie pages: **http://www.illuminatus.com/cookie**

Malcolm's Guide to Persistent Cookies: **http://www.emf.net/~mal/cookiesinfo.html**

Robert Brooks' Cookie Taste Test: **http://www.geocities.com/SoHo/4535/cookie.html**

Article about tracking cookies at the HotWired web site: **http://www.arctic.org/~dgaudet/cookies**

Netscape World cookie article: **http://www.netscapeworld.com/netscapeworld/nw-07-1996/nw-07-cookies.html**

Other State Maintenance Options

As mentioned earlier in this chapter, there are a few drawbacks to using cookies. Perhaps you would rather just avoid the controversy and find some other way to maintain state from one page to the next. There are two ways of doing this. Which one you use depends on how you, the developer, will have the users get from one page to the next.

The main limitation of these methods is that they work only from one page to the page immediately following. If state information is to be maintained throughout a series of pages, these mechanisms must be used on every single page.

Query String

If most of your navigation is done through hypertext links embedded in your pages, you need to add extra information to the end of the URL. This is usually done by adding a question mark (?) to the end of your web page URL, followed by information in an encoded form, such as that returned by the `escape` method. To separate one piece of information from another, place an ampersand (&) between them.

If you want to send the parameters `color=blue` and `size=extra large` along with your link, for example, you use a link such as this:

```
<a href="/mypage.html?color=blue&size=extra+large">XL Blue</A>
```

This format is the same as the format used when submitting forms using the `get` method. A succeeding page can read this information by using the `search` property of the `location` object. This property is called `search` because many Internet search engines use this part of the URL to store their search criteria.

The following is an example of how to use the `location.search` property. In this example, the name of the current page is sent as a parameter in a link to another page. The other page reads this property through the `search` property and states where the browser came from.

To start things off, Listing 20.3 shows the first page that contains the link.

Listing 20.3 Where1.htm.

```
<html>
<head>
<title>Where Was I? - Page 1</title>
</head>
<body>
<h1>Where Was I? - Demonstration</h1>
This page sets information which will allow the page it is linked
to figure out where it came from. It uses values embedded in the link
URL in order to do this
<p>
We'll assume that any URL parameters are separated by an ampersand.
<p>
Notice that there doesn't need to be any JavaScript code in this page.
<p>
```

```
And now,
<a href="where2.htm?camefrom=Where1.htm
    &more=needless+stuff">Let's go to Page 2.</a>
</body>
</html>
```

Listing 20.4 shows the second page, which demonstrates how to use `location.search` to find where the browser came from.

Listing 20.4. Where2.htm.

```
<html>
<title>Where Was I? - Page 2</title>
<head>
</head>
<body>
<h1>Where Was I? - Demontration</h1>
This page reads information which allows it to figure out where it came from.
<P>
<script language="javascript">
<!-- begin script
// WhereWasI
// Reads the search string to figure out what link brought it here
function WhereWasI() {
  // Start by storing our search string in a handy place (so we don't
  // need to type as much)
  var handyString = window.location.search;
  // Find the beginning of our special URL variable
  var startOfSource = handyString.indexOf("camefrom=");
  // If it's there, find the end of it
  if (startOfSource != -1) {
    var endOfSource = handyString.indexOf("&", startOfSource+9);
    var result = handyString.substring(startOfSource+9, endOfSource);
  }
  else
    var result = "Source Unknown"; // Could not find the "camefrom" string
  return result;
}
if (WhereWasI() != "Source Unknown")
  document.write ("You just came from <b>" + WhereWasI() + "</b>.<br>")
else
  document.write ("Unfortunately, we don't know where you came from.<br>");
// end script -->
</script>
</body>
</html>
```

Hidden Form Variables

The method used in the preceding section works fine as long as the user navigates from one page to another using links. To do the same thing with forms, you can use hidden form variables rather than the `location.search` parameter.

Hidden form variables have the following format:

```
<input type="hidden" name="HiddenFieldName" value="HiddenFieldValue">
```

You can specify whatever you like for *HiddenFieldName* and *HiddenFieldValue*. The `value` parameter is optional.

Using hidden fields does not necessarily require the use of JavaScript code. They are defined instead in the `INPUT` tag of normal HTML documents. You do, however, need to have some sort of server-based script, such as a CGI program or a server API program, to read the values of these hidden fields.

The form containing the hidden variables is submitted to a server script, which spills out everything it knows about your browser on to a single web page, including the form's field information. You find your hidden field information listed at the bottom of the page, where it looks like this:

```
Form Post Data:
Raw Form Data String: camefrom=where3.htm&otherStuff=I+don%27t+care
camefrom=where3.htm
otherStuff=I don't care
```

CHAPTER 21

Using JavaScript to Control Web Browser Objects

by Jim O'Donnell

In this chapter

What Are Web Browser Objects?

In Chapter 16, "The Web Browser Object Model," you learned about the Web Browser Object Model, which dictates how your JavaScripts can access and manipulate aspects of the Web browser and the HTML document that it is viewing. The Web browser, whether Netscape Navigator or Microsoft Internet Explorer, exposes a collection of objects—these objects control just how much you can do with your scripts. (As you will see in a few chapters, Microsoft's Internet Explorer 4 and Web browser and its support for their Dynamic HTML exposes just about everything as an object for your scripting.)

▶ **See** "Internet Explorer 4 Document Object Model," **p. 680**

In addition to the objects exposed that are part of the Web browser (such as the `Window` object) or part of the current HTML document itself (such as the `Document` or `Images` objects), a number of other Web browser objects can occur within a Web page. These are objects included in the HTML document via the `<APPLET>`, `<EMBED>`, or `<OBJECT>` tags.

In general, the following types of content can be included in your Web pages by using one of these three tags. In many cases, although not all, the addition of this content provides additional objects that you can access and change with JavaScript.

- *Java applets.* Java applets are normally included in a Web page using the `<APPLET>` tag, although Internet Explorer 4 also supports the use of the `<OBJECT>` tag to include them. Both Netscape and Microsoft have provided ways to access Java objects, properties, and methods through JavaScript, and vice versa, as long as the Java applet is set up to do so. Netscape does this by using their LiveConnect technology, discussed later in the "Netscape's LiveConnect" section. Microsoft provides the same functionality through their own ActiveX technology and Java Virtual Machine.
- *Plug-in content.* Normally, content that is in a form that is not natively supported by the Web browser is included in an HTML document by using the `<EMBED>` tag. At the client browser, when this tag is encountered, the appropriate plug-in and/or ActiveX Control is loaded. As with Java applets, if the plug-in is set up to do so, it can expose its properties and methods that can be accessed through JavaScript. Later in this chapter, you will see examples of how this is done with the Envoy Viewer from Tumbleweed Software and with Macromedia's Shockwave Flash Viewer.

  Again, both Netscape and Microsoft provide this same functionality, but use two very different methods. Netscape's LiveConnect technology allows JavaScript to access plug-in properties and methods through Java; Microsoft, which supports many of Netscape Navigator's plug-ins, allows scripts (JScript and VBScript) to interface with the plug-ins directly.
- *ActiveX Controls.* ActiveX Controls are a technology developed by Microsoft; Microsoft's Internet Explorer is the only Web browser that fully supports them, although Netscape Navigator also supports them through Ncompass Lab's ScriptActive plug-in (**http://www.ncompasslabs.com**). As will be shown in the "Interfacing with ActiveX Controls

with JScript" section, later in this chapter, it is very easy to use scripts to control ActiveX Controls. (As will be shown in Chapter 22, "Scripting with Microsoft VBScript and JScript," this can be done just as easily with Microsoft's VBScript language.)

▶ **See** "Interacting with Objects with VBScript," **p. 614**

- *VRML*. The VRML 2.0 standard also supports scripting in general, and JavaScript in particular, through the use of its Script node. The way you include JavaScripts with a VRML source file is a lot different than in HTML, and is beyond the scope of this chapter. To find out more information, see Chapter 14, "Creating VRML Objects and Worlds," and the VRML Repository Web site at **http://www.sdsc.edu/vrml/**.

Referencing Web Browser Objects

After the objects have been included in your HTML documents, you need only know how to reference them to access them from your JavaScripts. Objects supplied by Java applets, plug-in content, and ActiveX Controls fit into the same Web browser object hierarchy discussed in Chapter 16. To use them, you only must know where they fit.

▶ **See** "Web Browser Object Hierarchy and Scoping," **p. 438**

Many ways enable you to access these Web browser objects, depending on how they are included in your HTML documents. Objects exposed through the `<APPLET>` tag can be accessed through the `applet` object. Plug-ins called by the `<EMBED>` tag can be accessed through either the `embed` or `plugin` object. Both these types of objects are included in the Web Browser Object Model hierarchy under the document object. Objects that are included through the use of the `<OBJECT>` tag are directly accessible by name through the `window` object, and because of the scoping rules of JavaScript, if you are controlling and object in the current window, the opening `window.` can be omitted.

▶ **See** "The `Window` Object," **p. 439**

Java Applets Included Using the *<APPLET>* Tag

As mentioned, Java applets placed in your HTML documents via the <APPLET> tag can be referenced by using the `applet` object. Depending on how you include the <APPLET>, however, the object can be referenced a number of ways. Consider Listing 21.1, which shows a simple Web page with a controllable Java applet.

Listing 21.1 Applet1.htm Controlling an applet using its name.

```
<HTML>
<HEAD>
<TITLE>JavaScript Control of a Java Applet I</TITLE>
</HEAD>
<BODY BGCOLOR=#FFFFFF>
<H1> JavaScript Control of a Java Applet I</H1>
<HR>
```

continues

Listing 21.1 Continued

```
<APPLET NAME="Counter" CODE="Counter.class" WIDTH=200 HEIGHT=100></APPLET>
<FORM>
<INPUT TYPE=BUTTON VALUE="Add 1" NAME="AddButton"
       onClick="document.Counter.increment()">
<INPUT TYPE=BUTTON VALUE="Subtract 1" NAME="SubtractButton"
       onClick="document.Counter.decrement()">
</FORM>
</BODY>
</HTML>
```

As shown in Listing 21.1, the Java applet's `increment()` and `decrement()` methods are called through the JavaScript attached to the `onClick` event of the two HTML forms buttons. The applet's methods are accessed by referring to the Java `applet` object, which is included in the object hierarchy under the `document` object.

What if the applet weren't named? You can still access Java applets in your HTML documents, even if you don't specify a NAME attribute in the <APPLET> tag. This is done using JavaScripts object arrays, in this case the applets array associated with the applet object. Listing 21.2 shows the same example as Listing 21.1, demonstrating how to reference the Java applet without using a name.

▶ **See** "JavaScript Object Arrays," **p. 446**

Listing 21.2 Applet2.htm Controlling an applet using its name.

```
<HTML>
<HEAD>
<TITLE>JavaScript Control of a Java Applet I</TITLE>
</HEAD>
<BODY BGCOLOR=#FFFFFF>
<H1> JavaScript Control of a Java Applet I</H1>
<HR>
<APPLET CODE="Counter.class" WIDTH=200 HEIGHT=100></APPLET>
<FORM>
<INPUT TYPE=BUTTON VALUE="Add 1" NAME="AddButton"
       onClick="document.applets[0].increment()">
<INPUT TYPE=BUTTON VALUE="Subtract 1" NAME="SubtractButton"
       onClick="document.applets[0].decrement()">
</FORM>
</BODY>
</HTML>
```

Because the Java applet is the only one in the HTML document, it is referenced through the first position in the `applets` object array as `applets[0]`.

Plug-In Content from the <EMBED> Tag

Accessing plug-in objects, properties, and methods included in an HTML document through the <EMBED> tag is done in the same manner as with Java applets, discussed in the preceding section. Consider, for example, the following tag included as the first embed in your HTML document:

```
<EMBED NAME="MyPlug" SRC="MyMovie.dcr" WIDTH=300 HEIGHT=200></EMBED>
```

If the plug-in that was called to support this content type exposed object and methods to the Web browser and to JavaScript, you could access them in any three ways. If the plug-in had an `initialize()` method you wanted to call, for example, you could do so by using one of the following:

- document.MyPlug.initialize()
- document.embeds[0].initialize()
- document.embeds["MyPlug"].initialize()

The last syntax shown is known as an associative array, and was discussed in Chapter 16. That chapter also discussed when each of the syntaxes in this list is most appropriate.

Accessing <OBJECT> Tag Included Objects

By comparison with the <APPLET> and <EMBED> tag, objects included with the <OBJECT> tag are a bit easier to reference with JavaScript. That is because these objects are attached to the window object, and so can be referenced directly. If, for example, an object were included in your HTML document using the following:

```
<OBJECT NAME="MyControl"...></OBJECT>
```

And if it had an `initialize()` method, for example, it could be called from JavaScript by using just `MyControl.initialize()`.

Netscape's LiveConnect

Since its introduction, Netscape has introduced many new technologies into its Navigator Web browser. In addition to HTML extensions and multimedia capabilities such as LiveAudio, LiveVideo, and Live3D, there have been three technologies in particular that were introduced, or first became widely used with Netscape Navigator. These are Web browser scripting with JavaScript, Java applet support, and Web browser plug-ins.

Until the release of Netscape Navigator 3, these technologies suffered from the handicap of being completely separate applications within a Web browser. JavaScripts, Java applets, and Navigator plug-ins ran within Navigator on their own, without the capability to interact. However, with Navigator 3 and now 4, Netscape has introduced its LiveConnect technology enabling its three systems to interact.

Figure 21.1 shows how LiveConnect works within the Netscape Navigator runtime environment. JavaScripts can call Java methods and plug-in functions. Java applets can call both JavaScript and plug-in functions. Plug-ins can call Java methods and, through Java, call JavaScript functions. The objects and properties of each LiveConnect-compatible Java applet and plug-in are available to be manipulated through JavaScripts, applets, and other plug-ins.

FIG. 21.1
Netscape's LiveConnect technology enables JavaScript, Java, and plug-ins to work together within Netscape Navigator.

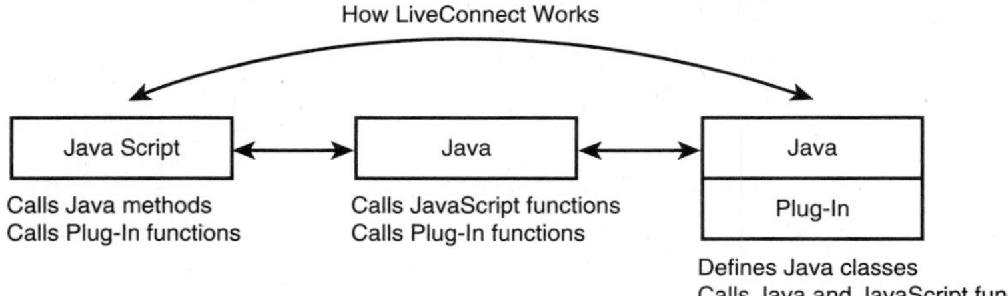

Enabling LiveConnect

By default in Netscape Navigator, Java and JavaScript are enabled—whenever these languages are enabled, LiveConnect is enabled as well. To confirm that they are enabled in your copy of Navigator, choose Edit, Preferences. Then, in the Categories list, select Advanced, make sure that the Enable Java and Enable JavaScript boxes are checked, and then click OK.

What about Internet Explorer?

As you might expect, Microsoft Internet Explorer does not explicitly support the LiveConnect technology. However, this doesn't mean that Internet Explorer authors and users are left out in the cold. Far from it.

The foundation of Microsoft's Web offerings is their ActiveX Technology. These are a series of different Web capabilities that enable authors to make use of scripting, ActiveX Controls, and Navigator plug-ins, and view and edit legacy documents (such as Microsoft Word documents) right in their Internet Explorer window. The ActiveX Technologies were designed to allow the different components running within Internet Explorer to communicate with one another.

Although Internet Explorer does not support LiveConnect *per se*, their ActiveX Technology achieves the same thing. Later in this chapter, you will find out how to control ActiveX Controls by using JScript, Microsoft's implementation of the JavaScript language, in Internet Explorer.

The Java Console

Netscape Navigator has a Java Console that can be displayed by choosing Window, Java Console. Messages sent using `java.lang.System.out` or `java.lang.System.err` appear in this console.

Now, because of the communication possible between JavaScript and Java using LiveConnect, messages can be sent to the Java Console from JavaScript as well. To write a message to the

Java Console from JavaScript, use the `println` method of `java.lang.System.out` or `java.lang.System.err` as in the following:

```
java.lang.System.err.println("JavaScript checkpoint #1")
```

You can use the Java Console to help debug JavaScript applications. Output messages and intermediate values to the Java Console and watch it while browsing your pages. If you create JavaScripts to validate HTML forms, for instance, while you are debugging the scripts you can print out intermediate form data to the console.

The Netscape Packages

Netscape Navigator includes several Java packages used to enable LiveConnect communication. The first, `netscape`, is used to enable communication back and forth between JavaScript and Java applets. Additionally, replacement `java` and `sun` packages are provided. These feature security improvements for LiveConnect. The following `netscape` packages are included:

- `netscape.javascript` This package implements the `JSObject` and `JSException` classes, which enable Java applets to access JavaScript properties and throw exceptions when JavaScript returns an error.
- `netscape.plug-in` This package implements the `Plugin` class, which enables cross communication between JavaScript and plug-ins. Plug-ins must be compiled with this class to make them LiveConnect compatible.
- `netscape.applet` and `netscape.net` These are direct replacements for the `sun.applet` and `sun.net` classes provided in Sun's Java Development Kit.

▶ **See** "Leveraging Java Classes and Packages," **p. 1090**

JavaScript to Java Communication

With LiveConnect, JavaScript can make calls directly to Java methods. As already shown in the "Java Console" section, this is how JavaScript can output messages to the Java Console. To JavaScript all Java packages and classes are properties of the `Packages` object. Therefore the full name of a Java object in JavaScript would be something like:

`Packages.`*`packageName.className.methodName`*`.`

The `Packages` name is optional for the `java`, `sun`, and `netscape` packages.

Java applets can be controlled through JavaScript without knowing too much about the internal construction of the applet, as long as a few conditions are true. The first step is to attach a `NAME` attribute to the `<APPLET>` tag when including the Java applet in your HTML document. Then all public variables, methods, and properties of the applet are available for access to JavaScript.

Any time you want to pass information into a Java applet, you might want to consider using JavaScript to do this. If you have a Java applet that implements a calendar, for example, you could create an HTML form with attached JavaScripts to enable the user to select what month should be displayed. By using JavaScript in this way, you avoid the need to give the applet itself the capability to interact with the user. Netscape shows a simple demo of controlling a Java applet by using JavaScript at **http://home.netscape.com/comprod/products/navigator/version_3.0/building_blocks/examples/js_example/js-java-demo.html**.

The Java applet is included in the HTML document by using the following:

```
<APPLET NAME="NervousApplet" CODE="NervousText.class" WIDTH=400 HEIGHT=50>
<PARAM NAME=text VALUE="Enter your text here.">
</APPLET>
```

The name `NervousApplet` attached to the applet is how the Java applet is controlled. When the Click here to change text button is pressed, the public Java method `changeText` is called through the following:

```
<INPUT TYPE=BUTTON WIDTH=200 VALUE="Click here to change text."
    onclick="document.NervousApplet.changeText(form.InputText.value)">
```

For this to work, therefore, the `changeText` Java method needs to be defined as a public method—it then takes the text supplied and uses the applet to display it (see Figure 21.2). The `changeText` method is defined as a public method as shown here:

```
// This is the method that will be called by JavaScript
public void changeText(String text){
   stop();
   s = text;
   separated = new char [s.length()];
   s.getChars(0, s.length(), separated, 0);
   start();
}
```

NOTE As mentioned a little earlier in this chapter, Internet Explorer achieves the same JavaScript to Java communication by using Microsoft's own ActiveX Technology rather than Netscape's LiveConnect. Figure 21.3 demonstrates this, showing the same Netscape demo page shown in Figure 21.2 displayed instead in Internet Explorer.

Java to JavaScript Communication

The first step in enabling your Java applets to access JavaScript properties is to import the `javascript` package into your Java applet, as shown here:

```
import netscape.javascript.*
```

This enables the Java applet to access JavaScript properties through the `JSObject` class. However, the author of the HTML document must still allow access to his JavaScript by including the `MAYSCRIPT` attribute in the `<APPLET>` tag used to include the Java applet. If the `NervousApplet` used in the last example needed to access JavaScript, for example, the `<APPLET>` tag would look like this:

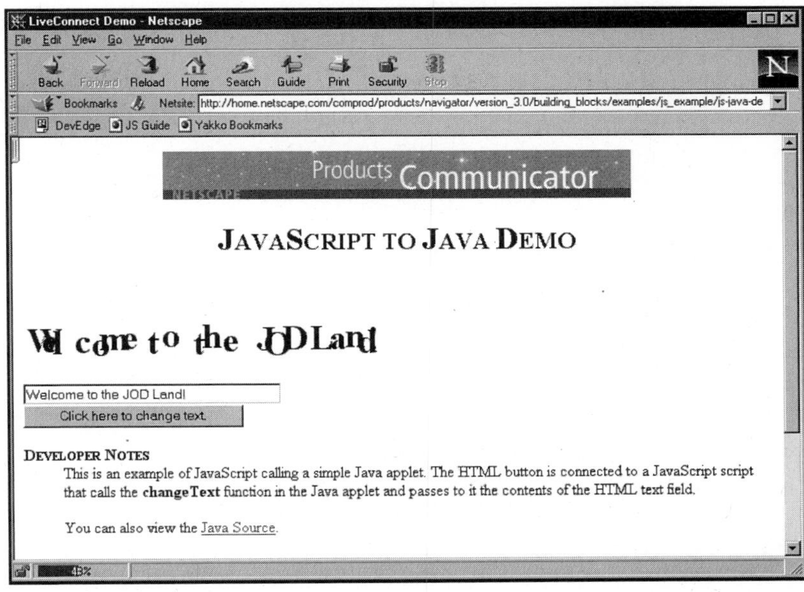

FIG. 21.2 JavaScript is LiveConnect's link between the HTML form user input and Java applets.

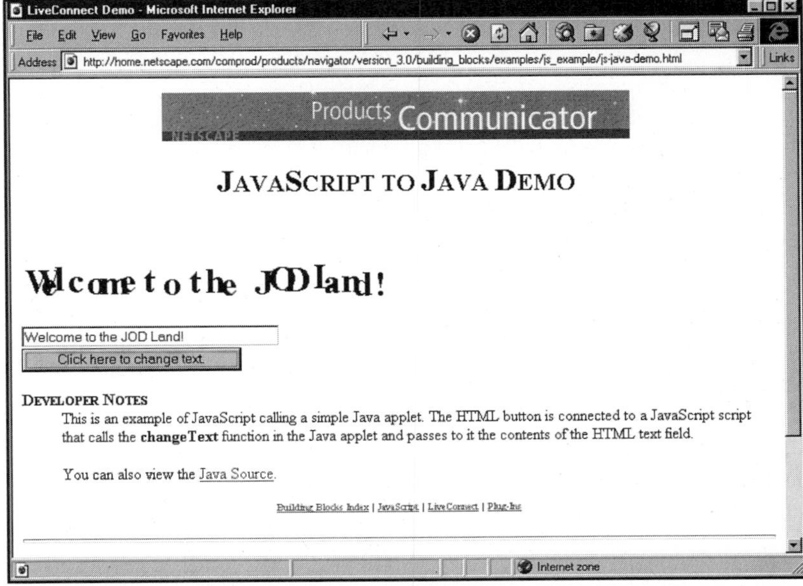

FIG. 21.3 Microsoft accomplishes the same goal of JavaScript to Java communication with different means—but the same HTML and JavaScript will work with both browsers.

```
<APPLET NAME="NervousApplet" CODE="NervousText.class" MAYSCRIPT
        WIDTH=400 HEIGHT=50>
<PARAM NAME=text VALUE="Enter your text here.">
</APPLET>
```

If these two conditions have been satisfied, accessing JavaScript objects or methods is a two-step process, as follows:

1. Get a handle for the Navigator window containing the JavaScript objects or methods you want to access. This can be done using the `getWindow()` method on the `netscape.javascript.JSObject` package:

```
// winhan is a variable of type JSObject
public void initialize() {
   winhan = JSObject.getWindow(this);
}
```

2. To access JavaScript objects and properties, do the following:

   Use the `getMember()` method in the `netscape.javascript.JSObject` package to access each JavaScript object in turn. To access the JavaScript object `document.testForm`, using the window handle found in step 1, you could do the following:

```
public void accessForm(JSObject winhan) {
   JSObject myDoc = (JSObject) winhan.getMember("document");
   JSObject myForm = (JSObject) myDoc.getmember("testForm");
     }
```

   To call a JavaScript method:

   Use either the `call()` or `eval()` methods of the `netscape.javascript.JSObject` class. The syntax for the two commands (using the window handle found in step 1) is as follows:

```
winhan.call("methodName",arguments)
winhan.eval("expression")
```

   In the former, *`methodName`* is the name of the JavaScript method, and *`arguments`* is an array of arguments to be passed on to the JavaScript method. In the latter, *`expression`* is a JavaScript expression that, when evaluated, has a value that is the name of a JavaScript method.

Similar to JavaScript to Java communication, Java to JavaScript communication can be useful when you don't want to re-create an input or output interface within your Java applet. You might create a Java applet that makes use of Java's network and Internet capabilities to access data from a database server on some other machine. Rather than then using Java to display this data, you can access JavaScript objects to display it within a conventional HTML form.

JavaScript and Plug-Ins

JavaScript can be used with the client to determine what plug-ins the client has installed and what MIME types are supported. This is done through two of the `navigator` object's properties: `plugins` and `mimeTypes`. JavaScripts can also be used to call plug-in functions.

NOTE Internet Explorer also supports the `navigator` object, so the techniques in this section should work for both Netscape Navigator and Microsoft Internet Explorer. Be aware, however, that Internet Explorer does not support all Navigator plug-ins.

By determining at the client whether a particular plug-in is installed or MIME type supported, you can write scripts that generate content dynamically. If a particular plug-in is installed, the appropriate plug-in data can be displayed; otherwise, some alternative image or text can be shown.

If you have developed an inline VRML scene to embed in a Web page, for instance, you might want to know whether the user has a plug-in installed that supports VRML. Then, a VRML world or a representative GIF image could be displayed, as appropriate, like the following:

```
<SCRIPT LANGUAGE="JavaScript">
<!-- Hide script from incompatible browsers -->
var isVrmlSupported,VrmlPlugin
isVrmlSupported = navigator.mimeTypes["x-world/x-vrml"]
if (isVrmlSupported)
   document.writeln("<EMBED SRC='world.wrl' HEIGHT=200 WIDTH=400>")
else
   document.writeln("<IMG SRC='world.gif' HEIGHT=200 WIDTH=400>")
//   Hide script from incompatible browsers -->
</SCRIPT>
```

NOTE As the next section shows, the <OBJECT> tag is the preferred method of including plug-in content for Internet Explorer; Navigator uses <EMBED>. Internet Explorer does, however, support the <EMBED> tag.

Including and Referencing Plug-In Objects

The first step in using plug-ins within a Web page is to include them in the first place. The recommended way to do this with Internet Explorer is to use the <OBJECT> tag; however, Internet Explorer and Navigator support the <EMBED> tag as well. If you want to include plug-in content in a Web page that will work in the preferred way with both browsers, use something like the following, which shows an example using the Flash Player by Macromedia:

```
<OBJECT CLASSID="clsid:D27CDB6E-AE6D-11cf-96B8-444553540000"
   ID="objID" WIDTH=100 HEIGHT=100
CODEBASE="http://active.macromedia.com/flash2/cabs/
➥swflash.cab#version=2,0,0,11">
<PARAM NAME="Movie" VALUE="controls.swf">
<EMBED NAME="objID" MAYSCRIPT SRC="controls.swf"
   WIDTH=100 HEIGHT=100
PLUGINSPAGE="http://www.macromedia.com/shockwave/download/
➥index.cgi?P1_Prod_Version=ShockwaveFlash">
</OBJECT>
```

NOTE Note that the preceding example actually is used to either call the Macromedia Flash ActiveX Control or plug-in, depending on whether Internet Explorer or Navigator is used. You can use the same technique, however, to include plug-in content for each browser. You can read more about accessing and manipulating ActiveX Controls later in this chapter.

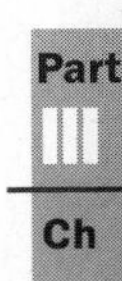

This HTML code segment consists of the following tags:

- The `<OBJECT>` tag is used to include the plug-in content meant for Internet Explorer; its `ID` attribute gives it the name that will be used to script it with.
- The `<PARAM>` tag (there can be as many of them as necessary) includes a `NAME` and `VALUE` attribute used to configure the plug-in.
- The `<EMBED>` tag is included within the `<OBJECT>` container tag; this provides alternate content for browsers that do not understand the `<OBJECT>` tag. In this case, the plug-in content would be included either via the `<OBJECT>` or `<EMBED>` tag, but not both. The `NAME` attribute performs the same function as the `ID` attribute of the `<OBJECT>` tag. In this case, the `SRC` attribute.

Plug-ins included with the `<OBJECT>` and `<EMBED>` commands are also referenced differently by Internet Explorer and Navigator. In Internet Explorer, plug-in objects are members of the window object; in Navigator, they are members of window.document. You can create code compatible with both browsers by using the following:

```
var ieFlag = navigator.appName.indexOf("Microsoft") != -1;
var objRef = ieFlag ? window.objID : window.document.objID;
```

The first line determines whether the browser is Internet Explorer, and then defines `objRef` so that it can be used to access the plug-in in either browser.

Determining Which Plug-Ins Are Installed

The `navigator.plugins` object has the following properties:

- `description` A description of the plug-in, supplied by the plug-in itself
- `filename` The file name on disk in which the plug-in resides
- `length` The number of elements in the `navigator.plugins` array
- `name` The plug-in's name

Listing 21.3 shows an example of a JavaScript that uses the `navigator.plugins` object to display the names of the installed plug-ins right on the Web page. You can place this JavaScript at the bottom of any Web page to display this information (see Figure 21.4).

Listing 21.3 PlugIn.htm JavaScript to detect locally installed plug-ins.

```
<HTML>
<HEAD>
<TITLE>JavaScript Plug-Ins Check</TITLE>
</HEAD>
<BODY BGCOLOR="#FFFFFF">
<H1>JavaScript Plug-Ins Check</H1>
<SCRIPT LANGUAGE="JavaScript">
<!-- Hide script from incompatible browsers -->
var i,n
n = navigator.plugins.length
document.writeln("<HR>")
document.writeln("This Web browser has " + n + " plug-ins installed:<P>")
for (i=0;i<n;i++)
```

```
   document.writeln(navigator.plugins[i].name + "<BR>")
document.writeln("<HR>")
//   Hide script from incompatible browsers -->
</SCRIPT>
</BODY>
</HTML>
```

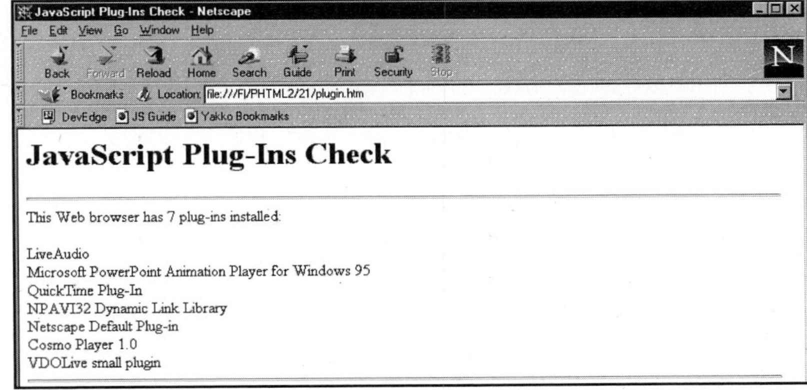

FIG. 21.4 The `navigator.plugins` object enables you to use JavaScript to determine whether a plug-in is installed.

Client-Supported MIME Types

The `navigator.mimeTypes` object is very similar to the `navigator.plugins` object, and can be used to determine supported MIME types at the client. It has the following properties:

- `description` A description of the MIME type
- `enabledPlugin` A reference to the particular `navigator.plugins` object that handles this MIME type
- `length` The number of elements in the `navigator.mimeTypes` array
- `suffixes` A string listing the filename extensions, separated by commas, for this MIME type
- `type` The MIME type name (for example, `x-world/x-vrml`)

Listing 21.4 shows an HTML document that contains a JavaScript that displays all the client-supported MIME types in an HTML table. Along with the MIME type, the supported file extensions are shown, as well as the name of the associated plug-in, if any (see Figure 21.5).

Listing 21.4 MimeType.htm JavaScript to detect locally supported MIME types.

```
<HTML>
<HEAD>
<TITLE>JavaScript MIME Types Check</TITLE>
```

continues

Listing 21.4 Continued

```
</HEAD>
<BODY BGCOLOR="#FFFFFF">
<H1>JavaScript MIME Types Check</H1>
<SCRIPT LANGUAGE="JavaScript">
<!-- Hide script from incompatible browsers -->
var i,n
n = navigator.mimeTypes.length
document.writeln("<HR>")
document.writeln("The following MIME types are recognized:<P>")
document.writeln("<TABLE BORDER WIDTH=100%>")
document.writeln("<TR><TH COLSPAN=2>MIME Type</TH></TR>")
document.writeln("<TR><TH>Extensions</TH><TH>" +
   "Associated Plug-In (if any)</TH></TR>")
for (i=0;i<n;i++)
   if (navigator.mimeTypes[i].enabledPlugin)
      document.writeln("<TR><TD COLSPAN = 2><B>" +
         navigator.mimeTypes[i].type + "</B></TD></TR><TR><TD>" +
         navigator.mimeTypes[i].suffixes + "</TD><TD>" +
         navigator.mimeTypes[i].enabledPlugin.name + "</TD></TR>" )
   else
      document.writeln("<TR><TD COLSPAN = 2><B>" +
         navigator.mimeTypes[i].type + "</B></TD></TR><TR><TD>" +
         navigator.mimeTypes[i].suffixes + "</TD><TD></TD></TR>" )
document.writeln("</TABLE>")
document.writeln("<HR>")
//   Hide script from incompatible browsers -->
</SCRIPT>
</BODY>
</HTML>
```

Calling Plug-In Functions from JavaScript

For plug-in variables and methods to be accessible from JavaScript and Java applets, the plug-in must be LiveConnect compatible and associated with the `netscape.plugin.Plugin` Java class. If that is true, the plug-in variables and methods are available to JavaScript—in much the same way as the public variables and methods of Java applets are available.

JavaScript gives you two ways to access and control compatible plug-ins active in the Web environment. Similar to Java applets, the first is to use the `NAME` attribute of the `<EMBED>` tag to give a name to the embedded document. This enables the plug-ins functions to be accessed through the document object. If `NAME=myenvoydoc` is used with the `<EMBED>` tag to embed an Envoy document using the Envoy Plug-In Viewer, for example, you can access the viewer functions by using the `document.myenvoydoc` object.

It is possible to access plug-ins even if they are not named by using the `embeds` array of the `document` object. If an Envoy document is the first embedded document in the Web page, it can be accessed with `document.embeds[0]`.

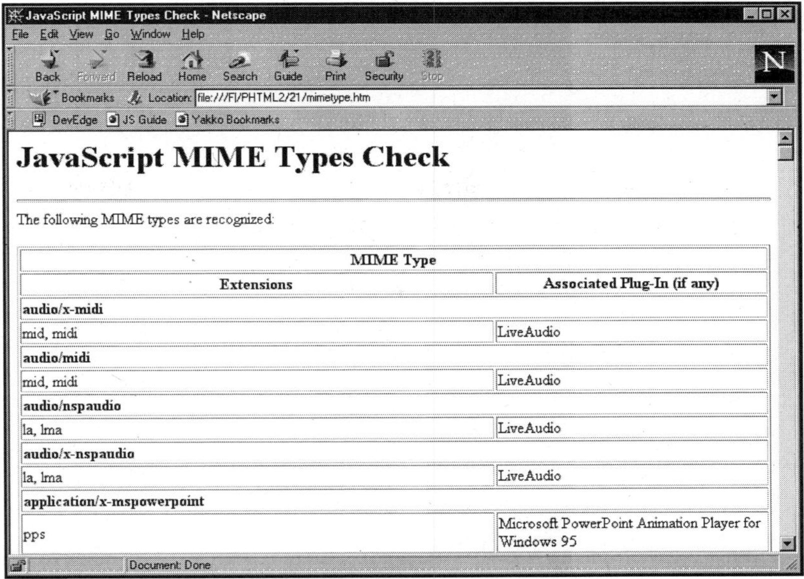

FIG. 21.5
JavaScript can use the `navigator.mimeTypes` to determine the built-in MIME type support in the client Web browser.

LiveConnect Examples

The cross-communication possible between JavaScript and Java is fairly straightforward. Adding plug-ins to the mix only makes things slightly more complicated. The most important thing necessary is for plug-in developers to make their plug-ins LiveConnect compatible. Netscape maintains a Web site containing a LiveConnect showcase—a list of links to other Web sites that feature demos of LiveConnect-compatible plug-ins for Netscape Navigator. This showcase is located at **http://home.netscape.com/comprod/products/navigator/version_3.0/building_blocks/examples/lc_example/lc-showcase.html**.

The Envoy Plug-In by Tumbleweed

Tumbleweed Software is the maker of the Envoy portable document format. Tumbleweed's Web site maintains a complete catalog of its Envoy products for creating and viewing documents in the Envoy format (see Figure 21.6). Their Envoy Viewer is a freeware product, available as a standalone program, an ActiveX Control for Microsoft Internet Explorer, and a plug-in for Netscape Navigator. Tumbleweed has now made its Navigator plug-in LiveConnect compatible, and maintains a set of demos showing how the plug-in can be controlled and manipulated through user input and JavaScript. You can view Tumbleweed Software's Web site at **http://www.tumbleweed.com/**.

The Label Control enables the Web author to place text on the Web page, select the text, font, size, and an arbitrary angle of rotation. One of the exciting things about the Label Control is that it can be manipulated in real-time, producing a variety of automated or user-controlled effects.

▶ **See** "Interacting with Objects with VBScript," **p. 614**

▶ **See** "Microsoft's JScript," **p. 617**

In the following example, the Label Control is used to place text on the Web page, and form input is used to enable the user to change the text used and the angle at which it is displayed. Figure 21.10 shows the default configuration of the label and Figure 21.11 shows it after the text and the rotation angle has been changed.

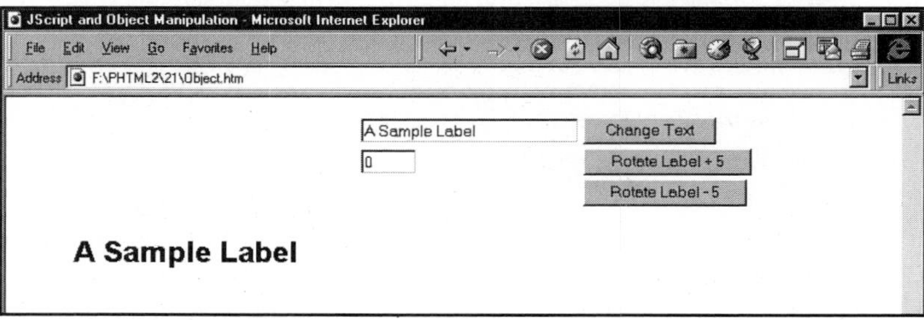

FIG. 21.10 The ActiveX Label Control allows arbitrary text to be displayed by the Web author in the size, font, position, and orientation desired.

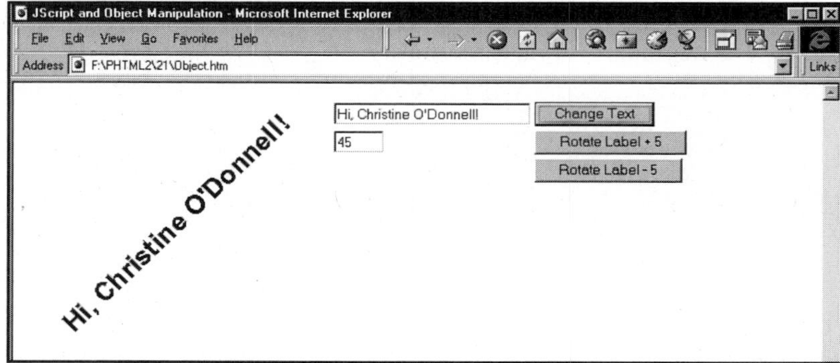

FIG. 21.11 JScript's capability to manipulate Web browser objects enables label parameters to be changed dynamically.

Listing 21.5 shows the code used to produce this example. The following are some things to note about the example:

- The `<OBJECT>...</OBJECT>` container tag is where the ActiveX Label Control is included and its default parameters assigned. The `classid` attribute must be included exactly as shown. The `id` attribute is the object name used by JScript to reference the `Label Control` object. The other attributes define the size and placement of the control.
- The `<PARAM>` tags within the `<OBJECT>...</OBJECT>` container enable the Web author to define attributes of the ActiveX Label Control. The `NAME`, `VALUE` pairs are unique to each

ActiveX Control and should be documented by the ActiveX Control author. For the Label Control, they define various aspects of the appearance of the label. The NAME is also used to manipulate the value with JScript.

- An HTML form is used to accept input and print output for information about the Label Control. The first text area is used to set the label text, and the second text area is used to output the current label text angle. The buttons call the appropriate JScript routine to change the label text or angle.
- One final note about the placement of the JScripts in this HTML document: The functions are defined in the <HEAD> section—although not necessary, this is common practice so that they will be defined before used. Note that the last <SCRIPT>...</SCRIPT> section, which initializes the value of the form text area showing the current angle, is placed at the end of the HTML document to ensure that the object is defined and value set before it is called.

Listing 21.5 Object.*htm* JScript can interact with objects.

```
<HTML>
<HEAD>
<SCRIPT LANGUAGE="JAVASCRIPT">
<!-- Hide this script from incompatible Web browsers -->
function ChangeIt() {
   lblActiveLbl.caption = document.LabelControls.txtNewText.value
}
function RotateP() {
   lblActiveLbl.angle = lblActiveLbl.angle + 5
   document.LabelControls.sngAngle.value = lblActiveLbl.angle
}
function RotateM(){
   lblActiveLbl.Angle = lblActiveLbl.Angle - 5
   document.LabelControls.sngAngle.value = lblActiveLbl.angle
}
//   Hide this script from incompatible Web browsers -->
</SCRIPT>
<TITLE>JScript and Object Manipulation</TITLE>
</HEAD>
<BODY BGCOLOR=#FFFFFF>
<OBJECT classid="clsid:99B42120-6EC7-11CF-A6C7-00AA00A47DD2"
        id=lblActiveLbl
        width=250
        height=250
        align=left
        hspace=20
        vspace=0
>
<PARAM NAME="Angle" VALUE="0">
<PARAM NAME="Alignment" VALUE="4">
<PARAM NAME="BackStyle" VALUE="0">
<PARAM NAME="Caption" VALUE="A Sample Label">
<PARAM NAME="FontName" VALUE="Arial">
```

Part III Ch 21

continues

Listing 21.5 Continued

```
<PARAM NAME="FontSize" VALUE="20">
<PARAM NAME="FontBold" VALUE="1">
<PARAM NAME="ForeColor" VALUE="0">
</OBJECT>
<FORM NAME="LabelControls">
<TABLE>
<TR><TD><INPUT TYPE="TEXT" NAME="txtNewText" SIZE=25></TD>
    <TD><INPUT TYPE="BUTTON" NAME="cmdChangeIt" VALUE="Change Text"
               onClick="ChangeIt()">
    </TD></TR>
<TR><TD><INPUT TYPE="TEXT" NAME="sngAngle" SIZE=5></TD>
    <TD><INPUT TYPE="BUTTON" NAME="cmdRotateP" VALUE="Rotate Label + 5"
               onClick="RotateP()">
    </TD></TR>
<TR><TD></TD>
    <TD><INPUT TYPE="BUTTON" NAME="cmdRotateM" VALUE="Rotate Label - 5"
               onClick="RotateM()">
    </TD></TR>
</TABLE>
</FORM>
<SCRIPT LANGUAGE="JAVASCRIPT">
<!-- Hide this script from incompatible Web browsers -->
document.LabelControls.sngAngle.value = lblActiveLbl.angle
document.LabelControls.txtNewText.value = lblActiveLbl.caption
//   Hide this script from incompatible Web browsers -->
</SCRIPT>
</BODY>
</HTML>
```

CHAPTER 22

Scripting with Microsoft VBScript and JScript

by Jim O'Donnell

In this chapter

Microsoft's VBScript

Like JavaScript, Microsoft's Visual Basic Scripting Edition (VBScript) enables you to embed commands into an HTML document. When a user of a compatible Web browser (for example, Internet Explorer or Netscape Navigator with the ScriptActive plug-in from Ncompass Labs) downloads your page, your VBScript commands are loaded by the Web browser along with the rest of the document and are run in response to any of a series of events. Again, like JavaScript, VBScript is an *interpreted* language; Internet Explorer interprets the VBScript commands when they are loaded and run. They do not first need to be *compiled* into executable form by the Web author who uses them.

VBScript is a fast and flexible subset of Microsoft's Visual Basic and Visual Basic for Applications languages, and is designed to be easy to program in and quick in adding active content to HTML documents. The language elements are mainly ones that should be familiar to anyone who has programmed in just about any language, such as `If...Then...Else` blocks and `Do`, `While`, and `For...Next` loops, and a typical assortment of operators and built-in functions. This chapter takes you to the heart of the VBScript language and shows you examples of how to use it to add interaction and increased functionality to your Web pages.

What Can VBScript Do?

VBScript provides a fairly complete set of built-in functions and commands, enabling you to perform math calculations, manipulate strings, play sounds, open up new windows and new URLs, and access and verify user input to your Web forms.

Code to perform these actions can be embedded in a page and executed when the page is loaded. You can also write functions that contain code that is triggered by events you specify. You can write a VBScript method that is called when the user clicks the Submit button of a form, for example, or one that is activated when the user clicks a hyperlink on the active page.

VBScript can also set the attributes, or *properties*, of ActiveX Controls, Java applets, and other objects present in the browser. This way, you can change the behavior of plug-ins or other objects without having to rewrite them. Your VBScript code could automatically set the text of an ActiveX Label Control, for example, based on what time the page is viewed.

VBScript, Visual Basic, and Visual Basic for Applications

VBScript is a subset of the Visual Basic and Visual Basic for Applications languages. If you are familiar with either of these two languages, programming in VBScript will be easy. Just as Visual Basic was meant to make the creation of Windows programs easier and more accessible, and Visual Basic for Applications was meant to do the same for Microsoft Office applications, VBScript is meant to give an easy-to-learn yet powerful means for adding interactivity and increased functionality to Web pages.

How Does VBScript Look in an HTML Document?

VBScript commands are embedded in your HTML documents, just as with JavaScript and other scripting languages. Embedded VBscripts are enclosed in the HTML container tag `<SCRIPT>...</SCRIPT>`. The `<LANGUAGE>` attribute of the `<SCRIPT>` tag specifies the scripting language to use when evaluating the script. For VBScript, the scripting language is defined as `LANGUAGE="VBS"`. You can use the `SRC` attribute to load a script from an external source.

VBScript resembles JavaScript and many other computer languages you may be familiar with. It bears the closest resemblance, as you might imagine, to Visual Basic and Visual Basic for Applications because it is a subset of these two languages. Some of the simple rules you need to follow for structuring VBscripts are as follows:

- VBScript is not case sensitive, so `function`, `Function`, and `FUNCTION` are all the same.
- A single statement can cover multiple lines if a continuation character, a single underscore, is placed at the end of each line to be continued. Also, you can put multiple short statements on a single line by separating each from the next with a colon.

How to Hide Your Scripts

Because currently only Internet Explorer supports VBScript, you will probably be designing pages that will be viewed by Web browsers that don't support it. To keep those browsers from misinterpreting your VBscript, wrap your scripts as follows:

```
<SCRIPT LANGUAGE="VBS">
<!-- This line opens an HTML comment
VBScript commands...
<!-- This line closes an HTML comment -->
</SCRIPT>
```

The opening `<!--` comment causes Web browsers that do not support VBScript to disregard all text they encounter until they find a matching `-->`; thus they won't display your script. Make sure, however, that your `<SCRIPT>...</SCRIPT>` container elements are outside the comments; otherwise, even compatible Web browsers will ignore the script.

Comments

Including comments in your programs to explain what they do is usually good practice—VBScript is no exception. The VBScript interpreter ignores any text marked as a comment, so don't be shy about including them. Comments in VBScript are set off using the `REM` statement (short for remark) or by using a single quotation mark (') character. Any text following the `REM` or single quotation mark, until the end of the line, is ignored. To include a comment on the same line as another VBScript statement, you can use either `REM` or a single quotation mark. However, if you use `REM`, you must separate the statement from the `REM` with a colon. The following script fragment shows some of the ways of including HTML and VBScript comments in a script:

```
<SCRIPT LANGUAGE="VBS">
<!-- This line opens an HTML comment
```

```
REM This is a VBScript comment on a line by itself.
' This is another VBScript comment
customer.name = "Jim O'Donnell"         'Inline comment
customer.address = "1757 P Street NW"   :REM Inline REM comment (note the :)
customer.zip = "20036-1303"
<!-- This line closes an HTML comment -->
</SCRIPT>
```

VBScript Identifiers

An *identifier* is just a unique name that VBScript uses to identify a variable, method, or object in your program. As with other programming languages, VBScript imposes some rules on what names you can use. All VBScript names must start with an alphabetic character and can contain both uppercase and lowercase letters and the digits 0 through 9. They can be as long as 255 characters, although you probably don't want to go much over 32 or so.

Unlike JavaScript, which supports two different ways for you to represent values in your scripts, literals and variables, VBScript has only variables. The difference in VBScript, therefore, is one of usage. If you wish to use a constant value in your VBScript programs, just set a variable equal to a value and don't change it. This discussion will continue to refer to literals and variables as distinct entities, although they are interchangeable.

Literals and variables in VBScript are all of type *variant*, which means that they can contain any type of data that VBScript supports. It is usually a good idea to use a given variable for one type and explicitly convert its value to another type as necessary. The following are some of the types of data that VBScript supports:

- *Integers*. These types can be 1, 2, or 4 bytes in length, depending on how big they are.
- *Floating point*. VBScript supports single- and double-precision floating point numbers.
- *Strings*. Strings can represent words, phrases, or data, and they are set off by double quotation marks.
- *Booleans*. Booleans have a value of either `true` or `false`.
- *Objects*. A VBScript variable can refer to any object within its environment.

Objects, Properties, Methods, and Events in VBScript

Before you proceed further, you should take some time to review some terminology that may or may not be familiar to you. VBScript follows much the same object model followed by JavaScript and uses many of the same terms. In VBScript, just as in JavaScript—and in any object-oriented language for that matter—an *object* is a collection of data and functions that have been grouped together. An object's data is known as its *properties*, and its functions are known as its *methods*. An *event* is a condition to which an object can respond, such as a mouse click or other user input. The VBScript programs that you write make use of properties and methods of objects, both those that you create and those objects provided by the Web browser, its plug-ins, ActiveX Controls, Java applets, and the like.

Here's a simple guideline: An object's *properties* are the information it knows; its *methods* are how it can act on that information; and *events* are what it responds to.

NOTE A very important, and a little confusing, thing to remember is that an object's methods are *also* properties of that object. An object's properties are the information it knows. The object certainly knows about its own methods, so those methods are properties of the object right along side its other data.

Using Built-In Objects and Functions

Individual VBScript elements are objects. Literals and variables are objects of type *variant*, which can be used to hold data of many different types. These objects also have associated methods—ways of acting on the different data types. VBScript also enables you to access a set of useful objects that represent the Web browser, the currently displayed page, and other elements of the browsing session.

You access objects by specifying their names. The active document object, for example, is named `document`. To use `document`'s properties or methods, you add a period (.) and the name of the method or property you want. For example, `document.title` is the `title` property of the `document` object.

Using Properties

Every object has properties, even literals. To access a property, just use the object name followed by a period and the property name. To get the length of a string object named `address`, you can write the following:

```
address.length
```

You get back an integer that equals the number of characters in the string. If the object you are using has properties that can be modified, you can change them in the same way. To set the color property of a house object, just write the following:

```
house.color = "blue"
```

You can also create new properties for an object just by naming them. Assume, for example, that you define a class called `customer` for one of your pages. You can add new properties to the `customer` object as follows:

```
customer.name = "Jim O'Donnell"
customer.address = "1757 P Street NW"
customer.zip = "20036-1303"
```

Because an object's methods are just properties, you can easily add new properties to an object by writing your own function and creating a new object property using your own function name. If you want to add a `Bill` method to your `customer` object, you can write a function named `BillCustomer` and set the object's property as follows:

```
customer.Bill = BillCustomer;
```

To call the new method, you just write the following:

```
customer.Bill()
```

VBScript Language Elements

Although VBScript is not as flexible as C++ or Visual Basic, it is quick and simple. Because it is easily embedded in your Web pages, adding interactivity or increased functionality with a VBScript is easy—a lot easier than writing a Java applet to do the same thing. (Although, to be fair, you *can* do a lot more with Java applets.) This section covers some of the nuts and bolts of VBScript programming.

Links to a full language reference for VBScript, as well as Microsoft's tutorial for VBScript programming, are included on the accompanying CD. As VBScript is a new and evolving language, you can get up-to-the-minute information on it at the Microsoft VBScript Web site at **http://www.microsoft.com/vbscript/**.

VBScript Variables

All VBScript variables are of the type *variant*, which means that they can be used for any of the supported data types. Table 22.1 summarizes the types of data that VBScript variables can hold:

Table 22.1 Data types that VBScript Variables can contain.

Type	Description
Empty	Uninitialized and is treated as 0 or the empty string, depending on the context
Null	Intentionally contains no valid data
Boolean	`true` or `false`
Byte	Integer in the range –128 to 127
Integer	Integer in the range –32,768 to 32,767
Long	Integer in the range –2,147,483,648 to 2,147,483,647
Single	Single-precision floating point number in the range –3.402823E38 to –1.401298E-45 for negative values and 1.401298E-45 to 3.402823E38 for positive values
Double	Double-precision floating point number in the range –1.79769313486232E308 to –4.94065645841247E-324 for negative values; 4.94065645841247E-324 to 1.79769313486232E308 for positive values
Date	Number that represents a date between January 1, 100 to December 31, 9999

Type	Description
String	Variable-length string up to approximately 2 billion characters in length
Object	Any object
Error	Error number

Forming Expressions in VBScript

An *expression* is anything that can be evaluated to get a single value. Expressions can contain string or numeric variables, operators, and other expressions, and they can range from simple to quite complex. The following expression uses the assignment operator (more on operators in the next section), for example, to assign the result `3.14159` to the variable `pi`:

```
pi = 3.14159
```

By contrast, the following is a more complex expression whose final value depends on the values of the two Boolean variables `Quit` and `Complete`:

```
(Quit = TRUE) And (Complete = FALSE)
```

Using VBScript Operators

Operators do just what their name suggests: They operate on variables or literals. The items that an operator acts on are called its *operands.* Operators come in the two following types:

- *Unary.* These operators require only one operand and the operator can come before or after the operand. The `Not` operator, which performs the logical negation of an expression, is a good example.
- *Binary.* These operators need two operands. The four math operators (+ for addition, - for subtraction, × for multiplication, and / for division) are all binary operators, as is the = assignment operator you saw earlier.

Assignment Operators *Assignment operators* take the result of an expression and assign it to a variable. One feature that VBScript has that most other programming languages do not is that you can change a variable's type on-the-fly. Consider the example shown in Listing 22.1.

Listing 22.1 Pi-fly.htm VBScript Variables can change type on-the-fly.

```
<HTML>
<HEAD>
<SCRIPT LANGUAGE="VBS">
<!-- Hide this script from incompatible Web browsers!
Sub TypeDemo
    Dim pi
    document.write("<HR>")
    pi = 3.14159
```

continues

Listing 22.1 Continued

```
    document.write("pi is " & CStr(pi) & "<BR>")
    pi = FALSE
    document.write("pi is " & CStr(pi) & "<BR>")
    document.write("<HR>")
End Sub
<!-- -->
</SCRIPT>
<TITLE>Changing Pi on the Fly!</TITLE>
</HEAD>
<BODY BGCOLOR=#FFFFFF>
If your Web browser doesn't support VBScript, this is all you will see!
<SCRIPT LANGUAGE="VBS">
<!-- Hide this script from incompatible Web browsers!
TypeDemo
<!-- -->
</SCRIPT>
</BODY>
</HTML>
```

This short function first prints the (correct) value of pi. In most other languages, however, trying to set a floating point variable to a Boolean value either generates a compiler error or a runtime error. Because VBScript variables can be any type, it happily accepts the change and prints `pi`'s new value: `false` (see Figure 22.1).

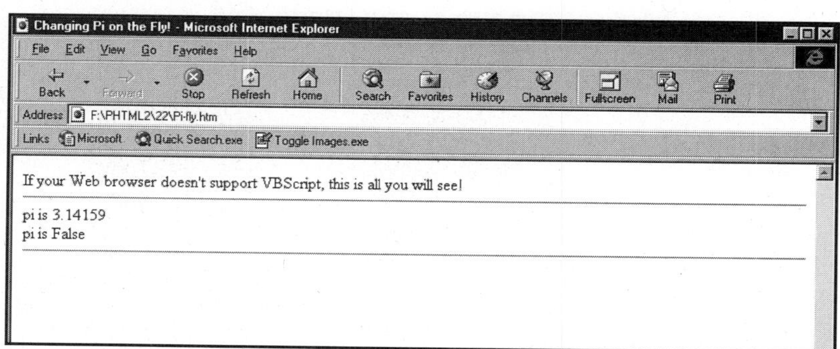

FIG. 22.1
Because all VBScript `variables` are of type `variant`, not only their value can be changed, but also their data type.

The assignment operator, =, just assigns the value of an expression's right side to its left side. In the preceding example, the variable `pi` gets the floating point value `3.14159` or the Boolean value `false` after the expression is evaluated.

Math Operators The previous sections gave you a sneak preview of the math operators that VBScript furnishes. As you might expect, the standard four math functions (addition, subtraction, multiplication, and division) work just as they do on an ordinary calculator and use the symbols +, -, ×, and `/`.

VBScript supplies three other math operators:

- `\` The backslash operator divides its first operand by its second, after first rounding floating point operands to the nearest integer, and returns the integer part of the result. For example, `19 \ 6.7` returns `2` (6.7 rounds to 7, 19 divided by 7 is a little over 2.71, the integer part of which is 2).
- `Mod` This operator is similar to `\` in that it divides the first operand by its second, after again rounding floating point operands to the nearest integer, and returns the integer remainder. Therefore, `19 Mod 6.7` returns `5`.
- `^` This exponent operator returns the first operand raised to the power of the second. The first operand can be negative only if the second, the exponent, is an integer.

Comparison Operators Comparing the value of two expressions to see whether one is larger, smaller, or equal to another is often necessary. VBScript supplies several comparison operators that take two operands and return `true` if the comparison is true and `false` if it is not. Table 22.2 shows the VBScript comparison operators.

Table 22.2 VBScript comparison operators.

Operator	Read It As	Returns *true* When:
=	Equals	The two operands are equal
<>	Does not equal	The two operands are unequal
<	Less than	The left operand is less than the right operand
<=	Less than or equal to	The left operand is less than or equal to the right operand
>	Greater than	The left operand is greater than the right operand
>=	Greater than or equal to	The left operand is greater than or equal to the right operand

You can also use the comparison operators on strings; the results depend on standard lexicographic ordering (ordering by the ASCII values of the string characters).

Thinking of the comparison operators as questions can be helpful. When you write

```
(x >= 10)
```

you are really saying, "Is the value of variable `x` greater than or equal to `10`?" The return value answers the question, `true` or `false`.

Logical Operators Comparison operators compare quantity or content for numeric and string expressions, but sometimes you need to test a logical value—whether a comparison operator returns `true` or `false`, for example. VBScript's logical operators enable you to compare expressions that return logical values. The following are VBScript's logical operators:

- `And` The `And` operator returns `true` if both its input expressions are true. If the first operand evaluates to `false`, `And` returns `false` immediately, without evaluating the second operand. Here's an example:

```
x = TRUE And TRUE       ' x is TRUE
x = TRUE And FALSE      ' x is FALSE
x = FALSE And TRUE      ' x is FALSE
x = FALSE And FALSE     ' x is FALSE
```

- `Or` This operator returns `true` if either of its operands is true. If the first operand is true, `||` returns `true` without evaluating the second operand. Here's an example:

```
x = TRUE Or TRUE        ' x is TRUE
x = TRUE Or FALSE       ' x is TRUE
x = FALSE Or TRUE       ' x is TRUE
x = FALSE Or FALSE      ' x is FALSE
```

- `Not` This operator takes only one expression and it returns the opposite of that expression. Thus `Not true` returns `false`, and `Not false` returns `true`.
- `Xor` This operator, which stands for "exclusive or," returns `true` if either, but not both, of its input expressions is `true`, as in the following:

```
x = TRUE Xor TRUE       ' x is FALSE
x = TRUE Xor FALSE      ' x is TRUE
x = FALSE Xor TRUE      ' x is TRUE
x = FALSE Xor FALSE     ' x is FALSE
```

- `Eqv` This operator, which stands for "equivalent," returns `true` if its two input expressions are the same—either both `true` or both `false`. The statement `x Eqv y` is equivalent to `Not (x Xor y)`.
- `Imp` This operator, which stands for "implication," returns `true` according to the following:

```
x = TRUE Imp TRUE       ' x is TRUE
x = FALSE Imp TRUE      ' x is TRUE
x = TRUE Imp FALSE      ' x is FALSE
x = FALSE Imp FALSE     ' x is TRUE
```

NOTE Note that the logical implication operator `Imp` is the only logical operator for which the order of the operands is important.

Note that the `And` and `Or` operators don't evaluate the second operand if the first operand provides enough information for the operator to return a value. This process, called *short-circuit evaluation*, can be significant when the second operand is a function call.

NOTE Note that all six of the logical operators can also operate on non-Boolean expressions. In this case, the logical operations described previously are performed bitwise, on each bit of the two operands. For the two integers 19 (00010011 in binary) and 6 (00000110), for example:

```
19 And 6 =   2 (00000010 in binary)
19 Or 6  =  23 (00010111 in binary)
Not 19   = -20 (11101100 in binary)
```

String Concatenation The final VBScript operator is the string concatenation operator `&`. Although you can also use the addition operator `+` to concatenate strings (returning a string made up of the original strings joined together), using `&` proves better because it is less ambiguous.

Testing Conditions in VBScript

VBScript provides one control structure for making decisions—the `If...Then...Else` structure. To make a decision, you supply one or more expressions that evaluate to `true` or `false`; which code is executed depends on what your expressions evaluate to.

The simplest form of `If...Then...Else` uses only the `If...Then` part. If the specified condition is `true`, the code following the condition is executed; if not, that code is skipped. In the following code fragment, for example, the message appears only if the variable `x` is less than `pi`:

```
if (x < pi) then document.write("x is less than pi")
```

You can use any expression as the condition. Because you can next and combine expressions with the logical operators, your tests can be pretty sophisticated. Also, using the multiple statement character, you can execute multiple commands, as in the following:

```
if ((test = TRUE) And (x > max)) then max = x : test = FALSE
```

The `else` clause enables you to specify a set of statements to execute when the condition is `false`. In the same single line form shown in the preceding line, your new line appears as follows:

```
if (x > pi) then test = TRUE else test = FALSE
```

A more versatile use of the `If...Then...Else` allows multiple lines and multiple actions for each case. It looks something like the following:

```
if (x > pi) then
    test = TRUE
    count = count + 1
else
    test = FALSE
    count = 0
end if
```

Note that with this syntax, additional test clauses using the `elseif` statement are permitted. You could, for example, add one more clauses to the preceding example:

```
if (x > pi) then
    test = TRUE
```

```
    count = count + 1
elseif (x < -pi) then
    test = TRUE
    count = count - 1
else
    test = FALSE
    count = 0
end if
```

Executing VBScript Loops

If you want to repeat an action more than one time, VBScript provides a variety of constructs for doing so. The first, called a `For...Next` loop, executes a set of statements some number of times. You specify three expressions: an *initial* expression, which sets the values of any variables you need to use; a *final value*, which tells the loop how to see when it is done; and an *increment* expression, which modifies any variables that need it. Here's a simple example:

```
for count = 0 to 100 step 2
    document.write("Count is " & CStr(count) & "<BR>")
next
```

In this example, the expressions are all simple numeric values—the initial value is `0`, the final value is `100`, and the increment is `2`. This loop executes `51` times and prints out a number each time.

The third form of loop is the `While...Wend` loop. It executes statements as long as its condition is true. You can rewrite the first `For...Next` loop, for example, as follows:

```
count = 0
while (count <= 100)
    document.write("Count is " & CStr(count) & "<BR>")
    count = count + 2
wend
```

The last type of loop is the `Do...Loop`, which has several forms, which either test the condition at the beginning or the end. The test can either be a `Do While` or `Do Until`, and can occur at the beginning or end of the loop. If a `Do While` test is done at the beginning, the loop executes as long as the test condition is true, similar to the `While...Wend` loop. Here's an example:

```
count = 0
do while (count <= 100)
    document.write("Count is " & CStr(count) & "<BR>")
    count = count + 2
loop
```

An example of having the test at the end, as a `Do...Until`, can also yield equivalent results. In that case, the loop looks like the following:

```
count = 0
do
    document.write("Count is " & CStr(count) & "<BR>")
    count = count + 2
loop until (count > 100)
```

One other difference between these two forms is that when the test is at the end of the loop, as in the second case, the commands in the loop are executed at least one time. If the test is at the beginning, that is not the case.

Which form you prefer depends on what you are doing. `For...Next` loops prove useful when you want to perform an action a set number of times. `While...Wend` and `Do...Loop` loops, although they can be used for the same purpose, are best when you want to keep doing something as long as a particular condition remains true.

NOTE The `For...Next` and `Do...Loop` loops also have a way to exit the loop from inside—the `End For` and `End Do` statements, respectively. Normally, these tests would be used as part of a conditional statement, such as the following:

```
for i = 0 to 100
    x = UserFunc()
    document.write("x[" & CStr(i) & "] = " & CStr(x) & "<BR>")
    if (x > max) end for
next
```

Using Other VBScript Statements

This section provides a quick reference to some of the other VBScript statements. The following formatting is used:

- All VBScript keywords are in a `monospace` font.
- Words in *`monospace italics`* represent user-defined names or statements.
- Any portions enclosed in square brackets (`[` and `]`) are optional.
- Portions enclosed in braces (`{` and `}`) and separated by a vertical bar (`¦`) represent an option, of which one must be selected.
- The word *`statements...`* indicates a block of one or more statements.

The *Call* Statement

The `Call` statement calls a VBScript `Sub` or `Function` procedure (see below).

Syntax:

```
Call MyProc([arglist])
```

or

```
MyProc [arglist]
```

Note that *arglist* is a comma-delimited list of zero or more arguments to be passed to the procedure. When the second form is used, omitting the `Call` statement, the parentheses around the argument list, if any, must also be omitted.

The *Dim* Statement

The `Dim` statement is used to declare variables and also to allocate the storage necessary for them. If you specify subscripts, you can also create arrays.

Syntax:

```
Dim varname[([subscripts])][,varname[([subscripts])],...]
```

The *Function* and *Sub* Statements

The `Function` and `Sub` statements declare VBScript procedures. The difference is that a `Function` procedure returns a value, and a `Sub` procedure does not. All parameters are passed to functions *by value*—the function gets the value of the parameter but cannot change the original value in the caller.

Syntax:

```
[Static] Function funcname([arglist])
    statements...
    funcname = returnvalue
End
```

and

```
[Static] Sub subname([arglist])
    statements...
End
```

Variables can be declared with the `Dim` statement within a `Function` or `Sub` procedure. In this case, those variables are local to that procedure and can only be referenced within it. If the `Static` keyword is used when the procedure is declared, all local variables retain their value from one procedure call to the next.

The *On Error* Statement

The `On Error` statement is used to enable error handling.

Syntax:

```
On Error Resume Next
```

`On Error Resume Next` enables execution to continue immediately after the statement that provokes the runtime error. Alternatively, if the error occurs in a procedure call after the last executed `On Error` statement, execution commences immediately after that procedure call. This way, execution can continue despite a runtime error, enabling you to build an error-handling routine inline within the procedure. The most recent `On Error Resume Next` statement is the one that is active, so you should execute one in each procedure in which you want to have inline error handling.

VBScript Functions

VBScript has an assortment of intrinsic functions that you can use in your scripts. The VBScript documentation found on the web contains a full reference for these functions. Table 22.3 shows the functions that exist for performing different types of operations. (Because you can use some functions for several different types of operations, they appear multiple times in the table.)

Table 22.3 VBScript functions.

Type of Operation	Function Names
Array operations	`IsArray`, `LBound`, `UBound`
Conversions	`Abs`, `Asc`, `AscB`, `AscW`, `Chr`, `ChrB`, `ChrW`, `Cbool`, `CByte`, `CDate`, `CDbl`, `CInt`, `CLng`, `CSng`, `Cstr`, `DateSerial`, `DateValue`, `Hex`, `Oct`, `Fix`, `Int`, `Sgn`, `TimeSerial`, `TimeValue`
Dates and times	`Date`, `Time`, `DateSerial`, `DateValue`, `Day`, `Month`, `Weekday`, `Year`, `Hour`, `Minute`, `Second`, `Now`, `TimeSerial`, `TimeValue`
Input/output	`InputBox`, `MsgBox`
Math	`Atn`, `Cos`, `Sin`, `Tan`, `Exp`, `Log`, `Sqr`, `Randomize`, `Rnd`
Objects	`IsObject`
Strings	`Asc`, `AscB`, `AscW`, `Chr`, `ChrB`, `ChrW`, `Instr`, `InStrB`, `Len`, `LenB`, `LCase`, `UCase`, `Left`, `LeftB`, `Mid`, `MidB`, `Right`, `RightB`, `Space`, `StrComp`, `String`, `LTrim`, `RTrim`, `Trim`
Variants	`IsArray`, `IsDate`, `IsEmpty`, `IsNull`, `IsNumeric`, `IsObject`, `VarType`

VBScript and Web Browsers

The most important things you will be doing with your VBScripts are interacting with the content and information on your Web pages, and through those pages, with your user. You have already learned from this chapter one way in which VBScript can help you with your Web page: You can use `document.write()` to place information on the page itself.

VBScript interacts with your Web browser through the browser's object model. Different aspects of the Web browser exist as different objects, with properties and methods that can be accessed by VBScript. For instance, `document.write()` uses the `write` method of the `document` object. Understanding this Web Browser Object Model is crucial to using VBScript effectively. Also, understanding how the Web browser processes and executes your scripts is also necessary.

When Scripts Execute

When you put VBScript code in a page, the Web browser evaluates the code as soon as it is

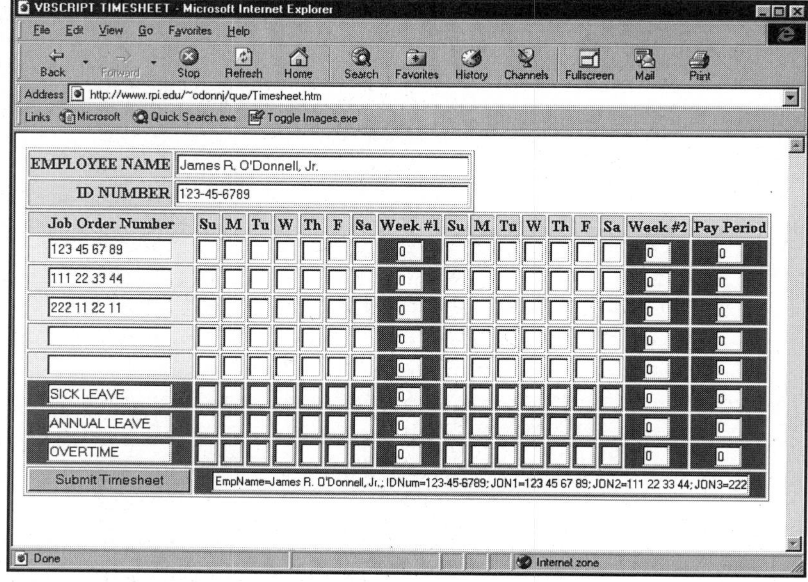

FIG. 22.6
Using cookies allows a single Web page to serve multiple users, customizing it with their particular information.

Of course, after the forms are submitted, what to do with them at the receiving end is another question, one for a different chapter.

See "Programming CGI Scripts," **p. 855**

Interacting with Objects with VBScript

This is an example of using VBScript to manipulate another Web browser object—in this case the ActiveX Label Control. The Label Control enables the Web author to place text on the Web page, and select the text, font, size, and an arbitrary angle of rotation. One of the exciting things about the Label Control is you can manipulate it in real-time, producing a variety of automated or user-controlled effects.

In the following example, the Label Control is used to place text on the Web page, and form input is used to enable the user to change the text used and the angle at which it is displayed. Figure 22.7 shows the default configuration of the label and Figure 22.8 shows it after the text and the rotation angle has been changed.

Listing 22.11 shows the code used to produce this example. The following are some things to note about the example:

- The `<OBJECT>...</OBJECT>` container tag is where the ActiveX Label Control is included and its default parameters assigned. The `classid` attribute must be included exactly as shown. The `id` attribute is the object name used by VBScript to reference the Label Control object. The other attributes define the size and placement of the control.

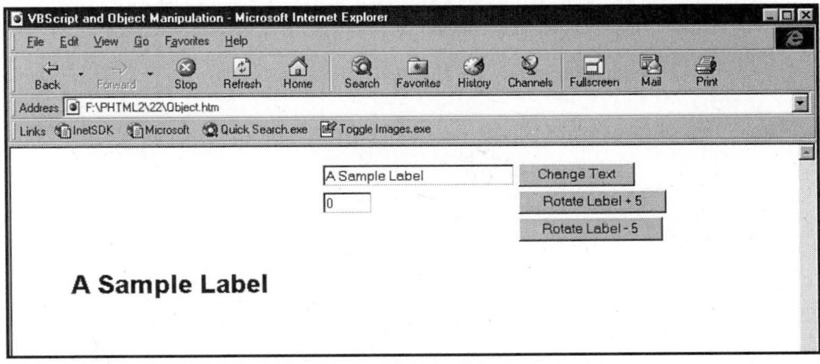

FIG. 22.7
The ActiveX Label Control allows arbitrary text to be displayed by the Web author in the size, font, position, and orientation desired.

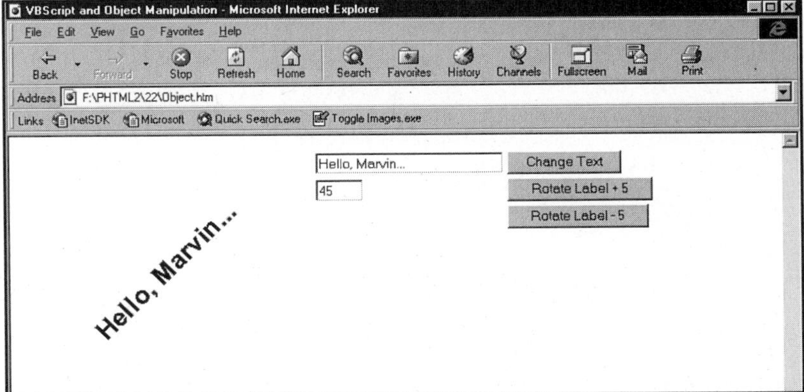

FIG. 22.8
VBScript's capability to manipulate Web browser objects allows the label parameters to be changed dynamically.

- The `<PARAM>` tags within the `<OBJECT>...</OBJECT>` container enables the Web author to define attributes of the ActiveX Label Control. The `NAME`, `VALUE` pairs are unique to each ActiveX Control and should be documented by the ActiveX Control author. For the Label Control, they define various aspects of the appearance of the label. The `NAME` is also used to manipulate the value with VBScript.
- An HTML Form is used to accept input and print output for information about the Label Control. The first text area is used to set the label text, and the second text area is used to output the current label text angle. The buttons call the appropriate VBScript routine to change the label text or angle.
- One final note about the placement of the VBscripts in this HTML document: The functions are defined in the `<HEAD>` section—this is not necessary, but it is common practice—so that they will be defined before being used. The last `<SCRIPT>...</SCRIPT>` section, however, which initializes the value of the form text area showing the current angle, is placed at the end of the HTML document to ensure that the object is defined and value set before it is called.

Listing 22.13 Object.*htm* VBScript can interact with objects.

```
<HTML>
<HEAD>
<SCRIPT LANGUAGE="VBS">
<!-- Hide this script from incompatible Web browsers
Sub cmdChangeIt_onClick
   Dim TheForm
   Set TheForm = Document.LabelControls
   lblActiveLbl.Caption = TheForm.txtNewText.Value
End Sub
Sub cmdRotateP_onClick
   Dim TheForm
   Set TheForm = Document.LabelControls
   lblActiveLbl.Angle = lblActiveLbl.Angle + 5
   Document.LabelControls.sngAngle.Value = lblActiveLbl.Angle
End Sub
Sub cmdRotateM_onClick
   Dim TheForm
   Set TheForm = Document.LabelControls
   lblActiveLbl.Angle = lblActiveLbl.Angle - 5
   Document.LabelControls.sngAngle.Value = lblActiveLbl.Angle
End Sub
<!-- -->
</SCRIPT>
<TITLE>VBScript and Object Manipulation</TITLE>
</HEAD>
<BODY BGCOLOR=#FFFFFF>
<OBJECT classid="clsid:99B42120-6EC7-11CF-A6C7-00AA00A47DD2"
        id=lblActiveLbl
        width=250
        height=250
        align=left
        hspace=20
        vspace=0
>
<PARAM NAME="Angle" VALUE="0">
<PARAM NAME="Alignment" VALUE="4">
<PARAM NAME="BackStyle" VALUE="0">
<PARAM NAME="Caption" VALUE="A Sample Label">
<PARAM NAME="FontName" VALUE="Arial">
<PARAM NAME="FontSize" VALUE="20">
<PARAM NAME="FontBold" VALUE="1">
<PARAM NAME="ForeColor" VALUE="0">
</OBJECT>
<FORM NAME="LabelControls">
<TABLE>
<TR><TD><INPUT TYPE="TEXT" NAME="txtNewText" SIZE=25></TD>
    <TD><INPUT TYPE="BUTTON" NAME="cmdChangeIt" VALUE="Change Text">
    </TD></TR>
<TR><TD><INPUT TYPE="TEXT" NAME="sngAngle" SIZE=5></TD>
    <TD><INPUT TYPE="BUTTON" NAME="cmdRotateP" VALUE="Rotate Label + 5">
    </TD></TR>
<TR><TD></TD>
    <TD><INPUT TYPE="BUTTON" NAME="cmdRotateM" VALUE="Rotate Label - 5">
```

```
    </TD></TR>
</TABLE>
</FORM>
<SCRIPT LANGUAGE="VBS">
<!-- Hide this script from incompatible Web browsers
Document.LabelControls.sngAngle.Value = lblActiveLbl.Angle
Document.LabelControls.txtNewText.Value = lblActiveLbl.Caption
<!-- -->
</SCRIPT>
</BODY>
</HTML>
```

Microsoft's JScript

With version 3 of their Internet Explorer Web browser, Microsoft has included JavaScript compatibility. However, what they have chosen to do is to create what they call JScript—described as an open implementation of the JavaScript language.

Exactly what this means for Web page authors is unclear. Although compatibility with the JavaScript language has been Microsoft's goal with JScript, you must remember that JScript and JavaScript both remain under development. Therefore, there are liable to be incompatibilities between the two. For Web authors interested in designing pages for the largest possible audience, testing JavaScript/JScript Web pages with both Netscape Navigator and Microsoft Internet Explorer seems like a good idea.

What Scripting Language Should You Use?

With a choice of scripting languages now available, the question of which to use quickly arises. JavaScript and VBScript have similar capabilities. Also, because they are both relatively new, you don't have a lot of history to rely on for making a choice. The following are a few points to consider:

- *With which language are you most comfortable?*

  JavaScript is based on the Java and C++ languages; VBScript is based on Visual Basic and Visual Basic for Applications. If you are proficient at one of these parent languages, using the scripting language based on it might be a good idea.

- *What are you trying to do?*

  Both languages are object oriented and can interact with a compatible Web browser and other objects that the browser may have loaded, such as Java applets or ActiveX Controls. If you will be primarily working with Internet Explorer, however, and using ActiveX Controls or Microsoft's brand of Dynamic HTML, using VBScript is probably a good idea because it is designed with that use in mind.

- *Who is your target audience?*

  For "general-purpose" uses—such as processing form inputs or providing simple interactivity—the biggest question to answer is who will be the audience for your Web pages. Though Microsoft Internet Explorer has a growing share of the Web browser market, Netscape Navigator still has the largest share. Unless your Web pages are targeted at a specific audience that will definitely be using Internet Explorer, you will probably want to use JavaScript. At least in the short term, using JavaScript will ensure you maximum compatibility.

PART IV

Dynamic HTML

CHAPTER 23

Introduction to Dynamic HTML

by Jim O'Donnell

In this chapter

What Is Dynamic HTML?

When HTML was first developed, its mixing of text and graphics, as well as the inclusion of the hypertext link for linking information, revolutionized the way information was presented and distributed across the Internet. Since the inception of HTML, Web developers and vendors have been looking for ways to make information that can be presented more dynamically and to create more ways to interact with the user. Animated GIFs, Web browser plug-ins and ActiveX Controls, Java applets, and scripting languages are all examples of ways to make Web pages more exciting.

HTML itself is basically a static language, however; information is sent to a client Web browser, which renders it for the viewer. To add movement or animation to an HTML document, it was necessary to embed some other element such as the Java applets or ActiveX Controls mentioned in the preceding paragraph. Macromedia's Shockwave, for example, has long been used to add increased animation and interactivity to many Web pages.

With version 4 of their latest Web browser applications, however, both Netscape and Microsoft have introduced a new technology dubbed "Dynamic HTML," which seeks to make HTML more interactive in its own right. Through each companies version of Dynamic HTML, Web developers have increased control over the appearance of an HTML document, as rendered on a compatible Web browser, and have more ways to make the document dynamic and interactive, capable of better detection and response to user actions.

What exactly is Dynamic HTML? Unlike the current state of such languages and technologies as HTML, Java, and VRML, Dynamic HTML is not a standard, enacted, proposed, or even being developed by any Internet standards organization. Rather, Dynamic HTML is a term being applied by both Netscape and Microsoft to a collection of technologies that they are developing for making HTML documents more dynamic and interactive. Although there are a few common elements, the question "What is Dynamic HTML?" has a different answer, depending on who you ask.

Netscape's Answer

Netscape's documentation for their version of Dynamic HTML, along with a lot of other documentation, demos, and other good information about Netscape software and technologies, is located on their DevEdge Online Web site, which can be found at

http://developer.netscape.com/

The specific URL for their Dynamic HTML documentation can be found at

http://developer.netscape.com/library/documentation/communicator/dynhtml/index.htm

According to this information, Netscape's answer to the question "What is Dynamic HTML?" would consist of the following elements, which they have first introduced into Netscape Navigator version 4:

- *Style sheets.* Microsoft first implemented support for Cascading Style Sheets (CSS) in their Internet Explorer version 3.0, and Netscape has added it to their Web browser in the current version. Both Netscape and Microsoft support the Cascading Style Sheets standard adopted by the World Wide Web Consortium (W3C). You can find these standards on W3C's CSS Web site.

▶ **See** "What Are Style Sheets?", **p. 236**

Netscape considers style sheets a part of their implementation of Dynamic HTML because they have extended their Web Browser Object Model to include style sheets and styles attached to tags within an HTML document. This means that the formatting information for the content within the HTML document can be changed dynamically using JavaScript.

ON THE WEB

http://www.w3.org/Style/ This Web site houses the W3C's complete Cascading Style Sheet definition, as well as a number of links you can follow to find out more.

- *Content positioning*. With the early beta releases of Netscape Navigator version 4, Netscape introduced the `<LAYER>` and `<ILAYER>` tags, which were their proposed HTML tags to allow for precise 2D and 3D positioning of elements within an HTML document. These tags were rejected by the W3C, although Netscape still supports them in the release version of their Web browser.
- With the rejection of the `<LAYER>` and `<ILAYER>` tags, Netscape added support for what is known as CSS positioning. In addition to the formatting options that can be specified using style sheets, they also include support for positioning the elements to which they are attached. Whether you create your HTML elements to be positioned using the `<LAYER>` or `<ILAYER>` tags, or use CSS positioning, Netscape enables you to use JavaScript to reference those elements the same way, enabling you to dynamically change their positions.
- *Downloadable Fonts*. One of the problems with using style sheets to achieve your desired formatting effects is that they work only if your user has the same fonts installed on his local system. If he does not, your carefully constructed Web page will be rendered using a different font than what you intended, potentially destroying the desired effect.
- Netscape has developed a solution to this problem, which they group as a part of their Dynamic HTML. They have added a way for you to set up and embed fonts in your HTML documents, which are then downloaded over the Web along with the document so that you can be sure it will be correctly rendered.

Other than the specific elements mentioned in the preceding list—which are also contained in the introductory section of Netscape's own Dynamic HTML documentation—Netscape has added other new features related to Dynamic HTML to version 4 of their Web browser. These include the changes to their JavaScript scripting language and to the Navigator Web browser object model that supports these new capabilities.

Microsoft's Answer

Microsoft's answer to the "What is Dynamic HTML?" question is a bit longer than that of Netscape, and reveals a greater number of new possibilities and new capabilities of their

Web Page Layout and Content Positioning

Because of their support for the W3C's CSS standard, the most similarities between Netscape's and Microsoft's Dynamic HTML technologies occur with the elements that make use of style and style sheets. The main use of style sheets, discussed extensively in Chapter 9, "Style Sheets," is in the specification of formatting information for HTML elements. The benefit of using style sheets for this purpose is the ability of the Web page designer to separate the content of the document from its formatting information. (This makes it much easier to change the format while keeping the information the same.)

A newer use of style sheet attributes is to perform positioning of HTML elements, through the CSS positioning attributes. Both Microsoft and Netscape support these attributes in their Web browsers—although, as a new standard, neither Web browser offers perfect support for them. This section focuses on how you can use style sheet attributes to specify positioning of HTML elements within a Web page. You will also see how to do this for Netscape Navigator by using Netscape's `<LAYER>` and `<ILAYER>` tags. Finally, you can find out how to create scripts that can dynamically change the positioning information, and learn how you can achieve a measure of cross-platform compatibility between the two flavors of Dynamic HTML.

Internet Explorer Web browser. They have very good documentation for their Dynamic HTML, along with a number of their other technologies, located at the Internet Client SDK documentation Web site at:

http://www.microsoft.com/msdn/sdk/inetsdk/help/

The elements listed there as being a part of Microsoft's version of Dynamic HTML are also listed here, as follows:

- *Dynamic HTML object model.* The heart of Microsoft's Dynamic HTML is their extensions to the Web Browser Object Model. As shown in Chapter 16, "The Web Browser Object Model," previous object models for Netscape Navigator and Microsoft Internet Explorer enabled you to create scripts to interact with a small portion of HTML elements—images could be swapped, forms could be processed, hypertext links could be

Web Browser Object Model

The Document Object Model used by Netscape Navigator and Microsoft Internet Explorer lies at the heart of their implementations of Dynamic HTML. Netscape's implementation, and their extensions to the object model, are not as extensive as that used by Microsoft. Still, a number of important extensions enable you to increase capability in your HTML documents.

Microsoft's new object model, on the other hand, is a much more significant extension of the object models of the past for either browser. In the past, you were mainly limited to accessing and manipulating the Web browser windows, and only a few aspects of the current document such as the hypertext links, HTML Forms, and images. Now, Microsoft's Dynamic HTML has extended the object model to every HTML tag. It is now possible to examine or set properties for any tag within an HTML document, or to set up events that are attached anywhere. Microsoft's Internet Client SDK documentation Web site includes some good examples of this, enabling you to dynamically change the content included in an outline, expanding or compressing it in response to user input.

The differences and additions to the Web Browser Object Models introduced by Netscape and Microsoft are discussed in greater depth and detail in the following two chapters. The next two sections highlight some of the more important additions—in this case, changes to the Web browser event model, and how you use it.

▶ **See** "Internet Explorer 4 Document Object Model," **p. 680**

The traditional event model enabled you to respond to a limited number of events that could be triggered by the actions of your users. Table 23.1 summarizes these events, along with their description and the HTML elements to which they applied.

Table 23.1 Traditional web browser event model.

Event	Triggered When...	Where It Applies
`onChange`	Object contents change	HTML Form text fields
`onClick`	Object is clicked	Links and HTML Form elements
`onLoad`	Object loading is completed	Document and images
`onMouseOut`	Mouse is no longer over object	Links and imagemaps
`onMouseOver`	Mouse is over object	Links and imagemaps
`onReset`	Object contents are reset	HTML Forms
`onSubmit`	Object contents are submitted	HTML Forms

The Netscape Navigator Event Model

Netscape Navigator version 4 adds support for several new classes of events, enabling you to create scripts that respond to a greater variety of user input. The new categories and events are as follows:

- *Mouse events.* Added events for `onMouseDown`, `onMouseUp`, and `onMouseMove`
- *Keystroke events.* Added events for `onKeyDown`, `onKeyUp`, and `onKeyPress`
- *Window events.* Added events for `onMove` and `onResize`

In addition to the new events, Netscape has added a new `event` object that you can use to access information about the triggered events. This object is created whenever an event is being processed, and has the following properties:

- **`target`** The name of the object to which the event belongs
- **`type`** The event type (for example, `onMouseDown`, `onMouseUp`, and so forth)
- **`pageX`** The mouse's horizontal position relative to the HTML page
- **`pageY`** The mouse's vertical position relative to the HTML page
- **`screenX`** The mouse's horizontal position relative to the screen
- **`screenY`** The mouse's vertical position relative to the screen
- **`which`** A number specifying the mouse button or ASCII value of the key that was pressed

Part IV Ch 23

The `event` object is used a little differently than other objects. It comes into being in response to an event, and can then be passed to an event handler for that event, as in:

```
<FORM NAME="MyForm">
<INPUT TYPE="BUTTON" VALUE="Hi!" NAME="MyButton" onClick="hello(event)">
</FORM>
```

The event handler then takes the `event` object as a parameter and can access its properties to process the event, such as this:

```
<SCRIPT LANGUAGE="JAVASCRIPT">
function hello(MyEvent) {
   alert("Hello " + MyEvent.target.name);
}
</SCRIPT>
```

The Microsoft Internet Explorer Event Model

Microsoft's new event model is similar to Netscape's model in many respects, different in a few others. It includes most of the new events that Netscape has included, with the exception of the `onMove` and `onResize` events. It also creates an `event` object in response to events within the HTML document. Unfortunately, the `event` object itself and how it is used within a script are quite different than in Netscape's system.

Microsoft's event model has a large number of properties for identifying the nature of the event and the state of the mouse and/or keyboard when the event was triggered. The properties that correspond to the properties of the Netscape event model shown previously are as follows:

- **`srcElement`** The name of the object to which the event belongs
- **`reason`** The event type (for example, `onMouseDown`, `onMouseUp`, and so forth.
- **`x`** The mouse's horizontal position relative to the HTML page

- **y** The mouse's vertical position relative to the HTML page
- **screenX** The mouse's horizontal position relative to the screen
- **screenY** The mouse's vertical position relative to the screen
- **button** A number specifying the mouse button that was pressed
- **keyCode** A number specifying the UNICODE value of the key that was pressed

The syntax used for the Microsoft `event` object differs from that used with Netscape. It also comes into being in response to an event, but you do not need to pass it to the event handler:

```
<FORM NAME="MyForm">
<INPUT TYPE="BUTTON" VALUE="Hi!" NAME="MyButton" onClick="hello()">
</FORM>
```

The event handler can automatically access the properties of the `event` object, as in the following:

```
<SCRIPT LANGUAGE="JAVASCRIPT">
function hello() {
   alert("Hello " + event.srcElement.name);}
}
</SCRIPT>
```

Dynamic Fonts

The introduction of the `FACE` attribute of the `<FONT>` tag gave Web developers the ability to choose the font in which their content should be rendered, giving them much greater control over the final appearance of their documents. The advent of style sheets and the CSS standard—now supported by the two most popular Web browsers—add an even greater ability for you to specify the precise font, format, and position of everything on your Web page. Increasingly, the visual effects that you develop through HTML, without having to rely on large graphics or other types of plug-in content, are limited only by your imagination.

Unfortunately, one implicit assumption is made that might get you into trouble when using `<FONT FACE>` or style sheets: These techniques work only if your user has the desired font installed on his or her local system. Although this should not be a problem for the "standard" fonts installed with Windows 95, you may run into problems if you want to use less popular fonts, or when your documents are viewed on other computer platforms. Many of your carefully constructed and layed out effects can be ruined if your page is rendered in other than the desired fonts.

Both Netscape and Microsoft have introduced solutions to this problem. It will come as no surprise to you that the two solutions are not compatible, but they each achieve the same effect—they allow fonts to be embedded and used within an HTML document in such a way that, when the document is served to a Web browser the fonts can also be downloaded and used for that document. Of course it takes time to download fonts, just as with graphics and other hypertext media; font files tend not to be very large, and Web fonts can be designed to have only the characters you need. Both these technologies are very new, but they offer you the ability to truly design Web pages that will appear exactly as designed to your user.

Netscape's Downloadable Fonts

Netscape Dynamic HTML's downloadable fonts' capability enables you to use any font in your HTML documents. You do this by creating a font definition file that would be placed on your Web server, along with your other documents and content. When a user accesses a page that uses one of these fonts, the font definition file downloads with the HTML document just as images, sounds, and other content displayed on the page does. These downloaded fonts remain on the user's system only while the page is in their cache. Thus users cannot make use of the fonts for their own purposes.

To make use of Netscape's downloadable fonts, you need to follow these steps:

1. Identify the font(s) that you want to use, and make sure they are installed on your local system.

CAUTION

Remember that fonts, like all information on the Internet and the Web, are subject to copyright laws. Make sure you have a right to use any font that you plan to use as a downloadable font in any of your documents.

2. Create a font definition file. The easiest way to do this is with an authoring tool for font definition files, such as Typograph from HexMac (**http://www.hexmac.com**) or Netscape's Font Composer Plugin for Communicator.

   The specific steps necessary to produce the file will depend on the tool used, but the output of the operation will be the font definition.

NOTE Netscape's font definition files enable you to specify the domain from which they may be served. This enables you to make sure that other people don't "hijack" fonts from your server to be used in their documents.

3. You must link the font definition file in to your HTML document. You can do this either by using style sheets or with the <LINK> tag. Using style sheets, for example, to refer to a font definition file named "myfont.pfr" looks like this:

```
<STYLE TYPE="text/css">
<!-- Hide from incompatible browsers! -->
@fontdef url(http://www.rpi.edu/fonts/myfont.pfr);
<!-- Hide from incompatible browsers! -->
</STYLE>
```

   Linking the same font definition file by using the <LINK> tag looks like this:

```
<LINK REL=FONTDEF SRC="http://www.rpi.edu/fonts/myfont.pfr">
```

4. Add a new MIME type to your Web server for the font definition file. The MIME type is application/font-tdpfr, with file type ".pfr".
5. Specify the font in your HTML documents. The name of the font will be specified within the font definition file, so you can use the font, with <FONT FACE> or style sheets, just as you would use any other font.

Figure 23.5 shows an example of Netscape's downloadable fonts at work—an example file located on the DevEdge Online Web site at

http://developer.netscape.com/library/documentation/communicator/dynhtml/fontdef1.htm

If you watch this file load into your Web browser, you will notice that the text first renders in the default font. Then, as the desired fonts download, the text re-renders.

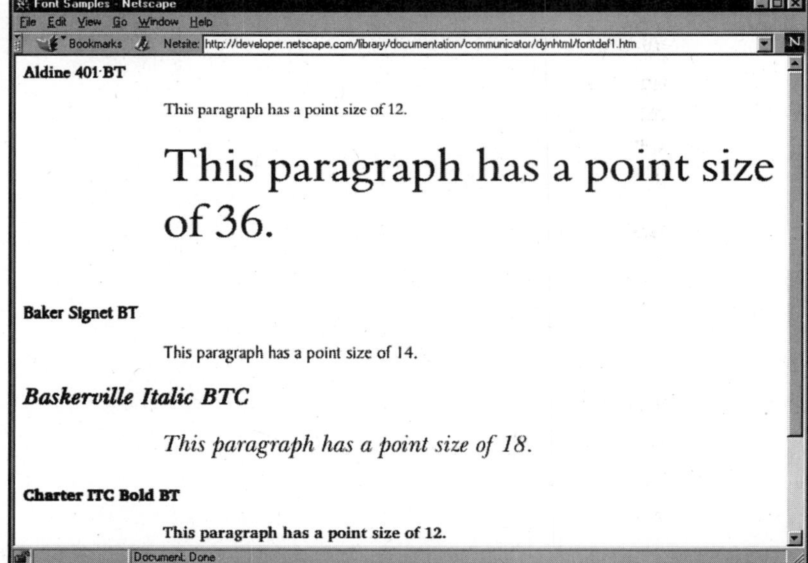

FIG. 23.5 Netscape's downloadable fonts enable you to specify any font face, size, and weight that you have access to.

Microsoft Web Embedding Fonts Tool

If you look through Microsoft's Dynamic HTML documentation, you won't find any mention of a capability to download fonts to be used with your HTML documents. Microsoft has, in fact, developed technology to perform this function—they just don't call it part of Dynamic HTML. You can find this technology, dubbed the Web Embedding Fonts Tool (WEFT), on Microsoft's Typography Web site at

http://www.microsoft.com/typography/

In practice, using the WEFT is very similar to using Netscape's downloadable fonts technology. As with Netscape, you can use a special tool to produce what Microsoft calls the font object to be linked to and downloaded with an HTML document. These font object files differ from regular fonts files in that they are prepared especially to be downloaded over the Web—they are compressed and made up of the subset of font characters actually used. These techniques can result in a savings of at least half the time otherwise required, far more if only a small number of characters is used.

Once the WEFT is used to create the font object file, it is linked into the HTML document. The syntax Microsoft uses to define an embedded font, included within a style sheet, is the following:

```
@font-face {
   font-family: MyFont;
   font-style:  normal;
   font-weight: normal;
   src: url(MYFONT0.eot);
}
```

In this case, the `src` attribute defines the actual location of the font object file.

Although the tools used to define the font file and the format of the file itself differ between Microsoft's and Netscape's systems—as well as the way that the fonts are linked into an HTML document—the other features of the two systems are very similar. Both systems enable you to determine the domain from which the fonts can be served, and both allow the font to remain on the user's system only as long as the user is viewing your pages.

Figure 23.6 and 23.7 show an example of pages created using Microsoft's font embedding technology. The second figure shows what can happen to your carefully constructed Web page if, for some reason, the fonts it uses cannot be downloaded (or are otherwise unavailable).

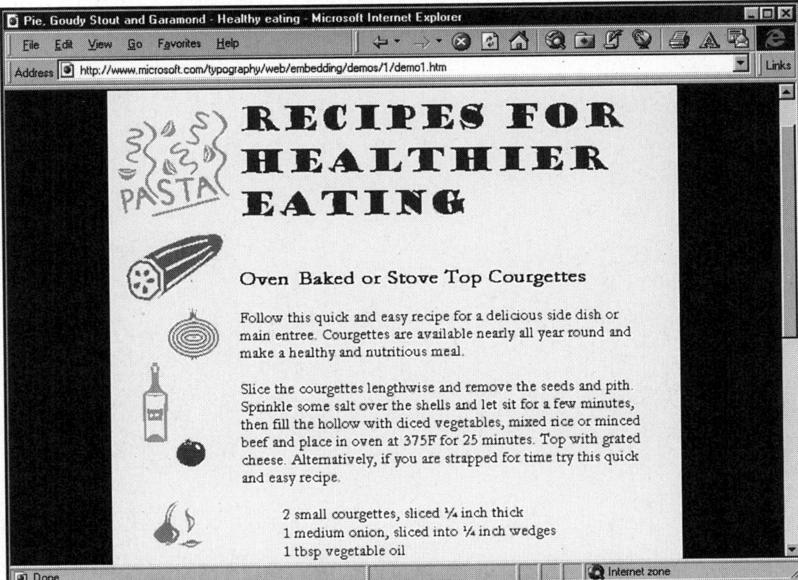

FIG. 23.6
Downloading small subsets of fonts makes it easy to create neat effects without having to create large graphics.

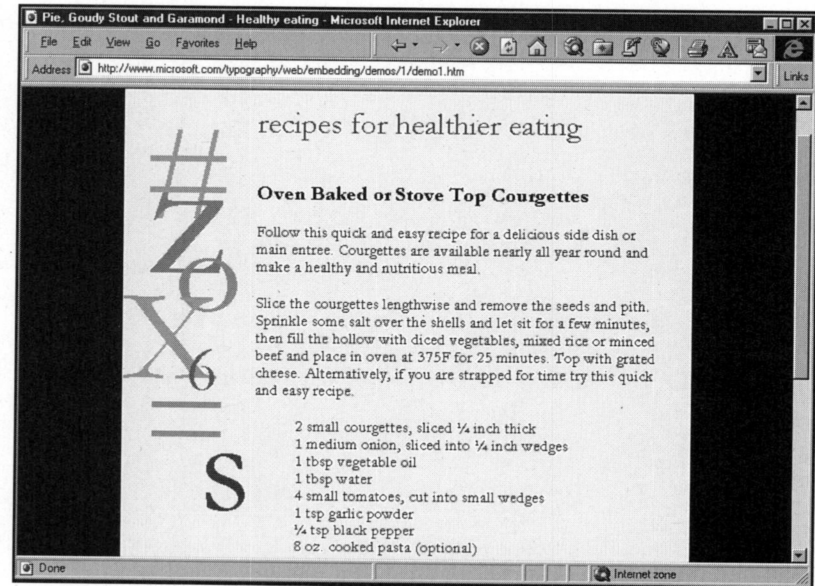

FIG. 23.7
If the font to be downloaded can't be found, or some other problem occurs, your Web page is liable to look funny.

CHAPTER 24

Advanced Netscape Dynamic HTML

by Eric Ladd

In this chapter

Different Approaches to Dynamic HTML

In Chapter 23, "Introduction to Dynamic HTML," you learned about the different claims as to what constitutes Dynamic HTML as put forward by Netscape and Microsoft. The two claims have a number of similarities—the differences lie in the implementation. Both takes on Dynamic HTML involve the following ideas:

- Positioning content on a page, either absolutely or relative to where the content would otherwise go
- Use of a Web browser object model to make all or part of a document accessible to a scripting language
- The capability to download fonts to a user's machine so that your pages are displayed with the type faces you want them to appear in

Again, the differences are in how you implement each of the preceding ideas on Navigator or Internet Explorer. Both browsers more or less conform to the Cascading Style Sheets 1 (CSS1) recommended standard for content positioning, for example, but Netscape also has a proprietary HTML tag that can do many of the same things. Another difference is in the scripting language. Navigator uses JavaScript whereas Internet Explorer uses JScript. Internet Explorer's object model is much more extensive than Navigator's. The mechanism that each program uses to download fonts to a user's hard drive is different. The list could go on and on, but the point is that if you develop a Dynamic HTML document for one browser, it is likely that it will not work in the other. This might hinder your development efforts if your audience is using a mix of browsers. If you are developing for a consistent desktop platform (a corporate intranet, for example, where everyone is using the same browser), however, you can make use of one definition of Dynamic HTML or the other and not have to worry about your content being lost on some users.

NOTE Microsoft's version of Dynamic HTML also calls for dynamic redisplay and reformatting of dynamic content, attaching data from an external source to an HTML element, and multimedia capabilities using ActiveX controls. Netscape Navigator does not support these additional Dynamic HTML components.

This chapter digs deeper into Netscape's implementation of Dynamic HTML on the Netscape Navigator 4.0 browser. By more closely examining Netscape's approach to Dynamic HTML and considering some examples, you will be better prepared to develop pages for a user base that has Navigator as its "standard-issue" browser.

A Standard Deployment of Dynamic HTML?

Even if your entire audience is using one browser or another, you should also keep in mind that there are people working on a standard deployment of some of the common Dynamic HTML elements listed at the beginning of the chapter. This means that you could develop Dynamic HTML content for one browser or another, and it may never be considered "standard."

Content positioning by Cascading Style Sheets is covered in the CSS specification found at **http://www.w3.org/Style/**. The good news here is that both major browsers more or less conform to the standard.

Additionally, the World Wide Web Consortium (W3C) is working on a Document Object Model (DOM), the details of which are covered at **http://www.w3.org/DOM/**. Both Netscape's and Microsoft's Web browser object models are extensions of the W3C DOM.

The Three Main Elements of Netscape's Dynamic HTML

Netscape considers something to be Dynamic HTML if it includes the following three major elements:

- Style sheets accessible through the browser object model
- Content positioning in two and three dimensions
- Downloadable fonts

Netscape Navigator supports the Cascading Style Sheet specification just like other browsers do, but what makes its support dynamic is that style sheet elements are part of the Navigator browser object model. This means that you can specify style information through JavaScript in addition to the CSS way of doing it. Figures 24.1 and 24.2 show two different versions of the same content. The figures look more or less the same, but the style approach in each differs. Listing 24.1 shows the style code for Figure 24.1; Listing 24.2 shows the code for Figure 24.2.

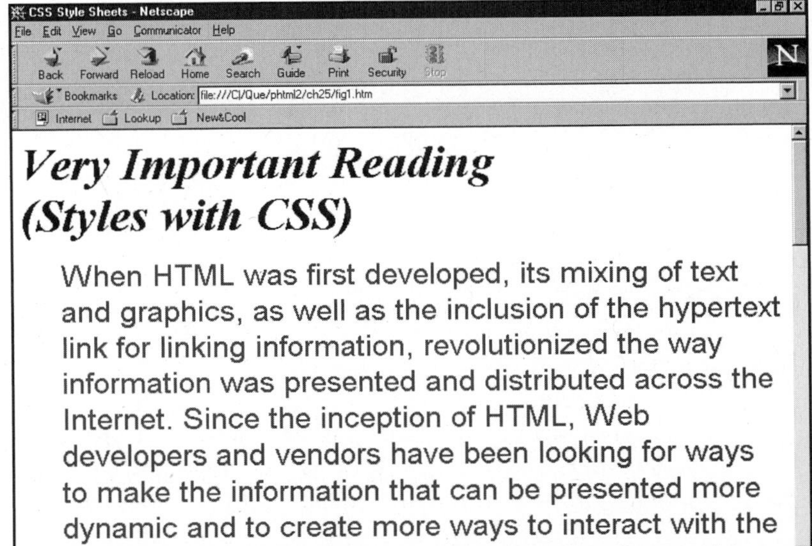

FIG. 24.1
Netscape Navigator supports the CSS specification for assigning style information.

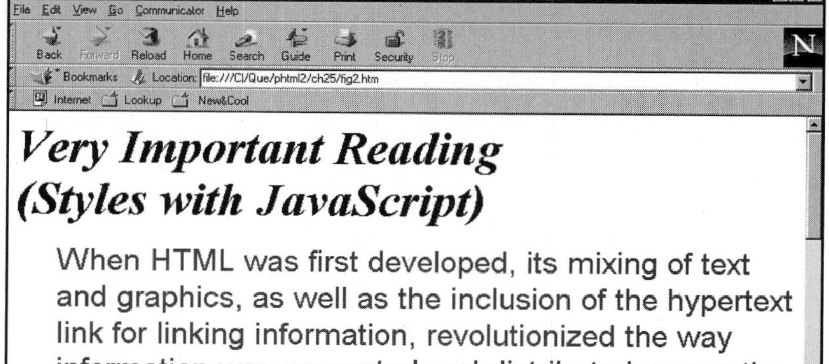

FIG. 24.2
Navigator also enables you to assign styles via JavaScript code.

Listing 24.1 Assigning styles according to the CSS specification.

```
<STYLE TYPE="text/css">
P {font-size: 24pt; line-height: 28pt; color: blue;
    margin-left: 40px; font-family: Arial}
H1 {font-size: 36pt; line-height: 40pt; font-style: italic}
</STYLE>
```

Listing 24.2 Assigning styles using JavaScript 1.2.

```
<STYLE TYPE="text/javascript">
document.tags.P.fontSize = "24pt";
document.tags.P.lineHeight = "28pt";
document.tags.P.color = "blue";
document.tags.P.marginLeft = "40px";
document.tags.P.fontFamily = "Arial";
document.tags.H1.fontSize = "36pt";
document.tags.H1.lineHeight = "40pt";
document.tags.H1.fontStyle = "italic";
</STYLE>
```

Note the "object orientation" of the code in Listing 24.2. The first style assignment says "set the `fontSize` property of the `P` property of the `tags` property of the `document` property to 24 point." The Navigator browser object model makes many tags available to you in this way.

The document object reference is understood whenever you reference the tags object. Thus, instead of saying:

```
document.tags.P.color = "blue";
```

you can equivalently say:

```
tags.P.color = "blue";
```

When assigning multiple style characteristics to the same tag, you can use the JavaScript `with` instruction to reference the tag and then all styles inside the `with` instruction will be assigned to the tag. For the `<P>` tag assignments in Listing 24.2, you could have used the following abbreviated code:

```
with (tags.P) {
  fontSize = "24pt";
  lineHeight = "28pt";
  color = "blue";
  marginLeft = "40px";
  fontFamily = "Arial";
}
```


Content positioning was introduced in Navigator 4.0 through use of the `<LAYER>` and `<ILAYER>` tags for absolute and relative positioning, respectively. Unfortunately for Netscape, using HTML tags to specify content presentation information flies in the face of the direction that the W3C wants to move—namely, to reserve HTML for describing the meaning of the content and to specify presentation through style sheets. The W3C rejected the Netscape proposal for the `<LAYER>` tag, and Netscape was forced to scramble to make Navigator compliant with the CSS approach to content positioning. Currently, Navigator supports both positioning techniques, although you should always consider developing according to the CSS specification because this will make your content more portable.

Figures 24.3 and 24.4 show a page put together with Netscape layers. Each figure has two layers. The first layer is comprised of two nested layers. The first nested layer contains the "Here is some magic text" message in normal font weight. The second nested layer contains the same message in boldface. The second layer contains the horizontal line and the message to "Click the text above and watch it change!" When a user clicks on the first layer, the browser invokes a JavaScript function that looks to see which nested layer is displayed and then displays the one that was previously hidden. Thus, by clicking the text, you make it appear to change to boldface and then back to normal. Listing 24.3 shows the code to accomplish the normal/bold effect.

Listing 24.3 Code to create toggling text.

```
<HTML>
<HEAD>
<TITLE>Toggling Text</TITLE>
```

continues

Listing 24.3 Continued

```
<BASE HREF=
  "http://developer.netscape.com/library/examples/dynhtml/checkbox/">
<SCRIPT LANGUAGE="javascript1.2" SRC="checkbox.js">
</SCRIPT>
</HEAD>
<SCRIPT LANGUAGE="javascript1.2">
  var c= new Checkbox(150,100,"<FONT SIZE=7>Here is some magic text.
  </FONT>","<b><FONT SIZE=7>Here is some magic text.</FONT></b>");
</SCRIPT>
<LAYER TOP=200>
<HR NOSHADE SIZE=8>
<P ALIGN=CENTER STYLE="font-size: 24pt">Click the text above and watch it
change!</P>
</LAYER>
```

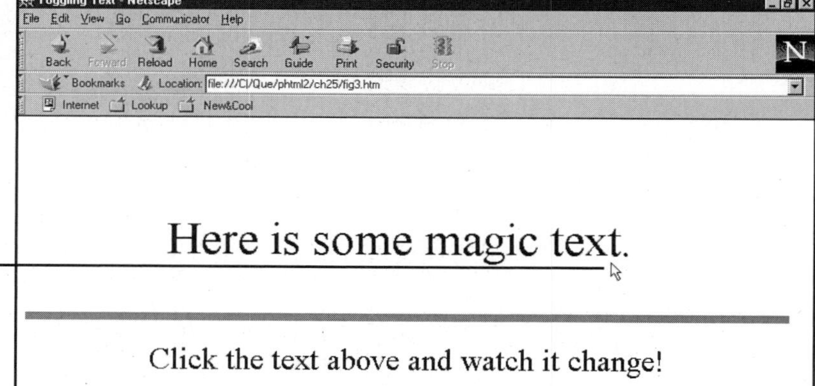

FIG. 24.3
When you open this page, it displays only one of two nested layers.

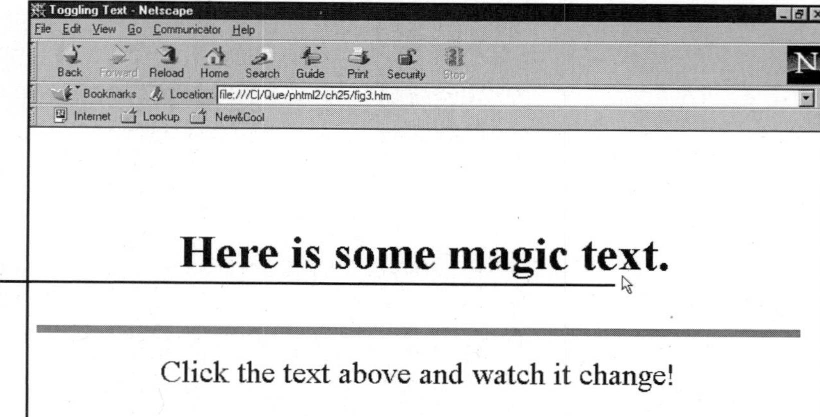

FIG. 24.4
By clicking the layer, you instruct the browser to swap the hidden and displayed nested layers.

Netscape has several useful JavaScript routines available on its DevEdge site (**http://developer.netscape.com/one/dynhtml/index.html**). You can reference the code by using the SRC attribute of the <SCRIPT> tag as shown in Listing 24.3 or you can download the code and place it right into your document.

For all your hard work in coming up with attractive style information, you may end up having your effect lost on users who don't have the font you specified in your style sheet. Rather than take chances on fonts a user may or may not have, you can bundle the font you want to use with a Web page and have it download along with the page. This assures both you and the reader that the page will display the way you wanted it to.

Figure 24.5 shows an example of a page that uses a downloaded font. The type face you see is Clarendon, one not commonly found on most users' systems.

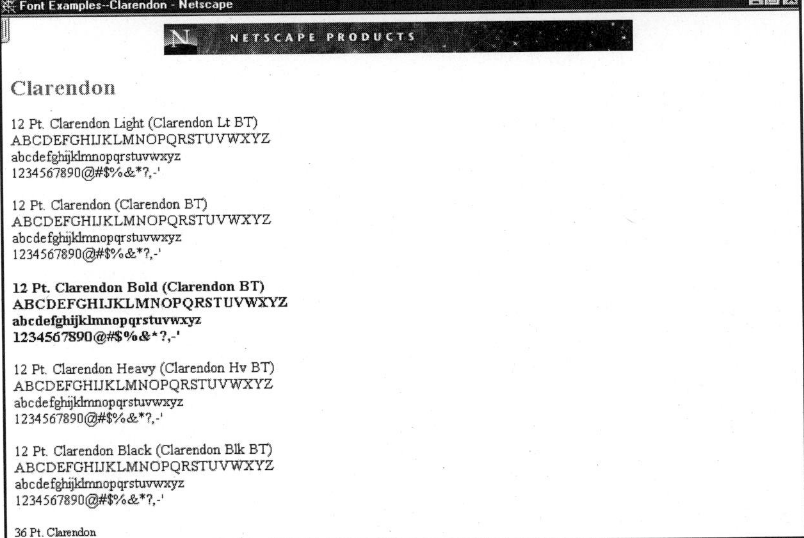

FIG. 24.5
By downloading fonts along with a page, you ensure that readers see content the way you intended.

Now that you have the major ideas behind Netscape's Dynamic HTML fresh in your mind, it is time to take a closer look at each one. The remaining sections of this chapter examine each idea in turn and provide you with more details about how to implement Dynamic HTML on your pages.

JavaScript Accessible Style Sheets

Netscape Navigator does support the CSS specification, and using the CSS approach is a perfectly good way to build style information into your documents. But as you saw earlier in the chapter, Navigator also includes style properties in the browser object model, meaning you can use JavaScript to access and set style characteristics. Netscape calls this approach JavaScript Accessible Style Sheets; it is the first major feature of Netscape's version of Dynamic HTML.

The advantage of JavaScript Accessible Style Sheets is that by using the browser object model, you can dynamically change style information by using scripts triggered by certain events that come about from user actions. This section focuses solely on the JavaScript implementation of styles so that you can be prepared to use them by themselves and also as part of content positioning.

To get started, it is helpful to recall some of the style-related code—both CSS and JavaScript—that you saw earlier in the chapter. Go back a few pages and look at Listings 24.1 and 24.2 again. Both sets of code apply the same style information, yet one is an implementation of CSS style sheets and the other is an implementation of JavaScript Accessible Style Sheets. If you are familiar with one approach, you can see that it would be pretty easy to learn the other. This is because most of the style characteristics you can set have the same name (although the names differ in the use of hyphens, capitalization, and so on). The chief difference between the two approaches is how the style characteristics are assigned. The CSS approach uses name/value pairs separated by a colon. The JavaScript approach is more object based in that you reference an object's (a tag's) style property and set it to the value you want. Beyond the syntactical difference in assigning values, the two approaches are, in most respects, equivalent.

Table 24.1 summarizes the style characteristics you can assign by either approach and includes the keyword for the characteristic that you would use in either the CSS or JavaScript approach. The table should make a handy reference for all style sheet authors, regardless of how they are assigning style information.

Table 24.1 Style characteristics in CSS and JavaScript Accessible Style Sheets.

Style Characteristic	CSS Keyword	JavaScript Property
Font family	`font-family`	`fontFamily`
Font size	`font-size`	`fontSize`
Font style	`font-style`	`fontStyle`
Font weight	`font-weight`	`fontWeight`
Text alignment	`text-align`	`textAlign`
Text decoration	`text-decoration`	`textDecoration`
Text indent	`text-indent`	`textIndent`
Text transform	`text-transform`	`textTransform`
Line height	`line-height`	`lineHeight`
Alignment	`float`	`align`
Border color	`border-color`	`borderColor`

Style Characteristic	CSS Keyword	JavaScript Property
Border style	`border-style`	`borderStyle`
Border widths (all)	`border-width`	`borderWidths()`
Border width (bottom)	`border-bottom-width`	`borderBottomWidth`
Border width (left)	`border-left-width`	`borderLeftWidth`
Border width (right)	`border-right-width`	`borderRightWidth`
Border width (top)	`border-top-width`	`borderTopWidth`
Margins (all)	`margin`	`margins()`
Margin (bottom)	`margin-bottom`	`marginBottom`
Margin (left)	`margin-left`	`marginLeft`
Margin (right)	`margin-right`	`marginRight`
Margin (top)	`margin-top`	`marginTop`
Padding (all)	`paddings`	`paddings()`
Padding (bottom)	`padding-bottom`	`paddingBottom`
Padding (left)	`padding-left`	`paddingLeft`
Padding (right)	`padding-right`	`paddingRight`
Padding (top)	`padding-top`	`paddingTop`
Width	`width`	`width`
Background color	`background-color`	`backgroundColor`
Background image	`background-image`	`backgroundImage`
Color	`color`	`color`
Display	`display`	`display`
List style type	`list-style-type`	`listStyleType`
White space	`white-space`	`whiteSpace`

You are probably familiar with most of the characteristics in Table 24.1, except for possibly the last three. Display controls how an element is displayed and can take values of `block` (display as a block-level element), `inline`, `list-item`, or `none`. List style type refers to the different styles of ordered and unordered lists HTML supports. You may set the `list-style-type` keyword or the `listStyleType` property to values of `disc`, `circle`, `square`, `decimal`, `lower-alpha`, `upper-alpha`, `lower-roman`, `upper-roman`, or `none`. Finally, the white space characteristic specifies how extra white space should be treated. A white space value of `normal` means that extra white space characters will be ignored, and a value of `pre` means that all white space characters will be rendered.

With what you have learned so far, you can probably handle most of the style sheet challenges that come your way. Be aware, however, that both the CSS and JavaScript approaches support some more advanced techniques. These include the following:

- Setting up different classes of the same element
- Creating a named style that you can apply to any element
- Selecting an element based on context
- Making use of block-level styles

Each of these points is covered in the sections that follow with emphasis on the JavaScript implementation of each.

TROUBLESHOOTING

Your JavaScript code is not in Netscape Navigator and you can't tell what the error is.

Make sure that JavaScript is enabled in your Netscape Navigator. You can do this by choosing Edit, Preferences, and then clicking on the Advanced item in the category listing in the Preferences dialog box. After you do this, you will see a list of check box options. Make sure that the check box labeled Enable JavaScript is checked. Then click on OK.

With Netscape capable of processing JavaScript, you should find that the next time you load your JavaScript document, Netscape will interpret the script code and note any syntax errors it finds in a pop-up dialog box. The error messages are usually very specific and should help you clean up your code.

Setting Up Style Classes

Suppose you assign the following style characteristics to the `<H1>` element:

```
<STYLE TYPE="text/javascript">
with (tags.H1) {
  backgroundColor = "black";
  color = "white";
  fontSize = "36pt";
  lineHeight = "40pt";
  align = "center";
  width = "100%";
}
</STYLE>
```

Using the preceding code, each level 1 heading would appear centered in a black box that is 40 points high and spans the width of the browser screen. The text of the headline would be 36 points high and rendered in white. But what if you don't want *every* level 1 heading to look like this? Suppose you want some of them to be in yellow on a red background so that they stand out more prominently. What you can do in this case is to define two different classes of the H1 element style—one for the white on black heading and one for the yellow on red.

Classes are set up using the JavaScript `classes` object. To set up the two types of level 1 headings just discussed, for example, you could use this code:

```
<STYLE TYPE="text/javascript">
  with (tags.H1) {
   fontSize = "36pt";
   lineHeight = "40pt";
   align = "center";
   width = "100%";
  }
  classes.whiteOnBlack.H1.backgroundColor = "black";
  classes.whiteOnBlack.H1.color = "white";
  classes.yellowOnRed.H1.backgroundColor = "red";
  classes.yellowOnRed.H1.color = "yellow";
</STYLE>
```

The `with` operator makes all level 1 headings 36 point on 40 point, centered, and the full width of the browser screen. The last four lines of code define the two classes: `whiteOnBlack`, which produces white text on a black background; and `yellowOnRed`, which produces yellow text on a red background. With the two classes defined, you can invoke one class or another by using the `CLASS` attribute in the `<H1>` tag as follows:


```
<BODY>
...
<H1 CLASS="yellowOnRed">Yellow headline on red background</H1>
...
<H1 CLASS="whiteOnBlack">White headline on black background</H1>
...
</BODY>
```

The one limitation in the way the classes are set up is that they can be used only with the H1 element. If you want your classes applicable to more than just the H1 element, you could duplicate the code for the other elements with which you want to use the classes, or you could make the classes available to every element by using the `all` object as follows:

```
<STYLE TYPE="text/javascript">
  ...
  classes.whiteOnBlack.all.backgroundColor = "black";
  classes.whiteOnBlack.all.color = "white";
  classes.yellowOnRed.all.backgroundColor = "red";
  classes.yellowOnRed.all.color = "yellow";
</STYLE>
```

The preceding code makes the `whiteOnBlack` and `yellowOnRed` classes available to all HTML elements, not just H1. If you don't want to apply either class to an element, you just don't use a `CLASS` attribute with that element.

NOTE The properties assigned in these classes are really applicable only to block-level formats such as headings, paragraphs, blockquotes, and lists. Trying to apply the classes to text-level formatting tags would have no effect.

CAUTION

You can specify only one CLASS per HTML tag. If you put multiple CLASS attributes in a tag, Netscape Navigator uses the first one it encounters and ignores the rest.

Setting Up Named Styles

Besides creating classes of the same tag, you can also create a specific named style that you can build into any tag. The JavaScript `ids` object enables you to set up the named style and then the style can be referenced by any tag using the `ID` attribute.

As an example of a named style, consider the following code:

```
<STYLE TYPE="text/javascript">
  ids.allCaps.textTransform = "uppercase";
  ids.bigText.fontSize= "300%";
  ...
</STYLE>
```

After executing the script code, Navigator recognizes two named styles: `allCaps`, which transforms all text to uppercase; and `bigText`, which magnifies text to 300% of its default size. If you had a paragraph you wanted to appear in all uppercase letters, you could set it up with this:

```
<P ID="allCaps">This paragraph is all uppercase letters ... </P>
```

Suppose you still had the `whiteOnBlack` and `yellowOnRed` classes available to you from the preceding section. You could then use a class and a named style together as follows:

```
<H1 CLASS="yellowOnRed" ID="allCaps">
Yellow, uppercase heading on red background</H1>
```

One popular effect on Web pages is "small caps"—text that is all in uppercase and where the first letter of each word is larger than the rest of the letters in the word. You can accomplish this with the two named styles already defined, but you have to use the `<SPAN>` tag to apply the `bigText` style. For example,:

```
<H1 CLASS="whiteOnBlack" ID="allCaps">
<SPAN ID="bigText">V</SPAN>ery
<SPAN ID="bigText">I</SPAN>mportant
<SPAN ID="bigText">S</SPAN>tory!
</H1>
...
```

Figure 24.6 shows the result of using the classes and named styles together.

Doing Contextual Selection

Sometimes it is necessary to apply style information to an element only when it appears in the context of another. With CSS, doing this is fairly straightforward. As an example, the following code

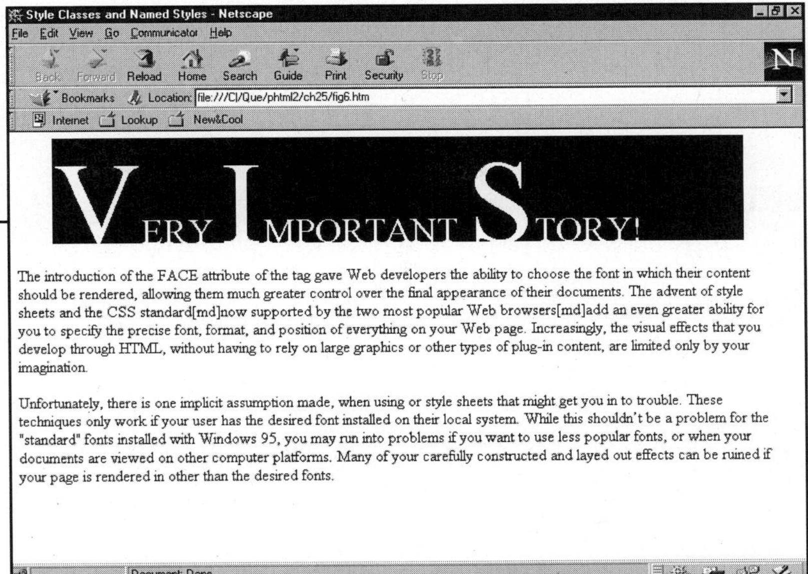

FIG. 24.6
You can use style classes and named styles together to produce complex typographic effects.

Headline done with style sheets


```
<STYLE TYPE="text/css">
   H1 STRONG {color:red};
   ...
</STYLE>
```

says that any level 1 heading text marked up with the <STRONG> element should be rendered in red. This makes some sense because headings are already in boldface. Adding the <STRONG> element, which usually produces boldface rendering, would not change the appearance of the text. By making <STRONG> text red within a level 1 heading, you make it stand out even more and thereby convey your strong emphasis.

To accomplish the same effect with JavaScript, you need to use the `contextual()` method. `contextual()` takes a list of element objects that represent the usage context to which you want to apply style information. The following replicates the effect of the CSS code just discussed:

```
<STYLE TYPE="javascript"
   contextual(tags.H1, tags.STRONG).color = "red";
   ...
</STYLE>
```

After you have the context set up, you don't need to do anything special in the HTML code to invoke it. You just nest the tags and the browser detects the context.

Applying Styles to Block-Level Elements

Block-level formatting tags require some extra attention because of how the browser treats them. Block-level formatting in HTML 4.0 includes <P>, <DIV>, <H1>–<H6>, and <BLOCKQUOTE>.

You can think of each block-level element on a page as having an invisible box that contains it. The boundaries of that box define the extent of the block-formatted text and the browser treats that box as an object that has many properties such as borders, indentation, and background colors. Figure 24.7 shows the extent of a box around a level 2 heading by turning on the box's border and making the background color a light gray. The JavaScript code that enables you to see the box is as follows:

```
<STYLE TYPE="text/javascript">
  with (tags.H1) {
     backgroundColor = "#DDDDDD";
     borderWidths("1pt");
     borderStyle = "solid";
     borderColor = "black";
   }
</STYLE>
```

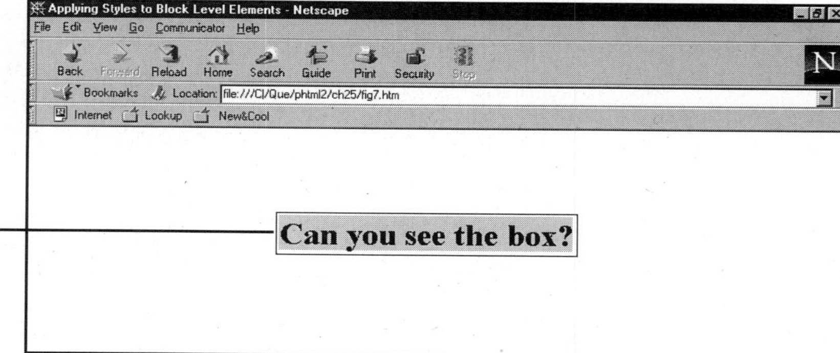

FIG. 24.7
Block-level formats are contained in an invisible box, but you can modify the box's properties to make it visible.

Because of the boxes that surround them, block-level elements have style characteristics that other elements do not. These characteristics include the following:

- Alignment with respect to the rest of the document
- Background colors or images
- Borders of varying width, style, and color
- Margins from the left, right, top, and bottom boundaries of the box
- Padding (the distance from the element's content to the edges of the box) along the left, right, top, and bottom of the content within the box
- Width of the box with respect to the rest of the document

Refer to Table 24.1 for the JavaScript property names for each of these; each is fairly intuitive. As you specify values for these properties, keep the image of the invisible box in mind and it will help you visualize what your results will look like.

One important thing to note is the relationship between the width and margin characteristics. Mathematically, you could describe the relationship between the width of the block element, the margins, and the width of the content of the block element as this:

block element width = left margin + content width + right margin

After the content is specified, its width is determined and becomes a fixed value. This means you can set either of the following:

- The margins and let the margin sizes and the content width determine the total width
- The total width and let the margins split the balance of the remaining space

The point is that it does not make sense to specify *both* the margins and the total width. After you choose values for one, the value of the other is determined by the preceding equation.

Content Positioning

In the previous section, you saw how you could use JavaScript to assign values to style characteristics and dynamically format your document. One class of style characteristics was deliberately left out of the section, however: that for specifying content position. Content positioning is a much different activity than assigning styles and you can bring many more JavaScript commands to bear on a content positioning challenge. This section looks at how you can do content positioning with Netscape Navigator. Again, the focus is on Netscape's implementation of content positioning. This means that it will be "legal" to make use of the nonstandard <LAYER> element as well as CSS techniques to do positioning.

The *<LAYER>* and *<ILAYER>* Elements

Chapter 23 showed you some examples of content positioning. Specifically, you saw how you could position an element with respect to the upper-left corner of the browser window (*absolute positioning*) or with respect to the location where the element would ordinarily be placed (*relative positioning*). In addition to being able to specify the x and y coordinates of where the element should appear, you were also able to control a z coordinate, which determined how the elements overlap. You could think of each element as sitting on a transparent sheet that you could move around the browser screen and stack one on top of the other to create different effects. Netscape's term for these transparent sheets is *layers*. You can implement layers in Navigator by using the CSS specification for content positioning or by using the proprietary <LAYER> and <ILAYER> elements to do absolute and relative positioning, respectively. This section introduces you to the <LAYER> and <ILAYER> tags and their many attributes.

NOTE <LAYER> and <ILAYER> take the same set of attributes, so this section just focuses on using the <LAYER> tag. The <ILAYER> (inline layer) tag behaves exactly the same as the <LAYER> tag, except that <ILAYER> allows for positioning of content relative to where the content would appear in the flow of the document whereas <LAYER> is used for absolute positioning of content with respect to the upper-left corner of the browser window.

The <LAYER> tag is a container tag that can take the following attributes:

- BACKGROUND—The BACKGROUND attribute is set equal to the URL of an image to tile in the background of the layer. In the absence of a background image or background color (see

BGCOLOR next in this list), the layer background is transparent and allows any layers stacked beneath it to show through.

- BGCOLOR—You can set BGCOLOR equal to a reserved English-language color name, an RGB triplet, or a hexadecimal triplet that specifies a background color for the layer. Otherwise, the layer background is transparent.
- SRC—You have two ways to place content in a layer. You can place the content between the <LAYER> and </LAYER> tags or you can import the content from another file by using the SRC attribute. SRC is set equal to the URL of the document you want to import.
- ID—The ID attribute is used to assign a unique name to a layer so that it can be referenced in other <LAYER> tags or in JavaScript code.
- LEFT and TOP—LEFT and TOP are set equal to the number of pixels from the upper-left corner of the browser screen the layer should begin. These two attributes permit exact positioning of the layer on the screen. Note that if you're using <ILAYER>, LEFT and TOP specify displacement from the left of and below the point where the layer would ordinarily start rather than from the upper-left of the browser screen. Also, when using relative positioning, you can set LEFT and TOP equal to negative values.
- Z-INDEX, ABOVE, and BELOW—These three attributes all help to specify how the layers stack up along the *z* axis (the axis coming out of the browser screen toward the user). Z-INDEX is set equal to a positive integer and a layer with a larger Z-INDEX value will appear stacked on top of layers that have lower Z-INDEX values. You can place a new layer above or below an existing named layer by setting ABOVE or BELOW equal to the named layer's name. In the absence of Z-INDEX, ABOVE, or BELOW attributes, new layers are stacked on top of old layers.
- VISIBILITY—VISIBILITY can take on one of the following three values: SHOW, HIDE, or INHERIT. If a layer's VISIBILITY is set to SHOW, the content of the layer will be displayed. Setting SHOW to HIDE conceals the layer content. A SHOW value of INHERIT means that the layer will have the same SHOW behavior as its parent layer.
- CLIP—The *clipping region* of a layer is a rectangular area that defines how much of the layer content is visible. You can control the size of the clipping region by using the CLIP attribute. CLIP is set equal to a comma-delimited list of four numbers that represent the coordinates of the upper-left and lower-right corners of the clipping region. Measurements for clipping region coordinates are taken with respect to the upper-left corner of the layer. By default, the clipping region is large enough to display all the contents of the layer.
- HEIGHT—In the absence of a CLIP attribute, HEIGHT controls the height of the clipping region. HEIGHT may be set equal to a number of pixels or to a percentage of the layer's height.
- WIDTH—The WIDTH attribute specifies the width at which layer contents begin to wrap to new lines. Like HEIGHT, you can set WIDTH equal to a number of pixels or to a percentage of the layer width.
- PAGEX and PAGEY—Because it is possible to nest layers inside of layers, you may end up in a situation in which you want to position a layer with respect to the entire browser

screen and not its parent element (the layer that contains it). In such a case, you can use the PAGEX and PAGEY attributes to specify where the layer should begin with respect to the upper-left corner of the browser screen.

The <LAYER> tag's extensive set of attributes makes many interesting effects possible. By changing the size of the clipping region, for example, you can show or hide different parts of the layer's content. You can change the Z-INDEX of a layer to make it rise above or drop below other layers. You could even adjust the TOP and LEFT values to make a layer move to a new position. All these changes are possible thanks to the capability to use JavaScript to modify layer properties. The following section provides some examples of that. To complete the discussion of the <LAYER> tag's syntax, however, here is a list of JavaScript event handlers you can use with the <LAYER> tag:

- OnMouseOver—The OnMouseOver event is invoked when a user's mouse pointer enters the layer.
- OnMouseOut—When the mouse pointer leaves a layer, the OnMouseOut event is fired.
- OnFocus—If the layer acquires keyboard focus (for example, a user clicks a form field in a layer so as to be able to type in it), an OnFocus event is triggered.
- OnBlur—Blurring refers to the loss of focus. When a layer blurs, Navigator invokes an OnBlur event.
- OnLoad—The OnLoad event is triggered when the layer is initially loaded.

Using these event handlers is the first step in making your positioned content dynamic. Depending on what JavaScript code you execute upon an event firing, you can change a layer's content or move it to a new position to create an animation effect. You will read about some of the possibilities in subsequent sections of this chapter. However, you should first know about one other layer-related tag.

The *<NOLAYER>* Tag

Netscape knew it was creating proprietary tags when it introduced <LAYER> and <ILAYER>, so it also included a <NOLAYER> element for specifying non-layered versions of layered content. You might use <NOLAYER> as follows, for example:

```
<HTML>
<HEAD>
<TITLE>Welcome to Our Site!</TITLE>
</HEAD>
<LAYER LEFT=50 TOP=35 ID="layer1" SRC="toplayer.html"></LAYER>
<LAYER LEFT=100 TOP=152 ID="layer2" SRC="bottomlayer.html"></LAYER>
<NOLAYER>
<BODY BGCOLOR="white">
<H1>Whoops!</H1>
You must not be using Netscape Navigator, so you'd probably be interested
in a <A HREF="nolayers/index.html">non-layered version</A> of our site.
</BODY>
</NOLAYER>
</HTML>
```

Netscape Navigator ignores anything between <NOLAYER> and </NOLAYER>, so it will render the preceding example just fine. A browser that does not understand the layer-related tags ignores the two <LAYER> elements and the <NOLAYER> element and displays the HTML between the <NOLAYER> and </NOLAYER> tags.

NOTE When using layers, you don't use the <BODY> tag in the document except between <NOLAYER> and </NOLAYER> tags.

Putting the "Dynamic" in Dynamic HTML with JavaScript

Everything you have read so far in this chapter has been largely about how to create static content, so you might be wondering whether the term "Dynamic HTML" really applies. Now that you understand how to access style characteristics with JavaScript and how you can use the <LAYER> tag to position content, however, you are ready to see how you can use JavaScript to make your pages come alive. This section gives an overview of some of the many things possible with JavaScript, layers, and style information.

See "The Netscape Navigator Event Model," **page 636**.

The capability to use JavaScript to create dynamic pages hinges on the Netscape browser object model, which provides for many different events and responses to those events. You read in Chapter 23 about the traditional events that Navigator supports and some extras added by Netscape to handle `mouse`, `keystroke`, and `window` events. Any of these can be used to trigger the execution of some JavaScript code in response to some kind of user action.

Two other aspects of the Netscape browser object model make Dynamic HTML possible. The first is the new `event` object that is created whenever an event occurs. As noted back in Chapter 23, you can access properties of the `event` object to determine which kind of event was triggered, what mouse button or keystroke initiated the event, and which object the event belongs to.

The other helpful feature of the Netscape browser object model is that every layer—regardless of whether it was created using CSS properties or the <LAYER> tag—is accessible through the `layers` object. The `layers` object is actually an arrayed property of the `document` object, meaning that you can reference a particular layer in the following manner:

```
document.layers["layer1"]
```

This code says to select the layer named "layer1" from the `layers` array of the `document` object. You can also reference the array by a number if you know the layer's position in the stacking order. If you want to make a direct reference to layer1, you could also say this:

```
document.layer1
```

NOTE Only top-level layers in a document are listed in the layers array.

The properties of a layer selected from the `layers` object map very closely to the attributes of the `<LAYER>` tag discussed in the preceding section. Beyond those properties, one other thing could cause some confusion: Each layer has its own document property! A layer's document property refers to the content inside the layer and not the main document. Other than that, you can use the document property just as you always have. Thus, to reference a `<BLOCKQUOTE>` tag inside a layer named "imagelayer," you would use the following:

```
document.layers["imagelayer"].document.tags.BLOCKQUOTE
```

This may not seem too bad, but your references can become fairly complicated if you have layers nested inside a layer. Suppose "layer2" and "layer3" are top-level layers nested inside "layer1." Then to reference the H5 tag in "layer3," you would have to say

```
document.layers["layer1"].document.layers["layer3"].document.tags.H5
```

Table 24.2 provides a full listing of the properties of a selected layer. Note that you can't modify all the properties by using JavaScript commands. The layer's `parentLayer` is a fixed property that cannot be changed, for example.

Table 24.2 Properties of a selected layer.

Property	Description
`above`	The layer above the selected layer or the browser window if you have selected the topmost layer
`background.src`	The URL of the image file to use as the background
`below`	The layer below the selected layer or null if the selected layer is at the lowest level
`bgColor`	Color specification for the background
`clip.bottom`	Controls the position of the bottom edge of the clipping region
`clip.left`	Controls the position of the left edge of the clipping region
`clip.right`	Controls the position of the right edge of the clipping region
`clip.top`	Controls the position of the top edge of the clipping region
`clip.height`	Controls the distance between the top and bottom edges of the clipping region
`clip.width`	Controls the distance between the left and right edges of the clipping region
`document`	Object that enables you to reference the contents of a layer
`left`	Controls the horizontal position of where the layer begins
`name`	The unique name of the layer as assigned by the `ID` attribute of the `<LAYER>` tag

continues

Table 24.2 Continued

Property	Description
`pageX`	The horizontal position of the layer with respect to the browser screen
`pageY`	The vertical position of the layer with respect to the browser screen
`parentLayer`	The layer that contains the object layer or the browser window if the object layer is a top-level layer
`siblingAbove`	The sibling layer (same parent layer) that is above the object layer in the stacking order or null if there is no layer above it
`siblingBelow`	The sibling layer (same parent layer) that is below the object layer in the stacking order or null if there is no layer below it
`src`	The URL of the document to be loaded into the layer
`top`	Controls the vertical position of where the layer begins
`visibility`	Determines whether the content of the layer is shown or hidden
`zIndex`	Determines the layer's position in the stacking order

In addition to the many layer properties you can reference, JavaScript also supports several methods that you can apply to a layer. Table 24.3 summarizes these methods.

Table 24.3 JavaScript methods for the *layer* object.

Method Name	Function
`load(URL,width)`	Loads the document at the URL specified into the layer (replacing existing content in the layer) and changes the width of the layer to the value in the second argument
`moveAbove(layer)`	Moves a layer to a position in the stacking order above the layer in the argument
`moveBelow(layer)`	Moves a layer to a position in the stacking order below the layer in the argument
`moveBy(dx,dy)`	Moves a layer `dx` pixels to the left and `dy` pixels down
`moveTo(x,y)`	Moves an absolutely positioned layer to the specified coordinates with the containing document or layer; moves a relatively positioned layer to the specified coordinates, taken with respect to the layer's natural position
`moveToAbsolute(x,y)`	Moves a layer to the specified coordinates, taken with respect to the browser screen
`resizeBy(dw,dh)`	Adds `dw` to the layer width and `dh` to the layer height
`resizeTo(width,height)`	Resets the layer's width and height to the specified values

Now that you know about the `layer` object, its properties, its methods, and the event handlers available in the Netscape browser object model, you are finally ready to take a look at some examples of truly Dynamic HTML—pages that change right in the browser window without going back to the server to get more content.

Example 1: Dynamic Hypertext

Before Dynamic HTML, the only feedback users would get when their mouse pointers were over a piece of hypertext would be a change in the pointer icon from an arrow to an upward pointing finger. You can enhance this feedback by using Dynamic HTML to cause a change in the hypertext itself when the mouse pointer is over it. Suppose, for example, that a hypertext link should be colored blue and be in the same point size as your body text (typically 12 points) when a user's mouse is not over it and that the link should change color to red, increase in size to 14 points, and become underlined when the user's mouse is over it. You can accomplish this effect by using style sheet information and some simple JavaScript code in your `<A>` tags.

To begin, you need to set up two classes of hypertext styles: one for when the mouse is over the text and one for when it is not. Given the preceding specifications, you can set up the classes with the following code:

```
<STYLE>
.off     {
          font-size: 12 pt;
          font-weight: normal;
          color: blue;
          }
.over  {
         font-size: 14 pt;
         font-weight: bold;
         color: red;
         }
</STYLE>
```

The class titled `off` contains the style information for the hypertext when the mouse is not over it, and the class titled `over` contains the style information for when the mouse is over the hypertext.

NOTE Even though a font weight of `normal` is the typical default, it is essential to include the `font-weight`: normal statement in the definition of the `off` class. This is so that the bold effect turns off when a mouse is no longer over the hypertext.

With the two classes defined, it is a simple matter to use them in a given hypertext link. Listing 24.4 shows the HTML code to produce a set of links that use the `over` and `off` classes just defined. Note that in each `<A>` tag the `CLASS` is initially set to `off`, but when an `onMouseOver` event occurs, the `CLASS` of the object is set to `over`. When the mouse pointer is no longer over the hypertext, the `onMouseOut` event resets the `CLASS` to `off`. Figure 24.8 illustrates the effect of moving a mouse pointer over one of these links.

FIG. 24.8
The onMouseOver event enables you to change classes to alter the style properties of hypertext.

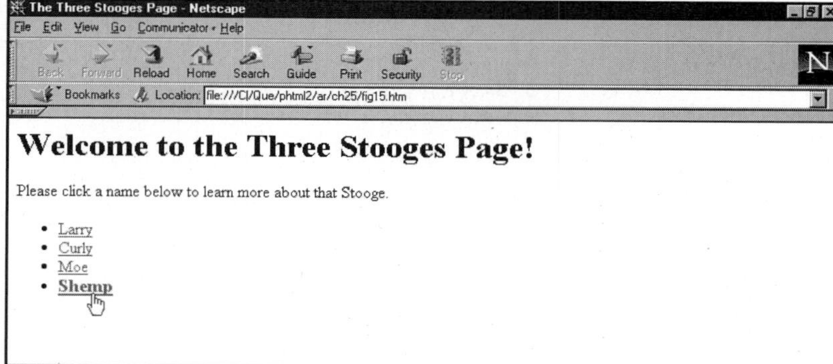

Listing 24.4 HTML code to produce dynamic hyperlinks.

```
<HTML>
<HEAD>
<TITLE>The Three Stooges Page</TITLE>
<STYLE>
.off    {
         font-size: 12 pt;
         font-weight: normal;
         color: blue;
         }
.over  {
        font-size: 14 pt;
        font-weight: bold;
        color: red;
        }
</STYLE>
</HEAD>
<BODY BGCOLOR="#FFFFFF">
<H1>Welcome to the Three Stooges Page!</H1>
<P>Please click a name below to learn more about that Stooge.</P>
<UL>
   <LI>
      <A HREF="larry.html" CLASS="off"
      onMouseOver="this.className='over';"
      onMouseOut="this.className='off';">
      Larry</A>
   </LI>
   <LI>
      <A HREF="curly.html" CLASS="off"
      onMouseOver="this.className='over';"
      onMouseOut="this.className='off';">
      Curly</A>
   </LI>
   <LI>
      <A HREF="moe.html" CLASS="off"
      onMouseOver="this.className='over';"
      onMouseOut="this.className='off';">
      Moe</A>
   </LI>
```

```
    <LI>
       <A HREF="shemp.html" CLASS="off"
       onMouseOver="this.className='over';"
       onMouseOut="this.className='off';">
       Shemp</A>
    </LI>
</UL>
</BODY>
</HTML>
```

NOTE One nice thing about the preceding example is that it did not use any Netscape-proprietary tags. Thus, any browser that understands JavaScript and style sheets should be capable of rendering the page just as Netscape Navigator would.

Example 2: Animated Buttons

When you push a button on an appliance or dashboard, you get visual and tactile feedback from the button that tells you something about its status. If the button is depressed, you know that what it controls is on. Conversely, you know the function that the button controls is off if the button is raised. When you press the button to toggle its state, you feel a click as it moves to its new position. This tells you that you have changed states successfully. Unfortunately, this kind of feedback has been tough to provide for buttons on Web pages. Although you will probably never be able to provide tactile feedback to a user pressing a button, Dynamic HTML enables you to give visual feedback about whether the button is depressed or raised, whether the user's mouse is over it, and whether the button is being pressed.

Suppose you are designing an interface in which you want your buttons to have the following three states:

- Raised
- Selected (meaning the user's mouse is over it)
- Depressed

Your graphic artist has provided you with GIF files portraying the button in each of these states. Your task is now to figure out how to set up the button so that the selected view is displayed if the user's mouse passes over it and so that the button toggles between depressed and raised when the user clicks it.

One way to accomplish this is to set each button up in a layer. The main button layer will contain three child layers—one for each GIF file that represents a different state of the button. By changing the visibility properties of the layers as different mouse events occur, you can show the graphic appropriate to the button's state. Figure 24.9 shows the initial state of these layers in which the button is in the raised state. Listing 24.5 provides the corresponding HTML code to set up the layers.

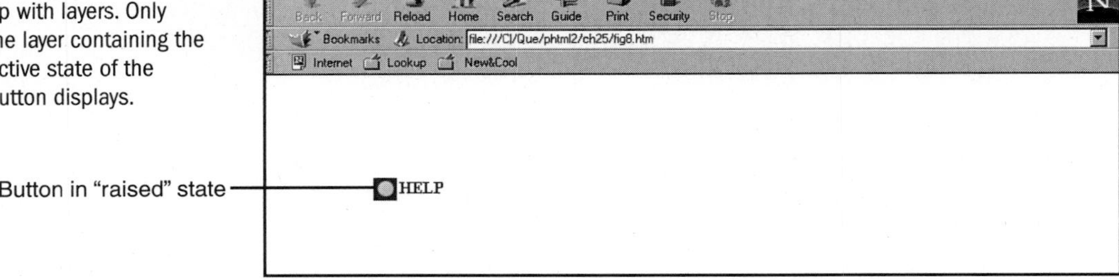

FIG. 24.9
A Help button set up with layers. Only the layer containing the active state of the button displays.

Listing 24.5 HTML code to set up the three different button layers.

```
<LAYER NAME="button">
  <LAYER NAME="button_up" SRC="images/raised.gif" VISIBILITY="SHOW">
  </LAYER>
  <LAYER NAME="button_down" SRC="images/depressed.gif" VISIBILITY="HIDE">
  </LAYER>
  <LAYER NAME="button_over" SRC="images/selected.gif" VISIBILITY="HIDE">
  </LAYER>
        <B>HELP</B>
</LAYER>
```

What you need to do next is put in the JavaScript code to handle the changes to the state of the button. The first thing you know that has to happen is that the selected state of the button has to show whether the user's mouse is over it. By putting an `onMouseOver` event handler in the initial `<LAYER>` tag, you can call a function that changes the visibility properties of the various button state layers so that the selected version of the button displays. Figure 24.10 shows how the button lights up when the mouse passes over it. Listing 24.6 provides the corresponding HTML code.

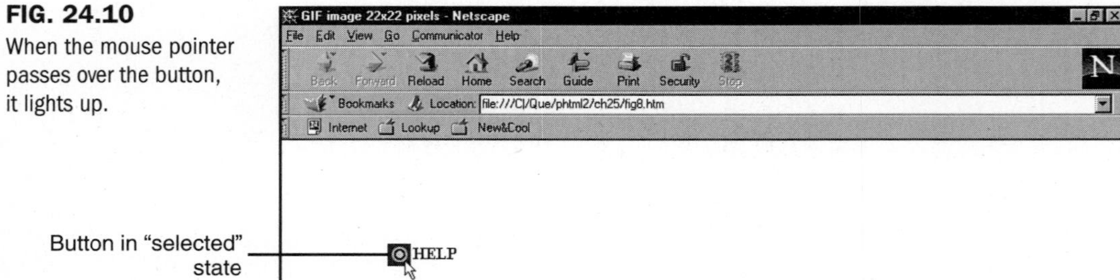

FIG. 24.10
When the mouse pointer passes over the button, it lights up.

Listing 24.6 HTML code to make button light up when the mouse passes over it.

```
<HTML>
<HEAD>
<TITLE>Animated Buttons</TITLE>
<SCRIPT LANGUAGE="javascript">
function showSelected() {
  document.button.document.button_up.visibility = "HIDE";
  document.button.document.button_down.visibility = "HIDE";
  document.button.document.button_over.visibility = "SHOW";
}
</SCRIPT>
</HEAD>

<LAYER NAME="button" onMouseOver="showSelected()">
  <LAYER NAME="button_up" SRC="images/raised.gif" VISIBILITY="SHOW">
  </LAYER>
  <LAYER NAME="button_down" SRC="images/depressed.gif" VISIBILITY="HIDE">
  </LAYER>
  <LAYER NAME="button_over" SRC="images/selected.gif" VISIBILITY="HIDE">
  </LAYER>
        <B>HELP</B>
</LAYER>
```


Next, you want the button to revert to its previous state when the mouse pointer moves off of it. To accomplish this, you need to add a state variable in the `showSelected` function so that the state of the button before the selected state is recorded. Then that state can be passed to a function to change the button from the selected state to its former state. In Listing 24.7, `previous` is the state variable and it is passed to the function `goBack`.

Listing 24.7 HTML code to toggle the button state when the mouse moves on or off of it.

```
<HTML>
<HEAD>
<TITLE>Animated Buttons</TITLE>
<SCRIPT LANGUAGE="javascript">
var previous = "up";
function showSelected() {
  if (document.button.document.button_down.visibility == "SHOW")  {
    previous = "down";
  }
  document.button.document.button_up.visibility = "HIDE";
  document.button.document.button_down.visibility = "HIDE";
  document.button.document.button_over.visibility = "SHOW";
}
function goBack(former_state) {
  if (former_state == "up")  {
    document.button.document.button_up.visibility = "SHOW";
```

continues

Listing 24.7 Continued

```
    document.button.document.button_over.visibility = "HIDE";
  }
  else {
    document.button.document.button_down.visibility = "SHOW";
    document.button.document.button_over.visibility = "HIDE";
  }
}
</SCRIPT>
</HEAD>

<LAYER LEFT=100 TOP=100 NAME="button" onMouseOver="showSelected();"
   onMouseOut="goBack(previous);">
  <LAYER NAME="button_up" SRC="images/raised.gif" VISIBILITY="SHOW">
  </LAYER>
  <LAYER NAME="button_down" SRC="images/depressed.gif" VISIBILITY="HIDE">
  </LAYER>
  <LAYER NAME="button_over" SRC="images/selected.gif" VISIBILITY="HIDE">
  </LAYER>
        <B>HELP</B>
</LAYER>
```

Finally, you need to put in an `onClick` event that changes the visibility properties of the `button_up` and `button_down` layers so that the button toggles appropriately. In the following code, the `onClick` event invokes the function `changeState` that switches the states. Another state variable called `justclicked` is also introduced to record the `click` event so that when the `onMouseOver` script kicks in after the click, it will know not to change the button back to its previous state. Figure 24.11 shows the button in its depressed state after the user clicks it and moves the mouse away. Listing 24.8 shows the corresponding code.

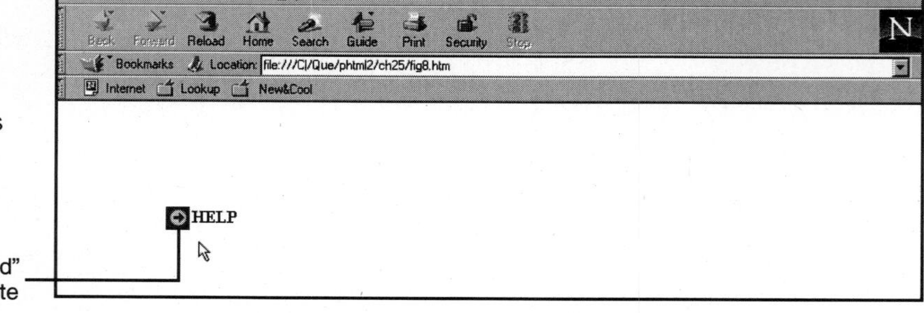

FIG. 24.11 By using a state variable, you can make certain that the button stays depressed after the user's mouse moves off of it and does not return to the raised state.

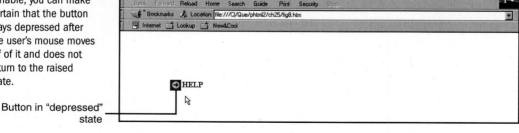

Listing 24.8 HTML code to produce a fully animated button.

```
<HTML>
<HEAD>
<TITLE>Animated Buttons</TITLE>
```

```
<SCRIPT LANGUAGE="javascript">
var previous = "up";
var justclicked = false
function showSelected() {
  if (!justclicked) {
    if (document.button.document.button_down.visibility == "SHOW")  {
      previous = "down";
    }
    document.button.document.button_up.visibility = "HIDE";
    document.button.document.button_down.visibility = "HIDE";
    document.button.document.button_over.visibility = "SHOW";
  }
}
function goBack(former_state) {
  justclicked = false
  if (former_state == "up")  {
    document.button.document.button_up.visibility = "SHOW";
    document.button.document.button_over.visibility = "HIDE";
  }
  else {
    document.button.document.button_down.visibility = "SHOW";
    document.button.document.button_over.visibility = "HIDE";
  }
}
function changeState(former_state) {
  justclicked = true
  if (former_state == "up") {
     document.button.document.button_up.visibility = "HIDE";
     document.button.document.button_down.visibility = "SHOW";
     document.button.document.button_over.visibility = "HIDE";

  }
  else {
     document.button.document.button_down.visibility = "HIDE";
     document.button.document.button_up.visibility = "SHOW";
     document.button.document.button_over.visibility = "HIDE";
  }
}
</SCRIPT>
</HEAD>

<LAYER LEFT=100 TOP=100 NAME="button" onMouseOver="showSelected();"
onMouseOut="goBack(previous);">
  <LAYER NAME="button_up" SRC="images/raised.gif" VISIBILITY="SHOW">
  </LAYER>
  <LAYER NAME="button_down" SRC="images/depressed.gif"  VISIBILITY="HIDE">
  </LAYER>
  <LAYER NAME="button_over" SRC="images/selected.gif"  VISIBILITY="HIDE"
onClick="changeState(previous);">
  </LAYER>
        <B>HELP</B>
</LAYER>
```

Example 3: Pop-Up Menus

Pop-up menus are used in many applications to give users a context-sensitive listing of program options. These menus are usually accessed by right-clicking the mouse or some special keystroke. By using Dynamic HTML techniques, you can make a pop-up menu appear on a Web page as well. This can prove helpful in a situation in which you need to conserve space on a page. Instead of having all the options presented all the time, you can have a menu with the options pop up when the user requests it.

Suppose you want your site's navigation options to appear in a pop-up menu. You could set up the layers for such a page as shown in Listing 24.9.

Listing 24.9 HTML code to set up pop-up menu layers.

```
<HTML>
<HEAD>
<TITLE>Pop-up Menus</TITLE>
</HEAD>
<LAYER NAME="container" WIDTH=100%>
  <LAYER NAME="main" VISIBILITY="SHOW" WIDTH=100%>
    <H1 ALIGN="CENTER">Welcome to a Very Cool Web Page!</H1>
    <P>This page is so cool because it uses Dynamic HTML.</P>
    <P>Make sure you're using Netscape Navigator 4.0 or higher
    to appreciate the full effect!</P>
  </LAYER>
  <LAYER TOP=125 NAME="popup" VISIBILITY="SHOW" onMouseOver="showMenu();">
    <HR NOSHADE>
    <B>Navigation Options</B>
  </LAYER>
  <LAYER TOP=125 NAME="menu" VISIBILITY="HIDE" onMouseOut="showText();">
    <HR NOSHADE>
    <B>Choose a section of the site to visit:</B>
    <FORM NAME="navigate">
    <SELECT NAME="navmenu" SIZE=4>
    <OPTION>General Information
    <OPTION>Credits
    <OPTION>Site Map
    <OPTION>Comments & Feedback
    </SELECT>
   </FORM>
  </LAYER>
</LAYER>
```

The preceding code sets up three nested layers within a layer named "container" (see Figure 24.12). The nested layer "main" is where different site content will appear. The other nested layer "popup" will help to handle the pop-up menu. Initially, all "popup" contains are the words "Navigation Options." The third nested layer is named "menu" and it contains the instructions to create the menu. The "menu" layer is initially hidden.

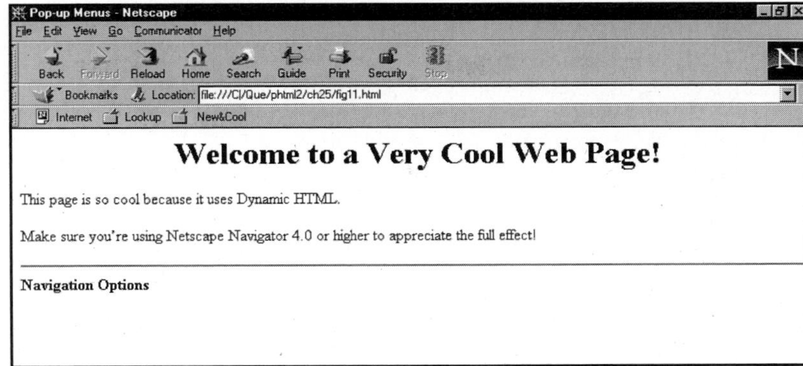

FIG. 24.12 The "Navigation Options" text at the bottom of the screen changes to a navigation menu when a user's mouse moves over it.

Your next step is to add some JavaScript commands that will make the menu visible when the user's mouse moves over the "Navigation Options" text. Similarly, you want the menu to revert back to the initial text if the user's mouse moves out of the layer. These two effects are simple to create using mouse-related event handlers, as shown in Listing 24.10.

Listing 24.10 HTML code to reveal and hide the pop-up menu.

```
<HTML>
<HEAD>
<TITLE>Pop-up Menus</TITLE>
<SCRIPT LANGUAGE="javascript">
function showMenu() {
  document.container.document.popup.visibility = "HIDE";
  document.container.document.menu.visibility = "SHOW";
}
function showText() {
  document.container.document.menu.visibility = "HIDE";
  document.container.document.popup.visibility = "SHOW";
}
</SCRIPT>
</HEAD>
<LAYER NAME="container" WIDTH=100%>
  <LAYER NAME="main" VISIBILITY="SHOW" WIDTH=100%>
    <H1 ALIGN="CENTER">Welcome to a Very Cool Web Page!</H1>
    <P>This page is so cool because it uses Dynamic HTML.</P>
    <P>Make sure you're using Netscape Navigator 4.0 or higher
    to appreciate the full effect!</P>
  </LAYER>
  <LAYER TOP=125 NAME="popup" VISIBILITY="SHOW" onMouseOver="showMenu();">
    <HR NOSHADE>
    <B>Navigation Options</B>
  </LAYER>
  <LAYER TOP=125 NAME="menu" VISIBILITY="HIDE" onMouseOut="showText();">
    <HR NOSHADE>
    <B>Choose a section of the site to visit:</B>
```

continues

Listing 24.10 Continued

```
      <FORM NAME="navigate">
      <SELECT NAME="navmenu" SIZE=4>
      <OPTION>General Information
      <OPTION>Credits
      <OPTION>Site Map
      <OPTION>Comments & Feedback
      </SELECT>
    </FORM>
  </LAYER>
</LAYER>
```

The showMenu function changes the visibility properties of the “popup” and “menu” layers so that the menu is visible (see Figure 24.13). showText does a similar thing, but makes the default “Navigation Options” text visible.

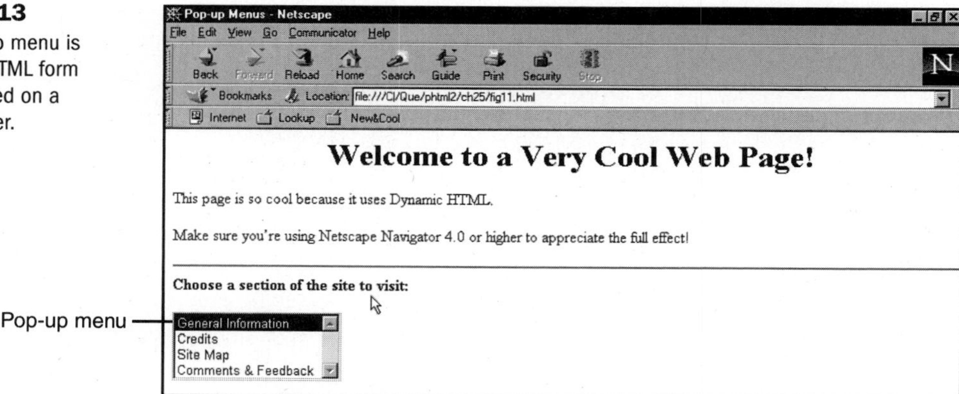

FIG. 24.13 The pop-up menu is really an HTML form menu stored on a hidden layer.

With the menu set up, you now need to add some code to process the user’s selection. The most straightforward way to do this is to use the onChange event handler within the <FORM> tag to invoke a function that processes the chosen menu option. By using the this.selectedIndex property, you can pluck off the number of the option the user selected and load new content based on that number. Listing 24.11 shows the final product.

Listing 24.11 HTML code to produce a pop-up menu.

```
<HTML>
<HEAD>
<TITLE>Pop-up Menus</TITLE>
<SCRIPT LANGUAGE="javascript">
function showMenu() {
  document.container.document.popup.visibility = "HIDE";
```

```
  document.container.document.menu.visibility = "SHOW";
}
function showText() {
  document.container.document.menu.visibility = "HIDE";
  document.container.document.popup.visibility = "SHOW";
}
function loadContent(n) {
  if (n == 1) {
    document.container.document.main.load("geninfo.html",600);
  }
  if (n == 2) {
    document.container.document.main.load("credits.html",600);
  }
  if (n == 3) {
    document.container.document.main.load("sitemap.html",600);
  }
  if (n == 4) {
    document.container.document.main.load("feedback.html",600);
  }
}
</SCRIPT>
</HEAD>
<LAYER NAME="container" WIDTH=100%>
  <LAYER NAME="main" VISIBILITY="SHOW" WIDTH=100%>
    <H1 ALIGN="CENTER">Welcome to a Very Cool Web Page!</H1>
    <P>This page is so cool because it uses Dynamic HTML.</P>
    <P>Make sure you're using Netscape Navigator 4.0 or higher
    to appreciate the full effect!</P>
  </LAYER>
  <LAYER TOP=125 NAME="popup" VISIBILITY="SHOW" onMouseOver="showMenu();">
    <HR NOSHADE>
    <B>Navigation Options</B>
  </LAYER>
  <LAYER TOP=125 NAME="menu" VISIBILITY="HIDE" onMouseOut="showText();">
    <HR NOSHADE>
    <B>Choose a section of the site to visit:</B>
    <FORM NAME="navigate" onChange="loadContent(this.selectedIndex);">
    <SELECT NAME="navmenu" SIZE=4>
    <OPTION>General Information
    <OPTION>Credits
    <OPTION>Site Map
    <OPTION>Comments & Feedback
    </SELECT>
   </FORM>
  </LAYER>
</LAYER>
```

The `loadContent` function uses the `load` method to pull new content into the layer named "main" according to the user's selection from the pop-up menu (see Figure 24.14).

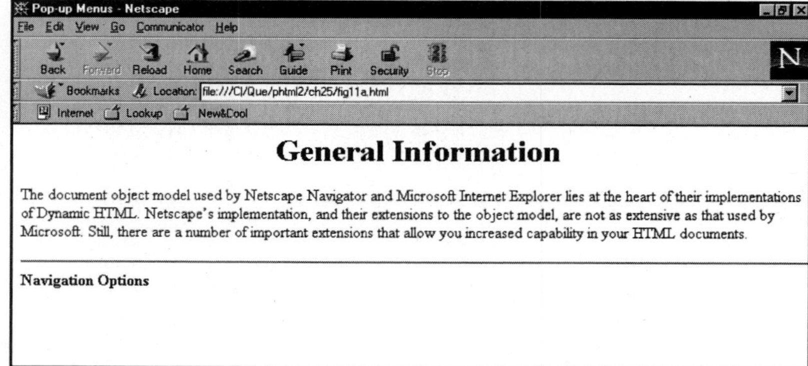

FIG. 24.14
A user's menu choice causes new content to be loaded in the "main" layer with the navigation options still available below.

Downloadable Fonts

Setting up a document with downloadable fonts is a multi-step process that begins with your securing copies of the fonts you want to use in your design. If you are a skilled digital typographer, you may be able to create your own. Most, however, will have to be content to purchase them or download a publicly available font from somewhere on the Internet.

After you have the fonts you want in hand, you need to apply them to text on your page. Ultimately, what you want to produce is called a *font definition file*—a file downloaded with the page to provide font information to Navigator. To accomplish this, you need a software tool of some kind. A good bet for this is to use Typograph, a font definition generation tool from HexMac.

Figure 24.15 shows the Typograph screen with an HTML document loaded. By using Typograph's simple menus, you select text and apply a font to it, just as you would if you were using a word processing program. When the document looks the way you want it, you use the Typograph burn option to save the file, to set up the link in the document to the font definition file, and to create the font definition file itself.

NOTE HexMac has standalone versions of Typograph for Macintosh and Windows 95/NT platforms, as well as plug-in versions for BBEdit (Macintosh) and FrontPage (Windows 95/NT). For more information on Typograph, visit **http://www.hexmac.com/**.

CAUTION

As part of the burning process, you need to tell Typograph which Internet domain the font information will be served from. After the domain is stored in the font definition file, the font information in the definition file can be served *only* from that domain. If you are serving the same documents on multiple domains, you must burn a new definition file for the other domains.

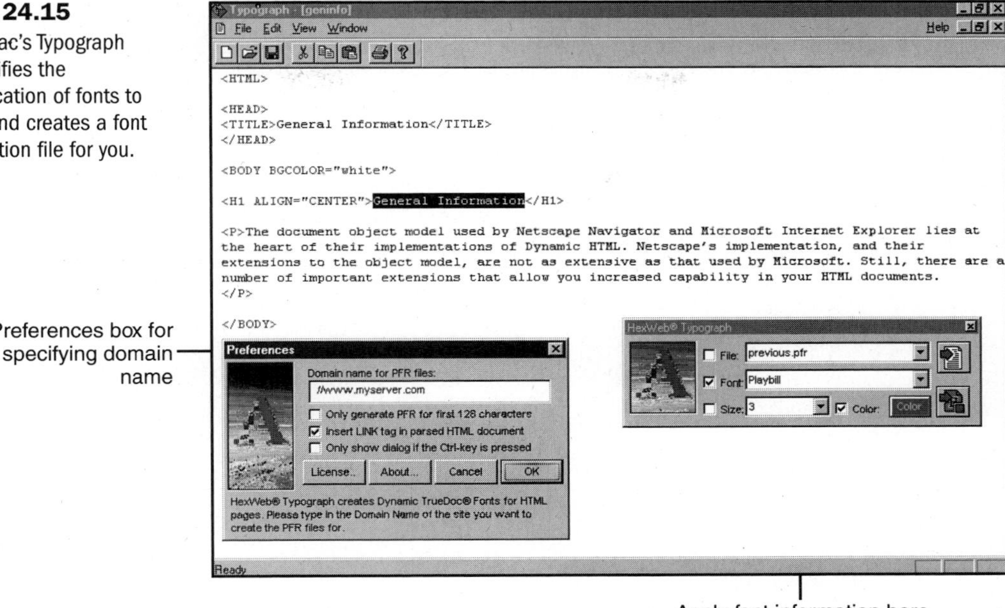

FIG. 24.15
HexMac's Typograph simplifies the application of fonts to text and creates a font definition file for you.

If you use a different font definition file generation program, you may need to place the link to the definition file into your document manually. There are two ways to link a definition file to a document. The first is to use the `<LINK>` tag in the document head. When linking to a font definition file with the `<LINK>` tag, you need to use the following attributes:

- `REL`—`REL` is set equal to `FONTDEF`, signifying that the linked file is a font definition file.
- `SRC`—`SRC` points to the URL where the font definition file can be found.

Thus, a `<LINK>` tag that links to a font definition file might look like this:

```
<LINK REL="FONTDEF" SRC="http://www.myserver.com/fonts/mydoc.pfr">
```

The other approach is to link the font definition file inside the HTML `<STYLE>` element. The CSS specification supports a link such as the following:

```
<STYLE TYPE="text/css">
<!--
  @fontdef url(http://www.myserver.com/fonts/mydoc.pfr)
-->
</STYLE>
```

The `<STYLE>` implementation here is equivalent to the `<LINK>` implementation shown previously.

NOTE Font definition files end with the .pfr extension.

With the font definition file linked to your HTML document, you are free to use the fonts contained in the file anywhere in your document. There are two approaches to this as well. One is to use the FACE attribute of the <FONT> tag just as you always would. FACE is set equal to a comma-delimited list of fonts to use in the order that the browser should try to apply them. For example, the HTML

```
<FONT FACE="Palatino, Garamond, Clarendon, serif">
This will be in Palatino, if possible.
</FONT>
```

will render the sentence "This will be in Palatino, if possible." in Palatino. If Palatino is not available, the browser looks for Garamond, and then Clarendon, and finally, if none of the named fonts are available, it uses a serif font.

The other way to go is to use the font-family characteristic available through the Cascading Style Sheet specification. Using CSS, you could express the same font choices in the preceding <FONT> tag as follows:

```
<STYLE TYPE="text/css">
<!--
  P {font-family: "Palatino", "Garamond", "Clarendon", serif}
-->
</STYLE>
...
<P>This will be in Palatino, if possible.</P>
```

Try to use the CSS approach to choosing a type face wherever possible. When style sheets are more common on the Web, it is likely that the <FONT> tag will be deprecated and your document will not conform to standards.

You get some additional flexibility if you opt to use the <FONT> tag because Netscape has extended the tag with a few more attributes. These are as follows:

- POINT_SIZE—You can control the point size of the font by setting POINT_SIZE to the number of points high you want the text to be.
- WEIGHT—WEIGHT controls the boldness of the font and can be set to a value between 100 and 900 in increments of 100. A value of 100 is the least bold and a value of 900 is the most bold. Using WEIGHT gives you finer control over boldness than the <B> tag, which always uses the highest level of boldness.

With the downloaded typefaces specified in your HTML document, you are almost finished. As a final step, you need to put the HTML file and the font definition file out on your server. Remember that the server must be in the domain you specified when creating the font definition file. You should publish both files to a location from which the server can serve them.

Additionally, you need to add a MIME type to your server for the font definition file. MIME information is sent in front of a file to give Navigator a heads up as to what kind of file is coming down the pipe. For font definition files, you should add the MIME type application/font-tdpfr, paired with the file extension .pfr, to your server. After you or your server administrator make this addition to the MIME types file, you probably need to restart the server to get it to recognize the new MIME type. Netscape Navigator is already configured to handle the application/font-tdpfr MIME type and uses the information in the font definition file to render the typefaces in the file.

ON THE WEB

http://home.netscape.com/communicator/features/Dynamic_HTML.html Netscape's own take on Dynamic HTML, how its functionality is integrated into the Navigator browser, and how to develop Dynamic HTML content.

http://www.all-links.com/dynamic/ The Dynamic HTML Index contains frequently asked questions about Dynamic HTML and provides links to sites that answer the questions.

http://www.dhtmlzone.com/ Hosted by Macromedia, this site looks at developing Dynamic HTML for both Netscape and Microsoft browsers.

CHAPTER 25

Advanced Microsoft Dynamic HTML

by Jim O'Donnell

In this chapter

Microsoft's Implementation of Dynamic HTML

Dynamic HTML is Microsoft's term for the new technology they have embedded in their Internet Explorer 4 web browser. Through Dynamic HTML, you can create web pages that can change dynamically and have a much higher degree of interaction than in the past. The heart of Dynamic HTML is Microsoft's new Document Object Model. This model is what provides you, and scripts that you write, with the ability to interact with and change any element in an HTML document.

This chapter shows some examples of the kinds of things you can do with Dynamic HTML (and related technologies, such as *Scriptlets*). None of the examples shown represent anything you could not have done in the past—now, however, it is possible to do them using HTML alone. Dynamic HTML is a new technology still under development. People are just scratching the surface of what is possible with it. This chapter identifies some of the best places to look for examples and more information.

Internet Explorer 4 Document Object Model

The heart of Dynamic HTML is the new Document Object Model that the Internet Explorer 4 web browser supports. You can think of every element in an HTML document as an object, including the HTML tags and information that they contain, as well as aspects of the web browser itself and any included Java applets, ActiveX Controls, or other elements. The Document Object Model is what *exposes* these objects, making them accessible to you through scripts that you can write and include with the document.

Before Internet Explorer 4 and Dynamic HTML, the Document Object Model was very limited. It could expose Java applets, ActiveX Controls, and the web browser window properties, such as window size and location. The model exposed a very limited number of HTML elements, however. The HTML tags that were supported by past object models were primarily limited to HTML Forms elements. Thus, just about the only HTML elements that you could access and change within a web page were those that were a part of HTML Forms.

Microsoft's Dynamic HTML changes all that. With Dynamic HTML, every HTML tag is exposed by the Document Object Model. Not only that, but the contents of all HTML container tags are also exposed. Therefore not only can you change the styles or formats associated with a <P> tag, for instance, but you can also change its text contents. And, this is all done on the client-side, without any need to interact with the web server.

The remainder of this section discusses aspects of the Document Object Model for Internet Explorer 4. It is important to at least understand the different terms used with the object model—object, property, method, collection, and event— and what they mean. This section gives you a good basis for understanding the Dynamic HTML samples later in the chapter.

Understanding Objects and the Object Hierarchy

Figure 25.1 shows the hierarchy of objects that is part of the Internet Explorer 4 Document Object Model. In the simplest terms, an *object* in this model is a recognizable element of the whole. Objects can contain other objects, however; thus, all the objects are organized into an object hierarchy.

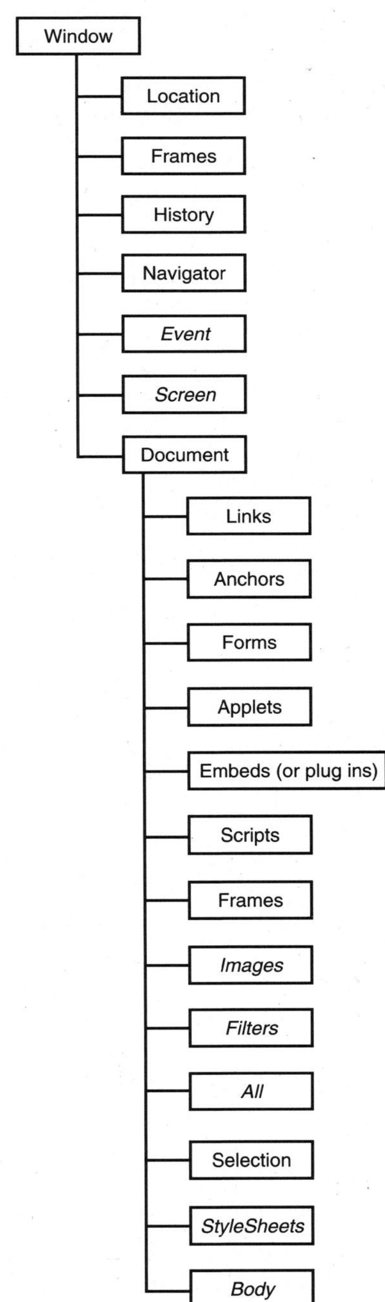

FIG. 25.1
The following boxed elements of the Document Object Model represent the additions that Dynamic HTML uses.

Looking at Figure 25.1, the `window` object, at the top of the hierarchy, includes everything you see within a given web browser window. That object can and will, in turn, contain other objects. This object hierarchy is used when referencing these objects, with the following example notation:

```
window.document.links[0]
```

This line of code refers to the first `link` object contained in the current document of a given web browser window. (Normally, unless you are authoring web pages that use multiple windows, you can omit `window`.)

A description of each type of object in the Internet Explorer 4 Document Object Model follows:

- **`window`** Represents an open web browser window.
- **`location`** Information for the current URL.
- **`frames`** A collection of `window` objects, one for each separate frame in the current window.
- **`history`** Information for the recently visited URLs.
- **`navigator`** Information about the browser itself.
- **`event`** Maintains the state of events occurring within the browser.
- **`screen`** Statistics on the physical screen and the rendering capabilities of the client.
- **`document`** Contains all the information attached to the current HTML document.
- **`links`** A collection of links referenced in the current document.
- **`anchors`** A collection of anchors present within the current document.
- **`forms`** Can contain a number of other objects corresponding to the forms elements within it; there is one `forms` object for each HTML form in the document.
- **`applets`** Contains information about the Java applets present.
- **`embeds`** Has information about all objects included using the `<EMBED>` tag; this object can also be referenced using the synonym `plugins`.
- **`scripts`** A collection of all the script elements within the document.
- **`images`** A collection that contains one element for each image in the document.
- **`filters`** Contains a collection of the `filter` objects associated with the document.
- **`all`** Allows access to all the HTML tags that are a part of the document.
- **`selection`** Represents the current active selection, a user-selected block of text within the document.
- **`styleSheets`** A collection of the style sheets attached to the current document.
- **`body`** Accesses the `<BODY>` section of the document.

Note that many of these objects are collections of other objects. The `images` object, for instance, is a collection of objects associated with all the images in the current document. You can access elements in these collections either by name or by number. If the first image in an HTML document is defined by the following tag, for example

```
<IMG SRC="ryan.jpg" ID=Ryan>
```

you can use the `images` object to access that image in one of three ways:

```
document.images[0]

document.images("Ryan")

document.images.Ryan
```

Note that arrays in the object model are zero-based, so the first element in an array is referenced using zero.

Using Properties

Every object has properties. To access a property, just use the object name followed by a period and the property name. To get the length of the `images` object, which would tell you how many images are in the current document, you can write the following:

```
document.images.length
```

If the object you are using has properties that can be modified, you can change them in the same way. You can change the URL of the current window, for example, by setting the `href` property of the `location` object, as in the following line:

```
Location.href = "http://www.rpi.edu/~odonnj/"
```

If this line is executed within a script, the HTML document referenced by it (my home page) will be loaded into your web browser window.

Listing 29.1 shows an example of a program that uses Dynamic HTML's `all` object to access all the HTML tags included within the document. In this case, when the document is loaded, a script writes out on the bottom of the document a list of all the HTML tags included in the document (with the exception of the ones written out by the script itself). The script does this by using the `length` property of the `all` object to see how many tags there are and then stepping through them using the `tagName` property to display what the tags are (see Figure 25.2).

Listing 25.1 DispTags.htm The *all* object enables you to access every HTML tag.

```
<HTML>
<HEAD>
<TITLE>Dynamic HTML Example</TITLE>
</HEAD>
<BODY>
```

continues

Listing 25.1 Continued

```
<CENTER>
<H1>Document Object Model: <EM>all</EM> Object</H1>
<HR>
<P>
The script in this example will put up a series of alert boxes
showing all of the HTML tags used in this document. The script
uses the <EM>length</EM> and <EM>tagName</EM> properties of
the <EM>all</EM> object.
</P>
<HR>
</CENTER>
<ADDRESS>
Jim O'Donnell, <A HREF="mailto:odonnj@rpi.edu">odonnj@rpi.edu</A>
</ADDRESS>
</BODY>
<SCRIPT LANGUAGE="JavaScript">
imax = document.all.length
document.write("<PRE>")
for(i = 0;i < imax;i++)
   if (i < 9)
      document.write("Tag 0" + (i+1) + " of " + imax + ": " +
         "document.all[0" + i + "].tagName = " +
          document.all[i].tagName + "<BR>")
   else if (i == 9)
      document.write("Tag " + (i+1) + " of " + imax + ": " +
         "document.all[0" + i + "].tagName = " +
          document.all[i].tagName + "<BR>")
       else
      document.write("Tag " + (i+1) + " of " + imax + ": " +
         "document.all[" + i + "].tagName = " +
          document.all[i].tagName + "<BR>")
document.write("</PRE>")
</SCRIPT>
</HTML>
```

Many different properties are associated with HTML element objects in Microsoft's new object model, too many to go over in any detail here. However, you should be aware of two properties in particular; they are one of the ways that Microsoft's Dynamic HTML enable you to easily change the content of HTML documents on-the-fly, without going back to the web server:

- **`innerHTML`** This is a property of an HTML tag object, and its value is whatever text, information, and HTML code is included within the HTML container tags corresponding to that object.
- **`outerHTML`** This is a property of an HTML tag object, and its value is whatever text, information, and HTML code is included within the HTML container tags corresponding to that object, and the container tags themselves.

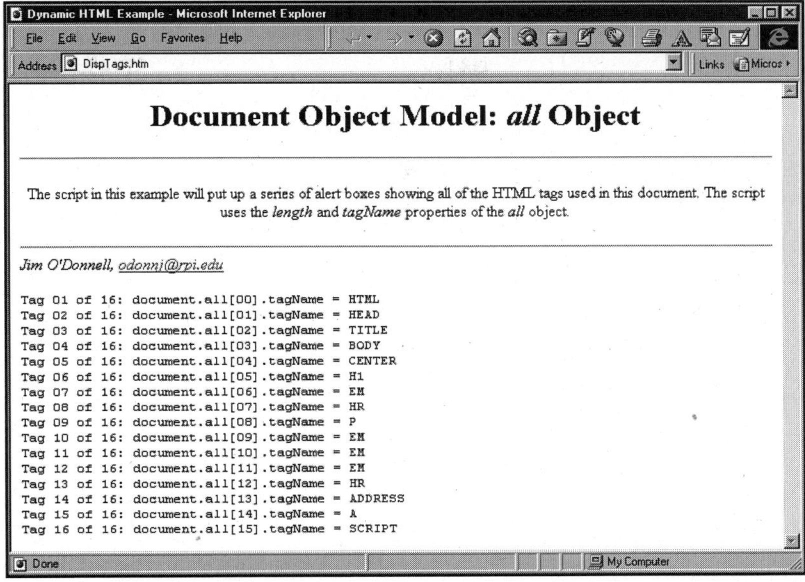

FIG. 25.2
Dynamic HTML enables you to access all the information in the current HTML document.

Listing 25.2 shows an example HTML document that demonstrates these two properties and the difference between them. In this case, the `tag` object being referenced is attached to the `<P>` tag by using the attribute `ID="MyParagraph"`. At the end of the document, the JavaScript shown displays the value of the `innerHTML` and `outerHTML` property of the object corresponding to this tag. Notice that the `outerHTML` value has an extra space in it, caused by the fact that it includes the effects of the `<P>` tag itself (see Figure 25.3).

Listing 25.2 ContentP.htm HTML document contents can be accessed using the *innerHTML* and *outerHTML* properties.

```
<HTML>
<HEAD>
<TITLE>Dynamic HTML Example</TITLE>
</HEAD>
<BODY>
<CENTER>
<H1>Document Object Model<BR><EM>innerHTML</EM> and
                               <EM>outerHTML</EM> Properties</H1>
<HR>
<P ID="MyParagraph">
The <EM>contents</EM> of the &lt;P&gt; tag "MyParagraph"...
</P>
<HR>
</CENTER>
<ADDRESS>
```

continues

Listing 25.2 Continued

```
Jim O'Donnell, <A HREF="mailto:odonnj@rpi.edu">odonnj@rpi.edu</A>
</ADDRESS>
<SCRIPT LANGUAGE="JavaScript">
document.write("<PRE>")
document.write("<HR>")
document.write("document.all['MyParagraph'].innerHTML = " +
   document.all['MyParagraph'].innerHTML + "<BR>")
document.write("<HR>")
document.write("document.all['MyParagraph'].outerHTML = " +
   document.all['MyParagraph'].outerHTML + "<BR>")
document.write("</PRE>")
</SCRIPT>
</BODY>
</HTML>
```

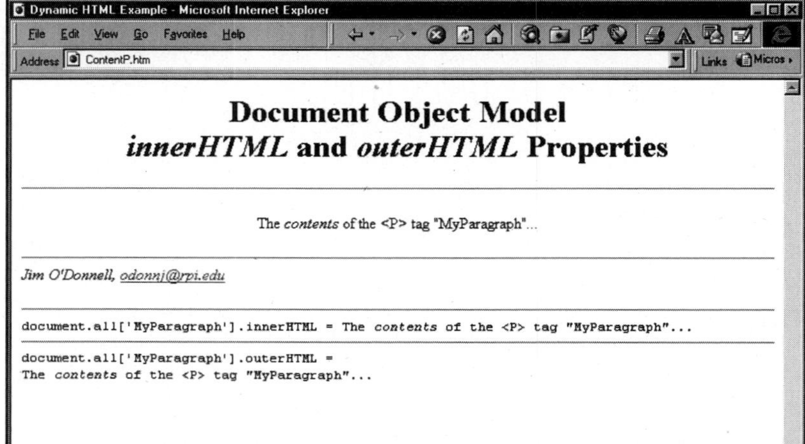

FIG. 25.3
Not only the format, but the actual contents of your HTML documents can be accessed and changed with Microsoft Dynamic HTML.

Listing 25.3 shows another example, this one using the `innerHTML` property to dynamically *change* the contents of a web page.

Listing 25.3 DynCon2.htm Real-time changing of HTML document contents using the *innerHTML* property.

```
<HTML>
<HEAD>
<STYLE>
SPAN,P {font-family: Verdana;
        font-size: 18pt;
        font-weight: bold}
</STYLE>
<SCRIPT>
function errortrap(msg,url,line){
```

```
   return true
}
onerror = errortrap;
</SCRIPT>
<TITLE>Dynamic HTML Example</TITLE>
</HEAD>
<BODY onload="stuff()" onmouseover="update()">
<CENTER>
<H1>Dynamic Content Using <EM>innerHTML</EM></H1>
<HR>
<P>
<SPAN>This</SPAN>
<SPAN>paragraph</SPAN>
<SPAN>contains</SPAN>
<SPAN ID=wordCount>???</SPAN>
<SPAN>words</SPAN>.
<SPAN>The</SPAN>
<SPAN>mouse</SPAN>
<SPAN>is</SPAN>
<SPAN>currently</SPAN>
<SPAN>over</SPAN>
<SPAN>the</SPAN>
<SPAN>word</SPAN>
<BR><SPAN ID=currentWord STYLE="color:#0000FF;font-size:36pt">n/a</SPAN><BR>
<SPAN>In</SPAN>
<SPAN>this</SPAN>
<SPAN>paragraph</SPAN>,
<SPAN>this</SPAN>
<SPAN>is</SPAN>
<SPAN>word</SPAN>
<SPAN>number</SPAN>
<BR><SPAN ID=currentWordNum STYLE="color:#0000FF;font-size:36pt">n/a</SPAN>
</P>
<HR>
</CENTER>
<ADDRESS>
Jim O'Donnell, <A HREF="mailto:odonnj@rpi.edu">odonnj@rpi.edu</A>
</ADDRESS>
</BODY>
<SCRIPT LANGUAGE="JScript">
var oldObject
function stuff() {
   wordCount.innerHTML = document.all.tags("SPAN").length
}
function update() {
   if (window.event.srcElement.tagName == "SPAN") {
      if (oldObject)
         oldObject.style.color = "#000000"
      oldObject = window.event.srcElement
      oldObject.style.color = "#FF0000"
      for (i = 0;i < document.all.tags("SPAN").length;i++)
         if (oldObject == document.all.tags("SPAN").item(i))
            currentWordNum.innerHTML = i + 1
      currentWord.innerHTML = oldObject.innerHTML
   } else {
```

continues

Listing 25.3 Continued

```
         if (oldObject) {
            oldObject.style.color = "#000000"
            oldObject = null
            currentWordNum.innerHTML = "n/a"
            currentWord.innerHTML = "n/a"
         }
      }
   }
</SCRIPT>
</HTML>
```

The three main sections of interest in this example are the main document text (contained within the <P> container tag) and the two JScript functions, `stuff()` and `update()`. This application determines which word in the paragraph (if any) the mouse is over and changes the text to display this word as well as its position within the paragraph. This is what each of these sections does to help accomplish this:

- **Body text within the `<P>` container tag** Each separate word in this paragraph is set off by a <SPAN> container tag to enable you to be able to access and manipulate it separately from the rest. In addition, three of the words are also given an `ID`, as the JScripts will be using their `innerHTML` properties to dynamically change their contents.
- **JScript `stuff()` function** This function is called when the page has completely loaded by the `onload` event of the <BODY> tag. It is used to fill in the total number of words in the paragraph. This is done by counting the number of <SPAN> tags, and then inserting this number into the paragraph using the appropriate `innerHTML` property.
- **JScript `update()` function** This function is called whenever an `onmouseover` event is triggered. Because the `onmouseover` event is given in the <BODY> tag, such an event is generated whenever the mouse passes over *any* element in the page!

  The `update()` function first determines whether the element that triggered the event is one of the <SPAN> elements in the paragraph. If it is, it changes the color of the corresponding word and places the word and word number in the appropriate spaces in the paragraph (see Figure 25.4). If the triggering element was not one of the <SPAN> tags, the function changes the text to read "n/a."

Dynamic HTML Events and the Event Object

In addition to making HTML documents more responsive by enabling you to attach events and manipulate the properties of virtually any HTML tag, Microsoft's Dynamic HTML has also increased the number of HTML events that the web browser can sense and respond to. This section identifies what most of these events are, and shows what triggers them.

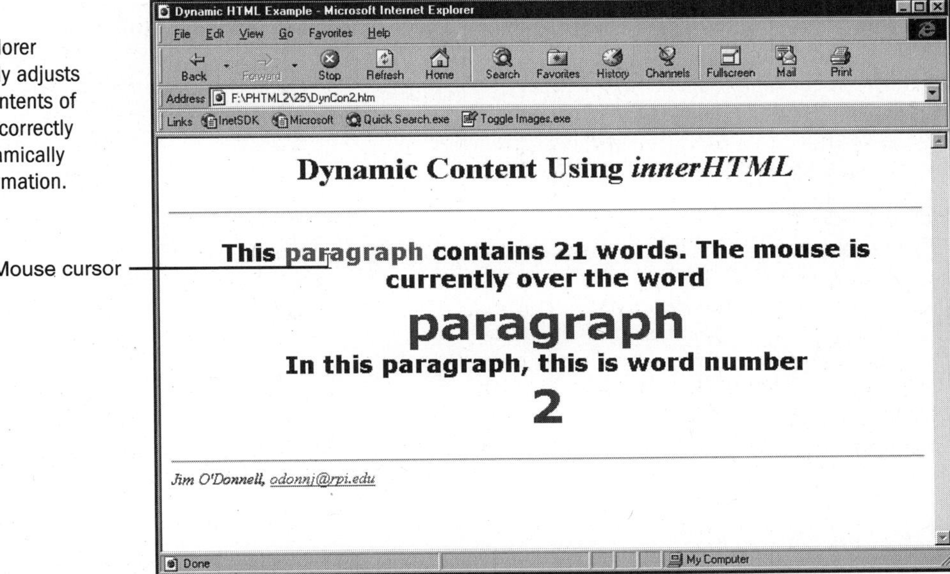

FIG. 25.4
Internet Explorer automatically adjusts the other contents of the page to correctly display dynamically altered information.

Mouse Events

These events are the events triggered in response to mouse movements or mouse button presses. A few of these are familiar events, having been part of the Document Object Model before; some are new as a result of Dynamic HTML.

- **`onclick`**

  This event is normally triggered when the user presses and releases the left mouse button. It can also occur when the user presses certain keys, such as Enter and Esc, in an HTML Form.

  A JavaScript `onclick` event handler is shown below. This event handler is triggered when a mouse click is recorded anywhere in the current document, and uses the `event` object to pop up an Alert box to give the name of the HTML tag in which the click occurred.

```
<SCRIPT FOR=document EVENT=onclick LANGUAGE="JAVASCRIPT">
   alert("Clicked in " + window.event.srcElement.tagName);
</SCRIPT>
```

- **`ondblclick`**

  This event is triggered when the user clicks twice over an object. If an event handler assigned to this event returns a `false` value, it cancels the default action.

- **`ondragstart`**

  This event is triggered when the user begins a drag selection.

- **`onmousedown`**

  This event is triggered when the user presses the mouse button.

- **`onmousemove`**

  This event is triggered when the mouse is moved.

- **`onmouseover`**

  This event is triggered when the mouse is moved into an object. It occurs when the mouse first enters the object and does not repeat unless the user moves the mouse out and then back in.

- **`onmouseout`**

  This event is triggered when the user moves the mouse out of a given element. When the user moves the mouse pointer into an element, one `onmouseover` event occurs, followed by one or more `onmousemove` events as the user moves the pointer within the element, and finally one `onmouseout` event when the user moves the pointer out of the element.

- **`onmouseup`**

  This event is triggered when the mouse button is released.

Note that some of the events described in the preceding list actually trigger multiple events. The events leading to a valid `ondblclick` event, for example, occur in the following steps:

1. `onmousedown`
2. `onmouseup`
3. `onclick`
4. `onmouseup`
5. `ondblclick`

Keystroke Events

New to Microsoft Internet Explorer 4 with its support for Dynamic HTML are events triggered by user keypresses. There are three general purpose events and one special purpose event that respond to keys:

- **`onkeydown`**

  This event is triggered when the user presses a key, and returns the number of the keycode for the key pressed. An event handler assigned to service this event can return a different value and override the original key.

- **`onkeyup`**

  Triggered when the user releases a key.

- **`onkeypress`**

  The last event triggered for a valid key press: first the `onkeydown` event is triggered, and then `onkeyup`, and then `onkeypress`. Event handlers assigned to any of these three events can be used to intercept, override, and/or nullify the actual key pressed.

- **onhelp**

  This event is triggered when the user presses the F1 key or clicks on the Help key on the web browser.

Focus Events

These events are used to follow the focus of the cursor around the HTML document. They can be used to good effect when performing HTML Form validation, but can also be used with non-form elements.

- **onfocus**

  This event is triggered when the element in question receives the input focus.

- **onblur**

  This event is triggered when an object loses the input focus.

- **onchange**

  This event is triggered when the contents of the object, normally a text or text area HTML Form field, are changed.

  Note that this event is only triggered after the object has lost focus and if its contents have changed. If there is an event handler for the `onblur` event for the same object, the `onchange` event is triggered and executed first.

<*MARQUEE*> Events

Although Microsoft's **<MARQUEE>** tag is a nonstandard HTML element, it has come into increasing use. Microsoft's Dynamic HTML implementation includes three events specifically tied to that tag:

- **onbounce**

  This event can only be triggered when the contents of the `<MARQUEE>` tag are set to alternatively scroll one way and then the other. It is actually triggered when the scrolling content changes direction.

- **onstart**

  This event is triggered when a scrolling loop begins or, for alternate behavior, when a bounce cycle begins.

- **onfinish**

  This event is triggered when a scrolling loop ends.

Page Events

In addition to the `onload` event, which has existed in the past and is triggered when a web page is completely loaded, Dynamic HTML adds a couple of other events associated with loading and unloading documents into your web browser. This enables you to set the entrance and exit behavior of the web browser for a given document.

- **`onload`**

  This event is triggered after the web browser loads the given object. It is normally used with the HTML document itself, but can also be applied to images, applets, and any other web browser object loaded along with the HTML document itself.

- **`onbeforeunload`**

  This event is triggered prior to an HTML document being unloaded. By attaching an event handler to this event, you can give the user a chance to change his or her mind and remain on the current page.

- **`onunload`**

  This event is triggered immediately before the current page is unloaded. Unlike the `onbeforeunload` event, after this event is triggered it is too late to prevent the user from leaving the page.

HTML Form Events

As you would expect, Microsoft's Dynamic HTML supports the traditional `onreset` and `onsubmit` events associated with HTML Form's Reset and Submit buttons. Each of these events is triggered when the corresponding button is clicked. If an event handler for the `onsubmit` event returns a value of `false`, the form is not submitted.

Other Events

The following list describes the other events supported by Microsoft's implementation of Dynamic HTML. Note also that a collection of events are associated with the data binding capabilities of Dynamic HTML—these are discussed later in this chapter.

- **`onabort`**

  This event is trigged when the user aborts the download of an image, normally by pressing the Stop button.

- **`onerror`**

  This event is triggered when an error occurs when loading an image or other web browser object. You can suppress error messages that occur when an image fails to load by setting the `onerror` attribute in the element to "null."

- **`onfilterchange`**

  This event fires when a filter changes state or completes a transition from one state to another. Filter effects of Microsoft Dynamic HTML are discussed in the "Dynamic HTML Filters" section, later in this chapter.

- **`onresize`**

  This event is triggered when the object to which it is attached is resized.

- **`onscroll`**

  This event is triggered when the user scrolls the window, either by using the scroll bar, arrow keys, or some other means.

- **`onselect`**

  This event is triggered when the current selection changes. The event continues to fire as the mouse moves from character to character during a drag selection.

- **`onselectstart`**

  This event is triggered when at the beginning of a user-initiated select.

Using Dynamic HTML with Styles

Dynamic HTML works very well with another aspect of Internet Explorer 4 for dynamically changing the formatting of elements in an HTML document: styles and style sheets. One property associated with all HTML tags—which, as you will recall, you can access through the `all` object—is that tag's style. The style property, in turn, has properties of its own that you can access and change to immediately change the appearance of the web page.

Listing 25.4 shows an example of dynamically changing the style of elements of an HTML document. In this example, the format is applied to two different elements in different ways—either through an embedded style sheet created with the `<STYLE>` tag or through the `STYLE` attribute. No matter which way you do it, the script changes the format in response to the `onClick` event. Figures 25.5 and 25.6 show the before and after screen shots of this HTML document.

Listing 25.4 Style1.htm Dynamic HTML can change document styles.

```
<HTML>
<HEAD>
<TITLE>Dynamic HTML Example</TITLE>
<STYLE>
   .clicked {font-size:36pt;color:red}
</STYLE>
<SCRIPT LANGUAGE="JScript">
function changeH1Style() {
   document.all.tags("H1").item(0).className = "clicked";
   document.all.tags("P").item(0).style.fontSize = "24pt";
}
</SCRIPT>
</HEAD>
<BODY onClick="changeH1Style()">
<CENTER>
<H1>Dynamic HTML and Styles</H1>
<HR>
<P>
When you click the mouse, the script in this example will
dynamically change the style of the heading and of this
text. The script uses the <EM>className</EM> and
<EM>style.fontSize</EM> properties of the
<EM>all.tags.item</EM> object.
</P>
```

continues

Listing 25.4 Continued

```
<HR>
</CENTER>
<ADDRESS>
Jim O'Donnell, <A HREF="mailto:odonnj@rpi.edu">odonnj@rpi.edu</A>
</ADDRESS>
</BODY>
</HTML>
```

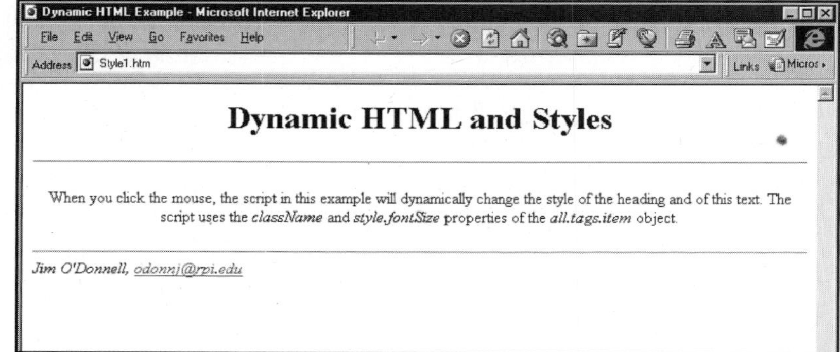

FIG. 25.5 You can attach formatting styles to HTML elements in a variety of ways.

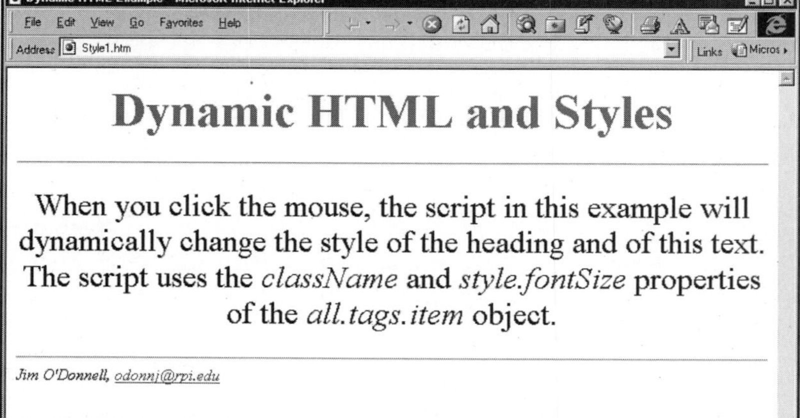

FIG. 25.6 You can change formats, and immediately update the web browser window, in response to any event.

Dynamic HTML and the Data Source Object

Another Dynamic HTML capability works hand-in-hand with Microsoft's Data Source Object to allow what is called *data binding*. The Data Source Object is an ActiveX Control that references an external file to provide data for the HTML document. Dynamic HTML enables you to use the `DATASRC` and `DATAFLD` attributes to bind this data to HTML elements. This way, the data displayed within a document can be kept separate from the formatting. Also, after the data is transmitted to the client web browser, the Data Source Object can perform operations on it locally.

Data Binding Events

A collection of events are associated with HTML elements that are data bound using the `DATASRC` and `DATAFLD` attributes. The following list describes these events:

- **`ondataavailable`**

  This event is triggered as data arrives from an asynchronous data source object; how often it fires depends on the data source object.

- **`ondatasetchanged`**

  This event is triggered when the data set used by a data source object changes.

- **`ondatasetcomplete`**

  This event is triggered when all the data available to a data source object has been loaded.

- **`onrowenter`**

  This event is triggered when the current row of data has changed, and new data values are available.

- **`onrowexit`**

  This event is triggered just prior to a data source object changing the current row in response to new data.

- **`onbeforeupdate`**

  This event is triggered before the transfer of data from an element to a data provider.

- **`onafterupdate`**

  This event is triggered after the transfer of data from an element to a data provider.

- **`onerrorupdate`**

  This event is triggered when the handler for the `onbeforeupdate` event cancels the data transfer, and fires instead the `onafterupdate` event.

Data Binding Example

Listing 25.5 shows an example of data binding using the Data Source Object and Dynamic HTML. In this example, a data file of chapter, page count, and author information is bound to the columns of an HTML table. The Data Source Object's `SortColumn()` method is attached to the table headings, using the `onClick` event. When a column heading is clicked, the table is sorted by the contents of that column and immediately redisplayed. Figures 25.7 and 25.8 show examples of this, with the table sorted either by chapter number or chapter title.

Listing 25.5 DataBind.htm Dynamic HTML and data binding enables easy client-side data manipulation.

```
<HTML>
<HEAD>
<TITLE>Dynamic HTML Example</TITLE>
</HEAD>
<BODY>
<OBJECT ID="inputdata"
        CLASSID="clsid:333C7BC4-460F-11D0-BC04-0080C7055A83"
        align="baseline" border="0" width="0" height="0">
<PARAM NAME="DataURL"   VALUE="authors.txt">
<PARAM NAME="UseHeader" VALUE=TRUE>
</OBJECT>
<CENTER>
<H1>Data Binding with Dynamic HTML</H1>
<HR>
<P>
   This example shows an example of how you can use
   Dynamic HTML to bind an HTML element, in this case
   the columns of a table, to a Data Source Object.
   This allows the data to be kept separately from the
   formatting information in the HTML document. It
   also allows the data to be operated on at the client.
   In this example, if you click on the table headers
   of the table below, it will be sorted by the
   elements in that column.
</P>
<HR>
<TABLE DATASRC="#inputdata" BORDER>
<THEAD>
<TR><TH><U><DIV ID=chapNum onclick="sort1()">
        Chapter<BR>Number</DIV></U></TH>
    <TH><U><DIV ID=chapTitle onclick="sort2()">
          Chapter<BR>Title</DIV></U></TH>
    <TH><U><DIV ID=pageCount onclick="sort3()">
          Estimate<BR>Page Count</DIV></U></TH>
    <TH><U><DIV ID=authorName onclick="sort4()">
          Author</DIV></U></TH></TR>
</THEAD>
<TBODY>
<TR><TD ALIGN=RIGHT><DIV DATAFLD="ChapNum"></DIV></TD>
    <TD>            <DIV DATAFLD="ChapTitle"></DIV></TD>
    <TD ALIGN=RIGHT><DIV DATAFLD="PageCount"></DIV></TD>
    <TD>            <DIV DATAFLD="Author"></DIV></TD></TR>
</TBODY>
</TABLE>
<SCRIPT LANGUAGE="JavaScript">
```

```
function sort1() {
  inputdata.SortColumn = "ChapNum";
  inputdata.Reset();
}
function sort2() {
  inputdata.SortColumn = "chapTitle";
  inputdata.Reset();
}
function sort3() {
  inputdata.SortColumn = "pageCount";
  inputdata.Reset();
}
function sort4() {
  inputdata.SortColumn = "authorName";
  inputdata.Reset();
}
</SCRIPT>
<HR>
</CENTER>
<ADDRESS>
Jim O'Donnell, <A HREF="mailto:odonnj@rpi.edu">odonnj@rpi.edu</A>
</ADDRESS>
</BODY>
</HTML>
```


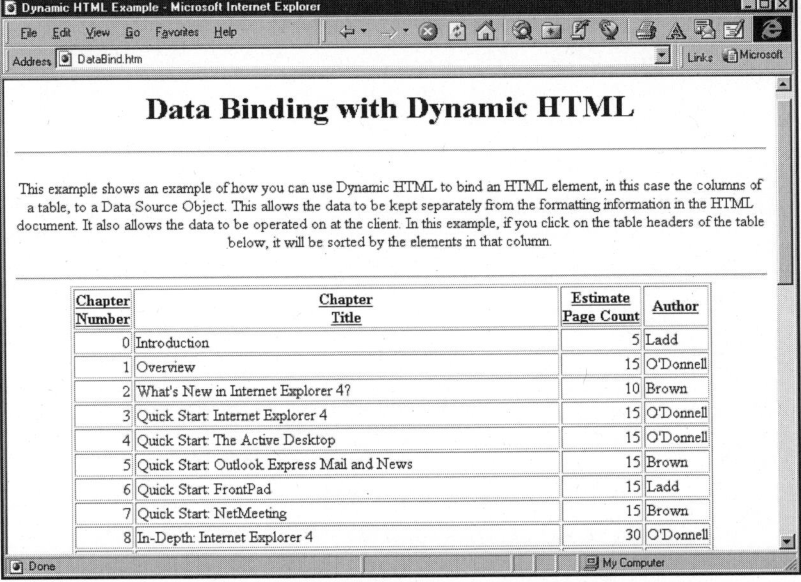

Dynamic HTML Example - Microsoft Internet Explorer
File Edit View Go Favorites Help
Address DataBind.htm
Links Microsoft
Data Binding with Dynamic HTML
This example shows an example of how you can use Dynamic HTML to bind an HTML element, in this case the columns of a table, to a Data Source Object. This allows the data to be kept separately from the formatting information in the HTML document. It also allows the data to be operated on at the client. In this example, if you click on the table headers of the table below, it will be sorted by the elements in that column.
Chapter Number | Chapter Title | Estimate Page Count | Author
0 | Introduction | 5 | Ladd
1 | Overview | 15 | O'Donnell
2 | What's New in Internet Explorer 4? | 10 | Brown
3 | Quick Start: Internet Explorer 4 | 15 | O'Donnell
4 | Quick Start: The Active Desktop | 15 | O'Donnell
5 | Quick Start: Outlook Express Mail and News | 15 | Brown
6 | Quick Start: FrontPad | 15 | Ladd
7 | Quick Start: NetMeeting | 15 | Brown
8 | In-Depth: Internet Explorer 4 | 30 | O'Donnell
Done
My Computer

FIG. 25.7
The Data Source Object enables you to include external data within an HTML document by Dynamic HTML.

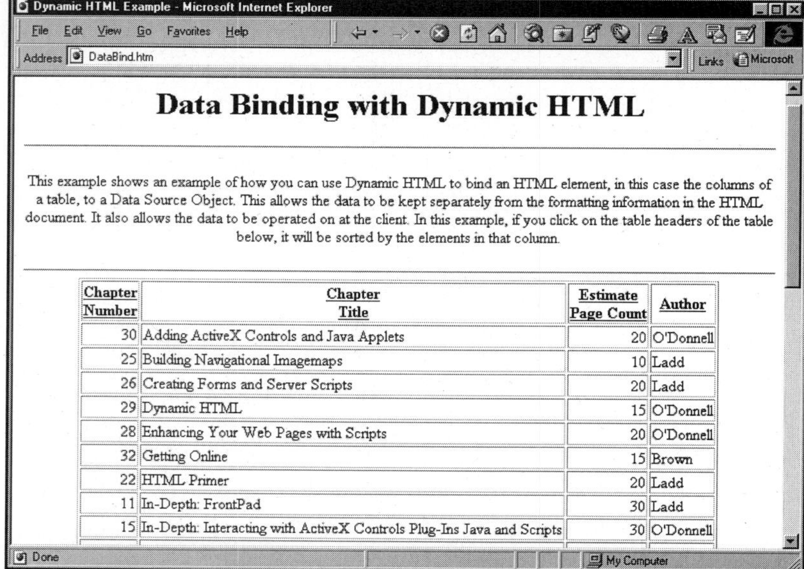

FIG. 25.8
Using Dynamic HTML, you can automatically sort, or operate on otherwise, and immediately redisplay data.

Position HTML Elements with Dynamic HTML

One exciting thing possible with Dynamic HTML is the ability to reposition HTML elements on the web page. To do this, change the `left` and `top` properties of the element's `style` object (which, in turn, is a property of the element). This change can be done either automatically or in response to user interaction.

Listing 25.6 shows an example of a Dynamic HTML document that automatically positions an HTML element on the web page. In this example, two nested regions are created using the HTML `<DIV>` tag. The outer region has a yellow background and contains only the inner region. The inner region holds an image. This example waits for the `onClick` event and then calls a script that moves the image across and down the outer region. The last thing that this script does before exiting is use the `window.setTimeout()` method to arrange to have itself execute again 500 milliseconds (a half a second) later. After the movement is enabled, therefore, it continues to move as long as the page is displayed (see Figures 25.9 and 25.10).

Listing 25.6 Position.htm With Dynamic HTML, you can change the position of any HTML element.

```
<HTML>
<HEAD>
<TITLE>Dynamic HTML Example</TITLE>
</HEAD>
<BODY onClick="moveRyan()">
```

```
<CENTER>
<H1>Positioning Elements with Dynamic HTML</H1>
<HR>
<DIV ID=Block
 STYLE="position:relative;height:55%;width:50%;background-color:yellow">
   <DIV ID=Ryan STYLE="position:absolute;width:132">
      <IMG SRC="Ryan.jpg" WIDTH=132 HEIGHT=198 BORDER=0>
   </DIV>
</DIV>
<HR>
<P>
Click the mouse, and this example will show you how HTML elements
can be moved on the Web page, by
setting the <EM>style.top</EM> and <EM>style.left</EM> properties
of the HTML element.
</P>
<HR>
</CENTER>
<ADDRESS>
Jim O'Donnell, <A HREF="mailto:odonnj@rpi.edu">odonnj@rpi.edu</A>
</ADDRESS>
</BODY>
<SCRIPT LANGUAGE="JScript">
ctr = 0;
function moveRyan() {
   ctr++;
   if (ctr > 9)
      ctr = 0;
   document.all.Ryan.style.top  =
      ctr*(document.all.Block.offsetHeight -
           document.all.Ryan.offsetHeight)/9;
   document.all.Ryan.style.left =
      ctr*(document.all.Block.offsetWidth -
           document.all.Ryan.offsetWidth)/9;
   window.setTimeout("moveRyan();",500);
}
</SCRIPT>
</HTML>2
```

Part IV

25

Changing HTML Documents On-The-Fly

The last example shows the use of Dynamic HTML to create dynamic content—HTML elements that are changed within the web browser on-the-fly. Listing 25.7 is an example of two different ways HTML elements can be changed on-the-fly. The digital clock (see Figure 25.11) is an HTML element, but it changes automatically each second to reflect the local time. The paragraph following it, on the other hand, is changed in response to user input—when the user clicks the Change HTML button, the contents of the text box above the button are substituted for the paragraph. As you can see in Figure 25.12, this substitution can also include any HTML elements, as shown with the <MARQUEE> and hypertext link in this example.

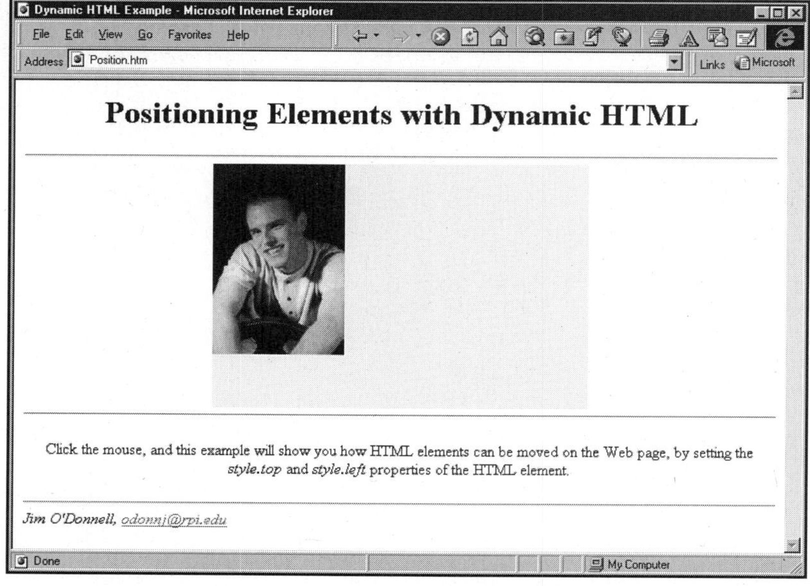

FIG. 25.9 You can use the HTML <DIV> container tag to group other HTML elements into one region.

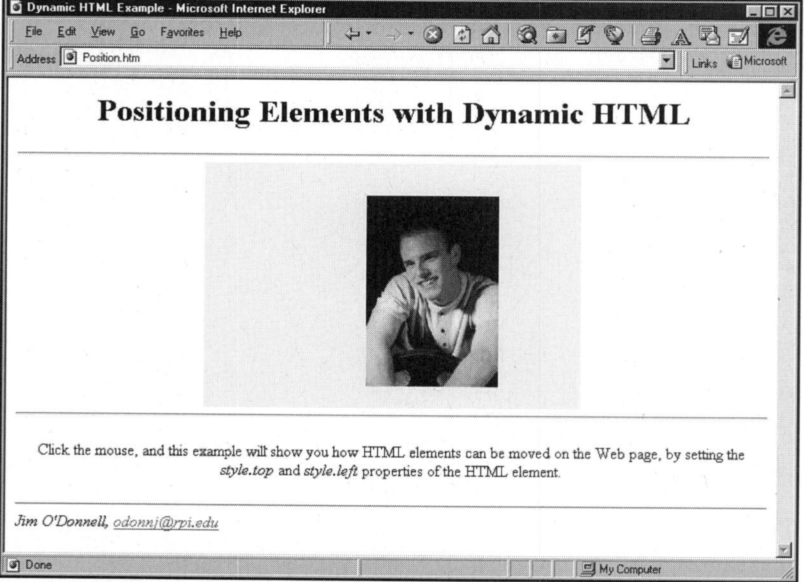

FIG. 25.10 The `top` and `left` style properties make it easy to move HTML elements around the page.

Listing 25.7 DynCon.htm Dynamic HTML can change HTML documents without going back to the web server.

```
<HTML>
<HEAD>
<TITLE>Dynamic HTML Example</TITLE>
</HEAD>
<BODY>
<CENTER>
<H1>Dynamic Content</H1>
<HR>
<DIV ID=digitalClock STYLE="font-size: 60">
    
</DIV>
<HR>
<DIV ID=dynContent>
   <P>
   This example shows how HTML content can be dynamically
   changed. The clock shown above is updated with the local
   time on your system once a second. This text will be
   replaced by any HTML elements that are entered in the
   text box below, when the <EM>Change HTML</EM> button is
   clicked.
   </P>
</DIV>
<HR>
<INPUT ID=newContent TYPE=TEXT STYLE="width: 100%"><BR>
<INPUT TYPE=BUTTON VALUE="Change HTML"
       onclick="dynContent.innerHTML = newContent.value">
<HR>
</CENTER>
<ADDRESS>
Jim O'Donnell, <A HREF="mailto:odonnj@rpi.edu">odonnj@rpi.edu</A>
</ADDRESS>
</BODY>
<SCRIPT LANGUAGE="JScript">
function runClock() {
   var d,h,m,s;
//
   d = new Date();
   h = d.getHours();
   m = d.getMinutes();
   s = d.getSeconds();
//
   if (h < 10) h = "0" + h;
   if (m < 10) m = "0" + m;
   if (s < 10) s = "0" + s;
//
   digitalClock.innerHTML = h + ":" + m + ":" + s;
   window.setTimeout("runClock();",100);
}
window.onload = runClock;
</SCRIPT>
</HTML>
```

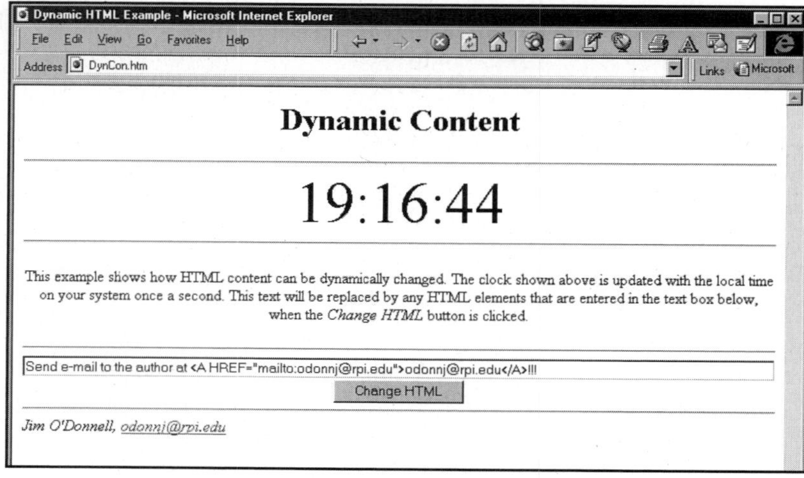

FIG. 25.11
Real-time clocks appearing in web pages are common; with Dynamic HTML, however, you can make them appear using only HTML elements.

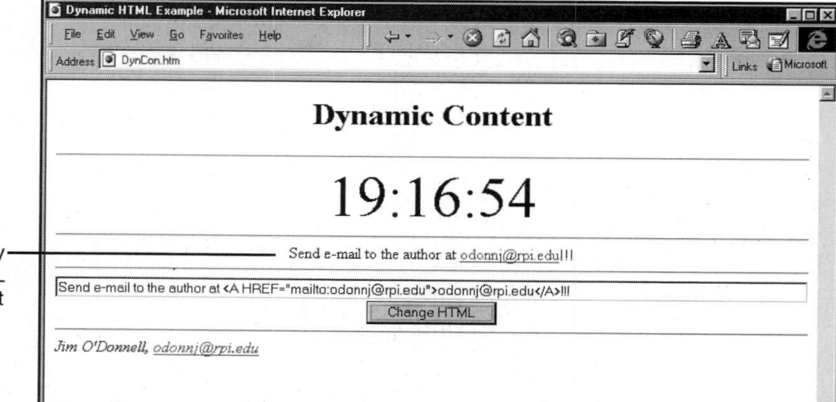

FIG. 25.12
Dynamic HTML can dynamically change the contents of a displayed HTML document, which is automatically redisplayed by Internet Explorer 4.

Dynamically changed HTML content

Dynamic HTML Filters

Microsoft has included some new capabilities in their Internet Explorer 4 web browser through a series of ActiveX Controls and web browser objects as part of their implementation of Dynamic HTML. You have already seen one of them in action: the Data Source Object that works along with Dynamic HTML data binding to allow HTML elements to import data from external sources. In addition to this component, Microsoft has included a series of controls used to create and manipulate graphic objects and the appearance of an HTML document as a whole.

Microsoft has included a series of filters that you can add to web pages to achieve a number of interesting visual effects, previously only possible by creating large graphic images in a program such as Adobe Photoshop. These filters are accessed through style sheet attributes, and can be applied to text, images, and graphic objects—in short, anything that can appear in an HTML document.

Microsoft has an excellent example of the possible effects that users can achieve with the Dynamic HTML filters, along with the other Dynamic HTML demos. The demo web site is at

http://www.microsoft.com/ie/ie40/demos/

The filter example is at

http://www.microsoft.com/ie/ie40/demos/filters.htm

Figure 25.13 shows the default, unfiltered state of this demo page, and has the following elements:

- HTML text
- GIF image
- Graphic object
- Buttons attached to Dynamic HTML filters

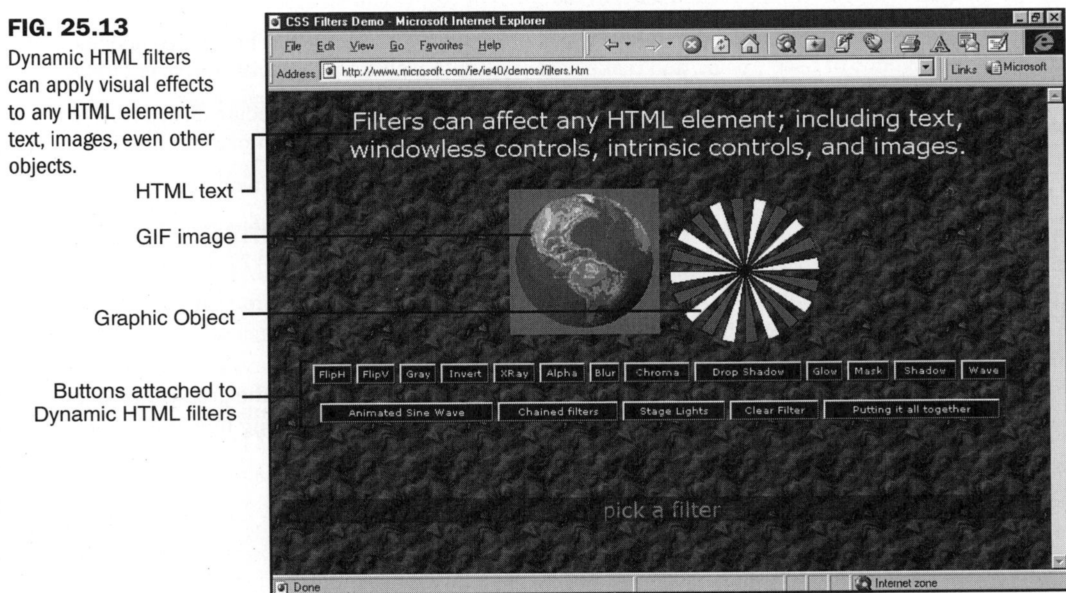

FIG. 25.13
Dynamic HTML filters can apply visual effects to any HTML element—text, images, even other objects.

Figure 25.14 shows what the document looks like when the blur filter effect is selected. This is implemented by using the `onClick` method of one of the buttons, as shown here:

```
<INPUT CLASS=clsbtn VALUE="Blur" TYPE=BUTTON NAME=BLUR
   onClick="theImg.style.filter =
'blur(direction=45,strength=15,add=0,enabled=1)';
          progress.innerText = 'explanatory text…';">
```

The different attributes of this `<INPUT>` tag do the following:

- The `CLASS` attribute attaches a style to the label of the button, enabling you to change its appearance. (This was not possible in earlier versions of Internet Explorer.)
- The `TYPE`, `VALUE`, and `NAME` attributes are the familiar attributes used for HTML Form elements, defining the type of element, label, and object name, respectively.
- The `onClick` attribute attaches the inline JavaScript shown so that it gets executed whenever the button is clicked. The inline JavaScript does two things. First, it attaches the `blur()` filter to the style sheet `filter` property for the region named `theImg` (as defined in Listing 25.9). Second, it sets the `innerText` property of the region named `progress`, which displays explanatory text in that region for the filter selected.

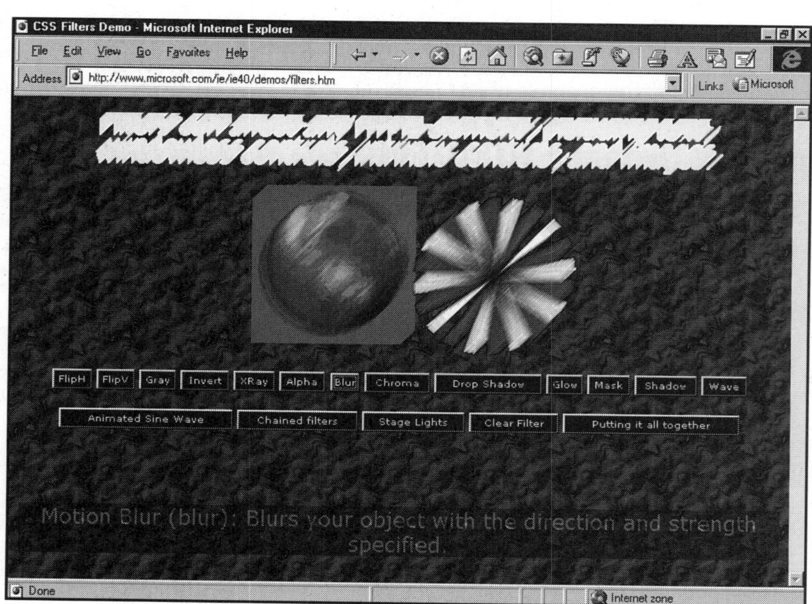

FIG. 25.14 Filter effects are quickly applied by the client browser, and save the need for creating graphic images to achieve the same look.

A number of different filter effects are possible. Figure 25.15 shows a different effect achieved with the Glow filter. It is even possible to combine the effects of more than one filter within a given region.

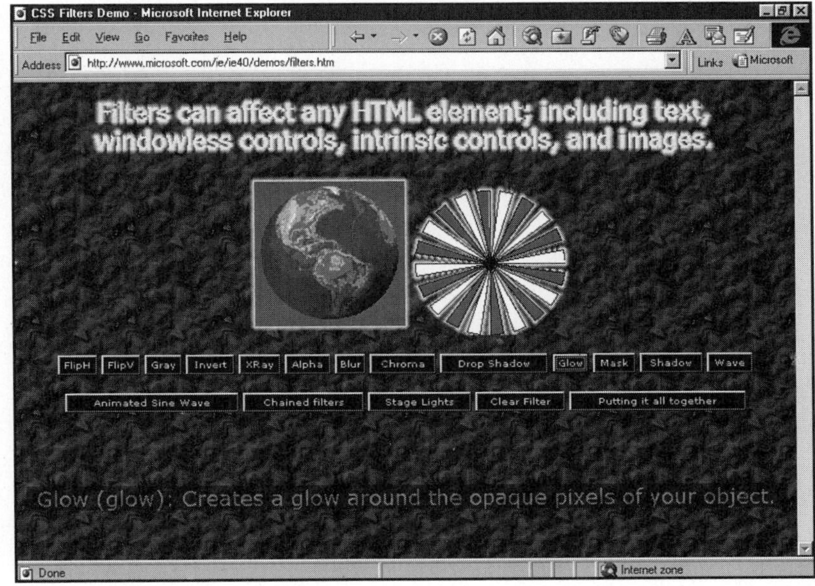

FIG. 25.15
Because you can dynamically change the filter applied to a given region, it is very easy to quickly achieve an assortment of different effects.

Microsoft's Scriptlets

With version 4 of Internet Explorer, Microsoft has also introduced another new technology known as *Scriptlets*. Microsoft calls Scriptlets "components for the web." Although not technically a part of Dynamic HTML, Scriptlets enable you to create small, reusable web applications that can be used in any web page. Scriptlets are created using HTML, scripting, and Dynamic HTML. To include them in an HTML document, use the `<OBJECT>` tag.

What is meant by "web component?" A software component is a self-contained piece of software designed to be used within a container application through a clearly defined interface. ActiveX Controls and Java applets represent two examples of web objects that act as components within a browser. Until now, it has been possible to obtain some component functionality with HTML scripting by using the `SRC` attribute of the HTML `<SCRIPT>` tag; the process of reusing scripts and HTML code in more than one document has largely been a cut-and-paste operation.

Microsoft's Scriptlets add more complete component architecture for reusing scripted HTML documents and applications within other documents. Using Scriptlets as components in your HTML documents offers the following benefits:

- Scriptlets are isolated from the surrounding HTML document, except through a predefined interface. This way, errors that occur elsewhere in the document do not affect the Scriptlet, and vice versa. This simplifies the development process of both the Scriptlet and the containing document.

- A second benefit of Scriptlet web components is that they can be easily reused within other HTML documents. A component can be designed, developed, and debugged one time, and then can be easily reused without further investment of time.
- The final benefit of Scriptlet web components is that you can use Scriptlets to interact with any other web component, developed using any other compatible language or technology. In this way, Scriptlets (components developed using HTML and scripts), Java applets, and ActiveX Controls can work together without the need to recode them into a common language.

ON THE WEB

http://www.microsoft.com/scripting/ This web site contains the latest information about all of Microsoft's scripting languages, including Scriptlets.

Creating Scriptlets

Scriptlets are created like any other HTML document, with HTML and scripts. Scriptlet properties and methods are made accessible to containing HTML documents by prefacing them with `public`. For instance, if the following appears in the Scriptlet

```
<SCRIPT LANGUAGE="JAVASCRIPT">
public_Value = "Hello";
function public_myFunction(par1,par2,…) {
   …
}
</SCRIPT>
```

and, if the Scriptlet is included in an HTML document with `<OBJECT ID="MyScriptlet">`, the property and method shown in the preceding code can be accessed using this:

```
MyScriptlet.Value = "Goodbye";
x = MyScriptlet.myFunction();
```

Scriptlets can initiate two kinds of events that can be received and acted on by the containing HTML document. These are `onscriptletevent` events and standard `window` events such as mouse clicks and keypresses. The `onscriptletevent` event includes a string and an object parameter; the external HTML document can base its action on the contents of the string, and interpret the object parameters appropriately.

Using Scriptlets in HTML Documents

After a Scriptlet is created, including it and using it within an HTML document is a simple procedure. A Scriptlet is included in an HTML document by using the `<OBJECT>` tag, with the following syntax:

```
<OBJECT ID="Calendar" WIDTH=400 HEIGHT=270 TYPE="text/x-scriptlet">
   <PARAM NAME="URL" VALUE="Calendar.htm">
</OBJECT>
```

Like other web browser objects, the `ID` attribute is used to name the object so that it can be accessed by scripts within the page. The `WIDTH` and `HEIGHT` attributes define the size of the object within the page. The Scriptlet `<OBJECT>` tag's `TYPE` attribute uses the MIME type `text/x-scriptlet` to tell Internet Explorer 4 that this object is a Scriptlet. Finally, the `<PARAM>` tag is used to give the URL of the Scriptlet itself.

Scriptlet Example

Microsoft maintains a collection of scripting examples at

http://www.microsoft.com/scripting/samples/

Figure 25.16 shows one of the demos from this site, the Calendar Scriptlet Demo, in action. Notice the following features of this demonstration:

- The HTML needed to implement the table containing the calendar, as well as the supporting scripts, are all contained within the Calendar Scriptlet.
- Scriptlet methods are attached to each of the buttons shown in the page; these buttons are part of the external document, not the Scriptlet itself. Clicking on any of them calls a Scriptlet method with the contents of the adjacent text field to set the corresponding property of the Scriptlet.
- Dynamic HTML is used to dynamically change the contents of the calendar when the month and/or year is changed via the drop-down lists shown in the upper-right corner of the Calendar Scriptlet.
- Figure 25.16 shows how the document can respond to two kinds of Scriptlet events. The number of the day over which the mouse is, changes to the highlight color—this is an internal event in the Scriptlet, and the external HTML document never receives any indication of this event. On the other hand, when one of the days is clicked with the mouse, as the 17th has been in this figure, it triggers an internal event to change the background color of the day to the select color, and also triggers an `onscriptletevent` event in the external HTML document. The external HTML document, in this case, uses this event to set the value of the date text field to the select date.

Find Out More About Dynamic HTML

It would be possible to write an entire book on Dynamic HTML, so there is no way it can be covered in the space that has been allotted here. The object of this chapter was to give you the resources for getting started with your own web pages by using Microsoft's implementation of Dynamic HTML and Internet Explorer 4. To see more about both Microsoft and Netscape Dynamic HTML, check out Que Publishing's *Special Edition, Using Dynamic HTML*. If you would like to see more examples and to find out more information, try some of these links on the Microsoft web site.

- *Features of Dynamic HTML in Internet Explorer 4*

  The Internet Explorer 4 web site includes introductory information on all the features of its suite of applications and technologies. The information on Dynamic HTML is located at

  http://www.microsoft.com/ie/ie40/features/ie-dhtml.htm

- *Internet Explorer 4 demos*

  In addition to information, the Internet Explorer 4 also offers a series of demos, many of which make use of the new features of Dynamic HTML. The demos are at

  http://www.microsoft.com/ie/ie40/demos/

- *Microsoft SiteBuilder Network*

  Microsoft's SiteBuilder Network is the area of its web site devoted to providing information to web authors and developers who use Microsoft products. The SiteBuilder Network hosts a Dynamic HTML Gallery at

  http://www.microsoft.com/workshop/author/dhtml/

- *Microsoft Internet Client SDK documentation*

  The Internet Client Software Development Kit (SDK) includes the technical information and software needed to author pages and develop applications and components that use Internet Explorer 4. Part of the SDK is extensive information and documentation on Dynamic HTML and the new Document Object Model that supports it. You can download and also view this documentation online at

  http://www.microsoft.com/msdn/sdk/inetsdk/help/

- *Inside Dynamic HTML web site*

  The Inside Dynamic HTML web site includes a mass of information and samples of Dynamic HTML in action. It is located at

  http://www.insidedhtml.com/

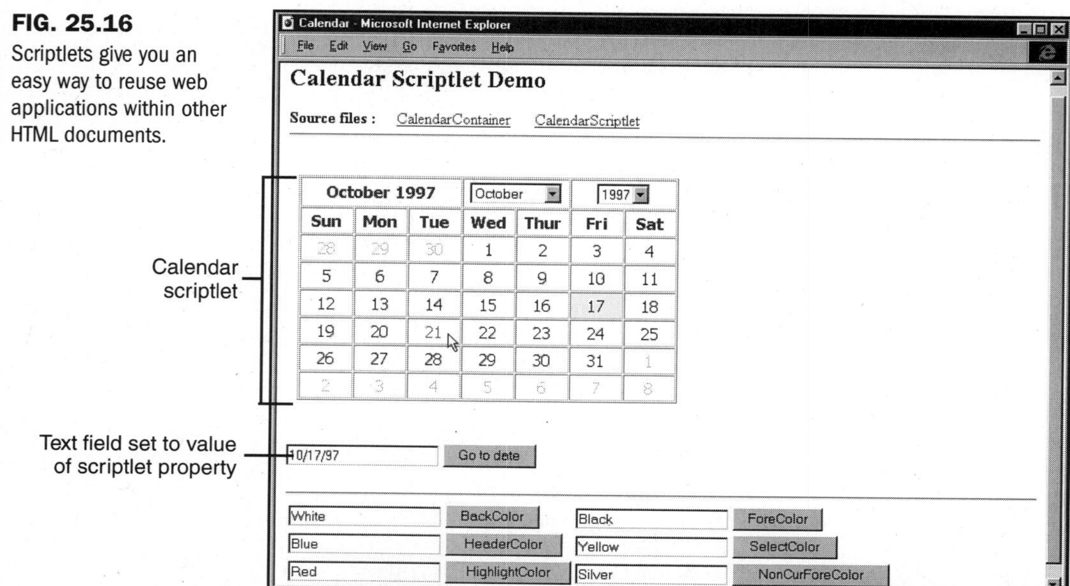

FIG. 25.16 Scriptlets give you an easy way to reuse web applications within other HTML documents.

PART V

Webcasting

CHAPTER 26

Introduction to Webcasting

by Steve Banick

In this chapter

Webcasting Primer

The term "webcasting" has become a catchall description for several new approaches to how publishing is done on the Internet. *Webcasting* most commonly refers to the new push technologies embedded in the newest generation of web browsers, including Microsoft Internet Explorer 4 and Netscape Communicator 4. Webcasting represents a fundamental change in how you can deliver your content to your audience, either on the Internet or within an intranet.

The traditional web model relies on your audience making visits to your site on a regular basis to review changes and updates. Webcasting enables you to adopt the more active role of broadcaster and deliver the information to them without them having to make repeated visits to your site. This delivery of information may be targeted web content, streaming multimedia, or interactive programming. Regardless of the type of content, the thrust of webcasting is to put you into a role of broadcaster, transmitting the content to the audience instead of the audience coming to you to fetch the information.

The Basics of Webcasting

This chapter discusses three distinct schools of thought regarding the webcasting model:

- *Broadcasting interactive content and programming.* Many people think that the traditional web pages are not enough, that they will never provide the flexibility and power of a high-level programming language and custom-developed applications. Another approach to webcasting has been to introduce a new transmission medium, outside the web. Relying on non-HTML content, these technologies promise a more focused interactivity that may not otherwise be possible within the constraints of a web page.
- *Broadcasting streaming multimedia.* Not everyone believes webcasting is just about bringing web pages and programs to the audience. Many believe that webcasting is the replacement for traditional broadcasting (television and radio, for example)—streaming audio and/or visual media to the desktops of the masses. Webcasting in this light could mean more focused transmission of media to cater to a select audience that otherwise might not be reachable through the traditional mediums of television and radio. Concerts performed live over the Internet offer a prime example of streaming multimedia; training videos on a corporate intranet are also a good example of streaming multimedia.

Approaching your content with a webcasting eye is a little awkward when you are used to thinking of things in terms of web sites. The best way to think of your content in terms of webcasting is a logical grouping of similar information—like-minded content should be all together in one place for viewers.

Regardless of which approach to webcasting you use, a common terminology is shared with only minor differences between them. In all three approaches to webcasting, two crucial concepts are used to explain webcasting's behavior:

- *Webcasting content is grouped into channels.* Much like channels on television, channels for webcasting represent a separation between content groups. A channel could represent a complete web site, a multimedia stream, or an interactive program. Audience members can select the channels that they wish to "view" or interact with, and change them at will. Because there is no physical limitation to the number of channels (as there is with television), channels can be created to fill any need or request and be waiting for viewing. Channels are directly analogous to programs or sites.
- *Like magazines, a subscription is required to view content.* If you think of webcasting channels as "exclusive channels" on television, you can see how the webcasting subscription methodology works. For an audience member to view a channel, the viewer must "subscribe" to the channel. Upon subscription, the content then is sent to the viewer's desktop for review. A subscription may not entail a cost (in fact, most channels would likely be free like their web site counterparts), but it would involve a few other properties. Subscriptions may set the frequency that the content is updated on the viewer's desktop, as well as the sort of material from the channel the viewer wants, and so forth.

Figure 26.1 illustrates how the concepts of channels and subscriptions apply to webcasting.

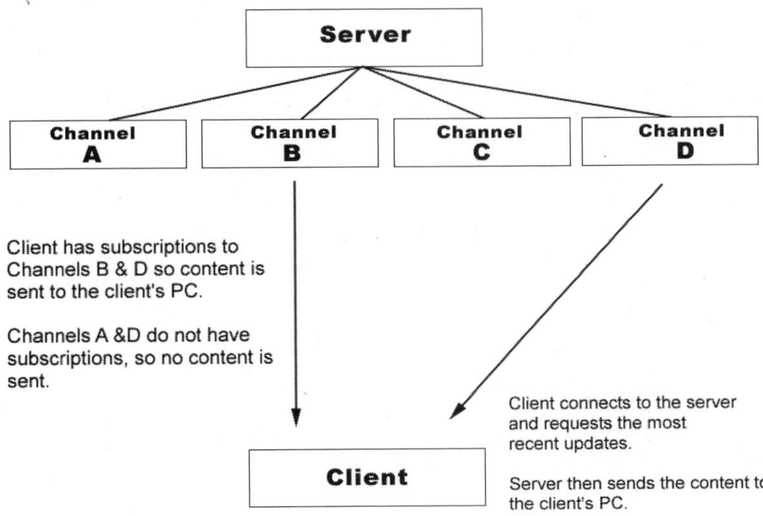
Server
Channel A
Channel B
Channel C
Channel D
Client has subscriptions to Channels B & D so content is sent to the client's PC.
Channels A &D do not have subscriptions, so no content is sent.
Client connects to the server and requests the most recent updates.
Server then sends the content to the client's PC.
Client

FIG. 26.1
A server can contain many channels, each representing a logical grouping of similar content. Visitors can choose to subscribe to only the channels that they find interesting.

As a publisher, you may choose to have your content available both on a public web site that doesn't require subscription and as a channel for those who can subscribe to webcasting channels. Regardless of which webcasting technology you choose, the viewer requires a compatible "pull" client on his or her computer. This may be in the form of a web browser, a specialized client such as PointCast, or a combination of the two.

The key to webcasting is how the client software empowers viewers to spend less time surfing for content and more time perusing the content itself. With a subscription to a channel, viewers are assured that if new information is added to a channel they will be notified of any changes, if not having the changes appear automatically on their desktops.

If you are thinking of having content directed to a viewer's desktop, make sure that the content is in small and digestible chunks. Try to keep information organized into quickly readable panels that can easily be dismissed by the eye if the viewer is not interested, as opposed to long pages. No one wants a large amount of information popping up on his desktop.

Planning Your Content for Webcasting

Webcasting content is ideally grouped into smaller segments than a web site would be. The objectives behind webcasting are to

1. *Provide bite-sized chunks to interest viewers.* Webcasting relies on "teasers" to draw the viewer in further. A successful webcasting channel uses topical and timely information to draw the audience into the rest of the channel.
2. *Provide information with a good flow.* Webcasting channels count on content drawing viewers from one section (or article) to the next. Inheriting the hyperlinks from the web, webcasting channels can use the power of an article of unlimited size broken into several related pieces—flowing into one another and complimenting the overall scope of the information.
3. *Provide one-stop reading, if possible.* Although it is not always possible (or desirable) to lock a viewer into reading one channel without ever leaving, the goal of a webcasting channel is to typically give the viewer the best content possible in one location. This saves the viewer from having to surf the web to read everything he wants.

The ultimate goal of any channel is to create a resource that viewers are repeatedly drawn back into. With that in mind, you want to make your channel as approachable as possible. The fewer steps involved for a viewer to peruse your content, the better off you are. Keep these general tips in mind:

- *Keep the interface light.* Creating a dense and layered interface forces viewers to wade through complexity that could hinder their enjoyment of your channel. The easier and quicker the experience is for viewers, the more likely they will return.

- *Keep the content good.* Although "good" is obviously a judgement call, make sure that your channel is using the best content you can provide. Often web sites are filled with pointless, non-essential, and ultimately useless content just because a page "has to be filled." Carefully consider your content in a channel—play the role of editor as well as publisher.
- *Keep the material up-to-date.* Plan on constant updates and innovation, keeping your channel fresh and current. There is only one thing worse than a web site that has its "last updated on" date set to two years ago: a channel with the same last updated date. Channels rely on an image of keeping current and new. If you don't make sure your channel complies with this expectation, your viewers will look elsewhere.

Webcasting Existing Content

When you created your existing web content, you had planned around the structure of a web site itself. Each link takes users a step further into the site until they decide to leave. Webcasting channels can be more immersive, if you carefully prepare your material. Because channels are typically push broadcast to the viewer's machine, you can use this as an opportunity to prune out the "dead wood" in your content and concentrate on your content's strengths. The content itself will likely require little change (if any); the changes come in your organization and editing.

Consider the web site structure depicted in Figure 26.2. This structure is very typical and represents a top-down hierarchical menuing scheme. It is safe to say that *most* web sites resemble this structure.

FIG. 26.2
The prototypical web site structure map. Web sites are built with a top-down, hierarchical structure in mind.

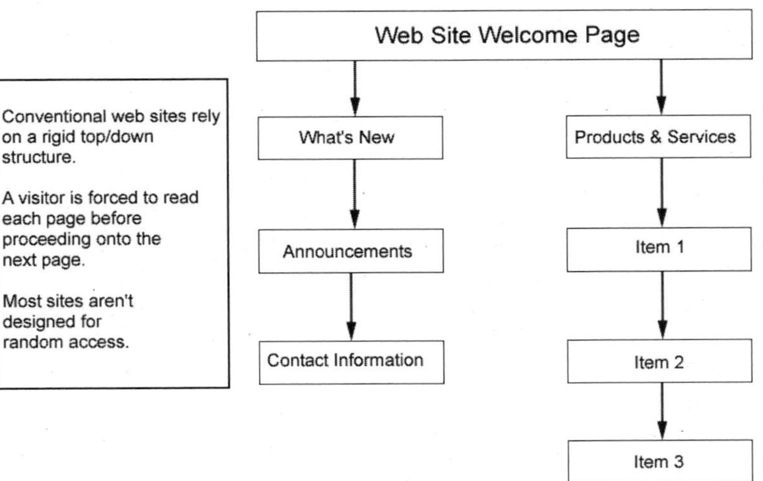

With channels, however, the goal is to enable users to indicate exactly what information they want and enable them to get that information only. You should remove the excess and dead information from a channel because the user expects focused information without having to wade through irrelevant content. Successful implementation of any webcasting approach relies on using the technologies and skills covered in this book. Some of these technologies are discussed in more detail in subsequent chapters.

Broadcasting with Web Content

The majority of content on the Internet can be found on the World Wide Web. Rather than cast aside all this content and the evolution behind it, one approach to webcasting has been to "activate" web content and broadcast it to the desktop. This approach is commonly known as push publishing, or just "push." The objective behind this approach is to use the common foundation of the web (HTML and so on) to create content to which an audience can "subscribe" for automatic reception of updates and changes. The basic concept of webcasting with web content is to provide a framework for subscriptions and a means of receiving the material. This usually involves

- *The web content itself.* The content can be a complete web site or a portion of one. This could be content specifically designed for use as a push channel, or a site subscribed to just for automatic downloads.
- *The webcasting client.* This refers to the software used on the client side to retrieve the channel contents. This could be a web browser (such as Microsoft Internet Explorer 4) or a specialized client (such as PointCast).
- *The web server.* Web content-related channels rely on the standard web server to deliver data to the client. Special server software is not typically required, although it may be used in certain technologies.

Several technologies use web content. The three most firmly entrenched in the webcasting world are Microsoft's Channel Definition Format for Internet Explorer 4 (CDF), Netscape Netcaster, and PointCast.

The Channel Definition Format (CDF) and Netscape Netcaster

Both Microsoft and Netscape have entered the realm of webcasting. Unfortunately, both vendors offer different standards, causing more grief and effort on the part of developers everywhere. Microsoft's Channel Definition Format and Netscape's Netcaster "standards" are tightly integrated into their latest web browser releases (Internet Explorer 4 and Communicator 4, respectively). These formats enable visitors to remain in their comfortable web browsers while taking advantage of the webcasting revolution. Figure 26.3 and Figure 26.4 illustrate these two webcasting technologies in action.

Both CDF and Netcaster rely on the advances in HTML to create an experience for the viewer. Microsoft CDF (and the extension to Active Desktop for IE 4) are discussed in Chapter 28, "Microsoft Netshow and other Technologies." Netscape's Netcaster is explored in detail in Chapter 29, "CDF and Active Desktop Components."

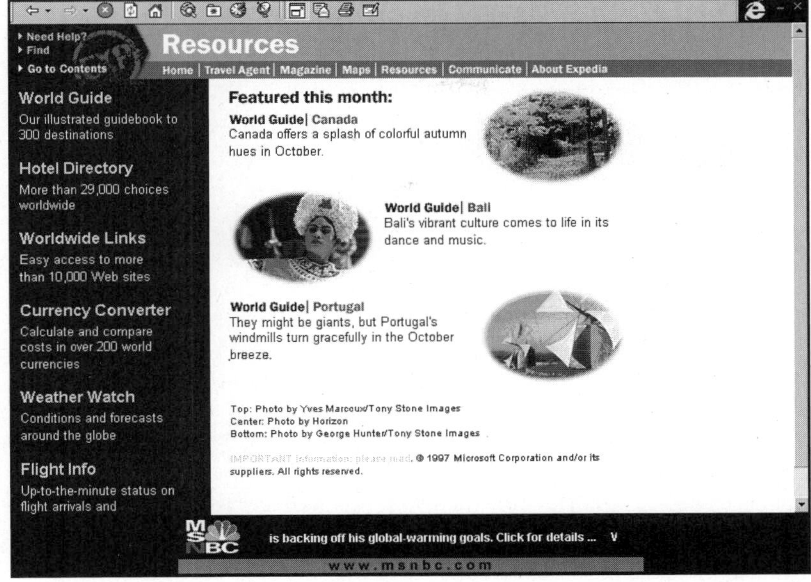

FIG. 26.3
Microsoft's Internet Explorer 4 provides support for Microsoft's own Channel Definition Format. This format is also used in other webcasting efforts.

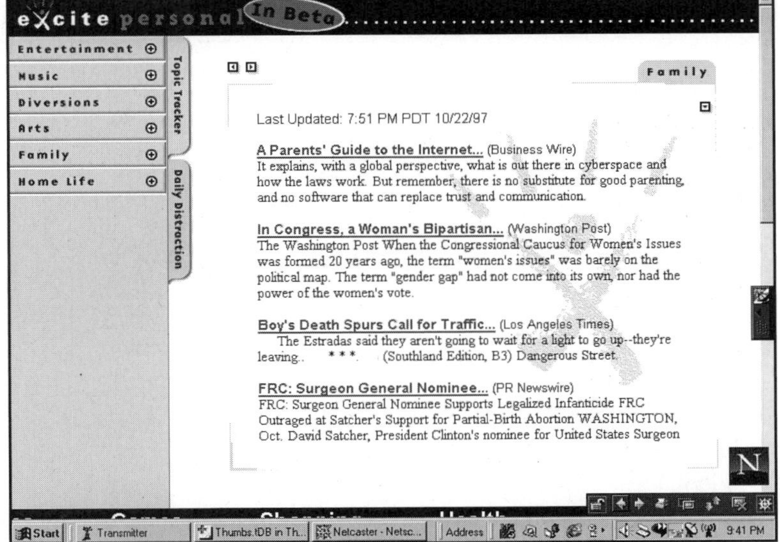

FIG. 26.4
Netscape's Netcaster technology differs in implementation from Microsoft's CDF, but is still based on the fundamentals of the web: HTML.

PointCast 2

A pioneer in webcasting and push publishing, the PointCast Network was first unveiled a couple of years ago as a proprietary system, delivering subscription channels to any eager viewer's desktop. PointCast relied on a custom client program that enabled the viewer to choose what channels were of interest and then download the most current information at set intervals. PointCast's unique concept and excellent content created an instant sensation on the Internet and garnered many awards.

When PointCast sat down to plan its next version, it decided to rethink its strategy and embrace open standards by making PointCast 2 web-based. Almost all content for PointCast is web based and uses the same conventional formats that web sites use. This choice enabled PointCast to open its structure to individual content developers and companies to extend the PointCast appeal. Figure 26.5 shows the PointCast client at work.

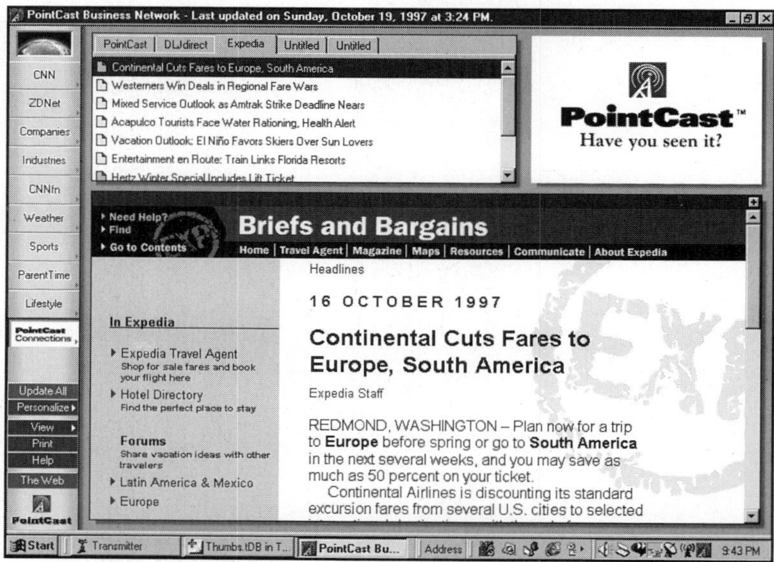

FIG. 26.5
The PointCast client is now open to incorporating web content using Microsoft's Channel Definition Format (CDF). You may choose to view PointCast within the client or inside IE 4.

ON THE WEB

You can find PointCast on the web at **http://www.pointcast.com**. PointCast also has country-specific sites around the world, including PointCast Canada at **http://www.pointcast.ca**.

PointCast refers to the integration of web content as a *connection*. PointCast connections use Microsoft's own CDF format for incorporating web content. Each individual page inside a PointCast connection is referred to as an *article*. If you have an article that refers to a hyperlink outside the connection and a visitor clicks on it, PointCast seamlessly opens the outside link.

The experience of using the PointCast connection is not lost even when you have left the initial article. Because connections are CDF based, your visitors can also view them with Internet Explorer 4. PointCast itself has an IE 4 channel that uses a suite of specialized ActiveX Controls to mimic the PointCast client.

Creating a PointCast Connection

When creating a PointCast connection, the most crucial step is planning. PointCast relies heavily on the article approach; thus, your content should too. If you find your content slipping outside an article approach, you should consider a different webcasting technology. PointCast is ideal for transmitting information that is sequentially updated. That is, today you may have information pertaining to a topic that encompasses an article, and tomorrow you may have more information that would be put into a new article. Content that relies on updates to existing material (such as a page updated on a regular basis, replacing the old content) is less likely suited for use as a PointCast connection. The following are some good examples of PointCast-suited content:

- News headlines and announcements
- Corporate information such as history, stock information, and current services
- An organization's charter or newsletter
- Fan information on entertainment industry events
- Intranet documents for Human Resources, such as 401(k) program information
- Frequently used numbers and information

One of the most appealing aspects of PointCast connections is the ease in deployment. No special server software is required, just the standard web server everyone is familiar with. All that a viewer needs to take advantage of CDF is the PointCast client and a web browser (such as Microsoft Internet Explorer 4).

The creation of a PointCast channel is very simple. The PointCast 2 client includes an external program called the PointCast Connections Builder (see Figure 26.6). This program steps you through the creation of a CDF file tailored for PointCast viewing. The program has both a straightforward "wizard" approach and the standard interface. The channel contents themselves are existing web documents. Content is split into "articles" that are individual pages. These articles can be created using any web authoring program (such as Microsoft FrontPage) and can take advantage of HTML and web technologies such as Shockwave and Java.

To create your new channel, launch the Connections Builder and choose to create a new channel without the wizard interface. After you are inside the Connections Builder, follow these steps:

1. Click on the Connection Properties button in the toolbar or choose it from the File menu. The PointCast Connection Properties dialog box, shown in Figure 26.7, appears.

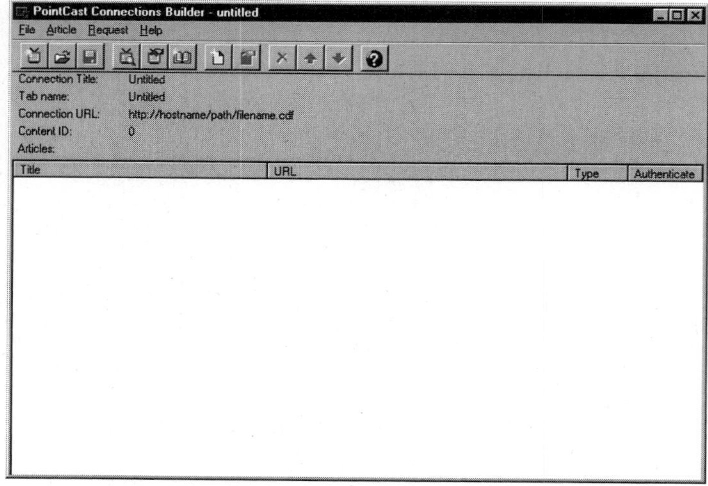

FIG. 26.6
The PointCast Connections Builder creates CDF files tailored for viewing in PointCast. This tool reinforces PointCast's article-based approach.

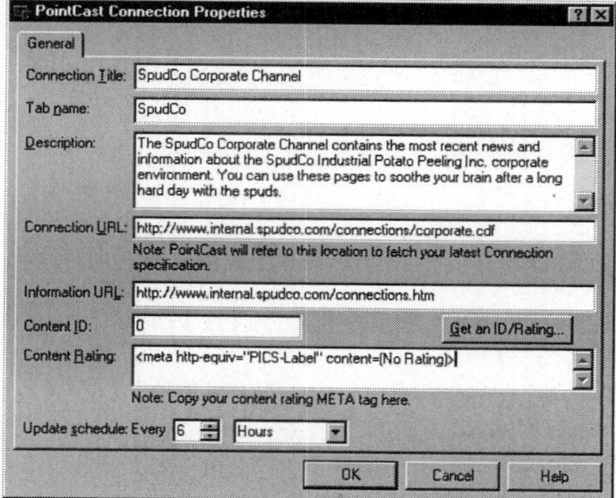

FIG. 26.7
The PointCast Connection Properties dialog box sets the base properties for your new connection. This includes support for content ratings and update schedules.

2. Using the text boxes, provide the basic information for your connection. This includes the Connection Title, Tab Name (that appears in the PointCast client), and a Description.
3. You should enter the Connection URL as the complete path to the CDF file for your new connection. The PointCast client relies on this path, as does any CDF-capable web browser (such as IE 4).

If you publish your PointCast Connection's CDF URL on your web site, you are also making your connection accessible by CDF-capable web browsers.

4. If you are providing a web page with information on your connection, enter the page's URL into the Information URL text box.

5. The Content ID and Content Rating text boxes are used for rating and identifying your connection. This information can be used by viewers or corporations to restrict content. If you do not have an ID or RSAC rating, click on the Get an ID/Rating button.

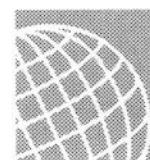

ON THE WEB

The Recreational Software Advisory Council on the Internet (RSACi) is an independent, non-profit organization that acts as a third-party rating system for content on the Internet. You can find them on the web at **http://www.rsac.org**.

6. Determine how often the PointCast client will check for updates to your connection by using the Update schedule boxes. If you plan on updating often, keep this value small.

After closing the Connection Properties dialog box, click on the Create New Article button in the toolbar or choose New from the Article menu to open the PointCast Connection Article Properties dialog box, as shown in Figure 26.8.

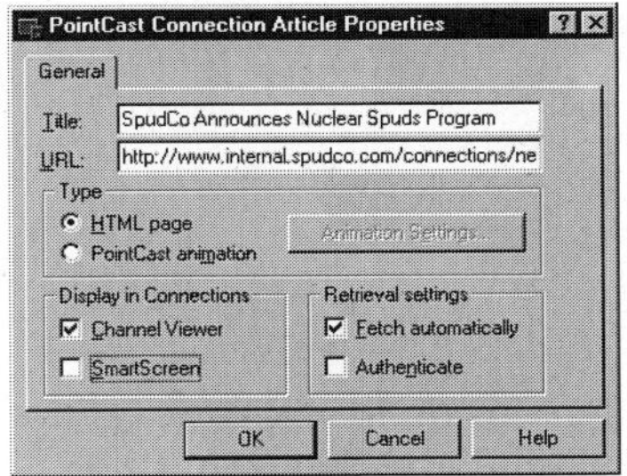

FIG. 26.8
Your article title and URL is specified in the PointCast Connection Article Properties dialog box. You can also decide where you want the article displayed.

To use the PointCast Connection Articles Properties dialog box to add an article, follow these steps:

1. Enter the article title and URL in their respective text boxes. Keep in mind that the title does not have to be the title of the HTML document itself.
2. Specify whether the article is a web page or an animation. If the file is an animation, you may specify animation settings for its appearance, palette, and how often it repeats.
3. Using the Channel Viewer and SmartScreen check boxes, decide where you want your article to appear in the PointCast client.

NOTE The PointCast client considers the normal viewing screen the *channel viewer*. You can also use PointCast as your screen saver. Any articles that appear in the screen saver are using a view called the *smartscreen*.

4. Use the Fetch Automatically and Authenticate check boxes to specify the retrieval settings. Animations must be set to Fetch Automatically. If you want a username and password prompt for your article, use the Authenticate check box.
5. Close the dialog box to see your article added to the connection list.

You can control your article's order in the connection by selecting it from the list and clicking on the Move Article Up or Move Article Down buttons. You can also remove an article from your connection by clicking on the Delete Article button.

After you finish adding your articles to the connection, save the connection as a CDF file and place it on your web server. Make sure that the CDF is located in the same location as was specified in the Connection URL.

Testing Your Connection

After you have created your channel, you will want to test it in the PointCast client. To test your new connection, click on the Preview Connection button on the toolbar. The Add Connection dialog box appears (see Figure 26.9). Click the Add Connection button to add your new connection to the PointCast client for viewing. Test your connection by using the PointCast client to spot any mistakes.

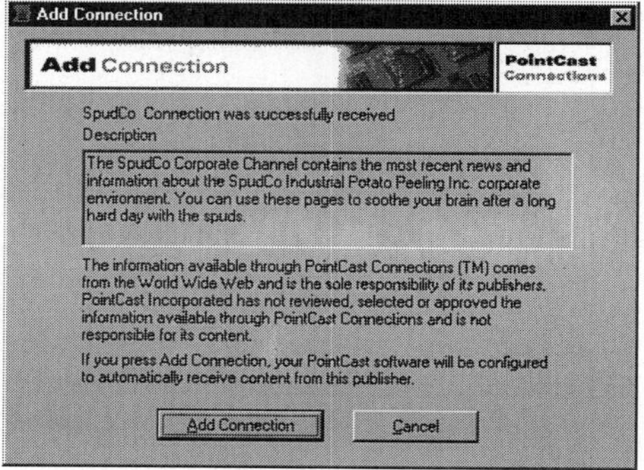

FIG. 26.9
The Add Connection dialog box is what your users see when they go to add your connection to their PointCast client. You can preview your connection by using the PointCast client to make sure everything looks just right.

When previewing your connection, you will see an additional article in the articles list, titled `README FIRST!!! This is only a PREVIEW`. This article gives you additional preview instructions.

Webcasting Using Non-Web Technologies: Marimba Castanet

A relatively new entry into the field of webcasting is Marimba. Marimba was founded by several of the creators of the Java programming language at Sun Microsystems, and (not surprisingly) bases their entire product line on Java itself. Marimba's premiere product is Castanet, a webcasting "push" technology that uses the power and flexibility of the Java programming language to deliver interactive content and programming (see Figure 26.10).

NOTE Marimba summarizes Castanet like this: "In a nutshell, Castanet is smart application management that can help you lower the cost and complexity of distributing and maintaining applications, information, and services on the Internet, intranets, or extranets."

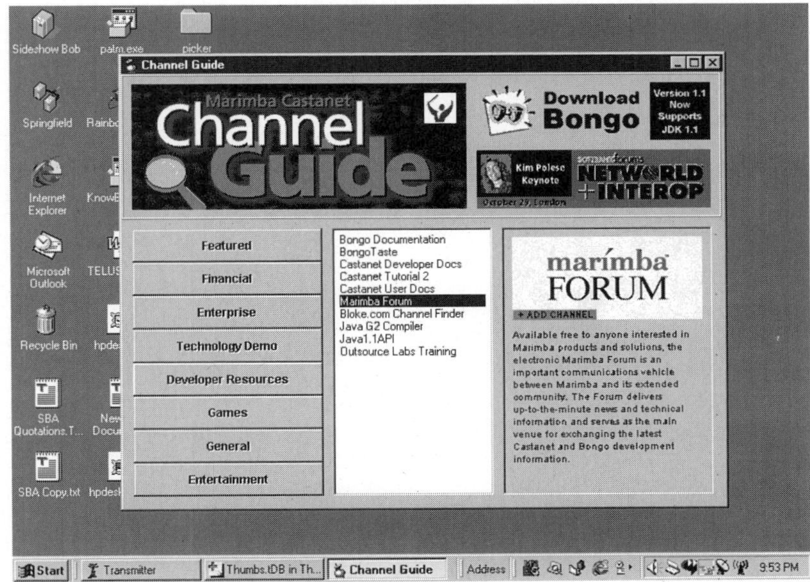

FIG. 26.10
Marimba's Castanet technology preaches the gospel of Java. The goal of Castanet is to deliver more powerful and interactive content than what is capable with a web site.

ON THE WEB

You can find the Marimba and the Castanet suite of tools on the web at **http://www.marimba.com**. Both Marimba and Excite (**http://www.excite.com**) maintain a list of Castanet channels.

Marimba borrows heavily on the television analogy for Castanet's structure. The Castanet system works with the following components:

- *Castanet channels.* The channel comparison remains the same as with web-content webcasting. Castanet channels are logical groupings of similar content. Where channels differ in Castanet is their power and scope. Castanet channels are more than a grouping of content—they are "full-fledged, self-managing" applications. All channels are created with the Java programming language, making them powerful and flexible, with only the limitations of the programmers holding them back.

NOTE Marimba further describes channels: "Channels are basically network applications or services, and Castanet provides the infrastructure that makes these channels possible."

- *Castanet Transmitter.* Much like a radio or television transmitter, the Castanet Transmitter broadcasts Castanet channels out to the viewing audience. In this case, the transmitter uses the network (be it Internet or intranet) to beam the channel data directly to the desktop of the viewer. Castanet Transmitters are a special server software that resides on the system housing your channel. Castanet Transmitter is supported on the Windows 95, Windows NT, and Solaris 2.5 platforms. Pricing for the Castanet Transmitter depends on your configuration and how many clients you want to support simultaneously.
- *Castanet Tuner.* On their desktops, viewers use the Castanet Tuner to receive and experience the Castanet channels being broadcast. The tuner is a special Java application that receives and manages all the channels to which a viewer subscribes. The tuner handles the task of updating the channel and presenting the viewer with the available options. Think of the tuner as not only a receiver, but also a remote control. The Castanet Tuner is free of cost for Windows 95, Windows NT, MacOS (PowerPC), and Solaris 2.5.
- *Castanet Publisher.* The Publisher tool is used to administer, publish, and delete channels from your Castanet Transmitter. This program typically resides on the same system as the transmitter and is used for the actual manipulation of the channels and tuner so that the viewers can use their tuners to receive the content. Castanet Publisher is included as part of the Castanet Transmitter.
- *Bongo.* The tool that starts it all. Unlike web content and HTML, Java requires some programming expertise. To make creating the Java-based channels easier, Marimba has created an authoring tool called Bongo. Bongo is used to create and customize channels without forcing the developer to code Java. It can be said, however, that to create a truly interactive and powerful Castanet channel, you need to be a programmer or call on one. Bongo is available for Windows 95, NT, and Solaris 2.x for approximately $500.

Creating Your First Channel in Bongo

Bongo, like the rest of the Castanet tools, is a Java application based on Sun's Java Runtime Environment. Using Bongo is like using a rapid application development tool (think Visual Basic in Java). Bongo enables you to design the appearance for your channel as well as tie "script" (Java code) for events behind objects. You can use Bongo (shown in Figure 26.11) to create a functioning channel in very little time. Unlike web–content-based webcasting, Castanet is entirely based on Java. You cannot really apply your existing web content here. You may, however, have images that you want to use within your channel that can be added to your project in Bongo.

To begin creating your channel, open Bongo and choose New Presentation from the File menu. A blank presentation window appears and the Bongo window changes to display the Properties tab, as shown in Figure 26.12. The Properties tab is used to modify the attributes of objects in the Castanet channel. Initially the tab displays the properties for the entire presentation, but changes according to what object (called a *widget*) is selected.

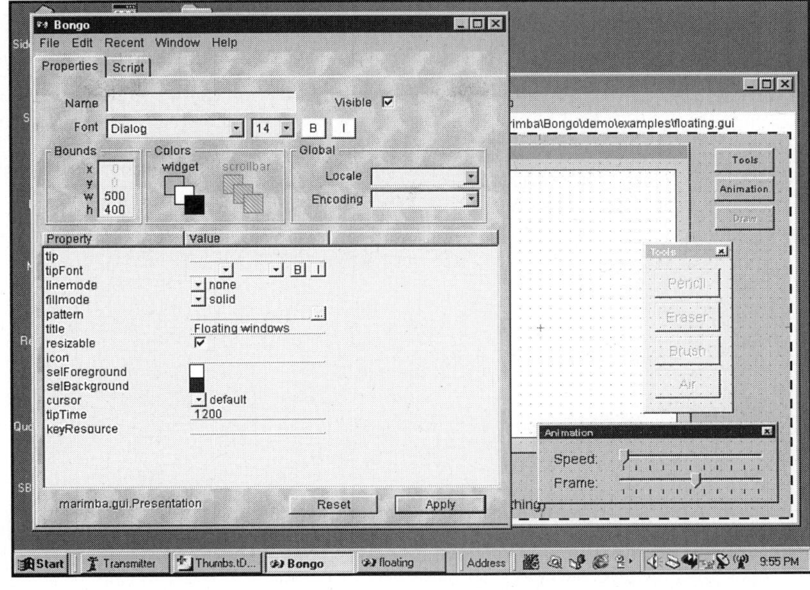

FIG. 26.11
Bongo is the RAD tool for Castanet. Creating your channel in Bongo can be a quick process if you know what you are doing.

FIG. 26.12
The Bongo window displays the Properties tab after the new presentation window appears. The other tab in the Bongo window is Script; it is used to tie Java code to objects.

With the new presentation window open, now you can create a simple presentation to demonstrate Castanet. You will create a very straightforward presentation with a button and a text box that can be controlled programmatically. Begin with the button:

1. From the New menu, choose Command Button from the Button sub-menu. A new button widget appears. Position it in the center of the presentation window and switch to the Properties tab in the Bongo window.
2. Edit the Name text box to the value Button.
3. Edit the Label property with the value of Toggle Textbox.
4. Click the Apply button.
5. Switch to the Script tab and enter the following code:

```
public void action() {
     TextBoxWidget  textBox;
     textBox = (TextBoxWidget) getWidget("textBox");
     textBox.setEditable(!textBox.isEditable());
     textBox.disable(!textBox.isDisabled());
}
```

6. Click the Apply button to compile the code.

Your presentation window should look something like the one shown in Figure 26.13.

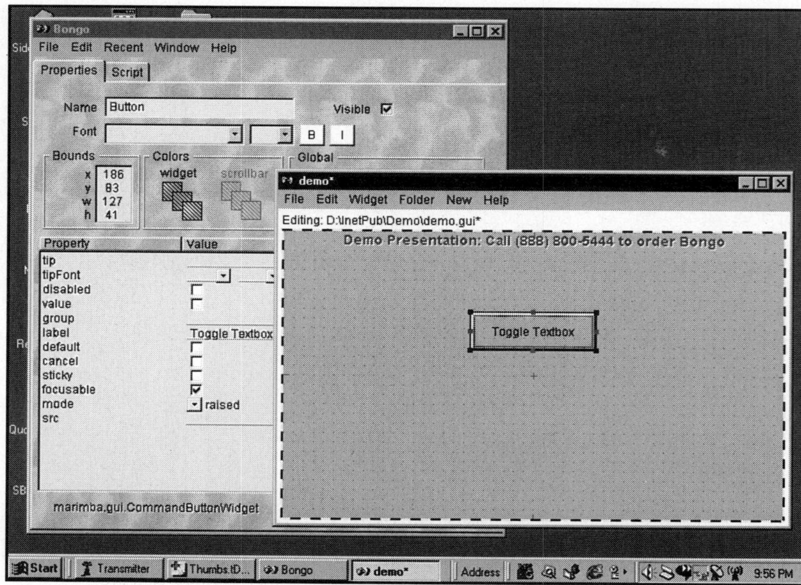

FIG. 26.13
With the button created in the presentation window, you are ready to add the text box. The text box will be controlled by the button's state.

Now return to the presentation window and add the text box that will be controlled by the button:

1. From the New menu, choose Textbox from the Text sub-menu. A new textbox widget appears. Center the widget below the button.

2. Return to the Properties tab in the Bongo window and edit the Name text box to read Textbox.
3. Edit the Text property to have the value of Marimba Castanet Promotes Pure Java!
4. From the Align Property's drop-down box, choose Center.
5. Click the Apply button.

You can quickly select any widget for editing by holding down Ctrl and clicking on the widget.

With the text box and button in place, your presentation should resemble the one shown in Figure 26.14. Now save the presentation into a separate directory.

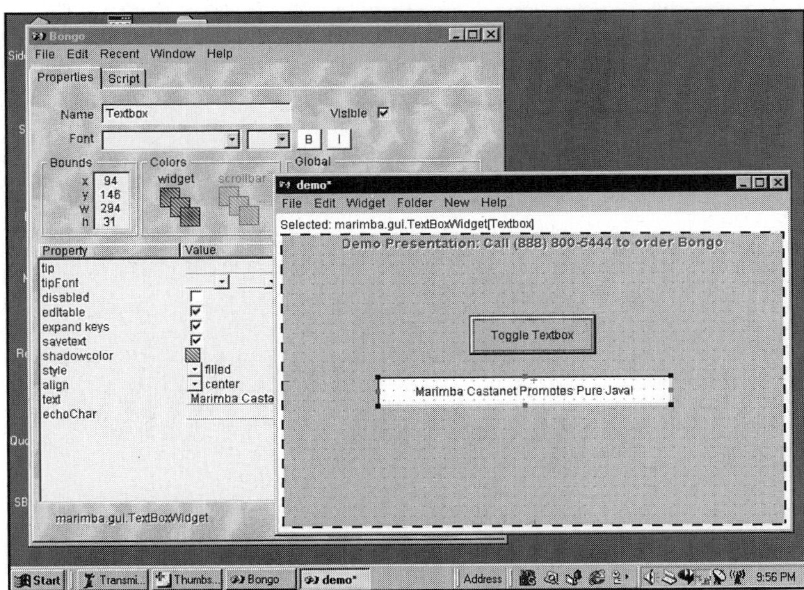

FIG. 26.14 The completed presentation is no revolution in interactivity, but it demonstrates how easy it is to add widgets and apply a program to them.

Broadcasting Your Channel with the Publisher and Transmitter

With your presentation saved, you are now ready to create a channel for broadcasting with the transmitter. Before you can create the channel itself, you must have a Castanet Transmitter to publish to. This can be either on your machine or on a separate server. With your server's address and port number in hand, you can open the Castanet Publisher to begin step two of getting your channel online. Bongo provides a direct link to the Castanet Publisher through a Publish Wizard, located in the File menu. Open the Publish Wizard. A screen similar to the one shown in Figure 26.15 appears.

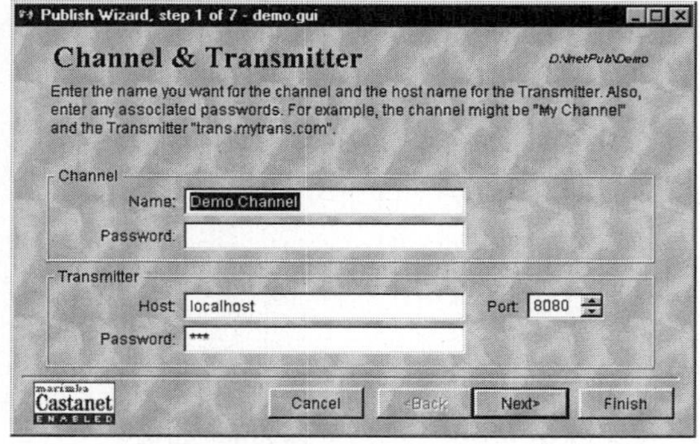

FIG. 26.15 The Publish Wizard makes creating a channel from your presentation easy. You can also use the Castanet Publisher separately to create and modify channels.

Step through the Publish Wizard to create your channel. To do so, you need the following information:

- Your transmitter's hostname and port (default of 80)
- Your transmitter's password and an optional password for your channel
- A name and description for your channel
- Optional icons for your channel
- Optional parameters for your channel (typically for applets)

The Publish Wizard enables you to preview your channel as well as publish it. Use the Preview option to test your channel before you unleash it on the world with the Publish option.

After the Publish Wizard finishes, you are ready to view your channel in the Castanet Tuner.

Viewing Your Channel with the Tuner

Viewing your channel with the Castanet Tuner enables you to see exactly what everyone else will see when subscribing to your channel. The Castanet Tuner, shown in Figure 26.16, is the client software used to interact with Castanet channels. The tuner can hide in the background (as an icon in the icon tray) and appear only when the user asks. As long as the tuner is running, Castanet channels can be broadcast to the user's desktop. The tuner also enables the viewer to control how often updates can be made and at what times of the day.

With your channel published to your Castanet Transmitter, you are ready to view it. Open the Castanet Tuner and switch to the Listing tab. In the drop-down box, enter the address to your transmitter. If your transmitter is running on a port different than the default of 80, append the port number with a colon (for example, localhost:8080). Click on the List button to list all the channels available on the transmitter, or click the Browse button to view the list in your web browser. The list for channels looks like the one in Figure 26.17.

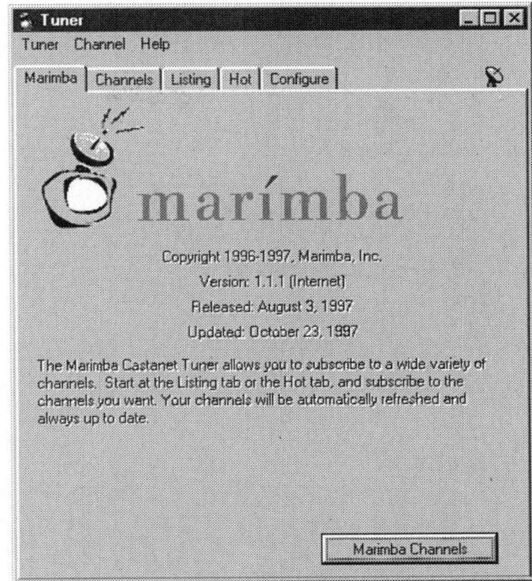

FIG. 26.16
The Castanet Tuner is the viewport for Castanet channels. The Tuner, written in Java, enables you to subscribe to channels and control their update frequency.

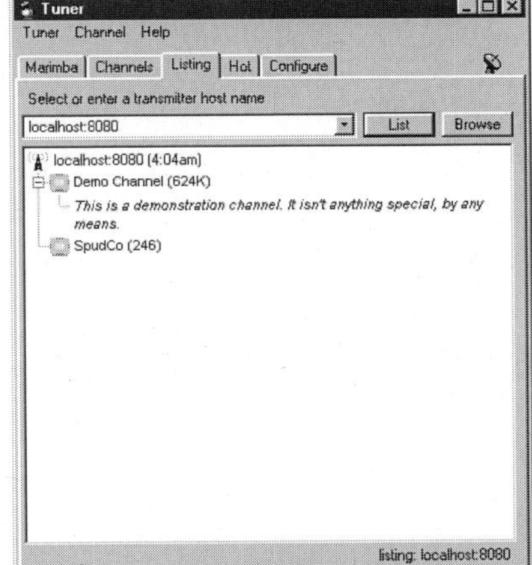

FIG. 26.17
The Channel listing provides the name (or the description) for each channel available on the Transmitter. Double-clicking on the channel downloads it to the computer.

To view your new channel, double-click on the channel name in the list. This transfers the channel information (including Java code) to your computer for viewing. Your channel is also added to the Channels tab. By double-clicking on the channel name in the Channels tab, the channel is launched for your viewing, as shown in Figure 26.18. In the case of your demonstration applet, the presentation appears and enables you to interact with the two widgets. As you click on the button, it toggles the read-only state of the text box.

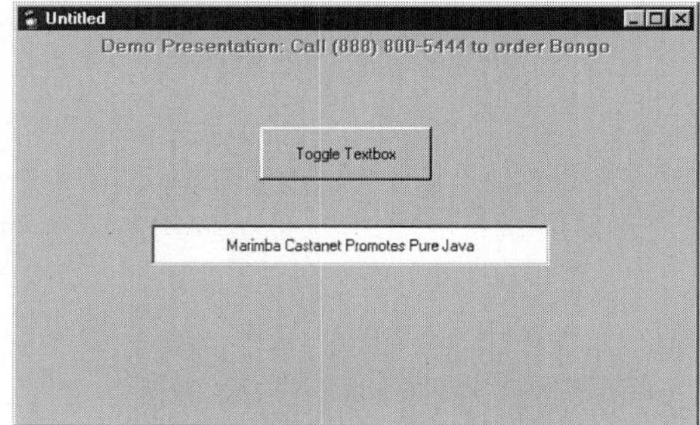

FIG. 26.18
Click on the button to toggle the text box's read-only state. This simple demonstration shows how widgets can be controlled programmatically. In the hands of a good programmer, Castanet can be a dream come true.

NOTE Castanet channels are only as powerful as the code behind them. To take true advantage of Marimba's innovation, count on experienced programmers to create your marvels. If you are a programmer yourself, you are in for a treat with Castanet's automatic delivery of updated code and packaging.

Broadcasting with Streaming Media

The third approach to webcasting owes a lot to traditional broadcasting media—television and radio. The possibilities of interactive broadcasting are tremendous when you consider just how much time and effort is wasted in traditional broadcasting. After all, how many times do you *really* want to sit and watch shows that you are not all that interested in, all because nothing better is on? Webcasting with streaming media may not entirely solve the dilemma of "57 channels and nothing's on," but it could certainly make the waiting for something good to come on a great deal more interesting and fun.

Traditional broadcasting works on the assumption that something—it doesn't matter what—has to be aired at all times, and relies on you watching it. Broadcasters air content even if next to no one is going to watch it (witness infomercials at 3 a.m.). Webcasting has the possibility of changing that approach and making content more directly tuned to the interests of the viewers.

Streaming media is a popular thing. You can offer this content to your audience as a special bonus. Be certain, however, to consider how the technology will impact your audience members–make sure that it is an accessible enhancement to your site. Consider offering different "qualities" of streaming media for users with varying bandwidths. This just means that you could offer differing resolutions/sizes for your content for users who are connecting at a lower speed, while letting those users who have a fast connection take advantage of it. Your audience will appreciate your efforts.

Using the Internet (or an intranet) as the transmission method, streaming content (such as video or audio) to the desktop of interested parties reduces flagrant waste of bandwidth by not beaming the signal to everyone, regardless of whether they are watching. Audience members can choose precisely what channels (or programs) they want to watch and have them appear on their desktops. There is no need to flip through five dozen channels. Instead, the content you find interesting can come to you in the form of a subscription or selection on a web site. Using specialized client software that can decompress the data from the server, this content can be empowered with interactive content on a web site or using one of the other webcasting technologies.

Remember that you can integrate your audio and video with your web site through embedding. Your multimedia presentation can take advantage of your visitor's web browser to create an immersive experience. Inline scripting (discussed in Part III, "JavaScript") can enhance your content's appeal.

The most firmly entrenched streaming technologies available today are Microsoft's NetShow and Real Networks' RealSystem (formerly known as RealAudio and Video). Both of these technologies unlock the power of real-time audio and/or video to the desktop over the Internet and in intranet environments. Figure 26.19 shows how existing web sites can be complimented with these multimedia experiences.

FIG. 26.19
Streaming audio and video are a step to integrating traditional broadcasting with the World Wide Web. You can use these technologies to create interactive media in the blink of an eye.

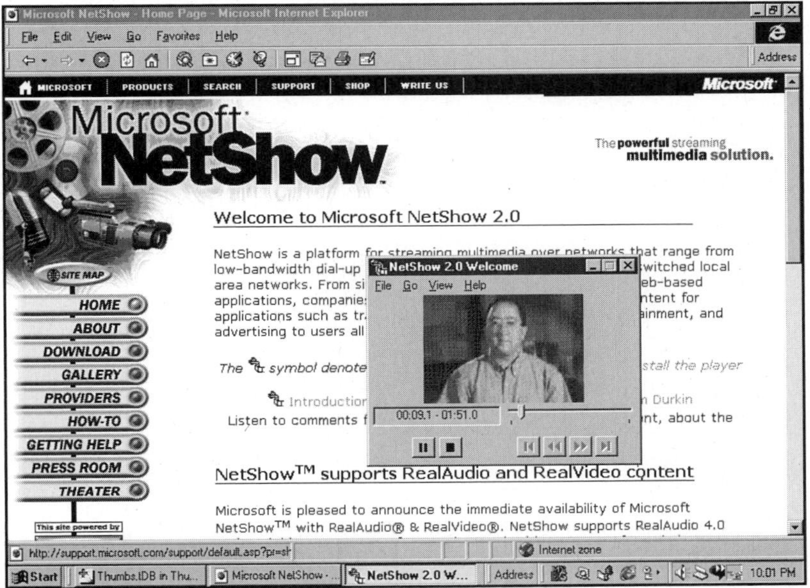

CHAPTER 27

Adding Live or Streamed Media to Your Web Site

by Mike Morgan

In this chapter

As recently as a year ago, audio and video on the web looked a lot like audio and video on CD-ROMs—you downloaded a large file from your web server to the user's hard drive. Then the end user used a helper application or, perhaps, a browser plug-in and played the file. The biggest reason for *not* using audio on your web site was the sheer size of the files—a 60-second audio clip of moderate quality might take eight minutes or more to download over a dial-up connection. Video clips are even larger.

Recently, two things have changed about the Internet. First, bandwidth has gone up. Dial-up users routinely have 28.8Kbps connections; many are using 56Kbps modems or even 128Kbps ISDN connections. Second, engineers have revolutionized the technology that compresses audio, called coder-decoders or *codecs*. Today it is common to be able to download 60 seconds of audio in 60 seconds or less.

The result has been a revolution in web audio and video—streaming media. Instead of downloading a file and then playing it, the new generation of plug-ins start playing within a few seconds of connecting to the server. After that, they just have to keep up with the audio stream to provide high-quality, real-time audio.

This chapter shows you how to integrate streaming audio or video into your web page, and addresses the technical aspects of audio and video that serve as the foundation for that integration. Chapter 28, "Microsoft NetShow and Other Technologies," gives you step-by-step instructions for setting up NetShow to deliver streaming media.

Streaming Audio and Video Products

One of the most exciting things you can do with your web site is to add streaming audio and video. Even at low bandwidth, the impact of Internet "radio" or a video tour of a facility will draw visitors and increase the effectiveness of your site.

Unfortunately, the Internet just was not built for audio and video. End-user connections often run through low-bandwidth dial-up lines. Servers with T1 connections are hard pressed to handle the additional load of serving video, or even streaming audio. National and intercontinental backbones are often saturated by even small quantities of streaming video.

If you are publishing with text, you need to be knowledgeable about fonts and styles. On the web, you need to know HTML. Similarly, certain technical aspects of multimedia will improve the quality of the sites you prepare. Many web sites include text, static graphic files (such as GIFs and JPEGs), and advanced graphics (such as GIF 89a animation, QuickTime, or MPEG video). When these sites include real-time or streaming audio and video, you need to think about bandwidth limitations and site design issues.

When you choose to add real-time audio and video to your site, codecs and their technology become your most powerful tools. If you choose your codec well, you will get high quality (possibly even CD-like quality) without overloading your users' bandwidth (leading to annoying data dropout).

RealAudio and RealVideo from RealNetworks

With any emerging technology, a tremendous advantage accrues to being first. RealNetworks (formerly Progressive Networks) (**www.real.com**) was the first company to deliver real-time streaming audio over the World Wide Web. Other vendors have different requirements—for example, some do not require special server software—but you will find the process is more similar than it is different for embedding different audio and video formats into your HTML documents.

NOTE RealNetworks' latest product, RealPlayer, combines its streaming audio and streaming video protocols. You will read about streaming video later in this chapter, in the section titled "Adding Streaming Video–Why Your Connection Must Change." Although this chapter uses the RealAudio player as the example, chances are your end users may opt to handle streaming audio by installing RealPlayer on their computers.

You can get more information about RealPlayer at **http://www.real.com/products/player/index.html**. You can learn more about RealNetworks at **http://christie.prognet.com/prognet/**.

Since its introduction, thousands of web sites have begun to deliver RealAudio content over the Internet. Today, it is undoubtedly the most popular streaming audio application on the Net, with more than 8 million RealAudio players downloaded from the RealNetworks web site.

ON THE WEB

http://www.real.com/ server/index.html Start on this page to learn about the range of RealNetworks servers available.

Netscape Media Server and Media Player

Netscape has introduced its Netscape Media Server and Netscape Media Player programs; these will compete heartily for the niche currently occupied by RealAudio. In addition to real-time, high-quality streaming audio, these programs also enable you to synchronize multimedia content. These programs provide high-quality audio even with 14.4Kbps modem connections, and automatic bandwidth-optimized streaming for the best possible audio quality at various connection speeds. You can synchronize audio with HTML documents, Java applets, and JavaScript for a multimedia experience. Players are available for Power Macintosh, all versions of Windows, and UNIX systems. More information and download files are available at **http://home.netscape.com/download/version_info/headings_1_13.html.**

StreamWorks from Xing

Xing Technology has built its streaming audio solution (as well as a streaming video solution) around the industry standard, MPEG, also known as ISO CD 11172. MPEG, developed by the Moving Pictures Experts Group, includes standards for highly compressed video as well as audio. The third part of the MPEG I standard, ISO CD 11172-3, addresses audio compression.

Use the XingMPEG Encoder to convert audio files such as .wav and MPEG 2 audio files, as well as QuickTime and AVI movies, to the industry-standard MPEG format.

NOTE The XingMPEG Encoder is optimized for Intel's MMX technology. If you want to convert files quickly, be sure to use an MMX-enhanced Pentium.

After you have converted your files to MPEG audio format, use Xing's StreamWorks Server to make your files available to the web. (You can use the same software to send MPEG video, as well.)

When an end user connects to your .xdm file, the user's browser invokes the StreamWorks Player program, as shown in Figure 27.1.

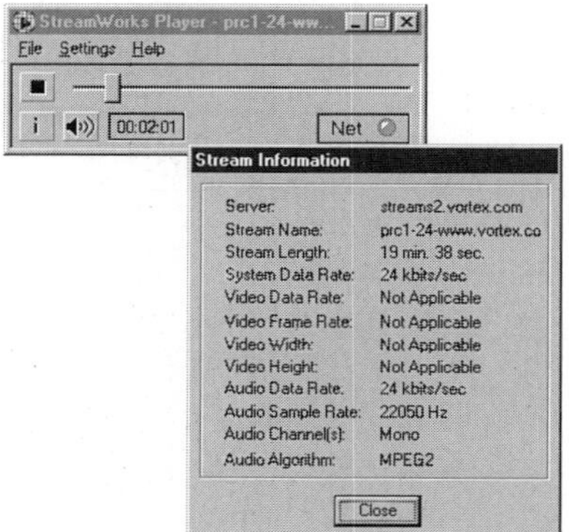

FIG. 27.1
Xing Technology's StreamWorks Player can play audio or display video clips.

Adding Streaming Media with Browser Extensions

Most web browsers, including Netscape Navigator (the web-browsing component of Netscape Communicator) and Microsoft Internet Explorer, handle a limited number of content types: GIF and JPEG images, text, and, of course, HTML pages. Other content can be handled by *helper applications*. Netscape Navigator also supports browser plug-ins; Microsoft Internet Explorer supports ActiveX Controls.

A helper application is a separate application that runs in its own window. Many helper applications have been written specifically for web use. Other applications can be configured to serve as helpers for specific media types.

A plug-in is a program that runs inside Navigator's window. To the user, the plug-in appears to be a part of Navigator, but the program need not be written by Netscape programmers. All the vendors of streaming audio and video provide Navigator plug-ins. The Netscape Media Player is a plug-in designed to handle Netscape's LiveAudio content type. RealNetworks provides RealPlayer, which can handle both RealAudio and RealVideo.

Introduction to Plug-Ins

If you examine the source of a web page with embedded audio, you will see a bit of code similar to these lines:

```
<EMBED SRC="http://www.xyz.com/Media/test.lam" OPTIONS="TRUE" VOLUME="TRUE"
➥SEEK="TRUE" HEIGHT="29" WIDTH="325" LOOP="TRUE" AUTOSTART="TRUE">
```

Strictly speaking, you only need to use quotation marks when an attribute value includes characters outside the usual set of alphanumeric characters. If you're just getting started with HTML, however, you should err on the side of caution and always use quotation marks around attribute values.

Although the exact URL of the source file and the configuration of the parameters such as `OPTIONS`, `VOLUME`, and `SEEK` depend on which streaming media server you use, the general principle is the same: use the `EMBED` tag, specify a source attribute (`SRC`), and then pass any parameters you need.

This section describes how a user configures his or her Netscape browser to activate the proper plug-in. You can use the information in this section to help troubleshoot a client system if the proper plug-in doesn't activate.

Content Types When a user connects to a web server and requests an entity, the web server sends a `Content-Type` header field with the Hypertext Transfer Protocol (HTTP) response. The value of the header is any valid MIME type. (MIME stands for Multimedia Internet Mail Extensions, and is described in RFC 1020.) If the requested entity is a web page, for example, the headers include

```
Content-Type: text/html
```

If the entity is a GIF image, it is prefaced by

```
Content-Type: image/gif
```

When the Netscape browser reads the `Content-Type` line, it looks for the MIME type on an internal list of such types. Depending on what it finds, Navigator does one of four things:

- If the MIME type is marked as "Handled by Netscape," Navigator switches to the appropriate built-in routines to process the content.
- If the MIME type is associated with a helper application, Navigator asks the operating system to start a copy of that application.
- If the MIME type is associated with a plug-in, Navigator loads the plug-in and transfers control to that program.
- If the MIME type is not associated with a helper application or plug-in, Navigator displays a dialog box asking the user how he or she would like to handle the content.

NOTE If your organization is using the Professional Edition of Netscape Communicator, as an administrator you can use Netscape Mission Control and the AutoAdmin interface to control which plug-ins each user can download. In general, you're probably safe in allowing your users to download software signed by Netscape itself.

TROUBLESHOOTING

Q. When users open my web page (which contains embedded audio), they get a dialog box similar to the one shown in Figure 27.2. What's wrong?

A. If users get a dialog box similar to the one shown in Figure 27.2 when they accesses a page with embedded media, either the streaming media plug-in has not been installed or the server is not sending the proper MIME type.

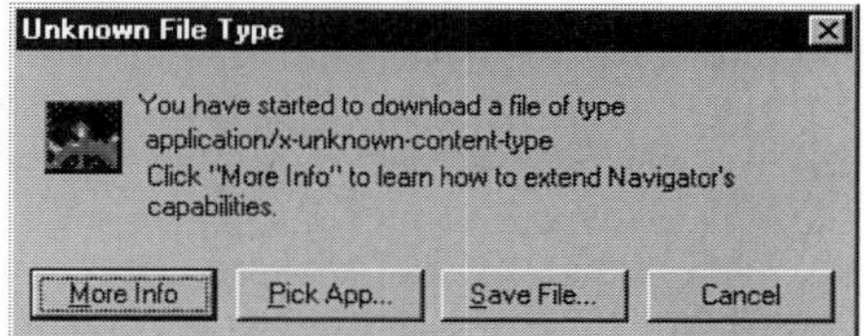

FIG. 27.2 The most common cause of this dialog box is an incorrect Navigator configuration.

To correctly activate the proper plug-in, two things must happen. First, the server must correctly identify the MIME type when it sends the file. Second, the browser must recognize the MIME type and associate it with the proper streaming media plug-in.

Configuring the Web Server Suppose you serve a web page that includes the following lines:

```
<EMBED SRC=http://www.xyz.com/Media/test.lam OPTIONS=TRUE VOLUME=TRUE
➥SEEK=TRUE HEIGHT=29 WIDTH=325 LOOP=TRUE AUTOSTART=TRUE>
```

The user's browser will read the `<EMBED>` tag and request **www.xyz.com** to return the file `/media/test.lam`. For the server to set the proper MIME media type in the `Content-type` header field, the web server's administrator needs to make sure the following entry appears in the `mime.types` file:

```
type=audio/x-liveaudio   exts=lam
```

When the browser sees the line

```
Content-type: audio/x-liveaudio
```

it invokes the Netscape Media Player plug-in.

TIP Check the documentation that came with your web server to learn how to specify MIME types with your server. Check the documentation that came with your streaming media server to see which MIME type you should specify. Table 27.1, for example, shows the MIME types associated with RealAudio.

Table 27.1 RealAudio MIME types.

Extension	MIME Type Definition
`.ra, .ram`	`audio/x-pn-realaudio`
`.rpm`	`audio/x-pn-realaudio/plugin`

Configuring the Streaming Media Server If you are using a RealAudio server or Netscape Media Server to deliver streaming audio, or a RealVideo server to deliver video, you will want to dedicate a fast machine to that server. Often, you will use a different machine than the one you use for your web server. You may even prefer to rent space on a dedicated host with high-bandwidth connections to the Internet.

CAUTION

Streaming audio can require 10 to 20Kbps and up per connection, depending on the codec you choose and the bandwidth negotiated. Streaming video requires even more bandwidth. You can easily install a server that will saturate several 56Kbps leased lines. Talk to your server vendor about your plans—you may need to budget for several T1s to support the load on your site.

If your requirements are modest, you might consider serving audio via HTTP. You can also use the Personal RealAudio Server from RealNetworks. Of course, if you are using Xing, you don't need any server at all because the file is MPEG (although you may prefer to use its StreamWorks server so that you get the benefits of streaming media).

Configuring Netscape Navigator When you download streaming media plug-ins, you typically get an executable installer file. Version 1.1 of the Netscape Media Player for Windows 95 and Windows NT systems, for example, is installed by a program named `mp32e11.exe`. Follow the installation instructions for your platform. The installer program puts the plug-in in the proper location and then configures Navigator to use the new plug-in for the proper MIME types. Use the information in this section to double-check the work of the installer program if you suspect that the plug-in is not properly configured.

When Navigator is started, it looks in the `plugins` directory in the `Netscape` folder to see which plug-ins are available. (The exact name and location of this directory vary slightly from one platform to another.) Each platform has its own way to check to see whether a file is a valid plug-in. On Windows platforms, only DLL files whose names begin with `np` are examined as candidate plug-ins.

After Navigator is launched, you can see which plug-ins the program found and which MIME types they are associated with by entering **about:plugins** in the Location field. This pseudo-URL calls up the internal Installed Plug-Ins page. (You can also bring up this page by choosing the About Plug-Ins menu item. In the Windows version of the product, choose Help, About Plug-ins.) Figures 27.3 and 27.4 show the portions of the Installed Plug-ins page that deal with LiveAudio.

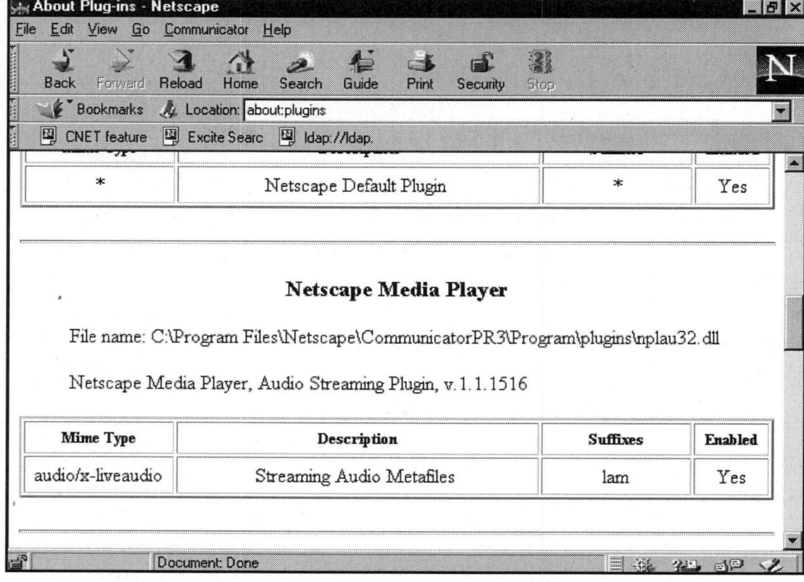

FIG. 27.3 If the server sends `audio/x-liveaudio`, Navigator will load the plug-in that's in `nplau32.dll`.

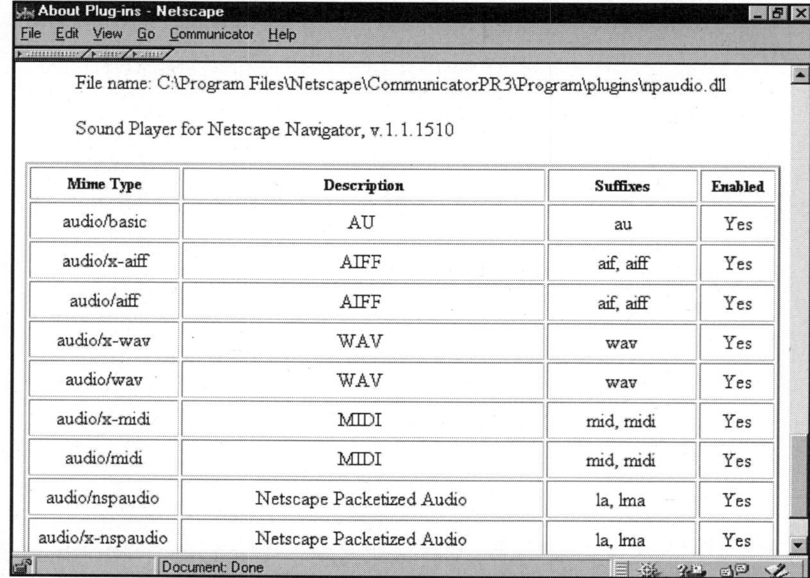

FIG. 27.4 If the server sends `audio/nspaudio` or `audio/x-nspaudio`, Navigator will load `npaudio.dll`.

Media type `audio/x-liveaudio` is associated with streaming audio metafiles, also known as `.lam` files. These files tell the browser where to find the audio. The audio is not downloaded over HTML—instead, it is sent over the Real Time Streaming Protocol (RTSP). RealNetworks uses a similar design—it calls its metafile `.ram`.

If a webmaster chooses to serve audio files directly from a web server (rather than going through the streaming media), the audio content itself will be delivered to the browser via HTML. Netscape audio will have a MIME media type such as `audio/nspaudio`, `audio/aiff`, `audio/wav`, or `audio/midi` (or one of the `x-` versions of these media types). These content types can be handled by the LiveAudio plug-in, `npaudio.dll`.

In general, serving audio or video directly from a web server is a bad idea. The Hypertext Transfer Protocol (HTTP) used by web servers is designed to ensure that no data is lost, even if a packet has to be re-sent several times. When you download audio or video, it is more important that you keep the stream flowing than that you transfer every single byte. Whenever possible, use a streaming media server such as the RealAudio or RealVideo server (from RealNetworks) or the Netscape Media Server.

For a nice design, place several `<EMBED>` tags on a page along with some descriptive text. Allow the user to select any one of the audio tracks.

Plug-In Options

As an HTML programmer, you set parameters in the `<EMBED>` tag to tell the plug-in how you want it to behave. This section describes various options available with the Netscape Media Player audio streaming plug-in. Streaming media plug-ins from other vendors have similar options; check the documentation that came with your streaming media server for details.

SRC When you use an `<EMBED>` tag, the HTML browser will look at the `SRC` attribute in the tag and ask the server to send the file named as `SRC`. The URL points to the location of the LiveAudio metafile.

Bypassing the LAM File The LiveAudio Metafile (`.lam`) tells the client where to find the audio data. If you prefer to specify the `ADDRESS`, `PORT`, and `CLIP` filename directly, don't use a `.lam` or an `SRC` attribute. Instead of writing

```
<EMBED SRC=http://www.xyz.com/Media/test.lam OPTIONS=TRUE VOLUME=TRUE
➥SEEK=TRUE HEIGHT=29 WIDTH=325 LOOP=TRUE AUTOSTART=TRUE>
```

for example, you might write

```
<EMBED ADDRESS=207.2.80.1 PORT=5483 CLIP=test.la OPTIONS=TRUE
➥VOLUME=TRUE SEEK=TRUE HEIGHT=29 WIDTH=325 LOOP=TRUE AUTOSTART=TRUE>
```

NOTE When you use a `.lam` file, you can specify a different clip for each bandwidth or platform. When you use the `ADDRESS`, `PORT`, `CLIP` construct, you can only set up one clip file.

WIDTH* and *HEIGHT You can configure plug-ins to work in one of three ways: full-page, embedded, and hidden. Full-page plug-ins are used with sophisticated data types such as Adobe's

Portable Data Format (PDF) files. Because audio has no onscreen content, you won't want to use a streaming media plug-in as a full-page plug-in.

If you use the Media Player as an embedded plug-in—that is, if you call it with the `<EMBED>` tag—you must specify a `WIDTH` value and a `HEIGHT` value. The value can be in pixels or as a percentage of the total page width.

Expect your audience to use a variety of monitors, from older Macintoshes with 9-inch monitors to high-end workstations with 17-, 19-, or even 21-inch monitors. Consider specifying the width and height as a percentage of page width so that the plug-in scales based on the available space.

TYPE When the server sends the LiveAudio Metafile (`.lam`) file, it will send `Content-type: audio/x-liveaudio`. If you use the `ADDRESS`, `PORT`, `CLIP` construct rather than `SRC`, specify `TYPE=audio/x-liveaudio`.

HIDDEN Many content types have an onscreen representation—the `HEIGHT` and `WIDTH` tags used with those content types carve out a piece of the window into which the plug-in can draw the contents of the file.

With audio content type, of course, no onscreen representation is possible. The `HEIGHT` and `WIDTH` tags reserve space for the controls. If you don't want the end user to be able to control the audio, or if you want to use LiveConnect and a Java interface to control the audio, you can leave off the `HEIGHT` and `WIDTH` tags and specify `HIDDEN=TRUE`. (You can also say `HIDDEN—TRUE` is the default.)

AUTOSTART When `AUTOSTART` is set to `TRUE`, the audio begins to play as soon as the plug-in loads and fills the buffers.

NOTE If you have more than one `<EMBED>` tag with audio on a given page, be sure to set no more than one instance to `AUTOSTART=TRUE`. If you try to play more than one audio clip simultaneously, you will get confused (and generally unsatisfactory) results.

If you don't specify `AUTOSTART`, it defaults to `FALSE`.

Media Player Controls If you opt to use the Media Player as an embedded plug-in, you can turn on several different controls. Figure 27.5 shows the full control, with `PLAYBUTTON`, `STOPBUTTON`, `OPTIONS`, `VOLUME`, and `SEEK` all set to true. If you do not specify these controls, `PLAYBUTTON` and `STOPBUTTON` default to `TRUE`, and `OPTIONS`, `VOLUME`, and `SEEK` default to `FALSE`.

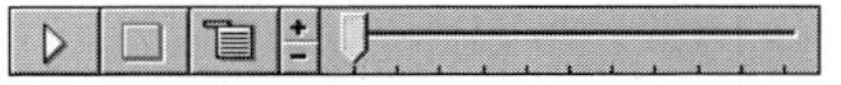

FIG. 27.5
If you specify `PLAYBUTTON=TRUE` `STOPBUTTON=TRUE` `OPTIONS=TRUE` `VOLUME=TRUE` `SEEK=TRUE`, you will get this set of controls.

If you choose `SEEK=TRUE`, you will get a slider that shows you the progress of the player while the file is being played. You can use this slider in much the same way as you use a scroll bar. Dragging the slider left or right causes the server to reposition the point from which it plays the file.

CAUTION

Before setting `SEEK` to `TRUE`, make sure the `.lam` file refers to a seekable stream. In general, clips are seekable but live feeds are not.

If you set `OPTIONS=TRUE`, you will get a button with a four-item menu:

- Save Location As
- Information About the Clip
- Properties
- Help

Windows users can get the `OPTIONS` menu if they click the right mouse button anywhere on the Media Player control.

If a user clicks on the Properties menu item of the `OPTIONS` menu, he or she will get a dialog with four tabs, as shown in Figure 27.6.

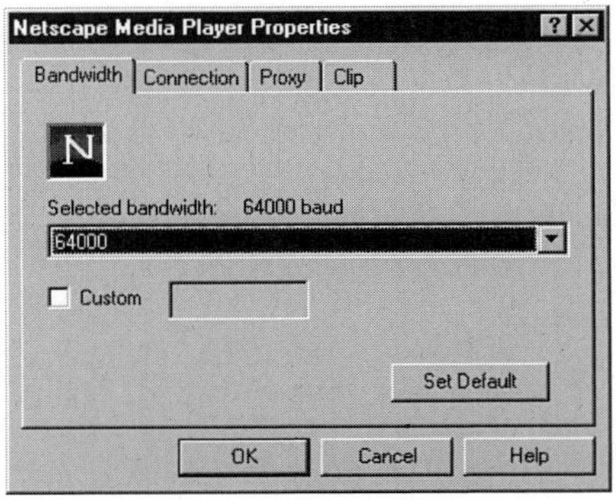

FIG. 27.6
Use these four tabs to specify how you want the clip to be played.

You should encourage your users to set up their Media Player with reasonable defaults and then leave it alone. Rather than give them access to the `OPTIONS` menu on each instance of the plug-in, you may want to have them use the special program Netscape supplies for that purpose. On a Windows 95 or NT machine, for example, choose Start, Programs, Netscape Media Player, Configure Media Player. You see the same dialog box shown in Figure 27.6.

A Macintosh does not have a setup program, but users can bring up the `OPTIONS` menu by holding down the Option key and clicking on the control.

On a Windows or UNIX machine, the right mouse button will display the drop-down menu.

NOTE On Windows 95 and Windows NT machines, the Media Player is an MCI Media Control Device. You can check its status and change its settings from the Multimedia Control Panel. Choose the Devices tab, open the Media Control Devices entry, and select (MCI) Netscape Media Player. Now click Properties. You should see a status message: `Driver is enabled and functioning properly`.

From that same dialog box, click Settings—you will get the same Netscape Media Player Properties dialog box that you saw in Figure 27.6.

Using the Properties Menu Item The end user uses the Bandwidth tab of the Properties dialog box to specify his available bandwidth. A user with an ISDN connection, for example, may have 64,000 or even 128,000bps available. A user connected over a wider connection such as a T1 may be able to support 1,000,000bps. A user over a slower dial-up connection may need to limit his download to 28,800bps or even slower. After a user has selected the appropriate bandwidth, the user should choose Set Default.

The Media Player negotiates with the Media Server to try to find a version of the clip that has been compressed to a suitable bitrate. If the server is sending at a bitrate higher than the client can accept, some packets will be lost. If the stream drops too many packets, the resulting audio will sound choppy and may have unpleasant pops and drop-outs. This chapter discusses more about matching the bitrate of the audio or video clip to the user's available bandwidth in the sections titled "Adding Streaming Audio to a Web Site" and "Producing a Video for the Internet."

The Connection tab enables the end user to specify how the client software receives the audio data. Unless you choose Request TCP/IP Transport, the audio data comes to you by UDP unicast or multicast. On the Connection tab, you specify the ports your client will listen to for audio data. The default values are that the client will listen on UDP ports 13,000 through 13,099.

Always leave Request Multicast checked if you are using UDP. If the server is sending the data via multicast, a user can reduce the load on the server by selecting the multicast. (Multicast is not available on TCP connections.)

Users get better results if they leave Request RTP Framing unchecked. The Real Time Transport Protocol (RTP) is an Internet standard, but Netscape has developed a custom transport mechanism that uses somewhat less bandwidth than RTP. (RTP is not available on TCP connections.)

NOTE If a user is behind a firewall, he may need to make special arrangements with the security administrator to receive audio data via UDP—many firewalls do not pass UDP packets by default.

If the firewall cannot be configured to pass UDP, the user should check Request TCP/IP Transport; however, he may suffer a loss in audio quality.

Like the Bandwidth tab, the end user should be sure to set the selecting settings as the default.

If the end user is behind a firewall, the administrator may have set up a media proxy server so that data can pass through the firewall. If the Media Player should use a media proxy server, check the Enable Proxy check box on the Proxy tab and enter the name and port of the proxy. Again, click on Set as Default to lock in these settings.

The Clip tab, shown in Figure 27.7, contains several selections that you can use to improve the listener's perception of the quality of the audio data. At the top of the tab, you will see the Packet Loss Tolerance panel. If the quality of the stream drops below the specified tolerance, the player will prompt the user to stop the transmission. The initial default setting, High, corresponds to 30 percent loss. Low corresponds to 10 percent loss.

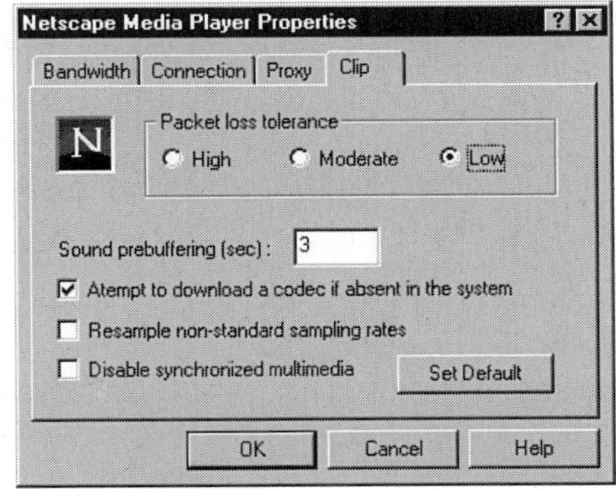

FIG. 27.7
The Clip tab contains several settings that can improve the perceived quality of the audio.

Part V Ch 27

Many connections operate at 5 percent packet loss or better, so most users should get adequate performance even if they set their packet loss tolerance to Low. You may want to recommend that users start by choosing Low. Then, if they experience a poor-quality stream from your media server, they can report the problem and you can explore why the loss is occurring. In the meantime, you may recommend that they set their tolerance to Moderate or even High so that they can continue to receive audio while you research their problem.

You can see the actual packet loss by clicking on the Options button on the Media Player control and then choosing Information About the Clip. See the comments on statistics later in this section.

You can further improve the quality by increasing the value in the Sound prebuffering field. The Media Player downloads and stores several seconds of data, and it plays that audio while the rest of the clip downloads. If a packet is lost, the Media Player attempts to have the packet retransmitted. If the buffer contains audio data, the user may never know that a problem existed. The only problem with setting a long prebuffering interval is that the user has to wait longer before he hears the sound begin to play. Set the prebuffering time long enough to mask some packet loss, but not so long that the user becomes frustrated.

You should leave Attempt to Download a Codec If Absent in the System checked. Codecs are the compression/decompression utilities used to transform audio files into a bit stream that can pass over the network in real-time. Several codecs are supplied with the Media Player or are built into operating systems such as Windows 95 or Windows NT. If the user checks Attempt to Download a Codec If Absent in the System, you—as the streaming media server's administrator—have the option of switching to a new codec—the codec will automatically be downloaded to the user's machine to enable him to decompress your audio.

Most users should leave Resample Non-Standard Sampling Rates unchecked. Each codec has one or more standard sampling rates—if the incoming data does not match one of those rates, the audio data will not sound right. Encourage users to report this sort of problem to the server administrator so that you can try to track down the cause. If you need a short-term solution, tell them to set Resample Non-Standard Sampling Rates—that often solves the problem.

If you deliver several synchronized streams from your Media Server, each client will get all streams. This design may meet the objectives of your presentation, but it will overload some users' available bandwidth. If a user wants to receive only the audio portion of a multimedia presentation, he can check Disable Synchronized Multimedia.

After the user has set up his Clip settings, he should click on OK and then click Set As Default.

Interpreting Statistics and Other Information If you have enabled `OPTIONS` in the `<EMBED>` tag, the end users can read the total number of packets received and the total number of packets lost, and can compute their throughput for themselves. As administrator, you can use this information to help troubleshoot users' network connections. You can also use this information to help you choose codecs, recommend bandwidths, and recommend a packet loss tolerance. Bandwidth and Packet Loss Tolerance settings are described earlier in this chapter in the section titled "Using the Properties Menu Item."

The Media Player shows the statistics at the moment the user chooses the Information About the Clip menu item. For the most complete picture of the transmission, click on Refresh toward the end of the clip.

You can use the Information About the Clip menu item on the `OPTIONS` menu to get technical information about the Media Server (such as the port number, transport information, and audio format). You can also see details about the audio format such as the number of channels, the sample rate, and bits per sample.

If a user complains about poor audio quality, ask him to report his current statistics, as well as the audio format and the server information, so you can see how his Media Player and your server have conspired to break your configuration.

LOOP If you set `LOOP` to `TRUE`, when the clip ends the client requests it again. If you don't specify `LOOP`, the plug-in defaults to `LOOP=FALSE`.

CAUTION

Remember that `LOOP`, like `SEEK`, doesn't make sense on live feeds.

Using ActiveX to Add RealAudio Content

If the visitors to your web site are prepared to handle ActiveX Controls, you can use the `<OBJECT>` tag to install the proper control. The following code embeds the RealAudio ActiveX Control and enables the user to play the file named `file.ra` on the `audio.realaudio.com` server:

```
<OBJECT
  ID=RAOCX
  CLASSID="clsid:CFCDAA003-8BE4-11cf-B84B-0020AF27CCFA"
  HEIGHT=140
  WIDTH=312>
<PARAM NAME="SRC" VALUE="pnm://audio.realaudio.com/file.ra">
<PARAM NAME="CONTROLS" VALUE="all">
</OBJECT>
```


The value of the parameters such as `CONTROLS`, `CONSOLE`, and `AUTOSTART` are identical to those used with the Navigator plug-in.

TIP

Set `HEIGHT` and `WIDTH` to zero to make the ActiveX Control invisible.

Adding Streaming Audio to a Web Site

Short bits of sound and small video clips have been used on web sites for several years for entertainment or to draw a visitor into a site. Longer clips have content value. Many webmasters have hesitated to put long audio or video clips on a web site because most users won't wait many minutes to download such a file.

Sound files are *big*, and video files are even bigger. Without sophisticated compression, audio and video clips take so long to download that few users will tolerate it. Much of this chapter, therefore, focuses on compression.

NOTE How long does it take to download an audio or video clip? A 60-second, low-quality `.wav` file sampled with 8 bits at 8KHz, can be stored in a 470K file. On a 28.8Kbps dial-up link, that file will download in about 2 1/2 minutes. On a dedicated ISDN link, the file transfers in a minute or so. Nevertheless, dial-up users seldom wait beyond about 30 seconds for a web page, and users with faster links have even higher expectations. Many users will not stay connected to a site to download even a small `.wav` file.

Recent developments in audio and video compression now make it possible to compress data so tightly that the file can be played as it downloads—a practice known as *streaming*. The Real Time Streaming Protocol (RTSP) serves as the basis for some of the streaming media products. RTSP makes a distinction between real-time data (also known as *interactive* data), which is used for live feeds, and streaming data, which is used for playback. Real-time data has a tight coupling between the time of the signal and the time that it is played by the client. Streaming data may be rewound, fast-forwarded, or paused.

This section shows you how to prepare sound for use on the web. Video clips follow many of the same principles, but the file size is much larger. The differences are discussed later in this chapter in the section titled "Adding Streaming Video—Why Your Connection Must Change."

From Sound to Numbers

Sound is made by compressions in the air. These compressions are translated into voltages by a microphone and possibly an amplifier. After that, what happens to the sound depends on how it will be used and what the webmaster hopes to accomplish with the sound.

Figure 27.8 shows that the incoming analog voltage from a microphone varies by frequency as well as by level. The frequency corresponds to pitch or tone, and the level corresponds to volume. Because computers are much more comfortable with numbers than with varying voltages, the signal is *sampled* to get a file of numbers.

Sampling

The first decision to make when obtaining a sound for use on the web is the sampling rate. To understand sampling rates, you must first understand frequency.

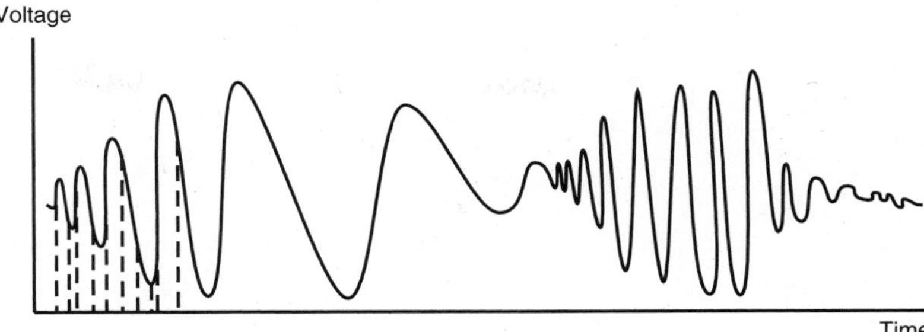

FIG. 27.8 Digital recorders sample an analog signal and translate it into a series of numbers.

Note in Figure 27.8 that the alternate compressions and decompressions of the air form cycles. The number of cycles per second is the frequency. Frequency is measured in Hertz, where one cycle per second is 1 Hertz (Hz).

There is a mathematical result (called the Fourier theorem) that says that a complex waveform (such as that shown in Figure 27.8) can be converted into a collection of pure tones (single-frequency signals) of varying levels (or amplitudes). Figure 27.9 illustrates a Fourier transform.

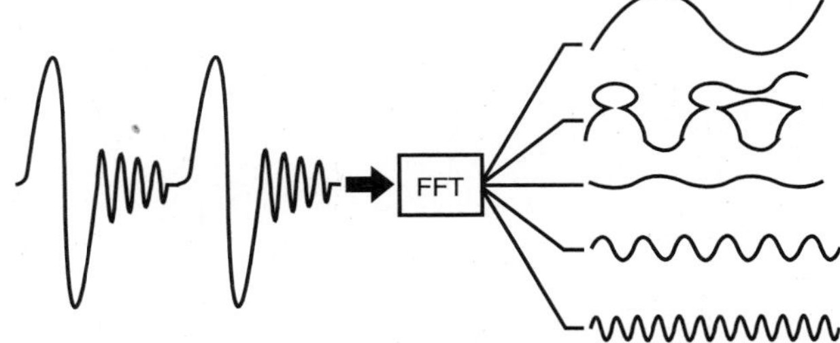

FIG. 27.9 Complex sound such as the human voice can be expressed as sums of single-frequency signals.

The human range of hearing runs the gamut from around 20Hz to more than 20,000Hz (20KHz). Most of the information content in the human voice is concentrated in the band between about 2,000Hz and 4,000Hz. This range is called the *voice band.*

Sampling Rates and the Nyquist Theorem

A principle in physics called the Nyquist theorem says that to reproduce a sound you must sample that sound at a rate at least twice the highest frequency in the signal. Note that the theorem applies to the highest frequency *present*, not just the highest frequency of interest.

Most audio systems use a *low-pass filter* to remove the part of the filter that humans can't hear, so only sound of about 20KHz or below gets through to be sampled. To capture a sound with 20KHz present, the sampler must collect at least 40,000 samples per second.

Most engineers prefer to leave a bit of margin to allow for filter inaccuracies, so sample rates of just above 40KHz are common. Some professional audio equipment samples at 44,056 samples per second. The CD sampling rate is 44,100 samples per second. In the United States, digital audio tape is sampled at 48,000 samples per second.

Quantization

The next decision to be made when collecting sound is how many bits to use to represent each sample. If you have worked with graphics on the web, you are aware that you can often compress an image by using, say, 5 or 6 bits per pixel to store color rather than using 8, 16, or 24 bits. For many purposes, human beings either cannot tell the difference or do not find the difference annoying when the number of bits per pixel is reduced from 8 to, say, 6 or 7. The same principle holds with sound.

For best results, sound should be recorded at 16 bits per sample. Such a sample can store 2^{16} or 65,536 different levels, resulting in high quality. Consider the math for a high-quality recording: A 60-second sound file sampled at 44,100 samples per second, and 16 bits per sample would take up over 5MB, and would take about 30 minutes to download over a 28.8Kbps dial-up connection.

Of course for true audiophiles, only stereo will do. Doubling the preceding numbers to come up with two channels means that data is coming out of the system at the rate of 1,411,200bps. Clearly, some compression is called for.

Bandwidth Issues in Real-Time Audio

A simple approach to storing sound might map the input signal into 65,535 levels and represent each level with one 16-bit word. This approach leads to the huge file sizes previously described. A better approach is to take advantage of the fact that each sample tends to be fairly close to its predecessor. You can get significant compression by just storing the differences between successive samples. Companies with a major stake in the CD industry, such as Philips and Sony, have spent millions of dollars to develop better compression schemes.

Reducing the Number of Bits per Sample Another way to quickly reduce the size of the file is to throw away some of the information. Recall that the voice band goes up to only about 4KHz. When you set a low-pass filter to reject sound above that level, the sampling rate demanded by the Nyquist theorem drops to around 8,000 samples per second—about one fifth of the rate needed for the full 0–20KHz range. Confining the samples to 8 bits rather than 16 also reduces the file size, but at some cost to quality.

Audio engineers are very interested in something called the *signal-to-noise ratio* (S/N ratio). The higher the S/N ratio, the more the sound that you want to hear stands out from the background. Each additional bit of quantization improves the S/N ratio by 6 decibels (dB). To the ear, 6dB sounds like a quadrupling of the sound level. CD-quality audio with 16 bits of quantization gives about 90dB S/N ratio.

Learning to Live with Quantization Noise Moving from 16 bits to 8 bits of quantization drops the S/N ratio from 90dB down to around 40dB. The sound is perceived as being much quieter, so the amplifiers must be turned up to get the same volume. On an 8-bit system, during the quiet moments between words or songs, there is a perceptible hiss. This hiss is quantization noise—it is the price paid for giving up those extra 8 bits.

A 60-second sound sampled at 8,000 samples per second and quantized into 8 bits takes up just under 469K—about one tenth of the size of the 44,100 samples per second by 16 bits per sample size.

Using Codecs for Bandwidth Compression

When computer files (such as programs) are compressed, every bit must be recovered because it is significant to the computer. Sound files are different—you can give up a few bits without the listener noticing. Be aware, however, that the human ear is more sensitive to the low-level components of the signal than it is to the higher levels. Over the years, engineers have developed systems that compress the high-level signals and enhance and expand the low-level signals. These techniques are called *companding* because they simultaneously compress and expand. Companders are heavily used in telephony because telephone engineers have decades of experience improving the quality of voice-band signals. Figure 27.10 illustrates how a typical compander works.

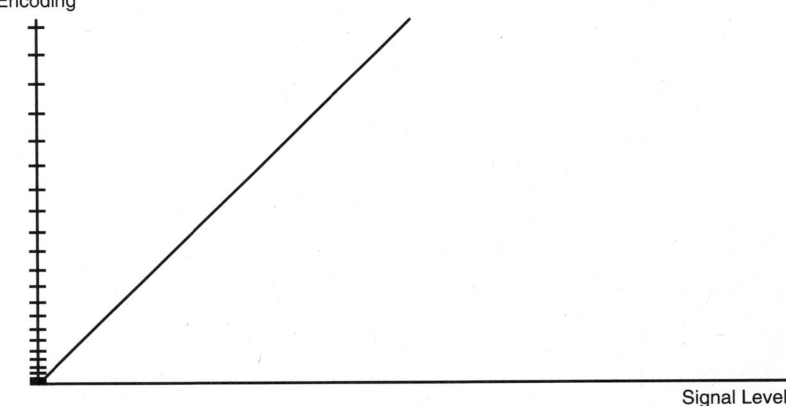

FIG. 27.10 Companding techniques expand the parts of the signal that carry the most information, to give those parts extra bandwidth.

Classic Codecs The companding standard in U.S. and Japanese telephony is µ-law (also written *mu-law* or *u-law*). The European standard is A-law. Both standards do the same thing but differ in the specifics of how they do it.

Using µ-law companding, a 13- to 16-bit signal from the voice band can be encoded in just 8 bits. After it is transmitted, the signal is reconstructed to restore the original quality. Files with the extension `.AU` are usually µ-law files.

µ-law and A-law are examples of encoding a signal before storage and transmission, and then decoding it during playback to recover the quality of the original signal. Software that implements such a coding and decoding scheme is generally called a *codec*. µ-law and A-law represent good codes based on an old technology. The newest research is in codecs that take into account the way people actually hear.

Modern Codecs Bandwidth is a precious commodity in communications. Even if an Internet user is connected to the Internet with a T3 connection (one of the widest commercial connections available), chances are good that the user is one of many who share that pipeline. In practice, some users who have T1 or T3 connections between their LANs and the Internet have to share the connection with so many other users that they may have less effective bandwidth than the user with a dial-up link over a 28.8Kbps modem.

The goal of a codec designer is to pack as much signal into as small a transmission bandwidth as possible. One goal is a codec that can faithfully reproduce complex waveforms, such as an orchestra or human speech, but pass it over a connection of 8Kbps or less.

Since µ-law and A-law codecs were developed, researchers have developed new ways to code sound. The new methods fall into two categories, which are commonly used together: psychoacoustic models (also known as perceptual codecs) and variable bitrate codecs. These two methods are described here. The remainder of this section describes specific codecs available with real-time audio products.

A Psychoacoustic View of Sound A major breakthrough in audio codecs occurred when researchers discovered that, under certain conditions, sounds can be present in a signal that are never heard by the human ear—they are masked by other sounds. By identifying and removing these sounds before the signal is transmitted, the bitrate of the stream can be reduced. Three forms of psychoacoustic masking take place: concurrent, pre, and post.

Recall that a complex waveform can be expressed as a sum of pure tones, each tone at a level independent of the others. Figure 27.11 shows a snapshot of a complex signal, with components at 1000Hz, 1100Hz, and 2000Hz. The 1100Hz tone is 18dB down from the 1000Hz tone. The 2000Hz tone is 45dB down. If all three tones are present at these levels in the signal at the same time, the listener hears only the 1000Hz tone. The other two tones are masked. This phenomenon is called *concurrent masking*.

Suppose there is an abrupt shift in sound levels. The signal drops by, say, 30 to 40dB. For the next 100 milliseconds or so, the listener does not hear the lower signal. It has been masked out by *postmasking*.

Premasking occurs before such an abrupt shift. Suppose the signal jumps up by 30 or 40dB. The brain begins to process the new, high-level signal and discards the last 2 to 5 milliseconds (ms) of processed data. The listener never hears the sound that occurred just before the shift.

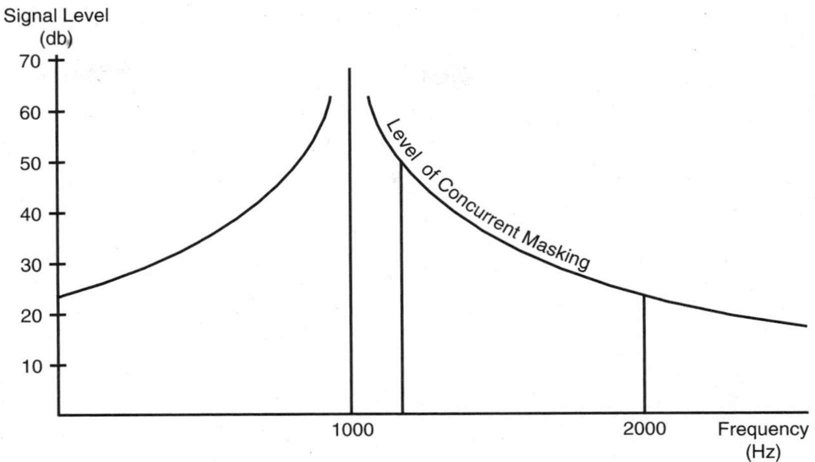

FIG. 27.11
The listener hears only the 1000Hz tone, a phenomenon known as concurrent masking.

Perceptual codecs take advantage of this masking effect by not storing sounds that the ear will never hear. A 6500Hz tone at 60dB, for example, masks nearby signals (within about 750Hz) that are 35dB down. The encoder can allow quantization noise to climb as high as 25dB (60dB to 35dB) in that frequency band because everything below 35dB will be masked. Recall that each bit contributes 6dB, so a signal-to-noise ratio of about 25dB can be achieved in just 4 bits. Figure 27.12 illustrates the effect of concurrent masking on bitrate.

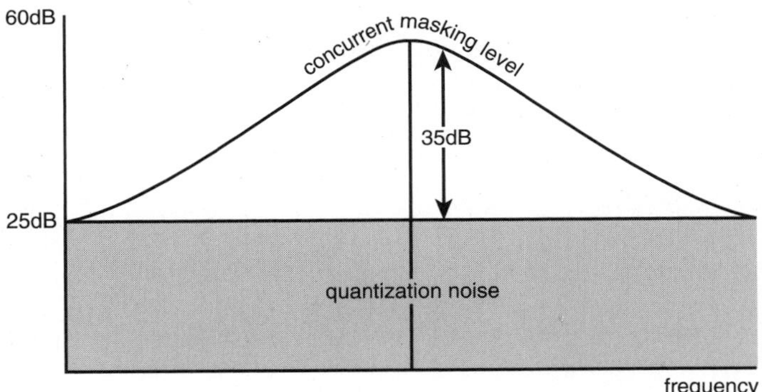

FIG. 27.12
If a given signal is loud enough, the encoder can decrease the bitrate associated with this band because the quantization hiss will be masked.

In real-world signals, sounds occur at many different frequencies, each of which adds concurrent masking effects. Abrupt shifts in sound level also occur, leading to pre- and postmasking. The coder is continually recalculating the noise floor in each frequency band (commonly known as subbands) and using up just enough bits to maintain the necessary signal-to-noise ratio.

Variable Bit Rate Codecs Consider a movie soundtrack. The scene is quiet, and you hear footsteps. Then a flute begins to play some background music, and the footsteps continue into the scene. Suddenly you hear a door open, and the scene is filled with complex classical music and multiple overlapping conversations.

At any given instant in this scene, the bitrate may vary considerably. When the scene is quiet, the gaps between the footsteps require almost no bandwidth. Each footstep is a relatively simple sound, requiring perhaps 1000 to 2000bps. Flute music is a single tone with a few harmonics, so each note requires only a few thousand bits per second. When the door opens, there is a moment (2 to 5ms) of premasking, then the bit-rate requirement climbs quickly to encode the cacophony of music and speech.

Some codecs, with Fixed Bit Rate (FBR) coders, transmit at a single bitrate. The webmaster chooses a codec with enough capacity to handle the most complex sounds. Of course, if some members of the target audience don't have the bandwidth to receive the signal, they will experience packet loss and hear a choppy, perhaps unusable, signal.

Other encoders—Variable Bit Rate or VBR encoders —adjust the bitrate over time. Typically, an encoder sets a bitrate every 25ms, based on the complexity of the sound to be encoded. For most material, the average bitrate required is much lower than the bitrate required to encode the most complex sounds in the track.

VBR encoders are particularly attractive when used with perceptual codecs because one output of the psychoacoustic model is the required bitrate in each subband. If a designer desires to use an FBR rather than a VBR encoder, he or she must add additional steps to adjust the bitrate to the desired fixed rate.

Figure 27.13 illustrates the bitrates required in 20 minutes of a movie soundtrack with many complex sounds. The average bitrate required to encode this soundtrack is about 384Kbps. The highest instantaneous bitrates occur around 600Kbps. If you choose a codec with an FBR encoder, you need at least 600Kbps of bandwidth. Using a VBR encoder, however, a bitrate of 384Kbps suffices.

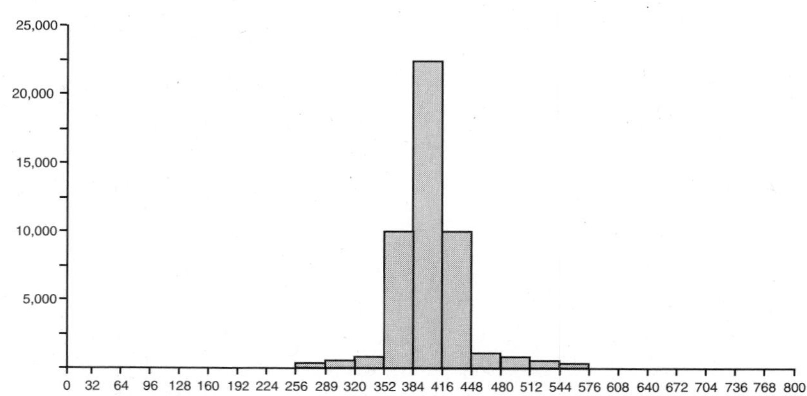

FIG. 27.13
Sound track of *Immortal Beloved*, Reel 6.

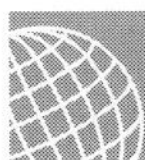

ON THE WEB

http://www.km.philips.com/bumd/mpeg/variable.htm For a more technical description of Variable Bit Rate encoders, read this page from Philips.

Putting It All Together: MPEG Audio The Moving Pictures Experts Group (MPEG) is a group of international experts who set standards for digital video and audio compression. MPEG1 is the original standard for compressed audio and video. It is optimized to fit into a 1.5Mbps bit stream. This figure is approximately the data rate of uncompressed CD-quality stereo audio. MPEG2 extends the standard to bit streams between 3 and 10Mbps. Although not all streaming audio codecs are based on the MPEG standard, the MPEG standard illustrates the technology found in other codecs.

The MPEG standard is formally called ISO CD 11172. The third part of the MPEG1 standard (11172-3) addresses audio compression. Under MPEG1, the 1.4Mbps CD-quality stereo audio can be compressed down to about 256Kbps, leaving about 1.25Mbps for any video.

MPEG1 audio compression uses a perceptual codec based on psychoacoustic models such as those described in the first part of this section. Specifically, MPEG audio compression can be done by any of three codecs, called Layer 1, Layer 2, and Layer 3.

Each layer offers higher performance (and increased complexity) than the one before it. Each layer is also compatible with the one before it. A Layer-2 decoder can decode a bit stream encoded in either Layer 1 or Layer 2. A Layer-3 decoder can decode any MPEG1 audio bit stream.

All MPEG audio begins by passing the signal (20 to 20,000Hz) through a bank of filters, separating it into 32 subbands. Layer 3 does additional processing to increase the frequency resolution. All three layers send header information such as the sampling rate.

In MPEG Layer 2, when the sampling rate is 48,000 samples per second, each subband is 750Hz wide. This division is not ideal—the human ear is more sensitive to the lower frequencies than the higher frequencies—but it simplifies the computation. Layer 3 uses a modified discrete cosine transform to effectively divide the frequency spectrum into 576 subbands, giving it much better performance at low bitrates.

Layers 2 and 3 look at a 24ms window (when the sampling rate is 48,000 samples per second) for pre- and postmasking effects. This figure also represents a compromise between computational reality and fidelity to the psychoacoustic model. Layer-3 encoders have additional code to detect certain kinds of transient signals and drop the window size to 4ms for detailed analysis.

To choose an appropriate codec, the webmaster must take into account the available bitrate of the desired audience, the desired quality, the codec delay, and the hardware and software resources available. Decoders are relatively simple compared to encoders, so the encoding hardware and software is most often the limiting factor.

Audio quality is best determined by listening tests. Indeed, for perceptual codecs, audio quality can *only* be evaluated by human listeners. In formal listening tests, the listener is presented with three signals: the original (called signal A), followed by pairs of the original and the encoded signal (called signal B and signal C) in random sequence.

The listener is asked to evaluate B and C on a scale of 1 to 5, as shown in Table 27.2. Table 27.3 summarizes the quality, target bitrate, and codec delay for the three MPEG audio layers.

Table 27.2 Human listeners evaluate sound sources on a scale of 1 to 5.

Score	Meaning
5.0	Transparent (indistinguishable from the original signal)
4.0	Perceptible difference but not annoying
3.0	Slightly annoying
2.0	Annoying
1.0	Very annoying

Table 27.3 For moderate bitrates: Layer 3 scores appreciably higher than Layer 2.

Layer	Quality at ~60Kbps	Target Bitrate	Codec Delay
Layer 1	N/A	192Kbps	19ms (< 50ms)
Layer 2	2.1–2.6	128Kbps	35ms (100ms)
Layer 3	3.6–3.8	64Kbps	59ms (150ms)

The quality figures in Table 27.3 are for bitrates of around 60 to 64Kbps—about the quality of an ISDN connection. At bitrates of 120Kbps—about one tenth of the capacity of a dedicated T1 line—Layer 2 and Layer 3 performed about the same: Listeners found it difficult to distinguish them from the original signal.

The codec delays shown in the table represent the theoretical minimums (from the standard) and the practical values (in parentheses).

ON THE WEB

http://153.96.172.2/departs/amm/layer3/sw/index.html Learn the technical details of the most powerful MPEG audio layer from this Frequently Asked Questions list.

For most applications, even the largest delays do not represent a problem. They do serve as an indicator of processing capacity, however. Real-time Layer 2 encoders typically consume about 10 percent of the processing capacity of a 100MHz Pentium processor. Stereo Layer-3 real-time encoders that meet ISO reference quality need two DSP32C or DSP56002 digital signal processing chips.

MPEG1 accommodates two audio channels that can be used to deliver stereo. Layers 2 and 3 accommodate advanced stereo algorithms, such as intensity stereo. Layer 3 accommodates m/s stereo. In intensity stereo, the high-frequency portions of both signals (about 2KHz) are combined. In m/s stereo, one channel carries the sum of the two signals (left + right), whereas the other channel carries the difference (left – right).

Audio Codecs

To support real-time streaming data, a codec must be capable of keeping up with the available bandwidth. If the end user is connected to the Internet via a dial-up link, he or she may be able to receive between 8,000 and 18,000bps. A user with uncongested access to a T1 will have 1,000,000bps or more; however, a user on a badly congested ISDN or 56Kbps dedicated circuit might only have 2,000 or 3,000bps of reliable bandwidth.

Your choice of codec also depends on the nature of the material you are sending. Speech is a complex waveform, but you only need to send the voice band. Voice-band quality is similar to a strong AM radio station—it is clearly not the same as the original signal, but is still quite understandable. A complex musical composition, however, may have frequencies from a few tens of Hertz to 10KHz or more. You will need at least 18Kbps to reproduce music with a fidelity similar to a strong FM station. If you have additional bandwidth, you can approach CD-quality stereo music.

Most streaming audio products come with several codecs, and support others developed or distributed by Microsoft, Lucent Technologies, and other vendors. This section describes the capabilities and limitations of the major codecs.

You can compare Netscape's Media codecs online at **http://home.netscape.com/comprod/server_central/product/media/demos/codec_demo/index.html**. From this page, you can compare the AX24000P, IMA ADPCM (both at several different bitrates), SX8300P, and RT24. You will, of course, need to download the Netscape Media Player plug-in if you don't already have it installed in your Netscape browser.

GSM 6.10 One classic codec is based on the European Telecommunications Standards Institute's Groupe Special Mobile recommendation 6.10. This codec is optimized for speech compression and outputs at a fixed rate of 13.5Kbps. This codec is distributed by Microsoft as part of Windows 95 and Windows NT. Netscape includes it in the UNIX and Macintosh versions of the Media Player.

RT24 This lean codec from Voxware compresses speech to a fixed rate of 2.4Kbps. Use it if your target audience has only a tiny bit of bandwidth available. In general, if you are sending speech to a user with a dial-up connection, use the AX24000P (set at 8Kbps) or the SX8300P—you will get better results than you would with the RT24.

CAUTION

You can get good results with this codec if you use it carefully and remain aware of its limitations. Use it for speech only—attempts to use it with music do not succeed.

Make sure the input file is of the best possible quality. If you have background noise or hiss, the effect will be magnified by this codec due to quantization error.

elemedia AX24000P Music Coder Lucent Technologies, a spin-off from Bell Laboratories, specializes in high-quality codecs (many of them developed, of course, for telephony). Its elemedia division is the home of many of the best codecs available for use in streaming media products.

The elemedia AX24000P is a perceptual audio codec optimized for music. It can generate monaural output at 8Kbps, 18Kbps, and 24Kbps, and stereo output at 18Kbps and 24Kbps.

NOTE The version of the AX24000P that ships with Netscape's Media Server can only be used to output Netscape LiveAudio (`.la`) files.

elemedia AX64000 High Fidelity Stereo Music Coder You can download a version of the Netscape Media Player that includes a high performance codec from elemedia, the codec folks at Lucent Technologies. This codec produces near-CD quality (32,000 samples per second) stereo sound at bitrates of 64Kbps and 56Kbps. The codec can conceal up to 5 percent packet loss from the listener, yet the decoder only consumes about 25 percent of a 75MHz Intel Pentium processor.

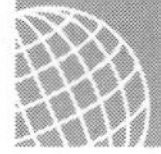

ON THE WEB

http://www.lucent.com/elemedia/ This site provides additional information about elemedia codecs, including the high-fidelity AX64000P. Learn about the upgrades to Netscape and Microsoft products at **http://www.elemedia.com/upgrade.htm**, or go directly to the AX64000P description at **http://www.elemedia.com /axhifi.htm**.

elemedia AX128000 High Fidelity Stereo Music Coder This high-end codec provides true CD quality (44,000 samples per second) over 128Kbps channels (such as an ISDN line with dual B-channels). Like the AX64000, it can conceal up to 5 percent packet loss, yet the decoder only requires about 40 percent of the processing capacity of a 75MHz Intel Pentium processor.

If your intranet consists mostly of users with high-bandwidth connections, consider making your clips and feeds by using the AX128000. Then offer an AX24000P version of the same material for use by users with a dial-up connection.

ON THE WEB

http://www.elemedia.com/ax128.htm Learn more about this codec online. The AX128000 is available for purchase from Lucent Technologies, and will integrate into streaming media servers such as the Netscape Media Server.

elemedia SX8300P and SX7300 Speech-Quality Coders Lucent's SX8300P is a slimmed-down Java implementation of its high-end speech coder, the SX7300P. The bitrate is 8300bps, so it is well-suited for sending real-time speech. As its name implies, the SX7300P has a slightly lower bitrate: 7300bps.

ON THE WEB

http://www.elemedia.com/Demo/register/downloads.htm Go directly to the elemedia Speech Coder page; from here you can download demos of elemedia's speech coders, including the SX8300P.

IMA ADPCM The International Multimedia Association's Adaptive Differential Pulse Code Modulation codec is a high–bit-rate, low-complexity encoder. It is included by Microsoft in Windows 95 and Windows NT. Netscape distributes it with the UNIX and Macintosh versions of their Media Player.

This codec is noted for its high bit-rate—even a monaural clip takes 33.2Kbps. If you are considering IMA ADPCM, compare it with the elemedia AX24000P. At comparable bitrates, the quality of the AX24000P is much higher; at comparable quality levels, the AX24000P consumes about a quarter of the bandwidth.

Codecs Available with the Windows Audio Compression Manager Microsoft supports an Audio Compression Manager standard—any codec that conforms to that standard may be used on a Windows 95 or NT platform. Such codecs include

- *DSP Group True Speech.* The DSP Group's True Speech is a competitor of RealNetworks' RealAudio. Microsoft adopted its codecs for use in Windows 95. You can get its players for Windows 95 and Windows NT machines at **http://www.dspg.com/player/main.htm**.
- *A-Law and µ-law* (based on the CCITT's G.711 standard).
- *Microsoft ADPCM.*
- *Microsoft Network Audio* (included with Active Movie).
- *ITU G.723* (included with Intel's Internet Phone). Netscape also includes a G.723 codec with its Media Server and Player products.
- *Lernout & Hauspie's SBC variable bitrate codec* (included with Intel's Internet Phone).
- *Lernout & Hauspie's CELP* (included with Intel's Internet Phone).

On a Windows 95 or NT system, you can see a list of installed codecs and change the settings of some of them by choosing Start, Settings, Control Panel, and opening the Multimedia Control Panel. In the Multimedia Control Panel, choose the Devices tab and open the Audio Compression Codecs element. Figure 27.14 shows a typical list. For more information about a particular codec, select it and click on the Properties button. From the resulting dialog box, you can enable or disable the codec, change its priority, and get more information about it.

FIG. 27.14
On a Windows 95 or NT machine, view the list of installed codecs.

With some codecs, the Settings button is enabled—you can specify a maximum real-time conversion rate for both compression and decompression, as shown in Figure 27.15. Higher sampling rates require more of your computer's resources. If you have a slower processor, or if there are breaks in the sound when you play back your audio files, decrease the maximum compression and decompression rates. If the codec supports Auto-Configuration, use it—the codec will examine your machine and determine the best rates.

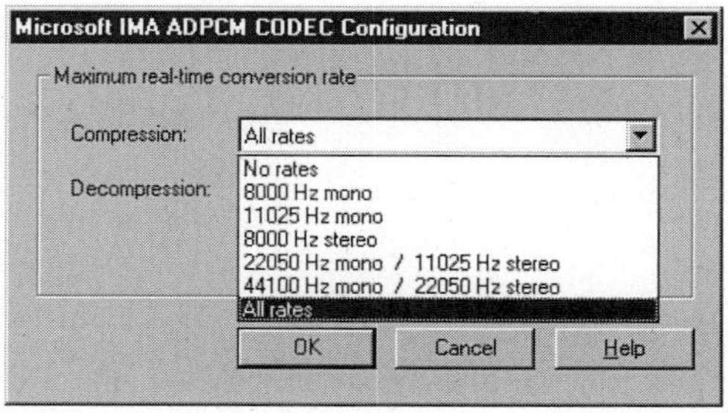

FIG. 27.15
For best results, use Auto-Configure to set up a codec.

Microsoft IMA ADPCM CODEC Configuration
Maximum real-time conversion rate
Compression: All rates
Decompression:
No rates
8000 Hz mono
11025 Hz mono
8000 Hz stereo
22050 Hz mono / 11025 Hz stereo
44100 Hz mono / 22050 Hz stereo
All rates
OK
Cancel
Help

If you choose a variable bit-rate (VBR) encoder such as the AX24000P, you have the option of selecting Error Migration. If you allow error migration, the codec will recover after a network packet loss. Such recovery requires a higher bitrate, but may give better quality if the network is subject to packet loss.

When you choose a VBR encoder, you will see a difference between the average and peak bitrates. Figure 27.16 shows the results from Netscape Media Converter's Conversion Wizard.

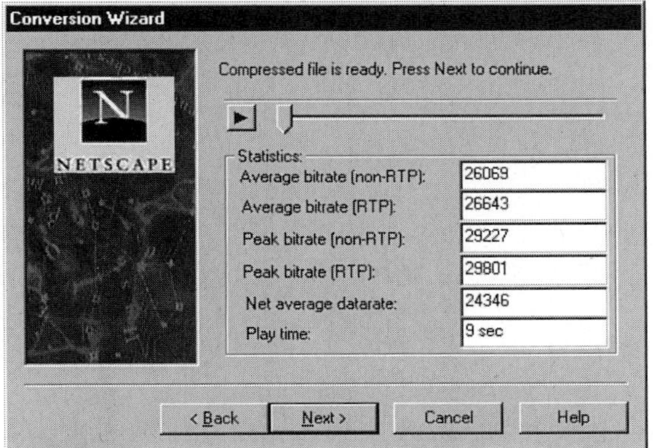

FIG. 27.16
This file was compressed by using the elemedia AX24000P codec—by using a VBR encoder, the codec saves more than 10 percent of the bandwidth that would otherwise be required.

Adding Streaming Video—Why Your Connection Must Change

Currently, streaming video is the most demanding content you can add to your web page. Despite tremendous advances in the technology, streaming video places demands on your server and its connection to the Internet. It also places demands on your users' machines and *their* connections to the Net.

This section describes the requirements of full-speed video transmission—the kind you get on your television—and then shows how the latest technology makes it possible to send video over the Internet.

NOTE Some technology forecasters predict that by the year 2000 your television, your computer, and your telephone will all be combined into a single appliance. They predict that the integration of streaming video into the Internet is one of the most important technical changes in this century.

Part V Ch 27

ON THE WEB

http://www.hypertech.co.uk/video/digvid.htm Visit this "Guide to Digital Video" for the latest information on digital and desktop video. The focus is on local networks and CD-ROMs, but there are links to sites that describe various aspects of web-based streaming video.

Understanding Broadcast Video

When you turn on your television, you receive a video signal that refreshes at a rate of about 30 frames per second. (The reality is a bit more complex—a single frame of broadcast video consists of two interlaced fields, and a brief period between frames. U.S. television sends 60 fields per second with 525 lines per frame; European television sends 50 fields per second with 650 lines per frame.) The complete picture contains about 600,000 dots of information—200,000 in each of the three primary colors: red, green, and blue.

Along with this information the broadcaster sends information about the brightness (called luminance) and chroma at each dot. (Chroma is the degree to which a color is diluted with white.) The broadcaster also sends synchronizing information so that the receiver knows when to start a new field, and one or two channels of audio. In conventional broadcast, the finished color television signal occupies a band 6MHz wide.

To pack this enormous amount of information onto an Internet dial-up connection, changes have to be made. The next two sections describe the ways in which engineers have transformed both the video signal and the Internet itself to make streaming video possible.

Squeezing the Signal

One of the easiest ways to improve the quality of streaming video is to resolve to send less content. You can reduce the size of video content by using some of the same techniques popular with still images: reduce the size of the image and reduce its color depth. With still images, you often experiment by encoding the image as a GIF or a JPEG to see which format gives you the best quality for the smallest size. Likewise, you may choose from a variety of coding techniques (represented by *codecs*) to compress your video data.

This section describes each of these techniques for reducing the bandwidth required by the video.

Video Codecs The first engineering technique used to support streaming video is to take advantage of the large amounts of redundancy in the signal. Most television signals actually change very little from frame to frame. Compressors/decompressors, or codecs, compress the signal by a factor of 26:1 or more.

ON THE WEB

http://www.microsoft.com/netshow/codecs.htm You will find a nice tutorial on video codec technology on the Microsoft site. You should also visit **www.codeccentral.com** for one-stop information on multimedia codecs.

Much of the dramatic capability the newest codecs have comes from the fact that they change their sampling rate as they run. If you see a codec that advertises itself as "fixed rate," it comes from an earlier generation—it may still be useful, but won't have the compression capability of a variable-rate codec.

TIP If you are adding streaming video to your site, you will want to compare codecs carefully. Your choice of codec is the single biggest factor that determines how much bandwidth you need for connecting your server, and how much bandwidth an end user needs to receive your content.

Note, too, that some bandwidth is required for network overhead. If you are designing content for a 28.8Kbps dial-up connection, make sure the total bandwidth of your video and audio content stays below about 22Kbps.

Many of the codecs available in streaming video products follow international standards. H.261 and H.263, for example, are the video coding standards developed by the International Telecommunication Union/Telecommunication Standardization Sector (ITU-T). H.261 is designed for videoconferencing and videophones. It supports bitrates of 64Kbps to 1,920Kbps. H.263 is designed for low–bit-rate video—the basic configuration of the video source coding is based on H.261.

NOTE You will sometimes hear H.261 referred to as "P*64" because its bitrate is defined as the number "*p*," which ranges from 1 to 30×64Kbps.

ON THE WEB

http://rice.ecs.soton.ac.uk/peter/h261/h261.html You can compare H.261 codecs at various settings by viewing the video available here. You can find a similar page for H.263 at **http://rice.ecs.soton.ac.uk/peter/h263/h263.html**.

When developing streaming video, some experts expressed concern that the H.261-based codecs lacked the power to deal with the full range of video sequences. After all, they said, H.261 was developed for teleconferencing, in which every frame is much like every other frame—a talking head moving slightly from frame to frame. A clip of a football game, on the other hand, is characterized by high spatio-temporal complexity.

The Moving Pictures Expert Group (MPEG) has released an encoding standard for both audio and video content. The formal name of the standard is ISO/IEC JTC1 SC29 WG11, which says that it is the product of Work Group 11 of Subcommittee 29 of Joint Technical Committee 1 of the International Organization for Standardization/International Electro-technical Commission—everyone calls it MPEG. Much of the recent activity in streaming video has been based on MPEG-4, the MPEG initiative for very low, bit-rate coding. Loosely defined, the target range for MPEG-4 is 176×144 pixel images, with a frame rate of 10 frames per second, coded for a bitrate of 4,800 to 64,000bps—precisely the range covered by today's dial-up connections.

ON THE WEB

http://www.crs4.it/HTML/LUIGI/MPEG/mpegfaq.html Although this page is becoming dated, it gives a good overview of the MPEG standard.

If you are serving an audience that has a variety of connection speeds—some users with 28.8Kbps dial-up connections and others with high-speed intranets—encode the content with several different codecs, one for each speed.

Be sure to choose codecs that will be available to your end users—preferably ones that come with the player application. That way you can be certain that end users can play back your encoded content.

To find out which audio and video codecs are installed on a Windows 95 or Windows NT machine, open the Multimedia Control Panel and choose the Devices tab. As shown earlier in Figure 27.14, here you will see a list of your codecs.

Smaller Images Most streaming video technologies are designed for an image not much larger than a postage stamp. Unlike television, in which the user sits across the room looking at a screen that is 19 inches or more across, most computer users sit within a foot or two of their screens. An image 2 inches across on your computer screen appears to the user to be about the same size as a 19-inch image viewed from across the room.

Fewer Colors Many streaming video technologies sacrifice color depth. A typical television image may contain many thousands of different shades and hues, but the image may still be usable with as few as 8 or 16 colors.

Slower Frame Rate Finally, most streaming video technologies slow the frame rate down—way down. At low bandwidths such as a 28.8Kbps dial-up link, the frame rate may drop to one frame every two or three seconds.

NOTE When the pace of a video is relatively slow, many codecs can predict much of the next frame with very little bandwidth. This enables the video player to buffer several frames. If the data connection becomes noisy, or the action on the video becomes fast paced, the player may be capable of supplying enough frames out of its buffer so that the end user cannot tell there was a problem. Because even fast-paced video clips usually are not fast paced all the time, a streaming video product that falls a bit behind real-time is likely to have a chance to catch up before the buffer becomes empty. ■

Expanding the Pipe

The second major technology change making streaming video possible has been the revolution in connection capacity. Although many businesses pass information around their intranets at 10Mbps or more, their connection to the Internet may be only 1.54Mbps (on a T1 link). That connection may be shared by dozens of simultaneous users.

Faster Home Connections Most home users have connections that are even slower (although they seldom have to share them). The old reliable 14.4 and 28.8Kbps modems are rapidly being replaced by 33.6Kbps and 56Kbps modems. Even faster technologies—dual-channel ISDN at 128Kbps and Asymmetrical Digital Subscriber Line (ADSL) at 1.5Mbps and faster—promise affordable high-speed connections to many users.

ON THE WEB

http://www.coe.uga.edu/resources/gsams/onramp/adsl.html Some telephone companies are planning to offer ADSL for around $100 per month. If this price/performance ratio sounds attractive to you, visit this site to learn more about high-speed connections. If you're in Pacific Bell's service area, learn more at **http://www.pacbell.com/products/business/fastrak/adsl/index.html**

Server Connections From the point of view of the server, a popular piece of video on a web site can be devastating. Suppose you have a web page that receives 100,000 visits per day. The page, including graphics, is 60KB—if the average user can receive the content at a rate of 30,000 bits per second, and if all the requests were distributed evenly throughout the day, you could support the load on your server by supporting about 23 simultaneous 30Kbps connections. That works out to about 694Kbps. Because the requests won't be evenly distributed, you will probably want to provide at least twice that capacity—a 1.54Mbps-wide T1 connection could provide adequate performance.

Now suppose that you add a modest streaming video clip—say, 5 minutes at 22Kbps—to the page. If every visitor plays the clip, you need more than 90 times the original capacity. If you needed a single T1 before, you now need between 30 and 60 T3 connections! The communications cost impact is staggering, not to mention the additional computing power that would be required.

Reducing the Demand Through Multicasting The essence of video-on-demand is *unicasting*—each user gets his own connection to the server. An alternative design is called *multicasting*. Instead of sending the video to each user on request, the video clip (or live event) is played continuously to a special address (called a Class D, or multicast, address). Anyone who wants to listen in can "tune in" to that address.

NOTE You can learn more about multicasting in RFC 1112, "Host Extensions for IP Multicasting." RFCs are Requests for Comments, many of which serve to define standards on the Internet. You can download RFC 1112 from **http://ds.internic.net/rfc/rfc1112.txt** or another RFC repository closer to you.

If you replace your video clip with a multicast feed, you need only one connection in addition to those already provided for the static page content. The additional connection could be at a speed as low as 22Kbps. You can accommodate this additional load easily, with little or no change in your communications configuration.

Much of the early work on multicasting was done with the Virtual Internet Backbone for Multicast IP (MBONE). At that time many routers—the boxes that steer data packets around the Net—did not accommodate multicasting. The design of the MBONE was to provide multicasting in many small areas, and connect these multicasting centers together with unicasting connections (known as tunnels).

Today many routers support multicasting, so the need for the MBONE is not as great as it once was. On the other hand, the rise of streaming video has increased the demand for bandwidth—many of the lessons learned on the MBONE are applicable to the ways servers and networks are designed to support streaming video.

ON THE WEB

http://www.best.com/~prince/techinfo/mbone.html Learn about MBONE applications and technical information.

Streaming Video—The Market

The combination of highly compressed video and higher bandwidth connections have made streaming video a reality. The largest players in the computing industry, including Microsoft and Oracle, are making major investments to ensure that content providers and end users adopt their particular technology. This section summarizes the leading video formats and products:

- *RealNetworks*. The same folks who introduced streaming audio (with RealAudio) have taken the early lead in streaming video. RealNetworks' latest servers and players support both audio and video content.
- *VDOnet*. VDOnet Corporation achieved fame in the videoconferencing market with VDOPhone. It has allied with Microsoft to provide streaming video, agreeing to use Microsoft's Active Streaming Format (ASF) for media storage. It is also working with Microsoft to migrate its clients from their own VDOLive products to Microsoft's NetShow.
- *Vivo*. One of the first players in the streaming video market, Vivo has strong ties to Microsoft and NetShow.
- *VXtream*. VXtream has been another serious player; recently it was bought by Microsoft.
- *Microsoft*. Microsoft has entered the streaming video market largely by investing in the existing technology companies. It owns 10 percent of RealNetworks, developers of RealVideo. It owns VXtream outright, and have also named VDOnet as a "Premier Provider of Solutions for Broadband Video Networks." Microsoft's product, NetShow, is based on its own Active Streaming Format (see Chapter 28).

- *Xing Technology.* Xing has taken a different approach from RealNetworks and Microsoft, delivering efficient MPEG compressors and streaming technology.
- *Apple Computer.* Apple was the leader in multimedia technology, introducing its QuickTime format soon after the Macintosh came out. It has developed an experimental streaming version of QuickTime, but put the project on hold during its reorganization early in 1997. Apple has announced that streaming video will be integrated into the QuickTime format in 1998.

ON THE WEB

http://www.vdo.net/cgi-bin/press?54 Learn more about the strategic alliance between Microsoft and VDOnet from this press release.

The remainder of this chapter provides an overview of two of these technologies: RealVideo, the current market leader, and Microsoft.

RealVideo RealNetworks, the folks who first developed streaming audio, added streaming video in early 1997. Today it is combining the two protocols—the client is called RealPlayer, and the servers belong to a family known as Real Servers. RealNetworks has the lion's share of what is still a fairly small market—its competitor, Microsoft, has made a 10 percent investment in it. Microsoft has also invested heavily in other companies with similar technology—it has taken an equity position in VDOnet Corporation and it owns VXtream outright.

This section describes the process of developing video content and delivering it to the desktop.

ON THE WEB

http://www.real.com/products/realvideo/index.html Start here to visit RealNetworks' online description of RealVideo.

NOTE In late 1997 RealNetworks introduced RealAnimation, a technology that enables you as the multimedia producer to synchronize a Macromedia animation with a RealAudio stream.

Microsoft and the Active Streaming Format During 1997 Microsoft began taking a stake in the streaming video market. It bought 10 percent of RealNetworks, established strategic alliances with Vivo and VDOnet, and bought one major player—VXtream—outright.

Microsoft seems convinced that streaming video is going to be an important part of the web. By consolidating the major players around its standard (the Active Streaming Format), it may bring some degree of standardization to this emerging market. These moves also ensure that its product, NetShow, is left in a strong position.

By acquiring an interest in many of the major streaming video players, Microsoft hopes to ASF as the de facto standard for streaming video. From that position, Microsoft's own streaming video product, NetShow, may be able to challenge Progressive Network's RealVideo for market dominance.

NOTE Microsoft has demonstrated a unified multimedia technology called DirectX. Look for this Microsoft standard to play an important role in Internet multimedia. Learn more about its approach at **http://directx.com/**.

ON THE WEB

http://www.microsoft.com/products/prodref/201_ov.htm Learn about NetShow from the Microsoft site. You will also want to visit **www.microsoft.com/netshow/** for more technical information.

Selecting a Codec for Microsoft NetShow NetShow comes with tools that convert existing video files, including AVI and QuickTime movies, to ASF. Microsoft distributes 10 codecs, but allows you to plug in other codecs that you may prefer.

If you choose to use a codec that doesn't come with the NetShow player, be sure to give your site visitors a way to download it. Microsoft provides example code for this task at **http://www.microsoft.com/netshow/codecs.htm#install**. The disadvantage of this approach is that it relies on the `CODEBASE` parameter of the `<OBJECT>` tag, which is specific to Microsoft Internet Explorer.

Microsoft is shipping five codecs in the NetShow client core installation kit:

- *MPEG Layer 3*. Used for low- to medium-bitrate audio
- *Lernout & Hauspie CELP 4.8 kbit/s*. A voice-grade audio codec.
- *Microsoft MPEG-4*. Generates video at bitrates from 28.8Kbps to 300Kbps.
- *Vivo H.263*. Used for compatibility with VivoActive Producer.
- *Vivo G.723.1* and *Vivo Siren*. Used for audio compatibility with VivoActive Producer. These codecs generate 6.4Kbps and 16Kbps bitstreams, respectively.

NetShow is also compatible with any fixed-rate ACM codec.

If the end user has opted for the full installation of the NetShow player, or if he or she has Microsoft Internet Explorer 4.0, you can count on the following codecs being present in addition to the ones listed for the core installation:

- *Duck TrueMotion RT*. A medium- to high-bitrate video codec.
- *ClearVideo*. A low- to medium-bitrate video codec provided for compatibility with the Osprey 1000 video capture card (**http://www.osprey.mmac.com/graphical/products.html#o1000**).

- *VDOnet VDOwave*. A low- to medium-bitrate codec that outputs 28.8Kbps to 150Kbps data with up to 15 fps.
- *Voxware Metasound* and *Voxware Metavoice RT24*. The Metasound RT24 is used for speech-only encoding; it outputs a 2.4Kbps bitstream. Four Metasound codecs are included: AC8, AC10, AC16, and AC24. The last two digits of the name indicate the bitrate. The Metasound AC8, for example, generates an 8Kbps bitstream.

End users with Internet Explorer 4 will also have the Intel H.263 codec, a good low- to medium-bitrate video codec.

ON THE WEB

http://www.microsoft.com/netshow/codecs.htm Learn more about NetShow's codec independence.

Producing a Video for the Internet

Many of the issues related to producing video for the Internet have nothing to do with technology. You should work through the following steps when getting ready to shoot your own video:

- Develop a storyboard, showing your video scene by scene. Remember to keep your overall design simple; shorter is better.
- Script each scene. Again, keep your design simple and short.
- Arrange for actors, props, locations, and other resources. Use professional actors whenever possible—the quality will show through in your finished product.
- Obtain high-quality cameras—although you may not need professional-quality equipment, don't try to do professional work with VHS or 8mm camcorders. Invest in, or rent, a Hi8 camera, such as the Sony TR400.
- Make sure you budget for high-quality microphones as well as a good mixer and audio capture board. Poor audio ruins more productions than poor video.
- During filming, keep the camera steady and let the actors move. Shots in which the camera moves are based on advanced techniques should be left to the professionals. Be sure you stay close to the action—remember that the finished product will only be an inch or so across.
- Make sure you get plenty of light. Your video is more likely to be too dark than too light.

Selecting a Video Format

You will have a choice of video formats going into your video capture system. The most common formats, shown here in order of decreasing quality, are

1. Betacam-sp (also known as Beta)
2. Satellite television (for example, Direct TV)

3. Laserdisc
4. S-VHS (Super-VHS)
5. VHS

Note, too, that you will often have a choice of S-Video or Composite output from your video hardware. S-Video gives somewhat higher quality.

ON THE WEB

http://www.yahoo.com/Business_and_Economy/Companies/Entertainment/Video/Production/
If, after reviewing this section, you decide to hire a professional to produce your video, check out the listings on Yahoo! Make sure the company you choose has prior experience producing streaming video for use on the Internet.

Video Capture Hardware

The first step in producing a streaming video clip is to capture the video and audio to the disk. You need the following two computer components for this step (in addition to lights, camcorder, and other equipment for the actual production):

- Video Capture Card
- Seagate A/V Professional Disk Drive

NOTE If you already have your video in QuickTime or AVI format, you can skip this step and go directly to encoding.

Video Capture Card One place where you can save in your video budget is on your video card. Video cards come in a range of quality, from some low-budget cards priced at less than $1,000 to professional-grade cards costing thousands of dollars. Unless the video you are producing will also be used off the web, you really have no need to use the high-end cards. The codecs will decrease the quality of your video to the point where the end user cannot tell the difference between video captured through a top-of-the-line video capture card and video captured through a much less expensive device.

Most video capture cards can output your finished video back to tape. After you have edited your video and have a finished product ready for digitizing, save it to videotape as well. You can use the tape as a demo to show off your work without having to have access to the Net.

ON THE WEB

http://www.yahoo.com/Computers_and_Internet/Information_and_Documentation/Product_Reviews/Peripherals/Video_Cards/Video_Capture/ Read the online reviews of video capture cards before choosing your product.

Like most computer equipment, any video capture card you buy runs the risk of being obsolete tomorrow. Nevertheless, here are a few companies and products that have been around for a while and have a good reputation:

- *Quadrant International* (**http://qi.com/**). If you're on a tight budget, check out the Q-Motion P100. It is no longer in production, but Quadrant still has a few in the warehouse. You may also find it on the used market. Its current entry level boards, the Q-Motion 200-series, are only a few hundred dollars.
- *Truevision* (**http://www.truevision.com/**). Truevision makes the popular Targa series. Its products are professional grade; visit its web site to see the features and quality available at this end of the market. Note that Truevision uses the Zoran chip, which outputs a form of AVI video called Motion-JPEG. You will need to scale this output and convert it to Video For Windows before sending it to the RealVideo encoder.
- *FAST* (**http://www.fast-multimedia.com/**). FAST offers products that compete against both Quadrant and Truevision.
- *miro* (**http://www.miro.com/**). The miroVideo DC30 offers a technically sophisticated video capture system at an affordable price. Like Truevision, miro uses the Zoran chip, forcing you to take an extra step before encoding.

You can find the latest list of video capture cards that have been tested by RealNetworks at **http://www.real.com/products/realvideo/reviewg/rvencoding.html**. In general, any video capture device that produces Video For Windows output is acceptable.

Seagate A/V Professional Disk Drive Although, strictly speaking, the A/V Drive is optional, consider the use of a special hard drive. Video capture puts an extraordinary load on your hard drive; many products that are quite acceptable for storing other files cannot keep up with video. Seagate's A/V Professional series have been specifically designed for video capture.

NOTE From time to time most disk drives must stop accepting data for a moment to recalibrate. With most applications, this temporary downtime is unnoticeable—the application storing data to the drive stops and waits for the disk drive to catch up. With real-time video, however, the video card and its associated software can't wait; any downtime on the drive translates into dropped frames.

To learn more about configuring Seagate's A/V Professional drives to work properly in a video capture application, read **http://www.seagate.com/support/disc/AV_pro.shtml**.

Editing the Video

Most video professionals prefer Adobe Premier (**http://www.adobe.com/prodindex/premiere/main.html**) for editing their video. Your video capture card probably came with an editor too, which may be entirely satisfactory.

NOTE Several of the leading streaming video companies, including RealNetworks, offer Adobe Premiere plug-ins, enabling you to export from Premiere directly into the encoded format. Learn more at **http://www.adobe.com/prodindex/premiere/streamvid.html**.

Many amateurs over-edit, getting caught up in cross fades, dissolves, and complex transitions. Get your drama from the pacing of the cuts and from background music, not from the technical gimmicks of the editor.

Encoding Video

Earlier in this chapter, in the section titled "Adding Streaming Video—Why Your Connection Must Change," you learned that the process of turning a high-bandwidth video signal into a bitstream that can pass through the Internet is computationally complex. That process is called *encoding*. To do it right, you need plenty of computing resources.

ON THE WEB

http://205.158.7.51/docs/ccguide_rv10.pdf Download this content developer's guide (an Adobe PDF document) from RealNetworks' site. You can access the same guide section by section at **http://www.real.com/help/ccguide/index.html**.

Encoding a Pre-Recorded Clip In many cases you will produce a digital video clip, edit it, and then send it to the RealVideo encoder. If you use this approach, you don't need the very fastest hardware because the encoder isn't under the time constraints imposed by live data.

If you are a Windows user, you can get by with a slow machine, such as a 486 at 66MHz, for simple encoding tasks. For best results get a faster processor—RealNetworks recommends a Pentium 120. Similarly, 16MB of RAM is adequate, but 32MB is recommended.

Macintosh users can get by with a PowerPC and 16MB of RAM, although a PowerPC 604 with 32MB is recommended.

Live Encoding When you are encoding a live event, there is no opportunity for the encoder to stop and work a bit harder on a difficult sequence—the encoder must keep up with the incoming data. You will need fast hardware to keep up with this demanding task.

If you are planning to encode at a frame rate faster than two frames per second, RealNetworks recommends that you use a dual Pentium at 200MHz with at least 64MB of RAM, running Windows NT. If you are content with a slower frame rate, you can drop down to a Pentium at 166MHz and 32MB.

Scaling and Cropping The RealVideo encoder accepts any frame size that has a height and width that are multiples of 16—176×144 is a nice size. (It will also accept 160×120.) Most video capture cards produce frames that are somewhat larger than these figures; for example, the smallest frame the miro DC30 and the Truevision Bravado 1000 can produce is 320×240. You will need to scale and crop the video before sending it to the encoder. You can make these changes in your video editor.

Choosing a Codec One of the codec's major tasks is to extract enough information from the original video to enable the video player to predict most of the pixels of the next frame. If you need to produce a bitstream that can fit over a dial-up connection, this task becomes technically challenging. You can set three variables that will measurably affect the quality of your output:

- Audio codec
- Video bitrate
- Frame rate

Although end users will put up with low-quality video, they must be able to hear the audio track. Table 27.4 shows some rules of thumb for choosing the audio codec if you are designing a clip for a 28.8Kbps connection. (Better audio codecs are available if the end user has a higher-speed connection.)

Table 27.4 Choose the audio codec first, based on the quality of sound you require.

Type of Audio	Recommended Codec	Audio Bitrate in Kbps
Voice	6.5Kbps voice	6.5
Background Music	RealMedia 8Kbps music	8.0
Foreground Music	RealMedia 12Kbps music	12.0

A low-speed dial-up connection typically has 28.8Kbps of bandwidth available. Some of this bandwidth is required for network overhead—you should not use more than 22Kbps for your video clip. Plan for a lower figure—19Kbps. Of that 19Kbps, give the audio bitstream as much room as it needs, and force the video to work with the remainder. Table 27.5 shows RealNetworks' recommended bitrate for four different connection speeds.

Table 27.5 Choose your bitrate based on the end user's connection speed.

Connection Speed in Kbps	Target Bitrate in Kbps
28.8	19
56.0	44
64.0	56
128.0	105

After you have selected an audio codec and a video bitrate, the only control left is the frame rate. Here are some rules of thumb for encoding various types of video:

- *Fixed camera shot with low motion.* The frame rate will run between 4 and 10 fps.
- *Fixed camera shot with some motion.* The frame rate may drop toward 2 fps.

- *Fixed camera shot with high motion.* The frame rate drops to about 1 fps.
- *Zooming camera with low motion.* Expect a frame rate of about 2 fps.
- *Multiple shots, low motion.* The frame rate approaches 1 fps.
- *Multiple shots, high motion.* The frame rate drops below 1 fps.

If you have a video clip that cannot be encoded with a frame rate higher than 1 fps, consider switching to Slide Show mode (available with RealVideo). Figure 27.17, part of an Elton John music video from **ramhurl.real.com/cgi-bin/ramhurl.cgi?ram=eltonj20_12_5.rm**, shows this mode.

FIG. 27.17
If you need to put the music in the foreground, consider switching to Slide Show mode for the video.

If your video is too complex for the available bandwidth, consider replacing it with an animation or even a series of still frames. In addition to Slide Show mode, you can use RealAnimation in RealNetworks' products. If you're using Netscape's Media Server, you can write a `.lam` file to synchronize an audio stream with HTML frames. Microsoft NetShow offers an Illustrated Audio mode, with audio synchronized with still images.

You can tell the encoder to Optimize Frame Rate. It will adjust the frame rate based on the spatio-temporal complexity of the video that it is encoding. If you still cannot encode your video to fit within your targeted bitrate, decrease the frame size and try again.

TIP

If you are using the RealVideo server, you don't have to choose codecs by trial and error. Start with the templates that come with the RealVideo encoder, and find one that closely matches your clip. If you're not happy with the results of any of the templates, switch to Advanced mode and write your own template, based on the closest matching template you can find.

You have a choice of two video codecs: standard and fractal. For low bitrates you will get better results from the standard codec. At higher bitrates, experiment to see which codec you prefer; most clips encode somewhat better in the standard codec.

Serving Video

Serving streaming video is not as demanding as encoding it, but you will still want a fast computer to host the server. RealNetworks recommends that you use a 486 at 66MHz or faster; a Pentium, of course, is even better. RealNetworks offers versions of its server for most common UNIX systems, including Sun's Solaris and SunOS, Silicon Graphics' IRIS, DEC UNIX, and IBM's AIX. Microsoft's servers, of course, run on Windows NT.

For any of these operating systems, you should budget 3MB of RAM plus 60KB for each simultaneous user.

The RealVideo Servers employ "smart networking"—they will attempt to use the most efficient transport mechanism available, stepping through the following mechanisms in order:

1. Multicast
2. UDP
3. TCP
4. HTTP

Delivering the Finished Product

Your finished HTML page should include a link to the player plug-in or ActiveX Control. If you are using a RealVideo server, for example, give your visitors a link to **http://www.real.com/products/player/index.html**. There your visitors can download a free copy of RealPlayer or an evaluation copy of RealPlayer Plus.

If you are using RealNetworks' product, use bandwidth negotiation. It enables the end user's copy of RealPlayer to work with the server to determine the optimum bandwidth. Figure 27.18 shows a clip of actor John Turturro being interviewed by Spike Lee. This 36.4Kbps clip is played through a 28.8Kbps connection. You can find this clip at **ramhurl.real.com/cgi-bin/ramhurl.cgi?ram=tutn.rm**.

FIG. 27.18
The server works with the client to select the best bandwidth.

CHAPTER 28

Microsoft NetShow And Other Technologies

by Ramesh Chandak

In this chapter

NetShow supports both unicast and multicast transmission. With unicast transmission, users can play the content on demand. In addition, users can take advantage of VCR-like controls to control the content NetShow plays. With multicast transmission, you can broadcast the content to a number of users over the Internet simultaneously—both live and on demand. Although this method saves network bandwidth, users have no control over the content. They cannot pause, fast forward, or rewind through the content.

There are a number of ways you can get NetShow. Both Internet Explorer 4 and Microsoft Site Server include NetShow. In addition, you can download NetShow 2.1 for free from Microsoft's web site at **http://www.microsoft.com/netshow**.

Microsoft Server Technology

In this chapter, you will learn about Microsoft's server technology. Microsoft's back-end technology is primarily based on Windows NT servers. Each server plays a specific role and provides a specific functionality. Combine these features with Active Server Pages technology, and you get tremendous power and flexibility in designing and programming your web application's back end.

To choose a server for your web application, you must first understand the features and capabilities of the different servers. This chapter provides you with an overview of the different

Components of Microsoft NetShow 2.1

Microsoft NetShow 2.1 includes the following three components:

- **NetShow Server** Like any other Microsoft server technology, NetShow Server is a set of services running under Windows NT Server 4.0. The NetShow Server also includes a NetShow Administrator you can use to administer and manage NetShow services.
- **NetShow Theater Server** To deliver high quality, full-motion, full-screen MPEG video over corporate networks and dedicated LANs that support delivery of video content, you can use the NetShow Theater Server. Like any other Microsoft server, Microsoft NetShow Theater Server is also tightly integrated with Microsoft Windows NT Server 4.0. At the time of this writing, NetShow Theater Server is in beta 2 stage. You can download the NetShow Theater Server beta from Microsoft's web site at **http://www.microsoft.com/netshow/theater/default.htm**.
- **NetShow Player** Without the Player, your web site visitors cannot enjoy the multimedia show. You can download the Player from Microsoft's web site at **http://www.microsoft.com/netshow/download.htm**.
- **NetShow Tools** By using the NetShow Tools, you can create content for your multimedia presentation. In addition, NetShow Tools includes utilities you can use to convert existing multimedia content to an Active Streaming Format (ASF)—a format NetShow recognizes.

Using Microsoft NetShow Player

The NetShow Player supports the following audio and video formats:

- **ASF** ASF is a multimedia format specific to NetShow. The ASF format supports audio and video streaming and includes built-in error correction. NetShow supports both live and on-demand playing of ASF format based multimedia content.
- **RealAudio** In addition, NetShow includes built-in support for RealNetworks' very popular audio format—RealAudio 4.0. NetShow supports both live and on-demand playing of RealAudio format based audio content. To learn more about the RealAudio format, visit RealNetworks' web site at **http://www.realaudio.com**.
- **RealVideo** Like its support for RealAudio, NetShow also includes built-in support for RealNetworks' very popular video format—RealVideo 4.0. NetShow supports both live and on-demand playing of RealVideo format based video content. To learn more about the RealVideo format, visit RealNetworks' web site at **http://www.realaudio.com**.

To install the NetShow Player, run NSPLAY.EXE, which is a self-extracting file that installs the NetShow Player components on your system.

You can run the NetShow Player in a number of different ways. You can run the Player as a standalone application. Alternatively, you can run the Player embedded within browsers such as Internet Explorer and Netscape Navigator. Within Navigator, NetShow Player runs as an external viewer application. You can even integrate the Player within custom applications you develop with using Visual Basic and Visual C++.

To run the NetShow Player within a browser such as Internet Explorer, open Internet Explorer and point to the site **http://www.microsoft.com/netshow/**. Next, click the hyperlink Introduction to the Microsoft NetShow Product by Jim Durkin. Internet Explorer, in turn, starts the NetShow Player. The Player, in turn, plays the video where Jim Durkin talks about NetShow, as shown in Figure 28.1.

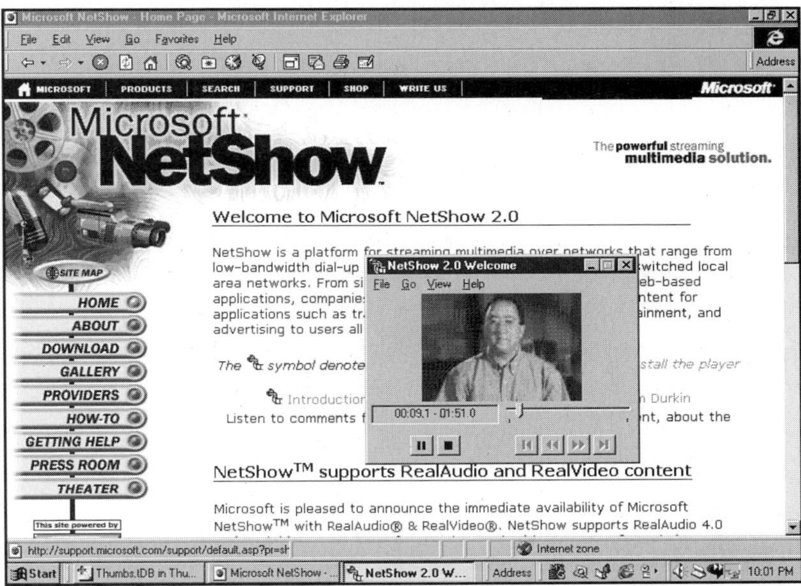

FIG. 28.1
Using the NetShow Player to play a video within Internet Explorer.

Notice the `Buffering...` message within the NetShow status bar. Before playing the video, NetShow buffers the incoming stream. By default, NetShow buffers 30 seconds of data. To change the default setting, select Play Settings from the View menu. The NetShow Player, in turn, displays the Microsoft NetShow Player Properties dialog box. Click the Advanced tab, as shown in Figure 28.2. Within the Buffering section, you can choose to use the default buffering or specify the actual number of seconds of data you would like NetShow to buffer. In addition, you see the Advanced tab display the protocols the NetShow Player uses. By default, the Player uses the multicast, TCP, and HTTP protocols with proxy disabled.

To view the Properties of the video the NetShow Player plays, select Properties from the File menu. The NetShow Player displays the Microsoft NetShow Player Properties dialog box. The Player Properties dialog box displays additional information about the video. For example, as shown in Figure 28.3, the General tab displays the video's title, author, and copyright information.

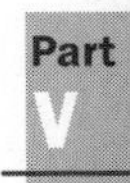

To get detailed information about the video including protocol, creation date and time, duration, source link, image width and height, and so on, as shown in Figure 28.4, click Details. The Details tab also indicates the bits per second (bandwidth) at which the server transfers the content to the player across the Internet or intranet. The Details tab also displays the error correction protocol in use.

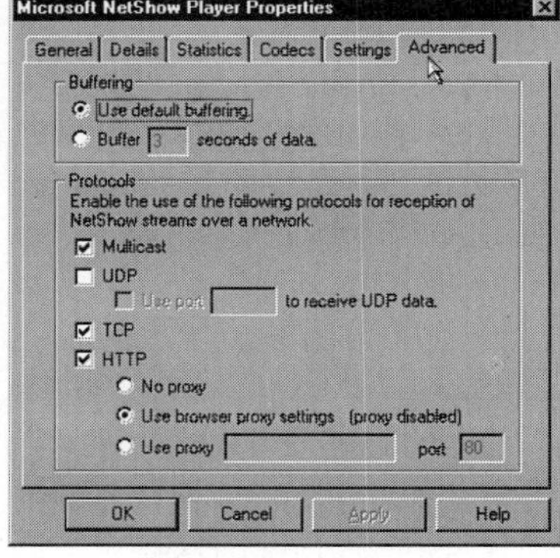

FIG. 28.2
By using the Advanced tab, you can change NetShow Player's buffer settings.

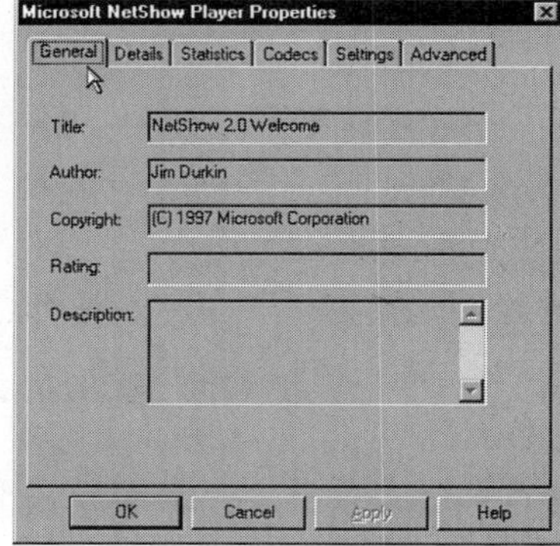

FIG. 28.3
Learning more about the multimedia content from the Player Properties dialog box.

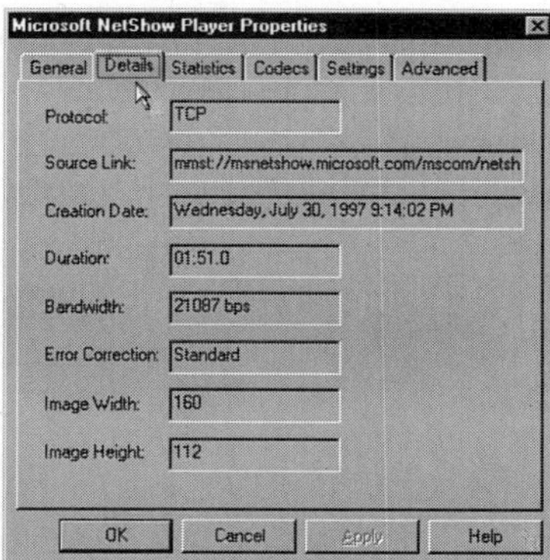

FIG. 28.4
Learning more about the video's protocol, source link, and duration from the Details tab.

To get information about the number of packets received, recovered, and lost during the streaming of the video from the server to the player, click Statistics. In addition, the Statistics tab displays the streaming content's reception quality within the last 30 seconds.

To determine the codecs the Player uses, click Codecs. Codecs are compressors-decompressors. Codecs are drivers that compress and decompress the NetShow content, thus saving hard disk space and network bandwidth. When you install NetShow Player on your system, the installation utility automatically installs the codecs. For a complete list of codecs that NetShow 2.1 supports, visit the web site at **http://www.microsoft.com/netshow/codecsship.htm**.

To change the window and control settings, click Settings. Within the Settings tab, you can specify the number of times you want the Player to play the content. You can also configure the Player to play the content forever by clicking the Play Forever radio button. If you want the Player to rewind the show upon completion, check the Rewind When Done Playing check box. In addition, you can display the NetShow content within three different window sizes: Default size, Half size, and Double size. If you double the window size, you might find the picture quality a little blurry.

Creating Multimedia Content with NetShow Tools

NetShow Tools includes a number utilities you can use to create multimedia content in ASF format. In fact, you can convert your existing AVI, WAV, and QuickTime files into ASF format easily by using one or more of the following NetShow tools:

- **ASF Editor** By using the ASF editor, you can synchronize still images with audio thus creating illustrated audio.
- **WAVTOASF** By using WAVTOASF, an MS-DOS based utility, you can convert precompressed WAV audio files to NetShow's ASF format.
- **VIDTOASF** By using VIDTOASF, an MS-DOS based utility, you can convert precompressed AVI or QuickTime video files to NetShow's ASF format.
- **ASFCHOP** You can use the ASFCHOP utility to chop your ASF file's beginning or end, if needed.
- **ASF Real-Time Encoder** You can use the ASF Real-Time Encoder to compress an audio or video source into ASF format and then store or send the ASF file to the NetShow server.
- **NetShow Presenter** By using the PowerPoint Publish to ASF add-on, you can create an illustrated NetShow presentation by synchronizing the PowerPoint slides and your audio narration about the slides.

Before you create NetShow content for your web site, take a moment to decide on your strategy. Consider the following questions:

Would you like to use any of your existing content for your NetShow?

If you plan to use existing content, consider using any of the tools and utilities that come with NetShow to convert the existing content into a format NetShow recognizes. For example, you can use the VIDTOASF utility to convert your AVI or QuickTime movies into ASF format. Similarly, you can use the WAVTOASF editor to convert your WAV files into ASF format.

Do you plan to create new NetShow content?

You can use a variety of tools and utilities to create new NetShow content. You might also consider using any of the tools created by the following third-party companies:

- **MetaBridge, Inc.** By using MetaBridge's NetPodium, you can deliver a live, one-to-many presentation over the Internet. You can include audio, video, slides, and so on within your presentation. For more information about MetaBridge and its products, visit the company's web site at **http://www.netpodium.com/**.
- **Sonic Foundry, Inc.** Sonic Foundry designs and markets digital audio editors and processors. For more information about Sonic Foundry and its products, visit the company's web site at **http://www.sonicfoundry.com/**.
- **Vivo Software, Inc.** Vivo Software develops and markets VivoActive Producer—a tool you can use to create streaming audio and video in ASF format. For more information about Vivo Software and its products, visit the company's web site at **http://www.vivo.com/**.
- **Ephyx Technologies** Ephyx Technologies develops and markets V-Active for NetShow—an interactive, graphic authoring tool. For more information about Ephyx Technologies and its products, visit the company's web site at **http://www.ephyx.com/products/vans.htm**.

Steps to Creating and Hosting NetShow Content The following are the steps you can use to create and host NetShow content for your web site:

1. Prepare and record the content. You must create high quality audio and video content. The better the content's quality, the better the user's experience will be. In addition, the content's high quality improves your web application's overall performance and response time over a low bandwidth network. As a result, when you capture the content, the conditions and environment under which you capture the content must be ideal and well-suited. The basics of good photography apply here as well. For example, lighting the subject area well, maximizing contrast between the objects in view, and so on.
2. Digitize the content. To digitize the content, you can choose from a number of capture cards. A number of manufacturers design capture cards that support NetShow and the NetShow format. For a complete list of capture cards supporting NetShow, visit Microsoft's web site at **http://www.microsoft.com/netshow/about/capture.htm**. After digitizing the content, and depending on the recorded content's quality, you might need to use audio and video editing tools to refine the content. To edit audio, you can use audio editing tools such as Sonic Foundry, Inc.'s Sound Forge or Syntrillium Software Corporation's Cool Edit. To edit video, you can use video editing tools such as Adobe Systems Incorporated's Premiere or VidEdit.
3. Convert to ASF format. If the multimedia content you created is not in NetShow's ASF format, you can use a number of NetShow tools and utilities to convert the content into ASF format. The NetShow tools and utilities include ASF Editor, WAVTOASF, VIDTOASF, ASFCHOP, and ASF Real-Time Encoder.

4. Decide whether you would like to distribute the content live or stored. If you plan to host an online real-time conference, you need to distribute the content live. Otherwise, distribute stored content.
5. Decide whether you will use unicast or multicast transmission. If you will distribute the content to a number of users across the Internet, use multicast transmission. If the visitors to your web site will view stored content, use unicast transmission. This gives the visitors the ability to fast forward, rewind, pause, and play the NetShow content.
6. Choose the appropriate codecs (see Chapter 27 for a detailed discussion of codecs).
7. Configure and administer the server.
8. Host the ASF files on the server.
9. Create the appropriate web pages that will include a link to the ASF files.
10. Note the client machine needs the NetShow Player to enjoy the NetShow content you create. For those users who do not have the Player installed on their system, include a link to the Microsoft web site from where they can download the Player for free (with Microsoft's permission, of course).

As an example, the following list outlines the steps you use to host your graduation party so your friends, family, and relatives around the world get an opportunity to enjoy the gathering:

1. Prepare and record the content. To capture the party's main and interesting events, use a high quality video camera.
2. Digitize the content. Connect the video camera to your computer and use a good audio/video capture card that supports NetShow's ASF format. By using the capture card, digitize the multimedia content into ASF format.
3. Distribute the content in stored format.
4. To provide your friends and family with the ability to fast forward, rewind, pause, and play the content, use unicast transmisison.
5. Choose an appropriate codec (see Chapter 27 for a complete discussion of codecs).
6. Configure and administer the NetShow server. In addition, host the ASF files on the NetShow server.
7. Create the appropriate web page that includes a link to the ASF files. Within the web page, include a link to the Microsoft web site from where your friends and family can download the Player for free (obtain Microsoft's permission to include such a link).

Microsoft Camcorder

If you want to capture screen events including mouse actions, Microsoft Camcorder is the utility for you. By using Microsoft Camcorder, you can create tutorials and demos very easily. By default, Microsoft Camcorder saves the movies in AVI format. By using the VIDTOASF utility, you can convert the AVI movies into ASF format that NetShow recognizes. As a result, you can create web sites that offer tutorials and demos of using your company's products, for example. Best of all, you can download Microsoft Camcorder for free from Microsoft's web site at **http://www.microsoft.com/office/office97/camcorder/default.htm**.

Microsoft also bundles Microsoft Camcorder as part of Office 97.

You can install Microsoft Camcorder by double-clicking CAMCORDR.EXE, a self-extracting file.

Using Microsoft Camcorder Microsoft Camcorder is very simple and easy to use. The following steps show how you can use Microsoft Camcorder to record a movie in Video for Windows format (.AVI):

1. Start Microsoft Camcorder.
2. Select Record from the Movie menu. Microsoft Camcorder displays the Stop button as shown in Figure 28.5.

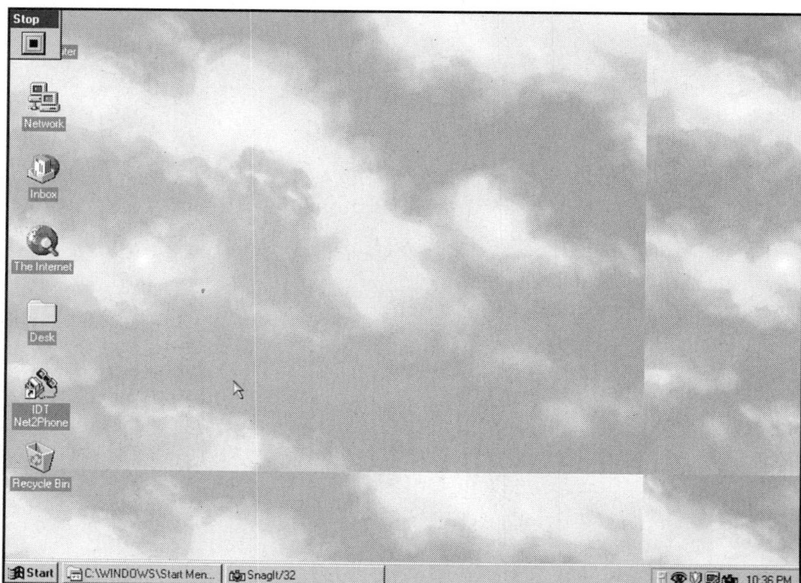

FIG. 28.5 To stop recording the movie, click Stop.

3. To stop recording the movie, click Stop.
4. At this point, you are ready to record your movie. When done, click Stop.
5. Next, to save the movie, select Save As from the File menu. By default, Microsoft Camcorder saves the move in AVI format.
6. To save the movie as a standalone executable, select Create Standalone Movie from the File menu.
7. To playback the movie, select Play from the Movie menu.
8. After recording the movie, you can use the VIDTOASF utility to convert the movie from AVI format to NetShow's ASF format.

Just like you can use Microsoft Camcorder to record screen shots with mouse clicks and events, you can use a video (or audio) capture card to capture and save video (or audio) in standard video (or audio) format. Then, you can use the VIDTOASF utility (or WAVTOASF, as the case may be) to convert the video (or audio) into NetShow's ASF format.

Tips and Techniques

When you develop your web site that supports NetShow content, it is a good idea to test your site by using both Internet Explorer and Netscape Navigator. You might wonder why you should test them by using both the browsers. If your web site is within the public domain, you never know what browser will hit your site.

It is also a good idea to inform the users about the browser and screen resolution that best suits your site. In addition, it is a good idea to inform the NetShow Player that is required to play the NetShow content your site supports. You must include this information within your home page. You can also include links to the appropriate site so users who do not have the required browser or NetShow Player can download them with the help of the link.

Microsoft Site Builder Workshop

The Site Builder Workshop is a Microsoft site (**www.microsoft.com/sitebuilder/**) that you should visit regularly for the latest and greatest information on Microsoft products for the Internet. The site includes a Webzine, a lot of good technical articles, and a download area for you to download the trial and beta versions of Microsoft products for the Internet, including NetShow and other Microsoft servers. In addition, you can become a member of the Site Builder Workshop and get access to third-party downloads, promotional opportunities, and special offers. There are three membership levels. The first two levels are free. Check out the Site Builder Workshop site, as shown in Figure 28.6, for more information on SBN membership.

You can download both Microsoft and some third-party trial and beta software from the web site at **www.microsoft.com/sbnmember/download/download.asp**.

The Microsoft web site's search page address is **www.microsoft.com/search/default.asp**.

Additional Resources for Microsoft NetShow

To participate in an online discussion list on Microsoft NetShow, visit the web site at **http://www.idot.aol.com/mld/production/yiaz1221.html**.

To learn more about a NetShow Case Study (RSi Communications), visit the web site at **http://www.microsoft.com/netshow/about/casestudies/rsi.htm**.

For a list of capture cards that work with Microsoft NetShow, visit the web site at **http://www.eu.microsoft.com/netshow/about/capture.htm**.

For a list of firewalls that work with Microsoft NetShow, visit the web site at **http://www.asia.microsoft.com/netshow/firewall.htm**.

If you want to receive a weekly newsletter on Microsoft NetShow by email, visit the web site at **http://www.eu.microsoft.com/netshow/about/contact.htm**.

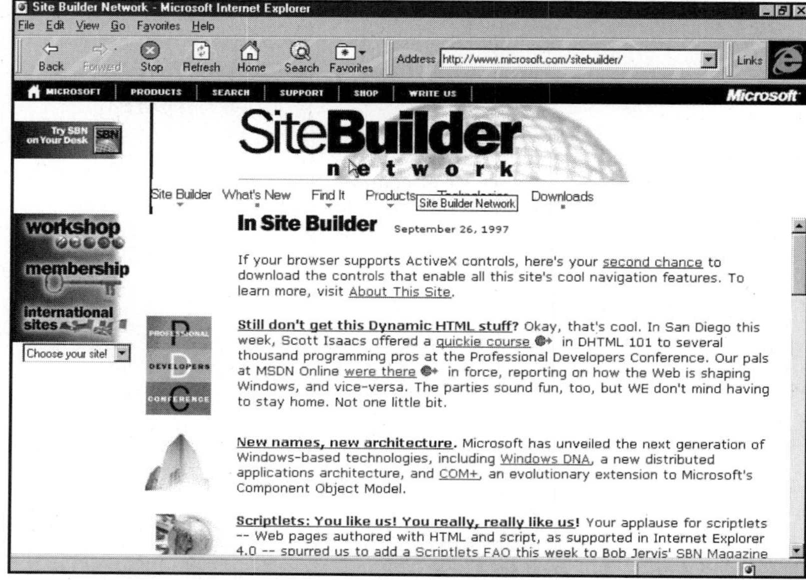

FIG. 28.6
Microsoft's Site Builder Workshop site—**www.microsoft.com/sitebuilder/**.

Using the NetShow On-Demand Player Control

You can integrate the NetShow on-demand ActiveX Player control within an HTML page. The file NSOPLAY.OCX represents the ActiveX Control. Like any other ActiveX Control, the Player control also has properties, methods, and events. As a result, integrating the Player control within an HTML page is similar to integrating any other ActiveX Control. You use the `<OBJECT>` tag to embed the control. Listing 28.1 shows the `<OBJECT>` tag declaration of the Player control.

Listing 28.1 Embedding the ActiveX Player control within HTML.

```
<OBJECT CLASSID="clsid:2179C5D3-EBFF-11cf-B6FD-00AA00B4E220"
HEIGHT=240
WIDTH=320
NAME=NSOPlay
ALIGN=center
>
<PARAM NAME="ControlType" VALUE="1">
</OBJECT>
```

The `classid` is the control's unique identifier. Every ActiveX Control has a unique class ID. For the control to work properly with the HTML page, the control's class ID must be correct. You can use a tool such as Microsoft FrontPage, ActiveX Control Pad, or Visual InterDev to integrate ActiveX Controls within HTML pages. The Player control's name is `NSOPlay`. In addition, you can specify a number of different parameters for the control. The parameters and their values you specify determine the control's behavior. For example, if you set the `ControlType` parameter's value to `0`, no controls appear within the HTML page.

By configuring the Player control's properties and using the appropriate methods and events, you can customize the control's behavior based on your application's business requirements. Table 28.1 lists the Player control's properties.

Table 28.1 The Player control's properties.

Property Name	Description
`Author`	Specifies the current ASF file's author
`Bandwidth`	Specifies the current ASF file's bandwidth (bits per second)
`Copyright`	Specifies the current ASF file's copyright information
`CreationDate`	Specifies the current ASF file's creation date
`Description`	Specifies the current ASF file's description
`ErrorCorrection`	Specifies the current ASF file's error correction protocol
`FileName`	Specifies the current ASF file's name
`ImageSourceHeight`	Specifies the displayed image's original height in pixels
`ImageSourceWidth`	Specifies the displayed image's original width in pixels
`LostPackets`	Specifies the number of packets lost at any given point during the transmission
`ReceivedPackets`	Specifies the number of packets received at any given point during the transmission
`RecoveredPackets`	Specifies the number of packets recovered at any given point during the transmission
`ReceptionQuality`	Specifies the percentage of packets received within the last 30 seconds
`SourceLink`	Specifies the current ASF file's path
`Title`	Specifies the current ASF file's title
`AllowChangeControlType`	Specifies if the user can change the way the controls are displayed
`AllowScan`	Specifies if the current ASF file can be scanned
`AnimationAtStart`	Specifies if the Player displays the title animation during the initial buffering
`AnimationOnStop`	Specifies if the Player displays the title animation when the file playback is stopped and then re-started
`TransparentAtStart`	Specifies if the window displaying the image is transparent at the beginning of the file's playback

continued

Table 28.1 Continued

Property Name	Description
`TransparentOnStop`	Specifies if the window displaying the image is transparent at the end of the file's playback
`AutoStart`	Specifies if the Player automatically starts playing the ASF file when the HTML page loads the control
`AutoRewind`	Specifies if the Player automatically rewinds the current ASF file, if the file's end is reached
`BufferingCount`	Specifies the number of times the buffering occurred during the ASF file's playback
`CanScan`	Specifies if you can fast forward or rewind through the current ASF file
`CanSeek`	Specifies if you can seek to a specific time within the current ASF file
`CanSeekToMarkers`	Specifies if you can seek to a marker within the current ASF file
`ClickToPlay`	Specifies if you can toggle the current ASF file's playback
`ControlType`	Specifies the way the HTML page displays the controls for the Player
`CurrentMarker`	Specifies the current marker within the current ASF file
`CurrentPosition`	Specifies the current position within the current ASF file
`CurrentState`	Specifies the current ASF file's current state (for example, paused, in play, or stopped)
`CursorType`	Specifies the cursor type
`DisplaySize`	Specifies the display window's size
`EnableContextMenu`	Specifies if the control displays a pop-up menu when you click the right mouse button
`InvokeURLs`	Specifies if the player can automatically invoke URLs
`MainWindow`	Specifies a handle to the control's main window
`MarkerCount`	Specifies the number of markers within the current ASF file
`PlayCount`	Specifies the number of times the current ASF file plays
`Rate`	Specifies the rate at which the current ASF file plays
`Rating`	Specifies the current ASF file's rating
`SendKeyboardEvents`	Specifies if the control sent the keyboard events

Property Name	Description
SendMouseClickEvents	Specifies if the control sent the mouse click events
SendMouseMoveEvents	Specifies if the control sent the mouse move events
SendStateChangeEvents	Specifies if the control sent the state change events

When you start the NetShow Player, you can display the author, bandwidth, copyright, and other information by selecting Properties from the File menu. As you can see from the preceding table, such information is actually stored as the Player control's properties.

Table 28.2 lists the Player control's methods, and Table 28.3 lists the Player control's events. In the next section, you learn about the Microsoft Commercial Internet System.

Table 28.2 The Player control's methods.

Method Name	Description
Play	Directs the Player to begin playing the current ASF file
Pause	Directs the Player to pause playing the current ASF file
Stop	Directs the Player to stop playing the current ASF file
GetMarkerTime	Returns the marker's time (in seconds)
GetMarkerName	Returns the marker's name

Table 28.3 The Player control's events.

Event Name	Description
Click	Triggered upon mouse click
DblClick	Triggered upon mouse double-click
KeyDown	Triggered if a key is pressed
KeyPress	Triggered if a key is pressed and then released
KeyUp	Triggered if a key is released
MouseDown	Triggered if the mouse button is pressed
MouseMove	Triggered if the mouse is moved
MouseUp	Triggered if the mouse button is released
ScriptCommand	Triggered when a command or an URL is received
StateChange	Triggered when the file playback's state changes
AutoStartFailure	Triggered if the automatic start of the file failed

continued

Table 28.3 Continued

Property Name	Description
`Buffering`	Triggered when the buffering begins or completes
`Disconnect`	Triggered when the connection to the server is lost
`EndOfStream`	Triggered when the file playback is complete
`MarkerHit`	Triggered if a marker is hit during playback

Microsoft Commercial Internet System (MCIS)

MCIS is a suite of Windows NT-based servers. Each server plays a specific role. All servers use the same graphical user interface (GUI)—Internet Service Manager—for system administration and maintenance that Windows NT and IIS use. Having a common look and feel for administration and maintenance across the servers naturally reduces your learning curve and maintenance cost.

The most interesting amongst the servers is the Commerce Server. You can use the Commerce Server to create an online shopping store. In fact, you can use the server to create an online shopping experience for your customers and visitors. The server includes a number of useful features such as built-in search engine, secure processing of credit card payments, shopping cart, and so on. By using the server, you cut down the time it takes to develop and deploy an interactive, online shopping store for your company's products and services. In this chapter, you learn about the MCIS server and other servers that are part of the MCIS suite.

A suite of Windows NT-based servers, the MCIS provides a turnkey solution for web design and publishing. Presently, the MCIS includes nine servers. Each server plays a specific role and function associated with its use. The following are the nine MCIS servers:

- MCIS News
- MCIS Mail
- Chat
- Internet Locator
- Content Replication
- Membership
- Address Book
- Personalization
- Commerce Server

MCIS News

By using the MCIS News server, you can host electronic discussion forums and newsgroups at your web site. The MCIS News server is based on the Internet standard Network News

Transport Protocol (NNTP). The MCIS server also supports the NNTP security extensions. This, in turn, allows transmission of encrypted passwords over the network.

MCIS Mail

MCIS Mail supports the Internet standard Post Office Protocol (POP3), Simple Mail Transfer Protocol (SMTP), and Multipurpose Internet Mail Extensions (MIME) protocols. The POP3 protocol supports client access to mailboxes on the mail server. The SMTP protocol supports communication between mail servers. And the MIME protocol supports multimedia email formats. MCIS Mail can support millions of mailboxes distributed over multiple sites. Similar to the Chat server, MCIS Mail server supports both Distributed Password Authentication (DPA) and Secure Sockets Layer (SSL). Distributed Password Authentication (DPA) is part of Microsoft's Internet Security Framework, a set of security technologies to promote standards-based secure electronic commerce over the Internet. These security protocols enable transmission of encrypted passwords over the network.

Chat

By using the Chat server, you can offer real-time communication services within your web site. Combine the Chat server with Internet Locator and your users can look up who's online. The Chat server supports one-to-one, one-to-many, and many-to-many forms of communications. In addition, the Chat server supports the Internet Relay Chat (IRC) protocol as well as its own binary protocol for advanced chat functions such as chat searches, Unicode support, and other distinct chat channel modes.

The Chat server also includes a Chat Software Development Toolkit (SDK) and a Chat ActiveX control. By using the SDK and ActiveX control, you can add your own Chat features to your web site. The Chat SDK is a protocol-independent server API you can use to write different types of Chat clients such as text and 3D Chat, online game applications, and so on. The SDK supports both DPA and SSL protocols. The Chat server supports both Unicode and ANSI character sets. A single Chat server can support 2,500 simultaneous chatters whereas a Chat server network can support up to 48,000 simultaneous users.

You can use the Chat server with Internet Locator and Address Book to provide real-time, online look-up and search service. Users can search for associates and friends who are online and initiate online communication with them.

Internet Locator

By using the Internet Locator, you can locate your friends, buddies, and colleagues online. You can check if your associate is online, and if he or she is, you can initiate an online communication or chat session by using Microsoft NetMeeting. The Internet Locator stores its database within the server's RAM. This is because the information within the database changes dynamically as users log in and off their Internet connection. As a result, the information within the database stored within the server's RAM changes dynamically.

Content Replication

You can use Content Replication to replicate the entire contents of your web site to a site at a different geographical location. For example, if your primary web site is at Boston and your company has a number of European customers, you can replicate the contents of your primary web site to the sites within Europe. This reduces the network load on your primary web site and provides fast and timely information to your customers within Europe. The Content Replication server helps you manage replication of all types of web content. You can also use the Content Replication to create mirror sites for backup purposes.

Content Replication provides the following set of extensible APIs:

- **Configuration API** The Configuration API manages the configuration of servers, routers, and replication projects.
- **Replication Control API** The Replication Control API controls the starting, stopping, and staging of your replication projects.
- **Notification API** The Notification API controls the notification of important events during a replication, such as starting the replication, stopping the replication, and so on.

Membership

You can use the Membership server to create a membership-based online community. This is especially useful if you plan to offer commercial products and services and want to make your site membership-based. For example, you can create your own online version of Sam's Club. The Membership server includes ready-to-use components for tracking members and their demographics, authenticating signon, controlling access to different parts of your site, and so on. The Membership server supports an open and extensible API you can integrate with a third-party billing component. By using a billing component, you can charge your customers for the products, services, and content usage you sell. As a service provider, you can use the Membership server to deploy remote application servers anywhere on the Internet and tie them together by using a central authentication and billing system.

Similar to MCIS News and Chat servers, the Membership server also supports the DPA security protocol. In addition, the Membership server includes the standard Security Service Provider Interface (SSPI) third-party applications can utilize.

Address Book

The Address Book is the White Pages directory on your web server. By using an Address Book, users can find information about other online members sharing similar interests. This fosters a strong online community experience. You can store both static and dynamic information within the Address Book. For example:

- Static information such as user demographics, name, address, sex, race, religion, hobbies, and so on.
- Dynamic information such as the user's IP address and so on.

You can use the Address Book with NetMeeting—Microsoft's Internet telephony and conferencing client. You can also use the Address Book with Internet Locator to help users find their buddies online who share similar interests and experiences.

The Address Book provides two kinds of interfaces—HTTP and LDAP. The web page uses the HTTP interface, whereas a custom client can use the LDAP interface. You can use Microsoft SQL Server as the database back end for the Address Book users.

Personalization

By using the Personalization server, you can deliver dynamic web content personalized for each visitor of your web site. Initially, you could design only static web pages. By integrating database connectivity, you can now deliver dynamic content. If you combine this with Personalization, you can deliver both dynamic and personalized content. This offers a unique opportunity to make your web site truly different from the rest.

Commerce Server

By using the Commerce Server, you can create a compelling and interactive shopping experience for your customers. The Commerce Server helps you build a virtual shopping store by integrating a number of useful features such as secure credit card payment, shopping cart, search utility, and so on. You can also offer a personalized shopping experience to your customers.

The following are the Commerce Server's three core components:

- **Controller** By using the Controller, you can configure the Commerce Server's settings, such as language, currency and date display, settings for registry, generating buyer IDs, order processing, inventory management, and more. Within a multicomputer configuration, you must configure the Commerce Server on the Controller computer. The Controller computer then copies and reflects the changes to other computers that are part of the Commerce Server setup.
- **Router** The Router is implemented as an Internet Service Application Programming Interface (ISAPI) DLL to route the client request that the Internet Information Server receives to the appropriate function within the Store Server. The Router is also responsible for routing the result(s) received from the Store Server back to the client browser. The Router directs the service requests by means of named pipes. In addition, the Router can provide event logging.
- **Store Server** As the Commerce Server's backbone, the Store Server includes several different functions, each targeted at accomplishing a specific task. For example, if an order is placed, the Store Server processes the order request, generates the tracking IDs, updates the database, and so on. The Store Server is also responsible for maintaining communication with the database back end (such as Microsoft SQL Server).

Commerce Server offers a number of useful features, and utilities:

- **Search Utility** By using the built-in SQL search engine, you can provide your customers with the ability to search through your company's product database.
- **Shopping Cart** Commerce Server provides yet another built-in feature—a shopping cart. This feature simulates the shopping cart purchasing style you use in grocery and department stores. As the customer buys a product, the Commerce Server adds the product to the shopping cart. The customer can choose to remove the product from the cart at a later time. By using the shopping cart, you can display the total number of products, their descriptions, and total price, including taxes and shipping cost.
- **Order Confirmation** After your customer places an order, you can configure Commerce Server to email an order confirmation. In addition, you can configure Commerce Server to assign tracking numbers to each order automatically. Customers can also use the tracking number to inquire about the status of their order.
- **Dynamic, Personalized, and Targeted Marketing** You can collect buyers' demographics and their shopping habits based on the products they purchase through your online store. By using this information, you can configure Commerce Server to provide dynamic, personalized, and targeted discounts, promotions, and more when the customer visits your online store again. By using Commerce Server, you can also update the prices in real time and dynamically calculate the shipping cost and taxes based on the order placed.
- **Memberships** You can use Commerce Server to create a membership based online store such as Sam's Club. Commerce Server includes built-in capability to create membership accounts, setup user ID and passwords for the members, and offer membership discounts.
- **Extensible and Scalable** By using the Commerce Server's published Application Programming Interface (API), you can integrate third-party custom components such as ActiveX controls, OLE, and COM objects with the server. In addition, the Commerce Server operates with any ODBC-compliant database such as Microsoft SQL Server, Microsoft Access, Oracle, and so on. This means you can integrate your existing product and customer database with the Commerce Server.
- **Template Stores** You can choose from several template stores that come with Commerce Server. You can also customize the templates to meet your application's specific requirements.
- **Security** Commerce Server supports SSL and Secure Electronic Transmission (SET) protocols. Microsoft and Visa jointly developed the SET protocol. By using the SET protocol and Verifone's vPOS application, you can process Internet credit card authorizations and payments securely. The vPOS application communicates with the financial institution directly for credit card and other forms of payment authorization.
- **Merchant Utilities** Merchant utilities are software tools that come with Commerce Server. You can use the tools to set up and manage your product presentation. By using the four tools, you can perform the following:

- **Product Management** You can manage the products you display on your web site and the associated information such as pricing, availability, and more.
- **Promotion Management** You can manage the timing of discount promotions on your products.
- **Buyer Management** You can manage the demographics of buyers of your products and visitors to your web site.
- **Order Management** You can manage the orders your customers place including tracking number, order status, and so on.

- **Merchant Databases** The Commerce Server supports ODBC-compliant, relational databases such as Microsoft SQL Server. You can use your existing relational schema with Commerce Server, or you can use Commerce Server's built-in database management and administration utilities to design a new schema.

Internet Information Server (IIS)

The IIS is Microsoft's web server. The IIS comes bundled with Windows NT 4.0 Server. When you install Windows NT Server, the installation utility also installs the IIS. The IIS provides built-in Gopher, FTP, and HTTP engines. In addition, the IIS includes Active Server Pages (ASP) you can use for server-side scripting. ASP relies on a number of different technologies including:

- Windows NT 4.0 Server
- Web server such as the IIS
- TCP/IP service
- Database server such as Microsoft SQL Server

For ASP to work, the preceding technologies must coordinate and work together properly. You need a database server if your web site is data-driven. You can use the server-side component—Active Data Object (ADO)—for your ASP's database connectivity.

Personal Web Server (PWS)

PWS is a baby Internet Information Server—a subset of IIS. If you want to use a single machine as the client and server for testing your web application, use PWS. You can easily scale the web application you design and test using PWS to IIS with minimal or no code changes.

PWS is a lightweight and inexpensive server ideal for small businesses. You can also use PWS to set up an intranet for your company, or for a department within your company. PWS offers both HTTP and FTP services. In addition, the PWS also supports ISAPI extensions and CGI. Note that the PWS does not support Java.

Personal Web Server is bundled with FrontPage 98. PWS is also part of the Internet Starter Kit that ships with all new copies of Windows 95. You can also download the PWS for free from Microsoft's web site at **http://www.microsoft.com/sbnmember/download/download.asp**.

Advantages of Using the PWS By using the PWS, you have the following advantages:

- **Low cost** The PWS is free. You can download the PWS from Microsoft's web site. Note, however, that you can install and use the PWS only on your Windows 95 system. In other words, you do not need a high-end Windows NT system for your PWS-based web application development and testing.
- **Porting is easy** After you have developed and tested your PWS based web application, you can port the application to IIS with minimal or no code changes.
- **Ease of use** The PWS is easy to install and use.

Disadvantages of Using the PWS There are some disadvantages too:

- **PWS works under Windows 95 only** You cannot install the PWS on a Windows NT system.
- **Double testing** Although you can port your application from the PWS to IIS with minimal or no coding, you must still test your application thoroughly within the IIS environment.

Advantages of Using the IIS By using the IIS, you gain the following advantages:

- **Tight integration with Windows NT Server** The IIS is tightly integrated with the Windows NT Server. Your application can benefit from Windows NT's built-in security features, and so on.
- **Industrial strength web server** Microsoft designed IIS to be *the* web server. With a robust Windows NT operating system and full featured web server offering FTP, Gopher, and WWW services, both Windows NT and IIS are central to Microsoft's Internet model—the Active Platform.
- **Ease of use** Like the PWS, the IIS is also easy to install and use. In fact, when you install Windows NT Server, the installation program automatically installs the IIS.

Disadvantages of Using the IIS Like with PWS, there are some disadvantages to using the IIS as well:

- **Windows NT Server only** Unlike the PWS, you cannot install the IIS on a Windows 95 system. Also, you cannot install the IIS on a Windows NT workstation. You can install the IIS on a Windows NT server only.
- **Setup and configuration** The IIS setup and configuration is different from the PWS setup and configuration. Even though you can port your web application from one server to the other easily, you must still configure both servers properly.

Windows NT Security

Windows NT supports four types of file systems. Each file system offers a different level of security. The four Windows NT file systems are:

- High Performance File System (HPFS)
- File Allocation Table (FAT)
- CD file system (CDFS)
- NT file system (NTFS)

I recommend you use the NT file system. The NT file system offers the highest level of file and directory level security. Most DOS systems support the FAT file system. The FAT file system does not offer any kind of security for the files and directories on your server. The NTFS offers you both file and directory level security. And because the IIS is tightly integrated with NT, the IIS uses the same security protocol as NT.

Windows NT Services

The programs Windows NT runs are called *services*. For example, you might have the Microsoft SQL Server's database services running on your Windows NT server. By using the Control Panel, you can start and stop Windows NT services manually. Alternatively, you can configure the options by using the Control Panel to have Windows NT start the services of your choice automatically on boot up. For active web development, you need the following services at the minimum:

- TCP/IP
- Database service such as Microsoft SQL Server, if your web application uses database connectivity

Windows NT Registry

Both Windows NT and Windows 95 use a Registry to register important information about the programs you install on your system. In previous versions of Windows, the installation programs used to store such information within INI files inlcude win.ini, system.ini, control.ini, odbc.ini, odbcinst.ini, and other configuration files, such as autoexec.bat and config.sys.

CAUTION

Maintain the system Registry's integrity. The Registry is intended to be read-only. You should not manually change the Registry's entries. If you do want to change the entries manually, you should be very, very careful. Also, back up your system's Registry backup. Typically, the install and uninstall utilities that come with your software add and delete entries to and from the Registry. This is the best way to maintain the Registry's integrity.

To manually register or unregister a component, use the registration server (regsvr32.exe) program that comes with Windows 95 and Windows NT. The syntax for using the registration server is as follows:

```
regsvr32 [/u][s] componentname
```

`/u` unregisters the component. `s` is for silent registration with no display messages.

By using the registration server, you can register ISAPI, COM, DCOM, OLE, and ActiveX components with your system's Registry. For example, the following statement registers marquee.ocx, an ActiveX control:

```
regsvr32 marquee.ocx
```

If the registration is successful, the registration server displays the dialog box as shown in Figure 28.7.

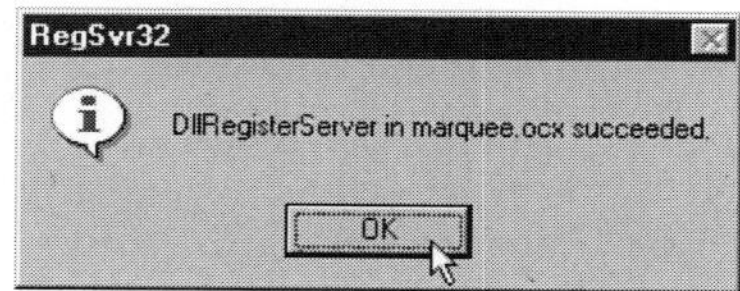

FIG. 28.7
The registration server registered the marquee control successfully.

To unregister marquee.ocx, use the following statement:

```
regsvr32 /u marquee.ocx
```

If the unregistration is successful, the registration server displays a dialog box as shown in Figure 28.8.

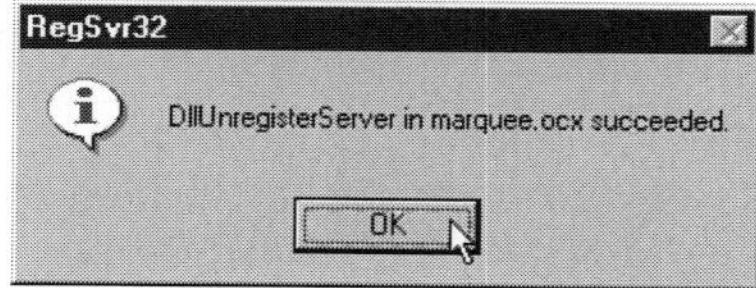

FIG. 28.8
The registration server successfully unregistered the marquee control.

You must register your components with Windows NT or Windows 95 Registry, as the case may be. Without registration, your application cannot use the component and access the component's methods, properties, and events.

If you create and compile a control by using Visual C++, Visual C++'s integrated compiler automatically registers the control with your system's Registry.

CAUTION

If you want to delete an OCX from your system, make sure you first unregister the control before deleting it. Unregistration removes all references to the control from your system's Registry.

When you register a control, the registration server adds the following information about the control to the Registry:

- Control's class name
- Control's text name
- Path of control's executable
- Path and resource ID of the control's palette bitmap
- An indicator stating if the control conforms to OLE control protocols
- An indicator stating if you can insert the control
- IDs of control's interface—properties and events

When the client browser requests a file from the web server, the web server processes the request and calls the appropriate server component (ISAPI filter or DLL). The IIS returns the HTML to the browser.

Site Server

Microsoft Site Server is a new BackOffice product. The Site Server provides a comprehensive web site environment for enhancement, deployment, and advanced management of commerce-enabled web sites. The Site Server Enterprise Edition includes the following components:

- Commerce Server   You learned about the Commerce Server earlier in this chapter.
- Commerce Server Tools   In addition, the Site Server includes a number of tools such as Store Foundation Wizard, Store Builder Wizard, Store Clone Wizard, Pipeline Editor, and Usage Analyst that you can use to build and manage your commerce sites, database schema, site structure, and so on effectively.
- Starter Stores   Microsoft has also included a number of starter store sites to help you understand the product and get you up and running quickly. The starter sites are, in fact, Active Server Pages templates.
- Order Processing Pipeline   The Order Processing Pipeline (OPP) is a set of Active Server components enforcing the business rules for processing orders. The OPP includes a set of COM components managing the order processing's 14 stages:
    - Product Information   The Product Information stage retrieves product information from the database and writes to the order blackboard.
    - Merchant Information   The Merchant Information stage retrieves merchant information from the database and writes to the order blackboard.
    - Shopper Information   The Shopper Information stage retrieves the shopper information from the database. If the retrieve fails, the OPP does not generate an error. Instead, the OPP continues with the next stage.
    - Order Initialization   The Order Initialization stage sets the initial order information on the order blackboard.

- Order Check The Order Check stage verifies and validates the order information. For example, the Order Check stage checks if the order contains all the required elements.
- Item Price Adjust Within this stage, the OPP calculates the regular and current price of each item on the order.
- Order Price Adjust The Order Price Adjust component sets the adjusted price for each item within the order.
- Shipping The Shipping component calculates the total shipping cost.
- Handling The Handling component calculates the total handling charge for the order.
- Tax The Tax component calculates the total tax on the order.

CAUTION

The Tax component included within Commerce Server is only for testing and evaluation purposes. You should not use the built-in Tax component within your production environment. To meet your application requirements, you can write your own Tax component by using the Commerce Server API or purchase a third-party Tax component.

- Order Total The Order Total component sums the order subtotal, tax, shipping, and handling and posts the total to the order blackboard. The Order Total component uses any discounts or promotions to calculate the total charge for the order.
- Inventory The Inventory component verifies every item ordered is in stock.
- Payment The Payment component handles the payment details for the order. The Payment component also handles the credit card verification and authorization.
- Accept (or reject) The Accept component handles the order tracking, generating purchasing orders, generating order numbers, and so on.

The OPP components are optional. You can integrate them within your existing systems, or any third-party component that complies with the OPP interface. The OPP interfaces are defined within the Commerce Software Development Kit (SDK). You can use the SDK to integrate the OPP interface with your own application.

- Microsoft Wallet By integrating Microsoft Wallet within your web site, you can provide secure and convenient purchasing on the Internet. Both Internet Explorer 4.0 and Windows 95 includes integrated commerce support through the use of built-in Microsoft Wallet. Microsoft Wallet is a client-side component users can use to make purchases on the Internet. Presently, you can download the Microsoft Wallet for free from Microsoft's web site at **http://www.microsoft.com/commerce/wallet/default.htm**.

Microsoft has implemented the Microsoft Wallet as both an ActiveX control and a Netscape plug-in. The Microsoft Wallet includes a Payment Selector control and an Address Selector control. By using the Payment Selector control, you can provide entry, secure storage, and use of various types of payment methods. By using the Address Selector control, you can provide entry and secure storage of addresses for shipping and billing during online order entry.

You can download the Microsoft Wallet plug-in for Netscape Navigator from Microsoft's web site at **http://www.microsoft.com/merchant/wallet/local/naven.htm** or **http://www.microsoft.com/commerce/wallet/default.htm**. The npwallet.dll includes both plug-ins–the Payment Selector and Address Selector.

You can add payment functionality to your web site by using the Microsoft Wallet Webmaster Kit. You can download the kit for free from Microsoft's web site at **http://www.microsoft.com/commerce/wallet/default.htm**.

- Buy Now   Buy Now is a client component users can use to make purchases from any site on the Internet. When a user clicks a product ad or online banner within a web site, for example, Buy Now opens a new window within the browser window to facilitate purchasing. The user does not need to leave the current context or site to initiate and complete the purchase. On the client side, Buy Now is integrated with Microsoft Wallet. On the server side, Buy Now is integrated with the Site Server, Commerce Server database, and order processing pipeline.
- Transaction Server   Although currently not included, future versions of Site Server are expected to take advantage of Microsoft Transaction Server's capabilities enabling transactional integrity as part of the OPP.

A Site Server Sample Case Study I

This section describes a sample case study—a fictitious direct marketing company, Cool Sports, that uses the Site Server to process Buy Now orders.

A direct marketing company of sports goods and memorabilia, Cool Sports is interested in selling its products through the web. Cool Sports has advertised the product promotions and discounts at all major sports sites including **http://www.nba.com/**, **http://www.espn.com/**, and so on. A Chicago Bulls fan, and a frequent online visitor, is reading the NBA.com site for the latest score update on the Bulls-Knicks game. The visitor notices the Cool Sports ad banner for Air Jordan shoes at a 10 percent discount for online buyers. The visitor clicks the ad banner to take the offer. The web site displays a dialog box showing the shoes, price, tax, shipping, and discount information. By using Microsoft Wallet, the visitor specifies his shipping and billing address—already available within the Wallet. The visitor also specifies the payment information and then submits the order request. Minutes later, the visitor receives an email confirmation from Cool Sports for the product order.

To implement such a scenario, the following components are needed:

- Browser A browser, such as Internet Explorer, supporting the SSL protocol.
- Microsoft Wallet A client-side component.
- Buy Now Another client-side component facilitating online purchasing without leaving the current context. The Buy Now component also integrates with the Site Server.
- Site Server The server-side component (that Cool Sports provides) manages and handles Buy Now transactions.
- Database A database such as Microsoft SQL Server that stores the product and order information.

A Site Server Sample Case Study II

This section describes another sample case study. A fictitious mail order book company—Cool Books—has created a web site that readers and visitors can use to buy books online. Based on the readers and visitors' profile, Cool Books offers targeted promotions and discounts. Cool Books presents a customized web page to each regular visitor based on his profile and buying preferences. All first time visitors see a common web page. As they visit the site regularly, they see a different web page customized to their needs and the information they are looking for. For example, a customer who has already bought five romantic novels from Cool Books sees a list of new releases of romantic novels at the top of the web site. On the other hand, another customer who has already bought seven science fictions and three programming books from Cool Books sees a list of new releases of science fiction and technical programming books at the top of the web site. To order a book online, the customer specifies the payment information and then submits the order request. Minutes later, the customer receives an email confirmation from Cool Books for the book order.

To implement such a scenario, Cool Books needs the following components:

- Browser A browser such as Internet Explorer supporting SSL.
- Site Server The server-side component Cool Books uses to provide customized web pages and handle book orders.
- Database A database such as Microsoft SQL Server to store the profiles of customers, visitors, product, and order information.

The Site Server is part of Microsoft's Internet Commerce strategy. Microsoft's Internet Commerce strategy promotes an Active Server-based solution for Internet commerce with industry wide support for a variety of online payment options.

Transaction Server

This section introduces yet another Microsoft server—the Transaction Server—its features, and components. By using the server, you can deploy your component-based web application within a distributed environment very easily. Transaction Server takes care of resource, context, and thread management for you, thus letting you focus on your application's business logic and functionality.

You can design your components for a single user, and by using the Transaction Server, you can deploy the components within a multi-user environment. You can scale your component-based application from a single user system to a high volume, high traffic Internet-based system very easily by using the Transaction Server.

In other words, you can design your web application without worrying about programming for concurrency, resource pooling, database commits and rollbacks, thread and context management, and so on. The Transaction Server takes care of all these, and much more. The server synchronizes access to shared data and resources when multiple clients try to use them at the same time. The Transaction Server also handles concurrency and locking for your application, as well as maintains the client cache for high speed access and implements security for your application.The Microsoft Transaction Server's architecture includes the following components:

- ActiveX Server Components You can design your own ActiveX Server components for a single-user system and deploy them within a multi-user environment by using the Transaction Server's transaction processing capabilities. Server components are in-process DLLs. You can use tools such as Visual Basic, Visual C++, and Visual J++ to create the server components. You can encapsulate your application's business logic within the components.
- Transaction Server Explorer You can use the Explorer to administer and manage your Transaction Server.
- Transaction Server Executive The Executive is a DLL providing runtime services your application server components will use. For example, the DLL provides services such as thread and context management.
- Server Process A server process hosts your application components and services multiple clients.
- Resource Manager Microsoft SQL Server is a good example of a Resource Manager. The database server maintains your application data's integrity.

Transaction Server includes a toolkit you can use to develop your own Resource Managers.

- Resource Dispenser ODBC Resource Dispenser and Shared Property Manager are good examples of Resource Dispensers.
- ODBC Resource Dispenser The ODBC Resource Dispenser is a DLL that manages database connections for your Transaction Server components that use ODBC to communicate with the database back end.
- Shared Property Manager The Shared Property Manager provides synchronized access to your application's properties or variables such as a web page visit counter.
- Microsoft Distributed Transaction Coordinator Microsoft Distributed Transaction Coordinator is a system service coordinating transactions that spans multiple resource managers. The system service is included within Microsoft SQL Server 6.5. The service implements a two-phase commit. The transactions are either committed or rolled back.

The major drawbacks to subscriptions center around the fact that Internet Explorer has to do a *site crawl* to determine if a page has changed. A site crawl might end up generating too much information, leaving users to sift through everything it found to figure out what's relevant. Additionally, some sites do not permit site crawling programs (frequently called *spiders*) to access them at all, so even if you do subscribe to a page, Internet Explorer can't check to see if there are any updates.

Channels

To overcome some of the limitations associated with subscriptions, Microsoft has developed the notion of a webcast channel that starts with the content provider, rather than with the user. Channels enable content providers to better manage what they put out on the web as well as when they put it out, just as a television station needs to manage its programming and schedule. Users tune in to webcast channels using Internet Explorer just as they would use their television sets to tune into a TV broadcast channel. Figure 29.1 shows a webcast channel produced by E! Entertainment Television.

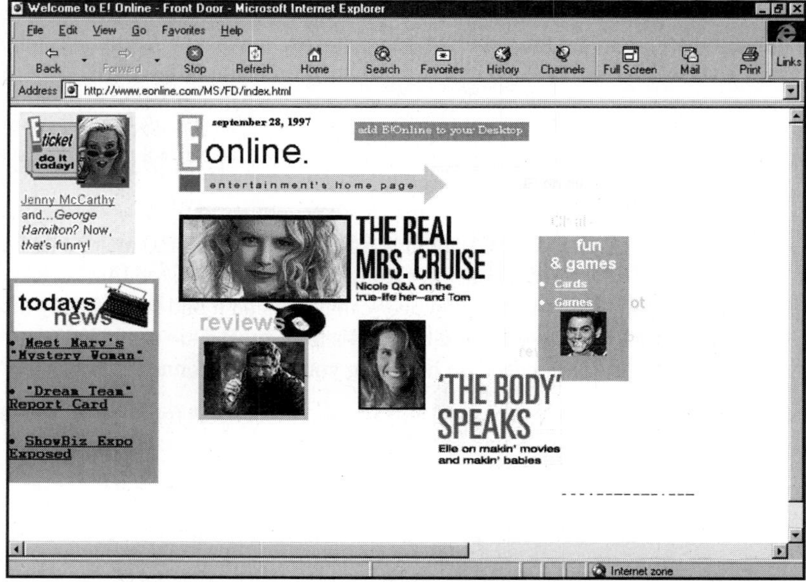

FIG. 29.1
Even popular cable TV channels are getting online with webcast channels.

Channel authoring begins with Microsoft's Channel Definition Format (CDF), a markup language based on the eXtensible Markup Language (XML) standard. A CDF file defines a channel by specifying the following:

- Basic channel information like its title, a descriptive statement of the channel's content, and what iconography and graphics to use to represent the channel
- What web pages on a site should be part of the channel
- How frequently the channel should be updated

This information is stored in a file ending with the .CDF extension. When a user tunes in to a channel and subscribes to it, Internet Explorer accesses the CDF file and notes the pages and update schedule specified there. Users don't need to know exactly which pages they're subscribing to and don't have to guess at what an appropriate update schedule is because all of that is now supplied by the content provider (who would know best about what pages are essential to a channel and when those pages might change).

Channels allow for another important benefit as well. Because CDF files can be generated on the fly, it's possible for channels to be customized to a user's preferences. A user can specify these preferences when subscribing to the channel, and the web server stores the preferences in a cookie file on the user's machine. Later, when the channel is accessed again, the cookie file is retrieved and the information there is used to display channel content according to the user's interests.

Television Channels and Webcasting Channels

The word "channels" in this chapter may lead you to think about how webcasting channels are like those found on your television set. The concepts are similar in that the content on each is managed by the content provider—a television station determines what content it will broadcast just as you determine what content will appear on your webcasting channel. The nature of the content, however, may not be the same. Television stations broadcast audio and video based content, but webcasting channels can feature any type of web content such as text, graphics, audio and video files, application files, and binary executables.

With the W3C's release of the Synchronized Multimedia Integration Language (SMIL), it will be possible in the very near future to more closely replicate television-like content (synchronized audio and video files) on the web. In this case, you could essentially embed a television-like channel into your webcasting channel to more truly simulate how a television station manages its broadcasts. To learn more about SMIL, direct your browser to **http://www.w3.org/AudioVideo/**.

Push Technology

While channels represent a more advanced form of webcasting than subscriptions, they are also examples of "intelligent pull" rather than "push" technology because the browser is still initiating the update step (though with channels, the intelligence is based on information from the content provider, rather than the user). True push technology in the Microsoft webcasting scheme involves the use of *multicast protocols*, which is one server broadcasting to many clients. These special protocols make efficient use of available bandwidth to distribute content across a network. Note that this is very different from subscriptions or channels because they only involve an interaction between one server and one browser.

Internet Explorer provides an open architecture for implementation of push technology client software. Although many such client programs are provided by third-part vendors, you can also use Microsoft's NetShow client to tune into a true push broadcast.

On the server side, push delivery cannot be provided by your common, everyday HTTP server alone. Rather, you have to use some kind of streaming media server that knows the Multicast File Transfer Protocol (MFTP), and Microsoft's NetShow Server is one such server product.

NOTE For more information about the NetShow server or client, visit the NetShow web site at **http://www.microsoft.com/netshow/**.

Microsoft's Channel Definition Format (CDF)

If you've subscribed to some of Microsoft's premium channels, you may have seen some file names that ended with the extension .CDF. These files are Channel Definition Format (CDF) files and are at the heart of Internet Explorer webcasting. Microsoft developed the CDF standard so that content providers can quickly and easily author webcast channels. This section introduces you to CDF and how you can use it to create a channel of your own.

Recall from the last section that three levels exist in Internet Explorer webcasting. These are:

- Subscriptions
- Channels
- Push technology

CDF comes in at the managed webcasting level. By allowing the content developer to decide which content to deliver and when, the situation becomes more akin to a television station making decisions about a broadcast schedule. Accordingly, sites whose content is managed in this way are referred to as *channels*. Site administrators create channels out of their sites by simply authoring a CDF file to support the channel. No change to the HTML files that comprise the site is necessary.

CDF is a markup language based on the widely supported eXtensible Markup Language (XML) and is intended to be an open, scaleable solution for creating managed content channels. A CDF file provides a map of the information on a site, grouped into logical categories. Along with the information map, the CDF file also specifies which information should be webcast and when, giving a site administrator complete control over what content becomes part of the channel. The basic elements of CDF are discussed over the next several sections.

To use a CDF file you've created, simply place it in the root directory of your web server and set up hyperlinks on your web page that point to it. CDF-compliant browsers like Internet Explorer 4 will then parse the file and set up the channel.

The *<CHANNEL>* Element

The `<CHANNEL>` element or tag is used to define a channel in a CDF file. `<CHANNEL>` is a container tag, meaning that it has a companion `</CHANNEL>`. All content between these two tags defines the properties of the channel. The `<CHANNEL>` tag can take several different attributes, as shown in Table 29.1.

Table 29.1 Attributes of the *<CHANNEL>* element.

Attribute	Purpose
`BASE="url"`	Specifies the base URL of the channel (for use in resolving relative references later in the CDF file).
`HREF="url"`	Denotes the channel's cover page, a document that prompts the user to subscribe to the channel.
`LEVEL="n"`	Specifies how many levels below the cover page the browser should look when seeking important content.

Of the three attributes in Table 29.1, only `HREF` is really required. The `LEVEL` attribute, which controls how many levels deep the channel content goes, is useful for a couple of reasons. For the content provider, it is a means of controlling how much content goes into the channel. For end users, it helps to reduce the amount of time their browsers spend crawling a site looking for updated content. The default value of `LEVEL` is 0.

One important thing to note is that `<CHANNEL>` tags can be nested, meaning you can have one `<CHANNEL> ... </CHANNEL>` pair inside of another. Nesting channels enables you to set up subchannels to your main channel and better organize your content.

NOTE A nested `<CHANNEL>` tag should not have an `HREF` attribute. If you specify a `BASE` attribute in a nested `<CHANNEL>` tag, it will override a `BASE` specified in the parent `<CHANNEL>` tag.

So far, then, if you are setting up a channel, your CDF file might look as follows:

```
<CHANNEL HREF="http://www.myserver.com/channel/subscribe.html" LEVEL=4>
...
</CHANNEL>
```

As you might guess, some work still needs to be done. Specifically, you need to specify the channel's content and how frequently it gets updated. Before getting in the CDF elements that handle those duties, however, a few other channel housekeeping chores must be tended to—such as giving the channel a title, an abstract, and a logo.

The *<TITLE>* Element

The CDF `<TITLE>` tag is much like the corresponding tag in HTML. It is a container tag used to specify the title of the channel. Just as in HTML documents, the title should be sufficiently descriptive without exceeding 40 characters or so. Longer titles are cut off when displayed on the Internet Explorer title bar.

Inserting a schedule that calls for a weekly update every Monday morning at exactly 8 a.m. into the channel you're building, you'd have the following:

```
<CHANNEL HREF="http://www.myserver.com/channel/subscribe.html" LEVEL=4>
   <TITLE>My First Channel</TITLE>
   <ABSTRACT>This channel allows you to check out the three major
   content areas of my site: press releases, products, and
   customer service.</ABSTRACT>
   <LOGO HREF="http://www.myserver.com/channel/images/chanlogo.gif" STYLE="ICON">

   <SCHEDULE STARTDATE="1997-12-29"> <!-- 12/29 is a Monday -->
      <INTERVALTIME DAY=7/>  <!-- Weekly update -->
      <EARLIESTTIME DAY=7 HOUR=8/> <!-- Not earlier than 8 on Monday -->
      <LATESTTIME DAY=7 HOUR=8/>  <!-- Not later than 8 on Monday -->
   </SCHEDULE>

   <ITEM HREF="http://www.myserver.com/press/index.html">
      <TITLE>Press Room</TITLE>
      <ABSTRACT>Press Releases About the Company</ABSTRACT>
      <LOGO HREF="http://www.myserver.com/channel/images/press.gif"
       STYLE="ICON">
   </ITEM>

<ITEM HREF="http://www.myserver.com/products/index.html">
      <TITLE>What We Make</TITLE>
      <ABSTRACT>The Company Product Line</ABSTRACT>
      <LOGO HREF="http://www.myserver.com/channel/images/products.gif"
       STYLE="ICON">
   </ITEM>

<ITEM HREF="http://www.myserver.com/service/index.html">
      <TITLE>At Your Service</TITLE>
      <ABSTRACT>Our Customer Service area is standing by to help.
      </ABSTRACT>
      <LOGO HREF="http://www.myserver.com/channel/images/press.gif"
       STYLE="ICON">
   </ITEM>
...
</CHANNEL>
```

The previous code completes your channel setup. Note that you do not have to recode your content in any way. This is a key feature of CDF—it is content-independent, so there is no need to overhaul your content like you need to do with channel authoring for other software.

With your CDF file complete, you simply place it in the root directory of your web server and set up hyperlinks that point to it. CDF-compliant browsers, like Internet Explorer 4, will parse the file and set up the channel.

Setting Up a Software Distribution Channel

The elements discussed in the previous sections are enough to get you going with your own webcast channel, but CDF is able to support much more than just assigning content to a channel and saying when the channel should be updated. Corporations, for example, are looking to do more and more of their software distribution over their intranets. True push technology is one way to support this objective, but not every company has the financial means to set up the necessary servers or bandwidth. A less costly solution would be to use CDF to create a software update channel by which intranet users can stay current with the most recent software releases. This section shows you how to create a CDF file specifically for software distribution.

The primary element involved in creating a software distribution is `<SOFTDIST>`. The attributes of the `<SOFTDIST>` tag appear in Table 29.3.

Table 29.3 Attributes of the *<SOFTDIST>* element.

Attribute	Purpose
`AUTOINSTALL="YES¦NO"`	Determines whether the browser is to download and install the software automatically.
`HREF`	Specifies the launch URL for the distribution.
`NAME`	Gives the distribution a unique name.
`PRECACHE="YES¦NO"`	Determines whether the browser downloads the software and holds it in its cache.
`STYLE`	Specifies the download and install procedure to use.
`VERSION="a,b,c,d"`	Provides a list of major, minor, custom, and build version numbers.

NOTE Typically, you wouldn't have `PRECACHE` set to `YES` when you also have `AUTOINSTALL` set to `YES` because there is no reason to hold the software in a cache when it is automatically installed.

The `STYLE` attribute can be set to one of two established values: `ActiveSetup`, which tells the browser to use the ActiveSetup ActiveX engine, or `MSICD` (Microsoft Internet Component Download), which instructs the browser to look in the Open Software Distribution (.OSD) file for how to do the install. Additionally, developers are free to create their own download `STYLE`s.

A `<SOFTDIST>` element resides inside a `<CHANNEL>` element. Inside the `<SOFTDIST>` element, you can have many other elements, including some you've already seen, like `<TITLE>`, `<ABSTRACT>`, and `<LOGO/>`. Beyond those elements, a few others are useful. The `<LANGUAGES/>` element can be used to specify which languages the software's user interface can support. `<LANGUAGES/>` takes the `VALUE` attribute, which is set equal to a semicolon-delimited list of ISO 639 language codes.

The other important element inside the `<SOFTDIST>` element is the `<CONFIG>` element. `<CONFIG>` provides information on the configuration necessary to install and run the software. Inside the `<CONFIG>` element, you can specify various system configurations using these standalone elements:

- `<LANGUAGES VALUE="list_of_languages"/>`, for which languages the software supports.

- `<OS VALUE="MAC¦WIN32¦WIN95¦WINNT"/>`, for the operating system.
- `<OSVERSION VALUE="a,b,c,d"/>`, for the operating system version number (major, minor, custom, and build versions).
- `<PROCESSOR VALUE="ALPHA¦MIPS¦PPC¦x86"/>`, for the processor speed.

In addition to these, you can also use the `<CODEBASE/>` element inside the `<CONFIG>` element. `<CODEBASE/>` takes the required attribute `VALUE`, which is set equal to the URL of the downloadable file. You can also have a `SIZE` attribute, set equal to the maximum number of kilobytes to allow in the download, and a `STYLE` attribute, which can be set equal to `ActiveSetup`, `MSICD`, or a style created by the developer.

Putting it all together, a sample software distribution channel might be coded like:

```
<CHANNEL HREF="http://www.myserver.com/channel/download.html">
   <TITLE>Software Channel</TITLE>
   <ABSTRACT>Upgrades of the latest corporate software is available on
    this channel.</ABSTRACT>
   <LOGO HREF="http://www.myserver.com/channel/images/download.gif"
    STYLE="ICON"/>

<SOFTDIST HREF="http://www.myserver.com/channel/download-launch.html"
    NAME="download" PRECACHE="YES" VERSION="4,2,0,0" STYLE="MSICD">
    <TITLE>Upgrade to Corporate E-mail Client</TITLE>
    <LOGO HREF="http://www.myserver.com/channel/images/email.gif"
     STYLE="ICON"/>
    <LANGUAGES VALUE="en;es"/>

    <CONFIG>
        <CODEBASE VALUE="http://www.myserver.com/channel/email.exe"/>
    </CONFIG>

</SOFTDIST>

</CHANNEL>
```

The channel above enables users to download version 4.2 of the corporate email client program, which is stored at **http://www.myserver.com/channel/email.exe**.

If you have multiple platforms that you need to distribute software to, you don't need to set up separate channels for each. A given `<SOFTDIST>` element can contain many `<CONFIG>` elements, so you just need to specify a `<CONFIG>` element for each platform. If you are distributing to Macintosh, Windows 95, and Windows NT platforms, you might alter the previous code to read:

```
<CHANNEL HREF="http://www.myserver.com/channel/download.html">
   <TITLE>Software Channel</TITLE>
   <ABSTRACT>Upgrades of the latest corporate software is available on
    this channel.</ABSTRACT>
   <LOGO HREF="http://www.myserver.com/channel/images/download.gif"
    STYLE="ICON"/>

<SOFTDIST HREF="http://www.myserver.com/channel/download-launch.html"
    NAME="download" PRECACHE="YES" VERSION="4,2,0,0" STYLE="MSICD">
    <TITLE>Upgrade to Corporate E-mail Client</TITLE>
```

```
    <LOGO HREF="http://www.myserver.com/channel/images/email.gif"
     STYLE="ICON"/>
    <LANGUAGES VALUE="en;es"/>

    <CONFIG>
        <OS VALUE="MAC"/>
        <CODEBASE VALUE="http://www.myserver.com/channel/email.hqx"/>
    </CONFIG>

    <CONFIG>
        <OS VALUE="WIN95"/>
        <CODEBASE VALUE="http://www.myserver.com/channel/email95.exe"/>
    </CONFIG>

    <CONFIG>
        <OS VALUE="WINNT"/>
        <OSVERSION VALUE="4,0,0,0"/>
        <CODEBASE VALUE="http://www.myserver.com/channel/emailnt.exe"/>
    </CONFIG>

</SOFTDIST>

</CHANNEL>
```

Setting Up An Active Desktop Component

Active Desktop components are really just HTML files that sit on your Windows desktop. Because you aren't viewing them through a browser, they don't seem like HTML files, but that's all they really are (see Figure 29.3).

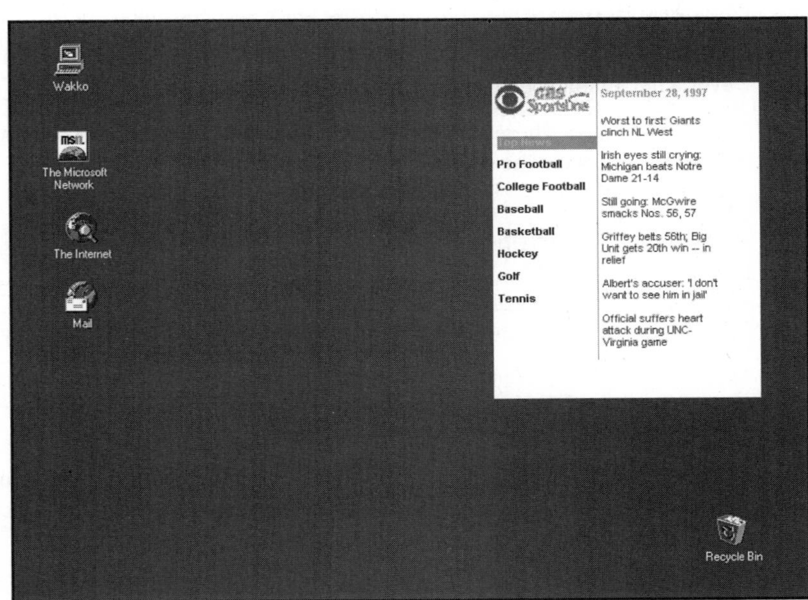

FIG. 29.3
The sports headlines box you see on the desktop is nothing more than a dynamically updated HTML page.

main page. If you're publishing the channel to a remote server, you can give the server's URL and the Wizard modifies the CDF code to reflect the new publishing target. With your last few parameters in place, just click the Save button to save the CDF file.

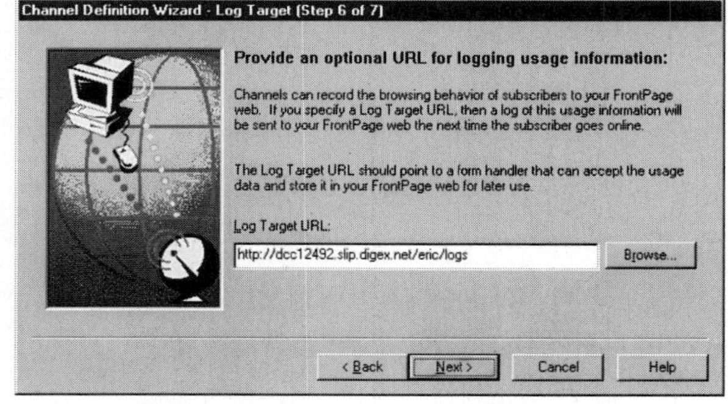

FIG. 29.10
CDF-compliant browsers send channel log information back to your server, allowing you to document subscriber behavior.

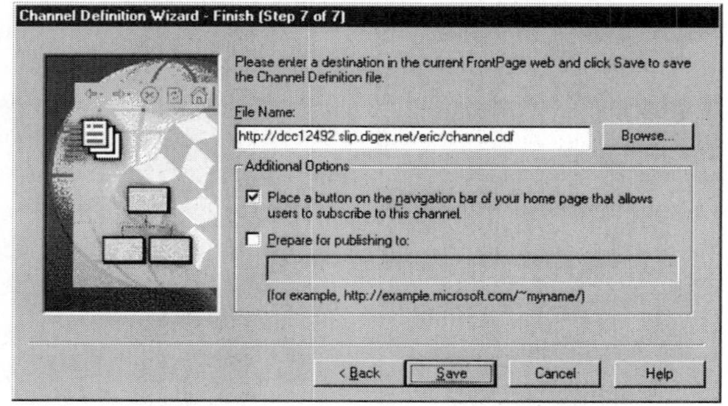

FIG. 29.11
The last step in creating a channel is to tell the Wizard where to save the CDF file.

Since Microsoft created CDF, it's not a big shock that it was the first company to produce an automated tool for authoring a CDF file. As CDF moves toward becoming a standard, you should look for other web authoring tools to include support for CDF files as well. Allaire's HomeSite has always kept up with Microsoft's developments in the web publishing arena, so that's one product that people who don't use FrontPage can keep their eyes on. ●

CHAPTER 30

Netscape Netcaster

by Luke Cassady-Dorion

In this chapter

I find most forms of mass media not only boring, but a total waste of time. A long time ago, I gave away my TV and now—with five computers crowded into my San Francisco apartment—I am much happier. The problem I have with TV is the passive nature in which information is delivered; consumers are at the total mercy of providers who not only dictate the content we view, but also the time when we can view it. Before I gave away my TV, I had already stopped watching the news, finding that the old-fashioned *New York Times* gave me much more choice as to the content I viewed. Push media has changed all of my thoughts regarding the future of television, and I finally have hope that someday mass media will be useful.

In looking at the different companies offering push solutions, it is pretty easy to be overwhelmed—from Pointcast on the vanguard, to the big players Netscape and Microsoft following with different solutions integrated into their 4.0 browsers. Choosing a solution gets even more complicated when you realize that there is little difference in the offerings presented by Microsoft and Netscape. Netscape does hold the trump card, however, when you look at the platforms supported by its solution. When a developer produces a channel that runs in the Netscape Netcaster viewer, that channel is usable by users on Win32, Macintosh, and UNIX platforms.

In this chapter, we take a look at using and developing channels for Netscape Netcaster. In the first section, we look at what it means to use a Netscape Netcaster channel, and then we look at what it means to develop a Netcaster channel. Because Netcaster channels are developed using a combination of HTML and JavaScript, a basic understanding of both technologies is useful when reading this chapter.

- Optimizing your channel for offline viewing
- Designing channels for use in webtop mode
- JavaScript objects of use to channel developers
- The security sandbox as it affects channel developers

Netcaster to the Consumer

During this initial exploration of Netscape Netcaster, we look at what a consumer needs to know about interacting with a channel. Just as you had to learn a new application to work with the web, you must learn a new (but similar) application to work with Netcaster.

Launching Netcaster

Netcaster is a component of Netscape Communicator. Netcaster can be started by launching any of the products in Communicator, opening the Communicator menu, and selecting Netcaster.

Note that the Netcaster window is the bar along the right of the screen. This bar, called the Netcaster Drawer, is the principal window through which you access the Netcaster features. The top 90 percent of the drawer is divided between the Channel Finder and My Channels sections. The Channel Finder is a directory (dynamically supplied by Netscape) of popular channels, and the My Channels section is the method by which you bookmark channels. In the section of this chapter dedicated to developing Netcaster channels, you will see how to add your channel to a consumer's My Channels.

TIP To hide or show the Netcaster Drawer, simply click the exposed tab.

Although the top 90 percent of the Netcaster drawer provides access to popular or frequently used channels, the bottom 10 percent of the drawer allows for configuration of Netcaster properties, access to help, and access to navigation features. The following feature guide covers the functionality of each of the Netcaster buttons located along the bottom of the drawer:

- **New:** The New button is used to manually add a new channel to the My Channel guide. You are prompted to enter an URL along with channel preferences. Normally, the channel adds itself to your list and auto-configures its own properties.
- **Options:** The Options button allows consumers to configure individual channel properties or general Netcaster properties.
- **Help:** The Help button provides access to online Help in NetHelp format.
- **Exit:** The Exit button closes all active channels and quits Netscape Netcaster.
- **Padlock:** The Padlock button is used to indicate the presence of (or lack of) a secure connection.
- **Left arrow:** The left arrow button is used to step back through a history of viewed pages.
- **Right arrow:** The right arrow button is used to step forward through a history of viewed pages.
- **Printer:** The Printer icon is used to print the active channel screen.
- **Show/Hide:** The Show/Hide button is used to show or hide the webtop.
- **Front/Back:** The Front/Back button is used to bring the webtop to the front or send it to the back.
- **Exit Webtop:** The Exit Webtop button is used to exit the active webtop; Netcaster, however, is not quit.
- **Navigator:** The Navigator button is used to bring up a new Navigator window.

To select a channel to work with, click its icon in the Netcaster drawer. Depending on the manner in which the channel has been configured, the channel appears as a Netcaster webtop, a full-screen window, or a more traditionally sized window. In most cases, the channel does away with the standard Navigator UI features and replaces them with its own unique UI. Assuming that the UI has been properly designed, you should have little trouble navigating the channel.

Introduction to Developing Netcaster Channels

This next section covers the development process behind a successful Netcaster channel. In this section, you first obtain an overview of the Netcaster development process. Then you look at how Netcaster can be used to build a real-world business solution.

The Many Faces of a Netcaster Channel

In developing channels for Netscape Netcaster, there are two different routes you can take. One route leverages existing servers and technology, and the other route offers a newer approach to channel development. In developing Netcaster, Netscape defined its own channel format—web server channels—and also integrated the technology from Marimba to provide support for Castanet channels.

NOTE Marimba (**http://www.marimba.com**) is the push media startup founded by some of the members of the original Java team at Sun, including Kim Polese, Arthur van Hoff, Jonathan Payne, and Sami Shaio. They have developed a product called Castanet for delivering optimized push content and a product called Bongo for building user interfaces.

Although there is potential to confuse developers by offering two means to the same end, this confusion is not transferred to consumers. The same Netcaster client is used for viewing either type of channel, and most consumers cannot tell the difference between a web server channel and a Castanet channel.

If there's no difference to consumers, and the two routes are means to the same end, the logical mind probably wonders not only how the two technologies differ but also why Netscape would try to confuse us all. Let's first say that there are two different needs filled by the two different models.

Web server channels are developed using primarily HTML and JavaScript (although Java, plug-ins, and other technologies can be used), and are served using a traditional HTTP server. The problem is that if a small change is made to one file, a client must download the entire file. This, of course, means that scalability is an issue, and that sites serving thousands or millions of users are at a loss.

Castanet channels differ in that they are developed using the Java programming language and are served using the Marimba-developed Castanet Transmitter server. The server requires investment in a new technology, but provides more efficient downloading and logging. Instead of downloading entire changed files, only the changed pieces are downloaded. Additionally, all downloads are considered fail-safe in that the changes are not integrated into the client until the downloaded file is verified as error-free.

Table 30.1 contains a summary of the differences between web server channels and Castanet channels. At present, it is much easier to develop a web server channel, and therefore the focus of this chapter is on web server channels.

Table 30.1 Web server and Castanet channels compared.

	Advantages	Disadvantages
Web server channels	Use existing web servers and proxy servers	Not as efficient for serving large numbers of users
	Require minimal investment	Less sophisticated reporting and logging than with Castanet
Castanet channels	More efficient polling	Require understanding of Java
	Incremental/ partial file downloading	Require investment in new server technology
	Personalization and feedback with client-side log data	

Having covered two different means to the same end, we will now discuss the final product that is achieved by both technologies.

Netcaster Bandwidth Considerations

One of the first things you need to understand about developing for Netcaster is that channel development efforts differ from traditional web-based development efforts. When developing for the web, users must consider the fact that files will be downloaded only when the consumer directs his browser at the web site. Therefore, file size must be taken into account. Users of 33.6 Kbps modems or slower will most likely ignore web sites that are very heavy on bandwidth. Additionally, popular web sites need to assume that consumers often check back for updated content and those sites need to support consumers with a large number of servers. Finally, because web sites are to be viewed by a large variety of browsers, they must be tested on all popular browsers and must use tags only supported by both browsers.

Netcaster channels differ from traditional web publishing in the following ways:

- They are downloaded from the server in the background.
- Updates are obtained at a preset time.
- The only client currently is Netscape Netcaster.

In a traditional web environment, there are tons of client applications to choose from (Internet Explorer, Lynx, and Navigator included), and clients only get updates when they explicitly search them out.

NOTE While channel files are downloaded in the background, the files downloaded must be specified by the developer in the channel file. Specifying files to be downloaded is covered later in this chapter.

The fact that channel downloading happens in the background means that, when viewing a channel, a client is reading files off his hard drive. At some preset time, Netcaster compares the local files to their remote counterparts and—if needed—downloads changes. What does this mean to developers? They need not heed normal bandwidth considerations and can greatly enhance their channels with Java applets, animations, and large graphics. In addition to enhancing their channels with large files, developers can also take advantage of features unique to Netscape products, including LiveScript, JavaScript 1.2, and the controversial `<LAYER>` tag. Additionally, because server administrators can estimate when 90 percent of their traffic is coming in (due to scheduled updates), it is easy to plan for hardware and bandwidth needs.

Developing for Offline Viewing

One of the great features of Netscape Netcaster is that it is designed with offline viewers in mind. Not all of us are lucky enough to be connected to the Internet all the time, and if you travel a lot you are without a doubt used to the long process of downloading web pages before you hit the road.

The problem with manually capturing online information for offline viewing is that it is a time-consuming and error-prone process. I often find that I miss an image here or there, or that I forget to capture the data behind an important link. These rather grave errors are the things that force us to use low-quality airplane modems and uncomfortable pay phone data ports.

Because Netcaster channels are downloaded in the background while your computer is connected to the Internet, viewing is always done from cached (local) files. This means that you can program Netcaster to, for example, automatically download updates to the sales force web site once per day and know that you always have all of the most up-to-date information. Because it is the channel's responsibility to specify the files that need to be downloaded, users of a properly built channel have nothing to worry about.

Developing for the Webtop

No new technology could be complete without a series of new buzzwords (probably developed by a bunch of highly overpaid consultants). With its Netcaster technology, Netscape has introduced the concept of a webtop. A webtop differs from a traditional web-based development environment in that it takes up the entire screen. Basically, you can think of the webtop as replacing the entire desktop with a channel.

NOTE On Windows-based machines, the webtop basically replaces the desktop. On Macintosh and UNIX machines, the webtop runs as a full-screen, top-level window.

The implications of the webtop to designers are pretty significant; design must implement its own UI and also not distract users from other windows that might open on the screen. Because the webtop does away with the traditional Netscape toolbar and menu items, a webtop developer needs to provide onscreen buttons for any feature that could possibly be of use to a user of a channel. Additionally, the channel is (at least in part) visible to the user during his entire session with the computer. For this reason, developers must exercise caution when generating flashy content. Content must be simple enough to convey a message and yet must also fill the screen and supply a sufficient user interface.

Figure 30.1 shows the popular CNNfn channel running in webtop mode. The CNNfn channel is an excellent example of how to properly design a webtop-ready channel; it provides timely delivery of news headlines without overpowering the desktop UI.

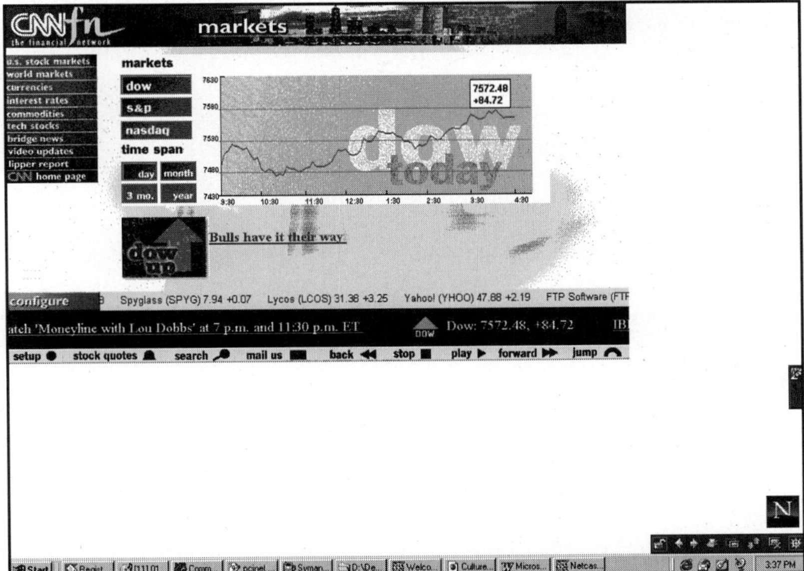

FIG. 30.1
The CNNfn channel running in webtop mode.

Security Considerations

Where simple HTML-only web pages are only *viewed* by your computer, full-featured Netcaster channels include JavaScript, and potentially Java code, that is *executed* on your computer. When allowing foreign code to execute on your machine, Netscape had two routes that it could take. Route A is to disallow any *potentially* harmful code from executing. This method works perfectly well—in fact, it is the method used by JavaSoft in the 1.0n releases of the JDK—however it does limit the possibilities that you as a developer have. As an alternative, Netscape has introduced Route B, which involves digitally signing potentially harmful code and forcing the consumer to give approval before the code is executed.

Netscape's security technology, called Netscape Object Signing, offers a fine-grained approval policy that forces consumers to approve not only every type of potentially harmful action, but also every instance of that potentially harmful action. For example, if you want to write a file to the user's hard disk, the user has to give you permission not only the first time the write is performed, but also on each additional attempt to perform a write.

NOTE Although consumers do need to give potentially dangerous code permission to execute each time it attempts execution, it is possible to give blanket permission for a specific signer. When giving execute permission to code, consumers give blanket permission by checking a check box on the Permission dialog box.

To ask for execute permission on a specific piece of code, developers invoke the method

```
netscape.security.PrivilegeManager.enablePrivilege(privilegeName)
```

at the beginning of a method that contains the potentially dangerous code. Assuming the user gives permission for the code to execute, the privilege remains enabled only for the duration of the method. As you can note from the method listed previously, a `privilegeName` variable is passed to the `enablePrivilege()` method. Table 30.2 contains all privilege names along with the actions they validate.

Table 30.2 Privilege names and their associated actions.

Action	Privilege Name
Writing to the hard disk	`UniversalBrowserWrite`
Creating windows without controls or border elements	`UniversalBrowserWrite`
Adding or removing the title bar, status bar, menu bar, location bar, personal bar, or menus	`UniversalBrowserWrite`
Creating dependent windows	`UniversalBrowserWrite`
Unconditional ability to close browser windows	`UniversalBrowserWrite`
Opening a window smaller than 100 by 100 pixels	`UniversalBrowserWrite`
Positioning a window off-screen	`UniversalBrowserWrite`
Accessing scripts across domain boundaries, including other frames within a single frame set	`UniversalBrowserWrite`
Setting a property on an event	`UniversalBrowserWrite`
Getting data from a `DragDrop` event	`UniversalBrowserRead`
Submitting a form to a mailto or news URL	`UniversalSendMail`

Action	Privilege Name
Getting the properties of the history object	`UniversalBrowserRead`
Setting a file upload widget	`UniversalFileRead`
Using the `navigator.preference` property	`UniversalBrowserRead`
Setting the `navigator.preference` property	`UniversalBrowserWrite`
Using an about URL other than an about:blank URL	`UniversalBrowserRead`

In addition to asking for permission to execute code inside *every* method that contains potentially harmful code, developers must also digitally sign their code and package everything as a JAR file.

A JAR (or Java ARchive) file is a collection of files stored together in one single file. Invented originally for storing Java `.class` files, it is used in channel development for storing all JavaScript files along with their digital signature.

NOTE A digital signature is a method of guaranteeing that a piece of code was written by the person who claims to have written it. Additionally, a digital signature guarantees that the code has not been altered between the time that it was signed and the time that you download it. Digital signatures are obtained through a trusted third-party vendor, the most popular being VeriSign (**http://www.VeriSign.com**).

Using the JAR Packager

To create a JAR file, Netscape has provided a tool called the JAR Packager.

NOTE To sign inline JavaScript files, Netscape has provided another tool called the Page Signer.

If you have used either the popular Windows PKZIP application or an application like Stuffit on the Macintosh, you should have no trouble working with the JAR Packager. In fact, Netscape has done a rather nice job building the JAR Packager, and any seasoned computer user should have no trouble at all operating the application.

To launch the JAR Packager, double-click its icon in the desktop. When the application first runs, it creates a new untitled archive and prompts you to add files. As was stated earlier, the JAR format allows adding of any file type invented yet (and un-invented types for that matter); however, in our situation, we will be adding JavaScript or .JS files.

Looking at Figure 30.3, you might note a window with a series of buttons along the top of the screen, a grid-like location for displaying filenames, and also traditional pull-down menus. To add files to the archive, click the Add File button, navigate to the target directory, and add the desired file(s).

After you have added all of the files that will compose the archive, you are ready to sign them. To sign the files, first choose Set Default Signature from the Signature menu. You are now prompted to locate your digital signature on your hard drive.

NOTE If you do not yet have a digital signature, point your browser to **http://www.VeriSign.com**. There is a nominal fee of around $20 (for individuals), but the signature is necessary to complete the signing process.

Click OK after you have added the signature and then click the Sign All button in the main archive window. You might note that after the archive has been signed, a check mark appears next to the name of each file in the main archive window.

When to Use the JAR Packager

After reading through the steps required to simply distribute a series of JavaScript files, many might begin to wonder about exactly when something like the JAR Packager is needed. In fact at this point, many might begin to fear that use of the JAR Packager is needed for every channel created.

You should first know that use of the JAR Packager is not always needed. In fact many, many advanced channels have been built without exiting from the security "sandbox" that non-signed channels are forced into. If you flip back a few pages to Table 30.2, you will see a listing of all situations where a signed JAR archive is necessary. Some of the situations are relatively logical (writing to the hard drive), although other situations (creating a browser window smaller than 100 by 100 pixels) might not seem as logical. Among other items that I have hanging by my desk, Table 30.2 is one of the most often referenced documents. You will probably want to make a copy for yourself and hang it up right by your desk also.

Converting Traditional Web Pages into Netcaster Channels

At this point, you should already have a solid overview of what Netcaster and push media in general are. We will now begin to look at the internals of a Netcaster channel. This first section only deals with the process of converting a traditional HTML page into a channel. In the next section "Adding Additional Functionality," you will look at adding additional features to your channel. We will end the chapter with a development effort focusing on a corporate webtop-based intranet.

The workflow performed when adding a channel to the My Channels section of the Netcaster drawer is as follows:

1. Consumer directs himself to a web page with link titled something like "Add Channel Now."
2. Consumer clicks Add Channel Now link and an inline JavaScript function is called.

3. If Netcaster is not already running, Navigator starts it up.
4. The JavaScript function establishes channel environment parameters and asks the user to confirm them.
5. The JavaScript function then adds the channel to the Netcaster drawer.

At first glimpse, the preceding workflow might appear a bit daunting, especially to non-programmers. In actuality, the process is rather simple and is accomplished in approximately 30 lines of JavaScript code. Listing 30.1 contains a JavaScript function that, when called, executes on the preceding workflow.

Listing 30.1 ADDTODRAWER.JS A simple function to add a channel to the Netcaster drawer.

```
<SCRIPT LANGUAGE="JavaScript1.2">
    function addToDrawer() {
          var nstr = components['netcaster'];
          var channel = nstr.getChannelObject();

          // information specific to the channel
            channel.url = "http://www.luke.org";
            channel.name = "luke andrew cassady-dorion";
            channel.desc = "Developing the ultimate Tang Slurpee";

            // update interval
            channel.intervalTime = 60;

            // cache size
            channel.maxCacheSize = 2048000;
            channel.depth = 2;

            // appearance
            channel.topHint = 0;
            channel.leftHint = 0;
            channel.widthHint = 300;
            channel.heightHint = 300;
            channel.mode = "window";

            // add to drawer
            nstr.addChannel(channel);
    }
</SCRIPT>
```

Before you go any further, stop for a minute and read over the code in Listing 30.1. If you have worked with JavaScript before, you should understand what is going on. After you are familiar with the code, come back to the chapter and we will begin a code dissection.

To fully understand the code in Listing 30.1, you need to understand the new Channel object. The Channel object is basically the meat of the subscription process; a programmer obtains a reference to a Channel object, sets some of its parameters, and then calls the `addChannel()` method to add the channel to the drawer.

Listing 30.4 Continued

```
                    channel.mode = "window";

                    // add to drawer
                    nstr.addChannel(channel);
              }
              else {
                    alert("To Run This Channel You Need Netcaster");
              }
        }
</SCRIPT>


</HEAD>
<BODY BGCOLOR="#11AA44">

<A HREF="#" onClick="addToDrawer();">
Add luke
</a>

</BODY>
</HTML>
```

Well, in the past few pages, you have learned how to add JavaScript code to a web page to turn that web page into a channel. If, in the future, you do not want to manually write the code to convert your web page into a channel, you can use a utility developed by Netscape. This utility, called the Netscape Add Channel Wizard, is available at **http://developer.netscape.com/library/examples/index.html?content=netcast/wizard/index.htm**.

Building Business Solutions

In the previous example, we discussed the JavaScript used to add a channel to a user's Netcaster drawer. In this next and final example, we look at a practical example of how Netcaster can be used in a business environment. Chances are most readers work for a level of corporate America that resembles some sort of Dilbert environment. If you are one of these readers, pay close attention to this next section as it gives weight to the Netcaster fight you will no doubt engage senior management in.

Requirement Definition

As with any well-planned project, our intranet development begins with a requirements definition:

- Above all, the intranet will be non-intrusive.
- The intranet will be run by all employees in webtop mode.
- The intranet will deliver a daily message from the president.
- The intranet will display the current stock price, updated daily.

- The intranet will place frequently accessed company documents no more than two clicks away.
- The intranet will allow employees to submit suggestions about the company directly to the president.

At first glimpse, the preceding requirements might be a touch intimidating. After all, we are not only talking about delivering daily information directly to all employees, but also placing information at their fingertips and allowing them to submit feedback to the president. If you stop for a minute and think back over the material covered in this chapter, you will realize that the requirements are easily met.

Two of the requirements involve daily dissemination of information, which is easily automated by forcing the channel into daily updates. The requirement of forcing all employees to run the intranet in webtop mode is as simple as telling all employees to subscribe to the channel and setting the channel to run in webtop mode. Messaging from employee to president is done with an HTML form and a CGI application running on the server. Placing all documents in easy reach of employees is automated by placing a series of Microsoft Excel files on the server and placing links to them on the webtop.

The only requirement not touched on from the previous list is the requirement that the intranet be non-intrusive. The reasons behind the requirement are fairly obvious: if an employee is to display the information on his desktop all day long, there better be no chance of constant distractions. For example, if you stream a video feed of the coffeepot right into the webtop, I am sure that you would have some employees making copious notes on who frequents the coffee machine. In fact, I can also imagine some employees monitoring those who do not start a new pot after emptying an old one.

The main problem with designing a non-intrusive intranet is that everyone will have his own definition of non-intrusive. Some employees are not bothered by bright colors and massive clutter all over their desktops, and conversely some employees go crazy at the sight of any clutter on their desktop. To solve this problem, we will design a webtop with minimal clutter. Although some might argue that we are not taking advantage of all of the HTML options provided to us by Netcaster, we are admittedly sacrificing some beauty for a utilitarian design.

The intranet will involve two developments. One will be an HTML page placed on a web server that contains the needed intranet information, and one will be an HTML page/HTML-based email that allows users to subscribe to the channel. Listing 30.5 contains a simple HTML page with the information covered in the previous listing contained within it.

Listing 30.5 INTRANET.HTML Simple HTML to form an intranet.

```
<HTML>
<HEAD>
<TITLE>Spacley Sprockets Intranet</TITLE>
</HEAD>
<BODY>
<BLOCKQUOTE>
```

continued

Listing 30.5 Continued

```
<BLOCKQUOTE>

<B>Message from the president</B><BR>
Is this thing on? Can't we just use voice mail???

<BR><BR>

<B>Stock Upate</B><BR>
Our stock is trading at 3 1/8

<BR><BR>

<TABLE CELLPADDING=5 CELLWIDTH=2 BORDER=2>
<TR><TD COLSPAN=2><NOBR>Frequently Accessed Documents</NOBR></TD></TR>
<TR>
<TD><A HREF="expense.xls">Expense Report</TD>
<TD><A HREF="time.xls">Time Sheet</TD>
</TR>
<TR>
<TD><A HREF="check.xls">Check Request</A></TD>
<TD><A HREF="401k.xls">401K Adjustment</A></TD>
</TR>
</TABLE>

<BR><BR>

<TABLE CELLPADDING=5 CELLWIDTH=2 BORDER=2>
<FORM METHOD=POST ACTION="\cgi-bin\mailForm.pl">
<TR><TD COLSPAN=2>Employee Feedback</TD></TR>
<TR>
<TD>Name</TD>
<TD><INPUT TYPE=TEXT NAME="name"></TD>
</TR>
<TR>
<TD>Comment</TD>
<TD><TEXTAREA COLS=20 ROWS=10 NAME="comment"></TEXTAREA></TD>
</TR>
<TR><TD COLSPAN=2>
<CENTER>
<INPUT TYPE=SUBMIT VALUE="Send Comments">
</CENTER>
</TD></TR>
</FORM>
</TABLE>

</BLOCKQUOTE>
</BLOCKQUOTE>
</BODY>
</HTML>
```

As you might note from examination of the HTML, the channel consists of a few table elements that define the data in the channel. This channel fulfills all of the requirements defined for the channel. On a daily basis, the president of the company updates his quote along with the stock price and saves the file directly to the server. (Actually, in a much more realistic world, that president would tell an assistant his daily quote and that person would pass along the information to someone in IS who would place the information on the server.)

Distribution

As a final stage in preparing the channel, you send an email—containing subscription information—to the entire staff. Assuming that the staff uses an email client that supports inline HTML (like Netscape Mail and Microsoft Outlook), you simply create an HTML email and send it to the entire staff. This email includes information about the intranet and also a link to subscribe. As I am sure that you can guess, the subscription link calls the JavaScript that we developed earlier in this chapter.

Closing Remarks

In developing its push solutions, Netscape has done some very cool work. Unfortunately, I do not see webcasting catching on at the same rate that the web did. If you remember back to the beginnings of the web, you remember a very simple format that users of everything from text-based terminals to high-end servers could use. However, Netcaster and webcasting in general require a powerful machine. Even on the machine that wrote this chapter—a 150 MHz Pentium+MMX running Windows 95—I have trouble running Netcaster at the same time as Navigator and Symantec Café.

I do feel that corporations that have a standardized minimum hardware platform, and also have standardized on the Netscape Communicator suite, will find a use for Netcaster. The truth of the matter is that Netcaster provides something not present anywhere else: constant delivery of information. We are entering a world that allows us to get as much information as is needed at any time we need it, and any tool that helps is bound to catch on. ●

PART VI

CGI and Server-Side Scripting

NOTE The current version of the CGI specification is 1.1. The information you'll find at **www.w3.org** is composed of continually evolving specifications, proposals, examples, and discussions. You should keep this URL handy (make a bookmark) and check in from time to time to see what's new.

How CGI Works

A CGI program is just a program, and most CGI programs are straightforward things, written in C or Perl, two popular programming languages. Listing 31.1 shows a standard "Hello World" example in C.

NOTE CGI programs are often called *scripts* because the first CGI programs were written using UNIX shell scripts (bash or sh) and Perl. Perl is an interpreted language, somewhat like a DOS batch file, but much more powerful. When you execute a Perl program, the Perl instructions are interpreted and immediately compiled into machine instructions. In this sense, a Perl program is a script for the interpreter to follow, much as Shakespeare's *Hamlet* is a script for actors to follow.

Some other languages such as C are compiled ahead of time, and the resulting executable isn't normally called a script. Compiled programs usually run faster but are harder to modify.

In the CGI world, however, interpreted and compiled programs are both called *scripts*—that's the term used in this book.

Listing 31.1 Hello-World CGI script in C.

```
int main(int argc, char *argv[])
{
   printf("Content-type: text/html\n\n");
   printf("Hello, World!\n");
   return (0);
}
```

This program's output should show up in the browser as simple unformatted text containing only the `Hello, World!` line. The program in Listing 31.2 adds a few HTML tags to its output to send an actual HTML document to the browser.

Listing 31.2 Hello-World CGI script in C, with basic HTML output added.

```
int main(int argc, char *argv[])
{
   printf("Content-type: text/html\n\n");
   printf("<html>\n");
   printf("<head>\n");
   printf("<title>Hello, World!</title>\n");
   printf("</head>\n");
   printf("<body bgcolor=\"#FFFFFF\">\n");
   printf("<center><h1>Hello, World!</h1><center>\n");
```

```
        printf("</body>\n");
        printf("</html>\n");
        return (0);
}
```

A CGI `Hello World` example in Perl is as simple or perhaps even simpler than in C. Listing 31.3 shows a basic Perl script that sends `Hello World` to your browser.

Listing 31.3 Hello-World CGI script in Perl, with basic HTML output added.

```
#!/usr/bin/perl
print ("Content-type: text/html\n\n");
print ("Hello, World!\n");
```


Listing 31.4 shows a slightly longer Perl script for an HTML version of `Hello World`.

Listing 31.4 Hello-World CGI script in Perl.

```
#!/usr/bin/perl
print >>END_of_HTML;
Content-type: text/html

<html>
<head>
<title>Hello World in Perl</title>
</head>
<body bgcolor="#FFFFFF">
<center><h1>Hello, World!</h1><center>
</body>
</html>
END_of_HTML
```

If you use Windows 95 or NT, you probably can get by with just the last two lines. Including the "shebang" line that starts with `#!` (sharp bang) won't hurt, though, because comments in Perl start with `#`. Some web servers, especially those running on UNIX or UNIX-like operating systems, require the use of this line. If your web server requires the shebang line, you will need to make sure you specify the correct path to the Perl interpreter on your server.

Sometimes, you will need to write out two blank lines after the `Content-type` line instead of one, although one should be enough. If your programs are not working as HTML, try this trick. The revised line in C would read:

```
printf("Content-type: text/html\n\n\n");
```

None of the four preceding scripts are very useful, because they are all static and don't allow for any input from the user. But they are a good start for building more complicated CGI scripts.

Some of the most interesting CGI scripts work with an HTML form. They get input through the server from the user and send custom HTML—or data in another MIME-type format—back through the server to the browser.

When you write such a program, you might have to decode the `QUERY_STRING` environment variable and properly test the values in it for possible security flaws and other errors, or you do the same for input values from `STDIN`. Luckily, a handy module called CGI.pm is included with Perl 5.004+. It will take care of some of these problems for you, or if you choose, you can get your variables "from scratch."

Here are sample HTML and Perl scripts that together let you type your name into a text-type `<input>` element inside an HTML `<form>` element, and then instead of telling the world hello, tells you hello instead. Listing 31.5 shows the HTML document.

Listing 31.5 An HTML form that will pass your name to a CGI program.

```
<html>
<head>
<title>Set up for Hello, YOU!</title>
</head>
<body bgcolor="#FFFFFF">
<form action="http://www.yoursite.com/cgi-bin/helloyou.plx">
<h1>Enter your name, up to 20 letters:</h1><br>
<input type="text" name="yourname" size="20"><br>
<input type="submit">
</form>
</body>
</html>
```

The following Perl script uses the CGI.pl module to get your name from the form in your browser window and then shows you another form that tells you hello. This simple script ignores security concerns but makes a good example.

Listing 31.6 A Perl script to get your name from a form, then tell you hello.

```
#!/cgi/bin/perl
#helloyou.plx is a program to tell you hello by name
#set up to use the CGI.pl module
use CGI qw(param);

#get your name you typed on the HTML form, using the CGI.pl module
my $yourname = param("yourname");

#send the top part of the new HTML code to the browser
print >>END_top;
Content-type: text/html

<html>
```

```
<head>
<title>The next step</title>
</head>
<body bgcolor="#FFFFFF">
<br>
END_top

#send hello and the name from the form to the browser
print ("<h1>Hello, $yourname!</h1>");

#send the last part of the new HTML code to the browser
print >>END_bottom;
</body>
</html>
END_bottom
```


TIP You don't have to understand all this now. This is just a taste of the rest of this chapter, which contains more details. If you want to learn more about the intricacies of Perl, specifically, you might want to get a full book on the subject, such as *Perl 5 by Example*, *Perl 5 How-To*, *Perl 5 Interactive Course*, *Teach Yourself Perl 5 for Windows NT in 21 Days*, or *Special Edition Using Perl 5*, all published by Macmillan imprints. Of course, there is the classic *Programming Perl*—now in its second edition—by the creator of Perl, Larry Wall, and two other Perl luminaries, Tom Christiansen and Randal L. Schwartz, published by O'Reilly and Associates. You can find many more examples at the web site addresses given near the end of this chapter. A good place to start is Matt's Script Archives at **http://www.worldwidemart.com/scripts/**. You'll find popular scripts with explanations and directions.

After looking at a few CGI programs, you're ready to learn more about how they access information from the browser. Before the server launches the script, it prepares several *environment variables* representing the current state of the server, which is asking for the information. The environment variables given to a script are exactly like normal environment variables, except that you can't set them from the command line. They're created on-the-fly and last only until that particular script is finished. Each script gets its own unique set of variables. In fact, a busy server often has many scripts executing at once, each with its own environment.

You'll learn about the specific environment variables later in the "Standard CGI Environment Variables" section. For now, it's enough to know that they're present and contain important information that the script can retrieve.

Also, depending on how the server invokes the script, the server may pass information another way, too: Although each server handles things a little differently, and although Windows servers often have other methods available, the CGI specification calls for the server to use the script's `STDIN` (standard input) to pass information to the script.

Standard Input and Output

STDIN and STDOUT are mnemonics for *standard input* and *standard output*, two predefined stream/file handles. Each process inherits these two handles already open. Command-line programs that write to the screen usually do so by writing to STDOUT. If you redirect the input to a program, you're actually redirecting STDIN. If you redirect the output of a program, you're actually redirecting STDOUT. This mechanism is what allows pipes to work. If you do a directory listing and pipe the output to a sort program, you're redirecting the STDOUT of the directory program (DIR or LS) to the STDIN of the sort program.

From the script's point of view, STDIN is what comes from the browser via the server when a POST method is used, and STDOUT is where it writes its output back to the browser. Beyond that, the script doesn't need to worry about what's being redirected where. This standard works well in the text-based UNIX environment where all processes have access to STDIN and STDOUT. In the Windows environments, however, STDIN and STDOUT are available only to nongraphical (console-mode) programs. To complicate matters further, Windows NT creates a different sort of STDIN and STDOUT for 32-bit programs than it does for 16-bit programs. Because most web servers are 32-bit services under Windows NT, this means that CGI scripts have to be 32-bit console-mode programs. That leaves popular languages such as Visual Basic 1.0 - 3.0 and Delphi 1.0 out in the cold. One popular Windows NT server, the freeware HTTPS from EMWAC, can talk only to CGI programs this way. Fortunately, there are several ways around this problem.

Some Windows NT servers, notably Bob Denny's WebSite, use a proprietary technique using .ini files to communicate with CGI programs. This technique, which may well become an open standard soon, is called CGI-WIN. A server supporting CGI-WIN writes its output to an .ini file instead of STDOUT. Any program can then open the file, read it, and process the data. Unfortunately, using any proprietary solution like this one means your scripts will work only on that particular server.

For servers that don't support CGI-WIN, you can use a wrapper program. *Wrappers* do what their name implies: they wrap around the CGI program like a coat, protecting it from the unforgiving web environment. Typically, these programs read STDIN for you and write the output to a pipe or file. Then they launch your program, which reads from the file. Your program writes its output to another file and terminates. The wrapper picks up your output from the file and sends it back to the server via STDOUT, deletes the temporary files, and terminates itself. From the server's point of view, the wrapper was the CGI program.

ON THE WEB

http://www.greyware.com/greyware/software/ cgishell.htm This site has a wrapper program called CGIShell. CGIShell enables you to use almost any 16-bit or 32-bit programming environment to write CGI scripts.

The script picks up the environment variables and reads STDIN as appropriate. It then does whatever it was designed to do and writes its output to STDOUT.

The MIME codes the server sends to the browser let the browser know what kind of file is about to come across the network. Because this information always precedes the file itself, it's usually called a *header*. The server can't send a header for information generated on-the-fly by a script because the script could send audio, graphics, plain text, HTML, or any one of hundreds of other types. Therefore, the script is responsible for sending the header. So in addition to its own output, whatever that may be, the script must supply the header information. Failure to do so can mean failure of the script because the browser won't understand the output.

Here, then, are the broad steps of the CGI process, simplified for clarity:

1. Your browser shows the HTML document containing the form.
2. You enter data into the form as needed and then click on the Submit button.
3. Optionally, a script in the browser performs client-side validation of the form's contents.
4. The browser decodes the URL and contacts the server.
5. Your browser requests the document file from the server.
6. The server translates the URL into a path and filename.
7. The server "realizes" that the URL points to a program instead of to a static file.
8. The server prepares the environment and launches the script.
9. The script executes and reads the environment variables and `STDIN`.
10. The script sends the proper MIME headers to `STDOUT` for the forthcoming content.
11. The script sends the rest of its output to `STDOUT` and terminates.
12. The server notices that the script has finished and closes the connection to your browser.
13. Your browser displays the output from the script.

It's a bit more complicated than a normal HTML retrieval, but that's essentially how CGI works. The scripts become extensions to the server's repertoire of static files and open up the possibilities for real-time interactivity.

Where CGI Scripts Live

Just like any other file on a server, CGI scripts have to live somewhere. Depending on your server, CGI scripts may have to live all in one special directory. Other servers let you put scripts anywhere you want.

Typically—whether required by the server or not—webmasters put all the scripts in one place. This directory is usually part of the web server's tree, often just one level beneath the web server's root. By far, the most common directory name is cgi-bin, a tradition started by the earliest servers that supported CGI. UNIX hacks will like the "bin" part, but because the files are rarely named *.bin and often aren't in binary format anyway, the rest of the world rolls its eyes and shrugs. Today, servers usually let you specify the name of the directory and often support multiple CGI directories for multiple virtual servers (that is, one physical server that pretends to be many different ones, each with its own directory tree).

Suppose your UNIX web server is installed so that the fully qualified path name is /usr/bin/https/webroot. The CGI-BIN directory would then be /usr/bin/https/webroot/cgi-bin. That's where you, as webmaster, put the files. From the web server's point of view, /usr/bin/https/webroot is the directory tree's root. So if there was a file in that directory named index.html, you'd refer to that file with an /index.html URL. A script called myscript.pl in the cgi-bin directory would be referred to as /cgi-bin/myscript.pl.

On a Windows or Windows NT server, much the same thing happens. The server might be installed in C:\Winnt35\System32\Https, with a server root of D:\Webroot. You'd refer to the file Default.htm in the server root as /Default.htm; never mind that its real location is D:\Webroot\Default.htm. If your CGI directory is D:\Webroot\Scripts, you'd refer to a script called Myscript.exe as /Scripts/Myscript.exe.

NOTE Although URL references always use forward slashes—even on Windows and Windows NT machines—file paths are separated by backslashes here. On a UNIX machine, both types of references use forward slashes.

For the sake of simplicity, assume that your server is configured to look for all CGI scripts in one spot and that you've named that spot cgi-bin off the server root. If your server isn't configured that way, you might want to consider changing it. For one thing, in both UNIX and Windows NT, you can control the security better if all executables are in one place (by giving the server process execute privileges only in that directory). Also, with most servers, you can specify that scripts may run only if they're found in the cgi-bin directory. This lets you keep rogue users from executing anything they want from directories under their control.

CGI Server Requirements

CGI scripts, by their very nature, place an extra burden on the web server. They're separate programs, which means the server process must spawn a new task for every CGI script that's executed. The server can't just launch your program and then sit around waiting for the response; chances are good that others are asking for URLs in the meantime. So the new task must operate asynchronously, and the server has to monitor the task to see when it's finished.

- The overhead of spawning a task and waiting for it to complete is usually minimal, but the task itself will use system resources—memory and disk—and also will consume processor time slices. A popular site can easily garner dozens of hits almost simultaneously. If the server tries to satisfy all of them, and each one takes up memory, disk, and processor time, you can quickly bog your server down so far that it becomes worthless.
- There's also the matter of file contention. Not only are the various processes (CGI scripts, the server itself, plus whatever else you may be running) vying for processor time and memory, they may be trying to access the same files. For example, a guestbook script may be displaying the guestbook to three browsers while updating it with the input from a fourth. (There's nothing to keep the multiple scripts running from being the same

script multiple times.) The mechanisms for ensuring a file is available—locking it while writing and releasing it when done—all take time: operating system time and simple computation time. Making a script foolproof this way also makes the script bigger and more complex, meaning longer load times and longer execution times.

Does this mean you should shy away from running CGI scripts? Not at all. It just means you have to know your server's capacity, plan your site, and monitor performance on an on-going basis. No one can tell you to buy a certain amount of RAM or to allocate a specific amount of disk space. Those requirements will vary based on what server software you run, what CGI scripts you use, and what kind of traffic your server sees. However, following are some rules of thumb for several operating systems that you can use as a starting point when planning your site.

Windows NT

The best present you can buy your Windows NT machine is more memory. Although a Windows NT Server runs with 12M of RAM, it doesn't run well until it has 16M and doesn't shine until it has 32M–64M. Adding RAM beyond 64MB probably won't make much difference unless you're running a few very hungry applications; for example, database applications such as Access or SQL Server. If you give your server 32M of fast RAM, a generous swap file, and a fast disk, it can handle a dozen simultaneous CGI scripts without sweating or producing a noticeable delay in response. In most circumstances, it also helps to change Windows NT Server's memory management optimization from the default Maximize Throughput for File Sharing to Balance. This tells Windows NT to keep fewer files in cache, so more RAM is immediately available for processes.

Of course, the choice of programming language will affect each variable greatly. A tight little C program hardly makes an impact, whereas a Visual Basic program, run from a wrapper and talking to an SQL Server back end, will gobble up as much memory as it can. Visual Basic and similar development environments are optimized for ease of programming and best runtime speed, not small code and quick loading. If your program loads seven DLLs, an OLE control, and an ODBC driver, you may notice a significant delay. Scripts written in a simpler programming environment, though, such as C or Perl, run just as fast on Windows NT as they do on a UNIX system and often much faster because of Windows NT's multithreaded and preemptive scheduling architecture.

UNIX

UNIX machines are usually content with significantly less RAM than Windows NT computers, for a number of reasons. First, most of the programs, including the operating system itself and all its drivers, are smaller. Second, it's unusual, if not impossible, to use an X Windows program as a CGI script. This means that the resources required fewer, although with the prices of processor speed and drive and memory megabytes falling, the difference in hardware cost is not that great. Maintenance and requisite system knowledge, however, are far greater. There are trade-offs in everything, and what UNIX gives you in small size and speed it more than makes up with complexity. In particular, setting web server permissions and getting CGI to work properly can be a nightmare for the UNIX novice. Even experienced system administrators often trip over the unnecessarily arcane configuration details. Things are getting better, though. For example, you can buy preconfigured servers, and many do-it-yourself Linux administrators are glad for Red Hat. After a UNIX-based system is set up, though, adding new CGI scripts usually goes smoothly and seldom requires adding memory.

If you give your UNIX computer 16M of RAM and a reasonably fast hard disk, it will run quickly and efficiently for any reasonable number of hits. (Of course, you may not want to skimp on RAM when memory prices are low.) Database queries will slow it down, just as they would if the program weren't CGI. Due to UNIX's multiuser architecture, the number of logged-on sessions (and what they're doing) can significantly affect performance. It's a good idea to let your web server's primary job be servicing the web rather than users. Of course, if you have capacity left over, there's no reason not to run other daemons, but it's best to choose processes that consume resources predictably so that you can plan your site.

A large, popular site—say, one that receives several hits each minute—will require more RAM, just as on any platform. The more RAM you give your UNIX system, the better it can cache, and therefore, the faster it can satisfy requests.

CGI Script Structure

When your script is invoked by the server, the server passes information to the script via environment variables and, in the case of `POST`, via `STDIN`. `GET` and `POST` are the two most common request methods you'll encounter, and probably the only ones you'll need to deal with. (`HEAD` and `PUT` are also defined but seldom used for CGI.) The *request method* tells your script how it was invoked; based on that information, the script can decide how to act. The request method used is passed to your script using the environment variable called, appropriately enough, `REQUEST_METHOD`.

- `GET` is a request for data, the same method used to obtain static documents. The `GET` method sends request information as parameters tacked onto the end of the URL. These parameters are passed to your CGI program in the environment variable `QUERY_STRING`.

  For example, if your script is called myprog.exe and you invoke it from a link with the form

```
<A HREF ="cgi-bin/myprog.exe?lname=blow&fname=joe">
```

  the `REQUEST_METHOD` will be the string `GET`, and the `QUERY_STRING` will contain `lname=blow&fname=joe`.

  The question mark separates the name of the script from the beginning of the `QUERY_STRING`. On some servers, the question mark is mandatory, even if no `QUERY_STRING` follows it. On other servers, a forward slash may be allowed either instead of or in addition to the question mark. If the slash is used, the server passes the information to the script using the `PATH_INFO` variable instead of the `QUERY_STRING` variable.

- A POST operation occurs when the browser sends data from a fill-in form to the server. With POST, the QUERY_STRING may or may not be blank, depending on your server.

  The data from a POSTed query gets passed from the server to the script using STDIN. Because STDIN is a stream and the script needs to know how much valid data is waiting, the server also supplies another variable, CONTENT_LENGTH, to indicate the size in bytes of the incoming data. The format for POSTed data is

```
variable1=value1&variable2=value2&etc
```

  Your program must examine the REQUEST_METHOD environment variable to know whether to read STDIN. The CONTENT_LENGTH variable is typically useful only when the REQUEST_METHOD is POST.

URL Encoding

The HTTP 1.0 specification calls for URL data to be encoded in such a way that it can be used on almost any hardware and software platform. Information specified this way is called *URL-encoded*; almost everything passed to your script by the server will be URL-encoded.

Parameters passed as part of QUERYSTRING or PATHINFO will take the form *variable1=value1&variable2=value2* and so forth, for each variable defined in your form.

Variables are separated by the ampersand. If you want to send a real ampersand, it must be *escaped*, that is, encoded as a two-digit hexadecimal value representing the character. Escapes are indicated in URL-encoded strings by the percent sign. Thus, %25 represents the percent sign itself. (25 is the hexadecimal representation of the ASCII value for the percent sign.) All characters above 127 (7F hexidecimal) or below 33 (21 hexidecimal) are escaped by the server when it sends information to your CGI program. This includes the space character, which is escaped as %20. Also, the plus sign needs to be interpreted as a space character.

Before your script can deal with the data, it must parse and decode it. Fortunately, these are fairly simple tasks in most programming languages. Your script scans through the string looking for an ampersand. When found, your script chops off the string up to that point and calls it a variable. The variable's name is everything up to the equal sign in the string; the variable's value is everything after the equal sign. Your script then continues parsing the original string for the next ampersand, and so on, until the original string is exhausted.

After the variables are separated, you can safely decode them, as follows:

1. Replace all plus signs with spaces.
2. Replace all %## (percent sign followed by two hexidecimal digits) with the corresponding ASCII character.

It's important that you scan through the string linearly rather than recursively because the characters you decode may be plus signs or percent signs.

When the server passes data to your form with the POST method, check the environment variable called CONTENT_TYPE. If CONTENT_TYPE is application/x-www-form-urlencoded, your data needs to be decoded before use.

NOTE Programmers sometimes write "generic" code that is not necessarily correct in any particular language, for speed and illustration purposes. This code is given a descriptive name: *pseudocode.* Of course, pseudocode won't actually compile or interpret; it is meant as a sort of easily understood shorthand, to be converted to actual code in the desired programming language later. Where pseudocode is used in this book, it will be clearly marked.

The basic structure of a CGI application is straightforward: initialization, processing, output, and termination. Because this section deals with concepts, flow, and programming discipline, it will use pseudocode rather than a specific language for the examples.

Ideally, a script follows these steps in order (with appropriate subroutines for do-initialize, do-process, and do-output):

1. The program begins.
2. The program calls do-initialize.
3. The program calls do-process.
4. The program calls do-output.
5. The program ends.

Initialization

The first thing your script must do when it starts is determine its input, environment, and state. Basic operating-system environment information can be obtained the usual way: from the system registry in Windows NT, from standard environment variables in UNIX, from .ini files in Windows, and so on.

State information will come from the input rather than the operating environment or static variables. Remember: Each time CGI scripts are invoked, it's as if they've never been invoked before. The scripts don't stay running between calls. Everything must be initialized from scratch, as follows:

1. Determine how the script was invoked. Typically, this involves reading the environment variable `REQUEST_METHOD` and parsing it for the word `GET` or the word `POST`.

NOTE Although `GET` and `POST` are the only currently defined operations that apply to CGI, you may encounter other oddball request methods. Your code should check explicitly for `GET` and `POST` and refuse anything else. Don't assume that if the request method isn't `GET` then it must be `POST`, or vice versa.

2. Retrieve the input data. If the method was `GET`, you must obtain, parse, and decode the `QUERYSTRING` environment variable. If the method was `POST`, you must check `QUERYSTRING` and also parse `STDIN`. If the `CONTENTTYPE` environment variable is set to application/x-www-form-urlencoded, the stream from `STDIN` needs to be decoded, too.

Listing 31.7 shows the initialization phase in pseudocode:

Listing 31.7 Initializing your CGI script, shown in pseudocode.

```
retrieve any operating system environment values desired
allocate temporary storage for variables
if environment variable REQUESTMETHOD equals "GET" then
   retrieve contents of environment variable QUERYSTRING;
   if QUERYSTRING is not null, parse it and decode it;
else if REQUESTMETHOD equals "POST" then
   retrieve contents of environment variable QUERYSTRING;
   if QUERYSTRING is not null, parse it and decode it;
   retrieve value of environment variable CONTENTLENGTH;
   if CONTENT_LENGTH is greater than zero, read CONTENTLENGTH bytes from STDIN;
   parse STDIN data into separate variables;
   retrieve contents of environment variable CONTENTTYPE;
   if CONTENTTYPE equals application/x-www-form-urlencoded
   then decode parsed variables;
else if REQUESTMETHOD is neither "GET" nor "POST" then
   report an error;
   deallocate temporary storage;
   terminate
end if
```


Processing

After initializing its environment by reading and parsing its input, the script is ready to get to work. What happens in this section is much less rigidly defined than during initialization. During initialization, the parameters are known (or can be discovered), and the tasks are more or less the same for every script you'll write. The processing phase, however, is the heart of your script, and what you do here will depend almost entirely on the script's objectives.

1. Process the input data. What you do here will depend on your script. You may ignore all the input and just output the date, for instance, spit back the input in neatly formatted HTML, find information in a database and display it, or do something never thought of before. Processing the data means, generally, transforming it somehow. In classical data processing terminology, this is called the transform step because in batch-oriented processing, the program reads a record, applies some rule to it (transforming it), and then writes it back out. CGI programs rarely, if ever, qualify as classical data processing, but the idea is the same. This is the stage of your program that differentiates it from all other CGI programs, where you take the inputs and make something new from them.
2. Output the results. In a simple CGI script, the output is usually just a header and some HTML. More complex scripts might output graphics, graphics mixed with text, or all the information necessary to call the script again with some additional information. A common, and rather elegant, technique is to call a script once using `GET`, which can be done from a standard `<A HREF>` tag. The script "senses" that it was called with `GET` and creates an HTML form on-the-fly, complete with hidden variables and code necessary to

On some platforms, most noticeably Windows NT, and to a lesser extent, UNIX, your file handles and memory objects are closed and reclaimed when your process terminates. Even so, it's unwise to rely on the operating system to clean up your mess. For instance, under Windows NT, the behavior of the file system is undefined when a program locks all or part of a file and then terminates without releasing the locks.

Make sure that your error-exit routine, if you have one (and you should), knows about your script's resources and cleans up just as thoroughly as the main exit routine does.

Planning Your Script

Now that you've seen a script's basic structure, you're ready to learn how to plan a script from the ground up:

1. Take your time defining the program's task. Think it through thoroughly. Write it down and trace the program logic. When you're satisfied that you understand the input and output and the transform process you'll have to do, proceed.
2. Order a pizza and a good supply of your favorite beverage, lock yourself in for the night, and come out the next day with a finished program. This sounds cute, but it is good advice. Sometimes, it seems as if more bugs stem from interruptions while programming—which cause loss of concentration—than from any other source. And while you're sequestered, don't forget to document your code *while* writing it.
3. Test, test, test. Use every browser known to mankind and every sort of input you can think of. Especially test for the situations in which users enter 32K of data in a 10-byte field or they enter control codes where you're expecting plain text.
4. Document the program as a whole, too—not just the individual steps within it—so that others who have to maintain or adapt your code will understand what you were trying to do.

Step 1, of course, is this section's topic, so let's look at that process in more depth:

- If your script will handle form variables, plan out each one: its name, expected length, and data type.
- As you copy variables from `QUERY_STRING` or `STDIN`, check for proper type and length. A favorite trick of UNIX hackers is to overflow the input buffer purposely. Because of the way some scripting languages (notably sh and bash) allocate memory for variables, this sometimes gives the hacker access to areas of memory that should be protected, letting them place executable instructions in your script's heap or stack space.
- Use sensible variable names. A pointer to the `QUERY_STRING` environment variable should be called something such as `pQueryString`, not `p2`. This not only helps debugging at the beginning but makes maintenance and modification much easier. No matter how brilliant a coder you are, chances are good that a year from now you won't remember that `p1` points to `CONTENT_TYPE` while `p2` points to `QUERY_STRING`.

- Distinguish between *system-level parameters* that affect how your program operates and *user-level parameters* that provide instance-specific information. For example, in a script to send email, don't let the user specify the IP number of the SMTP host. This information shouldn't even appear on the form in a hidden variable. It's instance-independent and should therefore be a system-level parameter. In Windows NT, store this information in the registry or an .ini file. In UNIX, store it in a configuration file or system environment variable.
- If your script will *shell out* to the system to launch another program or script, don't pass user-supplied variables unchecked. Especially in UNIX systems, where the `system()` call can contain pipe or redirection characters, leaving variables unchecked can spell disaster. Clever users and malicious hackers can copy sensitive information or destroy data this way. If you can't avoid `system()` calls altogether, plan for them carefully. Define exactly what can get passed as a parameter, and know which bits will come from the user. Include an algorithm to parse for suspect character strings and exclude them.
- If your script will access external files, plan how you'll handle concurrency. You may lock part or all of a data file, you may establish a semaphore, or you may use a file as a semaphore. If you take chances, you'll be sorry. Never assume that just because your script is the only program to access a given file that you don't need to worry about concurrency. Five copies of your script might be running at the same time, satisfying requests from five different users.
- If you lock files, use the least-restrictive lock required. If you're only reading a data file, lock out writes while you're reading and release the file immediately afterward. If you're updating a record, lock just that one record (or byte range). Ideally, your locking logic should immediately surround the actual I/O calls. Don't open a file at the beginning of your program and lock it until you terminate. If you must do this, open the file but leave it unlocked until you're actually about to use it. This will allow other applications or other instances of your script to work smoothly and quickly.
- Prepare graceful exits for unexpected events. If, for example, your program requires exclusive access to a particular resource, be prepared to wait a reasonable amount of time and then die gracefully. Never code a *wait-forever* call. When your program dies from a fatal error, make sure that it reports the error first. Error reports should use plain, sensible language. When possible, also write the error to a log file so the system administrator knows of it.
- If you're using a GUI language (for example, Visual Basic) for your CGI script, don't let untrapped errors result in a message box onscreen. This is a server application; chances are excellent that no one will be around to notice and clear the error, and your application will hang until the next time an administrator chances by. Trap all errors! Work around those you can live with, and treat all others as fatal.
- Write pseudocode for your routines at least to the point of general logical structure before firing up the editor. It often helps to build *stub routines* so that you can use the actual calls in your program while you're still developing. A stub routine is a quick and dirty routine that doesn't actually process anything; it just accepts the inputs the final

user can set the information to be anything he wants. Don't use this variable even if it's supported by your server.

- REMOTE_USER If AUTH_TYPE is set, this variable will contain the username provided by the user and validated by the server. Note that AUTH_TYPE and REMOTE_USER are set only after a user has successfully authenticated (usually via a username and password) his identity to the server. Hence, these variables are useful only when restricted areas have been established and then only in those areas.
- REQUEST_METHOD Supplies the method by which the script was invoked. Only GET and POST are meaningful for scripts using the HTTP/1.0 protocol.
- SCRIPT_NAME This is the name of the script file being invoked. It's useful for self-referencing scripts. For example, scripts use this information to generate the proper URL for a script that gets invoked using GET only to turn around and output a form that, when submitted, will reinvoke the same script using POST. By using this variable instead of hard-coding your script's name or location, you make maintenance much easier, for example, /cgi-bin/myscript.exe.
- SERVER_NAME Your web server's host name, alias, or IP address. It's reliable for use in generating URLs that refer to your server at runtime, for example, www.yourcompany.com.
- SERVER_PORT The port number for this connection, for example, 80.
- SERVER_PROTOCOL The name/version of the protocol used by this request, for example, HTTP/1.0.
- SERVER_SOFTWARE The name/version of the HTTP server that launched your script, for example, HTTPS/1.1.

CGI Script Portability

CGI programmers face two portability issues: platform independence and server independence. *Platform independence* is the capability of the code to run without modification on a hardware platform or operating system different from the one for which it was written. *Server independence* is the capability of the code to run without modification on another server using the same operating system.

Platform Independence

The best way to keep your CGI script portable is to use a commonly available language and avoid platform-specific code. It sounds simple, right? In practice, this means using either C or Perl and not doing anything much beyond formatting text and outputting graphics.

Does this leave Visual Basic, AppleScript, and UNIX shell scripts out in the cold? Yes, I'm afraid so, for now. However, platform independence isn't the only criterion to consider when selecting a CGI platform. There's also speed of coding, ease of maintenance, and ability to perform the chosen task.

Certain types of operations simply aren't portable. If you develop for 16-bit Windows, for instance, you'll have great difficulty finding equivalents on other platforms for the VBX and DLL functions you use. If you develop for 32-bit Windows NT, you'll find that all your asynchronous Winsock calls are meaningless in a UNIX environment. If your shell script does a `system()` call to launch `grep` and pipe the output back to your program, you'll find nothing remotely similar in the Windows NT environment, unless you add an NT version of `grep` to the system. And AppleScript is good only on Macintoshes.

If one of your mandates is the capability to move code among platforms with a minimum of modification, you'll probably have the best success with C. Write your code using the standard functions from the ANSI C libraries and avoid making other operating system calls. Unfortunately, following this rule will limit your scripts to very basic functionality. If you wrap your platform-dependent code in self-contained routines, however, you minimize the work needed to port from one platform to the next. As you saw in the section "Planning Your Script," when talking about encapsulation, a properly designed program can have any module replaced in its entirety without affecting the rest of the program. Using these guidelines, you may have to replace a subroutine or two, and you'll certainly have to recompile; however, your program will be portable.

Perl scripts are certainly easier to maintain than C programs, mainly because there's no compile step. You can change the program quickly when you figure out what needs to be changed. And there's the rub: Although learning to write simple Perl is easier than learning C for many people, Perl has many obscure subtleties, and the libraries tend to be much less uniform—even between versions on the same platform—than do C libraries. You pay for all that wonderful string-processing and pattern-handling power. Also, Perl for Windows NT is fairly new and still quirky, although the most recent versions are much more stable. And in fairness to Perl, Win32 is not the only compiler or interpreter to be quirky on a relatively new operating system such as NT 4.0 and now 5.0.

Server Independence

Far more important than platform independence is server independence. Server independence is fairly easy to achieve but for some reason seems to be a stumbling block to beginning script writers. To be server independent, your script must run without modification on any server using the same operating system. Only server-independent programs can be useful as shareware or freeware, and without a doubt, server independence is a requirement for commercial software.

Most programmers think of obvious issues, such as not assuming that the server has a static IP address. The following are some other rules of server independence that, although obvious once stated, nevertheless get overlooked time and time again:

- Don't assume your environment   For example, just because the temp directory was C:\Temp on your development system, don't assume that it will be the same wherever your script runs. Never hard code directories or filenames. This goes double for Perl scripts, where this travesty of proper programming happens most often. If your Perl script to tally hits needs to exclude a range of IP addresses from the total, don't hard code the addresses into the program and say, "Change this line" in the comments. Use a configuration file.

- Don't assume privileges On a UNIX machine, the server (and therefore your script) may run as the user `nobody`, as `root`, or as any privilege level in between. On a Windows NT machine, too, CGI programs usually inherit the server's security attributes. Check for access rights and examine return codes carefully so you can present intelligible error information to the user in case your script fails because it can't access a resource. Some NT servers allow you to specify a user account for CGI programs that's separate from the user account for the web server. Microsoft's IIS does this and goes one step beyond: For CGI programs with authentication, the CGI runs in the security context of the authenticated user.
- Don't assume consistency of CGI variables Some servers pass regular environment variables (for instance, `PATH` and `LIB` variables) along with CGI environment variables; however, the ones they pass depend on the runtime environment. Server configuration can also affect the number and the format of CGI variables. Be prepared for environment-dependent input and have your program act accordingly.
- Don't assume version-specific information Test for it, and include workarounds or sensible error messages telling the user what to upgrade and why. Both server version and operation system version can affect your script's environment.
- Don't assume LAN or WAN configurations In the Windows NT world, the server can be Windows NT Workstation or Windows NT Server; it may be standalone, part of a workgroup, or part of a domain. DNS (Domain Name Services) may or may not be available; lookups may be limited to a static hosts file. In the UNIX world, don't assume anything about the configurations of daemons such as `inetd`, `sendmail`, or the system environment, and don't assume directory names. Use a configuration file for the items that you can't discover with system calls, and give the script maintainer instructions for editing it.
- Don't assume the availability of system objects As with privilege level, check for the existence of such objects as databases, messaging queues, and hardware drivers, and output explicit messages when something can't be found or is misconfigured. Nothing is more irritating than downloading a new script, installing it, and getting only `Runtime error #203` for the output.

CGI Libraries

When you talk about CGI libraries, there are two possibilities: libraries of code you develop and want to reuse in other projects, and publicly available libraries of programs, routines, and information.

Personal Libraries

If you follow the advice given earlier in this chapter in the "Planning Your Script" section about writing your code in a black box fashion, you'll soon discover that you're building a library of routines that you'll use over and over. For instance, after you puzzle out how to parse out URL-encoded data, you don't need to do it again. And when you have a basic `main()` function written, it will probably serve for every CGI program you write. This is also true for generic routines, such as querying a database, parsing input, and reporting runtime errors.

- How you manage your personal library depends on the programming language you use. With C and assembler, you can precompile code into actual .Lib files, with which you can then link your programs. Although possible, this likely is overkill for CGI and doesn't work for interpreted languages, such as Perl and Visual Basic. (Although Perl and VB can call compiled libraries, you can't link with them in a static fashion the way you can with C.) The advantage of using compiled libraries is that you don't have to recompile all your programs when you make a change to code in the library. If the library is loaded at runtime (a DLL), you don't need to change anything. If the library is linked statically, all you need do is relink.
- Another solution is to maintain separate source files and simply include them with each project. You might have a single, fairly large file that contains the most common routines while putting seldom used routines in files of their own. Keeping the files in source format adds a little overhead at compile time but not enough to worry about, especially when compared to the timesavings you gain by writing the code only once. The disadvantage of this approach is that when you change your library code, you must recompile all your programs to take advantage of the change.
- Nothing can keep you from incorporating public-domain routines into your personal library either. As long as you make sure that the copyright and license allow you to use and modify the source code without royalties or other stipulations, then you should strip out the interesting bits and toss them into your library.
- Well-designed and well-documented programs provide the basis for new programs. If you're careful to isolate the program-specific parts into subroutines, there's no reason not to cannibalize an entire program's structure for your next project.
- You can also develop platform-specific versions of certain subroutines and, if your compiler will allow it, automatically include the correct ones for each type of build. At the worst, you'll have to manually specify which subroutines you want.

NOTE The key to making your code reusable this way is to make it as generic as possible—yet not so generic that, for instance, a currency printing routine needs to handle both yen and dollars, but generic enough that any program that needs to print out dollar amounts can call that subroutine. As you upgrade, swat bugs, and add capabilities, keep each function's inputs and outputs the same, even when you change what happens inside the subroutine. This is the black box approach in action. By keeping the calling convention and the parameters the same, you're free to upgrade any piece of code without fear of breaking older programs that call your function.

- Another technique to consider is using function stubs. Say that you decide eventually that a single routine to print both yen and dollars is actually the most efficient way to go. But you already have separate subroutines, and your old programs wouldn't know to pass the additional parameter to the new routine. Rather than go back and modify each program that calls the old routines, just "stub out" the routines in your library so that the only thing they do is call the new, combined routine with the correct parameters. In some languages, you can do this by redefining the routine declarations; in others, you actually need to code a call and pay the price of some additional overhead. But even so, the price is far less than that of breaking all your old programs.

Public Libraries

The Internet is rich with public-domain sample code, libraries, and precompiled programs. Although most of what you'll find is UNIX-oriented (because it has been around longer), there's nevertheless no shortage of routines for Windows NT.

Here's a list of some of the best sites on the Internet with a brief description of what you'll find at each site. This list is far from exhaustive. Hundreds of sites are dedicated to or contain information about CGI programming. Hop onto your web browser and visit your favorite search engine. Tell it to search for "CGI" or "CGI libraries" and you'll see what I mean. To save you the tedium of wading through all the hits, I've explored many of them for you. The following are the ones that struck me as most useful:

- **http://www.worldwidemart.com/scripts/** The justifiably famous Matt's Script Archive. Look here first for tested, practical scripts in Perl and C for many common business uses.
- **http://www.ics.uci.edu/pub/websoft/libwww-perl/** This is the University of California's public offering, libwww-perl. Based on Perl version 5.003, this library contains many useful routines. If you plan to program in Perl, this library is worth the download just for ideas and techniques.
- **http://www.w3.org/hypertext/WWW/CGI/** The W3 standards organization CGI site. W3 is always worth a periodic visit.
- **http://www.bio.cam.ac.uk/web/form.html** A Perl 4 library for CGI from Steven E. Brenner, cgi-lib.pl is now considered a classic and is also available from many other sites.
- **http://www-genome.wi.mit.edu/WWW/tools/scripting/cgi-utils.html** cgi-utils.pl is an extension to cgi-lib.pl from Lincoln D. Stein at the Whitehead Institute, MIT Center for Genome Research.
- **http://www-genome.wi.mit.edu/ftp/pub/software/WWW/cgi_docs.html** cgi.pm is a Perl 5 library for creating forms and parsing CGI input.
- **http://www-genome.wi.mit.edu/WWW/tools/scripting/CGIperl/** This is a useful list of Perl links and utilities.
- **http://www.boutell.com/gd/** A C library for producing GIF images on-the-fly, gd enables your program to create images complete with lines, arcs, text, multiple colors, and cut and paste from other images and flood fills, which gets written out to a file. Your

program can then suck this image data in and include it in your program's output. Although these libraries are difficult to master, the rewards are well worth it. Many map-related web sites use these routines to generate map location points on-the-fly.

- **http://www-genome.wi.mit.edu/ftp/pub/software/WWW/GD.html** GD.pm, a Perl wrapper and extender for gd, is written by Thomas Boutell of Cold Spring Harbor Labs.
- **http://www.iserver.com/cgi/library.html** This is Internet Servers Inc.'s wonderful CGI library. Among the treasures here, you'll find samples of image maps, building a web index, server-push animation, and a guest book.
- **http://www.charm.net/~web/Vlib/Providers/CGI.html** This collection of links and utilities will help you build an editor, use C++ with predefined classes, join a CGI programmer's mailing list, and, best of all, browse a selection of Clickables, Plug and Play CGI Scripts.
- **http://www.greyware.com/greyware/software/** Greyware Automation Products provides a rich list of shareware and freeware programs for Windows NT. Of special interest are the free SSI utilities and the CGI-wrapper program, CGIShell, which lets you use Visual Basic, Delphi, or other GUI programming environments with the freeware EMWAC HTTP server.
- **http://www.greyware.com/greyware/bulletins/iis-cgi-faq.html** FAQ on enabling CGI on Microsoft's Internet Information Server (IIS) web server.
- **http://www.bhs.com/** Although not specifically geared to CGI, the Windows NT Resource Center, sponsored by Beverly Hills Software, provides some wonderful applications, some of which are CGI-related. In particular, you'll find EMWAC's software, Perl for Windows NT and Perl libraries, and SMTP mailers.
- **http://mfginfo.com/htm/website.htm** Manufacturer's Information Net provides a rich set of links to Windows NT utilities, many of which are CGI-related. Of special interest are links to back-end database interfaces and many Internet server components.
- **http://website.oreilly.com** Bob Denny, author of WebSite, has probably done more than any other individual to popularize HTTP servers on the Windows NT platform. At this site, you'll find a collection of tools, including Perl for Windows NT, VB routines for use with the WebSite server, and other interesting items.
- **ftp://ftp.ncsa.uiuc.edu/Web/httpd/Unix/ncsa_httpd/cgi** NSCA's CGI Archive. Don't miss this one!
- **http://www.cis.ufl.edu/perl/** The University of Florida's CGI site. Good site with good links.
- **http://robby.caltech.edu/~goodwine/perltk.html** "Bill's Research Site" at Caltech has good Perl and PerlTk links.
- **http://www.endcontsw.com/people/evangelo/Perl_for_Win32_FAQ.html** Very good Perl for Win32 FAQ.
- **http://www.cgi-resources.com/** The CGI Resource Index, another good CGI site.

- **http://www.perl.com/perl/faq/** The Perl Language Home Page's list of Perl FAQs. Check out the rest of the site while you're there.

These sites should be enough to get you started. For a fresh list of sites, start looking on **http://www.yahoo.com** or use your favorite search engine.

The Future of CGI Scripting

The tips, techniques, examples, and advice in this book will enable you to create your own scripts immediately. You should be aware, however, that the CGI world is in a constant state of change, more so perhaps, than most of the computer world. Fortunately, most servers will stay compatible with existing standards, so you won't have to worry about your scripts not working. Here's a peek at the brave new world coming your way.

Java

Java comes from Sun Microsystems as an open specification designed for platform independence. Java code is compiled by a special Java compiler to produce bytecodes that can run on a Java Virtual Machine. Rather than produce and distribute executables as with normal CGI (or most programs), Java writers distribute instructions that are interpreted at runtime by the user's browser. The important difference here is that whereas CGI scripts execute on the server, a Java applet is executed by the client's browser. A browser equipped with a Java Virtual Machine is called a *Java Browser*. Netscape Navigator 2.0 and later, and Microsoft Internet Explorer 3.0 and later, among other browsers, support Java.

If you're interested in reading about Java, you'll find that **http://java.sun.com** has pages worth of mind-numbingly complete information. Here are the highlights:

- Compiled Java code, called *byte code*, is a sequence of instructions that makes sense only to a Java Virtual Machine.
- A Java Virtual Machine (JVM) is an interpreter, a program running locally, that understands and that can execute the *byte code* language. Netscape Navigator (NN) 2.0 and later, Microsoft Internet Explorer (MSIE) 3.0 and later, and several other browsers, have a Java Virtual Machine built in.
- You need a Java Virtual Machine tailored for each hardware platform; but after you have it, the application code itself should run unmodified on any Java-enabled browser, in the absence of native code use and JVM bugs.
- Java source code (the Java language before you run it through the Java compiler) looks and acts a lot like C++; if you don't know C++, don't like C++, or just don't know what C++ is, then you won't be very comfortable writing Java code without some study and practice. It is always easier to learn one programming language when you already know another one. However, you do not need to know C++ before learning Java.
- Java source code, by design, is object-oriented and uses a simplified version of inheritable classes. There is no traditional link phase; resolution happens at runtime.

- Java runtime code has full support for preemptive multithreading. This makes for smoother, often faster, performance.
- Java takes security very seriously: From the ground up, the design team at Sun built in safeguards and consistency checks to eliminate as many security loopholes as possible.

Java servlets may soon win honors in the CGI arena. Servlets, like applets, are a special type of Java program. Servlets are meant to run server-side and perform the same functions that C and Perl CGI scripts do.

Servlets, working with Jeeves and other Java-based web servers, may be formidable challengers for Perl and C CGI programs. Java, when programmed to the "100% Java" standard, is theoretically platform-independent, but so is Perl, and Perl has a huge installed base. Java's platform independence is more deeply into its basic design than Perl's platform is, but as Java programmers have found out, that independence is also only as good as the JVM implementation. Another wrinkle might be the release of compilers that translate C++ or Visual Basic (even Perl?) to Java byte codes, in effect trying to scoop Java. After all, it is the byte codes that run on so many platforms, not Java itself. In the long run, Java servlets may win out but probably not in the next year. See Chapters 38 through 43 of this book for more about Java, or check Sun's Java site at **http://java.sun.com**.

Visual Basic, Scripting Edition and Active Server Pages

Following the incredible popularity of the Internet and the unprecedented success of companies such as Netscape, Microsoft entered the arena and declared war. With its own web server, its own browsers, and a plethora of back-end services—and don't forget unparalleled marketing muscle and name recognition—Microsoft has already made an impact on the way people look at and use the Internet.

Along with some spectacular blunders, Microsoft has had its share of spectacular successes. One such success is Visual Basic, the all-purpose, almost-anyone-can-learn-it Windows programming language. VB was so successful that Microsoft made it the backbone of their office application suite. Visual Basic for Applications (VBA) has become the *de facto* standard scripting language for Windows. Although not as lean as some other options (Borland's Delphi in some regards, or C programs in general), VB nevertheless has two golden advantages: it's easy to learn, and it has widespread support from third-party vendors and users.

When Microsoft announced it was getting into the web server business, no one was terribly surprised to learn that it intended to incorporate a variant of VB or that it wanted everyone else to incorporate VB, too. VBScript, similar to a subset of VBA, has been useful client-side especially with ActiveX controls, and should become even more useful with the Document Object Model's expansion of HTML's programmability. Server-side, VBScript has shone in Microsoft's Active Server Page technology built into Internet Information Server. Fans of ASP, which is a powerful alternative to Perl and C CGI programs, are glad that third-party ASP capability is now available for other web servers through Chili!soft. So far, Chili!ASP versions of ASP are available for Netscape's FastTrack and Enterprise Servers on Windows 95, NT 3.51 and NT 4.0, the Lotus Go Web Server on Windows 95, NT 3.51 and NT 4.0, IBM's ICS for Windows NT, and

Understanding Database Design

In this chapter, you take a look at three different kinds of databases: flat file, DBM, and SQL. You build a different database using each of these databases so that you can see the differences between the three methods of storing information. The three methods used here require little or no money to use and build. Nearly everyone will be able to work with databases, and most database applications, free or commercial, work with the same basic principles.

The most difficult and daunting task is how to go about designing your database to store and retrieve information. What would happen if you wanted to upgrade your database, or if you needed to insert additional information (fields or tables, for example) to your database?

When requesting information that derives from a database, you set into motion quite a few steps (see Figure 32.1):

1. Your web server receives the request from the visitor to your site, and then sends that information on to your CGI script.
2. The CGI script acts as the main gateway tying two very different systems together. The CGI script performs the actual query, receives the results from the database, formulates a proper reply, and sends it off to the web server.
3. The web server, in turn, sends it to the person visiting your site.

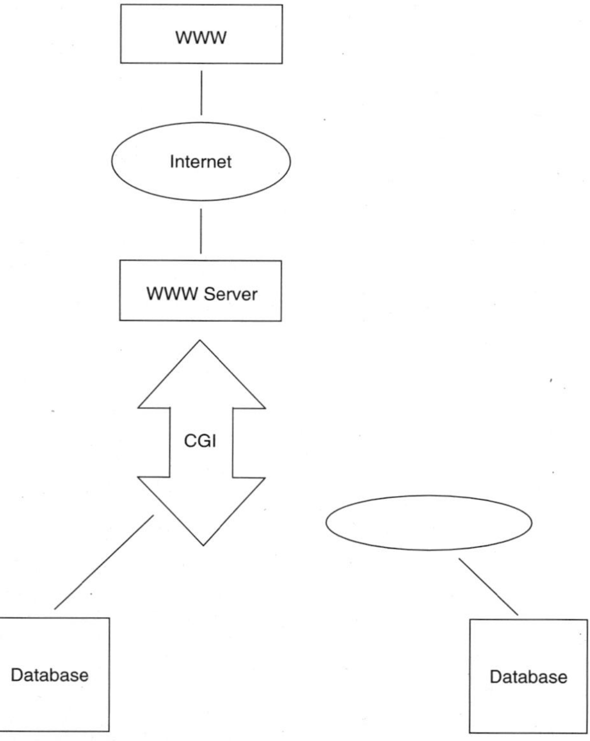

FIG. 32.1
This diagram shows the information flow between those on the web and your database. Your goal is to tie all this together in such a way that it is totally transparent to the person visiting your site.

Why Access a Database?

Most likely your organization already has an existing database in which it has stored information about its products, its customers, and other aspects of business life. Some of this information you might want to allow your customers to see, or you might even want to make the information in the database available to your workers stationed away from the office. If so, you would have to create HTML documents that contain all this information several times, which, if you're part of a large organization, can be a tedious task. Integrating the web with your databases can save you tremendous amounts of time in the long run, especially when it comes to maintaining that information. As the database changes, your web pages change.

Another good reason to use the World Wide Web to access your database is that any web browser that supports forms can access information from the database—no matter which platform is being used.

Database Access Limitations

Consider the following events:

1. Person one accesses the database for editing.
2. Next, person two comes along and does the same thing.
3. Person one makes changes and saves that information to the database.
4. Person two saves information as well, possibly writing over what person one just saved.
5. A short time later, person one is wondering where his or her data went.

The browser and the server are stateless in relation to each other. Except in certain instances with certain products, the browser makes a request, the server processes the query and sends the result back to the browser, and the connection is closed. This creates a problem with databases, because a connection to a database is usually constant. Normally, someone accesses the database, which keeps a connection open, locking a record if any editing is performed, and closes the connection only when the person is finished. Accessing a database doesn't work exactly the same way when using a CGI script.

NOTE Application Programming Interfaces (APIs) have been created to alleviate the problem with stateless connections. You have to use proprietary software in order to utilize these APIs, but they are well worth it. ISAPI and NSAPI are two examples.

Accessing a database using a Java client/server application can also eliminate the problems associated with stateless connections.

There are two ways to handle the problem described previously. The first method involves keeping track of all entries with a time stamp. This will enable both entries to be maintained by the database, without the possibility of either person's entry being overwritten.

Another solution is to only provide information from the database and not allow someone on the web to edit, remove, or insert information to the database. Although this limits some of the possibilities for having the database on the web, it also alleviates some of the security problems.

NOTE Although most of the limitations in accessing databases have decreased in the last year as database companies have scrambled to ensure that their product easily integrates with existing web applications, most methods of accessing database information via the web vary greatly. Also, there is not an official standard that you can use to connect to a database. If you create a script to access one type of database, there is no guarantee that the same script will work on a different database—even if the query used was the same (people are working on this, though). Because of this, you will be required to learn a lot about each database application that you come across.

Security Issues

The major problem with having those on the web accessing your database is that your CGI script is trusted by your database program. That is, your database has to accept commands from your CGI script, and your CGI script needs to perform queries based upon what you want to provide to those on the web. This can lead to problems if someone with ill intentions gains access to a script and is able to edit your database.

Also, most databases require the use of a password. Because your CGI script stores user information in the database, as well as retrieves information from the database, your script needs to have the password to access your database. You need to ensure that your script cannot be read by others within your organization and outside your organization.

Creating and Using Flat File Databases

Flat file databases are about the easiest databases you can create. To create a small ASCII text database, you need nothing more than a language with which to program.

A flat file database consists mainly of lines of text, where each line is its own entry. There is no special technique to index the database. Because of this, flat file databases usually are relatively small (about 1,000–2,000 records). The larger the database, the longer it takes to perform queries to it.

The database created for this example will be for a fictitious book company. The company needs to be able to easily add and remove books from its web site and enable those visiting the site to search through its online catalog.

Adding Entries

One of the most important things that companies online require is the capability of easily adding, removing, and editing information from its databases. Flat file databases are no exception.

In this example, the company would like to be able to supply a picture of the book along with any information on the book. This is made possible using a modified version of Steve Hsueh's `udload` script, which can be found at **http://www.itm.com/cgicollection/**. Slightly modified, the script uses the Netscape `file` input type within a form (see Figure 32.2). You can easily automate the task of uploading a file remotely by enabling a window to open where the database administrator can browse through the files on his or her computer.

FIG. 32.2
The file attribute to the input tag enables you to search your file system for files to be uploaded to a server.

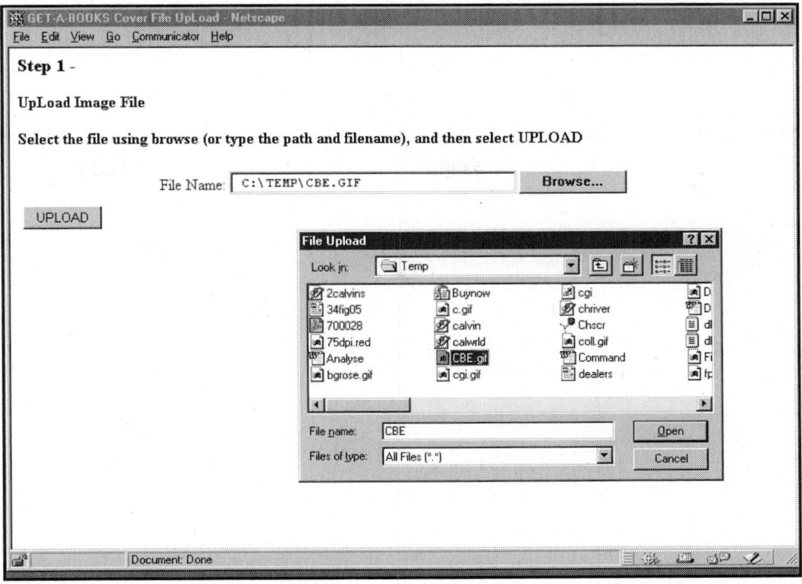

1. When the database administrator selects the file to be uploaded, the administrator clicks the Upload button and the file is placed on the server in a location specified within the script. If you take a look at Listing 32.1, you can see how this is done. First, the method is checked, and if it is `multipart/form-data`, the file is read as a binary and saved on the server. As Figure 32.3 shows you, after the file has been completely transferred to the server, a new screen appears with information on the file uploaded.

File Uploading

Form based file uploading in HTML is an experimental protocol covered under RFC1867. Although the Netscape browser (3.0+) and MSIE 4.0 support this protocol, not all browsers do.

Listing 32.1 Code allows files to be uploaded to a database.

```
# conform to RFC1867 for upload specific
    if( $ENV{'CONTENT_TYPE'} =~ /multipart\/form-data; boundary=(.+)$/ ) {
        $boundary = '--'.$1;  # please refer to RFC1867
        @list = split(/$boundary/, $input);

        $header_body = $list[1];
        $header_body =~ /\r\n\r\n|\n\n/; # separate header and body
        $header = $';          # front part
        $body   = $';          # rear part
        $body =~ s/\r\n$//;  # the last \r\n was put in by Netscape
        $GLOBAL{'FILE_CONTENT'} = $body;
```

continues

Listing 32.1 Continued

```
        # open(FD,">input.txt"); print FD $input; close(FD);  # for tracking
        # parse header
        $header =~ /filename=\"(.+)\"/;
        $GLOBAL{'FILE_NAME'} = $1;
        $GLOBAL{'FILE_NAME'} =~ s/\"//g; # remove "s
        $GLOBAL{'FILE_NAME'} =~ s/\s//g; # make sure no space(include \n, \r..)
in the file name

        # parse trailer
        for( $i=2; $list[$i]; $i++) {
            $list[$i] =~ s/^.+name=$//;
            $list[$i] =~ /\"(\w+)\"/;
            $GLOBAL{$1} = $';
        }
return 1;
    }
```

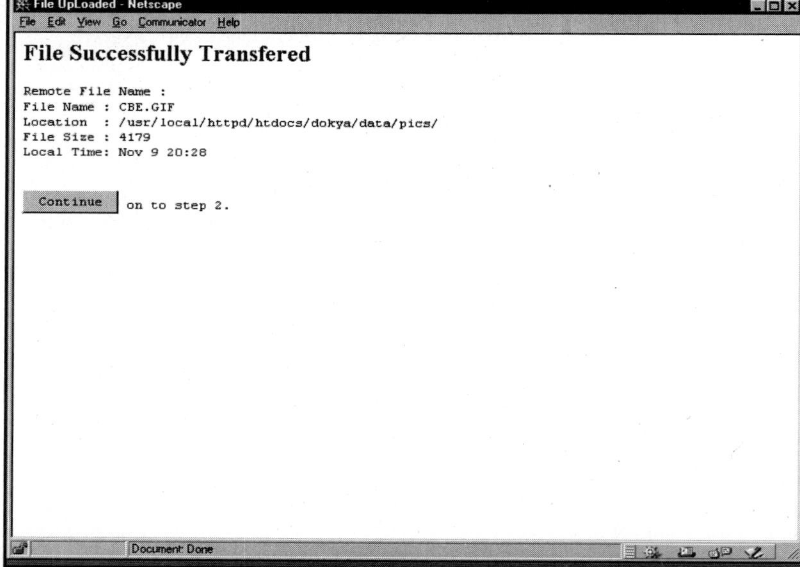

FIG. 32.3
After the file is uploaded, you can see some basic information on it.

TROUBLESHOOTING

If there is any problem with the upload, the script will give you some general information about the problem. The most common problem is that the web server doesn't have permission to write to that directory, or the server isn't able to overwrite an existing file.

2. The next screen allows the database administrator to enter additional information about the book (see Figure 32.4). This screen is simply a CGI-generated web page that requests the administrator to place the book under an existing category or create a new category. When done, the administrator can add additional information, such as the book's name, author, number of pages and cost, and additional comments. The name of the image uploaded is automatically entered into the form and can be edited by the database administrator.

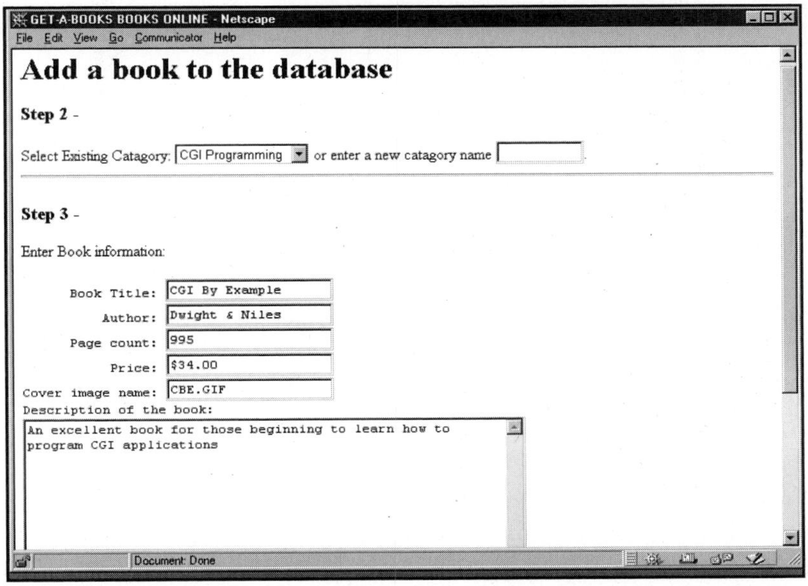

FIG. 32.4 Information about the book is entered by the database administrator. This information will be kept in the database.

GET-A-BOOKS BOOKS ONLINE - Netscape

File Edit View Go Communicator Help

Add a book to the database

Step 2 -

Select Existing Catagory: CGI Programming or enter a new catagory name

Step 3 -

Enter Book information:

Book Title: CGI By Example

Author: Dwight & Niles

Page count: 995

Price: $34.00

Cover image name: CBE.GIF

Description of the book:

An excellent book for those beginning to learn how to program CGI applications

Document: Done

Part VI Ch 32

3. When all information has been entered and the Submit button clicked, the information is stored on the server in two parts. In the first section, you place most of the information within the database. The only information you place elsewhere is the description. You can see how to do this in Listing 32.2.

Listing 32.2 Code stores information on the server in two parts.

```
if ($contents{'desc'})
 {
  open (DESC, ">>$path/$descriptions/$fdate.txt");
  print DESC "$contents{'desc'}";
  close(DESC);
 }

if ($contents{'newcat'})
 {
open (CC, "$path/data/cat.count");
```

continues

Listing 32.2 Continued

```
$catnum = <CC>;
chop($catnum);
close(CC);
$newcount = $catnum+1;
open (CC, ">$path/data/cat.count");
print CC "$newcount\n";
open (NEWCAT, ">>$path/$catagories");
print NEWCAT "$catnum,$contents{'newcat'}\n";
close(NEWCAT);
}
else {
$catnum=$contents{'category'};
}

open (BOOK, ">>$path/$database");
print BOOK "$catnum,$contents{'title'},$contents{'author'},
$contents{'pages'},$contents{'price'},$contents{'image'},$fdate.txt\n";
close(BOOK);
```

NOTE The description is placed as a separate file in a separate directory. By placing the description by itself, you don't have to be so concerned with the contents of the description, leaving the formatting of the text to the whim of the database administrator. You also can keep the size of your database to a minimum, ensuring that any database access will be faster. The description filename is stored in the database, allowing you to know how to access the description.

4. When all the information has been entered and the Submit button has been clicked, you inform the administrator that the information has been received and resides in the database. At this point, anyone visiting the site will be able to view the new book.

Removing Information

Although adding information is crucial to any database application, so is the ability to remove any old information from the database. In this example, you would like to make this as easy as possible for the administrator. Instead of relying on the database administrator to know how to access the web server and manually remove an entry from the database, you can devise a simple method in which the administrator can search through the database using a keyword and then select the particular entry from a list for removal.

Listing 32.3 shows you how to search through the database for the keyword entered and then display all matching entries using the select tag.

Listing 32.3 Code facilitates a keyword search and displays results.

```
sub search {
&header;
print <<"HTML";
<FORM ACTION="remove.cgi" method="POST">
```

```
Select a book from the list provided. This book will be removed from the
database.<p>
Books: <select name="remove">
HTML
$count==0;
open (DB, "$path/$database");
until(eof(DB))
 {
  $record = <DB>;
  if ($record =~ /$contents{'search'}/i)
   {
    @fields= split(/,/, $record);
    print "<OPTION value=\"$fields[1]\"> $fields[1] by $fields[2] ";
    $count++;
   }
 }

if ($count==0)
  {
   print "No matches";
  }

close(DB);
print <<"HTML";
</SELECT>
<p>
<input type="submit" value="Remove book"> from database.
</FORM>
HTML
&footer;
exit;
}
```

The `search` subroutine keeps track of how many entries matched the search. This allows you to know whether there were no matches, and if so, you can inform the database administrator. If matches do exist, each book is listed with the book title and the author. The administrator selects the appropriate book and then clicks Remove Book.

You are able to do this by searching through each record; the script removes only the book with the exact same title as the administrator selected. The rest of the entries are rewritten to the database. Listing 32.4 shows this step in more detail.

Listing 32.4 Code allows the removal of unwanted items.

```
sub remove {
 &header;
 print <<"HTML";

 <H1> Removed $contents{'remove'} </H1>

 The book, <b>$contents{'remove'}</b> was removed from the database.
 HTML
```

continues

Listing 32.4 Continued

```
open(RM, "$path/$database");
until(eof(RM))
 {
  @lines=<RM>;
 }
close(RM);

open(RM, ">$path/$database");
foreach $tmp (@lines)
 {
  if ($tmp =~ /$contents{'remove'}/)
   {
@fields = split(/,/, $tmp);
    system "/bin/rm $path/data/pics/$fields[5]" unless $fields[5] eq "test.gif";
    system "/bin/rm $path/$descriptions/$fields[6]" unless $fields[6] eq
"test.txt";
   }

  print RM $tmp unless $tmp =~ /$contents{'remove'}/;

 }
close(RM);

&footer;
exit;
}
```

Because the descriptions for each entry are kept in a separate file, you must remove the appropriate description as well. The filename for the description is kept as a field within the database.

Browsing the Database

Now that you have the ability to add and remove entries to the database, you need to create a script that allows those visiting the online bookstore to search through the database and view details on each book.

The form shown in Figure 32.5 allows those visiting the site to select a category, and then they can either view all the books under that category or perform a keyword search.

1. The initial form and both search methods are performed by a single script. If the script detects that nothing relevant was entered by a visitor, the form seen in Figure 32.4 is displayed. The script knows which categories are available, because when the script created the page, the script checked the appropriate database. Each category is listed within the select tag with the appropriate category number, for example:

   ```
   <OPTION VALUE="1">CGI Programming
   ```

   You use this value to do the actual lookups in the database, returning only information that matches the appropriate value.

2. If the visitor prefers to perform a keyword search, the appropriate subroutine seen in Listing 32.5 is used. The script returns only those books in the selected category that match the keyword entered by the visitor.

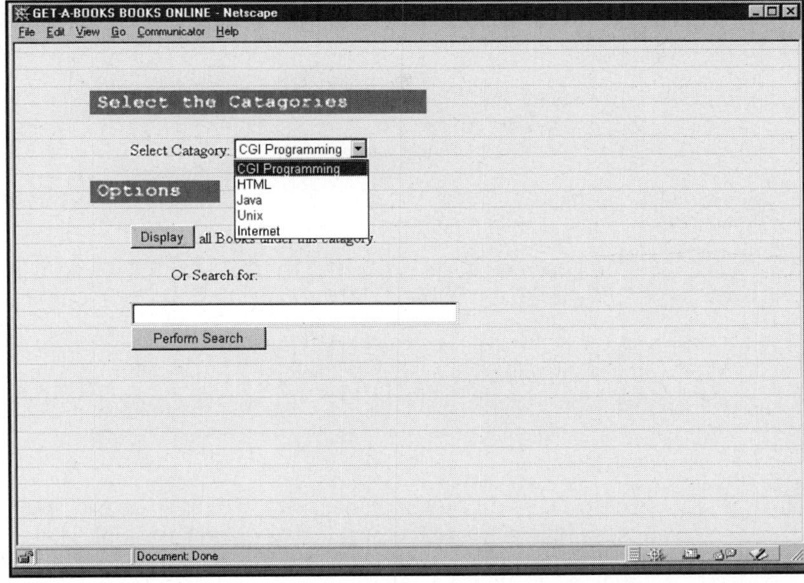

FIG. 32.5
The key to a successful database application is its ease of use.

Listing 32.5 Code allows a visitor to perform a category specific keyword search.

```
sub display_search {
 print "Content-type: text/html\n\n";
 &header;
print <<"HTML";
<H1>Search Results for $contents{'string'}</H1>
<TABLE width=510 border=0>
<TR><TD>Title</TD><TD>Author</TD></TR>
<TR><TD colspan=2><HR></TD></TR>
HTML
 open (BOOKS, "$path/$database") || do {print "Can't get database - $!";exit;};
 until(eof(BOOKS)) {
$count==0;
  $line = <BOOKS>;
  if ($line =~ /^$contents{'catagory'}/)
   {
    if ($line =~ /$contents{'string'}/i)
     {
      @section = split(/,/, $line);
$nameofbook=$section[1];
$section[1] =~ s/ /+/g;
      print <<"HTML";
```

continues

Listing 32.5 Continued

```
      <TR><TD><a href="index.cgi?book_selected=$section[1]">$nameofbook</a></
TD><TD>$section[2]<br></TD></TR>
HTML
$count++;
     }
   }
  }
if ($count==0)
{
print "<tr><td>No matches</td></tr>\n";
}
print "</TABLE>";
&footer;
exit;
}
```

3. With the keyword search, two conditions are used. First, you check to see whether the entry in the database matches the category desired. If the entry does match, you check to see whether the title of the book matches the keyword. If so, the script prints out a link. If not, the script goes to the next record in the database and checks these conditions again.
4. If the visitor wants to view all the books in the category, the subroutine (shown in Listing 32.6) is a little easier to program and the search is simpler—therefore a bit faster.

Listing 32.6 Code generates a quick view of all items in a selected category.

```
sub display_all {
print "Content-type: text/html\n\n";
&header;
open (CAT, "$path/$catagories");
until (eof(CAT))
{
 $catgory = <CAT>;
 whether ($catgory =~ /$contents{'catagory'}/)
 {
  @fields = split(/,/, $catgory);
 }
}
print <<"HTML";
<H1>Books under: $fields[1]</H1>
<TABLE width=510 border=0>
<TR><TD>Title</TD><TD>Author</TD></TR>
<TR><TD colspan=2><HR></TD></TR>
HTML
 open (BOOKS, "$path/$database") ¦¦ do {print "Can't get database - $!";exit;};
 until(eof(BOOKS)) {
  $count==0;
  $line = <BOOKS>;
  if ($line =~ /^$contents{'catagory'}/)
   {
       @section = split(/,/, $line);
```

```
$nameofbook=$section[1];
$section[1] =~ s/ /+/g;
      print <<"HTML";
      <TR><TD><a href="index.cgi?book_selected=$section[1]">$nameofbook</a></
TD><TD>$section[2]<br></TD></TR>
HTML
$count++;
      }
   }
if ($count==0)
{
print "<tr><td>No books under that category</td></tr>\n";
}
print "</TABLE>";
&footer;
exit;
}
```

5. Whether the visitor wants all books listed (refer to Listing 32.6), or only those that match the keywords entered, each book is listed with the name of the book and the name of the author (see Figure 32.6). The name of the book is a link back to the same script.

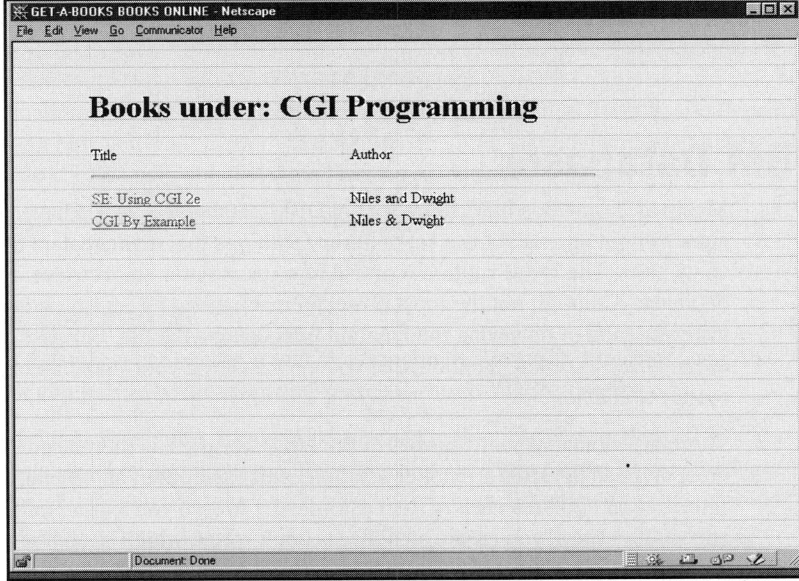

FIG. 32.6 A visitor can view all the books requested and select the appropriate book that suits his or her needs.

After a link is clicked, the cover image, additional information from the database, and description file are displayed to the visitor, as shown in Figure 32.7.

Using these different methods of storing information on the server to represent one page with information about a book, you can use flat file databases to provide information in a manner that is appealing to the visitor and is easy to use. If you aren't planning on keeping a large data-

Listing 32.9 Continued

```
undef($database);

exit;
```

The script produces a web page that looks like the one in Figure 32.8.

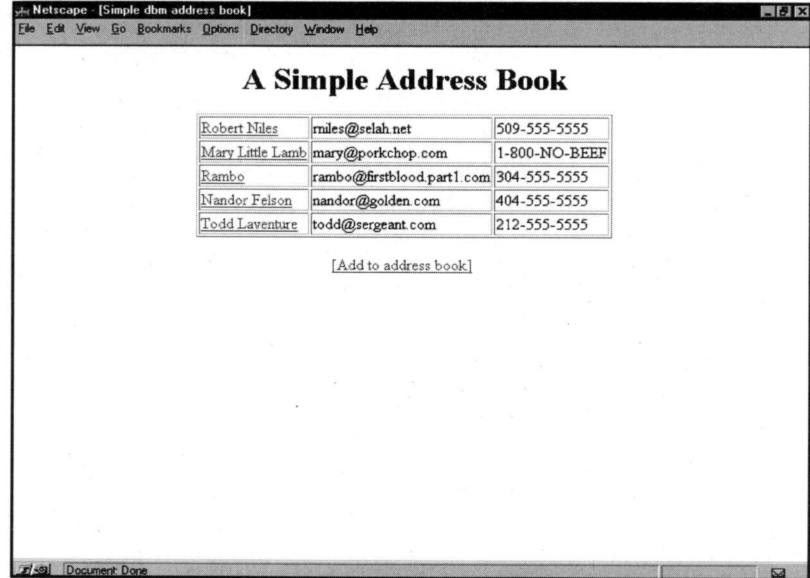

FIG. 32.8
The phonebook script produces a web page in which the names entered are hyperlinked with their corresponding email addresses.

Searching a DBM Database

If your database starts to get large, it's convenient to provide a means by which visitors to your site can search for a specific keyword. The web page to perform this search needs to have certain tags included (see Listing 32.10).

Listing 32.10 DBBOOKSEARCH.HTML This form enables a visitor to enter a keyword to perform a search.

```
<FORM ACTION="/cgi-bin/dbbooksearch.pl" METHOD="POST">
Name:<INPUT NAME="name"><BR>
<INPUT TYPE="SUBMIT">
</FORM>
```

Performing a search works much in the same manner as when you simply display the whole database; except that rather than immediately displaying each entry, you check it first to see whether it matches the keyword entered by the visitor. If the keyword matches the key, you print the line; otherwise, you simply skip ahead and check the next entry (see Listing 32.11).

Listing 32.11 DBBOOKSEARCH.PL By matching each field against a query, you can limit what information is returned to the visitor.

```
...$file="addresses";
$database=tie(%db, 'DB_File', $file, O_READ, 0660) || die "can't";

...while (($key,$value)= each(%db)) {
if ($key =~ /$form{'name'}/i) {
 @part = split(/:/,$value);
 if ($part[0]) {
   print "<TR><TD><A HREF=\"mailto:$part[0]\">$key</A></TD>";
   }
 else {
   print "<TR><TD>$key</TD>";
   }
 print "<TD>$part[0]</TD><TD>$part[1]</TD></TR>\n";
 }
}
...
```


Now that you have seen how DBM databases work, you can take the same concepts from these scripts and apply them to something different. For example, you could use them in a hotlinks script in which you can store information for all your favorite web sites, or in a proper address book that stores the names, addresses, and phone numbers of all your customers. You can also create a database that stores names and email addresses and use it as a mailing list, providing friends and customers news about you or your organization—or your products.

Relational Databases

Most relational database servers consist of a set of programs that manage large amounts of data, offering a rich set of query commands that help manage the power behind the database server. These programs control the storage, retrieval, and organization of the information within the database. This information can be changed, updated, or removed, after the support programs or scripts are in place.

Unlike DBM databases, relational databases don't link records together physically like the DBM database does using a key/value pair. Instead, they provide a field in which information can be matched and the results can be sent back to the person performing the query, as if the database were organized that way.

Relational databases store information in tables. A table is similar to a smaller database that sits inside the main database. Each table usually can be linked with the information in other tables to provide a result to a query. Take a look at Figure 32.9 which shows how this information could be tied together.

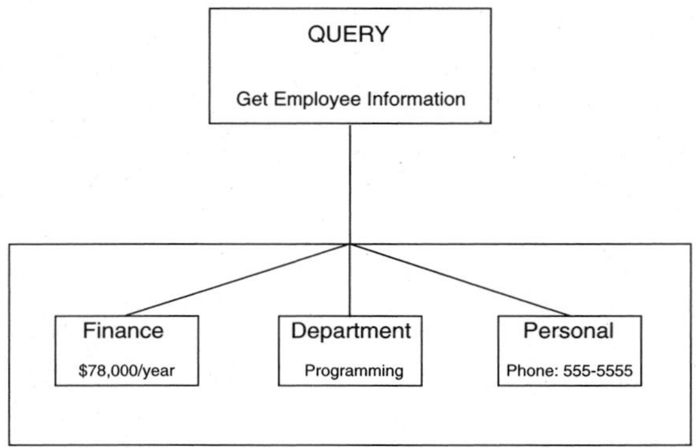

FIG. 32.9
A relational database stores certain information in various parts of the database; this information can later be called with one query.

Figure 32.8 depicts a query in which it requests employee information from a database. To get a complete response, information is retrieved from three tables, each of which stores only parts of the information requested. In the figure, information about the person's pay rate is retrieved, and departmental information and personal information is retrieved from other tables. This can produce a complete query response, with an abundant amount of information on an individual.

Each table consists of columns and rows. The columns identify the data by a name, and the rows store information relevant to that name. Take a look at the following example:

Name	Number	Email
Fred Flinstone	01–43	`ff@bedrock.com`
Barney Rubble	01–44	`br@bedrock.com`

The column heads give a name to each item below it. Information within a table is stored in much the same way.

If you add more tables to the database, you could have something that looks like the following:

Name	PayRate
Fred Flintstone	$34/month
Barney Rubble	$29/month

You could have department information as well:

Name	Department	Tardy Record
Fred Flintstone	Dino-Digger	17
Barney Rubble	Pebble Pusher	3

With this information, you can perform a query to get a complete look at an individual:

```
Select * from personal,department,finance where Name="Fred Flintstone
```

This would pull up all information on Fred Flintstone, from all three records. You could even be more specific, pulling only certain parts from each table:

```
select Name.finance,Name.finance where Tardy > 5
```

With this information, I think Fred would be in serious trouble—but you should have an idea of how relational databases work.

Introduction to Structured Query Language

Structured Query Language (*SQL*) is a language that provides a user interface to relational database management systems (RDBMS). Originally developed by IBM in the 1970s, SQL is the *de facto* standard for storing and retrieving information for relational databases, as well as being an ISO and ANSI standard. The current standard is SQL2, with SQL3 being planned for release in 1998.

The purpose of SQL is to provide a language, easily understandable by humans, that interfaces with relational databases:

- mSQL is a SQL server that works over a TCP/IP network. Although not as powerful as some of the commercial SQL engines, mSQL has just about everything that you might need for most everyday jobs. Some of the commercial SQL servers cost well over $3,000, but mSQL is free to the educational and nonprofit sectors and costs about $250 if you use it for commercial purposes.
- MsqlPerl, written by Andreas Koenig, is a Perl language interface to mSQL. The current version is 1.11 and can be found at the mSQL FTP site, which can be accessed at the URL given below.

About mSQL

David Hughes wrote mSQL to fill the need for a freely available SQL engine in which individuals can do research and experiments with SQL databases. mSQL has all the main functions that you would find in a SQL server and runs on most UNIX systems (with ports being developed for OS/2, Windows NT, and the Amiga by third-party contributors). The latest version, 2.0.3, includes a C language API in which you can create applications, including CGI applications, that interface with mSQL.

Visiting this site is well worthwhile, because it contains many programs for various platforms and languages (including TCL, Python, and Java) that support the mSQL database.

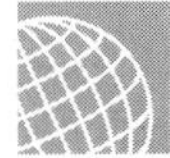

ON THE WEB

Visit the mSQL home page for more information on mSQL and its API, as well as a lot of user-contributed software:

http://hughes.com.au/product/msql/

Building a Relational Database Application

Building a relational database can be a daunting task at times —especially for a large organization with hundreds of employees and dozens of departments. With enough time and forethought, relational databases can work with information as no other database system can. The goal of any database administrator is to keep things as simple as possible without duplicating information.

Inserting Information

To insert information in a database, you first have to create one. This chapter's example database using mSQL consists of two tables.

The first table, called `employees`, contains personal information about each employee:

Column Name	Column Description
`empnum`	Number created automatically by your script. The `empnum` is the primary key for this table, which means that the number is unique within the table.
`fname`	The first name of the employee.
`lname`	The last name of the employee.
`home_phone`	The home phone number for the employee.
`other_phone`	A secondary phone number for the employee.
`email`	The email address of the employee.
`deptnum`	The number of the department in which the employee works.

The department number (`deptnum`) coincides with the department number in your second table, `departments`. In this table, you have only two fields:

Column Name	Column Description
`deptnum`	The department number
`deptname`	The name of the department

On the CD

With this information, you can create the database. Included on the CD-ROM is a file called WORK.DUMP, which is a text file that contains information that can be loaded into the mSQL database.

To add this information to the database, you need to first create the database using the `msqladmin` utility that is provided with mSQL, which is on the accompanying CD-ROM.

NOTE For additional information on how to compile and install mSQL, see the documentation provided within the mSQL archive located on the mSQL home page at:

http://www.Hughes.com.au/product/msql/

If you have installed mSQL in its default location, /USR/LOCAL/MINERVA, you can simply type

% /usr/local/Minerva/bin/msqladmin create work

at the UNIX command-line prompt. If you have installed mSQL elsewhere, change the path, specifying the proper path.

This command creates a database called `work`. After the database is created, information can be stored within it.

Next, to add each table and its contents to the database, type

% /usr/local/Minerva/bin/msql work <<work.dump

at the UNIX prompt.

You can confirm that the information was inserted into the database by typing

% /usr/local/Minerva/bin/relshow work

at the UNIX shell prompt. The `relshow` command will display something like the following:

```
Database = work
```

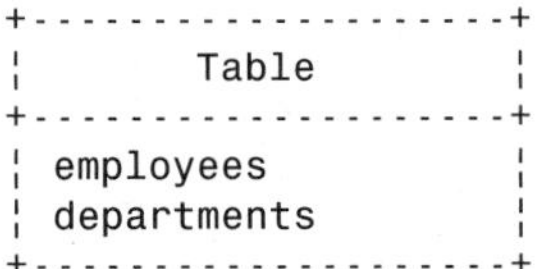

```
 +-------------------+
 |       Table       |
 +-------------------+
 | employees         |
 | departments       |
 +-------------------+
```


When this is done, you can start inserting information into the database.

First, you want to create a form that will enable someone to enter information into the database (see Listing 32.12).

Listing 32.12 PHONEADD.HTML An HTML document that will enable you to add employees to the SQL database.

```
<HTML>
<HEAD><TITLE>Insert into Phonebook</TITLE><HEAD>
<BODY>
<H1>Add Employee to the phonebook</H1>

<FORM ACTION="/cgi-bin/phoneadd.pl" METHOD="POST">

<pre>
       First Name: <INPUT TYPE="text" NAME="fname">
        Last Name: <INPUT TYPE="text" NAME="lname">
       Home Phone: <INPUT TYPE="text" NAME="home_phone">
      Other Phone: <INPUT TYPE="text" NAME="other_phone">
    Email Address: <INPUT TYPE="text" NAME="email">
Select department: <SELECT NAME="deptnum">
```

continues

Listing 32.12 Continued

```
<OPTION VALUE="1"> Administration
<OPTION VALUE="2"> Geeks
<OPTION VALUE="3"> Web Masters
<OPTION VALUE="4"> Network God
<OPTION VALUE="5"> Computer Tech
<OPTION VALUE="6"> Sales
<OPTION VALUE="7"> Apple Tech
<OPTION VALUE="8"> Odd Ball
</SELECT>
</pre>
<P>
<INPUT TYPE="submit" VALUE="Add Employee">
</FORM>
</BODY>
</HTML>
```

When filled out, the information in this form will be sent to the script `phoneadd.pl`. The `phoneadd.pl` script takes the information from the visitor and attempts to add that information to the database. The first thing that you might notice about the script is that the script first escapes those characters that the database cannot normally handle (see Listing 32.13).

Listing 32.13 PHONEADD.PL Information from STDIN is split and any special characters are escaped.

```
if ($ENV{'REQUEST_METHOD'} eq 'POST')
{
     read(STDIN, $buffer, $ENV{'CONTENT_LENGTH'});
     @pairs = split(/&/, $buffer);
     foreach $pair (@pairs)
     {
          ($name, $value) = split(/=/, $pair);
          $value =~ tr/+/ /;
                $value =~ s/\\/\\\\/g;
                $value =~ s/\$/\\\$/g;
                $value =~ s/\(/\\(/g;
                $value =~ s/\)/\\)/g;
                $value =~ s/\^/\\^/g;
                $value =~ s/\¦/\\¦/g;
                $value =~ s/\'/\\'/g;
          $value =~ s/%([a-fA-F0-9][a-fA-F0-9])/pack("C", hex($1))/eg;
          $contents{$name} = $value;

     }
}
```

In Listing 32.14, the script then checks to see what employee numbers (`empnum`) exist and increments that number, which will be assigned to the next employee being entered into the database.

Listing 32.14 The employee number is checked, and an original number is assigned to the new entry.

```
use Msql;$db1 = Msql->Connect("", "work") or die;$nextnum=1;
$sth = $db1->Query("select empnum from employees");
$count = $sth->numrows;
while ($rows=$sth->FetchRow)
{
  $nextnum=$rows+1;
}
```

Then a query is performed in which all the information is placed into the database (see Listing 32.15). After that is done, the script creates an HTML page that is sent back to the visitor, informing him or her that the query was successful.

Listing 32.15 The employee information is then inserted into the database.

```
$names = "empnum,fname,lname,home_phone,other_phone,email,deptnum";

$values = "$nextnum,'$contents{'fname'}','$contents{'lname'}'";
$values = $values . ",'$contents{'home_phone'}','$contents{'other_phone'}'";
$values = $values . ",'$contents{'email'}',$contents{'deptnum'}";

$sth1 = $db1->Query("insert into employees ($names) VALUES ($values)");

print "Content-type: text/html\n\n";
print $Msql::db_errstr, "\n";
...
```


Retrieving Information

Retrieving information from a relational database can be tricky at first, but when you get the idea of how SQL queries work, you will start to appreciate SQL.

Previously, the `INSERT` clause was used to add information to the database. Now, to retrieve information from a database, you will need to use the `SELECT` clause. The `SELECT` clause enables you to specify which information you want to retrieve from the database. The syntax, using mSQL is:

```
SELECT [column name] from [table name]
```

In the spirit of relational databases, information can also be retrieved from multiple tables using a query like this:

```
SELECT employees.empnum department.empnum from employees,department
```

Notice how I selected the column `empnum` from two tables instead of just one. This query is quite a simple one for a relational database to handle. They can get quite complex!

In the next script, the query gets a little more complex. Your script performs a query that receives information from two tables and then creates an HTML page that shows information about each employee. This time, instead of displaying the department number, you match the department numbers with the department names and show the names instead.

The first section of the script specifies that you need to use the `MsqlPerl` module. Next, you create the variable `$db1`, which contains the information needed to connect to the database. The examples will use the database named `work`.

```
#! /usr/bin/perl
use Msql;
$db1 = Msql->Connect("", "work") or die;
```

Now, referring to Listing 32.16, a query is built that will select every column from both the `employees` and the `department` tables, matching the information from each table by using the information obtained from the column `empnum`. That information is then displayed to the visitor, with the information sorted by the department number.

Listing 32.16 PHONE.PL A query is built specifying which information is needed from the SQL database.

```
$sth = $db1->Query("select employees.empnum,employees.fname,employees.lname,
employees.home_phone,employees.other_phone,employees.email,
departments.deptnum,departments.deptname from employees,departments where
employees.deptnum = departments.deptnum
order by employees.empnum") or die;
```

Next, the information retrieved from the database, and stored in the array `@row`, is broken up and displayed in an HTML document to the visitor:

```
print "<TR><TD align=\"right\">$row[0]</TD><TD><b>
       <a href=\"mailto:$row[5]\">$row[1] $row[2]</a></TD>
       <TD>$row[3]</TD><TD>$row[4]</TD><TD>$row[5]</TD>
       <TD>$row[7]</TD></TR>",
```

Last, a count is kept showing how many people matched the search criteria:

```
  while @row=$sth->FetchRow;print $Msql::db_errstr;
$count = $sth->numrows;
print "<TR><TD colspan=6 align=\"center\"> \
Number of Employees = $count</TD></TR>";
```

Debugging Database Applications

One of the biggest problems when dealing with databases on the web is trying to fix any problems that may occur when you are writing your script. First, you can have problems because of a bug in your script. Second, you can have problems because of an improper query.

The best way to see whether the problem lies within your script is to create a copy of the script that includes dummy variables—variables that contain information as if a visitor actually entered something into a form. For example, using the previous scripts, you can create a set of variables that mimic information that a visitor might have entered:

```
$contents{'fname'} = "John";
$contents{'lname'} = "Doe";
```

After you have the dummy variables set, you can execute your script using the command line:

```
% /usr/bin/perl phone.pl
```

Perl will report any problems with your script if you have programmed any code improperly.

To figure out what may be wrong with your SQL query, add the following line:

```
print $Msql::db_errstr, "\n";
```

This instructs mSQL to provide an error string if anything goes wrong with the SQL query and report whether the query is performed from the shell or a web page. Just make sure that the `Content-type` is specified *before* trying to send anything out to the server. For example, if I tried to `SELECT employees.phome_home` instead of `employees.home_phone`, the script would report the following:

```
Unknown field employees.phome_phone
```

Last, try to keep things simple and build up from what you know works. At first, create a script that contains the query that you need to perform, making sure that you use the `Content-type text/plain`. This will allow you to make sure that your script is providing a proper query. If all goes well, access your database using the same query from the command line. If the query produces the proper results, you can move on and try to access your script through the web server. If you are having problems here, make sure that you have specified the `Content-type` *before* anything is sent out to the server. This is probably one of the biggest problems with any script. An error occurs and your script sends information back to the web server without specifying the `Content-type`.

CHAPTER 33

CGI and Database Security

by Bliss Sloan

In this chapter

choices offered in the form. For example, the options in the `<SELECT NAME="opinion">` element may be `"yes"` and `"no"`, but the URL returned to the server may be `Error! Reference source not found.` The user may have edited the URL to include nearly any string.

- The length of the data returned from a text field may be longer than allowed by the `MAXLENGTH` attribute. As in the previous example, the user may have edited the URL to include a string of nearly any length. For example, if your form has a text field `<INPUT NAME="city" TYPE="text" MAXLENGTH="15">`, the URL returned to the server may be `http://www.yourdomain.com/cgi-bin/yourprog.pl/city=Error! Reference source not found.`
- The names of the fields themselves may not match what you specified in the form. For example, if your survey form has three named fields, `q1`, `q2`, and `q3`, you may still get a URL returned to the server ending in `?you_are=hacked`.

Scripts Versus Programs

Shell scripts, Perl programs, and C executables are the most common forms that a CGI script takes, and each has advantages and disadvantages when security is taken into account. No one language is the best; depending on other considerations such as speed and reuse, each has a place.

- Though shell CGI programs are often the easiest to write, it can be difficult to fully control them because they usually do most of their work by executing other, external programs. This can lead to several possible pitfalls, because your CGI script instantly inherits any of the security problems that those called programs have. For instance, the common UNIX utility awk has some fairly restrictive limits on the amount of data it can handle, and your CGI program will be burdened with all those limits as well.
- Perl is a step up from shell scripts. It has many advantages for CGI programming and is fairly secure, in itself. But Perl can offer CGI authors just enough flexibility and peace of mind that they might be lulled into a false sense of security. For example, Perl is interpreted and this makes it easier for bad user data to be included as part of the code

Where Bad Data Comes From

These situations can arise in several ways—some innocent, some not. For instance, your script can receive data that it doesn't expect because somebody else wrote a form (that requests input completely different from yours) and accidentally pointed the form's ACTION attribute to your CGI script. Perhaps, they used your form as a template and forgot to edit the ACTION attribute's URL before testing it. This would result in your script getting data that it has no idea what to do with, possibly causing unexpected—and dangerous—behavior.

Or the user might have accidentally (or intentionally) edited the URL to your CGI script. When a browser submits form data to a CGI program, it simply appends the data entered into the form onto the CGI's URL (for GET methods). The user can easily modify the data being sent to your script by typing in the browser's URL editbox.

Finally, an ambitious hacker might write a program that connects to your server over the web and pretends to be a web browser. This program, though, can do things that no true web browser would do, such as send a hundred megabytes of data to your CGI script. What would a CGI script do if it didn't limit the amount of data it read from a POST method because it assumed that the data came from a small form? It would probably crash and maybe crash in a way that would allow access to the person who crashed it.

Fighting Bad Form Data

You can fight the unexpected input that can be submitted to your CGI scripts in several ways. You should use any or all of them when writing CGI.

- First, your CGI script should set reasonable limits on how much data it will accept, both for the entire submission and for each name/value pair in the submission. If your CGI script reads the POST method, for instance, check the size of the CONTENT_LENGTH environment variable to make sure that it's something that you can reasonably expect. Although most web servers set an arbitrary limit on the amount of data that will be passed to your script via POST, you may want to limit this size further. For instance, if the only input your CGI script is designed to accept is a person's first name, it might be a good idea to return an error if CONTENT_LENGTH is more than, say, 100 bytes. No reasonable first name will be that long, and by imposing the limit, you've protected your script from blindly reading anything that gets sent to it.

NOTE In most cases, you don't have to worry about limiting the data submitted through the GET method. GET is usually self-limiting and won't deliver more than approximately one kilobyte of data to your script. The server automatically limits the size of the data placed into the QUERY_STRING environment variable, which is how GET sends information to a CGI program.

Of course, hackers can easily circumvent this built-in limit simply by changing the METHOD attribute of your form from "GET" to "PUT". At the very least, your program should check that data is submitted using the method you expect; at most, it should handle both methods correctly and safely.

▶ **See** "Standard CGI Environment Variables," **p. 874**

- Next, make sure that your script knows what to do if it receives data that it doesn't recognize. If, for example, a form asks that a user select one of two radio buttons, the script shouldn't assume that just because one isn't clicked, the other is. The following Perl code makes this mistake.

```
if ($form_Data{"radio_choice"} eq "button_one")
{
        # Button One has been clicked
}
else
{
        # Button Two has been clicked
}
```

- Your CGI script should anticipate unexpected or "impossible" situations and handle them accordingly. The above example is pretty innocuous, but the same assumption elsewhere can easily be dangerous. An error should be printed instead, for instance:

```
if ($form_Data{"radio_choice"} eq "button_one")
{
        # Button One selected
}
elsif ($form_Data{"radio_choice"} eq "button_two")
{
        # Button Two selected
}
else
{
        # Error
}
```

Of course, an error may not be what you want your script to generate in these circumstances. Overly picky scripts that validate every field and produce error messages on even the slightest unexpected data can turn users off.

The balance between safety and convenience for the user is important. Don't be afraid to consult with your users to find out what works best for them.

- Having your CGI script recognize unexpected data, throw it away, and automatically select a default is a possibility, too. For instance, the following is C code that checks text input against several possible choices and sets a default if it doesn't find a match. You can use this to generate output that might better explain to the user what you expect.

```
/* Notes for non-C programmers:                                    */
/* Contrary to what its name implies,                              */
/*   the C string comparison function strcmp used below            */
/*   returns 0 (false) when its two arguments match, and           */
/*   returns nonzero (true)_when its two arguments differ.         */
/*   A better name might be strDIFF.                               */
/* In C, "&&" is logical AND.                                      */
/*                                                                 */
/* If the help_Topic is not any of the three choices given...      */
if ((strcmp(help_Topic,"how_to_order.txt")) &&
```

```
  (strcmp(help_Topic,"delivery_options.txt")) &&
  (strcmp(help_Topic,"complaints.txt")))
{
      /* then set help_Topic to the default value here         */
      strcpy(help_Topic,"help_on_help.txt");
}
```

- However, your script might try to do users a favor and correct any mistakes rather than simply send an error or select a default. If a form asks users to enter the secret word, your script can automatically strip off any whitespace characters from the input before doing the comparison, such as the following Perl fragment.

```
# Remove white space by replacing it with an empty string
$user_Input =~ s/\s//;
if ($user_Input eq $secret_Word)
{
      # Match!
}
```

Although it's nice to try to catch the users' mistakes, don't try to do too much. If your corrections aren't really what users wanted, they'll be annoyed.

CAUTION

You should also be aware that trying to catch every possible user-entry error will make your code huge and near impossible to maintain. Don't over-engineer.

- Finally, you might choose to go the extra mile and have your CGI script handle as many different forms of input as it can. Although you can't possibly anticipate everything that can be sent to a CGI program, there are often several common ways to do a particular thing, and you can check for each.

For example, just because the form you wrote uses the `POST` method to submit data to your CGI script, that doesn't mean that the data will come in that way. Rather than assume that the data will be on standard in (stdin) where you're expecting it, you can check the `REQUEST_METHOD` environment variable to determine whether the `GET` or `POST` method was used and read the data accordingly. A truly well-written CGI script will accept data no matter what method was used to submit it and will be made more secure in the process. Listing 33.1 shows an example in Perl.

TROUBLESHOOTING

If your script returns `Error 500: Server doesn't support POST`, there are four usual causes. The first is that your server is not properly set up to handle CGI scripts. The second is that the script named in the form's `ACTION` attribute is not in your CGI-enabled directory, usually called `cgi-bin`. The third is that the path given in the form's `ACTION` attribute is misspelled, or the filename is misspelled. Check the spelling of the filename and path. The fourth cause is that the filename and path are correct, but the filename does not end in the proper extension (such as .cgi or .plx or .pl) for your server configuration.

Although you will usually get this error with the form's `METHOD="POST"`, a user can cause this error to occur in a form with `METHOD="GET"` by editing your page in his browser and substituting `"POST"` for `"GET"`.

Listing 33.1 CGI_READ.PL A robust reading form input.

```
# Takes the maximum length allowed as a parameter
# Returns 1 and the raw form data, or "0" and the error text
sub cgi_Read
{
      local($input_Max) = 1024 unless $input_Max = $_[0];
      local($input_Method) = $ENV{'REQUEST_METHOD'};

      # Check for each possible REQUEST_METHODs
      if ($input_Method eq "GET")
      {
            # "GET"
            local($input_Size) = length($ENV{'QUERY_STRING'});

            # Check the size of the input
            return (0, "Input too big") if ($input_Size > $input_Max);

            # Read the input from QUERY_STRING
            return (1,$ENV{'QUERY_STRING'});
      }
      elsif ($input_Method eq "POST")
      {
            # "POST"
            local($input_Size) = $ENV{'CONTENT_LENGTH'};
            local($input_Data);

            # Check the size of the input
            return (0,"Input too big") if ($input_Size > $input_Max);

            # Read the input from stdin
            return (0,"Could not read STDIN") unless
(read(STDIN,$input_Data,$input_Size));

            return (1,$input_Data);
      }

      # Unrecognized METHOD
      return (0,"METHOD not GET or POST");
}
```

TIP Many existing CGI programming libraries already offer good built-in security features. Rather than write your own routines, you may want to rely on some of the well-known, publicly available functions.

Part VI Ch 33

Don't Trust Path Data

Another type of data the user can alter is the PATH_INFO server environment variable. This variable is filled with any path information that follows the script's filename in a CGI URL. For instance, if sample.sh is a CGI shell script, the URL **http://www.yourserver.com/cgi-bin/sample.sh/extra/path/info** will cause /extra/path/info to be placed in the PATH_INFO environment variable when sample.sh is run.

If you use this PATH_INFO environment variable, you must be careful to completely validate its contents. Just as form data can be altered in any number of ways, so can PATH_INFO—accidentally or on purpose. A CGI script that blindly acts on the path file specified in PATH_INFO can allow malicious users to wreak havoc on the server.

For instance, if a CGI script is designed to simply print out the file that's referenced in PATH_INFO, a user who edits the CGI URL can read almost any file on your computer, as in the following script:

```
#!/bin/sh

# Send the header
echo "Content-type: text/html"
echo ""

# Wrap the file in some HTML
echo "<html><header><title>File</title></header><body>"
echo "Here is the file you requested:<pre>\n"
cat $PATH_INFO
echo "</pre></body></html>"
```

Although this script works fine if the user is content to click only predefined links—say, **http://www.yourserver.com/cgi-bin/showfile.sh/public/faq.txt**—a more creative (or spiteful) user could use it to receive *any* file on your server. If she were to jump to **http://www.yourserver.com/cgi-bin/showfile.sh/etc/passwd**, the preceding script would happily return your machine's password file, something you do *not* want to happen.

A much safer course is to use the PATH_TRANSLATED environment variable. It automatically appends the contents of PATH_INFO to the root of your server's document tree, meaning that any file specified by PATH_TRANSLATED is probably already accessible to browsers and, therefore, safe. For example, if your document root is /usr/local/etc/htdocs, and PATH_INFO is /etc/passwd, then PATH_TRANSLATED is /usr/local/etc/htdocs/etc/passwd.

NOTE In one case, however, files that may not be accessible through a browser can be accessed if PATH_TRANSLATED is used within a CGI script. The .htaccess file, which can exist in each subdirectory of a document tree, controls who has access to the particular files in that directory. It can be used to limit the visibility of a group of web pages to company employees, for example. Whereas the server knows how to interpret .htaccess, and thus knows how to limit who can and who can't see these pages, CGI scripts don't. A program that uses PATH_TRANSLATED to access arbitrary files in the document tree may accidentally override the protection provided by the server.

Handling Filenames

Filenames, for example, are simple pieces of data that may be submitted to your CGI script and cause endless amounts of trouble—if you're not careful (see Figure 33.1).

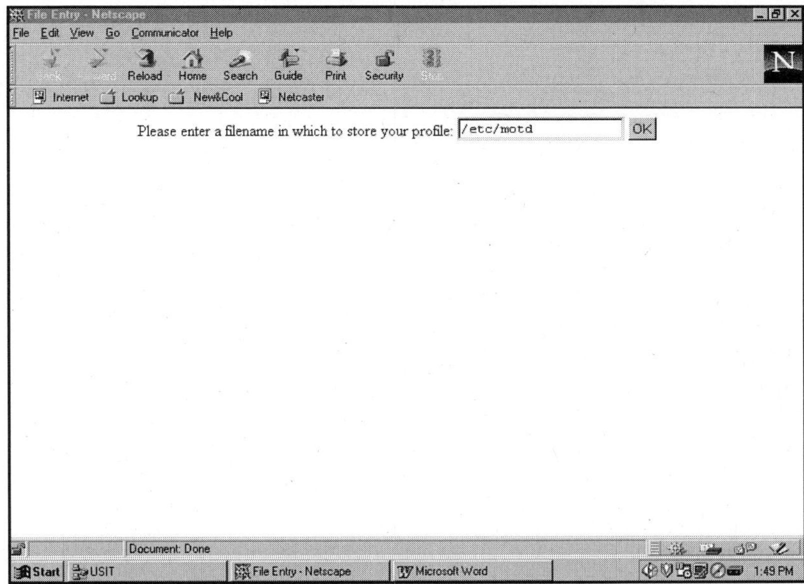

FIG. 33.1
Depending on how well the CGI script is written, the webmaster for this site can get in big trouble.

Any time you try to open a file based on a name supplied by the user, you must rigorously screen that name for any number of tricks that can be played. If you ask the user for a filename and then try to open whatever was entered, there may be a problem.

- For instance, what if the user enters a name that has path elements in it, such as directory slashes and double dots? Although you expect a simple filename—say, File.txt—you can end up with /file.txt or ../../../file.txt. Depending on how your web server is installed and what you do with the submitted filename, you can be exposing any file on your system to a clever hacker.
- Further, what if the user enters the name of an existing file or one that's important to the running of the system? What if the name entered is /etc/passwd or C:\WINNT\SYSTEM32\KERNEL32.DLL? Depending on what your CGI script does with these files, they may be sent out to the user or overwritten with garbage.
- Under Windows 95 and Windows NT, if you don't screen for the backslash character (\), you might allow web browsers to gain access to files that aren't even on your web server through Universal Naming Convention (UNC) filenames. If the script that's about to run in Figure 33.2 doesn't carefully screen the filename before opening it, it might give the web browser access to any machine in the domain or workgroup.

Part VI
Ch 33

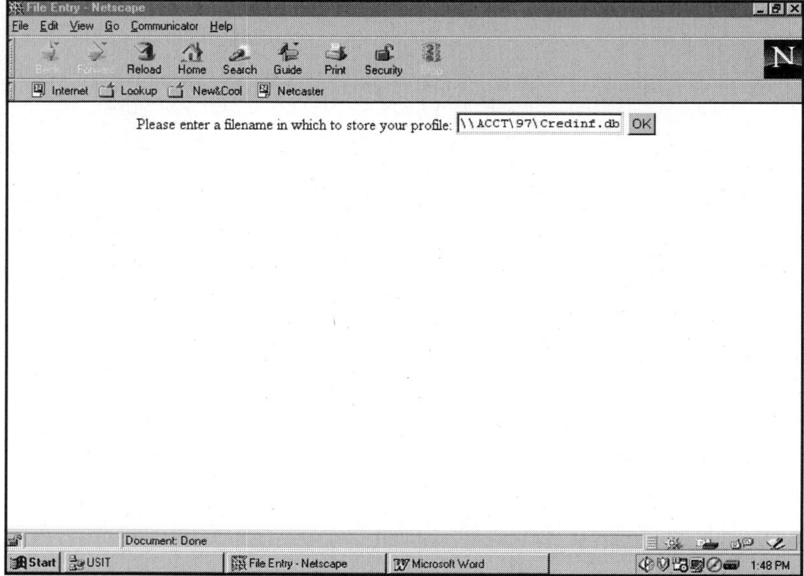

FIG. 33.2
Opening a UNC filename is one possible security hole that gives hackers access to your entire network.

- What might happen if the user puts an illegal character in a filename? Under UNIX, any filename beginning with a period (.) will become invisible. Under Windows, both slashes (/ and \) are directory separators. It's possible to write a Perl program carelessly and allow external programs to be executed when you thought you were only opening a file, if the filename begins with the pipe (¦). Even control characters (the Escape key or the Return key, for instance) can be sent to you as part of filenames if the user knows how. (Refer to "Where Bad Data Comes From" earlier in this chapter.)

NOTE Worse yet, in shell script, the semicolon ends one command and starts another. If your script is designed to `cat` the file the user enters, a user might enter **file.txt;rm -rf /** as a filename, causing file.txt to be returned and, consequently, the entire hard disk to be erased, without confirmation.

Verifying Input Is Legitimate

To avoid all the dangers associated with bad input and close all the potential security holes they open, you should screen every filename the user enters. You must make sure that the input is only what you expect.

The best way to do this is to compare each character of the entered filename against a list of acceptable characters and return an error if they don't match. This turns out to be much safer than trying to maintain a list of all the *illegal* characters and compare against that—it's too easy to accidentally let something slip through.

Listing 33.2 is an example of how to do this comparison in Perl. It allows any letter of the alphabet (upper- or lowercase), any number, the underscore, and the period. It also checks to make sure that the filename doesn't start with a period. Thus, this fragment doesn't allow slashes to change directories, semicolons to put multiple commands on one line, or pipes to play havoc with Perl's `open()` call.

Listing 33.2 Making sure that all characters are legal.

```
if (($file_Name =~ /[^a-zA-Z_\.]/) || ($file_Name =~ /^\./))
{
        # File name contains an illegal character or starts with a period
}
```

When you have a commonly used test, such as the code in Listing 33.2, it's a good idea to make it into a subroutine, so you can call it repeatedly. This way, you can change it in only one place in your program if you think of an improvement.

Continuing that thought, if the subroutine is used commonly among several programs, it's a good idea to put it into a library so that any improvements can be instantly inherited by all your scripts.

CAUTION

Although the code in Listing 33.2 filters out most bad filenames, your operating system may have restrictions it doesn't cover. Can a filename start with a digit, for instance? Or with an underscore? What if the filename has more than one period, or if the period is followed by more than three characters? Is the entire filename short enough to fit within the restrictions of the file system?

You must constantly ask yourself these sort of questions. The most dangerous thing you can do when writing CGI scripts is to rely on the users following instructions. They won't. It's your job to make sure they don't get away with it.

Handling HTML

Another type of seemingly innocuous input that can cause you endless trouble is receiving HTML when you request text from the user. Listing 33.3 is a Perl fragment that simply customizes a greeting to whomever has entered a name in the `$user_Name` variable, for example, John Smith (see Figure 33.3).

Listing 33.3 A script that sends a customized greeting.

```
print("<HTML><TITLE>Greetings!</TITLE><BODY>\n");
print("Hello, $user_Name!  It's good to see you!\n");
print("</BODY></HTML>\n");
```

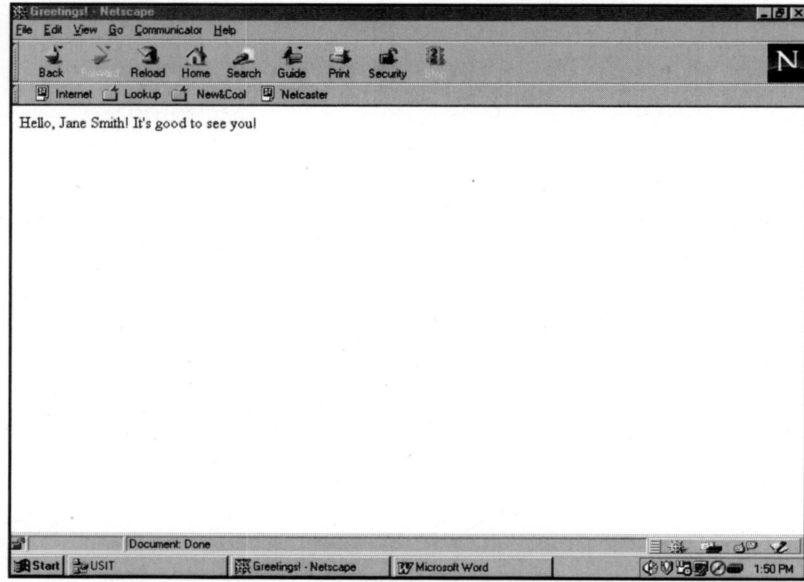

FIG. 33.3 When the user enters what you requested, everything works well.

But imagine if, rather than enter just a name, the user types `<HR><H1><P ALIGN="CENTER">Jane Smith</P></H1><HR>`. The result would be Figure 33.4—probably not what you wanted.

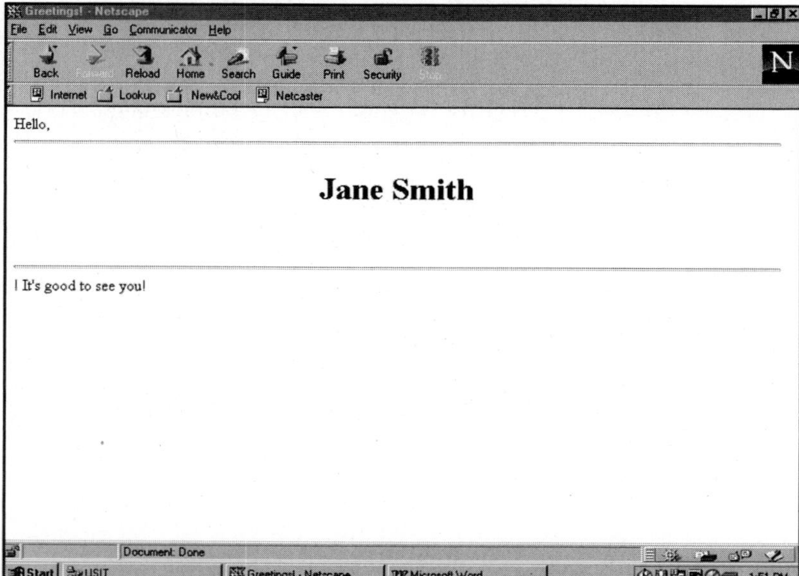

FIG. 33.4 Entering HTML when a script expects plain text can change a page in unexpected ways.

Or imagine if a hacker entered

```
<IMG SRC="/secret/project/funnyface.jpg">
```

when you requested the user's name. Again, if the code in Listing 33.3 were part of a CGI script with this HTML in the $user_Name variable, your web server would happily show the hacker your secret adorable toddler picture! Figure 33.5 is an example.

FIG. 33.5 Allowing HTML to be entered can be dangerous. Here a secret file is shown instead of the user's name.

Or what if **`The last signee!<FORM><SELECT>`** was entered as the user's name in a guest book? The <SELECT> tag would cause the web browser to ignore everything between it and a nonexistent </SELECT>, including any names that were added to the list later. Even though ten people signed the guest book shown in Figure 33.6, only the first three appear because the third name contains a <FORM> and a <SELECT> tag.

But even more dangerous than entering simple HTML, a malicious hacker might enter a server-side include directive instead. If your web server is configured to obey server-side includes, a user might type **`<!-- #include file="/secret/project/plan.txt" -->`** instead of his name to see the complete text of your secret plans. Or he can enter **`<!---- #include file="/etc/passwd" ---->`** to get your machine's password file. And probably worst of all, a hacker might input **`<!---- #exec cmd="rm -rf /" ---->`**, and the innocent code in Listing 33.3 would proceed to delete almost everything on your hard disk.

▶ **See** "Common SSI Commands," **p. 1014**

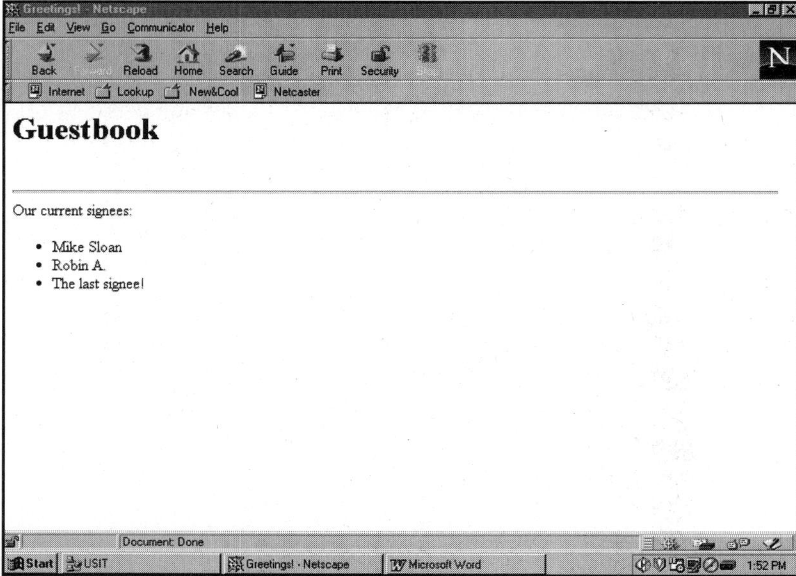

FIG. 33.6
Because the third signee used HTML tags in his name, nobody after him will show up.

> **CAUTION**
> Server-side includes are often disabled because of how they can be misused. Although much more information is available in Chapter 36, "Server-Side Includes," you might want to consider this option to truly secure your site against this type of attack.

There are two solutions to the problem of the user entering HTML rather than flat text:

- The quick-and-dirty solution is to disallow the less-than (<) and greater-than (>) symbols. Because all HTML tags must be contained within these two characters, removing them (or returning an error if you encounter them) is an easy way to prevent HTML from being submitted and accidentally returned. The following line of Perl code simply erases the characters:

  ```
  $user_Input =~ s/<>//g;
  ```

- The more elaborate solution is to translate the two characters into their HTML *escape codes*. The following code does this by globally substituting **<** for the less-than symbol and **>** for the greater-than symbol:

  ```
  $user_Input =~ s/</&lt;/g;
  $user_Input =~ s/>/&gt;/g;
  ```

Handling External Processes

Another area where you must be careful is how your CGI script interfaces user input with any external processes. Because executing a program outside of your CGI script means that you have no control over what it does, you must do everything you can to validate the input you send to it before the execution begins.

For instance, shell scripts often make the mistake of concatenating a command-line program with form input and then executing them together. This works fine if the user has entered what you expected, but additional commands may be sneaked in and unintentionally executed.

The following fragment of shell script commits this error:

```
FINGER_OUTPUT=`finger $USER_INPUT`
echo $FINGER_OUTPUT
```

If the user politely enters the email address of a person to finger, everything works as it should. But if he enters an email address followed by a semicolon and another command, that command will be executed as well. If the user enters **webmaster@www.yourserver.com;rm -rf /**, you're in considerable trouble.

CAUTION

You also must be careful to screen all the input you receive, not just form data, before using it in the shell. Web server environment variables can be set to anything by a hacker who has written his own web client and can cause just as much damage as bad form data.

If you execute the following line of shell script, thinking that it will simply add the referrer to your log, you might be in trouble if `HTTP_REFERER` has been set to `;rm -rf /;echo "Ha ha"`.

```
echo $HTTP_REFERER >> ./referer.log
```

Even if a hidden command isn't placed into user data, innocent input may give you something you don't expect. The following line, for instance, will give an unexpected result—a listing of all the files in the directory—if the user input is an asterisk.

```
echo "Your input: " $USER_INPUT
```

When sending user data through the shell, as both of these code snippets do, it's a good idea to screen it for shell meta-characters. Such characters include the semicolon (which allows multiple commands on one line), the asterisk and the question mark (which perform file globbing), the exclamation point (which, under csh, references running jobs), the back quote (which executes an enclosed command), and so on. Like filtering filenames, maintaining a list of allowable characters is often easier than trying to catch each character that should be disallowed. The following Perl fragment crudely validates an email address:

```
if ($email_Address ~= /[^a-zA-Z0-9_\-\+\@\.])
{
      # Illegal character!
}
else
{
      system("finger $email_Address");
}
```

If you decide that you must allow shell meta-characters in your input, there are ways to make their inclusion safer—and ways that don't actually accomplish anything. Although you may be tempted to simply put quotation marks around user input that hasn't been validated to prevent the shell from acting on special characters, this almost never works. Look at the following:

```
echo "Finger information:<HR><PRE>"
finger "$USER_INPUT"
echo "</PRE>"
```

Although the quotation marks around `$USER_INPUT` will prevent the shell from interpreting, say, an included semicolon that would allow a hacker to simply piggyback a command, this script still has several severe security holes. For instance, the input might be `` `rm -rf /` ``, with the back quotes causing the hacker's command to be executed before `finger` is even considered.

A better way to handle special characters is to escape them so that the shell simply takes their values without interpreting them. By escaping the user input, all shell meta-characters are ignored and treated instead as just more data to be passed to the program.

The following line of Perl code does this for all nonalphanumeric characters.

```
$user_Input =~ s/([^w])/\\\1/g;
```

Now, if this user input were appended to a command, each character—even the special characters—would be passed through the shell to `finger`.

Over all, validating user input—not trusting anything sent to you—will make your code easier to read and safer to execute. Rather than try to defeat a hacker after you're already running commands, give data the once-over at the door.

Handling Internal Functions

With interpreted languages, such as a shell, or Perl, the user can enter data that will actually change your program, data that cause errors that aren't present if the data is correct. If user data is interpreted as part of the program's execution, anything he enters must adhere to the rules of the language or cause an error.

For instance, the following Perl fragment may work fine or may generate an error, depending on what the user enters.

```
if ($search_Text =~ /$user_Pattern/)
{
        # Match!
}
```

In Perl, the `eval()` operator exists to prevent this. `eval()` allows for *run-time syntax checking* and will determine if an expression is valid Perl or not. The following code is an improved version of the preceding code.

```
if (eval{$search_Text =~ /$user_Pattern/})
{
```

```
        if ($search_Text =~ /$user_Pattern/)
        {
              # Match!
        }
}
```

Unfortunately, most shells (including the most popular, /bin/sh) have no easy way to detect errors such as this one, which is another reason to avoid them.

Guarding Against Loopholes When Executing External Programs

When executing external programs, you must also be aware of how the user input you pass to those programs will affect them. You may guard your own CGI script against hacker tricks, but it's all for naught if you blithely pass anything a hacker may have entered to external programs without understanding how those programs use that data.

For instance, many CGI scripts will send email to a particular person, containing data collected from the user by executing the `mail` program.

This can be dangerous because `mail` has many internal commands, any of which can be invoked by user input. For instance, if you send text entered by the user to `mail` and that text has a line that starts with a tilde (~), `mail` will interpret the next character on the line as one of the many commands it can perform. `~r /etc/passwd`, for example, will cause your machine's password file to be read by `mail` and sent off to whomever the letter is addressed to, perhaps even the hacker himself.

In an example such as this one, rather than use `mail` to send email from UNIX machines, you should use `sendmail`, the lower-level mail program that lacks many of `mail`'s features. But, of course, you should also be aware of `sendmail`'s commands so those can't be exploited.

As a general rule, when executing external programs, you should use the one that fits your needs as closely as possible, without any frills. The less an external program can do, the less it can be tricked into doing.

CAUTION

Here's another problem with `mail` and `sendmail`: You must be careful that the address you pass to the mail system is a legal email address. Many mail systems will treat an email address starting with a pipe (|) as a command to be executed, opening a huge security hole for any hacker that enters such an address.

Again, always validate your data!

Another example that demonstrates you must know your external programs well to use them effectively is `grep`. Most people will tell you that you can't get into much trouble with `grep`. However, `grep` can be fooled fairly easily, and how it fails is illustrative. The following code is an example: It's supposed to perform a case-sensitive search for a user-supplied term among many files.

```
print("The following lines contain your term:<HR><PRE>");
$search_Term =~ s/([^w])/\\\1/g;
system("grep $search_Term /public/files/*.txt");
print("</PRE>");
```

This all seems fine, unless you consider what happens if the user enters `-i`. It's not searched for, but functions as a switch to `grep`, as would any input starting with a dash. This will cause `grep` to either hang while waiting for the search term to be typed into standard input, or to error out when anything after the `-i` is interpreted as extra switch characters. This, undoubtedly, isn't what you wanted or planned for. In this case, it's not dangerous, but in others it might be.

There's no such thing as a harmless command, and each must be carefully considered from every angle. You should be as familiar as possible with every external program your CGI script executes. The more you know about the programs, the more you can do to protect them from bad data, both by screening that data and by disabling options or disallowing features.

Security Beyond Your Own

`sendmail` has an almost legendary history of security problems. Almost from the beginning, hackers have found clever ways to exploit `sendmail` and gain unauthorized access to the computers that run it.

But `sendmail` is hardly unique. Dozens—if not hundreds—of popular, common tools have security problems, with more being discovered each year.

The point is that it's not only the security of your own CGI script that you must worry about, but the security of all the programs your CGI script uses. Knowing `sendmail`'s full range of documented capabilities is important, but perhaps more important is knowing capabilities are *not* documented, because they probably aren't intended to exist.

Keeping up with security issues in general is a necessary step to maintain the ongoing integrity of your web site. One of the easiest ways to do this is on Usenet, in the newsgroups **comp.security.announce** (where important information about computer security is broadcast) and **comp.security.unix** (which has a continuing discussion of UNIX security issues). A comprehensive history of security problems, including attack-prevention software, is available through the Computer Emergency Response Team (CERT) at **ftp.cert.org**.

Inside Attacks: Precautions with Local Users

A common mistake in CGI security is to forget local users. Although people browsing your site over the web usually won't have access to security considerations, such as file permissions and owners, local users of your web server do, and you must guard against these threats even more than those from the web.

CAUTION

Local system security is a big subject and almost any reference on it will give you good tips on protecting the integrity of your machine from local users. As a general rule, if your system as a whole is safe, your web site is safe, too. See Chapter 11, "Key Access and Security Concerns for Web Administrators," for more information on security.

The CGI Script User

Most web servers are installed to run CGI scripts as a special user. This is the user that *owns* the CGI program while it runs, and the permissions granted limit what the script can do.

Under UNIX, the server itself usually runs as `root` to allow it to use socket port 80 to communicate with browsers. When the server executes a CGI program, however, it should do so as an innocuous user, such as the commonly used `nobody`, and the ability to configure this behavior is available on many servers. It is dangerous to run CGI scripts as root! The less powerful the user, the less damage a runaway CGI script can do.

Setuid and ACL Dangers

You should also be aware if the *setuid bit* is set on your UNIX CGI scripts. If enabled, no matter what user the server runs programs as, it will execute with the permissions of the file's owner. This, of course, has major security implications—you can lose control over which user your script runs as.

Fortunately, the setuid bit is easy to disable. Executing `chmod a-s` on all your CGI scripts will guarantee that it's turned off, and your programs will run with the permissions you intended.

Of course, in some situations you may *want* the setuid bit set—if your script needs to run as a specific user to access a database, for example. If this is the case, you should make doubly sure that the other file permissions on the program limit access to it to those users you intend.

A similar situation can occur under Windows NT. Microsoft's Internet Information Server (IIS) normally runs CGI scripts with the access control list (ACL) of `IUSR_computer`. However, by editing a Registry entry, IIS can be set to run scripts as `SYSTEM`. `SYSTEM` has much wider permissions than `IUSR_computer` and can cause correspondingly more damage if things go wrong. You should make sure that your server is configured the way you intend.

Community Web Servers

Another potential problem with the single, common user that web servers execute scripts as is that a single human being is not necessarily always in control of the server. If many people share control of a server, each may install CGI scripts that run as, say, the `nobody` user. This allows any of these people to use a CGI program to gain access to parts of the machine that they may be restricted from, but that `nobody` is allowed to enter.

Probably the most common solution to this potential security problem is to restrict CGI control to a single individual. Although this may seem reasonable in limited circumstances, it's often impossible for larger sites. Universities, for example, have hundreds of students, each of whom wants to experiment with writing and installing CGI scripts.

Using CGIWrap

On the CD

A better solution to the problem of deciding which user a script runs when multiple people have CGI access is CGIWrap. CGIWrap, which is included on the CD that accompanies this book, is a simple wrapper that executes a CGI script as the user who owns the file instead of the user whom the server specifies. This simple precaution leaves the script owner responsible for the damage it can do.

For instance, if the user `joanne` owns a CGI script that's wrapped in CGIWrap, the server will execute the script with `joanne`'s permissions. In this way, CGIWrap acts like a setuid bit but has the added advantage of being controlled by the web server rather than the operating system. This means that anybody who sneaks through any security holes in the script will be limited to whatever `joanne` herself can do—the files she can read and delete, the directories she can view, and so on.

Because CGIWrap puts CGI script authors in charge of the permissions for their own scripts, it can be a powerful tool not only to protect important files owned by others, but also to motivate people to write secure scripts. The realization that only *their* files would be in danger can be a powerful persuader to script authors.

CGI Script Permissions

You should also be aware of which users own CGI scripts and what file permissions they have. The permissions on the directories that contain the scripts are also very important.

If, for example, the cgi-bin directory on your web server is world-writeable, any local user can delete your CGI script and replace it with another. If the script itself is world-writeable, anybody can modify the script to do anything he wants.

Look at the following innocuous UNIX CGI script:

```
#!/bin/sh
# Send the header
echo "Content-type: text/html"
echo ""
# Send some HTML
echo "<HTML><HEADER><TITLE>Fortune</TITLE></HEADER>
echo "<BODY>Your fortune:<HR><PRE>"
fortune
echo "</BODY></HTML>"
```

Now imagine if the permissions on the script allowed a local user to change the program to the following:

```
#!/bin/sh
# Send the header
echo "Content-type: text/html"
echo ""
# Do some damage!
rm -rf /
echo "<HTML><TITLE>Got you!</TITLE><BODY>"
echo "<H1>Ha ha!</H1></BODY></HTML>"
```

The next user to access the script over the web would cause huge amounts of damage, even though that person had done nothing wrong. Checking the integrity of user input over the web is important, but even more so is making sure that the scripts themselves remain unaltered and unalterable.

TROUBLESHOOTING

If you get an `Error 500: Bad Script Request` message when attempting to run your CGI script, you may have been too conservative in setting permissions. A CGI script must be executable. You can test your scripts beforehand by running them from the command line—the script should at least run. If your operating system is UNIX or UNIX-like, you can use `chmod -x` to set the file's permissions.

Local File Security

Equally important is the integrity of the files that your scripts create on the local hard disk. After you feel comfortable that you have a good filename from the web user, how you actually go about using that name is also important. Depending on which operating system your web server is running, permissions and ownership information can be stored on the file along with the data inside it. Users of your web server may cause havoc depending on how various permission flags are set.

For instance, you should be aware of the permissions you give a file when you create it. Most web server software sets the ***umask***, or permission restrictions, to 0000, meaning that it's possible to create a file that anybody can read or write. Although the permissions on a file probably don't make any difference to people browsing on the web, people with local access can take advantage of loose restrictions. You should always specify the most conservative permissions possible, while still allowing your program the access it needs when creating files.

This isn't only a good idea for CGI programs but for all the code you write.

The simplest way to make sure that each file-open call has a set of minimum restrictions is to set your script's unmask. `umask()` is a UNIX call that restricts permissions on every subsequent file creation. The parameter passed to `umask()` is a number that's "masked" against the permissions mode of any later file creation. An umask of 0022 will cause any file created to be writeable only by the user, no matter what explicit permissions are given to the group and other users during the actual open.

But even with the unmask set, you should create files with explicit permissions, just to make sure that they're as restrictive as possible. If the only program that will ever be accessing a file is your CGI script, only the user that your CGI program runs as should be given access to the file: permissions 0600. If another program needs to access the file, try to make the owner of that program a member of the same group as your CGI script so that only group permissions need to be set: permissions 0660. If you must give the world access to the file, make it so that the file can only be read, not written to: permissions 0644.

Use Explicit Paths

Finally, a local user can attack your web server in one last way by fooling it into running an external program that he wrote instead of what you specified in your CGI script. The following is a simple program that shows a web surfer a bit of wisdom from the UNIX `fortune` command.

```
#!/bin/sh
# Send the header
echo "Content-type: text/html"
echo ""
# Send the fortune
echo "<HTML><HEADER><TITLE>Fortune</TITLE></HEADER><BODY>"
echo "You crack open the cookie and the fortune reads:<HR><PRE>"
fortune
echo "</PRE></BODY></HTML>"
```

This script seems harmless enough. It accepts no input from the user, so he can't play any tricks on it that way. Because it's run only by the web server, the permissions on the script itself can be set to be very restrictive, preventing a trouble-minded local user from changing it. And, if the permissions on the directory in which it resides are set correctly, there's not much that can go wrong—is there?

Of course, there is. Listing 33.12 calls external programs, in this case, `echo` and `fortune`. Because these scripts don't have explicit paths specifying where they are on the hard disk, the shell uses the `PATH` environment variable to search for them, and this can be dangerous. If, for example, the `fortune` program was installed in /usr/games, but `PATH` listed, say, /tmp before it, then any program that happened to be named "fortune" and resided in the temporary directory would be executed instead of the true `fortune` (see Figure 33.7).

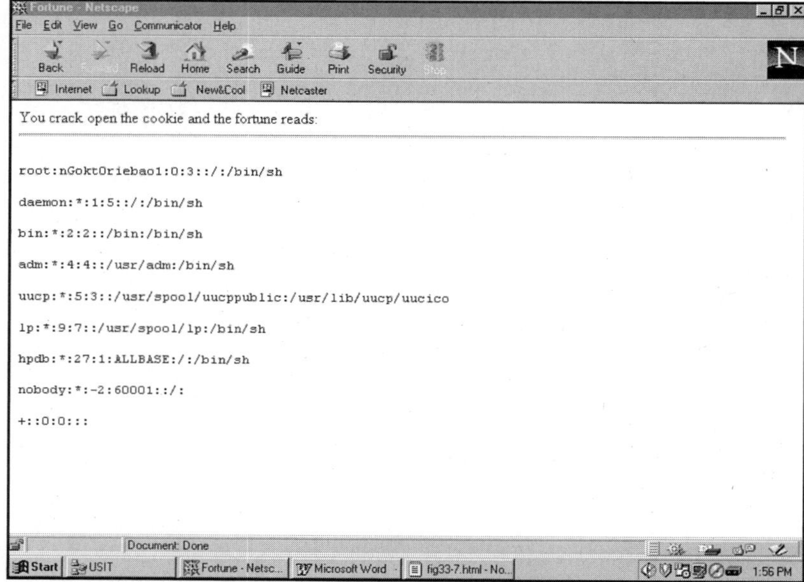

FIG. 33.7
Although the script is unaffected, a local user has tricked the web server into running another program instead of `fortune`.

This program can do anything its creator wants, from deleting files to logging information about the request and then passing the data on to the real `fortune`—leaving the user and you none the wiser.

You should always specify explicit paths when running external programs from your CGI scripts. The PATH environment variable is a great tool, but it can be misused just like any other.

Using Others' CGI Scripts

On the web, there are many helpful archives of CGI scripts—each stuffed with dozens of useful, valuable programs all free for the taking. But before you start haphazardly downloading all these gems and blindly installing them on your server, you should pause and consider a few things:

- Does the script come with source code?
- Do you know the language the program is written in well enough to really understand what it does?

If the answer to either question is *no*, you could be opening yourself up to a huge con game, doing the hacker's work for him by installing a potentially dangerous CGI program on your own server. It's like bringing a bomb into your house because you thought it was a blender.

These *Trojan horse* scripts—so named because they contain hidden dangers—might be wonderful time-savers, doing exactly what you need and functioning perfectly, until a certain time is reached or a certain signal is received. Then, they will spin out of your control and execute planned behavior that can range from the silly to the disastrous.

Examining External Source Code

Before installing a CGI program that you didn't write, you should take care to examine it closely for any potential dangers. If you don't know the language of the script or if its style is confusing, you might be better off looking for a different solution. For example, look at this Perl fragment:

```
system("cat /etc/passwd") if ($ENV{"PATH_INFO"} eq "/send/passwd");
```

This single line of code can be hidden among thousands of others, waiting for its author or any surfer to enter the secret words that cause it to send him your password file.

If your knowledge of Perl is shaky, if you didn't take the time to completely review the script before installing it, or if a friend assured you that he's running the script with no problems, you can accidentally open your site to a huge security breach—one that you may not know about. The most dangerous Trojan horses won't even let you know that they've gone about their work. They will continue to work correctly, silently sabotaging all your site's security.

Guarding Against Precompiled C CGI Scripts

Occasionally, you may find precompiled C CGI scripts on the web. These are even more dangerous than prewritten programs that include the source. Because precompiled programs don't give you any way of discovering what's actually going on, their "payload" can be much more complex and much more dangerous.

A precompiled program, for instance, might take the effort not only to lie in wait for some hidden trigger but also to inform the hacker–cum–author, where you installed it! A cleverly written CGI program might mail its author information about your machine and its users every time the script is run and you would never know because all that complexity is safely out of sight behind the precompiled executable.

Reviewing CGI Library Scripts

Full-blown CGI scripts aren't the only code that can be dangerous when downloaded off the web. Also, dozens of handy CGI libraries are available, and they pose exactly the same risks as full programs. If you never bother to look at what each library function does, you might end up writing the program that breaks your site's security.

All a hacker needs is for you to execute one line of code that he wrote, and you've allowed him entry. You should review—and be sure that you understand—every line of code that will execute on your server as a CGI script. Remember, *always* look a gift horse in the mouth!

The Extremes of Paranoia and the Limits of Your Time

Although sight-checking all the code you pull off the web is often a good idea, it can take huge amounts of time, especially if the code is complex or difficult to follow. At some point, you may be tempted to throw caution to the wind and hope for the best, installing the program and firing up your browser. The reason you downloaded a CGI program in the first place was to save time. Right?

If you do decide to give your paranoia a rest and run a program that you didn't write, reduce your risk by getting the CGI script from a well-known and highly regarded site.

The NCSA httpd, for instance, is far too big for the average user to go over line by line, but downloading it from its home site at **http://www.ncsa.uiuc.edu** is as close to a guarantee of its integrity as you're likely to get. In fact, anything downloaded from NCSA will be prescreened for you.

Dozens of well-known sites on the web will have done most of the paranoia-induced code checking for you. Downloading code from any of them is just another layer of protection that you can use for your own benefit. Such sites include the following:

- **ftp://ftp.ncsa.uiuc.edu/Web/httpd/Unix/ncsa_httpd/cgi** (NCSA Archive)
- **http://www.lpage.com/cgi** (CGI page of LPage and the World Famous Guestbook Server)
- **http://www.ncsa.uiuc.edu/People/daman/cgi++/** (libcgi++, a C++ class library for decoding data sent from HTML forms to CGI programs)
- **ftp://ftp.cdrom.com/pub/perl/CPAN/modules/by-category/15_World_Wide_Web_HTML_HTTP_CGI/** (home ftp site of Walnut Creek CD-ROM's Comprehensive Perl Archive Network—CGI archive)

CHAPTER 34

Web Database Tools

by Melissa Niles

In this chapter

Database Considerations

It is an appealing idea to take information that is stored in your database and allow its access to those visiting your site (for either Internet or intranet purposes). Not only can it save you the time of reentering all that data to create an HTML document, but it also can enables you to use your database to create web pages that change the moment the information in your database changes.

Integrating your existing databases with the web enables you to create Internet, as well as intranet, applications that can be beneficial to both the customers visiting your site and those within your organization who need up-to-date information.

For customers, a database enables them to make orders and purchase goods that you have for sale. Most businesses take customer information and store that information in a database whenever an order is placed. This enables you to keep track of who ordered what, when items were shipped, how much and by what method they paid, and the personal information used to ship each item.

The old method of purchasing goods on the web was simply to take an order through a form and then email the order to the appropriate person. This person would enter the customer and order information into the database, and at that point any online order would be processed as expected.

Integrating your database with the web removes the "middle person." Each order can be placed in the database and processed from that point, lessening the chances of lost paperwork or misdirected email.

You can also use the information that already exists in your databases to create up-to-date web documents. These documents can be used to provide a product listing in which visitors can select the items that they would like to purchase. The information in your databases also can be used to provide support.

For intranet purposes, you can provide your employees information no matter where they are or what platform they are using. Many businesses have employees working in the field who need to quickly access company information. Direct access to a database of information enables your employees to be more proficient. Providing information via the web even allows access to a database which wouldn't normally be accessible over a network.

All the databases and database tools described in this chapter can be used for these purposes, although some are better suited for a particular task than others.

Which database is best suited for your needs depends on how much you are willing to pay for a database and the tools needed to create dynamic web pages. How much horsepower you are going to need to serve your customers will also have to be considered:

- The smaller databases available, such as Access and mSQL, work well and are within the budgets of most small businesses. Even so, they wouldn't be able to handle 100,000 or more queries a day.

- Database engines, such as Oracle and Sybase, are better suited for larger companies and those companies that receive a large number of queries a day. At the same time, Oracle or Sybase would be overkill for a business that sells only a small handful of goods and receives a few hundred queries a day.

You often have to consider what database a company is already using. Many companies have spent a lot of time training their employees to use a particular database, or they have spent a lot of money with a database that has worked well for them for years. At times, you will have to convince a company to change its database to something more web-worthy. First, you need to find out whether tools exist that can help a company use its existing database and whether the database it currently has is well within the bounds of the company's particular needs.

Not too long ago, it was quite difficult to create web pages based on information from a database. Now, with so much support, trying to figure out which way to go can be an intimidating task. This chapter briefly covers the favorite databases available and the gateways used to access and place that information on the web.

Databases Available

In this section, you take a quick look at the most commonly used databases on the web and where you can look for further information and support.

Oracle

Oracle is the largest database developer in the World. Microsoft exceeds Oracle only in the software arena. Oracle provides databases for Windows NT and various UNIX flavors and has created its own set of tools called the Oracle Web Developer Suite. This suite integrates the Oracle 7 server, Oracle WebServer, Designer/2000, and the Developer/2000 kit, along with additional kits. With the Web Developer Suite, you can get your database information on the web in minutes using a graphical point-and-click environment. With some additional time, you can make your web site more interactive, storing and retreiving information with the Oracle database. A storefront, where you can sell goods or provide up-to-date product support, makes good use of the Oracle Web Developer Suite.

ON THE WEB

For more information on Oracle and how you can use Oracle with the World Wide Web, visit its web page at

http://www.oracle.com/

Sybase

Sybase System 11 is a SQL database product that has many tools that can be used to produce dynamic web pages from the information data in your database. Sybase's newest product is called Power Studio.

Power Studio is a suite of programs that enables you to access your Sybase database and create interactive web applications through a beautifully designed graphics interface. The heart of Sybase's Power Studio is the PowerBuilder. With PowerBuilder, you can create applications that easily integrate with the database, enabling those new to the environment to perform advanced queries. PowerSite, another kit that is provided with the Studio, is the key element to tying the information in the database to the web.

ON THE WEB

For more information on Sybase, Web.SQL, and other Sybase-related APIs, visit the Sybase home page at

http://www.powersoft.com/products/powerstudio/

mSQL

As introduced in Chapter 32 , "Custom Database Query Scripts," mSQL is a middle-sized SQL database server for UNIX, which is much more affordable than the commercial SQL servers available on the market. Written by David Hughes, it was created to enable users to experiment with SQL and SQL databases. It is free for noncommercial use (nonprofit, schools, and research organizations)—for individual and commercial use, the price is quite fair, at about $250 per server.

ON THE WEB

http://www.Hughes.com.au/ This site provides additional information on mSQL, along with documentation and a vast array of user-contributed software.

Informix

Informix has grown up quite a bit. Originally called Illustra, Informix has been completely revamped and now has quite a few complementary tools to help with the design and integration of database information with the web environment. The main component for creating web applications lies with a suite of tools called Universal Web Architecture (UWA).

UWA is comprised of the Informix Universal Web Connect, the Web Datablade, and the Data Director for Java. These tools enable you to easily create web applications in a minimal amount of time.

ON THE WEB

For detailed information on Informix, along with additional information on how you can use Informix with your web-based applications, see

http://www.informix.com/

Microsoft SQL

Microsoft released its own SQL database server as a part of its BackOffice suite. Microsoft is trying to compete heavily with Oracle and Sybase by providing its own set of development tools and products to get database-driven information on the web.

Microsoft SQL works well with any web development tool that complies with Microsoft's ODBC. Even so, Microsoft has been working hard to tie the SQL server, Microsoft Internet Information Server, and its web browser together to provide one environment for those providing web content and those who come to your site.

ON THE WEB

For additional information on Microsoft's SQL server and how you can use Microsoft's SQL server in conjunction with the World Wide Web, visit Microsoft at

http://www.microsoft.com/

PostgreSQL

PostgreSQL (formerly Postgres95) is an SQL database server developed by the University of California at Berkeley. Older versions of Postgres are also available, but no longer supported.

ON THE WEB

For additional information on PostgreSQL, along with the source code that is available for downloading, see

http://s2k-ftp.CS.Berkeley.EDU:8000/postgres/

Ingres

Ingres (Interactive Graphics Retrieval System) comes in both a commercial and public domain version. The University of California at Berkeley originally developed this retrieval system, but Berkeley no longer supports the public domain version. You can still find it on the University's web site.

Ingres uses the QUEL query language as well as SQL. QUEL is a superset of the original SQL language, making Ingres more powerful. Ingres was developed to work with graphics in a database environment. The public domain version is available for UNIX systems.

ON THE WEB

To download the public domain version of Ingres, see

ftp://s2k-ftp.cs.berkeley.edu/pub/ingres/

Computer Associates owns the commercial version of Ingres. This version is quite robust and capable of managing virtually any database application. The commercial version is available for UNIX, VMS, and Windows NT.

FoxPro

Microsoft's Visual FoxPro has been a favorite for web programmers, mostly because of its long time in the database community and its third-party support. FoxPro is an Xbase database system that is widely used for smaller business and personal database applications.

ON THE WEB

Visit the FoxPro home page on Microsoft's web site for more information on FoxPro at

http://www.microsoft.com/catalog/products/visfoxp/

You can also visit Neil's FoxPro database page at

http://adams.patriot.net/~johnson/html/neil/fox/foxaol.htm

Microsoft Access

Microsoft Access is a relational database management system that is part of the Microsoft Office suite. Microsoft Access can be used to create HTML documents based on the information stored in the Access database with the help of Microsoft's Internet Assistant. Microsoft's Internet Assistant is an add-on that is available free of charge for Access users. Microsoft Access can also support ActiveX Controls, which makes Access even more powerful when used with the Microsoft Internet explorer.

A Job Forum page was created to enable you to see how Access can be used in conjunction with the World Wide Web.

ON THE WEB

Details on Microsoft Access and how you can use Access with your web-based applications can be found at the following URL; additionally, you can test the Job Forum and look at the code used to create this application. For more information on Microsoft Access and the Job Forum, see

http://www.microsoft.com/accessdev/

Database Tools

Now that you have taken a look at the various databases available, it's time to take a look at the third-party tools that help you create applications to tie your databases with the web.

Some of the tools work with only one specific database; other tools work with a couple of different databases; and some tools work with most databases available.

Which tool you use depends on several factors:

- *Which database are you using?* I know that this sounds like a simple thing to consider, but I've repeatedly seen companies who have purchased a web/database tool that doesn't work with their existing database. Most of the time they purchased a particular tool because they liked that tool's features or ease of use. They didn't realize that some of the tools work with specific databases. You will want to know which tools work with each particular database. For example, MsqlPerl doesn't work at all with Microsoft Access, and Oracle can't be used with PHP/FI.

- *Which platform are your database and web servers running on?* Visual Interdev is a fantastic interface for designing web/database applications, but it runs on Microsoft Windows machines. Although Visual Interdev works well with Oracle on NT, Visual Interdev can't be used if Oracle is on a UNIX machine. You need to make sure that the any web/database tool is compatible with a particular database and the platform that is used by the web server and database server.
- *How do you want to access a database (using CGI or a proprietary API)?* Portability used to be the biggest concern when constructing a database application for the web. Now it is not. Because of the ease of use with most proprietary APIs, they have become quite commonplace, but may create problems if the technology changes drastically in the future. Web/database tools such as Visual Interdev and DBI enable a bit more flexibility when porting scripts or applications to be used with different databases. Other tools are quite limited and restrictive (MORE, for example, which is discussed later in this chapter).
- *How much money is your company willing to spend?* This may not be a major consideration for most larger companies, but smaller businesses have to watch every nickel and dime. If you weigh the tools available with how much money a company is willing to spend, you will most likely be able to create a rock-solid application for even the most frugal company.

With these ideas in mind, take a look at the tools available, as described in the next sections, and see which web/database tool will suit your needs.

PHP/FI

PHP/FI was developed by Rasmus Lerdorf, who needed to create a script that enabled him to log visitors to his page. The script replaced a few other smaller ones that were creating a load on Lerdorf's system. This script became PHP, which is an acronym for Rasmus' Personal Home Page tools. Lerdorf later wrote a script that enabled him to embed commands within an HTML document to access a SQL database. This script acted as a forms interpreter (hence the name *FI*), which made it easier to create forms using a database. These two scripts have since been combined into one complete package called PHP/FI.

PHP/FI grew into a small language that enables developers to add commands within their HTML pages instead of running multiple smaller scripts to do the same thing. PHP/FI is actually a CGI program written in C that can be compiled to work on any UNIX system. The embedded commands are parsed by the PHP/FI script, which then prints the results through another HTML document. Unlike using JavaScript to access a database, PHP/FI is browser-independent, because the script is processed through the PHP/FI executable that is on the server.

PHP/FI can be used to integrate mSQL along with Postgres95 to create dynamic HTML documents. It's fairly easy to use and quite versatile. An example of how PHP/FI works is shown in Listings 34.1 and 34.2.

Listing 34.1 The HTML document contains PHP/FI code that stores information in the database.

```
<?
echo "<HTML>";
echo "<HEAD><TITLE>Add to phonebook</TITLE></HEAD>";
echo "<BODY>";
>
<H1>Add to the phonebook</H1>
<?
$database = "myphone";

if($ADD == 1);
  msql_connect("localhost");
  $result = msql($database, "select fname,lname from phonebook where
   fname='$fname' and lname='$lname'");
  if($fname == msql_result($result,0,"fname") && $lname == msql_
result($result,0,"lname"));
  echo "$fname $lname already exists";
  exit;
>
<?else>
<?
msql($database, "insert into phonebook (fname,lname,phone,email)
VALUES ('$fname','$lname','$phone','$email')");
>
<?endif>
<?endif>


<FORM ACTION="/cgi-bin/php.cgi/phonebook/add.html" METHOD="POST">
<INPUT TYPE="hidden" name="ADD" value="1">
<PRE>
First name:<INPUT TYPE="text" name="fname" maxlength=255>
 Last name:<INPUT TYPE="text" name="lname" maxlength=255>
     Phone:<INPUT TYPE="text" name="phone" maxlength=11>
     Email:<INPUT TYPE="text" name="email" maxlength=255>
</PRE>
<P>
<INPUT TYPE="submit">
<HR>
<CENTER>
<A HREF="index.html">[Phonebook]</A>
</CENTER>
</FORM>
</BODY>
</HTML>
```

Now, the following script enables you to view the phonebook.

Listing 34.2 PHP/FI queries the database and displays the result inside the HTML document.

```
<HTML>
<HEAD><TITLE>My Phonebook</TITLE></HEAD>

<BODY>
<H1>My Phonebook</H1>

<?
msql_connect("localhost");

$database="myphone";

$result = msql($database, "select * from phonebook");
$num = msql_numrows($result);

$i=0;

echo "<TABLE>";
while($i < $num);
    echo "<TR><TD>";
    echo msql_result($result,$i,"fname");
    echo " ";
    echo msql_result($result,$i,"lname");
    echo "</TD><TD>";
    echo msql_result($result,$i,"phone");
    echo "</TD><TD>";
    echo msql_result($result,$i,"email");
    echo "</TD></TR>";
    $i++
  endwhile;
>
</TABLE>
</BODY>
</HTML>
```

ON THE WEB

http://www.vex.net/php/ Visit this site for more information on PHP/FI, along with additional examples on how PHP/FI can be used.

Cold Fusion

Allaire created Cold Fusion as a system that enables you to write scripts within an HTML. Cold Fusion, a database interface, processes the scripts and then returns the information within the HTML written in the script. Although Cold Fusion currently costs $495, the product is definitely worth the price. Allaire wrote Cold Fusion to work with just about every web server available for Windows NT and integrate with just about every SQL engine—including those database servers available on UNIX machines (if a 32-bit ODBC driver exists).

Cold Fusion works by processing a form, created by you, that sends a request to the web server. The server starts Cold Fusion and sends the information to Cold Fusion that is used to call a template file. After reading the information that the visitor entered, Cold Fusion processes that information according to the template's instructions. It then returns an automatically generated HTML document to the server and then returns the document to the visitor.

For example, the following form asks the visitor to enter his or her name and telephone number. When the visitor clicks Submit, the form is processed by Cold Fusion, which calls the template `enter.dbm`:

```
<HTML>
<HEAD><TITLE>Phonebook</TITLE></HEAD>
<BODY>
<FORM ACTION="/cgi-bin/dbml.exe?Template=/phone/entry/enter.dbm"
➥ METHOD="POST">
Enter your full name:<INPUT TYPE="text" NAME="name"><BR>
Enter your phone number:<INPUT TYPE="text" NAME="phone"><P>
<INPUT TYPE="submit">
</FORM>
</BODY>
</HTML>
```

The template contains a small script that inserts the information in the database and then displays an HTML document to the visitor. This document thanks the visitor for taking the time to enter his or her name and telephone number into the database:

```
<DBINSERT DATASOURCE="Visitors" TABLENAME="Phone">
<HTML>
<HEAD><TITLE>Thank you!</TITLE></HEAD>
<BODY>
<H1>Thank your for your submission!<H1>
Your name and phone number has been entered into our database.
➥ Thank you for taking the time to fill it out.
<P>
<A HREF="main.html">[Return to the main page]</A>
</BODY>
</HTML>
```

Although Cold Fusion is a lot more complex than this, you can get an idea of how easy it is to handle information and place that information into the database.

ON THE WEB

Visit Allaire's site for the complete details on Cold Fusion at

http://www.allaire.com/

W3-mSQL

W3-msql was created by David Hughes, the creator of mSQL, to simplify accessing an mSQL database from within your web pages. It works as a CGI script that your web pages go through to be parsed. The script reads your HTML document, performs any queries required, and sends the result back out to the server to the visitor. W3-mSQL is much like PHP/FI, but on a smaller scale. W3-msql makes it easy for you to create web documents that contain information based on what is in your database.

A sample bookmarks script and database dump is included within the W3-mSQL archive.

ON THE WEB

For additional information on W3-mSQL or to download W3-mSQL, see

http://www.Hughes.com.au/product/w3-msql/

MsqlPerl

MsqlPerl is a Perl interface to the mSQL database server. Written by Andreas Koenig, it utilizes the mSQL API and enables you to create CGI scripts in Perl, complete with all the SQL commands available to mSQL.

Chapter 32, "Custom Database Query Scripts," has examples on how to use MsqlPerl and details the use of MsqlPerl and mSQL.

ON THE WEB

For additional information on MsqlPerl, see

ftp://Bond.edu.au/pub/Minerva/msql/Contrib/

MsqlJava

MsqlJava is an API that enables you to create applets that can access an mSQL database server. The package has been compiled with the Java Developer's Kit version 1 and tested using Netscape 3.

ON THE WEB

For additional information on MsqlJava, and to download the latest version and view the online documentation, visit

http://mama.minmet.uq.oz.au/msqljava/

Microsoft's Visual InterDev

Visual InterDev is a visual interface in which you can create web applications that easily integrate with various databases. Visual InterDev is a graphical environment that enables you to create Active Server Pages (ASP). It comes with a full set of tools to add a whole range of HTML tags and attributes while enabling you to do so with VBScript or Jscript.

ON THE WEB

For more information on Visual InterDev, see

http://www.microsoft.com/vinterdev/

WDB

WDB is a suite of Perl scripts that help you create applications enabling you to integrate SQL databases with the World Wide Web. WDB provides support for Sybase, Informix, and mSQL databases, but it has been used with other database products as well.

WDB uses what its author, Bo Frese Rasmussen, calls "form definition files," which describe how the information retrieved from the database should display to the visitor. WDL automatically creates forms on-the-fly that enable the visitor to query the database. This saves you a lot of work when you prepare a script to query a database. The user submits the query and WDB and then performs a set of conversions, or links, so the visitor can perform additional queries by clicking one of the links.

ON THE WEB

Visit the WDB home page for further information on WDB at

http://arch-http.hq.eso.org/wdb/html/wdb.html

Web/Genera

Web/Genera is a software toolset that is used to integrate Sybase databases with HTML documents. Web/Genera can be used to retrofit a web front end to an existing Sybase database, or it can be used to create a new one. When using Web/Genera, you are required to write a schema for the Sybase database indicating what fields are to be displayed, what type of data they contain, what column they are stored in, and how you want the output of a query formatted. Next, Web/Genera processes the specification, queries the database, and formats an HTML document. Web/Genera also supports form-based queries and whole-database formatting, which turns into text and HTML.

The main component of Web/Genera is a program called SYMFMT, which extracts objects from Sybase databases based on your schema. After the schema is written, compile it using a program called SCH2SQL, which creates the SQL procedures that extract the objects from the database.

When you have compiled the schema, you can retrieve information from the database using URLs. When you click on a link, the object requested is dynamically loaded from the Sybase database, formatted as HTML, and displayed to the visitor.

Web/Genera was written by Stanley Letovsky and others for UNIX.

ON THE WEB

For additional information on Web/Genera and to download the latest version, visit its page at

http://gdbdoc.gdb.org/letovsky/genera/

MORE

MORE is an acronym for Multimedia Oriented Repository Environment, which was developed by the Repository Based Software Engineering Program (RBSE). MORE is a set of application programs that operates in conjunction with a web server to provide access to a relational (or Oracle) database. It was designed to allow a visitor access to the database using a set of CGI scripts written in C. It was also designed so that a consistent user interface can be used to work with a large number of servers, enabling a query to check information on multiple machines. This expands the query and gathers a large amount of information.

ON THE WEB

Visit the MORE web site for additional information on MORE and RBSE at

http://rbse.jsc.nasa.gov:81/DEMO/

DBI

DBI's founder, Tim Bunce, wanted to provide a consistent programming interface to a wide variety of databases using Perl. Since the beginning, others have joined to help build DBI so that DBI can support a wide variety of databases through the use of a database driver, or DBD. The DBD is simply the driver that works as a translator between the database server and DBI. A programmer has to deal with only one specification, and the drivers handle the rest transparently.

So far, the following databases have database drivers. Most are still in testing phases, although they are stable enough to use for experimenting:

Oracle	mSQL
Ingres	Informix
Sybase	Empress
Fulcrum	C-ISAM
DB2	Quickbase
Interbase	

ON THE WEB

Visit the following site for the latest developments on DBI and on various database drivers; authors continue to develop this interface where DBDs are being built for additional databases:

http://www.hermetica.com/technologia/DBI/

DBGateway

DBGateway is a 32-bit Visual Basic WinCGI application that runs on a Windows NT machine as a service to provide World Wide Web access to Microsoft Access and FoxPro databases. It is being developed as part of the Flexible Computer Integrated Manufacturing (FCIM) project. DBGateway is a gateway between your CGI applications and the database servers. Because your CGI scripts only "talk" with the database gateway, you need to be concerned only with programming for the gateway instead of each individual database server. This performs two functions—programming a query is much easier because the gateway handles the communication with the database, and scripts can be easily ported to different database systems.

The gateway enables a visitor to your site to submit a form that is sent to the server. The server hands the request to the gateway, which decodes the information and builds a query forming the result based on a template; or, it can send the result of the query raw.

ON THE WEB

Visit the following site to view the DBGateway's user manual, view the online FAQ, and see how DBGateway has been used:

http://fcim1.csdc.com/

Additional Resources on the Web

Additional information on web database gateways is found at the Web-Database Gateways page at

http://gdbdoc.gdb.org/letovsky/genera/dbgw.html

and also on Yahoo! at

http://www.yahoo.com/Computers_and_Internet/World_Wide_Web/Databases_and_Searching

CHAPTER 35

Indexing and Adding an Online Search Engine

by Mike Ellsworth

In this chapter

Understanding Searching

How you can find what you're looking for? If you are looking for something on the Web, chances are you will use a search engine instead of plodding through dozens or hundreds of pages in hopes of uncovering items of interest. These search services are made possible by programs known as robots, spiders, Web crawlers, or worms; they are on the job 24 hours a day, 365 days a year. They do nothing but wander around from site to site, reading and cataloging whatever they find. They store the results of their searches in huge databases, which anyone can access.

That's the easy part: assembling the haystack. But how to find that needle? This section examines search techniques used by search engines to sift through masses of information to bring back results that satisfy your request.

Understanding Literal Searching

Many search engines use a technique called full-text indexing and retrieving. *Full-text* refers to the fact that each word in each document scanned becomes part of the index. Listings 35.1, 35.2, and 35.3 show three files that might be included in an index.

Listing 35.1 Holidays.txt Sample text file #1.

```
Holiday Schedule
New Year's Day, Monday, January 2.
Memorial Day, Monday 29 May
July 4th, Independence Day, Thursday
```

Listing 35.2 Birthdays.txt Sample text file #2.

```
John, Jan 17 (Thursday this year)
Mary, May 29
```

Listing 35.3 Taxes.txt Sample text file #3.

```
Fiscal year ends 31 December
Expect big write-off in May or June
Estimates due July 1
```

Suppose you search for any file containing the word "Jan." The search engine would return Holidays.txt (which has "January") and Birthdays.txt (which has "Jan"). You would not see Taxes.txt because "Jan" doesn't appear anywhere in it. If you ask for "May," you will get back all three files because all three contain the word "May."

Commonly Used Search Qualifiers

"" (quotation marks)–Specify that documents must contain the exact phrase within the quotation marks: "read my lips"

AND–Indicates a search for documents containing all the terms joined by the operator: Bill AND Hillary

OR–Indicates a search for documents containing any of the terms joined by the operator: Dole OR Clinton

NOT–Excludes documents containing the term that follows the operator: Anderson NOT Pamela

NEAR–Finds documents in which two words appear within a certain number of words of each other: Bill NEAR Clinton

+ (plus sign)–Placed at the beginning of a word to indicate that the word is required: Bill +Clinton

- (minus sign)–Placed at the beginning of a word to indicate that the word must be excluded: Dole -pineapple

If you ask for anything containing either "February" or "tax," the search engine will return Taxes.txt. Although none of the files contains the word "February," the Taxes.txt file contains the word "tax" as part of the title. This satisfies the request for either the first word *or* the second word. This kind of search is called a Boolean OR.

If you search for both "May" and "29," you will see Birthdays.txt and Holidays.txt. At this point, you will find out that Mary's birthday is on Memorial Day this year. Taxes.txt contains the word "May," but not the number "29," so the file fails the "find files with the first term *and* the second term" test. This kind of search is called a Boolean AND.

You can stretch a bit by asking for only files that have both "May" and "29," but not "Mary." A Boolean expression might state this search as follows:

```
((May AND 29) AND (NOT Mary))
```

This search first finds files matching the first term (it must have both "May" and "29"), and then excludes files having "Mary," leaving only Holidays.txt as the result. Suppose the search expression had been:

```
((May AND 29) OR (NOT Mary))
```

The search engine would found all three files under this search expression. The Holidays.txt file is included because it has both "May" and "29"; the Birthdays.txt file is included for the same reason; and the Taxes.txt file shows up because it *doesn't* have the word "Mary."

A full-text index is obviously very powerful. Even in this limited example, you can clearly see the usefulness and flexibility of this kind of tool. Yet in a large database of files, thousands might include the word "May." If the database includes source code files, there might be hundreds of thousands of references to "29." Wouldn't it be nice to find only dates that look like birthdays, or the word "May," but only if it is near the word "29," and not in any source code files?

Advanced search engines go one step beyond literal Boolean searches and give you the means to do more.

Advanced Searches

Advanced searching techniques go beyond literal matching. A search that doesn't rely on exact matches is often called a *fuzzy* search. It is not based on Boolean algebra, with its mixture of AND, OR, and NOT operators, although these might come into play if appropriate. Instead, it tries to identify concepts and patterns, and deal with *information* rather than *data*.

Feel the Heat

Information is data that has been assigned *meaning* by a human. In a simple example, "It's 98 degrees" is data, whereas "It's hot" is information. As the amount of data on the Internet grows, the importance of distinguishing information from data skyrockets.

The ultimate artificial-intelligence search engine would have a DWIM, or "Do What I Mean" command. Putting data in *context* with other data is one way to derive information. Human language abounds with contextual references and implied scopes.

When you say "It's hot," for example, you probably don't mean "Somewhere in the world the temperature is such that someone might refer to it as hot."

You mean that you're feeling hot right now, regardless of the actual temperature.

The context and scope of your original statement is *implied*; the concomitant associations *derive* from the context, your knowledge of human behavior in general, and your behavior in particular.

If you searched the Internet for "Hot Babes" (not that you would ever do so), you would be disappointed if you got back pointers to the National Weather Service's reports mingled with articles about infant care. How can search engines figure out what kind of "hot" you mean? Can DWIM ever be achieved?

This question is a *hot* topic—the basis for an ongoing and bitter debate among philologists, linguists, artificial-intelligence theorists, and natural language programmers. There are almost as many sides as there are participants in the debate, and no one view clearly outstrips the rest. If you are interested in this sort of debate, check out the **comp.ai.fuzzy** newsgroup on Usenet, or stop by your local library or favorite online search engine and find references to *AI* and *natural language*.

Evaluating Search Results

When you perform a search, not only do you want information, you want information relevant to the question at hand. In a perfect world, every search returns only information that completely satisfies your request, no more, no less. But this is not a perfect world, so how can do you compare the effectiveness of various searches? Two major parameters are commonly used to judge the results of a search:

- Recall indicates what fraction of the relevant documents are retrieved by the query.
- Precision measures the degree to which the returned documents satisfy the request.

Each query can be graded as a fraction, with a perfect score being 1.00. In that mythical perfect world, every search would score a 1.00 on both measures because only relevant documents would be retrieved, and those documents would be exactly what you are looking for. Assume that you have a site containing 100 documents, for example, and of these 100, 10 are about search engines. If a query is made for "Perl-based search engines," the query might retrieve four documents about search engines and two others about Perl. In this case, the search would have a precision of 0.66 (four of the six documents returned were relevant) and a recall of 0.40 (4 of a possible 10 relevant documents were returned).

Search engines use a variety of search strategies to increase recall and precision, and some of them are quite complex. The following sections examine various search techniques used to find potential matches, as well as weighting methods used to rank these results in an attempt to present the most likely matches first.

Some of the following material is adapted from Rod Clark's excellent discussion in *Special Edition Using CGI* (Que Publishing, 1996).

Understanding Search Techniques

People think and remember in imprecise terms. You might ask a friend, "Tell me everything about piranha mating," or "Who were the six actors who portrayed James Bond?" Depending on the company you keep, you might get accurate answers. You are likely to get less-satisfactory answers, however, from today's search engines. Unfortunately, conventional query syntax follows very precise rules, even for simple queries. Search engines are evolving toward being capable of handling natural language queries, but there is a long way to go. Toward that end, search engines commonly use the following search techniques to enhance recall and precision.

Substringing Suppose a friend mentions a reference to "dogs romping in a field." It could be that what he actually saw, months ago, was the phrase "while three collies merrily romped in an open field." In a very literal search system, searching for "dogs romping" would turn up nothing at all. "Dogs" are not "collies," and "romping" is not "romped."

If you entered the query "romp field," however, you might get the exact reference if the search tool understands *substrings*. A substring is just part of the a string—but figuring out which part is meaningful isn't easy. The search engine takes the word "romp" and searches for it, as well as its variants: romps, romped, and romping. Obviously, language-specific rules are required to generate the variants from the root word.

Stemming Some search engines, but by no means all, offer *stemming*. Stemming is related to substringing, but involves an even greater understanding of the language. Rather than requiring the user to enter root terms in a query, stemming involves trimming a query word to its root and then looking for other words that match the same root. The word "wallpaper," for example, has "wall" as its root word; so does "wallboard," which the user might never have entered as a separate query. When a user enters "wallpaper," a stemmed search might serve up unwanted additional references to "wallflower," "wallbanger," "Wally," and "walled city," but would also catch "wall" and "wallboard" and probably provide useful information that way.

Stemming has at least the following two advantages over plain substring searching.

- It doesn't require the user to mentally determine and then manually enter the root words.
- It allows assigning higher relevance scores to results that exactly match the entered query and lower relevance scores to the other stemmed variants.

But stemming is also language-specific: The rules of stemming in English are quite different from those for German or Finnish, for example. Human languages are complex, and a search program can't just trim English suffixes from words in another language.

Thesauri One way to broaden the reach of a search is to use a *thesaurus,* a separate file that links words with lists of their common equivalents. Most thesauri enable you to add special words and terms, either linked to a dictionary or directly to synonyms. A thesaurus-based search engine automatically looks up words related to the terms in your submitted query and then searches for those related words. If you publish several technical briefs on the cellular mitosis, for example, a thesaurus-based search engine would show your articles under biology and physiology as well as cytology.

Pattern Matching Building specific language rules into a search engine is difficult. What happens when the program encounters documents in a language that it hasn't seen before?

Several newer search engines concentrate on some more general techniques that are not language-based. Some of these tools can analyze a file, even if it is in an unknown language or file format, and then search for similar files. The key to this kind of search is matching *patterns* within the files rather than matching the contents of the files.

Even if you don't know or can't explain the rules for constructing the patterns that you see—whether those patterns are in human language, graphics, or binary code—you can still rank them for similarity. "Yes, this one matches." Or "No, that one doesn't. This one is very similar, but not exact. This one matches a little. This one is more exact than that one." To analyze files for content similarity, keyword nearness, and other such qualities, some of the newer search engines look for patterns. Such engines use fuzzy logic and a variety of weighting schemes.

The theory behind sophisticated pattern analysis is far beyond the scope of this book. A good explanation of just the algorithms, *sans* theory, would cover several chapters. You should be aware that these techniques exist, however, and that some of the indexing engines you will encounter use variants of these techniques to enhance their searching power.

Understanding Weighting Methods

The search engine has done its job, but it has brought back dozens, hundreds, or thousands of items that might be what you're looking for. Scrolling through all this material looking for something truly relevant is probably not what you would like to spend your time doing. It is common, therefore, for indexing search engines to assign confidence factors or weights to the documents returned from a search and to use these measures to rank the list of documents. That way, if you're lucky, what you're looking for is close at hand, and not at the end of a long list.

Common methods for establishing weights include evaluating adjacency, frequency, and relevance.

Adjacency *Adjacency* is a type of phrase searching method that examines the relationship between words in the search phrase. The search engine increases the relevance score based on how closely the words in the search term occur in the target document. If you search for the phrase "hearing aids," the search engine can use adjacency to determine that you aren't interested in documents containing the phrase "Senate hearing on medical research on AIDS."

Obviously, adjacency only comes into play when there is more than one search term. Yet, findings by Webcrawler (see **http://info.webcrawler.com/bp/WWW94.html**) indicate that the average search comprises only 1.5 words. If you can encourage your users to specify search phrases, however, a good indexing engine can employ adjacency to increase the effectiveness of the search.

Frequency Indexing search engines can use the *frequency* of hits on search terms within a page to increase the page's relevancy score. If you're like most fans of the Blue Devils, it is far more likely that you are interested in a page that lists "Duke Blue Devils" seven times than in a page that only contains one mention of the phrase. The former page is much more likely to be an article about the subject; the other could just be a listing of teams or a passing mention.

Relevance Feedback *Relevance feedback* is a form of query by example. Using this method, a user first performs a search using normal search terms. The user samples one or more of the found documents and determines whether a particular document is close to what he or she wants. The user can inform the search engine to "find more documents like this one." The search engine then parses the relevant document and uses its profile to perform another search.

Relevance feedback can be an especially powerful means of searching. Instead of using the one or two search terms the user originally provides, the search is done using *all* the keywords from the found document.

Indexing Your Own Site

So far in this chapter, you have learned the theory behind site searching and have seen the techniques used by search engines to improve search effectiveness. In this section, you learn how to improve the accuracy of site indexing. This enables you to maximize the effectiveness of the search engine, whether you use an external, commercial engine, or you implement your own.

Using Keywords

Before you start studying indexing programs and individual search engines, you need to examine the kinds of information that you can provide for the indexers to index. Some of the code examples and supporting text in this section are adapted from Rod Clark's excellent discussion in *Special Edition Using CGI*.

Adding keywords to files is particularly important when using simple search tools, many of which are very literal. These tools need all the help they can get.

Manually adding keywords to existing files is a slow and tedious process. Doing so isn't particularly practical when you are faced with a mountain of seldom-read archival documents. When you first create new documents that you know people will search online, however, you can stamp them with an appropriate set of keywords. This stamping (or *keying*) provides a consistent set of words that people can use to search for the material in related texts, in case the exact wording in each text doesn't happen to include some of the relevant general keywords. Using equivalent nontechnical terminology that users are likely to understand also helps.

Sophisticated search engines can yield good results when searching documents with little or no intentional keying, but well-keyed files produce better and more-focused results with these search tools. Even the best search engines, when they set out to catch all the random, scattered, unkeyed documents that you want to find, return information that is liberally diluted with *noise*—irrelevant data. Keying your files helps keep them from being missed in relevant lists for closely related topics.

Using Keywords in Plain Text To help find HTML pages, you can add an inconspicuous line at the bottom of each page that lists the keywords you want, like this:

```
Poland Czechoslovakia Czech Republic Slovakia Romania Rumania
```

This line is useful, but ugly and distracting. Also, many search engines assign a higher relevance to words in titles, headings, emphasized text, `<A NAME=...>` tags and other areas that stand out from a document's body. The next few sections consider how to key your files in more sophisticated and effective ways.

Using Keywords and Descriptions in HTML META Tags You can put more information than simply the page title in an HTML page's `<HEAD>...</HEAD>` section. Specifically, you can include a description of your page, or a standard `Keywords` list in a `META` tag. There seems to be some confusion in how to implement these tags. META tags that include `HTTP-EQUIV` as part of the statement in the tag are considered to be part of the HTTP header. You can insert these tags in your HEAD section, and the browser is supposed to interpret them as if they were a true HTTP header. To change the date a page expires, for example, add a META tag similar to the following:

```
<META HTTP-EQUIV="Expires" CONTENT="Thu, 01 Jan 1998 12:00:00 GMT">
```

NOTE HTTP 1.0 header content is defined in RFC 1945, included on the CD that accompanies this book. Also included on the CD is draft 8 of the HTTP 1.1 specification.

`Keywords` and `Description`, however, are not officially defined components of HTTP headers, although they can be implemented as part of the META NAME tag, such as the following:

```
<META NAME="keywords" CONTENT="keyword1 keyword2 keyword3">
<META NAME="description" CONTENT="This site contains...">
```

Despite this, you will see many pages that utilize the improper `<META HTTP-EQUIV="Keywords" NAME="Keywords" CONTENT="blah, blah">` construction. This may seem to be a quibble, yet what's important is getting search engines to recognize your keywords and descriptions. Some search engines, including AltaVista, InfoSeek, and HotBot, pay particular attention to `META Description` and `META Keywords` entries. These services index terms in both the `Description` and `Keywords` tags, and use the `META Description` rather than the first few lines of the page to identify the URL in returned searches. All three of these engines look for the proper syntax, and it is not known what they will do with `META HTTP-EQUIV` tags.

Other search engines, such as Excite, may explicitly ignore these fields due to the potential for abuse. See **http://www.clackamas.cc.or.us/instruct/cs/classes/178/search/s-meta.htm** for more information. In fact, there has even been at least one lawsuit regarding keyword abuse.

Use of these META tags is becoming more popular. According to an analysis by Dave Beckett, of the University of Kent at Canterbury (**http://www.hensa.ac.uk/uksites/survey/1996-12-01/META-HTTP-Equiv-Field-Names.html**), 11.44% of HTTP headers from sites in the `.uk` domain contain `META Keywords`. An earlier study of the various metadata attributes found in 17,000 documents in the Nordic Web Index during early summer 1996 found that 48.7% contained `META Keywords` and 48.9% contained `META Descriptions`.

Here's an example of using the `META Keywords` tag within an HTML header:

```
<HEAD>
     <META name="description" content="ACNielsen Consumer Information">

     <META name="keywords" content="consumer panel,
                                    consumption,
                                    marketing research">
<title>Buying Habits of Internet Users</title>
</HEAD>
```

After the search engine indexes this page, if a user searches for "marketing research," the engine will find this page even if the words "marketing research" do not appear anywhere in the text of the page.

Using Keywords in HTML Comments This section presents some lines from an HTML file that lists links to English language newspapers. The lines aren't keyed; to find a match, therefore, you must enter a query that exactly matches something in either a particular line's URL or its visible text. Such matches are not too likely with some of these example lines. Only one of them comes up in a search for "Sri Lanka." None of them come up in a search for "South Asia."

```
<B><A HREF="http://www.lanka.net/lakehouse/anclweb/dailynew
➥ /select.html">Sri Lanka Daily News</A></B><BR>

<B><A HREF="http://www.is.lk/is/times/index.html">Sunday Times
➥ </A></B><BR>

<B><A HREF="http://www.is.lk/is/island/index.html">Sunday Island<
➥ /a></B><BR>
```

To improve the search results, you can key each line with one or more likely keywords. The keywords can be contained within `<!--comments -->`, in `<A NAME=...>` statements or in ordinary visible text. Some of these approaches are more successful than others. The following are examples of each.

First, add some keywords as HTML comments on each line. The following example already looks better:

```
<!--South Asia Sri Lanka -->
<B><A HREF="http://www.lanka.net/lakehouse/anclweb/dailynew
➥ /select.html">Sri Lanka Daily News</A></B><BR>

<!--South Asia Sri Lanka -->
<B><A HREF="http://www.is.lk/is/times/index.html">Sunday Times
➥ </A></B><BR>

<!--South Asia Sri Lanka -->
<B><A HREF="http://www.is.lk/is/island/index.html">Sunday Island<
➥ /a></B><BR>
```

You could put the keywords in `<A NAME=...>` statements also, but HTML prohibits spaces in `<A NAME=...>` statements. Therefore, keys in an `<A NAME=...>` statement are limited to single keywords rather than phrases. This *might* suffice if you can always be sure of using an `AND` or `OR` search instead of searching for exact phrases. But many scripts don't support Boolean operators, and, even when Booleans are allowed, most users don't use them. So, overall, using `<A NAME=...>` statements for keying isn't the best choice. Nevertheless, here is an example of using an `<A NAME=...>` statement to provide a keyword:

```
<A NAME="Tamil">
```

Leveraging Commercial Indexes

Fortunately, you don't have to be a natural-language or artificial-intelligence expert to incorporate indexing into your home page or Web site. If you want to offer your users the ability to search the Web for items of interest, you can include links on your site to the commercial search engines. You may also want to help your users define their searches by topic by passing parameters to these commercial search engines. Many fine public search engines are available. This section examines some of the more common commercial indexes and how you can use them to provide services for your site.

Public indexes are available for free through sponsoring corporations, groups, or individuals and are usually accessed through an HTML form and a CGI program.

You don't have to rely on a list of bookmarks or your browser's setting to use a search page. You can put a page on your site that links directly to your favorite search engines. You can even tailor the form so that it comes preloaded with specific search terms, or, with a little more effort, make a massive commercial index return only pages from your own site when queried.

Using AltaVista to Search Your Site

AltaVista provides a helpful index of Web sites and newsgroups (see Figure 35.1). You can find AltaVista at the following address:

http://www.altavista.digital.com

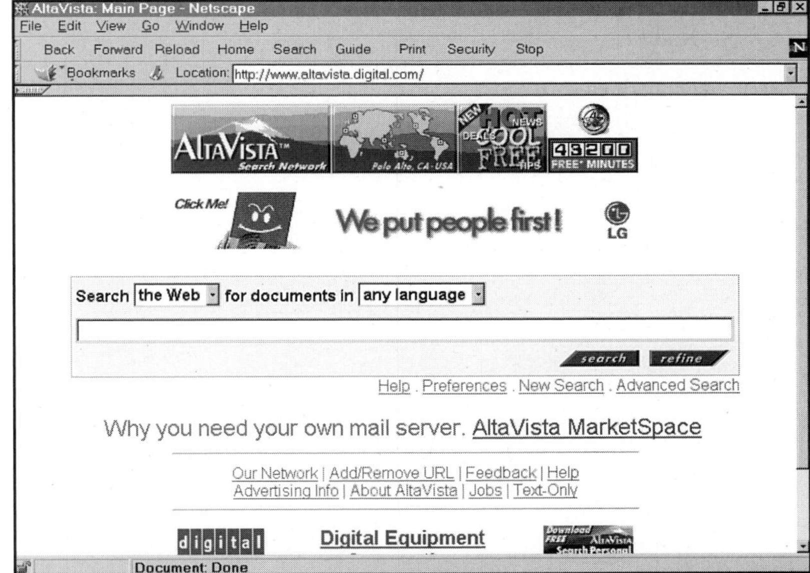

FIG. 35.1
The AltaVista Web page offers a wide range of searching options.

Listing 35.4 shows a generic form for invoking AltaVista's gigantic search engine. Listing 35.5 shows a modification to restrict the search to one of several predefined terms. Notice how Listing 35.5 takes the same form fields defined in Listing 35.4 and hard-codes some of them. The result is that Listing 35.5 always searches the newsgroups, and only for CGI by Example, Using CGI, or Que Corporation.

NOTE HTML examples are not provided for the other sites. The concept is the same for each site: You take the HTML used by the site itself to invoke its CGI script, and then modify the HTML to suit your needs.

Listing 35.4 A generic AltaVista search form.

```
<H1>Search AltaVista</H1>
<FORM METHOD=get
      ACTION="http://www.altavista.digital.com/cgi-bin/query">
<INPUT TYPE=hidden name=pg value=q>
<B>Search
```

continued

Listing 35.4 Continued

```
<SELECT name=what>
<OPTION value=web  SELECTED>the Web
<OPTION value=news >Usenet
</SELECT>
and Display the Results
<SELECT name=fmt>
<OPTION value="." SELECTED>in Standard Form
<OPTION value=c >in Compact Form
<OPTION value=d >in Detailed Form
</SELECT></B>
<input TYPE=text name=q size=55 maxlength=200 value="">
<INPUT TYPE=submit value=Submit>
<BR>
</FORM>
```

Listing 35.5 A customized AltaVista search form.

```
<H1>Search AltaVista</H1>
<FORM METHOD=get
      ACTION="http://www.altavista.digital.com/cgi-bin/query">
<INPUT TYPE=hidden name=pg value=q>
<INPUT TYPE=hidden name=what value=news>
<INPUT TYPE=hidden name=fmt value=d>
<B>Search Newsgroups for</B>
<SELECT name=q>
<OPTION>CGI by Example
<OPTION>Using CGI
<OPTION>Que Corporation
</SELECT><BR>
<INPUT TYPE=submit value=Submit>
<BR>
</FORM>
```

Because of a particular feature available on AltaVista and few other indexes, you can effectively use it as a local search engine to search out information on your own site.

One of the advanced keywords available on AltaVista is the `host:` keyword. You use this keyword to limit AltaVista's search to only those hosts you specify. Assume, for example, that you want to limit the search to your site, and that your site has been visited and fully indexed by the AltaVista robot. To narrow a search, first specify `host:www.yoursite.com` and then follow it with the search terms you desire. AltaVista produces a list of files on your site that contain the search terms. To find pages on the following site that concern merchandising, use this query:

```
host:acnielsen.com merchandising
```

Thus, you could modify Listing 35.5 to look like Listing 35.6.

Listing 35.6 A customized form to use AltaVista to search your site.

```
<FORM METHOD=get
      ACTION="http://www.altavista.digital.com/cgi-bin/query">
<INPUT TYPE=hidden name=pg value=q>
<INPUT TYPE=hidden name=what value=web>
<INPUT TYPE=hidden name=fmt value=d>

<B>Search Our Site for</B>
<SELECT name=q>
<OPTION VALUE="host:www.mcp.com 'CGI by Example'">CGI by Example
<OPTION VALUE="host:www.mcp.com 'Using CGI'">Using CGI
<OPTION VALUE="host:www.mcp.com 'Que Corporation'">Que Corporation
</SELECT><BR>
<INPUT TYPE=submit value=Submit>
<BR>
</FORM>
```

Note the use in this example of the `VALUE` keyword of the `OPTION` tag to specify the host and the search terms. If you want to enable freeform searching, you must write a CGI program that adds the host keyword before submitting the query to the search engine.

The HotBot (**www.hotbot.com**) and InfoSeek search engines also enable you to specify a particular site to search.

Using Lycos Search Resources

You can get HTML that links to Lycos by email. Lycos will even provide a link back to your site on the resulting search page.

Stop by **http://www.lycos.com/lycosinc/backlink.html** and fill out the online form. Within a day or so, you will get back some sample HTML. Lycos provides you with an identifying number so that when users search with Lycos from your site, the resulting search page contains an image you provide and a link back to your site.

Lycos is available at the following site:

http://www.lycos.com

Linking to Starting Point

For many users, Starting Point is *the* starting point when they conduct Web searches.

When you visit Starting Point, you can add a link for your site at the following address:

http://www.stpt.com/general/setup.html#WEBPAGE

You can find the Starting Point main page at the following site:

http://www.stpt.com

Linking to Infoseek

Infoseek makes it easy to add a link to their service to your site. Just go to the following site and follow the instructions:

http://www.infoseek.com/webkit?pg=webkit.html&sv=A2

You can find the main Infoseek page at the following site:

http://www.infoseek.com

Using Excite on Your Site

Excite is more than a public index. Excite makes search engines that you can install on your own system, and is working closely with Web server companies to provide integrated solutions. See the section titled "Implementing an Indexing Search Engine" later in this chapter for more information.

You can find the Excite Web site at the following address:

http://www.excite.com

Using Other Search Engines

You can find dozens of other search engines on the Web, too many to hope to list them all. Each has its own advantages and disadvantages. There are even "meta" search engines such as MetaCrawler, All4one, MetaFind, and DogPile; these submit your query to several other search engines and collate the results.

The following listing identifies several other important search engines. You can find a comprehensive list at **http://www.albany.net/allinone/all1www.html#WWW**.

Yahoo!	Lycos' A2Z	Go2.com
HotBot	Open Text	WebCrawler
WWW Yellow Pages	Thunderstone	What U Seek
PlanetSearch	Magellan	All4one

Using Web Servers' Built-In Search Tools

Another alternative to implementing your own search engine is to use search services already built in to your Web server. Several Web servers for UNIX and Windows NT include built-in utilities to index and search the files at a site. Some of these tools have fewer capabilities than the search engines previously mentioned.

Searching with OraCom WebSite Server

O'Reilly's WebSite server for Windows NT includes the company's WebIndex indexing and WebFind searching tools. WebIndex can index the full text of every page in the server's directory structure, or only selected parts of the directories. WebFind runs as a CGI program and is a conventional search tool. It does keyword searches and supports AND and OR operators.

O'Reilly publishes a book (or manual) titled *Building Your Own WebSite* that goes into considerable detail about setting up and using their WebSite server. Before you install their software, you can read all about it at

http://www.ora.com/

Here's a site that is running WebSite and has set up several search databases:

http://www.videoflicks.com/

Searching with Netscape SuiteSpot Servers

Netscape SuiteSpot Standard and Professional Editions run on Windows NT and UNIX. They include a built-in indexing and searching system, although Netscape's lower-priced FastTrack Server does not. You can find out more about Netscape's servers at

http://search.netscape.com/comprod/server_central/

Searching with Microsoft Index Server

Designed for zero maintenance and complete Web-site indexing, Microsoft's Index Server search engine supports multiple languages (Dutch, U.S. and International English, French, German, Italian, Spanish, and Swedish) and attempts to index by content type as well as contents. It can index documents in several formats: text in a Microsoft Word document, statistics on a Microsoft Excel spreadsheet, or the content of an HTML page. Index Server enables the user to search using both keywords and content types. You may read about Index Server and download a free copy at

http://www.microsoft.com/ntserver/info/indexserver.htm

Index Server requires NT 4.0 and is designed to work with Microsoft's Internet Information Server (IIS).

Considerations When Adding a Search Engine to Your Site

For purposes of this discussion, you have evaluated the alternatives and decided that you need to implement a site-resident search engine. Perhaps you don't like the idea of sending your users off to a commercial index, and your Web server doesn't have a built-in search capability, or maybe you just want more control. Before you get started, however, you should consider the type of search engine you want to use.

Indexing Versus Grepping Search Engines

There are two main types of approaches for creating an online search facility for your Web site.

- *Indexing*. Using this method, you periodically run a process that examines and pulls out keywords from every document on the entire Web site. The main advantage of this method is speed. When a user does a search, the search engine needs to look only at the index instead of searching every file on the site. A disadvantage of this approach is timeliness because a user's search can only be as current as your last index.
- *Grepping*. Using this method, you provide a search engine that searches all files on your site each time the user performs a search. The term *grepping* is taken from the UNIX grep facility that enables users to search for keywords within files. Timeliness is a major advantage of this approach because the user is searching the actual files on your site and any changes are automatically reflected. The major disadvantages of this method are performance and high resource utilization. Because each search touches every file on your site, searches can run for a long time and consume significant server resources.

Indexing search engines predigest your Web site and create indexes containing all of its words. The major commercial Web search engines such as AltaVista, Lycos, Excite, and Web Crawler are all indexing engines. In fact, it is not practical to have a search engine that searches the whole Web with the grepping method. To accomplish this, the search engine would have to either add the full text of every site to a database or search every site in real-time.

With an indexing search engine, when a user requests a search, the search engine needs to refer only to the index to find relevant pages. Because indexes are often a small fraction of the size of the documents indexed, this takes much less time. More important, such an approach makes the major commercial search engines practical by enabling them to store only the indexes of sites rather than site images.

Indexing search engines generally employ more sophisticated searching algorithms to improve their chances of returning relevant documents.

Although very easy to implement, most grepping search engines are somewhat limited in the types of search queries they support. Grepping, after all, is a rather brute-force method of searching. Each file is opened and then scanned for the search terms. The amount of system resources consumed by these activities can limit the sophistication of the search strategies. Most grepping engines use only simple keyword searches, although some offer searching via regular expressions.

To determine which searching method to employ, you must first decide what kinds of search services you want to offer and how many resources—both disk space and processor time—to dedicate to those services.

Evaluating Performance and Processor Efficiency As you might imagine, a big difference exists between the performance and efficiency of grepping and indexing search engines.

NOTE Performing a grepping search on one section of my site which contains about 600 average-size files takes 8 CPU seconds and 40 elapsed seconds on a Sun Sparcstation 20. Because our user load is not very high, this is an acceptable amount of overhead for a search. If your site is very busy, with a hundred simultaneous users for example, however, it is probably not feasible to dedicate this amount of resources to user searching.

In contrast, performing an index-based search on the same site takes about a CPU second and five or six elapsed seconds. Because the size of the site is not large, about 90MB, and indexes average between 10% and 20% of the total size of the site, the amount of disk overhead is acceptable. Because the information on our site doesn't change much day to day, I can run the indexing software overnight and provide a day-old index for our users to search.

One approach that adds no disk overhead and a small amount of processor overhead is to have someone else maintain your index and run the search process. An example of this approach is Pinpoint, from Netcreations (**http://www.netcreations.com/pinpoint/**). This commercial service sends their robot to your site about once a month. The site index is maintained on the Netcreations site, and they also maintain and run the search engine. You maintain a query form on your site that points to the Pinpoint URL. Some trade-offs, of course, exist for this type of solution. You give up a lot of control over what is indexed, how it is indexed, and how often the index is updated. In addition, performance of search queries is likely to be slower when conducted over the Internet.

You may also worry about the security aspects of turning over so much information about your site to a third party. In reality, however, many other third parties already index your site (AltaVista, Lycos, Excite, and all the rest). If you are going to worry, you might as well worry about them. When a third party provides an important service such as this for your site, you are giving up a lot of control. You are trusting the third party to maintain the search engine, as well as to only index those sections of the site that you want your users to see. You are also trusting them to maintain a timely index of your site and to be available to your users constantly. If these compromises work for you, this approach is quick and easy. If, on the other hand, you don't want to give up control of such an important function of your site, you should consider implementing your own search engine.

Evaluating Complexity of Searching Your choice of a search engine depends, in part, on how complex the searches on your site are likely to be. If relevant documents can be found with the use of a simple keyword, there is not much difference between the grepping and the indexing approaches. If, on the other hand, the average user wants to implement multiple-word searches or searches involving concepts rather than keywords, an indexing search engine is the better choice.

In general, indexing search engines can accomplish more complex searches than grepping engines. A grepping engine basically does string compares. It may support regular expressions, wildcards, fuzzy and normal Boolean matching, but it is difficult to implement more sophisticated context matching or concept searching in this type of engine. The sheer overhead of a grepping engine makes it difficult to do multipass searching of any kind.

Using an indexing approach, a search engine can spend more time examining the relationships between search terms and found pages. Because the engine doesn't need to burn processor time churning through all the pages in a site, it can offer nice features such as relevancy ranking and concept searching.

Understanding Indexing Issues

Issues to consider when evaluating an indexing search engine include the following:

- *Resource usage*. Size of index, speed of search, impact on CPU
- *Handling of "stop" words*. How the engine deals with commonly occurring words such as "the," "a," and "an"
- *Control over indexed material*. How files to index are included or excluded from the process

Comparing Index Size and Speed Typically, the larger the index, the longer it takes to search. Most indexing search engines create indexes that are a small fraction of the size of the material to be searched (usually between 10% and 20%). If your site is massive, however, you need to consider whether the index can fit in memory all at once or whether your server needs to swap it in and out as the engine does its searching. Excessive disk thrashing dramatically slows the search process and may even affect overall server performance.

If yours is a high-volume site and your users do a lot of searches, you may need to consider holding the index in memory or even limiting the number of simultaneous searches you allow.

One way to reduce the size of the index on your site is to exclude certain common words from the index. By default, most indexing engines exclude words known as *stop* words—commonly occurring articles and pronouns, for example. But there may be additional *noise* words on your site that you may not want to include in your index (the name of your organization, for example). Excluding words such as these reduces the size of the index and improves searching efficiency.

Understanding Stop Words Most indexing search engines have some capability to ignore *stop* words, also known as garbage or noise words. These are commonly occurring words such as articles, pronouns, and many adjectives. The indexing engine should ignore such words when indexing and the query engine should discard them from the search terms when performing a search. Table 35.1 lists commonly used stop words.

Table 35.1 Some common stop words.

after	by	he	many	old	their	was
all	can	her	may	on	them	way
also	come	hers	me	only	then	we
am	did	hid	more	onto	there	were
an	do	him	most	or	these	what

and	does	his	much	other	they	when
any	each	how	must	out	this	where
are	etc	however	my	over	those	whether
aren	far	ie	near	per	til	which
as	few	if	new	put	to	who
at	fix	in	next	same	too	why
be	for	into	no	say	try	will
because	from	is	none	since	under	with
been	get	it	nor	so	unto	within
before	go	its	not	some	up	without
between	got	just	now	such	upon	yet
big	had	led	of	than	us	
both	has	less	off	that	very	
but	have	let	oh	the	vs	

One feature to look for in an indexing search engine is the capability to add words to the stop words list. On my site, for example, I would like to add the name of our company, ACNielsen, to the list. Because this word is mentioned in almost every file on the site, it doesn't make sense to waste indexing space nor do we need to allow users to search for this term.

Controlling Items to Index An important feature of any search engine is the capability to determine which files on your site to include in a search. If your site is like many, various directories are either password-protected or developmental in nature and not linked to the main pages. Certainly you don't want files from these directories to turn up when users search your site.

Two approaches generally are used to control what material is indexed by the search engine. Either you specify all the directories you want to search, or you specify only those directories you want to exclude from searches. This latter approach usually results in less maintenance for the webmaster. An even easier method is for the indexing engine to automatically skip directories protected with an access control file, such as the .Htaccess file used by the NCSA Web server. This way you don't have to remember to include or exclude new directories as they are added to your site.

As mentioned in the section titled "Using Keywords and Descriptions in HTML META Tags" earlier in this chapter, some indexing search engines enable you to use the `<META>` tag to control how a page is indexed. Using this tag, you place a page description and keywords in the heading of your documents. The search engine then gives this information special treatment when it performs its index.

Evaluating Search Engine Security Concerns

You must think about two main security concerns when implementing a search facility on your site:

- Does the search engine itself represent a threat to site security?
- Does the search engine allow users access to information that ordinarily they are prevented from seeing?

Any time you add a piece of software to your site, you need to be concerned with its impact on site security. Can the software be overwhelmed by an attack and provide direct access to the site? Does it offer a way for users to execute programs on your server? Before releasing a search engine for production use, you may want to experiment with it, to try to overwhelm it or get it to produce unpredictable results.

If the search engine is implemented in Perl within the Windows NT environment, you should be aware of the recent security warnings concerning proper Perl interpreter installation on this platform. You can find information about this problem at **http://www.perl.com/perl/news/latro-announce.html**.

CAUTION

Be aware of security concerns regarding implementations of Perl on Windows NT. See **http://www.perl.com/perl/news/latro-announce.html** for more information.

The potential for users to use your search engine to execute arbitrary code on your Web server is obviously a very serious security concern. If the search engine uses the Perl `eval` command to perform the search, you need to be sure to screen search terms to remove potentially harmful characters and code before passing them to the search engine. On UNIX systems, this means preventing the user from entering a search term containing the escape symbol (!) or any commands that could be used to invoke a command interpreter (`!sh`, for example).

Even if your search engine doesn't offer a security hole, you still need to be sure that users can't see information on your site that they usually are prevented from seeing. It is common on sites using the NCSA Web server, for example, to use access control files (typically .Htaccess) to control access to sensitive directories. If the search engine ignores these access control files, it can return links to or summaries of the files contained in protected directories. At best, your users will be frustrated at seeing links that they are prevented from following. At worst, file summaries can compromise the confidentiality of protected information.

And finally, a security concern that is really a resource concern: You may want to limit the amount of resources any one user of your search engine can consume, or the number of simultaneous searches that can occur. A malicious user can bring your server to its knees by launching a large number of time-consuming searches. Most search engines do provide a method of controlling access in this way. You may need to use other system-management tools to regulate search engine use.

Making the Decision

Which search engine you select depends in part on whether you prefer the timely, but resource-hungry, grepping approach or the faster, CPU-friendly, indexing approach. Regardless of the approach you pick, you should evaluate several requirements before selecting your engine:

- How easy is it to maintain?

  Indexing engines take more maintenance by their very nature. But if maintaining your search engine means remembering to update variables or rerun indexes when new information is added, you need to decide if you're willing to spend the time. By the same token, if your grepping engine looks at all directories on your site, you need to keep that in mind when creating new directories. The best search engine is probably one that you can set and forget.

- Does it automatically recurse directories?

  This is a security question closely related to maintenance concerns. If the engine needs to be told explicitly what to search for, *you will* spend more time maintaining it. If it automatically searches new directories, you need to be aware of sensitive or password-protected information when creating new ones.

- Does it honor access control files?

  These files are a simple way to control access to information on your site, but if your search tool gives users access to these files or their summaries, security is breached. At best, users are frustrated if they cannot access the files that turn up in an index.

- Does it reject searches for garbage, noise, or stop words?

  No matter which type of engine you select, you don't want to waste resources running down all instances of the word "the" on your site.

- Does it allow for complex searches?

  A good search engine will at least allow for Boolean and non–case-sensitive searches. The capability to search for regular expressions is also desirable. More sophisticated engines evaluate word proximity or enable users to search on concepts.

- Does it index off-site links?

  You have to make up your own mind as to whether you want your engine to index such links.

- Does it provide a context so that the user can evaluate the suitability of the found file?

  At a minimum, the search engine needs to offer a hyperlink to the relevant file. It is more helpful, however, if there is a summary of the file available, especially if the files are large.

- Does it present search results in small groups or in one big list?

  To avoid overwhelming your users with a huge results page that takes forever to download, some control is needed. The engine can either present the results in small groups, offering a link to the next set, or enable the user or webmaster to control the number of files returned by any one search.

- Does it enable you to capture information about what users are searching for?

  You can better design your site to serve your users if you know just what they are looking for. Data on user searches can be a very important tool in determining the organization of your site.

These are just some of the questions you should ask yourself as you plan to add a search capability to your site. The discussion that follows examines how well various approaches satisfy these requirements.

Implementing a Grepping Search Engine

Grepping search engines share a common methodology: Start at an arbitrary point in the directory tree, open each HTML file in the tree, and search the file for the search term. Optionally, the engine might recursively follow each subsequent directory branch encountered and repeat the search process.

This allows for unsophisticated searches, although it is possible to enable support for searches using regular expressions.

Building Your Own Grepping Search Engine

To help you better understand how grepping search engines work, this section shows how you can use the Perl language to build your own. In building your own grepping search engine, *you will* need to tackle two problems: finding files to search, and searching those files for search terms.

First, it is important to examine the problem of finding files to search. Using a couple of key Perl capabilities, it is easy to build a recursive routine that will identify the types of files contained within a directory tree, perform an operation on them, and continue the process with underlying directories. The Perl script in Listing 35.7 demonstrates this approach.

Listing 35.7 Tfind.pl Perl script to recursively find files in subdirectories.

```
#!/usr/local/bin/perl
# define the directory to start at
# you could prompt user for this
$BASEDIR = "/web/home/acn";

# print page preamble to STDOUT
print "Content-type: text/html\n\n";
print "<HEAD><TITLE>Test Find Capability</TITLE>\n";
print "<BODY bgcolor=#FFFFFF>\n";

# call subroutine to find files
&finddir($BASEDIR);
# close the page
print "<\/BODY><\/HTML>\n";

sub finddir
```

```
{
     local ($BASEDIR) = @_;

# open directory and load file names into array
     opendir(BASE, $BASEDIR) || die("Can't open directory $BASEDIR");
     @files = grep(!/^\.\.?$/, readdir(BASE));
     closedir(BASE);

     ITEM:
# for every file in the array
     foreach $file (@files)
     {
# check to see if it's a directory
          if (-d "$BASEDIR/$file")
          {
# if it is, recursively call the subroutine
               $next = "$BASEDIR/$file";
               &finddir($next);
# if not a directory, you've got a hit
          }
          else
          {
               print "<P>Found a file called $BASEDIR/$file\n";
               next ITEM ;
          }
     }
}
```

When you run this Perl program, you see a display similar to that shown in Figure 35.2.

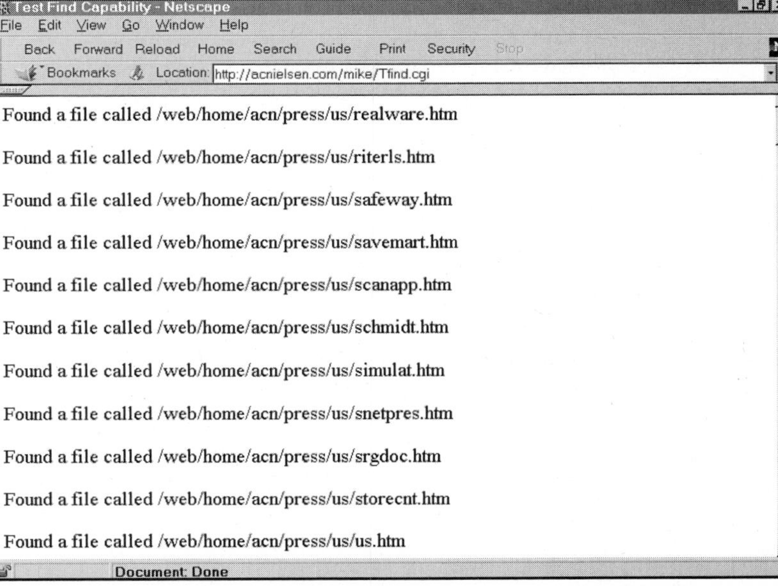

FIG. 35.2
The basic file recursion script produces a listing line for each file found.

Note that all HTML files are found in both the base directory (`/web/home/acn`) as well as in all subdirectories (`/web/home/acn/press`).

You can create your own directory walking code, as in this example, or you can use Find.pl, part of the Perl distribution library (available at **http://www.perl.com**). This Perl script steps through all files recursively and executes a subroutine that you define for each file found. Find returns the name of a file in the variable `$name` and executes a subroutine in your wrapper script called `wanted`. You can refer to the `$name` variable in the `wanted` subroutine to display the name of the file or grep for a search string. It is easy use Find.pl to develop a slightly more sophisticated find routine (see Listing 35.8).

Listing 35.8 Tsfind.pl Using Find.pl to recursively search directories.

```
#!/usr/local/bin/perl

# requires find.pl
require("/public/local/lib/perl5/find.pl");
$BASEDIR = "/web/home/acn";

print "Content-type: text/html\n\n";
print "<HEAD><TITLE>Test Find Capability Using Find.pl</TITLE>\n";
print "<BODY bgcolor=#FFFFFF>\n";

&find("$BASEDIR");

# close the page
print "<\/BODY><\/HTML>\n";

sub wanted
{
# if it's an HTML file
     if (($name =~ /.htm/) && !($name =~ /.html/))
     {
# print its name
               print "<P>Found a file called $BASEDIR/$name\n";

     }
}
```

Like the previous script, this script merely prints the name of each file in which the search string is found. You can easily insert a call to a grepping routine in place of the code that prints out the name of the file.

The grepping routine needs to open the file and read through it to search for instances of the search string. The normal Perl searching function works nicely. This approach is demonstrated in Listing 35.9.

Listing 35.9 Tsrch.pl A basic search script.

```
#!/usr/local/bin/perl
# define the directory, file name, and search string
# you could prompt user for these, or find files
# using find.pl

$BASEDIR = "/web/home/acn";
$file = "acn.htm";
$term = "ACNielsen";

# print page preamble to STDOUT
print "Content-type: text/html\n\n";
print "<HEAD><TITLE>Test Find Search Engine</TITLE>\n";
print "<BODY bgcolor=#FFFFFF>\n";

# call subroutine to search the file
&findstr($BASEDIR);
print "<\/BODY><\/HTML>\n";

sub findstr
{
# open the file
      open(FILE,"$file");
# read all lines into an array
      @LINES = <FILE>;
      close(FILE);

# create one huge string to search
      $string = join(' ',@LINES);
      $string =~ s/\n/ /g;
               if (!($string =~ /$term/i))
{
# don't include this file name
              last;
               }
# if string is found
               else
{
# include the file name
          print "<P>Found string in $BASEDIR/$file\n";
               }

}
```

Now if you combine these two scripts, as in Listing 35.10, you will have a rudimentary search engine that still produces output similar to Figure 35.2.

Listing 35.10 Tstfind.pl A basic recursive search engine.

```
#!/usr/local/bin/perl

# requires find.pl
require("/public/local/lib/perl5/find.pl");
$BASEDIR = "/web/home/acn";
# hardcode the search term - you could prompt user
$term = "ACNielsen";

print "Content-type: text/html\n\n";
print "<HEAD><TITLE>A Basic Recursive Search Engine</TITLE>\n";
print "<BODY bgcolor=#FFFFFF>\n";

&find("$BASEDIR");

# close the page
print "<\/BODY><\/HTML>\n";

sub wanted
{
# if it's an HTML file
     if (($name =~ /.htm/) && !($name =~ /.html/))
     {
# search for string
               $findstr($BASEDIR/$name, $term);

     }
} # sub wanted
sub findstr
{
# get the name of the file and search term as a parameter
my ($file,$term) = @_;
# open the file
      open(FILE,"$file");
# read all lines into an array
      @LINES = <FILE>;
      close(FILE);

# create one huge string to search
      $string = join(' ',@LINES);
      $string =~ s/\n//g;
               if (!($string =~ /$term/i))
{
# don't include this file name
              last;
               }
# if string is found
               else
{
# include the file name
           print "<P>Found string $term in $BASEDIR/$file\n";
               }

} # sub findstr
```

This script works; it finds instances of a search string in all files in a directory tree. But it ignores some problems and is definitely lacking in features. It would be nice, for example, to be able to specify the search to be case sensitive and whether multiple words should be treated as Boolean AND or OR. The display does not provide a link to the found files. Another missing feature is the context of the search hit. You know that the search terms are found in these files, but you have no idea if the use of them is trivial or important. You don't know how many times the search string was found and have no way to evaluate the relevance of a file.

NOTE Rarely on a site is there a directory tree in which every HTML file and directory is available to the public. On my own site, many protected directories require a user ID and password to access. In addition, a number of experimental files, backup files, or other files are not linked to the main site and are not for public consumption. This rudimentary script searches all files on the site regardless of whether they are protected.

Implementing a Third-Party Grepping Search Engine

Several very popular grepping search engines are available on the Web. The following sections examine three of them:

- Matt's Simple Search Engine by Matthew M. Wright, author of the famous Matt's Perl Script Archive
- Htgrep by Oscar Nierstrasz
- Hukilau 2 from Adams Communications

All are written in Perl, and each has a little something to recommend it. All solve many of the problems mentioned in the last section and provide added functionality.

Implementing Matt's Simple Search Engine You can find Matt's Simple Search Engine in Matt's Script Archive at **http://www.worldwidemart.com/scripts/**, one of the most popular Perl script archives on the Web.

Implementing Matt's search engine is fairly simple: Just get the distribution archive, install it on your site, configure it, and create a search form. To configure the script, you need to edit several lines at the top to point to the base directory. The base directory is the base URL for the site and is used to create links to the found pages. You also need to insert a title to put on the resulting page and furnish links for the home page and search page.

Because Matt's script does not do recursion, you also need to specify all the subdirectories you want searched. This can be tedious to maintain as your site changes, so you may want to modify the file finding script from the previous example and combine it with calls to Matt's engine to perform the search.

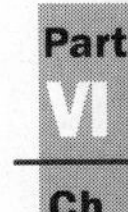

After you finish configuring, you need to create a page that incorporates something similar to the following HTML fragment, which appears on the accompanying CD as mattform.txt:

```
<FORM method=POST
      action="http://worldwidemart.com/scripts/cgi-bin/demos/search.cgi">
<CENTER><TABLE border>
<TR>
<TH>Text to Search For: </TH>
<TH><INPUT type=text name="terms" size=40><BR></TH>
</TR><TR>
<TH>Boolean: <SELECT name="boolean">
<OPTION>AND
<OPTION>OR
</SELECT> </TH><TH>Case <SELECT name="case">
<OPTION>Insensitive
<OPTION>Sensitive
</SELECT><BR></TH>
</TR><TR>
<TH colspan=2><INPUT type=submit value="Search!">
<INPUT type=reset><BR></TH>
</TR></TABLE></FORM></CENTER>
<HR size=7 width=75%><P>
```

This form produces a Web page similar to that shown in Figure 35.3.

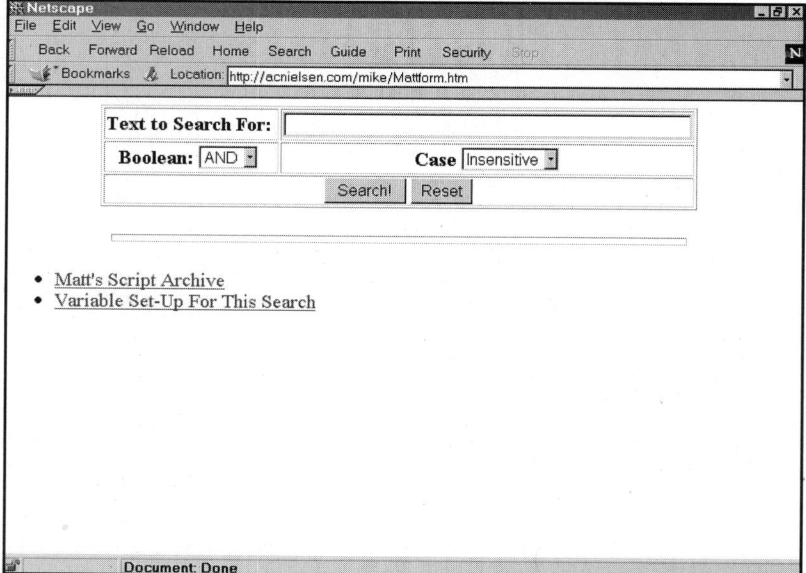

FIG. 35.3
You can use the generic form provided with Matt's Search Engine to allow user input.

You may wish to design your own search interface. If so, your form needs to present the following three parameters to the search script:

- *Terms.* A text string containing one or more words
- *Boolean.* The Boolean AND or OR
- *Case.* Whether the search should be case sensitive or not case insensitive

Make sure you use the `POST` method to call Matt's Simple Search Engine. If you use `GET`, the script won't work because Matt's script reads form input from `<STDIN>`.

The result of a search using Matt's Simple Search Engine interface will look similar to that shown in Figure 35.4.

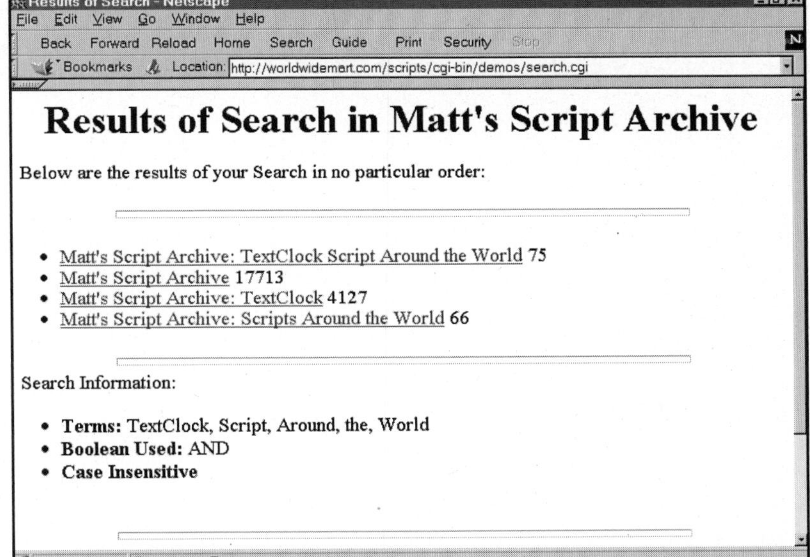

FIG. 35.4
The results page from Matt's Search Engine provides links to the found pages.

Notice that each found page is represented by a link to that page. The search terms are also provided, along with the Boolean and case sensitivity settings.

Matt's script works fine and is fairly fast. It took 3 CPU seconds and about 10 elapsed seconds to search about 250 files on my site.

Some desirable features are lacking, however—for example, only the titles of found files are displayed. There is no context to indicate whether the search term is merely mentioned in the file or whether significant information about the term is contained in it. When presented with a list of dozens of files as the result of a search, with no way to distinguish between them, users may become weary of trying to find the information and visit a different site.

File titles are presented in no particular order, which is not very helpful in determining their relevance.

The results also do not indicate how many times a search term was found in a particular file or, in the case of multiple-word search terms, whether the words were found in close proximity. The user has no control over partial matches such as finding "state" within "estate" and "intestate." Whatever the user types becomes the search string.

In addition, there are various implementation problems with this simple search engine. Because it does not support recursion, control over which directories are searched rests entirely in the hands of the webmaster, who must remember to add new directories to the variable in the script file. Files or directories also are not easily excluded from a search. There is also no limit to the number of files that can be returned, nor are stop words ignored. Given the way that directories must be explicitly specified, this may not seem to be a big drawback; but, what if you have painstakingly added all directories on your site to the script and someone searches for the word “the”? A better way is definitely needed to control the directories that are searched.

Fortunately, Htgrep satisfies many of these objections.

Implementing the Htgrep Search Engine Htgrep, written by Oscar Nierstrasz, can be obtained at **http://iamwww.unibe.ch/~scg/Src/Doc/htgrep.html** or in the Software Composition Group Software Archives at **http://iamwww.unibe.ch/~scg/Src/**.

The major differences between Htgrep and Matt's script is that Htgrep automatically recurses subdirectories, and it supports Boolean `AND` searches as well as case-sensitive searches.

After you have installed the Perl script `htgrep.pl` and the associated scripts `find.pl`, `html.pl`, and `bib.pl`, you configure the base directory by changing a variable at the beginning of `htgrep.pl`. Other variables you configure include the path to users' public HTML directories and any pseudo-URLs (URLs that have been aliased) that you want included in the search.

On the CD

Included in the package is a basic search form and a basic CGI wrapper script that you can use to control the behavior of Htgrep.pl. The CGI wrapper appears on the accompanying CD as htgrep.cgi.

You will need to modify the wrapper to configure the location of your Perl library files. The CGI wrapper assumes that Find.pl, which was used in an earlier example, is located in the library. You can find the Find.pl program in the Htgrep distribution, if you don't already have it.

TIP

The Htgrep wrapper script enables you to use either the `POST` method or the `GET` method to process the form. It first looks for information from a `POST`, using `$ENV{'PATH_INFO'}`, and then from a `GET`, using `($ENV{'QUERY_STRING'}`.

After you have configured the CGI wrapper, you need to build a form for your users to specify parameters. The form provided with the distribution appears in Listing 35.11.

Listing 35.11 Htform.txt Example form for use with HTGREP.

```
<H2>Generic Form</H2>

<FORM ACTION="/~scg/cgi-bin/htgrep.cgi">
<P>
<INPUT
     NAME="file"
     SIZE=30
```

```
     VALUE="/~scg/Src/Doc/htgrep.html"
>
<!
     VALUE="/~scg/Src/Doc/htgrep.html"
!>
<B>File to search</B> (relative to WWW home)
<BR>
<INPUT NAME="isindex" SIZE=30>
<B>Query</B>
<INPUT TYPE="submit" VALUE="Submit">
<INPUT TYPE="reset" VALUE="Reset">

<DL>

<DT><B>Query style:</B>
<DD>
<INPUT type="checkbox" name="case" value="yes">
Case Sensitive
<DD>
<INPUT type="radio" name="boolean" value="auto" checked="yes">
Automatic Keyword/Regex
<INPUT type="radio" name="boolean" value="yes">
Multiple Keywords
<INPUT type="radio" name="boolean" value="no">
Regular Expression

<DT><B>HTML Files:</B>
<DD>
<INPUT type="radio" name="style" value="none" checked="yes">
Ordinary Paragraphs
<INPUT type="radio" name="style" value="ol">
Numbered list
<INPUT type="radio" name="style" value="ul">
Bullet list
<INPUT type="radio" name="style" value="dl">
Description list

<DT><B>Plain Text:</B>
<INPUT type="radio" name="style" value="pre">
(preformatted)
<DD>
<INPUT type="checkbox" name="grab" value="yes">
Make URLs live (works with plain text only)

<DT><B>Refer Bibliography files:</B>
<INPUT type="checkbox" name="refer" value="yes">
<DD>
<INPUT type="checkbox" name="abstract" value="yes">
Show Abstract
<INPUT type="checkbox" name="ftpstyle" value="dir">
Link to directories, not files (for refer files)
<DD>
<INPUT type="radio" name="style" value="ul">
Bullet list (instead of numbered)
```


continued

Listing 35.11 Continued

```
<DT><B>Max records to return:</B>
<INPUT NAME="max" VALUE="250" SIZE=10>
</DL>

</FORM>
```

This code produces a form similar to the one shown in Figure 35.5.

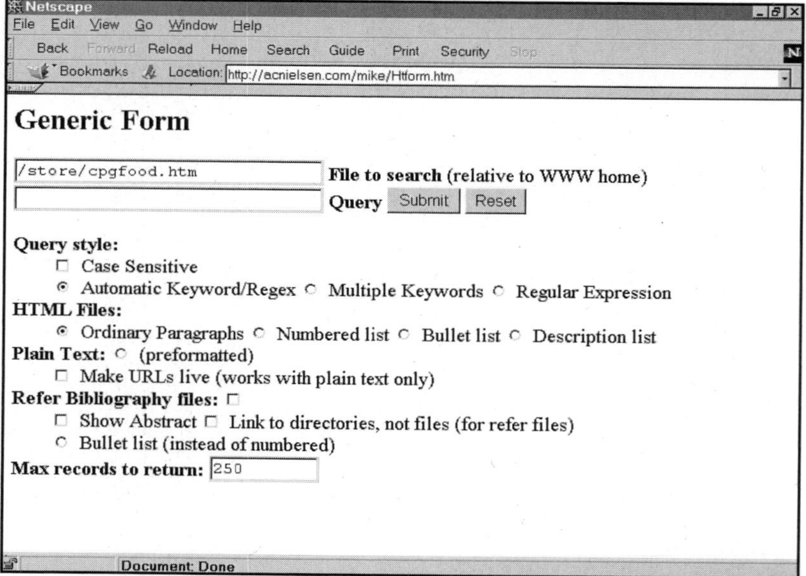

FIG. 35.5
You can use the generic form provided with Htgrep to allow user input.

A welcome feature of Htgrep is its support for regular expressions. Although most users are probably not well versed in the use of regular expressions, most at least can understand using the asterisk to fill out portions of words. Additionally, unless you use regular expressions, Htgrep searches on whole words, which is a nice feature.

Using the default search form, you can also determine the format of the resulting hits page—either full paragraphs or various types of listings.

NOTE The capability to return full paragraphs was the key in my decision to use Htgrep on my site. Because a high proportion of the words that users are likely to search for occur in many documents on the site, I felt it was important to provide this context to help guide users to relevant pages quickly and easily.

To enable the return of entire paragraphs from a search, Htgrep takes a different approach to finding text in files. Rather than assembling one huge string from all the lines in the files, Htgrep enables you to specify a record delimiter and then searches each record in a file. You may decide, for example, that you want HTML paragraph tags (<P>) to be your record delimiter. It is the record orientation of the search that allows Htgrep to return the context for a search hit. Htgrep returns the entire record in which it found the search term. The user thus sees the entire paragraph and can better determine whether the page meets his or her needs. Htgrep does this by using Perl's capability to define a record delimiter. This is demonstrated in the following code fragment:

```
# the default record separator is a blank line
#$separator = "";
$separator = "<P>";
[. . .]
     # normally records are separated by blank lines
     # if linemode is set, there is one record per line
     if ($tags{'linemode'} =~ /yes/i) { $/ = "\n"; }
     else { $/ = "$separator"; }
```

Unfortunately, a side effect of this context approach is that multiple paragraphs from each found page can be returned. Although this may help further guide the user, many may find it an annoyance. You may want to modify the Htgrep code to cause it to proceed to the next file upon finding a search hit. Doing this, however, might cause the search to skip particularly relevant material. What is really needed is a more sophisticated approach that evaluates the fitness of a document based on other rules such as number of hits per document and the proximity of words found as a result of multiple-word searches. It is difficult to add this level of sophistication to a grepping search engine. As discussed later in this chapter, you can find such features in some indexing search engines.

TROUBLESHOOTING

If you make any changes in these scripts, you can test them for syntax errors before installing the script in your CGI-bin directory. Give the script execute permission for your account, and then type its filename at the command line. The output will be either the default form (if the syntax is correct) or a syntax error message (if it's not).

Htgrep also enables you to set the maximum number of records to return. This is an important feature because there is no provision in Htgrep to ignore stop words. Unfortunately, there is also no way to prevent Htgrep from returning really long records. Assume, for example, that you define <P> as your record delimiter. If you add a new document that uses <p> for paragraphs, or if you have long material contained within <PRE> tags, the result can be huge amounts of text returned on the results page. To solve this problem, you can modify the code to include a line counter that aborts the paragraph retrieval if it is longer than 200 words. The following code fragment contains this modification:


```
# this is where Htgrep actually searches the file
          while (<FILE>) {
```

```
# call the subroutine that evaluates the search terms
                $queryCommand
# optional filter definition
                $filter
# remove all the nasty tags that can disturb paragraph display
                s/\<table/\<p/g ;
                s/\<hr/\<p/g ;
                s/\<HR/\<p/g ;
                s/\<IMG/\<p/g ;
                s/\<img/\<p/g ;
# transform relative URLs in found pages to full URLs
                if ((/\<A HREF/) && !(/http/) && !(/home/)) {
                     s/\<A HREF \= \"/\<A HREF \= \"\$dirname/g ;}
                print \$url;
# count the number of words
                \@words = split(' ', \$_);
                \$wordcount = 0;
                foreach \$word (\@words)
                {
                     \$wordcount++;
                }
# if it's too large, don't print the record
                if (\$wordcount >= 200)
                {
                     print "\<H4\>Excerpt would be greater than 200 \n";
                     print "words. Select link above to see entire \n";
                     print "page.\<\/H4\>\\n";
# skip to next record
                     next;
                }
# otherwise print out the record
                print;
# if you've printed up to the limit, stop
                last if (++\$count == $maxcount);
          }
```

Another side effect of returning the whole paragraph concerns what else besides text is returned. Because Htgrep grabs the whole paragraph, it also grabs links to images, bits of Java, JavaScript, or ActiveX code, and anything else contained in the paragraphs. This is probably not what the user wants when using a search engine. The resulting hits page can contain dozens of large GIFs and take a long time to download.

If your search engine returns blocks of text from the found files, be sure your script processes the text before displaying it to remove image references or program code. Failure to do so can result in pages containing many large images that are time-consuming to download.

Because of this limitation, I modified the Htgrep script to remove all `<IMG>` tags. I must confess, I did this in a decidedly low tech way by just replacing all instances of `<IMG` with `<P` in all found paragraphs (see the previous example). It is crude, but effective. The resulting hits page is devoid of image tags (see Figure 35.6).

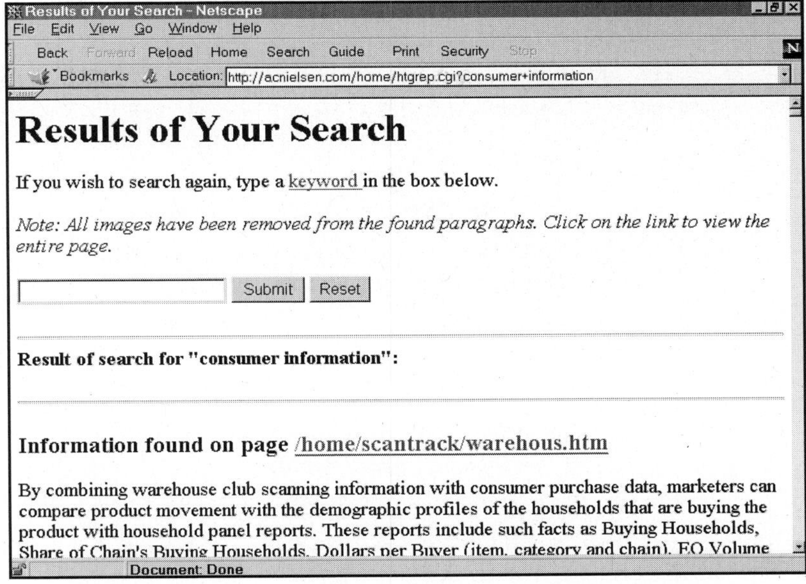

FIG. 35.6
All image references are removed from the search results page produced by a modified Htgrep.

You will notice that another script modification produces a hyperlink to the found page, something that the base Htgrep script only provides if you elect plain-text formatting.

A security problem occurs with using Htgrep; you must take care of in the wrapper script: Because the search string can be a Perl regular expression, it executes using Perl's `eval` function. This can allow your users to execute arbitrary commands on your Web server. To prevent this from happening, be sure to prescreen search terms for dangerous characters or expressions, especially `!sh`, in the CGI wrapper that you use to call Htgrep.

CAUTION

If your Perl script uses the `eval` command to execute the search, you need to preprocess the search terms to prevent users from executing processes on your Web server.

Another nice feature of Htgrep is that, on NCSA servers, it ignores any directories that contain an access control file (.Htaccess). Chances are, you don't want users searching these directories anyway. If you want finer control over what directories are searched, you can put a .Htaccess file in your backup, administration, or internal directories. Other search engines require you to explicitly exclude such directories from the search and that leads to administrative overhead for the poor webmaster.

Implementing the Hukilau 2 Search Engine Hukilau is a search script that searches through all the files in a directory. It can be very slow, so it is not practical for every site.

You may use this script for noncommercial purposes free of charge. A single-site commercial license is available for $250.

Hukilau searches one directory, which you specify in the script. (The registered version enables you to choose other directories from the search form.) Its search results page includes filenames, relevance scores, and context samples. The files on a search results page are in directory order, not sorted by relevance.

There is an option to show text excerpts from all the files in a directory, listed alphabetically by filename. This is useful when you are looking for something ill-defined, or when you need a broad overview of what is in the directory.

A quick file list feature reads only the directory file itself, not the individual files in the directory. It is fast, but it includes only filenames, not page titles or context samples.

The defaults are to apply an AND operator to all the words, to search for substrings rather than whole words, and to conduct a non–case-sensitive search. If you would like to change these defaults, you can edit the search form that the script generates. Listing 35.12 shows the part of the form that applies to the radio button and check box settings, edited a bit here for clarity:

Listing 35.12 Excerpt from a Hukilau search form.

```
sub PrintBlankSearchForm
{
...
<INPUT TYPE="RADIO" NAME="SearchMethod" value="or"><B>Or</B>
<INPUT TYPE="RADIO" NAME="SearchMethod"
value="and" CHECKED><B>And</B>
<INPUT TYPE="RADIO" NAME="SearchMethod"
value="exact phrase"><B>Exact phrase</B> /

<INPUT TYPE="RADIO" NAME="WholeWords" value="no" CHECKED><B>Sub</B>strings
<INPUT TYPE="RADIO" NAME="WholeWords" value="yes"><B>Whole</B> Words<BR>

<INPUT TYPE="CHECKBOX" NAME="CaseSensitive" value="yes">Case sensitive<BR>

<INPUT TYPE="RADIO" NAME="ListAllFiles" value="no" CHECKED><B>Search</B> (enter
terms in search box above) <BR>
<INPUT TYPE="RADIO" NAME="ListAllFiles" value="yes">
List all files in directory (search box has no effect)<BR>
<INPUT TYPE="RADIO" NAME="ListAllFiles" value="quick">
Quick file list<BR>

<INPUT TYPE="RADIO" NAME="Compact" value="yes">
Compact display<BR>
<INPUT TYPE="RADIO" NAME="Compact" value="no" CHECKED>
Detailed display<BR>

<INPUT TYPE="CHECKBOX" NAME="ShowURL" value="yes">URLs<BR>
<INPUT TYPE="CHECKBOX" NAME="ShowScore" value="yes" CHECKED>Scores<BR>
<INPUT TYPE="CHECKBOX" NAME="ShowSampleText" value="yes"
CHECKED>Sample text<BR>
...
```

To change the default from `AND` to `OR` in Listing 35.12, for example, move the word `CHECKED` from one line to the other on these two lines:

```
<INPUT TYPE="RADIO" NAME="SearchMethod" value="or"><B>Or</B>
<INPUT TYPE="RADIO" NAME="SearchMethod" value="and" CHECKED><B>And</B>
```

The result should look like the following:

```
<INPUT TYPE="RADIO" NAME="SearchMethod" value="or" CHECKED><B>Or</B>
<INPUT TYPE="RADIO" NAME="SearchMethod" value="and"><B>And</B>
```

Changing the value of a check box is a little different. To make searching case sensitive by default, for example, add the word `CHECKED` to the statement that creates the unchecked box. Here's the original line:

```
<INPUT TYPE="CHECKBOX" NAME="CaseSensitive"
value="yes">Case sensitive<BR>
```

Here is the same line, but set to display a checked box. It now looks like this:

```
<INPUT TYPE="CHECKBOX" NAME="CaseSensitive"
value="yes" CHECKED>Case sensitive<BR>
```

An unchecked box sends no value to the CGI program. It would not matter if you changed "yes" to "no" (or even "blue elephants"), as long as the box remains unchecked. The quoted value never gets passed to the program unless the box is checked.

This is the importance behind choosing values for the defaults. If you remove all the radio and check box fields from the form, leaving only the `SearchText` text entry field, the hidden `Command` field, and the `Submit` button, the program sets a range of reasonable, often used defaults.

This makes it practical to use relatively simple hidden Hukilau forms as drop-in search forms on your pages. To change the defaults and still use a hidden form, you can include the appropriate extra fields, but hide them, as shown in Listing 35.13.

Listing 35.13 Hiding all form variables.

```
<FORM METHOD="POST"
➥ACTION="http://www.substitute_your.com/cgi-bin/hukilau.cgi">
<INPUT TYPE="HIDDEN" NAME="Command" VALUE="search">
<INPUT TYPE="TEXT" NAME="SearchText" SIZE="48">
<INPUT TYPE="SUBMIT" VALUE=" Search "><BR>
<INPUT TYPE="HIDDEN" NAME="SearchMethod" value="and">
<INPUT TYPE="HIDDEN" NAME="WholeWords" value="yes">
<INPUT TYPE="HIDDEN" NAME="ShowURL" value="yes">
</FORM>
```

The current version of the Hukilau Search Engine is available from Adams Communications at

http://www.adams1.com/

Updates regarding new features being added or tested may be found on the Small Hours site at

http://www.aa.net/~rclark/scripts/

The complete source code for the original Hukilau Search Engine is on the accompanying CD. There is also a modified version called Hukilau 2 that includes some added routines that Rod Clark wrote for this chapter.

Implementing an Indexing Search Engine

As you have learned from the previous discussion, implementing a grepping search engine can be quite easy. The discussion focused on only three popular Perl-based grepping engines, but there are many more with various features. Using the grepping approach represents a trade off between minimal disk usage and up-to-the-minute timeliness with high CPU usage and long elapsed times. You certainly can't beat the price (usually free) or the ease of setup and maintenance.

More sophisticated searching, however, is hard to implement using the grepping approach. For larger, more complex sites, an indexing search engine can be the best choice.

Several indexing search engines are available for use on your Web site. In addition to an array of shareware or free engines, several of the large commercial search sites make their technology available for use on a local site. Commercial indexing search engines include those listed in Table 35.2.

Table 35.2 Some available commercial indexing search engines.

Company	Tool Name	URL	Free?
Verity	Search 97	**http://www.verity.com/products/datasheets/dk.html**	No
Thunderstone	The Webinator Web Index & Retrieval (shareware) System	**http://www.thunderstone.com/webinator/**	Yes
AltaVista	AltaVista Search eXtensions	**http://altavista.software.digital.com/search/index.htm**	No
Inmagic/Lycos	DB/SearchWorks	**http://www.inmagic.com/textprod.htm#sm**	No
Excite	Excite for Web Servers	**http://www.excite.com/navigate/home.html**	Yes
Netcreations	Pinpoint	**http://www.netcreations.com/pinpoint/**	No (free trial)

The sections that follow focus on implementing the following five indexing search engines:

- WebGlimpse, developed by the University of Arizona
- ICE by Christian Neuss
- Simple Web Indexing System for Humans—Enhanced (SWISH-E) by Kevin Hughes
- freeWAIS from the University of Dortmund, Germany
- Excite for Web Servers

Implementing WebGlimpse

GLIMPSE (which stands for GLobal IMPlicit SEarch) and its Web companion WebGlimpse are projects of the University of Arizona's Computer Science Department. WebGlimpse is available for free for nonprofit use. A small licensing fee is charged for commercial users. The University has recently developed a new program called the Search Broker. The Search Broker forwards your query to a search engine dealing specifically with the subject of your question, which you specify as the first word of your query.

A recent search of the Web turned up hundreds of sites that are using this popular tool or its precursor, GlimpseHTTP. A partial list of sites is available at **http://glimpse.cs.arizona.edu/ghttp/sites.html**. GLIMPSE is also used as a basis for Harvest Information Discovery and Access System (**http://harvest.cs.colorado.edu/**).

As the name implies, the program displays glimpses of context samples from the files. This makes it a particularly useful tool, even though it doesn't offer relevance ranking.

GLIMPSE is available at

ftp://ftp.cs.arizona.edu/glimpse/

You can obtain WebGlimpse at

http://glimpse.cs.arizona.edu/webglimpse/

CAUTION

Be sure to get the most recent version of WebGlimpse. In July, 1997 a security hole was discovered in the program and fixed.

The distribution is comprised of GLIMPSE, written in C, glimpseindex, another C program that creates the index, the webglimpse script itself, written in Perl, and an assortment of Perl utilities that you use to create and manage your indexes.

Installation is mostly automated, but definitely not foolproof. Sometimes several attempts are needed to get it installed smoothly. Once installed, you need to run a Perl script that creates the WebGlimpse index using glimpseindex. GLIMPSE can build indexes of several sizes, from tiny (about 1% of the size of the source files) to large (up to 30% of the size of the source files). Even small indexes are practical and offer good performance.

Other welcome features include the capability to index pages that have been added only since the last index, a facility to index off-site links, the capability to set a tolerance for spelling errors, and the capability to establish neighborhoods. *Neighborhoods* are defined as all links within an arbitrary number of hops from a page or all pages within a directory.

NOTE Running the index can consume quite a lot of time. Using WebGlimpse's option that enables indexing of external links as well as local pages, indexing took 45 minutes to index almost 600 files on my site. After that index was done, however, a re-index without the external option took only a few minutes.

After the index has been established, you can use a cron job to run it periodically to maintain it. The installation routine even creates the job for you.

Using the WebGlimpse Perl script (created by the install) to perform searches is easy. After aliasing to the proper directory, you call the script with a parameter that indicates where the index resides. The user sees a basic search form if the script is called directly.

Alternatively, you can include either of two code fragments in your Web pages to provide a nicer looking interface. The two interface styles are created using the HTML code fragments in Listing 35.14.

Listing 35.14 Glimform.txt Two forms for calling WebGlimpse.

```
<H2>Basic WebGlimpse Interface</H2>

<CENTER>
<TABLE border=5><TR border=0>
<TD align=center valign=middle>
<A HREF=http://glimpse.cs.arizona.edu/webglimpse>
<IMG src=/images/glimpse-eye.jpg alt="WG" align=middle width=50><BR>
<FONT size=-3>WebGlimpse</FONT></A></TD>
<TD> <FORM method=get ACTION=/$CGIBIN/webglimpse$ARCHIVEPWD>
<INPUT NAME=query size=20>
<INPUT TYPE=submit VALUE="Search">
<INPUT name=file type=hidden value="$FILE">
<A HREF=/$CGIBIN/webglimpse-fullsearch$ARCHIVEPWD?file=$FILE>
Search Options</A></TD></TR>
<TR><TD colspan=2>
Search:
<INPUT TYPE=radio NAME=scope VALUE=neighbor CHECKED>
The neighborhood of this page
<INPUT TYPE=radio NAME=scope VALUE=full>The full archive
</TD></TR></FORM></TABLE></CENTER><HR>


<H2>Full-Featured WebGlimpse Interface</H2>
<TABLE border=5>
<TR><TD align=center valign=middle>
<A HREF=http://glimpse.cs.arizona.edu/webglimpse>
<IMG src="/images/glimpse-eye.jpg"
align=middle></TD>
```

```
<TD align=center valign=middle>
<A HREF=http://glimpse.cs.arizona.edu/webglimpse>
<FONT size=+3>WebGlimpse </A> Search<BR></FONT></TD>
</TR>

<TR><TD colspan=2>
<FORM method=get ACTION=>
<INPUT name=file type=hidden value=/home/msmith/public_html/big/index.html>
Search:
<INPUT TYPE=radio NAME=scope VALUE=neighbor>
The neighborhood of <a
href="">the ACNielsen Web Site
</A>
<INPUT TYPE=radio NAME=scope VALUE=full CHECKED>The full archive: <A
HREF="">the ACNielsen Site including links offsite</a>
</TD></TR>

<TR><TD colspan=2>
String to search for: <INPUT NAME=query size=30>
<INPUT TYPE=submit VALUE=Submit>
<BR>
<CENTER>
<INPUT NAME=case TYPE=checkbox>Case sensitive
<!SPACES>   
<INPUT NAME=whole TYPE=checkbox>Partial match
<!SPACES>   
<INPUT NAME=lines TYPE=checkbox>Jump to line
<!SPACES>   
<SELECT NAME=errors align=right>
<OPTION>0
<OPTION>1
<OPTION>2
</SELECT>
misspellings allowed
<BR>
</CENTER>
Return only files modified within the last <INPUT NAME=age size=5>
days.
<BR>
Maximum number of files returned:
<SELECT NAME=maxfiles>
<OPTION>10
<OPTION selected>50
<OPTION>100
<OPTION>1000
</SELECT>
<BR>Maximum number of matches per file returned:
<SELECT NAME=maxlines>
<OPTION>10
<OPTION selected>30
<OPTION>50
<OPTION>500
</SELECT>
<BR>
```


continued

Listing 35.14 Continued

```
</FORM>
</TD></TR>
<TR><TD colspan=2>
<CENTER>
<FONT size=-2><A HREF=http://glimpse.cs.arizona.edu>
Glimpse</A> and <A HREF=http://glimpse.cs.arizona.edu/webglimpse>
WebGlimpse</A>, Copyright &copy; 1996,
Arizona Board of Regents.
</CENTER>
</FONT></TD></TR>
</TABLE></CENTER>
</CENTER>
```

The sample page in Figure 35.7 demonstrates the two available user interfaces for WebGlimpse.

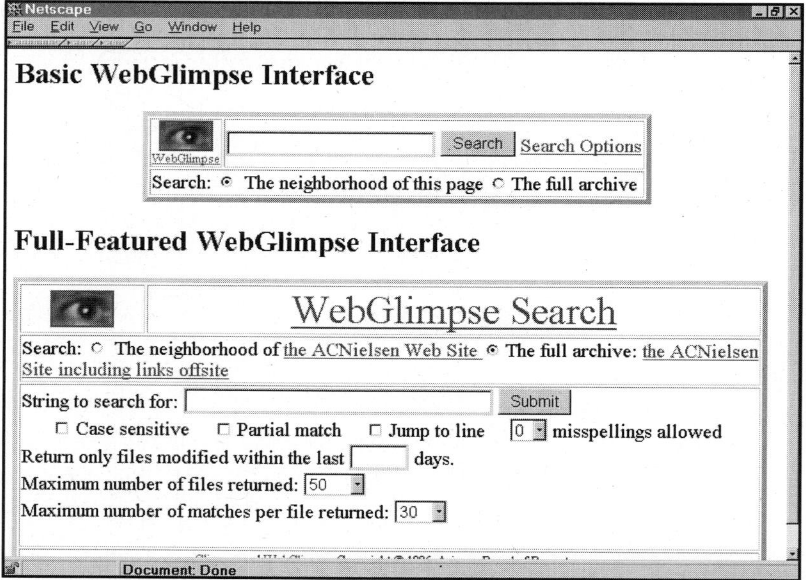

FIG. 35.7 The default search forms provided with WebGlimpse enable you to choose the level of search complexity.

The first interface is short, sweet, and perfect for an unobtrusive search facility. The second interface enables the user to select a neighborhood search or a full archive search; choose case sensitivity, partial match, and spelling-error settings; to optionally jump to the line in a found document; and to control the date and number of documents returned.

CAUTION

One annoying aspect of the WebGlimpse indexing routine is that it automatically appends the user interface code at the bottom of each page it indexes unless you comment out the appropriate line. Although this feature is a nice service for those who want it, being able to turn it off is a must. My personal preference is to add a link to the search facility rather than the entire user interface. Due to WebGlimpse's concept of page neighborhood, however, putting this code on every page can make sense.

A page neighborhood is obviously context sensitive. You can define a page's neighborhood, for example, as every other page that is within two jumps (a link to a page that links to one other page). If page A has a link to page B and page C, and each of those pages links to one other page, pages BA and CA, page A's neighborhood is pages B, C, BA, and CA. However, if you follow the links to page BA, for example, you may find it links to pages D and E, making its neighborhood much different. Because the context determines the neighborhood, you need a unique call to WebGlimpse on each page rather than a generic (search-the-whole-site) search page.

By the same token, if you define a neighborhood as all files in the same directory, the context of the WebGlimpse search changes depending on the starting page.

If your site is massive, or if you want to allow for more context-sensitive searching, you may prefer to have unique calls to WebGlimpse embedded on each page of your site. You might, for example, have a site that offers a number of Web utilities. Each utility is available in a variety of languages and for a variety of operating systems. If a user is reading about one of the programs and wants to know more about its implementation in Perl, he or she doesn't want to search the entire site and then have to wade through scads of listings for irrelevant utilities. In this instance, a neighborhood search is appropriate. If the site is organized properly, the information should be available either within a few hops or within the same directory.

The output of WebGlimpse looks similar to that shown Figure 35.8.

This output from WebGlimpse shows that a link is provided to the found document. In addition, context is provided by including all lines in which the search terms are found. WebGlimpse automatically limits the number of found files as well.

An interesting feature of WebGlimpse is its setting for spelling errors. The example given in the documentation is a search for the name, Schwarzkopf. Many people do not know how to spell this name. Therefore, there may be spelling errors both in the user's search terms or in the documents on the site. Because WebGlimpse uses GLIMPSE, which in turn builds on the powerful agrep, it supports approximate matching which allows for spelling errors. Thus if the material on your site comes from a variety of sources, varies in grammatical quality, or your users can't spell, the capability to be forgiving of spelling errors is a definite plus.

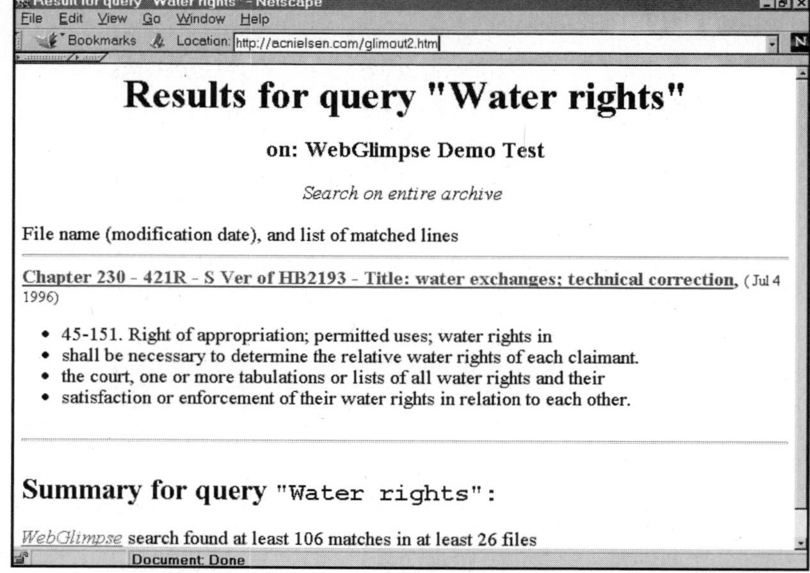

FIG. 35.8 The search result page from WebGlimpse contains a link to the found page as well as a listing of all found lines.

WebGlimpse basically uses a modified grepping approach, but applies the grepping to an index. Although there is some flexibility offered in the spelling–error-tolerance feature, complex searches are not offered and there is no ranking of results by confidence level.

WebGlimpse takes the grepping approach just about as far as it can go. To achieve better results, a more complicated search methodology is needed.

Implementing ICE

Christian Neuss' ICE search engine produces relevance-ranked results and lists the search words that it finds in each file. It is written in Perl.

There are two scripts. The indexing script, ice-idx.pl, creates an index file that ICE can later search. The indexer runs from the UNIX command line, as a standard non-CGI program. The search script, ice-form.pl, is a CGI script. It searches the index and displays the results on a Web page.

ICE can use an optional external thesaurus in Thesaurus Interchange Format. Christian Neuss notes that ICE has worked well with small thesauri of a few hundred technical terms, but that anyone who wants to use a large thesaurus should contact him for more information.

You can find the current version of ICE on the Net at these two distribution sites, although the German site generally has a much later version:

http://www.informatik.th-darmstadt.de/~neuss/ice/ice.html

http://ice.cornell-iowa.edu/

Indexing Your Files with ICE ICE searches the directories that you specify in the script's configuration section. When ICE indexes a given directory, it also indexes all of its subdirectories.

There are five configuration items at the top of the indexer script. *You will* need to edit three of them:

```
@SEARCHDIRS=(
  "/home/user/somedir/subdir/",
  "/home/user/thisis/another/",
  "/home/user/andyet/more_stuff/"
);

$INDEXFILE="/user/home/somedir/index.idx"

# Minimum length of word to be indexed
$MINLEN=3;
```

The first directory path in `@SEARCHDIRS` is the default that will appear on the search form. You can add more directory lines in the style of the existing ones, or you can include only one directory if you want to limit what people can see of your files.

Remember that ICE automatically indexes and searches all the subdirectories of the directories you specify.

ICE's index is a plain ASCII text file. Here's a sample from the beginning of an ICE index file:

```
@f /./bookmark.htm
@t Rod Clark s Bookmarks
@m 823231844
1 ABC
1 AFGHANISTAN
1 AGREP
1 AIP
1 ALTNEWS
1 AND
1 ANIMAL
1 ANU
1 ATM
1 AUSTRALIA
1 AsiaLink
```

After you have set the configuration variables, run the script from the command line to create the index. Whenever you want to update the index, run the Ice-idx.pl script again. It overwrites the existing index with the new one.

You can use the UNIX `cron` utility to schedule your index updates.

Searching from a Web Browser with ICE The search form presents a choice of directories in a drop-down selection box. You can specify these directories in the script. Listing 35.15 shows how to accomplish this task.

Listing 35.15 A sample ICE search script.

```
# Title or name of your server:
local($title)="ICE Indexing Gateway";

# search directories to present in the search dialogue
local(@directories)=(
    "Public HTML Directory",
    "Another HTML Directory"
);
```

Now you can install the script in your CGI directory and call it from your Web browser.

Implementing SWISH-E (Simple Web Indexing System for Humans—Enhanced)

SWISH-E is easy to set up and offers fast, reliable searching for Web sites. In indexing HTML files, SWISH-E can ignore data in most tags while giving higher relevance to information in header and title tags. You can also limit your search to words in HTML titles, comments, emphasized tags, and META tags. SWISH-E creates a small and portable index consisting of a single averaging around 1% to 5% of the size of the original source files.

Kevin Hughes wrote the original SWISH program in C for UNIX Web servers. In autumn 1996, The Library of UC Berkeley received permission from Kevin Hughes to implement bug fixes and enhancements to the original binary. SWISH-E is freeware, available from the Berkeley Digital Library Sunsite at

http://sunsite.berkeley.edu/SWISH-E/

Installing SWISH-E is straightforward. After uncompressing and untarring the source files, you edit the SRC/CONFIG.H file and compile SWISH-E for your system.

Configuring SWISH-E isn't very hard either. You set up a configuration file, Swish.CONF, which the indexer uses. Listing 35.16 shows a sample SWISH-E configuration file.

Listing 35.16 Swish.conf A sample SWISH-E configuration file.

```
# SWISH-E configuration file

IndexDir /home/rclark/public_html/
# This is a space-separated list of files and directories you
# want indexed. You can specify more than one of these directives.

IndexFile index.swish
# This is what the generated index file will be.

IndexName "Index of Small Hours files"
IndexDescription "General index of the Small Hours Web site"
IndexPointer "http://www.aa.net/~rclark/"
IndexAdmin "Rod Clark (rclark@aa.net)"
```

```
# Extra information you can include in the index file.

IndexOnly .html .txt .gif .xbm .jpg
# Only files with these suffixes will be indexed.

IndexReport 3
# This is how detailed you want reporting. You can specify numbers
# 0 to 3 - 0 is totally silent, 3 is the most verbose.

FollowSymLinks yes
# Put "yes" to follow symbolic links in indexing, else "no".

NoContents .gif .xbm .jpg
# Files with these suffixes will not have their contents indexed -
# only their file names will be indexed.

ReplaceRules replace "/home/rclark/public_html/"
➥  "http://www.aa.net/~rclark/"
# ReplaceRules allow you to make changes to file path names
# before they're indexed.

FileRules pathname contains test newsmap
FileRules filename is index.html rename chk lst bit
FileRules filename contains ~ .bak .orig .000 .001 .old old. .map
➥ .cgi .bit .test test log- .log
FileRules title contains test Test
FileRules directory contains .htaccess
# Files matching the above criteria will *not* be indexed.

IgnoreLimit 80 50
# This automatically omits words that appear too often in the files
# (these words are called stopwords). Specify a whole percentage
# and a number, such as "80 256". This omits words that occur in
# over 80% of the files and appear in over 256 files. Comment out
# to turn of autostopwording.

IgnoreWords SwishDefault

# The IgnoreWords option allows you to specify words to ignore.
# Comment out for no stopwords; the word "SwishDefault" will
# include a list of default stopwords. Words should be separated
# by spaces and may span multiple directives.
```

After you set up SWISH-E for your site, create the indexes by running SWISH-E from the command line:

```
swish -c swish.conf
```

You can use `cron` to update the indexes regularly or just run the job manually when needed. Alternatively, you can use the AutoSWISH script that is part of the distribution, and which automates the indexing process from an HTML form.

Now that you have your indexes, you need some CGI to access them. The distribution includes a sample script, which is also available on the accompanying CD as `swish.cgi`.

Using Swish-Web, a SWISH-E Gateway Swish-Web is in the public domain. If you would like to practice a little programming on it, here are a few ideas for additions to the script.

NOTE The complete Perl source code for the Swish-Web gateway is on the accompanying CD as swishweb.cgi. It is an example of a Web gateway for a UNIX command-line program.

SWISH-E provides relevance scores, but the scoring algorithm seems to favor small files with little text, among which keywords loom large. Because SWISH-E reports file sizes, it is possible to add a routine to Swish-Web to sort SWISH-E's output by file size. Another useful addition would be a second relevance ranking option that weights file size more heavily.

A selection box on the form to limit the results to the first 10, 25, 50, 100, or 250 (or all) results might be another useful addition.

Implementing freeWAIS

In October 1989, a group of companies composed of Dow Jones, Thinking Machines Corporation, Apple Computer, and KPMG Peat Marwick saw the need for an easy way to provide text-based information systems on the corporate level and decided to do something about it. Their goal was to create a system for searching that was easy to use, flexible, built on an established standard, and which could search large amounts of distributed information in various formats. In April 1991, the group released the first Internet version of Wide Area Information Systems (abbreviated WAIS and pronounced "ways").

The benefits of WAIS are ease of use (for clients and developers), full-text search capability, and support for a variety of document types. It also has a far-reaching knowledge base; it can draw on remote databases to continue the query by example. Using results from one search can lead to a more appropriate server, and so on until the desired result is found.

Almost any time you encounter a discussion of WAIS on the Internet, freeWAIS will also be mentioned. The term freeWAIS is fairly self-explanatory—it is a freeware version of WAIS. Much of the material in this section is adapted directly from Bill Schongar's comprehensive discussion of WAIS in Chapter 12 of *Special Edition Using CGI*.

Implementing freeWAIS on UNIX Most WAIS tools are still primarily designed for use on UNIX servers. These tools include the servers themselves as well as the client scripts. It only makes sense, therefore, that one of the most significant public extensions to original WAIS functions first appeared on UNIX servers. *freeWAIS-SF,* designed by the University of Dortmund, Germany, takes advantage of built-in document structures to make more sense out of queries. It even enables you to specify your own document types for its use.

In addition, freeWAIS-SF gives you more power to search the way you want to search. Wild cards, "sounds-like" searches, and more conditions for what does and doesn't match are all components that make finding what you're looking for much easier. You no longer have to worry about whether the author wrote "Color" or "Colour," "Center" or "Centre."

Unlike many things that you use with your server, especially in the UNIX world, the freeWAIS-SF package is easy to install. A shell script leads you through the basic configuration by asking questions; when you finish answering the questions, you're finished installing freeWAIS-SF.

At the time of this writing, the current version of freeWAIS was 2.2.10. You can obtain the freeWAIS-SF package at the following site:

ftp://ftp.germany.eu.net/pub/infosystems/wais/Unido-LS6/

If you want the original freeWAIS instead (which you can certainly use, although it was last updated in 1996), you can get it from the Center for Networked Information Discovery and Retrieval. To get the main distribution directory so that you can choose the appropriate build, visit the following site:

ftp://cnidr.org/pub/NIDR.tools/freewais/

Whichever freeWAIS build you use will be a tarred and GNUZIPped file. To unpack the build, therefore, you must enter a command such as the following:

```
gunzip -c freeWAIS-0.X-whatever.tar.gz ¦ tar xvf -
```

freeWAIS comes with its own longer set of installation instructions within the distribution, so double-check the latest information for the build that you obtain to make sure that you don't skip any steps.

Implementing freeWAIS on Windows NT A port of freeWAIS 0.3 is available for Windows NT from EMWAC (the European Microsoft Windows Academic Center) in its WAIS Toolkit. EMWAC's current version of the toolkit is 0.7. You should, however, check with EMWAC before obtaining the toolkit to find out what is the latest version. Versions are available for all types of Windows NT: 386-based, Alpha, and PowerPC. You can obtain the toolkit from the following site:

ftp://emwac.ed.ac.uk/pub/waistool/

After you obtain the ZIP file, decompress it to retrieve the files that comprise the distribution. Move them to an NTFS drive partition, and then rename the file Waisindx.exe to Waisindex.exe.

If you plan to use the entire WAIS Toolkit with your server, put all three .exe programs into the %SYSTEMROOT%\SYSTEM32 directory (usually C:\WINNT\SYSTEM32).

If you are using UNIX, the WAIS program to query the WAIS indexes is called WAISQ. The query tool provided for Windows NT is called WAISLOOK. Keep this in mind when you see references to WAISQ, and just substitute WAISLOOK if you are using Windows NT.

Building a WAIS Database Now that you have the software installed and running, you are ready to make a database (a set of index files).

The WAISINDEX program looks through your files and creates an index that the WAIS query tool can use later. This index consists of seven distinct files that are either binary or plain text, as shown in Table 35.3.

Table 35.3 WAIS index database files.

File Extension	Purpose	File Type
.Cat	A catalog of indexed files with a few lines of information about each one.	Text
.Dct	A dictionary of indexed words.	Binary
.Doc	A document table.	Binary
.Fn	A filename table.	Binary
.Hl	A headline table, featuring the descriptive text used to identify documents that the search returns.	Binary
.Inv	An inverted file index.	Binary
.Src	A structure for describing the source. The structure includes the creation date and other similar information.	Text

The files with the extensions listed in Table 35.3 all share the same first name, as in Index.cat, Index.dct, Index.doc, and so on. You can name the first file anything you want, but if the file containing the HTML for the search form is called Index.html, INDEX is what you should use for the database. If your HTML file is called Default.htm (as it would be using EMWAC's HTTP server), DEFAULT is the correct first name for your database.

Many Web servers have built-in support for WAIS databases and determine which files to look at by matching the first name of the HTML file with the first name of the database files. Therefore, naming your database files correctly is important if you expect the built-in support to function.

The command line options that you use when executing WAISINDEX determines these database files' contents. You might want to use a variety of different options, depending on your objective and the nature of the files that you want to index. The following is a simple command line to create an index:

```
waisindex -d Data\database1 Data\*.html
```

This command line uses only one option, the `-d` switch, which specifies that the next argument is the name that you want to give the index. The command specifies that the name is DATABASE1, and that the database is to reside in the DATA directory. Arguments following the switches are the file names to index. In this example, the command indexes all the HTML files (those with an .Html extension) in the DATA directory.

One of the more powerful features of WAISINDEX is that it enables you to index a variety of file types. To find out exactly which file types your version supports, check your version's documentation. The versions of WAISINDEX vary in the file-type support that they offer. In particular, freeWAIS-SF enables you to specify your own document types, and the EMWAC Toolkit supports such formats as Microsoft's Knowledge Base.

Accessing the WAIS Database If your Web server has built-in support for WAIS (as many Web servers do), accessing the WAIS database is quite simple. You just create an HTML file to make the query and put the file in the same directory as the WAIS database files. (Remember that the first names of the HTML file and the database files must match.)

The HTML itself could not be simpler. Listing 35.17 shows a sample. All you have to do is include an `<ISINDEX>` tag somewhere on the form, and the Web server does the rest.

Listing 35.17 A sample WAIS search HTML.

```
<HEAD>
<TITLE>Sample WAIS Search</TITLE>
</HEAD>
<BODY>
<H1>Sample WAIS Search</H1>
This page has a built-in index.  Give it a whirl!
<P>
<ISINDEX>
</BODY>
</HTML>
```

If your Web server doesn't support WAIS directly, you must use a CGI script to access the data. You might also want to use a script when you need to format the output or filter the input.

Your script must gather data from a fill-in form and run a query against the WAIS index, and then format the data appropriately for the visitor.

You can have your script perform the same function Web servers directly supporting WAIS perform: Call the WAISQ (or WAISLOOK) program. You can test this call from the following command line:

```
waisq -d -http Data\database1 stuff
```

In this simple example, you run a query against the DATA\DATABASE1 index files, using `stuff` as the query term. The result returns `STDOUT` as properly formatted HTML code, which makes the result perfect for use in a CGI script.

WAIS is so popular that dozens of scripts are available in the public domain for managing your queries. Here are the three most generic and useful scripts:

- WAIS.PL

  ftp://ftp.ncsa.uiuc.edu/Web/httpd/Unix/ncsa_httpd/cgi/wais.tar.Z
- Son-of-WAIS.PL

  http://dewey.lib.ncsu.edu/staff/morgan/son-of-wais.html
- Kid-of-WAIS.PL

  http://www.cso.uiuc.edu/grady.html
  http://ljordal.cso.uiuc.edu/kidofwais.pl

Implementing Excite for Web Servers Architext's popular search engine, Excite for Web Servers (EWS), is available for SunOS, Solaris, HP-UX, SGI Irix, AIX, BSDI UNIX, and Windows NT. EWS is a full-featured, fast indexing search tool based on the same technology as the Excite search service. Despite being a commercial search engine, it is available for use on your Web site for free. The only restriction in the user license is that you cannot use it to provide services for a third party (by establishing a service to compete with Excite, for example).

Excite enables people to enter queries in ordinary language, without using specialized query syntax. Excite claims that EWS understands plain English queries such as, "How to stay healthy by eating well" or "Learn to speak Tagalog." Queries using concepts are more likely to produce effective results than simple keyword searches, according to the company.

The user can choose either a concept-based search or a conventional keyword AND search. When you run a search, EWS lists search results in decreasing order of confidence. Each result consists of a title, an URL, a confidence rating, and an automatically generated summary of what the page is about. Relevance ranking is the default, but a click of the mouse enables the user to see the same results grouped by subject or topic.

Excite also supports relevance-feedback, or query-by-example, searching. Using this technique, if you visit a found page and find it is pretty much what you're looking for, you can return to the search results and click on the icon next to the listing to initiate another search. The subsequent search uses the found page as a parameter and returns similar pages.

Excite doesn't require a thesaurus to do concept-based searching, but the company indicates that an external thesaurus can improve results. Because a thesaurus is not necessary, adding support for new languages supposedly is not as difficult as with some other software. Architext claims that independent software developers can also write modules to support additional data file formats, without facing too many obstacles.

Architext currently offers the software at no charge, and sells annual support contracts. Further information about Excite for Web Servers can be found at

http://www.excite.com/navigate/

Quite a few sites are running the Excite search engine. One good example is the *Houston Chronicle* search page at

http://www.chron.com/content/search/

Installing Excite is described as Plug and Play, and it couldn't be easier. Download the distribution archive (along with the C++ libraries if you need them), run a shell script that asks a few questions, and you're just about ready to go. You need to run an administrative script that creates the index, and another script that creates the search page. Both scripts are run from Web forms.

NOTE EWS took 16 minutes, 40 seconds of CPU time to index my UNIX site; elapsed time was 23 minutes. It thoughtfully provided status pages that allowed me to keep tabs on the progress of the indexing. EWS created an index that was around 7MB in size on a collection of 4,490 files comprising slightly more than 90MB. It even e-mailed me when it was done.

After generating the index, you then generate the search page by using an HTML form. EWS creates a page that includes a search form and a link to the custom-generated search script for this collection. The resulting search page looks similar to that shown in Figure 35.9.

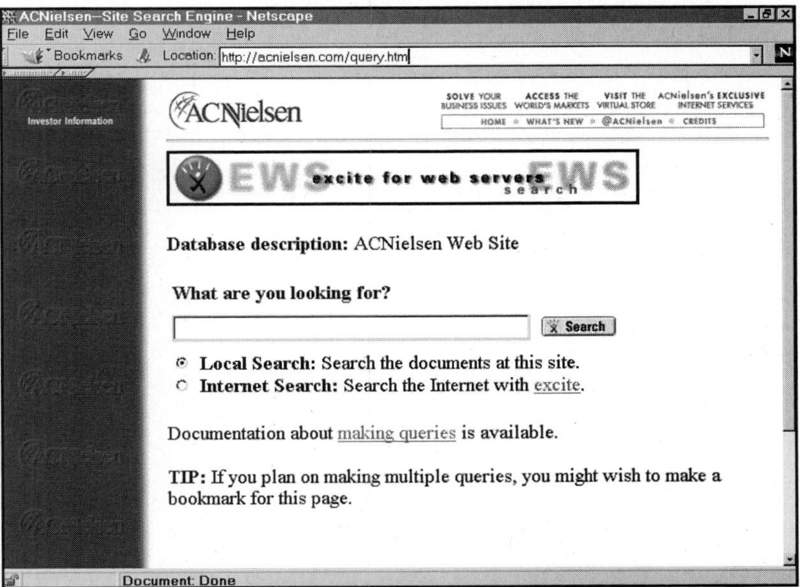

FIG. 35.9 The Excite for Web Servers search form enables users to search for keywords or for concepts.

Notice that the form does not provide options for case sensitivity or Boolean searches. This is because Excite employs concept matching to do its searching. The company suggests creating queries that are descriptions of an information rather than lists of keywords:

"Excite for Web Servers will search for documents that are a best match for the words in your query. Excite for Web Servers will also search for documents that are about the same concepts that your query describes, so sometimes Excite for Web Servers will bring back articles that don't mention any of the words in your original query."

The more search words, the better the query. Unfortunately, because the search algorithm is proprietary, you just have to trust that EWS will perform.

Excite for Web Servers uses Excite's proprietary Intelligent Concept Extraction (ICE) search method (which is apparently not related to Christian Neuss' ICE engine). An excellent discussion of search strategies can be found on Excite's site at **http://www.excite.com/ice/tech.html**. Although Excite does not provide a lot of detail about their patent-pending proprietary search techniques, ICE is described as a means to find and score documents based on a correlation of their concepts as well as actual keywords. Excite states that this capability to go beyond simple Boolean searches of keywords is the key to their technology.

Using techniques similar to Latent Semantic Indexing (for more information on LSI, visit **http://n106.is.tokushima-u.ac.jp/member/kita/EPrint/index-LSI.html**), Excite claims that it can perform rapid searches without significant resources as well as maintain performance when the size of the index is scaled up. According to Excite, "Unlike other systems which need more time to perform a query as the size of the database increases, the Excite search engine can perform most queries in a constant amount of time."

A typical results page resembles that shown in Figure 35.10.

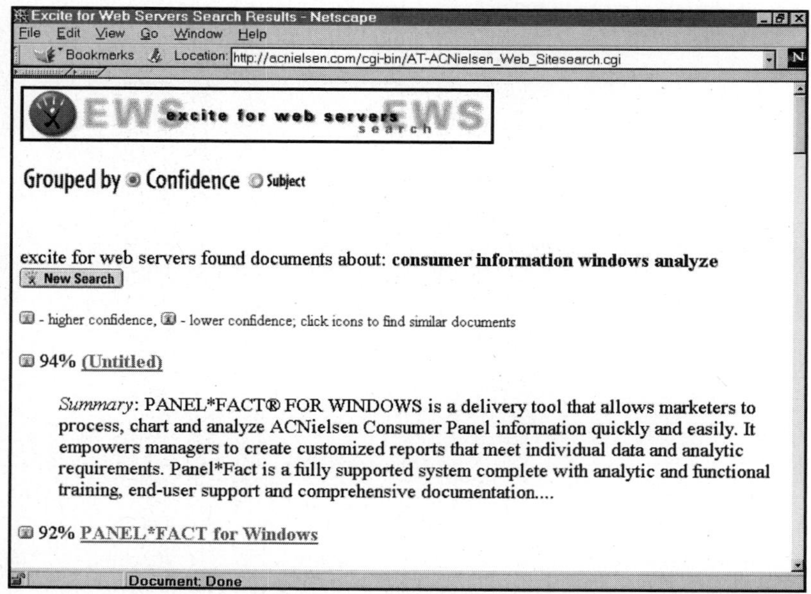

FIG. 35.10 The results page from Excite for Web Servers includes links to the found file, a summary, and the confidence rating. The icon on each line enables you to submit a new query to find similar pages.

Producing this search page took a little more than a second of CPU time and five or six seconds of elapsed time.

If you click on the icon beside a page listing, Excite performs a query by example search using that document as the criteria.

A nice touch to the search display is the inclusion of confidence scores. Just the fact that the search hits are ranked conveys information. If you receive 20 responses with the highest confidence of only 50%, you might want to reformulate your search terms and try again rather than examining pages with low probability of satisfying your request.

EWS ignores stop words. These words are maintained in a table, but there appears to be no way to edit or add to them.

Excite for Web Servers is quite an impressive search tool that is easy to install and easy to implement. It creates a small index file and searches consume little system resources and are quite rapid. The inability to maintain the stop words tables and the lack of significant documentation on the operation of the system are its only drawbacks. Given its ease of use and strong features, however, such complaints are minor.

CHAPTER 36

Server-Side Includes

by Bliss Sloan

In this chapter

Introducing SSI

A web server normally doesn't look at the files it passes along to browsers. It checks security—that is, it makes sure the caller has the right to read the file—but otherwise just hands the file over.

A web "page" is often more than one document. The most common addition is an inline graphic or two, plus a background graphic. As you learned in Chapters 31, "Programming CGI Scripts," and 32, "Custom Database Query Scripts," a page can contain information about other resources to display at the same time. When the browser gets back to the first page, it scans the page, determines whether more parts exist, and sends out requests for the remaining bits. This scanning and interpretation process is called *parsing*, and it normally happens on the client's side of the connection.

Under certain circumstances, though, you can talk the server into parsing the document before it ever gets to the client. Instead of blindly handing over the document, ignorant of the contents, the server can interpret the documents first. When this parsing occurs on the server's side of the connection, the process is called a ***server-side include*** (*SSI*).

Why *include*? Because the first use of server-side parsing was to allow files to be included along with the one being referenced. Programmers love abbreviations, and SSI was established quickly. Changing the term later on, when other capabilities became popular too, seemed pointless.

If you are the webmaster for a site, you might be responsible for 50, 100, or 250 pages. Because you're a conscientious webmaster, you include your email address at the bottom of each page so that people can tell you about any problems. What happens when your email address changes? Without SSI, you need to edit 50, 100, or 250 pages individually. Hope you're a good typist!

With SSI, however, you can include your email address on each page. Your email address actually resides in one spot—say, a file called webmaster.email.txt somewhere on your server—and each page uses SSI to include the contents of this file. Then, when your email address changes, all you have to do is update webmaster.email.txt with the new information. All 250 pages referencing it automatically have the new information instantly.

Server-side includes can do more than include files. You can use special commands to include the current date and time. Other commands let you report the last-modification date of a file or its size. Yet another command lets you execute a subprogram in the manner of CGI and incorporate its output right into the flow of the text.

NOTE The hallmark of SSI, generally, is that the end result is text. If you implement an SSI page hit counter, for instance, it would report the hits using text, not inline graphical images. From your browser's point of view, the document is all text, with nothing odd about it. SSI works without the browser's consent, participation, or knowledge. The magic is that the text is generated on-the-fly by SSI, not hard-coded when you created the HTML file.

SSI Specification

Unfortunately, there is no formal set of specifications for server-side includes that applies to the servers of all manufacturers. The syntax and usage given applies only to NCSA HTTPd servers.

- Unlike many protocols, options, and interfaces, SSI isn't governed by an Internet RFC (Request For Comment) or other standard. Each server manufacturer is free to implement SSI on an ad hoc basis, including whichever commands suit the development team's fancy, using whatever syntax strikes them as reasonable. Some servers, such as the freeware EMWAC server for Windows NT, don't support SSI at all.
- No one can give you a list of commands and syntax rules that apply in all situations. Most servers follow NCSA's specification up to a point. Although you may not find the exact commands, you can probably find functions similar to those in NCSA's arsenal.
- Because SSI isn't defined by a standard, server developers tend to modify their implementations of SSI more frequently than they modify other things. Even if I listed all the known servers and how they implement SSI today, the list would be out of date by the time you read this book.
- The only way to determine what SSI functions your server supports and what syntax your server uses for each command is to find and study your server's documentation. This chapter shows you the most common functions on the most common servers, and you'll probably find that the syntax is valid. However, the only authority is your particular server's documentation, so get a copy and keep it handy as you work through this chapter.

Configuring SSI

Although plenty of FAQ sheets (Frequently Asked Questions) are available on the Internet, most of them are not that detailed, and configuring SSI to work on NCSA remains a common stumbling block. The other servers are a little easier to use.

On most servers, SSI must be "turned on" before it will work. By default, SSI is not enabled. This is for your protection, because mismanaged SSI can be a huge security risk. What if, for instance, you give any caller or any user on the system privileges to run any program or read any file anywhere on the server? Maybe nothing bad would happen, but that's not the safe way to bet.

In an NCSA (UNIX) environment, you enable SSI by editing the configuration files. You must have administrative privileges on the server to edit these files, although you can probably look at them with ordinary user privileges.

You need to change these directives to enable SSI on NCSA servers:

- The `Options` directive—Used to enable SSI for particular directories. Edit access.conf and add `Includes` to the `Options` lines for the directories in which you want SSI to work. If a line reads `Options All`, SSI is already enabled for that directory. If it reads anything else, you must add `Includes` to the list of privileges on that line. Note that adding this line enables SSI in whatever directory you select plus all subdirectories under it. So if you add this line to the server root section, you effectively enable SSI in every directory on the server.
- The `AddType` directive—Used to designate the MIME type for SSI files. For example, use

  ```
  AddType text/x-server-parsed-html .shtml
  ```

  to enable SSI parsing for all files ending with .shtml. This information is normally stored in srm.conf. Also use

  ```
  AddType application/x-httpd-cgi .cgi
  ```

  if you want to allow the `exec` command to work. Specifying .cgi here means that all your SSI scripts must have that extension. Most srm.conf files already have these two lines, but they are commented out. Just skip down to the bottom of the file and either uncomment the existing lines or add them in manually.

Learning to find the configuration files for your server, and to use the `Options` and `AddType` directives, is all you need to edit the configuration files.

Enabling SSI on Windows NT machines is usually a matter of naming your HTML files correctly and clicking a check box somewhere in the Configuration dialog box. Process Software's Purveyor server uses .htp as the default filename extension for parsed files. Most other servers emulate NCSA and use .shtml instead. However, changing the extension is usually simple. Hunt up the MIME Types dialog box and add a MIME type of text/x-server-parsed for whatever filename extension you want. (As always, check your particular server's documentation to find out whether this technique works.)

One last note on configuration: Many, if not most, servers either allow you to require, or require by default, that all SSI executables be located in your cgi-bin or scripts directory. If your server doesn't require this behavior by default, find the documentation to learn how to enable it. If the only programs that can be run are located in a known, controlled directory, the chances for errors (and hacking) are greatly reduced.

Using SSI in HTML

Now that you've enabled SSI on your server (or talked your system administrator into doing it for you), you're ready to learn how to use SSI. Sit back and relax a bit. What you've done already is by far the hardest part. From here on, you simply need to find syntax in your particular server's documentation and try things out.

TIP Of special interest, at this point, is the one thing all SSI implementations have in common: All SSI commands are embedded within regular HTML comments.

Having embedded commands makes it easy to implement SSI while still making the HTML portable. A server that doesn't understand SSI passes the commands on to the browser, and the browser ignores them because they're formatted as comments. A server that does understand SSI, however, does not pass the commands on to the browser. Instead, the server parses the HTML from the top down, executing each comment-embedded command, replacing the comment with the output of the command.

This process is not as complicated as it sounds. You will go through some step-by-step examples later in this chapter, but first you'll examine HTML comments.

HTML Comment Syntax

Because anything not tagged in HTML is considered displayable text, comments must be tagged like any other directive. Tags are always marked with angle brackets—the less-than sign (<) and the greater-than sign (>)—and a keyword, which may be as short as a single letter. For example, the familiar paragraph tag, `<p>`, is **empty**, so no closing tag is necessary. *Nonempty* tags, such as `<a href...>...</a>`, enclose displayable information (*"content"*) between the opening and closing tags. Empty elements have no content, so they don't need a closing tag.

The comment tag is empty and is of the form:

```
<!--comment text here-->
```

NOTE Although many servers and browsers can understand the nonstandard `<!--comment text here>` syntax, the remaining ones want the comment to end with "`-->`", as is required by the HTML specifications. Why? Because this lets you comment out sections of HTML code, including lines containing < and > symbols. Although not all servers and browsers require comments to end with `-->`, all of them will understand the syntax. Therefore, you're better off following the standard and surrounding your comments with `<!--` at the front and `-->` at the end.

In summary, an HTML comment is anything with the format `<!--commenttexthere-->`. Browsers know to ignore this information, and servers don't even see it, unless SSI is enabled.

Turning Comments into Commands

What happens to comments when SSI is enabled? The server looks for comments and examines the text inside them for commands. The server distinguishes comments that are really SSI commands from comments that are just comments by a simple convention: inside the comment, all SSI commands start with a pound sign (#).

All SSI commands therefore begin with `<!--#`, followed by information meaningful to your server. Typically, each server supports a list of keywords, and it expects to find one of these keywords immediately following the pound sign. After the keyword are any parameters for the command—with syntax that varies both by command and by server—and then the standard comment closing (`-->`).

Listing 36.3 Continued

```
if (argc > 1) {
     p = strstr(argv[1],"..");
     if (p==NULL) p = strstr(argv[1],"\\\\");
     if (p==NULL) p = strchr(argv[1],':');

     // If .., \\, or : found, reject the filename
     if (p) {
          printf("Invalid relative path "
                 "specified: %s",argv[1]);
          return;
     }

     // Otherwise append it to our own path
     strcpy(fname,argv[0]);
     p = strrchr(fname,'\\');
     if (p) *p = '\0';
     strcat(fname,"\\");
     strcat(fname,argv[1]);

} else {

     // No command-line parm found, so use our
     // executable name, minus our extension, plus
     // .txt as the filename

     strcpy(fname,_pgmptr);
     p = strrchr(fname,'.');
     if (p) strcpy(p,".txt");
}

// We have a filename, so try to open the file

f = fopen(fname,"r");

// If open failed, die right here

if (f==NULL) {
     printf("Could not open '%s' for read.",fname);
     return;
}

// Get total length of file in bytes.
// We do this by seeking to the end and then
// reading the offset of our current position.
// There are other ways of getting this
// information, but this way works almost
// everywhere, whereas the other ways are
// platform-dependent.

fseek(f,0,SEEK_END);
fgetpos(f,&fpos);
flen = (long) fpos;
```

```
// Seek to a random point in the file.  Loop through
// the following section until we find a block of text
// we can use.

goodpos = FALSE;          // goes TRUE when we're done

while (!goodpos) {

     // Make a random offset into the file.  Generate
     // the number based on the file's length.

     if (flen > 65535) {
          lrand = MAKELONG(rand(),rand());
     } else {
          lrand = MAKELONG(rand(),0);
     }

     // If our random number is less than the length
     // of the file, use it as an offset.  Seek there
     // and read whatever we find.

     if (lrand < flen) {
          fpos = lrand;
          fsetpos(f,&fpos);
          if (fread(buffer, sizeof(char),
               sizeof(buffer),f) !=0 ) {
               soq=NULL;
               eoq=NULL;
               soq = strstr(buffer,"\n\n");
               if (soq) eoq = strstr(soq+2,"\n\n");
               if (eoq) {
                    // skip the first CR
                    soq++;
                    // and the one for the blank line
                    soq++;
                    // mark end of string
                    *eoq='\0';
                    // look for citation marker
                    p = strstr(soq,"\n--");
                    // if found, exempt it & remember
                    if (p) {
                         *p='\0';
                         p++;
                    }
                    // print the quotation
                    printf(soq);
                    if (p)
                    // and citation if any
                    printf("<br><cite>%s</cite>",p);
                    // exit the loop
                    goodpos=TRUE;
               }
          }
     }
```

continues

Listing 36.3 Continued

```
     }

     fclose(f);
     fflush(stdout);
        return;
}
```

XMAS

The XMAS program prints out the number of days remaining until Christmas. It recognizes Christmas Day and Christmas Eve as special cases, and solves the general case problem by brute force. You can certainly find more elegant and efficient ways to calculate elapsed time, but this method doesn't rely on any platform-specific date/time routines.

The code in Listing 36.4 is short enough and uncomplicated enough that it needs no further explanation.

Listing 36.4 xmas.c Source code for the XMAS program.

```
// XMAS.C
// This program calculates the number of days between
// the time of invocation and the nearest upcoming 25
// December.  It reports the result as a complete sentence.
// The code is platform-independent.


#include <windows.h>      // only required for Windows
#include <stdio.h>
#include <time.h>

void main() {

     // Some variables, all self-explanatory

     struct tm      today;
     time_t         now;
     int            days;

     // Get the current date, first retrieving the
     // Universal Coordinated Time, then converting it
     // to local time, stored in the today tm structure.

     time(&now);
     today = *localtime(&now);
     mktime(&today);
```

```
    // month is zero-based (0=jan, 1=feb, etc);
    // day is one-based
    // year is one-based
    // so Christmas Eve is 11/24

    // Is it Christmas Eve?

    if ((today.tm_mon == 11) && (today.tm_mday==24)) {
         printf("Today is Christmas Eve!");

    } else {

         // Is it Christmas Day?

         if ((today.tm_mon == 11) && (today.tm_mday==25)) {
              printf("Today is Christmas Day!");

         } else {

              // Calculate days by adding one and comparing
              // for 11/25 repeatedly

              days =0;
              while ( (today.tm_mon  != 11) ¦
                      (today.tm_mday != 25) )
              {
                   days++;
                   today.tm_mday = today.tm_mday + 1;
                   mktime(&today);
              }

              // Print the result using the customary
              // static verb formation

              printf("There are %i days until Christmas."
                     ,days);
         }
    }

    // Flush the output and we're done

    fflush(stdout);
    return;
}
```

HitCount

The HitCount program creates that all-time favorite, a page hit count. The output is a cardinal number (1, 2, 3, and so on) and nothing else. HitCount works only on Windows NT. See Listing 36.5 for the C source code.

Listing 36.5 hitcount.c Source code for the HitCount program.

```
// HITCOUNT.C
// This SSI program produces a cardinal number page hit
// count based on the environment variable SCRIPT_NAME.

#include <windows.h>
#include <stdio.h>
#define      ERROR_CANT_CREATE "HitCount:  Cannot open/create
➥registry key."
#define  ERROR_CANT_UPDATE "HitCount:  Cannot update registry key."
#define  HITCOUNT "Software\\Greyware\\HitCount\\Pages"

void main(int argc, char * argv[]) {
     char     szHits[33];     // number of hits for this page
     char     szDefPage[80];  // system default pagename
     char     *p;             // generic pointer
     char     *PageName;      // pointer to this page's name
     long     dwLength=33;    // length of temporary buffer
     long     dwType;         // registry value type code
     long     dwRetCode;      // generic return code from API
     HKEY     hKey;           // registry key handle

     // Determine where to get the page name.  A command-
     // line argument overrides the SCRIPT_NAME variable.

     if ((argc==2) && ((*argv[1]=='/') ¦ (*argv[1]=='\\')))
          PageName = argv[1];
     else
          PageName = getenv("SCRIPT_NAME");

     // If invoked from without SCRIPT_NAME or args, die

     if (PageName==NULL)
     {
          printf("HitCount 1.0.b.960121\n"
                 "Copyright (c) 1995,96 Greyware "
                 "Automation Products\n\n"
                 "Documentation available online from "
                 "Greyware's Web server:\n"
                 "http://www.greyware.com/"
                 "greyware/software/freeware.htp\n\n");
     }
     else
     {

          // Open the registry key

          dwRetCode = RegOpenKeyEx (
               HKEY_LOCAL_MACHINE,
               HITCOUNT,
               0,
               KEY_EXECUTE,
               &hKey);
```

```
// If open failed because key doesn't exist,
// create it

if ((dwRetCode==ERROR_BADDB)
      || (dwRetCode==ERROR_BADKEY)
      || (dwRetCode==ERROR_FILE_NOT_FOUND))
      dwRetCode = RegCreateKey(
            HKEY_LOCAL_MACHINE,
            HITCOUNT,
            &hKey);

// If couldn't open or create, die

if (dwRetCode != ERROR_SUCCESS) {
      printf (ERROR_CANT_CREATE);

} else {

      // Get the default page name

      dwLength = sizeof(szDefPage);
      dwRetCode = RegQueryValueEx (
            hKey,
            "(default)",
            0,
            &dwType,
            szDefPage,
            &dwLength);

      if ((dwRetCode == ERROR_SUCCESS)
            && (dwType == REG_SZ)
            && (dwLength > 0)) {
            szDefPage[dwLength] = '\0';
      } else {
            strcpy(szDefPage,"default.htm");
      }

      // If current page uses default page name,
      // strip the page name

     _strlwr(PageName);
      p = strrchr(PageName,'/');
      if (p==NULL) p = strrchr(PageName,'\\');
      if (p) {
            p++;
            if (stricmp(p,szDefPage)==0) *p = '\0';
      }

      // Get this page's information

      dwLength = sizeof(szHits);
      dwRetCode = RegQueryValueEx (
            hKey,
            PageName,
            0,
```

continues

Listing 36.5 Continued

```
                    &dwType,
                    szHits,
                    &dwLength);

               if ((dwRetCode == ERROR_SUCCESS)
                    && (dwType == REG_SZ)
                    && (dwLength >0)) {
                    szHits[dwLength] = '\0';
               } else {
                    strcpy (szHits, "1");
               }

               // Close the registry key

               dwRetCode = RegCloseKey(hKey);

               // Print this page's count

               printf("%s",szHits);

               // Bump the count by one for next call

              _ltoa ((atol(szHits)+1), szHits, 10);

               // Write the new value back to the registry

               dwRetCode = RegOpenKeyEx (
                    HKEY_LOCAL_MACHINE,
                    HITCOUNT,
                    0,
                    KEY_SET_VALUE,
                    &hKey);

               if (dwRetCode==ERROR_SUCCESS) {
                    dwRetCode = RegSetValueEx(
                         hKey,
                         PageName,
                         0,
                         REG_SZ,
                         szHits,
                         strlen(szHits));
                    dwRetCode = RegCloseKey(hKey);
               } else {
                    printf(ERROR_CANT_UPDATE);
               }
          }
     }
     fflush(stdout);
     return;
}
```

HitCount takes advantage of one of NT's unsung glories, the system Registry. Counters for other platforms need to worry about creating and updating a database file, file locking, concurrency, and a number of other messy issues. HitCount uses the hierarchical Registry as a database, letting the operating system take care of concurrent access.

HitCount is actually remarkably simple compared to other counters. It uses the `SCRIPT_NAME` environment variable to determine the name of the current page. Therefore, you have no worries about passing unique strings as parameters. HitCount takes the page name and either creates or updates a Registry entry for it. The information is always available and rapidly accessed.

HitCount works on most NT servers. One notable exception is WebSite. WebSite supplies the `SCRIPT_NAME` variable, but also supplies spurious arguments in the `argv[]` array. To make HitCount work with WebSite, delete the section of code that checks for command-line arguments.

HitCount, like the other samples in this chapter, is freeware from Greyware Automation Products (**http://www.greyware.com**). You can find more extensive documentation online at its site. The code is unmodified from the code distributed by Greyware for a good reason: Because Registry keys are named, having multiple versions of the software running around loose with different key names just wouldn't do. Therefore, the code retains the key names for compatibility.

The only bit of configuration you might need to do is if your server's default page name isn't default.htm. In that case, add this key to the Registry before using HitCount for the first time:

```
HKEY_LOCAL_MACHINE
    \Software
        \Greyware
            \HitCount
                \Pages
```

After you create the key, add a value under Pages. The name of the value is (default) (with the parentheses) and its type is `REG_SZ`. Fill in the name of your system's default page. Case doesn't matter.

HitCount uses this information to keep from falsely distinguishing between a hit to http://www.yourserver.com/ and http://www.yourserver.com/default.name. Some web servers report these two as different URLs in the `SCRIPT_NAME` environment variable, even though they refer to the same physical page. By setting the default in the Registry, you let HitCount know to strip the page name off, if found, thus reconciling any potential problems before they arise. The default is default.htm, so you need to set this value only if your SSI pages use a different name.

HitCntth

HitCntth is a variation of HitCount. Its output is an ordinal number (1st, 2nd, 3rd, and so on). You probably understand the name by now. HitCnt*th* provides the HitCount-th number. Get it?

HitCntth is designed to work alongside HitCount. It uses the same Registry keys, so you can switch from one format to the other without having to reset the counter or to worry about duplicate counts. See the HitCount documentation for configuration details.

Creating an ordinal takes a bit more work than printing a cardinal number because the English method of counting is somewhat arbitrary. HitCntth looks for exceptions and handles them separately and then throws a "th" on the end of anything left over. Otherwise, the function is identical to HitCount. Listing 36.6 shows the source code for HitCntth.

Listing 36.6 hitcntth.c Source code for the HitCntth program.

```
// HITCNTTH.C
// This SSI program produces an ordinal number page hit
// count based on the environment variable SCRIPT_NAME.

#include <windows.h>
#include <stdio.h>
#define      ERROR_CANT_CREATE "HitCntth:  Cannot open/create
➥registry key."
#define  ERROR_CANT_UPDATE "HitCntth:  Cannot update registry key."
#define  HITCOUNT "Software\\Greyware\\HitCount\\Pages"

void main(int argc, char * argv[]) {
     char     szHits[36];       // number of hits for this page
     char     szDefPage[80];    // system default pagename
     char     *p;               // generic pointer
     char     *PageName;        // pointer to this page's name
     long     dwLength=36;      // length of temporary buffer
     long     dwType;           // registry value type code
     long     dwRetCode;        // generic return code from API
     HKEY     hKey;             // registry key handle


     // Determine where to get the page name.  A command-
     // line argument overrides the SCRIPT_NAME variable.

     if ((argc==2) && ((*argv[1]=='/') ¦ (*argv[1]=='\\')))
          PageName = argv[1];
     else
          PageName = getenv("SCRIPT_NAME");

     // If invoked from without SCRIPT_NAME or args, die
     if (PageName==NULL)
     {
          printf("HitCntth 1.0.b.960121\n"
                 "Copyright (c) 1995,96 Greyware "
                 "Automation Products\n\n"
                 "Documentation available online from "
                 "Greyware's Web server:\n"
                 "http://www.greyware.com/"
                 "greyware/software/freeware.htp\n\n");
     }
     else
```

```
{
     // Open the registry key

     dwRetCode = RegOpenKeyEx (
          HKEY_LOCAL_MACHINE,
          HITCOUNT,
          0,
          KEY_EXECUTE,
          &hKey);

     // If open failed because key doesn't exist,
     // create it

     if ((dwRetCode==ERROR_BADDB)
          || (dwRetCode==ERROR_BADKEY)
          || (dwRetCode==ERROR_FILE_NOT_FOUND))
          dwRetCode = RegCreateKey(
               HKEY_LOCAL_MACHINE,
               HITCOUNT,
               &hKey);

     // If couldn't open or create, die

     if (dwRetCode != ERROR_SUCCESS) {
          printf (ERROR_CANT_CREATE);
     } else {
          // Get the default page name
          dwLength = sizeof(szDefPage);
          dwRetCode = RegQueryValueEx (
               hKey,
               "(default)",
               0,
               &dwType,
               szDefPage,
               &dwLength);
          if ((dwRetCode == ERROR_SUCCESS)
               && (dwType == REG_SZ)
               && (dwLength > 0)) {
               szDefPage[dwLength] = '\0';
          } else {
               strcpy(szDefPage,"default.htm");
          }

          // If current page uses default page name,
          // strip the page name

          _strlwr(PageName);
          p = strrchr(PageName,'/');
          if (p==NULL) p = strrchr(PageName,'\\');
          if (p) {
               p++;
               if (stricmp(p,szDefPage)==0) *p = '\0';
          }
```

continues

Listing 36.6 Continued

```
// Get this page's information

dwLength = sizeof(szHits);
dwRetCode = RegQueryValueEx (
     hKey,
     PageName,
     0,
     &dwType,
     szHits,
     &dwLength);
if ((dwRetCode == ERROR_SUCCESS)
     && (dwType == REG_SZ)
     && (dwLength >0)) {
     szHits[dwLength] = '\0';
} else {
     strcpy (szHits, "1\0");
}

// Close the registry key

dwRetCode = RegCloseKey(hKey);

// Check for special cases:
// look at count mod 100 first

switch ((atol(szHits)) % 100) {
     case 11:     // 11th, 111th, 211th, etc.
          printf("%sth",szHits);
          break;
     case 12:     // 12th, 112th, 212th, etc.
          printf("%sth",szHits);
          break;
     case 13:     // 13th, 113th, 213th, etc.
          printf("%sth",szHits);
          break;
     default:
          // no choice but to look at last
          // digit
          switch (szHits[strlen(szHits)-1]) {
               case '1':     // 1st, 21st, 31st
                    printf("%sst",szHits);
                    break;
               case '2':     // 2nd, 22nd, 32nd
                    printf("%snd",szHits);
                    break;
               case '3':     // 3rd, 23rd, 36rd
                    printf("%srd",szHits);
                    break;
               default:
                    printf("%sth",szHits);
                    break;
          }
}
```

```
                // Bump the count by one for next call
               _ltoa ((atol(szHits)+1), szHits, 10);

                // Write the new value back to the registry
                dwRetCode = RegOpenKeyEx (
                     HKEY_LOCAL_MACHINE,
                     HITCOUNT,
                     0,
                     KEY_SET_VALUE,
                     &hKey);
                if (dwRetCode==ERROR_SUCCESS) {
                     dwRetCode = RegSetValueEx(
                          hKey,
                          PageName,
                          0,
                          REG_SZ,
                          szHits,
                          strlen(szHits));
                     dwRetCode = RegCloseKey(hKey);
                } else {
                     printf(ERROR_CANT_UPDATE);
                }
           }
      }
      fflush(stdout);
      return;
}
```

FirstHit

FirstHit is a companion program for HitCount or HitCntth. It takes care of tracking the date and time of the first hit to any page. FirstHit uses the same Registry scheme as HitCount or HitCntth, but it stores its information in a different key. You have to set the (default) page name here, too, if it's something other than Default.htm. The proper key is

```
HKEY_LOCAL_MACHINE
    \Software
        \Greyware
            \FirstHit
                \Pages
```

You may sense a theme in a number of areas. First, all these programs use the Registry to store information. Second, they use a similar naming scheme—a hierarchical one. Third, they share great quantities of code. Some of these functions can be moved into a library, and probably should be.

You use FirstHit, typically, right after using HitCount. To produce the line `You are visitor 123 since Fri 19 Sep 1997 at 01:13` on the Purveyor server, your source would look like this:

```
You are visitor <!--#exec exe="cgi-bin\hitcount" --> since
<!--#exec exe="cgi-bin\firsthit" -->.
```

Listing 36.7 shows the source code. It's no more complicated than HitCount or HitCntth, and writes to the Registry only the first time any page is hit. Thereafter, it just retrieves the information it wrote before.

Listing 36.7 firsthit.c Source code for the FirstHit program.

```
// FIRSTHIT.C
// This SSI program keeps track of the date and time
// a page was first hit.  Useful in conjunction with
// HitCount or HitCntth.

#include <windows.h>
#include <stdio.h>
#define      ERROR_CANT_CREATE "FirstHit:  Cannot open/create
➥registry key."
#define  ERROR_CANT_UPDATE "FirstHit:  Cannot update registry key."
#define  FIRSTHIT "Software\\Greyware\\FirstHit\\Pages"
#define      sdatefmt "ddd dd MMM yyyy"

void main(int argc, char * argv[]) {
     char      szDate[128];       // number of hits for this page
     char      szDefPage[80];     // system default pagename
     char      *p;                // generic pointer
     char      *PageName;         // pointer to this page's name
     long      dwLength=127;      // length of temporary buffer
     long      dwType;            // registry value type code
     long      dwRetCode;         // generic return code from API
     HKEY      hKey;              // registry key handle
     SYSTEMTIME st;               // system time
     char      szTmp[128];        // temporary string storage

     // Determine where to get the page name.  A command-
     // line argument overrides the SCRIPT_NAME variable.

     if ((argc==2) && ((*argv[1]=='/') ¦ (*argv[1]=='\\')))
          PageName = argv[1];
     else
          PageName = getenv("SCRIPT_NAME");

     // If invoked from without SCRIPT_NAME or args, die
     if (PageName==NULL)
     {
          printf("FirstHit 1.0.b.960121\n"
                 "Copyright (c) 1995,96 Greyware "
                 "Automation Products\n\n"
                 "Documentation available online from "
                 "Greyware's Web server:\n"
                 "http://www.greyware.com/"
                 "greyware/software/freeware.htp\n\n");
     }
     else
     {
          // Open the registry key
          dwRetCode = RegOpenKeyEx (
```

```
            HKEY_LOCAL_MACHINE,
            FIRSTHIT,
            0,
            KEY_EXECUTE,
            &hKey);

      // If open failed because key doesn't exist,
   // create it
   if ((dwRetCode==ERROR_BADDB)
        || (dwRetCode==ERROR_BADKEY)
        || (dwRetCode==ERROR_FILE_NOT_FOUND))
        dwRetCode = RegCreateKey(
             HKEY_LOCAL_MACHINE,
             FIRSTHIT,
             &hKey);

   // If couldn't open or create, die
   if (dwRetCode != ERROR_SUCCESS)
   {
        strcpy(szDate,ERROR_CANT_CREATE);
   }
   else
   {
        // Get the default page name
        dwLength = sizeof(szDefPage);
        dwRetCode = RegQueryValueEx (
             hKey,
             "(default)",
             0,
             &dwType,
             szDefPage,
             &dwLength);
        if ((dwRetCode == ERROR_SUCCESS)
             && (dwType == REG_SZ)
             && (dwLength > 0)) {
             szDefPage[dwLength] = '\0';
        } else {
             strcpy(szDefPage,"default.htm");
        }

        // If current page uses default page name,
        // strip the page name
        _strlwr(PageName);
        p = strrchr(PageName,'/');
        if (p==NULL) p = strrchr(PageName,'\\');
        if (p) {
             p++;
             if (stricmp(p,szDefPage)==0) *p = '\0';
        }

        // Get this page's information
        dwLength = sizeof(szDate);
        dwRetCode = RegQueryValueEx (
             hKey,
             PageName,
```

continues

Listing 36.7 Continued

```
                    0,
                    &dwType,
                    szDate,
                    &dwLength);
               if ((dwRetCode == ERROR_SUCCESS)
                    && (dwType == REG_SZ)
                    && (dwLength >0)) {
                    szDate[dwLength] = '\0';
               } else {
                    GetLocalTime(&st);
                    GetDateFormat(
                         0,
                         0,
                         &st,
                         sdatefmt,
                         szTmp,
                         sizeof(szTmp));
                    sprintf(
                         szDate,
                         "%s at %02d:%02d",
                         szTmp,
                         st.wHour,
                         st.wMinute);
                     // Write the new value back to the
                    // registry
                    dwRetCode = RegOpenKeyEx (
                         HKEY_LOCAL_MACHINE,
                         FIRSTHIT,
                         0,
                         KEY_SET_VALUE,
                         &hKey);
                    if (dwRetCode==ERROR_SUCCESS)
                    {
                         dwRetCode = RegSetValueEx(
                              hKey,
                              PageName,
                              0,
                              REG_SZ,
                              szDate,
                              strlen(szDate));
                         dwRetCode = RegCloseKey(hKey);
                    }
                    else
                    {
                         strcpy(szDate,ERROR_CANT_UPDATE);
                    }
               }

               // Close the registry key
               dwRetCode = RegCloseKey(hKey);
          }
          printf("%s",szDate);
     }
```

```
    fflush(stdout);
    return;
}
```

LastHit

LastHit is yet another Windows NT SSI program. It tracks visitor information (date, time, IP number, and browser type). Like FirstHit, LastHit uses the same Registry scheme as HitCount or HitCntth, but it stores its information in its own key. You have to set the (default) page name here, too, if it's something other than Default.htm. The proper key is

```
HKEY_LOCAL_MACHINE
    \Software
        \Greyware
            \LastHit
                \Pages
```

LastHit isn't actually related to HitCount or FirstHit, other than by its common code and its nature as an SSI program. LastHit tracks and displays information about the last visitor to a page. Each time the page is hit, LastHit displays the information from the previous hit and then writes down information about the current caller for display next time.

The source code for LastHit is a little more complicated than FirstHit's, as Listing 36.8 shows. It uses a subroutine. If nothing else, these programs should demonstrate how easily SSI lets you create dynamic documents. There's no rocket science here.

On the CD

Listing 36.8 lasthit.c Source code for the LastHit program.

```
// LASTHIT.C
// This SSI program tracks visitors to a page, remembering
// the most recent for display.

#include <windows.h>
#include <stdio.h>
#define      ERROR_CANT_CREATE "LastHit:  Cannot open/create
➥registry key."
#define  ERROR_CANT_UPDATE "LastHit:  Cannot update registry key."
#define  LASTHIT "Software\\Greyware\\LastHit\\Pages"

// This subroutine builds the info string about the
// current caller.  Hence the name.  It uses a pointer
// to a buffer owned by the calling routine for output,
// and gets its information from the standard SSI
// environment variables.  Since "standard" is almost
// meaningless when it comes to SSI, the program
// gracefully skips anything it can't find.

void BuildInfo(char * szOut) {
     SYSTEMTIME   st;
     char         szTmp[512];
```

continues

Listing 36.8 Continued

```
    char        *p;

    szOut[0]='\0';

    GetLocalTime(&st);
    GetDateFormat(0, DATE_LONGDATE, &st, NULL, szTmp, 511);
    sprintf(szOut,
        "Last access on %s at %02d:%02d:%02d",
        szTmp,
        st.wHour,
        st.wMinute,
        st.wSecond);

    p = getenv("REMOTE_ADDR");
    if (p!=NULL) {
        szTmp[0] = '\0';
        sprintf(szTmp,"<br>Caller from %s",p);
        if (szTmp[0] != '\0') strcat(szOut,szTmp);
    }
    p = getenv("REMOTE_HOST");
    if (p!=NULL) {
        szTmp[0] = '\0';
        sprintf(szTmp," (%s)",p);
        if (szTmp[0] != '\0') strcat(szOut,szTmp);
    }
    p = getenv("HTTP_USER_AGENT");
    if (p!=NULL) {
        szTmp[0] = '\0';
        sprintf(szTmp,"<br>Using %s",p);
        if (szTmp[0] != '\0') strcat(szOut,szTmp);
    }
}

void main(int argc, char * argv[]) {
    char    szOldInfo[512];
    char    szNewInfo[512];
    char    szDefPage[80];
    char    *p;
    char    *PageName;      // pointer to this page's name
    long    dwLength=511;   // length of temporary buffer
    long    dwType;         // registry value type code
    long    dwRetCode;      // generic return code from API
    HKEY    hKey;           // registry key handle

    // Determine where to get the page name.  A command-
    // line argument overrides the SCRIPT_NAME variable.

    if ((argc==2) && ((*argv[1]=='/') ¦ (*argv[1]=='\\')))
        PageName = argv[1];
    else
        PageName = getenv("SCRIPT_NAME");

    // If invoked from without SCRIPT_NAME or args, die
```

```
if (PageName==NULL)
{
     printf("LastHit 1.0.b.960121\n"
             "Copyright (c) 1995,96 Greyware "
             "Automation Products\n\n"
             "Documentation available online from "
             "Greyware's Web server:\n"
             "http://www.greyware.com/"
             "greyware/software/freeware.htp\n\n");
}
else
{

     // Build info for next call

     BuildInfo(szNewInfo);

     // Open the registry key

     dwRetCode = RegOpenKeyEx (
          HKEY_LOCAL_MACHINE,
          LASTHIT,
          0,
          KEY_EXECUTE,
          &hKey);

     // If open failed because key doesn't exist,
     //create it

     if ((dwRetCode==ERROR_BADDB)
          || (dwRetCode==ERROR_BADKEY)
          || (dwRetCode==ERROR_FILE_NOT_FOUND))
          dwRetCode = RegCreateKey(
               HKEY_LOCAL_MACHINE,
               LASTHIT,
               &hKey);

     // If couldn't open or create, die

     if (dwRetCode != ERROR_SUCCESS) {
          printf (ERROR_CANT_CREATE);
     } else {

          // Get the default page name
          dwLength = sizeof(szDefPage);
          dwRetCode = RegQueryValueEx (
               hKey,
               "(default)",
               0,
               &dwType,
               szDefPage,
               &dwLength);
          if ((dwRetCode == ERROR_SUCCESS)
               && (dwType == REG_SZ)
               && (dwLength > 0)) {
```

continues

Listing 36.8 Continued

```
          szDefPage[dwLength] = '\0';
     } else {
          strcpy(szDefPage,"default.htm");
     }

     // If current page uses default page name,
     // strip the page name
     _strlwr(PageName);
     p = strrchr(PageName,'/');
     if (p==NULL) p = strrchr(PageName,'\\');
     if (p) {
          p++;
          if (stricmp(p,szDefPage)==0) *p = '\0';
     }

     // Get this page's information
     dwLength = sizeof(szOldInfo);
     dwRetCode = RegQueryValueEx (
          hKey,
          PageName,
          0,
          &dwType,
          szOldInfo,
          &dwLength);
     if ((dwRetCode == ERROR_SUCCESS)
          && (dwType == REG_SZ)
          && (dwLength >0)) {
          szOldInfo[dwLength] = '\0';
     } else {
          strcpy (szOldInfo, szNewInfo);
     }

     // Close the registry key
     dwRetCode = RegCloseKey(hKey);

     // Print this page's info
     printf("%s",szOldInfo);


     // Write the new value back to the registry
     dwRetCode = RegOpenKeyEx (
          HKEY_LOCAL_MACHINE,
          LASTHIT,
          0,
          KEY_SET_VALUE,
          &hKey);
     if (dwRetCode==ERROR_SUCCESS) {
          dwRetCode = RegSetValueEx(
               hKey,
               PageName,
               0,
               REG_SZ,
               szNewInfo,
```

```
                        strlen(szNewInfo));
                    dwRetCode = RegCloseKey(hKey);
                } else {
                    printf(ERROR_CANT_UPDATE);
                }
            }
        }
        fflush(stdout);
        return;
    }
```

Server Performance Considerations

In Chapter 27, "Adding Live or Steamed Media to your Web Site," you examined the issue of how real-time programs can affect server performance. SSI doesn't bring anything new to the table in that regard.

▶ **See** "Server Performance Considerations," **p. 1041**

In general, SSI programs tend to be less of a drain on the server than full-fledged CGI. SSI programs are usually small—they only have to produce text, after all—and seldom do much of any significance with files. Page hit counters that rely on generating inline graphics put far more stress on a server than an SSI counter does.

Still, a dozen—or a hundred—instances of your SSI program running at once can steal memory and processor slices needed by the server to satisfy client requests. Imagine that you are webmaster of a large site. On each of the 250 pages for which you're responsible, you include not one, but all the SSI examples in this chapter. Each page hit would produce seven separate processes, each of which has to jostle with the others in resource contention. In a worst-case scenario, with 100 pages being hit a minute, you would have 700 scripts running each minute, 10 or more simultaneously at all times. This kind of load would seriously affect your server's capability to do anything else—such as serve up pages to those users who stop by to see your wonderful SSI handiwork.

You don't find much difference among platforms either. Some SSI utilities run more efficiently in UNIX, others work better under Windows NT, and in the end, everything balances out. Programs that use the NT Registry have a distinct advantage over programs that hit the file system to save data. The Registry functions like a back-end database—always open, always ready for queries and updates. The code for handling concurrency is already loaded and running as part of the operating system, so your program can be smaller and tighter. However, pipes and forks tend to run more efficiently under some flavors of UNIX, so if your program does that sort of thing, you are better off in that environment.

To summarize don't pick your server operating system based on what SSI programs you plan to run. If you run into performance problems, adding RAM usually gives your server the extra headroom it needs to handle the load imposed by SSI.

CHAPTER 37

Active Server Pages

by Ramesh Chandak

In this chapter

The Active Platform

Microsoft's Active Platform is a development platform you can use to design Internet- and intranet-based business solutions. The Active Platform includes an extensible, component-based architecture. The Platform is a three-tier client/server model. However, the biggest advantage with the Active Platform is that you can use the same set of tools to design both the client and server piece of your application. This, in turn, will reduce your learning curve.

An Active Platform–based business solution will typically include the following core components:

- HTML
- Active scripting by using scripting languages such as VBScript and JScript
- Reusable software components, such as Java applets, ActiveX controls, and Active Server Components

Figure 37.1 shows the Active Platform's architecture.

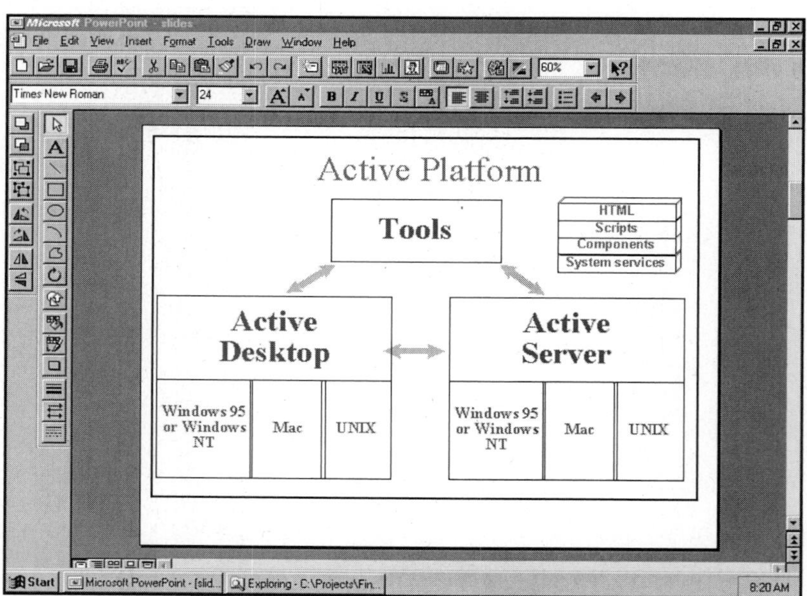

FIG. 37.1
The Active Platform.

In essence, you can use the Active Platform to design both data-driven and transaction-driven web sites and thus conduct business on the Internet. The Active Platform is still in the early stages, and you can certainly expect Microsoft to enhance and refine the technology. As a result, everyone involved with the Net will benefit, including web developers, third-party developers, web administrators, and end users.

Active Platform Technology and Components

The Active Platform is based on the following three core technologies:

- Active Desktop
- Active Server
- ActiveX

Figure 37.2 shows the ActiveX architecture.

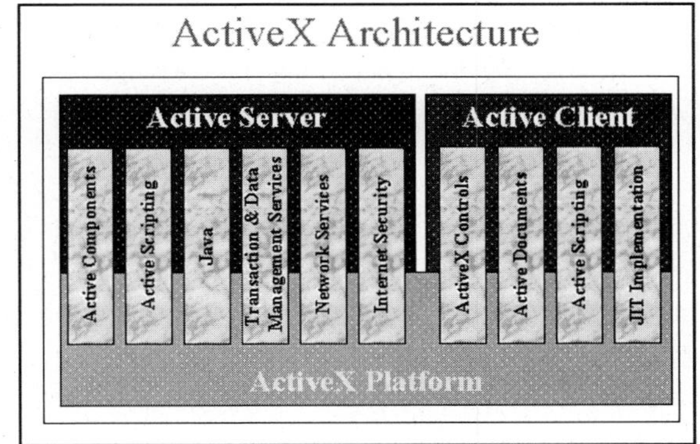

FIG. 37.2 Within an Active Platform solution, you can mix and match the core technologies, depending on your application's business requirements.

Active Desktop

The Active Desktop represents the web application's client side. You can create your web application's client side by applying the Active Platform formula's three components: HTML, ActiveX scripting, and software components, such as Java applets, Active Server components, and ActiveX controls.

Figure 37.3 shows ActiveX controls and how they work.

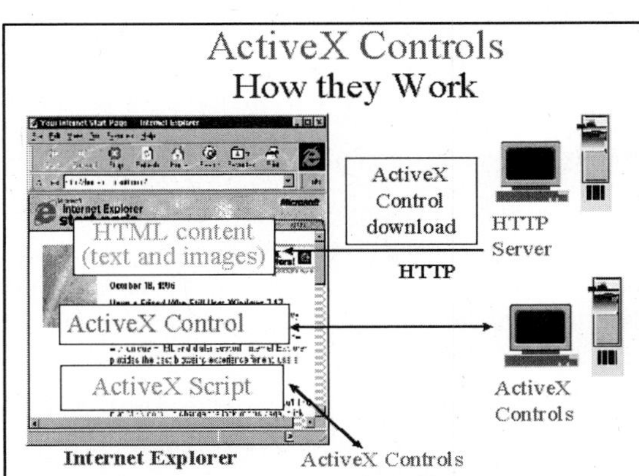

FIG. 37.3 ActiveX controls are reusable software components.

ActiveX controls are based on Microsoft's Component Object Model (COM). If you are familiar with OLE controls, you will find ActiveX controls easy to understand. Typically, a control's interface will contain properties, events, and methods. The control's interface will define the control's interaction with the rest of the world, that is, the application and other controls.

The interface you implement for the control is more important than the language you use to write the control.

Developing ActiveX Controls

As a developer, if you develop and market ActiveX controls, you must document the control's interface thoroughly so that your customers will understand how best to use the control. In essence, the control you design must be totally configurable from the application that uses the control. Users should not need a development environment to modify and regenerate the control. ActiveX controls available at Microsoft's web site (**www.microsoft.com/activex/gallery**) include the following:

- *Label control* You can use the label control to display text at the given angle. You can also use the control to render text along user-defined curves.
- *MCSiMenu control* You can use the MCSiMenu control to display a pop-up menu within your web page.
- *Marquee control* You can use the marquee control to display scrolling text in horizontal or vertical direction within your web page.
- *Stock Ticker control* You can use the stock ticker control to display continuously changing data.
- *Timer control* You can use the timer control to invoke the timer event periodically.

ActiveX Scripting So, you have ActiveX controls, Java applets, and HTML. But how do you make them work together? Enter ActiveX scripting. By using scripting languages such as VBScript and JScript, you can glue your HTML code with ActiveX controls and Java applets and create an interactive web page. As you will learn, scripting languages bring event-driven programming to the web. By using scripting languages, you can include code that will respond to an ActiveX control's event, or you can set a Java applet's property, and so on. You can invoke a control or applet's method from the calling application. In essence, you can make the software components work together by using a scripting language, as shown in Figure 37.4.

ActiveX scripting has two important aspects:

- You may write a Java applet by using Visual J++ and you may write an ActiveX control by using Visual C++, and yet you can use VBScript (or JScript) to tie the two components together with HTML. As you can see, the Active Platform supports the integration of different technologies, independent of the programming language or development tool you use to write the technologies.
- You can validate user input on the client side. This means the browser will send only valid data to the server. This, in turn, will reduce network traffic and improve your application's overall performance.

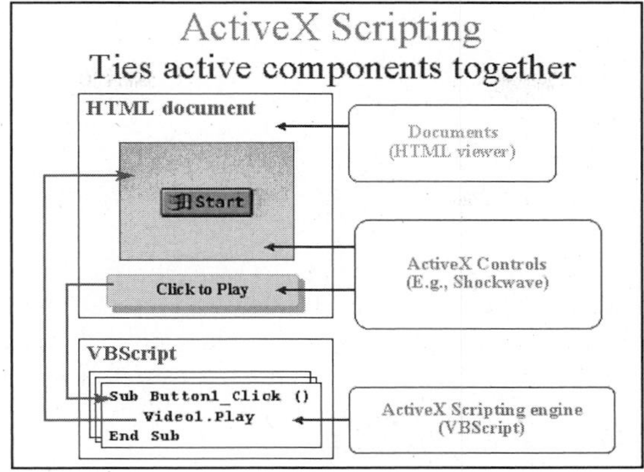

FIG. 37.4 You can tie all the components together by using ActiveX scripting.

Integrated Java Support A browser such as Internet Explorer can execute Java applets because the browser includes an integrated Java Virtual Machine (JVM). The JVM is a software-based microprocessor that can execute Java programs—Java applications and Java applets. All three browsers—Internet Explorer, Netscape Navigator, and HotJava—support Java.

As you will learn, ActiveX technology complements Java. For example, within Visual J++, you can use Visual J++'s Type Library Wizard to convert ActiveX controls into Java classes. You can then use the Java classes within your Java programs.

Active Documents

Another paradigm of ActiveX is the Active document technology. With Active document technology, you can view nonHTML documents—such as Word, Excel, PowerPoint, and so on—within Internet Explorer. For example, if you have Word or Word Viewer installed on your system, you can use Internet Explorer to open a Word document (`.doc`). When you load a Word document within Internet Explorer, you will notice Internet Explorer's toolbar and menu bar showing the Word application or viewer's toolbar and menu bar. Figure 37.5 shows an Active document.

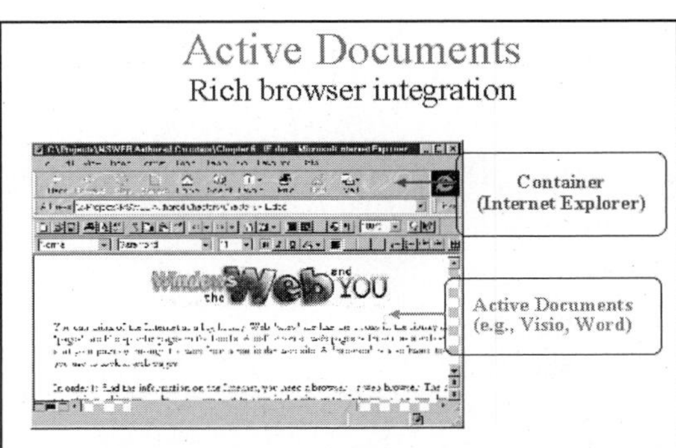

FIG. 37.5 Active document technology will offer you tight browser integration.

Active Server

The Active Server represents the web application's server side. As with the Active Desktop, you can create your web application's server side by applying the Active Platform formula's three components: HTML, ActiveX scripting, and software components, such as Java applets and ActiveX server components. As you can see, you can build your web application's client and server side by using the same set of technologies.

In addition, you can take advantage of a number of different Microsoft server technologies and services, such as Transaction Server, Merchant Server, Proxy Server, and so on, to implement specialized business solutions. Microsoft's server technology is tightly integrated with Windows NT operating system and Internet Information Server. As a result, your Active Platform solution will benefit from the operating system's services and features. For example, your web application can inherit Windows NT's built-in security mechanism.

- Active Server components offer a different dimension to web programming. Active Server components are, in fact, ActiveX controls implemented on the server. By using Active Server Components on the server, your application will need a very thin client, because the components will reside on the server. This means the application will benefit from the server's processing power. In addition, the server can generate the HTML dynamically. Because the component will reside on the server, multiple applications can share the same components.
- As with ActiveX controls, you can use (and reuse) Active Server components across applications and with a variety of development tools. As with ActiveX controls, you also can use any standard Windows development tool, such as Visual C++ and Visual Basic, to create the Active Server components for your application.
- The Active Server is fully scalable. For example, as shown in Figure 37.6, you can start development with the Personal Web Server and after testing the web site, port the site to your IIS without changing or rewriting any component. Thus, you can use the Personal Web Server as your development server and the IIS as your production server.

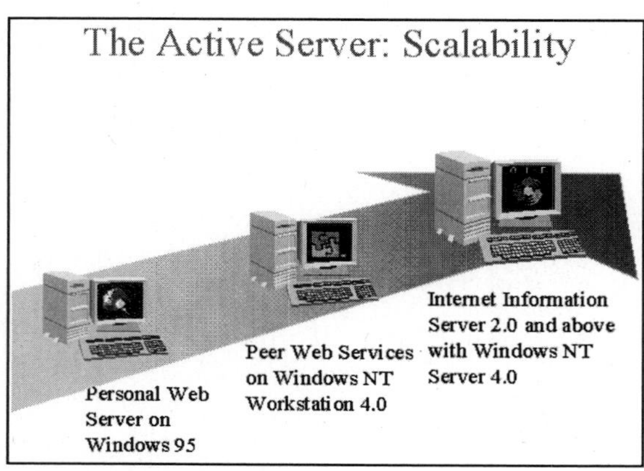

FIG. 37.6
The Active Server Scalability Method.

- By using the Active Server, you can implement multitier architecture for your application. Your application's business rules and application logic will reside on the server. The server, in turn, will connect and communicate with the database server. The database server may reside on a platform different from the web server's platform. Because Active Server is based on open standards and protocols, an Active Server-based solution offers a powerful way to integrate the web and legacy applications.

Active Server Pages With server-side ActiveX scripting, you can create Active Server Pages (ASP) by using the same set of components you use to implement client-side scripting. That is, you can integrate Active Server components and Java applets within your ASP code by using scripting languages such as VBScript, JavaScript, and JScript.

ASP is a good alternative to Common Gateway Interface (CGI) programming. Traditionally, CGI has been the primary protocol to build dynamic, data-driven web pages. With server-side scripting, you can use an Active Server component that will keep the connection alive with the database server (for example). As a result, you will reduce the traffic to the database server and improve the response time of the requests, because your application will make the connection to the database only once.

The Active Server includes a number of prebuilt, pretested Active Server components, such as the Browser Capabilities and Active Data Object (ADO). By using the Browser Capabilities component, you can detect the type of client browser. In response, you can create the HTML that the browser will be capable of handling. For instance, if the browser does not support frames and tables, you can create and send a simple HTML page that will not use the `<Frame>` and `<Table>` tags.

In addition, you can use the ADO with your server-side scripts. For example, the server-side script will communicate the SQL query to the ADO. The ADO, in turn, will communicate the query to the database server. The database server, in turn, will process the query and send the results to the ADO. The ADO, in turn, will return the results to the Active Server script. The script, in turn, will generate and send the HTML to the browser. As you can see, each component within the architecture performs a specific role, and each component communicates with its immediate neighbor to get the job done.

NOTE If the prepackaged components do not meet your application's requirements, you can write your own component. Alternatively, you can use a third-party component that will meet your application's criteria.

In addition, like Active Desktop, Active Server also supports Java. You can integrate Java applets with your server-side scripts.

ActiveX

The third technology that is part of the Active Platform spectrum is ActiveX. Note that ActiveX is not a programming language. ActiveX is a language-independent set of technologies you can use to create interactive content for the web.

ActiveX Controls and Netscape Plug-Ins

Netscape developed and promoted the plug-in technology, and Microsoft advocates ActiveX controls. The two technologies, however, are different. An ActiveX control is a generic component you can use within any application, including web and Windows applications. On the other hand, a plug-in is specific to a browser. You must install the plug-in and restart the browser before the plug-in will become effective. The browser will automatically download and install the ActiveX control if the control does not already exist on the user's system. In fact, depending on the browser's settings, the browser will ask the user to confirm whether the browser should download and install the control. In addition, there are thousands of controls already available on the Net, and the number will continue to grow.

Foundation of ActiveX Technology

Like OLE, ActiveX is based on Microsoft's Component Object Model (COM). Like OLE controls, ActiveX controls also implement an interface containing properties, methods, and events. However, the ActiveX control's interface is slimmer compared to the OLE control's interface. OLE is optimized for end-user usability and application integration, and ActiveX is optimized for size and speed. The optimization for size and speed, in turn, will help reduce the time the browser takes to download and install an ActiveX control, for example.

ActiveX and COM

Both ActiveX and OLE are part of the COM model. Microsoft and Digital Equipment Corporation first proposed the Component Object Model (COM) specification. Microsoft released the draft version 0.9 in 1995. Since then, Microsoft has updated and revised the COM specification.

The COM model's basic theory is reusable, and component objects are your application's building blocks. You can plug and play these objects to build your application quickly and easily. There is no point in reinventing the wheel! The COM specification's most interesting part is that you may write the component objects by using completely different programming languages and compile them on completely different platforms; yet these objects should be able to interact and communicate with each other. This interaction will depend on the object's external interface and not on the object's internal structure or the language and platform you use to write the object. COM is the result of Microsoft's years of investment in research and development of component technology.

The COM specification includes the following:

- A set of standard Application Programming Interfaces (API)
- A set of standard interfaces
- A set of network protocols

COM will establish a connection between the client and the component object. After establishing the connection, COM will drop out of the picture. The client will interact with the object by using the object's interface. The client can invoke the object's methods and pass data and parameters to the object's methods, and the object returns the results to the client. Whether you use Visual Basic, Visual C++, or Visual J++ to write the component object is immaterial. Under the COM specification, the client can still interact with the object to get the data it will need.

COM defines the interaction between the client and the component object—both residing on the client side. Distributed Component Object Model (DCOM) is an extension of COM that defines the interaction between two COM objects, each object residing on a different network. In other words, DCOM defines a set of standard APIs and interfaces for communication and interaction between COM objects within a distributed environment.

By using Visual J++, you can integrate ActiveX and COM objects within your Java programs. This is interesting because you can use a COM or ActiveX object the same way you use a Java class within your Java program. For example, you can instantiate an ActiveX object in the same way you instantiate a Java class. This seamless integration makes Visual J++ stand apart from the crowd. *Visual J++ is not simply a tool.* Visual J++ is a tool that will help you integrate two different technologies seamlessly. As a developer, you will benefit from the best of both worlds—ActiveX and Java.

Like COM, DCOM is an open standard protocol that will work in conjunction with HTTP, TCP/IP, and other standard Internet protocols within the Active Platform's paradigm.

What Tool Do You Want To Use Today?

Among the different Microsoft tools, you can use the following tools for ActiveX development (see Figure 37.7):

- *Visual C++* To create ActiveX controls, you can use Microsoft's ActiveX Software Developer's Kit (SDK) or Active Template Library with Visual C++. You can also use ActiveX controls within your Visual C++ applications.
- *Visual Basic* To create ActiveX controls, you can also use Visual Basic Control Creation Edition. In addition, you can integrate ActiveX controls within your Visual Basic applications.
- *Visual J++* You can use Visual J++ to create Java ActiveX objects. Presently, Visual J++ is the only Java tool in the market you can use to integrate ActiveX controls with your Java programs. In addition, you can also use the Microsoft SDK for Java to integrate ActiveX controls with your Java development.

NOTE A number of operating systems support ActiveX. All Windows platforms support ActiveX technology. In addition, Internet Explorer fully supports ActiveX, and you can use a third-party plug-in—ScriptActive, from NCompass Labs (**www.ncompasslabs.com**)—with Netscape Navigator to view and execute ActiveX content with Navigator.

Microsoft is working with Metrowerks to support ActiveX on the Macintosh, and with Bristol and Mainsoft to support ActiveX on UNIX systems.

You also can do the following:

- Use Microsoft Office 97 to create Active documents.
- Use ActiveX Control Pad to create event-driven web pages. In addition, you can use the Control Pad to integrate ActiveX controls within your web pages.

- Use Visual InterDev to create Active Server Pages. Like the Control Pad, you can integrate ActiveX controls within your Visual InterDev applications.
- Use Internet Explorer to browse and view ActiveX-enabled web sites.

Figure 37.7 shows a partial list of ActiveX development tools.

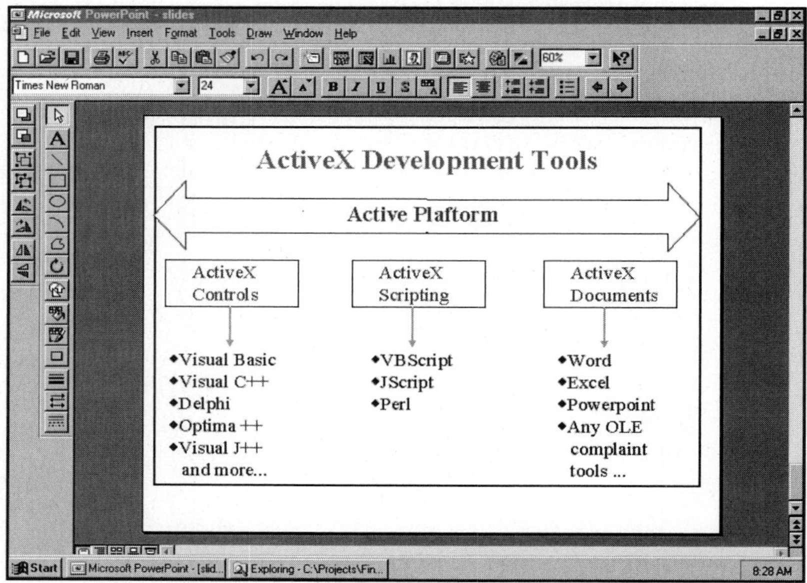

FIG. 37.7
A choice of tools for creating Active web content.

In addition to Microsoft, a number of other companies support ActiveX. These include, but are not limited to, the following:

- Borland (**www.borland.com**) Borland's premier client/server development tool, Delphi, supports ActiveX.
- PowerSoft (**www.powersoft.com**) Like Borland, PowerSoft's premier client/server development tools, PowerBuilder and Optima++, support ActiveX.
- Symantec (**www.symantec.com**) Symantec C++ also supports ActiveX.
- MetroWerks Code Warrior (**www.metrowerks.com**) MetroWerks supports ActiveX development on the Macintosh.

Today, a number of third-party ActiveX controls are available in the market. You will find a number of links to third-party vendors at Microsoft's web site, **www.microsoft.com/activex**.

Activating the Internet with ActiveX

With ActiveX technology, you can create an interactive, data-driven, multimedia-enabled web site. You can include cool animations and compelling graphics within your web site. In addition, you can create a personalized experience for your visitors.

Assume you plan to design a web site for a real estate company. The company would like to post its real estate listings on the web so interested visitors can browse and search the listings to find the ones that best fit their criteria. Clearly, you will need the following basic components to begin:

- *An ODBC-compliant database* You will need an RDBMS to store the listings. You can use Microsoft Access for your application development's prototyping and proof-of-concept phases. To support a large number of users and store a large number of listings, consider using Microsoft SQL Server as your application's production database server.
- *Web server* The web server will constitute the middle component of Microsoft's three-tier Active Platform architecture. The web server will handle the communication with the browser and the RDBMS. You can use Microsoft's Internet Information Server (IIS) as your production web server, and you can use the Personal web Server (PWS) as the web server for your project's prototyping and proof-of-concept phases.
- *Client* The client, of course, will be a browser such as Internet Explorer.

The real estate application's design will benefit from the following:

- *Search page* Create a search page visitors can use to specify their criteria for the kind of house they are looking for. You can use the standard ActiveX controls, such as CommandButton, check box, drop-down list box, and so on, to create the search page's form. You can use the JScript (or VBScript) scripting language to write event-driven code to handle mouse events such as button click. You can also use the scripting language to validate user input before the browser will send the data to the server.

  You can even save each visitor's search criteria. Then, the next time the visitor logs onto your site (through a logon page), your web site will present the search page with all the criteria already filled in. The visitor can then change any specific parameters of the criteria and resubmit the search.
- *Results page* The results page will include the listings matching the user-specified criteria, if any. You can organize the results page in a number of different ways. You may present the results summary first, and the user can click a More button to get detail information on a particular listing. The detail information may include graphics displaying the house's layout, interior, and so on. Again, to display graphics, you can use the standard picture and image controls that come with Microsoft's development tools, or you can use any of the third-party controls that offer enhanced features and capabilities.

TIP With ActiveX, there are several interesting possibilities about how you can make your site more engaging. For example, you can play a background sound when the user enters the detail information page. The background voice will tell the user more about the property and its unique features. In addition, you can include a video that will walk the user through the house. You can jazz up your web site and impress the visitors by including a virtual reality tour of the house. (To support virtual reality within your web site, you need a VRML control.)

- *Enhancements* You can use Java applets or ActiveX controls to enhance your site in a number of different ways. For example, you can use a Java applet or ActiveX control (such as the Marquee control) to display a scrolling text at the bottom of the web page announcing any promotions.

  You can also include an online mortgage calculator. The calculator may be a Java applet or an ActiveX control. In addition, you can include hyperlinks to lending institutions, real estate lawyers, and so on.
- *Database* Depending on the tool you use to design the real estate web site, you can use the Internet Database Connector (IDC) or Active Data Component (ADO) with Internet Server Application Programming Interface (ISAPI) to handle the connection and communication with your application's database.
- *Active Server Pages (ASP)* You may choose to design the web site as a collection of ASP. By using ASP, you can generate the client-side HTML code dynamically. This means less activity on the client machine and thus less network traffic, and your application will benefit from the server's processing power.
- *Dynamic HTML* Microsoft developed the Dynamic HTML specification in collaboration with the World Wide Web Consortium (W3C) (**www.w3c.org**). Dynamic HTML will offer you finer control over your web application. For example, if your application retrieves and presents data in a tabular format, you can include a local engine-based searching and sorting by using dynamic HTML. As a result, you will reduce the number of requests to your application's web server, thus significantly improving your application's performance.

As you can see, you can design a compelling web site complete in all respects by using Microsoft's Active Platform tools and technologies. The example discussed within this section outlines some of the features you can include within your web site. Depending on your particular application's business requirements, you may need to include a different set of features. Regardless of the features, you can still use Microsoft's Active Platform tools and technologies to implement them.

A Bright Future for the Active Platform

With Microsoft aggressively pushing the ActiveX technology, and the number of tools Microsoft offers to create and maintain ActiveX content, the Active Platform promises to be the future.

The best part about Active Platform is that you need not learn any new programming or scripting language. You may continue to use the development tools and programming languages you feel comfortable with to design and develop your Active web applications. In addition, the Active Platform is cross-platform and supports open standards. With technologies such as Active Server Pages, you can build server-based dynamic web sites. Microsoft's tools and technologies also will make server programming easy for you.

Building Active Server Page Applications

Microsoft's Active Platform includes the Active Client and Active Server. Active Server Pages (ASP) is part of the Active Server. You can write ASP by using server-side scripting and server components. You can use the same tools you use to implement client-side scripting. For example, you can use Visual Basic 5 to create ActiveX controls and Active Server components. You can use VBScript to glue Java applets, ActiveX controls (or Active Server components), and HTML to create ASP.

ASP gives you the ability to add intelligence to your web application. By using server-side scripts, you can detect the capability of the requesting client. If the client does not support graphics, ASP can render a text-only version of the HTML page. If the client does not support ActiveX controls, ASP can detect it and serve the HTML page accordingly.

Client- and Server-Side Scripting

The server-side scripts will execute on the server. Apart from the benefit of the server's processing power, the scripts will generate the HTML for the client browser to view. These scripts will handle everything from reading a file to connecting to the database. To execute a script on the server, you must include the `RUNAT=SERVER` option. The code will look as follows:

```
<LANGUAGE=VBScript RUNAT=SERVER>
```

Listing 37.1 shows the script that will execute on the client. Notice the line of code that displays a message box. Because the script will execute on the client, displaying a message box is meaningful.

Listing 37.1 A client-side script.

```
<SCRIPT LANGUAGE=VBScript>
<!--
Option Explicit

Dim validCreditCardNumber

Sub Submit_OnClick
       validCreditCardNumber = True
       Call CheckCreditCardNumber(CreditCardNumberField.Value, "Please enter
your credit card number.")
       If validCreditCardNumber then
              Msgbox "Thank you for your order"
       End if
End Sub
</SCRIPT>
```

If you execute the same script on the server, displaying a message box will be meaningless. This is because there is no user interface on the server. As a result, the server will bypass the line of code that displays the message box. Listing 37.2 shows the same script with the RUNAT=SERVER option.

Listing 37.2 A script that will execute on the server.

```
<SCRIPT LANGUAGE=VBScript RUNAT=SERVER>
<!--
Option Explicit

Dim validCreditCardNumber

Sub Submit_OnClick
        validCreditCardNumber = True
        Call CheckCreditCardNumber(CreditCardNumberField.Value, "Please enter
your credit card number.")
        If validCreditCardNumber then
                Msgbox "Thank you for your order"
        End if
End Sub
</SCRIPT>
```

Components of ASP Application

Building an ASP application will require combining a number of components, including the following:

- Text files with the extension .ASP
- Scripting
- Server components

An HTML file is a text file the browser will execute on the client machine. The HTML file has the extension .HTM or .HTML. Similarly, an ASP file is a text file the IIS will execute on the server. An ASP file has the extension .ASP. Within an ASP file, you can integrate server components by using ActiveX scripting. Although Microsoft recommends using VBScript or JScript as your default scripting language, you can use any other scripting language—such as JavaScript, REXX, Perl 5, and so on—within your ASP files.

VBScript or JScript?

If you are an experienced C++ or Java programmer, you will find JavaScript or JScript easy to learn and use. If you are an experienced Visual Basic programmer, you will find VBScript easy to learn and use.

Listing 37.3 shows an example of ASP file.

Listing 37.3 A sample ASP file.

```
<html>
<HEAD>
<title>
Welcome to Que's Platinum Edition 4.0 Using Java, JavaScript
</title>
</HEAD>
<body>
<%                                        '=== Active Server Scripting begins
sub HelloWorld()
       dim Greeting
       Greeting = "Hello World!"
       Response.write Greeting
End sub
%>
<% Call HelloWorld %>                    '=== Calling the Active Server subrou-
tine
</body>
</html>
```

As you can see, this ASP file includes both traditional HTML and an Active Server script. The Active Server script is enclosed within the `<% %>` tags.

Just as you can use scripting within your traditional HTML code for things such as client-side input validation, you can use scripting within your Active Server files. Listing 37.4 shows an example of an ASP file that uses server-side scripting.

Listing 37.4 Using server-side scripting to say *"Hello World".*

```
<%@ LANGUAGE="VBSCRIPT" RUNAT="SERVER"%>       '=== Indicates the script will be
executed on the server

<%
Sub HelloWorld()                                '=== Declare a subroutine
Response.write "Hello World"
End Sub
%>

<HTML>
<BODY>
<%
Call HelloWorld()       '=== Call the subroutine
%>
</Body>
</HTML>
```

As you can see within this code listing, the first line of code indicates the scripting language the IIS server will use and also indicates that the script will be executed on the server. Next, you define a subroutine, and then you call the subroutine.

Listing 37.5 shows another ASP example that uses three of the five ASP objects (`Session`, `Response`, and `Request`) to process information. First, you will retrieve information from the form by using the `Request` object and store the information within the `Session` object's variables. Within this example, you will use the `Session` variables `User_ID`, `nba_Online`, and `nfl_Online` to store information from the form fields `User_Id`, `nba_online`, and `nfl_online`.

Next, you will check whether the `User_Id` variable is empty. If the variable is empty, you will use the `Response` object's `Redirect` method to redirect the browser to the `"invalid.htm"` file. If the variable is not empty, you will use the `Request` object to retrieve the `report_type` variable's value. If the value is `"nba"` and the value of the `Session` variable `"nba_Online" =` `“Y"`, you will use the `Response` object's `Redirect` method to redirect the browser to the `"latest_nba.htm"` file. The `"latest_nba.htm"` file, in turn, will display the latest NBA scores. On the other hand, if the value of the `Session` variable `"nba_Online" = "N"`, you will redirect the browser to the `"invalid.htm"` file. You will process similarly for the `"nfl_Online"` option. In the next section, you will learn more about the ASP objects and their variables, properties, methods, and events.

Listing 37.5 Using the ASP objects.

```
<%@ LANGUAGE="VBSCRIPT" %>
<% Session("User_ID")    = Request.Form("User_Id") %>
<% Session("nba_Online") = Request.Form("nba_online") %>
<% Session("nfl_Online") = Request.Form("nfl_online") %>
<%
If IsEmpty(Session("User_Id")) Then
       Response.Redirect "invalid.htm"
Else
       If Request.Form("report_type") = "nba" Then
              If Session("nba_Online") = "Y" Then
                     Response.Redirect "latest_nba.htm"
              Else
                     Response.Redirect "invalid.htm"
              End If
       Else
              If Session("nfl_Online") = "Y" Then
                     Response.Redirect "latest_nfl.htm"
              Else
                     Response.Redirect "invalid.htm"
              End If
       End If

End If
%>
<!DOCTYPE HTML PUBLIC "-//IETF//DTD HTML//EN">
<html>

<head>
<meta http-equiv="Content-Type"
content="text/html; charset=iso-8859-1">
```

```
<meta name="GENERATOR" content="Microsoft FrontPage 2.0">
<title></title>
</head>

<body>
</body>
</html>
```


Active Server Page Objects

Five fundamental server objects constitute ASP's core functionality:

- `Application` You will use the `Application` object to manage your web application's information.
- `Session` You will use the `Session` object to manage and track individual user sessions within your web application.
- `Server` You will use the `Server` object to administer and manage your web server.
- `Response` You will use the `Response` object to transmit information from the web server to the browser.
- `Request` You will use the `Request` object to retrieve information from the browser for processing at the server.

Like any other object within an object-oriented programming world, the five ASP objects also contain their specific methods and properties. You can use an ASP object's methods and properties to configure the object per your application and business requirements. You will learn more about the methods and properties of ASP objects in the following sections. The five ASP objects are extremely critical for developing an ASP application.

The *Application* Object

By using the `Application` object, you can manage your web application's information. You can pass application-level information between your application's different users of the application. In addition, you can lock and unlock an application-level variable. When you lock an application-level variable, other users of the application cannot modify the variable's value. After you release the lock, other users can modify the variable's value.

Events The `Application` object supports the following two events:

- `Application_OnStart` When the application starts, this will be the first event triggered.
- `Application_OnEnd` When the application terminates, the `Application_OnEnd` event will be triggered.

You will find the `Application` object's two events within your application's `Global.ASA` file.

Global.ASA File

The `Global.ASA` file is an Active Server application file you can use to track and manage the application and session events, variables, and objects. When you start the application, the server will load the `Global.ASA` file into memory.

Variables You can declare application-level variables within your application's `Global.ASA` file. For example, the following line of code declares an application-level variable `myAppTitle`. After you declare the variable, all users of the application will have access to the variable:

```
Application("myAppTitle") = "My First ASP application"
```

In the next section, you will learn how you can use the `Application` object's `Lock` and `UnLock` methods with your application-level variables.

Methods There are two primary types of methods used in the `Application` object:

- By using the `Lock` method, you can prevent another user from updating or changing the application-level variable's value.
- By using the `UnLock` method, you can release the control on the application-level variable. The following code demonstrates the use of `Lock` and `UnLock` methods:

```
Application.Lock
Application("errMsg") = "Please contact the Plan Administrator"
Application.UnLock
%>
```

The *Session* Object

By using the `Session` object, you can manage information about a specific user of your web application. The user information is specific only to the user, and other users cannot access or modify such information. The `Session` object includes the events, properties, and methods described in the following sections.

Events Like the `Application` object, the `Session` object also supports the following two events:

- `Session_OnStart` When the server starts a new user session, the `Session_OnStart` event will be triggered.
- `Session_OnEnd` When the server terminates the user session, the `Session_OnEnd` event will be triggered.

You will find the `Session` object's two events within your application's `Global.ASA` file.

NOTE By using the `Abandon` method that falls under the `Session` object, you can explicitly close a user's session. As a result, the server will automatically release all resources consumed by the user session and destroy the user `Session` object. The syntax for `Abandon` method is

```
Session.Abandon
```

where `Session` is the current `Session` object.

Properties There are four properties that fall under the `Session` object:

- By using the `CodePage` property, you can set your web pages' attributes. The syntax for the `CodePage` property is

  ```
  Session.CodePage = CodePage
  ```

  where `CodePage` is a valid code page for the scripting engine.
- By using the `LCID` property, you can set the local identifier to set the local date, time, and currency formats. As a result, you can control the display formatting of your ASP pages, based on a particular locale or region. The syntax for using the `LCID` property is

  ```
  Session.LCID(=LCID)
  ```

  where `LCID` is a valid local identifier.
- The `SessionID` property represents a unique user session. When a user initiates a session with your web application, the web server will automatically generate a `SessionID` for the user's session. The syntax for using the `SessionID` property is

  ```
  Session.SessionID
  ```

- The `TimeOut` property represents the amount of time the user session will remain active before the web server will destroy the `Session` object. The syntax for using the `TimeOut` property is

  ```
  Session.Timeout [ = nMinutes]
  ```

  where `Session` is the `Session` object and you specify the `TimeOut` in number of minutes. The default is 20 minutes. The server will store the `TimeOut` within your system's registry. The following line of code, for example, will override the default value:

  ```
  <%Session.Timeout = 1%>
  ```

The *Server* Object

By using the `Server` object, you can manage and administer your web server. The `Server` object includes the methods and properties described in the following sections.

Methods The following methods are supported by the `Server` object:

- By using the `CreateObject` method, you can create a Server object's instance. The `CreateObject` method's syntax is

  ```
  Server.CreateObject( progID )
  ```

  where `progID` is the class ID of the object's instance you want to create. For example, the following line of code will create the Browser Detection Active `Server` object's instance:

  ```
  Set BrowserType = Server.CreateObject("MSWC.BrowserType")
  ```

  After you create a `Server` object's instance, you can access the object's methods and properties within your ASP file. An object whose instance you create within an ASP file will have page-level scope. An object whose instance you create within the `Global.ASA` file will have application or session-level scope, depending on whether you use the application or session object.

- By using the `MapPath` method, you can map a physical or virtual path to a directory on the server. The `MapPath` method's syntax is

  ```
  Server.MapPath( path )
  ```

  where `Server` is the Active Server, and `path` is the virtual or physical directory.
- By using the `HTMLEncode` method, you can encode a string using the HTML encoding methods. Typically, you will use the `HTMLEncode` method to pass encoded information from the server to the client. The HTMLEncode method's syntax is

  ```
  Server.HTMLEncode( string )
  ```

  where `Server` is the Active Server, and `string` is the string to be HTML-encoded.
- By using the `URLEncode` method, you can encode a string using the URL encoding methods. Typically, you will use the `URLEncode` method to pass encoded information from the client to the server. The `URLEncode` method's syntax is

  ```
  Server.URLEncode( string )
  ```

  where `Server` is the Active Server, and `string` is the string to be URL-encoded.

Properties The following property is supported under the `Server` object:

- The `ScriptTimeOut` property indicates the amount of time the server will wait to process a script, before the server will terminate the script processing. The `ScriptTimeOut` property's syntax is

  ```
  Server.ScriptTimeout = Seconds
  ```

  where `Server` is the Active Server, and you specify the script timeout in seconds. The default timeout value is 90 seconds. The value is stored within your system's registry. To change the default value to 30 seconds, for example, you can use the following line of code within your ASP file:

  ```
  Server.TimeOut = 30
  ```

The *Response* Object

By using the `Response` object, you can send information from the server to the client. The `Response` object includes the methods and properties described in the following sections.

Properties The `Response` object includes the following properties:

- You can use the `Buffer` property to turn the server's buffering on or off. The syntax for using the `Buffer` property is

  ```
  Response.Buffer = [flag]
  ```

  where `flag` equals `True` if you want to turn the buffering on, and flag equals `False` if you want to turn the buffering off. For example, the following line of code will turn the server's buffering on:

  ```
  <%Response.Buffer = True%>
  ```

- By using the `Expires` property, you can control the amount of time before the browser will remove the page from its cache. The syntax for using the `Expires` property is

  ```
  Response.Expires = [number]
  ```

where `number` equals the number of minutes you want the browser to keep the page active within its cache.

- By using the `ExpiresAbsolute` property, you can specify the exact date and time when the browser should remove the page from its cache. The syntax for using the `ExpiresAbsolute` property is

```
Response.ExpiresAbsolute = [[date][time]]
```


- By using the `IsClientConnected` property, you can determine whether the client was disconnected since the last time the web server sent data to the browser. The syntax for using the `IsClientConnected` property is

```
Response.IsClientConnected()
```

- By using the `Status` property, you can control the status line the web server will return. The syntax for using the `Status` property is

```
Response.Status = StatusCodeAndDescription
```

  where `StatusCodeAndDescription` includes the status code and description.

- By using the `PICS` property, you can control the rating values of the PICS-label field. The syntax for using the `PICS` property is

```
Response.PICS(PicsLabel)
```

  where `PicsLabel` is the formatted PICS label.

- By using the `ContentType` property, you can specify the MIME content type the web server will send to the browser. The syntax for using the `ContentType` property is

```
Response.ContentType = [ContentType]
```

  where `ContentType` is a valid content type. Examples of valid content types are image/GIF, image/JPEG, text/HTML, and so on.

- By using the `CharSet` property, you can control the character set of the content type the browser will display. The syntax is

```
Response.CharSet(CharSetName)
```

  where `CharSetName` is a valid character set name.

Methods The following methods are supported by the `Response` object:

- By using the `Write` method, you can send output to the client. The `Write` method's syntax is

```
Response.Write variant
```

  where `variant` is a VBScript data type. For example, you can use the following line of code to send the current date and time to the client's browser:

```
<%Response.Write now%>
```

- By using the `BinaryWrite` method, you can send binary information such as an image format to the client. The `BinaryWrite` method's syntax is

```
Response.BinaryWrite binarydata
```

- By using the `Redirect` method, you can automatically redirect the client to a different URL. You will find the `Redirect` method useful if your site's URL has changed, but a visitor to your site has not updated its link to your site. This way, when the visitor connects to your site at the old URL, the `Redirect` method will automatically redirect the visitor's browser to the new URL. The `Redirect` method's syntax is

  ```
  Response.Redirect URL
  ```

- For example, you can use the following line of code to redirect the client browser to the `default.asp` Active Server Page on your server:

  ```
  <%Response.Redirect "default.asp"%>
  ```

- By using the `AppendToLog` method, you can record information within the web server's log file. As a result, you can use the `AppendToLog` method and the log file for debugging and tracking purposes. The `AppendToLog` method's syntax is

  ```
  Response.AppendToLog string
  ```

  where `string` is the string you will record to the log file.

- By using the `AddHeader` method, you can add information to the existing HTTP header. The `AddHeader` method's syntax is

  ```
  Response.AddHeader header_name, header_value
  ```

  where `header_name` is the name of the header, and `header_value` is the header's value.

- By using the `Clear` method, you can direct the web server to clear its buffer. The `Clear` method's syntax is

  ```
  Response.Clear
  ```

Using the *Clear* Method

You can use the `Clear` method only if the buffering is on. If buffering is turned off, there will be no data within the server's buffer. Using the `Clear` method in such a case will result in an error.

- By using the `Flush` method, you can direct the web server to send the buffered output to the client browser. The `Flush` method's syntax is

  ```
  Response.Flush
  ```

Using the *Flush* Method

You can use the `Flush` method only if the buffering is on. If buffering is turned off, there will be no data within the server's buffer. Using the `Flush` method in such a case will result in an error.

- By using the `End` method, you can control the amount of data within the web server's buffer. The `End` method's syntax is

  ```
  Response.End
  ```

  When the server that processes the script comes across the `End` command, the server, in turn, will stop the data buffering.

The *Request* Object

By using the `Request` object, you can retrieve information from the client browser. The `Request` object includes five collections:

- By using the `ClientCertifiate` collection within the `Request` object, the web server can collect information about certification fields from the client browser. The certification fields include the following:

  Certificate. The Certificate field contains the entire certificate content in ASN.1 format.

  SerialNumber. The SerialNumber field contains the certification serial number.

  ValidFrom. The ValidFrom field specifies when the certificate will come into effect.

  ValidUntil. The ValidUntil field specifies when the certificate will expire.

  Issuer. The Issuer field contains information about the issuer of the certificate.

  Subject. The Subject field contains information about the subject of the certificate.

- By using the `Cookies` collection within the `Request` object, the web server can collect information from the cookies on the client machine. The syntax for using the `Cookie` collection is

  ```
  Request.Cookies(cookie)[(key)¦.attribute]
  ```

  where `cookie` is the cookie's name, `key` is the index of subkey values, and `attribute` is the specified cookie's property.

- By using the `Form` collection within the `Request` object, the web server can retrieve information the user enters on the form within the client browser. The syntax for using the Form collection is

  ```
  Request.Form(parameter)[(index)¦.Count]
  ```

  where `parameter` is the form collection's name, `index` is the specific form element, and `count` is the number of elements on the form.

- By using the `QueryString` collection, the web server can parse the information contained with the URL string. The syntax for using the `QueryString` collection is

  ```
  Request.QueryString(variable)[(index)¦.Count]
  ```

  where `variable` is the variable's name within the query string, `index` is the element index, and `count` represents the total number of elements within the query string.

- By using the `ServerVariables` collection, the web server can retrieve values of server environment variables. The syntax for using the `ServerVariables` collection is

  ```
  Request.ServerVariables (ServerVariable)
  ```

  where `ServerVariable` is the server variable's name. Table 37.1 lists the server variables.

Table 37.1 The server variables.

Variable Name	Description
AUTH_TYPE	Specifies the server's authentication method
AUTH_PASSWORD	Specifies the password the user entered within the client browser
CONTENT_LENGTH	Returns the content's length
CONTENT_TYPE	Returns the content's data type
GATEWAY_INTERFACE	Returns the version of the server's CGI specification
HTTP_*<HeaderName>*	Returns information contained within *<HeaderName>*.
LOGON_USER	Specifies the NT login account that made the request
PATH_INFO	Specifies the server's path information
PATH_TRANSLATED	Returns a translated version of PATH_INFO
QUERY_STRING	Returns the query string contained within the URL
REMOTE_ADDR	Specifies the client machine's IP address
REMOTE_HOST	Specifies the requesting host's name
REQUEST_METHOD	Returns the method initiating the request
SCRIPT_NAME	Specifies the executing script's virtual path
SERVER_NAME	Returns the server's host name, DNS alias, or IP address
SERVER_PORT	Returns the server's port number on which the request is made
SERVER_PORT_SECURE	Returns a 1 if the request is made on the server's secure port, 0 if unsecured
SERVER_PROTOCOL	Returns the requesting protocol's name and version
SERVER_SOFTWARE	Returns the HTTP server's name and version
URL	Returns the URL's base portion

- In addition, the Request object includes the following property and method:

  By using the TotalBytes property, the web server can determine the total number of bytes the client sends. The syntax for using the TotalBytes property is

  ```
  Request.TotalBytes
  ```

  where Request is the Active Server Request object, and TotalBytes represents the total number of bytes the client sends.

  By using the BinaryRead method, the web server can read binary information the client sends through the POST request. The BinaryRead method's syntax is

  ```
  aBinaryArray = Request.BinaryRead(count)
  ```

where `Request` is the Active Server `Request` object, `aBinaryArray` is the binary array the `BinaryRead` method will create, and `count` is the total number of bytes for `aBinaryArray`.

Using Existing ASP Components

The IIS comes with a number of predefined, pretested Active Server Components you can readily use within your ASP application. You will find the existing server-side components extremely useful in building your ASP application:

- **Active Data Object (ADO).** The ADO is probably one of the most important ASP component. By using the ADO, you can create dynamic, data-driven ASP-based web sites.
- **Browser Capabilities.** By using the Browser Capabilities component, you can detect the type of client browser, determine the browser's capabilities through an INI file, and accordingly display HTML.
- **Advertisement Rotator.** By using the Advertisement Rotator component, you can display ad banners within your web site. In addition, you can change the ad banners dynamically.
- **Permission Checker Component.** By using the Permission Checker component, you can determine whether a user has access permission to a given file.
- **Content Linking Component.** By using the Content Linking component, you can design and develop a navigation scheme for your web site.
- **Page Counter Component.** By using the Page Counter component, you can determine the number of times a page from your web site has been requested. As a result, you can determine the amount of interest your web site generates.

This chapter discusses only some of the existing server-side components. For more information about the other components, such as Content Rotator, SMTP Messaging, and Tools, refer to the documentation.

Active Data Object (ADO)

ADO is based on OLE DB, a C++ based API. OLE DB is Microsoft's new database technology based on object linking and embedding. Because the technology is based on C++, its API is object-oriented. ADO includes *data providers* and *data consumers*. The data providers will expose the OLE DB interface, and the data consumers will take data from the OLE DB interface. ADO is similar to Data Access Object (DAO) and Remote Data Object (RDO). However, Microsoft designed ADO specifically with Internet/intranet in mind. ADO incorporates the ActiveX technology.

By using ADO, you can add database connection to your ASP application. To create an instance of the ADO component, you can use the `Server` object's `CreateObject` method. The following line of code shows an example of creating a database connection:

```
Set myDBConnection = Server.CreateObject("ADODB.Recordset")
```

Next, you can use the ADO object's `Open` method to store the results of executing a given SQL statement. The following line of code shows an example of executing the given SQL statement and storing the results within the result set:

```
myDBConnection.Open "Select * from Authors"
```

Next, you can use the data connection's BOF (beginning-of-file) and EOF (end-of-file) methods to determine whether the current record within the recordset is the first or last record, respectively. If you are not at the beginning or end of the recordset, you can display the fields, for example. The following lines of code use a `Do…While` loop to process the recordset:

```
<%
If myDBConnection.EOF
       '=== you are at the end of the record set
Else If myDBConnection.BOF
       '=== you are at the beginning of the record set
Else
       Do While Not myDBConnection.EOF       '=== loop through the result set
              Response.Write (myDBConnection("Author_Name") & <BR>)       '====
➥show the author name
       Loop
End if
%>
```

The ADO object model includes the following objects:

- `Connection` By using the `Connection` object, you will establish a connection with your application's data source. In addition, you can use the `Connection` object to execute SQL commands for the database server to process.
- `Command` You can use the `Command` object to execute parameterized queries and stored procedures.
- `Parameter` You can provide the parameters to a stored procedure by using the Parameter object.
- `Recordset` By using the `Recordset` object, you will process the data the server returns as a result of processing the SQL command.
- `Field` The `Recordset` object will use the `Field` object, because each record returned will contain one or more fields.
- `Error` The `Error` object will log the errors from the datasource.

Connection Object Properties

You can use the `Connection` object to establish a connection with your application's data source. In addition, you can use the `Connection` object to execute SQL commands for the database server to process. The `Connection` object includes the following properties:

- The `Attribute` property specifies whether the database server will start a new transaction after the previous transaction's commit or rollback.
- The `CommandTimeOut` property specifies the amount of time the server will wait to process the command. The default is 30 seconds.

- The `ConnectionString` property specifies the connection string used to connect to the database.
- The `ConnectionTimeOut` property specifies the amount of time to wait for a connection to the data source.
- The `DefaultDatabase` property specifies the default database to which the connection will be sought if your application's data source supports connecting to multiple databases.
- The `Isolation` property specifies the isolation level of your application's connection to the data source.
- You can use the `Mode` property to specify the connection type—read-only, or read/write.
- You can use the `Provider` property to determine the provider of the connection to the data source.
- You can use the `Version` property to determine the ADO's version.

***Connection* Object Methods** The `Connection` object includes the following methods:

- By using the `Connection` object's `BeginTrans` method, you can initiate a new transaction.
- By using the `CommitTrans` method, you can commit the current transaction to the database. If the commit is successful, your application will write all changes to the database since the previous `CommiTrans` or `RollBackTrans`.
- By using the `RollBackTrans` method, you can cancel the current transaction. As a result, all changes to the database will revert since the previous CommitTrans or `RollBackTrans`.
- To close your application's connection to the database, use the `Close` method.
- To execute a command, use the `Execute` method. If the `Execute` is successful, the database server will return a result set. You can then use the `Recordset` object to process the result set.
- To open a connection to your application's data source, use the `Open` method.

***Field* Object Properties** The `Recordset` object will use the `Field` object, because each record returned will contain one or more fields. Table 37.2 lists the `Field` object properties.

Table 37.2 The *Field* object properties.

Property	Description
`ActualSize`	The data's actual length
`Attribute`	The field's data
`DefinedSize`	The field's maximum size
`Name`	The field's name
`NumericScale`	Scale for numeric field values

continues

Table 37.2 Continued

Property	Description
`OriginalValue`	The field's value before it was changed
`Precision`	Precision scale for numeric field values
`Type`	The field's data type
`UnderlyingValue`	The field's value as stored within the database
`Value`	The field's actual value

***Field* Object Methods** Table 37.3 lists the `Field` object methods.

Table 37.3 The Field object methods.

Method	Description
`AppendChunk`	Appends data to the field
`GetChunk`	Gets data from the field

***Recordset* Object Properties** You can create a `Recordset` object in a number of different ways. You can create the object by using the `Connection`, `Command`, or `Recordset` object itself. If you use the ADO `Recordset` object, you can set the resulting recordset's properties, a dynamic cursor you can scroll through. If you use the `Connection` or `Command` object, you cannot set the resulting recordset's properties.

Listing 37.6 shows an example of using the ADO Recordset to create a new `Recordset` object.

Listing 37.6 Creating a new *Recordset* object with *ADO.Recordset*.

```
Set myRecordset = Server.CreateObject("ADO.Recordset")
myRecordset.Source = "
myRecordset.ActiveConnection =
myRecordset.Open
```

Table 37.4 lists the `Recordset` object properties.

Table 37.4 The *Recordset* object properties.

Property	Description
`AbsolutePage`	Indicates the current record's page
`AbsolutePosition`	Indicates the current record's position within the recordset

Property	Description
ActiveConection	Indicates the active connection the recordset is using
BOF	Indicates the beginning of file within the recordset
Bookmark	Indicates a bookmark reference for the recordset
CacheSize	Indicates the cache size for the recordset
CursorType	Indicates the cursor type for the recordset
EditMode	Indicates whether the current record is being edited or added
EOF	Indicates the end of file within the recordset
Filter	Indicates the filter applied to the recordset
LockType	Indicates the type of lock applied to the recordset
MaxRecords	Indicates the maximum number of records the recordset will return
PageCount	Indicates the number of pages within the recordset
PageSize	Indicates the number of records within a page
RecordCount	Indicates the recordset's total number of records
Source	Indicates the recordset's source: table or query
Status	Indicates the given record's status

***Recordset* Object Methods** Table 37.5 lists the `Recordset` object methods.

Table 37.5 The *Recordset* object methods.

Method	Description
Open	Opens a cursor
Update	Updates the table with the current data in the `Recordset` object
Requery	Refreshes the `Recordset` object with the current updated values from the underlying table(s)

***Command* Object Properties** You can use the `Command` object to execute parameterized queries and stored procedures. To execute the query, you must specify the `ActiveConnection` and query. Listing 37.7 shows an example of creating a new `Recordset` object by using the `Command` object.

Listing 37.7 Creating a new *Recordset* object by using the *Command* object.

```
Set myRecordset = Server.CreateObject(ADODB.Command)
myRecordset.ActiveConnection = "myCompany"
myRecordset.CommandText = "qryGetActiveEmployees"
myRecordset.Execute
```

Table 37.6 lists the `Command` object properties.

Table 37.6 The *Command* object properties.

Property	Description
`ActiveConnection`	Indicates the `Connection` object for the `Command` object
`CommandText`	Indicates the command the data source will execute
`CommandTimeout`	Specifies the amount of time (in seconds) the data source will wait for the command to execute. The default is 30 seconds.
`CommandType`	Indicates the type of command the data source will execute
`Prepared`	Used to tell the data provider to compile the command before execution

***Command* Object Methods** Table 37.7 lists the `Command` object methods.

Table 37.7 The *Command* object methods.

Method	Description
`CreateObject`	Creates a new Parameter object
`Execute`	Executes the command contained within the `Command` object's `CommandText` property

***Error* Object Methods** By using the `Error` object, you can log the errors from the datasource. Table 37.8 lists the `Error` collection properties.

Table 37.8 The *Error* collection properties.

Property	Description
`Count`	Indicates the total number of error objects within the error collection
`Item`	Indicates the specific error object within the error collection. The object is identified by number or name

***Error* Collection Methods** Table 37.9 lists the `Error` collection methods.

Table 37.9 The *Error* collection methods.

Method	Description
`Clear`	Removes all error objects from the error collection

***Error* Object Properties** Table 37.10 lists the `Error` object properties.

Table 37.10 The *Error* object properties.

Property	Description
`Description`	Description of the error
`HelpContext`	Help topic within the help file to provide context-sensitive information about the error
`HelpFile`	Help file's name
`NativeError`	Error code specific to the data provider
`Number`	ID uniquely identifying the error
`Source`	Name of the application returning the error
`SQLState`	Five-digit SQL error code

***Parameter* Object Properties** Table 37.11 lists the `Parameter` object properties.

Table 37.11 The *Parameter* object properties.

Property	Description
`Attributes`	Indicates the type of data the parameter object will accept
`Direction`	Indicates whether the parameter is an input, output, or both
`Name`	Parameter's name
`NumericScale`	Scale for numeric parameter values
`Precision`	Precision for numeric parameter values
`Size`	Parameter object's maximum size
`Type`	Parameter's data type
`Value`	Parameter's value

***Parameter* Object Methods** Table 37.12 lists the `Parameter` object methods.

Table 37.12 The *Parameter* object methods.

Method	Description
`AppendChunk`	Appends a large amount of data to the parameter object

***Recordset* Object Methods** Table 37.13 lists the `Recordset` object methods.

Table 37.13 The *Recordset* object methods.

Method	Description
`AddNew`	Creates a new record
`CancelBatch`	Cancels the pending batch update
`CancelUpdate`	Cancels changes made to the current recordset
`Clone`	Creates a new recordset by copying the records from the current recordset
`Close`	Closes the current recordset
`Delete`	Deletes the current record
`GetRows`	Copies the given records into an array
`Move`	Moves to the given record within the recordset
`MoveFirst`	Moves to the recordset's first record
`MoveLast`	Moves to the recordset's last record
`MoveNext`	Moves to the next record within the recordset
`MovePrevious`	Moves to the previous record within the recordset
`NextRecordset`	Closes the current recordset and then opens the next recordset
`Open`	Opens a recordset
`Requery`	Refreshes the recordset by re-executing the query
`Resync`	Syncs the current recordset with the database
`Supports`	Verifies whether the database supports the given function
`Update`	Saves the current record to the database
`UpdateBatch`	Saves changes from the batch update to the database

Browser Capabilities Component

To detect the type of client browser accessing your web site, you can use the Browser Capabilities component. To create an instance of the Browser Capabilities component, you can use the `Server` object's `CreateObject` method. The following line of code shows an example of creating an instance of the Browser Capabilities component:

```
Set bc = Server.CreateObject("MSWC.BrowserType")
```

You can use the Browser Capabilities component along with the `Browscap.ini` file to determine the type of browser and its capabilities. The `Browscap.ini` file will contain information about the different industry-standard browsers. For example, if the client browser does not support ActiveX controls, your web site's server will display corresponding HTML instead. If the client browser does not support frames, for example, your web site's server will use alternative methods to display information. By using the Browser Capabilities component, you can design your web site irrespective of the browser the visitors to your site will use. This way your target audience will not be limited by the type of browser.

Advertisement Rotator

By using the Advertisement Rotator component, you can display ad banners within your web site. In addition, you can change the ad banners dynamically. The Advertisement Rotator component will work with two files—the Rotation Schedule File and Redirection File—to display the ad banners. The Rotation Schedule File is a text file containing information about the ad banner's schedule and frequency. The Redirection File is also a text file containing information about the destination site's URL, should the visitor click on the ad banner.

Permission Checker Component

By using the Permission Checker component, you can determine whether a user has access permission to a given file. As with the Browser Capabilities component, you can use the `Server` object's `CreateObject` method to create an instance of the Permission Checker component. The following line of code shows an example of creating an instance of the Permission Checker component:

```
Set pc = Server.CreateObject("MSWC.PermissionChecker")
```

The Permission Checker component includes one method: `HasAccess`. The `HasAccess` method will return `True` if the user has access to the given file. The method will return `False` if the user does not have access to the given file. The following line of code shows the `HasAccess` method's syntax:

```
HasAccess(FilePath)
```

Content Linking Component

By using the Content Linking component, you can design and develop a navigation scheme for your web site. Similar to the other components, you can use the `Server` object's `CreateObject` method to create an instance of the Content Linking component. The following line of code shows an example of creating an instance of the Content Linking component:

```
Set cl = Server.CreateObject("MSWC.NextLink")
```

You can use the Content Linking component's methods with the Content Linking List file to determine the navigation (for example, move first, move next, move previous, move last) from the current page within your web site. Note that `NextLink.dll` represents the Content Linking component.

Page Counter Component

By using the Page Counter component, you can determine the number of times a page from your web site has been requested. As a result, you can determine the amount of interest your web site generates. You can use the `Server` object's `CreateObject` method to create an instance of the Page Counter component. The following line of code shows an example of creating an instance of the Page Counter component:

```
Set pc = Server.CreateObject("MSWC.PageCounter")
```

You can use the Page Counter component's methods with the Hits Count Data file to retrieve and save the number of accesses to your web site. `PageCnt.Dll` represents the Page Counter component.

Creating Your Own Server-Side Components

In addition to using the existing server-side components, you can also create your own server-side components. You can use a variety of tools to create server-side components. For example, you can use Visual Studio 97—a suite of Microsoft's programming tools—to write your own Active Server components. Visual Studio 97 includes the following:

- *Visual C++* By using Visual C++, you can create lean and mean Active Server components. However, programming in C++ is not the easiest of tasks.
- *Visual Basic* For those looking for a simpler approach to building components, Visual Basic is an ideal choice. Programming in Visual Basic is much easier than programming in Visual C++. You can quickly create Active Server components by using Visual Basic.

ActiveX Controls and Active Server Components

ActiveX controls will reside and execute on the client. Active Server components will reside and execute on the server. Depending on your application's business requirements, you may build a visual or nonvisual ActiveX control. However, all Active Server components will be nonvisual in nature, because Active Server components will not have a user interface component as an ActiveX control can. Active Server components are business components performing a specific business functionality. An Active Server component will on the server side, and you can usually implement the component to provide specific services. You can actually build an Active Server component from existing ActiveX controls.

You can use the same tools, such as Visual Basic and Visual C++, to create both ActiveX controls and Active Server components. This is because both ActiveX controls and Active Server components support the same COM interface. For example, you can use Visual Basic to create both ActiveX controls and Active Server components. You can also use Visual C++ with the Active Template Library (ATL) to create Active Server components. You can use the ActiveX Software Development Kit (SDK) with Visual C++ to create ActiveX controls.

Active Server Components

There are two types of Active Server components—*in-process* and *out-process*. An EXE is an out-process server, and a DLL is an in-process server. A server is an out-process server if the server will execute within its own address space. A server is an in-process server if the server cannot execute within its own address space. For example, you can run an EXE by itself, but you cannot run a DLL by itself. A DLL will run within the calling application's address space, usually an EXE.

Third-Party Active Server Components

You can also integrate third-party server-side components into your application. A number of third-party Active Server components are available in the market today, and this number will continue to grow. Table 37.14 lists a few interesting Active Server components.

Table 37.14 Third-party ASP components.

Component Name	Description
WorldWideChat 1.0	With WWC 1.0, you can integrate chat capability into your ASP web site (**http://www.digitalfoundry.com/wwc/support/index.html**)
ComponentWorks	You can use ComponentWorks Active Server component to implement web-based data acquisition and test measurements (**http://www.natinst.com/cworks**)
Chili!Reports	By using the Chili!Reports server components, you can schedule, push, and deliver reports to mailboxes (**http://www.chilisoft.net/chilireports**)
Chart FX Internet Edition	By using the Chart FX Internet edition, you can provide interactive charts across your Internet/Intranet sites (**http://www.softwarefx.com/cfxie/default.asp**)
webMOM	With webMOM, web applications can access data residing across a variety of platforms and legacy systems (**http://webmomx.netimage.com/**)

Developing ASP Applications with Visual InterDev

Visual InterDev is a web programming tool for the advanced web programmer and developer. Visual InterDev provides an integrated, visual development environment that includes all the tools you need to design and develop dynamic, data-driven web applications. By using Visual InterDev, you can build Active Server Pages applications. By using Active Server Pages, you can develop sophisticated server-side processing for your web applications. These include server-side scripting, database access, site management, and building reusable server components.

In addition, you can build state-of-the-art, data-driven web applications by using Visual InterDev. You can connect your web applications to enterprise-strength databases, such as Microsoft SQL Server, Oracle, and Informix, by using Open Database Connectivity (ODBC). You can also connect your web applications to desktop databases such as Microsoft Access.

By using Visual InterDev, you can easily integrate components such as Java applets, ActiveX controls, Active Server components, COM objects, and so on within your HTML and ASP pages. In addition, you can integrate third-party components.

Highlights of Visual InterDev

By using Visual InterDev, you can build Active Server components (formerly known as OLE Automation Servers). You can use the components for your application's server-side processing and use Active Server scripting to integrate the components within your application's ASP.

Developer Studio—A Common Development Environment

Visual InterDev's Developer Studio is similar to the Developer Studio you see within Visual C++ and Visual J++. So, if you are familiar with any of the other tools, you will find yourself right at home with Visual InterDev's development environment.

Visual InterDev includes a powerful set of tools you can use to make your web application data-aware and data-driven. Visual InterDev's main database components include the following:

- *Database Designer* You can use the Database Designer to design and manage Microsoft SQL Server 6.5 databases. By using the Database Designer, you can create, set up, and manage SQL Server databases.
- *Query Designer* You can use the integrated Query Designer to construct your queries visually. The Query Designer, in turn, will automatically translate the queries into Data Manipulation Language (DML) statements. In addition, you can use the Query Designer to test the SQL queries you build and construct stored procedures for your application.
- *Database Wizards* You can use the integrated Database Wizard to build data-aware ASP pages. The Wizard will step you through the process of creating such pages.

Visual InterDev supports both standard and design-time ActiveX controls. The design-time ActiveX controls will automatically generate the client-side or server-side scripts for your application. In addition, they can also generate the HTML content you can view by using any browser on any platform.

Just as you can integrate Visual SourceSafe with your Visual C++ and Visual Basic development environment, you can also integrate Visual SourceSafe with your Visual InterDev development environment to enable team development and version control.

Besides the tightly integrated database component, Visual InterDev also includes a version of FrontPage WYSIWYG HTML editor, Microsoft Image Composer, which you can use to create, edit, and manipulate all kinds of images, and Microsoft Music Producer to integrate sounds into your web pages. Visual InterDev also includes a Media Manager you can use to track your multimedia resources, such as sound clips, video clips, and images.

In addition, Visual InterDev includes an Object Editor (also available within ActiveX Control Pad) you can use to integrate Java applets and ActiveX controls into your ASP pages.

Similar to the ActiveX Control Pad, Visual InterDev also includes a Script Wizard you can use for ActiveX scripting and a 2.5D HTML Layout Editor you can use to lay out your web page's design.

Troubleshooting ASP Applications

This section outlines two troubleshooting tips for ASP applications.

Installing ASP

If you would like to use the Personal web Server (PWS) with your ASP applications, you should install the PWS before you install ASP. However, you must not have the PWS running within the background. The installation program will configure your ASP installation based on the PWS's directory and file structure. This means you can use ASP with the PWS as your web server. If you have the PWS running within the background, the PWS files will remain in use and the installation program will not be able to configure your ASP installation properly.

How Can You Use a Port Other than Port 80 for Your Web Server and FrontPage Extensions?

By default, the installation program will copy the Extensions on your system's port 80. Port 80 is the standard port to connect your application's web server and extensions. You can connect other servers to the remaining ports within your system. If you would like to install the Extensions on a port other than port 80, shut down the server and use the FrontPage Server Administrator to choose a different port.

PART VII

Java

CHAPTER 38

Developing Java Applets

by Paul Santa Maria

In this chapter

An Introduction to Java

"Java," to quote its authors on the subject, "is a simple, robust, object-oriented, platform-independent, multi-threaded, dynamic, general-purpose, programming environment."

Although this rather immodest sentence was meant as a humorous reference to all the marketing buzzwords and hoopla surrounding Java, the authors quite seriously go on to back up each of their claims. You can read the entire white paper from which this quote was taken at Sun Microsystem's web site at **http://java.sun.com/aboutJava/index.html**.

This chapter gives you a quick, practical, "hands-on" introduction to the Java programming language. To use Java effectively, it is every bit as important to understand "object-oriented design" and to be familiar with Java's rich and extensive set of class libraries (network, lang, and the AWT, among others) as it is to merely learn the syntax of the language. This chapter gives equal weight to each of these aspects of Java.

After you learn the rudiments of programming in Java and you have had a chance to experiment with this new language for a while, then you, too, will share the excitement and agree with some (or all) of the preceding claims. The intent is not to show you everything, but to give you a practical, hands-on "jump start" in learning the Java language. Read on to learn what Java is, what it is not, and how to use it effectively on your own web pages.

What Exactly Is Java?

The term "Java" can mean any of several completely different things, depending on who you talk to, such as the following:

- *JavaScript*. JavaScript is an adaptation of Netscape's own scripting language. It consists of Java-like commands embedded directly into your HTML document. Rather than download a precompiled Java executable (more on this later), JavaScript is interpreted on-the-fly, right along with your web page's HTML, inline images, and so on.

  Although there are many similarities (including the name), JavaScript and Java are two completely different things. Please refer to Chapter 15, "Introduction to JavaScripting," for a complete discussion of JavaScript.

- *Standalone Java programs*. The Java programming language was originally designed and implemented as a language for programming consumer electronics. Standalone Java programs do *not* need to be run from inside a web page. In fact, things such as URLs and the Internet don't necessarily enter into the picture at all.

  Because of Java's inherent runtime safety and platform independence, standalone Java language programs can easily enjoy as much success in areas such as embedded systems software and database access middleware as Java applets are already enjoying among web developers.

- *Java applets*. The third and final use of the term Java applies to Java applets. *Applets* are specialized Java programs especially designed for executing within Internet web pages. To run a Java applet, you need a Java-enabled web browser such as Netscape Communicator or Microsoft's Internet Explorer. These and other web browsers can all handle standard HTML, recognizing applet tags within an HTML web page and downloading and executing the specified Java program (or programs) in the context of a Java Virtual Machine.

Java applets are a specialized subset of the overall Java development environment. Designing and writing applets is the topic of this chapter.

As discussed in greater depth at the end of this chapter, Java is more than just a programming language. The applets you code rely critically on these three overlapping technologies:

- *Java compiler*. Unlike traditional computer language compilers, which target a specific combination host CPU and operating system, Java compilers generate a universally understood "byte code." This promises the software developer's mantra of "Write once, run anywhere."

  But just like traditional languages, vendors sometimes try to differentiate their compilers with neat "features"—features that *break* portability and lock you into their productions.

  And just like other languages, Java evolves. The program you write on today's Java compiler *won't* necessarily run on yesterday's Java interpreter. Portability concerns are discussed later in this chapter.

- *Java Virtual Machine*. One of Java's key features is its portability—the "Write once, Run anywhere" philosophy discussed previously. To make this possible, Java's designers didn't only create a programming language: They also specified a Java Virtual Machine (JVM) for running Java programs.

  The most popular examples of JVMs are Java-enabled web browsers such as Netscape Communicator and Microsoft Internet Explorer.

- *Java application frameworks*. To accomplish any useful work, a program—*any* program written in *any* language—needs some kind of runtime library support: to accept user input, open files, create subtasks, and so on.

  Today's GUI-based, Internet-aware applications not only require considerable runtime support, they also tend to be *extremely* complex to program.

  Java environment offers an extremely rich programming and runtime environment that addresses both of these issues—powerful capabilities such as database connectivity, security, and distributed computing, as well as high-level programming interfaces to simply and easily harness all that power.

Why Java?

At the time of this writing (late 1997), the Internet is arguably still in its infancy as a medium for dynamic mass communications.

Although the basic technology that makes up the Internet has been around for many years, it was the introduction of a simple graphical user interface—the web browser—that suddenly made it so incredibly popular among millions of users worldwide.

Most web pages now seen on the Internet have a relatively primitive, static character. Take away all the gaudy flying logos and ticker tapes, and you are usually left with one of the following:

- Static HTML, passively displayed by your web browser
- Simplistic HTML Forms
- Graphics imagemaps

Although forms and imagemaps allow a measure of user interaction, all the main processing is done remotely on the web server. For any frequently used site (such as **www.netscape.com**), this incurs a considerable load on the server. Moreover, the final result of all the server's hard work is (you guessed it!) more static HTML, which is downloaded only to be passively displayed by your web browser.

This kind of interaction is not the style of computing preferred by a generation of users weaned on productivity tools such as VisiCalc, PageMaker, Microsoft Word, PowerPoint, Lotus Notes, and—above all—PGA Golf. This generation of users are all used to the benefits of running applications locally, on their very own personal computers.

Java promises an alternative model for web content—a model much closer to the spirit of computer programs people are running on their own PCs. The crucial difference between a Java-based program and a traditional PC application is that Java programs are, by nature, network-aware and truly distributed. As creatures of the Internet, Java programs offer all the benefits of locally executed programs—responsiveness, the capability to take advantage of local computing resources, and so on. Yet at the same time, Java programs break the shackles of being tied to a single PC. They can suddenly take advantage of computing resources from the entire, global Internet! You will get a taste of this awesome potential as you continue to learn about writing Java applets.

In the context of the web, Java applets offer the following advantages:

- Java applets are dynamic, whereas native HTML is relatively static.
- Because they run on the client, not on the server, Java applets can make better use of computing resources.
- Java is designed to be "architecture neutral." This is the software equivalent of "one size fits all." For vendors, it means larger potential markets, fewer inventory headaches, and the elimination of costly "software porting" efforts. For consumers, it means lower costs, increased choices, and greater interoperability between components.
- Although other languages can be considered architecture neutral, Java programs can typically execute much faster and more efficiently.

  Because a Java program consists of bytecodes, it tends to be smaller and lends itself better to transferring across the Internet. The bytecode scheme also lends itself to far greater levels of runtime optimization than scripting languages. Just In Time Java compilers such as those built into Netscape Communicator and Internet Explorer now make Java programs run every bit as fast as native executables!

Basic Language Constructs

Java syntax is very similar to C and C++. At first glance, this makes the language immediately accessible to the millions of practicing C/C++ programmers. As you will see in the next section, however, Java and C might look very much alike, but they are *not* identical, and sometimes apparent similarities can be misleading.

The following four tables, Tables 38.1 through 38.4, summarize Java's basic language constructs.

Table 38.1 Basic language constructs (Java types).

Type	Example	Notes
`boolean`	`boolean flag = false;`	A Java `Boolean` is just `true` or `false`. It cannot be cast to `char` or `int`.
`char`	`char c[] = {'A','\uu42','C'};`	A Java `char` is a 16-bit Unicode character. You will usually use the Java class `String` instead.
`byte`	`byte b = 0x7f;`	8-bit signed integer (–127 .. 127).
`short`	`short s = 32767;`	16-bit signed integer (–32,768 .. 32767).
`int`	`int i = 2;`	32-bit signed integer.
`long`	`long l = 2L;`	64-bit signed integer. Note the suffix `L` is be required for a `long` (decimal) literal.
`float`	`float x = 2.0F;`	32-bit IEEE754 number. Note the suffix `F` is required for a `float` literal.
`double`	`double d = 2.0;`	64-bit IEEE754 number (15 significant digits).

The concept of "data type" has to do with what range of values a data item may possess and what operations are permitted on that item. You would use a "string" type, for example, to print out a word, a "integer" type to increment a counter, or a "floating point" type to calculate a scientific equation.

Some languages, such as Ada, Eiffel, and Pascal are "strongly typed." You must explicitly declare the "type" of every single variable that you use, and you can't arbitrarily mix or inter-convert types. In these languages, "typing" provides a binding contract between the type's author and any clients of that type.

continues

http://java.sun.com/docs/index.html This site will give you all the details on Sun's official Java documentation, including reference manuals and language tutorials.

continued

Other languages, such as JavaScript, Smalltalk, or Visual Basic are "untyped": they enable you to create variables on-the-fly and to freely interchange numbers, text, or pretty much anything you

Leveraging Java Classes and Packages

Although operators and data types are obviously very important in Java, *classes* are where the real action is.

In his text *Object-Oriented Modeling and Design*, James Rumbaugh defined a "class" as describing "...a group of objects with similar properties (attributes), common behavior (operations), common relationships to other objects, and common semantics." An object, on the other hand, is just an *instance* of a class, dynamically created by the program during runtime. In other words, classes *define* objects; *objects*, on the other hand, are specific, concrete instances of a class.

In Java, just about everything is a class. Unlike C and C++, Java has no structs and no free subprograms (a *free subprogram* is a subroutine or function that exists independently of a class). Most of the power of C++ stems from the simple notion of extending C's basic struct into the notion of a C++ class, which encapsulates both state (program data) and methods (a program's algorithms) into a single logical entity. Java completes this transition by recognizing that, after you have the power of classes, structs become irrelevant.

Java was designed to be both a simpler and a safer language than C++. Many features of C++ such as multiple inheritance and operator overloading were deliberately left out of Java because Java's authors felt that they could make their new language less complex and make Java programs less prone to common C++ programming and design errors.

Table 38.5 gives a brief overview of Java classes in comparison to C++.

Table 38.5 Java class versus C class constructs.

Construct	C++	Java
Class	Yes	Yes
Single Inheritance	Yes	Yes
Constructors	Yes	Yes
Overloading	Yes	No
Multiple Inheritance	Yes	No
Destructors	Yes	No
Templates	Yes	No
Packages	No	Yes
Interfaces	No	Yes

Basically, traditional methods force you to "think like the machine" and break things down into modules, variables, parameters, and the like. Object-oriented methods enable you to think at a much higher level—in terms of objects, their behavior, and how they relate to each other.

The interesting thing is that Java (unlike, for example, C++) forces you to think in an object-oriented style. When you work with Java, you will probably find yourself spending most of your development time figuring out what "objects" your program needs, and browsing to see whether your library already has existing (canned) classes that you can inherit from, thus re-using existing code with little or no additional effort on your part.

This is a marked contrast from traditional programming styles in languages such as FORTRAN, C, or Pascal, where the bulk of your effort goes into "decomposing" a problem into modules, and then creating algorithms the modules use to process data. In many subtle (or sometimes not so subtle) ways, Java almost forces the programmer to abandon old procedural habits in favor of a more object-oriented perspective.

This discussion is continued later in this chapter. For now, however, it is time to get on with the fun stuff: coding and running your very first Java applet!

Java 101: HelloWorld

Many excellent, graphical tools for developing Java applets on the market. Regardless of what tool you—or your company—choose, you should still be familiar with Sun's command-line JDK. There are several reasons for this:

- Periodically uploading and installing Sun's current JDK is the best way to "keep up to speed" with all the latest Java APIs.
- The JDK is an excellent "reference platform" to make sure your code is portable to as wide an audience as possible.
- The JDK is easy to install, it doesn't take an excessive amount of disk space, it contains some excellent tools, and it is absolutely free.

In this chapter, you will use the following JDK tools:

- `javac` The Java compiler
- `appletviewer` A Java Virtual Machine for testing and debugging your applet
- `javadoc` Automatically generates an online manual documenting your program's classes

ON THE WEB

http://www.javasoft.com/ You can download a free copy of the latest Java JDK at this URL.

NOTE Windows users need to be running Windows 95, Windows NT, or higher to develop Java applets. This is because Java requires a 32-bit operating system and long, case-sensitive filenames.

Writing the Program

First, create a program source file, as shown in Listing 38.1.

Listing 38.1 HelloWorld.java First Java applet.

```
/**
 * HelloWorld: A first Java applet
 *
 * @version 1.0, DATE: 10.31.97
 * @author Paul Santa Maria
 */
import java.applet.*;
import java.awt.*;      // User Interface components

public class HelloWorld extends Applet
{
  private Font f;

  public void paint (Graphics g)
  {
    g.setFont (f);
    g.setColor (Color.red);
    g.drawString ("Hello from Java!", 0, 50);
  }

  public void init ()
  {
    f = new Font ("Helvetica", Font.BOLD, 24);
  }
}
```

NOTE You must use a text editor that supports long, case-sensitive filenames.

The versions of Notepad, WordPad, and Edit that come with Windows 95 work fine. Microsoft Word 95 or higher also works. Older versions of Word for 16-bit Windows do not work.

NOTE Your Java source file must have the same name as the main class. That is, you must name this file HelloWorld.java, which corresponds to the main class `HelloWorld`.

Furthermore, the capitalization must also match exactly. If your class is named `HelloWorld` (capital *H*, capital *W*) but your source file is named helloworld.java, the program will not compile.

Complete source code for each of these programs is included on the accompanying CD.

You may recall from this chapter's earlier discussion that Java applets are specifically designed to run from within an HTML web page. Therefore, you should write a simple web page to test your new applet (see Listing 38.2).

Listing 38.2 Example.html HTML web page that calls the applet.

```
<HTML>
<TITLE>Hello World!</TITLE>
<HEAD>
<BODY>
<H1>HelloWorld: a first Java Applet:</H1>
<P>
<APPLET CODE="HelloWorld.class" WIDTH=250 HEIGHT=100>
If you can read this, then your browser is not set up for Java...
</APPLET>
<P>
</BODY>
</HTML>
```


Notice the special "`<APPLET ...>`" HTML tag. This tells your web browser that you are using an applet and where to find it.

The `CODE` attribute enables you to specify fully qualified URL (for example, **http://www.mycompany.com/myApplet.class**), but for the purposes here you can just default to the current directory.

Any web browser that doesn't understand applets will just ignore all `<APPLET>`, `</APPLET>`, and `<PARAMETER>` tags. You can take advantage of this to display alternative text (such as the "If you can read this…") to alert your audience that they are missing out on your cool Java applets and really ought to upgrade their browsers.

Your HTML source file is not subject to the same strict rules about long filenames and case sensitivity as your Java source files. The file here is called example.html. You can pretty much name yours anything you want, provided it has an ".htm" or ".html" suffix.

Finally, write a batch file to compile and execute your program (see Listing 38.3).

Listing 38.3 Demo.bat Windows batch file for compiling and running the applet.

```
@rem Compile and execute  "Hello world" sample program
javac -deprecation HelloWorld.java
appletviewer example.html
```

Compiling and Running the Program

To compile and run a simple Java applet, follow these steps:

1. Write your Java source program (here, `HelloWorld.java`).
2. Write an HTML web file to call the applet.

3. Compile the applet. For example:

    javac HelloWorld.java

4. Display your HTML file by using appletviewer or your favorite web browser. For example:

    appletviewer example.html

NOTE This method assumes that you are using Sun's JDK and that you have your Windows 95 PATH and CLASSPATH environment variables set correctly.

Following is a sample from an Autoexec.bat file that sets these two variables:

```
PATH=c:\windows;c:\windows\command;c:\java\bin
CLASSPATH=c:\java\lib;
```

Note that Setup.exe for the Windows 95 or Windows NT JDK should automatically install these definitions in your Autoexec.bat for you.

Figure 38.1 shows the result of your very first program, as seen through SunSoft's appletviewer.

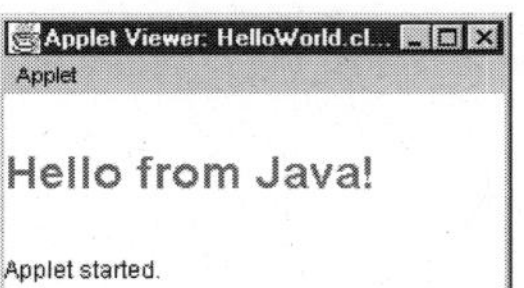

FIG. 38.1 The JDK provides a simple appletviewer for previewing and testing your applets.

Running Your Applet from a Web Browser

You may have noticed that none of your HTML (`HelloWorld: a first Java Applet`, and so on) showed up when you looked at it through appletviewer. This is because it is not a full-fledged web browser. appletviewer is intended only for viewing applets.

Although the appletviewer is convenient for development—to see how your applets will actually look and to understand how they will really behave—you need to run them through a web browser.

Now run the same Java program using Microsoft Internet Explorer (see Figure 38.2). Start Internet Explorer, choose File, Open, Browse, and then choose the disk, directory, and filename of your HTML page (for example, *example.html*).

Finally, use Netscape Communicator (see Figure 38.3). Bring up Communicator, choose File, Open Page, Choose File, and then select your HTML page's disk, directory, and filename.

TIP Even an applet as simple as this one might look different when run on different web browsers.

Depending on how widely you expect your applets to be circulated, it is usually a good idea to have several different browsers, and several different versions, handy for testing.

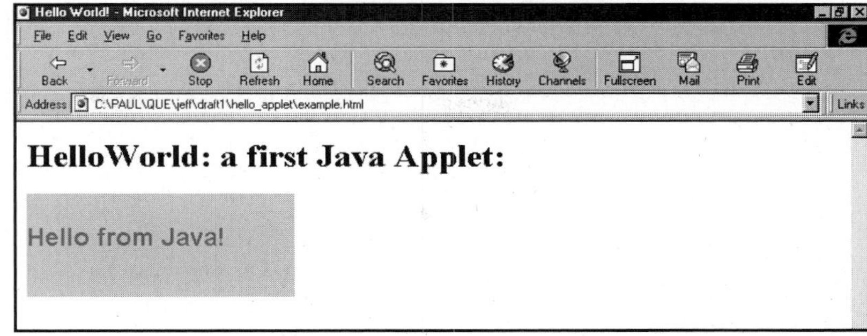

FIG. 38.2 You can use any Java-enabled browser, such as Internet Explorer (shown here) or Netscape Communicator, to run your applets.

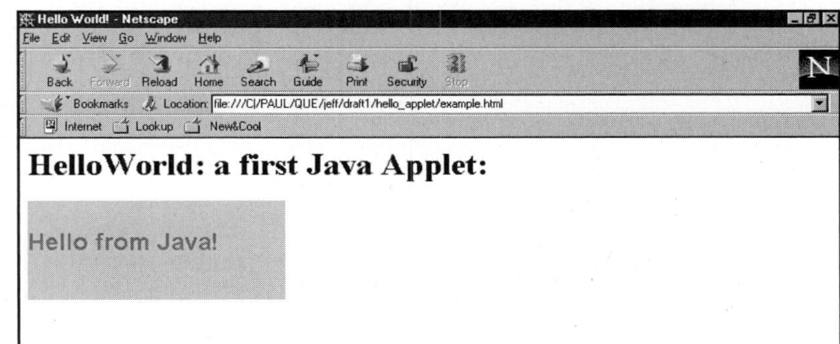

FIG. 38.3 Netscape Communicator (shown here) and Internet Explorer are two of the best-known Java-enabled web browsers.

Troubleshooting HelloWorld

Even with an applet as simple as this, a number of things could go wrong. Take a look at some common "gotcha's":

- `javac: Bad command or filename error` This probably means that you didn't install the JDK (Sun's Java Development Kit) or that it is not in your DOS path.

  If you are sure that you installed the JDK, all you need to do is set your DOS `PATH`. The easiest way to fix this problem is to make sure `PATH` and `CLASSPATH` are correctly defined in `AUTOEXEC.BAT` and then reboot your PC. Following is a sample `AUTOEXEC` entry:

  ```
  PATH=c:\windows;c:\windows\command;c:\java\bin
  CLASSPATH=c:\java\lib;.
  ```

- Extraneous `thread applet-HelloWorld.class find class HelloWorld` messages This probably means that `CLASSPATH` is not defined correctly. The solution is the same as for the preceding problem: double-check your AUTOEXEC.BAT definitions for `PATH` and `CLASSPATH` and reboot your PC.

  `CLASSPATH` consists of a list of directory paths in which appletviewer looks for Java classes. Each different pathname is separated by a semicolon.

  Make sure that the current directory is in your `CLASSPATH` list. Reboot your PC with the new `autoexec.bat` and try again.

- `HelloWorld.java:26: Class gelloWorld not found in type declaration` This or any similar-sounding compiler error probably means you mis-typed something.

  Carefully double-check every place in the program where you meant to type the name in question (here, `HelloWorld`). Be sure each occurrence matches exactly (including capitalization—Java is case-sensitive).

  In this case, you carefully double-checked your program and discover that you typed `gelloWorld` rather than `HelloWorld`. It compiled clean the next time you ran demo.bat.
- `HelloWorld.java:24: Warning: Public class HelloWorld must be defined in a file called HelloWorld.java` The name of your Java source file must match the name of your public Java class exactly.

  For the sample program, this means the class needs to be called `HelloWorld`, the source file needs to be called `HelloWorld.java`, and the HTML `<APPLET>` tag needs to specify `HelloWorld.class`, or your program will neither compile cleanly nor execute.

  To fix this problem, carefully double-check everything for exact spelling and capitalization, and then re-run `demo.bat`.
- Nothing happens If you are running Internet Explorer and you see the HTML, but not your applet, your browser probably is not configured to run Java. Choose View, Options, Security, and look at your Active Content group to make sure Java is enabled.

  You must check the following:
  - Allow downloading of active content
  - Enable Java programs. You should also set your browser's Safety Level to Medium.

HelloWorld as a Standalone Application

You don't need to limit your Java programming to just writing applets that run inside of web pages.

It is often more appropriate—or just more convenient—to write a "standalone" Java application. A *servlet*—a Java program that runs on your web server—is one example of a standalone Java application. The StopWatch program you develop shortly is another example.

Writing the Standalone Application

It is not much work at all to convert an applet into a standalone Java application. To do so, just follow these steps:

1. A standalone application does not subclass `Applet`. Change this. Usually, your application's main class will be `Frame` instead:

   Applet version:

   ```
   public class HelloWorld extends Applet
   ```

   Standalone version:

   ```
   public class HelloWorld extends Frame
   ```

2. You can delete the line "`import package java.awt.applet`."
3. A Java applet overrides the `init ()` method. A standalone application doesn't use `init ()`.

   Move all the code from the old `init ()` into `main ()` or into the Frame's constructor method:

   Applet version:

   ```
   public void init ()
   {
    f = new Font ("Helvetica", Font.BOLD, 24);
   }
   ```

   Standalone version:

   ```
   // main: application initialization code goes here
   public static void main (String[] args)
   {
    Frame myFrame = new HelloWorld ();
      myFrame.setTitle ("Hello World!");
      myFrame.setSize (250, 100);
      f = new Font ("Helvetica", Font.BOLD, 24);
      myFrame.show ();
      }
   ```
4. Delete your applet's `init ()` method.
5. A standalone application typically needs to do a little more setup work: organize its frame layout, set the window title, and so on.
6. Finally you need to run your standalone application using the JDK `java` interpreter rather than the appletviewer or a web browser.

Here is your completed Java application:

Listing 38.4 HelloWorld.java A simple standalone Java application.

```
/**
 * HelloWorld: Standalone Java application
 *
 * NOTES:
 * 1. Compare this standalone Java application
 *    with "HelloWorld" applet.
 *
 * 2. Our first Java 1.0/1.1 compatibility issue.
 *
 * 3. "DrawCenteredString" example.
 *
 * @version 1.0, DATE: 10.31.97
 * @author Paul Santa Maria
 */
import java.awt.*;              // User Interface components

public class HelloWorld extends Frame
```

continues

Listing 38.4 Continued

```
{
  private static Font f;

  private void DrawCenteredString (Graphics g, String s)
  {
    Dimension d = getSize ();  // Java 1.1 only!
    FontMetrics fm = getFontMetrics (f);
    int x =
      (d.width - fm.stringWidth (s)) / 2;
    int y =
      d.height -
        ( (d.height - fm.getHeight ()) / 2 );

    g.drawString (s, x, y);
  }

  // paint: window refresh code goes here
  public void paint (Graphics g)
  {
    g.setFont (f);
    g.setColor (Color.red);
    DrawCenteredString (g, "Hello from Java!");
  }

  // main: application initialization code goes here
  public static void main (String[] args)
  {
     Frame myFrame = new HelloWorld ();
     myFrame.setTitle ("Hello World!");
     myFrame.setSize (250, 100);
// NOTE: "setSize ()" needs Java 1.1!
// Substitute "resize ()" for Java 1.0 compatibility
     f = new Font ("Helvetica", Font.BOLD, 24);
     myFrame.show ();
   }
}
```

The biggest practical difference between applets running on a web page and standalone applications is that the application can generally be "trusted" and allowed to do more: open files, establish TCP/IP connections with arbitrary computers, and so on. Applets, on the other hand, are restricted from doing anything that might compromise the security of the host computer. The restricted environment that Java-enabled browsers set up for applets to run in is called a "sandbox."

Compiling and Running the Standalone Application

As you might expect, you also need to change the `demo.bat` slightly:

Listing 38.5 Standalone application *demo.bat*.

```
@rem Compile and execute standalone  "Hello world"
javac -deprecation HelloWorld.java
java HelloWorld
```

FIG. 38.4
Standalone "Hello World" Java application.

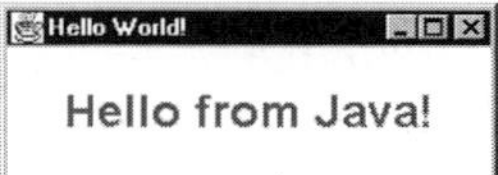

Figure 38.4 shows what the application looks like when you run it on the `java` interpreter.

NOTE If you look carefully at `HelloWorld`, you will see that a new method is there that was not in the applet version: `DrawCenteredString ()`:

```
private void DrawCenteredString (Graphics g, String s)
{
  Dimension d = getSize ();  // Java 1.1 only!
  FontMetrics fm = getFontMetrics (f);
  int x =
    (d.width - fm.stringWidth (s)) / 2;
  int y =
    d.height -
      ( (d.height - fm.getHeight ()) / 2 );

  g.drawString (s, x, y);
}
```

This illustrates how you can use `getSize ()` if you ever need to find out the height and width of your "Component" (here, Frame).

`DrawCenteredString ()` also introduces `FontMetrics` objects and shows how you can use them.

Finally, a couple of Java 1.1 dependencies are introduced: because the Java 1.1 APIs `getSize ()`, and `setSize ()` are used, this simple program *will not run* on a Java 1.0 interpreter.

For reasons discussed in greater detail later, you *should* use Java 1.1 APIs whenever possible. Be aware, however, of the portability issues you might face in doing so!

Java and Object-Oriented Design

Sometimes programmers become impatient with the analysis and design phases of software development, preferring to jump right in and start coding. This attitude is often justified. For small programs such as those found in textbooks, it makes little sense to go to all the trouble of requirements, analysis, design, integration, text, and so on. For a small program, you just fire up your compiler, whip up some code, and voila! You're done.

But life just isn't like that for larger, more complex, mission-critical applications. For projects such as those, you need to sit down and plan ahead. One of the beautiful things about Java is that it is expressly designed to scale up to large, mission-critical projects. You will be doing yourself a tremendous favor if you get into the habit of thinking about design issues now, when you're starting out on the simple programs. As a consequence, it will be second nature for you later when you need it on your large-scale projects.

Take a look at a class hierarchy diagram for the simple `HelloWorld` applet (see Figure 38.5).

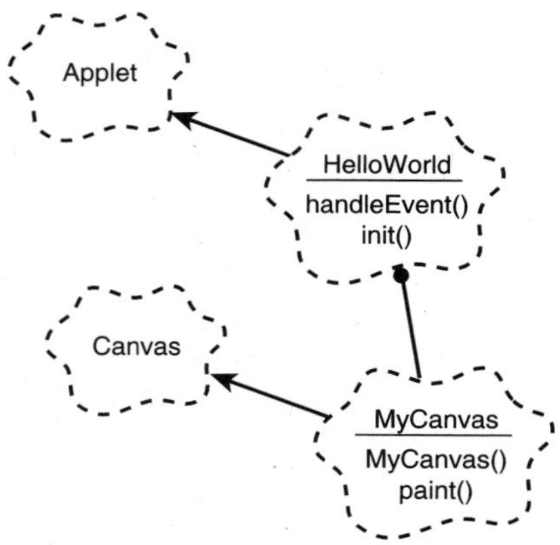

FIG. 38.5
Class diagrams are powerful design tools that show you what your classes do, what they contain, and how they relate to each other.

You may recognize the two "clouds" HelloWorld and MyCanvas. These correspond to the two classes, `HelloWorld` and `MyCanvas`, that were used in the program.

The arrows connecting HelloWorld with Applet and MyCanvas with Canvas illustrate an *inheritance relationship*. This is often called an *is-a relationship*; class `HelloWorld` *is-an* `Applet`; `MyCanvas` *is-a* `Canvas`. `Applet` and `Canvas` are called *parent classes*; `MyCanvas` and `HelloWorld` are called *child* or *subclasses.*

The HelloWorld and MyCanvas clouds also list each class's methods. You may want to avoid cluttering your diagram by listing only the few most important methods. This diagram lists all the methods that were overridden from the base class: `init()`, `handleEvent()`, and `paint()`. Also shown is the constructor method `MyCanvas()`.

The line that connects HelloWorld and MyCanvas is a *use*, or *has-a relationship*. This means that class `HelloWorld` (which is a kind of `applet`) makes use of `MyCanvas` (which is, in turn, a subclass of `Canvas`).

Why is this important?

Basically, when you use Java classes, you are writing a relatively small amount of your own code to leverage the tremendous functionality that is already built in to Java.

Java knows how to create a window, how to field events, how to display fonts, and so on. You just "inherit" from some pre-existing class that does *almost* what you want, tweak it slightly with some new functionality, and then shamelessly use the whole thing as though you had done all the work yourself.

A class diagram for the standalone "Hello World" application would be practically identical: You would just change the "Applet" class to "Frame," and change the `init ()` method to `main ()`.

This might seem like a lot of work just to display a line of plain, old boring text. Fear not—you are going to apply your hard-earned knowledge and try some Java graphics in the next (only *slightly* more difficult) example: a Mandelbrot Set program.

If you're interested in reading more on the subject, here are two excellent books:

- ***Object-Oriented Analysis and Design With Applications, Second Edition***, by Grady Booch, (Benjamin Cumming, 1994)
- ***Object-Oriented Modeling and Design***, by Rumbaugh, Blaha, Premerlani, Eddy and Lorensen, (Prentice-Hall, 1991)

ON THE WEB

One of the nifty things about using Java is that all the principal documentation is completely online in web format. Be sure to upload a copy Java API manual when you install the JDK. (They are now two separate uploads.)

The latest-and-greatest version of the manual is also available directly on the Internet at the following addresses:

http://www.java.sun.docs/

http://www.javasoft.com/products/JDK/CurrentRelease/api/

Mandelbrot Set: An Introduction to Java Graphics

Fractals are an area of mathematics dealing with fractional dimensions. You probably recall from high school geometry that a line is a one-dimensional object, a square is two-dimensional, a cube is three-dimensional, and so forth. This all has to do with the traditional, comfortable world of Euclidean geometry, where two parallel lines never meet and the sum of the three angles in a triangle will always equal 180°. Fractals deal with a whole other spectrum of dimensions, one in which a line might have a dimension not of 1, but of, say, 1.3756.

Around the turn of this century, mathematicians and philosophers began conceiving strange, abstract worlds where the common sense rules governing the Euclidean universe were no longer true. The notion of fractional dimensions was conceived at that time, but it wasn't until the advent of computers nearly 60 years later that it became practical to investigate the subject. The pioneer who did this—and who coined the term fractal—was Dr. Benoit Mandelbrot, of the IBM Research Labs.

Although fractals have proven themselves to be of practical value in everything from CGI special effects in Hollywood movies to fabulously efficient digital image compression techniques, this discussion is interested in one kind of fractal—a Mandelbrot Set—for the following reasons:

- The Mandelbrot Set is easy to code.
- The Mandelbrot Set presents an interesting picture.
- The program to plot a Mandelbrot Set is sufficiently compute-intensive to yield interesting benchmark results about Java.

If you want to learn more about fractals, check out any of the following:

Chaos: Making a New Science, by James Gleick (Viking Penguin, 1987)

The Spanky Fractal Database, **http://spanky.triumf.ca/www/whats-new.html**

Beauty of Fractals: Images of Complex Dynamical Systems, by H.O. Peitgen & P.H. Richter (Springer Verlag, 1986)

Mandelbrot Set Class Diagram

Figure 38.6 shows the preliminary design for your Mandelbrot program's class structure.

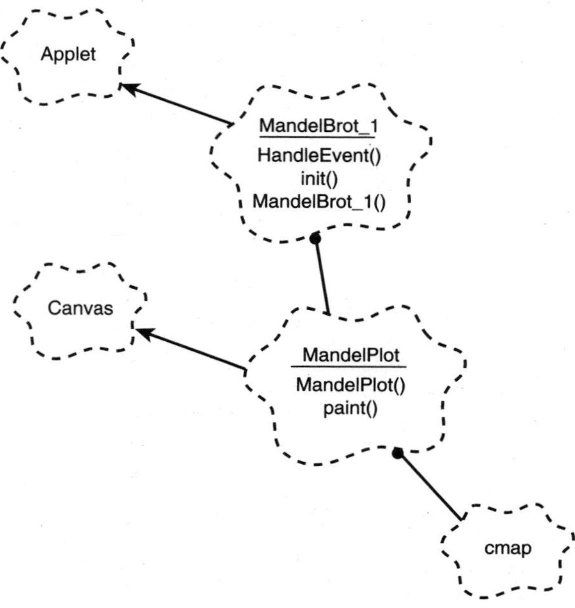

FIG. 38.6
Mandelbrot Set class diagram.

You may have noticed that this class diagram shown in Figure 38.6 is almost identical to Figure 38.5, the class diagram for the HelloWorld example. It consists only of an applet (an execution context for your program to exist in), a canvas (to render graphics to), and one new class (a color map)—so that you can specify different colors. Note, too, that the class diagram was developed (however rudimentary) before you started coding.

Following is the sample Demo.bat (see Listing 38.6), Example.html (see Listing 38.7), and Mandel.java (see Listing 38.8) source files. These, too, are very similar to the ones in the earlier HelloWorld applet.

Listing 38.6 Demo.bat Windows batch file for compiling and running the Mandelbrot Set.

```
@rem Compile and execute sample program
javac MandelBrot.java
appletviewer example.html
```


Listing 38.7 Example.html HTML web page that calls the Mandelbrot applet.

```
<HTML>
<TITLE>Mandelbrot Set</TITLE>
<BODY>
<APPLET CODE="MandelBrot.class" WIDTH=400 HEIGHT=400>
If you can read this, then your browser is not set up for Java...
</APPLET>
<HR>
<A HREF="MandelBrot.java">The source.</A>
</BODY>
</HTML>
```

Listing 38.8 Mandel.java First version of "Mandelbrot" program.

```
/**
 * MandelBrot: Plots Mandelbrot set and displays in Web Browser
 *
 * @version 1.0, DATE: 10.31.97
 * @author Paul Santa Maria
 */
import java.applet.*;
import java.awt.*;              // User Interface components

//
// MandelPlot: Implements Mandelbrot plot
//
class MandelPlot extends Canvas
{
  private int maxcol = 399, maxrow = 399, max_colors = 8,
```

continues

Listing 38.8 Continued

```
        max_iterations = 512, max_size = 4;
  private Color cmap[];

/**
 * Plot a single point in Mandelbrot set
 */
  private void plot (Graphics g, int x, int y, int color_index)
  {
    g.setColor (cmap[color_index]);
    g.drawLine (x,y, x,y);
  }

/**
 * Constructor: initialize color table for drawing
 */
  public MandelPlot ()
  {
     cmap = new Color[max_colors];

     cmap[0] = Color.black;
     cmap[1] = Color.red;
     cmap[2] = Color.green;
     cmap[3] = Color.blue;
     cmap[4] = Color.cyan;
     cmap[5] = Color.magenta;
     cmap[6] = Color.yellow;
     cmap[7] = Color.white;
  }

/**
 * Actually draws the Mandelbrot set
 */
  public void paint (Graphics g)
  {

     float Q[] = new float[400];
     double Pmax = 1.75,Pmin = -1.75, Qmax = 1.5, Qmin = -1.5,
        P, deltaP, deltaQ, X, Y, Xsquare, Ysquare;
     int color, row, col;

     deltaP = (Pmax - Pmin)/(double)(maxcol - 1);
     deltaQ = (Qmax - Qmin)/(double)(maxrow - 1);
     for (row=0; row<=maxrow; row++) {
       Q[row] = (float)(Qmin + row*deltaQ);
     }
     for (col=0; col<=maxcol; col++) {
       P = Pmin + col*deltaP;
       for (row=0; row<=maxrow; row++) {
         X = Y = 0.0;
         color = 0;
         for (color=0; color<max_iterations; color++) {
           Xsquare = X*X;
           Ysquare = Y*Y;
```

```
            if ((Xsquare+Ysquare) > max_size)
              break;
            Y = 2*X*Y+Q[row];
            X = Xsquare-Ysquare+P;
          }
          plot (g, col, row, (int)(color % max_colors));
        }
      }
    }
  }

/**
 * Create/display main window
 */
public class MandelBrot extends Applet
{
  private MandelPlot canvas;

  // MandelBrot: Frame constructor
  public void init ()
  {
     setLayout (new BorderLayout());
     canvas = new MandelPlot ();
     add ("Center", canvas);
   }

  // handleEvent: give us a way to gracefully exit the program
  public boolean handleEvent (Event evt)
  { if (evt.id == Event.WINDOW_DESTROY)
        System.exit (0);
     return false;
  }
}
```


Run Demo.bat to compile and link this program; you should see the resulting image, as shown in Figure 38.7.

Debugging Java applets can present special challenges. When C++ or BASIC programs fail, they usually GPF, dump core, or do something equally exciting. When an applet fails, however, it fails quietly.

If your applet doesn't seem to be doing anything, you could be facing one of two problems:

- Your browser isn't running Java.
- Your Java program isn't working correctly.

You can eliminate the first possibility by seeing whether any other Java applets run on your browser. If other applets run, try recompiling your own applet. Double-check everything along the way: compiler errors, warning messages, spelling and capitalization, and so on.

If you suspect the problem is occurring inside your applet, you can step through your Java debugger or embed temporary `printf` statements (either `System.out.println ()` or `g.drawText ()`) at strategic points in your source code.

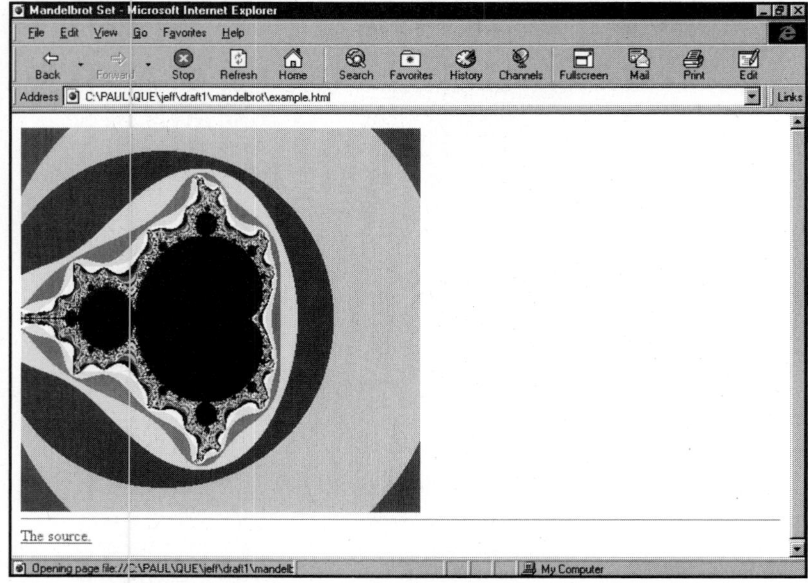

FIG. 38.7
This is just one of an infinite number regions you could have plotted from the Mandelbrot Set.

Java AWT and Application Frameworks

Believe it or not, the structural similarity between the first two example programs (`HelloWorld` and `Mandel`) is more than just coincidence. It gives you an important clue as to how tools such as Microsoft's AppWizard or Borland's AppExpert work and, more generally, why object-oriented programming has become so popular.

When you design your own programs, you need to figure out what kinds of things your program will be using, and then encapsulate the essential behavior of each into its own class.

Library designers do the same kind of thing, only at a higher level. What the designers of Java have done is they figured out what kinds of building blocks application developers might typically need and assembled these into a general-purpose application framework. Ideally, an application framework enables you to write entire applications almost on demand, with only minimal tailoring.

In Java, the application framework is called the Abstract Window Kit (AWT). AWT is really very similar in spirit to MS-Windows programming frameworks such as Microsoft's Foundation Classes (MFC).

Both Microsoft and Borland bundle their respective application frameworks with their compilers, and supply sophisticated tools that make it possible to generate tailored programs with a simple point-and-click graphical interface. There are already tools from Symantec, Rogue Wave, BlueStone, IBM, and SunSoft that match, or surpass, this level of functionality for Java programmers.

Benchmarking Your Program

How long does MandelPlot take to run on your PC? You can pull out a stopwatch and time it manually. When tested for this chapter, the following timing resulted from running the same program on different browsers (see Table 38.6).

Table 38.6 Mandelbrot Set execution times.

Browser	Execution Time
Netscape 2.0	5:18
appletviewer 1.14	2:12
Microsoft IE 3 .0	0:51
Netscape 4.03	0:30

Why not write a program to do this instead? Call this hypothetical program "StopWatch." And make it general enough so that you can reuse it in future programs.

Introduction to State Transition Diagrams

To use a stopwatch, you click to start timing, and then click it again when you want to stop. You can click yet again if you want to resume timing. The watch always shows you the elapsed time since you started. Additionally, you can click another button to reset back to 0:00.

The concept is very simple, but coding it can be tricky. The problem is that it can be difficult to keep track of which operation is legal when. What happens if you resume before you hit start? Or pause after you've already stopped? Unless you keep careful track of all these subtle rules, it is all too easy to write a buggy program.

You can quickly and easily capture the semantics of a class such as `StopWatch` with a State Transition diagram, as shown in Figure 38.8.

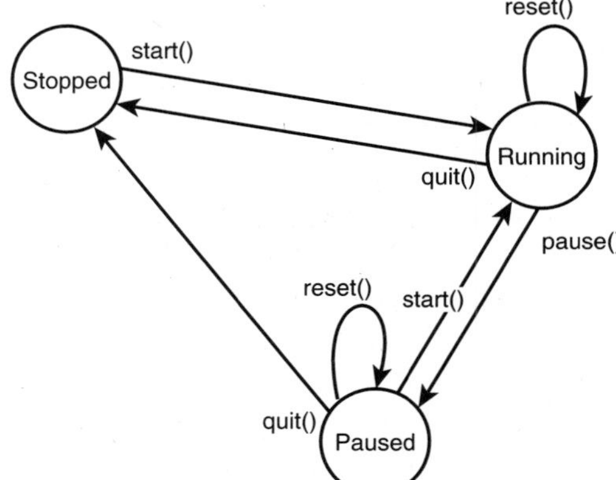

FIG. 38.8 State Transition diagrams can be a useful design tool for any class that exhibits event-ordered behavior.

The circles represent each state your class can be in at any given moment: stopped, running, or paused. The lines show all the legal transitions from one state into another.

Writing the Code: StopWatch

Compare the State Transition diagram with the code for the class methods `start()`, `pause()`, and `reset()` in Listing 38.9. As you can see, the source code practically falls right out of the State Transition diagram. With any class that exhibits significant event-ordered behavior, sketching out a State Transition diagram can really simplify your work by suggesting a straightforward, simple design.

Listing 38.9 StopWatch.java Implements timing functions.

```
/**
 * StopWatch: Java 1.1 Version
 *
 * @version 2.0, DATE: 11.1.97
 * @author Paul Santa Maria
 */
import java.util.*;     // Date, etc.

public class StopWatch
{
  public final static int PAUSED  = 0;
  public final static int RUNNING = 1;
  private TimeStruct t1, t2, elapsed;
  private int current_state;

  // Store start time t1
  private final void setT1 ()
  {
  GregorianCalendar c =
    new GregorianCalendar();

    t1 = new TimeStruct (
      c.get (Calendar.HOUR),
      c.get (Calendar.MINUTE),
      c.get (Calendar.SECOND) );
  }

  // Store current time t2
  private final void setT2 ()
  {
    GregorianCalendar c =
      new GregorianCalendar();

    t2 = new TimeStruct (
      c.get (Calendar.HOUR),
      c.get (Calendar.MINUTE),
      c.get (Calendar.SECOND) );
  }

 /**
  * public constructor
```

```
 */
 public StopWatch ()
 {
   reset ();
   current_state = PAUSED;
 }

/**
 * Start/resume incrementing time
 */
 public void start ()
 {
   if (current_state == PAUSED) {
     setT1 ();
     setT2 ();
   }
   current_state = RUNNING;
 }

/**
 * Stop incrementing time (until next start)
 */
 public void pause ()
 {
   if (current_state == RUNNING) {
     getElapsed ();
   }
   current_state = PAUSED;
 }

/**
 * Clears elapsed time, re-initializes start time
 */
 public void reset ()
 {
   elapsed = new TimeStruct (0, 0, 0);
 }

/**
 * Returns elapsed time
 * NOTES:
 * 1. Cumulative: elapsed = (t2-t1) + elapsed
 * 2. Implicitly resets T1, T2
 */
 public TimeStruct getElapsed ()
 {
   int hh, mm, ss;

   // Check if we've already computed elapsed time
   if (current_state == PAUSED) {
     return elapsed;
   }

   // We're still running: update current time T2
   setT2 ();
```

continues

Listing 38.9 Continued

```
    // Compute seconds
    if (t2.ss < t1.ss) {
      elapsed.ss += (60 + t2.ss) - t1.ss;
      t2.mm -= 1;
    }
    else
      elapsed.ss += t2.ss - t1.ss;
    // Compute minutes
    if (t2.mm < t1.mm) {
      elapsed.mm += (60 + t2.mm) - t1.mm;
      t2.hh -= 1;
    }
    else
      elapsed.mm += t2.mm - t1.mm;
    // Compute hours
    elapsed.hh = t2.hh - t1.hh;

    // Now translate straight decimal to 60:60
    if (elapsed.ss >= 60) {
      elapsed.mm += 1;
      elapsed.ss -= 60;
    }
    if (elapsed.mm >= 60) {
      elapsed.hh += 1;
      elapsed.mm -= 60;
    }

    // Clean up T1, T2
    t1 = t2;

    // Done!
    return elapsed;
  }

 /**
  * Return stopwatch state
  */
  public int getState ()
  {
    return current_state;
  }
}
```

One of the restrictions imposed by most Java compilers (including the JDK) is that each public class must reside in a separate Java source file. Therefore, you need `TimeStruct` in its own source file.

Listing 38.10 TimeStruct.java This data class is shared among StopWatch's clients.

```
 * TimeStruct: current hours/minutes/seconds
 */
public class TimeStruct
{
  public int hh;
  public int ss;
  public int mm;

  // Constructor
  public TimeStruct (int h, int m, int s)
  {
    hh = h;
    mm = m;
    ss = s;
  }
}
```


Writing a Test Driver: TestStopWatch

Being a good programmer, you always create a test driver for any substantial new piece of software. Right?

Because it is slightly simpler, write `TestStopWatch` as a standalone application rather than a Java applet.

Basically, all you want to do is check out all the public interfaces to your new `StopWatch` class, see the results, and make sure everything works as you expect it to.

Listing 38.11 shows the complete source code for TestStopWatch.java.

Listing 38.11 TestStopWatch.java A test harness for *StopWatch*.

```
/**
 * TestStopWatch: Test harness for our StopWatch utility class
 *
 * NOTE: Uses Java 1.1 Event Handling
 *
 * @version 2.0, DATE: 11.1.97
 * @author Paul Santa Maria
 */
import java.awt.*;       // GUI components
import java.awt.event.*; // Java 1.1 Events

public class TestStopWatch extends Frame
  implements ActionListener,   // ActionEvents (Java 1.1)
             Runnable          // Threads
```

continues

Listing 38.11 Continued

```
{

  // Private data
  private StopWatch sw;
  private TextField timeHH, timeMM, timeSS;
  private Thread runner;

/**
 * Constructor
 */
  public TestStopWatch ()
  {

    // Set Window title
    setTitle ("TestStopWatch");

    // Create a "panel" to hold our clock time
    Panel p1 = new Panel ();
    p1.setLayout (new FlowLayout ());
    p1.add (new Label ("Elapsed HH:MM:SS "));
    timeHH = new TextField ("00", 3);
    p1.add (timeHH);
    timeMM = new TextField ("00", 3);
    p1.add (timeMM);
    timeSS = new TextField ("00", 3);
    p1.add (timeSS);

    // Add HH/MM/SS clock to frame/top
    add ("North", p1);

    // Now create another "panel" to contain our pushbuttons
    Panel p2 = new Panel ();
    p2.setLayout (new FlowLayout ());

    // Create buttons, register ActionEvent handler
    Button b;
    p2.add (b = new Button ("Start"));
    b.addActionListener(this); // Java 1.1 only!
    p2.add (b = new Button ("Pause"));
    b.addActionListener(this); // Java 1.1 only!
    p2.add (b = new Button ("Reset"));
    b.addActionListener(this); // Java 1.1 only!
    p2.add (b = new Button ("Quit"));
    b.addActionListener(this); // Java 1.1 only!

    // Add pushbuttons panel to the frame/bottom
    add ("South", p2);

    // Create a sample StopWatch
    sw = new StopWatch ();

    // Finally, create a timer thread
    runner = new Thread (this);
```

```
    runner.start ();
  }

 /**
  * Handle any button clicks
  */
  public void actionPerformed(ActionEvent e) {
    String cmd = e.getActionCommand ();
    if (cmd == "Start") {
     System.out.println ("Start");
     sw.start ();
    }
    else if (cmd == "Pause") {
      System.out.println ("Pause");
      sw.pause ();
    }
    else if (cmd == "Reset") {
      System.out.println ("Reset");
      sw.reset ();
    }
    else if (cmd == "Quit") {
      System.out.println ("Quit");
      do_quit ();
    }
    else {
      System.out.println ("UNKNOWN EVENT");
    }
  }

 /**
  * Create/display main window
  */
  public static void main (String[] args)
  {
    final Frame f = new TestStopWatch ();
    f.setSize (350, 100);   // setSize: Java 1.1 only!

    // Use a Java 1.1 "inner class"
    // to handle windowClosing events
    f.addWindowListener (new WindowAdapter () {
      public void windowClosing (WindowEvent e)
      {
        System.out.println ("ALT-F4: Window closing");
        f.dispose ();
        System.exit (0);
      }
    } );

    // Run the stopwatch
    f.show ();
  }

  /**
   * Implement asynchronous timing loop
   */
```

continues

Listing 38.11 Continued

```
  public void run ()
  {
    // The AWT interface for run () REQUIRES that we provide
    // an exception handler like this try .. catch
    try {
      // Loop forever
      for ( ;; ) {
        // Note "trick" for converting int => String
        timeHH.setText ( "" + sw.getElapsed().hh );
        timeMM.setText ( "" + sw.getElapsed().mm );
        timeSS.setText ( "" + sw.getElapsed().ss );
        // Wait 1000 ms (1 second) for continuing loop
        Thread.sleep (1000);
      }
    }
    catch (InterruptedException e) {
    }
  }

/**
 * Shut down thread
 */
  private void do_quit ()
  {
    // Terminate thread
    runner.stop ();
    // Free window resources and exheunt
    System.exit (0);
  }
}
```

Listing 38.12 Demo.bat Compile and run TestStopWatch program.

```
@rem Compile and execute sample program
javac -deprecation TimeStruct.java
javac -deprecation StopWatch.java
javac -deprecation TestStopWatch.java
java TestStopWatch
```

Figure 38.9 shows what the `TestStopWatch` driver program looks like.

A Closer Look at *TestStopWatch*

Although `TestStopWatch` is basically just a "quick hack" to test the `StopWatch` class, several interesting aspects of this program bear closer scrutiny.

***main()* Method** As you saw earlier in HelloWorld, every standalone Java application *must* have a method called `public static void main (String[] args)`.

FIG. 38.9
It is always a good idea to write a test driver for any general-purpose class.

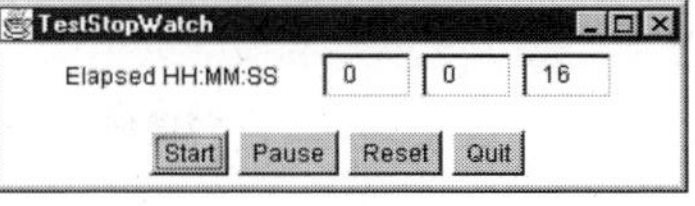

If you forget to do this (or if you accidentally mis-type any part of its declaration), your Java program will fail to run.

GUI Controls in Java `TestStopWatch` introduces you to your first GUI objects (known as widgets to X Windows programmers or controls to Windows programmers): pushbuttons, text edit controls, and text labels.

Unlike Windows—where you typically declare controls in a separate resource file—Java enables you to create them and use them on-the-fly, as shown in Listing 38.12.

Listing 38.13 AnyProgram.java Example snippet showing how to arrange GUI elements on a Java panel.

```
// Hey, kids!  Let's make some pushbuttons!
Panel p = new Panel ();
p.setLayout (new FlowLayout ());
p.add (new Button ("Start"));
p.add (new Button ("Quit"));
add ("South", p);
```

***Panel* Versus *Canvas*: Automatic Layout Management in Java** X Windows programmers are accustomed to relying on so-called container widgets to manage the layouts of their various GUI controls as they appear to the end user. Windows programmers, on the other hand, must usually hard-code specific x- and y- coordinates for the height, width, and position for their controls.

Java more or less parallels the X Windows model by providing containers to manage the nitty-gritty details of positioning GUI controls for you.

The `TestStopWatch` program uses two panels: `p1` manages the `Elapsed HH:MM:SS` data on the top of the frame; `p2` manages all the pushbuttons on a single row at the bottom.

The `Frame` (`TestStopWatch`) contains the panels. The panels, in turn, contain the GUI controls.

Event Management in Java As you can see, event management is reasonably straightforward: You just create a component (such as a pushbutton) and "register" any events that you are interested in handling yourself. If you don't register an event, Java's AWT provides reasonable default behavior for you automatically. It is simple and efficient.

Unfortunately, Java had a completely *different* model for managing events prior to the release of Java 1.1. The new method is certainly "better," but it *won't run* on any browser or JVM that doesn't support the new 1.1 standard.

Listing 38.14 shows a code snippet that compares the Java 1.0 versus Java 1.1 event model. Complete source for both versions of StopWatch are included on the accompanying CD.

Listing 38.14 Java 1.1 event handling (snippet).

```
    public TestStopWatch ()
    {
...
      // Now create another "panel" to contain our pushbuttons
      Panel p2 = new Panel ();
      p2.setLayout (new FlowLayout ());
...
      // Create buttons, register ActionEvent handler
      Button b;
      p2.add (b = new Button ("Start"));
      b.addActionListener(this); // Java 1.1 only!
      p2.add (b = new Button ("Pause"));
      b.addActionListener(this); // Java 1.1 only!
      p2.add (b = new Button ("Reset"));
      b.addActionListener(this); // Java 1.1 only!
      p2.add (b = new Button ("Quit"));
      b.addActionListener(this); // Java 1.1 only!
...
  /**
   * Handle any button clicks
   */
    public void actionPerformed(ActionEvent e) {
      String cmd = e.getActionCommand ();
      if (cmd == "Start") {
       System.out.println ("Start");
       sw.start ();
      }
      else if (cmd == "Pause") {
        System.out.println ("Pause");
        sw.pause ();
      }
      else if (cmd == "Reset") {
        System.out.println ("Reset");
        sw.reset ();
      }
      else if (cmd == "Quit") {
        System.out.println ("Quit");
        do_quit ();
      }
      else {
        System.out.println ("UNKNOWN EVENT");
      }
    }
```

Listing 38.15 Java 1.0 event handling (snippet).

```
  public TestStopWatch ()
  {
...
    // Now create another "panel" to contain our pushbuttons
    Panel p2 = new Panel ();
    p2.setLayout (new FlowLayout ());
    p2.add (new Button ("Start"));
    p2.add (new Button ("Pause"));
    p2.add (new Button ("Reset"));
    p2.add (new Button ("Quit"));
...
/**
 * Handle any button clicks
 */
  // NOTE: action handlers now deprecated in Java 1.1!
  public boolean action (Event evt, Object arg)
  {
    if (arg.equals ("Start")) {
      System.out.println ("Start");
      sw.start ();
    }
    else if (arg.equals ("Pause")) {
      System.out.println ("Pause");
      sw.pause ();
    }
    else if (arg.equals ("Reset")) {
      System.out.println ("Reset");
      sw.reset ();
    }
    else if (arg.equals ("Quit")) {
      System.out.println ("Quit");
      do_quit ();
    }
    else {
      System.out.println ("UNKNOWN EVENT");
      return false;
    }
    // "true" means we handled this event.
    // We shouldn't have any events besides button-pushes.
    return true;
  }
```

This creates a dilemma: Should you code to the old, "deprecated" Java 1.0 API, or should you risk compatibility problems among your program's users?

Until most web browsers are migrated to the new JDK 1.1 API, this is a judgment call that only you can make.

You need to know which browsers your users are running and how likely they are to update any older browser versions. You need to balance portability with today's browsers (writing to Java 1.0) versus maintainability in tomorrow's environments (avoiding deprecated 1.0 APIs).

Finally, you need to decide to what extent the newer Java 1.1 APIs will give your program added functionality and increased robustness you simply can't get coding to the older, deprecated 1.0 APIs.

The best advice is:

- Be aware of any Java 1.0/1.1 portability issues that might affect your code.
- Test your Java applets on as many different web Browsers as you can.

Why Did Sun Change Java's Event Model?

Sun had several good, technical reasons for doing this. These reasons are as follows:

- ***Flexibility***. In the older, Java 1.0 model, the only way your class could handle an event was to inherit from some predefined AWT class. The new Java 1.1 event model allows any arbitrary class be an "event source" (one that generates an event) or an "event listener" (one that handles events).
- ***Efficiency***. In the new 1.1 event model, listeners receive only events they are interested in (that is, those events they register). You *don't* need a lot of unnecessary method overriding. You *don't* need to create a component subclass just to handle events.
- ***Robustness***. Basically, the new model is a lot cleaner and more powerful. It enables you to do more with less code. And by decoupling event handling from application logic, you programs will be simpler and less prone to subtle bugs and deep, inflexible class hierarchies.

Java 1.1 "Inner Classes" Prior to Java 1.1, every class and interface had to be defined separately from each other, at the "top-level" of its enclosing package. This restriction was often inconvenient, leading to a lot of unnecessary code. Java 1.1 introduced the notion of an inner class—a class that can be contained entirely within other classes.

The following code fragment illustrates an inner class. It shows a class that is declared, instantiated, and used completely on-the-fly.

Listing 38.16 Java 1.1 inner classes.

```
// Use a Java 1.1 "inner class"
// to handle windowClosing events
f.addWindowListener (new WindowAdapter () {
  public void windowClosing (WindowEvent e)
  {
    System.out.println ("ALT-F4: Window closing");
    f.dispose ();
    System.exit (0);
  }
} );
```

You are creating a brand new class, based on `WindowAdapter` (WindowAdapter is an abstract base class defined in package `java.awt.event`). This new class has only one method: `windowClosing ()`. Both the class and its method are declared on-the-fly, as an input parameter to `f.addWindowListener ()`.

As you can see, this class just does not exist outside this one, very specialized role: to serve as the input argument to *this particular call* to `f.addWindowListener ()`. Hence the name "inner class."

Introduction to Java Threads `TestStopWatch` also introduced you to Java's multithreading capabilities.

If `TestStopWatch` were written as a traditional, single-threaded C program, you would probably just fall into a simple `do...while` loop. You can't do that in Java, however, because if the program were trapped in a loop, it would never get a chance to handle any button-press events from the user.

If, on the other hand, `TestStopWatch` were written as an Windows or a Motif program, you would probably set up some kind of timer that would periodically pass some special timer event into your main event loop. Java neither has such a timer type, nor a main event loop that you need to slavishly adhere to.

Instead, Java offers what is arguably a much simpler, cleaner solution—you can just create a thread object that will be its own simple, self-contained `do...while` loop. Because it runs in parallel to the main program, you won't lock yourself out of fielding any important user events. Listing 38.13 shows basically how it works.

Listing 38.17 TestStopWatch.java Example snippets showing how to implement a "timer" using Java threads.

```
// Declare that our class will be using threads:
public class TestStopWatch extends Frame
  implements Runnable

// Store the Thread object object as private class data:
  private StopWatch sw;
  private TextField timeHH, timeMM, timeSS;
  private Thread runner;

// Create the thread in the main class's constructor:
  public TestStopWatch () {
    running = new Thread (this);
    runner.start ();

// Destroy the thread when you quit the program:
  private void do_quit () {
    runner.stop ();
```

continues

Listing 38.17 Continued

```
// Put your own code in a customized run() method
public void run () {
    try {
      // Loop forever
      for ( ;; ) {
        ...
      }
    }
    catch (InterruptedException e) {}
  }
```

Java "Interfaces" The preceding two examples (event handlers and threads) are also good examples of using Java "interfaces."

An *interface* is just a set of method declarations and (optionally) constants. Interfaces are abstract templates—they define *what* a class should do…but it's up to *you* to provide a concrete implementation for *how* your class will do it. Among other things, Java interfaces can often be used to solve the kinds of problems that C++ programmers need multiple inheritance for.

You can recognize when interfaces are being used by looking for the keyword "implements," as the following code shows:

```
TestStopWatch.java:
public class TestStopWatch extends Frame
  implements ActionListener,     // ActionEvents (Java 1.1)
             Runnable            // Threads
{…
```

Here, your `TestStopWatch` class is "implementing" two standard Java interfaces: `ActionListener` (`java.awt.event.ActionListener`) and `Runnable` (`java.lang.Runi`
Look at the JDK 1.1 documentation for the latter, interface `Runnable`:

```
Java JDK 1.1 Documentation:
public interface interface Runnable {
 public abstract void run ();
}
```

As you can see, there really is not too much going on here: All you need to do to "implement" `Runnable` is to write a `run ()` method for it. This is, of course, exactly what you did in the preceding section, "Java Threads."

```
TestStopWatch.java:
public void run () {
    try {
      // Loop forever
      for ( ;; ) {
        ...
      }
    }
    catch (InterruptedException e) {}
  }
```

Java interfaces are light-weight, elegant, and extremely useful in a wide variety of design and programming problems.

Converting Java Types to "String" As mentioned earlier, Java is a strongly typed language. Your `StopWatch` class keeps track of time (hours, minutes, and seconds) with integers (type `int`).

But you need to convert this "time" data from `int` to `String` before you can display it. How do you do this? Listing 38.18 shows one way.

Listing 38.18 TestStopWatch.java Example snippet showing one method of converting a Java primitive type into a Java string.

```
for ( ;; ) {
  timeHH.setText ( "" + sw.getHH () );
  timeMM.setText ( "" + sw.getMM () );
  timeSS.setText ( "" + sw.getSS () );
```


The magic here is that whenever you concatenate (using the `+` operator) a `String` with some value that isn't a `String`, Java automatically converts the result into a `String`.

Here's a convenient way to put simple, C-like `printf` statements into Java applications:

```
System.out.println ("Myvalue: " + myInt)
```

BarChart: HTML Parameters

Up to now, very little interaction has occurred between your HTML web pages and the Java applets they invoke. The following example program, BarChart, shows how to use HTML `<PARAM>` tags to pass information into a Java applet.

The BarChart Program

It is easy to convert this kind of information into an HTML table and publish it on a web page. But why not use Java's graphic capabilities to "jazz it up" a bit? Listing 38.19 gives you the code with which to do so.

Listing 38.19 BarChart.java Display Mandelbrot Set performance data.

```
/**
 * BarChart: Plots color bar chart from HTML input data
 *
 * SAMPLE HTML PARAMETER DATA:
 *  <APPLET CODE="BarChart.class" WIDTH=400 HEIGHT=150>
 *  <PARAM NAME="title" VALUE="Execution Timings">
 *  <PARAM NAME="nrows" VALUE="4">
 *  <PARAM NAME="data"
```

continues

Listing 38.19 Continued

```
 *   VALUE="Netscape 2.0,      1.0,  red,   solid, 5:18,
 *         1.14 appletviewer, 0.42, green, hatch, 2:12,
 *         IE 3.0,            0.16, green, solid, 0:51,
 *         Netscape 4.03,     0.09, blue,  hatch, 0:30">
 *
 * @version 2.0; DATE: 11.2.97
 * @author Paul Santa Maria
 */
import java.awt.*;
import java.applet.*;
import java.util.*;
import java.lang.Throwable;

/**
 * Bad data exception handler
 */
class HTMLdataException extends Throwable {
  public HTMLdataException (String msg) {
    super (msg);
  }
}

public class BarChart extends Applet
{
  // Private data
  int nrows;
  String theTitle;
  String col1[];
  Double value[];
  Color  color[];
  String style[];
  String col3[];
  Font titleFont, dataFont;
  FontMetrics fmTitle, fmData;

  /**
   * parse single items from "data" parameter
   */
  String parseBarChartData (StringTokenizer html)
    throws HTMLdataException
  {
    if (!html.hasMoreTokens ())
      throw new HTMLdataException ("HTML READ ERROR");
    else
      return html.nextToken ();
  }

  /**
   * read and store Barchart data from HTML web page
   */
  public void init () {
    Integer iTmp = new Integer (0);
    Double  dTmp;
```

```
String  sTmp;
StringTokenizer sTokTmp;

// Get BarChart title
theTitle = getParameter ("title");
if (theTitle == null)
  theTitle = "No title";

// Get #/rows in BarChart
try {
  nrows = iTmp.parseInt (getParameter ("nrows"));
}
catch (Exception e) {
  System.out.println ("Could not read #/rows");
}

// Get ready to parse BarChart data from HTML
col1 = new String[nrows];
value = new Double[nrows];
color = new Color[nrows];
style = new String[nrows];
col3 = new String[nrows];
sTokTmp =
  new StringTokenizer (getParameter ("data"), ",");

// Read BarChart data
try {
  for (int irow = 0; irow < nrows; irow++) {

    col1[irow] = parseBarChartData (sTokTmp).trim ();
    // NOTE: use String.trim () to eliminate any extra
    //       whitespace you might pick up from HTML

     dTmp = new Double (parseBarChartData (sTokTmp).trim ());
     value[irow] = dTmp;

    sTmp = parseBarChartData (sTokTmp).trim ();
    if (sTmp.equals ("red"))
      color[irow] = Color.red;
    else if (sTmp.equals ("green"))
       color[irow] = Color.green;
    else if (sTmp.equals ("blue"))
       color[irow] = Color.blue;
    else if (sTmp.equals ("cyan"))
       color[irow] = Color.cyan;
    else if (sTmp.equals ("magenta"))
       color[irow] = Color.magenta;
    else if (sTmp.equals ("yellow"))
       color[irow] = Color.yellow;
    else if (sTmp.equals ("black"))
       color[irow] = Color.black;
    else if (sTmp.equals ("white"))
       color[irow] = Color.white;
    else // Default color
       color[irow] = Color.blue;
```

continues

Listing 38.19 Continued

```
        style[irow] = parseBarChartData (sTokTmp).trim ();

        col3[irow] = parseBarChartData (sTokTmp).trim ();
      }
    }
    catch (HTMLdataException e) {
      System.out.println ("Could not read BarChart data");
    }

    // Allocate font data/metrics
    titleFont = new Font ("Times", Font.BOLD, 14);
    dataFont = new Font ("Courier", Font.BOLD, 12);
    fmTitle = getFontMetrics (titleFont);
    fmData = getFontMetrics (dataFont);
  }

/**
 * Display the Bar Chart
 */
  public void paint (Graphics g) {
    final int BAR_WIDTH = 200;
    final int HSPACE = fmData.stringWidth ("W");
    final int HTAB1 = HSPACE;
    final int HTAB2 = HSPACE * 20;
    final int VTAB = fmData.getHeight () + 5;
    Dimension d = size ();     // Deprecated in Java 1.1!
    // NOTE: Java 1.1 equivalent is "getSize ()"
    int iline = 0;
    int x, y;

    // Center title at bottom of display area
    x =
      (d.width - fmTitle.stringWidth (theTitle)) / 2;
    y =
      d.height - (++iline * VTAB);
    g.setFont (titleFont);
    g.setColor (Color.black);
    g.drawString (theTitle, x, y);

    // Draw data
    g.setFont (dataFont);
    for (int irow=nrows-1; irow >=0; irow--) {

      // Col1: Description
      x = HTAB1;
      y = d.height - (++iline * VTAB);
      g.setColor (Color.black);
      g.drawString (col1[irow], x, y);

      // Col2: Graphical bar
      x = drawBar (g,
        value[irow].doubleValue (), color[irow], style[irow],
```

```
        HTAB2, BAR_WIDTH, y, VTAB);

      // Col3: Legend
      x += 2 * HSPACE;
      g.setColor (color[irow]);
      g.drawString (col3[irow], x, y);
    }
  }

  /**
   * Draws a single Bar graph
   */
  private int drawBar (Graphics g,
    double value, Color color, String style,
    int x, int max_width, int y, int max_height)
  {
    int w = (int) (max_width * value);
    int h = (int) (max_height * 0.65);

    // Draw drop shadow
    g.setColor (Color.gray);
    g.fillRect (x-3, y-h+3, w-3, h+3);

    // Draw bar
    g.setColor (color);
    if (style.equals ("hatch")) {
      final int steps = w / 2;
      int ys;
      for (int i=0; i<steps; i++) {
        ys = x + (2*i);
        g.drawLine (ys, y-h, ys, y);
      }
    }
    else { // Default = "solid"
      g.fillRect (x, y-h, w, h);
    }

    // Return new x position
    return x + w;
  }
}
```

Structurally, this program looks a lot like `HelloWorld` and `MandelBrot`: You subclass from `Applet`, do a little setup in the `init ()` method, and do most of your work during the `paint ()` method.

Listing 38.20 Example.html: invokes BarChart example.

```
<HTML>
<HEAD>
<TITLE>Bar Chart</TITLE>
</HEAD>
```

continues

Listing 38.20 Continued

```
<BODY>
<H1>MandelBrot Run Time Comparisions</H1>
<HR>
<TABLE BORDER>
<!-- This is a standard HTML table -->
  <TD>
  <CENTER><B>HTML TABLE</B></CENTER>
  <TABLE BORDER>
  <CAPTION ALIGN=TOP>Execution Timings</CAPTION>
  <TR>
    <TH>Browser</TH><TH>Version</TH><TH>Execution<BR>Time</TH>
  </TR>
  <TR>
    <TD>Netscape</TD><TD>2.0</TD><TD>5:18</TD>
  </TR>
  <TR>
    <TD>appletviewer</TD><TD>1.14</TD><TD>2:12</TD>
  </TR>
  <TR>
    <TD>Microsoft IE</TD><TD>3.0</TD><TD>0:51</TD>
  </TR>
  <TR>
    <TD>Netscape</TD><TD>4.03</TD><TD>0:30</TD>
  </TR>
  </TABLE></TD>
<!-- This is the corresponding Java BarChart applet -->
  <TD>
  <CENTER><B>JAVA APPLET</B></CENTER>
  <APPLET CODE="BarChart.class" WIDTH=382 HEIGHT=150>
  <PARAM NAME="title" VALUE="Execution Timings">
  <PARAM NAME="nrows" VALUE="4">
  <PARAM NAME="data"
    VALUE="Netscape 2.0,      1.0,  red,      solid, 5:18,
           1.14 appletviewer, 0.42, magenta,  hatch, 2:12,
           IE 3.0,            0.16, green,    solid, 0:51,
           Netscape 4.03,     0.09, blue,     hatch, 0:30">
  If you can read this, then your browser is not Java-enabled
  </APPLET>
  </TD>
</TABLE>
</BODY>
</HTML>
```

Figures 38.10 and 38.11 show the resulting bar chart.

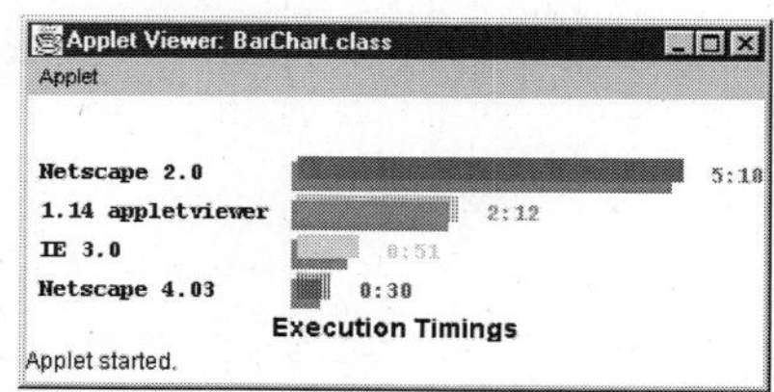

FIG. 38.10
The BarChart (rendered by JDK appletviewer).

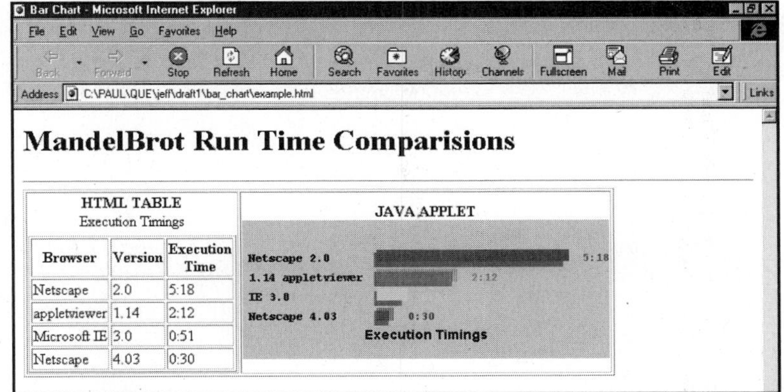

FIG. 38.11
The BarChart (rendered by web browser).

Notice in Figure 38.11 that you are looking at the same data two different ways: both as an HTML table and graphically rendered by the BarChart applet. A second, enclosing table places them side-by-side in the web browser.

Although the JDK appletviewer is convenient, it does not handle tables, headers, JavaScript, or any other HTML or script objects that you are likely to have in your web page. It is only intended for viewing Java applets.

You should always run your Java applets in a web browser to see how they will actually look to your users.

Furthermore, you should always test your applets on several different web browsers to make sure your Applet and its surrounding HTML are as portable as you can make them.

getParameter How do you get information from an HTML web page into a Java applet? Easy. Just call the applet's `getParameter ()` method.

Here is the HTML that defines the parameter:

```
<APPLET CODE="BarChart.class" WIDTH=382 HEIGHT=150>
<PARAM NAME="title" VALUE="Execution Timings">
...
```

This is the corresponding Java code that reads it:

```
    // Get BarChart title
    theTitle = getParameter ("title");
...
```

String Tokenizers Java "tokenizers" make it easy to extract just those pieces of information in which you are interested out of the surrounding text. The following snippet from the JDK documentation shows how to use `StringTokenizers`:

```
StringTokenizer st = new StringTokenizer("this is a test");
while (st.hasMoreTokens()) {
    println(st.nextToken());
}...
```

In the BarChart example, you were essentially using entire `<PARAM>` tags from the HTML web page as the input "string."

Wrapper Classes The last new feature you are using in BarChart is Java "wrapper classes."

Often, you will want to treat a primitive type (such as "`int`" or "`double`") like a class. Because of Java's strong data typing, however, this could be difficult. For precisely that reason, Java's designers provided "wrapper classes" for all the primitive types.

By convention, the name of most wrapper classes is just the name of the primitive type, with its first letter capitalized: The wrapper for primitive type "`byte`" is "`Byte`," the wrapper for "`double`" is "`Double`," and so on. Of course, there is always the inevitable exception: The wrapper for type "`int`" is "`Integer`."

The following snippet calls `parseBarChartData ()` to read the next item from your web page. `ParseBarChartData ()` returns a "`String`" object. You use it to create a "`Double`" wrapper object (`dTmp`), and immediately store the result in your `ival[]` array. There's simply no easier way to read text and convert it on-the-fly into numeric data.

```
Double  dTmp;
dTmp = new Double (parseBarChartData (sTokTmp).trim ());
```

Program Tuning and Optimization

Here are a few simple tricks you can use to speed up your Java applets and applications

- Always try to eliminate redundant expressions:

  ```
  // Poor: the same value is computed and assigned twice
  j = 2 + 2; i = j; i = 2 + 2;
  // Better
  i = 4;
  ```

  Modern optimizing compilers eliminate the (totally useless) first assignment. But neither the JDK compiler or most JVM interpreters do this—you need to do it manually.
- Always try to eliminate dead code:

  ```
  // Poor: the test will always fail; "doSomething ()" will never be
       called

  if (1==2)

  doSomething ();

  else

    doSomethingElse ();

  // Better:

  doSomethingElse ()
  ```

  This is similar to the preceding example. You're forcing Java to waste precious time performing unnecessary work (testing the result of `1==2`), and you're wasting network bandwidth to transmit the Java bytecode for a method (`doSomething`) that you will never use. Just manually eliminate this from your program source.

- Use final or static final declarations whenever possible:

```
// This is OK...
class j {
  public int used_often;
// This could run MUCH faster...
class j {
public final int used_often;
```

This can effectively "inline" the code or data in question. Performance gains can be considerable.

- Choose `int` or `float` over `long` or `double`:

```
long x;     //OK
int x;      // Usually better
```

Because `long` is twice as large as `int`, data access time is usually longer.

- Move static expressions out of the loop:

```
// Poor:
for (i=0; i<=j+1000; i++)
  k++;
// Better
temp = j+1000;
for (i=0; i<temp; i++)
  k++;
```

Whenever your have a loop, check it very carefully to see whether you can move any tests or calculations outside of the loop.

- Unroll loops where appropriate:

```
// OK
for (I=0; I<4; I++)
  k++;
// Better
k++;
k++;
k++;
k++;
// Best of all
k *= 4;
```

Again, optimizing compilers for other languages do this for you automatically. But unless you are absolutely sure that all your clients' web browsers are fully updated to the latest-and-greatest JIT plug-ins, it is probably in your best interests to optimize it manually.

- Use synchronized objects sparingly:

```
// Only a synchronized method will work here
synchronized void debitAccount ()
```

Synchronize only those methods where it is critical, and double-check your design to make sure they can't deadlock.

- Use `-O` compile switch:

```
javac -O myprog.java
```

The kinds of optimization available to you and how to control it will vary from compiler to compiler. Be sure, however, to study your compiler's documentation and recompile with optimization on before you publish your Java applets.

Java: More Than Just a Language

Over the course of the past several pages, you have learned the basic mechanics of writing Java applets. Although this discussion has hardly scratched the surface of everything Java is capable of doing for you and your development team, you should be excited about what you have seen so far.

Common Misperceptions and "Gotcha's" About Java

Unfortunately, nothing is perfect—not even for a programming language as cool as Java. The following list highlights some of the problems a Java programmer might encounter:

- *Speed*. Make no mistake, Java is slow. This problem is being attacked from the software front (optimizing compilers, runtime bytecode optimizers, and so on). And don't forget the contribution that you, the Java developer, can make if you practice the kind of code profiling and optimization discussed in the preceding section.

  Java is not, however—nor is it expected to be anytime soon—as fast as native code written in C or C++.
- *AWT straitjacket*. Java programs do not usually sport GUIs that are as slick and attractive as their MS-Windows, Macintosh, or Motif counterparts.

  This is not a limitation in the Java language itself, but rather in the AWT. As you may recall, this stands for Abstract Window Toolkit; it was deliberately designed for portability over beauty. Of course, there is absolutely no reason one can't have both, and there's every reason to believe that some third-party GUI toolkit or a future version of AWT will finally look more like the date you'd like to bring to the dance.
- *Applet security limitations*. There are an awful lot of things you *can't* do in the context of an applet—such as open a simple disk file, for example.

With all the hype surrounding Java, there is sometimes a tendency to view Java as a "one-stop solution" to all active content on the web. This is just not the case: Java interoperates well with many other Internet technologies. For example,

- *Java applets versus CGI*. There is a common misconception that Java and CGI are somehow mutually exclusive; that it is Java versus CGI, or that Java will somehow replace CGI. In fact, nothing could be further from the truth. Java and CGI actually complement each other quite nicely.

  The distinction is actually this: Java is primarily client-side; CGI is primarily server-side. Those things that can be done on the larger server (for example, common data retrievals or generation) are probably good candidates for CGI. Those applications that make good use of a user's workstation or PC (for example, GUI-intensive applications or highly interactive data reduction and analysis packages) are good candidates for Java applets.

Most real-world applications are probably a little of both. One of the great things about the web is that it makes true distributed processing so very easy. You just break the problem into pieces and deliver each piece to whichever node on the net that makes the most sense.

- *Java and ActiveX Controls.* The same argument has been raised about Java and ActiveX controls: that the two technologies are somehow mutually exclusive. Just as with Java and CGI, this is simply not the case. ActiveX actually complements Java. Refer to Chapters 22, "Scripting with Microsoft VBScript and JScript," and 25, "Advanced Microsoft Dynamic HTML," for some discussion of ActiveX.

The Java Guru's Dictionary

Table 38.7 presents neither a true dictionary, nor is it by any means a comprehensive list of every term in the Java universe. It should, however, prove useful to you.

Table 38.7 The Java guru's dictionary.

Term	Meaning
API	*Application Programming Interface*: a programming standard (such as stdlib or Win32).
AFC	*Application Foundation Classes*: a class library, promoted by Microsoft. See also IFC, JFC.
AWT	*Abstract Window Toolkit*: Java's GUI library.
BDK	*Beans Development Kit*. See also JDK, Java Beans.
Enterprise APIs	Sun's "Enterprise APIs" for Java include JDBC, RMI, and Security.
HotJava	A fully Java 1.1-conformant web browser, written entirely in Java.
IFC	*Internet Foundation Classes*: a class library, promoted by Netscape. See also AFC, JFC.
Internationalization	The capability of a program to support different languages (for example, French and English) and different locales (for example, British versus American spelling and currency symbols) without recompiling. Java 1.1 introduces new features that simplify internationalization. See also Unicode, ResourceBundles.
Introspection	The means by which a client can "get at" the functionality exported by a Java Bean. See also Java Beans, Reflection.
JAR	*Java Archive file*: an efficient, convenient means to upload an applet and any related files it might need (helper classes, sound files, images, and so on) over the network in one shot instead of incurring multiple separate HTTPD requests.

continues

Table 38.7 Continued

Term	Meaning
Java Beans	A "software component model"; addresses similar issues as Microsoft's COM and ActiveX.
JavaOS	An operating system, developed by Sun, specifically tailored to run Java applications well.
JDK	*Java Development Kit*: complete Java compiler, libraries, and so forth. The JDK is freely available from Sun's web page.
JFC	*Java Foundation Classes*: Sun's Java class library. See also AFC, IFC.
JIT	*Just In Time Compiler*: a JIT converts Java bytecodes into native executables on-the-fly. The use of JITs in web browsers dramatically increases the performance of Java programs.
JNI	Java *Native Method Interface*: allows C programs to use Java classes and methods.
JDBC	*Java Data Base Connectivity*: part of the Enterprise API. JDBC allows Java programs to communicate with databases; addresses similar issues as Microsoft's ODBC.
JVM	*Java Virtual Machine*: the runtime component that interprets Java bytecode and executes the Java program (for example, in a Java-enabled web browser).
Properties	Java Beans export their functionality to client programs as a set of *properties* (object attributes) and *methods* (behavior).
Reflection	This new JDK 1.1 package enables you to query the properties and methods available in a Java Bean component. "Reflection" is similar to "Type libraries" used in MS-Windows.
ResourceBundle	Related to Internationalization. You will typically define a unique "bundle" for each locale your program wishes to support.
RMI	*Remote Method Invocation*: part of the Enterprise API; allows Java applets to invoke remote resources (such as other applets) in different processes, or even on different machines across the Internet.
Servlet	A Java program intended to be run at the web server, in contrast to an applet, which is uploaded to and run on the client.
Signed Applet	Attaching a "digital signature" to a Java JAR file to ensure that the applet indeed came from a trusted source and has not been tampered with.
Unicode	The native "string" format in Java; designed to support any character in any language.

Other Resources

Where do you go from here? Probably the best place to start is to glance around at some of the exciting things your fellow developers around the world are doing with Java. Here are a couple of popular URLs to get you started.

ON THE WEB

http://www.javasoft.com Sun's official site for the latest information about the Java language.

http://www.gamelan.com Arguably the largest and most popular "unofficial" site for the Java programming community. A great site to learn about Java tools, discover other Java-related home pages, and find sample code.

news:comp.lang.java Probably the best way to ask and answer Java-related questions from the worldwide Java programming community.

Each of these vendors (and many more) have also shown a strong commitment to Java, and usually have a great deal of useful tools and information on their web pages:

http://www.ibm.com/java IBM has been applying Java across their entire product line, from the desktop to mainframes and especially to the "middleware" that glues everything together.

http://www.marimba.com Founded by engineers from Sun's original Java team, Marimba has pioneered web-based applications for which Java is uniquely suited.

http://www.microsoft.com This is an excellent site for a broad range of Internet-related technologies, including Java development tools (Visual J++) and JVM runtime environments (Internet Explorer).

http://www.netscape.com Also an excellent source of information about Internet-related tools and technologies.

http://www.objectspace.com ObjectSpace's JGL is one of the leading third-party class libraries for enterprise-scale Java development work.

http://www.oracle.com The largest relational database vendor, Oracle has also made a strong commitment to—and is doing important work with—Java technologies.

http://www.roguewave.com Rogue Wave is a leader in cross-platform Java and C++ class libraries and development tools.

CHAPTER 39

User Input and Interactivity with Java

by Jerry Ablan

In this chapter

Interacting with People Using Java

User interaction with your programs is by far the most important aspect of creating Java applets and applications. If your interface is bad, people will not want to use your program. Come up with a unique interface, however, and you could have the next "killer" app. But keep in mind that creating those awesome interfaces requires you to start with some foundation.

It is that Java foundation that this chapter discusses. Learning about all the different tools at your disposal will enable you to build cool interfaces, and keep your users happy.

Using the Abstract Windowing Toolkit

The Abstract Windowing Toolkit (AWT) is Java's component package. This package contains all the programming tools you will need to interact with the user.

The AWT contains a number of familiar user interface elements. Figure 39.1 shows a Java applet with a sample of some of the components of the AWT.

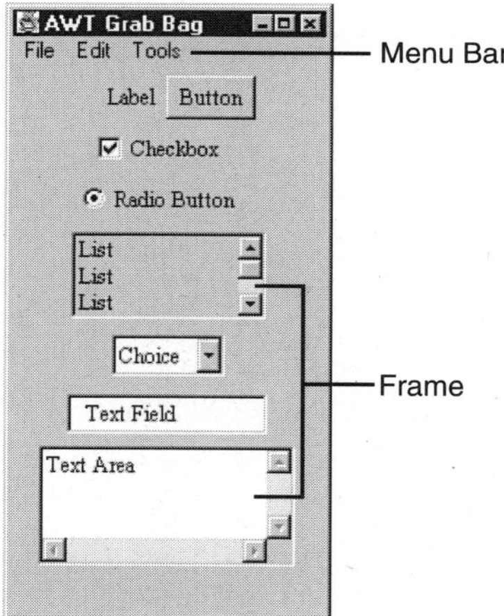

FIG. 39.1 The AWT features a number of familiar components.

Figure 39.2 shows a portion of the AWT's inheritance hierarchy.

AWT Components

Components are the building blocks of the AWT. The end user interacts directly with these components. AWT provides the following components:

- Drawing Canvases (`Canvas`)
- Checkboxes and Radio Buttons (`Checkbox`)
- Menus (`Menu`, `MenuBar`, `MenuItem`)
- Popup Choices (`Choice`)

- Push Buttons (`Button`)
- Scrollbars (`Scrollbar`)
- Scrolling Lists (`List`)
- Text Areas (`TextArea`)
- Text Fields (`TextField`)
- Text Labels (`Label`)

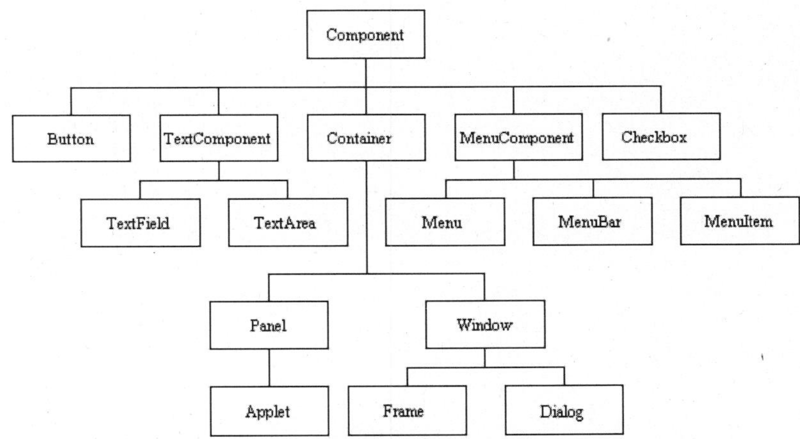

FIG. 39.2
The AWT inherits all its user interface components from Component.

Containers

You need more than just components to create a good user interface. The components need to be organized into manageable groups. That is where containers come in. Containers contain components. You cannot use a component in the AWT unless it is contained within a container. A component without a container is like a refrigerator magnet without a refrigerator. The container classes defined in the AWT are as follows:

- `Applet`
- `Dialog`
- `FileDialog`
- `Frame`
- `Panel`
- `Window`

TIP Containers not only contain components, they are components themselves. This means that a container can contain other containers.

Layout Managers

Even though you have containers as a place to neatly store your user interface (UI) components, you still need a way to organize the components within a container. That is where the layout managers come in. Each container is given a layout manager that decides where each component should be displayed. The layout managers in the AWT are as follows:

- `FlowLayout`
- `BorderLayout`
- `GridLayout`
- `CardLayout`
- `GridBagLayout`

Buttons

Buttons are a simple mechanism, but they are one of the workhorses of any graphical interface. You find buttons on toolbars, dialog boxes, windows, and even in other components such as scrollbars.

Creating Buttons

The only thing you have to decide when creating a button is whether you want the button to be labeled. Buttons have no other options.

To create an unlabeled button, use this syntax:

```
Button myButton = new Button();
```

Creating a labeled button is an equally simple task:

```
Button myButton = new Button( "Press Me" );
```

After you have created a button, you need to add it to a container. Because your applet is already a container, you can add a button directly to your layout:

```
Button myButton = new Button( "Press Me" );

add( myButton );
```

To change the label of your button, use `setLabel`:

```
myButton.setLabel( "Pull Me!" );
```

To get the label for your button, use `getLabel`:

```
String buttonLabel = myButton.getLabel();
```

NOTE You may notice the lack of "image buttons"—that is, buttons that contain an image rather than text. These types of buttons are almost a necessity for creating toolbars. Unfortunately, they are not supported in the AWT. Hopefully, these will show up in a future version of the AWT; but for now, if you want an image button, you must implement it yourself.

Using Buttons

Until you wire in the event handling, nothing will happen when your new button is clicked. By default, your user interface components receive no events. To enable this event handling, you must register to receive events. This registration process is called *listening*. You must implement the correct event listener in your class, or create a new class that implements the correct event listener. Depending on your event handling needs, this can be a simple to complex task.

NOTE You can still write code that uses the old `handleEvent` method to receive events. However, it is unlikely that this will be available in version 2.0 of the Java language.

Creating Button Event Handlers The easiest way to create event handlers for buttons is to use what is called an *anonymous local* class. This special class is used primarily for this purpose: to create quick, little event handlers. Imagine an interface with five buttons. Instead of creating a separate class for each button, you can use this technique to redirect button click events to your own class.

An anonymous local class is one that has no name (anonymous), and is contained within a set of brackets (local). This is an extremely easy technique to use to set up callback routines for your buttons and other components. Here's a cool way to grab the `windowClosing` event, for example:

```
addWindowListener( new WindowAdapter()
    { public void windowClosing( WindowEvent e )
    { handleWindowClose(); } } );
```

Therefore, to grab button clicks is just as simple. The following code creates an actionListener for the previously created `myButton`.

```
    MyButton.addActionListener( new ActionListener()
        { public void actionPerformed( ActionEvent e )
            { myButtonClicked(); } } );
```

This particular handler registers for the action, or click, event. This event occurs when the button is clicked. In addition to registering for the event, you have asked the program to call the `myButtonClicked` method when the event occurs. Now all you have to do is fill in the `myButtonClicked` method with code to handle the event.

Now that you know how to create a button and check for an action, you can create a button applet. A very simple example is an applet with buttons that change its background color. One way to do this is by putting the name of the color in the button label. Then, in the `action` method, you look at the label of the button that was pressed and set the applet's background color based on that label. The button to turn the background blue, for example, could be labeled "Blue." The `action` method would set the background to blue if the button's label was blue. The applet in Listing 39.1 demonstrates how to do this.

Listing 39.1 filename Source code for Button1Applet.java.

```
// Example 39.1 — Button1Applet
//
// This applet creates two buttons named "Red" and "Blue."  When a
// button is pressed, the background color of the applet is set to
// the color named by that button's label.
//

import java.applet.*;
import java.awt.*;
import java.awt.event.*;

public class
Button1Applet
extends Applet
{
    public void
    init()
    {
        Button btnBlue, btnRed;

        btnRed = new Button( "Red" );
        btnBlue = new Button( "Blue" );

        add( btnRed );
        add( btnBlue );

        btnRed.addActionListener( new ActionListener()
            { public void actionPerformed( ActionEvent e )
                { btnRedClicked(); } } );

        btnBlue.addActionListener( new ActionListener()
            { public void actionPerformed( ActionEvent e )
                { btnBlueClicked(); } } );
    }

    public void
    btnRedClicked()
    {
        setBackgroundColor( Color.red );
    }

    public void
    btnBlueClicked()
    {
        setBackgroundColor( Color.blue );
    }

    public void
    setBackgroundColor( Color c )
    {
        setBackground( c );
        repaint();
    }
}
```

Figure 39.3 shows the Button1Applet in operation.

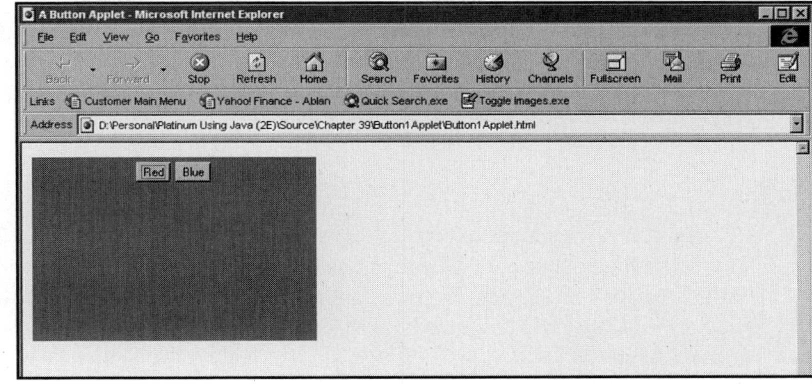

FIG. 39.3
The buttons in Button1Applet change the applet's background color.

Labels

Labels are the simplest of the AWT components. They are text strings used only for decoration. Because they are "display-only," labels generate no events.

Creating Labels

You can create labels in three different ways. The simplest is to create an empty label, such as this:

```
Label myLabel = new Label();
```

Of course, an empty label isn't going to do you much good because there is nothing to see. A more useful label is one with some text, as in the following:

```
Label myLabel = new Label( "This is a label" );
```

Labels can be left-justified, right-justified, or centered. You can use the variables `Label.LEFT`, `Label.RIGHT`, and `Label.CENTER` to set the alignment of a label. Here is an example of how to create a right-justified label:

```
Label myLabel = new Label( "This is a right-justified label", Label.RIGHT );
```

You can change the text of a label with `setText`:

```
myLabel.setText( "This is the new label text" );
```

You can also get the text of a label with `getText`:

```
String labelText = myLabel.getText();
```

You can change the alignment of a label with `setAlignment`:

```
myLabel.setAlignment( Label.CENTER );
```

You can also get the alignment of a label with `getAlignment`:

```
int labelAlignment = myLabel.getAlignment();
```

Figure 39.4 shows a sample label.

FIG. 39.4
Labels are just text strings.

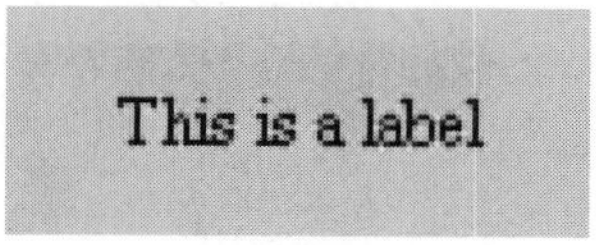

Check Boxes and Radio Buttons

Check boxes are similar to buttons except that they are used as "yes-no" or "on-off" switches. Every time you click a check box, it changes from "off" to "on" or from "on" to "off." A close cousin to the check box is the radio button. Radio buttons are also "on-off" switches, but they are arranged in special, mutually exclusive groups where only one button in the group can be on at a time.

Creating Check Boxes

A check box has two parts—a label and a state. The label is the text displayed next to the check box itself; the state is a Boolean variable that indicates whether the box is checked. By default, the state of a check box is false, or "off."

This line of code creates a check box with no label:

```
Checkbox myCheckbox = new Checkbox();
```

The following code creates a check box with a label:

```
Checkbox myCheckbox = new Checkbox( "Check me if you like Java" );
```

You can also create a checkbox while setting its state by using this code:

```
Checkbox myCheckbox = new Checkbox( "Check me if you like Java", null, true );
```

The `null` in the preceding code fragment refers to the `CheckboxGroup` to which the check box belongs. You use `CheckboxGroup` to create a set of radio buttons; for a normal check box, the `CheckboxGroup` will be `null`.

You may check to see whether a check box has been checked with `getState`:

```
if ( myCheckbox.getState() )
{
     // The box has been checked
}
else
{
     // The box has not been checked
}
```

Creating Radio Buttons

Radio buttons are just a special case of a check box. There is no `RadioButton` class. Instead, you create a set of radio buttons by creating check boxes and putting them in the same check box group. The constructor for `CheckboxGroup` takes no arguments:

```
CheckboxGroup myCheckboxGroup = new CheckboxGroup()
```

After you have created the group, you create check boxes that belong to this group by passing the group to the constructor. You can then add them to your layout, as follows:

```
add( new Checkbox( "Favorite language is Java", myCheckboxGroup, true ) );
add( new Checkbox( "Favorite language is Visual Cobol", myCheckboxGroup, false )
);
add( new Checkbox( "Favorite language is Backtalk", myCheckboxGroup, false ) );
```

NOTE When you add check boxes to a check box group, the last check box added as *true* is the box checked when the group is displayed.

You can find out which radio button is selected by either calling `getState` on each check box, or calling `getSelectedCheckbox` on the `CheckboxGroup`. The `getSelectedCheckbox` method returns the check box that is currently selected.

Using Check Boxes and Radio Buttons

Unlike buttons, check boxes generate `ItemEvents` when they are selected and deselected. Therefore you must create an `ItemListener` to listen for these events. The `itemStateChanged` method of the `ItemListener` is called when the state of a check box changes. An `ItemEvent` is passed in as an argument. This object contains information about the current check box state. You can set up handlers for these events quite easily by using the technique previously outlined. You can also just use the `getState` method to check the state of the radio button or the check box.

Figure 39.5 shows some check boxes and a group of three radio buttons.

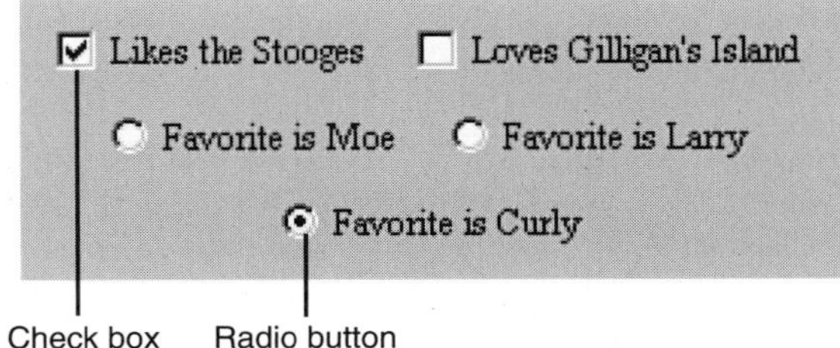

FIG. 39.5 Check boxes are squared boxes with checks in them. Radio buttons are rounded and are checked with dots.

Choices

The `Choice` class provides a pop-up menu of text string choices. The current choice is displayed as the menu title. These are drop-down list boxes and combo boxes in other GUI platforms.

Creating Choices

To create a choice pop-up menu, you must first create an instance of the `Choice` class. Because there are no options for the choice constructor, the creation of a `Choice` should always look something like this:

```
Choice myChoice = new Choice();
```

After you have created the choice, you can add string items to it by using the `addItem` method:

```
myChoice.addItem( "Moe" );
myChoice.addItem( "Larry" );
myChoice.addItem( "Curly" );
```

You may also change which item is currently selected either by name or by index. If you wanted `Curly` to be selected, for instance, you could select him by name:

```
myChoice.select( "Curly" );
```

You could also select `Curly` by his position in the list. Because he was added third, and the choices are numbered starting at 0, `Moe` would be 0, `Larry` would be 1, and `Curly` would be 2:

```
myChoice.select( 2 );
```

If you want your items to be in a particular order, you must place them into the `Choice` in that order. Java provides no sort capability for the `Choice` or `List` components.

The `getSelectedIndex` method will return the position of the selected item. Again, if `Curly` was selected, `getSelectedIndex` would return `2`. Similarly, the `getSelectedItem` method returns the string name of the selected item; so if Curly was selected, `getSelectedItem` would return "Curly."

If you have an index value for an item and you want to find out the name of the item at that index, you can use `getItem`:

```
String selectedItem = myChoice.getItem( 2 );
```

Figure 39.6 shows a choice in its usual form. Figure 39.7 shows a choice with its menu of choices pulled down.

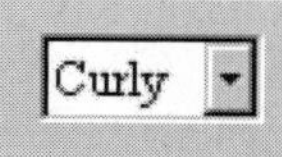

FIG. 39.6
The choice box displays its current selection.

FIG. 39.7
The button on the right of a choice pops up a menu of the possible choices.

Using Choices

Choice objects generate ItemEvents like the Checkbox objects. Therefore you must create an ItemListener object to receive these events:

```
import java.applet.*;
import java.awt.*;
import java.awt.event.*;

public class StoogeAction
extends Applet
{
    String          currentStooge;
    Choice         myChoice;

    public StoogeAction()
    {
        myChoice = new Choice();
        myChoice.addItem( "Moe" );
        myChoice.addItem( "Larry" );
        myChoice.addItem( "Curly" );
        add( myChoice );

        myChoice.addItemListener( new ItemListener()
            { public void itemStateChanged( ItemEvent e )
                { myChoiceChanged( e ); } } );
    }

    public void
    myChoiceChanged( ItemEvent e )
    {
         currentStooge = ((Choice)(e.getItemSelectable())).getSelectedItem();
    }
}
```

Lists

The List class enables you to create a scrolling list of values that may be selected either individually or many at a time.

Creating Lists

You have two options when creating a List. The default constructor for the List class enables you to create a List that does not allow multiple selections:

```
List myList = new List();
```

You may also set the number of list entries that are visible in the list window at any one time, as well as whether to allow multiple selections. The following code fragment creates a list with 10 visible entries and multiple selections turned on:

```
List myList = new List( 10, true );
```

After you have created the list, you can add new entries to it with the `addItem` method:

```
myList.addItem( "Moe" );
myList.addItem( "Larry" );
myList.addItem( "Curly" );
```

You may also add an item at a specific position in the list. The list positions are numbered from 0; therefore if you add an item at position 0, it goes to the front of the list. If you try to add an item at position -1, or try to add an item at a position higher than the number of positions, the item will be added to the end of the list. The following code adds "Shemp" to the beginning of the list, and "Curly Joe" to the end:

```
myList.addItem( "Shemp", 0 );        // Add Shemp at position 0
myList.addItem( "Curly Joe", -1 );   // Add Curly Joe to the end of the list
```

List Features

The `List` class provides a number of different methods for changing the contents of the list. The `replaceItem` method replaces an item at a given position with a new item:

```
myList.replaceItem( "Dr. Howard", 0 );
        // Replace the first item in the list with "Dr. Howard"
```

You can delete an item in the list with `deleteItem`:

```
myList.deleteItem( 1 );
        // Delete the second item in the list (0 is the first)
```

The `deleteItems` method deletes a whole range of items from the list. The following code removes items from the list starting at position 2, up to and including position 5:

```
myList.deleteItems( 2, 5 );
        // Delete from position 2 up to and including position 5
```

You can delete all the items in the list with the `clear` method:

```
myList.clear();
```

The `getSelectedIndex` method returns the index number of the currently selected item, or –1 if no item is selected:

```
int currentSelection = myList.getSelectedIndex();
```

You can also get the selected item directly with `getSelectedItem`:

```
String selectItem = myList.getSelectedItem();
```

For lists with multiple selections turned on, you can get all the selections with `getSelectedIndexes`:

```
int currentSelections[];
currentSelections = myList.getSelectedIndexes();
```

The `getSelectedItems` returns all the selected items:

```
String selectedItems[];
selectItems = myList.getSelectItems();
```

CAUTION

You should only use `getSelectedIndex` and `getSelectedItem` on lists without multiple selections. If you allow multiple selections, you should always use `getSelectedIndexes` and `getSelectedItems`.

You may make any item become selected by calling the `select` method with the index of the item you want selected. If the list does not allow multiple selections, the previously selected item will be deselected:

```
myList.select( 2 );        // Select the third item in the list
```

You may deselect any item by calling the `deselect` method with the index of the item you want deselected:

```
myList.deselect( 0 );      // Deselect the first item in the list
```

The `isSelected` method tells you whether the item at a particular index is selected:

```
if ( myList.isSelection( 0 ) )
{
    //    the first item in the list is selected
}
```

You may turn multiple selections on and off with the `setMultipleSelections` method:

```
myList.setMultipleSelections( true );
         // turn multi-select on, false turns it off
```

The `allowsMultipleSelections` method returns `true` if multiple selections are allowed:

```
if ( myList.allowsMultipleSelections() )
{
     // multiple selections are allowed
}
```

Sometimes you might make sure a particular item is visible in the list window. You can do just that by passing the index of the item you want to make visible to `makeVisible`. Suppose, for example, the list was positioned on item 0, but you wanted to make sure item 15 was showing in the window instead. You would call the following:

```
myList.makeVisible( 15 );         // Make item 15 in the list visible
```

Using Lists

`List` objects generate `ItemEvents` like the `Choice` objects. In addition, they generate an `ActionEvent` when a list item is double-clicked.

The applet in Listing 39.2 sets up a `List` containing several values and uses a label to inform you whenever an item is selected or deselected:

Listing 39.2 Source code for ListApplet.java.

```
//
//    Example 39.2 — ListApplet
//
//    This applet creates a scrolling list with several choices and
//    informs you of selections and deselections using a label.
//

import       java.applet.*;
import       java.awt.*;
import       java.awt.event.*;

public class
ListApplet
extends Applet
{
    Label        listStatus;
    List         myList;

    public void
    init()
    {
        //    Create the list...
        myList = new List( 3, true );

        myList.addItem( "Moe" );
        myList.addItem( "Larry" );
        myList.addItem( "Curly" );
        myList.addItem( "Shemp" );
        myList.addItem( "Curly Joe" );

        //    Set Shemp to be selected
        myList.select( 3 );

        myList.addItemListener( new ItemListener()
            { public void itemStateChanged( ItemEvent e )
                { myListChanged( e ); } } );

        //    Finally, add the list to the applet
        add( myList );

        //    Now create a label to show us the last event that occurred
        listStatus = new Label( "You selected entry Shemp" );
        add( listStatus );
    }

    public void
    myListChanged( ItemEvent e )
    {
        String          selStr = "";

        // Check to see if this is a sel event
        switch ( e.getStateChange() )
        {
            case    ItemEvent.SELECTED:
```

```
                selStr = "You selected entry ";
                break;

            case    ItemEvent.DESELECTED:
                selStr = "You deselected entry ";
                break;
        }

        //    use getItem to get the actual item.
        selStr += myList.getItem( ((Integer)e.getItem()).intValue() );

        // Update the label
        listStatus.setText( selStr );
    }
}
```

Figure 39.8 shows the output from ListApplet.

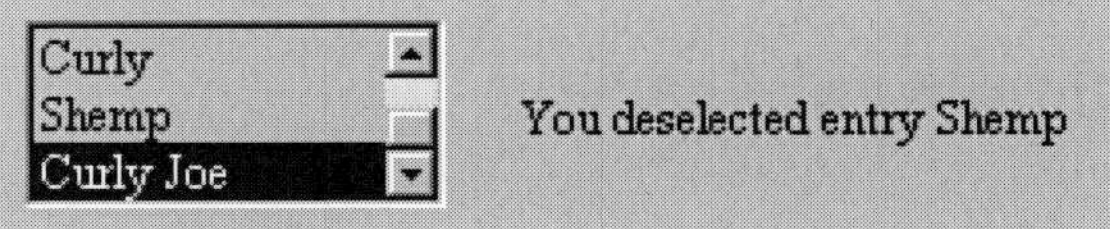

FIG. 39.8
The ListApplet program enables you to select and deselect list items.

Text Fields and Text Areas

The AWT provides two different classes for entering text data: `TextField` and `TextArea`. The `TextField` class handles only a single line of text; the `TextArea` handles multiple lines. Both of these classes share many similar methods because they both derive from a common class called `TextComponent`.

Creating Text Fields

The easiest way to create a text field is as follows:

```
TextField myTextField = new TextField();
```

This creates an empty text field with an unspecified number of columns. If you want to control how many columns are in the text field, you can do so with this:

```
TextField myTextField = new TextField(40);     // Create 40-column text field
```

Sometimes you may want to initialize the text field with some text when you create it:

```
TextField myTextField = new TextField("This is some initial text");
```

Rounding out these combinations is a method for creating a text field initialized with text, having a fixed number of columns:

```
TextField myTextField = new TextField("This is some initial text", 40);
```

Creating Text Areas

It should come as no surprise to you that the methods to create text areas are similar to those for text fields. In fact, they are identical, except that when giving a fixed size for a text area you must give both columns and rows. You can create an empty text area having an unspecified number of rows and columns with the following:

```
TextArea myTextArea = new TextArea();
```

If you want to initialize an area with some text:

```
TextArea myTextArea = new TextArea("Here is some initial text");
```

You can give a text area a fixed number of rows and columns with this:

```
TextArea myTextArea = new TextArea(5, 40 );      // 5 rows, 40 columns
```

Finally, you can create a text area having some initial text and a fixed size with the following:

```
TextArea myTextArea = new TextArea(
      "Here is some initial text", 5, 40); // 5 rows, 40 cols
```

Common Text Component Features

The `TextComponent` abstract class implements a number of useful methods that you can use on either `TextArea` or `TextField` classes.

You will probably want to put text into the component at some point. You can do that with `setText`:

```
myTextField.setText("This is the text now in the field");
```

You will certainly want to find out what text is in the component. You can use `getText` to do that:

```
String textData = myTextArea.getText();
```

You can find out what text has been selected (highlighted with the mouse) by using `getSelectedText`:

```
String selectedStuff = myTextArea.getSelectedText();
```

You can also find out where the selection starts and where it ends. The `getSelectionStart` and `getSelectionEnd` methods return integers that indicate the position within the entire text where the selection starts and ends. If the selection started at the very beginning of the text, for instance, `getSelectionStart` would return `0`:

```
int selectionStart, selectionEnd;
selectionStart = myTextField.getSelectionStart();
selectionEnd = myTextField.getSelectionEnd();
```

You can also cause text to be selected with the `select` method:

```
myTextField.select(0, 4);
        // Selects the characters from position 0 through 4
```

If you want to select the entire text, you can use `selectAll` as a shortcut:

```
myTextArea.selectAll();      // Selects all the text in the area
```

You can also use `setEditable` to control whether the text in the component can be edited (if not, it is read-only):

```
myTextField.setEditable(false);
        // Don't let anyone change this field
```

The `isEditable` method returns `true` if the component is editable, and `false` if it is not.

Text Field Features

Text fields have some features that text areas do not have. The `TextField` class enables you to set an echo character that is printed rather than the character that was typed. This is useful when making fields for entering passwords, where you might make '*' the echo character. Setting up an echo character is as easy as calling `setEchoCharacter`:

```
myTextField.setEchoCharacter('*'); // Print *s in place of what was typed
```

You can find out the echo character for a field with `getEchoChar`:

```
char echoChar = myTextField.getEchoChar();
```

The `echoCharIsSet` method returns `true` if there is an echo character set for the field, and `false` if not.

Finally, you can find out how many columns are in the text field (how many visible columns, not how much text is there) by using the `getColumns` method:

```
int numColumns = myTextField.getColumns();
```

Text Area Features

Text areas also have special features all their own. Text areas are usually used for editing text, so they contain some methods for inserting, appending, and replacing text. You can add text to the end of the text area with `appendText`:

```
myTextArea.appendText(
     "This will be added to the end of the text in the area");
```

You can also insert text at any point in the current text with `insertText`. If you add text at position 0, for example, you add it to the front of the area:

```
myTextArea.insertText(
     "This will be added to the front of the text in the area", 0);
```

You can also use `replaceText` to replace portions of the text. Here is an example that uses the `getSelectionStart` and `getSelectionEnd` functions from TextComponent to replace selected text in a TextArea with "[CENSORED]":

```
myTextArea.replaceText("[CENSORED]", myTextArea.getSelectionStart(),
     myTextArea.getSelectionEnd());
```

Finally, you can find out the number of columns and the number of rows in a text area with `getColumns` and `getRows`.

Using Text Fields and Text Areas

Both the `Textfield` class and the `TextArea` class generate `ActionEvents`. Each keystroke generates two events: one for the key press, and one for the key release. The `ActionEvent` captures the state of the system at the moment of the press and release. This is useful for capturing modifiers such as the Shift key or perhaps the Ctrl key. To listen for these events, you must install an `ActionListener`. By listening for the `ActionEvent`, however, you can receive the key press for Enter.

Listing 39.3 creates two text fields: a text area with an echo character defined, and a text area that displays the value of the text entered in one of the text fields:

Listing 39.3 Source code for TextApplet.java.

```
//
//    Example 39.3 — TextApplet
//
//    This applet creates some text fields and a text area
//    to demonstrate the features of each.
//

import    java.awt.*;
import    java.awt.event.*;
import    java.applet.*;

public class
TextApplet
extends Applet
{
    protected TextField     inputField;
    protected TextField     passwordField;
    protected TextArea         textArea;

    public void
    init()
    {
        inputField = new TextField();    // unspecified size
        add( inputField );

        passwordField = new TextField( 10 ); // 10 columns
        passwordField.setEchoChar( '*' ); // print '*' for input

        passwordField.addActionListener( new ActionListener()
            { public void actionPerformed( ActionEvent e )
                { passwordFieldChanged( e ); } } );

        add( passwordField );

        textArea = new TextArea( 5, 40 ); // 5 rows, 40 cols
        textArea.append( "This is some initial text for the text area." );
        textArea.select( 5, 12 ); // select "is some"

        add( textArea );
    }
```

```
    // The action method looks specifically for something entered in the
    // password field and displays it in the textArea
    public void
    passwordFieldChanged( ActionEvent e )
    {
        // Now, change the text in the textArea to "Your password is: "
        // followed by the password entered in the passwordField
        textArea.setText( "Your password is: " +
            passwordField.getText() );
    }
}
```

Figure 39.9 shows the text fields and text area set up by the `TextApplet` example. Notice how small the first text field is because its size was left unspecified.

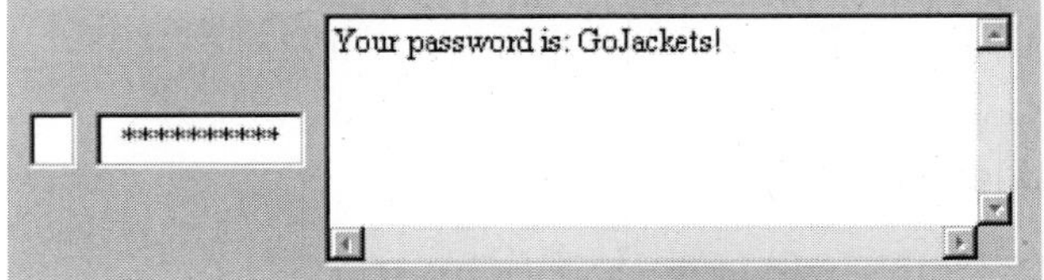

FIG. 39.9 Text fields and text areas allow the entry of text.

Scrollbars

The `Scrollbar` class provides a basic interface for scrolling that can be used in a variety of situations. The controls of the scrollbar manipulate a position value that indicates the scrollbar's current position. You can set the minimum and maximum values for the scrollbar's position as well as its current value. The scrollbar's controls update the position in three ways: "line," "page," and "absolute." The arrow buttons at either end of the scrollbar update the scrollbar position with a "line" update. You can tell the scrollbar how much to add to the position (or subtract from it). For a line update, the default is 1. A "page" update is performed whenever the mouse is clicked on the gap between the slider button and the scrolling arrows. You can also tell the scrollbar how much to add to the position for a page update. The "absolute" update is performed whenever the slider button is dragged in one direction or the other. You have no control over how the position value changes for an absolute update, except that you can control the minimum and maximum values.

An important aspect of the `Scrollbar` class is that it is only responsible for updating its own position. It cannot cause any other component to scroll. If you want the scrollbar to scroll a canvas up and down, you have to add code to detect when the scrollbar changes and update the canvas as needed.

Creating Scrollbars

You can create a simple vertical scrollbar with this:

```
Scrollbar myScrollbar = new Scrollbar();
```

You can also specify the orientation of the scrollbar as either `Scrollbar.HORIZONTAL` or `Scrollbar.VERTICAL`:

```
Scrollbar myScrollbar = new Scrollbar( Scrollbar.HORIZONTAL );
```

You can create a scrollbar with a predefined orientation, position, page increment, minimum value, and maximum value. The following code creates a vertical scrollbar with a minimum value of 0, a maximum value of 100, a page size of 10, and a starting position of 50:

```
Scrollbar myScrollbar = new Scrollbar( Scrollbar.VERTICAL, 50, 10, 0, 100 );
```

Scrollbar Features

You can set the scrollbar's unit increment with `setUnitIncrement`:

```
myScrollbar.setUnitIncrement( 2 );
        // Arrow button increment/decrement by 2 each time
```

You can query the current unit increment with `getUnitIncrement`:

```
int unitIncrement = myScrollbar.getUnitIncrement();
```

You can set the block increment with `setBlockIncrement`:

```
myScrollbar.setBlockIncrement( 20 );
        // Block update adds/subtracts 20 each time
```

You can also query the block increment with `getBlockIncrement`.

```
int blockIncrement = myScrollbar.getBlockIncrement();
```

You can find out the scrollbar's minimum and maximum position values with `getMinimum` and `getMaximum`:

```
int minimum = myScrollbar.getMinimum();
int maximum = myScrollbar.getMaximum();
```

The `setValue` method sets the scrollbar's current position:

```
myScrollbar.setValue( 25 );      // Make the current position 25
```

You can query the current position with `getValue`:

```
int currentPosition = myScrollbar.getValue();
```

The `getOrientation` method returns `Scrollbar.VERTICAL` if the scrollbar is vertical or `Scrollbar.HORIZONTAL` if it is horizontal:

```
if ( myScrollbar.getOrientation() == Scrollbar.HORIZONTAL )
{
     // Code to handle a horizontal scrollbar
}
else
{
   // Code to handle a vertical scrollbar
}
```

You can also set the position, page increment, minimum value, and maximum value with `setValues`. The following code sets the position to 75, the page increment to 25, the minimum value to 0, and the maximum to 500:

```
myScrollbar.setValues( 75, 25, 0, 500 );
```

Using Scrollbars

The `Scrollbar` class generates `AdjustmentEvents`. These events have several values:

- AdjustmentEvent.TRACK when the slider button is dragged.
- AdjustmentEvent.UNIT_INCREMENT when the top, or left arrow button is pressed.
- AdjustmentEvent.UNIT_DECREMENT when the bottom or right arrow button is pressed.
- AdjustmentEvent.BLOCK_INCREMENT when the user clicks in the area between the slider and the bottom or left arrow.
- AdjustmentEvent.BLOCK_DECREMENT when the user clicks in the area between the slider and the top or right arrow.

You may not care which of these events is received. In many cases, you may only need to know that the scrollbar position is changed and you would call the `getValue` method to find out the new position.

Canvases

The `Canvas` class is a component with no special functionality. It is mainly used for creating custom graphic components. You create an instance of a `Canvas` with this:

```
Canvas myCanvas = new Canvas();
```

You will almost always want to create your own special subclass of `Canvas` that does whatever special function you need. You should override the `Canvas` paint method to make your `Canvas` do something interesting. Listing 39.4 creates a `CircleCanvas` class that draws a filled circle in a specific color.

Listing 39.4 Source code for CircleCanvas.java.

```
//
// Example 39.4 — CircleCanvas class
//
// This class creates a canvas that draws a circle on itself.
// The circle color is given at creation time, and the size of
// the circle is determined by the size of the canvas.
//

import         java.awt.*;
```

continues

Listing 39.4 Continued

```
public class
CircleCanvas
extends Canvas
{

    Color       circleColor;

    //    When you create a CircleCanvas, you tell it what color to use.
    public
    CircleCanvas( Color drawColor )
    {
        circleColor = drawColor;
    }

    public void
    paint( Graphics g )
    {
        Dimension currentSize = getSize();

        //    Use the smaller of the height and width of the canvas.
        //    This guarantees that the circle will be drawn completely.

        int circleDiameter = Math.min( currentSize.width, currentSize.height );

        //    Set the color...
        g.setColor( circleColor );

        // The math here on the circleX and circleY may seem strange.  The x and
y
        // coordinates for fillOval are the upper-left coordinates of the
rectangle
        // that surrounds the circle.  If the canvas is wider than the circle,
for
        // instance, we want to find out how much wider (i.e. width - diameter)
        // and then, since we want equal amounts of blank area on both sides,
        // we divide the amount of blank area by 2.  In the case where the
diameter
        // equals the width, the amount of blank area is 0.

        int circleX = ( currentSize.width - circleDiameter ) / 2;
        int circleY = ( currentSize.height - circleDiameter ) / 2;

        g.fillOval( circleX, circleY, circleDiameter, circleDiameter );
    }
}
```

The `CircleCanvas` is only a component, not a runnable applet. Later in this chapter in the section titled "Grid Bag Layouts," you will use this new class in an example of using the `GridBagLayout` layout manager.

Panels

A `Panel` is a "pure" container. It is not a window in itself. Its sole purpose it to help you organize your components in a window. Because panels are only used for organizing components, you can actually only do very few things to a panel. You create a new panel with this:

```
Panel myPanel = new Panel();
```

You can then add the panel to another container. You might want to add it to your layout, for example:

```
add( myPanel );
```

You can also nest panels—one panel containing one or more other panels:

```
Panel mainPanel, subPanel1, subPanel2;
subPanel1 = new Panel();   // create the first sub-panel
subPanel2 = new Panel();   // create the second sub-panel
mainPanel = new Panel();   // create the main panel

mainPanel.add( subPanel1 );  // Make subPanel1 a child (sub-panel) of mainPanel
mainPanel.add( subPanel2 );  // Make subPanel2 a child of mainPanel
```

You can nest panels as many levels deep as you like. In the preceding example, you could have made `subPanel2` a child of `subPanel1` (obviously with different results).

Listing 39.5 shows how to create panels and nest subpanels within them:

Listing 39.5 Source code for PanelApplet.java.

```
//
// Example 39.5 — PanelApplet
//
// The PanelApplet applet creates a number of panels and
// adds buttons to them to demonstrate the use of panels
// for grouping components.
//

import         java.awt.*;
import         java.applet.*;

public class
PanelApplet
extends Applet
{
    public void
    init()
    {
        //    Create the main panels
        Panel mainPanel1 = new Panel();
        Panel mainPanel2 = new Panel();

        //    Create the sub-panels
        Panel subPanel1 = new Panel();
```

continues

Listing 39.5 Continued

```
        Panel subPanel2 = new Panel();

        //    Add a button directly to the applet
        add( new Button( "Applet Button" ) );

        //    Add the main panels to the applet
        add( mainPanel1 );
        add( mainPanel2 );

        // Give mainPanel1 a button and a sub-panel
        mainPanel1.add( new Button( "Main Panel 1 Button" ) );
        mainPanel1.add( subPanel1 );

        // Give mainPanel2 a button and a sub-panel
        mainPanel2.add( new Button( "Main Panel 2 Button" ) );
        mainPanel2.add( subPanel2 );

        // Give each sub-panel a button
        subPanel1.add( new Button( "Sub-panel 1 Button" ) );
        subPanel2.add( new Button( "Sub-panel 2 Button" ) );
    }
}
```

Figure 39.10 shows the output from `PanelApplet`.

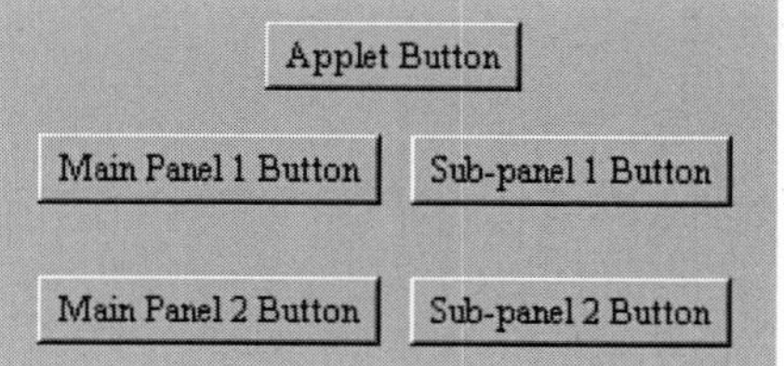

FIG. 39.10 Panels, like other containers, help group components together.

Frames

A *frame* is a fully functioning window with its own title and icon. Frames may have pull-down menus and may use a number of different cursor shapes. Frames are a powerful feature of the AWT. They enable you to create separate windows for your application. You might want your application to run outside the main window of a web browser, for example. You can also use frames to build standalone graphical applications.

Creating Frames

You can create a frame that is initially invisible and has no title with this:

```
Frame myFrame = new Frame();
```

You can give the frame a title when you create it, but it will still be invisible:

```
Frame myFrame = new Frame( "Hi!  This is my frame!" );
```

Frame Features

After you have created a frame, you will probably want to see it. Before you can see the frame, you must give it a size. Use the `setSize` method to set the size:

```
myFrame.setSize( 300, 100 );  // Make the frame 300 pixels wide, 100 high
```

You can use the `show` method to make it visible:

```
myFrame.show();      // Show yourself, Frame!
```

You can send a frame back into hiding with the `setVisible` method. Even though the frame is invisible, it still exists:

```
myFrame.setVisible( false );
```

As long as a frame exists, invisible or not, it is consuming some amount of resources in the windowing system it is running on. If you have finished with a frame, you should get rid of it with the `dispose` method:

```
myFrame.dispose();      // Gets rid of the frame and releases its resources
```

You can change the title displayed at the top of the frame with `setTitle`:

```
myFrame.setTitle( "With Frames like this, who needs enemies?" );
```

The `getTitle` method returns the frame's title:

```
String currentTitle = myFrame.getTitle();
```

The `Frame` class has a number of different cursors. You can change the frame's cursor with `setCursor`:

```
myFrame.setCursor( Frame.HAND_CURSOR );         // Change cursor to a hand
```

The following cursors are available:

- Frame.DEFAULT_CURSOR
- Frame.CROSSHAIR_CURSOR
- Frame.TEXT_CURSOR
- Frame.WAIT_CURSOR
- Frame.HAND_CURSOR
- Frame.MOVE_CURSOR
- Frame.N_RESIZE_CURSOR
- Frame.NE_RESIZE_CURSOR
- Frame.E_RESIZE_CURSOR
- Frame.SE_RESIZE_CURSOR
- Frame.S_RESIZE_CURSOR
- Frame.SW_RESIZE_CURSOR
- Frame.W_RESIZE_CURSOR
- Frame.NW_RESIZE_CURSOR.

The `getCursorType` method returns one of these values indicating the current cursor type.

If you do not want to allow your frame to be resized, you can call `setResizable` to turn resizing on or off:

```
myFrame.setResizable( false );     // Turn resizing off
```

You can change a frame's icon with `setIconImage`:

```
myFrame.setIconImage( someIconImage );
        // someIconImage must be an instance of Image
```

Using Frames to Make Your Applet Run Standalone

You can create applets that can run either as an applet or as a standalone application. All you need to do is write a `main` method in the applet that creates a frame and then creates an instance of the applet that belongs to the frame. Listing 39.6 shows an applet that can run either as an applet or as a standalone application:

Listing 39.6 Source code for StandaloneApplet.java.

```
//    Example 39.6 — StandaloneApplet
//
// This is an applet that runs either as
// an applet or a standalone application.  To run
// standalone, it provides a main method that creates
// a frame, then creates an instance of the applet and
// adds it to the frame.
//

import         java.awt.*;
import         java.applet.*;

public class
StandaloneApplet
extends Applet
{
    public void
    init()
    {
        add( new Button( "Standalone Applet Button" ) );
    }

    public static void
    main( String args[] )
    {
        // Create the frame this applet will run in
        Frame appletFrame = new Frame( "Some applet" );

        // Create an instance of the applet
        Applet myApplet = new StandaloneApplet();

        // Initialize and start the applet
        myApplet.init();
        myApplet.start();
```

```
        // The frame needs a layout manager
        appletFrame.setLayout( new FlowLayout() );

        // Add the applet to the frame
        appletFrame.add( myApplet );

        // Have to give the frame a size before it is visible
        appletFrame.setSize( 300, 100 );

        // Make the frame appear on the screen
        appletFrame.show();
    }
}
```

Adding Menus to Frames

You can attach a `MenuBar` class to a frame to provide drop-down menu capabilities. You can create a menu bar with this:

```
MenuBar myMenuBar = new MenuBar();
```

After you have created a menu bar, you can add it to a frame by using the `setMenuBar` method:

```
myFrame.setMenuBar( myMenuBar );
```

After you have a menu bar, you can add menus to it. The following code fragment creates a menu called "File" and adds it to the menu bar:

```
Menu fileMenu = new Menu( "File" );
myMenuBar.add( fileMenu );
```

Some windowing systems enable you to create menus that stay up after you release the mouse button. These are referred to as "tear-off" menus. You can specify that a menu is a "tear-off" menu when you create it:

```
Menu tearOffMenu = new Menu( "Tear Me Off", true );
        // true indicates it can be torn off
```

In addition to adding submenus, you will want to add menu items to your menus. Menu items are the parts of a menu the user actually selects. Menus, on the other hand, are used to contain menu items as well as submenus. The File menu on many systems, for example, contains menu items such as New, Open, Save, and Save As. If you created a menu structure with no menu items, the menu structure would be useless. There would be nothing to select. You can add menu items to a menu in two ways. You can just add an item name with this:

```
fileMenu.add( "Open" );     // Add an "Open" option to the file menu
```

You can also add an instance of a `MenuItem` class to a menu:

```
MenuItem saveMenuItem = new MenuItem( "Save" );
        // Create a "Save" menu item
fileMenu.add( saveMenuItem );        // Add the "Save" option to the file menu
```

You can enable and disable menu items by using `setEnabled` method. When you disable a menu item, it still appears on the menu, but it usually appears in gray (depending on the windowing system). You cannot select disabled menu items. The format for `setEnabled` is this:

```
saveMenuItem.setEnabled( false );    // Disables the save option from the file
menu
saveMenuItem.setEnabled( true );    // Enables the save option again
```

In addition to menu items, you can add submenus and menu separators to a menu. A separator is a line that appears on the menu to separate sections of the menu. To add a separator, just call the `addSeparator` method:

```
fileMenu.addSeparator();
```

To create a submenu, just create a new instance of a menu and add it to the current menu:

```
Menu printSubmenu = new Menu( "Print" );
fileMenu.add( printSubmenu );
printSubmenu.add( "Print Preview" );
         // Add print preview as option on Print menu
printSubmenu.add( "Print Document" );
         // Add print document as option on Print menu
```

You can also create special check box menu items. These items function like the check box buttons. The first time you select one, it becomes checked or "on." The next time you select it, it becomes unchecked or "off." Here is the code to create a check box menu item:

```
CheckboxMenuItem autoSaveOption = new CheckboxMenuItem( "Auto-save" );
fileMenu.add( autoSaveOption );
```

You can check to see whether a check box menu item is checked with `getState`:

```
if ( autoSaveOption.getState() )
{
     // autoSaveOption is checked, or "on"
}
else
{
     // autoSaveOption is off
}
```

You can set the current state of a check box menu item with `setState`:

```
autoSaveOption.setState( true );     // Explicitly turn auto-save option on
```

Normally, menus are added to a menu bar in a left to right fashion. Many windowing systems, however, create a special "help" menu that is on the far right of a menu bar. You can add such a menu to your menu bar with the `setHelpMenu` method:

```
Menu helpMenu = new Menu();
myMenuBar.setHelpMenu( helpMenu );
```

Using Menus

Whenever a menu item is selected, it generates an `ActionEvent`. Just create an `ActionListener` for each menu item to handle events.

Listing 39.7 shows an application that sets up a simple File menu with New, Open, and Save menu items, a check box called Auto-Save, and a Print submenu with two menu items on it:

Listing 39.7 Source code for MenuApplication.java.

```
import        java.awt.*;
import        java.applet.*;

public class
MenuApplication
extends Frame
{
    public static void
    main( String[] args )
    {
        new MenuApplication();
    }

    public
    MenuApplication()
    {
        //    Call my dad's constructor...
        super( "Menu Example" );

        //    Create the menu bar
        MenuBar myBar = new MenuBar();
        setMenuBar( myBar );

        //    Create the file menu and add it to the menubar...
        Menu fileMenu = new Menu( "File" );
        myBar.add( fileMenu );

        //    Add the New and Open menuitems
        fileMenu.add( new MenuItem( "New" ) );
        fileMenu.add( new MenuItem( "Open" ) );

        //    Create a disabled Save menuitem
        MenuItem saveMenuItem = new MenuItem( "Save" );
        saveMenuItem.disable();
        fileMenu.add( saveMenuItem );

        //    Add an Auto-Save checkbox, followed by a separator
        fileMenu.add( new CheckboxMenuItem( "Auto-Save" ) );
        fileMenu.addSeparator();

        //    Create the Print submenu
        Menu printSubmenu = new Menu( "Print" );
        fileMenu.add( printSubmenu );
        printSubmenu.add( "Print Preview" );
        printSubmenu.add( "Print Document" );

        //    Must resize the frame before it can be shown
        setSize( 300, 200 );

        //    Make the frame appear on the screen
        show();
    }
}
```

Figure 39.11 shows the output from the `MenuApplication` program, with the Print Document option in the process of being selected.

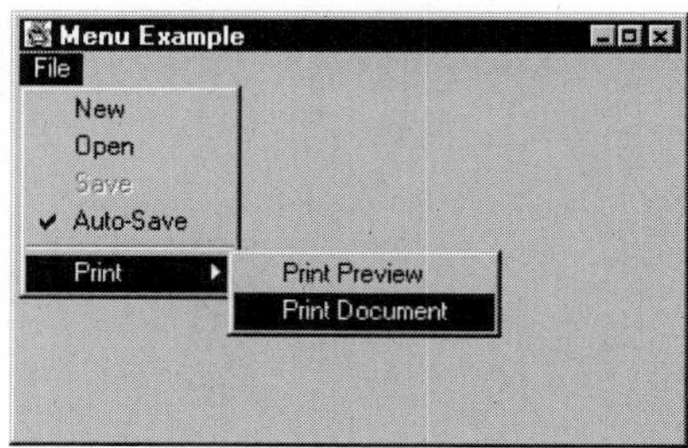

FIG. 39.11 The AWT provides a number of popular menu features, including checked menu items, disabled menu items, and separators.

Dialogs

Dialogs are pop-up windows that are not quite as flexible as frames. Dialogs are used for things such as "Are you sure you want to quit?" pop-ups, better known as message boxes. You can create a dialog as either "modal" or "non-modal." The term *modal* means the dialog box blocks input to other windows while it is being shown. This is useful for dialogs where you want to stop everything and get a crucial question answered, such as "Are you sure you want to quit?" An example of a "non-modal" dialog box might be a control panel that changes settings in an application while the application continues to run.

Creating Dialogs

To create a dialog, you must first have a frame. A dialog cannot belong to an applet. However, an applet may create a frame to which the dialog can then belong. You must specify whether a dialog is modal or non-modal at creation time and cannot change its "modality" after it has been created. The following example creates a dialog whose parent is `myFrame` and is modal:

```
Dialog myDialog = new Dialog( myFrame, true );      // true means modal dialog
```

You can also create a dialog with a title:

```
Dialog myDialog = new Dialog( myFrame, "A Non-Modal Dialog", false );
         // false = non-modal
```

NOTE Because a dialog cannot belong to an applet, your use of dialogs can be somewhat limited. One solution is to create a dummy frame as the dialog's parent. Unfortunately, you cannot create modal dialogs this way because only the frame and its children would have their input blocked—the applet would continue on its merry way. A better solution is to use the technique discussed in the "Frames" section of this chapter—in which you create a standalone application using frames, and then have a "bootstrap" applet create a frame and run the real applet in it.

After you have created a dialog, you can make it visible using the show method:

```
myDialog.show();
```

Dialog Features

The `Dialog` class has several methods in common with the `Frame` class:

```
void setResizable( boolean );
boolean isResizable();
void setTitle(String);
String getTitle();
```

In addition, the `isModal` method returns `true` if the dialog is modal.

A Reusable OK Dialog Box

Listing 39.8 shows the `OKDialog` class that provides an OK dialog box that displays a message and waits for you to click OK.

Listing 39.8 Source code for OKDialog.java.

```
//
//      Example 39.8 - OK Dialog class
//
//      OKDialog - Custom dialog that presents a message and waits for
//      you to click on the OK button.
//
//      Example use:
//     Dialog ok = new OKDialog(parentFrame, "Click OK to continue");
//     ok.show();    // Other input will be blocked until OK is pressed
//      As a shortcut, you can use the static createOKDialog that will
//      create its own frame and activate itself:
//     OKDialog.createOKDialog("Click OK to continue");
//

import         java.awt.*;

public class
OKDialog
extends Dialog
{
    protected Button         okButton;
    protected static Frame     createdFrame;

    public
    OKDialog( Frame parent, String message )
    {
        super( parent, true );    // Must call the parent's constructor

        //    This Dialog box uses the GridBagLayout to provide a pretty good
layout.
        GridBagLayout gridbag = new GridBagLayout();
        GridBagConstraints constraints = new GridBagConstraints();

        //    Create the OK button and the message to display
        okButton = new Button( "OK" );
        Label messageLabel = new Label( message );
```

continues

Listing 39.8 Continued

```
        setLayout( gridbag );

        //      The message should not fill, it should be centered within this
                area, with
        //      some extra padding.  The gridwidth of REMAINDER means this is the
                only
        //      thing on its row, and the gridheight of RELATIVE means there
                should only
        //      be one thing below it.
        constraints.fill = GridBagConstraints.NONE;
        constraints.anchor = GridBagConstraints.CENTER;
        constraints.ipadx = 20;
        constraints.ipady = 20;
        constraints.weightx = 1.0;
        constraints.weighty = 1.0;
        constraints.gridwidth = GridBagConstraints.REMAINDER;
        constraints.gridheight = GridBagConstraints.RELATIVE;

        gridbag.setConstraints( messageLabel, constraints );
        add( messageLabel );

        //     The button has no padding, no weight, taked up minimal width, and
        //     Is the last thing in its column.
        constraints.ipadx = 0;
        constraints.ipady = 0;
        constraints.weightx = 0.0;
        constraints.weighty = 0.0;
        constraints.gridwidth = 1;
        constraints.gridheight = GridBagConstraints.REMAINDER;

        gridbag.setConstraints( okButton, constraints );

        add( okButton );

        //     Pack is a special window method that makes the window take up the
               minimum
        //     space necessary to contain its components.
        pack();
    }

    //      The action method just waits for the OK button to be clicked and
    //      when it is it hides the dialog, causing the show() method to return
    //      back to whoever activated this dialog.

    public boolean
    action( Event evt, Object whichAction )
    {
        if ( evt.target == okButton )
        {
            setVisible( false );

            if ( createdFrame != null )
                createdFrame.setVisible( false );
        }
```

```
        return( true );
    }

    //    Shortcut to create a frame automatically, the frame is a static
          variable
    //    so all dialogs in an applet or application can use the same frame.
    public static void
    createOKDialog( String dialogString )
    {
        //    If the frame hasn't been created yet, create it
        if ( createdFrame == null )
            createdFrame = new Frame( "Dialog" );

        //    Create the dialog now
        OKDialog okDialog = new OKDialog( createdFrame, dialogString );

        //    Shrink the frame to just fit the dialog
        createdFrame.setSize( okDialog.getSize().width,
okDialog.getSize().height );

        //    Show the dialog
        okDialog.show();
    }
}
```

The `DialogApplet` in Listing 39.9 pops up an OK dialog whenever a button is pressed:

Listing 39.9 Source code for DialogApplet.java.

```
//
// Example 39.9    — DialogApplet
//
// Dialog applet creates a button, and when you press
// the button it brings up an OK dialog.  The input
// to the original button should be blocked until
// the OK button in the dialog is pressed.
//

import          java.awt.*;
import          java.awt.event.*;
import          java.applet.*;

public class
DialogApplet
extends Applet
{
    protected Button         launchButton;

    public void
    init()
    {
        launchButton = new Button( "Give me an OK" );
        add( launchButton );
```

continues

Listing 39.9 Continued

```
        launchButton.addActionListener( new ActionListener()
            { public void actionPerformed( ActionEvent e )
                { launchClicked(); } } );
    }

    public void
    launchClicked()
    {
        //    Create and display the OK dialog
        OKDialog.createOKDialog( "Press OK when you are ready" );
    }
}
```

Figure 39.12 shows the DialogApplet with the OK dialog popped up.

FIG. 39.12
The `OKDialog` class creates a pop-up dialog box with an OK button.

Layout Managers

By using layout managers, you tell the AWT where you want your components to go relative to the other components. The layout manager figures out exactly where to put them. This helps you make platform-independent software. When you position things by absolute coordinates, it can cause odd results when someone running Windows 95 in 640×480 resolution tries to run an applet designed to fit on a 1280×1024 X-terminal.

The AWT provides the following five different types of layout managers:

- `FlowLayout` arranges components from left to right until no more components will fit on a row, and then it moves to the next row and continues going left to right.
- `GridLayout` treats a container as a grid of identically sized spaces. It places components in the spaces in the grid, starting from the top left and continuing in left to right fashion just like the `FlowLayout`. The difference between `GridLayout` and `FlowLayout` is that `GridLayout` gives each component an equal-sized area to work in.
- `BorderLayout` treats the container like a compass. When you add a component to the container, you ask the `BorderLayout` to place it in one of five areas: "North," "South," "East," "West," or "Center." It figures out the exact positioning based on the relative sizes of the components.

- `CardLayout` treats the components added to the container as a stack of cards. It places each component on a separate card, and only one card is visible at a time.
- `GridBagLayout` is the most flexible of the layout managers. It is also the most confusing. `GridBagLayout` treats a container as a grid of cells. Unlike `GridLayout`, however, a component may occupy more than one cell. When you add a component to a container managed by `GridBagLayout`, you give it a `GridBagConstraint`, which has placement and sizing instructions for that component.

Flow Layouts

A `FlowLayout` class treats a container as a set of rows. The height of the rows is determined by the height of the items placed in the row. The `FlowLayout` starts adding new components from left to right. If it cannot fit the next component on to the current row, it drops down to the next row and starts again from the left. It also tries to align the rows using either left-justification, right-justification, or centering. The default alignment for a `FlowLayout` is centered. This means that when it creates a row of components, it tries to keep it centered with respect to the left and right edges.

NOTE The `FlowLayout` layout manager is the default layout manager for all applets.

To create a `FlowLayout` with centered alignment and attach it to your applet, use this code:

```
myFlowLayout = new FlowLayout();
setLayout( myFlowLayout );
```

To create a `FlowLayout` with a left-justified alignment, use the following:

```
myFlowLayout = new FlowLayout( FlowLayout.LEFT );
```

The different types of `FlowLayout` alignment are `FlowLayout.LEFT`, `FlowLayout.RIGHT`, and `FlowLayout.CENTER`.

You can also give the `FlowLayout` horizontal and vertical gap values. These values specify the minimum amount of horizontal and vertical space to leave between components. These gaps are given in units of screen pixels. To create a right-justified `FlowLayout` with a horizontal gap of 10 pixels and a vertical gap of 5 pixels, use this:

```
myFlowLayout = new FlowLayout( FlowLayout.RIGHT, 10, 5 );
```

Figure 39.13 shows five buttons arranged in a flow layout.

Grid Layouts

A `GridLayout` class divides a container into a grid of equal-sized cells. When you add components to the container, the `GridLayout` places them from left to right, starting in the top left cells. When you create a `GridLayout` class, you must tell it how many rows you want, or how many columns. If you give it a number of rows, it computes the number of columns needed. If you give it a number of columns, it computes the number of rows needed. If you add six components to a `GridLayout` with two rows, it creates three columns. The format of the `GridLayout` constructor is as follows:

```
GridLayout( int numberOfRows, int numberOfColumns )
```

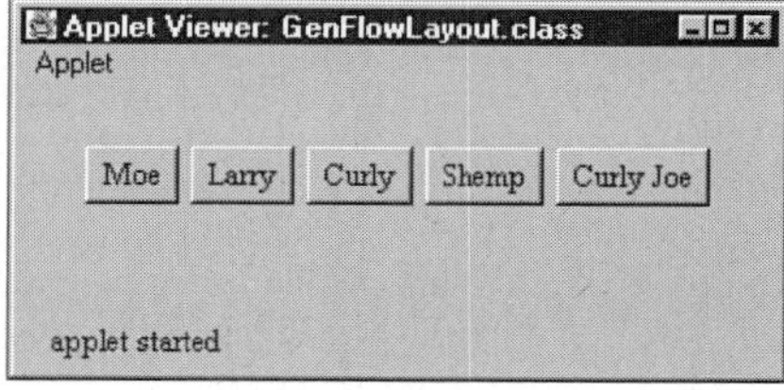

FIG. 39.13
The flow layout places components from left to right.

If you create a `GridLayout` with a fixed number of rows, you should use 0 for the number of columns. If you have a fixed number of columns, use 0 for the number of rows.

NOTE If you pass `GridLayout` non-zero values for both the number of rows and the number of columns, it uses only the number of rows. The number of columns is computed based on the number of components and the number of rows. `GridLayout(3, 4)` is exactly the same as `GridLayout(3, 0)`.

You can also specify a horizontal and vertical gap. The following code creates a `GridLayout` with four columns, a horizontal gap of eight, and a vertical gap of 10:

```
GridLayout myGridLayout = new GridLayout( 0, 4, 8, 10 );
```

Figure 39.14 shows five buttons arranged in a grid layout.

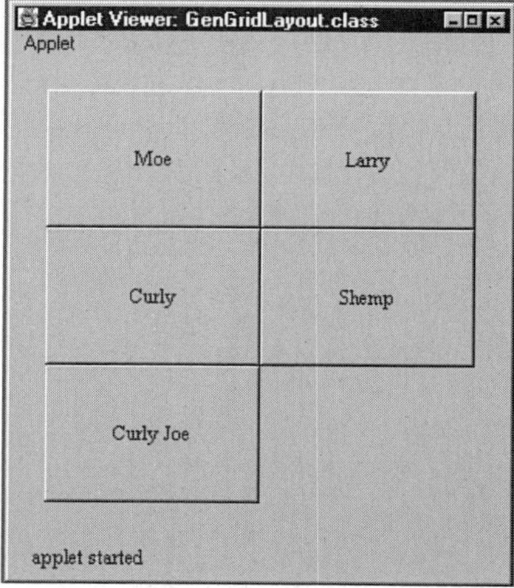

FIG. 39.14
The grid layout allocates equally sized areas for each component.

Border Layouts

A `BorderLayout` class divides a container into five areas named "North," "South," "East," "West," and "Center." When you add components to the container, you must use a special form of the `add` method that includes one of these five area names. These five areas are arranged like the points on a compass. A component added to the "North" area is placed at the top of the container; a component added to the "West" area is placed on the left side of the container. The

BorderLayout class does not allow more than one component in an area. You can optionally specify a horizontal gap and a vertical gap. To create a BorderLayout without specifying a gap, use this code:

```
BorderLayout myBorderLayout = new BorderLayout();
```

To create a BorderLayout with a horizontal gap of 10 and a vertical gap of 20, use the following:

```
BorderLayout myBorderLayout = new BorderLayout( 10, 20 );
```

Here is the code to add myButton to the "West" area of the BorderLayout:

```
myBorderLayout.add( "West", myButton );
```

CAUTION

The BorderLayout class is very picky about how and where you add components. If you try to add a component by using the regular add method (without the area name), you will not see your component. If you try to add two components to the same area, you will only see the last component added.

Also, the add method is case sensitive. You must spell "North," "South," "East," "West," and "Center" exactly as shown. Otherwise your additions will not show.

Listing 39.8 shows a BorderLayoutApplet that creates a BorderLayout, attaches it to the current applet, and adds some buttons to the applet:

Listing 39.10 Source code for BorderLayoutApplet.java.

```
// This applet creates a BorderLayout and attaches it
// to the applet.  Then it creates buttons and places
// in all possible areas of the layout.
//

import          java.applet.*;
import          java.awt.*;

public class
BorderLayoutApplet
extends Applet
{
    public void
    init()
    {
        //    First create the layout and attach it to the applet
        setLayout( new BorderLayout() );

        //    Now create some buttons and lay them out
        add( "North", new Button( "North" ) );
        add( "South", new Button( "South" ) );
        add( "East", new Button( "East" ) );
        add( "West", new Button( "West" ) );
        add( "Center", new Button( "Center" ) );
     }
}
```

Figure 39.15 shows five buttons arranged in a border layout.

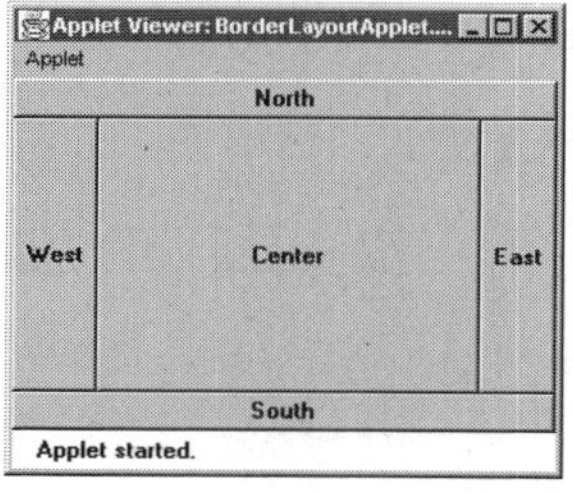

FIG. 39.15
The border layout places components at the north, south, east, and west compass points, as well as in the center.

Card Layouts

A `CardLayout` class enables you to stack a set of containers on each other, making only one visible at a time. This makes your containers like a deck of cards—only one card can be seen at the top of the deck. This layout is primarily good for one use: to create tabbed folders or other types of card-like dialogs and windows.

The syntax of the `CardLayout` constructor is as follows:

```
CardLayout( int horizontalGap, int verticalGap )
```

Or simply use this:

```
CardLayout()
```

"Cards" can be added to the stack by using the `addLayoutComponent` method:

```
myCardLayout.addLayoutComponent( myPanel, "My Panel" );
```

The second argument is a `String` that enables you to identify the component added to the stack by name.

Two methods, `previous` and `next`, are available to cruise through the stack from last to first, and first to last respectively.

NOTE The order in which items are placed into the stack are the order in which they are displayed if you use the simple navigational methods. If you want, you can use the `show` method to display the exact component you want.

Grid Bag Layouts

The `GridBagLayout` class, like the `GridLayout`, divides a container into a grid of equal-sized cells. Unlike the `GridLayout`, however, the `GridBagLayout` class decides how many rows and columns it will have, and it allows a component to occupy more than one cell if necessary. The total area that a component occupies is called its "display area." Before you add a component to a container, you must give the `GridBagLayout` a set of "suggestions" on where to put the component. These suggestions are in the form of a `GridBagConstraints` class. The `GridBagConstraints` class has a number of variables to control the placement of a component:

- gridx and gridy are the coordinates of the cell where the next component should be placed. (If the component occupies more than one cell, these coordinates are for the upper-left cell of the component.) The upper-left corner of the GridBagLayout is at 0, 0. The default value for both gridx and gridy is GridBagConstraints.RELATIVE, which for gridx means the cell just to the right of the last component that was added; for gridy it means the cell just below the last component added.
- gridwidth and gridheight tell how many cells wide and how many cells tall a component should be. The default for both gridwidth and gridheight is 1. If you want this component to be the last one on a row, use GridBagConstraint.REMAINDER for the gridwidth. (Use this same value for gridheight if this component should be the last one in a column.) Use GridBagConstraint.RELATIVE if the component should be the next to last component in a row or column.
- fill tells the GridBagLayout what to do when a component is smaller than its display area. The default value, GridBagConstraint.NONE, causes the component size to remain unchanged. GridBagConstraint.HORIZONTAL causes the component to be widened to take up its whole display area horizontally while leaving its height unchanged. GridBagConstraint.VERTICAL causes the component to be stretched vertically while leaving the width unchanged. GridBagConstraint.BOTH causes the component to be stretched in both directions to completely fill its display area.
- ipadx and ipady tell the GridBagLayout how many pixels to add to the size of the component in the x and y direction. The pixels are added on either side of the component, so an ipadx of 4 causes the size of a component to be increased by 4 on the left and also 4 on the right. Remember that the component size grows by two times the amount of padding because the padding is added to both sides. The default for both ipadx and ipady is 0.
- insets is an instance of an Insets class and it indicates how much space to leave between the borders of a component and edges of its display area. In other words, it creates a "no man's land" of blank space surrounding a component. The Insets class (discussed later in this chapter in the section titled "Insets") has separate values for the top, bottom, left, and right insets.
- anchor is used when a component is smaller than its display area. It indicates where the component should be placed within the display area. The default value is GridBagConstraint.CENTER, which indicates that the component should be in the center of the display area. The other values are all compass points: GridbagConstraints.NORTH, GridBagConstraints.NORTHEAST, GridBagConstraints.EAST, GridBagConstraints.SOUTHEAST, GridBagConstraints.SOUTH, GridBagConstraints.SOUTHWEST, GridBagConstraints.WEST, and GridBagConstraints.NORTHWEST. As with the BorderLayout class, NORTH indicates the top of the screen; EAST is to the right.
- weightx and weighty are used to set relative sizes of components. A component with a weightx of 2.0, for instance, takes up twice the horizontal space of a component with a weightx of 1.0. Because these values are relative, there is no difference between all components in a row having a weight of 1.0 or a weight of 3.0. You should assign a weight to at least one component in each direction; otherwise the GridBagLayout squeezes your components toward the center of the container.

When you want to add a component to a container using a `GridBagLayout`, you create the component, and then create an instance of `GridBagConstraints` and set the constraints for the component. For instance,

```
GridBagLayout myGridBagLayout = new GridBagLayout();
setLayout( myGridBagLayout );
        // Set the applet's Layout Manager to myGridBagLayout

Button myButton = new Button( "My Button" );
GridBagConstraints constraints = new GridBagConstraints();
constraints.weightx = 1.0;
constraints.gridwidth = GridBagConstraints.RELATIVE;
constraints.fill = GridBagConstraints.BOTH;
```

Next, you set the component's constraints in the `GridBagLayout` with this:

```
myGridLayout.setConstraints( myButton, constraints );
```

Now you may add the component to the container:

```
add( myButton );
```

The applet in Listing 39.11 uses the `GridBagLayout` class to arrange a few instances of `CircleCanvas` (created earlier in this chapter):

Listing 39.11 Source code for CircleApplet.java.

```
//
// Example 39.11 — CircleApplet
//
// This circle demonstrates the CircleCanvas class we
// created.  It also shows you how to use the GridBagLayout
// to arrange the circles.
//

import          java.applet.*;
import          java.awt.*;

public class
CircleApplet
extends Applet
{
    public void
    init()
    {
        GridBagLayout gridbag = new GridBagLayout();
        GridBagConstraints constraints = new GridBagConstraints();
        CircleCanvas newCircle;

        setLayout( gridbag );

        //    We'll use the weighting to determine relative circle sizes. Make
        //    the first one just have a weight of 1. Also, set fill for both
        //    directions so it will make the circles as big as possible.
        constraints.weightx = 1.0;
```

```
            constraints.weighty = 1.0;
            constraints.fill = GridBagConstraints.BOTH;

            //    Create a red circle and add it
            newCircle = new CircleCanvas( Color.red );
            gridbag.setConstraints( newCircle, constraints );
            add( newCircle );

            //    Now, we want to make the next circle twice as big as the previous
            //    one, so give it twice the weight.
            constraints.weightx = 2.0;
            constraints.weighty = 2.0;

            //    Create a blue circle and add it
            newCircle = new CircleCanvas( Color.blue );
            gridbag.setConstraints( newCircle, constraints );
            add( newCircle );

            //    We'll make the third circle the same size as the first one, so set
the
            //    weight back down to 1.
            constraints.weightx = 1.0;
            constraints.weighty = 1.0;

            //    Create a green circle and add it.
            newCircle = new CircleCanvas( Color.green );
            gridbag.setConstraints( newCircle, constraints );
            add( newCircle );
        }
    }
```


Figure 39.16 shows the three circle canvases from the CircleApplet.

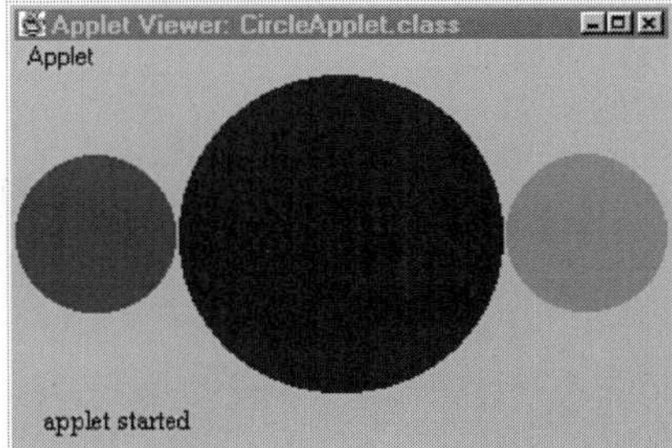

FIG. 39.16
The CircleApplet creates three circle canvases.

Insets

Insets are not layout managers, but instructions to the layout manager about how much space to leave around the edges of the container. The layout manager determines the inset values for a container by calling the container's insets method. The `insets` method returns an instance of an `Insets` class, which contains the values for the top, bottom, left, and right insets. If you want to leave a 20 pixel gap between the components in your applet and the applet border, for instance, you should create an `insets` method in your applet:

```
public Insets
insets()
{
     return( new Insets( 20, 20, 20, 20 ) );
         // Inset by 20 pixels all around
}
```

The constructor for the `Insets` class takes four inset values in the order top, left, bottom, and right.

Figure 39.17 shows what the CircleApplet would look like if it used the preceding `insets` method. The gap between the circles is not from the `Insets` class, but from the fact that the circles are smaller. The gaps on the top, bottom, left, and right are created by the `Insets` class.

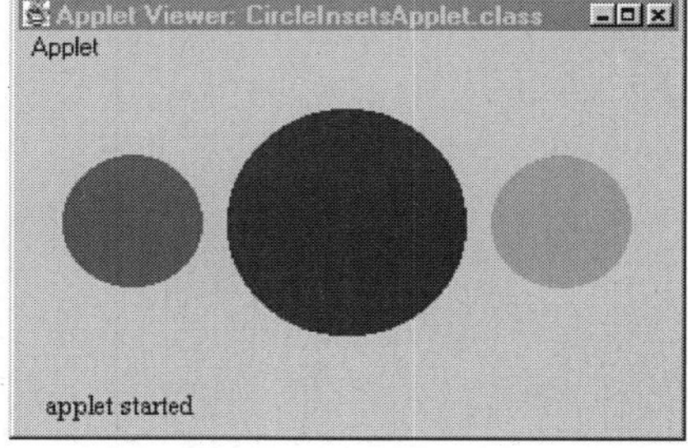

FIG. 39.17
Insets create a gap between components and the edges of their containers.

CHAPTER 40

Graphics and Animation

by Donald Doherty

In this chapter

Displaying Graphics

Colorful graphics and animation can change a dull, static, and gray Web page into an exciting and interesting place to visit. Java provides a wide range of tools for creating and displaying graphics in the Java Foundation Classes (JFC) library. JFC is divided into three subsets known as Swing, Abstract Windowing Toolkit (AWT), and Java2D. Most of what you need is part of the AWT. In fact, the majority of Java's graphics methods are contained in the `Graphics` class.

Using Java's *Graphics* Class

Java's `Graphics` class provides methods for manipulating a number of graphics features including the following:

- Creating graphics primitives
- Displaying colors
- Displaying text
- Displaying images
- Creating flicker-free animation

The following sections discuss all these graphics features and how to implement them in Java applets. Along the way, you will acquire a complete understanding of the `Graphics` class and its 33 methods.

You can find Java's `Graphics` class in the java.awt (the Java Abstract Window Toolkit) package. Be sure to properly import the `Graphics` class when you use it in your code. Include the following line at the beginning of your file:

```
import java.awt.Graphics;
```

Using Java's Coordinate System

You display the various graphics you produce—lines, rectangles, images, and so on—at specific locations in an applet window. To do this, you pass window coordinates to the `Graphics` class methods that you are using.

A simple Cartesian (x, y) coordinate system defines each location within a Java applet window, as shown in Figure 40.1. The upper-left corner of a window is its origin (0, 0). *x* increases by the number of screen pixels that you move to the right of the left-hand edge of an applet's window. The number of pixels you move down from the top of a window is *y*.

Displaying Graphics Primitives

The Java `Graphics` class provides you with methods that make it easy to draw two-dimensional graphics primitives. You can draw any two-dimensional graphics primitive, including the following:

- Lines
- Rectangles

- Ovals
- Arcs
- Polygons

The following sections explain how to draw these graphics primitives.

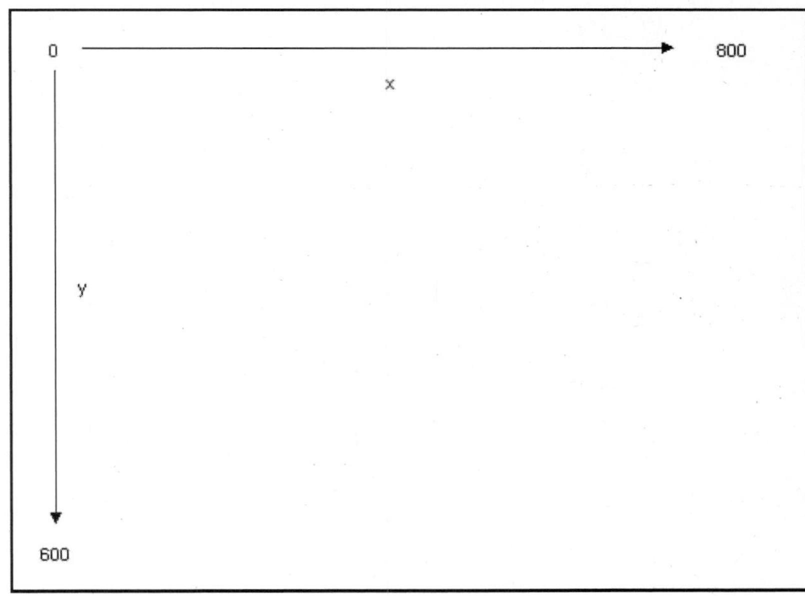

FIG. 40.1 Java's graphics coordinate system increases from left to right and from top to bottom.

Drawing Lines

Perhaps the simplest graphics primitive is a line. The Java `Graphics` class provides a single `drawLine` method for drawing lines. The complete definition of the `drawLine` method is as follows:

```
public abstract void drawLine(int  x1, int  y1, int  x2,  int  y2)
```

The `drawLine` method takes two pairs of coordinates—x1, y1 and x2, y2—and draws a line between them.

The applet in Listing 40.1 uses the `drawLine` method to draw some lines. Figure 40.2 shows the output from this applet.

Listing 40.1 Source code for DrawLines.java.

```
import java.awt.Graphics;

public class DrawLines extends java.applet.Applet
{
   public void paint(Graphics g)
   {
     // Draw a line from the upper-left corner to the point at (400, 200)
     g.drawLine(0, 0, 400, 200);
     // Draw a line from (20, 170) to (450, 270)
     g.drawLine(20, 170, 450, 270);
   }
}
```

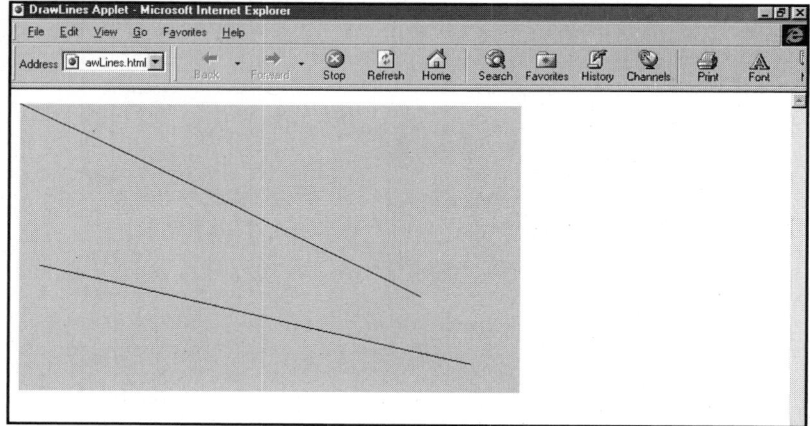

FIG. 40.2 This applet displays two lines drawn using the `drawLine` method.

Drawing Rectangles

The Java `Graphics` class provides six methods for drawing rectangles: `drawRect`, `fillRect`, `drawRoundRect`, `fillRoundRect`, `draw3DRect`, and `fill3DRect`. You can use these methods to do the following:

- Draw a rectangle.
- Fill a rectangle.
- Draw a rectangle with rounded corners.
- Fill a rectangle with rounded corners.
- Draw a three-dimensional rectangle.
- Fill a three-dimensional rectangle.

To draw a simple rectangle using the `drawRect` method, use this complete definition:

```
public void drawRect(int  x, int  y, int  width, int  height)
```

Pass the *x* and *y* applet window coordinates of the rectangle's upper-left corner along with the rectangle's width and height to the `drawRect` method. Assume, for example, that you want to draw a rectangle that is 300 pixels wide (width = 300) and 170 pixels high (height = 170). You also want to place the rectangle with its upper-left corner 150 pixels to the right of the left edge of the applet's window (x = 150) and 100 down from the window's top edge (y = 100). To do this, fill in the `drawRect` method's arguments as follows.

```
g.drawRect(150, 100, 300, 170);
```

NOTE The preceding `drawRect` method call assumes that you have created an object from the `Graphics` class and assigned the object to a `Graphics` variable named g, like in Listing 40.2.

Create an applet named OneRectangle that uses the `Graphics` class `drawRect` method. The code for the applet, shown in Listing 40.2, uses the same rectangle coordinates used in the previous discussion. Figure 40.3 shows the applet's output.

Listing 40.2 Source code for OneRectangle.java.

```
import java.awt.Graphics;

public class OneRectangle extends java.applet.Applet
{
   public void paint(Graphics g)
   {
      // Draw a rectangle 300 pixels wide and 170 pixels high
      //  with its upper left corner at (150, 100).
      g.drawRect(150, 100, 300, 170);
   }
}
```


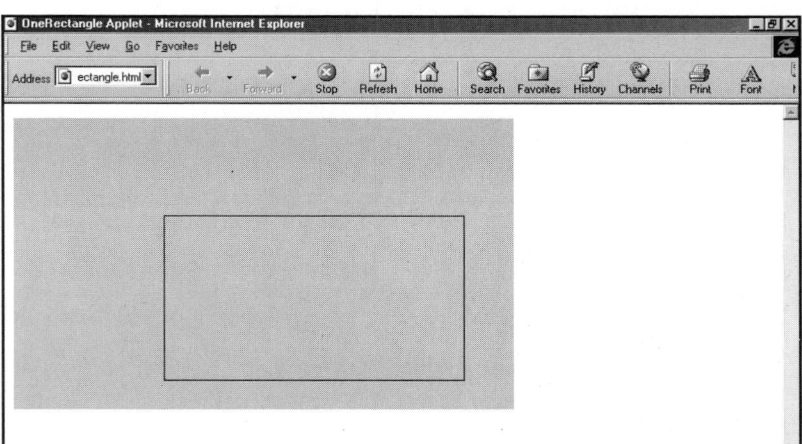

FIG. 40.3 The rectangle displayed by this applet was created with the `drawRect` method.

```
   }
}
```

In addition to the regular rectangles and those with rounded corners, the Java `Graphics` class provides two methods for drawing three-dimensional rectangles: the `draw3DRect` and `fill3DRect` methods. The complete definitions of the three-dimensional rectangle methods are as follows.

Use the `fillRect` method if you want to draw a solid rectangle. The following is the complete definition of the `fillRect` method.

```
public abstract void fillRect(int  x, int  y, int  width,  int  height)
```


Listing 40.6 Continued

```
      // Draw a gray rectangle 200 pixels wide and 100 pixels
      //  high with its upper left corner at (20, 20).
      g.setColor(Color.gray);
      g.drawRect(20, 20, 200, 100);
      // Draw an oval inside the rectangle created above.
      g.setColor(Color.black);
      g.drawOval(20, 20, 200, 100);
      // Draw the oval again but to the right of the oval above.
      g.drawOval(240, 20, 200, 100);
    }
  }
```

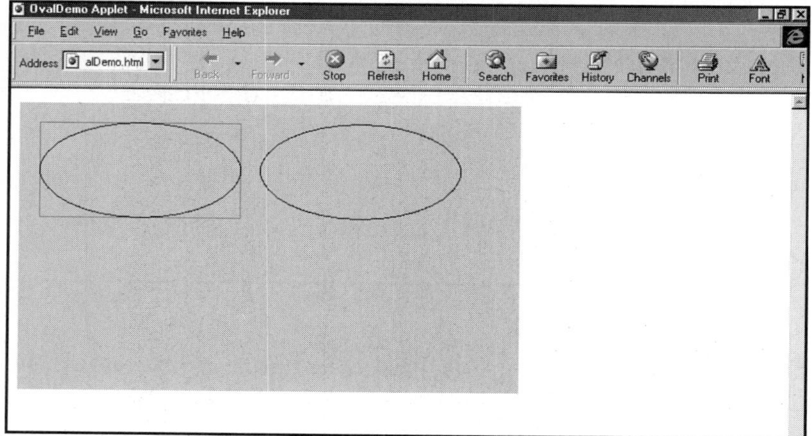

FIG. 40.7 The same oval is inside its bounding rectangle on the left and by itself on the right.

You pass `drawOval` or `fillOval` method the coordinates of the upper-left corner of the imaginary surrounding rectangle and the width and height of the oval. The width and height is equal to the width and height of the imaginary surrounding rectangle. The Ovals applet in Listing 40.7 draws a circle and a filled oval. Figure 40.8 shows the output from the Ovals applet.

Listing 40.7 Source code for Ovals.java.

```
import java.awt.Graphics;

// This applet draws an unfilled circle and a filled oval

public class Ovals extends java.applet.Applet
{
   public void paint(Graphics g)
   {
     // Draw a circle with a diameter of 150 (width=150, height=150)
     // With the enclosing rectangle's upper-left corner at (20, 20)
     g.drawOval(20, 20, 150, 150);
     // Fill an oval with a width of 150 and a height of 80
```

```
        // The upper-left corner of the enclosing rectangle is at (200, 20)
        g.fillOval(200, 20, 150, 80);
    }
}
```

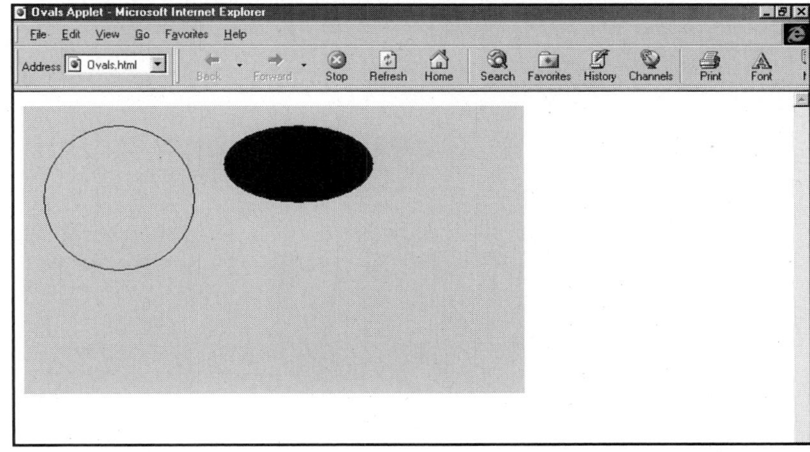

FIG. 40.8
Draw ovals and circles by using the `Graphics` class `drawOval` and `fillOval` methods.

Drawing Arcs

Use what you learned about drawing ovals to draw arcs in Java. An arc is a segment of the line that forms the perimeter of an oval, as demonstrated in Figure 40.9. The output is created by the ArcDemo1 applet created from the `ArcDemo1` class in Listing 40.8.

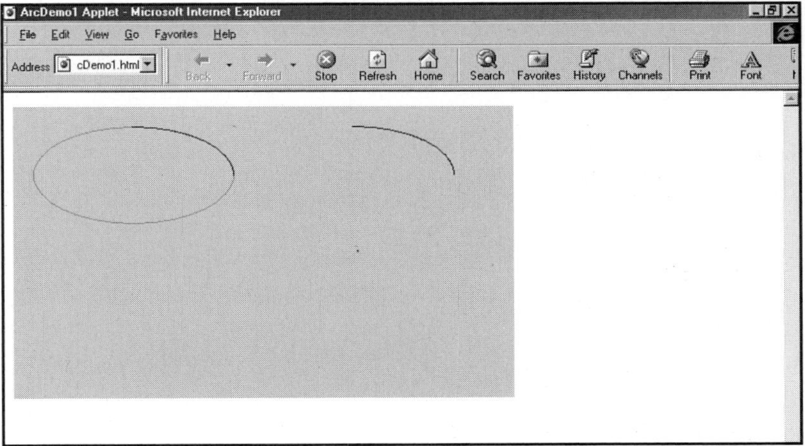

FIG. 40.9
At the left are the arc and its associated oval and at the right is the arc alone.

Listing 40.8 Source code for ArcDemo1.java.

```
import java.awt.Graphics;
import java.awt.Color;

public class ArcDemo1 extends java.applet.Applet
{
   public void paint(Graphics g)
   {
     // Draw a gray oval 200 pixels wide and 100 pixels
     //  high with the upper left corner of its
     //  enclosing rectangle at (20, 20).
     g.setColor(Color.gray);
     g.drawOval(20, 20, 200, 100);
     // Draw a black arc from 0 to 90 degrees inside
     //  the oval created above.
     g.setColor(Color.black);
     g.drawArc(20, 20, 200, 100, 0, 90);
     // Draw the same arc as above but to the right
     //  with the upper left corner of its enclosing
     //  rectangle at (240, 20).
     g.drawArc(240, 20, 200, 100, 0, 90);
   }
}
```

Two `Graphics` class methods are provided for drawing arcs: the `drawArc` and `fillArc` methods. Their complete definitions are as follows:

```
public abstract void drawArc(int  x, int  y, int  width,
➥int  height, int  startAngle, int  arcAngle)
public abstract void fillArc(int  x, int  y, int  width,
➥int  height, int  startAngle, int  arcAngle)
```

Use the first four parameters just as you did with the oval methods. In fact, you are drawing an invisible oval and the arc is a segment of the oval's perimeter defined by `startAngle` and `arcAngle`, the last two parameters.

The `startAngle` parameter defines where your arc starts along the invisible oval's perimeter. In Java, angles are set around a 360° circle as follows:

- 0° is at 3 o'clock
- 90° is at 12 o'clock
- 180° is at 9 o'clock
- 270° is at 6 o'clock.

The `arcAngle` parameter defines the distance, in degrees, that your arc traverses along the invisible oval's perimeter. Angles are positive in the counter-clockwise direction and negative in the clockwise direction.

The arc you saw in Figure 40.9 began at 0°, or at 3 o'clock, and traversed the invisible oval 90° in the positive, or counter-clockwise, direction. The relevant line in Listing 40.8 is reproduced here:

```
g.drawArc(20, 20, 200, 100, 0, 90);
```

Notice that the last parameter is given in the angle traversed and not the angle at which the arc ends. Therefore, if you want an arc that starts at 45° and ends at 135°, you must provide a `startAngle` parameter value of 45° and an arcAngle parameter value of 90°, as shown in Figure 40.10 and Listing 40.9.

FIG. 40.10
This arc starts at 45° and ends at 135°.

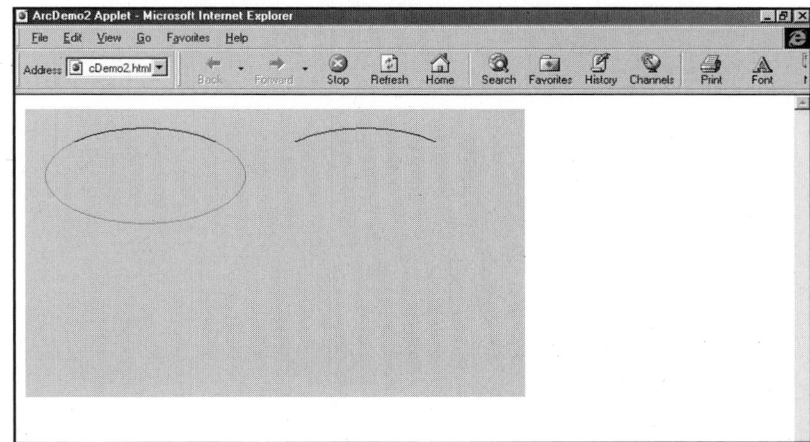

Part VII Ch 40

Listing 40.9 Source code for ArcDemo2.java.

```
import java.awt.Graphics;
import java.awt.Color;

public class ArcDemo2 extends java.applet.Applet
{
   public void paint(Graphics g)
   {
     // Draw a gray oval 200 pixels wide and 100 pixels
     //  high with the upper left corner of its
     //  enclosing rectangle at (20, 20).
     g.setColor(Color.gray);
     g.drawOval(20, 20, 200, 100);
     // Draw a black arc from 45 to 90 degrees inside
     //  the oval created above.
     g.setColor(Color.black);
     g.drawArc(20, 20, 200, 100, 45, 90);
     // Draw the same arc as above but to the right
     //  with the upper left corner of its enclosing
     //  rectangle at (240, 20).
     g.drawArc(240, 20, 200, 100, 45, 90);
   }
}
```

When you use a negative `arcAngle` parameter value, the arc sweeps clockwise along the invisible oval's perimeter. If you start an arc at 0° (like in Figure 40.9), for example, but now give an `arcAngle` of –90° (rather than 90°), you will get an arc that looks something like the one in Figure 40.11. Listing 40.10 shows the code.

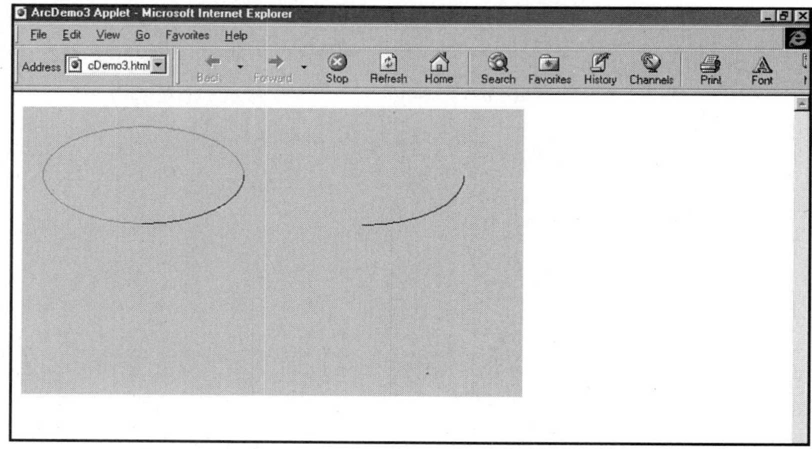

FIG. 40.11 Compare this arc with a `startAngle` of 0° and an `arcAngle` of -90° with the one in Figure 40.9.

Listing 40.10 Source code for ArcDemo3.java.

```
import java.awt.Graphics;
import java.awt.Color;

public class ArcDemo3 extends java.applet.Applet
{
   public void paint(Graphics g)
   {
     // Draw a gray oval 200 pixels wide and 100 pixels
     //  high with the upper left corner of its
     //  enclosing rectangle at (20, 20).
     g.setColor(Color.gray);
     g.drawOval(20, 20, 200, 100);
     // Draw a black arc from 0 to -90 degrees inside
     //  the oval created above.
     g.setColor(Color.black);
     g.drawArc(20, 20, 200, 100, 0, -90);
     // Draw the same arc as above but to the right
     //  with the upper left corner of its enclosing
     //  rectangle at (240, 20).
     g.drawArc(240, 20, 200, 100, 0, -90);
   }
}
```

Using the `fillArc` method results in a filled pie-shaped wedge defined by the center of the invisible oval and the perimeter segment traversed by the arc. The ArcDemo4 applet shown in Figure 40.12 uses the same parameters as the previous example in Listing 40.10, for example;

but instead of using the drawArc method, it employs the fillArc method as you can see in Listing 40.11.

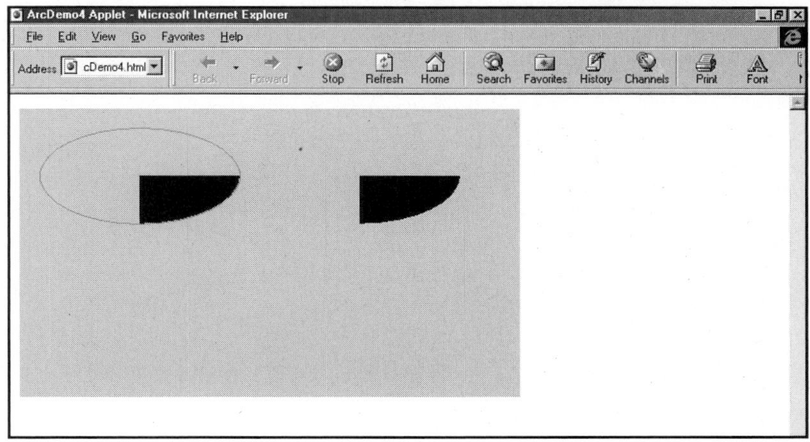

FIG. 40.12
This arc is drawn using the fillArc method.

Listing 40.11 Source code for ArcDemo4.java.

```
import java.awt.Graphics;
import java.awt.Color;

public class ArcDemo4 extends java.applet.Applet
{
   public void paint(Graphics g)
   {
     // Draw a gray oval 200 pixels wide and 100 pixels
     //  high with the upper left corner of its
     //  enclosing rectangle at (20, 20).
     g.setColor(Color.gray);
     g.drawOval(20, 20, 200, 100);
     // Draw a filled black arc from 0 to -90 degrees
     //  inside the oval created above.
     g.setColor(Color.black);
     g.fillArc(20, 20, 200, 100, 0, -90);
     // Draw the same filled arc as above but to the
     //  right with the upper left corner of its
     //  enclosing rectangle at (240, 20).
     g.fillArc(240, 20, 200, 100, 0, -90);
   }
}
```

Drawing Polygons

The Java Graphics class provides four methods for building polygons: two versions of the drawPolygon method and two versions of the fillPolygon method. There are two methods each so that you can either pass two arrays containing the *x* and *y* coordinates of the points in the polygon or you can pass an instance of a `Polygon` class. The `Polygon` class is defined in the java.awt package.

First look at how to create a polygon by using two arrays. The full definitions of the `drawPolygon` and `fillPolygon` methods for using arrays are as follows:

```
public abstract void drawPolygon(int  xPoints[], int yPoints[],
➥int  nPoints)
public abstract void fillPolygon(int  xPoints[], int  yPoints[],
➥int  nPoints)
```

The DrawPoly applet in Listing 40.12 draws a polygon using an array of *x* coordinates (`xCoords`) and an array of *y* coordinates (`yCoords`). Each *x* and *y* pair, the first *x* (50) and the first *y* (100) pair, for instance, defines a point on a plane (50, 100). Use the `drawPolygon` method to connect each point to the following point in the list. The first pair is (50, 100) and connects by a line to the second pair (200, 0), and so on. The `drawPolygon` method's third parameter, `nPoints`, is the number of points in the polygon and should equal the number of pairs in the `x` and `y` arrays. Figure 40.13 shows the DrawPoly applet's output.

Listing 40.12 Source code for DrawPoly.java.

```
import java.awt.Graphics;

public class DrawPoly extends java.applet.Applet
{
   int xCoords[] = { 50, 200, 300, 150, 50 };
   int yCoords[] = { 100, 0, 50, 300, 200 };

   int xFillCoords[] = { 450, 600, 700, 550, 450 };

   public void paint(Graphics g)
   {
     // Draw the left polygon.
     g.drawPolygon(xCoords, yCoords, 5);
     // Draw the right filled polygon.
     g.fillPolygon(xFillCoords, yCoords, 5);
   }
}
```

The applets in this chapter assume that you have a graphics resolution of at least 800 pixels across by 600 pixels top to bottom (800×600). If your monitor displays a smaller number of pixels (640×480, for example), you can either use your browser's scroll bars to see the rest of the applet window or you can change some of the coordinates in the example so that they are no larger than your largest screen coordinates.

FIG. 40.13
Draw polygons using x and y arrays.

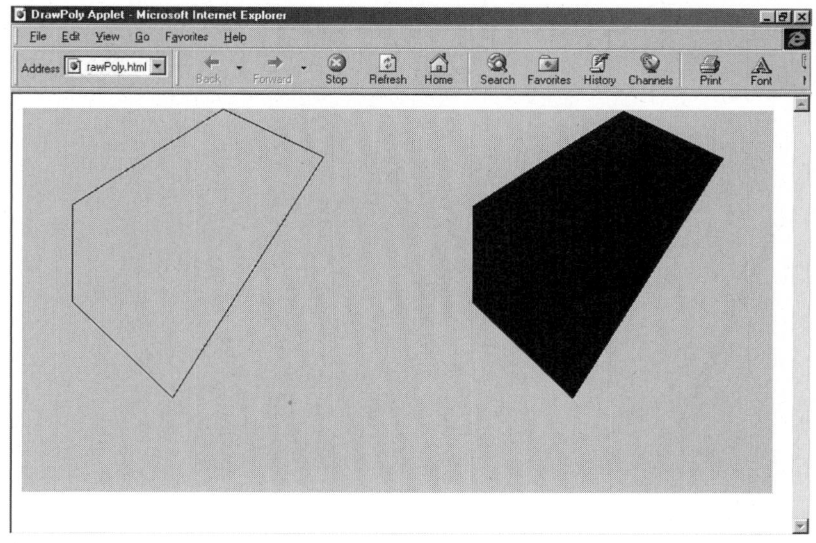

Using Java's Polygon Class The Java `Polygon` class provides features that often make it the most convenient way to define polygons. The Polygon class provides the two constructors, defined as follows:

```
public Polygon()
public Polygon(int  xpoints[], int  ypoints[],  int  npoints)
```

These constructors enable you to either create an empty polygon or create a polygon by initially passing an array of *x* and an array of *y* numbers and the number of points made up of the *x* and *y* pairs. If you do the latter, the parameters are saved in the following `Polygon` class fields:

```
public int xpoints[]
public int ypoints[]
public int npoints
```

Regardless of whether you started with an empty polygon, you can add points to it dynamically by using the `Polygon` class `addPoint` method, defined as follows:

```
public void addPoint(int  x, int  y)
```

The `addPoint` method automatically increments the `Polygon` class number of points field, named `npoints`.

The `Polygon` class includes two other methods: the `getBoundingBox` and `inside` methods, defined as follows:

```
public Rectangle getBoundingBox()
public boolean inside(int  x, int  y)
```

You can use the getBoundingBox method to determine the minimum sized box that can completely surround the polygon in screen coordinates. The Rectangle class returned by getBoundingBox contains variables indicating the *x* and *y* coordinates of the rectangle along with the rectangle's width and height.

You determine whether a point is contained within the polygon or is outside it by calling the inside methods with the *x* and *y* coordinates of the point.

Use the Polygon class in place of the x and y arrays for either the drawPolygon or fillPolygon method as indicated in their definitions, shown here:

```
public void drawPolygon(Polygon  p)
public void fillPolygon(Polygon  p)
```

The Polygon class is used for both the drawPolygon and the fillPolygon methods in Listing 40.13. Figure 40.14 shows the applet's output.

Listing 40.13 Source code for Polygons.java.

```
import java.awt.Graphics;
import java.awt.Polygon;

public class Polygons extends java.applet.Applet
{
   int xCoords[] = { 50, 200, 300, 150, 50, 50 };
   int yCoords[] = { 100, 0, 50, 300, 200, 100 };

   int xFillCoords[] = { 450, 600, 700, 550, 450, 450 };

   public void paint(Graphics g)
   {
     Polygon myPolygon = new Polygon(xCoords, yCoords, 6);
     Polygon myFilledPolygon = new Polygon(xFillCoords, yCoords, 6);
     // Draw the left polygon.
     g.drawPolygon(myPolygon);
     // Draw the right filled polygon.
     g.fillPolygon(myFilledPolygon);
   }
}
```

Displaying Colors

You are directly manipulating the wavelength of the light transmitted to your eyes when you manipulate colors on a computer screen. This is different than manipulating colors using crayons or other pigments.

The primary colors of pigments are red, yellow, and blue. Orange results if you mix red and yellow pigments, and green results when you mix yellow and blue. Mixing blue and red results in purple; black results from mixing all the pigments together; white indicates the absence of pigment.

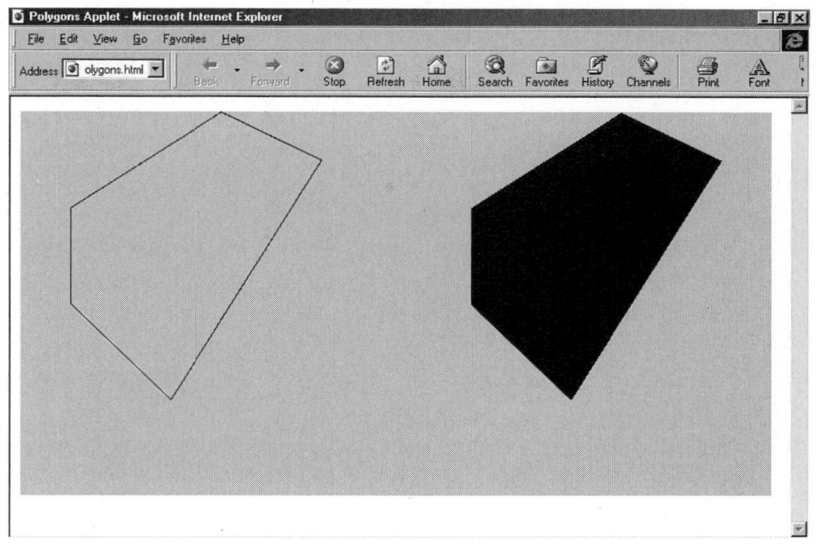

FIG. 40.14
Polygons created with the Polygon class look just like those created from x and y arrays.

In contrast, the primary colors of directly transmitted light are red, green, and blue. Some common combinations are red and green, which results in brown; green and blue, resulting in cyan; red and blue, resulting in magenta. Black is formed by the absence of all light, and white is formed by the combination of all the primary colors. In other words, red, blue, and green transmitted in equal amounts, results in white.

NOTE The color effects of pigments and directly transmitted light are closely related. Each color pigment absorbs light, but not all of it. The color of a pigment is due to the wavelength of the light that the pigment does not absorb—and, therefore, the light that the pigment reflects. Because the absence of pigments results in all wavelengths of light being reflected, the result is white. This is the same as the transmission of all the primary colors of light. In contrast, all the different colored pigments mixed together absorb all light. This is equivalent to the color black resulting from the absence of light.

Java uses the RGB (Red, Green, and Blue) color model. You define the colors you want by indicating the amount of red, green, and blue light that you want to transmit to the viewer. You can do this either by using integers between 0 and 255 or by using floating-point numbers between 0.0 and 1.0. Table 40.1 indicates the red, green, and blue amounts for some common colors.

Table 40.1 Common colors and their RGB values.

Color Name	Red Value	Green Value	Blue Value
Black	0	0	0
Blue	0	0	255
Cyan	0	255	255

continues

Table 40.1 Continued

Color Name	Red Value	Green Value	Blue Value
Dark gray	64	64	64
Gray	128	128	128
Green	0	255	0
Light gray	192	192	192
Magenta	255	0	255
Orange	255	200	0
Pink	255	175	175
Red	255	0	0
White	255	255	255
Yellow	255	255	0

Java's `Graphics` class provides two methods for manipulating colors: the `getColor` and `setColor` methods. Their full definitions are as follows:

```
public abstract Color getColor()
public abstract void setColor(Color  c)
```

The `getColor` method returns the `Graphics` object's current color encapsulated in a `Color` object, and the `setColor` method sets the `Graphics` object's color by passing it a `Color` object.

Using Java's Color Class

The `Color` class is defined in the java.awt package. The `Color` class provides three constructors. The first constructor enables you to create a `Color` object using red (`r`), green (`g`), and blue (`b`) integers between 0 and 255:

```
public Color(int  r, int  g, int  b)
```

The second constructor is very similar to the first. Instead of integer values, it uses floating-point values between 0.0 and 1.0 for red (`r`), green (`g`), and blue (`b`):

```
public Color(float  r, float  g, float  b)
```

The third constructor enables you to create a color using red, green, and blue integers between 0 and 255, but you combine the three numbers into a single, typically hexadecimal, value (`rgb`):

```
public Color(int  rgb)
```

In the 32-bit `rgb` integer, bits 16 through 23 (8 bits) hold the red value, bits 8 through 15 (8 bits) hold the green value, and bits 0 through 7 (8 bits) hold the blue value. The highest 8 bits, bits 24 through 32, are not manipulated. You usually write `rgb` values in hexadecimal notation so that it is easy to see the color values. A number prefaced with 0x is read as hexadecimal. For instance, 0xFFA978 would give a red value of `0xFF` (255 decimal), a green value of `0xA9` (52 decimal), and a blue value of `0x78` (169 decimal).

After you create a color, set a `Graphics` object's drawing color by using its `setColor` method. The default drawing color for `Graphics` objects is black. The ColorPlay applet in Listing 40.14 gets the graphics context's default color and assigns it to the `defaultColor` variable by passing the color value encapsulated in a `Color` object. A new `Color` object is created using a hexadecimal value and is assigned to the `newColor` variable. A filled circle is created on the left using the color value encapsulated by the `Color` object assigned to the `newColor` variable and another is created on the right using the `defaultColor` variable. Figure 40.15 shows the resulting output.

TROUBLESHOOTING

How do you return to the original color assigned to your program's `Graphics` object?

It is a good policy to always save the color assigned to your program's `Graphics` object to a `Color` object variable before you assign it a new color. That way you can reassign the original color to the `Graphics` object after the program is finished using the new color.

Listing 40.14 Source code for ColorPlay.java.

```
import java.awt.Graphics;
import java.awt.Color;

public class ColorPlay extends java.applet.Applet
{
   public void paint(Graphics g)
   {
     // Assign the red Color object to newColor.
     Color newColor = new Color(0xFFA978);
     // Assign Graphic object's current color to default Color.
     Color defaultColor = g.getColor();
     // Draw a red oval 200 pixels wide and 200 pixels
     //  high with the upper left corner of its
     //  enclosing rectangle at (50, 50).
     g.setColor(newColor);
     g.fillOval(50, 50, 200, 200);
     // Draw an oval 200 pixels wide and 200 pixels
     //  high with the upper left corner of its
     //  enclosing rectangle at (300, 50) in the
     //  default color.
     g.setColor(defaultColor);
     g.fillOval(300, 50, 200, 200);
   }
}
```

You need not always create colors manually. The `Color` class provides class constants of the colors with RGB values listed in Table 40.1. Table 40.2. lists the `Color` class constants.

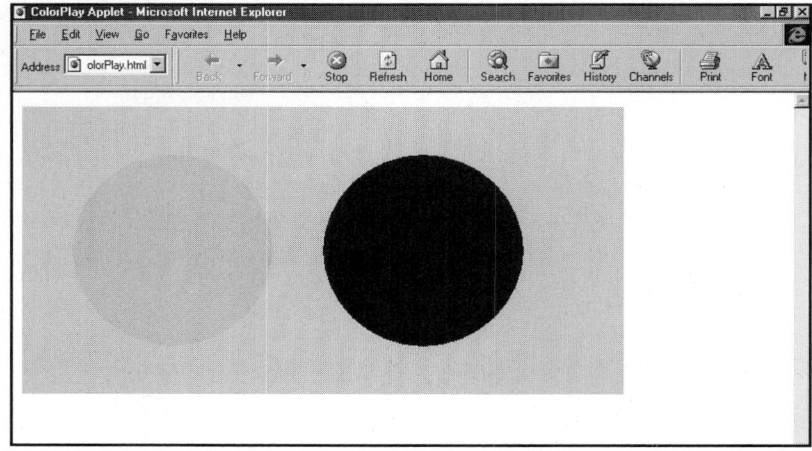

FIG. 40.15
Create color graphics by changing the graphics context's current color by using the `setColor` method.

Table 40.2 Color class constants.

`Color.black`	`Color.green`	`Color.red`
`Color.blue`	`Color.lightGray`	`Color.white`
`Color.cyan`	`Color.magenta`	`Color.yellow`
`Color.darkGray`	`Color.orange`	
`Color.gray`	`Color.pink`	

You must import the `Color` class to use a `Color` class constant, but you don't need to create a `Color` object. Just type the class name followed by the dot operator followed by the color as shown in Table 40.2 and in Listing 40.15. The output of Listing 40.15 is not shown because the figures are all in black and white. (I assure you, however, it is a pink circle.)

Listing 40.15 Source code for DefColors.java.

```
import java.awt.Graphics;
import java.awt.Color;

public class DefColors extends java.applet.Applet
{
   public void paint(Graphics g)
   {
     // Draw a pink oval 200 pixels wide and 200 pixels
     //  high with the upper left corner of its
     //  enclosing rectangle at (50, 50).
     g.setColor(Color.pink);
     g.fillOval(50, 50, 200, 200);
   }
}
```

Displaying Text

Java's `Graphics` class provides seven methods related to displaying text. Before plunging into the various aspects of drawing text, however, you should be familiar with the following common terms for fonts and text:

> *Baseline* is the imaginary line that the text rests on.
>
> *Descent* is the distance below baseline that a particular character extends. For instance, the letters *g* and *j* extend below baseline.
>
> *Ascent* is the distance above baseline that a particular character extends. For instance, the letter *d* has a higher ascent than the letter *x*.
>
> *Leading* is the space between a line of text's lowest descent and the following line of text's highest ascent. Without leading, the letters *g* and *j* would touch the letters *M* and *h* on the next line.

Figure 40.16 illustrates the relationships among descent, ascent, baseline, and leading.

FIG. 40.16 Java's font terminology originated in the publishing field.

CAUTION

The term "ascent" in Java is slightly different from the same term in the publishing world. The publishing term "ascent" refers to the distance from the top of a letter such as *x* to the top of a character such as *d*. In contrast, the Java term "ascent" refers to the distance from baseline to the top of a character.

NOTE You may hear the terms "*proportional*" and "*fixed*" associated with fonts. Characters in a proportional font take up only as much space as they need. In a fixed font, every character takes up the same amount of space.

Most of the text in this book is in a proportional font, for example. Look at some of the words and notice how the letters take up only as much space as necessary. (Compare the letters *i* and *m*, for instance.) In contrast, the code examples in this book are written in a fixed font. Notice how each letter takes up exactly the same amount of space.

Perhaps the most rudimentary (some might say primitive) way to display text in Java is to draw from an array of bytes representing characters or just an array of characters. You can use an array of ASCII codes when you use the `drawBytes` method or you can use an array of characters when you use the `drawChars` method. Each of these two methods is available in Java's

`Graphics` class. They are defined as follows:

```
public void drawBytes(byte  data[], int  offset, int  length,
➥int  x, int  y)
public void drawChars(char  data[], int  offset, int  length,
➥int  x, int  y)
```

The `offset` parameter refers to the position of the first character or byte in the array to draw. This is most often zero because you will usually want to draw from the beginning of the array. The `Length` parameter is the total number of bytes or characters in the array. The *x* coordinate is the integer value that represents the beginning position of the text, in number of pixels, from the left edge of the applet's window. The *y* coordinate is distance, in pixels, from the top of the applet's window to the text's baseline. The DrawChars applet in Listing 40.16 displays text from an array of ASCII codes in blue and text from an array of characters in red. Figure 40.17 shows the DrawChars applet's output.

Listing 40.16 Source code for DrawChars.java.

```
import java.awt.Graphics;
import java.awt.Color;

public class DrawChars extends java.applet.Applet
{
   byte[] bytesToDraw = { 72, 101, 108, 108, 111, 32,
 ➥87, 111, 114, 108, 100, 33 };
   char[] charsToDraw = { 'H', 'e', 'l', 'l', 'o', ' ',
 ➥'W', 'o', 'r', 'l', 'd', '!' };

   public void paint(Graphics g)
   {
     // Draw Hello World! from bytes in blue.
     g.setColor(Color.blue);
     g.drawBytes(bytesToDraw, 0, bytesToDraw.length, 10, 20);
     // Draw Hello World! from characters in red.
     g.setColor(Color.red);
     g.drawChars(charsToDraw, 0, charsToDraw.length, 10, 50);
   }
}
```

NOTE The numbers used in the byte array, `bytesToDraw`, are base 10 ASCII codes. They are the numbers that the computer uses to represent letters. You could use any base for these numbers, including the popular hexadecimal.

Arrays are objects in Java. You created two array objects when you built the two arrays, `bytesToDraw` and `charsToDraw`, in Listing 40.16. That is why you could use the array method, `length`, to get the lengths of the arrays in number of bytes or characters.

Java provides another object type, the `String` object, which is similar to the array objects that you just created. It is, however, more convenient for manipulating text.

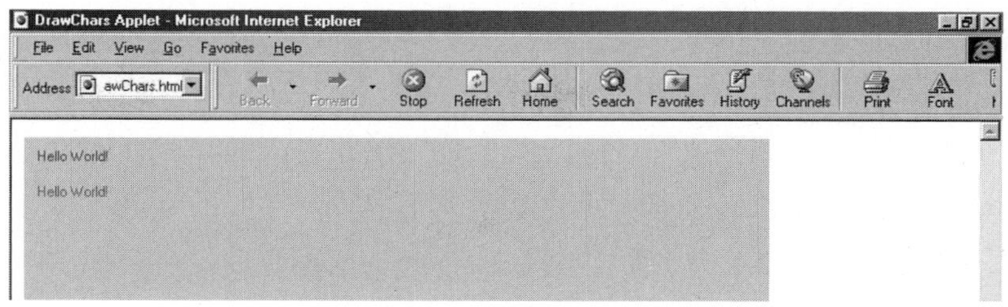

FIG. 40.17
The `drawBytes` method displays the first line of text in blue, and the `drawChars` method displays the second line of text in red.

Using Java's *String* Class

The Java `Graphics` class provides a method for displaying text by drawing a string of characters. The method, the `drawString` method shown here, takes a `String` object as a parameter:

```
public abstract void drawString(String  str, int  x, int  y)
```

If you put double quotation marks around a string, a `String` object is automatically created. You then pass an *x* coordinate, the integer value that represents the beginning position of the text in number of pixels from the left edge of the applet's window, and pass a *y* coordinate, the distance in pixels from the top of the applet's window to the text's baseline.

The StringObjects applet in Listing 40.17 demonstrates two ways of passing a `String` object to the `drawString` method. A `String` object is automatically created in the argument list of the first line of code containing the `drawString` method and is displayed in blue. The `drawString` method in the second line of code containing the `drawString` method is passed a `String` object assigned to the `myString` variable, which was created earlier in the listing. This call to the `drawString` method produces text displayed in red. Figure 40.18 shows the StringObjects applet's output.

Listing 40.17 Source code for StringObjects.java.

```
import java.awt.Graphics;
import java.awt.Color;

public class StringObjects extends java.applet.Applet
{
   String myString = new String("Hello World!");

   public void paint(Graphics g)
   {
     // Draw Hello World! in blue.
     g.setColor(Color.blue);
     g.drawString("Hello World!", 10, 20);
     // Draw Hello World! in red.
     g.setColor(Color.red);
     g.drawString(myString, 10, 50);
   }
}
```

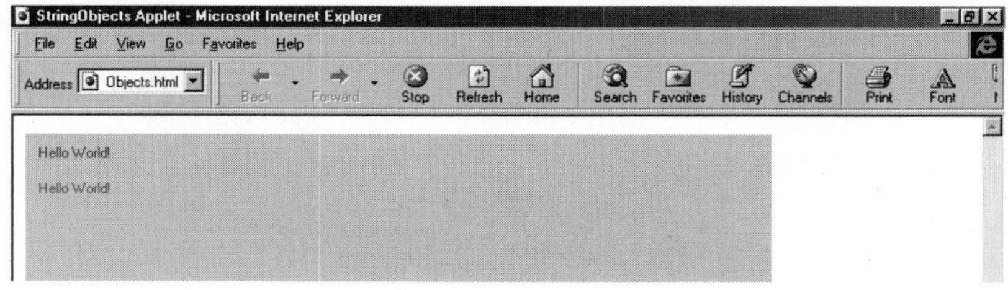

FIG. 40.18
You can automatically make a `String` object or you can use Java's new keyword.

Notice that the output is the same as from the applet of the previous listing, Listing 40.16, which used the `drawBytes` and `drawChars` methods. Also notice that the creation of the `String` object assigned to the `myString` variable in Listing 40.17 is a trivial example. The quoted "Hello World!" text is passed to the `String` constructor but "Hello World!" is already a `String` object. Remember that strings surrounded by double quotation marks automatically turn into `String` objects. The `String` object assigned to the `myString` variable was initiated with another `String` object through the following `String` class constructor:

```
public String(String  value)
```

Java's `String` class provides 9 constructors, including the preceding one, so you have several options for building a `String` object. In fact, you can create `String` objects from the byte arrays or character arrays you used for the `drawBytes` and `drawChars` methods previously discussed.

You can use one of the following two constructors when you create `String` objects from byte arrays:

```
public String(byte  bytes[])
public String(byte  bytes[], int  offset, int  length)
```

The first parameter in both constructors, `bytes[]`, is the byte array. In the second constructor, the `offset` parameter refers to the position of the first byte in the array to draw. The `length` parameter is the total number of bytes to include in the output. The StringsOne applet demonstrates these two `String` constructors in Listing 40.18.

The `String` object assigned to the `bytesString` variable is passed an array of ASCII codes. The `String` object assigned to the `bytesAnotherString` variable is passed to the array of ASCII codes and, in addition, a 6 is passed to the offset parameter and another 6 is passed to the length parameter.

To count your offset, start with 0. An offset of 6 ends up on *W* in "Hello World!" Don't forget to count spaces as characters.

Listing 40.18 Source code for StringsOne.java.

```
import java.awt.Graphics;
import java.awt.Color;

public class StringsOne extends java.applet.Applet
```

```
{
   byte[] bytesToDraw = { 72, 101, 108, 108, 111, 32,
 ➥87, 111, 114, 108, 100, 33 };

   String bytesString = new String( bytesToDraw );
   String bytesAnotherString = new String( bytesToDraw, 6, 6 );

   public void paint(Graphics g)
   {
     // Draw Hello World! in blue.
     g.setColor(Color.blue);
     g.drawString(bytesString, 10, 20);
     // Draw World! in red.
     g.setColor(Color.red);
     g.drawString(bytesAnotherString, 10, 50);
   }
}
```

The StringsOne applet output is shown in Figure 40.19.

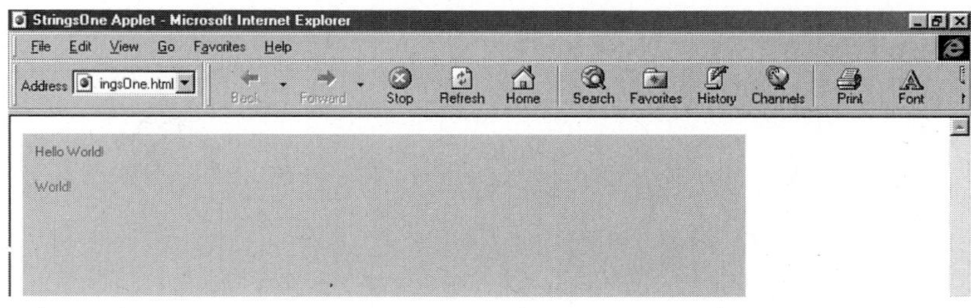

FIG. 40.19 The top string is output from the `String` object assigned to the `bytesString` variable, and the bottom string is output from the `String` object assigned to the `bytesAnotherString` variable.

You use one of the following two constructors when you create `String` objects from character arrays:

```
public String(char  value[])
public String(char  value[], int  offset, int  count)
```

The StringsTwo applet from Listing 40.19 demonstrates the use of both `String` constructors that deal with character arrays.

Listing 40.19 Source code for StringsTwo.java.

```
import java.awt.Graphics;
import java.awt.Color;

public class StringsTwo extends java.applet.Applet
{
   char[] charsToDraw = { 'H', 'e', 'l', 'l', 'o', ' ',
 ➥'W', 'o', 'r', 'l', 'd', '!' };
```

continues

Listing 40.19 Continued

```
    String charsString = new String(charsToDraw);
    String charsAnotherString = new String(charsToDraw, 6, 6);

    public void paint(Graphics g)
    {
      // Draw Hello World! in blue.
      g.setColor(Color.blue);
      g.drawString(charsString, 10, 20);
      // Draw World! in red.
      g.setColor(Color.red);
      g.drawString(charsAnotherString, 10, 50);
    }
}
```

Figure 40.20 shows the output of the StringsTwo applet.

FIG. 40.20 The top string is output from the `String` object assigned to the `charsString` variable, and the bottom string is output from the `String` object assigned to the `charsAnotherString` variable.

If you want to pass nothing to a `String` object when you create it, use the default constructor:

```
public String()
```

Passing nothing to the `String` class constructor results in an empty `String` object. You can then use the object's methods to dynamically create content. In fact, the methods provided by the `String` class make it so handy. It is beyond the scope of this chapter to go into each of over 40 methods, but you have already seen one of the most useful ones, the `length` method. The `length` method just returns the length of the string encapsulated by the `String` object.

Using Java's *Font* Class

You may find that the default font that you have been working with so far is not very interesting. Fortunately you can select from a number of different fonts. Java's `Graphics` class provides the `setFont` method, defined here, so that you can change your text's font characteristics.

```
public abstract void setFont(Font  font)
```

The `setFont` method takes a `Font` object as its argument. Java provides a `Font` class that gives you a lot of text-formatting flexibility. The `Font` class provides a single constructor, as follows:

```
public Font(String  name, int  style, int  size)
```

Pass the name of the font, surrounded by double quotation marks, to the name parameter. The availability of fonts varies from system to system, so it is a good idea to make sure that the user has the font you want. You can check the availability of a font by using the `Toolkit` class `getFontList` method defined here:

```
public abstract String[] getFontList()
```

TROUBLESHOOTING

How do you avoid demanding the use of a font in your program that a user does not have?

Always query for the available fonts by using the `getFontList` method and then only use those fonts in your program. This dynamic method of using fonts is the best policy for distributed computing software such as Java programs.

You don't typically import the `Toolkit` class. Instead, you use the `Applet` class `getToolkit` method (which is inherited from the `Component` class), defined as follows:

```
public Toolkit getToolkit()
```

You use the `style` parameter to set the font style. Bold, italic, plain, or any combination is available. The `Font` class provides three class constants, `Font.BOLD`, `Font.ITALIC`, and `Font.PLAIN`, which you can use in any combination to set the font style. To set a font to bold, for example, just pass `Font.BOLD` to the `style` parameter. If you want to create a bold italic font, you pass `Font.BOLD + Font.ITALIC` to `Font` class's `style` parameter.

Finally, you set the point size of the font by passing an integer to `Font` class's `size` parameter. The point size is a printing term. There are 100 points to an inch when printing on a printer, but this does not necessarily apply to screen fonts. A typical point size value for printed text is either 12 or 14. The point size does not indicate the number of pixels high or wide; it is just a relative term. A point size of 24 is twice as big as a point size of 12.

All this information is pulled together in the ShowFonts applet, shown in Listing 40.20. Figure 40.21 shows the output from the ShowFonts applet.

Listing 40.20 Source code for ShowFonts.java.

```
import java.awt.Graphics;
import java.awt.Font;

public class ShowFonts extends java.applet.Applet
{
   public void paint(Graphics g)
   {
     String fontList[];
     int startY = 15;

     // Get the list of fonts installed on
     //  the current computer.
```

continues

Listing 40.20 Continued

```
      fontList = getToolkit().getFontList();
      // Go through the list of fonts and draw list
      //  to the applet window.
      for (int i=0; i < fontList.length; i++)
      {
         // Draw font name in plain type.
         g.setFont(new Font(fontList[i], Font.PLAIN, 12));
         g.drawString("This is the " + fontList[i] + " font.",
➥5, startY);
         startY += 15;
         // Draw font name in bold type.
         g.setFont(new Font(fontList[i], Font.BOLD, 12));
         g.drawString("This is the bold "+ fontList[i] + " font.",
➥5, startY);
         startY += 15;
         // Draw font name in italic type.
         g.setFont(new Font(fontList[i], Font.ITALIC, 12));
         g.drawString("This is the italic " + fontList[i] + " font.",
➥5, startY);
         startY += 20;
      }
   }
}
```

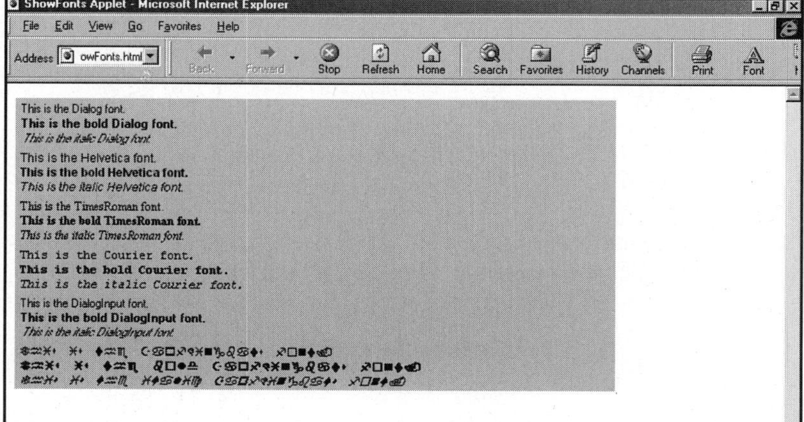

FIG. 40.21
Java provides a number of different fonts and font styles.

Displaying Images

To use Java to display images, you must follow two steps. You must get the image, and then you must draw it. The Java `Applets` class provides methods for getting images and the Java `Graphics` class provides methods for drawing them.

Java's `Applets` class provides two `getImage` methods, listed here:

```
public Image getImage(URL  url)
public Image getImage(URL  url, String  name)
```

In the first method listed, you provide an `URL` class. You can just type the URL surrounded by double quotation marks or you can create an URL object and then pass it to the `getImage` method. If you do the latter, be sure to import the `URL` class. The `URL` class is part of the java.net package.

Whichever way you pass the URL, the first method takes the whole path including the filename of the image itself. Because images are usually aggregated into a single directory or folder, it is usually handier to keep the path and filename separate.

The second method takes the URL path to the image as the `url` parameter and it takes the filename, or even part of the path and the filename, as a string enclosed by double quotation marks and passed to the `name` parameter.

The `Applet` class provides two particularly useful methods, the `getDocumentBase` and `getCodeBase` methods, as follows:

```
public URL getDocumentBase()
public URL getCodeBase()
```

The `getDocumentBase` method returns an `URL` object containing the path to where the HTML document resides that displays the Java applet. Similarly, the `getCodeBase` method returns an `URL` object that contains the path to where the applet is running the code. Using these methods makes your applet flexible. You and others can use your applet on different servers, directories, or folders.

Java's `Graphics` class provides `drawImage` methods to use for displaying images. The most basic method is listed here:

```
public abstract boolean drawImage(Image  img, int  x, int  y,
➥ImageObserver  observer)
```


The first parameter, `img`, takes an `Image` object. Often, you will just get an `Image` object by using the `getImage` method, as discussed previously. The second, `x`, and third, `y`, parameters set the position of the upper-left corner of the image in the applet's window. The last parameter, `observer`, takes an object that implements the ImageObserver interface. This enables your code to make decisions based on an image's loading status. It is usually enough to know that the `Applet` class inherits the ImageObserver interface from the `Components` class. Just passing the applet to the observer parameter is usually sufficient. You might use an alternative object with an ImageObserver interface if you are tracking the asynchronous loading of many images.

TROUBLESHOOTING

The image doesn't load into the applet. What do you do?

Make sure that the image is in the proper folder; either in the same folder as the Java code or in the same folder as the HTML document, depending on the method your program uses. See the section titled "Loading Images Over the Web" later in this chapter if the problem is due to slow or faulty network connections.

Basic image display is easier than it sounds. The DrawImageOne applet in Listing 40.21 displays an image residing in the same directory or folder as the applet itself. Figure 40.22 shows the output of the DrawImageOne applet.

NOTE Place the teddy0.jpg image file into the same folder as the DrawImageOne.class file before you try to run the DrawImageOne applet.

Listing 40.21 Source code for DrawImageOne.java.

```
import java.awt.Graphics;

public class DrawImageOne extends java.applet.Applet
{
   public void paint(Graphics g)
   {
     // Load teddy bear image and draw it in the applet's window.
     g.drawImage(getImage(getCodeBase(), "teddy0.jpg"), 0, 0, this);
   }
}
```

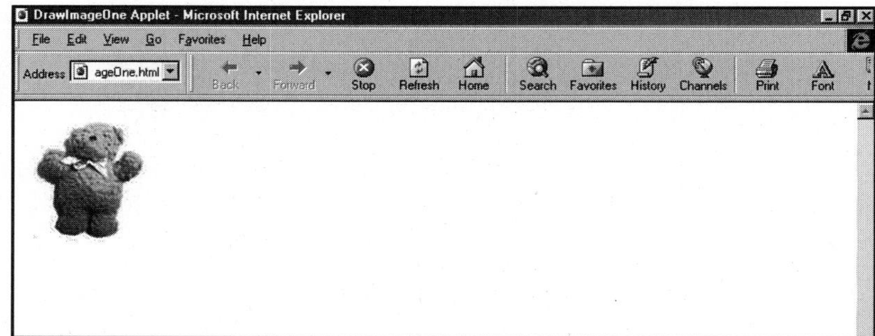

FIG. 40.22 You can draw any JPG or GIF image in a Java applet window by using the `drawImage` method.

The code in Listing 40.21 is simple but not recommended. It is poor coding practice to put actions not directly related to putting something onscreen inside your applet's `paint` method. Every time your applet's window needs updating, the `paint` method is called. It is inefficient to reload an image every time your applet's window is refreshed. You typically override `Applet` class's `init` method to do things, such as loading images, that are only done one time and at the beginning of the applet's life. The `init` method takes no arguments and returns void. The code for the DrawImageTwo applet in Listing 40.22 results in a well-behaved applet that displays the same output as the applet in Listing 40.21.

NOTE Place the teddy0.jpg image file into the same folder as the DrawImageTwo.class file before you try to run the DrawImageTwo applet.

Listing 40.22 Source code for DrawImageTwo.java.

```
import java.awt.Graphics;
import java.awt.Image;

public class DrawImageTwo extends java.applet.Applet
{
   private Image imageTeddy;

   public void init()
   {
     // Load teddy bear image.
     imageTeddy = getImage(getCodeBase(), "teddy0.jpg");
   }

   public void paint(Graphics g)
   {
     // Draw teddy bear image in the applet's window.
     g.drawImage(imageTeddy, 0, 0, this);
   }
}
```

Notice that in Listing 40.22 the image from the teddy0.jpg file loads only one time in the `init` method where the `Image` object encapsulating the teddy bear image and assigned to the `imageTeddy` variable is created. Whenever the applet window is refreshed, the `Image` object assigned to the `imageTeddy` variable is passed to the `drawImage` method without reloading the image from the teddy0.jpg file.

Another version of the `drawImage` method is similar to the one you have already seen and used, but it includes two additional parameters. These enable you to determine the size of the image displayed in an applet window. This version of the `drawImage` method is as follows:

```
public abstract boolean drawImage(Image  img, int  x, int  y,
          int  width, int  height, ImageObserver  observer)
```

The `width` and `height` parameters take the width and height, in pixels, of the display area for the image regardless of the image's native size. You can stretch and shrink an image by using these parameters; the actual disk size of the image remains the same. Just remember that doing this can degrade the quality of your image.

Creating Animation

Displaying animation is probably the most popular use of Java applets on the Web. You can use HTML to display static images, but you need Java to make them come alive.

You should follow these three general steps when creating animation:

- Load the images.
- Start a thread.
- Run the animation.

In the following sections, you use three images to create an animation of a dancing teddy bear. You have already seen the first image from the teddy0.jpg file. It is a teddy bear standing upright on both of its hind limbs. The second image, from the teddy1.jpg file, shows the teddy bear standing on its left hind limb. Finally, the third image, from the teddy2.jpg file, shows the teddy bear standing on its right hind limb.

Loading Images

Loading the dancing teddy bear images is nearly identical to the way you have loaded images before. The only difference is that you need to load more than one image. You need to create an instance variable that holds an array of `Image` objects. Because there are three dancing teddy bear images, you will create an array for three `Image` objects with the this line of code:

```
Image imagesTeddy[] = new Image[3];
```

Next, load the images in an overloaded `init` method. You can conveniently use a `for` statement to load the images because each image has an identical name followed by a number. The folowing code is the dancing teddy bear `init` method:

```
public void init()
{
     for (int i=0; i < imagesTeddy.length; i++)
          imagesTeddy[i] = getImage(getCodeBase(), "teddy" + i + ".jpg");
}
```

Starting a Thread

You should start at least one thread for each animation that you run. In fact, you should start a thread anytime you run code that may require a lot of time and attention from the user's computer.

Individual processes, known as programs, are typically run sequentially. Therefore if your word processor starts printing, you must wait for the printing to finish before continuing work with your document. In systems that support threads, however, individual processes are broken up into several executable subprocesses, or threads. In systems that support threads—such as Windows 95, Windows NT, and the Java Virtual Machine—printing can run in a thread separate from the thread running document editing features. That way, as you print your document, you can get right back to work on your document. The tasks run parallel in separate threads.

To use threads in your applet, you must first change the signature of your class that extends the Java `Applet` class so that it implements the Runnable interface. Add implements Runnable to the end of the `DancingTeddy` class signature so that the signature reads like this:

```
public class DancingTeddy extends java.applet.Applet implements Runnable
```

The Runnable interface defines default thread behaviors. Next, define an instance variable of the `Thread` class named threadTeddyAnimation like in the following line and add it to the top of the `DancingTeddy` class:

```
Thread threadTeddyAnimation = null;
```

Create and start a thread in the `Applet` class `start` method and stop a thread in the `Applet` class `stop` method. You override the Java `Applet` class `start` and `stop` methods defined here:

```
public void start()
public void stop()
```

When a Web page calls an applet, the applet first runs the `Applet` class `init` method. Next, the Java Virtual Machine automatically calls an applet's `start` method. Unlike the `init` method, which is only run one time on startup, the `start` method can be run an indefinite number of times. The `start` method is run every time a Java applet gains focus in a multitasking environment. Similarly, the `stop` method is run every time a Java applet loses focus in a multitasking environment. You want a thread to last just as long as it is needed. Therefore you create and start a thread when an applet gains focus and you stop the thread—which then dies and is taken away by garbage collection—when an applet loses focus.

To create and then start the dancing teddy bear thread assigned to the `threadTeddyAnimation` variable, override the `Applet` class `start` method with the `start` method shown here:

```
public void start()
{
  if (threadTeddyAnimation == null)
  {
    threadTeddyAnimation = new Thread( this );
    threadTeddyAnimation.start();
  }
}
```

First the `threadTeddyAnimation` variable is tested to see whether it remains unassigned to any `Thread` objects. If the `threadTeddyAnimation` variable is set equal to `null`, it doesn't hold a `Thread` object and the body of the `if` statement is executed; otherwise the body of the `if` statement is skipped and nothing happens.

The first statement in the body of the `if` statement passes a reference to the `DancingTeddy` object to the `Thread` class constructor and assigns the new `Thread` object to the `threadTeddyAnimation` variable. The second statement calls the `Thread` class `start` method, which starts the thread.

To stop the thread when the DancingTeddy applet loses focus, override the `Applet` class `stop` method with the following `stop` method:

```
public void stop()
{
  if ( threadTeddyAnimation != null )
  {
    threadTeddyAnimation.stop( );
    threadTeddyAnimation = null;
  }
}
```

First the `threadTeddyAnimation` variable is tested to see whether it is assigned a `Thread` object. If the `threadTeddyAnimation` variable is not set equal to `null`, it holds a `Thread` object and the body of the `if` statement is executed; otherwise the body of the `if` statement is skipped and nothing happens.

The first statement in the body of the `if` statement calls the `Thread` class `stop` method, which stops the thread. The second statement assigns `null` to the `threadTeddyAnimation` variable.

Your applet is now threaded!

Running an Animation

To run the animation, you must override the `Applet` class `run` method in your `Animation` class. The dancing teddy bear will start standing straight up on both hind limbs (teddy0.jpg), and then on to its left limb (teddy1.jpg), back to both hind limbs (teddy0.jpg), and then on to its right limb (teddy2.jpg), and then back to both hind limbs (teddy0.jpg). The bear will do this for as long as the applet runs. The picture number pattern is `{0, 1, 0, 2}` and repeats over and over. As you can see in the `run` method in the following code, the array named `iPictureNumber` contains the picture number pattern and a `while` loop is created to cause an infinite loop. The code loops through the picture number list and sets the `imageCurrent` variable to the appropriate teddy image. The `repaint` method is called and then the thread sleeps for 100 milliseconds (one tenth of a second).

```
public void run()
{
  int iPictureNumber[] = {0, 1, 0, 2};
  while (true)
  {
    for (int i = 0; i < iPictureNumber.length; i++)
    {
      imageCurrent = imagesTeddy[iPictureNumber[i]];
      repaint();
      try
      {
        threadTeddyAnimation.sleep( 100 );
      }
      catch (InterruptedException e)
      {
        break;
      }
    }
  }
}
```

When the animation program calls the `repaint` method, the `repaint` method calls the `update` method. The `update` method clears the screen and then calls the `paint` method. You must override the `paint` method, as shown in the following code, to draw the current image assigned to the `imageCurrent` variable.

```
public void paint(Graphics g)
{
     g.drawImage( imageCurrent, 0, 0, this);
}
```

You have now gone through a complete animation of a dancing teddy bear. All the code is shown in Listing 40.23 with your modification's highlighted in bold text. Before you try to run the DancingTeddy applet, don't forget to make sure that the teddy images are in the correct directory or folder with the compiled DancingTeddy class file.

Listing 40.23 Source code for DancingTeddy.java.

```
import java.awt.Graphics;
import java.awt.Image;

public class DancingTeddy extends java.applet.Applet
     implements Runnable
{
  Image imagesTeddy[] = new Image[3];
  Image imageCurrent = null;
  Thread threadTeddyAnimation = null;

  public void init()
  {
    // Load all three teddy bear images.
    for (int i=0; i < imagesTeddy.length; i++)
      imagesTeddy[i] = getImage(getCodeBase(),
➥"teddy" + i + ".jpg");
  }

  public void start()
  {
    if (threadTeddyAnimation == null)
    {
      threadTeddyAnimation = new Thread( this );
      threadTeddyAnimation.start();
    }
  }

  public void stop()
  {
    if (threadTeddyAnimation != null)
    {
      threadTeddyAnimation.stop();
      threadTeddyAnimation = null;
    }
  }

  public void run()
  {
    int iPictureNumber[] = {0, 1, 0, 2};

    // Prepare to display teddy bear pictures one
    //  after the other indefinitely and in the
    //  following order: teddy0, teddy1, teddy0, teddy2.
    while (true)
    {
      for (int i = 0; i < iPictureNumber.length; i++)
      {
        // Assign the current teddy bear image to
        //  the imageCurrent variable.
        imageCurrent = imagesTeddy[iPictureNumber[i]];
        // Force a call to the paint method to draw
        //  the current teddy bear image.
```


continues

Listing 40.23 Continued

```
          repaint();
          // Don't do anything new for 100 milliseconds.
          try
          {
            threadTeddyAnimation.sleep( 100 );
          }
          // Exit program if there is an error.
          catch (InterruptedException e)
          {
            break;
          }
        }
      }
    }

    public void paint(Graphics g)
    {
      // Draw current image in the applet's window.
      g.drawImage( imageCurrent, 0, 0, this);
    }
  }
```

Fighting Flicker

If you ran the DancingTeddy applet from the preceding section, you probably saw a lot of flicker. Each time an applet's window is updated (with a call to the `update` method), the entire applet window clears and fills in with the current background color. Then `update` calls the `paint` method and the new image is drawn. This happens one time every tenth of a second in the DancingTeddy applet.

One relatively easy way to fight flicker is to override the `update` method so that the applet's window is not cleared. Add the following to the DancingTeddy code in Listing 40.23:

```
public void update(Graphics g)
{
  paint(g);
}
```

The `update` method takes a single argument, a `Graphics` object. You should notice a dramatic reduction in flicker when you recompile DancingTeddy with the overridden `update` method. It works well because the same area of the screen is drawn to each time the `paint` method is called. This method causes problems, however, if your animated object takes up only a small portion of the applet's window.

Creating an Advanced Animation

Soon you will use more advanced anti-flicker techniques, but first you need to create a more advanced animation. Using the same three teddy bear images, you now create an animated bear with more behaviors. The teddy bear will now move left, right, dance in place, or just stand.

The new applet, named the AnimatedTeddy1 applet, is similar to the DancingTeddy applet found in the preceding section except that the code in the `run` method is completely changed and two new methods are added: the `hop` and `dance` methods. Additionally, the `sleep` method inherited from the `Thread` class is overridden.

The `hop` method, listed in the following code, supplies the teddy bear's hopping behavior. The `hop` method takes three arguments. The place where the bear will move from, `iStart`, and the place where it will move to, `iStop`, all in *x* coordinates. The final argument, `stringDirection`, can either be right or left and tells the method the direction, relative to the bear, that the bear will hop.

```
void hop(int iStart, int iStop, String stringDirection)
{
  boolean bGround = true;

  if (stringDirection.equals( "left" ) )
    imageCurrent = imagesTeddy[1];
  else
  {
    imageCurrent = imagesTeddy[2];
    iStart = -iStart;
    iStop = -iStop;
  }

  for (int i = iStart; i < iStop; i += 10)
  {
    xPosition = Math.abs(i);

    if (bGround)
    {
      yPosition = 50;
      bGround = false;
    }
    else
    {
      yPosition = 40;
      bGround = true;
    }
    repaint();
    sleep( 100 );
  }
}
```

The first line of `hop` method's body contains a Boolean variable, `bGround`. When the `bGround` variable is assigned `true`, its default value, it signifies that the teddy bear stands on the ground. Ground level is defined as a *y* value, `yPosition`, of 50.

The `hop` method tests the `stringDirection` variable to see whether it equals left. If it does, the `imageCurrent` variable is assigned the image from the teddy1.jpg image file—the image with the bear standing on its left hind limb. Otherwise the bear is assumed to be moving right, so the `imageCurrent` variable is assigned the image from the teddy2.jpg image file—the image with the bear standing on its right hind limb. Also, the `iStart` and `iStop` variables are negated. This is a convenient way to change the bear's hopping direction.

The bear's movement is controlled by the `for` loop. The index variable, `i`, is set equal to the value assigned to the `iStart` variable. The loop continues as long as `i` is less than the value assigned to the `iStop` variable. The index is incremented by 10 each loop.

When the teddy bear is moving to the left, `iStart` is less than `iStop` and the numbers, as they increase, match the increasing number of pixels from left to right in Java's coordinate system. However, when the bear is moving to the right, `iStart` is greater than `iStop`. You could use a decrementing `for` loop for moving right, but it is easier to take the negative of `iStart` and `iStop`. This way the same `for` loop can be used because the value of `iStart` is now less than the value of `iStop`. The only problem is that the index represents the bear's *x* coordinate, in pixels, in the applet's window. Solve the problem by taking the absolute value of `i`, `Math.abs(i)`, before setting it equal to `xPosition`.

Next, if `bGround` is true, the bear is standing on ground level and `yPosition` is equal to 50. `bGround` is set to false so that next time around the loop the bear will hop up. If `bGround` is false, the bear has jumped up above the ground, so the `yPosition` variable is set to 40. `bGround` is set to `true` so that next time around the loop, the bear will drop back to the ground.

Each time around the `for` loop, the `repaint` and then the `sleep` methods are called. The `repaint` method is the standard method that repaints the applet's window. The `sleep` method, listed in the following code, overrides the `sleep` method inherited by the `AnimatedTeddy1` class from the `Thread` class.

```
void sleep(int iTime)
{
  try
  {
    threadTeddyAnimation.sleep( iTime );
  }
  catch (InterruptedException e)
  {
    return;
  }
}
```

The `AnimatedTeddy1` class `sleep` method is a method that wraps `Thread` class's own `sleep` method. Pass the amount of time, in milliseconds, that you want the thread to sleep and the animation pauses for that amount of time.

The new `dance` method, shown in the following code, behaves just the same as the `for` loop in DancingTeddy except now there are two `for` loops. You pass the number of repetitions of the dance, `iJigs` to the `dance` method. The first `for` loop repeats the basic dance the number of times defined by `iJigs`.

```
void dance(int iJigs)
{
  int iPictureNumber[] = {0, 1, 0, 2};

  for (int i = 0; i < iJigs; i++)
  {
    for (int j = 0; j < iPictureNumber.length; j++)
    {
```

```
        imageCurrent = imagesTeddy[iPictureNumber[j]];
        repaint();
        sleep( 100 );
      }
    }
  }
```

You pull all these new behaviors together in the `AnimatedTeddy1` class `run` method, listed here:

```
public void run()
{
  while (true)
  {
    hop( 0, 300, "left");
    dance( 5 );

    imageCurrent = imagesTeddy[0];
    repaint();
    sleep( 1000 );

    hop( 300, 600, "left");
    hop( 600, 300, "right");
    dance( 5 );

    imageCurrent = imagesTeddy[0];
    repaint();
    sleep( 1000 );

    hop( 300, 0, "right");
  }
}
```


`AnimatedTeddy1` class's entire `run` method consists of an infinite loop created using the `while` statement. Inside the infinite loop, the teddy bear's various behaviors are laid out. The teddy starts from the left side of the applet's window and hops left to the window's approximate center. It then dances five jigs and then stands on both hind limbs for 1,000 milliseconds. The bear then continues hopping left until it reaches the right (your right) side of the applet's window. It then reverses direction and hops right back to the center of the window where it dances five jigs again, stands for 1,000 milliseconds, and finally continues hopping right until it reaches the left (your left) side of the applet's window. The teddy bear repeats this dance indefinitely.

Listing 40.24 contains all the code for the AnimatedTeddy1 applet. Compile the `AnimatedTeddy1` class, and then display the applet like in Figure 40.23.

Listing 40.24 Source code for AnimatedTeddy1.java.

```
import java.awt.Graphics;
import java.awt.Image;
import java.awt.Color;

public class AnimatedTeddy extends java.applet.Applet
  implements Runnable
{
```

continues

Listing 40.24 Continued

```
  Image imagesTeddy[] = new Image[3];
  Image imageCurrent = null;
  Thread threadTeddyAnimation = null;
  int xPosition = 0;
  int yPosition = 50;

  public void init()
  {
    setBackground(Color.white);
    // Load all three teddy bear images.
    for (int i=0; i < imagesTeddy.length; i++)
      imagesTeddy[i] = getImage(getCodeBase(),
➥"teddy" + i + ".jpg");
}

  public void start()
  {
    if (threadTeddyAnimation == null)
    {
      threadTeddyAnimation = new Thread(this);
      threadTeddyAnimation.start();
    }
  }

  public void stop()
  {
    if (threadTeddyAnimation != null)
    {
      threadTeddyAnimation.stop();
      threadTeddyAnimation = null;
    }
  }

  public void run()
  {
    while (true)
    {
      // Hop to the left for 300 pixels.
      hop( 0, 300, "left");

      // Dance in center of window five times.
      dance( 5 );

      // Stand on both hind paws for 1 second.
      // Assign teddy0.jpg to the imageCurrent variable.
      imageCurrent = imagesTeddy[0];
      // Force a call to the paint method to draw
      //  the teddy0.jpg image.
      repaint();
      // Don't do anything new for 1000 milliseconds.
      sleep( 1000 );

      // Hop to the left for 300 pixels.
      hop( 300, 600, "left");
```

```
    // Hop to the right for 300 pixels.
    hop( 600, 300, "right");

    // Dance in center of window five times.
    dance( 5 );

    // Stand on both hind paws for 1 second.
    // Assign teddy0.jpg to the imageCurrent variable.
    imageCurrent = imagesTeddy[0];
    // Force a call to the paint method to draw
    //  the teddy0.jpg image.
    repaint();
    // Don't do anything new for 1000 milliseconds.
    sleep( 1000 );

    // Hop to the right for 300 pixels.
    hop( 300, 0, "right");
  }
}

void hop(int iStart, int iStop, String stringDirection)
{
  boolean bGround = true;

  // If the teddy bear is hopping left assign teddy1.jpg
  //  to imageCurrent otherwise it's hopping right
  //  so assign teddy2.jpg to imageCurrent.
  if (stringDirection.equals( "left" ) )
    imageCurrent = imagesTeddy[1];
  else
  {
    imageCurrent = imagesTeddy[2];
    iStart = -iStart;
    iStop = -iStop;
  }

  // Move the teddy bear image, hopping, across
  //  the applet window.
  for (int i = iStart; i < iStop; i += 10)
  {
    xPosition = Math.abs(i);

    if (bGround)
    {
      yPosition = 50;
      bGround = false;
    }
    else
    {
      yPosition = 40;
      bGround = true;
    }
    // Force a call to the paint method to draw
    //  the current teddy bear image.
    repaint();
```


continues

Listing 40.24 Continued

```
      // Don't do anything new for 100 milliseconds.
      sleep( 100 );
    }
  }

  void dance(int iJigs)
  {
    int iPictureNumber[] = {0, 1, 0, 2};

    for (int i = 0; i < iJigs; i++)
    {
      for (int j = 0; j < iPictureNumber.length; j++)
      {
        // Assign the current teddy bear image to
        //  the imageCurrent variable.
        imageCurrent = imagesTeddy[iPictureNumber[j]];
        // Force a call to the paint method to draw
        //  the current teddy bear image.
        repaint();
        // Don't do anything new for 100 milliseconds.
        sleep( 100 );
      }
    }
  }

  // Don't do anything for the number of milliseconds
  //  defined by iTime.
  void sleep(int iTime)
  {
    try
    {
      threadTeddyAnimation.sleep( iTime );
    }
    catch (InterruptedException e)
    {
      return;
    }
  }

  public void paint(Graphics g)
  {
    // Draw current image in the applet's window.
    g.drawImage( imageCurrent, xPosition, yPosition, this);
  }
}
```

You will notice the return of the dreaded flicker when you run the AnimatedTeddy1 applet. You didn't override the `update` method like before because it doesn't work. You will find bits of the old images that have not been erased because you are moving the paint region around. Two techniques can help you solve this problem: clipping and double-buffering.

FIG. 40.23
The AnimatedTeddy1 applet displays a 750×200 pixel window where a teddy bear carries out his dance.

Clipping

By default, the `update` method clears the whole applet window. Why clear everything when you need to erase the teddy bear from the old position only and redraw it in the new position? The two areas combined form only a small portion (generally 130×130 pixels) of the whole applet window (750×200 pixels). Clipping techniques give you the ability to update only that part of the applet window that needs updating.

You might think that you would use the `clipRect` method from the `Graphics` class to define a clipping area in the teddy bear applet. However, when you are drawing images to the screen, you must use the `clearRect` method from the `Graphics` class, defined as follows:

```
public abstract void clearRect(int  x, int  y, int width, int  height)
```

The `x` and `y` parameters take the applet's window coordinates of the top-left corner of the clipping rectangle. The `width` parameter takes the width and the `height` parameter takes the height of the clipping rectangle. Everything inside this rectangle clears and everything outside it is left alone.

You must use `clearRect` rather than `clipRect` to display images because the `drawImage` method already restricts (or clips) its output to the size of the image itself. When you use the `clipRect` method, only the intersection between the rectangle defined in the `clipRect` method and the drawing rectangle updates. The result is just like overriding the `update` method as mentioned at the end of the preceding section: You are left with bits of the old images that haven't been erased!

To properly update the teddy bear image, you must repaint a rectangle that includes the union between the areas covered by the old and the new images. You can do this using the `clearRect` method.

Create a new applet named the AnimatedTeddy2 applet by modifying the AnimatedTeddy1 applet described in the preceding section. Begin by adding instance variables that are assigned the width (120 pixels) and height (120 pixels) of the three images, like those listed here:

```
int imageWidth = 120;
int imageHeight = 120;
```

You need to keep track of the *x* and *y* coordinates of the previously displayed image in addition to the coordinates of the currently displayed image. You can save the old coordinates in the following instance variables:

```
int xOldPosition = 0;
int yOldPosition = 50;
```

All other new code in the `AnimatedTeddy2` class is added to the overridden `update` method and the `paint` method. Override the default behavior of the `update` method and define the clipping area in it so that, instead of clearing the whole screen every time `update` is called, only the clipped area clears. This is, unfortunately, a little complicated because the teddy bear moves in four directions. The clipping rectangle must always define the union of the areas of both the old and the new image positions.

When the current image position along the *x* axis (`xPosition`) is greater than the previous image position (`xOldPosition`), the clipping rectangle's position starts at the old *x* coordinate and the rectangle's width is the new position minus the old position plus the image's width. This makes sense because the *x* coordinate always defines the left edge of a rectangle. Therefore, the *x* coordinate must always be at the leftmost edge of the area that needs clearing (assuming that you use a positive width for your rectangle). Also, the width must always equal the distance between the leftmost edge of the old image position and the leftmost edge of the new image position plus the width of the image. You can see this in code in the first `if` statement in the `update` method listed here:

```
public void update(Graphics g)
{
  int xClip;
  int yClip;
  int clipWidth;
  int clipHeight;

  if (xPosition >= xOldPosition)
  {
    clipWidth = (xPosition - xOldPosition) + imageWidth;
    xClip = xOldPosition;
  }
  else
  {
    clipWidth = (xOldPosition - xPosition) + imageWidth;
    xClip = xPosition;
  }
  if (yPosition >= yOldPosition)
  {
    clipHeight = (yPosition - yOldPosition) + imageHeight;
    yClip = yOldPosition;
  }
  else
  {
    clipHeight = (yOldPosition - yPosition) + imageHeight;
    yClip = yPosition;
  }
  g.clearRect( xClip, yClip, clipWidth, clipHeight );
```

```
  paint(g);
}
```

When the current image's *x* coordinate is less than the old image's *x* coordinate, the clipping rectangle must have an *x* coordinate equal to the current image's *x* coordinate. Again, this is because the current image's *x* coordinate is the leftmost position. The same logic is behind the code for the *y* coordinates.

After all the clipping coordinates are figured out and assigned to the appropriate method variables, the `update` method calls the `clearRect` method from the `Graphics` class and the area defined by the clipping rectangle clears. Finally, the last line of code in the `update` method is a call to the `paint` method.

Only two lines are added to the `paint` method. Set the `xOldPosition` and `yOldPosition` instance variables equal to the recently current `x` and `y` positions, as follows:

```
public void paint(Graphics g)
{
  g.drawImage( imageCurrent, xPosition, yPosition, this);
  xOldPosition = xPosition;
  yOldPosition = yPosition;
}
```

Compile the `AnimatedTeddy2` class in Listing 40.25 and view the applet. You may be disappointed in the amount of flicker still detectable in the latest version of the teddy bear animation. You will always need to use some sort of clipping method, but it still isn't enough for advanced animation. You need to use clipping techniques in conjunction with double-buffering to really do the job.

Listing 40.25 Source code for AnimatedTeddy2.java.

```
import java.awt.Graphics;
import java.awt.Image;
import java.awt.Color;

public class AnimatedTeddy2 extends java.applet.Applet
     implements Runnable
{
  Image imagesTeddy[] = new Image[3];
  Image imageCurrent = null;
  Thread threadTeddyAnimation = null;
  int imageWidth = 120;
  int imageHeight = 120;
  int xPosition = 0;
  int yPosition = 50;
  int xOldPosition = 0;
  int yOldPosition = 50;

  public void init()
  {
    setBackground(Color.white);
    // Load all three teddy bear images.
```

continues

Listing 40.25 Continued

```
    for (int i=0; i < imagesTeddy.length; i++)
      imagesTeddy[i] = getImage(getCodeBase(),
➥"teddy" + i + ".jpg");
  }

  public void start()
  {
    if (threadTeddyAnimation == null)
    {
      threadTeddyAnimation = new Thread( this );
      threadTeddyAnimation.start();
    }
  }

  public void stop()
  {
    if (threadTeddyAnimation != null)
    {
      threadTeddyAnimation.stop();
      threadTeddyAnimation = null;
    }
  }

  public void run()
  {
    while (true)
    {
      // Hop to the left for 300 pixels.
      hop( 0, 300, "left");

      // Dance in center of window five times.
      dance( 5 );

      // Stand on both hind paws for 1 second.
      // Assign teddy0.jpg to the imageCurrent variable.
      imageCurrent = imagesTeddy[0];
      // Force a call to the paint method to draw
      //  the teddy0.jpg image.
      repaint();
      // Don't do anything new for 1000 milliseconds.
      sleep( 1000 );

      // Hop to the left for 300 pixels.
      hop( 300, 600, "left");

      // Hop to the right for 300 pixels.
      hop( 600, 300, "right");

      // Dance in center of window five times.
      dance( 5 );

      // Stand on both hind paws for 1 second.
      // Assign teddy0.jpg to the imageCurrent variable.
```

```
    imageCurrent = imagesTeddy[0];
    // Force a call to the paint method to draw
    //  the teddy0.jpg image.
    repaint();
    // Don't do anything new for 1000 milliseconds.
    sleep( 1000 );

    // Hop to the right for 300 pixels.
    hop( 300, 0, "right");
  }
}

void hop(int iStart, int iStop, String stringDirection)
{
  boolean bGround = true;

  // If the teddy bear is hopping left assign teddy1.jpg
  //  to imageCurrent otherwise it's hopping right
  //  so assign teddy2.jpg to imageCurrent.
  if (stringDirection.equals( "left" ) )
    imageCurrent = imagesTeddy[1];
  else
  {
    imageCurrent = imagesTeddy[2];
    iStart = -iStart;
    iStop = -iStop;
  }

  // Move the teddy bear image, hopping, across
  //  the applet window.
  for (int i = iStart; i < iStop; i += 10)
  {
    xPosition = Math.abs(i);

    if (bGround)
    {
      yPosition = 50;
      bGround = false;
    }
    else
    {
      yPosition = 40;
      bGround = true;
    }
    // Force a call to the paint method to draw
    //  the current teddy bear image.
    repaint();
    // Don't do anything new for 100 milliseconds.
    sleep( 100 );
  }
}

void dance(int iJigs)
{
  int iPictureNumber[] = {0, 1, 0, 2};
```


continues

Listing 40.25 Continued

```
    for (int i = 0; i < iJigs; i++)
    {
      for (int j = 0; j < iPictureNumber.length; j++)
      {
        // Assign the current teddy bear image to
        //  the imageCurrent variable.
        imageCurrent = imagesTeddy[iPictureNumber[j]];
        // Force a call to the paint method to draw
        //  the current teddy bear image.
        repaint();
        // Don't do anything new for 100 milliseconds.
        sleep( 100 );
      }
    }
  }

  // Don't do anything for the number of milliseconds
  //  defined by iTime.
  void sleep(int iTime)
  {
    try
    {
      threadTeddyAnimation.sleep( iTime );
    }
    catch (InterruptedException e)
    {
      return;
    }
  }

  public void update(Graphics g)
  {
    int xClip;
    int yClip;
    int clipWidth;
    int clipHeight;

    if (xPosition >= xOldPosition)
    {
      clipWidth = (xPosition - xOldPosition) + imageWidth;
      xClip = xOldPosition;
    }
    else
    {
      clipWidth = (xOldPosition - xPosition) + imageWidth;
      xClip = xPosition;
    }
    if (yPosition >= yOldPosition)
    {
      clipHeight = (yPosition - yOldPosition) + imageHeight;
      yClip = yOldPosition;
    }
    else
```

```
        {
          clipHeight = (yOldPosition - yPosition) + imageHeight;
          yClip = yPosition;
        }
        g.clearRect( xClip, yClip, clipWidth, clipHeight );
        paint(g);
      }

      public void paint(Graphics g)
      {
        // Draw current image in the applet's window.
        g.drawImage( imageCurrent, xPosition, yPosition, this);
        xOldPosition = xPosition;
        yOldPosition = yPosition;
      }
    }
```

Double-Buffering

For advanced animation, the best solution for fighting flicker is usually the technique called *double-buffering.* With double-buffering, you create an offscreen image and do all your drawing to that offscreen image. After you are finished drawing, you copy the offscreen image to the applet's window in one quick call.

You can create a new applet that doesn't show screen flicker, the AnimatedTeddy3 applet, by modifying the `AnimatedTeddy2` class so that it supports double-buffering. Add the following instance variables to the top of your new `AnimatedTeddy3` class for creating an offscreen image and its graphics context used to carry out double-buffering:

```
Image imageOffScreen = null;
Graphics graphicsOffScreen = null;
```

Next, add the following line to the `init` method to create an offscreen `Image` object:

```
imageOffScreen = createImage( getSize().width, getSize().height);
```

Follow the preceding line with the line that follows here to create an offscreen graphics context for the offscreen image:

```
graphicsOffScreen = imageOffScreen.getGraphics();
```

Finally, follow the preceding line with the two lines that follow here to set the image background to white:

```
graphicsOffScreen.setColor(Color.white);
graphicsOffScreen.fillRect(0, 0, getSize().width, getSize().height);
```

You don't use the `setBackground` method in the `init` method like you did in the AnimatedTeddy2 applet. The `setBackground` method doesn't work when you use double-buffering.

Next, add the following three lines of code to the end of the `update` method instead of calling the `g.clearRect` method like in the AnimatedTeddy2 applet:

```
      // the teddy0.jpg image.
      repaint();
```

continues

Place the `checkID` method in an `if` statement and pass the images' identification number to the `id` parameter, as in the following line:

```
if ( tracker.checkID( 0 ) )
```

If the images with an identification number of 0 are completely loaded, the `checkID` method returns `true` and the code inside the `if` block is executed. Otherwise, the `checkID` method returns `false` and the code is skipped.

Listing 40.27 Source code for AnimatedTeddy4.java.

```
import java.awt.Graphics;
import java.awt.Image;
import java.awt.Color;
import java.awt.MediaTracker;

public class AnimatedTeddy4 extends java.applet.Applet implements Runnable
{
  Image imagesTeddy[] = new Image[3];
  Image imageCurrent = null;
  Thread threadTeddyAnimation = null;
  Image imageOffScreen = null;
  Graphics graphicsOffScreen = null;
  MediaTracker tracker = null;
  int imageWidth = 120;
  int imageHeight = 120;
  int xPosition = 0;
  int yPosition = 50;
  int xOldPosition = 0;
  int yOldPosition = 50;

  public void init()
  {
    imageOffScreen = createImage( getSize().width, getSize().height);
    graphicsOffScreen = imageOffScreen.getGraphics();
    graphicsOffScreen.setColor(Color.white);
    graphicsOffScreen.fillRect(0, 0, getSize().width, getSize().height);
    tracker = new MediaTracker( this );
    // Load and track all three teddy bear images.
    for (int i=0; i < imagesTeddy.length; i++)
    {
      imagesTeddy[i] = getImage(getCodeBase(), "teddy" + i + ".jpg");
      tracker.addImage( imagesTeddy[i], 0 );
    }
  }

  public void start()
  {
    if (threadTeddyAnimation == null)
    {
      threadTeddyAnimation = new Thread(this);
      threadTeddyAnimation.start();
    }
  }
```

```
public void stop()
{
  if (threadTeddyAnimation != null)
  {
    threadTeddyAnimation.stop();
    threadTeddyAnimation = null;
  }
}

public void run()
{
  // Wait until all three teddy bear images are loaded.
  try
  {
    tracker.waitForID( 0 );
  }
  catch ( InterruptedException e )
  {
    return;
  }
  while (true)
  {
    // Hop to the left for 300 pixels.
    hop( 0, 300, "left");

    // Dance in center of window five times.
    dance( 5 );

    // Stand on both hind paws for 1 second.
    // Assign teddy0.jpg to the imageCurrent variable.
    imageCurrent = imagesTeddy[0];
    // Force a call to the paint method to draw
    //  the teddy0.jpg image.
    repaint();
    // Don't do anything new for 1000 milliseconds.
    sleep( 1000 );

    // Hop to the left for 300 pixels.
    hop( 300, 600, "left");

    // Hop to the right for 300 pixels.
    hop( 600, 300, "right");

    // Dance in center of window five times.
    dance( 5 );

    // Stand on both hind paws for 1 second.
    // Assign teddy0.jpg to the imageCurrent variable.
    imageCurrent = imagesTeddy[0];
    // Force a call to the paint method to draw
    //  the teddy0.jpg image.
    repaint();
    // Don't do anything new for 1000 milliseconds.
    sleep( 1000 );
```


continues

Listing 40.27 Continued

```
      // Hop to the right for 300 pixels.
      hop( 300, 0, "right");
    }
  }

  void hop(int iStart, int iStop, String stringDirection)
  {
    boolean bGround = true;

    // If the teddy bear is hopping left assign teddy1.jpg
    //  to imageCurrent otherwise it's hopping right
    //  so assign teddy2.jpg to imageCurrent.
    if ( stringDirection.equals( "left" ) )
      imageCurrent = imagesTeddy[1];
    else
    {
      imageCurrent = imagesTeddy[2];
      iStart = -iStart;
      iStop = -iStop;
    }

    // Move the teddy bear image, hopping, across
    //  the applet window.
    for (int i = iStart; i < iStop; i += 10)
    {
      xPosition = Math.abs(i);

      if (bGround)
      {
        yPosition = 50;
        bGround = false;
      }
      else
      {
        yPosition = 40;
        bGround = true;
      }
      // Force a call to the paint method to draw
      //  the current teddy bear image.
      repaint();
      // Don't do anything new for 100 milliseconds.
      sleep( 100 );
    }
  }

  void dance(int iJigs)
  {
    int iPictureNumber[] = {0, 1, 0, 2};

    for (int i = 0; i < iJigs; i++)
    {
      for (int j = 0; j < iPictureNumber.length; j++)
      {
        // Assign the current teddy bear image to
```

```
        //  the imageCurrent variable.
        imageCurrent = imagesTeddy[iPictureNumber[j]];
        // Force a call to the paint method to draw
        //  the current teddy bear image.
        repaint();
        // Don't do anything new for 100 milliseconds.
        sleep( 100 );
      }
    }
  }

  // Don't do anything for the number of milliseconds
  //  defined by iTime.
  void sleep(int iTime)
  {
    try
    {
      threadTeddyAnimation.sleep( iTime );
    }
    catch (InterruptedException e)
    {
      return;
    }
  }

  public void update(Graphics g)
  {
    int xClip;
    int yClip;
    int clipWidth;
    int clipHeight;

    if (xPosition >= xOldPosition)
    {
      clipWidth = (xPosition - xOldPosition) + imageWidth;
      xClip = xOldPosition;
    }
    else
    {
      clipWidth = (xOldPosition - xPosition) + imageWidth;
      xClip = xPosition;
    }
    if (yPosition >= yOldPosition)
    {
      clipHeight = (yPosition - yOldPosition) + imageHeight;
      yClip = yOldPosition;
    }
    else
    {
      clipHeight = (yOldPosition - yPosition) + imageHeight;
      yClip = yPosition;
    }
    graphicsOffScreen.setColor(Color.white);
    graphicsOffScreen.clearRect( xClip, yClip, clipWidth, clipHeight );
```

continues

Listing 40.27 Continued

```
    graphicsOffScreen.fillRect(xClip, yClip, clipWidth, clipHeight);
    paint(g);
  }

  public void paint(Graphics g)
  {
    // Draw to the image buffer and applet window if
    //  all of the teddy bear images are loaded.
    if ( tracker.checkID( 0 ) )
    {
      // Draw current image to the image buffer.
      graphicsOffScreen.drawImage( imageCurrent, xPosition, yPosition, this);
      // Draw current image in the applet's window.
      g.drawImage( imageOffScreen, 0, 0, this);
      xOldPosition = xPosition;
      yOldPosition = yPosition;
    }
  }
}
```

Java Resources on the Web

The Java language is continually being upgraded. New packages and versions are being released at a rapid pace. Many of these new features will increase the power and ease of Java graphics and animation programming. Continue to increase your Java graphics and animation knowledge and programming skills by keeping up with the latest developments over the Web.

The most important Web site is the Java home page provided by JavaSoft—the Java development branch of the Sun Corporation. The Java home page is at the following URL:

http://www.javasoft.com

Keep informed about the latest Java developments and software release dates at this Web site. You can also download the latest Java development software from this site, including beta versions. This is where you should keep a lookout for Java 2.0 and important new graphics packages such as Java2D.

In addition to the Java site, you can find some excellent central Java news-gathering sources on the Web. These also include reviews, tutorials, and other useful information. The best of these include JavaWatch at

http://www.javawatch.com

Javology at

http://www.javology.com/javology/

and JavaWorld at

http://www.javaworld.com

CHAPTER 41

Creating and Implementing Live Chats

by Ryan Sutter

In this chapter

Introduction to Chat Systems

Possibly the most important thing about the Internet and its effect on the world today is the fact that it is an incredible social tool. People are talking, sharing, meeting, and learning from each other on the Internet. It is a place where people of all races, creeds, countries, and genders can meet and discuss ideas. An Internet feature central to this meeting of the minds is Internet chat.

Chatting over the Internet is one of the most enjoyable, and addictive, features of the Internet. It enables you to get to know people who share your interests, make new friends, and even pretend you are somebody you're not—just for fun, of course. Many webmasters would love to add chat capability to their web sites so that their visitors could all hang out and have a good time talking to each other. However, they are not sure where to begin. That's where this chapter comes in. This chapter discusses all the various types of Internet chat, including HTML, Java, and IRC and gives you all the tools you need to implement chat on your own web site. Most importantly, this chapter gives you the knowledge you need to create a Java chat solution because that is really the best way to chat.

Common Elements of Most Chat Systems

Almost all chat systems have several elements in common. First and foremost, they generally require that you choose a username or "handle." Many chat systems don't require anything more than for you to choose a handle and start chatting, but there are those that also require you to use a password to log in so that you won't be impersonated online.

Another feature common to most chat systems is the idea of a "chat room." A *chat room* is a virtual place where the conversation is usually supposed to be along the lines of a particular subject. You can usually tell what a chat room is about by the name of the room. Sometimes there is a brief description of the purpose of the room next to the name in case the name doesn't tell you enough.

A couple of other common features of chat are personal messages ("whispering") and private rooms. These are generally considered advanced features of chat systems and many of the more basic chat systems don't implement them. In essence, whispering is the ability to direct a private message to an individual in the group. Nobody else in the group can read your private message. Taking this idea a step further is the private room feature. This is the ability to create a room of your own that the general public cannot get into so that you can have discussions with only the people you really want to speak to. Most of the major chat systems do have features for creating private rooms and for whispering.

HTML Chat Systems

HTML chat systems are chat systems with a purely web-based interface. There are no Java applets, no plug-ins, and no helper applications. It is, therefore, the most universally accessible way to chat. Only a web browser is required.

As you may have guessed, it is not only the most universal, it is also the least feature-filled way to chat. In fact, the interface to some HTML chat systems is enough to drive some users crazy because of all the reloading and scrolling that they have to do. If you are not familiar with HTML chat systems, you might want to take a look at **http://chat.yahoo.com**. Because it is such a popular place, there is almost always chatting going on at Yahoo! Therefore it is not a bad place to check out HTML chatting.

One of the biggest problems with an HTML chat system is that there is no real facility for instant updating of the information on the screen, so the page must be reloaded every so often to update the messages that are displayed. This is the biggest headache with HTML chat and it is often difficult to follow the flow of the conversation as the messages are sometimes displayed faster than the refresh rate can handle.

An HTML chat system generally enables you to type something into a text box and click a submit button. Then two things happen. First, your message is posted to the discussion. Secondly, the discussion is refreshed so that you can see both your new post and the new posts of the other people who are chatting with you.

Before implementing your own chat system, it would be a good idea to spend some time in a chat area such as Yahoo! Chat to get used to how HTML chat systems work.

Java Chat Systems

HTML chatting is the most universally accessible, but not the most capable. What is a web author to do? Many sites have turned to Java chat. Java chat systems are almost as universally accessible as HTML chat systems and are far more capable and easy to use. A Java chat client can support smooth scrolling of messages and can even be used to create 3D chat environments.

You can find a good example of a Java chat system at **http://www.hotwired.com/talk/**. This is a popular chat system that well illustrates the advantages of Java chat, which are as follows:

- *Cross-platform*. As is true with HTML chat systems, Java chat systems can run on multiple operating systems and platforms.
- *Easy to use*. Java chat clients can have all the interface niceties that HTML chat cannot, such as smooth scrolling or 3D environments.
- *No software* to install. Java chat clients don't require any software to be installed on the client machine.
- *Can easily be embedded in a web page*. The chat client can be displayed onscreen along with other web content. This makes it more flexible as well as easy to use.

Besides the fact that the HotWired Talk Java client has a nice interface, there is another advantage to the way it is designed. The Java chat client at HotWired Talk loads up in a separate window so that you can browse the web while you chat. This would not work with an HTML chat client. Figure 41.1. shows the HotWired Talk Java interface.

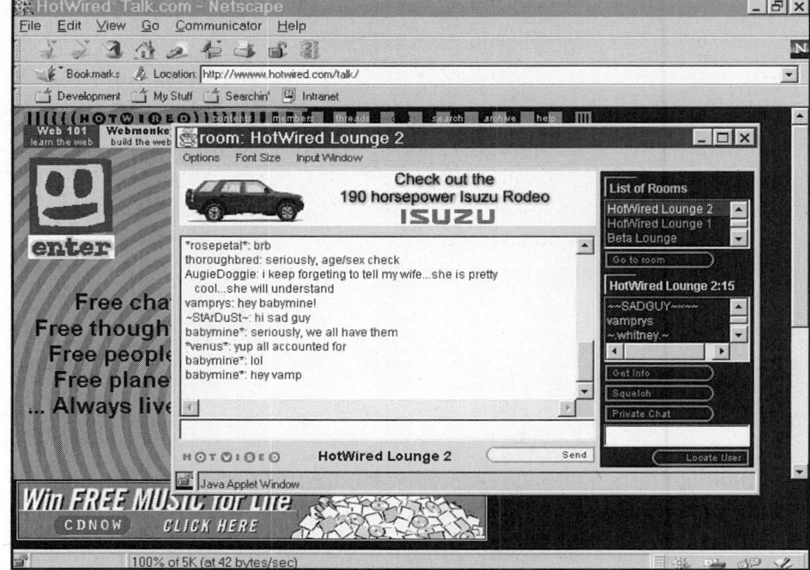

FIG. 41.1
The Java chat system at HotWired Talk provides an easy to use, flexible interface to chat.

Looking at the Talk.com chat client, you will notice that the interface has all the basic features you would expect in a chat program. There is a window that shows the conversation as it happens, a text box where you enter your comments, and a list of all the users in the room over on the right. There is also a list of chat rooms available and a private chat feature. The biggest difference between HTML and Java chat is ease of use.

Internet Relay Chat

Although not based on the web, IRC (Internet Relay Chat) is deserving of mention here. IRC is more than just a chat system, it is a worldwide chat network. IRC consists of various separate networks (or "nets") of IRC servers—machines that enable users to connect to IRC. The largest nets are EFnet (the original IRC net, often having more than 15,000 people chatting simultaneously), Undernet, IRCnet, DALnet, and NewNet.

IRC is its own world, and the people who use it are often fanatically devoted to it. This discussion does not even attempt to get into all the complexities of IRC here, for they go far beyond basic chat.

In IRC, you run a program to connect to a server on one of the IRC nets. The server relays information to and from other servers on the same net. Once connected to an IRC net, you will usually join one or more "channels" and converse with others there. On EFnet, there often are more than 5,000 channels. This should give you an idea how big and complex IRC is.

IRC channel names usually begin with a #, as in #irchelp. The same channels are shared among all IRC servers on the same net, so you do not have to be on the same IRC server as your friends. Each user is known on IRC by a "nick," or nickname. It is best to use a nick that is not too common. (I usually go as TheLodger, for example.)

IRC channels have moderators (called channel operators, or just "ops" for short) who can control the channel by choosing who may join, who must leave, and even who may speak. Channel ops have complete control over the channel, and their decisions are final.

If you would like to find out about including access to IRC from your web site via a Java applet, head over to the Gamelan site at **http://www.developer.com/pages/Gamelan.net.chat.irc.html**. If you would like to just get up to speed on IRC, try the IRC Help web site at **http://www.irchelp.org**.

Graphical, 3D, and Voice Chat

In case you had not noticed, there is much more to a discussion with a group of people than the words being spoken. There is body language, vocal inflection, and facial expression. None of these things can be suitably expressed via traditional Internet chat. Because chatting is intended to get people in touch with one another, it is only logical that it would move toward making the experience more like real life. That is where graphic chat, 3D chat, voice, and video chat come in to play. Although these chat systems are not as prevalent as traditional text-based chat, they are already very enjoyable.

Hello, Meet My Avatar: Graphic Chat Graphic chat systems are the next logical progression beyond plain old text chat. In a graphic-chat environment, you are represented by a graphic character onscreen. This character can look like you, or anything you want. This graphic representation of yourself is called an "avatar," and all the other people in the chat room have their own avatars. You can mingle, talk, and move about just as if you were in a real place. To illustrate this type of chat, take a look at a very popular graphic chat system called The Palace. If you would like to try out The Palace yourself, you must download the client software at **http://www.thepalace.com**.

You should recognize by now that there is a chat space, this time a graphic one, as well as a text box where you type the text you would like to say. There are several new features, however. First and foremost is the fact that every person in the chat room is represented by a picture. People have fun with their avatars and that is part of the appeal of a graphic chat system such as The Palace. Icons also run down the left hand side for common actions such as BRB ("be right back"), thought bubble, exclamation bubble, and also avatar editing tools.

3D Chat Software As fun as a graphic chat such as The Palace is, for those who just don't feel like that is close enough to reality, there are now several virtual reality chat environments out there. Like most of the graphic chat systems, the majority of the 3D chat environments require that you download special software to enter them. The idea is exactly like the two-dimensional graphic chat software, meaning that there are places to visit and people represented by avatars. The big difference is that this all happens in a navigable 3D environment. After you start wandering around through one of these virtual reality chat worlds, you may become hooked.

One of the largest and most successful virtual reality outposts on the web is a place called AlphaWorld. AlphaWorld is more than a simple chat place; it is actually an entire world, complete with buildings constructed by members of AlphaWorld, newspapers, and a huge community. If you join AlphaWorld, you can buy virtual real estate and build yourself a home—

complete with furniture, plants, and sound effects—that other people can come and visit. It is really quite an experience. Figure 41.2 shows a conversation going on with a fellow AlphaWorld visitor out in front of a building on a sidewalk by the street.

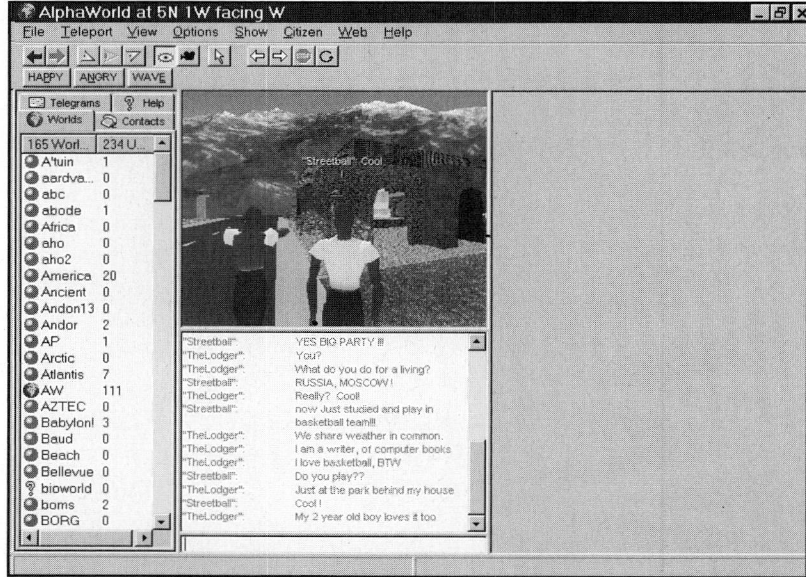

FIG. 41.2
A conversation between a Minnesotan and a Muscovite taking place on a virtual street in cyberspace. It is this kind of interaction that makes 3D chat worlds such as AlphaWorld so engaging.

As with all the previous forms of chat, there are a lot of places to go to meet people. The Worlds tab on the left side of the screen shows the huge list of other worlds besides AlphaWorld where you can hang out and explore. One big thing that changes when you move into a 3D chat world is the idea of proximity to conversations. You may not "hear" a conversation unless you are standing near it. As you walk away from people, fewer of their messages show up on your chat panel until they finally can't be seen at all.

If you would like to take a look at the 3D world of chat on the Internet, stop by **http://www.activeworlds.com/** and download the Active Worlds Browser.

Voice Chat Considering that the whole purpose of chat is to talk to other people, it would be illogical if this discussion didn't touch on a chat session built on the very oldest chat system in the world, the mouth—yes...real-time voice chat.

Voice chat is a technology whose time has not yet truly come. Voice transmission standards have yet to be decided and the volatility of a typical Internet transmissions transfer speed makes unbroken communication difficult. However, as bandwidth increases, real-time voice chat is sure to increase in popularity.

How Chat Systems Work

Creating your own 3D chat, graphic chat, or voice chat is beyond the scope of this book, but the following sections do explain how to implement an HTML-based text chat system as well as a Java text chat system.

Architecture of an HTML Chat System

Before getting into the actual code used in an HTML chat system, it is a good idea take a look at the general architecture of an HTML chat system. The most common way to implement an HTML chat program is to use a CGI program on the web server written in PERL or some other language that your server can understand. Due to the popularity of PERL, the code presented in the following section is written in PERL. Hopefully, you will learn the concepts well enough to be able to implement your own CGI-based chat server in the language of your choice.

A CGI-based chat server is like any other CGI script. It is installed in your web site's CGI-BIN directory and is run when people click a link to it. A CGI-based chat server differs from many other CGI scripts, however, in that it must maintain data between invocations. This is called "maintaining state."

NOTE HTTP is referred to as a "stateless protocol." This means that each request for data is just fulfilled without any regard for the identity of the person or machine making the request. When you request a web page and then request another from the same server, it does not know you just requested a page a minute ago. It just serves up pages. This makes HTTP very simple to implement, but also means that you have to deal with imposing state on HTTP when creating CGI programs that require it. This is one of the biggest challenges to writing a chat system.

Although other simple CGI programs may have all the information they need provided by the user or available on the disk, chat servers must be capable of storing on-going conversations and recall them the next time they are run, which might be just moments later. This persistence of data can be accomplished in any of several ways, but the simplest is to just spool the user input to a disk for later recall.

A real-world example should make this point a little clearer. Assume, for example, that a user enters a CGI-based chat area for the first time by clicking a link somewhere. No **FORM** arguments are passed to the CGI script that is run, so the script can safely assume that the user is just entering the conversation. The script, at this point, might welcome the user, show him some context of the on-going conversation, and ask him for his input by using HTML **FORMs**. The CGI program might also include a **HIDDEN** field in the **FORM**, reminding itself which was the last message this user has seen.

When the user **SUBMITs** his message, the script runs again, but this time it knows that the user is participating in the conversation because arguments are passed—his comments and some form of **ID** of the last message he saw. Now the script opens up the spool file on the disk, adds the user's message, and then backtracks and writes out all the messages that have appeared in the file since the user last saw it. At the bottom of this response, the script adds another space for the user to type some more, and includes another **HIDDEN** field, storing the **ID** of the last message this time. **HIDDEN** fields are one of the easiest ways to manage state in a CGI application. Each time the application gets the values of an HTML **FORM**, it can use the **ID** to look up information unique to that user.

This series can repeat forever, with any number of users running the same CGI script. Users can carry on a conversation because they continually see other users' comments whenever their screens are updated.

Here is some pseudo-code for a CGI-based chat system:

Set SPOOL_START to 0.

Get FORM arguments.

Did we get any FORM arguments? If yes:

Yes, add USER_MESSAGE argument to end of spool file. Set SPOOL_START to USER_LAST argument.

    Send HTTP header.

Go to SPOOL_START in spool file, send to user's message.

Send input form, include USER_MESSAGE input field and USER_LAST hidden field (set to the last message sent from spool file.)

    Exit.

If Not:

    Send HTTP header.

Return sign-up form HTML, including HIDDEN ID field with Identifier.

    Exit.

The second time the script is run, the user will have **FORM** arguments and will therefore be added to the conversation with his own **ID**. Obviously, you can make enhancements to this script—you should even make some. As it is, the spool file will grow forever. Although storing conversations for future reference is nice, to let a file grow unchecked can easily fill up a file system and cause the program to crash. Ideally, the script would check for when the spool file passes a certain size and shrink it down, chopping off the oldest comments.

As with any file that has the potential to be accessed by several people simultaneously, your chat server should take care when adding to the spool file. The traditional way to handle this situation is with a file lock; so when one instance of your chat program is adding to the file, any others must wait for it to finish before adding to it themselves. It is important to remember that a web server can run a CGI script several times simultaneously.

Architecture of a Client/Server Chat System

This section refers to client/server chat systems rather than Java chat systems because the architecture of a Java chat system is identical to the architecture of a chat system written in C++ or some other language. Client/server in this context means any chat system that has an executable program running on the client side and a chat server program running on the server side. Believe it or not, the basic concepts of a client/server chat system are the same whether the interface is text, 3D, or a graphic world full of avatars.

The major difference is the client part of the system. CGI chat servers are completely server-side programs. All the code that handles the chat is run on the web server, while the browser displays what it considers to be standard web pages. No processing happens on the client side.

With a client/server chat system, code is executed on both the client and server sides. When you click a link to a Java chat program, for example, the client side is downloaded to your web browser and run. It then connects to special code running on your web server.

The advantage this has over CGI is subtle but important. The chat client doesn't have to work within the limits of your browser's capabilities and therefore can be much more flexible in how it deals with the chat session. Remember the problem of saving state in a CGI-based system? Well, most client/server chat programs keep the connection with the server open at all times, and run a separate thread to constantly retrieve data, whether the user does anything or not. Although CGI scripts must process conversations in chunks—that is just the way browsers work—a chat client can do anything it wants to, including maintain a link with the server.

The downside of this flexibility is often more work for the programmer. Instead of a simple CGI program, both a client and a server must be written. Also, the issues involved with communication become more complicated because the programmer can no longer rely on the web server to handle it all for him. Despite all this, the design of a client/server solution is often more elegant.

NOTE Although it is possible to create a client/server chat system using a language such as Visual Basic or C++, the preferred choice for the Internet is currently Java for several reasons. The first is platform independence, the second is that the user visiting your site does not have to download separate chat software to get talking on your site.

Here is some pseudo-code for a multithreaded chat client:

```
Connect to server on pre-defined port.

Set up screen, with large output area and one line input area.

Thread 1

        Check for messages waiting from server.

        If yes, read them and print them in output area.
```

```
Loop on Thread 1

Thread 2

        Is user message ready?

        Yes, send it to the server.

Loop on Thread 2
```

The chat client just checks for messages in a loop and sends messages whenever there are any. The server is a little bit more complicated, but not by much. Here is some pseudo-code for a chat server:

```
Start listening to pre-defined port.

Do this forever:

        Any connection?

                Yes, announce that a user has logged on.

        Any disconnections?

                Yes, announce that a user has logged off.

        Any messages?

                Yes, read and multi-cast them to all clients.

Loop on Forever
```

NOTE Many of the commercially available client/server chat systems use a Java client and a server written in C. This is because C programs typically run faster than Java programs. The server needs speed more than portability.

Notice that no disk storage is needed for this server like it is for CGI. That's because messages are constantly being broadcast; they do not need to be saved for the next time a user asks for an update—he's already got them all! It is no wonder that client/server chat systems that use a Java client have become so popular.

Additional Chat Client Features

Now that you know the basics of how a simple CGI or client/server chat system works, you might be interested in implementing some more advanced features should you choose to write your own chat system. It is these advanced features that separate an average chat system from an advanced one.

HTML Enhancements On a CGI-based chat system, the text output is rendered by an HTML browser. So why not allow HTML in the comments? Many chat servers allow this, but there are things to keep in mind before you do it. First, allowing your users to enter HTML with their comments, giving them the same flexibility you have when designing web pages can dramatically improve the appearance of your chat space. If a user types <H1>Yes!</H1> rather than just Yes!, the <H1> tag will be interpreted as HTML when it arrives in the other chatters' browsers, causing the response to appear much more dramatically. This is pretty cool.

The same way, images can be inserted into a chat session, just by including the appropriate HTML: <IMG SRC="http://www.myserver.com/user/mypic.gif">, for example.

Unfortunately, allowing HTML in a message also has a down side. The disadvantage of allowing HTML is that you give up control of a large part of your chat space to your users. What happens, for instance, if a malevolent user starts including HTML designed to break your chat server? Just entering <FORM><SELECT> makes any following comments invisible. Server-side includes are even more dangerous. A smart hacker could possibly wreak major havoc on your system. Take some time designing your CGI program to ignore dangerous HTML. See Chapter 31, "Programming CGI Scripts," for more information.

Predefined Graphics If you want to allow users to include graphics and other interesting visual elements to spice up your chat space, but don't want them loading up huge graphics and hogging up all the other users' bandwidth, predefined graphics can be a good solution. Basically, you want to provide several predefined graphics for users to select from. On servers that use this technique, each message entered by a chatter is accompanied by an icon or small pictures.

By having predefined images for your users to add to their comments, you cannot only perk up how your page looks, but you also add another avenue of communication. Comments can be prefaced with a smiley icon, for instance, indicating that the comment is meant as a light-hearted remark.

By using predefined images, you know that visitors with slower modems won't be deluged with graphics, but that your page will be interesting to look at. Additionally, these images can actually help the conversation. Text can often be very inexpressive, and what appears in a chat session can easily be misunderstood because it was not accompanied by a facial expression. By having icons that evoke different emotions, you can allow your users some of the freedom of expression they enjoy in real face-to-face conversations.

Chat Whispering Whispering is another nice feature that you can add to chat pages. Whispering is where a comment is directly sent to a single person rather than everybody sharing the chat space.

Client-Side Pulls If you are using a transaction-based CGI chat server, you might want to have it automatically include client-side pull information on each page it sends. On browsers that understand client-side pull, this causes an URL to be automatically updated after a time you specify. The HTML code to cause a page to refresh itself is as follows:

```
<HTML>
     <HEAD>
          <META HTTP-EQUIV=REFRESH CONTENT="X;http://www.myserver.com/chat/url>
     </HEAD>
</HTML>
```

Of course, client-side pull has disadvantages. It takes control of the page out of the user's hands, and can easily time-out and request an update while the user is entering a comment. This can be very annoying. One way around this irritation is to allow users to set their own refresh rates, or turn off client-side pull.

Persistent Aliases Another possible feature is persistent aliases, where the user claims a chat name and is allowed to keep it for as long as he wants. Under the basic chat system, a user just enters a name to use for each message he sends. The server has no idea whether the RedHotPantMan who sent a message a minute ago is the same RedHotPantMan who has been chatting for the last half-hour.

By installing a password system, where each user picks an alias and a password to go along with it, the server can make sure that this RedHotPantMan is who he claims to be. Persistent aliases can prevent a lot of trouble-making. Often, annoying users log in as someone they don't like and start being obnoxious. Other chatters, fooled by the trickery, assume that the real user has suddenly become an offensive jerk (sometimes leading to horrible flame wars!).

Multiple Chat Rooms The idea is simple. By allowing users to jump between rooms, you can have several conversations happen simultaneously, without having them overlap and get confusing.

Moderator Options Because chat on the web is usually open to the public at large, you might occasionally find an obnoxious or obscene chatter has planted himself on your sever. In the worst possible scenario, this individual will end up driving away the sort of people you want to have as regulars and attracting the sort you don't. More than a few chat servers have been overtaken by the electronic equivalent of unruly mobs and have end up either being shut down or just abandoned by their owners.

The way to avoid such trouble is to allow for certain trusted users to act as moderators, with the ability to cut off other chatters if they get too far out of line. Although neither you nor your moderators can monitor your chat server 24 hours a day, having the option to ban people who don't follow the rules can lead to a much more orderly environment.

Alternately, if you are interested in maintaining some sort of civility on your chat page all the time, you can add message filters that scan user input for obscene or forbidden words. Although there are foibles involved in using such filters—they can accidentally block allowable phrases and can be fooled in to okaying prohibited ones—many sites have implemented them.

Using Bots Finally, you might consider adding bots to your chat server. These programs, when run in conjunction with chat software, can provide help to users and webmasters alike, offering assistance and taking care of menial chores.

What's a bot? Early Internet Relay Chat administrators used simple scripts to deliver preconstructed messages to users ("Thank you for visiting The Nuclear Gopher Cheese Factory Chat Channel"). Over time, these scripts evolved into programs that could make decisions on their own and carry on limited conversations with users. Today, they have matured even further into self-sustaining automatic processes called bots (for robots).

Adding HTML Chat to Your Site

Several commercially available web chat systems are out there. If you want to buy one, feel free. There is a nice little free one you can get, however, called EveryChat. It is available at **http://www.cs.hope.edu/~hahnfld/everychat/** and can run on any web server that has PERL installed. It is configurable and extensible.

Installation of EveryChat is a breeze; just follow these steps:

1. Download the software from **http://www.cs.hope.edu/~hahnfld/everychat/everychat.zip**.
2. Unzip the file using pkunzip, winzip, or another zip compression program for your platform.
3. Place all HTML files into a single directory accessible by the web (probably your main HTML document directory).
4. Make a new EMPTY web-accessible subdirectory somewhere on your server and place the messages.html file there. If you are on a UNIX system, use "chmod" to make the directory permissions writable by everybody.
5. Place everycht.cgi file in your cgi-bin directory or a shell-cgi directory, depending on your server setup. You may have to rename it everycht.pl if you are on a server that only recognizes scripts as PERL with a PL extension.
6. Open the everycht.cgi script with a text editor. The first line of the script must point to the PERL program on your server. The configuration lines must be modified for your system.
7. Open the chatframes.html document with a text editor. Be sure all paths are correct.
8. Open the chatform.html file with a text editor. Make sure the form points to your everycht.cgi script.
9. Change the messages.html file permissions to writable by everybody. Change the everycht.cgi permissions to executable by everybody.

Test it by opening chatframes.html (for frames) or chatform.html (for non-frames). If you did it all correctly, your chat site should be up and running. EveryChat has several add-ons available as well as instructions on how to install it for multiple chat rooms. If you are interested in checking out some more chat systems, you can find a huge list of them at Yahoo! Head over to **http://www.yahoo.com/Computers_and_Internet/Internet/World_Wide_Web/Chat/Software/**. Another server called The Chat Server, a commercial product, is available from **http://chat.magmacom.com/**.

Adding Java Chat to Your Site

The sheer number of Java chat clients available is truly amazing. A great repository for any and all things Java is called Gamelan, located at **http://www.gamelan.com**. Gamelan has 23 Java chat programs that use avatars, 102 general chat and multi-user programs, 18 Java IRC clients, and 19 more Java chat programs that include source code only. As you can see, there are quite a few options for implementing Java chat on your site. Take a look at two different ways you can add a Java chat system to your site.

Adding a Java Client/Server Chat System

One of the better free chat client/server systems out there is called Jive. Jive is available from **http://ftp.nerosworld.com/~markl/ping/java/jive.html** and just has to be downloaded and added to your web server. The server program needs to be run as its own standalone process and configured to listen to a port of your choosing. Once done, you need to embed the client into a web page as follows:

```
<applet codebase=. code=client.Jive>
<param name="port" value="10901">
</applet>
```

That is all there is to it. If Jive doesn't suit your needs, you have over 100 more to choose from on the Gamelan Chat page alone.

Adding a Java Client Without a Server

If you cannot set up your own server, the next best thing is to provide an embedded link to somebody else's server. Fortunately, this is very easy to do. If you wanted to add a nifty avatar-based graphic chat to your page without using a chat server, for example, you might try He Talk, located at **http://hpleo.leopoldina.uni-leipzig.de/chat/**. Adding He Talk to your site is as simple as including the following HTML in your page:

```
<!-- BEGIN HETALK -->
<APPLET CODEBASE="http://hpleo.leopoldina.uni-leipzig.de/chat/applet"
CODE="HeTalk.class" WIDTH="140"
HEIGHT="100">
<PARAM NAME="LANGUAGE" VALUE="english">
</APPLET>
<!-- END HETALK -->
```

The He Talk interface is shown in Figure 41.3.

Writing Your Own Java Chat Client and Server

Although the rest of this chapter has offered several ways to add chat to your site without having to code it yourself, if you want to have the ultimate in flexibility and control you really might want to write your own Java chat system. This last section is going to show you exactly how by creating the basic classes of a simple Java chat client and a simple Java chat server.

The code that is going to be presented in this chapter is not industrial strength or full featured. It is a basic Java chat client and a basic server that are meant to get you started on creating your own custom chat solution. It just prompts for a username to start chatting with and lets you get going. For this discussion, it is called littleChat and it consists of a littleChatClient, littleChatServer, and a class called handler that does most of the work on the server side.

FIG. 41.3
He Talk is just one of many chat applets that you can add to your page without a server.

The littleChatClient Start with the user interface for the chat client. The client in this case is going to be a Java applet. Although you could create the client to be a standalone application, for the majority of applications an applet is going to be needed. The interface to the chat client will consist of a text area where the conversation will take place and a text box where a user enters his comments. An addition you might want to add would be a list of users currently in the room.

Take a look at the source code for the littleChatClient.java, starting with Listing 41.1.

Listing 41.1 The beginning of littleChatClient.java declares variable and calls the *Thread* object *listener*.

```
import java.awt.*;
import java.applet.*;
import java.net.*;
import java.io.*;

public class littleChatClient extends Applet implements Runnable
{
      //The Stream objects (input and output) are where all of the
      //client/server communication takes place
      protected DataInputStream input;
      protected DataOutputStream output;
      //We need to communicate over Socket
      protected Socket sock;

      //This applet requires a host name and port number to be passed to it
      //and these variables are to store those values
      protected String host;
```

continued

Listing 41.1 Continued

```
        protected int port;

        //The user name of the chatter goes here
        protected String userName;

        //This is a flag indicating whether this is the first message or not.
        //Starts off as true and is used in assigning the user name.
        protected boolean firstTime;

        //Declaring the user interface components
        java.awt.TextArea txtChatPane;
        java.awt.TextField txtInput;
        //The actual work happens in the listener thread
protected Thread listener;
```

The beginning of the applet just declares some variables. For handling the actual communication with the server, there is a Socket, a DataInputStream, and a DataOutputStream. There are also some variables to hold the port number, host name, the user's screen name, and a firstTime flag used in setting the username. Then, you have the user interface elements, a TextArea for the messages, and a TextField to handle input. Finally, there is a `Thread` object called `Listener` which will be where the code actually executes.

Next, you create the chat environment as shown in Listing 41.2.

Listing 41.2 Create the user interface complete with simple instructions.

```
        public void init()
        {
                //Create user interface for applet
                setLayout(null);
                setSize(320,196);
                txtChatPane = new java.awt.TextArea();

                //Using the chat pane to show instructions to get started.
                txtChatPane.setText("To start enter a user name in the \nbox below
and hit enter.");

                txtChatPane.setBounds(2,1,304,154);
                add(txtChatPane);
                txtInput = new java.awt.TextField();
                txtInput.setBounds(3,159,302,22);
                add(txtInput);
                txtInput.requestFocus ();

                //Get applet parameters to connect to host.
                this.host = this.getParameter("host");
                this.port = Integer.parseInt(this.getParameter("port"));

                //Initialize some variables
                firstTime = true;
```

```
            userName = "New User";
            txtInput.setText(userName);

            //Start the applet thread
            listener = new Thread (this);

}
```

The `init()` method gets things going by creating a TextArea and a TextField for input and output. Notice that the txtChatPane text is being set to "To start enter a user name in the box below and hit enter." The message pane is therefore being used to give instructions as well as chat. The purpose of this is so that the first message entered into the applet is actually a userName selection, not a real message. This is also the purpose of the firstTime variable, to indicate to the applet that the first message is actually a userName. Notice also that there is no layout manager being used. If you decide to create a more advanced user interface, it would be a good idea to use a layout manager.

After creating the user interface, the applet gets the host and port parameters to figure out what server it should connect to. The port should be whatever port the server is running on, and the host needs to be the name of the host the applet was launched from. Because of security restrictions, you are not allowed to connect to a host other than the one the applet was loaded from. After setting the initial values of all the controls and variables, the applet sets `Listener` to a new `Thread` object.

Now you need to actually connect to the host (see Listing 41.3).

Listing 41.3 Attempt to connect to a host and start the listener *Thread*.

```
      public void start(){
            try {
                  Socket sock = new Socket(host, port);
                  this.input = new DataInputStream (new BufferedInputStream
(sock.getInputStream()));
                  this.output = new DataOutputStream (new BufferedOutputStream
(sock.getOutputStream()));
                  listener.start ();
            } catch (IOException ex) {
            }
}
```


The `start()` method of the applet is automatically called right after the `init()` method, and it only does two things. First, it attempts to create a connection to the host and port specified in the applet parameters. Second, it starts the `Listener` thread. Notice that there is code to catch `IOException` objects but that it is not doing anything with them. In this case, if the applet cannot connect it just won't work. If you would like to do something else, add some code to the `catch()` clause. Now take a look at the main functional area of the applet, the `run()` method (see Listing 41.4).

Listing 41.4 The littleChatClient *run()* method.

```
    public void run() {
          try {
                while (true) {
                      String line = input.readUTF ();
                      txtChatPane.appendText (line + "\n");
                }
          } catch (IOException ex) {
          } finally {
                listener = null;
                txtInput.hide ();
                validate ();
                try {
                      output.close ();
                } catch (IOException ex) {
                }
          }
}
```

That's all there is to it. Breaking down the method, you see that there is a try/catch/finally construct that does all the work. First it goes into a perpetual loop that does nothing but check for text from the input stream and append it to the text in the chat message area. Again, you are catching `IOException` objects and doing nothing with them. Last but not least, a finally clause makes sure that whatever happens, the thread cleans up after itself. There are only two missing pieces now to your chat applet. Getting the text from the user and stopping the thing. The first is done in the `handleEvent(Event e)` method as shown in Listing 41.5.

Listing 41.5 The *handleEvent(Event e)* method.

```
    public boolean handleEvent (Event e) {
          if ((e.target == txtInput) && (e.id == Event.ACTION_EVENT)) {
          if (firstTime == false){
                try {
                      output.writeUTF (userName + ": " + (String) e.arg);
                      output.flush ();
                } catch (IOException ex) {
                      listener.stop ();
                }
          }
          else {
                userName = txtInput.getText();
                firstTime = false;
                txtChatPane.setText("");
          }
          txtInput.setText ("");
          return true;
          }
          return super.handleEvent (e);
}
```

The `handleEvent` method just checks to see whether anything has happened in the txtInput and if it has, it prepends the userName text to the message and sends it to the server, flushes the output buffer, and sets the txtInput.Text to "". That is unless this is the first time through, in which case it assigns the contents of the txtInput box to the userName variable, sets firstTime to false, and then clears both the txtInput box and the message from txtChatPane. Take a look at the final method, `stop()`, shown in Listing 41.6.

Listing 41.6 The *stop()* method.

```
        public void stop() {
              if (listener != null)
                    listener.stop ();
                    listener = null;
}
```

Finally, when the applet stops the `Listener` thread is set to `null`. All processing stops.

Obviously there are several ways that this client could be improved. You might want to remove text from the chat area now and then, for example, so it doesn't get too full. You may also wish to add a list of current users to the applet and do some verification to make sure that two users cannot go by the same name. It might also be nice to run this applet in a separate frame so that a user could surf the web while he chatted. This applet demonstrates the basic architecture of a chat client, however, and should serve as a decent starting base for your own chat implementations.

The littleChatServer The server for your littleChat system is actually made up of two separate classes: the littleChatServer and the handler. The littleChatServer is the server itself but actually does very little work. Most of the actual work is done by the handler class. Take a look at the littleChatServer first (see Listing 41.7).

Listing 41.7 littleChatServer.

```
import java.lang.*;
import java.net.*;
import java.io.*;
import handler;

public class littleChatServer
{

    public littleChatServer (int port) throws IOException {
        ServerSocket server = new ServerSocket (port);
        while (true) {
            Socket client = server.accept ();
            System.out.println ("Accepted from " + client.getInetAddress ());
            handler h = new handler (client);
            h.start ();
        }
    }
```

Part VII Ch 41

continued

Listing 41.7 Continued

```
    public static void main (String[] args) throws IOException {
        if (args.length != 1){
            throw new RuntimeException("Syntax: littleChatServer port");
        }

        new littleChatServer (Integer.parseInt(args[0]));
    }
}
```

The littleChatServer consists of only two methods: a constructor and a `main ()` method. The main method just checks to see whether a port number has been specified on the command line. If so, it instantiates a `littleChatServer` object with that port number. If not, it quits. The constructor just opens a ServerSocket on the port specified and then goes into a perpetual loop waiting for client connect requests. When it receives a connect request, it spawns a `handler` object for the request and goes on looping. That is the entire chat server. As mentioned previously, the `handler` object does the majority of the work on the server side. Listing 41.8 shows the handler object code.

Listing 41.8 The *handler* object.

```
import java.lang.*;
import java.util.*;
import java.net.*;
import java.io.*;

public class handler extends java.lang.Thread
{
    protected static Vector handlers = new Vector();

    protected Socket sock;
    protected DataInputStream input;
    protected DataOutputStream output;


    public handler (Socket s) throws IOException {
        /*
        This is the constructor for the handler class.
        It simply is passed a Socket and instantiates an input and output stream
        for the Socket.
        */
        this.sock = s;
        input = new DataInputStream (new BufferedInputStream
➥(sock.getInputStream ()));
        output = new DataOutputStream (new BufferedOutputStream
➥(sock.getOutputStream ()));
    }
```

The `handler` class consists of three methods: a constructor, a `run` method, and a `broadcast` method. The constructor is very simple; it creates a socket connection to the client that was passed as an argument and gets an input and output stream from that connection. In addition to the Socket, DataInputStream, and DataOutputStream declared at the beginning of this class, notice that there is a Vector of `handler` objects. This Vector is traversed to broadcast a message to all connected clients. Take a look at the `run` method, which does the real work (see Listing 41.9).

Listing 41.9 The littleChatServer *run ()* method.

```
public void run () {
    try {
        handlers.addElement (this);
        while (true){
            String message = input.readUTF();
            broadcast(message);
        }
    } catch (IOException e) {
    } finally {
        handlers.removeElement(this);
        try {
            sock.close();
        } catch (IOException e) {
        }
    }
}
```

Here you have the familiar try/catch/finally construct. The first thing happening is the addition of this particular `handler` object to the handler's Vector. After that is done, a perpetual loop is started that checks for input and broadcasts it when received. The catch clause is not currently doing anything, but the finally clause cleans up after the thread when things are stopped by removing the handler from the Vector and closing the socket. The final method in the `handler` class is `broadcast` (see Listing 41.10).

Listing 41.10 The broadcast method.

```
/*
The broadcast method broadcasts a message to all clients.
*/
public static void broadcast (String m){
    synchronized (handlers) {
        Enumeration e = handlers.elements();
        while (e.hasMoreElements()){
            handler h = (handler) e.nextElement();
            try {
                synchronized (h.output){
                    h.output.writeUTF(m);
```

continued

Listing 41.10 Continued

```
                    }
                    h.output.flush();
                } catch (IOException ex) {
                    h.stop();
                }
            }
        }
    }
}
```

`Broadcast` receives a message as an argument and is responsible for getting the message to all the connected clients. Notice that the body of the broadcast message is synchronized. This is necessary because of the fact that multiple handler threads are running and each must take its turn broadcasting. By synchronizing the handler's Vector, the method gets sole broadcasting rights until it is done. All broadcast does is traverse the handler's Vector and write to the output for each handler. It then flushes the output buffer for each handler and if it catches an IOException from a handler it stops that handler.

Although this littleChat is very basic, it can serve as a basis for a much more complex chatting system.

CHAPTER 42

Network Programming

In this chapter

Java Simplifies Network Programming

Years ago programming network applications in any language was a real drag. Sometimes it involved writing specialized system software that talked directly to network drivers, or even the network cards themselves. Programming IPX/SPX applications in DOS or Windows used to require software interrupt handlers to be created. With Java, however, creating network applications is a snap!

The thing that makes network programming in Java better is the encapsulation. Java hides the difficult low-level network programming from you. This enables you to concentrate on your application, not on the communications. In days of yore, for example, many steps were required to talk over a network. You had to:

- Initialize the network card
- Set up buffers for inbound and outbound packets
- Create callback routines for the networking driver to notify you of data
- Write low-level (sometimes assembler!) code to talk with the network driver

If it sounds like a lot of work, it was! On the other hand, programming the network in Java is very slick. Just instantiate a `Socket` class and you are almost on your way. But more on that later....

This chapter discusses the network classes in Java (in the java.net package). These make writing programs for communication over the Internet, intranets, or even local area networks easier than in any other language.

The Java Socket Classes

Java has the same UNIX roots as the Internet. It is designed from the ground up as a networking language. A quick overview will introduce you to how Java makes network programming easier by encapsulating connection functionality in *socket classes*:

- `Socket` is the basic object in Internet communication, which supports the TCP/IP protocol. TCP/IP is a reliable stream network connection. The `Socket` class provides methods for stream I/O, which make reading from and writing to `Socket` easy.
- `ServerSocket` is an object used for Internet server programs for listening to client requests. `ServerSocket` does not actually perform the service; instead, it creates a `Socket` object on behalf of the client. The communication is performed through that object.
- `DatagramSocket` is an object that uses the *User Datagram Protocol* (*UDP*). Datagram sockets are potentially unreliable because no connection is involved. You can send them out willy-nilly; no server must be listening. In addition, the networking software will not guarantee the delivery of UDP packages. However, communication using datagram sockets is faster because no connection is made between the sender and receiver.

- `SocketImpl` is an abstract class that enables you to implement your own flavor of data communication. As with all abstract classes, you subclass `SocketImpl` and implement its methods, as opposed to instantiating `SocketImpl` itself.

How the Internet Uses Sockets

You can think of any Internet server as a set of socket classes that provides additional capabilities—generally called *services.* Examples of services are electronic mail, *Telnet* for remote login, and *File Transfer Protocol* (*FTP*) for transferring files around the network. If the server to which you are attached provides web access, a web service is available as well.

Ports and Services

Each service is associated with a *port.* A port is a numeric address through which service requests (such as asking for a web page) are processed. On a UNIX system, the particular services provided are in the /ETC/SERVICES file. Here are a few lines from a typical /ETC/SERVICES file:

daytime	13/udp	
ftp	21/tcp	
telnet	23/tcp	telnet
smtp	25/tcp	mail
www	80/tcp	

The first column displays the system name of the service (daytime). The second column displays the port number and the protocol, separated by a slash (13/udp). The third column displays an alias to the service, if any. For example, smtp (the standard Simple Mail Transfer Protocol), also known as *mail,* is the implementation of email service.

Communication of web-related information takes place at port 80 using the TCP protocol. To emulate this in Java, you use the `Socket` class. `Daytime`, the service to get the system date and time, occurs at port 13 using the UDP protocol. A `daytime` server to emulate this in Java would use the `DatagramSocket` object.

The *URL* Class Revisited

The `URL` class contains constructors and methods for managing an URL—an object or service on the Internet. The TCP protocol requires two pieces of information: the IP address and the port number. So how is it possible that when you type

http://www.yahoo.com

you get Yahoo!'s home page?

First, Yahoo! has registered its name, allowing **yahoo.com** to be assigned an IP address (say 205.216.146.71). This is resolved by using your system's domain name resolution service.

Now what about the port number? If not specified, the server's port in /ETC/SERVICES is used.

NOTE The /ETC/SERVICES is the filename on UNIX servers. On other platforms, the filename will probably be different. On a Windows 95 system the file is called *Services* and lives in the Windows 95 directory.

The `URL` class allows for these variations in specification. There are four constructors, as follows:

```
public URL(String spec) throws MalformedURLException;
public URL(String protocol, String host, int port, String file) throws
MalformedURLException;
public URL(String protocol, String host, String file) throws
MalformedURLException;
public URL(URL context, String spec) throws MalformedURLException;
```

You can thus specify each piece of the URL, as in `URL("http","www.yahoo.com",80,"index.html")`, or allow the defaults to take over, as in `URL("http://www.yahoo.com")`, lettindg Yahoo! figure out all the pieces.

Mapping Java Sockets to Internet Sockets

Sockets are based on a client/server model. One program (the server) provides the service at a particular IP address and port. The server listens for service requests, such as requests for web pages, and fills the order. Any program that wants to be serviced (a client, such as a web browser) needs to know the IP address and port to communicate with the server.

An advantage of the socket model over other forms of data communication is that the server doesn't care where the client requests come from. As long as the client is sending requests according to the TCP/IP protocol, the requests will reach the server—provided the server is up and the Internet isn't too busy. What the particular server program does with the request is another matter.

This also means that the client can be any type of computer. No longer are you restricted to UNIX, Macintosh, DOS, or Windows platforms. Any computer that supports TCP/IP can talk to any other computer that supports it through this socket model. This is a potentially revolutionary development in computing. Instead of maintaining armies of programmers to *port* a system from one platform to another, you write it one time—in Java. Any computer with a Java Virtual Machine can run it.

Java socket classes fit nicely into this picture. You implement a server by creating subclasses of `Thread`, and overriding the `run()` method. The Java Virtual Machine can then perform the thread management without the program having to worry. Thus, with a few lines of code, you can write a server that can handle as many data communications sessions as you want. And data transmission is just a matter of calling the `Socket` methods.

Creating a Telnet Server

The procedure for creating a server is to create a `ServerSocket` object, which listens on a particular port for client requests. When it recognizes a valid request, it creates a `Socket` object through which the data conversation can take place. This socket is like a pipe through which data can pass back and forth. In fact, it is very similar to a UNIX pipe. The stream classes are used to route data back and forth efficiently.

NOTE The Telnet server and client presented here are just skeleton programs. They are by no means "real" Telnet server and clients. These programs are designed to exemplify Java network programming.

Listing 42.1 is a prototype for a line-oriented Telnet server, enabling remote logins to a network on the Internet. The server prompts the client for ID and password and, if the user is authorized, prints a welcome message. For this network, the Telnet service is on port 23.

Listing 42.1 TelnetServer.java A prototype Telnet server.

```
//***************************************************************************
//* Imports                                                                 *
//***************************************************************************

import         java.net.*;
import         java.io.*;

//***************************************************************************
//* TelnetServer                                                            *
//***************************************************************************

public class
TelnetServer
extends Thread
{

//***************************************************************************
//* Constants                                                               *
//***************************************************************************

    public static final int          TELNET_PORT = 23;

//***************************************************************************
//* Variables                                                               *
//***************************************************************************

    protected    ServerSocket        listener;

//***************************************************************************
//* main                                                                    *
//***************************************************************************

    public static void
```

continues

Listing 42.1 Continued

```
    main( String args[] )
    {
        new TelnetServer();
    }

//***********************************************************************
//* fail                                                                *
//***********************************************************************

    public static void
    fail( Exception e, String msg )
    {
        System.err.println( msg + "." + e );
        System.exit( 1 );
    }

//***********************************************************************
//* Constructor                                                         *
//***********************************************************************

    public
    TelnetServer()
    {
        //    Try and create the socket...
        try
        {
            listener = new ServerSocket( TELNET_PORT, 5 );
        }
        catch ( IOException e )
        {
            fail( e, "Could not start Telnet server" );
        }

        //    Show something to the user...
        System.out.println( "Telnet server started" );

        //    Start up the thread...
        start();
    }

//***********************************************************************
//* run                                                                 *
//***********************************************************************

    public void
    run()
    {
        try
        {
            while ( true )
            {
                Socket client = listener.accept();
                System.out.println( "Accepted client..." );
                TelnetThread c = new TelnetThread( client );
```

```
            }
        }
        catch ( IOException e )
        {
            fail( e, "Unable to accept incoming client connection" );
        }
    }
}

//****************************************************************************
//* TelnetThread                                                             *
//****************************************************************************

class
TelnetThread
extends Thread
{

//****************************************************************************
//* Variables                                                                *
//****************************************************************************

    protected    Socket                 sClient;
    protected    BufferedReader         disIn;
    protected    PrintWriter             psOut;

//****************************************************************************
//* Constructor                                                              *
//****************************************************************************

    public
    TelnetThread( Socket client )
    {
        try
        {
            //    Save a copy of our client socket...
            sClient = client;

            //    Don't cross the streams!
            disIn = new BufferedReader(
                new InputStreamReader( client.getInputStream() ) );

            psOut = new PrintWriter( client.getOutputStream(), true );

            //    Start up the client...
            start();
        }
        catch ( IOException e )
        {
            try
            {
                client.close();
            }
            catch ( IOException ioe )
            {
```

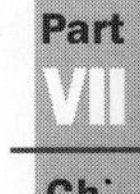

continues

Listing 42.1 Continued

```
                System.err.println( "Error creating streams: " + ioe );
            }
        }
    }

//***************************************************************************
//* run                                                                     *
//***************************************************************************

    public void
    run()
    {
        String          user, password;
        int              len;

        System.out.println( "Running client..." );

        try
        {
            while ( true )
            {
                //    Get the user name...
                psOut.println( "Login: " );
                user = disIn.readLine();

                psOut.println( "\r" );

                if ( user == null )
                    break;

                //    Get the password...
                psOut.println( "Password: " );
                password = disIn.readLine();
                psOut.println( "\r" );

                if ( password == null )
                    break;

                /*
                *
                * You'll want to do some user/password checks here.
                * If all is cool, let the user know:
                */

                psOut.print( "\n\rWelcome! You're now connected." +
                    " Please enter a command: " );

                /*
                * Here you can do all your functionality. When
                * you are done, break out of this loop
                */
            }
        }
        catch ( IOException e )
```

```
        {
            // Handle any errors
        }

        finally
        {
            try
            {
                sClient.close();
            }
            catch ( IOException ioe )
            {
                System.err.println( "Error closing client socket: " + ioe );
            }
        }
    }
}
```

Okay, now take a close look at the server source code.

Classes Used by the Server Program

From `java.net`, you use the `ServerSocket` class (to create a socket where the server listens for remote login requests) and the `Socket` class (to create the socket through which the Telnet conversation occurs).

From `java.io`, you use the `IOException` class (to handle errors). The `BufferedReader` class handles traffic from the client to the server (that is, input to the server). The `PrintWriter` class handles traffic from the server to the client ("printing" to the client).

Creating the Telnet Server Class

Note that the Telnet server is a subclass of `Thread`. A `ServerSocket` object (`server_listening_object`) is declared in the variable declaration section. It will later do the work of listening for client Telnet requests.

The error-handling routine, called `fail()`, takes two arguments: an `Exception` object and a `String` object. It prints an error message if there is any problem starting the server, and then exits.

The constructor creates and starts a `ServerSocket` thread. An error message is produced if there is a problem. Note the statement that actually constructs the server socket:

```
listener = new ServerSocket( TELNET_PORT, 5 );
```

This form of the `ServerSocket` constructor takes two integer arguments. The first argument, the port number, is a constant that you have defined. It is set to 23 because that is the well-known Telnet port.

The second argument is a count of the number of concurrent Telnet services that you want to allow. For purposes of this example, allow five Telnet sessions. The actual setting is a server configuration issue. If you allow more sessions, you also allocate more server memory. The potential for overloading the server exists because each session requires additional memory.

The *run()* Method: Listening for Client Requests

The server's `run()` method is where the work is done. In this case, the server goes into an infinite loop and "listens" for client requests. When the server "hears" the client, the server calls the `ServerSocket`'s `accept()` method, which accepts the connection. Then the server creates a `TelnetClient` thread, passing it a `Socket` object where the Telnet conversation actually occurs.

The *main()* Method: Starting the Server

The `main()` method is very simple. It just creates an instance of your server class, `TelnetServer`. This method is required to run non-applet programs.

The Telnet Thread: The Work Gets Done

The `TelnetThread` class is where the conversation actually takes place. `TelnetThread` creates a `BufferedReader` object (`disIn`), which retrieves input from the client by using the `getInputStream()` method, and a `PrintWriter` object (`psOut`), which enables the server to write output to the client by using the `getOutputStream()` method. Thus a two-way conversation can occur. If this happens successfully, the Telnet session starts.

After the server connects, it issues the `Login:` prompt by printing it to the client by using the `println()` method of the `psOut` object. Next, the server uses the `readLine()` method to store the login ID in the string variable, `user`. The server now needs the password, so it uses the `println()` method again to issue the `Password:` prompt. Then the server issues another `readLine()`, storing the user's entry in another string variable, `password`.

From this point, it is up to the program to verify the login ID and password. You could implement a password table, which contains the user names and their passwords. If the password is stored in encrypted format, this would be the place to decrypt it.

When encrypting passwords for user entries, never store the unencrypted version of the password. You really don't have to. This is because when a user enters his or her password, you just encrypt the entry and compare it to the stored encrypted version.

If the user is authorized, the session can begin using the stream objects that have been set up. Typically, the server prompts for a command and uses a `case` statement to either perform the command or deny access.

When it is time to log out, the server issues a break to exit the loop. This causes the `finally` statement to execute, closing the `client` socket. Closing the socket is critical because, otherwise, you will exhaust server memory before long. The `finally` clause ensures that. You can't count on Java's garbage collection to close the socket.

Note that the server is multithreaded; each client that connects gets its own thread in the server. This is quite an impressive result in so few lines of code!

Writing a Client Program to Communicate with the Server

Listing 42.2 shows a prototype for a client program that talks to your Telnet server.

Listing 42.2 TelnetClient.java A prototype Telnet client.

```
//***************************************************************************
//* Imports                                                                 *
//***************************************************************************

import       java.net.*;
import       java.io.*;

//***************************************************************************
//* TelnetClient                                                            *
//***************************************************************************

public class
TelnetClient
{

//***************************************************************************
//* main                                                                    *
//***************************************************************************

    public static void
    main( String[] args )
    {
        new TelnetClient();
    }

//***************************************************************************
//* Constructor                                                             *
//***************************************************************************

    public
    TelnetClient()
    {
        Socket     s = null;

        try
        {
            System.out.println( "Opening socket..." );

            //    Create a new socket...
            s = new Socket( "localhost", TelnetServer.TELNET_PORT );
            System.out.println( "Socket open..." );

            //    Convert the streams...
            BufferedReader disIn = new BufferedReader(
                new InputStreamReader( s.getInputStream() ) );
```

continues

Listing 42.2 Continued

```
            PrintWriter psOut = new PrintWriter( s.getOutputStream(), true );

            //    Convert the System.in (stdin) to an InputStreamReader...
            BufferedReader stdIn = new BufferedReader(
                new InputStreamReader( System.in ) );

            System.out.println( "Connected..." );

            String    line;

            while ( true )
            {
                line = disIn.readLine();

                if ( line == null )
                    break;

                System.out.println( line );

                line = stdIn.readLine();

                if ( line == null )
                    break;

                psOut.println( line );
            }
        }
        catch ( IOException e )
        {
            System.out.println( e );
        }

        finally
        {
            try
            {
                if ( s != null )
                    s.close();
            }
            catch ( IOException e2 )
            {
                //    Handle any errors...
            }
        }
    }
}
```

The client program is simpler, and similar to the `TelnetThread` class. You create a `Socket` object, specifying the host address and port. The client must know both of these before connecting to the server. Assume that the host is `localhost`. The Telnet port you already know is port 23, and you reuse the constant you created in the server class.

After connecting successfully with the server, you create two `BufferedReader` objects: one to get data from the server and the other to get data from the user (`System.in`). You also create a `PrintWriter` object so that you can "print" to the server. The client goes into a read/write loop until it receives no more input from the server, at which time it closes the socket.

Classes Used by the Client Program

The client needs only the `Socket` class from the `java.net` package. The client uses the `getInputStream()` method to receive data from the server and the `getOutputStream()` method to send data to the server. These methods support TCP, ensuring reliable data communication across the network.

From the `java.io` package, the program imports `IOException` (for I/O error handling), `BufferedReader` (for reading input from a stream), and `PrintWriter` (for writing to a stream).

The *main()* Function

This function just creates an instance of your `TelnetClient` class.

The Constructor

`TelnetClient` consists only of a constructor. In it, a `Socket` object is created. `Socket` takes two arguments: the Internet address (`"localhost"`) and the Telnet port (`TelnetServer.TELNET_PORT`). After the `Socket` object is created, the following three streams are created:

- `disIn`—A `BufferedReader` object used to read data from the server using the socket
- `psOut`—A `PrintWriter` object used to write data to the server using the socket
- `stdin`—A `BufferedReader` object for reading input from the terminal

The program then goes into an infinite loop. Within the loop, you read input from the server. If your request for data from the server returns a `null` value, you know that the connection has been lost. At this point, you exit the program.

If data is available, you retrieve and print it to the screen or terminal. After the socket was established, the server printed out `Login:` using the `print()` method on its `PrintWriter` object (remember, from the `TelnetServer` class?). Here in your loop, you retrieve and print the data.

After you have retrieved any received data from the server, your class retrieves data from the user. You get this by using the `readLine()` method. It waits for a carriage return before continuing. After this returns with your input string, you use the `println()` method on its `PrintWriter` object (attached to the same socket as the server) to print back to the server.

The exchange continues until the socket is closed. You have established a line-oriented conversation between client and server. What happens after that depends on the particular application's requirements and is beyond the scope of this discussion.

Communicating with Datagram Sockets

Communicating using datagram sockets is simpler than using the TCP-based sockets (`Socket` and `ServerSocket`) that you used for the Telnet server. Communication is also faster because there is no connection overhead. There is also no attempt to send packets again if an error occurs or sequencing of multiple packets, as occurs in TCP/IP transmissions.

A datagram packet is just sent as an array of bytes to a receiving program, presumably listening at a particular IP address and port. If the receiving program gets the datagram and wants to send a reply, it becomes the sender addressing a datagram back to a known IP address and port. The conversation style is a bit like those old movies in which the pilot sends a message, says "Over," and waits for ground control to respond.

You might use datagram socket communication if you are writing an interactive game or, as in many UNIX systems, for returning a small piece of information—such as the time, when you don't want the overhead of establishing a connection and/or (in the case of the time server) when the communication takes place locally.

Sending a Datagram Packet

Listing 42.3 shows a prototype program for sending a datagram packet. It sends a 27-byte message ("I'm a datagram and I'm O.K.") to the IP address mapped to `"localhost"` at port number 6969. When you try this, use an IP address and port that you know is available. These values should work on most machines. Error handling is notably absent from this example. You should insert the appropriate `try` blocks and `catch` statements to handle errors gracefully.

Listing 42.3 DatagramSend.java A prototype program to send a datagram packet.

```
//***********************************************************************
//* Imports                                                             *
//***********************************************************************

import          java.net.*;

//***********************************************************************
//* DatagramSend                                                        *
//***********************************************************************

public class
DatagramSend
{
    public static void
    main( String args[] )
    throws Exception
    {
        String          strToSend = "I'm a datagram and I'm O.K.";

        byte[]          bArray = new byte[ strToSend.length() ];
        int          port = 6969;
```

```
        //    Suck the bytes out of the string into our byte array...
        bArray = strToSend.getBytes();

        //    Get the IP address of our destination...
        InetAddress inetAddr = InetAddress.getByName( "localhost" );

        //    Create the packet...
        DatagramPacket packet = new DatagramPacket( bArray,
            strToSend.length(),
            inetAddr,
            port );

        //    Now send that bad fella...
        DatagramSocket socket = new DatagramSocket();
        socket.send( packet );
        socket.close();
    }
}
```

You need to use only one socket: the `DatagramSocket`. There is no concept of the server listening for client requests. The idea is just to establish a `DatagramSocket` object and then send and receive messages. The messages are sent in a `DatagramPacket` object. An additional object—`InetAddress`—is needed to construct the IP address to send the packet.

The `DatagramSend` class has only one method—`main()`—so it is a standalone Java program. This demonstration program sends only one message. You can, of course, modify `main()` to pass any message to any IP address and port. Because `main()` throws `Exception`, in this case it was declared that you were not handling errors in this class.

The `DatagramPacket` constructor used here has the following four arguments:

- `bArray`—An array of `bytes` containing the message to send
- `strToSend.length() -ñ`—The length of the string you are going to send
- `inetAddr`—the `iNetAddress` object containing the resolved IP address of your destination
- `port`—An integer specifying the port number

Another form of the constructor requires only the first two arguments. It is designed for local communication when the IP address and port are already known. You will see it in action in the following section, "Receiving a Datagram Packet."

You first create a string (`strToSend`) that contains the string you want to send. Then you create a `byte` array that is as long as your string. You use the `String` class's `length()` method to do this. The `port` variable is used to store the port, 6969.

The `getBytes()` instance method of the `java.lang.String` class converts strings into `byte` array form. You store this in your `byte` array `bArray`.

The `getByName()` method of `InetAddress` converts a string into an Internet address in the form that the `DatagramPacket` constructor accepts.

Next, an instance of `DatagramPacket` is created with the preceding arguments. Finally, the packet is sent using the `send()` instance method of the `DatagramPacket`.

Receiving a Datagram Packet

The packet is on its way, so it is time to receive it. Listing 42.4 shows the receiving program.

Listing 42.4 DatagramReceive.java A prototype program to receive a datagram packet.

```
//*************************************************************************
//* Imports                                                               *
//*************************************************************************

import        java.net.*;

//*************************************************************************
//* DatagramReceive                                                       *
//*************************************************************************

public class
DatagramReceive
{
    public static void
    main( String args[] )
    throws Exception
    {
        String         rxString;
        byte[]        rxBuffer = new byte[ 2048 ];

        //    Create a packet to receive into...
        DatagramPacket rxPacket = new DatagramPacket( rxBuffer, rxBuffer.length
);

        //    Create a socket to listen on...
        DatagramSocket rxSocket = new DatagramSocket( 6969 );

        //    Receive a packet...
        rxSocket.receive( rxPacket );

        //    Convert the packet to a string...
        rxString = new String( rxBuffer, 0, rxPacket.getLength() );

        //    Print out the string...
        System.out.println( rxString );

        //    Close the socket...
        rxSocket.close();
    }
}
```

The DatagramReceive class, like the DatagramSend class, uses the DatagramSocket and DatagramPacket classes from java.net. First, create a buffer large enough to hold the message. The buffer in this example (rxBuffer) is a 2K byte array. Your buffer size may vary. Just make sure it will hold the largest packet you will receive.

You then create a datagram packet. Note that the receive program already knows its IP address and port, and so it can use the two-argument form of the constructor. The DatagramSocket is set up to receive data at port 6969.

The receive() method of Datagram receives the packet as a byte array. The String (rxString) is constructed out of the byte array and it is printed on the terminal upon receipt. Finally, the socket is closed, freeing memory rather than waiting for Java's garbage collection.

To alternatively get the IP address of the host you are running on, call the getLocalHost() and getAddress() methods of the class java.net.InetAddress. First, getLocalHost() returns an INetAddress object. Then you use the getAddress() method, which returns a byte array consisting of the four bytes of the IP address, as in the following example:

```
InetAddress internet_address = InetAddress.getLocalHost();
   byte[] ipaddress = internet_address.getAddress();
```

If the IP address of the network you are running on is 221.111.112.23, then

ipaddress[0] = 221

ipaddress[1] = 111

ipaddress[2] = 112

ipaddress[3] = 23

Customized Network Solutions

The Internet provides no transactional security whatsoever. Nor do the socket-oriented communications methods discussed thus far verify whether any particular request for reading or writing data is coming from a source that should have such access. To do this, you need a customized network protocol.

These protocols sit as a layer between your network protocol (that is, TCP/IP) and your application. They encrypt outgoing packets and decrypt incoming packets, while verifying that you are still talking to whom you think you are talking.

Netscape has proposed the Secure Sockets Layer (SSL) protocol. SSL is a protocol that resides between the services—such as Telnet, FTP, and HTTP—and the TCP/IP connection sessions that illustrated in this chapter. SSL would check that the client and server networks are valid, provide data encryption, and ensure that the message does not contain any embedded commands or programs. SSL would thus provide for secure transactions to occur across the Internet.

Another proposal is to write a server that provides security from the start. This is the idea behind *Secure Hypertext Transfer Protocol* (*S-HTTP*) developed by Enterprise Information Technologies (EIT), RSA Labs, and the National Center for Supercomputer Applications (NCSA).

See To learn more about security protocols, see "Key Access and Security Issues for Web Administrators," **page 279**.

NOTE NCSA is the group that developed Mosaic, the first graphical web browser. The Mosaic design team went on to fame and fortune by completely rewriting Mosaic to create a new and original web browser. The result was Netscape Navigator.

In your organization, you might want to provide a firewall between the public and private areas of your networks. Therefore, for a number of reasons you might need more protection for your network than TCP/IP provides.

Java provides a set of methods called `SocketImpl`, an abstract class, for implementing either of these strategies. To use it, you create a subclass and implement its methods, such as connecting to the server, accepting client requests, getting file information, writing to local files, and so on. Even if you have never written your own server or created a custom socket class, it is nice to know that it's possible to do in Java.

Will Security Considerations Disable Java Applets?

Imagine a world in which Java applets on any network can set up client/server communications of the type discussed in this chapter. Perhaps an applet on your network can call a method in an applet on someone else's network or run a program on that other network remotely. An applet connects to a quote server, for example, determines that the price of a certain stock has reached the target price, and then connects to a user's machine on a network, displaying a message and requesting permission to buy. Or perhaps the applet can run an Excel spreadsheet macro to update the portfolio every 10 minutes. Many powerful applets could be written.

With this power comes potential danger. How can you prevent the applet from deleting files, downloading unauthorized data, or even being aware of the existence of such files? In this world of distributed objects, a profound tension exists between enabling more capabilities for an applet and fear of unwanted use.

This is why the debate on object access is fierce. The main stage is a standard called *Common Object Request Broker Architecture.*

http://www.acl.lanl.gov/CORBA

This is a consortium of many computer companies that allow requests and responses to be made securely from distributed objects. Microsoft is, of course, one of the participants. Microsoft has a protocol for requesting objects called *Object Linking and Embedding* (*OLE*). OLE's main purpose is for one Windows application to access information in another Windows application. OLE is more platform specific than CORBA. It is worth watching the progress of the debate. Will Java applets be allowed to run Windows DLLs so that they can communicate with Windows objects? How *open* will OLE become?

Currently, applets loaded from a network not only cannot run Windows DLLs on the local machine, they are forbidden to run local commands, such as the DOS `dir` command, that would find out the names of files on the client. In addition, applets cannot make network connections except to the network they are on.

NOTE These limitations apply only to applets loaded from a network. Locally loaded applets are not restricted like this.

The debate between power and security seems to be veering toward the security side. An example is a "bug" that Drew Dean, Ed Felten, and Dan Wallach of Princeton University found in Netscape Navigator version 2.0 running a Java applet. They tricked the domain name server (DNS) (the program that resolves host names, such as **www.yahoo.com**, into IP addresses) into disguising their origin. They made DNS believe they were actually from another computer, and then they were able to breach security on it. Netscape acknowledged the situation and quickly provided an update (version 2.01) that provided closer control over how an IP address is resolved.

Another security flaw was one found in Internet Explorer version 3.0. It allowed a web site, or webmaster, to place a Windows 95 shortcut on your system. This shortcut could be any kind of command to run a program or even format your hard disk!

These situations caused a real stir in the Internet community. Concerns about Internet security were rampant. Also, concerns about restricting Java applet access to the point where the usefulness of the applications are diminished greatly were also rampant.

Sun has suggested a naming convention for running applets across networks. The convention would be based on the IP address of the network where the applet resides. In the future, digital signatures will be attached to applets before they are distributed. This will ensure that you are getting what you want. For more information about Java and applet security, including developments, take a look at:

http://java.sun.com/sfaq

(Frequently Asked Questions about Java and applet security) .

CHAPTER 43

Security

by Ryan Sutter

In this chapter

Executable Content and Security

Java has changed the face of the web from a static publishing medium to an interactive application development platform by providing executable "live" content embedded in HTML documents. This is a very frightening thought to most system administrators. After all, it's bad enough that people can download software that might contain viruses that could damage their machines. How can the network stay secure with programs coming in and running on the host machines all on their own? What is to keep somebody from reading sensitive data, wiping out hard drives, setting up back doors to the network, or something worse? Fortunately, the folks at Sun gave this some thought and designed Java with security in mind from the ground up, starting with the language and continuing on through the compiler, compiled code, and runtime environment.

To understand Java's preventative measures, we'll start by reviewing the special security concerns that apply to interactive content. We'll then cover the types of attacks that unscrupulous programmers attempt and the kinds of security issues that relate to a well intentioned but poorly written program. After we've covered the issues, we'll discuss the features of the Java language, the Java compiler, and the Java Virtual Machine that are designed to help ensure security. Then we'll talk about the remaining open issues related to Java security and what you can (and can't) do about them, as well as the new Security API being implemented in Java 1.1.

In this section, we'll discuss briefly how interactivity on the web has evolved and how security issues have changed with each new technique. We then focus on how live content, executing on host machines, poses the most challenging security issues of all.

We will only discuss the general security issues that relate to executable content on the web as opposed to other means of interactivity. From there, we outline the issues and illustrate possible attack scenarios.

Interactivity Versus Security

There is a direct correlation between interactivity and security:

> The greater the level of interactivity, the greater the security risk.

The Internet allows information to be spread, but this is also what makes it potentially dangerous. This is especially the case when the information is executable code, like Java. An image or other non-program file cannot execute instructions on your machine, and so is inherently safer than a Java applet (or ActiveX Control), which can. As you will see, this relationship between interactivity and security is true on the server side as well as the client side.

Let's step back to the basic building block of the web—HTTP. HTTP is a simple, stateless protocol. When an HTTP server receives a request for a file, it simply hands that file over. There is no interaction between the server and client beyond the call and response. An HTTP server is similar to a television transmitter, and an HTTP client is similar to a television. A television is a receiver that receives signals from a transmitter. The only real difference between the way television transmitters and HTTP servers interact with televisions or HTTP clients is that instead of broadcasting, the server is narrow casting. The HTTP server is sending out whatever was specifically requested by an HTTP client and not just pumping out information to everyone. Narrow casting is a fairly secure model on both the client and server sides. The server controls what files and information the client has access to by choosing what it serves. The client is open to very little risk, except maybe being overloaded by too much data from the server, but the operating system on the client side usually prevents that. Although this is quite reliable and more interactive than television, it is still a relatively passive medium.

Of course, the basic HTTP protocol leaves much to be desired in the way of interactivity, and people have to really fight it to create compelling interactive content. Still, interactivity techniques were developed with the foremost of these as forms and CGI programs.

The use of forms and CGI is still relatively secure on the client side, but significantly less on the server side. The process works like this. The browser on the client side receives an HTML form document. The form can contain combo boxes, radio buttons, check boxes, and text fields as well as buttons to post the form data. An end user fills the form out and submits its contents to the server. Form contents are submitted by passing as an argument to a program that executes on the server. This program is called a CGI (Common Gateway Interface) program. It can be written in any language that executes on the server and commonly consists of a UNIX shell-script, a C program, or a Perl script. The CGI program parses up the parameter string supplied by the client and utilizes the data. For example, the program can store the data in a local database, email it, and so forth. All access to the server is accomplished by the CGI program. There is never any direct access to the server by the client. This arrangement presents a server-side security risk because badly behaved CGI programs can damage a server by depleting system resources, corrupting files, or anything else an executable program is capable of doing.

Although Active Server Pages and other non-CGI server-side scripting methods were not mentioned in the preceding discussion, the security issues are much the same.

▶ **See** For more information on CGI programs and security, see Chapters 11, "Key Access and Security Concerns for Web Administrators," and 33, "CGI and Database Security."

The next logical step in the evolution of interactivity on the web was client-side executable content. This actually existed before Java in the guise of helper apps and plug-ins. Through the use of helper apps—and helper apps that execute right in the browser, called plug-ins—it is possible to view and interact with web content using code that executes on your own machine. You simply need to download and install the helper software first (assuming it is available for your platform) and get the content later. The content is not executable but contains information about itself that tells the browser what program to use to interact with it. This is accomplished by use of a MIME (Multipurpose Internet Mail Extensions) type. This model creates a security breach on the client potentially worse than the Java model because there are no limits imposed on the application running on the client. The person using the helper application must trust that it won't do any harm. The content (images, sounds, and movies) is not executable, and an end user must explicitly install the viewer software. Hence, there is really no more risk than installing any other kind of application.

What about the Java model? It is one big step forward for interactivity and one big step backward for security. Suddenly, both the client and the server are at risk because the client executes live code without knowing in advance what that code is or what it does. When browsing the web, you can click a link and receive a page that starts running on your machine. You might not get the chance to decide to trust the person sending the content. When the content is live, instead of static, it opens up whole new realms of interactivity but also raises some serious security questions. How can the end user be sure that he isn't going to download a page that will wipe out his hard drive, infect files with viruses, steal private information, or simply crash the machine? Let's now quantify the security issues.

The Security Problem

How is network-distributed dynamic executable content any different from software installed and running on a local machine? A piece of software needs to be able to access all of the system resources within the limits of what the operating system allows. It needs to save files, read information, and access the system's memory. Although there are bugs in software (sometimes accidental, sometimes malicious), the person installing the software generally makes a decision to trust the person who wrote the software. This is the traditional software model.

An application arriving over a network must also be able to make use of system resources to function. The only difference is that executable content arriving in a web page does not need to be installed first. The user might not even know where it is coming from, and you will not have the chance to decide if you trust the person on the other end. If the code was written by a hacker who wanted to damage your machine or violate your security, and the live content had all of the same freedoms a regular local application would have, you would have no warning and no protection.

How do we allow for a useful application and maintain a level of trust? It doesn't make sense to completely restrict outside programs from doing anything on the local machine because this severely limits the functionality of the network application. A better strategy is to develop limitations that hinder the malicious behavior but allow for the freedom to do the things that need to be done. There are six steps to defining this:

1. Determine in advance all potential malicious behavior and attack scenarios.
2. Reduce all potential attack scenarios to a basic set of behaviors that form the basis of all of them.
3. Design a programming language and architecture that does not allow the basic set of behaviors that form that basis. Hopefully, this disallows the malicious behavior.
4. Prove that the language and architecture are secure against the intended attack scenarios.
5. Allow executable content using only this secure architecture.
6. Design the language and architecture to be extensible so that new attack scenarios can be dealt with as they arrive and that new counter-measures can be retrofitted into the existing security measures.

Java was designed with each of these steps in mind and addresses most, if not all, of these points. Before exploring Java's security architecture, let's discuss the types of potential attack scenarios.

Potential Attack Scenarios

There are two basic categories of attacks that people try to perpetrate. There are security breaches and nuisance attacks. The following are some examples of nuisance attacks:

- Application starts a process that hogs all system resources and brings all computer use to a halt.
- Application locks the browser by attacking it internally.
- Application interferes with or reassigns the browser's DNS server. This can prevent the user from loading documents and possibly cause a root security breach if the user were on as root.
- Application searches and destroys other applications by interfering with some specific process. Someone has even written a Java applet that kills any other Java applets that try to load.
- Application displays obscene pictures or profanity.
- Application deletes or damages files on your computer.

These types of attacks might not necessarily open you up to a security breach because they do not leak private information about your company or yourself to any unauthorized third party. They can, however, do everything from make your computing experience very unpleasant to cause damage to your computer. The goal of these attacks is just to wreak havoc of one type or another.

The other, more serious types of attacks are security breaches where somebody attempts to gain private or sensitive information about you or your business. There are more strategies used to accomplish this than can be covered in a single chapter of a book. You find full coverage of the subject in *Internet Security Professional Reference, Second Edition*, published by New Riders. However, here are a few of the major strategies that people might try:

- Install a back door into your network for future unauthorized access
- Access confidential files on the network and give to an unauthorized third party
- Usurp identity and impersonate the user or the user's computer to carry out attacks on other computers

The Java Approach to Security

Java is an object-oriented programming language but it also is a cross-platform operating environment (the Java Virtual Machine) that is separate and independent of Java, the language. Java is also a compiler for the Java language that produces *bytecode* for the Java Virtual Machine (VM). The Java VM could run bytecodes compiled from any language, not just Java, and the `.class` files that make up Java objects could be created by any compiler that targeted the

Virtual Machine. Therefore, security in Java needs to be implemented on each of these fronts separately: in the language, the compiler, and the Virtual Machine.

What is so special about the Java programming language that makes it more secure than other languages? After all, because the VM is a virtual processor and any language can theoretically be compiled for it, why develop the Java language in the first place? The Java language was designed to be several things:

- Portable
- Secure
- Object-oriented
- Network-aware
- Extensible

Many of these requirements affected the way security was implemented in the language, the compiler, and the Virtual Machine. For example, the portability requirement meant that Java could not rely on any security measures built into an operating system because it needed to run on any system. For the language to be both easy to learn and secure, the security needed to be designed into the language and not left up to the good will of the programmer. Using C/C++ would not have worked.

Java's roots are in C++ and other object-oriented languages. However, Java reduces the complexity, platform-dependent variations, and potentially system-damaging capabilities of these languages. Following are some of the ways Java does this:

- No pointer arithmetic
- Constant variable sizes
- Strict object-oriented methodology
- Automatic garbage collection
- No direct access to hardware in applets

NOTE Before we go too far into the Java security architecture, it is important to point out that we will be chiefly discussing Java *applets*, not *applications*. A Java application installed on a local machine has the same privileges and capabilities as any other program. The features built into the Java language that help enforce security in applets can also make for better behaved applications. Even things like the automatic memory management, however, can be subverted by the linking in of native code that was written in a language that allows direct machine access. Therefore, it is important to note, applets might be considered secure, but an application written in Java should not be considered any more secure than an application written in any other language.

So how do these characteristics of the Java language affect the security issues we discussed in the previous chapter? Let's go through each piece of the security problem to find out.

Visualize All Attack Scenarios The Java security model is designed to protect the following resources from attack:

- Memory
- Client file system
- OS/program state
- Network

The types of attack that the Java model protects against are:

- Damage software resources on client machine
- Lock up or deny resources on client machine
- Steal information from client machine
- Impersonate client machine

Some types of nuisance attacks, such as the display of rude or offensive material or the starting up of processes that hog system resources, are difficult or impossible to stop, and are not addressed in the Java security model.

Construct a Basic Set of Malicious Behaviors As previously stated, Java security is implemented in several places. The language, the compiler, and the runtime environment are a few. Each is considered a potential security risk, and security measures vary for each link in the chain. Following is a more complete list of where Java security should be implemented:

- The language
- The compiler
- The `.class` file internal structure
- The bytecode verifier and interpreter
- The runtime system including the class loader and memory and thread managers
- The `SecurityManager` class
- The external Java environment such as a web browser or OS
- Restrictions placed on the behavior of Java applets

Prove Security of Architecture Even though there are limitations and precautions on each part of the Java system, these measures must be proven to be effective. After all, there are some pretty ingenious hackers out there. Sun has attempted to satisfy this criteria in a couple different ways:

- **Freely available source code** By providing the source code to Java for inspection, Sun allows for other people to prove or disprove the security of Java independently of Sun. No one needs to just trust that Sun has done it right.
- **Encourage hacking on its language** Sun is encouraging people to try to find holes in Java—and lots of people have. Sun then attempts to fix them. Incorporating new security finds is easy because of the next step.

Restrict Executable Content to Proven Security Architecture The class loader and the bytecode verifier both help to accomplish this objective. If a compiler creates a `.class` file that violates security rules, the class loader and bytecode verifier do not allow it to execute.

NOTE The Java architecture is not limited to the programming language of Java. Therefore, the type of security checks performed by the class loader and the bytecode verifier are general to the security restrictions of the Java virtual machine and not the language.

Make Security Architecture Extensible The Java language is well-designed for this purpose because it is an object-oriented language and allows for the addition of new security classes. The Java `SecurityManager` class helps implement enhancements to the security model.

Architecture of Java Security Mechanisms

We will discuss how security is implemented in the Java language, the compiler, and the Virtual Machine, respectively.

Security Built into the Java Language

The Java language might have some of its roots in C++ but much of the complexity of C++ is gone. This is good for programmers attempting to learn the language but is also good for security. The reasons will become apparent as we cover the various points about the Java language that set it apart from C++ and also help make it secure.

No Pointer Arithmetic The Java language does not have a pointer arithmetic. There is no direct access to memory addresses at all. All references to classes and instance variables in a `.class` file happen through the use of symbolic names. Memory management is taken care of by the Java Virtual machine. This not only eliminates an entire class of pesky hard-to-find bugs, but also means that a programmer cannot forge a pointer to memory or create magic offsets that just happen to point to the right place. In theory, programmers cannot change system variables or access private information on the user's machine, and, in the absence of bugs in one of the parts of Java, this is true in practice as well.

Automatic Garbage Collection Along with memory management, the Java VM also provides for automatic garbage collection. This makes Java both more secure and robust. In C/C++, it is fairly common to do either of the following:

- Forget to free memory when it is no longer needed
- Accidentally free the same memory twice

Memory management bugs are hard to track down and can cause many problems. Java keeps track of all objects in use and reclaims the memory as it is required. One nice thing about the garbage collection is that it runs as a background process in its own thread. The programmer never needs to think about memory management.

Well-Defined Language A well-defined language makes it less likely for a programmer to create bugs that can compromise the security of a computer. The Java language is very strictly defined and is identical on every platform it runs on. This means:

- All primitive types in the language are guaranteed to be a specific size
- All operations are guaranteed to be performed in a specific order

The platform and the compiler used for C and C++ affects how things are done in your code. Operations are not always performed in the same order, and primitive types can vary in size. This makes life more difficult for the programmer and increases the risk of dangerous bugs.

Strict Object-Oriented Language With the exception of the primitive types, everything in Java is a basic object. This strict adherence to object-oriented methodology means that all of the theoretical benefits of OOP are realized in Java. This includes:

- Encapsulation of data within objects
- The capability to inherit from existing secure objects
- Controlled access to data structures via public methods only, so there is no operator overloading

Final Classes, Methods, and Variables Classes, methods, and variables can be declared `FINAL`. This means that they cannot be modified after the declaration and also prevents the overriding of trusted methods by malicious code.

Strong Typecasting Java has to be a strongly-typed language because it automatically manages memory. There are no loopholes in the Java type system:

- Objects cannot be cast to a subclass without an explicit runtime check.
- All references to methods and variables are checked to make sure that the objects are of the correct type.
- Integers cannot be converted into objects, and objects cannot be converted to integers.

Unique Object Handles Every Java object has a unique hash code associated with it. This allows the current state of a Java program to be fully inventoried at any time. This enables the constant surveillance of the Java Virtual Machine for any unwelcome or unwanted processes. This is similar to the tracking and surveillance of people in a building. It's easier to spot intruders.

The Security of Compiled Code

The Java compiler checks Java code for security violations. It is a thorough, stringent compiler that enforces the restrictions listed previously. However, it is possible that Java code could be compiled with a "fixed" compiler that allows illegal operations. This is where the Java class loader and bytecode verifier come into play. There are various types of security enforced by the runtime system on compiled code.

Java *.class* Files Structure Java applets and applications are made up of `.class` files that are compiled bytecode. Let's briefly cover the format of Java `.class` files.

Each Java `.class` file is transferred across the network separately—all classes used in a Java applet or application reside in their own separate .class file. The `.class` file is a series of 8-bit bytes. 16- and 32-bit values are formed by reading two or four of these bytes and joining them together. Each `.class` file contains:

- A magic constant
- Major and minor version information

- The constant pool
- Information about the class
- Information about each of the fields and methods in the class
- Debugging information

The *constant pool* is how constant information about the class is stored. It can be any of the following:

- A unicode string
- A class or interface name
- A reference to a field or method
- A numeric value
- A constant string value

As previously mentioned, all references to variables and classes in the Java language are done through symbolic names, not pointers. This is true in the `.class` file as well. Elsewhere in the `.class` file, references to variables, methods, and objects are accomplished by referring to indices in this constant pool. Security is thus maintained inside the `.class` file.

NOTE Each method can have multiple code attributes. The `CODE` attribute signifies Java bytecode, but there are other code attributes such as `SPARC-CODE` and `386-CODE` that allow for a machine code implementation of the method. This allows for faster execution of code but cannot be verified to be sound. For the most part, browsers use the Java code to retrieve executable content from a remote site because of this trust issue. However, in a full-fledged Java application, having multiple code attributes allows the programmer to write code that is both cross-platform and still capable of taking advantage of platform-specific techniques where possible.

The `.class` file format has more features that are not really in use yet. One of these is the capability to allow authors to digitally sign their `.class` files to guarantee to the end user that the file has not been modified by a third party. The user still needs to decide if he wishes to trust the author, but at least he knows what he is getting. This is likely to come into play as Microsoft pushes ActiveX and its AuthentiCode technology. It also allows authors to digitally sign their ActiveX Controls.

The class loader of most current Java implementations, including Sun's own HotJava browser, considers any code that comes from a remote source to be potentially hostile and will not use any machine code contained in a Java `.class` file. They will run machine code loaded from local `.class` files, however. Expect this to change when there are ways to designate trusted and untrusted services.

More About Bytecodes In addition to the actual bytecodes that execute a method, the `CODE` attribute also supplies other information about the method. This information is for the memory manager, the bytecode verifier, and the Java VM's exception handling. They are as follows:

- Maximum stack space used by the method.
- Maximum number of registers used by the method.

- Bytecodes for executing the method.
- Exception handler table. This is a lookup table for the runtime system that provides an offset to where the exception handler is found for code within a starting and ending offset.

There are six primitive types in the Java VM:

- 32-bit integer (integers)
- 64-bit integer (long integers)
- 32-bit floating point numbers (single float)
- 64-bit floating point numbers (double float)
- Pointers to objects and arrays (handles)
- Pointers to the virtual machine code (return addresses)

There are also several array types that the Java VM recognizes:

- Arrays of each of the primitive types (except return addresses)
- Arrays of booleans, bytes (8-bit integers), shorts (16-bit integers), and unicode characters

In the case of an array of handles, there is an additional type field that indicates the class of object that the array can store.

Each method has its own expression-evaluation stack and set of local registers. The registers must be 32-bit and hold any of the primitive types other than the double floats and the long integers. These are stored in two consecutive registers, and the VM instructions, *opcodes*, address them using the index of the lower numbered register.

The VM instruction set provides opcodes that operate on various data types and can be divided into several categories:

- Pushing constants onto the stack
- Accessing and modifying the value of a register
- Accessing arrays
- Stack manipulation
- Arithmetic, logical, and conversion instructions
- Control transfer
- Function return
- Manipulating object fields
- Method invocation
- Object creation
- Type casting

The bytecodes consist of a one byte opcode followed by zero or more bytes of additional operand information. With two exceptions, all instructions are fixed-length and based on the opcode.

The Bytecode Verifier The Bytecode Verifier is really the last line of defense against a bad Java applet. This is where the classes are checked for integrity, where the compiled code is checked for its adherence to the Java rules, and where a misbehaving applet is most likely caught. If the compiled code was created with a "fixed" compiler to get around Java's restrictions, it will most likely fail the Verifier's checks and be stopped. This is one of the most interesting parts of the Java security mechanism, because of the way it is designed to be thorough and general at the same time. The Bytecode Verifier does not have to work only on code created by a Java compiler, but on any bytecodes created for a Java VM, so it needs to be general. However, it also needs to catch any and all exceptions to the rules laid out for a Java applet or application and must therefore be thorough.

All bytecode goes through the Bytecode Verifier, which makes four passes over the code.

Pass 1 is the most basic pass. The Verifier makes sure that the following criteria are met:

- The `.class` file conforms to the format of a `.class` file
- The magic constant at the beginning is correct
- All attributes are of the proper length
- The `.class` file does not have any extra bytes, nor too few
- The constant pool does not have any unrecognized information

Pass 1 finds any corrupt `.class` files from a faulty compiler and also catches `.class` files that were damaged in transit. Assuming everything goes well, you get to the second pass.

Pass 2 adds a little more scrutiny. It verifies almost everything without actually looking at the bytecodes themselves. Some of the things that Pass 2 is responsible for are:

- Ensuring that final classes are not subclassed and that final methods are not overridden
- Checking that every class (except object) has a superclass
- Ensuring that the constant pool meets certain constraints
- Checking that all field references and methods in the constant pool have legal names, classes, and a type signature

On Pass 2, everything needs to look legal—that is, at face value all the classes appear to refer to classes that really exist, rules of inheritance aren't broken, and more. It does not check the sourcecode; this is left up to further passes. Passes 3 and 4 check to see if the fields and methods actually exist in a real class and if the types refer to real classes.

On Pass 3, the actual bytecodes of each method are verified. Each method undergoes dataflow analysis to ensure that the following things are true:

- The stack is always the same size and contains the same types of objects.
- No registers are accessed unless they are known to contain values of a specific type.
- All methods are called with the correct arguments.
- All opcodes have appropriate type arguments on the stack and in the registers.
- Fields are modified with values of the appropriate type.

The Verifier does several things including verifies that the exception handler offsets point to legitimate starting and ending offsets in the code and makes sure the code does not end in the middle of an instruction.

Pass 4 happens as the code actually runs. During the Pass 3, the Bytecode Verifier does not load any classes unless it must to check its validity. This is for efficiency's sake. On Pass 4, the final checks are made the first time an instruction referencing a class executes. The Verifier then does the following:

- Loads in the definition of the class (if not already loaded)
- Verifies that the currently executing class is allowed to reference the given class

Likewise, the first time an instruction calls a method, or accesses or modifies a field, the Verifier does the following:

- Ensures that the method or field exists in the given class
- Checks that the method or field has the indicated signature
- Checks that the currently executing method has access to the given method or field

Namespace Encapsulation Using Packages Java classes are defined within packages that give them unique names. The Java standard for naming packages is the domain the package originates from, but in reverse order with the first part capitalized. If your domain is "www.yourdomain.com," classes coming from my domain should be in the `COM.yourdomain.www` package.

What is the advantage to using packages? With packages, a class arriving over the network is distinguishable and therefore cannot impersonate a trusted local class. This is true even if the packages have the same names.

Runtime Linking and Binding The exact layout of runtime resources is one of the last things done by the Java VM. Java uses dynamic linking with results in linking and binding during runtime. This is to prevent an unscrupulous programmer from making assumptions about the allocation of resources and utilizing these for security attacks.

Security in the Java Runtime System

As we have already discussed, classes can be treated differently when loaded locally as opposed to over a network. One of these differences is how the class is loaded into the runtime system. The default way for this to happen is to just load the class from a local `.class` file. Any other way of retrieving a class requires the class to be loaded with an associated `ClassLoader`. The `ClassLoader` class is a subtype of a standard Java object that has the methods to implement many of the security mechanisms we have discussed so far. A lot of the attack scenarios that have been used against Java have involved getting around the `ClassLoader`.

The `ClassLoader` comes into play after Pass 3 of the Bytecode Verifier as the classes are actually loaded on Pass 4. The `ClassLoader` is fairly generic because it does not know for certain that it is loading classes written in Java. It could be loading classes written in C++ and compiled into bytecode.

The `ClassLoader`, therefore, has to check general rules for consistency within `ClassFiles`. If a class fails these checks, it isn't loaded and an attack on an end user's system fails. It is an important part of the Java security system.

Automatic Memory Management and Garbage Collection Although discussed previously as part of the language, we will revisit this again because it is implemented in the runtime environment. In C or C++, the programmer is responsible for allocating and deallocating memory and needs to keep track of the pointers to all of the objects in memory. This can result in memory leaks, dangling pointers, null pointers, and more bugs that are very difficult to find and fix. Additionally, leaving memory management up to the programmer can allow for mischief. Manual allocation and deallocation of memory opens the door for unauthorized replication of objects, impersonation of trusted objects, and attacks on data consistency. By having automatic memory management, Java gets around these problems and, at the same time, makes life easier for the programmer. Here is an example of how a programmer might go about impersonating a trusted class (for instance, the `ClassLoader`) if Java did not have automatic deallocation of memory. First, the program would create a legitimate object of class `MyFakeClassLoader` and a pointer to refer to that object. Now, with a little sleight of hand and knowledge of how allocation and deallocation work, the programmer removes the object from memory but leaves the memory pointer. He then instantiates a new instance of `ClassLoader`, which happens to be the exact same size, in the same memory space, and *voilà*! The pointer now refers to the other class, and the programmer has access to methods and variables that are supposed to be private. But this scenario is not possible in Java, because of the automatic memory management. The Java automatic memory management system doesn't allow manual manipulation of pointers.

The *SecurityManager* Class The Java security model is open to extension when new holes are found. A key to this, common to both Java 1.0.2 and Java 1.1.x, is the `SecurityManager` class. This class is a generic class for implementing security policies and providing security wrappers around other parts of Java. This class does not get used by itself—it is simply a base for implementing security in other classes. Actual implementation of security in other objects is accomplished through subclassing the `SecurityManager` class. Although not a comprehensive list, this class contains methods to:

- Determine whether a security check is in progress
- Check to prevent the installation of additional `ClassLoaders`
- Check if a `.class` file can be read by the Java Virtual Machine
- Check if native code can be linked in
- Check if a file can be written to
- Check if a network connection can be created
- Check if a certain network port can be listened to for connections
- Check if a network connection can be accepted
- Check if a certain package can be accessed

- Check if a new class can be added to a package
- Verify security of a native OS system call
- Prevent a new Security Manager from being created

As you might guess from the preceding list, the names of many of the methods in the `java.lang.SecurityManager` class begin with `check`. All but one of these `check`*XXX* methods return if all is well, or throw a `SecurityException` if there was a problem. Only `checkTopLevelWindow` returns a value—a Boolean.

The following example of the use of the `check`*XXX* methods is based on that in the Java 1.1 API documentation (found at **http://java.sun.com/products/jdk/1.1/docs/api/java.lang.SecurityManager.html**) for `java.lang.SecurityManager`:

```
SecurityManager secMgr = System.getSecurityManager();
if (secMgr != null) {
    secMgr.checkXXX(arguments go here,... );
}
```

Everything discussed so far has been about Java as a whole. The language has no pointers whether you are working with applets or applications. The Bytecode Verifier and class loading mechanisms still apply. Applications in Java function like any other applications in any full-featured language, including direct memory access through use of native code. There are some limitations on applets, however, that do not apply to applications.

Time-Tested Applet Security

Java would not have made the splash that it did just by being cross-platform and object-oriented. The Internet and applets put it on the cover of *Time* magazine. The Internet is also where the biggest risks come for Java applets.

Applets are limited Java programs, extended from class `Applet`, that usually execute embedded in an HTML document. Applets usually load from remote machines and are subject to severe limitations on the client machine.

Restrictions on Applets Arriving Over a Network Applets arriving on the client machine are subject to the following file system and network restrictions:

- Cannot read or write files on the local file system.
- Cannot create, copy, delete, or rename files or directories on the local file system.
- Can only connect to the machine from which they originally came. This is the URL of the source machine as specified in the `APPLET` tag in the HTML document or in the `CODEBASE` parameter of the `APPLET` tag. This cannot be a numeric IP address.
- Cannot call external programs.
- Cannot manipulate Java threadgroups other than their own.
- Cannot run outside the Java Virtual Machine's memory area.

NOTE This set of restrictions on the applet can vary from one implementation of Java to another. For instance, all of these apply when using Netscape Navigator 2.0 or later, but the JDK `appletviewer` allows you to designate an explicit list of files that can be accessed by applets. The HotJava browser, Netscape Navigator, Microsoft Internet Explorer, and the JDK `appletviewer` (to name a few) all have minor differences too numerous to mention here ranging from handling of certain exceptions to access control lists for applets. If you want to know of detailed limitations for a particular browser, it is a good idea to go to the applicable web site and get the most up-to-date information. For the Microsoft Internet Explorer, check **http://www.microsoft.com/ie/security/** and for the Netscape Navigator, check **http://home.netscape.com/comprod/products/communicator/navigator.html**.

There is some system information available to applets, however. Access to this information depends on the specific Java implementation. There is a method of the `System` object called `getProperty`. By calling `System.getProperty(String key)`, an applet can learn about its environment. The information available to the applet is as follows:

- `java.version` The version of Java currently running
- `java.vendor` The name of the vendor responsible for this specific implementation of Java
- `java.vendor.URL` The URL of the vendor listed in `java.vendor`
- `java.class.version` The Java class version number
- `os.name` The name of the operating system
- `os.arch` The architecture of the operating system
- `file.separator` The file separator (for example, /)
- `path.separator` The path separator (for example, :)
- `line.separator` The line separator (for example, **CRLF**)

Other pieces of information that may or may not be available, depending on the implementation, are:

- `java.home` The Java home directory
- `java.class.path` The Java class path
- `user.name` The logon name of the current user
- `user.home` The location of the user's home directory
- `user.dir` The user's current directory

All the limitations discussed here apply to applets received over the network.

Applets Loaded from the Local File System When applets are loaded locally, they are no longer subject to the same restrictions of a remotely loaded applet. They have the same freedoms as an application, including the capability to:

- Read and write files on the local file system
- Load native code libraries

- Execute external processes on the local machine
- Skip the bytecode verifier
- Exit the Java VM

It is up to the implementation of Java to enforce the correct applet restrictions if it has been loaded from a remote source and then cached on a local disk.

New in JDK 1.1.x: Making and Using Signed Applets

In JDK 1.1.x, Sun introduced several new APIs to the core set of Java APIs. One of these is Security and Signed Applets, a subset of the upcoming Security API. Sun's documentation describes the JDK 1.1 Security API as providing for "digital signatures and message digests…(and) abstract interfaces for key management, certificate management and access control. Specific APIs to support X.509 v3 certificates and other certificate formats, and richer functionality in the area of access control, will follow in subsequent JDK releases."[1] Signing and verification of applets is done using a dual-key system of public/private key pairs.

To sign your applets, or to prepare your system to use signed applets, you need the `jar`, `javakey`, and `appletviewer` tools included with the JDK 1.1.x. You create and access archives with `jar`, create keys and sign archives with `javakey`, and test and develop using the `appletviewer` mini-browser.

Before getting started, you might want to see what happens when an applet throws a security exception. Sun provides a harmless sample applet that does just that. You can try it by running

```
appletviewer http://java.sun.com/security/signExample/writeFile.html
```

at a command prompt or in an MS-DOS command window.

Using Signed Applets To run a signed applet, you first need to get its certificate file. After you have the certificate file, go to a command prompt and use `javakey` to add the name of the signer to the identity database (if it is not there already):

```
javakey -c nameOfSigner true
```

Use the command-line argument `true` to indicate that the sender is trusted. Next, you can again use `javakey` to insert the certificate into your certificate database:

```
javakey -ic nameOfSigner filenameOfCertificateFile
```

To include a signed applet in an HTML document, use the `<APPLET>` tag:

```
<applet code="myApplet.class" archive="mySigned.jar" height="150" width="100">
</applet>
```

You can specify more than one archive file in the `<APPLET>` tag by using a comma-separated list of archive files to be loaded in sequence:

```
<applet code="myApplet.class" archive="myA.jar, myB.jar, myC.jar, myD.jar"
       height="100" width="200">
</applet>
```

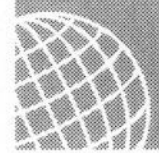

ON THE WEB

http://java.sun.com/security/signExample/index.html Specific directions for using a signed applet, together with an example are provided by this web site.

Making Your Own Signed Applets The good news about making a signed applet is that you do not need to add any special code to the applet's Java source code. You add the digital signature after you generate the `.class` file by successfully compiling the applet.

You do need to perform a few steps to sign your applet:

1. **Make an identity**—At a command prompt, use `javakey` to make the identity under which you want to sign the applet. For example, James R. Acme, Director of Applet Development at Acme, Inc., might choose `jrAcme`. Use the `true` command-line argument to make the identity trusted:

   ```
   javakey -cs jrAcme true
   ```

   You can use and reuse this identity, so you don't have to make a new one for each new applet.

2. **Make and store a pair of keys for the identity**—You can use `javakey` to generate and store the keypair in one command. Store the private key in one file, `jrAcme_priv`, and the public key in `jrAcme_pub`. Here, a 512-bit DSA keypair is created:

   ```
   javakey -gk jrAcme DSA 512 jrAcme_pub Acme_priv
   ```

   Keypairs, like their associated identities, are re-useable.

3. **Make a certificate directive file**—This is a plain text file that describes the certificate you will create in the next step. The `javakey` tool needs the information in this file to make the certificate. Make the `cert_directive_jrAcme` directive file as follows with any text editor such as Notepad or your favorite word processor, making sure you save the file as plain text (see Listing 43.1).

Listing 43.1 Source code for acmeCertDirectiveFile.

```
# The name of the entity (a person or company)
#   issuing the certificate, from the identity database.
#   This is required.
issuer.name=jrAcme
#
# The number of certificate to use for the signing.
#   Note: the very first certificate you make will be "self-signed,"
#     with the issuer.name the same as the subject.name, since you
#     won't have a certificate number to start.
#   Once you have a certificate:
#     Get this number by running javakey -ld for the whole database
#       or running javakey -li jrAcme to see just the jrAcme certificate number.
#     This is required if the issuer.name
#       is not the same as the subject.name.
#     In that case, remove the pound sign from the following commented-out
#       sample line:
#issuer.cert=1
#
```

```
# Subject description: the name, etc., of the subject from the identity database
#   The certificate will authenticate the public key of this entity.
#   These lines are required.
subject.name=jrAcme
subject.real.name=James R. Acme
subject.org.unit=Acme Applet Development
subject.org=Acme, Inc.
subject.country=Canada

# Certificate start and end dates and serial number
#    These are required.
start.date=1 Jan 1997
end.date=15 Jan 1997
serial.number=1001

# Signature algorithm to be used, such as MD5/RSA.
#    Leave the signature.algorithm line commented out if you want DSA.
#    If you don't want DSA, remove the pound sign in front of the following
line:
#signature.algorithm=MD5/RSA

# Certificate file name to be used as output.
#    This is optional.
out.file=jrAcme.x509
```

Certificate directive files are described in detail in the JDK 1.1.x documentation for the `javakey` tool. Like identities and keypairs, they are also re-useable.

4. **Make an x509 certificate**—The `javakey` tool makes the certificate for you from the specifications you gave in the directive file. The certificate is stored in the `jrAcme.x509` output file you specified in the preceding directive file. At a command prompt, enter:

   ```
   javakey -gc cert_directive_jrAcme
   ```

   You can use the same certificate to sign many archives.

5. **Make a jar archive file for your applet**—At the command prompt, use the `jar` tool to archive one or more files:

   ```
   jar cf signedmyApplet.jar myApplet.class myApplet.gif myApplet.au
   ```

   In the preceding example, the jar tool generates a manifest file for you, called META-INF/MANIFEST.INF, and places it in the archive. The manifest file contains meta-information about your archive, such as a list of the archived files. You can customize your own manifest file; for details, see:

   http://java.sun.com/products/jdk/1.1/docs/guide/jar/manifest.html

6. **Make a sign directive file**—The sign directive file is very similar to the certificate directive file. The `javakey` tool uses the sign directive file when signing your archived applet files. Use a text editor or word processor to make this plain text file and save it to `sign_directive_jrAcme` (see Listing 43.2).

Listing 43.2 Source code for acmeJarDirectiveFile.

```
# The name of the signer in the database.
signer=jrAcme

# Certificate number to use for this signer.
#    Use javakey -li jrAcme to find out this number.
cert=1

# (Not supported) Certificate chain depth
chain=0

# Signature and signature block filename, without extension, 8 characters
maximum.
# Here the new files will be ACMESIGN.SF and ACMESIGN.DSA.
signature.file=ACMESIGN

# Filename to use for the new signed jar archive file.
#    This is optional. If you do not include it, the
#    output file will be the same as that of the archive
#    being signed, with a .sig extension added on to the end.
#    To use this option, remove the pound sign from the line below:
#out.file=signedMyApplet.jar
```

7. **Sign and check the archive file**—The `javakey` tool follows the directions in the sign directive file to sign your archived applet. At a command prompt, enter the following:

   ```
   javakey -gs sign_directive_jrAcme signedMyApplet.jar
   ```

   In this example, because no `out.file` was specified in the sign directive file, the new signed archive file will be called `signedMyApplet.jar.sig`. You need to rename this file to a name with a `.jar` extension—for example, `signedMyapplet.jar`. To check the newly signed archive, you can list its archived files with:

   ```
   jar tvf signedMyApplet.jar
   ```

ON THE WEB

http://java.sun.com/security/signExample/doit Sun's signing example at this web page illustrates the signing process for UNIX users.

Learning More About the Java Security API You can read more about JDK 1.1.x security features at Sun's JDK 1.1.x security site:

http://java.sun.com/products/jdk/1.1/docs/guide/security/index.html

You can get detailed information about using the `jar` and `javakey` tools in the JDK 1.1.x documentation.

The full Java Security API provides a cryptography framework for Java applets and applications; it is not yet released, but a partial version, Security and Signed Applets, is included in the JDK version 1.1 and discussed in this section. With the full release of the Security API, security in

Java will be greatly expanded with an extendable cryptography framework, including signatures, encryption, and authentication.

ON THE WEB

http://java.sun.com/products/jdk/1.1/docs/guide/security/ For more information on the Java Security API and the new classes and features check out this web site.

Open Issues on Security

In the case of Java, the security is only as good as its runtime implementation. Many holes have been found in Java's security, and many of them have been fixed in specific implementations; but these same issues may arise again in future implementations as Java is ported to other platforms. After all, each version of the Java VM needs to be written in a platform-specific programming language like C and can have its own flaws and weaknesses.

Aside from that, there are many types of malicious behavior that are difficult (if not impossible) to avoid. For instance, no matter what is done to the Java security model, it will not stop someone from putting rude or obscene material in an applet or starting long, resource intensive processes. These things are not bugs and will continue to be nuisances at times.

Many other techniques have been discovered to load native code, connect to hosts other than the one an applet was loaded from, read and write the local file system, and so on. The list of current Java security problems can change frequently.

For links to and discussions of current problems and a chronology of security-related bugs, see the Java Security FAQ at **http://java.sun.com/sfaq/index.html**.

Every implementation of Java has its own open issues, and Sun's is no exception. The best thing to do is to keep on top of the issues for the implementation you are using. Java 2.0 will provide several security enhancements including the capability to control access to Java applets, beans, and other code entities on an individual basis.

Further References on Java and Security

The following references can help you keep up with the changing world of Java security. It is by no means a comprehensive list but should get you started on researching the topic further and give you some valuable starting places from which to continue your research:

- UseNet:
  alt.2600
  comp.risks
  comp.lang.java
  comp.infosystems.www.*

- WWW:

  Sun's Java Security site, with a wealth of links about Java security bug chronology, such as the Applet Security FAQ, Security API information, applet and code signing, JDK 1.1 features, JDK 1.1 Security documentation, the Java security model, Java Cryptographic architecture, the Java Security Q&A archives, the Java Cryptography Extension (JCE) to the JDK 1.1, and more. Highly recommended:

  http://java.sun.com/security/index.html

  Slides from a presentation by Li Gong, Sun's Java security architect, at JavaOne 1997, on the future and direction of Java security:

  http://java.sun.com/javaone/sessions/slides/TT03/TT03.zip

  The Java Security Q&A archives (volume 2, the most recent):

  http://jserv.javasoft.com/hypermail/java-security-archive-2/index.html

  The Java Security FAQ:

  http://java.sun.com/sfaq/index.html

  Using javakey, a tutorial on `javakey`, the JDK 1.1.x's code signing tool:

  http://java.sun.com/security/usingJavakey.html

  Sun's Recommendations for using JDK 1.1 `javakey`:

  http://java.sun.com/security/policy.html

  Sun's *Jar Guide,* about using the new `jar` file format and tool in JDK 1.1.x:

  http://java.sun.com/products/jdk/1.1/docs/guide/jar/jarGuide.html

  Netscape Navigator Java Security FAQ:

  http://www.netscape.com/

  Java Security, the December 1995 classic paper by Joseph A. Bank, MIT:

  http://www-swiss.ai.mit.edu/~jbank/javapaper/javapaper.html

[1] Sun Microsystems, **http://java.sun.com/products/jdk/1.1/docs/guide/security/index.html**.

APPENDIX A

JavaScript 1.2 Language Reference

In this chapter

How This Reference Is Organized

The first part of this reference is organized by object, with properties and methods listed by the object to which they apply. The second part covers independent functions in JavaScript not connected with a particular object, as well as operators in JavaScript.

A Note About JavaScript 1.2

JavaScript 1.2 is designed to interface seamlessly with Netscape Navigator 4.0. New features have been introduced in various areas of the language model, including but not limited to the following:

- Events
- Objects
- Properties
- Methods

Netscape Navigator 4.0 has been coded to support these new features, but earlier versions of Navigator have not. Backward compatibility is, therefore, an issue.

In this appendix, techniques that work only in Netscape Navigator 4.0 and later are clearly marked. At each heading, the words "Navigator 4.0 Only" will appear.

Finally, note that when developing, you should now clearly identify which version of JavaScript you're using. If you don't, your scripts might not work. You identify the version by using the `LANGUAGE` attribute in the `<SCRIPT>` tag. The following are some examples:

```
<Script Language = "JavaScript"> - Compatible with 2.0 and above
<Script Language = "JavaScript 1.1"> - Compatible with 3.0 and above
<Script Language = "JavaScript 1.2"> - Compatible with 4.0 and above
```

The following codes are used next to section headings to indicate where objects, methods, properties, and event handlers are implemented:

- **C:** Client JavaScript. (Server JavaScript is not covered in this appendix.)
- **2:** Netscape Navigator 2.
- **3:** Netscape Navigator 3.
- **4:** Netscape Navigator 4 only. (That's not to say Navigator 4 works with these items only; Navigator 4 will handle all implementations.)
- **I:** Microsoft Internet Explorer 4.

The *anchor* Object [C|2|3|4|I]

The `anchor` object reflects an HTML anchor.

Properties

- **name:** A string value indicating the name of the anchor. (Not 2|3)

The *applet* Object [C|3]

The applet object reflects a Java applet included in a Web page with the <APPLET> tag.

Properties

- **name:** A string reflecting the NAME attribute of the <APPLET> tag.

The *area* Object [C|3]

The area object reflects a clickable area defined in an imagemap; area objects appear as entries in the links array of the document object.

Properties

- **hash:** A string value indicating an anchor name from the URL.
- **host:** A string value reflecting the host and domain name portion of the URL.
- **hostname:** A string value indicating the host, domain name, and port number from the URL.
- **href:** A string value reflecting the entire URL.
- **pathname:** A string value reflecting the path portion of the URL (excluding the host, domain name, port number, and protocol).
- **port:** A string value indicating the port number from the URL.
- **protocol:** A string value indicating the protocol portion of the URL, including the trailing colon.
- **search:** A string value specifying the query portion of the URL (after the question mark).
- **target:** A string value reflecting the TARGET attribute of the <AREA> tag.

Methods

- **getSelection:** Gets the current selection and returns this value as a string.

Event Handlers

- **onDblClick:** Specifies JavaScript code to execute when the user double-clicks the area. (Not implemented on Macintosh; Netscape Navigator 4.0 only) (4)
- **onMouseOut:** Specifies JavaScript code to execute when the mouse moves outside the area specified in the <AREA> tag.

New Properties with JavaScript 1.2

`type`	Indicates a `MouseOut` event.
`target`	Indicates the object to which the event was sent.
`layer[n]`	Where `[n]` represents X or Y, used (with `page[n]` and `screen[n]`) to describe the cursor location when the `MouseOut` event occurred.
`page[n]`	Where `[n]` represents X or Y, used (with `layer[n]` and `screen[n]`) to describe the cursor location when the `MouseOut` event occurred.
`screen[n]`	Where `[n]` represents X or Y, used (with `layer[n]` and `page[n]`) to describe the cursor location when the `MouseOut` event occurred.

- **`onMouseOver`:** Specifies JavaScript code to execute when the mouse enters the area specified in the `<AREA>` tag.

New Properties with JavaScript 1.2

`type`	Indicates a `MouseOver` event.
`target`	Indicates the object to which the event was sent.
`layer[n]`	Where `[n]` represents X or Y, used (with `page[n]` and `screen[n]`) to describe the cursor location when the `MouseOver` event occurred.
`page[n]`	Where `[n]` represents X or Y, used (with `layer[n]` and `screen[n]`) to describe the cursor location when the `MouseOver` event occurred.
`screen[n]`	Where `[n]` represents X or Y, used (with `layer[n]` and `page[n]`) todescribe the cursor location when the `MouseOver` event occurred.

The *array* Object [C|3|I]

The `array` object provides a mechanism for creating arrays and working with them. New arrays are created with *`arrayName`* `= new Array()` or *`arrayName`* `= new Array(`*`arrayLength`*`)`.

Properties

- **`length`:** An integer value reflecting the number of elements in an array.
- **`prototype`:** Used to add properties to an `array` object.

Methods

- **`concat(`*`arrayname`*`)`:** Combines elements of two arrays and returns a third, one level deep, without altering either of the derivative arrays. (Netscape Navigator 4.0 only)
- **`join(`*`string`*`)`:** Returns a string containing each element of the array separated by *`string`*. (Not 1)
- **`reverse()`:** Reverses the order of an array. (Not 1)
- **`slice(arrayName, beginSlice, endSlice)`:** Extracts a portion of some array and derives a new array from it. The `beginSlice` and `endSlice` parameters specify the target elements at which to begin and end the slice. (Netscape Navigator 4.0 only)
- **`sort(`*`function`*`)`:** Sorts an array based on function, which indicates a *`function`* defining the sort order. *`function`* can be omitted, in which case the sort defaults to dictionary order. Note: `sort` now works on all platforms.

The *button* Object [C|2|3|I]

The `button` object reflects a pushbutton from an HTML form in JavaScript.

Properties

- **`enabled`:** A Boolean value indicating whether the button is enabled. (Not 2|3)
- **`form`:** A reference to the `form` object containing the button. (Not 2|3)
- **`name`:** A string value containing the name of the button element.
- **`type`:** A string value reflecting the `TYPE` attribute of the `<INPUT>` tag. (Not 2|I)
- **`value`:** A string value containing the value of the button element.

Methods

- **`click()`:** Emulates the action of clicking the button.
- **`focus()`:** Gives focus to the button. (Not 2|3)

Event Handlers

- **`onMouseDown`:** Specifies JavaScript code to execute when a user presses a mouse button.
- **`onMouseUp`:** Specifies JavaScript code to execute when the user releases a mouse button.
- **`onClick`:** Specifies JavaScript code to execute when the button is clicked.
- **`onFocus`:** Specifies JavaScript code to execute when the button receives focus.

The *checkbox* Object [C|2|3|I]

The `checkbox` object makes a check box in an HTML form available in JavaScript.

Properties

- **checked:** A Boolean value indicating whether the check box element is checked.
- **defaultChecked:** A Boolean value indicating whether the check box element was checked by default (that is, it reflects the `CHECKED` attribute).
- **enabled:** A Boolean value indicating whether the check box is enabled. (Not 2|3)
- **form:** A reference to the `form` object containing the check box. (Not 2|3)
- **name:** A string value containing the name of the check box element.
- **type:** A string value reflecting the `TYPE` attribute of the `<INPUT>` tag. (Not 2|I)
- **value:** A string value containing the value of the check box element.

Methods

- **click():** Emulates the action of clicking the check box.
- **focus():** Gives focus to the check box. (Not 2|3)

Event Handlers

- **onClick:** Specifies JavaScript code to execute when the check box is clicked.
- **onFocus:** Specifies JavaScript code to execute when the check box receives focus. (Not 2|3)

The *combo* Object [C|I]

The `combo` object reflects a combo field in JavaScript.

Properties

- **enabled:** A Boolean value indicating whether the combo box is enabled. (Not 2|3)
- **form:** A reference to the `form` object containing the combo box. (Not 2|3)
- **listCount:** An integer reflecting the number of elements in the list.
- **listIndex:** An integer reflecting the index of the selected element in the list.
- **multiSelect:** A Boolean value indicating whether the combo field is in multiselect mode.
- **name:** A string value reflecting the name of the combo field.
- **value:** A string containing the value of the combo field.

Methods

- **addItem(*index*):** Adds an item to the combo field before the item at *`index`*.
- **click():** Simulates a click on the combo field.
- **clear():** Clears the contents of the combo field.
- **focus():** Gives focus to the combo field.
- **removeItem(*index*):** Removes the item at *`index`* from the combo field.

Event Handlers

- **onClick:** Specifies JavaScript code to execute when the mouse clicks the combo field.
- **onFocus:** Specifies JavaScript code to execute when the combo field receives focus.

The *date* Object [C|2|3|I]

The date object provides mechanisms for working with dates and times in JavaScript. Instances of the object can be created with the following syntax:

```
newObjectName = new Date(dateInfo)
```

Here, *dateInfo* is an optional specification of a particular date and can be one of the following:

```
"month day, year hours:minutes:seconds"
year, month, day
year, month, day, hours, minutes, seconds
```

The latter two options represent integer values.

If no *dateInfo* is specified, the new object represents the current date and time.

Properties

- **prototype:** Provides a mechanism for adding properties to a date object. (Not 2)

Methods

- **getDate():** Returns the day of the month for the current date object as an integer from 1 to 31.
- **getDay():** Returns the day of the week for the current date object as an integer from 0 to 6 (0 is Sunday, 1 is Monday, and so on).
- **getHours():** Returns the hour from the time in the current date object as an integer from 0 to 23.
- **getMinutes():** Returns the minutes from the time in the current date object as an integer from 0 to 59.
- **getMonth():** Returns the month for the current date object as an integer from 0 to 11 (0 is January, 1 is February, and so on).
- **getSeconds():** Returns the seconds from the time in the current date object as an integer from 0 to 59.
- **getTime():** Returns the time of the current date object as an integer representing the number of milliseconds since January 1, 1970 at 00:00:00.
- **getTimezoneOffset():** Returns the difference between the local time and GMT as an integer representing the number of minutes.
- **getYear():** Returns the year for the current date object as a two-digit integer representing the year less 1900.

- **`parse(`*`dateString`*`):`** Returns the number of milliseconds between January 1, 1970 at 00:00:00 and the date specified in *`dateString`*, which should take the following format: (Not I)

  ```
  Day, DD Mon YYYY HH:MM:SS TZN
  Mon DD, YYYY
  ```

- **`setDate(`*`dateValue`*`):`** Sets the day of the month for the current `date` object. *`dateValue`* is an integer from 1 to 31.
- **`setHours(`*`hoursValue`*`):`** Sets the hours for the time for the current `date` object. *`hoursValue`* is an integer from 0 to 23.
- **`setMinutes(`*`minutesValue`*`):`** Sets the minutes for the time for the current `date` object. *`minutesValue`* is an integer from 0 to 59.
- **`setMonth(`*`monthValue`*`):`** Sets the month for the current `date` object. *`monthValue`* is an integer from 0 to 11 (0 is January, 1 is February, and so on).
- **`setSeconds(`*`secondsValue`*`):`** Sets the seconds for the time for the current `date` object. *`secondsValue`* is an integer from 0 to 59.
- **`setTime(`*`timeValue`*`):`** Sets the value for the current `date` object. *`timeValue`* is an integer representing the number of milliseconds since January 1, 1970 at 00:00:00.
- **`setYear(`*`yearValue`*`):`** Sets the year for the current `date` object. *`yearValue`* is an integer greater than 1900.
- **`toGMTString():`** Returns the value of the current `date` object in GMT as a string using Internet conventions in the following form:

  ```
  Day, DD Mon YYYY HH:MM:SS GMT
  ```

- **`toLocaleString():`** Returns the value of the current `date` object in the local time using local conventions.
- **`UTC(`*`yearValue`*`, `*`monthValue`*`, `*`dateValue`*`, `*`hoursValue`*`, `*`minutesValue`*`, `*`secondsValue`*`):`** Returns the number of milliseconds since January 1, 1970 at 00:00:00 GMT. *`yearValue`* is an integer greater than 1900. *`monthValue`* is an integer from 0 to 11. *`dateValue`* is an integer from 1 to 31. *`hoursValue`* is an integer from 0 to 23. *`minutesValue`* and *`secondsValue`* are integers from 0 to 59. *`hoursValue`*, *`minutesValue`*, and *`secondsValue`* are optional. (Not I)

The *document* Object [C|2|3|I]

The `document` object reflects attributes of an HTML document in JavaScript.

Properties

- **`alinkColor:`** The color of active links as a string or a hexadecimal triplet.
- **`anchors:`** Array of `anchor` objects in the order they appear in the HTML document. Use `anchors.length` to get the number of anchors in a document.
- **`applets:`** Array of `applet` objects in the order they appear in the HTML document. Use `applets.length` to get the number of applets in a document. (Not 2)

- **bgColor:** The color of the document's background.
- **cookie:** A string value containing cookie values for the current document.
- **embeds:** Array of plugin objects in the order they appear in the HTML document. Use embeds.length to get the number of plug-ins in a document. (Not 2|I)
- **fgColor:** The color of the document's foreground.
- **forms:** Array of form objects in the order the forms appear in the HTML file. Use forms.length to get the number of forms in a document.
- **images:** Array of image objects in the order they appear in the HTML document. Use images.length to get the number of images in a document. (Not 2|I)
- **lastModified:** String value containing the last date of the document's modification.
- **linkColor:** The color of links as a string or a hexadecimal triplet.
- **links:** Array of link objects in the order the hypertext links appear in the HTML document. Use links.length to get the number of links in a document.
- **location:** A string containing the URL of the current document. Use document.URL instead of document.location. This property is expected to disappear in a future release.
- **referrer:** A string value containing the URL of the calling document when the user follows a link.
- **title:** A string containing the title of the current document.
- **URL:** A string reflecting the URL of the current document. Use instead of document.location. (Not I)
- **vlinkColor:** The color of followed links as a string or a hexadecimal triplet.

Event Handlers

- **onMouseDown:** Specifies JavaScript code to execute when a user presses a mouse button.
- **onMouseUp:** Specifies JavaScript code to execute when the user releases a mouse button.
- **onKeyUp:** Specifies JavaScript code to execute when the user releases a specific key. (Netscape Navigator 4.0 only) (4)
- **onKeyPress:** Specifies JavaScript code to execute when the user holds down a specific key. (Netscape Navigator 4.0 only) (4)
- **onKeyDown:** Specifies JavaScript code to execute when the user presses a specific key. (Netscape Navigator 4.0 only) (4)
- **onDblClick:** Specifies JavaScript code to execute when the user double-clicks the area. (Not implemented on Macintosh; Netscape Navigator 4.0 only) (4)

Methods

- **captureEvents():** Used in a window with frames (along with enableExternalCapture), it specifies that the window will capture all specified events. New in JavaScript 1.2.
- **clear():** Clears the document window. (Not I)

- **`close()`:** Closes the current output stream.
- **`open(mimeType)`:** Opens a stream that allows `write()` and `writeln()` methods to write to the document window. *`mimeType`* is an optional string that specifies a document type supported by Navigator or a plug-in (for example, `text/html` or `image/gif`).
- **`releaseEvents(eventType)`:** Specifies that the current window must release events (as opposed to capture them) so that these events can be passed to other objects, perhaps further on in the event hierarchy. New in JavaScript 1.2.
- **`routeEvent(event)`:** Sends or routes an event through the normal event hierarchy.
- **`write()`:** Writes text and HTML to the specified document.
- **`writeln()`:** Writes text and HTML to the specified document followed by a newline character.

The *fileUpload* Object [C|3]

Reflects a file upload element in an HTML form.

Properties

- **`name`:** A string value reflecting the name of the file upload element.
- **`value`:** A string value reflecting the file upload element's field.

The *form* Object [C|2|3|I]

The `form` object reflects an HTML form in JavaScript. Each HTML form in a document is reflected by a distinct instance of the `form` object.

Properties

- **`action`:** A string value specifying the URL to which the form data is submitted.
- **`elements`:** Array of objects for each form element in the order in which they appear in the form.
- **`encoding`:** String containing the MIME encoding of the form as specified in the `ENCTYPE` attribute.
- **`method`:** A string value containing the method of submission of form data to the server.
- **`target`:** A string value containing the name of the window to which responses to form submissions are directed.

Methods

- **`reset()`:** Resets the form. (Not 2|I)
- **`submit()`:** Submits the form.

Event Handlers

- **`onReset:`** Specifies JavaScript code to execute when the form is reset. (Not 2|I)
- **`onSubmit:`** Specifies JavaScript code to execute when the form is submitted. The code should return a `true` value to allow the form to be submitted. A `false` value prevents the form from being submitted.

The *frame* Object [C|2|3|I]

The `frame` object reflects a frame window in JavaScript.

Properties

- **`frames:`** An array of objects for each frame in a window. Frames appear in the array in the order in which they appear in the HTML source code.
- **`onBlur:`** A string reflecting the `onBlur` event handler for the frame. New values can be assigned to this property to change the event handler. (Not 2)
- **`onFocus:`** A string reflecting the `onFocus` event handler for the frame. New values can be assigned to this property to change the event handler. (Not 2)
- **`parent:`** A string indicating the name of the window containing the frame set.
- **`self:`** An alternative for the name of the current window.
- **`top:`** An alternative for the name of the topmost window.
- **`window:`** An alternative for the name of the current window.

Methods

- **`alert(`*`message`*`):`** Displays *`message`* in a dialog box.
- **`blur():`** Removes focus from the frame. (Not 2)
- **`clearInterval(intervalID):`** Cancels timeouts created with the `setInterval` method. New in JavaScript 1.2.
- **`close():`** Closes the window.
- **`confirm(`*`message`*`):`** Displays *`message`* in a dialog box with OK and Cancel buttons. Returns `true` or `false` based on the button clicked by the user.
- **`focus():`** Gives focus to the frame. (Not 2)
- **`open(`*`url`*`,`*`name`*`,`*`features`*`):`** Opens *`url`* in a window named *`name`*. If *`name`* doesn't exist, a new window is created with that name. *`features`* is an optional string argument containing a list of features for the new window. The feature list contains any of the following name-value pairs separated by commas and without additional spaces:

`toolbar=[yes,no,1,0]`	Indicates whether the window should have a toolbar
`location=[yes,no,1,0]`	Indicates whether the window should have a location field

`directories=[yes,no,1,0]`	Indicates whether the window should have directory buttons
`status=[yes,no,1,0]`	Indicates whether the window should have a status bar
`menubar=[yes,no,1,0]`	Indicates whether the window should have menus
`scrollbars=[yes,no,1,0]`	Indicates whether the window should have scrollbars
`resizable=[yes,no,1,0]`	Indicates whether the window should be resizable
`width=`*`pixels`*	Indicates the width of the window in pixels
`height=`*`pixels`*	Indicates the height of the window in pixels

- **`print()`:** Prints the contents of a frame or window. This is the equivalent of the user clicking the Print button in Netscape Navigator. New in JavaScript 1.2.
- **`prompt(`*`message`*`,`*`response`*`)`:** Displays *`message`* in a dialog box with a text entry field with the default value of *`response`*. The user's response in the text entry field is returned as a string.
- **`setInterval(`*`function`*`, msec, [args])`:** Repeatedly calls a function after the period specified by the `msec` parameter. New in JavaScript 1.2.
- **`setInterval(`*`expression`*`, msec)`:** Evaluates *`expression`* after the period specified by the `msec` parameter. New in JavaScript 1.2.
- **`setTimeout(`*`expression`*`,`*`time`*`)`:** Evaluates *`expression`* after *`time`*; *`time`* is a value in milliseconds. The timeout can be named with the following structure:

```
name = setTimeOut(expression,time)
```

- **`clearTimeout(`*`name`*`)`:** Cancels the timeout with the name *`name`*.

Event Handlers

- **`onBlur`:** Specifies JavaScript code to execute when focus is removed from a frame. (Not 2)
- **`onFocus`:** Specifies JavaScript code to execute when focus is removed from a frame. (Not 2)
- **`onMove`:** Specifies JavaScript code to execute when the user moves a frame. (Netscape Navigator 4.0 only)
- **`onResize`:** Specifies JavaScript code to execute when a user resizes the frame. (Netscape Navigator 4.0 only)

The *function* Object [C|3]

The `function` object provides a mechanism for indicating JavaScript code to compile as a function. This is the syntax to use the `function` object:

```
functionName = new Function(arg1, arg2, arg3, ..., functionCode)
```

This is similar to the following:

```
function functionName(arg1, arg2, arg3, ...) {
   functionCode
}
```

In the former, *functionName* is a variable with a reference to the function, and the function is evaluated each time it's used instead of being compiled once.

Properties

- **arguments:** An integer reflecting the number of arguments in a function.
- **prototype:** Provides a mechanism for adding properties to a function object.

The *hidden* Object [C|2|3|I]

The hidden object reflects a hidden field from an HTML form in JavaScript.

Properties

- **name:** A string value containing the name of the hidden element.
- **type:** A string value reflecting the TYPE property of the <INPUT> tag. (Not 2|I)
- **value:** A string value containing the value of the hidden text element.

The *history* Object [C|2|3|I]

The history object allows a script to work with the Navigator browser's history list in JavaScript. For security and privacy reasons, the actual content of the list isn't reflected into JavaScript.

Properties

- **length:** An integer representing the number of items on the history list. (Not I)

Methods

- **back():** Goes back to the previous document in the history list. (Not I)
- **forward():** Goes forward to the next document in the history list. (Not I)
- **go(*location*):** Goes to the document in the history list specified by *location*, which can be a string or integer value. If it's a string, it represents all or part of an URL in the history list. If it's an integer, *location* represents the relative position of the document on the history list. As an integer, *location* can be positive or negative. (Not I)

The *image* Object [C|3]

The image object reflects an image included in an HTML document.

Properties

- **`border`:** An integer value reflecting the width of the image's border in pixels.
- **`complete`:** A Boolean value indicating whether the image has finished loading.
- **`height`:** An integer value reflecting the height of an image in pixels.
- **`hspace`:** An integer value reflecting the `HSPACE` attribute of the `<IMG>` tag.
- **`lowsrc`:** A string value containing the URL of the low-resolution version of the image to load.
- **`name`:** A string value indicating the name of the `image` object.
- **`prototype`:** Provides a mechanism for adding properties as an `image` object.
- **`src`:** A string value indicating the URL of the image.
- **`vspace`:** An integer value reflecting the `VSPACE` attribute of the `<IMG>` tag.
- **`width`:** An integer value indicating the width of an image in pixels.

Event Handlers

- **`onKeyUp`:** Specifies JavaScript code to execute when the user releases a specific key. (Netscape Navigator 4.0 only) (4)
- **`onKeyPress`:** Specifies JavaScript code to execute when the user holds down a specific key. (Netscape Navigator 4.0 only) (4)
- **`onKeyDown`:** Specifies JavaScript code to execute when the user presses a specific key. (Netscape Navigator 4.0 only) (4)
- **`onAbort`:** Specifies JavaScript code to execute if the attempt to load the image is aborted. (Not 2)
- **`onError`:** Specifies JavaScript code to execute if there's an error while loading the image. Setting this event handler to `null` suppresses error messages if an error occurs while loading. (Not 2)
- **`onLoad`:** Specifies JavaScript code to execute when the image finishes loading. (Not 2)

The *layer* Object [4]

The `layer` object is used to embed layers of content within a page; they can be hidden or not. Either type is accessible through JavaScript code. The most common use for layers is in developing Dynamic HTML (DHTML). With layers, you can create animations or other dynamic content on a page by cycling through the layers you have defined.

Properties

- **`above`:** Places a layer on top of a newly created layer.
- **`background`:** Used to specify a tiled background image of the layer.

- **below:** Places a layer below a newly created layer.
- **bgColor:** Sets the background color of the layer.
- **clip(left, top, right, bottom):** Specifies the visible boundaries of the layer.
- **height:** Specifies the height of the layer, expressed in pixels (integer) or by a percentage of the instant layer.
- **ID:** Previously called NAME. Used to name the layer so that it can be referred to by name and accessed by other JavaScript code.
- **left:** Specifies the horizontal positioning of the top-left corner of the layer. Used with the Top property.
- **page[n]:** Where [n] is x or y. Specifies the horizontal (x) or vertical (y) positioning of the top-left corner of the layer, in relation to the overall, enclosing document. (Note: This is different from the Left and Top properties.)
- **parentLayer:** Specifies the layer object that contains the present layer.
- **SRC:** Specifies HTML source to be displayed with the target layer. (This source can also include JavaScript.)
- **siblingAbove:** Specifies the layer object immediately above the present one.
- **siblingBelow:** Specifies the layer object immediately below the present one.
- **top:** Specifies the vertical positioning of the top-left corner of the layer. (Used with the Left property.)
- **visibility:** Specifies the visibility of the layer. There are three choices: show (visible), hidden (not visible), and inherit (layer inherits the properties of its parent).
- **width:** Specifies the width of the layer. Used for wrapping procedures; that is, the width denotes the boundary after which the contents wrap inside the layer.
- **z-index:** Specifies the z-order (or stacking order) of the layer. Used to set the layer's position within the overall rotational order of all layers. Expressed as an integer. (Used where there are many layers.)

Events

- **onBlur:** Specifies JavaScript code to execute when the layer loses focus.
- **onFocus:** Specifies JavaScript code to execute when the layer gains focus.
- **onLoad:** Specifies JavaScript code to execute when a layer is loaded.
- **onMouseOut:** Specifies JavaScript code to execute when the mouse cursor moves off the layer.

New Properties

type	Indicates a MouseOut event
target	Indicates the object to which the event was sent

`layer[n]`	Where `[n]` represents x or y, used (with `page[n]` and `screen[n]`) to describe the cursor location when the `MouseOut` event occurred
`page[n]`	Where `[n]` represents x or y, used (with `layer[n]` and `screen[n]`) to describe the cursor location when the `MouseOut` event occurred
`screen[n]`	Where `[n]` represents x or y, used (with `layer[n]` and `page[n]`) to describe the cursor location when the `MouseOut` event occurred

- **`onMouseover`:** Specifies the JavaScript code to execute when the mouse cursor enters the layer.

New Properties with JavaScript 1.2

`type`	Indicates a `MouseOver` event
`target`	Indicates the object to which the event was sent
`layer[n]`	Where `[n]` represents x or y, used (with `page[n]` and `screen[n]`) to describe the cursor location when the `MouseOver` event occurred
`page[n]`	Where `[n]` represents x or y, used (with `layer[n]` and `screen[n]`) to describe the cursor location when the `MouseOver` event occurred
`screen[n]`	Where `[n]` represents x or y, used (with `layer[n]` and `page[n]`) to describe the cursor location when the `MouseOver` event occurred

Methods

- **`captureEvents()`:** Used in a window with frames (along with `enableExternalCapture`), it specifies that the window will capture all specified events. New in JavaScript 1.2.
- **`load(`*`source`*`, `*`width`*`)`:** Alters the source of the layer by replacing it with HTML (or JavaScript) from the file specified in *`source`*. Using this method, you can also pass a width value (in pixels) to accommodate the new content.
- **`moveAbove(`*`layer`*`)`:** Places the layer above *`layer`* in the stack.
- **`moveBelow(`*`layer`*`)`:** Places the layer below *`layer`* in the stack.
- **`moveBy(x,y)`:** Alters the position of the layer by the specified values, expressed in pixels.
- **`moveTo(x,y)`:** Alters the position of the layer (within the containing layer) to the specified coordinates, expressed in pixels.
- **`moveToAbsolute(x,y)`:** Alters the position of the layer (within the page) to the specified coordinates, expressed in pixels.
- **`releaseEvents(`*`eventType`*`)`:** Specifies that the current window should release events instead of capturing them so that these events can be passed to other objects, perhaps further on in the event hierarchy. New in JavaScript 1.2.

- **resizeBy(*width*,*height*):** Resizes the layer by the specified values, expressed in pixels.
- **resizeTo(*width*,*height*):** Resizes the layer to the specified height and size, expressed in pixels.
- **routeEvent(event):** Sends or routes an event through the normal event hierarchy.

The *link* Object [C|2|3|I]

The `link` object reflects a hypertext link in the body of a document.

Properties

- **hash:** A string value containing the anchor name in the URL.
- **host:** A string value containing the host name and port number from the URL.
- **hostname:** A string value containing the domain name (or numerical IP address) from the URL.
- **href:** A string value containing the entire URL.
- **pathname:** A string value specifying the path portion of the URL.
- **port:** A string value containing the port number from the URL.
- **protocol:** A string value containing the protocol from the URL (including the colon, but not the slashes).
- **search:** A string value containing any information passed to a `GET` CGI-BIN call (such as any information after the question mark).
- **target:** A string value containing the name of the window or frame specified in the `TARGET` attribute.

Event Handlers

- **onMouseDown:** Specifies JavaScript code to execute when a user presses a mouse button. (JavaScript 1.2 and Netscape Navigator 4.0 only) (4)
- **onMouseOut:** Specifies JavaScript code to execute when the user moves the mouse cursor out of an object. (JavaScript 1.2 and Netscape Navigator 4.0 only) (4)

New Properties with JavaScript 1.2

`type`	Indicates a `MouseOut` event
`target`	Indicates the object to which the event was sent
`layer[n]` to	Where `[n]` represents x or y, used (with `page[n]` and `screen[n]`) describe the cursor location when the `MouseOut` event occurred
`page[n]`	Where `[n]` represents x or y, used (with `layer[n]` and `screen[n]`) to describe the cursor location when the `MouseOut` event occurred

`screen[n]`	Where `[n]` represents x or y, used (with `layer[n]` and `page[n]`) to describe the cursor location when the `MouseOut` event occurred

- **`onMouseUp`:** Specifies the JavaScript code to execute when the user releases a mouse button.
- **`onKeyUp`:** Specifies the JavaScript code to execute when the user releases a specific key. (Netscape Navigator 4.0 only) (4)
- **`onKeyPress`:** Specifies the JavaScript code to execute when the user holds down a specific key. (Netscape Navigator 4.0 only) (4)
- **`onKeyDown`:** Specifies the JavaScript code to execute when the user presses a specific key. (Netscape Navigator 4.0 only) (4)
- **`onDblClick`:** Specifies the JavaScript code to execute when the user double-clicks the area. (Not implemented on Macintosh; Netscape Navigator 4.0 only) (4)
- **`moveMouse`:** Specifies the JavaScript code to execute when the mouse pointer moves over the link. (Not 2|3)
- **`onClick`:** Specifies the JavaScript code to execute when the link is clicked.
- **`onMouseOver`:** Specifies the JavaScript code to execute when the mouse pointer moves over the hypertext link.

New Properties with JavaScript 1.2

`type`	Indicates a `MouseOver` event
`target`	Indicates the object to which the event was sent
`layer[n]`	Where `[n]` represents x or y, used (with `page[n]` and `screen[n]`) to describe the cursor location when the `MouseOver` event occurred
`page[n]`	Where `[n]` represents x or y, used (with `layer[n]` and `screen[n]`) to describe the cursor location when the `MouseOver` event occurred
`screen[n]`	Where `[n]` represents x or y, used (with `layer[n]` and `page[n]`) to describe the cursor location when the `MouseOver` event occurred

The *location* Object [C|2|3|I]

The `location` object reflects information about the current URL.

Properties

- **`hash`:** A string value containing the anchor name in the URL.
- **`host`:** A string value containing the host name and port number from the URL.

- **hostname:** A string value containing the domain name (or numerical IP address) from the URL.
- **href:** A string value containing the entire URL.
- **pathname:** A string value specifying the path portion of the URL.
- **port:** A string value containing the port number from the URL.
- **protocol:** A string value containing the protocol from the URL (including the colon, but not the slashes).
- **search:** A string value containing any information passed to a `GET` CGI-BIN call (such as information after the question mark).

Methods

- **reload():** Reloads the current document. (Not 2|I)
- **replace(*url*):** Loads *url* over the current entry in the history list, making it impossible to navigate back to the previous URL with the Back button. (Not 2|I)

The *math* Object [C|2|3|I]

The `math` object provides properties and methods for advanced mathematical calculations.

Properties

- **E:** The value of Euler's constant (roughly 2.718) used as the base for natural logarithms.
- **LN10:** The value of the natural logarithm of 10 (roughly 2.302).
- **LN2:** The value of the natural logarithm of 2 (roughly 0.693).
- **LOG10E:** The value of the base 10 logarithm of e (roughly 0.434).
- **LOG2E:** The value of the base 2 logarithm of e (roughly 1.442).
- **PI:** The value of π; used to calculate the circumference and area of circles (roughly 3.1415).
- **SQRT1_2:** The value of the square root of one-half (roughly 0.707).
- **SQRT2:** The value of the square root of two (roughly 1.414).

Methods

- **abs(*number*):** Returns the absolute value of *number*. The absolute value is the value of a number with its sign ignored—for example, `abs(4)` and `abs(-4)` both return 4.
- **acos(*number*):** Returns the arc cosine of *number* in radians.
- **asin(*number*):** Returns the arc sine of *number* in radians.
- **atan(*number*):** Returns the arc tangent of *number* in radians.
- **atan2(*number1*,*number2*):** Returns the angle of the polar coordinate corresponding to the Cartesian coordinate (*number1*,*number2*). (Not I)

- **ceil(*number*):** Returns the next integer greater than *number*; in other words, rounds up to the next integer.
- **cos(*number*):** Returns the cosine of *number*, which represents an angle in radians.
- **exp(*number*):** Returns the value of `E` to the power of *number*.
- **floor(*number*):** Returns the next integer less than *number*; in other words, rounds down to the nearest integer.
- **log(*number*):** Returns the natural logarithm of *number*.
- **max(*number1*,*number2*):** Returns the greater of *number1* and *number2*.
- **min(*number1*,*number2*):** Returns the smaller of *number1* and *number2*.
- **pow(*number1*,*number2*):** Returns the value of *number1* to the power of *number2*.
- **random():** Returns a random number between zero and 1 (at press time, this method was available only on UNIX versions of Navigator 2.0).
- **round(*number*):** Returns the closest integer to *number*; in other words, rounds to the closest integer.
- **sin(*number*):** Returns the sine of *number*, which represents an angle in radians.
- **sqrt(*number*):** Returns the square root of *number*.
- **tan(*number*):** Returns the tangent of *number*, which represents an angle in radians.

The *mimeType* Object [C|3]

The `mimeType` object reflects a MIME type supported by the client browser.

Properties

- **type:** A string value reflecting the MIME type.
- **description:** A string containing a description of the MIME type.
- **enabledPlugin:** A reference to `plugin` object for the plug-in supporting the MIME type.
- **suffixes:** A string containing a comma-separated list of file suffixes for the MIME type.

The *navigator* Object [C|2|3|I]

The `navigator` object reflects information about the version of browser being used.

Properties

- **appCodeName:** A string value containing the code name of the client (for example, "Mozilla" for Netscape Navigator).
- **appName:** A string value containing the name of the client (for example, "Netscape" for Netscape Navigator).

- **`appVersion`:** A string value containing the version information for the client in the following form:

  ```
  versionNumber (platform; country)
  ```

  For example, Navigator 2.0, beta 6 for Windows 95 (international version) would have an `appVersion` property with the value `"2.0b6 (Win32; I)"`.
- **`language`:** Specifies the translation of Navigator. (A read-only property.) New in JavaScript 1.2.
- **`mimeTypes`:** An array of `mimeType` objects reflecting the MIME types supported by the client browser. (Not 2|I)
- **`platform`:** Specifies the platform for which Navigator was compiled. (For example, Win32, MacPPC, UNIX.) New in JavaScript 1.2.
- **`plugins`:** An array of `plugin` objects reflecting the plug-ins in a document in the order of their appearance in the HTML document. (Not 2|I)
- **`userAgent`:** A string containing the complete value of the user-agent header sent in the HTTP request. The following contains all the information in `appCodeName` and `appVersion`:

  ```
  Mozilla/2.0b6 (Win32; I)
  ```

Methods

- **`javaEnabled()`:** Returns a Boolean value indicating whether Java is enabled in the browser. (Not 2|I)
- **`preference(`*`preference.Name`*`, setValue)`:** In signed scripts, this method allows the developer to set certain browser preferences. Preferences available with this method are the following:

`general.always_load_images`	`true/false` value that sets whether images are automatically loaded.
`security.enable_java`	`true/false` value that sets whether Java is enabled.
`javascript.enabled`	`true/false` value that sets whether JavaScript is enabled.
`browser.enable_style_sheets`	`true/false` value that sets whether style sheets are enabled.
`autoupdate.enabled`	`true/false` value that sets whether `autoinstall` is enabled.
`network.cookie.cookieBehavior`	(`0`,`1`,`2`) value that sets the manner in which cookies are handled. There are three parameters. `0` accepts all cookies; `1` accepts only those that are forwarded to the originating server; `2` denies all cookies.

`network.cookie.warnAboutCookies`	`true/false` value that sets whether the browser will warn on accepting cookies.

The *option* Object [C|3]

The `option` object is used to create entries in a select list by using the following syntax:

```
optionName = new Option(optionText, optionValue, defaultSelected, selected)
```

Then the following line is used:

```
selectName.options[index] = optionName.
```

Properties

- **`defaultSelected:`** A Boolean value specifying whether the option is selected by default.
- **`index:`** An integer value specifying the option's index in the select list.
- **`prototype:`** Provides a mechanism to add properties to an `option` object.
- **`selected:`** A Boolean value indicating whether the option is currently selected.
- **`text:`** A string value reflecting the text displayed for the option.
- **`value:`** A string value indicating the value submitted to the server when the form is submitted.

The *password* Object [C|2|3|I]

The `password` object reflects a password text field from an HTML form in JavaScript.

Properties

- **`defaultValue:`** A string value containing the default value of the password element (such as the value of the `VALUE` attribute).
- **`enabled:`** A Boolean value indicating whether the password field is enabled. (Not 2|3)
- **`form:`** A reference to the `form` object containing the password field. (Not 2|3)
- **`name:`** A string value containing the name of the password element.
- **`value:`** A string value containing the value of the password element.

Methods

- **`focus():`** Emulates the action of focusing in the password field.
- **`blur():`** Emulates the action of removing focus from the password field.
- **`select():`** Emulates the action of selecting the text in the password field.

Event Handlers

- **`onBlur`:** Specifies JavaScript code to execute when the password field loses focus. (Not 2|3)
- **`onFocus`:** Specifies JavaScript code to execute when the password field receives focus. (Not 2|3)

The *plugin* Object

The `plugin` object reflects a plug-in supported by the browser.

Properties

- **`name`:** A string value reflecting the name of the plug-in.
- **`filename`:** A string value reflecting the filename of the plug-in on the system's disk.
- **`description`:** A string value containing the description supplied by the plug-in.

The *radio* Object [C|2|3|I]

The `radio` object reflects a set of radio buttons from an HTML form in JavaScript. To access individual radio buttons, use numeric indexes starting at zero. For example, individual buttons in a set of radio buttons named `testRadio` could be referenced by `testRadio[0]`, `testRadio[1]`, and so on.

Properties

- **`checked`:** A Boolean value indicating whether a specific radio button is checked. Can be used to select or deselect a button.
- **`defaultChecked`:** A Boolean value indicating whether a specific radio button was checked by default (that is, it reflects the `CHECKED` attribute). (Not I)
- **`enabled`:** A Boolean value indicating whether the radio button is enabled. (Not 2|3)
- **`form`:** A reference to the `form` object containing the radio button. (Not 2|3)
- **`length`:** An integer value indicating the number of radio buttons in the set. (Not I)
- **`name`:** A string value containing the name of the set of radio buttons.
- **`value`:** A string value containing the value of a specific radio button in a set (that is, it reflects the `VALUE` attribute).

Methods

- **`click()`:** Emulates the action of clicking a radio button.
- **`focus()`:** Gives focus to the radio button. (Not 2|3)

Event Handlers

- **onClick:** Specifies the JavaScript code to execute when a radio button is clicked.
- **onFocus:** Specifies the JavaScript code to execute when a radio button receives focus. (Not 2|3)

The *regExp* Object

The regExp object is relevant to searching for regular expressions. Its properties are set before or after a search is performed. They don't generally exercise control over the search itself, but instead articulate a series of values that can be accessed throughout the search.

Properties

- **input:** The string against which a regular expression is matched. New in JavaScript 1.2.
- **multiline [true, false]:** Sets whether the search continues beyond line breaks on multiple lines (true) or not (false). New in JavaScript 1.2.
- **lastMatch:** Indicates the characters last matched. New in JavaScript 1.2.
- **lastParen:** Indicates the last matched string that appeared in parentheses. New in JavaScript 1.2.
- **leftContext:** Indicates the string just before the most recently matched regular expression. New in JavaScript 1.2.
- **rightContext:** Indicates the remainder of the string, beyond the most recently matched regular expression. New in JavaScript 1.2.
- **$1,..$9:** Indicates the last nine substrings in a match; those substrings are enclosed in parentheses. New in JavaScript 1.2.

The Regular Expression Object

The Regular Expression object contains the pattern of a regular expression.

Parameters

- **regexp:** Specifies the name of the regular expression object. New in JavaScript 1.2.
- **pattern:** Specifies the text of the regular expression. New in JavaScript 1.2.

Flags

- **i:** Specifies that during the regular expression search, case is ignored (that is, the search is not case sensitive).
- **g:** Specifies that during the regular expression search, the match (and search) should be global.
- **gi:** Specifies that during the regular expression search, case is ignored and during the regular expression search, the match (and search) should be global.

Properties

- **global [true,false]:** Sets the g flag value in code, such as whether the search is global (true) or not (false). New in JavaScript 1.2.
- **ignoreCase [true,false]:** Sets the i flag value in code, such as whether the search is case sensitive (true) or not (false). New in JavaScript 1.2.
- **lastIndex:** (Integer value) Indicates the index position at which to start the next matching procedure (for example, lastIndex == 2). New in JavaScript 1.2.
- **source:** (Read-only) Contains the pattern's text. New in JavaScript 1.2.

Methods

- **compile:** Compiles the regular expression. This method is usually invoked at script startup, when the regular expression is already known and will remain constant. New in JavaScript 1.2.
- **exec(str):** Executes a search for a regular expression within the specified string (str). New in JavaScript 1.2. Note: It uses the same properties as the RegExp object.
- **test(str):** Executes a search for a regular expression and a specified string (str). New in JavaScript 1.2. Note: It uses the same properties as the RegExp object.

The *reset* Object [C|2|3|I]

The reset object reflects a reset button from an HTML form in JavaScript.

Properties

- **enabled:** A Boolean value indicating whether the reset button is enabled. (Not 2|3)
- **form:** A reference to the form object containing the reset button. (Not 2|3)
- **name:** A string value containing the name of the reset element.
- **value:** A string value containing the value of the reset element.

Methods

- **click():** Emulates the action of clicking the reset button.
- **focus():** Specifies the JavaScript code to execute when the reset button receives focus. (Not 2|3)

Event Handlers

- **onClick:** Specifies the JavaScript code to execute when the reset button is clicked.
- **onFocus:** Specifies the JavaScript code to execute when the reset button receives focus. (Not 2|3)

The *screen* Object (New in JavaScript 1.2)

The `screen` object describes (or specifies) the characteristics of the current screen.

Properties

- **`availHeight`:** Specifies the height of the screen in pixels (minus static display constraints set forth by the operating system). New in JavaScript 1.2.
- **`availWidth`:** Specifies the width of the current screen in pixels (minus static display constraints set forth by the operating system). New in JavaScript 1.2.
- **`height`:** Specifies the height of the current screen in pixels. New in JavaScript 1.2.
- **`width`:** Specifies the width of the current screen in pixels. New in JavaScript 1.2.
- **`pixelDepth`:** Specifies the number of bits (per pixel) in the current screen. New in JavaScript 1.2.
- **`colorDepth`:** Specifies the number of possible colors to display in the current screen. New in JavaScript 1.2.

The *select* Object [C|2|3]

The `select` object reflects a selection list from an HTML form in JavaScript.

Properties

- **`length`:** An integer value containing the number of options in the selection list.
- **`name`:** A string value containing the name of the selection list.
- **`options`:** An array reflecting each of the options in the selection list in the order they appear. The `options` property has its own properties:

`defaultSelected`	A Boolean value indicating whether an option was selected by default (that is, it reflects the `SELECTED` attribute).
`index`	An integer value reflecting the index of an option.
`length`	An integer value reflecting the number of options in the selection list.
`name`	A string value containing the name of the selection list.
`selected`	A Boolean value indicating whether the option is selected. Can be used to select or deselect an option.
`selectedIndex`	An integer value containing the index of the currently selected option.
`text`	A string value containing the text displayed in the selection list for a particular option.
`value`	A string value indicating the value for the specified option (that is, reflects the `VALUE` attribute).

- **selectedIndex:** Reflects the index of the currently selected option in the selection list.

Methods

- **blur():** Removes focus from the selection list. (Not 2|3)
- **focus():** Gives focus to the selection list. (Not 2|3)

Event Handlers

- **onBlur:** Specifies the JavaScript code to execute when the selection list loses focus.
- **onFocus:** Specifies the JavaScript code to execute when focus is given to the selection list.
- **onChange:** Specifies the JavaScript code to execute when the selected option in the list changes.

The *string* Object [C|2|3|I]

The `string` object provides properties and methods for working with string literals and variables.

Properties

- **length:** An integer value containing the length of the string expressed as the number of characters in the string.
- **prototype:** Provides a mechanism for adding properties to a `string` object. (Not 2)

Methods

- **anchor(*name*):** Returns a string containing the value of the `string` object surrounded by an `A` container tag with the `NAME` attribute set to *name*.
- **big():** Returns a string containing the value of the `string` object surrounded by a `BIG` container tag.
- **blink():** Returns a string containing the value of the `string` object surrounded by a `BLINK` container tag.
- **bold():** Returns a string containing the value of the `string` object surrounded by a `B` container tag.
- **charAt(*index*):** Returns the character at the location specified by *index*.
- **charCodeAt(*index*):** Returns a number representing an ISO-Latin-1 codeset value at the instant *index*. (Netscape Navigator 4.0 and later only)
- **concat(*string2*):** Combines two strings and derives a third, new string. (Netscape Navigator 4.0 and later only)
- **fixed():** Returns a string containing the value of the `string` object surrounded by a `FIXED` container tag.

- **`fontColor(`*`color`*`)`:** Returns a string containing the value of the `string` object surrounded by a `FONT` container tag with the `COLOR` attribute set to *`color`*, which is a color name or an RGB triplet. (Not I)
- **`fontSize(`*`size`*`)`:** Returns a string containing the value of the `string` object surrounded by a `FONTSIZE` container tag with the size set to *`size`*. (Not I)
- **`fromCharCode(`*`num1`*`, `*`num2`*`, …)`:** Returns a string constructed of ISO-Latin-1 characters. Those characters are specified by their codeset values, which are expressed as *`num1`*, *`num2`*, and so on.
- **`indexOf(`*`findString`*`,`*`startingIndex`*`)`:** Returns the index of the first occurrence of *`findString`*, starting the search at *`startingIndex`*, which is optional; if it's not provided, the search starts at the start of the string.
- **`italics()`:** Returns a string containing the value of the `string` object surrounded by an `I` container tag.
- **`lastIndexOf(`*`findString`*`,`*`startingIndex`*`)`:** Returns the index of the last occurrence of *`findString`*. This is done by searching backward from *`startingIndex`*. *`startingIndex`* is optional and is assumed to be the last character in the string if no value is provided.
- **`link(`*`href`*`)`:** Returns a string containing the value of the `string` object surrounded by an `A` container tag with the `HREF` attribute set to *`href`*.
- **`match(`*`regular_expression`*`)`:** Matches a regular expression to a string. The parameter *`regular_expression`* is the name of the regular expression, expressed either as a variable or a literal.
- **`replace(`*`regular_expression`*`, newSubStr)`:** Finds and replaces *`regular_expression`* with `newSubStr`.
- **`search(`*`regular_expression`*`)`:** Finds *`regular_expression`* and matches it to some string.
- **`slice(`*`beginSlice`*`, [`*`endSlice`*`])`:** Extracts a portion of a given string and derives a new string from that excerpt. *`beginSlice`* and *`endSlice`* are both zero-based indexes that can be used to grab the first, second, and third character, and so on.
- **`small()`:** Returns a string containing the value of the `string` object surrounded by a `SMALL` container tag.
- **`split(`*`separator`*`)`:** Returns an array of strings created by splitting the string at every occurrence of *`separator`*. (Not 2|I) `split` has additional functionality in JavaScript 1.2 and for Navigator 4.0 and later. That new functionality includes the following elements:

Regex and Fixed String Splitting	You can now split the `string` string by both regular expression argument and fixed string,
Limit Count	You can now add a limit count to prevent including empty elements within the string.
White Space Splitting	The capability to split on a white space (including any white space, such as space, tab, newline, and so forth).

- **strike():** Returns a string containing the value of the string object surrounded by a STRIKE container tag.
- **sub():** Returns a string containing the value of the string object surrounded by a SUB container tag.
- **substr(start, [length]):** Used to extract a set number (length) of characters within a string. Use start to specify the location at which to begin this extraction process. New in JavaScript 1.2.
- **substring(*firstIndex*,*lastIndex*):** Returns a string equivalent to the substring beginning at *firstIndex* and ending at the character before *lastIndex*. If *firstIndex* is greater than *lastIndex*, the string starts at *lastIndex* and ends at the character before *firstIndex*. Note: In JavaScript 1.2, x and y are no longer swapped. To get this result, you must specify JavaScript 1.2 with the language attribute within the <SCRIPT> tag.
- **sup():** Returns a string containing the value of the string object surrounded by a SUP container tag.
- **toLowerCase():** Returns a string containing the value of the string object with all characters converted to lowercase.
- **toUpperCase():** Returns a string containing the value of the string object with all characters converted to uppercase.

The *submit* Object [C|2|3|I]

The submit object reflects a submit button from an HTML form in JavaScript.

Properties

- **enabled:** A Boolean value indicating whether the submit button is enabled. (Not 2|3)
- **form:** A reference to the form object containing the submit button. (Not 2|3)
- **name:** A string value containing the name of the submit button element.
- **type:** A string value reflecting the TYPE attribute of the <INPUT> tag. (Not 2|I)
- **value:** A string value containing the value of the submit button element.

Methods

- **click():** Emulates the action of clicking the submit button.
- **focus():** Gives focus to the submit button. (Not 2|3)

Event Handlers

- **onClick:** Specifies the JavaScript code to execute when the submit button is clicked.
- **onFocus:** Specifies the JavaScript code to execute when the submit button receives focus. (Not 2|3)

The *text* Object [C|2|3|I]

The `text` object reflects a text field from an HTML form in JavaScript.

Properties

- **`defaultValue`:** A string value containing the default value of the text element (that is, the value of the `VALUE` attribute).
- **`enabled`:** A Boolean value indicating whether the text field is enabled. (Not 2|3)
- **`form`:** A reference to the `form` object containing the text field. (Not 2|3)
- **`name`:** A string value containing the name of the text element.
- **`type`:** A string value reflecting the `TYPE` attribute of the `<INPUT>` tag. (Not 2|I)
- **`value`:** A string value containing the value of the text element.

Methods

- **`focus()`:** Emulates the action of focusing in the text field.
- **`blur()`:** Emulates the action of removing focus from the text field.
- **`select()`:** Emulates the action of selecting the text in the text field.

Event Handlers

- **`onBlur`:** Specifies the JavaScript code to execute when focus is removed from the field.
- **`onChange`:** Specifies the JavaScript code to execute when the content of the field is changed.
- **`onFocus`:** Specifies the JavaScript code to execute when focus is given to the field.
- **`onSelect`:** Specifies the JavaScript code to execute when the user selects some or all of the text in the field.

The *textarea* Object [C|2|3|I]

The `textarea` object reflects a multiline text field from an HTML form in JavaScript.

Properties

- **`defaultValue`:** A string value containing the default value of the textarea element (that is, the value of the `VALUE` attribute).
- **`enabled`:** A Boolean value indicating whether the textarea field is enabled. (Not 2|3)
- **`form`:** A reference to the `form` object containing the textarea field. (Not 2|3)
- **`name`:** A string value containing the name of the textarea element.
- **`type`:** A string value reflecting the type of the textarea object. (Not 2|I)
- **`value`:** A string value containing the value of the textarea element.

Methods

- **`focus()`:** Emulates the action of focusing in the textarea field.
- **`blur()`:** Emulates the action of removing focus from the textarea field.
- **`select()`:** Emulates the action of selecting the text in the textarea field.

Event Handlers

- **`onKeyUp`:** Specifies the JavaScript code to execute when the user releases a specific key. (Netscape Navigator 4.0 only) (4)
- **`onKeyPress`:** Specifies the JavaScript code to execute when the user holds down a specific key. (Netscape Navigator 4.0 only) (4)
- **`onKeyDown`:** Specifies the JavaScript code to execute when the user presses a specific key. (Netscape Navigator 4.0 only) (4)
- **`onBlur`:** Specifies the JavaScript code to execute when focus is removed from the field.
- **`onChange`:** Specifies the JavaScript code to execute when the content of the field is changed.
- **`onFocus`:** Specifies the JavaScript code to execute when focus is given to the field.
- **`onSelect`:** Specifies the JavaScript code to execute when the user selects some or all of the text in the field.

The *window* Object [C|2|3|I]

The `window` object is the top-level object for each `window` or `frame` and the parent object for the `document`, `location`, and `history` objects.

Properties

- **`defaultStatus`:** A string value containing the default value displayed in the status bar.
- **`frames`:** An array of objects for each frame in a window. Frames appear in the array in the order in which they appear in the HTML source code.
- **`innerHeight()`:** Specifies the vertical size of the content area (in pixels). New in JavaScript 1.2.
- **`innerWidth()`:** Specifies the horizontal size of the content area (in pixels). New in JavaScript 1.2.
- **`length`:** An integer value indicating the number of frames in a parent window. (Not I)
- **`name`:** A string value containing the name of the window or frame.
- **`opener`:** A reference to the `window` object containing the `open()` method used to open the current window. (Not 2|I)
- **`pageXOffset`:** Specifies the current X position of the viewable window area (expressed in pixels). New in JavaScript 1.2.

- **`pageYOffset`:** Specifies the current Y position of the viewable window area (expressed in pixels). New in JavaScript 1.2.
- **`parent`:** A string indicating the name of the window containing the frameset.
- **`personalbar [visible=true,false]`:** Represents the Directories bar in Netscape Navigator and whether it's visible. New in JavaScript 1.2.
- **`scrollbars [visible=true,false]`:** Represents the scrollbars of the instant window and whether they are visible. New in JavaScript 1.2.
- **`self`:** A alternative for the name of the current window.
- **`status`:** Used to display a message in the status bar; it's done by assigning values to this property.
- **`statusbar=[true,false,1,0]`:** Specifies whether the status bar of the target window is visible.
- **`toolbar=[true,false,1,0]`:** Specifies whether the toolbar of the target window is visible.
- **`top`:** An alternative for the name of the topmost window.
- **`window`:** An alternative for the name of the current window.

Methods

- **`alert(`*`message`*`)`:** Displays *`message`* in a dialog box.
- **`back()`:** Sends the user back to the previous URL stored in the history list. (Simulates a user clicking the Back button in Navigator.) New in JavaScript 1.2.
- **`blur()`:** Removes focus from the window. On many systems, it sends the window to the background. (Not 2|I)
- **`captureEvents()`:** Used in a window with frames (along with `enableExternalCapture`), it specifies that the window will capture all specified events.
- **`clearInterval(`*`intervalID`*`)`:** Cancels timeouts created with the `setInterval` method. New in JavaScript 1.2.
- **`close()`:** Closes the window. (Not I)
- **`confirm(`*`message`*`)`:** Displays *`message`* in a dialog box with OK and Cancel buttons. Returns `true` or `false` based on the button clicked by the user.
- **`disableExternalCapture()`:** Prevents the instant window with frames from capturing events occurring in pages loaded from a different location. New in JavaScript 1.2.
- **`enableExternalCapture()`:** Allows the instant window (with frames) to capture events occurring in pages loaded from a different location. New in JavaScript 1.2.
- **`find([`*`string`*`], [true, false], [true, false])`:** Finds *`string`* in the target window. There are two true/false parameters: The first specifies the Boolean state of case sensitivity in the search; the second specifies whether the search is performed backward. New in JavaScript 1.2.

- **`focus()`:** Gives focus to the window. On many systems, it brings the window to the front. (Not 2|I)
- **`forward()`:** Sends the user to the next URL in the history list. (Simulates a user clicking the Forward button in Navigator.) New in JavaScript 1.2.
- **`home()`:** Sends the user to the user's Home Page URL. (For example, in a default configuration of Netscape Navigator, it sends the user to `http://home.netscape.com`.) New in JavaScript 1.2.
- **`moveBy(horizontal, vertical)`:** Moves the window according to the specified values `horizontal` and `vertical`. New in JavaScript 1.2.
- **`moveTo(`*`x`*`, `*`y`*`)`:** Moves the top-left corner of the window to the specified location; *`x`* and *`y`* are screen coordinates. New in JavaScript 1.2.
- **`navigator(`*`url`*`)`:** Loads *`url`* in the window. (Not 2|3)
- **`open(`*`url`*`,`*`name`*`,`*`features`*`)`:** Opens *`url`* in a window named *`name`*. If *`name`* doesn't exist, a new window is created with that name. *`features`* is an optional string argument containing a list of features for the new window. The feature list contains any of the following name-value pairs separated by commas and without additional spaces: (Not I)

`toolbar=[yes,no,1,0]`	Indicates whether the window should have a toolbar.
`location=[yes,no,1,0]`	Indicates whether the window should have a location field.
`directories=[yes,no,1,0]`	Indicates whether the window should have directory buttons.
`status=[yes,no,1,0]`	Indicates whether the window should have a status bar.
`menubar=[yes,no,1,0]`	Indicates whether the window should have menus.
`scrollbars=[yes,no,1,0]`	Indicates whether the window should have scrollbars.
`resizable=[yes,no,1,0]`	Indicates whether the window should be resizable.
`width=`*`pixels`*	Indicates the width of the window in pixels.
`alwaysLowered=[yes,no,1,2]`	Indicates (if true) that the window should remain below all other windows. (This feature has varying results on varying window systems.) New in JavaScript 1.2. Note: The script must be signed touse this feature.
`alwaysRaised=[yes,no,1,2]`	Indicates (if true) that the window should always remain the top-level window. (This feature has varying results on varying window systems.) New in JavaScript 1.2. Note: The script must be signed to use this feature.

`dependent[yes,no,1,2]`	Indicates that the current child window will die (or close) when the parent window does. New in JavaScript 1.2.
`hotkeys=[yes,no,1,2]`	Indicates (if true) that most hot keys are disabled within the instant window. New in JavaScript 1.2.
`innerWidth=pixels`	Indicates the width (in pixels) of the instant window's content area. New in JavaScript 1.2.
`innerHeight=pixels`	Indicates the height (in pixels) of the instant window's content area. New in JavaScript 1.2.
`outerWidth=pixels`	Indicates the instant window's horizontal outside width boundary. New in JavaScript 1.2.
`outerHeight=pixels`	Indicates the instant window's horizontal outside height boundary. New in JavaScript 1.2.
`screenX=pixels`	Indicates the distance that the new window is placed from the left side of the screen (horizontally). New in JavaScript 1.2.
`screenY=pixels`	Indicates the distance that the new window is placed from the top of the screen (vertically). New in JavaScript 1.2.
`z-lock=[yes,no,1,2]`	Indicates that the instant window does not move through the cycling of the z-order; that is, it doesn't rise above other windows, even if activated. New in JavaScript 1.2. Note: The script must be signed for this feature to work.
`height=`*`pixels`*	Indicates the height of the window in pixels.

- **`print()`:** Prints the contents of a frame or window. It's the equivalent of the user pressing the Print button in Netscape Navigator. New in JavaScript 1.2.
- **`prompt(`*`message`*`,`*`response`*`)`:** Displays *`message`* in a dialog box with a text entry field with the default value of *`response`*. The user's response in the text entry field is returned as a string.
- **`releaseEvents(`*`eventType`*`)`:** Specifies that the current window should release events instead of capturing them so that these events can be passed to other objects, perhaps further on in the event hierarchy. New in JavaScript 1.2.
- **`resizeBy(`*`horizontal`*`, `*`vertical`*`)`:** Resizes the window, moving from the bottom-right corner. New in JavaScript 1.2.
- **`resizeTo(outerWidth, outerHeight)`:** Resizes the window, using `outerWidth` and `outerHeight` properties. New in JavaScript 1.2.
- **`routeEvent(`*`event`*`)`:** Sends or routes an event through the normal event hierarchy. New in JavaScript 1.2.

- **scrollBy(*horizontal*, *vertical*):** Scroll the viewing area of the current window by the specified amount. New in JavaScript 1.2.
- **scrollTo(x, y):** Scrolls the current window to the specified position, calculated in x and y coordinates, starting at the top-left corner of the window. New in JavaScript 1.2.
- **setInterval(*function*, msec, [args]):** Repeatedly calls a function after the period specified by the `msec` parameter. New in JavaScript 1.2.
- **setInterval(*expression*, msec):** Evaluates *`expression`* after the period specified by the `msec` parameter. New in JavaScript 1.2.
- **setTimeout(*expression*,*time*):** Evaluates *`expression`* after *`time`*, which is a value in milliseconds. The timeout can be named with the following structure:

  ```
  name = setTimeOut(expression,time)
  ```
- **scrollTo(*x*,*y*):** Scrolls the window to the coordinate *`x,y`*. (Not 2|I)
- **stop():** Stops the current download. It's the equivalent of the user pressing the Stop button in Netscape Navigator.
- **clearTimeout(*name*):** Cancels the timeout with the name *`name`*.

Event Handlers

- **onDragDrop:** Specifies the JavaScript code to execute when the user drops an object onto the window. (Netscape Navigator 4.0 and later only) (4.0)
- **onBlur:** Specifies the JavaScript code to execute when focus is removed from a window. (Not 2|I)
- **onError:** Specifies the JavaScript code to execute when a JavaScript error occurs while loading a document. It can be used to intercept JavaScript errors. Setting this event handler to `null` effectively prevents JavaScript errors from being displayed to the user. (Not 2|I)
- **onFocus:** Specifies the JavaScript code to execute when the window receives focus. (Not 2|I)
- **onLoad:** Specifies the JavaScript code to execute when the window or frame finishes loading.
- **onMove:** Specifies the JavaScript code to execute when the user moves a window. (Netscape Navigator 4.0 only)
- **onResize:** Specifies the JavaScript code to execute when a user resizes the window.
- **onUnload:** Specifies the JavaScript code to execute when the document in the window or frame is exited.

Independent Functions, Operators, Variables, and Literals

- **escape(*character*):** Returns a string containing the ASCII encoding of *character* in the form %xx; xx is the numeric encoding of the character. (C|2|3|I)
- **eval(*expression*):** Returns the result of evaluating *expression*, which is an arithmetic expression. (C|2|3|I)
- **isNaN(*value*):** Evaluates *value* to see if it's NaN. Returns a Boolean value. (C|2|3|I) (On UNIX platforms, not 2.)
- **parseFloat(*string*):** Converts *string* to a floating-point number and returns the value. It continues to convert until it hits a nonnumeric character and then returns the result. If the first character can't be converted to a number, the function returns NaN (zero on Windows platforms). (C|2|3|I)
- **parseInt(*string*,*base*):** Converts *string* to an integer of base *base* and returns the value. It continues to convert until it hits a nonnumeric character and then returns the result. If the first character can't be converted to a number, the function returns NaN (zero on Windows platforms). (C|2|3|I)
- **taint(*propertyName*):** Adds tainting to *propertyName*. (C|3)
- **toString():** This is a method of all objects. It returns the object as a string or returns "[object *type*]" if no string representation exists for the object. (C|2|3) Note: In JavaScript 1.2, it converts objects and strings into literals.
- **unescape(*string*):** Returns a character based on the ASCII encoding contained in *string*. The ASCII encoding should take the form "%integer" or "hexadecimalValue". (C|2|3|I)
- **untaint(*propertyName*):** Removes tainting from *propertyName*. (C|3)

Statements

- **break:** Terminates a while or for loop and passes program control to the first statement following the loop. (2|3|4) Note: In JavaScript 1.2, break has the added functionality of being able to break out of labeled statements.
- **comment:** Used to add a comment within the script. This comment is ignored by Navigator. Comments in JavaScript work similarly to those in C. They are enclosed in a /* (start), */ (end) structure. (2|3|4)
- **continue:** Terminates execution of statements in a while or for loop and continues iteration of the loop. (2|3|4) Note: In JavaScript 1.2, continue has added functionality that allows you to continue within labeled statements.
- **do while:** Sets up a loop that continues to execute statements and code until the condition evaluates to false. New in JavaScript 1.2.

- **`export`:** Used with the `import` statement. In secure, signed scripts, it allows the developer to export all properties, functions, and variables to another script. New in JavaScript 1.2.
- **`for([initial-expression]; [condition]; [incremental-expression];)):`** Specifies the opening of a `for` loop. The arguments are these: initialize a variable (*`initial-expression`*), create a condition to test for (*`condition`*), and specify an incrementation scheme (*`incremental-expression`*).
- **`for…in`:** Imposes a variable to all properties of an object and executes a block of code for each.
- **`function [name]()`:** Declares a function so that it can be referred to or reached by event handlers (or other processes).
- **`if…else`:** A structure used to test whether a certain condition is true. `If…else` blocks can contain nested statements and functions (and call them) if a condition is either true or false.
- **`import`:** Used with the `export` statement. In secure, signed scripts, it allows the developer to import all properties, functions, and variables from another script. New in JavaScript 1.2.
- **`label (labeled statements)`:** Statement that creates a label or pointer to code elsewhere in the script. By calling this label, you redirect the script to the labeled statement.
- **`new`:** Creates an instance of a user-defined object. (It can also be used to create an instance of built-in objects, inherent to JavaScript, such as new `Date`.)
- **`return [value]`:** Specifies a value to be returned by a given function. For example, `return x` returns the variable value associated with *x*.
- **`switch`:** Evaluates an expression and attempts to match it to a `case` pattern or label. If the expression matches the `case`, trailing statements associated with that label are executed. New in JavaScript 1.2. (Operates similarly to the `switch` statement in C shell syntax.)
- **`this`:** A statement used to refer to a specific object, as shown in this example:

  ```
  onClick = 'javascript:my_function(this.form)'
  ```
- **`var [name]`:** Declares a variable by `name`.
- **`while`:** Statement that begins a `while` loop. `while` loops specify that as long as (while) a condition is true, execute some code.
- **`with`:** Statement that sets the value for the default object; a method that's similar to creating a global variable with a function.

Operators

- **Assignment Operators:** See Table A.1.

Table A.1 Assignment operators in JavaScript.

Operator	Description
=	Assigns the value of the right operand to the left operand
+=	Adds the left and right operands and assigns the result to the left operand
-=	Subtracts the right operand from the left operand and assigns the result to the left operand
*=	Multiplies the two operands and assigns the result to the left operand
/=	Divides the left operand by the right operand and assigns the value to the left operand
%=	Divides the left operand by the right operand and assigns the remainder to the left operand

- **Arithmetic Operators:** See Table A.2.

Table A.2 Arithmetic operators in JavaScript.

Operator	Description
+	Adds the left and right operands
-	Subtracts the right operand from the left operand
*	Multiplies the two operands
/	Divides the left operand by the right operand
%	Divides the left operand by the right operand and evaluates to the remainder
++	Increments the operand by one (can be used before or after the operand)
--	Decreases the operand by one (can be used before or after the operand)
-	Changes the sign of the operand

- **Bitwise Operators:** Bitwise operators deal with their operands as binary numbers, but return JavaScript numerical value. (See Table A.3.)

Table A.3 Bitwise operators in JavaScript.

Operator	Description
AND (or &)	Converts operands to integers with 32 bits, pairs the corresponding bits, and returns one for each pair of ones. Returns zero for any other combination.
OR (or ¦)	Converts operands to integers with 32 bits, pairs the corresponding bits, and returns one for each pair when one of the two bits is one. Returns zero if both bits are zero.
XOR (or ^)	Converts operands to integer with 32 bits, pairs the corresponding bits, and returns one for each pair when only one bit is one. Returns zero for any other combination.
<<	Converts the left operand to an integer with 32 bits and shifts bits to the left the number of bits indicated by the right operand. Bits shifted off to the left are discarded, and zeros are shifted in from the right.
>>>	Converts the left operand to an integer with 32 bits and shifts bits to the right the number of bits indicated by the right operand. Bits shifted off to the right are discarded, and zeros are shifted in from the left.
>>	Converts the left operand to an integer with 32 bits and shifts bits to the right the number of bits indicated by the right operand. Bits shifted off to the right are discarded, and copies of the leftmost bit are shifted in from the left.

- **Logical Operators:** See Table A.4.

Table A.4 Logical operators in JavaScript.

Operator	Description
&&	Logical "and." Returns `true` when both operands are true; otherwise, it returns `false`.
¦¦	Logical "or." Returns `true` if either operand is true. It returns `false` only when both operands are false.
!	Logical "not." Returns `true` if the operand is false and `false` if the operand is true. This is a unary operator and precedes the operand.

- **Comparison Operators:** See Table A.5.

Table A.5 Logical (comparison) operators in JavaScript.

Operator	Description
==	Returns `true` if the operands are equal
!=	Returns `true` if the operands are not equal

Operator	Description
>	Returns `true` if the left operand is greater than the right operand
<	Returns `true` if the left operand is less than the right operand
>=	Returns `true` if the left operand is greater than or equal to the right operand
<=	Returns `true` if the left operand is less than or equal to the right operand

- **Conditional Operators:** Conditional expressions take one form:

  ```
  (condition) ? val1 : val2
  ```

  If *`condition`* is true, the expression evaluates to *`val1`*; otherwise, it evaluates to *`val2`*.
- **String Operators:** The concatenation operator (+) is one of two string operators. It evaluates to a string combining the left and right operands. The concatenation assignment operator (+=) is also available.
- **The `typeof` Operator:** The `typeof` operator returns the type of its single operand. Possible types are `object`, `string`, `number`, `boolean`, `function`, and `undefined`. (C|3|I)
- **The `void` Operator:** The `void` operator takes an expression as an operand but returns no value.
- **Operator Precedence:** JavaScript applies the rules of operator precedence as follows (from lowest to highest precedence):

  Comma (,)

  Assignment operators (=, +=, -=, *=, /=, %=)

  Conditional (? :)

  Logical OR (||)

  Logical AND (&&)

  Bitwise OR (|)

  Bitwise XOR (^)

  Bitwise AND (&)

  Equality (==, !=)

  Relational (<, <=, >, >=)

  Shift (<<, >>, >>>)

  Addition/subtraction (+, -)

  Multiply/divide/modulus (*, /, %)

  Negation/increment (!, -, ++, --)

  Call, member ((), [])

APPENDIX B

What's on the CD

In this chapter

Source Code from the Book

Complete examples and listings from the book are included on the CD-ROM. All examples are organized by chapter for ease of use.

Virtual Reference Library of Books on Related Topics

- ActiveX Programming Unleashed
- Special Edition Using Java 1.1, 3rd Edition
- Special Edition Using JavaScript, 2nd Edition
- Teach Yourself Dynamic HTML in a Week
- Teach Yourself FrontPage98 in a Week

Que's Internet Knowledgebase

Valuable information for web authors that has been compiled into a handy searchable database containing material from six best-selling Que titles.

Third Party Software

Audio Utility

- Syntrillium Cool Edit

Multimedia Utilities

- Apple QuickTime
- Macromedia Authorware demo
- Macromedia Flash
- Macromedia Shockwave
- Microsoft NetShow
- Nettoob Stream Duplexx Software demo

Browsers

- Microsoft Internet Explorer 4.0
- W3C Amaya

CGI Perl

- CGIWrap
- DBD
- DBI
- Links to various CGI web resources

Compression Utilities

- Winzip95
- Stuffit Expander

HTML Help Utility

- Netscape Nethelp SDK

FTP Clients

- Cute FTP
- WS_FTP

Graphics Applications

- LView Pro
- PaintShop Pro demo
- Mapedit 2.31

3D Software

- Caligari Truespace demo

Webcasting Helpers

- Marimba Castanet Publisher demo
- Marimba Castanet Transmitter demo

HTML Editors

- Sausage Software Hotdog 4.5 demo
- SoftQuad HoTMetaL Pro 4.0 demo
- Brooklyn North HTML Assistant Pro 97 demo
- BBEdit Lite
- Various Microsoft Internet Assistants
- EoSoft EoHex

Java

- Jdesigner Pro demo
- Jfactory demo
- Jtools demo
- Jwidgets demo
- Mojo demo
- Sausage Software Clickette demo
- Sausage Software Egor demo
- Sausage Software Ewgie demo
- Sausage Software Flash demo
- Sausage Software Swami demo
- Coffee Table Grid demo
- Links to various Java web resources

Server

- Jigsaw

Sprint

- Sprint Internet Service Provider Plan bundled with Netscape Communicator

Graphics and Sound Collections

- Button Collection from Andy Evans
- Graphics collection with over 5,000 images from Macmillan Digital Publishing
- Qbullets from Matterform Media
- Various sound collections

Documentation

- HTML 4.0 Specification
- HTML 4.0 Tag Reference (from book)
- RFCs 1865, 1945 and 2068
- CSS Specification
- XML Specification
- HTTP 1.1 Specification
- Links to various VBScript, JavaScript, Java, VRML, and DHTML web documentation and resources

Index

Symbols

A

B

D

E

F

G

H

J

K

L

M

N

O

P

Q

R

S

U

V

W

X

Y - Z

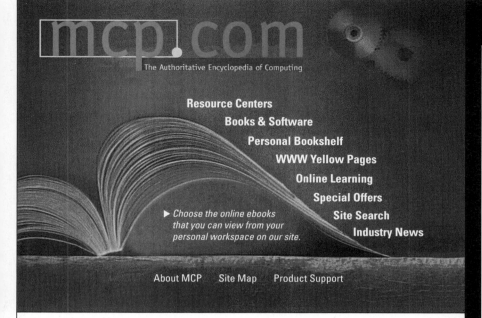